Using

Sage 50 Accounting 2013

M. PURBHOO

Covers both Sage 50 Premium Accounting® 2013 and Sage 50 Pro Accounting® 2013

Canadian Edition

(Formerly Sage Simply Accounting)

PEARSON

Toronto

Vice-President, Editorial Director: Gary Bennett
Editor-in-Chief: Nicole Lukach
Acquisitions Editor: Megan Farrell
Marketing Manager: Claire Varley
Developmental Editor: Megan Burns
Production Editor: Leanne Rancourt
Copy Editor: Leanne Rancourt
Proofreader: Susan Bindernagel
Lead Project Manager: Avinash Chandra
Page Layout: Mary Purbhoo
Art Director: Julia Hall
Interior and Cover Designer: Anthony Leung
Cover Image: veer.com

Credits
Page 466 and Appendix K, screen shots from Canada Revenue Agency Web site: Canada Revenue Agency and the Minister of Public Works and Government Services Canada, 2013.

---

10 9 8 7 6 [EBM]

Printed and Printed and bound in the United States of America.

Library and Archives Canada Cataloguing in Publication

Purbhoo, Mary, 1949–, author
Using Sage 50 accounting 2013 / Mary Purbhoo. — Canadian edition.

Includes index.
ISBN 978-0-13-340125-7 (pbk. : spiral binding)

1. Sage 50 accounting (Computer file).
2. Small business—Accounting—Computer programs. I. Title. II. Title: Sage 50 accounting 2013

HFP5679.8868 2013 657.9042028553 C2013-902031-4

PEARSON

ISBN 978-0-13-340125-7

CONTENTS

PREFACE

NOTES
In 2013, Sage renamed the Sage Simply Accounting program to Sage 50 Accounting, Canadian Edition. The US Edition of Sage 50 Accounting replaces Sage Peachtree.

Using Sage 50 Accounting 2013 provides full coverage of Sage 50 Premium Accounting 2013 and Sage 50 Pro Accounting 2013. The 2013 Student version (Release 1) is also a Premium version program, so all users can learn the program using the same release the author used to create the data files, screens and keystrokes. Although we do not address the Quantum version of Sage 50, the book is also compatible with this version. Because Sage offers the Sage 50 Student version program only as a download from its Web site, we provide simple download instructions in an access card packaged with this book and detailed instructions for downloading, installing and activating the Student version in Appendix A.

We have introduced some changes in this edition.

As in last year's edition, the keystrokes and source documents are integrated throughout each chapter but, in response to user feedback, we modified the format to make these source documents stand out. We made the check box larger, included the source document number in the check box, added colour to the source document text and removed the coloured sidebars.

No new topics were added in this edition, but we created two new applications and made changes to others. Phoebe's Photo Studio (Chapter 6 and Appendix H on cash-basis accounting) and Flabuless Fitness (Chapter 10) are new for this text. Air Care Services has been revised to become the setup application for Chapter 7 and we added inventory to Stratford Country Inn in Chapter 17.

But we maintained the aspects of previous editions that have been well-received:

- a diversity of companies and business situations, including non-profit, service and inventory businesses
- comprehensive and current tax coverage for different provinces, including GST, HST, PST and QST, and tax remittances
- the realistic approach
- easy-to-follow, step-by-step keystroke instructions and screen illustrations, updated for Version 2013
- the currency of our information
- several company setup chapters increasing in complexity and a separate setup for payroll, all with keystroke instructions
- delayed introduction of advanced Accounts Receivable and Payable topics
- realistic source documents throughout the text to give you the "feel" of actual company transactions

The Student DVD with Data Files included with the text has the following resources:

- Pro and Premium version data files for all applications (except Chapter 17)
- review questions and cases for each chapter (Appendix D)
- additional appendices with supplementary materials (Appendices E – O)
- the interactive Accounting Cycle Tutorial, which introduces basic accounting terms and concepts

We continue to provide options for automatically installing data from the Student DVD: backup data files for both Premium and Pro versions, and full Premium version data files for all source document applications in the text. Supplementary files are provided only as backup files. Of course, we still include detailed instructions on restoring backups. These alternatives have additional advantages — if computer speed and time permit, users can install the full data files; otherwise, the smaller backup files can be copied quickly or backup files can be restored to your hard disk directly from the DVD one at a time. Premium version users can install both the full and backup sets of files. Backup files may be restored as often as needed without reinstalling.

The removable page-length bookmark attached to the back cover has a mini index and a ruler-marked edge to help you refer to specific lines on a page. This bookmark should help to manage page-flipping, which is inevitable because most keystrokes for a transaction go beyond the page with the transaction.

In this edition, we continue to work with module windows in the Enhanced view throughout the text, create user-specific customized shortcuts to access journals in other modules and use the industry-specific terms for the different applications. Classic View margin notes like the following are included for users who prefer this approach:

CLASSIC VIEW
Notes for Classic view users

These notes describe how icons, keystrokes or terms in the Classic view are different from those in the Enhanced view.

The basic organization of the text is unchanged. Part One provides an overview and introduction to Sage 50 and sales taxes. Data applications that can be completed with both Pro and Premium versions are located in Part Two. We introduce the six ledgers of Sage 50 (General, Payables, Receivables, Payroll, Inventory and Division) in separate applications. Budgeting and account reconciliation procedures are covered in two more applications. Advanced Receivables and Payables features (orders and quotes, tax remittances, sales to foreign customers and Internet links) are demonstrated in two other separate chapters. An online banking simulation (in Appendix I on the Student DVD) allows you to download a bank statement that integrates with data from the text. The required data files for all these chapters are set up in advance, and for each new type of transaction we provide detailed keystrokes and matching screens.

Four applications cover setting up a computerized accounting system using Sage 50. Again, detailed instructions with screen illustrations are given for each setup as you learn to design, convert and implement a complete accounting system.

- Chapter 4: set up a non-profit organization that uses only the General Ledger
- Chapter 7: set up an organization using the General, Payables and Receivables ledgers
- Chapter 9: add payroll to a data file that already has the General, Payables and Receivables ledgers
- Chapter 16: set up a comprehensive retail organization that uses the General, Payables, Receivables, Payroll and Inventory ledgers

In the final application in Part Two (Stratford Country Inn, Chapter 17), you set up a computerized accounting system on your own. All source documents in this chapter are realistic and descriptive.

Time & Billing and Departmental Accounting, advanced features available only in the Premium version, are covered in Part Three. Separate chapters and data files are prepared for these. All Part Three pages are edged with a blue stripe so that you can find them quickly.

For reference or further study, we include three appendices in Part Four of the text and 12 more on the Student DVD in PDF format — placing them on the DVD allows us to cover extra features. The appendices on the Student DVD are available for you to read or print. These supplementary appendices are provided as reference material that should prove to be useful in any working environment.

USING THIS BOOK

The accounting applications in this text were prepared using the Sage 50 Premium Accounting 2013, Canadian Edition, and Sage 50 Pro Accounting 2013, Canadian Edition (Release 1) of the Sage 50 software published by The Sage Group PLC. The Windows 7 operating system was used to create and test the screen images and keystrokes.

You must have a hard disk and DVD drive or a network system with Windows installed. If you do not have your own copy of the Sage 50 program, you can download the Student Premium software from the Sage Web site (refer to page xiii and Appendix A). Network system users should work with the site administrator to ensure complete data access.

In addition, you should have a standard accounting text for reviewing accounting principles. The text provides some accounting principles and procedures, and the Review of Basic Accounting (Appendix O) and the Accounting Cycle Tutorial on the Student DVD also provide an introduction. However, these are not intended to replace the breadth and depth of most standard accounting texts. You should also consult the built-in Help features of Sage 50.

The text is as simple and straightforward as we could make it, but familiarity with computers and some fundamentals of troubleshooting will make your progress through this text easier.

Student Resources

The Student DVD with Data Files

The Student DVD has an autorun feature that should open the Student DVD home page automatically when you insert the DVD into your DVD drive. From this home page you can choose to install data files, view the supplementary appendices (PDF format), run the Accounting Cycle Tutorial or browse the DVD. The Student DVD home page will remain open for you to make another selection until you close it.

Complete instructions for installing and accessing the files on the Student DVD are provided in Chapter 1.

Separate data sets with separate installation programs will help you install the data set you need and make it easy for all users to follow the text. To choose the correct data set, you must know what version of Sage 50 you are using. You can get this information from the program package, from the program CD or from the Welcome and Select Company window in the program (see page 7). SAGE 50 PRO ACCOUNTING 2013 or SAGE 50 PREMIUM ACCOUNTING 2013 appears in the Home window title bar for all data files. If you accepted the default installation settings, the program folder name in Program Files also matches the version. The Student version for 2013 is a Premium version program, Release 1.

Use the following chart to help you install the data set you need from the Install Data screen:

FOR VERSION	**Pro Version 2013**
CLICK INSTALL BUTTON	Install Pro Version Backup Files
DATA SET (FOLDER ON DVD)	Pro_Backup_Version
FOR VERSIONS	**Student Version 2013** **Premium Version 2013** and **Quantum Version 2013**
CLICK INSTALL BUTTON	Install Premium Version Full Files
DATA SET (FOLDER ON DVD)	Premium_Full_Version_Data
	or
CLICK INSTALL BUTTON	Install Premium Version Backup Files
DATA SET (FOLDER ON DVD)	Premium_Backup_Version

All installation programs create a data folder named SageData13 on drive C (Local Disk C: or [OS] C:). If you need to work with another location for your data files, refer to page 6 in this text. You can install the data as often as you need to. We recommend renaming the previous folder to prevent overwriting all your previous files.

You can restore backup files directly from the Student DVD to your hard disk. However, we recommend installing the backup files to your hard disk and keeping the original DVD safe for later use.

If you are using Sage 50 Quantum Accounting, the Sage 50 Upgrade Company wizard will convert the Premium data files when you open them or restore them. Because the DVD files remain unchanged, you can install the same files later and use the Premium version.

Supplementary Data Files

In addition to the data files needed to work through the keystroke applications in the text, we provide supplementary files with all installation options. Backup files are included for online bank reconciliation (Appendix I on the Student DVD) and importing accounting transactions from an Accountant Edition (Chapter 12). These backup files will be located in the Bank and ACCOUNTANT folders in SageData13, respectively, when you install the data files. The ACCOUNTANT folder also has the text file that you import. The Logos folder includes company and inventory logos for the setup chapters and new inventory items.

Passwords

We have not added passwords to any data files to ensure maximum accessibility. However, if you are using the program in a multi-user or network environment that includes users and passwords, you will need to enter your user name and password before you can open the data files. Ask your instructor or site administrator for the user name and password that you should use. Refer to Chapter 16, page 686, and Appendix G on the Student DVD for instructions on working with passwords.

Working with Different Versions of Sage 50

Windows Version

We used Windows 7 for all screenshots and keystrokes for this text and to create and test the data files. Fortunately, the screens and functionality of Sage 50 are the same for different versions of Windows. They differ only at the interface between Windows and Sage 50 — in the screens for browsing, opening and saving files. For example, My Computer and its File menu in Windows XP are named Computer and Organize menu in Windows Vista and Windows 7. Sage 50 is also compatible wiith Windows 8. A basic Windows text will include the information you need to successfully complete this text.

Pro Version

Although we have written this text primarily for the Premium version and show Premium version screens, you can use the Student DVD data files with the 2013 Pro, Premium, Quantum and Premium Student versions of Sage 50, Release 1 or later.

Therefore, we have tried to make version differences, such as differences in features, terminology and labels, as clear as possible. We use margin notes identified by a specific Pro Version heading and icon:

PRO VERSION
Notes for Pro version users

These notes for Pro version users describe how screens, terms or keystrokes in the Pro version are different from those in the Premium version.

Student Version of Sage 50

The Student Premium version of Sage 50 must be downloaded from the Sage Web site. All copies of the 2013 Student version program have the same **serial number — 242P1U2-1000004**. The actual installation is the same as it is for the regular retail CD version of the program, as described in Appendix A in the text. Detailed instructions for downloading, installing and activating or registering your Student version of Sage 50 are also included in Appendix A.

Students needing help with the program should work with their instructor. Additional help for students is available online from the following Web site: **www.sageforstudents.com/forums**. Please note that you may have limited access to technical support if you are using an older version of the program.

About the Student Version Program

The Student version is a fully functional Premium version that you can use for 14 months after installation, but you cannot restore or open data files from previous versions with it. If you have already installed a Trial version, the date you installed it will count toward this 14-month limit. You can install only one version of Sage 50 Accounting 2013 on your computer. If you are using the Pro version or a Trial version and you want to install the Student Premium version, you must first completely uninstall the Pro or Trial version from the Control Panel in Windows (refer to Appendix A, page A–14). After you use a data set with the

Student version for 14 months, you must use a regular retail licensed version of the program to access that data.

None of the data files were created with a Student or Trial version, so the data itself will not expire. If you have used the data with a Student version for 14 months, however, you may see a data expired message.

If you see a message that the program has expired when you try to install it or to open a data set, and you have not yet used the program for 14 months, you should refer to page A-14 and ask your instructor for assistance.

The differences between the Student version and the retail Premium version are very small, but where they occur we have identified them with margin notes as shown here:

STUDENT VERSION
Notes for Student version users

These notes describe how the Student version differs from the regular or retail Premium version.

Earlier Versions

If you try to access the data files with earlier versions of Sage Simply Accounting (2012 and earlier), Sage 50 displays an error message. In this case, you should download and install the Student version. Refer to Appendix A, page A–10, for information on downloading and installing the Student version.

Later Versions

Although the data files can be used with later versions of the software, you may see changes in screens, keystrokes and payroll tax amounts. Before you open a data file with a later version, the Sage 50 conversion wizard will update the data file to match the later version you are using. Always refer to the manuals and update notices for later versions. Once the file has been updated, you will no longer be able to use it with the earlier version or release, unless you reinstall the data files from the Student DVD.

For this reason, we recommend that you turn off the Automatic Updates feature so that you do not update your program beyond Release 1 until you have finished working with the data files in the text. Refer to Appendix A, page A–7, for information on automatic updates. Automatic updates are not available for the Student version.

Quantum Version

This text can be used with Sage 50 Quantum Accounting. All the features covered in the text are available in the Quantum version, though you may see small variations in the screens. The Quantum version includes features that are not available in the Premium version — these advanced features are not covered in this text. If you are using the Quantum version, the Sage 50 data conversion wizard will convert the Premium data files when you open them or restore them. Because the DVD files remain unchanged, you can install and use the same files later using the Premium version.

Working Through the Applications

Keystroke Instruction Style

We have incorporated different paragraph styles for different kinds of statements in the text to help you identify the instructions that you must follow to complete the transactions correctly and see the screens that we present. These different styles are illustrated below:

Press enter or **press** the **Add button** to start the Add Account wizard. (Keystroke command line — command word is in bold and the object of the command, what you press, is in colour. Commands are indented and spaced apart. Additional text or information for the line is shown in plain text.)

Type `Foothills Hardware`
(Keystroke command line with text you type in a special font.)

Or you can click the Comment field to advance the cursor. (Alternative keystroke sequence that you may want to use later. Paragraph is indented in block style and plain text style is used.)

Regular text is presented in normal paragraphs, like this one. **Key words** are shown in colour to make it easy to identify the topics. Names of icons, fields, text and tool buttons that you will see on-screen have all initial letters capitalized (for example, Adjust A Previously Posted Invoice tool or E-mail Confirmation Of Invoices And Quotes). Account names included in regular text paragraphs are italicized (for example, *Revenue from Sales* or *Cost of Goods Sold*).

✓ 12 **Purchase Invoice #FG-642** **Dated Aug. 1/15**

From Fundy Gift House, $800 plus $104 HST for eight tea service sets. Invoice total, $904. Terms: net 30.
(Source document — with all text in colour — that you should enter using Sage 50. The ✓ in the check box indicates that keystroke instructions are provided. The number in colour in the lower part of the check box shows the source document number.) All source documents are numbered in sequence.

25 **Purchase Invoice #BF-2987** **Dated Aug. 15/15**

From Bathurst Food Supplies, $800 weekly invoice for pastries, breads, condiments and other foods. Terms: 1/10, n/30. Recall the stored entry.
(Source document — with all text in colour — that you should enter on your own using Sage 50. No keystroke instructions are provided — the upper part of the check box is empty and the lower part contains the source document number in colour.)

In addition to the different types of margin notes already described for the Pro and Student versions and the Classic view, the text includes regular margin Notes that contain additional important information for all users and warning notes when extra attention is needed:

NOTES Regular Notes.	Regular Notes for all users providing additional general information.
WARNING! Warning notes	Warning notes point out common errors or things to watch out for! All users should read these notes carefully.

Order of Applications

Setup applications are introduced early in the text. Advanced users should have no difficulty working through the applications in the order given and may even choose to skip some applications. However, at a minimum, we recommend working through all keystroke transactions (the ones with a ✓ in the check box beside them) so that you become familiar with all the journals before starting the more comprehensive applications.

There are alternatives if the text is used at introductory and advanced levels for different courses. In this case, students can complete the General, basic Payables, basic Receivables, Payroll and Inventory transaction applications (Chapters 3, 5, 6, 8 and 10) in the introductory course and the remaining chapters later. Chapters 11 and 12 may be completed at any time after Chapter 6 because these chapters do not have payroll or inventory transactions. Chapters may also be completed in a different sequence, as outlined below and on the following page:

1. Read and work through the two Getting Started chapters in Part One.
2A. Complete the ledger applications in order: Muriel's Murals (General), Chai Tea Room (basic Payables), Phoebe's Photo Studio (basic Receivables), Helena's Academy (Payroll), Adrienne Aesthetics (Inventory), Andersson Chiropractic Clinic and Maple Leaf Rags (advanced features of the first three ledgers) and Truman Tires* (Division or Project).
2B. (Premium version only) Complete the Part Three applications in any order: Ryder's Routes (Time & Billing) and Able & Associates (departmental accounting).
3. Complete Tesses Tresses (Chapter 15, account reconciliation and deposit slips) and Village Galleries (Chapter 14, budgeting).
4. Complete the four setup applications in order: Toss for Tots (General), Air Care Services (three ledgers), Lime Light Laundry (adding the Payroll ledger) and VeloCity (five ledgers).
5. Complete the Stratford Country Inn setup application with realistic source documents. Users may want to attempt this setup with the help of the setup wizards from the Setup menu in the Home window.
6. Complete the cash-basis accounting application in Appendix H at any time after Chapter 6.

* Truman Tires (Division Ledger, Chapter 13) may be completed at any time after these chapters because it does not introduce keystrokes required for any other application. Later chapters may be completed before Truman Tires.

This order is shown graphically in the chart on the following page:

AN ALTERNATIVE SEQUENCE FOR WORKING THROUGH THE APPLICATIONS

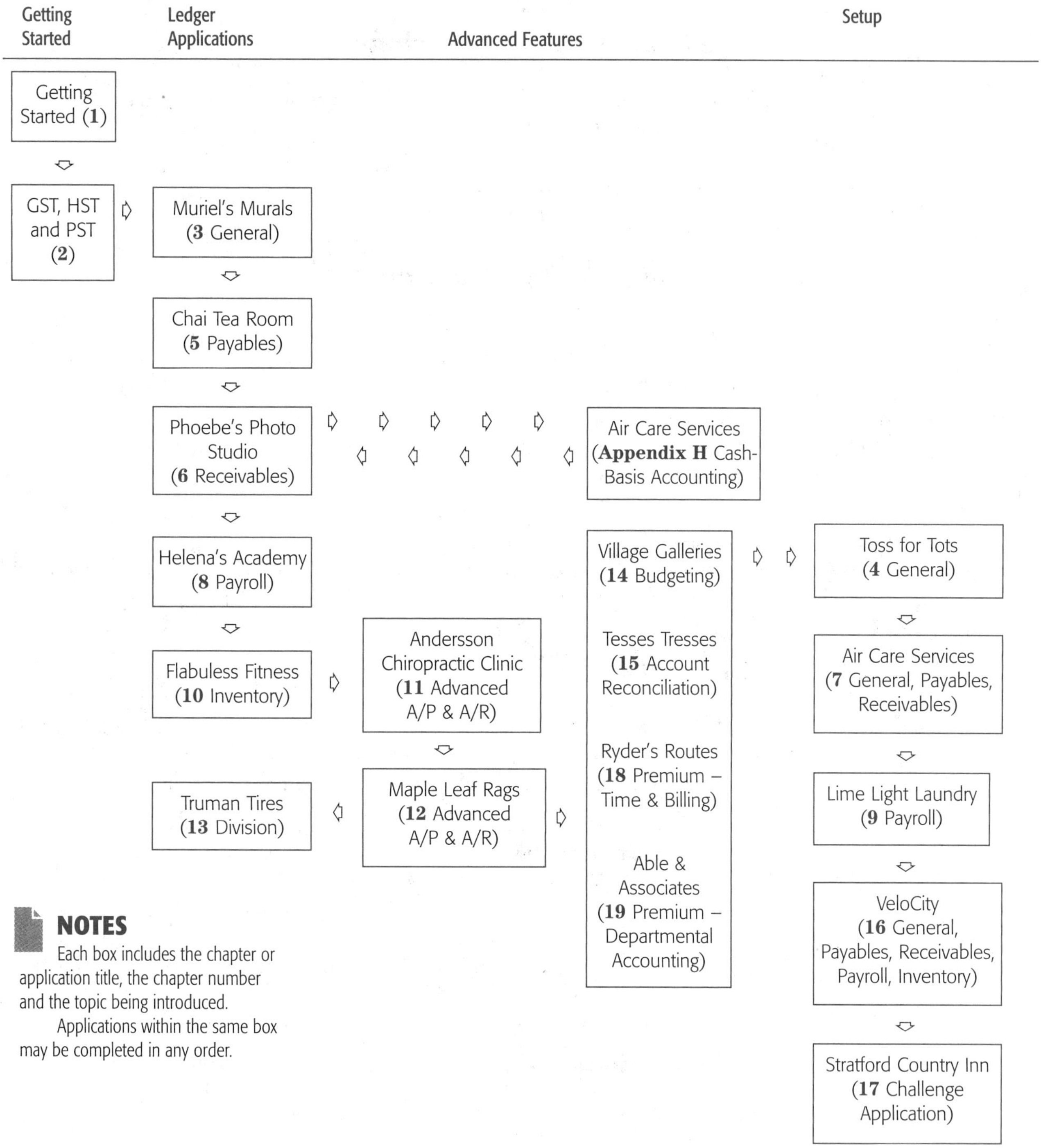

NOTES

Each box includes the chapter or application title, the chapter number and the topic being introduced.

Applications within the same box may be completed in any order.

Supplements

The Student Text Enrichment Site

A text enrichment site accompanies this text: www.pearsoncanada.ca/text/purbhoo2013. This site has an online banking simulation for VeloCity in Chapter 16, including the bank statement that you can download for reconciliation. Instructions for accessing the site and completing the simulation are in Appendix I on the Student DVD.

CourseSmart for Students

NOTES
The author wishes to advise users of this text that the information about CourseSmart for Students (first paragraph) and CourseSmart for Instructors is provided by CourseSmart.

CourseSmart goes beyond traditional expectations — providing instant, online access to the textbooks and course materials you need at an average savings of 60%. With instant access from any computer and the ability to search your text, you'll find the content you need quickly, no matter where you are. And with online tools such as highlighting and note-taking, you can save time and study efficiently. See all of the benefits at www.coursesmart.com/students.

CourseSmart students will download the Premium Version Backup files to work with the text. The additional appendix files that are on the Student DVD will be included as chapters with the text for online access. The Accounting Cycle Tutorial is not included with the CourseSmart version of the text.

Instructor Supplements

- **Solutions** Solutions for all applications in the text are available as Sage 50 Premium Accounting backup files. These files have all the source document transactions in the text completed. The files must be restored with the Sage 50 program and all reports may be displayed or printed.
- **Additional Setup Files** Backup files for the setup chapters (Chapters 4, 7, 9, 16 and 17) are provided with setup completed and ready for entry of source documents. Two additional files are provided for Chapter 16 — for journal entry beginning in the second and third month of the applications. Files for bank reconciliation are also included: February bank reconciliation for Tesses Tresses; Case 8 in Appendix D for VeloCity; and Case 2 in Appendix D for Stratford Country Inn. Appendix D is on the Student DVD.
- **Source Documents** Source document files for all chapters are available. These PDF-formatted source document files do not include any keystrokes and are available only from your Pearson sales representative.
- **Instructor's Manual** The Instructor's Manual is offered in two parts. The first is a file in PDF format with information about all the instructor resource materials, teaching and testing suggestions and some troubleshooting tips. The second part, Answers to Review Questions and Cases, includes answers to all the end-of-chapter questions and cases (Appendix D on the Student DVD). This part is available as a PDF and a Microsoft Word document so that instructors may choose or modify individual answers.
- **Test Item File** Multiple-choice tests (with over 500 questions) organized by textbook chapter and several applied tests that require students to set

up company files and enter source documents using Sage 50 are provided. The applied tests have alternate versions and may be completed as intermediate or end-of-course tests. All test files are provided in Microsoft Word format and may be modified by instructors. Solutions are included for all test items. For increased flexibility, the applied test solutions are Sage 50 backup files at two stages of completion: with the setup completed but history not finished and with all source transactions completed. The setup solution files may be given as separate tests (entering source transactions only) or they may be modified to create your own tests.

All instructor supplements except the source document files may be downloaded from the Instructors' Resource Site. Information about access to the Instructors' Resource Site can be obtained from your Pearson Canada sales representative.

- **CourseSmart for Instructors** CourseSmart goes beyond traditional expectations — providing instant, online access to the textbooks and course materials you need at a lower cost for students. And even as students save money, you can save time and hassle with a digital eTextbook that allows you to search for the most relevant content at the very moment you need it. Whether it's evaluating textbooks or creating lecture notes to help students with difficult concepts, CourseSmart can make life a little easier. See how when you visit www.coursesmart.com/instructors.

ACKNOWLEDGMENTS

As this project is winding down, it is time to recognize all the people who helped make it happen. This is the most important page in the book. On a day-to-day basis, we often do not take enough time to say thank you, so I hope to make up for some of these oversights now.

Having fewer new faces on the project at Pearson Canada also meant fewer glitches. Megan Burns returned from a leave to resume her role as developmental editor. She has recently accepted a position elsewhere and I will miss the opportunity to work with her in the future. Megan Farrell, acquisitions editor, negotiated contracts including the coordination with Sage. Avinash Chandra, project manager, brings experience and calm support to his work and has been a pleasure to work with again. Anthony Leung's creative efforts never seem to end. Each year, working within the constraints provided by the software and a title that changes very little, his results are original, artistic and professional in appearance. Anthony, this design is one of my favourites. Gary Bennet, Vice-President and Editorial Director, operates quietly in the background at the head of this team, but his busy schedule always finds time for our chats and offers a sympathetic ear when I need to air my grievances.

In her second year of working on this text, Leanne Rancourt in her dual roles as copy editor and production editor has been an invaluable resource — professional, efficient and effective — fixing errors while remaining open to suggestions. Thank you once again Leanne. Susan Bindernagel proofread the entire manuscript in the very short timeframe available for this stage, and Efren Barrato checked all the keystrokes and worked through all the accounting transactions, providing the additional pairs of eyes that, as usual, find things that others have missed. However, any remaining errors are my responsibility — without the efforts of this team there would be many more.

The support of employees at Sage, especially Simon Gatto and Jim Collins, have been helpful throughout this project. We are also grateful for the cooperation of Sage Payment Solutions, Beanstream and Right Networks — by providing access to their programs students are able to see how Sage 50 can reach even further into the business world.

Kathleen McGill also filled an important role. As sponsoring editor at Pearson Canada she sought out instructors to complete surveys and compiled the results from this feedback. And I want to thank the instructors who took the time to complete the surveys, providing the feedback that helped to shape this text.

Part 1
Getting Started

CHAPTER ONE

Getting Started

OBJECTIVES

After completing this chapter, you should be able to

- ***start*** the Sage 50 program
- ***open*** a working copy to access the data files for a business
- ***restore*** backup files to access data files for a business
- ***understand*** the help feature in Sage 50
- ***save*** your work
- ***back up*** your data files
- ***finish*** your session
- ***change*** default date format settings

GETTING STARTED

WARNING!

In 2013, Sage Simply Accounting was renamed Sage 50.

You will be unable to open the data files with Sage Simply Accounting 2012 or earlier versions.

The Student DVD with Data Files will be referred to as the Student DVD throughout the text.

NOTES

The instructions in this chapter for starting the program and copying files refer to Windows 7 procedures. If you are using a different version of Windows, please refer to Sage 50 and Windows Help and manuals for assistance with these procedures.

Sage 50 works best when Internet Explorer is your default browser and you keep your Internet connection open.

Data Files and Abbreviations

The applications in this workbook were prepared using Windows 7 and the Sage 50 Premium Accounting 2013 and Sage 50 Pro Accounting 2013 (Release 1) software packages produced by Sage. Before 2013, this program was named Sage Simply Accounting (Premium and Pro). You will be unable to open the data files with Sage Simply Accounting 2012 or earlier versions. Later releases and versions of the software use later income tax tables and may have changes in screens or keystrokes. If you have a version other than 2013 Release 1, you can download and install the Sage 50 Premium Accounting – Student Version program to work through the applications. Refer to Appendix A, page A–10, if you are installing the Student version.

The instructions in this workbook have been written for a stand-alone PC with a DVD drive and a hard drive with Windows correctly installed. Your printer(s) should be installed and accessible through the Windows program. Refer to Windows Help and manuals for assistance with these procedures.

This workbook reflects the author's approach to working with Sage 50. There are alternative approaches to setting up company accounts and working with the software. Refer to Sage 50 and Windows Help and manuals for further details.

DATA APPLICATION FILE NAMES AND LOCATIONS (All folders and files are located in C:\SageData13\)			
Company	Full File Installation	Backup File Installation	Chapter
Getting Started	Start\start.SAI	start1.CAB	1
Muriel's Murals	Murals\murals.SAI	murals1.CAB	3
Toss for Tots	Template\skeleton.SAI	skeleton1.CAB	4
Chai Tea Room	Chai\chai.SAI	chai1.CAB	5
Phoebe's Photo Studio	Photo\photo.SAI	photo1.CAB	6
Air Care Services	user setup required	user setup required	7
Helena's Academy	Helena\helena.SAI	helena1.CAB	8
Lime Light Laundry	Limelite\limelite.SAI	limelite1.CAB	9
Flabuless Fitness	Flabuless\flabuless.SAI	flabuless1.CAB	10
Andersson Chiropractic Clinic	Andersson\andersson.SAI	andersson1.CAB	11
Maple Leaf Rags	Maple\maple.SAI	maple1.CAB	12
Truman Tires	Truman\truman.SAI	truman1.CAB	13
Village Galleries	Village\village.SAI	village1.CAB	14
Tesses Tresses	Tess\tess.SAI	tess1.CAB	15
VeloCity	user setup required	user setup required	16
Stratford Country Inn	user setup required	user setup required	17
Ryder's Routes (Prem.)	Ryder\ryder.SAI	ryder1.CAB	18
Able & Associates Inc. (Prem.)	Able\able.SAI	able1.CAB	19
Phoebe's Photo Studio (Cash-Basis)	Cash\photo-cash.SAI	cash1.CAB	Appendix H

The applications increase in complexity. Each one introduces new ledgers, setups or features as shown in the following chart:

DATA APPLICATION	**LEDGER USED**						**OTHER**
	GL	**AP**	**AR**	**PAY**	**INV**	**DIV**	
Muriel's Murals	*						
Toss for Tots	*						2
Chai Tea Room	*	*					
Phoebe's Photo Studio	*	*	*				3
Air Care Services	*	*	*				2, 3
Helena's Academy	*	*	*	*			
Lime Light Laundry	*	*	*	*			2
Flabuless Fitness	*	*	*	*	*		3
Andersson Chiropractic Clinic	*	*	*				
Maple Leaf Rags	*	*	*				3, 4, 7
Truman Tires	*	*	*	*	*	*	3, 7, 9
Village Galleries	*	*	*	*	*		3, 5, 7
Tesses Tresses	*	*	*		*		6
VeloCity	*	*	*	*	*		2, 3, 4, 7
Stratford Country Inn	*	*	*	*	*		1, 3, 7, 8
Ryder's Routes	*	*	*	*	*		PREMIUM 1
Able & Associates Inc.	*	*	*	*	*		PREMIUM 2
Phoebe's Photo Studios (Appendix H)	*	*	*				10

LEDGERS

GL = General Ledger
AP = Accounts Payable
AR = Accounts Receivable
PAY = Payroll
INV = Inventory
DIV = Division or Project Allocations

Other:
1 All realistic source documents (most chapters have some realistic source documents)
2 Setup application with keystrokes
3 Credit cards
4 Internet links
5 Budgeting
6 Account reconciliation
7 Foreign currency transactions
8 Setup application without keystrokes
9 Credit card processing
10 Cash-basis accounting

PREMIUM 1 Time & Billing; Build from Bill of Materials; Inventory locations (Premium version only)
PREMIUM 2 Departmental Accounting (Premium version only)

NOTES

Applications in Chapters 1 through 17 can be completed with both the Pro and the Premium versions. For the applications in Chapters 18 and 19, you must use the Premium version.

Data files for the applications in Chapters 4, 7, 9, 16 and 17 – the setup chapters – are not set up in advance. You must create those files on your own.

In addition to the data files, the Student DVD includes data files for cash-basis accounting in Appendix H (Cash folder or cash1.CAB backup file) and a backup file velobank1.CAB (Bank folder) for online banking in Appendix I. Appendices H and I are on the Student DVD as PDF files.

The Sage 50 Program

Sage 50 is an integrated accounting program with many features that are suitable for small and medium-sized businesses. It includes several ledgers and journals that work together so that data entered in one part of the program will be linked to and available in other parts of the program. Thus ledgers are automatically updated from journal entries, and reports always include the most recent transactions and ledger changes. A business can use one or more of the accounting modules: General, Payables, Receivables, Payroll, Inventory, Project and, for the Premium and Quantum versions, Time & Billing. You need to set up only the features you use. Thus, if payroll is not used, there is no need to set up the Payroll module, and it can be hidden from view. A more complete description of the program and its features is presented in Chapter 16, pages 621–622.

Sage 50 Program Components

NOTES
For assistance with installing the Sage 50 program, refer to Appendix A.

NOTES
You can access the Sample Data file from the Sage 50 Welcome Select Company screen shown on page 7.

When you select the Typical Installation option, several components will be installed:

- **Sage 50 Program**: the program that you will need to perform the accounting transactions for your company.
- **Sample Data**: complete records for a sample company — Universal Construction.
- **Templates**: predefined charts of accounts and settings for a large number of business types.
- **Crystal Reports Print Engine**, **Customizable Forms** and **Management Reports**: a variety of commonly used business forms and reports and the program to access and print them.
- **Microsoft Office Documents**: a variety of Microsoft Office documents designed for integrated use with Sage 50.
- **Manuals & Tutorials**: documentation and videos to help you learn the program.
- **Add-in for Microsoft Outlook**: a program link that connects your data with Microsoft Outlook.
- **Sage 50 Business Intelligence**: a program that allows more extensive customization of reports. The Reports menu has a link to this program, but you must purchase the licence to use it after the initial 30-day trial period.

NOTES
The Pro version does not have the add-in for Microsoft Outlook.
The Student version does not have Sage 50 Business Intelligence.

The Student Data DVD

NOTES
Sage 50 writes directly to your working data file as you enter transactions. Therefore, you cannot use read-only files as your working copy. All CD and DVD files are read-only files, so you cannot open the Sage 50 data files from the Student DVD.

Before you begin the applications, you must copy the data to your hard drive. The Student DVD has both full data files and Sage 50 backup files. The full data files are large and will take longer to install, so we provide only backup files for supplementary data files (refer to page xii) and for Pro users. Furthermore, you cannot work from CD or DVD files because they are read-only files. Keep the Student DVD in a safe place in case you need to start over from the original files. The following instructions will copy all the files to your hard drive and create the necessary folders.

Installing Your Data

WARNING!
Unless you have experience working with Windows folders, we recommend using the auto-install feature on the Student DVD to install your data set.

The Student DVD contains Pro and Premium versions of the data files and several supplementary files for the book. It also has programs that will automatically copy the data to a new SageData13 folder on your hard drive (drive C:). If you want to use a different location for your data files, proceed to page 6.

You must work with the correct version of the data set. If you are working with the Pro version, install the Pro data files — you cannot open Premium version files. If you are working with the Premium (or Student) version, install the Premium data files.

If you are using the **Pro version**, refer to Pro Version margin notes throughout the text for the differences between the Pro 2013 and Premium 2013 versions.

Insert the **Student DVD** into your DVD drive. The home page appears:

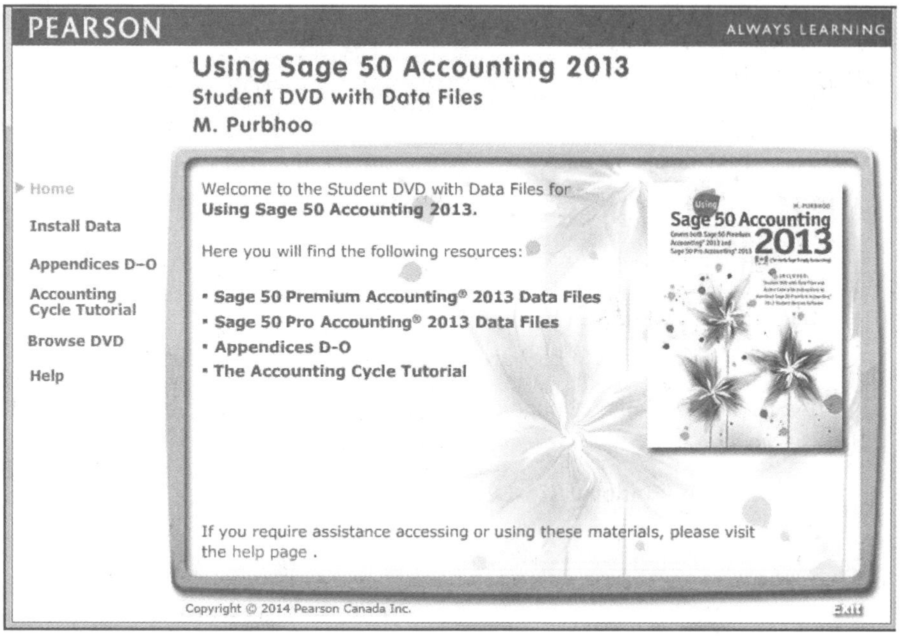

This page shows your options for installing data files and viewing the additional resources and allows you to access these options from the left-hand side pane.

Click **Install Data** to see your data installation options:

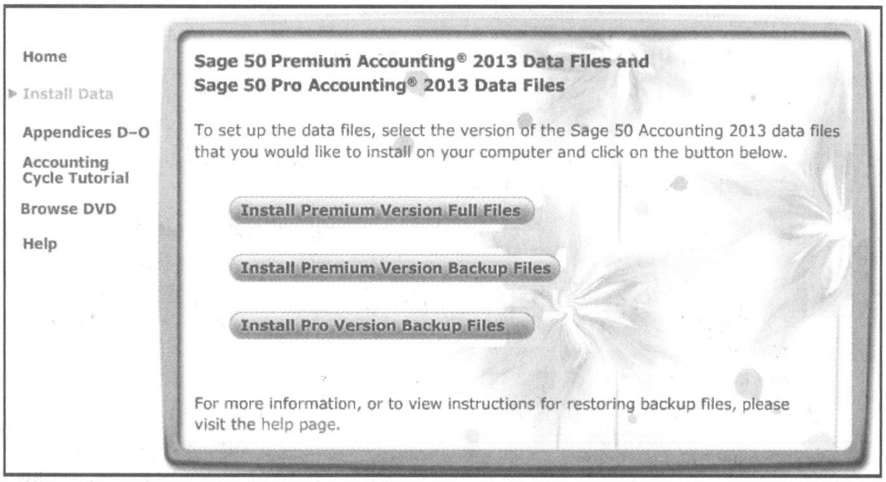

All data installation options will create the SageData13 folder on your hard drive Local Disk C: or OS C:, and all files will be placed in this new folder.

The **Install Premium Version Full Files** option (~550 MBytes) will copy folders and files for each company data set in the primary keystroke chapters. In addition, you will have backup files for online banking and importing entries from an accountant. This installation requires substantially more time for copying the files.

The **Install Premium Version Backup Files** option (~60 MBytes) will install backup files for all the applications in the text except the setup chapters. When you restore these with Sage 50, the default location will be the same as that for the Full File Installation option. If you are working on a slower computer, we recommend this option.

NOTES

If you are working with the Quantum version, you should install the Premium version files. Your program will automatically upgrade the files to the Quantum version when you open or restore them.

NOTES

If the Student DVD does not start automatically, open your Computer or Windows Explorer window. Right-click the DVD and click Explore. Double-click Start.exe to run the DVD.

Clicking Browse DVD on the DVD home page (in the left navigation bar) will open the DVD directory and list all the files on the Student DVD.

NOTES

The Student DVD also has an appendix that reviews accounting principles and an interactive Accounting Cycle Tutorial that introduces basic accounting procedures for manual accounting.

NOTES

You will see a black DOS Command screen scrolling through all the files as they are being copied to your hard drive. There are thousands of individual files in the full version data set, so this will take some time.

All data files will be copied to C:\SageData13\, the starting point we use throughout the text.

If you reinstall the files, you will be prompted to replace the older files. Your options are to replace all (type A), replace just this one file (type Y) or do not replace this one file (type N). Press (enter) after making your choice. Choosing All (typing A) will automatically replace all the files and you will not see this same prompt for each of the thousands of individual files.

The **Install Pro Version Backup Files** option will install backup files for the applications for Pro users. Pro version files are provided only in backup format. Instructions for restoring backup files begin on page 22.

Click **Install Pro Version Backup Files** to copy the data set for Pro 2013.

For Premium, Student Premium and Quantum version data files,

Click **Install Premium Version Full Files**, or

Click **Install Premium Version Backup Files**.

While the files are being copied, you will see a black DOS window that scrolls through all the files being copied. This will take some time if you are installing the Premium Version Full Files, so please be patient. (Read the margin Notes.)

When all the files have been copied, you will see the following message:

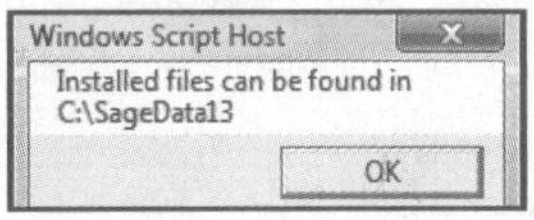

Click **OK**. The data files are located in C:\SageData13. The DOS window closes.

If the Student DVD home page does not open automatically when you insert the Student DVD,

Click the **Windows Start icon**  on your desktop task bar. **Type** `run` in the Search field and **press** (enter) to open the Run window.

Type `d:\start.exe` (where D: is the drive letter for your DVD drive).

Click **OK**.

You can also view the supplementary files on the DVD. You can save these PDF files to your hard drive or print them if you want.

Click **Appendices D–O** and then **click** the **file** you want.

Close the **PDF file** when you have finished viewing or printing it.

Click **Exit** to close the Student DVD window.

All the data files for the book are now located in the new SageData13 folder in drive C:. We will use the shorthand C: instead of Local Disk C: or OS C:. We will open and restore the backups from this folder and use it as our working data folder.

NOTES

Keystroke instructions that you must use are shown with highlighted text in indented paragraphs, like the ones on this page starting with **Click**, **Type** and **Close**.

The command words are in **bold black** type and the object of the command is shown in **colour**.

Text you should type or key in is shown in `Courier font` after the command word **Type**.

Working with Other File Locations

You can copy the files to a different location by copying the data from the DVD just as you would copy other files to your hard drive. Choose the correct version of the data set (Pro or Premium), and be sure to copy the entire folder for each data set to include both the SAJ folder and the .SAI file. These must be kept together for Sage 50 to be able to open the data file.

NOTES

Alternative instructions or commands that you may need to use are shown in indented paragraphs without highlighting, like the paragraph beside this note, beginning with "You can copy the files to."

You cannot open a Sage 50 data file directly from a CD or DVD, but you can restore a Sage 50 backup file from a CD or DVD. You must save the file on your hard drive before you can work with the data.

You can also work on a removable USB drive in Sage 50 because this is a rewritable medium.

Starting Sage 50

From your Windows desktop, if you are using Windows 7,

Click **Start**  (on the task bar) so the pop-up menu appears.

If you have opened the program recently, its name may be pinned to the shortcuts list above All Programs:

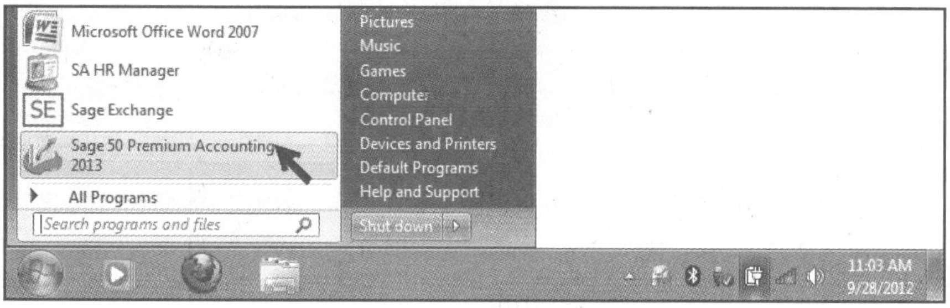

In this case, you can click Sage 50 Premium Accounting 2013. Otherwise,

Point to All Programs.

Click **Sage** and **Sage 50 Premium Accounting 2013** and **point to Sage 50 Premium Accounting 2013** as shown in the following screen:

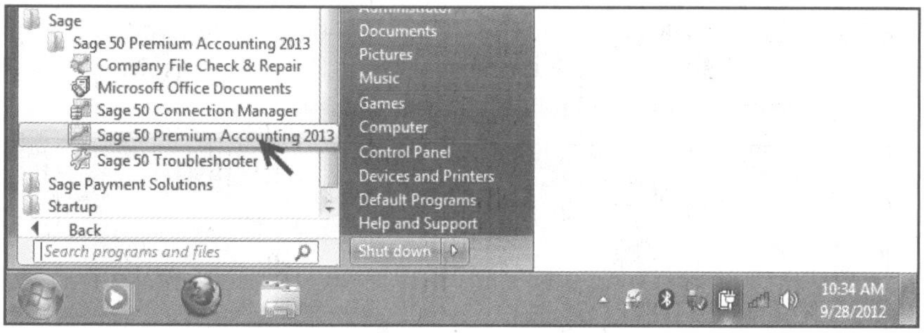

Click **Sage 50 Premium Accounting 2013** from this submenu.

You will open the registration screen the first time you use the program. Otherwise, you will see the Sage 50 Welcome and Select Company screen:

If you have not yet registered the program, refer to Appendix A, pages A-5–A-7 in the text. Until you register and activate the program, you will be allowed to use the program only for a limited time. The Student version must be activated before you can use it. Refer to Appendix A, pages A-12–A-14.

If you are restoring the backup file, refer to page 22 for instructions.

Opening a Data File

The opening Sage 50 Welcome and Select Company screen gives you several options: working with the sample company files, creating new company files, restoring backup files or working with existing data files. The next time, because we will have worked with the program before, the option to Open The Last Company You Worked On will be

PRO VERSION

The desktop shortcut is labelled Sage 50 Pro Accounting 2013.

You will choose Sage 50 Pro Accounting 2013 in the Programs list and then click Sage 50 Pro Accounting 2013 to open the Select Company Welcome screen.

NOTES

If you added a desktop shortcut when you installed the program, you can double-click 

to open Sage 50.

WARNING!

You will be allowed to use the program only for a limited time before entering the registration validation codes.

Remember to activate Payroll as well. Refer to Appendix A in this text. You must have a payroll ID code in order to use the Payroll features of the program.

You must register the Student version before you can use it, but you will not need to activate payroll.

Refer to Appendix A for information about registering and activating your program.

NOTES

The Select Company window shows the version you are using. This window has Premium added to the program name.

In Chapter 4, we show the location of the Select Company window option in the View menu.

NOTES

If you are restoring backup files, refer to the instructions on page 22.

added with the name of the file you used (see page 22). If you choose this option when you use the same data set for several work sessions, you will bypass the Open Company window (shown below).

Click **Select An Existing Company**. **Click OK**.

The Sage 50 – Open Company window appears next. The following screen shows the drives in List view:

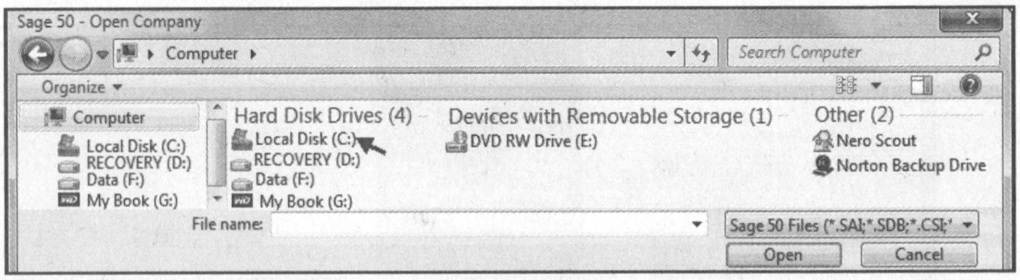

The initial path shown will be for the file you used most recently and it will be selected for you to accept or to change. If this is the first time you are opening a data file, your path will be determined by your program and system settings. Therefore, the file name you see on your screen may be different from the ones we show.

Click **Computer** in the left pane list or in the file path field on top to open the screen we show.

Click **Local Disk (C:)** or the name for the local hard drive C: on your computer and **click Open** to list the folders on this drive. The following screen shows the folders in Details view:

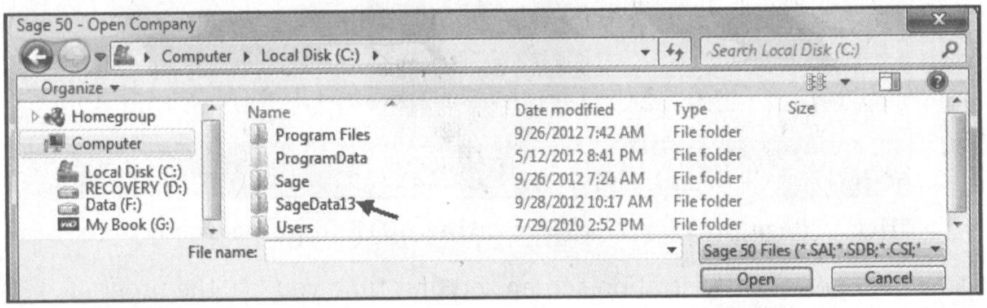

Click **SageData13**. (Click the SageData13 folder icon  if your viewing mode is icons.) Then **click Open** to see the files you installed from the Student DVD. The following screen shows the folders in List view:

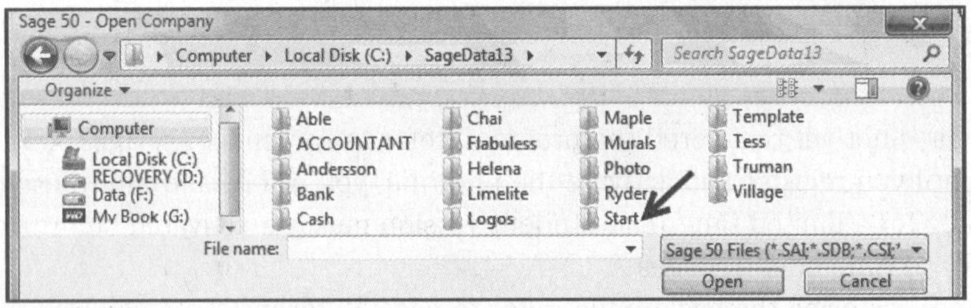

Click **Start** (or its folder icon ) and then **click Open**:

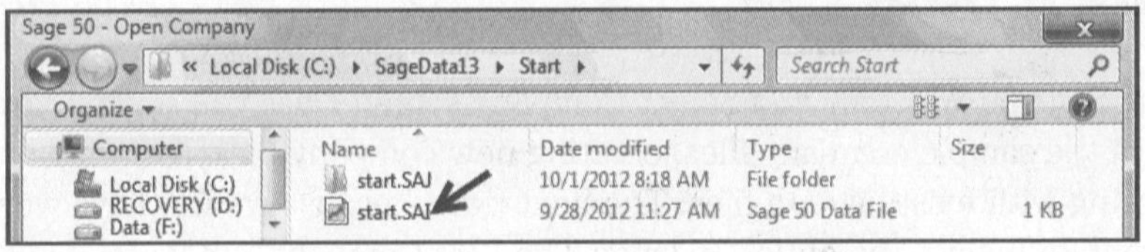

WARNING!
Each application has many files containing different parts of the accounting information. All files must be contained in the same folder. If any file is missing, you will be unable to access the information. The auto-install procedure keeps the necessary files together.

NOTES
Your screens may look different if you have selected different viewing options, such as displaying the folders as icons, details or lists. The viewing options can be changed from the View icon drop-down menu.

NOTES
The path for the most recently used company file will be shown initially. Therefore, we cannot be certain what your screen will show in the path field. Our instructions should direct you to the data files from any location.

NOTES
We show the default location for the Sage 50 program and for the data files from the automatic installation. If you installed the files to a different location, choose the drive for your setup.

PRO VERSION
The first folder on the list is ACCOUNTANT. Refer to page 22 for instructions on restoring backup files.

You can gain access to the company records only from the ***.SAI** file. Sage 50 recognizes this file extension as a Sage 50 format. The remaining data files for the company are in the SAJ folder. Both the .SAI file and the SAJ folder that are part of the data set must be located in the same folder. The complete data path [(C:)>SageData13>Start] is added to the path field near the top of the screen.

Click **start** (or the start icon ), or click **start.SAI** (if you show file extensions) to select it and add it to the File Name field as shown:

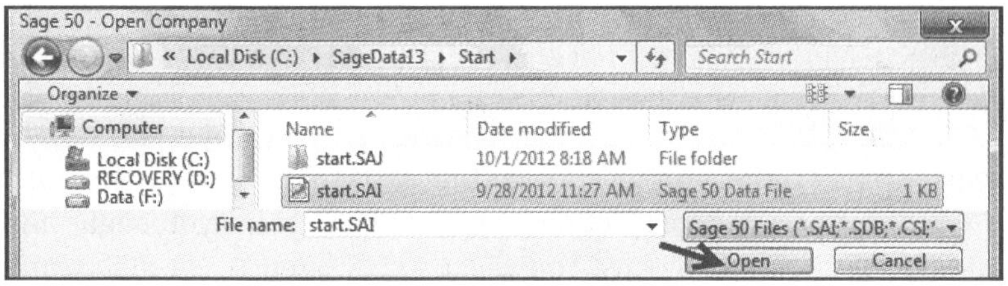

Click **Open** to see the session date screen:

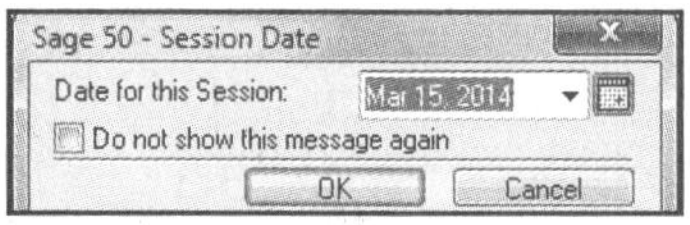

Click **OK** to accept the date and open the Home window. The session date is explained in Chapter 3.

If passwords have been set up for the file, you will see this password entry screen before the session date window:

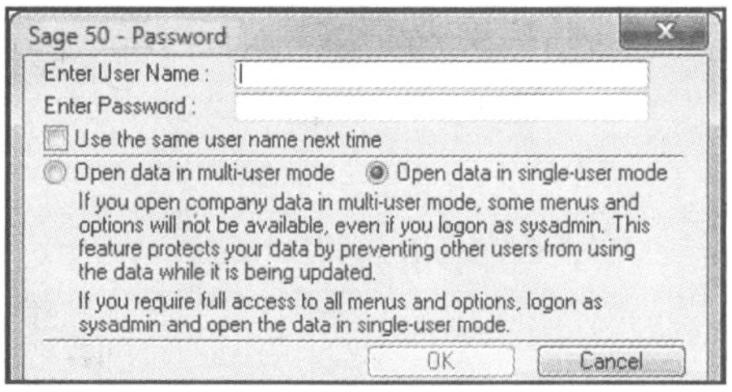

Ask your instructor or site administrator for the name and password to use. Enter your user name and password. Open the file in Single-User Mode. Click OK to open the session date screen. Refer to Chapter 16, page 686, and Appendix G on the Student DVD.

If you see a screen advising that the data has been updated to a new file format, your program may be an earlier version than 2013, and you will be unable to open the data file.

The first time you use the program, you will see a message about automatic program updates (see page A-7). **Do not update your program yet.** Later updates will download later versions and your answers may not match the screens we show.

Do not choose **automatic updates**.

NOTES
Showing the complete file path as we do is a Windows option. The open folder is named in the Search field.

WARNING!
If you are not showing file extensions, you will click start. Do not click the Start.SAJ folder. The folder has a small folder icon beside the name. The .SAI file you need has a Sage 50 program icon beside the name.

NOTES
The session date is explained in Chapter 3, where you will also learn how to change the session date.
The session date drop-down list includes the current session date, the end of the fiscal period and the start of the next fiscal period. The list for any date field includes the dates commonly selected.

NOTES
We have not set passwords for any data files in this text, but your site administrator for the network may have done so. Refer to Appendix G for more information about passwords.

PRO VERSION
You will see an additional message about upgrading to the Premium version of Sage 50.

NOTES
If your update is later than Release 1, you can download the Student Premium Version Release 1 program.

NOTES
You can download updates periodically (from the Help menu) when you have finished working through the applications in this text.

NOTES
The contents of the Getting Started screen will change to match the industry or business type of your company data set.

The Sage 50 Getting Started Welcome screen opens:

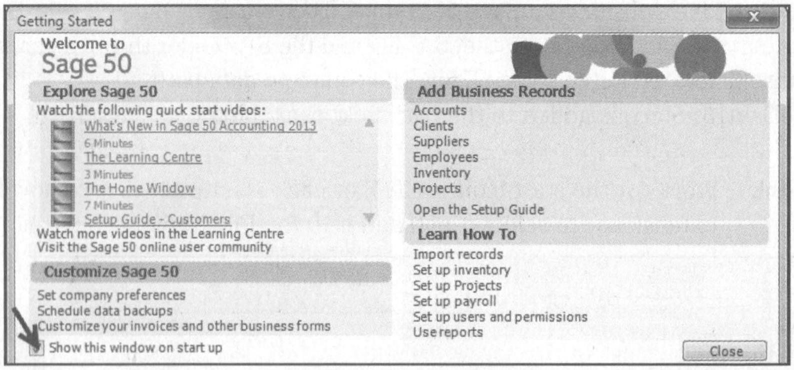

PRO VERSION
The terms Customers and Vendors will replace Clients and Suppliers.

This screen outlines various options for getting assistance with the program. These include brief video tutorials and instructions for some basic steps you might need when setting up data files for a new company. You will see this screen each time you open a data file in Sage 50 2013, unless you have turned it off. After reading the options, you can close this screen now so that it will not appear each time you open this file. For other data files in this text, we have already turned off the selection.

Click **Show This Window On Start Up** to remove the ✓.

Click **Close** to continue.

Sage 50 Dashboard

The main Sage 50 Dashboard Home window should now be open:

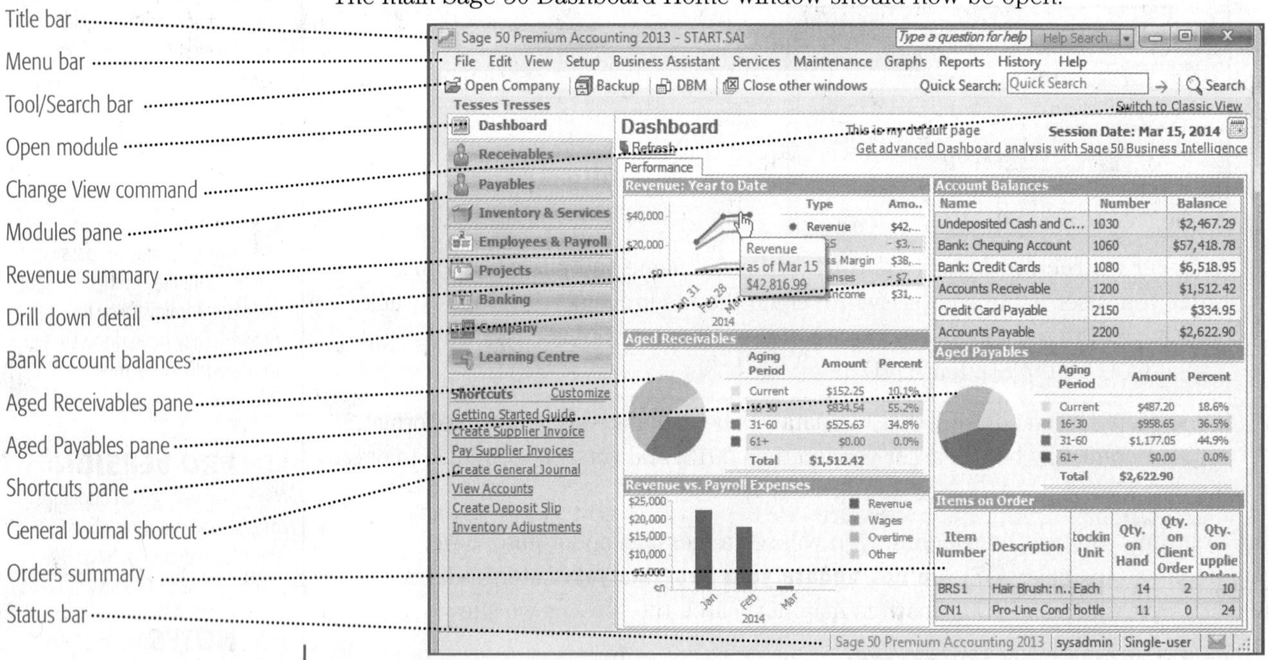

PRO VERSION
The program name in the title bar is Sage 50 Pro Accounting 2013.

The **title bar** is at the top of the Home window, and it contains the program name, Sage 50 Premium Accounting 2013, the file name, START.SAI (or START), the Help Search field, Control Menu icon and the size buttons. The **main menu bar** comes next with the **tool bar** below. Tool buttons provide quick access to commonly used menu items and the **search** function. The Search field enables you to look up information in any journal or ledger. Different windows in the program have different buttons on the tool bar. Below the tool bar, you will find the command to **Switch To Classic View** (see pages 13–14).

The Dashboard provides several key performance indicators in the various panes, including both graphic views and tables. Account balances for all bank, credit card, receivable and payable accounts show the cash position of the company. The first graph — for Revenue — has revenue and cost of goods sold and other expense information providing both gross margin income and net income for the fiscal year to date. The Receivables and Payables graphs are pie charts with the totals divided among the different aging periods defined for the business. The proportion of the total that is overdue in each case is immediately apparent. The final two charts on the Dashboard show the relation between payroll expenses and total revenue and the items on order. This particular company has no employees, so the payroll expenses are zero.

Click the **Revenue line** to see the amount represented in this line.

Click some **other graph segments** to see the amounts they represent.

For all graphs, details will appear in a bubble when you click on part of the graph. In the screen on the previous page, the information for total revenue is provided. Double-clicking any part of the graph will open the detailed Sage 50 report for that information.

Sage 50 graphs and reports are covered further in later chapters for each module.

Click **Receivables** in the Modules pane.

Sage 50 Window (Enhanced View)

The Receivables module window is usually the default Home window:

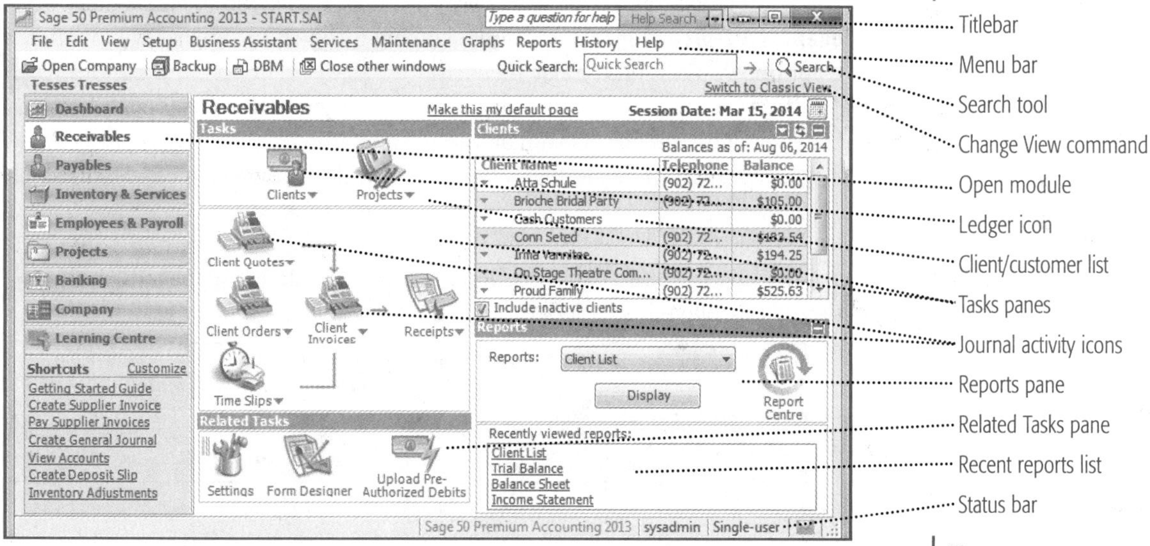

The module Home window is divided into several panes. The **Modules pane** lists all the modules available for this company data set. The open module — Receivables in this illustration — has a lighter background. The Receivables module is the default Home window for most of our chapters, but you can choose any module as the Home window. Activities for the module are represented by separate icons. The Modules pane also has access to the **Learning Centre**. To access a function or activity, click the related icon.

Below the list of modules, the **Shortcuts pane** allows one-click access to as many as 10 different tasks and activities that you set up or customize for each user.

The next column has all the icons you need to complete the activities for the module. The **upper Tasks pane** has the **ledger icon** that allows you to create and modify customer records from the Customers (Clients) window and Project records in the Projects window. The **lower Tasks pane** has the icons for **journal activities** or **transactions**. Use these icons to enter the accounting transactions in this text. Clicking the icon opens the journal directly for that type of transaction.

PRO VERSION

Icon labels do not change. Customers will replace the Clients label for the ledger icon and list. Sales Invoices replaces Client Invoices.

You will not see the Time Slips icon. Time & Billing is a Premium version feature.

NOTES

Appendix B shows a complete chart of alternative terms used in Sage 50 for different types of industries.

In the Premium version, the icon labels change to suit the type of company. For the service company illustrated here, the ledger icon is labelled Clients.

Many ledger and journal icons have a **shortcuts drop-down list arrow**. Clicking an entry in an icon shortcuts list will access the activity directly and bypass the main task window. For example, you can begin adjusting an invoice to make a correction if an entry was posted in error, bypassing the first step of opening the journal.

Click the **shortcuts drop-down list arrow for Client Invoices**:

PRO VERSION
The Pro version does not have the Time Slips icon.

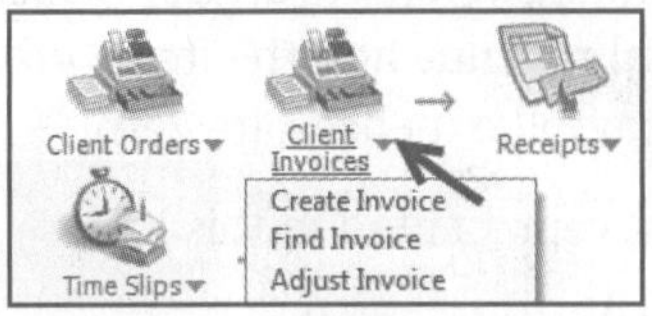

Click some **other shortcuts list arrows** to see the choices.

Below the ledger and journal icons, you will find the **Related Tasks pane**. From the icons in this pane, you can perform other ledger-related activities, such as entering settings for the open ledger.

NOTES
You can hide the telephone number and Balance columns for increased security.

The right-hand column also has three different panes. The first has a **list of ledger accounts** for the selected module. For the Receivables module, the list shows clients or customers with the phone number and outstanding balance. The Payables ledger will show the list of suppliers or vendors. You can hide the extra details.

Below the list of customers or clients, the **Reports pane** allows quick access to all reports for the ledger from the **Reports drop-down list** and to the **Report Centre**, from which you can access all reports. Reports that you displayed most recently are listed in the **Recently Viewed Reports** section. Clicking a report in this list will open it with the report options you selected most recently.

NOTES
In other windows, the status bar describes the purpose of the icon or field that has the pointer.

The **status bar** appears last. In the Enhanced View, the status bar shows the program name and version as well as the user's name.

To work with another module, click the module you want in the Modules pane list.

Click **Employees & Payroll** in the Modules pane.

This module now becomes the Home window, so its icons for ledger and journal activities are displayed. The ledger icon is now labelled Employees, as shown:

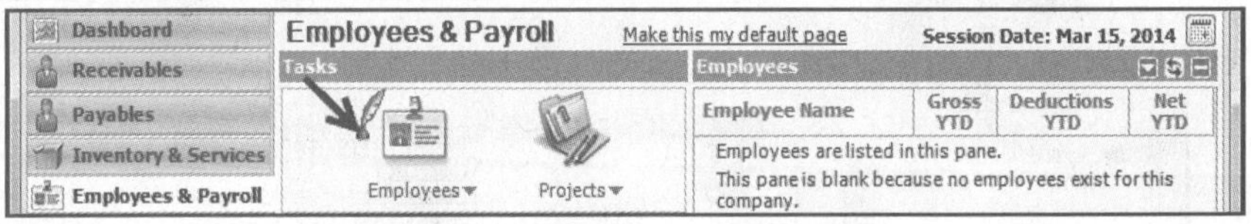

In this module, the quill pen symbol shows that the Payroll Ledger is not set up — the history is not finished. When ledgers are not finished, you can add and change historical data. When you create new company data files, all ledgers have this symbol.

Your Muriel's Murals Home window (in Chapter 3) will show the Company Module with access only to the General Ledger and journals — Chart of Accounts and General Journal. Icons for unused features and ledgers that are not set up will be hidden.

Open and **close** some **other module windows** to see their activity icons.

NOTES
Many Sage 50 windows include a Home window tool that brings the Home window to the front without closing the other windows.

Sage 50 on the Windows Desktop

Click **Receivables** in the Modules pane list. **Click Make This My Default Page** beside the Receivables module heading.

Now each time you open this data file, the Receivables module will be the starting point.

Click **Create General Journal** in the Shortcuts pane list. This will open the General Journal.

Click the **Entry menu**. Your desktop should now look like the one that follows:

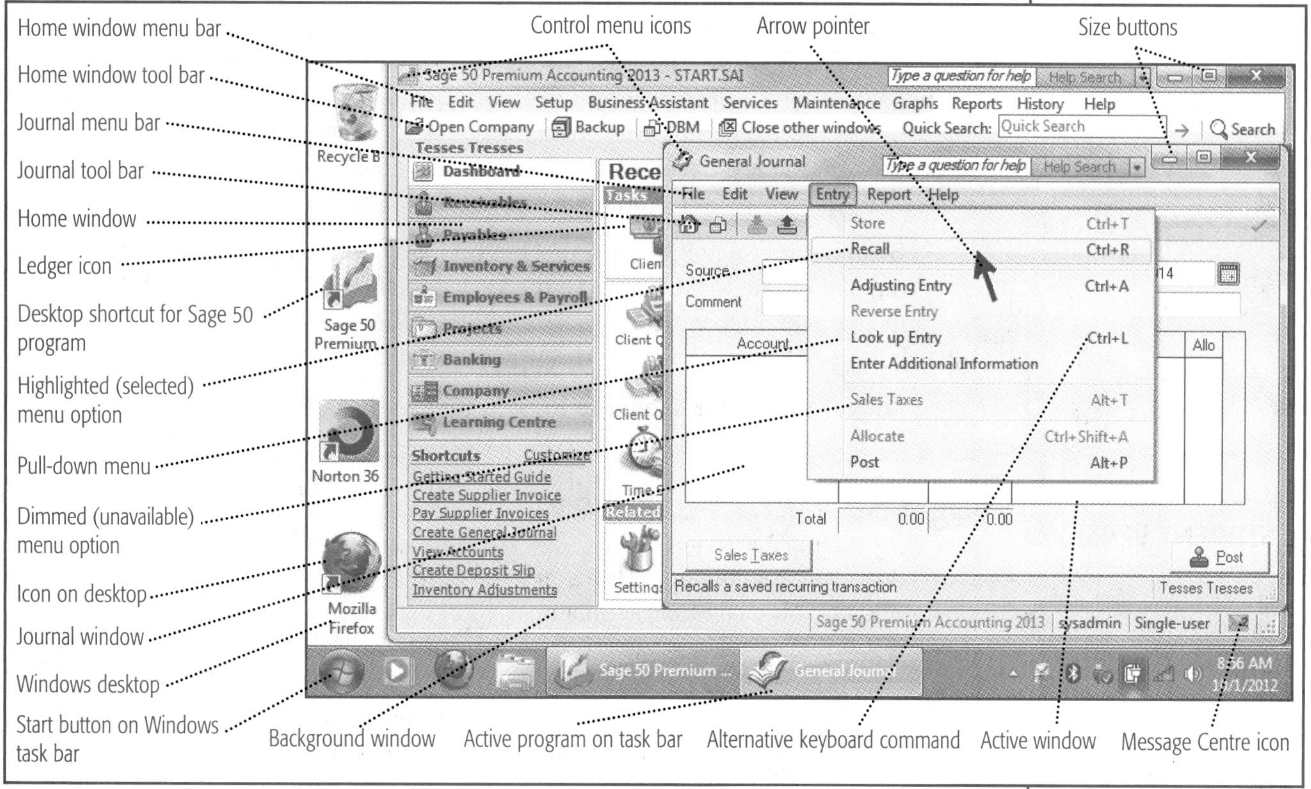

If you have messages from Sage for your account, the message centre icon will have a number in it. Connect to the Internet and then click this icon to see your messages.

Click ☒ to close the Journal window and return to the Home window.

NOTES

We used Windows 7 to illustrate this desktop. If you have a different version of Windows or use different Windows settings, your desktop may look different from the one we show.

Sage 50 Classic View Home Window

Throughout this text, we will work from the Enhanced view Home window. However, we will provide alternate instructions for using the Classic view in the Classic View margin notes.

Click **Switch To Classic View** to change the Home window:

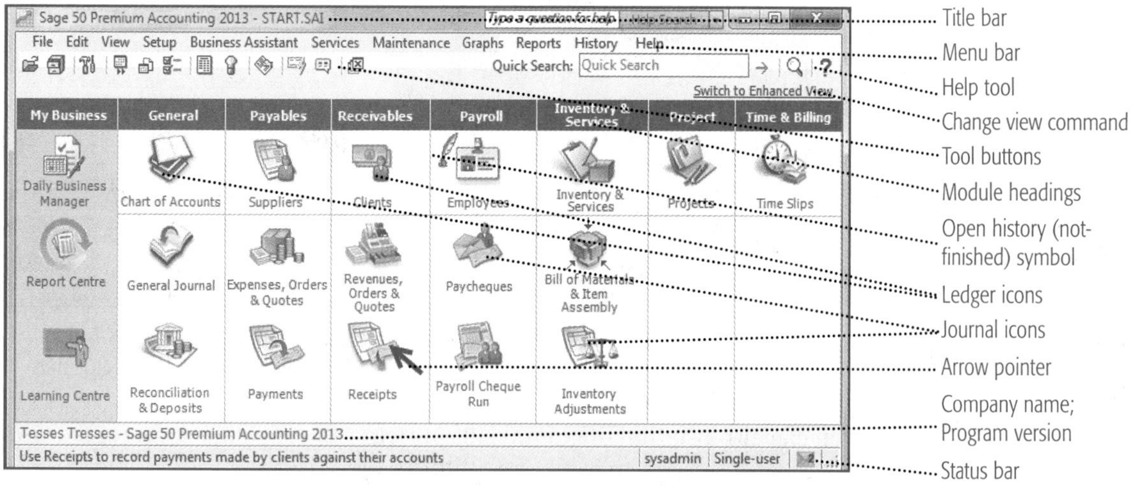

The tool bar in the Classic view has more items than in the Enhanced view. The **ledger** or module names come next with their respective icons filling up the major part of the window. The ledger icons in the top row are below the ledger or module name, and the **journal icons** are under their respective ledgers in the last two icon rows of the window. All journals and ledgers can be accessed from the icons in this single Classic view Home window. Below the journal icons are two more information lines: the company name and the **status bar**. In this example, the status bar describes the purpose of the Receipts Journal because the pointer is on the Receipts icon.

The icons in the **My Business tab column** allow quick access to the Daily Business Manager, Report Centre and Learning Centre.

Hold the mouse pointer on a tool button for a few seconds to see the name or function of the tool button and the keyboard shortcut if there is one. Hold the mouse over an icon to see its description or function in the status bar at the bottom of the window.

Click **Switch To Enhanced View** to change Home window views again.

Sage 50 Help Features

STUDENT VERSION
Student version users may obtain assistance by posting their questions online at <www.SageforStudents.com/forum>.

Sage 50 provides program assistance in several different ways. You can display or print Help information on many topics. General accounting information, advice topics and Sage 50 software assistance are included. You can access Help from the Home window at any time.

The most immediate form of help comes from the **status bar** at the bottom of many program windows. It offers a one-line description of the icon or field that the mouse is pointing to. As you move the mouse around the screen, the status bar information changes accordingly. The message in the status bar is connected to the mouse position only. This may not be the same as the position of the cursor or insertion point, which is located wherever the mouse was when you last clicked the mouse button.

Many settings or options windows include a **Help button** that offers context-sensitive help for the procedure you are using.

Sage 50 Help can be accessed in several ways.

NOTES
The Support Info button on the About Sage 50 screen (from the Help menu) shows your complete registration details.

Click **Learning Centre** in the Modules pane:

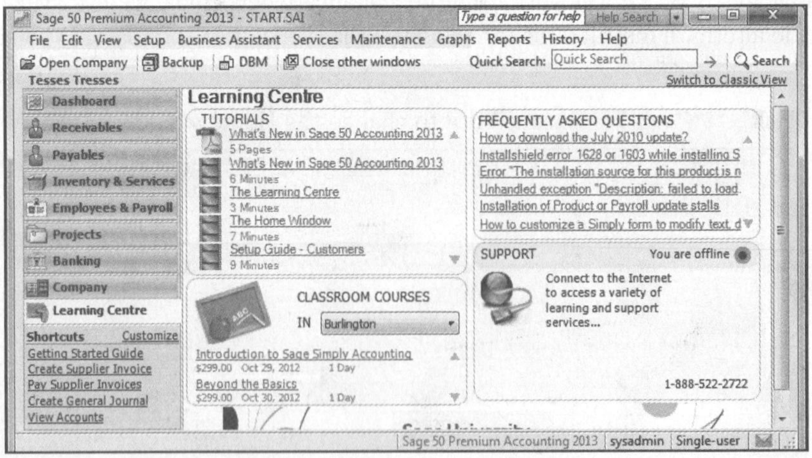

From this centre you can get different types of assistance: access online assistance, run a tutorial, learn about courses and training, look for answers to frequently asked questions, contact a Sage 50 expert or provide feedback to Sage.

You can also use the program's built-in Help.

Click the **Help menu** in the Home window as shown:

The options on this menu include access to Help, the Learning Centre and its options, a description of new features for version 2013 and the Getting Started Guide. In addition you can update the program to a later release, upgrade the program to Premium from Pro (or to Quantum) and see the version number and serial number for your program (About Sage 50 Premium Accounting).

Choose the **Help menu** and **click Search Help** as shown above to open the Sage 50 Help Welcome screen:

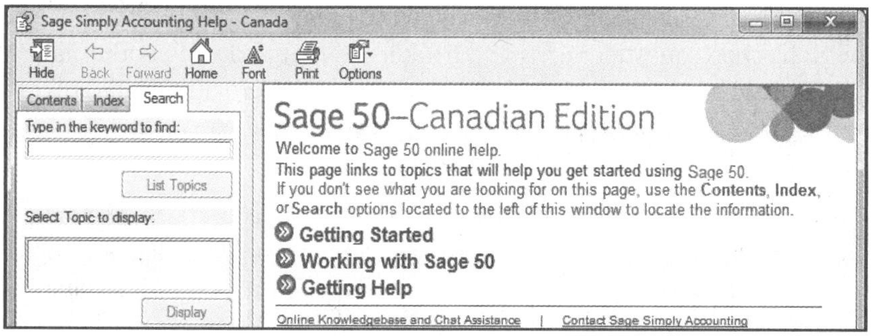

The Help Welcome screen opens with links to several introductory topics and sources of assistance. The **Search tab** is selected in the Options pane on the left-hand side and the information pane is on the right. Initially, the topic fields will be blank.

In the pull-down Help menu shown above, **Use Online Help** is selected (has a ✓).

If your Internet connection is active when you click Search Help and Use Online Help is selected, your starting Help screen will look like the following one:

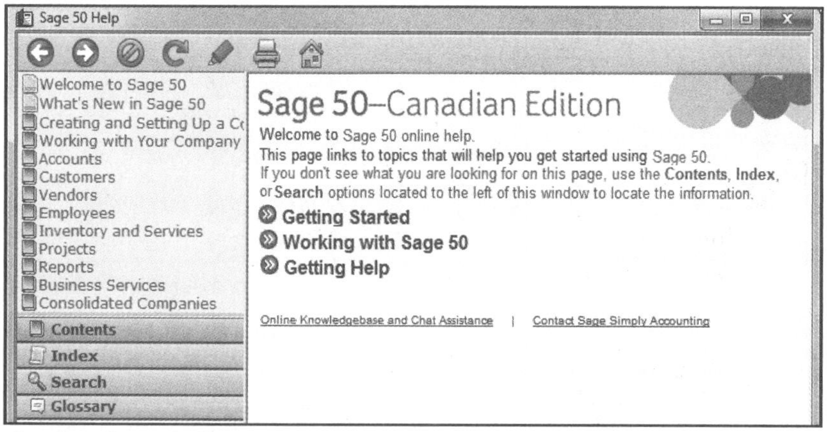

The shortcut icons below the title bar look different, but most of them serve the same purpose. Both windows include Previous, Next, Home window and Print icons. The pen icon replaces the Font icon and an icon for Internet Explorer is added.

Tabs in the upper screen are replaced by function bars in the Online Help window, and Glossary is added as a separate option. Icons in the left-hand side contents pane also look different.

CLASSIC VIEW

Click the Help tool ? on the tool bar or press f1.

NOTES

If your Internet connection is active and Internet Explorer is your default browser, you will have access to online help information. The Help features we show here do not require an Internet connection.

Internet Explorer is the preferred default browser for working with Sage 50.

Click the **Contents tab** in the Options pane, or **click** the **Contents bar** in the lower left-hand side options pane of the Online Help screen:

NOTES

If a topic has subtopics it will have a book icon; you must choose a subtopic with the question or page icon to display. If there are still multiple entries, you will see an additional book icon and you can choose from the list that Sage 50 offers at this stage.

Major topics in the Contents menu have a **book icon** beside them (or in the online version).

Click **Vendors** or click (or or) beside Vendors in the Table of Contents pane to open a list of subtopics.

The book icon beside Vendors has changed to an **open book** icon. The second list of topics has both question icons and book icons that indicate another level of subtopics. Clicking an arrow beside a heading in the information pane will expand the list of topics. The screen above has the Getting Started topic expanded. Clicking an underlined subtopic will open detailed information for it.

When a topic has a **question icon** (or a page icon in the online version) beside it, there is detailed help on that subject. Click the topic or the question icon to display information on that subject in the right-hand side information display pane of the Help window.

Click a book title (or or) to close the book and hide the list of subtopics.

Click **Purchases** or (or) to view the second list of subtopics.

Click **Paying Vendors (Payments)** or (or) to see the next list of subtopics.

Click **Paying A Vendor** (with or beside it):

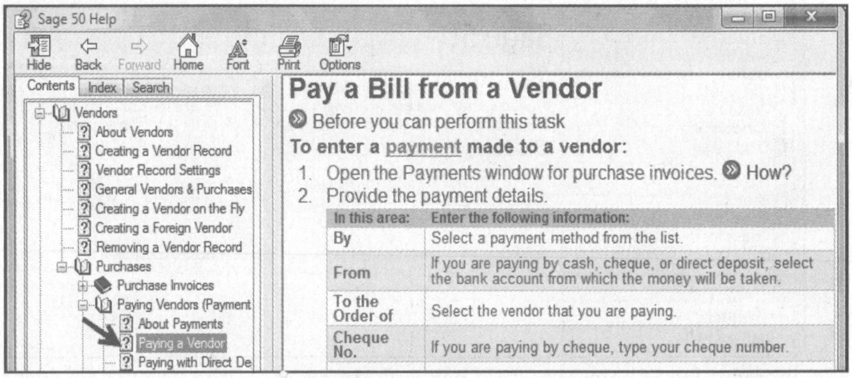

Click any underlined topic in the information pane to display the information for that newly selected topic. Clicking an arrow in the information pane expands the topic.

Click the **Search tab** at the top of the Options pane:

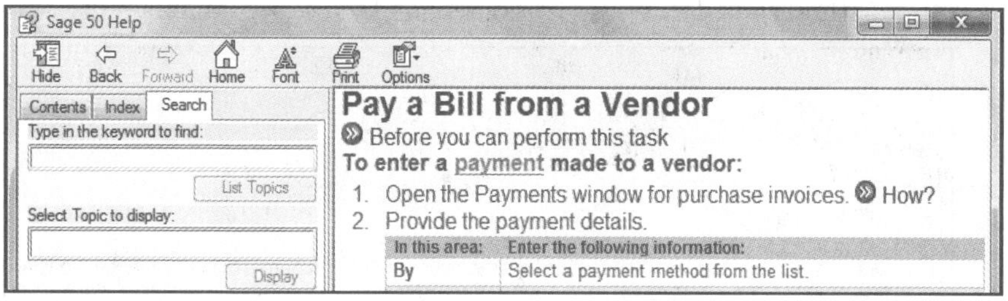

The help information from your previous search is still displayed. A Search field has opened below the Options pane tabs.

Click the **Search field**. **Type** `purchase orders`

Click the **List Topics button** below the Search field:

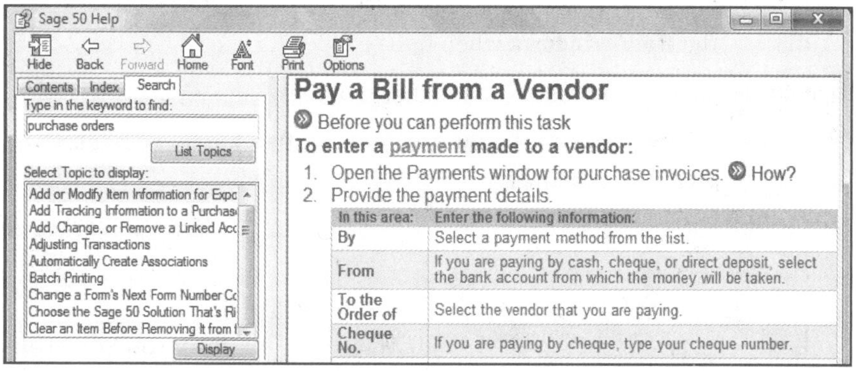

An alphabetic list of topics including your key words is listed. The previous help information remains displayed until a new topic is selected.

Scroll down and **click Enter A Purchase Order**.

Click the **Display button** below the list to see the help on this topic:

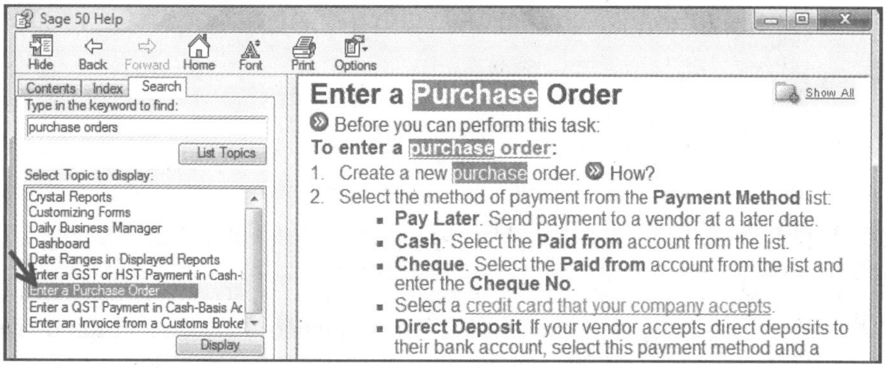

Type `Glossary` in the Search field. **Click List Topics** and then **click Display**. **Click Glossary** in the list of topics. The information pane now includes an alphabetic list of terms.

Click an **underlined entry** to see its definition added below the term:

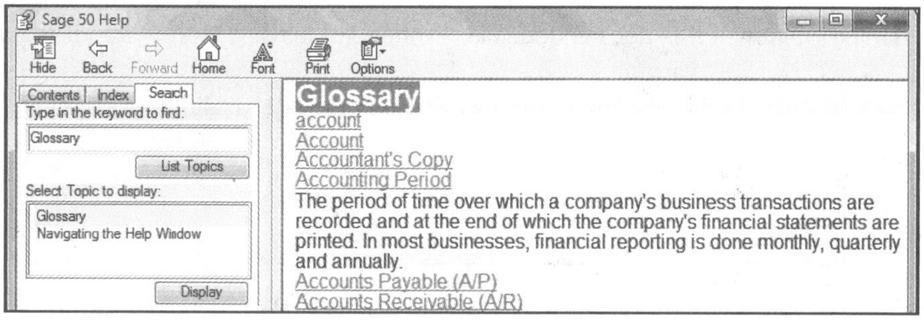

NOTES

The information from your previous search always remains on display until you choose to display another topic.

NOTES

If you have Online Help activated and your Internet connection is open, click the Glossary function bar.

Click the **Index tab** in the Options pane to see an alphabetic list of entries:

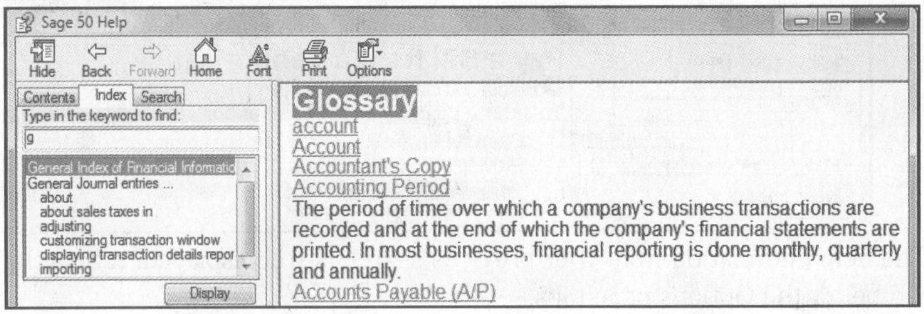

Click an index topic to open the help information. Type a letter in the text field above the list to advance the alphabetic list quickly.

Search for **information** on other topics in the different option screens.

Close the **Help windows** when finished.

Sage 50 also includes **Advice** on a number of topics.

Choose the **Business Assistant menu**, then **click Business Advice** and **All Modules** as shown:

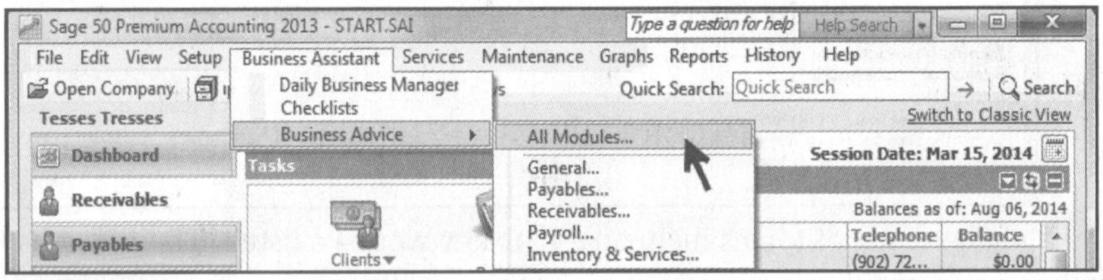

CLASSIC VIEW

In the Classic view, you can click the Advice tool .

Both General Advice and Management Reports will be available.

If a Home window ledger or journal icon is selected when you click the Advice tool, you will see the list of Management Reports for only that module or ledger.

A list of topics opens:

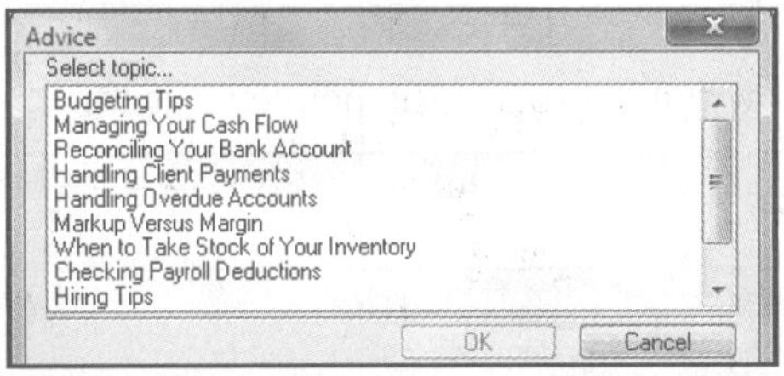

NOTES

If you have not installed the Crystal Report Engine and the customizable forms, Management Reports will not be available.

These topics provide general business information or accounting practices.

Management Reports, available from the Reports menu in the Home window, also provide advice, but the information is specific to the company data set that is open.

Management Reports are available only for ledgers that are not hidden, so the list you see is not always complete. These reports combine the company data with forms and reports provided through the Crystal Report Engine. Management Reports are covered with other reports for each module in the following chapters.

PRO VERSION

Remember that you will see the term Customers instead of Clients.

Click the **topic** you want and then **click OK**. **Close** the **advice report windows** when finished.

A final source of general assistance is available as **automatic advice**. This feature can be turned off from the Setup menu (User Preferences, View, shown on page 82) in the Home window if it is not needed. We recommend leaving it on. When it is turned on, Sage 50 will provide warning statements.

For example, for a customer who has exceeded the credit limit, you will see the following warning:

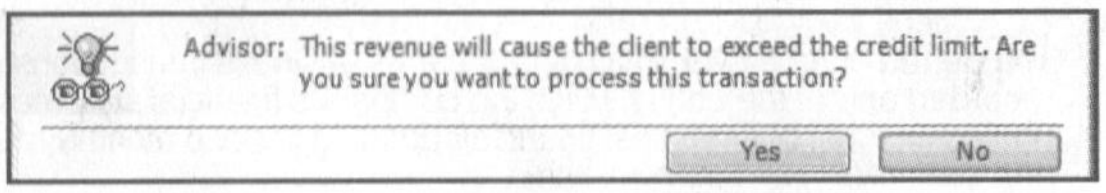

NOTES

If you try to post a sale (client invoice) for any of the listed customers for $10 000, you will see the message about credit limits.

If you try to enter a sale to Irma Vanitee, you will see the message about the customer who pays late.

To proceed, you must make a decision in order to close the advice screen. In the example shown here, you can click Yes to proceed with the sale or No to return to the invoice and make a change (perhaps by asking for a deposit).

Another warning appears when you choose a customer with a history of making late payments:

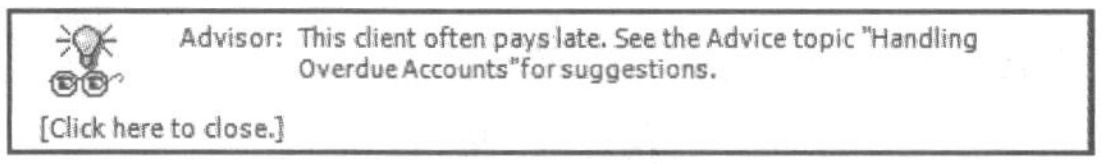

To close this message, click the Advisor icon as indicated [Click Here To Close].

The program also warns when year-end is approaching and it is time to complete year-end adjustments, when your chequing account is overdrawn or when inventory items reach the reorder point.

Click **Receivables** in the Modules pane.

Date Formats and Settings

Before closing the program we will review date format settings. Date accuracy is very important because dates are used for discounts, payment terms and many reports.

Sage 50 has date format control settings within each file that are independent of the display date settings for Windows. When you enter dates using a series of two digits for month, day and year, it is important to know how these will be interpreted. For example, when you type 12-06-05, this date may be June 12, December 6 or June 5 in the year 2005, 1905, 1912 or 2012, depending on whether month, day or year comes first and whether your computer defaults to 1900 dates or is preset for 2000 dates.

Fortunately, Sage 50 allows you to enter and display dates as text. Thus, you can type June 5, 2012, in a date field. And if you want, you can display this date as Jun 05, 2012, even if you enter numbers in the date field. Sage 50 uses three letters to display the month when the text option is selected.

All date fields also have a **Calendar icon** that you can click to access a month-by-month calendar from which you can select a date. These two options will help you avoid making date errors from incorrect orders. To access the date settings,

Click the **Settings icon** in the Related Tasks pane, or **choose** the **Setup menu**, then **click Settings**.

Click **Company** in the list of modules on the left to open the main Company Settings window:

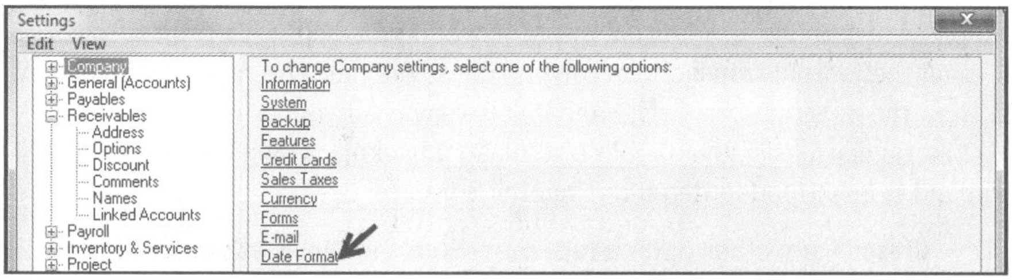

Each entry in the list opens the Settings screen for a different part of the program.

NOTES
Sage 50 allows you to enter earlier session dates but warns you first. If you have advanced the date incorrectly, you can reverse the decision as long as you have not moved to a new fiscal year. Warnings are also given when you advance the date by more than one week or when you try to move to a new fiscal period. These warnings should serve as signals that you may have made a mistake.

CLASSIC VIEW
Right-click the Chart of Accounts icon and then click the Setup tool icon to open the General Settings window. Click Company.

NOTES
When you click the ⊞ beside Company, the list expands beneath the heading. You can click Date Format in either list to open the Date Format Settings window.

Click **Date Format** to open the Settings window for dates:

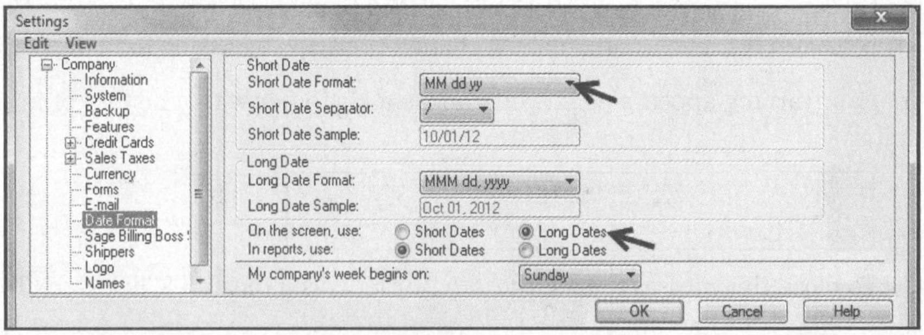

> **NOTES**
> Sage 50 displays only the first three letters of a month when you choose the long or text date format (shown as MMM in the selection list). Therefore, Oct is displayed for October; Jun will be displayed for June, and so on.

Each field has a drop-down list of format options. The **Short Date Format** uses two digits each for month and day. For the year, you can choose a two-digit or four-digit format. You can choose to begin with month, day or year — the Short Date Format shows which comes first. The **Short Date Separator** character may be a slash, dash or period. This is the character that will appear on the screen regardless of how you entered the date. The sample shows the appearance for the current date from your selections.

The **Long Date Format** shows the month as a three-letter text abbreviation. Either the month or the day can be the first character in the long date style. The sample shows the current date with your selected format.

The next section allows you to select the short or long date styles for your screen and reports. You can select different date styles for your reports and screen displays.

We will use the long date format settings on screen for all files to avoid any confusion about dates when the numeric entry might be ambiguous. For reports you can use long or short date formats. For the files we provided in the data set, the month-day-year order is already selected for short and long formats.

To change date format settings,

> **NOTES**
> Showing a four-digit year will ensure that you see whether you are using 1900 or 2000 year dates.
> A final date option allows you to indicate the normal first weekday for the business.

Click the **Short Date Format field list arrow**.

Click **MM dd yyyy**. Be sure that Month (MM) is the first part of the entry.

Click the **Long Date Format field list arrow**.

Click **MMM dd, yyyy**.

Click **Long Dates** beside the option On The Screen, Use. **Click OK** to save the settings.

Saving and Backing Up Your Work

Sage 50 saves your work automatically when you are working with the program. For example, when you post a journal entry or when you display or print reports, Sage 50 writes all the journal transactions to your file to compile the report you want. When you exit from the program properly, Sage 50 also saves all your work.

On a regular basis, you should also make a backup copy of your files. The Backup command is described in detail in Chapter 3.

> **NOTES**
> You can also start the Backup wizard from the Company module window by clicking the Data Management icon or by choosing Backup from the icon's drop-down list of shortcuts.

Close any other open **windows**. (**Click** the **Close Other Windows tool**.)

Click the **Backup tool** or **choose** the **File menu** and **click Backup** to start the Backup wizard.

The wizard will create a separate backup folder inside your current working folder so that the backup will remain separate from your working copy.

While **Backup** creates compressed copies of the files that must be restored with the Restore command before you can use them, the next two options create new complete working copies of your data files that can be opened directly. Both save the file under a different file name so that you will have two working copies of the files — the original and the copy. You can create backups on a CD but not on a DVD with the Backup command.

Save As makes a copy, closes the original file and lets you continue to work with the new copy. Because the new file becomes your working file, you can use Save As to copy to any medium that you can also work from in Sage 50 — your hard drive or a removable memory stick or flash drive, but not a CD. **Save A Copy** makes a copy of the file and then allows you to continue working with the original file. You can use Save A Copy to save your files to a CD (but not to a DVD). You must copy the CD files back to your hard drive and remove the read-only property before working with these files.

NOTES
You may want to use the Save A Copy or Save As command when you are unsure how a journal entry will be posted and you want to experiment with different methods of entering the same transactions.

NOTES
To remove the read-only property, right-click the file name or icon in the Computer window and choose Properties from the pop-up menu. Click Read-Only to remove the ✓.

Because the data files are very large, we recommend using the Backup procedure described in Chapter 3 rather than Save As or Save A Copy for regular backups.

Choose the **File menu** and **click Save A Copy** to open the file name window.

You can save the copy in the same folder as the original by entering a different file name or use a different folder. We recommend using different folders.

Click a **different folder in the file path** to change folders.

Double-click a **folder** in the name and folders pane to open it. To create a new folder inside the one that you have open,

Click **New Folder** (in the tool bar). **Click Browse Folders** first if necessary to reveal the New Folder option. **Type** a **new name** to replace New Folder, the selected text. **Click** the **folder's icon** to select it. **Click Open**.

Double-click the file name **NEW** or **NEW.SAI** if you show file extensions.

Type the **new file name**. **Click Save**. You will return to your original file and you can continue working.

To save the file under a different name and work with the new file, use **Save As**.

Choose the **File menu** and **click Save As** to open the file name window.

The remaining steps are the same as Save A Copy. Change folders, create a new folder, rename the folder, open the new folder, type a file name for the copy and click Save. Remember to return to your original working copy before entering any transactions if you use the Save As command.

You can also back up all your data files at the same time by using Windows (in the Windows Explorer or Computer windows) Copy and Paste commands. In this way, you can save the files to a different folder on your hard drive or on a CD.

NOTES
You can also use the Windows Copy command to make CD copies of your data, but you must close the Sage 50 data file before you start to copy. Remember to copy the data folders when you copy from Windows to ensure that you keep all necessary files (the .SAI file and the SAJ folder) together.

You must use a DVD-writing program to copy your data files to a DVD.

You cannot open the data files from the CD or DVD. You must first copy them back to your hard drive and remove the read-only property.

Finishing a Session

Choose the **open window Control Menu icon** and **click Close** or **click** to close the journal input form or display window you are working in.

Click the **Close Other Windows tool** if you have several windows open. You will return to the main Home window.

Choose the **Sage 50 Control Menu icon** and **click Close**, or **click** or **choose** the **File menu** and **click Exit** to close the Home window. **Click No** to close the backup prompt.

Your work will be saved again automatically when you complete this step. You should now be in the Windows desktop.

Opening a Data File from a Backup

Click 

, the desktop icon, or **start** the **Sage 50 program** from the Start icon or menu (see page 7) to open the Welcome and Select Company window:

> **NOTES**
> The first time you start the program, the option to Open The Last Company You Worked On will not be included. See the Welcome and Select Company screen on page 7.

The opening window gives you several options: working with the sample company files, creating new company files, restoring backup files or working with existing data files. If you have worked with the program before, the option to **Open The Last Company You Worked On** appears with the name of the file you used most recently (as shown here). We need to restore a backup file.

If your working files are lost or damaged, you will also need to restore backup files. You can also restore files from the Home window File menu of any data file, including the Sample Company file, or from the Company window Data Management shortcuts list.

Click **Restore From Backup**.

Click **OK** to start the Sage 50 Restore From Backup wizard:

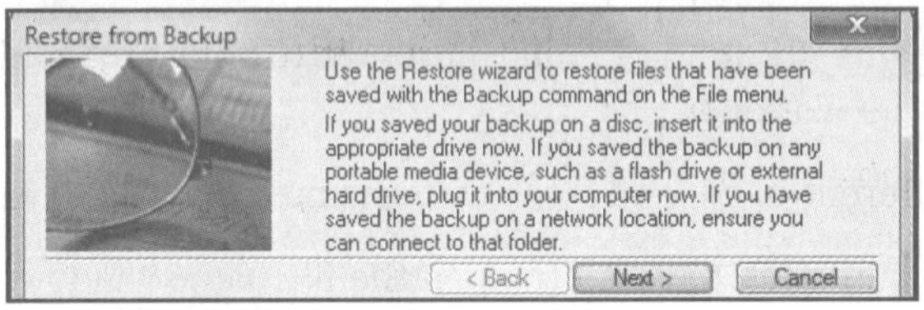

> **NOTES**
> You can also start the Restore wizard from any open Sage 50 data file. From any Home window, choose the File menu and click Restore to start the Restore wizard.
> Or, from the Company module window, start the wizard from the Data Management icon shortcuts list. Click the icon's list arrow and choose Restore.

Click **Next** to begin:

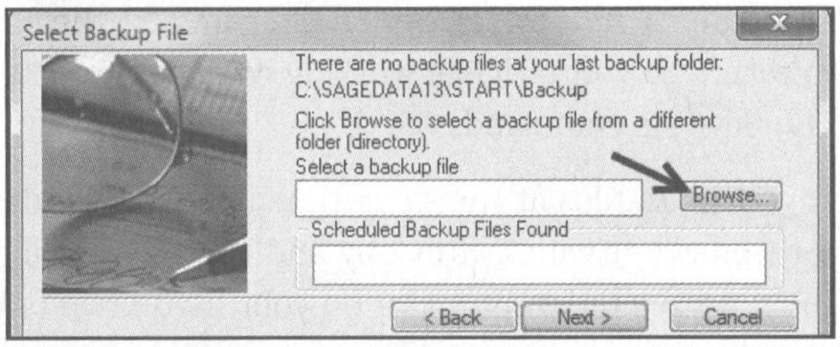

The first time you restore a backup, no default location or backup files are entered.

Click **Browse** to open the folder you worked in most recently.

The folder names in your Look In field and Browse windows may be different from the ones we show. Sage 50 uses a folder under Libraries\Documents as the default location for files, so you may see this as the selected folder initially. If you have opened another data file, you may see the folder where that file is stored. To ensure consistency in file names and locations for our instructions, we always work with the folder we created when installing the data files, that is, C:\SageData13.

Click **Computer** in the path field at the top of the screen or in the left pane list of links, drives and folders.

All the drives on your computer will be listed:

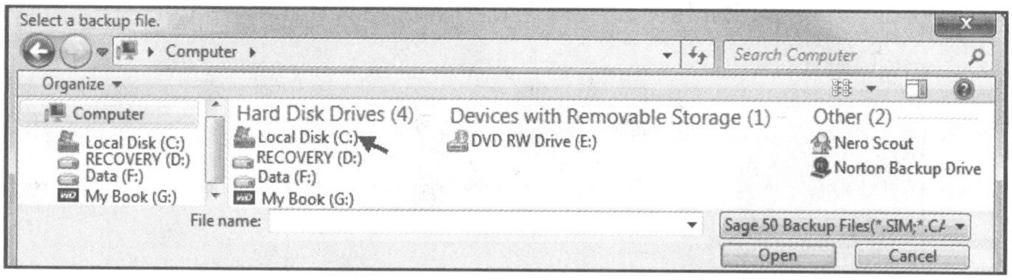

Double-click **Local Disk (C:)** to show the files and folders in this drive:

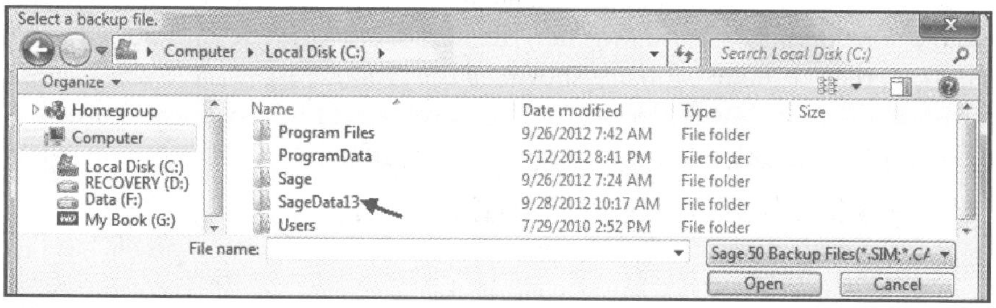

Click **SageData13** to select it, or click the SageData13 folder icon 

.

Click **Open** to see the list of files you copied from the Student DVD:

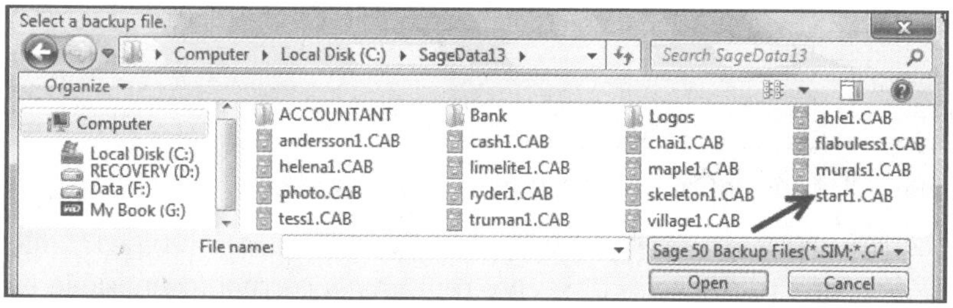

Only Sage 50 format backup files and folders are listed because we are working with the Restore Backup wizard.

Click **start1.CAB** to select it or click the start1.CAB icon 

if you are in icon view. (Click **start1** if you are not showing file extensions.) Start1 is added to the File Name field.

Click **Open**. You will return to the wizard.

Backup files are now listed in the Select A Backup File text box with start1.CAB selected, as shown:

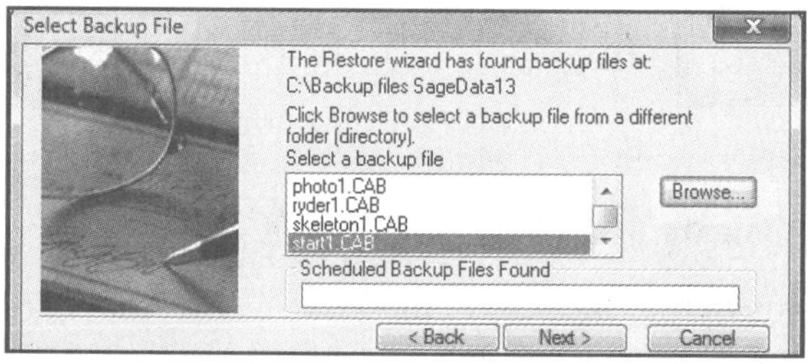

Click **Next** to continue, showing the selections you have made:

NOTES

Your screens may look different if you have selected different viewing options such as displaying the folders as lists or icons. The viewing options can be changed from the Views icon drop-down menu.

NOTES

We show the default location for the data files from the automatic installation. If you installed the files to a different location, choose the drive and folder for your setup.

PRO VERSION

The first backup file listed is andersson1.CAB.

WARNING!

If you are not showing file extensions, click start1. The file name has a filing cabinet icon beside it  (like the ones you see on this page).

NOTES

The original location of the file used to create the backup will be the default name and restore location for your backup.

> **NOTES**
> The original name and location are the ones we used to create the initial backup file. The default for the restored file will be C:\SageData13\Start\start.SAI.

If the information is incorrect, click Back to return to the file selection screen.

Click **Next** to continue if the information is correct:

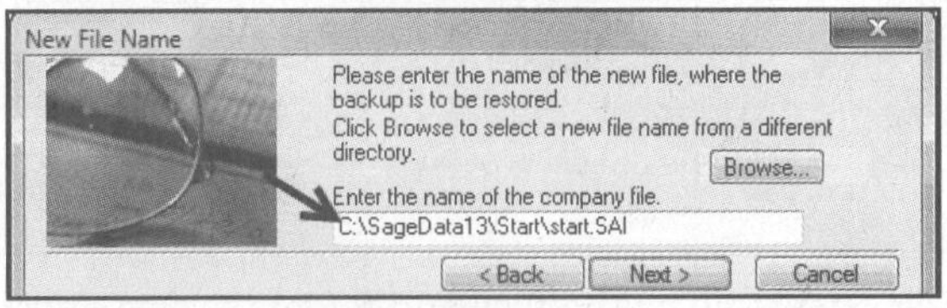

At this stage, you should enter the name of the file you are restoring. If you have created the backup from your own file, the name and location of the original file from which you created the backup are shown as the default.

We will create a new folder for each data set in this text. We will continue to work in the SageData13 folder. If the name you see is different from the one shown above,

Type `C:\SageData13\Start\start`

Click **Next**.

You can choose a different location and file name by clicking Browse to access your folders. Enter the location and file name you want to use.

You will see a screen advising you that you are using folder and file names that are new. Sage 50 will create the new folders and files for you:

Click **Yes** to confirm and continue.

If you are replacing a file, you will see a warning when you type the file name and location file. Click Yes if you are replacing a corrupt or unusable file.

Sage 50 now confirms that all the data required have been entered:

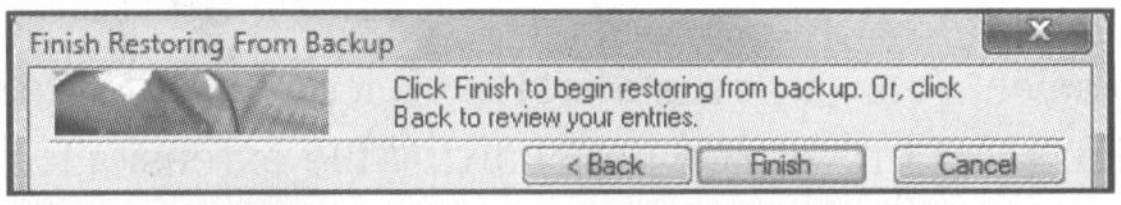

This is your last chance to change information by clicking Back.

Click **Finish** to begin restoring the file. You should see the screen that prompts you to enter the session date:

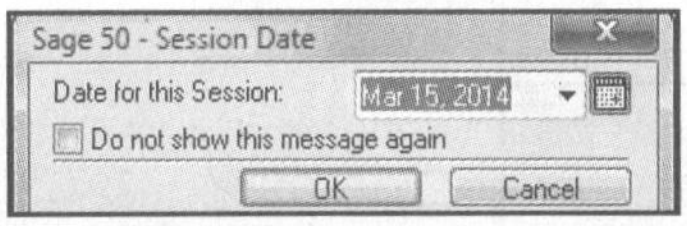

Click **OK** to open the Getting Started window.

Click **Show This Window On Start Up** to remove the ✓.

Click **Close** to continue to the Home window.

Continue with the instructions on page 10.

REVIEW

The Student DVD with Data Files includes Review Questions for this chapter.

CHAPTER TWO

GST, HST and PST

OBJECTIVES

After completing this chapter, you should be able to

- ***understand*** the terms relevant to the federal Goods and Services Tax
- ***understand*** the different methods of calculating the GST
- ***understand*** Harmonized Sales Tax in relation to GST
- ***understand*** how to file for GST or HST remittances or refunds
- ***understand*** other provincial sales taxes in relation to GST

GENERAL TAX INFORMATION

Definition of GST

NOTES
Provinces may or may not include GST in the price on which they calculate Provincial Sales Tax (PST). Provincial tax rates vary from province to province. See page 30.

The Goods and Services Tax (GST) is levied by the federal government at the rate of 5 percent on most goods and services in Canada. Retailers pay the GST to their wholesalers and vendors but are allowed to deduct any GST they pay from the GST they collect from customers. Retailers remit the difference, GST owing, to the Receiver General for Canada or claim a refund with monthly or quarterly returns.

GST Registration Any business with annual sales exceeding $30 000 per year must register for GST collection and must collect GST on all applicable sales. Registration is optional for most smaller businesses. Businesses that are not registered for GST do not charge GST on sales to their customers, but they also cannot recover the GST they pay on business-related purchases.

NOTES
GST collected on sales is reduced by the GST on sales returns.

Collecting the GST The business must collect GST for those goods and services sold that are not zero rated or tax exempt. The business must remit GST at regular intervals, filing GST returns monthly, quarterly or annually and paying instalments, depending on annual income and GST owing.

Zero Rated Goods and Services Zero rated goods and services are those on which the tax rate is zero. These goods include basic groceries, prescribed medical devices, prescribed drugs, exported goods and services, agricultural products and fish products. A business selling only zero rated goods and services does not collect GST on sales, but it can still claim a refund for GST it pays for purchases.

NOTES
Unlike rent on personal residences, rent on business property is subject to GST.

Tax Exempt Goods and Services Tax exempt goods and services are those on which tax is not collected. These goods and services include health care, dental care, daycare services and rent on personal residences. Most educational and financial services are also included in this group. These businesses are not able to claim refunds for GST paid for business purchases related to selling tax exempt goods and services.

NOTES
The input tax credit is reduced by the amount of GST for purchases returned.

Paying the GST A business must pay GST for purchases made for business purposes, unless the goods or services purchased are zero rated or tax exempt. The business can use the GST paid as an input tax credit by subtracting the amount of GST paid from the amount of GST collected and remitting GST owing or claiming a refund. GST amounts paid on purchases for personal use do not qualify as input tax credits.

NOTES
Purchases of goods and services on a reserve that are made by businesses or by individuals registered as Status Indians are also usually exempt from GST and HST.

Bank and Financial Institution Services Most bank products and services are not taxable. Exceptions include safety deposit box rentals, custodial and safekeeping services, personalized cheques, self-administered registered savings plan fees, payroll services, rentals of night depository, rentals of credit card imprinters and reconciliation of cheques. Banks remit the full amount of GST they collect from customers. Because most bank services are not taxable, banks cannot claim input tax credits for GST they pay on business-related purchases.

NOTES
Visitors to Canada can request a refund for GST paid on goods purchased in Canada that they are taking home with them. They cannot claim a refund for goods and services they consumed in Canada, such as entertainment and dining.

GST on Imported and Exported Goods GST is not charged on exported goods. Customers in other countries who import goods from Canada do not pay GST. However, businesses in Canada must pay GST on the items they import or purchase from other countries. The GST is collected by the Canada Revenue Agency (CRA) when the goods enter Canada based on the purchase price (plus import duty) and current exchange rates. Businesses must pay this GST and other import duties before the goods are released to them.

Administering the GST

The federal government has approved different methods of administering the GST; the regular method is most commonly used.

The Regular Method

The regular method of administering the GST requires the business to keep track of GST paid for all goods and services purchased from vendors (less returns) and of GST collected for all goods and services sold to customers (less returns). It then deducts the GST paid from the GST collected and files for a refund or remits the balance owing to the Receiver General on a monthly or quarterly basis.

Accounting Examples Using the Regular Method (without PST)

NOTES
GST Paid on Purchases is a contra-liability account because it normally has a debit balance while most liability accounts have a credit balance. Therefore, GST Paid on Purchases reduces the total GST liability to the Receiver General.

SALES INVOICE Sold goods to customer for $200 plus $10 GST collected (5%). Invoice total, $210.

Date	Particulars	Debit	Credit
02/15	Accounts Receivable	210.00	
	GST Charged on Sales		10.00
	Revenue from Sales		200.00

PURCHASE INVOICE Purchased supplies from vendor for $300 plus $15 GST paid (5%). Invoice total, $315.

Date	Particulars	Debit	Credit
02/15	Supplies	300.00	
	GST Paid on Purchases	15.00	
	Accounts Payable		315.00

The GST owing is further reduced by any GST adjustments — for example, GST that applies to bad debts that are written off. If the debt is later recovered, the GST liability is also restored as an input tax credit adjustment.

Other Methods of Calculating GST

Certain small businesses may be eligible to use simpler methods of calculating their GST refunds and remittances that do not require them to keep a separate record for GST on each individual purchase or sale. The simplified accounting method, the streamlined accounting method and the quick method are examples of these alternatives.

NOTES

Under the quick method, the GST remittance or refund amount is based on a flat-rate percentage of total sales, including GST. The remittance rate varies for different types of businesses. GST paid on purchases of capital is an input tax credit to reduce the amount owing (or increase the refund).

These alternative methods of calculating GST are not used in the applications in this workbook.

Calculating GST Refunds or Remittances

The following example uses the regular method for a retailer who is filing quarterly:

Quarterly Total Sales (excluding GST)	$50 000.00	
Quarterly Total Qualifying Purchases	29 700.00	
5% GST Charged on Sales		$2 500.00
Less: 5% GST Paid on Purchases		
Cash Register (cost $1 000)	50.00	
Inventory (cost $25 000)	1 250.00	
Supplies (cost $500)	25.00	
Payroll Services (cost $200)	10.00	
Store Lease (cost $3 000)	150.00	
Total GST Paid		- 1 485.00
GST Remittance		$1 015.00

GST Remittances and Refunds

The business must file returns that summarize the amount of GST it has collected and the amount of GST it has paid. CRA may require reports monthly, quarterly or yearly, depending on total sales. Yearly reports usually require quarterly instalments.

GST Collected on Sales	>	GST Paid on Purchases	=	GST Owing
GST Collected on Sales	<	GST Paid on Purchases	=	GST Refund

Accounting Examples for Remittances

Usually a business will make GST remittances because sales usually exceed expenses — the business operates at a profit. The following example shows how the GST accounts are cleared and a liability (*Accounts Payable*) is set up to remit GST owing to the Receiver General for Canada. In this case, the usual one, the Receiver General becomes a vendor for the business so that the liability can be entered and the payment made.

NOTES

The rules concerning the GST may change periodically, as in the 2006 federal budget when the rate changed from 7 percent to 6 percent. In the 2007 budget, the rate was reduced again to 5 percent. Always refer to current guidelines.

Date	Particulars	Debit	Credit
03/31	GST Charged on Sales	2 500.00	
	GST Paid on Purchases		1 485.00
	A/P - Receiver General		1 015.00
03/31	A/P - Receiver General	1 015.00	
	Cash in Bank		1 015.00

Accounting Examples for Refunds

The example below shows how the GST accounts are cleared and a current asset account (*Accounts Receivable*) is set up for a GST refund from the Receiver General for Canada. In this case, the Receiver General owes money to the business; that is, it acts like a customer, so a customer record is set up to record and collect the refund.

Date	Particulars	Debit	Credit
03/31	GST Charged on Sales	1 500.00	
	A/R - Receiver General	500.00	
	GST Paid on Purchases		2 000.00
04/15	Cash in Bank	500.00	
	A/R - Receiver General		500.00

Harmonized Sales Tax: HST

Five provinces have adopted the Harmonized Sales Tax (HST) method of taxing goods and services: Prince Edward Island, Ontario, New Brunswick, Nova Scotia and Newfoundland and Labrador. When HST applies, the GST and provincial taxes are harmonized at a single rate. In all provinces, 5 percent of the HST rate is the federal portion, or GST, while the remainder is the provincial portion. Provincial retail sales tax rates vary from one province to another, so the HST rates also vary. In Prince Edward Island, the HST rate is 14 percent (9 percent provincial); in Ontario, New Brunswick and Newfoundland and Labrador, the HST rate in 2013 is 13 percent (8 percent provincial) and in Nova Scotia the rate is 15 percent (10 percent provincial). The HST replaces the former separate GST and PST, and unlike those separate taxes, it is administered entirely at the federal level. This removes some administrative work both from the provincial Ministries of Finance and from the businesses that charge taxes to their customers. They have only one tax to calculate and remit.

NOTES

Prices shown to customers may have the HST included (tax-inclusive pricing), but they must show either the amount of HST included in the price or the HST rate. Most retailers show prices before taxes are included.

The full 13, 14 or 15 percent Harmonized Sales Tax (HST) operates much like the basic GST: HST is applied at each level of sale and resale, and manufacturing; has the same business registration requirement of annual sales exceeding $30 000; is applied to the same base of goods and services; and is collected in the same way. HST returns and remittances are also calculated in the same way as GST returns and remittances. The business remits any excess of HST collected over HST paid for its business expenses, or claims a refund when HST paid exceeds the HST collected from customers.

The following example illustrates the application in Ontario (or New Brunswick or Newfoundland and Labrador), where the HST rate is 13 percent.

Ontario business sold goods on account for $565, including HST at 13% ($500 base price).

HST = (0.13 × 500) = $65
Total amount of invoice = $565

Date	Particulars	Debit	Credit
02/15	Accounts Receivable	565.00	
	HST Charged on Sales		65.00
	Revenue from Sales		500.00

A single remittance for the full 13 percent is made to the Receiver General; the provincial portion of the HST is not tracked or collected separately by the business.

The following examples show the journal entries for an HST remittance and an HST refund:

Remittance: A New Brunswick business calculates and pays HST Owing

For Sales of $50 000 plus 13% HST; Qualifying purchases of $30 000 plus 13% HST

Date	Particulars	Debit	Credit
03/31	HST Charged on Sales	6 500.00	
	A/P - Receiver General		2 600.00
	HST Paid on Purchases		3 900.00
04/15	A/P - Receiver General	2 600.00	
	Chequing Bank Account		2 600.00

Refund: A New Brunswick business qualifies and applies for an HST Refund

For Sales of $30 000 plus 13% HST; Qualifying purchases of $42 000 plus 13% HST

Date	Particulars	Debit	Credit
03/31	HST Charged on Sales	3 900.00	
	A/R - Receiver General	1 560.00	
	HST Paid on Purchases		5 460.00
04/15	Chequing Bank Account	1 560.00	
	A/R - Receiver General		1 560.00

Goods and Services Exempt for HST

Under the HST method, all items that are exempt for GST or are zero rated are also exempt for HST or are zero rated for HST. In addition, each province has decided that some items will be exempt for HST and subject only to GST. For example, books and children's clothing are exempt for HST but not for GST. For these goods, the customer pays only the 5 percent GST portion of the tax. At the retail level, for these special items a separate tax code for GST only is applied. When the business files its HST return, it will remit the HST collected plus the GST collected, less the amounts of GST plus HST paid on qualifying business-related purchases on a single return.

The following example shows these calculations for a book seller who also sells music CDs in Nova Scotia. HST at the rate of 15 percent (including a provincial portion of 10 percent) applies to the sale of CDs, while GST at the rate of 5 percent applies to the sale of books.

Quarterly Total Sales (excluding taxes)	$92 000	
Quarterly Total Qualifying Purchases (excluding taxes)	$52 000	
HST Charged on Sales (15% × 41 000)	$6 150	
GST Charged on Sales (5% × 51 000)	2 550	
Total GST/HST collected		$8 700
Less: GST Paid on Purchase of books for resale (5% × 21 000)	1 050	
HST Paid on other Purchases (15% × 31 000)	4 650	
Total HST Credits		–5 700
HST Remittance		$3 000

NOTES

Instead of applying different tax rates, retailers who sell PST exempt goods may also charge the full HST rate but provide an immediate point-of-sale rebate to the customer for the provincial portion. They will then claim an adjustment for the rebate amount on their HST return to reduce the amount remitted.

The net effect of the two methods is the same for the customer and for the merchant.

GST and Other Provincial (Retail) Sales Taxes

NOTES
If a business purchases inventory for resale but later uses the inventory within the business instead, it must remit PST on this internal transaction. The business has become the final consumer of the products.

NOTES
Services may be exempt or taxable for PST. PST is usually charged on services, such as repairs, that are applied to goods that are themselves taxable for PST.
Insurance, such as for home and automobile, is one of the few services that is taxable for PST and not for GST.

The rules governing provincial sales taxes vary from province to province in terms of the tax rate, the goods and services that are taxed and whether Provincial Sales Tax (PST) is applied to the GST as well as to the base purchase price (that is, whether GST is taxable). The following examples assume that the item sold has both GST and PST applied.

Although GST is applied at each level of sale and resale (including the stages of manufacturing), PST is a retail sales tax and, therefore, is paid only by the final consumer of a product or service. Therefore, it is generally referred to as a Retail Sales Tax by the provincial governments, and the terms RST and PST are equivalent. Thus, a business purchasing inventory to sell to customers will not pay PST on these purchases. When the same business buys supplies or services for its use in conducting business, it must pay PST because it has become the final consumer of these goods or services.

PST applies only to sales within a province, not to sales to customers in a different province or in a different country. HST and GST do apply to interprovincial sales. If the consumer's province applies HST, the consumer pays HST on purchases from other provinces. All consumers in Canada pay GST.

Alberta, the Northwest Territories, Yukon and Nunavut

Alberta, the Northwest Territories, Yukon and Nunavut do not have Provincial Sales Taxes. Customers in these regions pay only the 5 percent GST on their purchases. Thus, the examples provided earlier without PST illustrate the application of GST for these regions.

PST in Manitoba, Saskatchewan, British Columbia and Quebec

NOTES
In 2013, three provinces changed their provincial tax system. Prince Edward Island adopted the Harmonized Sales Tax to replace the separate GST and PST. Quebec changed its taxation method so that the provincial sales tax was not calculated on the base price plus GST (QST is no longer charged on GST). British Columbia stopped using HST and now applies separate GST and PST.

These four provinces apply PST to the base price of the sale, the amount without GST included. In Manitoba and British Columbia, the retail sales tax rate is 7 percent; in Saskatchewan, the rate is 5 percent, in Quebec the rate is 9.975 percent. The following example illustrates the application in Manitoba:

Manitoba business sold goods on account for $500. GST charged is 5% and PST charged is 7%.

GST = (0.05 × 500) = $25
PST in Manitoba = (0.07 × 500) = $35
Total amount of invoice = $500 + $25 + $35 = $560

Date	Particulars	Debit	Credit
02/15	Accounts Receivable	560.00	
	GST Charged on Sales		25.00
	PST Payable		35.00
	Revenue from Sales		500.00

NOTES
In July, 2013, Manitoba changed its provincial tax rate to 8 percent. This change was announced too late to be incorporated into the current text.

The full amount of PST collected on sales is remitted to the provincial Minister of Finance (less any applicable sales tax compensation).

Part 2
Applications

CHAPTER THREE

Muriel's Murals

OBJECTIVES

After completing this chapter, you should be able to

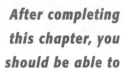

- ***access*** the data files for the business
- ***open*** the General Journal
- ***enter*** transactions in the General Journal
- ***edit*** and ***review*** General Journal transactions
- ***post*** transactions
- ***create*** new General Ledger accounts
- ***adjust*** journal entries after posting
- ***display*** and ***print*** General Ledger and General Journal reports
- ***graph*** General Ledger reports
- ***display*** and ***print*** comparative financial reports
- ***customize*** reports
- ***back up*** your data files
- ***advance*** the session date
- ***finish*** an accounting session

COMPANY INFORMATION

Company Profile

NOTES
Muriel's Murals
66 Collage Avenue
Edmonton, AB T4P 4C2
Tel 1: (780) 763-4127
Tel 2: (800) 455-4127
Fax: (780) 765-4842
Business No.: 743 647 397

Muriel's Murals is owned and operated by Muriel Missoni in Edmonton, Alberta. She shares studio space with her sister Maria, owner of Missoni Marbleworks. While studying art and interior design at university and community college, Missoni learned that she enjoys the physical aspects of art as well as the creative parts. Therefore, she started her own business as an interior painter specializing in unique wall textures, collages and murals for private homes and public places. For customers who want three-dimensional wall friezes, she collaborates with Maria, her sister the sculptor, who creates moulds for plaster appliques based on Muriel's drawings. Muriel applies and paints the plaster friezes. Her superior colour sense has encouraged her to keep an inventory of base paints that she can colour as needed. Her customers, especially those with young children, appreciate her insistence on VOC-free paints (free of volatile organic compounds) and are willing to pay the premium prices for the non-toxic products. For large murals, she enlists the assistance of senior art students who work from her drawings.

Some of her customers have set up accounts with Muriel's Murals, and she has set up accounts with her regular vendors and suppliers.

To convert her accounting records to Sage 50 in April, she has used the following:

- Chart of Accounts
- Trial Balance
- Accounting Procedures

CHART OF POSTABLE ACCOUNTS

MURIEL'S MURALS

ASSETS
1080 Chequing Account
1200 A/R - Alberta Jasper
1220 A/R - Kananaskis Mall
1240 A/R - Silver Birch Inn
1320 Prepaid Insurance
1360 Paint & Supplies
1540 Computer Equipment
1550 Tools & Equipment
1570 Van ▶

▶LIABILITIES
2100 A/P - Foothills Hardware
2120 A/P - Western Sky Interiors
2180 A/P - Chinook Promotions
2650 GST Charged on Services
2670 GST Paid on Purchases

EQUITY
3100 M. Missoni, Capital
3150 M. Missoni, Drawings
3600 Net Income ▶

▶REVENUE
4100 Revenue from Painting Contracts
4150 Revenue from Consultation
4200 Interest Revenue

EXPENSE
5020 Advertising & Promotion
5040 Bank Charges
5060 Hydro Expense
5080 Interest Expense ▶

▶5100 Maintenance & Repairs
5110 Paint & Supplies Used
5120 Rental Expenses
5140 Telephone Expenses
5160 Wages Expenses

NOTES: The Chart of Accounts includes only postable accounts and the Net Income or Current Earnings account. Sage 50 uses the Net Income account for the Income Statement to calculate the difference between revenue and expenses before closing the books.

TRIAL BALANCE

MURIEL'S MURALS

April 1, 2015		Debits	Credits
1080	Chequing Account	$ 34 000	
1200	A/R - Alberta Jasper	2 400	
1220	A/R - Kananaskis Mall	3 600	
1320	Prepaid Insurance	2 100	
1360	Paint & Supplies	2 050	
1540	Computer Equipment	2 500	
1550	Tools & Equipment	14 500	
1570	Van	32 000	
2120	A/P - Western Sky Interiors		$ 1 200
2650	GST Charged on Services		1 500
2670	GST Paid on Purchases	940	
3100	M. Missoni, Capital		80 160
3150	M. Missoni, Drawings	900	
4100	Revenue from Painting Contracts		21 000
4150	Revenue from Consultation		4 000
5020	Advertising & Promotion	2 000	
5040	Bank Charges	160	
5060	Hydro Expense	300	
5100	Maintenance & Repairs	400	
5110	Paint & Supplies Used	4 400	
5120	Rental Expenses	1 650	
5140	Telephone Expenses	360	
5160	Wages Expenses	3 600	
		$107 860	$107 860

> **NOTES**
> Most bank and financial institution services used in this text are exempt from GST charges.
> Alberta does not levy a provincial sales tax.

Accounting Procedures

GST

Muriel's Murals has chosen the regular method for remittance of the Goods and Services Tax (GST). She records the GST collected from customers as a liability (credit) in the *GST Charged on Services* account. She records GST that she pays to vendors in the *GST Paid on Purchases* account as a decrease (debit) to her liability to the Canada Revenue Agency. Her GST remittance or refund is calculated automatically in the *GST Owing (Refund)* subtotal. You can see these accounts when you display or print the Balance Sheet. Missoni files her GST remittances or requests for refunds with the Receiver General for Canada on the last day of each fiscal quarter. (For details, please read Chapter 2 on the Goods and Services Tax.)

> **NOTES**
> In these instructions, our starting point for opening the file is the Start file in Chapter 1 as the last company you worked on.
> For detailed instructions on restoring data files, refer to Chapter 1, page 22.

INSTRUCTIONS

1. **Open** or **restore** the **data for Muriel's Murals**. Keystroke instructions begin below.
2. **Enter** the **source documents for April** in the General Journal in Sage 50 using the Chart of Accounts and Trial Balance for Muriel's Murals. The procedures for entering each new type of transaction for this application are outlined step by step in the Keystrokes section with the source documents. These transactions have a ✓ in the completion check box beside the source document. The source documents are numbered — the number is placed below or in the lower part of the check box.
3. **Print** the **reports and graphs** indicated on the printing form below after you have completed your entries. Keystrokes for reports begin on page 51.

REPORTS

Accounts
- ☐ Chart of Accounts
- ☐ Account List
- ☑ General Journal Entries: Apr 1 to Apr 30

Financials
- ☑ Comparative Balance Sheet dates: Apr 1 and Apr 30 with difference in percentage
- ☑ Income Statement from Jan 1 to Apr 30
- ☑ Trial Balance date: Apr 30
- ☑ General Ledger accounts: 1080 2650 3100 4100 from Apr 1 to Apr 30

Management Reports
- ☐ General

GRAPHS
- ☐ Revenues by Account
- ☐ Expenses by Account
- ☑ Expenses and Net Profit as % of Revenue

> **NOTES**
> To start from the backup file, click Restore From Backup on the Welcome Getting Started screen.
> Click OK and click Next. Click Browse and locate the folder C:\SageData13 where you installed the data. Double-click SageData13. Click murals1.CAB or murals1 to select the file you need. Click Open. Click Next and confirm the details. Click Next.
> Type C:\SageData13\Murals\murals in the Name field if this is not the default entry. Click Next and click Yes to confirm the creation of the new folder and file.
> Click Finish and wait for the session date to appear.

KEYSTROKES

Opening Data Files

Double-click the **Sage 50 desktop shortcut**, or

Choose **Start** then **choose** **All Programs** and **Sage 50 Premium Accounting 2013**. **Click** **Sage 50 Premium Accounting 2013**.

Click **Select An Existing Company** and **click OK**.

Locate the folder **C:\SageData13** where you installed the data.

Double-click the **SageData13 folder** to open it.

Double-click the **Murals folder** to open it.

Click **murals** or **murals.SAI** to select the file you need. **Click** **Open**.

Refer to Chapter 1, page 7, for detailed instructions on opening data files.

The following screen appears, asking (prompting) you to enter the session date for this work session:

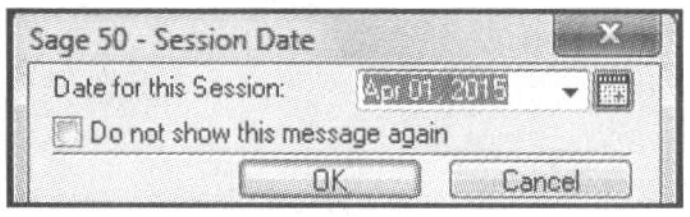

The date format on your screen is controlled by the Date Format Settings options in Sage 50, not by the format you use to enter the date. (Refer to page 19.)

The session date is the date of your work session — the date on which you are recording the accounting transactions on the computer. A business with a large number of transactions may record these transactions at the end of each day. One with fewer transactions may enter them once a week. In this workbook, transactions are entered once a week for most applications so we update the session date one week at a time. The session date may or may not be the same as the date on which the transaction actually took place.

The session date for your first session is April 7, 2015. Since this is not the default shown on the screen, you must change the date. Every date field has a Calendar icon.

Click the **Calendar icon** to open the calendar:

The calendar has the current session date highlighted with a blue background. The calendar for any date field also shows the range of dates that will be accepted based on the settings chosen for the company files. The arrows allow you to move forward to a later month or back to a previous month. The calendar stops at the dates that indicate the range you may use. Click a date on the calendar to enter it or use one of the following alternative formats. For consistency, we use the same order of month, day and year throughout the text. Entering the year is optional in most date fields.

- use different characters to separate numbers: 04-07-15 or 04/07/15
- omit leading zeros or the year: 4/7/15 or 4-7
- leave spaces between numbers instead of separating characters: 04 07 15 or 4 7
- type lower- or upper-case text: April 7, 2015 or APRIL 7, 2015
- use three-letter abbreviations for the month: Apr 7 -15 or apr 7 15
- use three-letter abbreviations for the month with the day first: 7 apr or 7Apr
- other non-alpha or non-numeric separating characters may also be used
- in most date windows, you can omit the year

We will use a variety of date formats throughout this workbook, but we always show the dates on-screen in the text format to minimize entering incorrect dates. Using the calendar to choose a date or using a text version to enter a date will also prevent an incorrect date entry.

Click **7** on the April date calendar or

Type `april 7 or 7apr`

Click **OK**.

NOTES
Many screens include a Cancel button. If you click Cancel, you will return to your previous screen without entering any changes.

NOTES
When you click , the dimmed back arrow in the date calendar, nothing happens because the earliest date you can use for Muriel's Murals s April 1.

NOTES
When you enter the date as text, the date is not ambiguous, so you can enter the day first. Similarly, you do not need to leave a space between the month and day because there is no ambiguity.

NOTES
Refer to Chapter 1, page 19, and Chapter 4, page 79, for instructions on changing date format settings.

NOTES
Keystrokes that you must use are shown in command statements like these:

Type `april 7`

or

Click **OK**

Instruction lines are indented; command words are in **boldface**; text you type is shown in a special font (`Courier`); and things that you must click on or select are in **colour and bold**. This format makes it easy to find the instruction statements in the text.

Your screen shows the following Company module Home window:

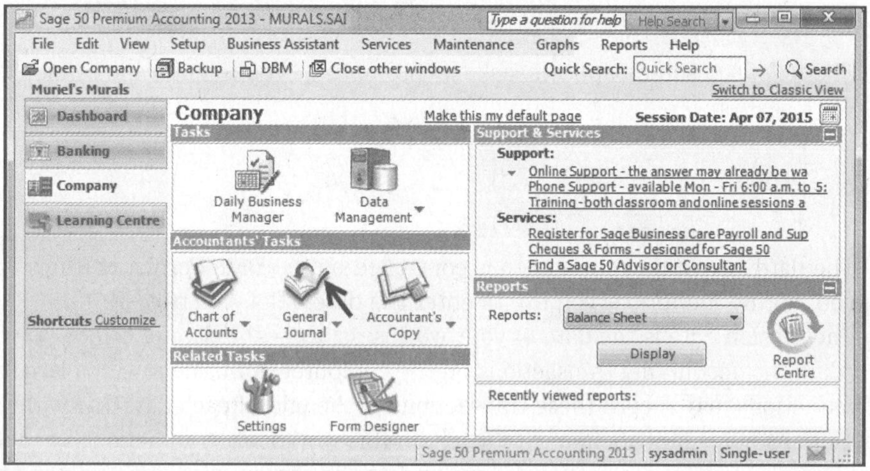

PRO VERSION

The program name in the title bar will be Sage 50 Pro Accounting 2013. The status bar will not include the single-user status. The Pro version is a single-user program.

CLASSIC VIEW

The Classic view Home window includes an icon for the Reconciliation and Deposits Journal. In the Enhanced view, Banking is listed as a separate module and the Reconciliation and Deposits Journal is accessed from it.

NOTES

Maximize the Home window if necessary. Refer to Chapter 1 for a more detailed description of the Home window.

NOTES

Although the Banking module is not used, it cannot be hidden if you want to use the General Journal.

NOTES

The Daily Business Manager is used in Chapter 11. The Learning Centre was introduced in Chapter 1. The Accountant's Copy is covered in Chapter 12.

For Muriel's Murals, the Company module is the default page. Only the General Ledger and Journal can be accessed for this file. When ledger icons are hidden, all main menu options related to those ledgers are also hidden or unavailable. (Click [maximize button] to maximize the window if necessary.) The Home window has the title bar on top with the program and file names, control menu icon and size buttons; the main menu bar comes next and the tool bar follows. Tool buttons permit quick access to commonly used menu items. The Home window tools (with their alternative pull-down menu locations) include Open Company and Backup (File menu), DBM — Daily Business Manager — (Business Assistant menu) and Close Other Windows (View menu). The Search function and tool (Edit menu) are located on the far right for easy access.

The major part of the window is divided into three columns of panes or sections — the **Modules** and **Shortcuts** panes on the left; task panes in the middle (**Accountants' Tasks** with Ledger and Journal icons and **Related Tasks**); and the **Support** and **Reports** panes on the right. Instead of ledgers in the upper Tasks pane, the Company window has access to the **Daily Business Manager** and **Data Management** tasks such as backing up files, restoring files and checking the integrity of the data files. For the Company module, the upper right pane has access to support services for Sage 50. For other modules, this pane lists the ledger accounts. The session date and the change date calendar icon are located above the Support pane.

Below these panes is the status bar with the program name and version and the user name (sysadmin) and status (Single-user). In most windows, the status bar shows the purpose of the field or icon that has the pointer on it.

Entering General Journal Transactions

All transactions for Muriel's Murals are entered in the General Journal in the Accountants' Tasks pane, indicated by the pointer in the following screen:

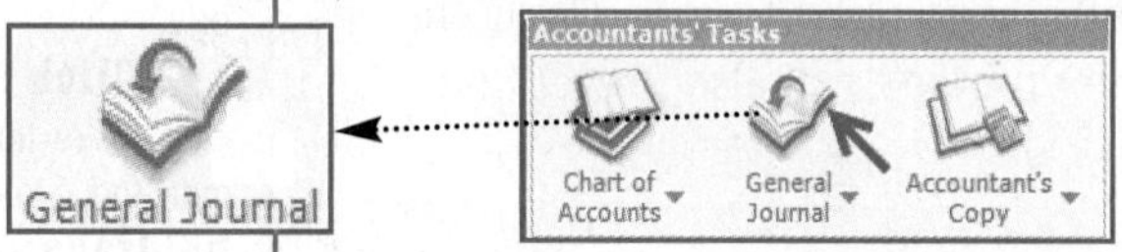

Click the **General Journal icon** in the Accountants' Tasks pane of the Company module Home window to open the General Journal.

The General Journal input form that follows appears on your screen:

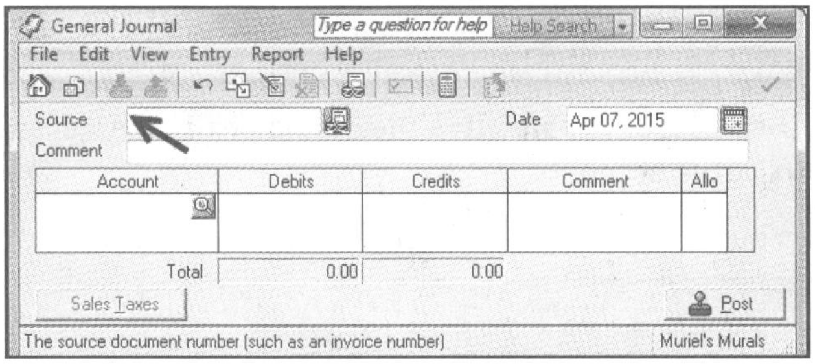

You are now ready to enter the first transaction in the General Journal input screen.

✓ 1 **Purchase Invoice #FH-161** **Dated April 2, 2015**

From Foothills Hardware, $795 plus $39.75 GST paid for cordless power drill with sander attachments. Purchase invoice total $834.75. Terms: net 30 days.

The cursor, a flashing vertical line, is blinking in the Source field, ready to receive information — up to 20 characters, including spaces. The Source field identifies the reference document from which you obtain the information for a transaction, in this case, the invoice number.

Type FH-161

Press *tab* to advance to the Look Up Entry icon. **Press** *tab* again.

The cursor advances to the next field, the Date field. You should enter the transaction date here. The program enters the session date by default. It is highlighted, ready to be accepted or changed. Because the work was completed on April 2, 2015, the session date of April 7 is incorrect and must be changed.

Type 04-02

Press *tab* to move to the Calendar icon.

Notice that the text form of the date is displayed, even though we entered the date as numbers. The year is added to the date.

If you click the Calendar icon in the Date field now, the session date has a frame around it. The current transaction date has a solid blue background.

Press *tab* again to accept the date and advance to the Comment field.

In the Comment field, you should enter a description of the transaction to make the permanent record more meaningful. You may enter up to 75 characters, including spaces.

Type Foothills Hardware **Press** *tab*.

The cursor moves forward to the first line of the Account field, creating a dotted box for the first account.

Sage 50 organizes accounts into financial statement sections or categories using the following boundaries for numbering:

- 1000–1999 Assets
- 2000–2999 Liabilities
- 3000–3999 Equity
- 4000–4999 Revenue
- 5000–5999 Expense

This system makes it easy to remember the first digit of an account. Double-clicking the Account field will display the list of accounts. If you type the first digit of an

NOTES

The Refresh tool applies to multi-user use of the program, so it is dimmed for the single-user examples we show. This feature is not available in the Pro version.

NOTES

A check box with a ✓ inside indicates that keystroke instructions are provided for this source document.

The lower part of the check box contains the source document number (**1**).

NOTES

Use the bookmark attached to the back cover to mark the page with the source document.

WARNING!

Unless you change the date, the session date will become the posting date for the entry.

Remember that you can use any date format listed on page 35 and you may also omit the year.

NOTES

When you press *tab* after typing a date in the Date field, you will advance to the Calendar icon. You must press *tab* again to advance to the next input field. That is, you must press *tab* twice. If you choose a date from the calendar, pressing *tab* once will move the cursor to the next input field.

NOTES

Although Sage 50 allows you to use more than four digits for account numbers in the Premium version, we will use only four-digit numbers for the applications in Part Two of the text.

account number then double-click or press (enter) while the cursor is flashing in any account field, the program will advance the list to accounts beginning with that digit.

Click the **List icon**, or **double-click** the dotted box in the **Account column** to list the accounts.

The following list of accounts appears on your journal screen:

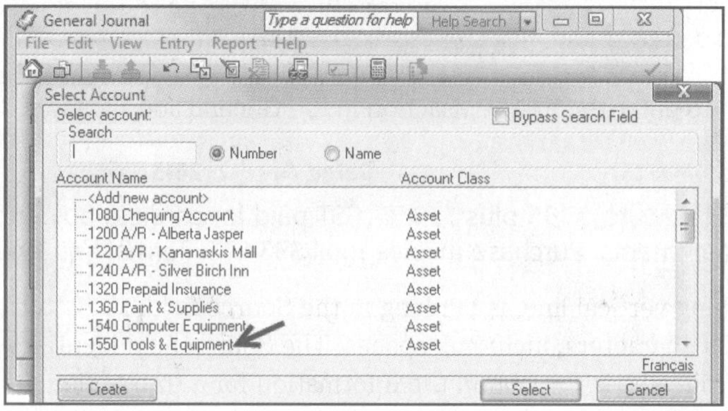

The beginning of the account list is displayed. The list includes only postable accounts, those that can be debited or credited in journal entries. The cursor is in the Search field. If you want to place the cursor in the account list directly from the Account field, you can choose the **Bypass Search Field** option. We will not select this option. Typing a number in the Search field selects the first account with that number. Following usual accounting practice, we enter the account to be debited first.

Click **1550 Tools & Equipment** to select this asset account.

Click the **Select button**. (A darker frame or an inner dotted box shows that a button is selected.)

You can also double-click a selected account or press (enter) to add it directly to your journal entry form. Instead of using the selection list, you can find the number in the Chart of Accounts, type it in and press (tab).

Notice that the account number and name have been added to your input form, so you can easily see whether you have selected the correct account. If the screen does not display the entire account title, you can see the rest of the account title by clicking anywhere on the part that is showing.

Your cursor is now positioned in the Debits field. The amount 0.00 is selected, ready to be changed. All journals include a **Windows Calculator tool** that opens the calculator directly for easy calculation of amounts if needed.

Click the Display The Windows Calculator tool to open the calculator. You can leave it open in the background for easy access.

Type amounts without dollar signs. You do not need to type decimals when you enter whole numbers. Sage 50 ignores any non-numeric characters that you type in an amount field.

Type `795`

Press (tab).

The cursor moves to the Comment field. You can add a comment for each account line in the journal. Account line comments are optional. You can add a comment for each line, for some lines or for none of the lines, but the extra details will be included in the journal report and will give you more information about the transaction.

Type `power drill + attachments`

NOTES

Many fields that allow you to select an account or other information from a list have the Select or List icon to provide quick access to the list. Showing the List icon is an option that you select as a user preference setting.

Other fields have list arrows that provide a drop-down or pop-up list.

NOTES

If the cursor is in the Account field, you can also press (enter) to open the Select Account list.

NOTES

Command statements that are indented but do not have the boldfaced command words show alternative keystrokes or optional instructions.

"You can also double-click..." is an example of an alternative command statement.

Press (tab). Your input form should now appear as follows:

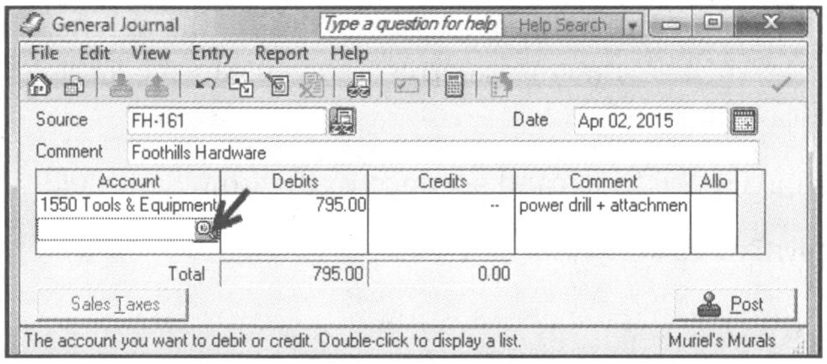

The cursor has advanced to the next line of the Account field, creating a new dotted box for the next account for this transaction — the liability account *GST Paid on Purchases*. Remember, liability accounts start with 2. However, we will type 3 to include the end of the 2000-level accounts in the selection list.

NOTES
If you know that the account you need is closer to the end of its numbered section, typing the next higher number shows you the end of the section you want. For example, typing 3 advances to 3100 and includes 2670 in the display. In this way, your account is more likely to be included in the display. Typing 2 will show the list with 2100 at the end and you will have to scroll down to include 2670.

Type 3

Click the **List icon** to advance your list to the 3000 accounts as shown:

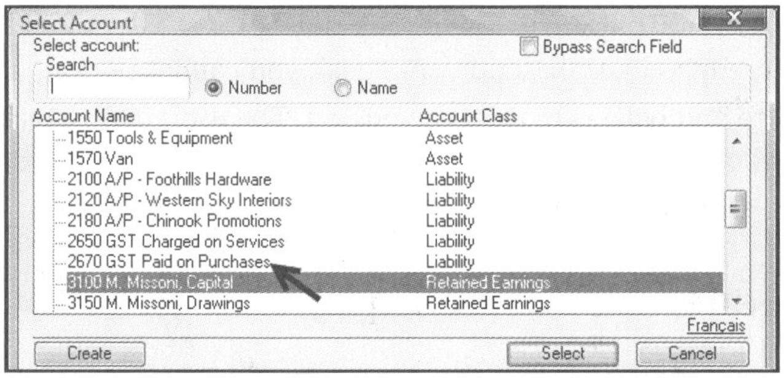

We have bypassed the Search field and selected the first account with the number we typed. This method quickly moves you to a later position in the list.

Click **2670 GST Paid on Purchases** from the displayed list to highlight it. If necessary, click a scroll arrow (▼ or ▲) to move through the account list to include *2670* in the display.

Press (enter).

Again, the account number and name have been added to your transaction form. The cursor has advanced to the Credits field, which shows 795.00 as the default amount because this amount will balance the entry. The amount is highlighted to indicate that you may edit it. This is a compound entry. You must change the amount to separate the GST, and you must delete the credit entry because the GST account is debited.

NOTES
Typing a negative number (adding a minus sign) in the Credits field will move the number to the Debits field. Typing a negative number in the Debits field will create a Credit entry.

Press (del) to delete the credit entry.

Click the **Debits field** on the second journal line below 795.00 to move the cursor.

Type 39.75

Press (tab) to advance to the optional Comment field.

Type GST @ 5%

Press (tab). The cursor moves to the next line in the Account field.

Press (enter) to open the Select Account list. The cursor is in the Search field.

Type 2

The list advances to the 2000 accounts. The liability account *2100 A/P - Foothills Hardware*, the account we need, is selected because it is the first 2000-level account.

Click **Select** to enter it and return to the journal.

The cursor advances to the Credits field again, where 834.75, the amount that will now balance the entry, is shown. The amount is correct, so you can accept it. The total for the Credits column is still displayed as zero.

Press tab to update the totals and advance to the Comment field.

Type `terms: net 30`

> **NOTES**
> The Sales Taxes button will be covered in Chapter 5. Sales taxes are not set up for Muriel's Murals so the button remains dimmed.

Your completed input form should appear as follows:

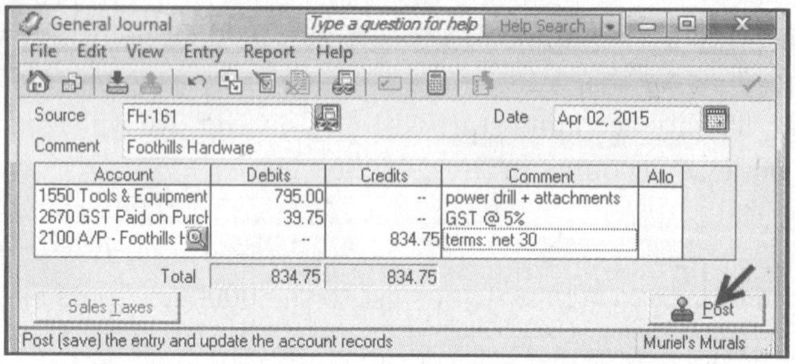

> **NOTES**
> We will use the Store tool button in the Chai Tea Room application (Chapter 5).

Until the debits and credits of a transaction are equal, you cannot post an entry. Once the entry is complete and balanced, it can be posted. The Store ( ) tool, for recurring entries, is also darkened. Before you proceed either to store or to post an entry, you should review the transaction.

Reviewing the General Journal Entry

> **NOTES**
> Pressing ctrl + J will also display the journal entry in any journal. Refer to Appendix B for a list of Sage 50 keyboard shortcuts.

Choose the **Report menu** and then **click Display General Journal Entry** as shown:

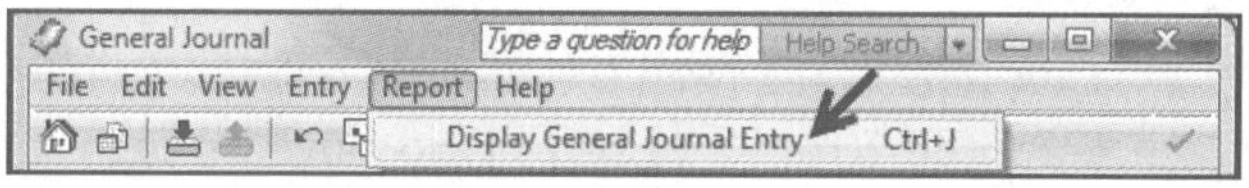

> **NOTES**
> If your display includes scroll arrows, you can use them to see more of your transaction.
> We use the short date format as the default for dates in reports.

The journal entry that will be posted for the transaction is displayed as follows:

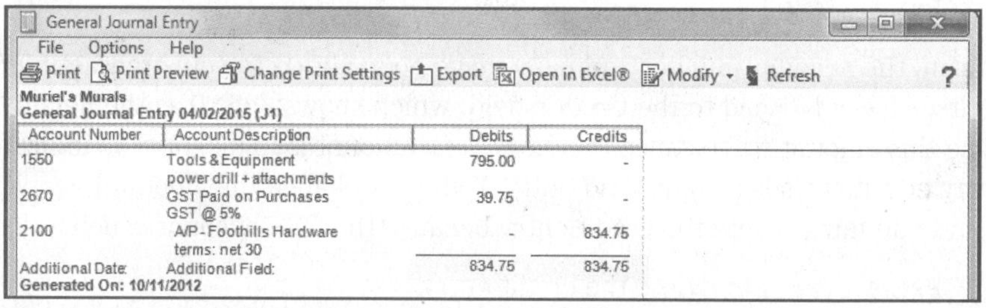

> **NOTES**
> The Additional Date and Field can be used to add more information to a journal entry. The Additional Information feature is available in all journals and will be introduced in Chapter 11.

Click the **Maximize button** to change your display to full screen size if your transaction does not fit on the screen.

To return to your input form,

Click or **choose** the entry's **Control Menu icon** and **click Close**.

> **NOTES**
> Refer to page 43 for assistance with correcting errors after posting.

CORRECTING THE GENERAL JOURNAL ENTRY BEFORE POSTING

Press tab to advance to the field that has the error. To move to a previous field, **press** shift and tab together (that is, while holding down shift, **press** tab). The field will be highlighted, ready for editing. **Type** the **correct information** and **press** tab to enter it.

You can also use the mouse to **point** to a field and **drag through** the **incorrect information** to highlight it. You can highlight a single number or letter, or the entire field. **Type** the **correct information** and **press** tab to enter it.

continued...

CORRECTING THE GENERAL JOURNAL ENTRY BEFORE POSTING CONTINUED

To correct an account number, **click** the **incorrect account number** (or **name**) to select the field. **Press** *enter* to display the list of accounts. **Click** the **correct account**. **Click Select. Press** *tab* to advance the cursor and enter the correction.

Click an **incorrect amount** to highlight it. **Type** the **correct amount** and **press** *tab*.

You can insert a line or remove a line by clicking the line that will be moved down or removed. Then **choose** the **Edit menu** and **click Insert Line** or **Remove Line**.

To discard the entry and begin again, **click** (Close) to close the journal or **click** (Undo on the tool bar) to open a blank journal window. When Sage 50 asks whether you want to discard the entry, **click Yes** to confirm your decision.

Posting

Once you are sure that all the information is correct, you are ready to post the entry.

Click the **Post button** Post in the lower right-hand corner of the General Journal (the one that looks like a stamp) or **choose** the **Entry menu** and then **click Post**.

We have chosen the option to confirm when a transaction is posted successfully, so you will see a confirmation message each time you post or record a transaction:

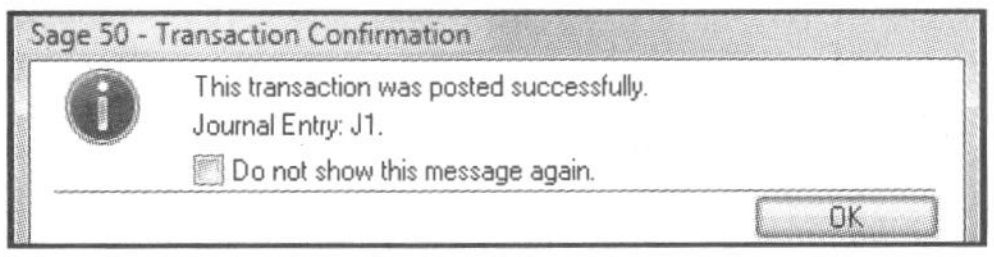

Click **OK** to open a new blank General Journal input form.

You can now enter the next transaction for this session date.

WARNING!
Don't post the transaction until you make sure that it is correct. Always review a transaction before posting it.

NOTES
This confirmation does not mean that you have entered the correct details, only that the entry could be posted – debits and credits were equal and data for required fields were included.

Adding a New Account

The bank credit memo on April 3 uses an account that is not listed in your Chart of Accounts. Often a company will need to create new accounts as it expands or changes direction. These future needs are not always foreseen when the accounts are first set up. You must add the account *2300 Bank Loan* to enter the bank credit memo transaction.

NOTES
You can add new accounts from the Account field in any journal or in the Accounts Ledger (Chart of Accounts). The Accounts Ledger is introduced in Chapter 4.

✓ 2 **Bank Credit Memo #AT-C3104** **Dated April 3, 2015**

From Alberta Trust Company, $8 000 bank loan secured for purchase of new customized work table. Loan deposited into bank account. Create new Group account 2300 Bank Loan.

First, enter the Source for the memo.

Type `AT-C3104`

Press *tab* **twice** to advance to the Date field. The date of the previous journal entry becomes the default date until you close the journal.

Click the **Calendar icon** and then **click 3**.

Press *tab* to advance to the Comment field.

Type `Alberta Trust - new loan`

Double-click the **Account field**.

NOTES
When you close the journal and open it later, the session date becomes the default again.

Double-click Chequing Account.

Type `8000` (the amount of the loan) as the debit part of the transaction.

Press *tab* to advance to the Comment field for the account.

Type `loan for customized work table`

Press *tab* to advance to the Account field on the second journal line.

Click the **List icon** or **press** *enter* to see the Select Account list.

Click **Add New Account**, the first entry in the list, and **click Select** or **click** the **Create** button.

This will begin the wizard for adding a General Ledger account:

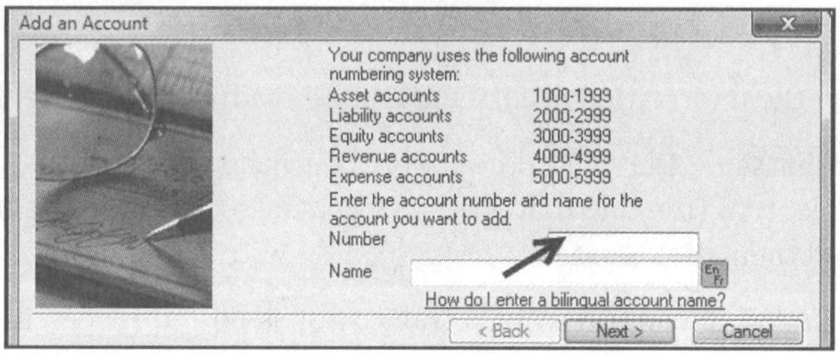

WARNING!
Enter account numbers carefully. You cannot change them after you post to the account in a journal entry.

The first screen prompts you for the account number and name. The cursor is in the Number field.

Type `2300`

Press *tab*.

Type `Bank Loan`

Click **Next** or **press** *enter* to continue.

NOTES
Next is selected so you can press *enter* repeatedly to advance through the wizard screens that you do not need to change.

The next screen asks for the **GIFI code**. This is the four-digit account number assigned by the Canada Revenue Agency for this category of account to use in electronically filed business returns. GIFI codes are not used in this workbook. They are described in Appendix K.

Click **Next** to skip this screen and continue.

The next screen asks whether this account is to be used as a **Heading** or **Total** in the financial statements. *Bank Loan* is an ordinary postable account that has a balance, so the default selection, No, is correct. A partial balance sheet illustrates account types.

Click **Next** to accept the default and continue.

WARNING!
Account types must be set correctly or you will get the error message that accounts are not in logical order when you try to display financial reports. If you see one of these messages, you can edit the account type. See Chapter 4, page 92, for help with creating and editing accounts.

The following screen deals with another aspect of the **account type**. Accounts may be **subtotalled** within their group of accounts. For example, if you have several bank accounts, you will want your Balance Sheet report to include the total cash deposited in all of them together. Different account types will be explained fully in the Toss for Tots application (Chapter 4), where you will set up the accounting records for a new company.

Bank Loan is a Group account. It is not subtotalled with any other account, so the default selection, No, is correct.

Click **Next** to continue.

The next wizard screen refers to the **account class**. Account classes are explained in Chapter 7. The default selection is the name of the section. Therefore, for account *2300*, Liability is the section and the default class. Generally, you can accept the default selection.

Click **Next** to continue.

Now you are being asked whether you want to **allocate** the balance of the account to different projects or divisions. Projects are not set up for Muriel's Murals, so the default selection, set at No for Balance Sheet accounts, is correct.

Click **Next** to continue.

The next setting screen asks whether you want to include or **omit** this account **from financial statements** when it has a zero balance. Choosing Yes means that if the balance in this account is zero, the account will not be included in your financial statements. If you choose No, the account will be printed even if it has a balance of zero. Some accounts, such as *Chequing Account*, should always be printed in financial statements. In Chapter 4 we explain this setting. The default setting, to include accounts (not to omit), is never wrong.

Click **Next** to continue to the final screen, like the one shown here:

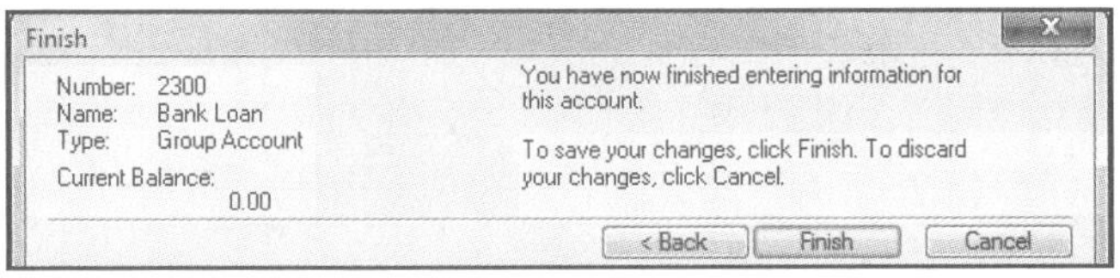

This final screen shows the selections you have made.

Check your **work**. **Click Back** until you reach the screen with the error. **Make** the **correction** and **click Next** until you reach this final screen again.

When all the information is correct, you must save the new account information.

Click **Finish**.

You will return to the General Journal window with the new account added to the account field. Notice that the cursor has not yet advanced, so you can change your account selection if you need to.

Click the **Credits field**. The balancing amount, $8 000, is added.

Press *tab* to accept the amount and advance to the Comment field.

Type `Alberta Trust loan`

Display the **journal entry** to see whether it is correct.

Close the **display**. **Make corrections** if you find errors.

Click **Post** [Post] to save the information. **Click OK** to confirm.

Enter the **next sale transaction** on your own.

3	**Sales Invoice #MM-40**	**Dated April 3, 2015**
	To Alberta Jasper, $3 500 plus $175 GST charged to design and paint animal theme mural in nursery as per contract. Sales invoice total $3 675. Terms: net 30 days.	

Adjusting a Posted Entry

Sometimes after posting a journal entry you discover that it had an error. You can make corrections directly in the General Journal by adjusting the previously posted transaction. Sage 50 allows you to make the correction by adjusting the entry without completing a reversing entry. The program creates the reversing and correcting journal

NOTES
For Muriel's Murals, the title for Projects is changed to Job Sites.

NOTES
Some reports have omitting accounts with zero balances as a report option.

NOTES
You can use the wizard in any account field to create a new account at any time. You do not need to use the account after creating it when you return to the journal.

NOTES
[3] A check box without a ✓ indicates that keystroke instructions are not provided for this source document.
The lower part of the check box contains the source document number (**3**).
If you use MM-xx as the source for sales, you can apply the report filter we show in Appendix E.

entries when you post the correction so that the audit trail is complete. The purchase from Foothills Hardware on April 2 was posted with an incorrect amount.

The General Journal should still be open.

✓ 4

Memo #1 **Dated April 4, 2015**

From Owner: The invoice from Foothills Hardware was entered incorrectly. The cost of the drill was $820 plus $41 GST paid. The revised purchase invoice total is $861. Adjust the posted invoice to make the correction.

Click the **Adjust A Previously Posted Entry tool** in the tool bar, or

choose the **Entry menu** and **click Adjusting Entry**.

> **NOTES**
> Pressing ctrl + A will also start the adjust entry process in any journal when the option is available.

The Search screen opens:

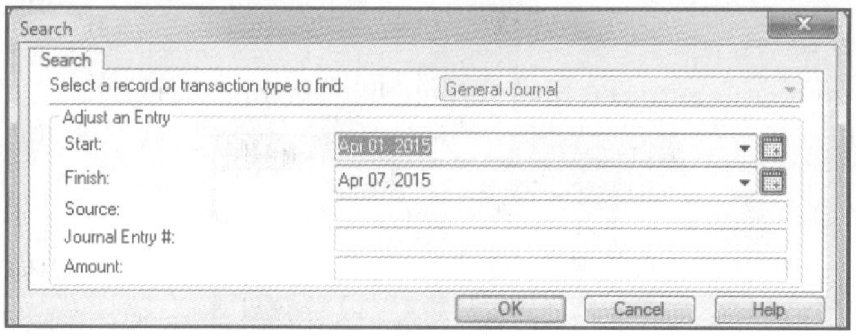

The Adjust An Entry and Search functions are combined. Because we selected the Adjust option, the Search section of the screen is dimmed, but General Journal is indicated as the search area. If you begin from the Home window Search option, the cursor will be placed in the Search part of the window. Finding a transaction is the same for both functions. You can select a range of journal entry dates to search. The date we converted the data files to Sage 50 and the session date are the default start and finish dates for the list. If you know the Source or the journal entry number, you can enter it in the Source or Journal Entry # field, respectively, and access the transaction entry directly by clicking OK.

We can accept the default dates because they include the transaction we need.

Click **OK** to list the journal entries:

> **NOTES**
> You should choose the order that makes it easiest to find your entry. That will depend on what information you entered and what you remember as well as how many entries you have.

All journal entries are listed with the most recent one at the top of the list (Z...A+ order for Date). You can choose the way the journal entries are sorted.

Click the **list arrow** beside the Date entry for **View Entries By**:

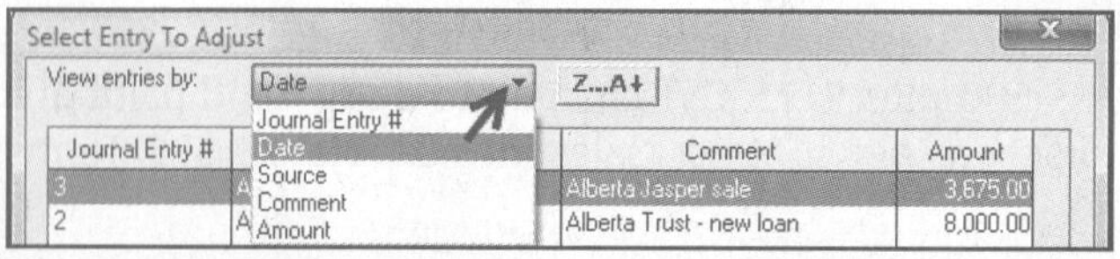

> **NOTES**
> Although Journal Entry #1 is highlighted, the cursor is still on the A...Z+ button, so pressing enter does not open the journal because of the keystroke sequence we used.
> You can also double-click anywhere on the line for an entry to open the transaction.

You can organize the list of entries by journal entry number, date, source number, comment or amount. The Z...A+ button lets you choose ascending or descending order.

Click **Journal Entry #**.

Click Z...A+ to reverse the order. The one we want is now first in the list.

Click **Journal Entry #1, FH-161** to select it.

Click **Select** or **double-click** to open the journal entry as it was posted:

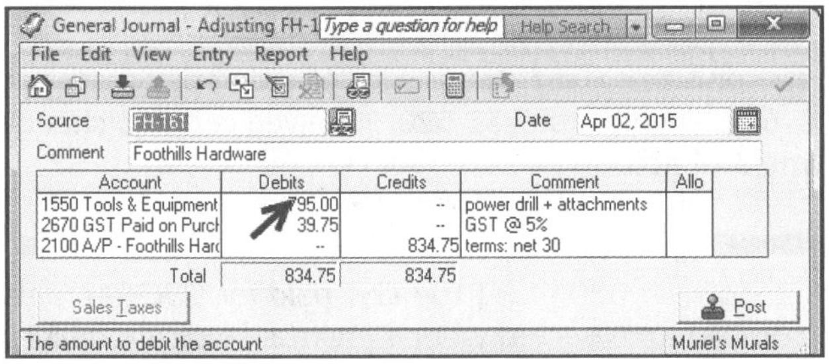

All fields may now be edited, just as if you had not yet posted the transaction. Notice that the title bar entry has changed to General Journal – Adjusting FH-161.

Click **795.00**, the amount in the Debit column for *Tools & Equipment*, to select it for editing.

Type 820

Click **39.75** or **press** ⇩ to select the Debit column amount for *GST Paid on Purchases*.

Type 41

Click **834.75**, the Credit column amount for *A/P - Foothills Hardware*.

Type 861 **Press** *tab* to update the totals with the correct amounts.

We will also modify the source to show that this entry is the correction for the memo.

Click the **Source field** before the current entry (**before F**).

Type (COR)

You can change the date for the correcting entry to April 4 if you want. We have not changed the date for this correction.

Review the **entry** to see the correct transaction and **close** the **display**. **Make corrections** if necessary.

Click **Post** Post. **Click OK** to confirm the posting. Notice that the entry is J5. (J4 is the reversing entry created by the program.)

When you display the General Journal Report with Corrections selected (refer to page 59), you will see three entries for the purchase invoice — the original incorrect entry, a reversing adjusting entry created by the program (ADJFH-161) and the correct entry (COR) FH-161 — providing a complete audit trail for the transaction and correction. See the partial General Journal Report display on page 59.

REVERSING A GENERAL JOURNAL ENTRY AFTER POSTING

If you need to reverse an entry instead of making changes to it, **click** the **Reverse Entry tool** in the tool bar of the General Journal – Adjusting window, or **choose** the **Entry menu** and **click Reverse Entry**. You will see a confirmation message before the action is taken. **Click Yes** to confirm and continue. Sage 50 does not delete the original entry. Instead it adds the reversing entry to the journal report for a complete audit trail. You can hide reversing entries in journal reports by not showing corrections.

Continue with the **journal entries** for the April 7 session date.

5 **Payment Cheque #48** **Dated April 5, 2015**

To Western Sky Interiors, $1 200 in payment of invoice #WSI-129.

6 **Cash Receipt #20** **Dated April 5, 2015**

From Alberta Jasper, cheque #828 for $2 400 in payment of invoice #MM-37.

NOTES

Usually clicking a number in a field will select the entire number. Sometimes, however, depending on exactly where you click, only part of the number is selected or an insertion point is added. Double-clicking will always select the entire number in the field so that you can edit it.

NOTES

You can change the date for the final correct entry but not for the adjusting or reversing entry.

NOTES

If you use Cheque #*xx* as the source for cheques, you can apply the report filter we show in Appendix E.

7

Cash Sales Invoice #MM-41 **Dated April 6, 2015**

To Rolf Kleinje, $2 400 plus $120 GST charged for plaster repair work and painting two rooms. Sales invoice total $2 520. Received certified cheque #AT-603 in full payment of account.

8

Purchase Invoice #WSI-611 **Dated April 6, 2015**

From Western Sky Interiors, $2 080 plus $104 GST paid for VOC-free paint and colour additives to complete contracted work. Purchase invoice total $2 184. Terms: net 30 days.

Advancing the Session Date and Backing Up Files

NOTES

We have set up the data files for Muriel's Murals so that future-dated transactions are not allowed.

NOTES

Refer to page 20 for information on the Save As and Save A Copy commands.

A complete data set is more than 25 Megabytes in size, while its backup file is about 2 Megabytes. The Save As and Save A Copy options require more disk storage space because the copy is not compressed.

When you have finished all the entries for the April 7 session date, the date for the next transaction is later than April 7. Therefore, you must advance the session date before you can continue. If you do not advance the date before posting the April 8 transaction, you will receive an error message.

Before advancing the date, however, close all open windows and then save and back up your work because you have already completed one week of transactions. Although Sage 50 saves automatically each time you post an entry or exit the program, it is important to know how to save and back up your work directly to a separate file and location or disk because your working files may become damaged and unusable.

Click or **choose** the **File menu** for the journal and **click Close** to close the General Journal.

To save a working copy of the file under a different file name, choose the File menu and click Save A Copy to continue working with the original files or Save As to open a new working copy of the file.

The data files for this workbook have been prepared with the default warning to back up your work weekly. Since we also advance the session date by one week at a time, you will be reminded to back up each time you advance the session date. You are now ready to advance the session date to April 14.

WARNING!

You must close all windows before you can advance the session date or before you make a backup.

You can click , the Home window Close Other Windows tool, or close each window separately. You also must be working in single-user mode to change the session date.

Click the **Calendar icon** beside **Session Date: Apr 07, 2015** on the right-hand side of the Home window:

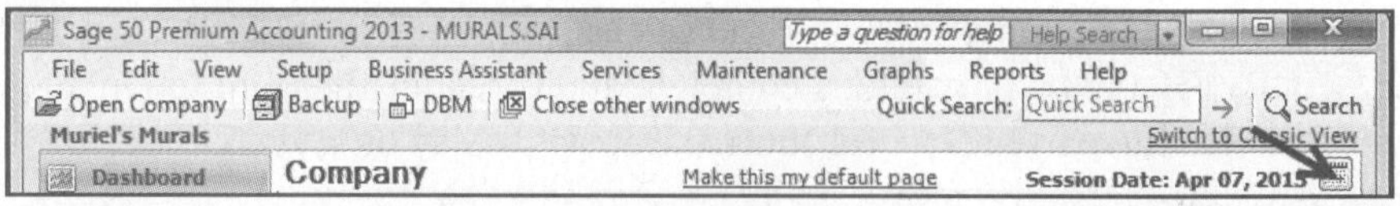

Or **choose** the **Maintenance menu** and **click Change Session Date** as shown:

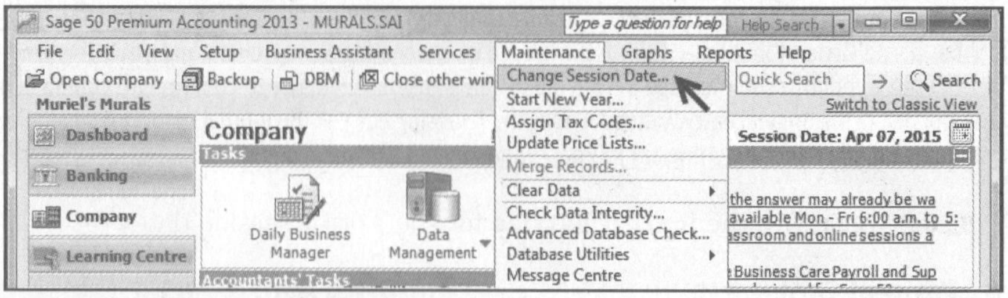

The Change Session Date window opens with the current session date highlighted:

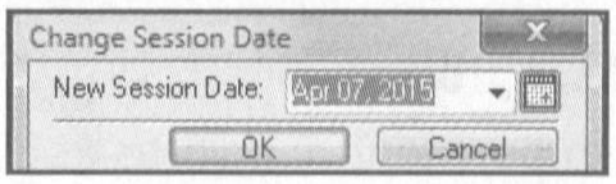

Type 04-14-15 (or click the calendar icon and click 14).

Click **OK** to accept the new date.

The following message advises you that you have not yet backed up your work:

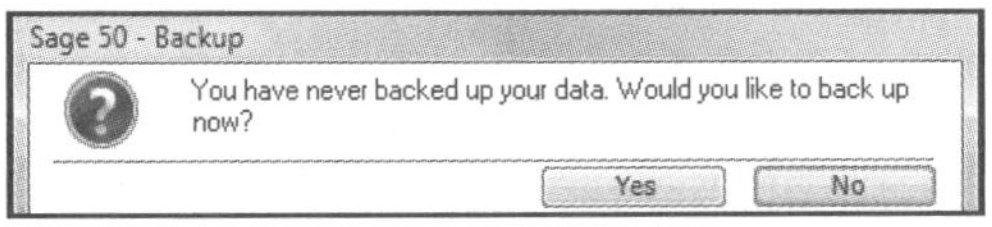

Click **Yes** to proceed with the backup. The next screen asks for a file name for the backup:

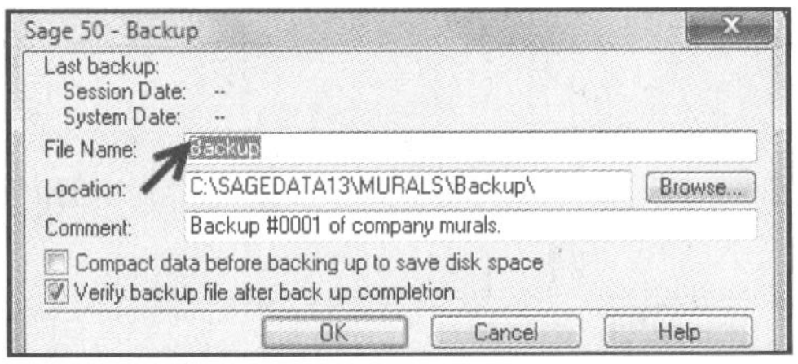

Sage 50 will create a file named Backup1 inside a new Backup subfolder of the folder that contains your working data files. You can edit the file name, location and comment. The name Backup is selected so you can change the name.

Type `murals`

If you want to change the location of the backup, click Browse, select a folder and file name and click OK.

Click **OK** to proceed.

When you name a new folder, you will see the following advisory message:

The program recognizes that the name is new and offers to create the folder. If you have typed the correct name and location,

Click **Yes** to accept the information and continue.

The backup file is different from the one you create by copying or using the Save A Copy or Save As command. The Save A Copy and Save As commands create a complete working copy of your data that you can access with the Sage 50 program directly. Backup creates a compressed file that must first be restored before you can use it to enter transactions. This file has 1 and the .CAB file extension added to the name

After a brief interval, you will see the message that the backup is complete:

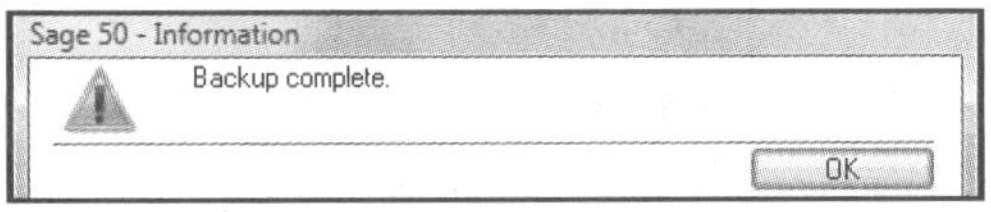

Click **OK** to proceed. You may now enter transactions for this session date.

If you have already created a backup for this data file, or when you change the session date again, you will be advised of the most recent backup date when you are prompted to back up again:

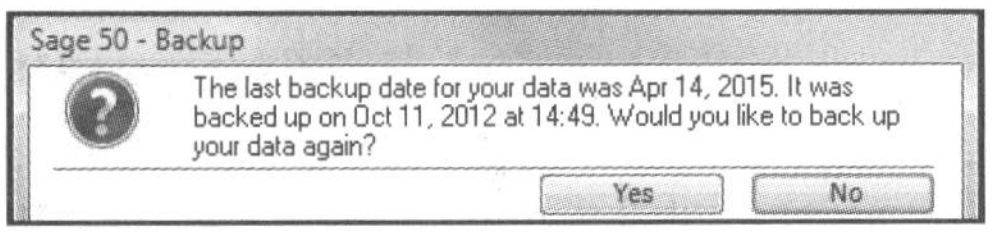

Click **Yes** to continue.

NOTES
You cannot create backups when working in multi-user mode.

WARNING!
Be sure to back up each time you are prompted to do so or each time you advance the session date. If your files are damaged, your work will be lost unless you have a backup.

NOTES
For later backups, you will see a backup message that shows the previous backup file name and date. In this case the backup # will also be increased as shown in the example on page 48.

WARNING!
You cannot use the same name for the backup and the file if they are in the same folder. If you want to use the same name, you must use a different folder. By using the Backup folder, we can name the backup file murals.

NOTES

When you change the session date again, the prompt to back up the file will include the session date and calendar date and time of the previous backup.

WARNING!

We recommend updating the backup name by adding a date or number to the name. For example, type murals2 for the next backup, then murals3 and so on. This will provide backups for different stages to return to if you later find errors.

Sage 50 will provide the same file name and location that you used for your most recent backup. The backup number in the Comment field will be updated.

Your backup information screens will look like the one we show, but with different system dates — the ones from your own computer:

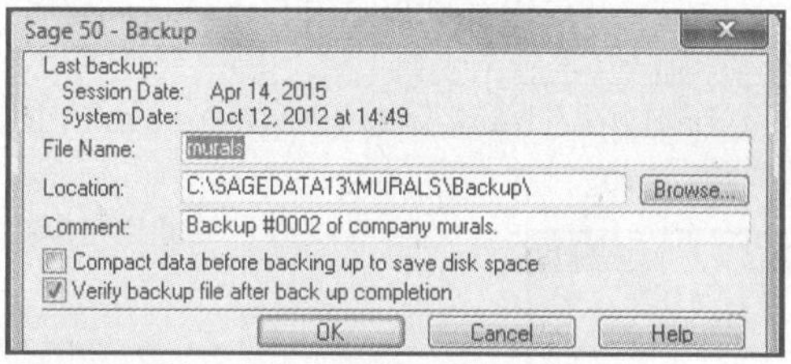

Click **OK**, or **make** the **changes** you want. Again, you can change the file name, its location or the comment.

Click **OK**.

If you use the same backup file name, you will be asked to replace the previous file:

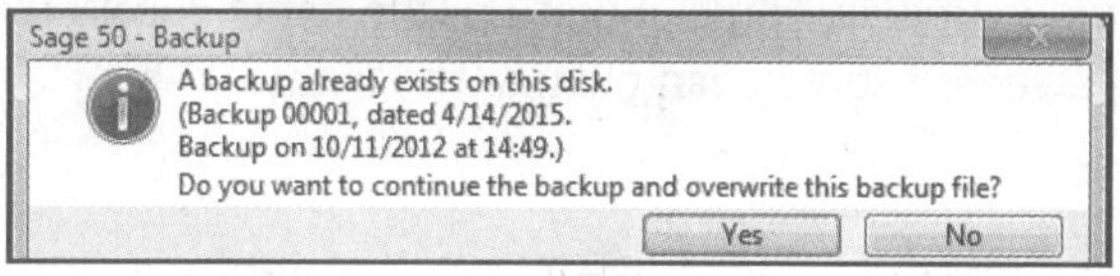

Clicking No will result in the message that the backup was unsuccessful. Then click OK to return to the Backup File Name screen.

Click Yes to continue with the replacement or click No to enter a different name.

Enter the **remaining transactions for April**.

9

Bank Debit Memo #AT-D3691 **Dated April 8, 2015**

From Alberta Trust Company, $49 for bank service charges.

10

Purchase Invoice #WMM-4499 **Dated April 10, 2015**

From West Mall Mechanical, $840 plus $42 GST paid for maintenance work on van. Purchase invoice total $882. Terms: net 10 days. Create new Group account 2190 A/P - West Mall Mechanical.

11

Memo #2 **Dated April 11, 2015**

Missoni paid her business hydro and telephone bills from her personal chequing account. She wrote cheque #49 for $361.20 to reimburse herself for these expenses. The hydro bill was $160 plus $8.00 GST and the telephone bill was $184 plus $9.20 GST.

12

Bank Credit Memo #AT-C3421 **Dated April 11, 2015**

From Alberta Trust Company, $240 semi-annual interest earned on bank account.

13

Cash Receipt #21 **Dated April 12, 2015**

From Kananaskis Mall, cheque #58821 for $3 600 in full payment of invoice #MM-38.

14

Sales Invoice #MM-42 **Dated April 14, 2015**

To Kananaskis Mall, $2 500 plus $125 GST charged for consultations and design additions for existing park theme mural. Sales invoice total $2 625. Terms: net 30 days.

SESSION DATE – APRIL 21, 2015

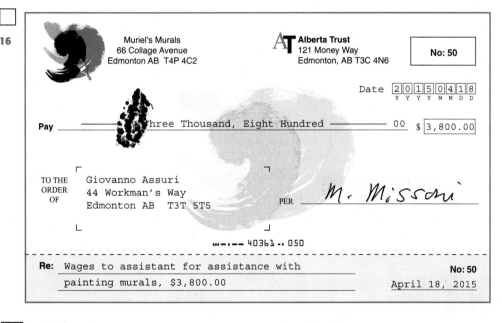

15

To: Muriel's Murals
66 Collage Avenue
Edmonton, AB
T4P 4C2

DEVON EQUIPMENT CO.
68 CUTTERS ROAD EDMONTON, AB T4C 3N6
TEL: 780-775-6116

Date: April 15, 2015

No: DE-1141

Description of item	
Large stainless steel work table with power supply	8,000.00

GST # 651 034 271	**Terms:** net 30 days	**Subtotal**	8,000.00
Signature M. Missoni		**GST**	400.00
		Total	$8,400.00

16

Muriel's Murals
66 Collage Avenue
Edmonton AB T4P 4C2

Alberta Trust
121 Money Way
Edmonton, AB T3C 4N6

No: 50

Date 20150418
Y Y Y Y M M D D

Pay ———Three Thousand, Eight Hundred ——— 00 $ 3,800.00

TO THE ORDER OF
Giovanno Assuri
44 Workman's Way
Edmonton AB T3T 5T5

PER M. Missoni

⑈—⑈— 40361 ⑈ 050

Re: Wages to assistant for assistance with painting murals, $3,800.00

No: 50
April 18, 2015

17 **Sales Invoice #MM-43** **Dated April 19, 2015**

To Lindbrook Estates, $1 600 plus $80 GST charged for consultation and design of frieze and mural for home office. Sales invoice total $1 680. Terms: net 10 days. Create new Group account 1280 A/R - Lindbrook Estates.

18 **Payment Cheque #51** **Dated April 20, 2015**

To West Mall Mechanical, $842 in payment of account. Reference invoice #WMM-4499.

NOTES

Create new Group account: 2210 A/P - Devon Equipment

NOTES

Use the General Journal for the payroll transaction in this application.

19 **Sales Invoice #MM-44** **Dated April 20, 2015**

To Sherwood Park Estates (new customer), $6 000 plus $300 GST charged to prepare and paint bedroom walls and ceilings, as per contract. Sales invoice total $6 300. Terms: net 10 days. Create new Group account 1260 A/R - Sherwood Park Estates.

20 **Cash Receipt #22** **Dated April 21, 2015**

From Lindbrook Estates, cheque #189 for $1 680 in payment of invoice #MM-43.

SESSION DATE – APRIL 28, 2015

21 **Sales Invoice #MM-45** **Dated April 24, 2015**

To Silver Birch Inn, $4 100 plus $205 GST charged to paint mural in dining room as per contract. Sales invoice total $4 305. Terms: net 30 days.

22 **Purchase Invoice #BT-2194** **Dated April 25, 2015**

From Beaumont Tekstore, $810 plus $40.50 GST paid for external hard drive for computer. Purchase invoice total $850.50. Terms: net 10 days. Create new Group account 2220 A/P - Beaumont Tekstore.

23 **Cash Purchase Invoice #BAA-719** **Dated April 25, 2015**

From Bon Accord Advertising, $400 plus $20 GST paid for printing and copying advertising flyers. Purchase invoice total $420. Terms: cash on receipt. Invoice paid in full with cheque #52.

24 **Cheque #53** **Dated April 28, 2015**

To Fonteyn Dance Studio, $390 for one session of dance lessons for daughter. Use Drawings account.

SESSION DATE – APRIL 30, 2015

25 **Memo #3** **Dated April 30, 2015**

Missoni used $1 450 of paint and supplies to complete projects in April.

26

Sherwood Park Estates
900 Sherwood Park Rd.
Edmonton, AB
T4J 4S6

No: 223

Date 20150430
Y Y Y Y M M D D

Pay to the order of Muriel's Murals $ 6,300.00

Six thousand three hundred 00 /100 **Dollars**

Royal Bank
69 Royalty Avenue
Edmonton, AB T3P 7C6

Robin Sherwood
Signature

⑈--- 393214 -⑈ 0223

Re: Reference Invoice #MM-44, $6,300.00 **No: 223**
In full payment of account. $6,300.00 April 30, 2015

27

April 30, 2015

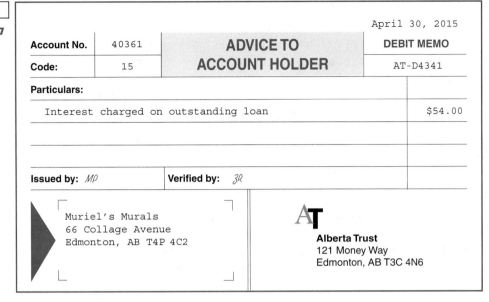

Account No.	40361	ADVICE TO ACCOUNT HOLDER	DEBIT MEMO
Code:	15		AT-D4341

Particulars:

Interest charged on outstanding loan	$54.00

Issued by: MP **Verified by:** JR

Muriel's Murals
66 Collage Avenue
Edmonton, AB T4P 4C2

AT
Alberta Trust
121 Money Way
Edmonton, AB T3C 4N6

28 **Memo #4** **Dated April 30, 2015**

Cheque #51 for $842 to West Mall Mechanical was entered with an incorrect cheque amount. The cheque amount was $882. Adjust the entry to change the amount.

Displaying General Reports

A key advantage to using Sage 50 rather than a manual system is the ability to produce financial reports quickly for any date or time period. Sage 50 allows you to enter accounting data accurately so you can prepare the reports you need for reporting to government and investors and for business analysis.

Reports that are provided for a specific date, such as the Balance Sheet, can be produced for any date from the time the accounting records were converted to the computerized system up to the latest journal entry. Reports that summarize a financial period, such as the Income Statement, can be produced for any period between the beginning of the fiscal period and the latest journal entry.

Reports are available from multiple locations: the Accounts window, the Home window Reports menu, the Display tool in the Classic view, and from the Reports list and the Report Centre in the Reports pane of the Home window.

The Reports Menu

From the Home window Reports menu, most General Ledger reports are located under the Financials option as shown:

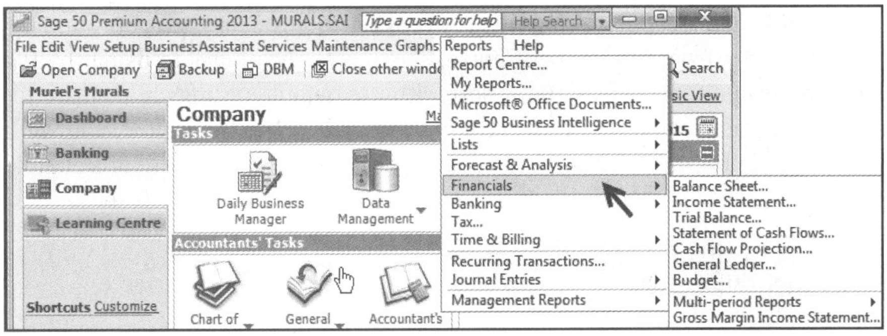

NOTES
Report analysis is beyond the scope of this text.

NOTES
If you have data for more than one fiscal period, you can display and print reports for the previous fiscal periods.

NOTES
The Home window Reports menu shows only the General Ledger reports because the other ledgers are hidden.

PRO VERSION
Sage 50 Business Intelligence, Forecast & Analysis, Multi-Period reports and Time & Billing reports are not available in the Pro version.

Accounts Window Reports Menu

Click the Chart of Accounts icon in the Home window (Classic view or Enhanced view) to open the Accounts window. All General Ledger reports will be available from the Reports menu in this window.

The Display Tool in the Classic View

CLASSIC VIEW
Right-click a Classic view Home window icon to select it without opening the journal or ledger.

The Display tool (on the Classic view Home window tool bar) provides a shortcut to displaying reports related directly to the ledger and journal icons. These include lists related to the ledgers such as the Chart of Accounts, supplier and employee lists, as well as all journal reports. The Display tool works in three different ways:

1. If a ledger or journal icon is selected but not open, the options window for that report is displayed immediately when you click the Display tool. The label for the Display tool changes to name the report for a selected icon.
2. If no icon is highlighted, clicking the Display tool produces the Select Report window that lists all journal reports and ledger lists. Click the list arrow and choose a report from this list. Click Select to display the report options window.
3. When the Accounts window is open, clicking the Display tool provides a Select A Report window that lists all the reports for the General Ledger. Click the list arrow, choose from this list and click Select to display the report or its options window. In other ledger windows, the reports list will include the reports related to that ledger.

NOTES
Financial, Account and Banking reports are all available from the Reports menu and Display tool list in the Accounts window.

The Reports Pane and Report Centre

PRO VERSION
You will not see Multi-Period reports in the list.

The Reports pane allows access to reports in three ways: from the Report Centre, from the list of recently viewed reports or from the drop-down list of reports for the module you have open. The Company module Reports list is shown here:

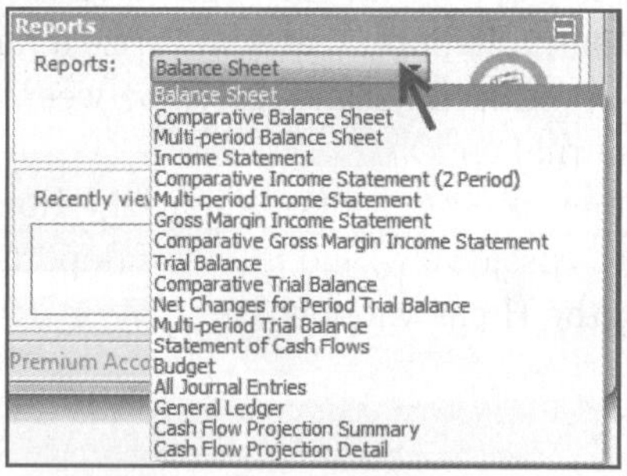

Clicking a report in this list will display it with the default report settings. Once you have displayed a report, it will be added to the Recently Viewed Reports pane list. Clicking the report in this list will display it with the settings you used most recently. If you have modified a report, using this list provides quick access to your modified report.

We will work from the Report Centre. There are advantages to using the Report Centre: you can either display the report with the default settings immediately or display the Options windows. Furthermore, before opening the report, you will see the purpose and a brief description of the report you want and a display of a sample report.

Click the **Report Centre icon** in the Reports pane.

Click **Financials** in the Select A Report Type list:

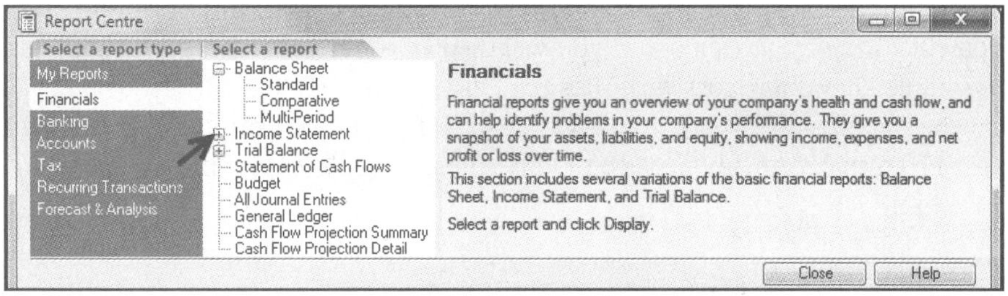

As from the Reports menu, reports for ledgers that are hidden are not available. Financial reports are selected because we started from the Company module Home window, and a list of the different financial reports is added. You can see that several of the reports have a ⊞ beside them, indicating that there are different forms of the report. A brief explanation of Financial Reports appears.

Read the **description**.

Click the ⊞ beside each report type to expand the list.

Click **Balance Sheet** to see a general description of balance sheets:

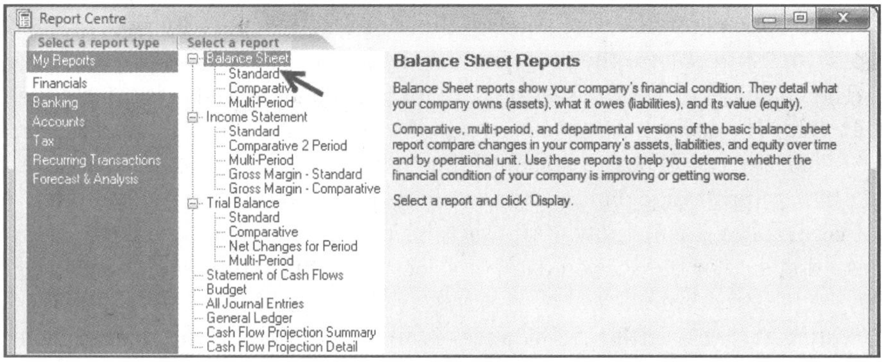

Because Balance Sheet is selected, the description now applies to that report. Standard (single-period) and Comparative (two-period) reports are available. When you have data for more than two months, you can also display Multi-Period Balance Sheets to compare reports for periods ranging from one to 12 months.

Displaying the Balance Sheet

The Balance Sheet shows the financial position of the business on the date you select for the report. You can display the Balance Sheet at any time.

Click **Standard** below Balance Sheet:

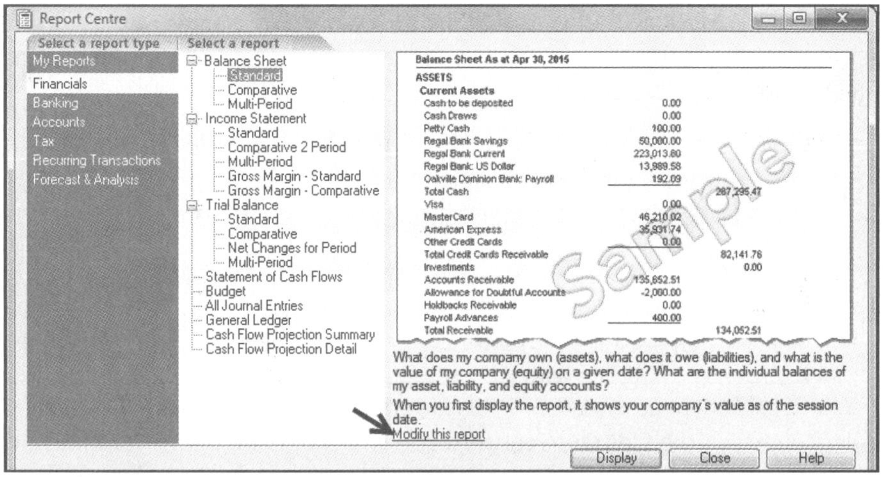

NOTES

When you open the Report Centre from a module window, the first report for that module is selected and you will see the description for it. Balance Sheet – Standard and its description may be displayed initially from the Company module window. Clicking Financials will return you to the general description of Financial Reports and its list.

PRO VERSION

The Pro version does not have Forecast & Analysis reports, and you will not see entries for Multi-Period reports.

You now see a sample of a standard Balance Sheet with its description and purpose. If you click **Display** at this point, you will display the report with the default settings. The sample shows a report with these default settings. To change the settings or to see what the defaults are, you can use the **Modify This Report** option. We will use this approach so that you can learn to modify the settings to suit your specific needs.

Click **Modify This Report** to open the Balance Sheet options window:

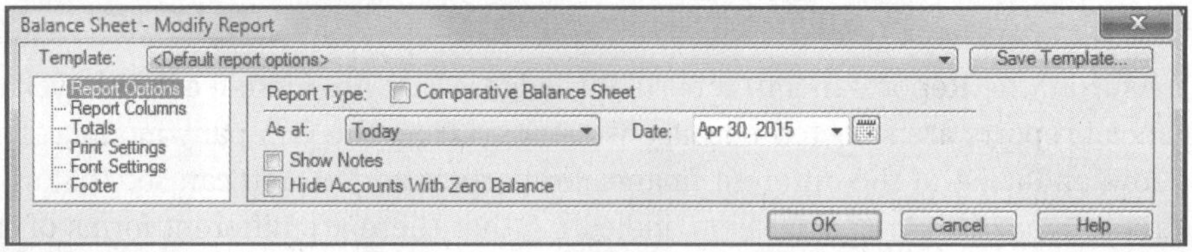

You can also choose the Reports menu, then choose Financials and click Balance Sheet. The report options window will open.

Default Report Options appears as the template the first time you view a report. The next time you open this window, the Last Used Report Options will display as the template. This selection allows you to see the same report without re-entering dates and other options. At any time you can choose **Default Report Options** on the Template drop-down list to restore the program default settings.

The default is to use the session date for the report — Today is selected in the **As At** field. The session date is entered in the Date field to match the selection in the As At field. You can choose a standard time period from the As At drop-down list, or you can enter a specific date in the Date field. In the **Date** field, you can select from a list that includes the first day of transactions entered in the program, the latest transaction date or the session date, or select a date from the Calendar icon to the right of the Date field.

NOTES
When you have postdated transactions, the latest transaction date will be later than the session date. Both dates will be on the drop-down list for the Date field.

Hiding accounts with zero balances is another option for the report. When you choose to omit zero balance accounts in the General Ledger (see page 90), you must select the option for each account individually, and the selection will apply to all reports showing that account. Here, you can choose the option selectively for different reports.

Click the **As At field list arrow** to see the options:

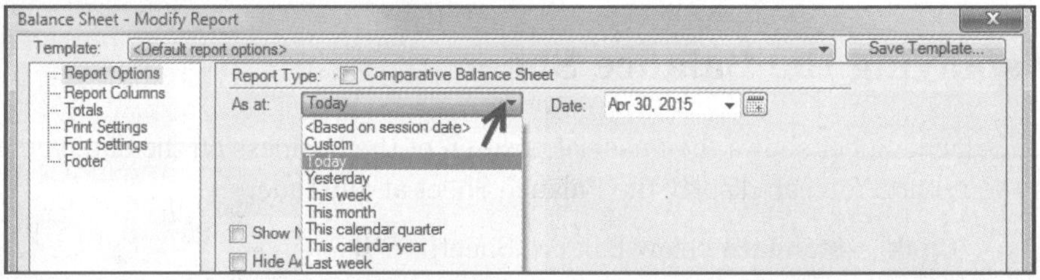

If you want to show the Balance Sheet for two different dates at the same time, you can use the Comparative Balance Sheet. Remember that this was also one of the options in the Report Centre window.

NOTES
Later applications use comparative statements for analysis purposes.

Click **Comparative Balance Sheet** to select this style of report and open the second date field as follows:

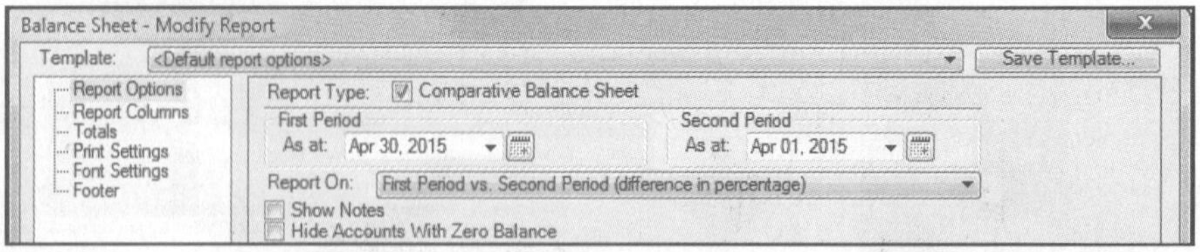

Your most recent session date is displayed in the first date field. The second date is the date on which the files were converted to Sage 50, the earliest transaction date.

Press tab to highlight the first date if you want to change it.

Click the **Calendar icon** to the right of the date (As At) field.

To enter a date, click and choose a date, select a date from the list or type the date you want using any accepted date format.

Press tab or **press** tab **twice** if you type the date.

Type the **second date** or choose from the date list or calendar.

Click the **Report On field** to display the report types in the drop-down list:

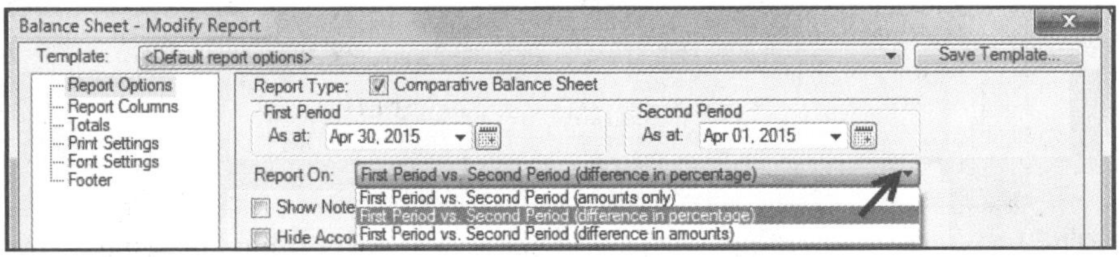

Choose **Amounts Only** if you want only the dollar balances for both dates. Choose **Difference In Percentage** if you want the dollar balances as well as the percentage increase from the second, earlier period amount to the first period amount. Choose **Difference In Amounts** if you want the dollar balances together with the difference between them in dollars. The second, earlier period amount is subtracted from the first to calculate the difference.

Click the report **contents** you want.

Click **OK** to display the Balance Sheet.

From any displayed report, you can change report options to create different reports.

Click the **Modify tool** and **choose Report Options** or **choose** the **Options menu** and **click Modify Report** to re-open the report options screen.

Click when you have finished to return to the Report Centre.

Displaying the Income Statement

The Income Statement is a summary of how much a business has earned — after expenses — in the interval you select for the statement. You can view the Income Statement at any time from the Report Centre or the Reports menu. We will continue from the Report Centre. The Income Statement list should still be expanded. You can see that the options are to display a Standard (single-period), Comparative (two-period) or Multi-Period statement. If inventory costs are tracked, Gross Margin Statements that separate the cost of goods sold from other expenses can also be displayed.

Click **Income Statement** and then **Standard** under Income Statement in the Select A Report list to see the report sample.

Click **Modify This Report** to open the report options window:

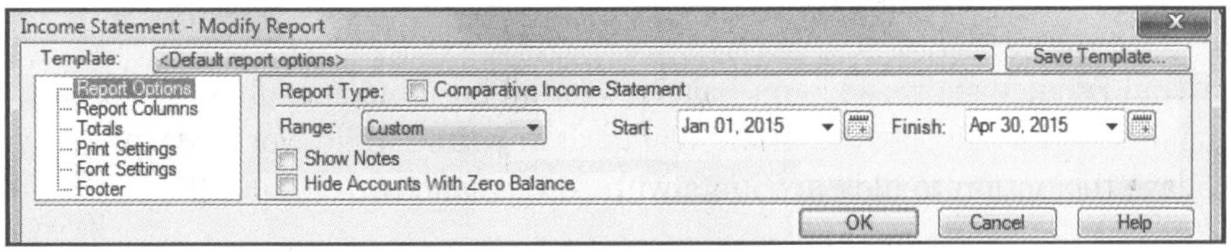

From the Home window, choose the Reports menu, then choose Financials and click Income Statement to open the Modify Report window.

NOTES

If you want a single Balance Sheet only, do not click Comparative Balance Sheet (the check box does not have a ✓ in it). Your most recent session date is displayed by default and highlighted. Choose from the calendar, choose from the date field list or type in the date you want. Click OK to display the Balance Sheet.

If you have accounting data for more than one fiscal period, you can display reports for the previous period as well as for the current period.

NOTES

The date list provided by the list arrow includes the earliest transaction date, the latest session date and the latest transaction date. The earliest transaction date and session date are frequent choices for the start and finish dates in reports.

NOTES

All reports include the option to modify them so you can change your report options easily. Modifying reports is covered more extensively in Appendix E on the Student DVD.

NOTES
The default report range is for the fiscal year up to the session date.

As for the Balance Sheet, you can hide accounts with zero balances. You can select the range of dates for the statement from the Range field list or from the Start and Finish field drop-down lists. You can also enter your own choices for the date range (Custom) by typing them in the Start and Finish fields or selecting other dates from the Calendar for those fields. The default range is the fiscal year to date.

Click the **Range field list arrow**:

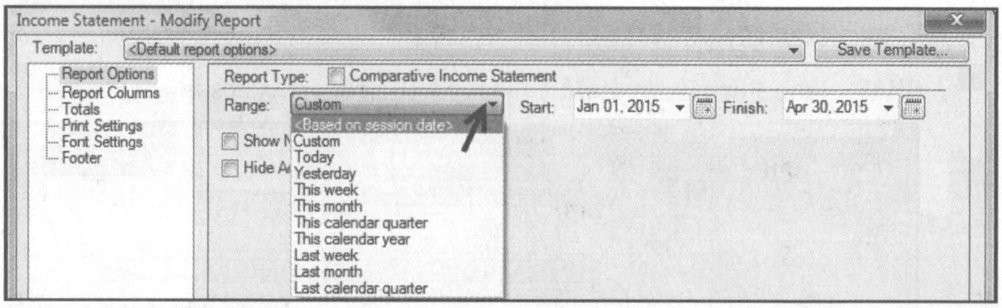

NOTES
If you have data for two fiscal periods, the dates for these two periods will be the defaults for comparative income statements.

The Income Statement also has a comparative report option, allowing comparisons between two different periods. You might want to compare the income for two months, quarters or years. For the comparative report, you have the same amount and difference options as the Balance Sheet.

Click **Comparative Income Statement** to select this option:

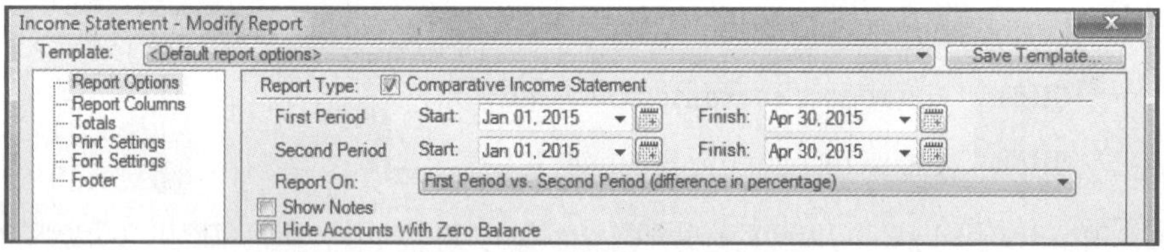

NOTES
When other modules are used, the Home window Reports menu in the Premium version includes a Business Reports option with several analysis reports. One of these is a Comparative Income Statement – YTD To Last Year. The menu label for these reports changes to match the industry type.

By default, the fiscal start date is provided as the start date for the first period and the second period. The session date is the finish date for both periods when you select the comparative report.

You must enter beginning and ending dates for the period (or periods) you want your Income Statement to cover. You may accept the defaults, choose a date from the calendar, choose from the date field list or type in the dates.

Click the **Start date field** and **enter** the **date** on which your Income Statement period begins.

Press *tab* (**twice** if you type the date).

Enter the **date** that your Income Statement period ends.

Enter the **Start** and **Finish dates** for the second period and **choose** the report **content** for comparative reports.

Click **OK**.

Click ☒ to close the display window when you have finished.

Displaying the Trial Balance

The Trial Balance shows account balances for all postable accounts in debit and credit columns. You can display the Trial Balance at any time while working with the software and have the option to hide accounts with zero balances.

Click **Trial Balance** and then **Standard** under Trial Balance in the Select A Report list to display the sample Trial Balance.

Click **Modify This Report** to see the report options window:

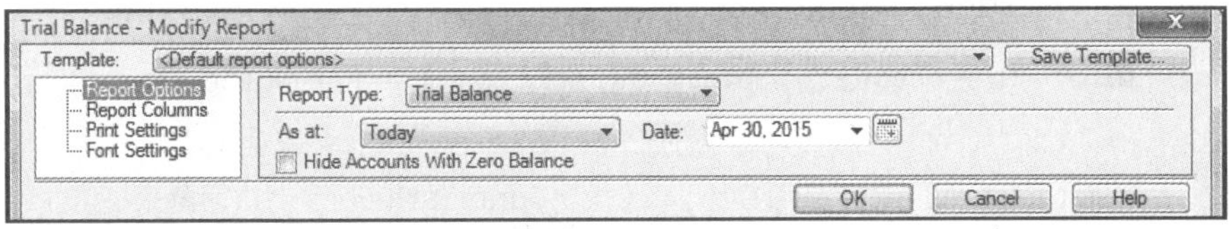

From the Home window choose the Reports menu, then choose Financials and click Trial Balance to open the report options window.

Click the **default date** and **enter** the **date** for which you want the Trial Balance or choose from the calendar.

Choose whether you want to **hide accounts with zero balances**.

Click **OK** to display the Trial Balance.

Click to leave the display and return to the previous screen or window.

Displaying the General Ledger Report

The General Ledger Report lists all transactions for one or more accounts in the selected interval. You can display the General Ledger at any time.

Click **General Ledger** in the Select A Report list to display the sample report.

Click **Modify This Report** to see the report options window:

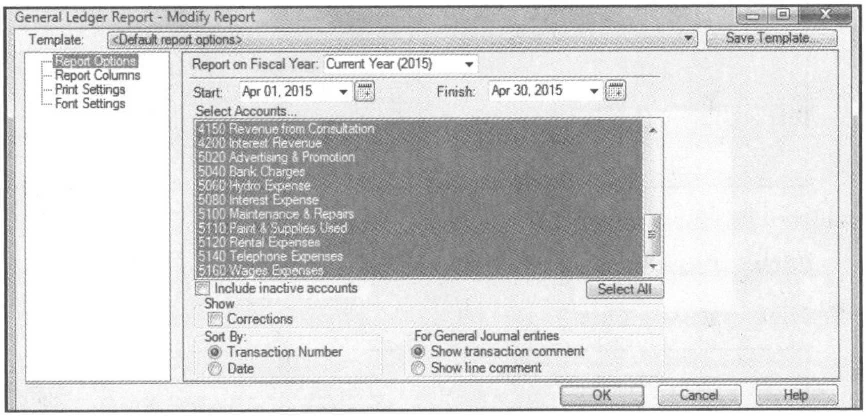

From the Home window choose the Reports menu, then choose Financials and click General Ledger to display the report options.

The General Ledger Report can be sorted in order of the transaction number (journal entry number) or the transaction date. The report includes account balances and transaction or account line comments. The earliest transaction and session dates are the default Start and Finish dates. All accounts are selected for the report initially. You can include or omit the corrections (adjusting and reversing entries) you made to journal entries with the **Show Corrections** option.

Click an **option** to select it or to change the default choices.

Enter the **starting date** for your General Ledger Report, choose a date from the calendar or choose a date from the Start field drop-down list.

Press *tab* (**twice** if you type the date).

Enter the **ending date** for your General Ledger Report.

The **Select All** option works like a toggle switch. When all accounts are selected, clicking Select All will remove all selections. With one or more

NOTES

The Trial Balance is also available in two other formats from the Report Type drop-down list: a Comparative Report with the same options as the Balance Sheet, and a report that shows the Net Changes for the selected period. Click the selection you want, enter the first and second dates, choose the report contents from the Report On list and click OK.

NOTES

When you do not show corrections, only the final correct entry is included in reports.

accounts selected or with no selections, clicking Select All will include all accounts for the reports.

Click the **account**, or **press** and **hold** ctrl and **click** the **accounts** you want to include.

Use the scroll arrows to see more accounts if the one you want is not visible. Click a selected item again to turn off the selection.

To select several accounts in a row, click the first one and then press and hold shift and click the last one you want to include in the list.

Choose the sorting method (date or journal entry) and the type of comment (transaction or account line) to include in your report.

Click **OK** to view the report.

Click to close the **display window** after viewing it.

Displaying the Chart of Accounts

The Chart of Accounts is a list of all accounts with the account number, name and account type and class.

CLASSIC VIEW
From the Home window, right-click the Chart of Accounts icon to select it. Click , the Display tool on the tool bar, to open the report options.
Right-click an icon in the Home window (click the right mouse button) to select it without opening the ledger or journal. Clicking the left mouse button will open the journal or ledger.

NOTES
When you have data for more than one fiscal period, you can display the Chart of Accounts for any of these years. For Muriel's Murals, only the Current Year is available.

Click **Accounts** in the Select A Report Type list (the list on the left) to expand the Select A Report list:

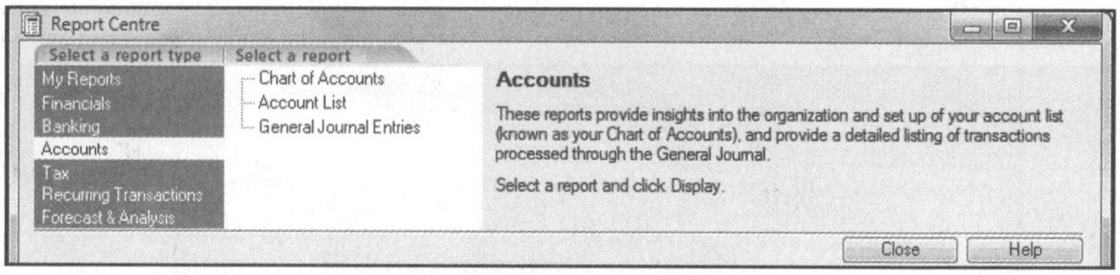

A brief description for the class of Accounts reports appears with the expanded list.

Click **Chart of Accounts** in the Select A Report list to display the sample.

Click **Modify This Report** to see the report options window:

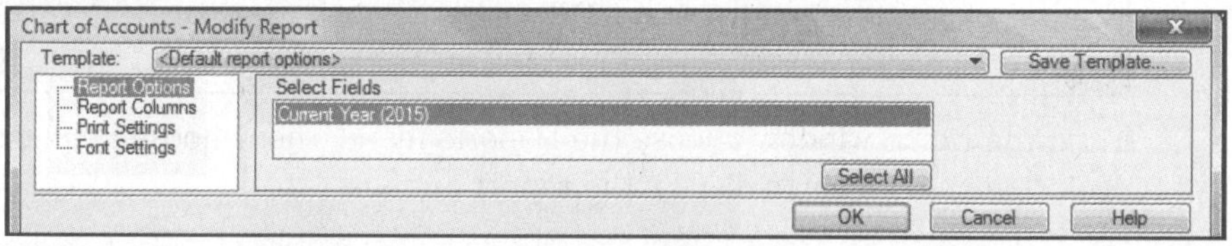

Or choose the Reports menu, then choose Lists and click Chart Of Accounts to display report options.

Choose the **Template** and the **year** (in the Select Fields list).

Click **OK** to see the chart. **Close** the **display** when you have finished.

Displaying the Account List

If you want to display the Chart of Accounts with account balances or other selected details, you can use the Account List. For example, you could create an account list with only GIFI numbers or account balances as the additional information.

Click **Account List** in the Select A Report list to display the sample.

Click **Modify This Report** to see the report options window:

From the Home window, choose the Reports menu, then choose Lists and click Accounts to see the report options.

Click **OK** to view the report. The default report shows the account number and name, balance, account type and account class.

Click [X] to close the **display window** after viewing it.

Displaying the General Journal

Click **General Journal Entries** in the Select A Report list to display the sample.

Click **Modify This Report** to see the report options window:

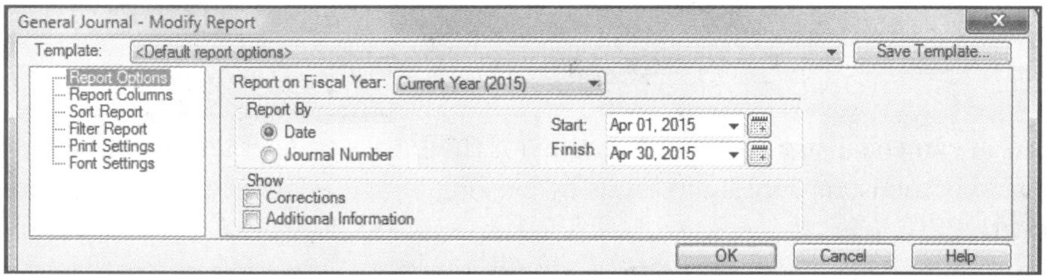

Or choose the Reports menu, then choose Journal Entries and click General to display the report options.

Journal reports may include correcting or adjusting entries or may omit them. You may select entries for the report either by the (posting) **Date** of the journal entries or by journal entry number. When you choose **Journal Number**, you must enter the first and last numbers for the entries you want to display. If you do not know the journal numbers, the date method is easier. Furthermore, your journal entry numbers might not match the ones we use if you have made any additional or correcting journal entries. Therefore, all reports in this workbook are requested by date — the default setting.

The earliest transaction and the latest session date are given by default for the period of the report.

Click **Corrections** to include the adjusting entries.

You can choose any dates for the Journal Report between the earliest transaction date and the last journal entry, including postdated entries if there are any.

Accept **April 1** and **April 30** as the dates for your journal report.

Click **OK** to display the report. A partial report is included here:

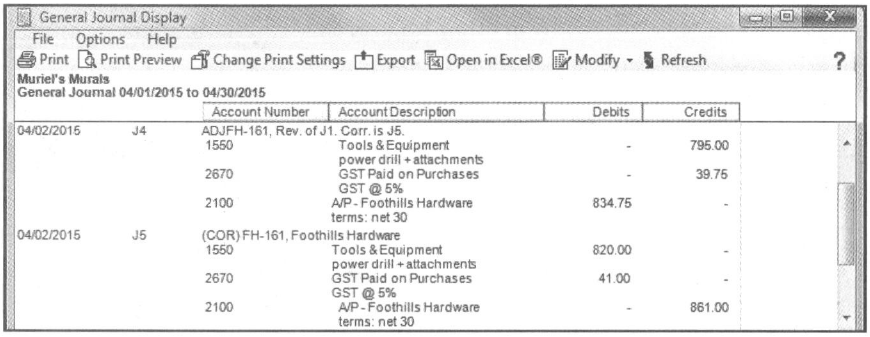

Muriel's Murals
General Journal 04/01/2015 to 04/30/2015

		Account Number	Account Description	Debits	Credits
04/02/2015	J4	ADJFH-161, Rev. of J1. Corr. is J5.			
		1550	Tools & Equipment power drill + attachments	-	795.00
		2670	GST Paid on Purchases GST @ 5%	-	39.75
		2100	A/P - Foothills Hardware terms: net 30	834.75	-
04/02/2015	J5	(COR) FH-161, Foothills Hardware			
		1550	Tools & Equipment power drill + attachments	820.00	-
		2670	GST Paid on Purchases GST @ 5%	41.00	-
		2100	A/P - Foothills Hardware terms: net 30	-	861.00

NOTES

You can select different details for the Account List Report by modifying the Report Columns. Refer to Appendix E on the Student DVD.

CLASSIC VIEW

From the Home window, right-click the General Journal icon [General Journal] to select it.

Click [Display], the Display tool on the tool bar, to open the report options.

NOTES

Since we have only General Journal entries for Muriel's Murals, this report will be the same as the one for All Journal Entries that you select from the Financials report list.

WARNING!

If you do not choose Show Corrections, the journal report will include only the latest corrected version of all entries. Showing the corrections will include the original incorrect entry, the reversing entry and the final correct one, thus providing a complete audit trail.

NOTES

From the Options menu in a displayed report, you can use the Find In This Report option to search for specific information. When you select the option, a Find field opens at the bottom of the report for you to enter the text you want to find. The Options menu also has a Find Next entry so you can continue searching for the next occurrence of the text.

> **NOTES**
> Sometimes, depending on who will see the report, you may want to omit the corrections.

The reversing and the final corrected entry for Memo #1 on page 44 are shown here. J1 (not shown) has the original incorrect entry. If corrections were not included, only J5, the final correct entry, would be shown. The complete report shows the audit trail.

Customizing Reports

> **NOTES**
> For example, you could create a journal report that displays only cheques by filtering on the Source field to match the word Cheque (or the entry you used for these transactions). We show this in Appendix E on the Student DVD.

When we selected dates, comparative options or correcting journal entries, we were customizing reports. Modify Report windows also include customization options in the pane on the left. You can change the columns or fields in the report, sort reports and filter them. Sorting reports changes the order in which data are presented, while filtering reports selects the records to include according to the data fields used as selection criteria. Printing options may also be modified.

Reports already on display may also be modified. You can choose the elements you want to change from the Modify tool drop-down list as shown:

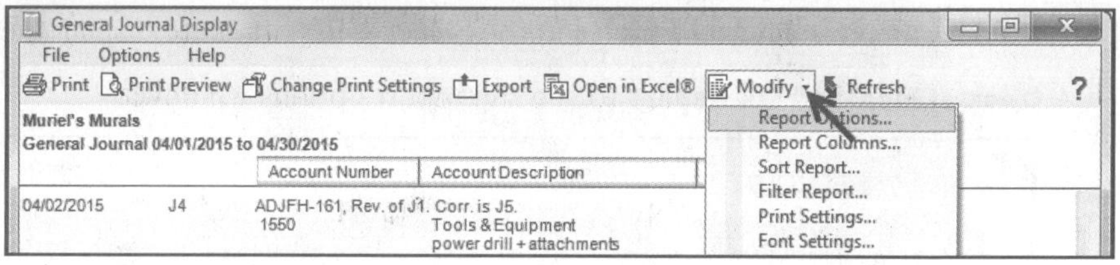

> **PRO VERSION**
> The option to show only totals or to collapse the amounts is not available in the Pro version.

You can collapse individual amounts for the Balance Sheet and Income Statement to show only totals, or only some totals by clicking a ⊟ beside an account heading in the report:

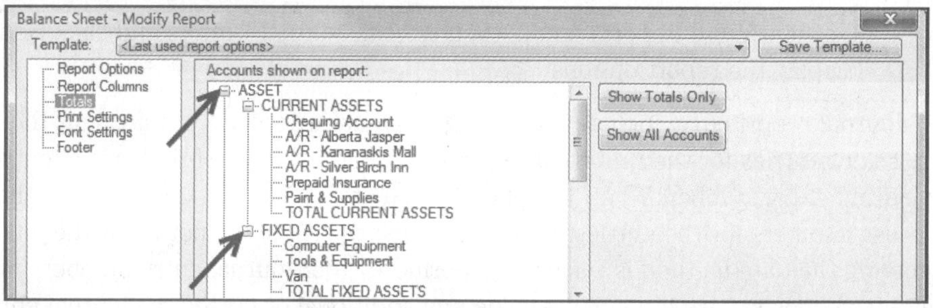

> **NOTES**
> Clicking ⊞ beside a collapsed amount will expand the account display again.
> You can collapse all amounts at once by clicking Show Totals Only. Clicking Show All Amounts will expand the totals and restore all individual amounts.

The ⊟ will change to a ⊞ to show the amounts have been collapsed.

You can also modify columns directly in the display. For example, you can widen a column by dragging the header margin to the right or remove a column by dragging it to the left. Clicking a column head will sort the report by the contents of that column, if the report can be sorted. Report modifications are covered further in Appendix E.

Close the **displayed report** when finished.

Drill-Down Reports

Some reports can be accessed from other reports that you have opened or displayed. These are cross-referenced or drill-down reports.

Whenever the pointer changes to 🔍 (a magnifying glass icon with a plus sign inside it), the additional reports can be displayed. When the other ledgers are used, detailed customer, vendor and employee reports are also available from the General Ledger Report and from the General Journal.

Move the **mouse pointer** over various items in the first report. The type of second report available may change. The name of the second report will appear in the status bar.

Double-click while the magnifying glass icon is visible to display the second report immediately. The first report stays open in the background.

The General Ledger Report for a specific account can be accessed from the Balance Sheet, Income Statement, Trial Balance, Chart of Accounts or General Journal when you double-click an account number, name or balance amount. The General Ledger record for an account can be accessed from the General Ledger Report.

While you have the additional drill-down report displayed, you may print it or drill down to other reports. (See Printing General Reports below.)

Close the **second report** and then **close** the **first report** when you have finished viewing them. **Close** the **Report Centre**.

Displaying Management Reports

Management reports provide accounting information that is specific to the company data file. When the other ledgers are used, the menu also includes management reports for these ledgers.

Management reports are available from the Reports menu — they are not available from the Report Centre or the Reports drop-down lists in the Reports pane.

Choose the **Reports menu**, then **choose Management Reports** and **click General** to see the display of available reports:

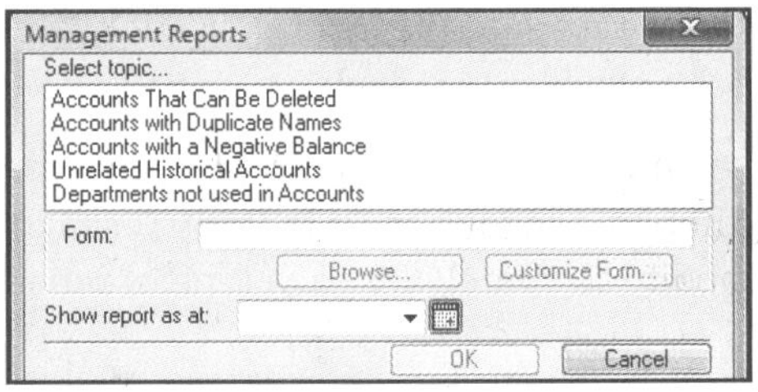

To see a report, click a topic to select it. The date field may be dimmed, depending on the topic selected. If it is not, type the date for the report in the Show Report As At field. The program will select a default report form from the ones you installed with the program. Generally, the default is the best choice. You can click Browse to see other report forms available and select the one you need. If you have the appropriate software program, you may customize the report form. Click OK to display the report.

For example, click the advice topic Accounts With A Negative Balance. Click OK. Your report should include *GST Paid on Purchases* and *M. Murals, Drawings* because these contra-accounts normally have negative balances.

Close the **display** when you have finished.

Printing General Reports

Display the **report** you want to print by following the instructions in the preceding pages on displaying reports.

There are overall print settings for the company file. These are available from the Home window and from any open report. From the displayed report,

Click the **Change Print Settings tool** or **choose** the **File menu** and **click Reports & Forms**.

CLASSIC VIEW
You can also access Management Reports from the Advice tool in the Classic view Home window tool bar.

NOTES
The Crystal Reports Print Manager is needed to view Management Reports. The Crystal Reports program is required to modify these reports.

PRO VERSION
The Unrelated Historical Accounts and Department reports are not available in the Pro version.

NOTES
Accounts that can be deleted are those that have zero balances and have not been used in journal transactions.

WARNING!
Always check that the file location in the Form field for the report is correct for your program setup. The file should be in the Forms folder, a subfolder of your Sage 50 Premium Accounting 2013 folder.

WARNING!
Always check that the correct printer is selected before printing reports. The printer selection is saved with the data file and may be incorrect for your setup.

The Report & Form Options screen opens:

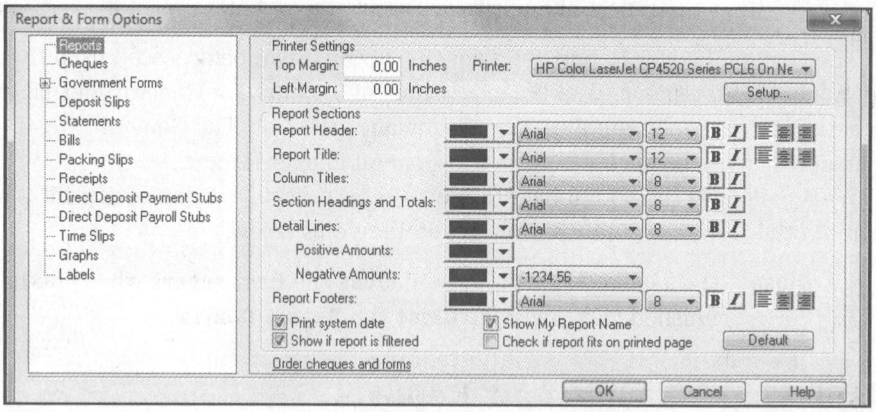

From the Home window, choose the Setup menu and click Reports & Forms.

These company settings become the defaults for all company reports.

From this window, you can select a printer, set the margins and choose the default style for different parts of the report. You can also add the computer system date to the report and indicate whether the report is filtered. The Default button will restore the original program default settings for the report.

Choose your **printer** from the drop-down list in the Printer field.

Click **OK** to save your changes and return to the display or **click Cancel** if you do not want to save the changes you made.

If you want to change the appearance only for the displayed report, you should modify the displayed report. The Modify Report windows include Print Settings and Font Settings as elements that you can modify separately for each type of report.

NOTES
From the Setup or other option buttons, you can choose advanced settings for the report and printer.

PRO VERSION
pro
Packing Slips and Time Slips will not appear on the list in the Pro version. The term Invoices replaces Bills.

NOTES
Refer to Appendix E for more detail on modifying Print Settings for individual reports.

Graphing General Reports

Graphs are available only from the main menu in any Home window.

Expenses and Net Profit as % of Revenue

Choose the **Graphs menu**, then **click Expenses And Net Profit As % Of Revenue** to display the following report options:

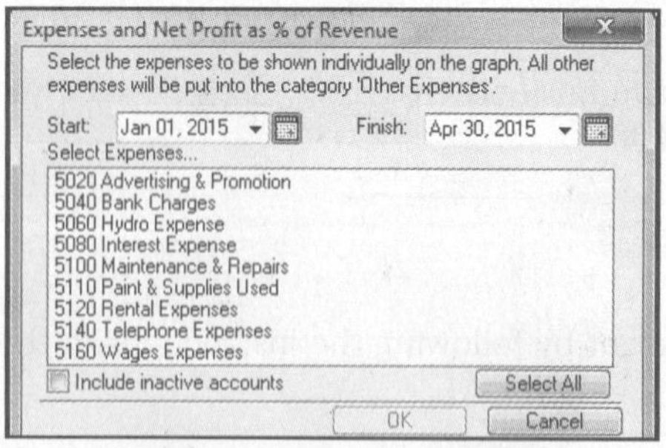

Double-click the **default Start date** and **enter** the **beginning date** of the period for your graph.

Press *tab* (**twice** if you type the date).

Type the **ending date** of the period for your graph.

NOTES
The default start and finish dates for the graph are the fiscal start date and the session date.

Press and **hold** ctrl and **click each expense account you want** included in the graph or **click Select All** to include all accounts.

Click **OK** to display the graph:

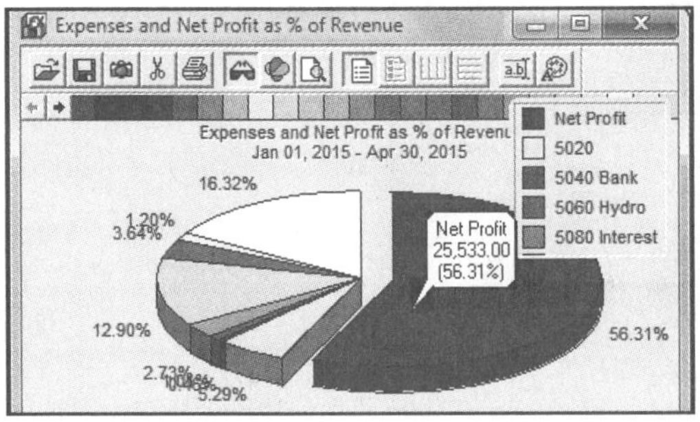

The pie chart shown above includes all expense accounts for the period from January 1 to April 30 and is a form of the Income Statement. You have several options regarding the graph at this stage. The tool bar options are the same for all graphs. By selecting the appropriate button on the tool bar, you can import a graph, export the displayed graph, copy it to the clipboard as a bitmap or a text file, print the graph, change the view from 3-D to 2-D, hide the legend, edit or add titles and so on. Hold the mouse pointer over a tool button for a few seconds to see a brief description of the tool's purpose. Most tool buttons lead to an additional options or control window requiring your input.

In addition, you can change colours by dragging the colour you want to the pie section you want to change, expand or shrink the legend by dragging its bottom border down or up respectively or pull out a section of the pie chart by dragging it away from the rest of the chart. The graph displayed has the Net Profit portion pulled out for emphasis.

Double-click a portion of the graph to see the name of the account, the dollar amount and the percentage of the total.

Double-click the legend to make it larger and to add the account names. Double-click the expanded legend to reduce it.

Right-click the legend to view a set of options for positioning the legend on the graph page. To move the legend to the new position, click the new legend position option. Double-click the legend to restore the original size and position.

Close the **graph** when you have finished.

NOTES

You can copy the graph as a .BMP file to the clipboard and then paste it into the Paint program for full editing capabilities.

You can include an exported graph in a Word, Excel or PowerPoint file.

Revenues by Account

Choose the **Graphs menu**, then **click Revenues By Account** to display the following report options:

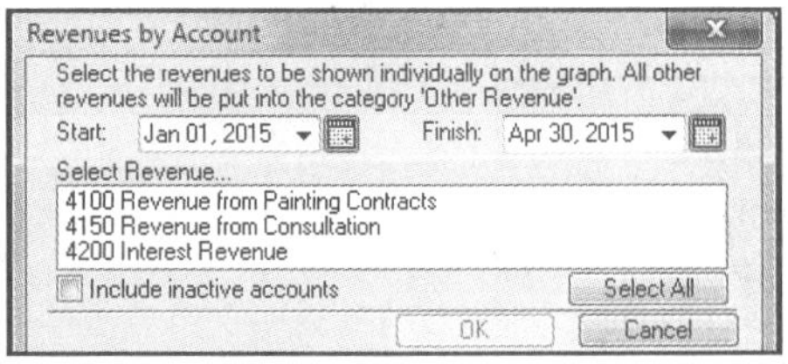

Enter the **beginning date** of the period for your graph.

Press tab (**twice** if you type the date).

Enter the **ending date** of the period for your graph.

Press ctrl and **click each revenue account you want** included in the graph or **click Select All** to include all accounts in the graph.

Click **OK** to display the pie chart as shown:

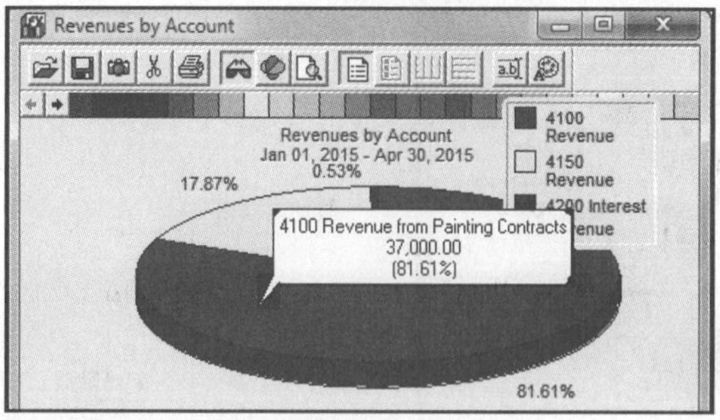

The pie chart has each revenue account represented by a different piece of the pie. You can see that most of the revenue comes from painting contracts. If you double-click a section of the pie, the amount and percentage for that account are shown in a bubble.

You have the same options for this graph as you do for the Expenses and Net Profit as % of Revenue graph.

Double-click a **pie section** to show its account, amount and percentage.

Close the **graph** when you have finished.

Expenses by Account

Choose the **Graphs menu**. **Click Expenses By Account** to display the options:

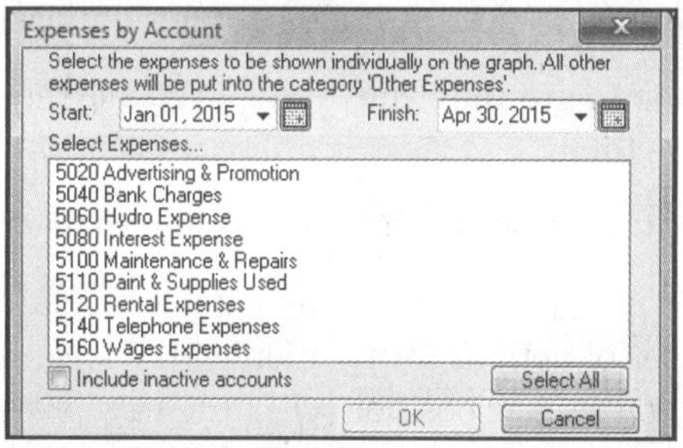

Enter the **beginning date** of the period for your graph.

Press tab (**twice** if you type the date).

Enter the **ending date** of the period for your graph.

Press ctrl and **click each expense account you want** included in the graph.

As usual, clicking **Select All** will include all accounts in the graph.

Click **OK** to see the graph:

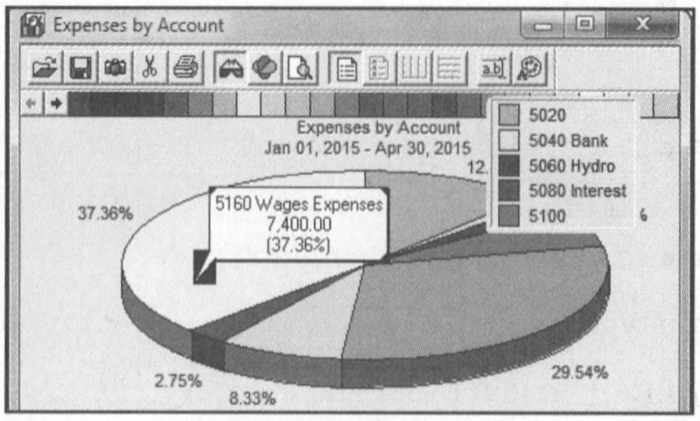

Each expense account that was selected is represented as a separate piece of the pie. The accounts not selected are grouped together in the **Other** category. The expenses graph makes it easy to identify at a glance the items that make up the largest share of expenses — paint & supplies and wages in this example.

Close the **graph** when finished.

Finishing a Session

Finish the last transaction you are working on for this session.

Click to close the transaction window (such as journal input or display) to return to the Home window.

You can click the Close Other Windows tool in the Home window if you have more than one open window. To restore the Home window,

Click the **Home window tool** in an open journal window. Or,

Click the **Sage 50 button** on the desktop task bar.

Click the **Close Other Windows tool** in the Home window.

Click **Exit** to close the program.

You will see the following message about backing up the data file:

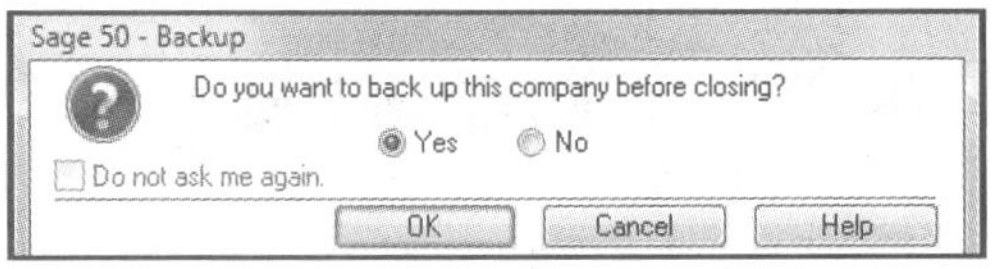

If you did not back up the file after the last set of transactions, you should do so now.

Click **OK** to start the backup procedure. Follow the instructions on page 47 to complete the backup.

After the backup is complete, the file will close.

Sage 50 will automatically save your work when you finish your session and exit properly. You can now turn off your computer — or take a coffee break.

R E V I E W

The Student DVD with Data Files includes Review Questions and Supplementary Cases for this chapter.

CHAPTER FOUR

Toss for Tots

OBJECTIVES

After completing this chapter, you should be able to

- ***plan*** and ***design*** an accounting system for a non-profit organization
- ***prepare*** a conversion procedure from manual records
- ***understand*** the objectives of a computerized accounting system
- ***create*** company files using the skeleton starter file
- ***change*** the default home window
- ***set up*** the organization's accounts
- ***enter*** historical account information
- ***finish*** entering accounting history to prepare for transactions
- ***enter*** fiscal end adjusting transactions
- ***close*** the books and start a new fiscal period
- ***enter*** transactions for a previous fiscal period

COMPANY INFORMATION

Company Profile

NOTES
Toss for Tots
North Toronto, PO Box 42665
Toronto, ON M5N 3A8
Tel: (416) 489-2734
Fax: (416) 489-6277
Business No.: 127 362 644 RR0001

Toss for Tots is a charitable organization created to raise awareness and to support research on cancer in children. One salaried event manager, assisted by a large group of volunteers, organizes a basketball free-throw tournament to raise money for children's cancer research and family support. The tournament uses a ladder-style elimination to determine the championship. During the first two weekends, a first round of 20 free throws determines the basic skill level of each participant for the initial pairing. The subsequent one-on-one free-throw elimination rounds take place over the next two weekends. Two basketball courts are rented, allowing eight participants to play at the same time for the early rounds — two at a time at each end of the two courts. One thousand people are expected to participate in the initial rounds. Professional basketball players are not permitted to compete.

Funds are raised in several ways during the event: each participant pays an entry fee of $50 and receives a $30 tax receipt; each participant is expected to get sponsors who can donate a fixed amount or an amount for each successful basketball throw; spectators pay an admission fee to watch the tournament — $10 for one day, $15 for one weekend or $25 for both weekends; snacks and drinks are sold to spectators and participants; surprise bags are sold for $10 each; and photos of participants on the court are sold for $10 each. Prizes, donated by various corporations, are offered to participants who collect large donation amounts, and a cash prize of $1 000 is awarded to the tournament champion.

Volunteers handle all the registrations, monitor the contest and determine placements or pairings for successive rounds on the ladder. Costs are also minimized by the large number of merchandise donations for the surprise packages and prizes. The organization does incur some expenses, including the event manager's salary; rental of the basketball courts; a computer to record all registrations, donations and ladder sequence; office supplies; promotional materials; telephones; drinks; snacks and so on.

At the start of the tournament, many of the participants have already paid their registration fees and most of the merchandise has been purchased or received. The organization has been operating for several months to prepare for the tournament.

The bank account has been set up for the early cash donations and registrations and to write cheques for pre-tournament expenses. Some cash is also kept on hand at the tournament to make change for on-site sales and for immediate purchases. Most of the cash and cheques received from registrations and admissions is deposited immediately for security purposes.

Toss for Tots has decided to use Sage 50 to keep the accounting records for the tournament in July 2015, partway through its current fiscal year. The charity requires only General Ledger accounts. The following information is available to set up the accounts using the General Ledger:

- Chart of Accounts
- Income Statement
- Balance Sheet
- Trial Balance
- Accounting Procedures

NOTES

For $10, spectators and players can purchase surprise bags that contain a variety of donated items such as gift certificates, magazines, books and games. The items are hidden from view, but the value of each package is never less than $10.

CHART OF ACCOUNTS

TOSS FOR TOTS

ASSETS
1000 CURRENT ASSETS [H]
1020 Bank: Toss for Tots [A]
1100 Cash on Hand [A]
1150 Total Cash [S]
1200 Surprise Bag Supplies
1300 Food Supplies
1320 Office Supplies
1360 T-shirts
1390 TOTAL CURRENT ASSETS [T]

1400 FIXED ASSETS [H]
1420 Fax/Telephone
1450 Computer
1500 Digital Camera
1590 TOTAL FIXED ASSETS [T] ▶

▶LIABILITIES
2000 CURRENT LIABILITIES [H]
2100 Bank Loan
2200 A/P - Designs U Wear
2300 A/P - Quiq Kopy
2350 A/P - Central College
2400 A/P - Snack City
2670 HST Paid on Purchases
2690 TOTAL CURRENT LIABILITIES [T]

EQUITY
3000 EQUITY [H]
3560 Accumulated Surplus
3600 Net Income [X]
3690 TOTAL EQUITY [T] ▶

▶REVENUE
4000 REVENUE [H]
4020 Revenue: Registrations
4040 Revenue: Sponsors
4080 Revenue: Surprise Bags
4100 Revenue: Admissions
4120 Revenue: Food Sales
4390 TOTAL REVENUE [T]

EXPENSE
5000 ADMIN EXPENSES [H]
5020 Court Rental Expense
5200 Office Supplies Used
5220 Non-refundable HST
5240 Postage Expense
5280 Printing & Copying ▶

▶5300 Telephone Expense
5320 Publicity & Promotion
5400 Wages - Manager
5420 Miscellaneous Expenses
5440 TOTAL ADMIN EXPENSES [T]

5450 MERCHANDISE & FOOD EXPENSES [H]
5500 Cost of T-shirts
5520 Cost of Surprise Bags
5550 Cost of Food
5690 TOTAL MERCHANDISE & FOOD EXPENSES [T]

NOTES: The Chart of Accounts is based on the current expenses and accounts. Account types are marked in brackets for subgroup Accounts [A], Subgroup totals [S], Headings [H], Totals [T] and Current Earnings [X]. All unmarked accounts are postable Group [G] accounts. The explanation of account types begins on page 85.

INCOME STATEMENT

TOSS FOR TOTS

For the Nine Months Ending June 30, 2015

Revenue	
4000 REVENUE	
4020 Revenue: Registrations	$20 000.00
4040 Revenue: Sponsors	2 000.00
4390 TOTAL REVENUE	$22 000.00
TOTAL REVENUE	$22 000.00
Expense	
5000 ADMIN EXPENSES	
5020 Court Rental Expense	$15 000.00
5200 Office Supplies Used	640.00
5240 Postage Expense	450.00
5280 Printing & Copying	2 000.00
5300 Telephone Expense	360.00
5320 Publicity & Promotion	4 000.00
5400 Wages - Manager	6 000.00
5440 TOTAL ADMIN EXPENSES	$28 450.00
TOTAL EXPENSE	$28 450.00
NET INCOME (LOSS)	($6 450.00)

NOTES: Because the event has not yet started, some expenses are still at zero. Because most of the funds have not yet come in, the Income Statement shows a net loss.

BALANCE SHEET

TOSS FOR TOTS

July 1, 2015

Assets		
1000 CURRENT ASSETS		
1020 Bank: Toss for Tots	$18 550.00	
1100 Cash on Hand	1 000.00	
1150 Total Cash		$19 550.00
1200 Surprise Bag Supplies		500.00
1300 Food Supplies		1 200.00
1320 Office Supplies		750.00
1360 T-shirts		800.00
1390 TOTAL CURRENT ASSETS		$22 800.00
1400 FIXED ASSETS		
1420 Fax/Telephone		500.00
1450 Computer		2 400.00
1500 Digital Camera		900.00
1590 TOTAL FIXED ASSETS		$ 3 800.00
TOTAL ASSETS		$26 600.00 ▶

▶ Liabilities	
2000 CURRENT LIABILITIES	
2100 Bank Loan	$ 15 000.00
2200 A/P - Designs U Wear	800.00
2300 A/P - Quiq Kopy	150.00
2350 A/P - Central College	11 300.00
2400 A/P - Snack City	900.00
2670 HST Paid on Purchases	−1 850.00
2690 TOTAL CURRENT LIABILITIES	$26 300.00
TOTAL LIABILITIES	$26 300.00
Equity	
3000 EQUITY	
3560 Accumulated Surplus	$ 6 750.00
3600 Net Income	−6 450.00
3690 TOTAL EQUITY	$ 300.00
TOTAL EQUITY	$ 300.00
LIABILITIES AND EQUITY	$26 600.00

TRIAL BALANCE

TOSS FOR TOTS

July 1, 2015		Debits	Credits
1020	Bank: Toss for Tots	$18 550.00	
1100	Cash on Hand	1 000.00	
1200	Surprise Bag Supplies	500.00	
1300	Food Supplies	1 200.00	
1320	Office Supplies	750.00	
1360	T-shirts	800.00	
1420	Fax/Telephone	500.00	
1450	Computer	2 400.00	
1500	Digital Camera	900.00	
2100	Bank Loan		$15 000.00
2200	A/P - Designs U Wear		800.00
2300	A/P - Quiq Kopy		150.00
2350	A/P - Central College		11 300.00
2400	A/P - Snack City		900.00
2670	HST Paid on Purchases	1 850.00	
3560	Accumulated Surplus		6 750.00
4020	Revenue: Registrations		20 000.00
4040	Revenue: Sponsors		2 000.00
5020	Court Rental Expense	15 000.00	
5200	Office Supplies Used	640.00	
5240	Postage Expense	450.00	
5280	Printing & Copying	2 000.00	
5300	Telephone Expense	360.00	
5320	Publicity & Promotion	4 000.00	
5400	Wages - Manager	6 000.00	
		$56 900.00	$56 900.00

Accounting Procedures

HST

Registered charities have two options with respect to the HST. Like regular for-profit businesses, they can register, charge HST on all sales and membership fees and claim all HST paid as input tax credits to reduce the liability to the Receiver General. The second option, used by Toss for Tots, does not require collection of HST but permits a partial rebate of HST paid. Periodically, the charity submits an application for refunds, listing the total of all HST paid toward its operating expenses. Fifty percent of the GST amount and 82 percent of the PST portion are eligible for the rebate in Ontario. Therefore, Toss for Tots records all General Journal entry purchases with the amount paid for HST separated from the total and debited to *HST Paid on Purchases*. This account is cleared with a credit entry as the application for a rebate is submitted. The debit entries to the *HST Refund Receivable* and the *Non-refundable HST* expense accounts will balance the journal entry.

Bank Accounts

The proceeds from the registrations and from the sale of merchandise are entered into the bank account. This account is used for all cheques to suppliers and to cover operating and administrative expenses and merchandise — drinks, snacks, T-shirts and surprise bag items. During the tournament, a *Cash on Hand* account is set up for day-to-day expenses incurred by the volunteer staff. Transfers are made from the *Bank: Toss for Tots* account to *Cash on Hand* by writing cheques to the event manager.

NOTES

A charity must apply for a business number to receive the rebate. The federal portion of the rebate – 50 percent of the 5 percent GST paid (form GST66) – is separated from the provincial portion – 82 percent of the 8 percent PST paid (Ontario form RC7066SCH). We have completed these calculations for Toss for Tots to avoid complicating the General Journal entries with separate tax amounts.

The provincial rebate percentage varies among the different HST provinces and for different types of non-profit organizations.

INSTRUCTIONS

1. **Set up** the **company accounts for Toss for Tots** in the General Ledger in Sage 50 using all the information provided in this application. Detailed keystroke instructions follow the instructions.
2. **Back up your work frequently** when working through this application to keep your backups updated.

   You may finish your session at any time while completing the setup. Simply open the Toss for Tots data file again, accept the session date and continue from where you left off.

   If you are using a different location for your data files, substitute the appropriate data path, including the drive and folder for your data setup.
3. **Enter** the **source documents** that begin on page 96 in the General Journal in Sage 50 using the Chart of Accounts and other information provided.
4. **Print** the **following reports** after you have completed your entries — choose Previous Year (2015) as the reporting period:
   a. General Journal from July 1 to September 30
   b. Comparative Balance Sheet at September 30 and October 1 (amounts)
   c. Income Statement for the period October 1, 2014, to September 30, 2015

KEYSTROKES FOR SETUP

The following are the five key stages in preparing the Sage 50 program for use by a company:

1. creating company files
2. preparing the system
3. preparing the ledgers
4. printing reports to check your work
5. backing up your files and finishing the company history

The following keystroke instructions are written for a stand-alone PC with a hard drive. The keystroke instructions provided in this application demonstrate one approach to setting up company accounts. Always refer to the Sage 50 and Windows manuals and Help for further details.

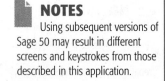

NOTES
Using subsequent versions of Sage 50 may result in different screens and keystrokes from those described in this application.

NOTES
You must work in single-user mode to set up new company files. Access to most settings is restricted in multi-user mode.

Creating Company Files

The following instructions assume that you installed the Sage 50 data files on your hard disk in drive C: in the SageData13 folder.

Sage 50 provides both templates and starter files to make it easier to create files for a new company. These files contain different sets of accounts that match the needs of different kinds of businesses. By starting with one of these files, you eliminate the need to create all the accounts for your business from scratch.

There are many templates that work with the setup wizards to define not only accounts, but also a number of settings for the different ledgers. These settings and accounts are suited to the type of business named by the files.

NOTES
The non-profit template has many more accounts, modules and features than are needed for Toss for Tots. This file, therefore, would require substantially more modification to make it match the company profile in this chapter.

In addition, Sage 50 includes two starter files — inteplus (Integration Plus) and skeleton. The starter files contain only a set of basic accounts. Starter files are opened like any other company file. You should work with a copy of these files so that you can use the original files for future applications.

The Skeleton starter has only General Ledger accounts, whereas the Integration Plus starter is suitable for a variety of business types because it has the basic linked accounts for all the ledgers.

NOTES
We want to illustrate different ways of creating company files. Therefore, the method of creating your company files from scratch is described in the Air Care Services setup application in Chapter 7.

You will have to customize any of these starter files to your particular company. Rarely are accounts identical for any two businesses. The files that are best suited to the Chart of Accounts for Toss for Tots are the Skeleton starter files (skeleton.SAI). These files contain only a few General Ledger accounts, headings and totals. They contain no linked accounts that link General Ledger accounts to the subsidiary ledgers. This is appropriate for Toss for Tots, which uses only the General Ledger.

The starter files are located in the Template folder in the Sage 50 Premium Accounting 2013 folder — the folder that contains your Sage 50 program.

This starter file is a Simply Basic 2005 A version file that must be upgraded before you can use it. The Student Premium version of Sage 50 cannot open files from previous version years, so we have created a 2013 Pro version of the Skeleton file. We will open this file (skeleton.SAI) from the SageData13\Template folder.

NOTES
If you use the Skeleton file located in C:\Program Files\Sage 50 Premium 2013\Template\, you will be upgrading from Simply Basic 2005 A to Premium (or Pro) 2013 Release 1. Make a backup of this file before changing settings and accounts.
Use the File menu Save As command to create and open the new file C:\SageData13\Toss\toss.SAI.

Start the **Sage 50 program** to access the Select Company window.

Click **Select An Existing Company** to access the Open Company window:

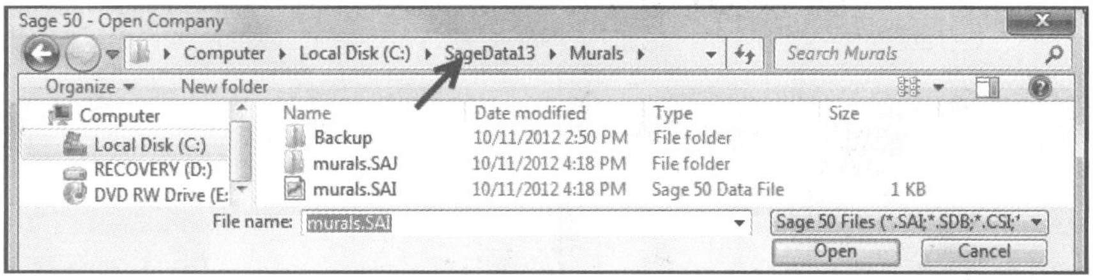

Click **SageData13** in the file path field to return to this folder and see all the folders you installed from the Student DVD.

Double-click **Template** to open this folder.

Click **skeleton** (or **skeleton.SAI**) to select this data file. **Click Open** to start the Upgrade Company Wizard:

NOTES
If you are using backup files, restore SageData13\skeleton1.CAB or skeleton1 to SageData13\Toss\toss. Sage 50 will create the necessary new folder. Refer to page 22 for assistance with restoring backup files.
If you start from the backup file, you will not need to complete the additional step of saving the file after the Upgrade wizard has completed.

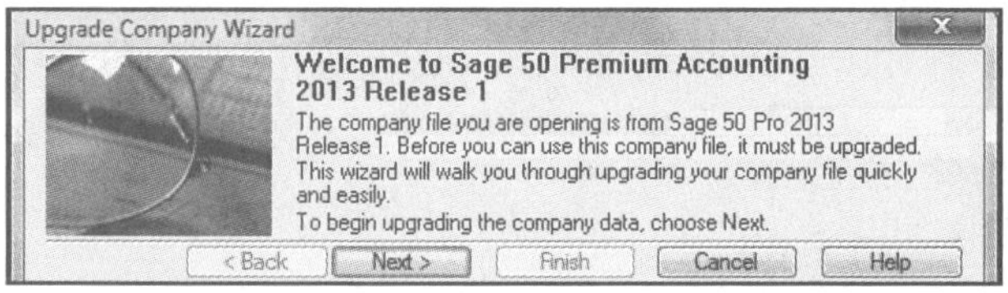

The Pro version Skeleton starter file must be converted to Premium Release 1.

Read the **introduction** to the wizard and **click Next** to continue:

PRO VERSION
The file will not be converted. You will see the session date screen on page 72 immediately.

This screen shows the name and location of the working file and the version changes that will be made if you proceed.

Click **Next**:

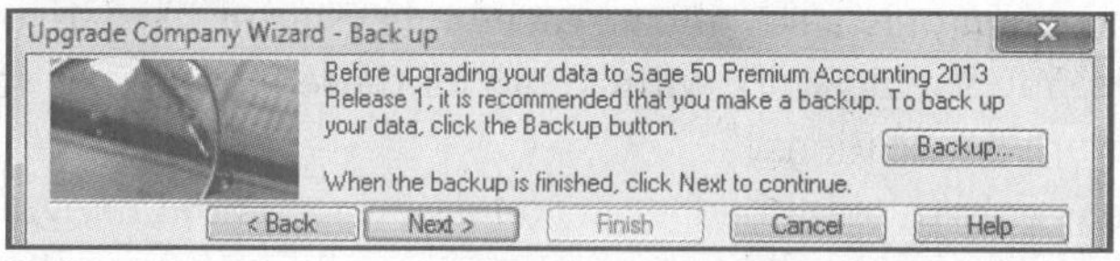

You can now back up the Skeleton file before proceeding. The program will check your data file for problems and repair them if you choose this option.

Click **Next** to see the final warning about converting files:

This final screen warns you of the changes you are making. After this step you cannot cancel the conversion. File conversions cannot be reversed — once you convert a file you will be unable to open it in the earlier version.

Click **Finish** to begin the conversion.

You will now be asked to indicate the type of company you are working with. Different company types have different icon and journal labels in the Premium version.

Click the **list arrow beside Other**, the default entry, to see the types:

Click **Non-Profit** and then **click OK**.

The Session Date window appears with January 1, 2000, as the session date:

Click **OK** to accept the date for now. We will update it later.

The Getting Started Welcome screen and the Daily Business Manager open. One window may be open in the background behind the other.

Click **Show This Window On Startup** to remove the ✓ and then **click** the **Close button** to close the Getting Started window.

Click  to close the Daily Business Manager window.

WARNING!
If you make a backup at this stage, it will be a Premium Version 2013 Release 1 backup.

NOTES
When you upgrade to a later release, you will see a reminder about payroll tax changes because new releases of Sage 50 are tied to tax table changes that usually occur every six months.

NOTES
Click the Sage 50 icon on your Windows desktop task bar to see the Sage windows that are open. Click the one you need to make it active and bring it to the front.

The Home window opens and all ledgers are available in the list of modules.

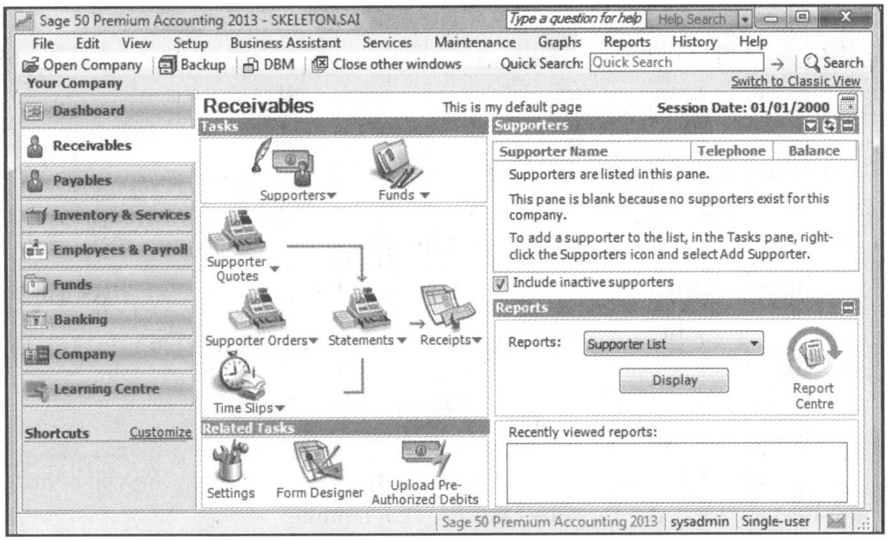

PRO VERSION

Sage 50 Pro Accounting 2013 is displayed as the program name in the title bar.

The ledger icon labels are Customers and Projects. Sales Invoices replaces Statements and Sales replaces Supporter for the journal labels. You will not see the Time Slips icon.

The ledger icon is labelled Supporters because we selected Non-Profit as the company type. For other types of companies, this icon may be labelled Customers or Clients. Projects are labelled Funds for non-profit companies.

The ledgers are not set up. An open history (quill pen) symbol  appears beside Supporters, the ledger icon, indicating that you can enter historical data for the ledger. If you open the other modules, you will see the same symbol for each ledger. Although you can make journal entries at this stage, you should first save this file under your company name, enter all the necessary company information and finish entering the history.

PRO VERSION

The open history symbol appears with the Customers icon.

First we will copy the template files so we can use this original again if we need to.

Choose the **File menu** and **click Save As** so that we can work with the new copy:

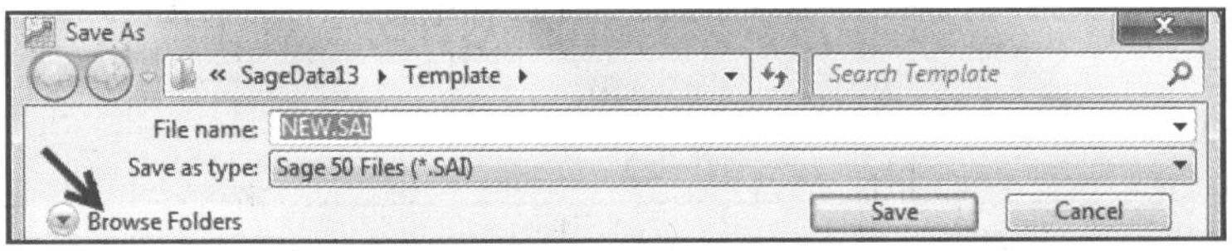

The Save As window opens. The path <C:\SageData13\Template> shows the location of the open skeleton file. NEW.SAI (or NEW) is the default name for the new data file. We need to create a new data folder for Toss for Tots, but we want this under the SageData13 level.

Click **SageData13** in the file path field. We need to return to the SageData13 folder where we will create the new data folder.

Click **Browse Folders** if necessary to expand the window and include the New Folder option:

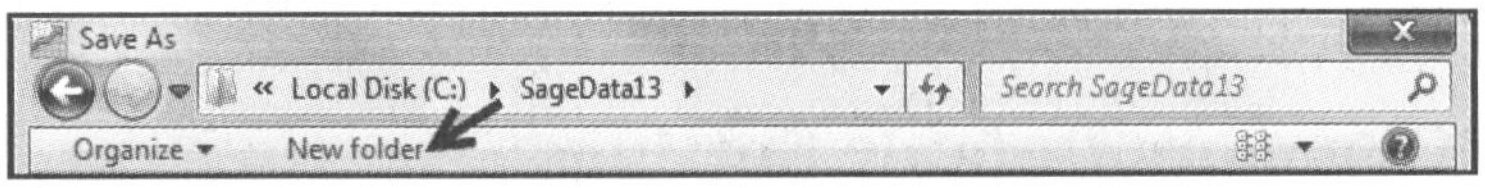

Click **New Folder**. The name New Folder is selected as the folder name so we can change it.

Type Toss

Click the **Toss folder** and then **click Open** or **double-click** the **Toss folder**:

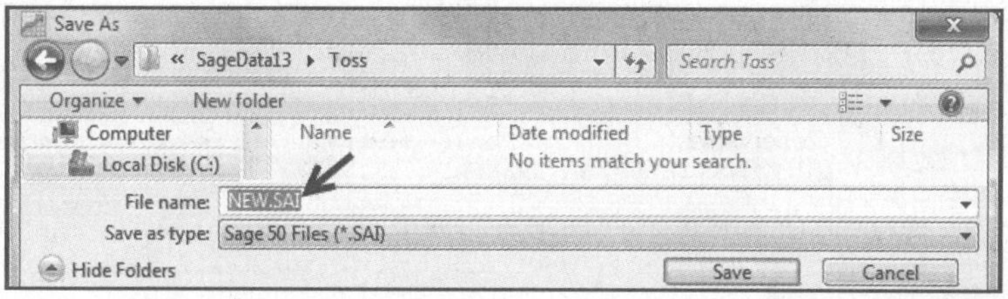

We can now enter the name for the new company file. NEW.SAI may be selected.

Click **NEW.SAI** (or **NEW**) if necessary. **Type** `toss` and **click Save**.

You should see the same Home window with the file name TOSS.SAI (or TOSS) in the title bar:

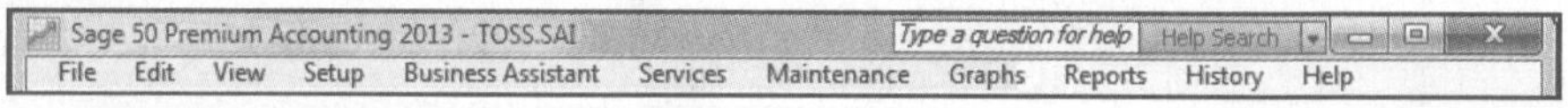

The Receivables module is the default for the Home window. We will change this default because Toss for Tots does not use this module.

Changing the Default Home Window

Toss for Tots uses only the General Ledger (Company module) so we will make this the Home window. The Receivables module has This Is My Default Page beside the name.

Click **Company** in the list of modules on the left to change the Home window.

Now we have the Chart of Accounts and the General Journal available. Notice that the message beside Company has changed to Make This My Default Page. Clicking this option for any module will select the displayed module as the default Home window.

Click **Make This My Default Page**.

The Company heading now has This Is My Default Page beside it as shown:

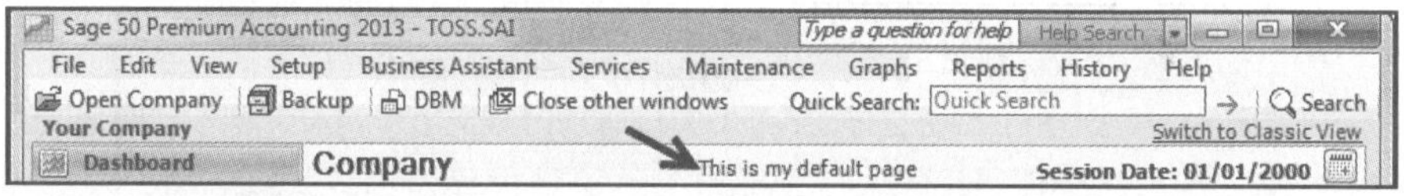

NOTES
You cannot complete the setup in multi-user mode.

Preparing the System

Before entering financial records for a new company, you must prepare the system for operation. This involves changing the default settings to reflect the Toss for Tots company information such as the company name and address, fiscal dates, screen display preferences and Chart of Accounts. Some initial defaults will not be suitable for Toss for Tots. You must also provide other information, such as the printer(s) that you will be using and the printing formats. This process of adding, deleting and modifying information is called customizing the system.

NOTES
The Sage 50 Setup menu includes a Setup Guide for modifying and creating ledger records.

The Setup menu also has wizards for linked accounts, adding users and updating HST. Because none of these wizards modify the company settings, we do not use them.

Changing Company Default Settings

Click the **Settings icon** in the Related Tasks pane, or **choose** the **Setup menu** and **click Settings**:

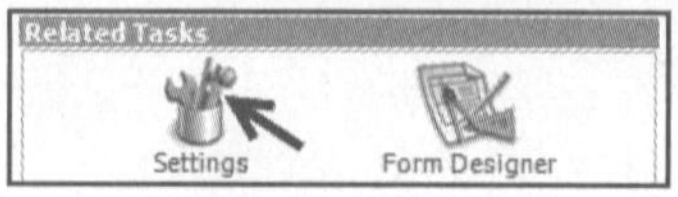

The Company Settings main menu window opens:

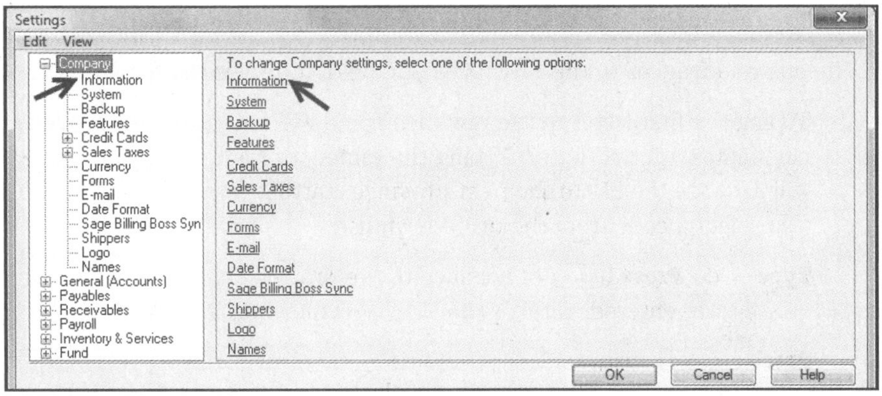

NOTES

If another module is open when you choose Settings, you will see the settings for that ledger. Click Company and then click Information to see the Information screen.

NOTES

As of December 2012, Sage no longer provided the Billing Boss program.

Most settings for a data file are entered from this central Settings screen. Some apply to features and modules not used by Toss for Tots. We will skip the screens that do not apply. They will be introduced in later chapters.

The modules are listed on the left. The remaining modules have a ⊞ beside them indicating there are multiple settings. The larger right-hand pane begins with the same expanded list of entries for the selected module as the expanded list on the left. The open Company module has a ⊟ beside it.

NOTES

Clicking the ⊟ beside a module name will collapse the expanded list.

Clicking a ⊞ beside an entry will expand the list and change the icon to ⊟. Clicking an entry in the list on the left without a ⊞ beside it or in the list on the right-hand side will open the options window for that entry.

Entering Company Information

Company settings apply to all modules of the company for all users of the data file.

Click **Information** (in either the left-hand side or right-hand side list) to see the following information screen:

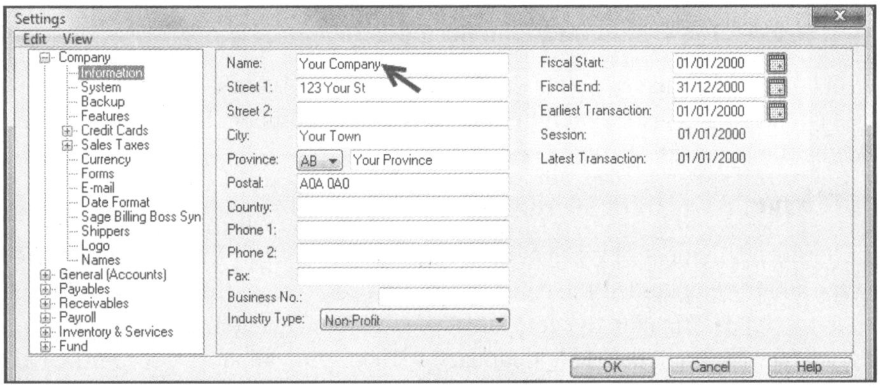

WARNING!

The initial date format for this file is day/month/year. This is evident from the Fiscal End date.

The Name field contains the information "Your Company" to let you know that this is where you should enter the name of your company.

Press `tab` or **drag through Your Company** to select this text.

Type `Toss for Tots` (add your own name). **Press** `tab`.

NOTES

You can personalize your files by adding your own name to this field (e.g., Toss for Tots – Sabeena) so that all reports printed will include your name for easy identification.

The cursor moves to the Street 1 field, the first address field. You can enter the address immediately because the current contents are already highlighted.

Type `North Toronto`

Press `tab` to advance to the second street address line (Street 2 field).

Type `PO Box 42665` **Press** `tab`.

The cursor advances to and highlights the contents of the City field.

Type Toronto **Press** tab.

The cursor advances to the Province code field. It, too, is ready for editing.

Typing the first letter of the province name will enter the first province beginning with that letter. Typing the same letter again or clicking the list arrow will advance the list to the next province starting with the same letter. You can also select a code from the drop-down list.

Type O **Press** tab to advance to the province name field. ON and Ontario are entered as this is the only province beginning with "O."

Press tab again to accept Ontario as the province.

The cursor is now placed in the highlighted Postal (postal code) field. You do not have to type the capitals or spaces in postal codes.

Type m5n3a8

The program automatically corrects the postal code format when you enter a Canadian postal code pattern.

In this case, all addresses will be in Canada, so we can leave the Country field blank. Now enter the telephone and fax numbers for the business. There is only one phone number so the Phone 2 field will remain blank. You do not need to type brackets or hyphens for phone numbers. Sage 50 will correct the format when you enter a seven- or ten-digit phone number.

Click the **Phone 1 field**. The postal code format is corrected.

Type 4164892734

Click the **Fax field**. The telephone number format is corrected.

Type 4164896277

Press tab to move to the Business No. field.

All companies must use a single Canada Revenue Agency business number that also serves as the HST registration number. All business numbers have an R*x* extension that indicates the business area for tax purposes.

Type 127362644 RR0001 **Press** tab.

There are a number of types of companies to choose from in the program. We selected the type when we upgraded the data file. You can select from the **Industry Type** list to change the type. Changing the company type will also change the icon labels.

Sage 50 will accept dates after January 1, 1900. You can store 100 years of accounting records.

The **Fiscal Start** field contains the date at which the current fiscal year begins. This date usually defines the beginning of the fiscal year for income tax purposes.

The **Fiscal End** is the date at which the company closes its books, usually one year after the fiscal start, and the end of the fiscal year used for income tax reporting purposes. For Toss for Tots, the fiscal end is two months after the tournament, when all the accounting information for the event has been entered.

The **Earliest Transaction** date is the date on which the company converts its manual accounting records to the computerized system. Entries before this date are historical entries. The earliest transaction date must not be earlier than the fiscal start and not later than the fiscal end. The earliest transaction date will be the first session date when you are ready to enter journal transactions. Sage 50 automatically advances the earliest transaction date when you start a new fiscal year.

NOTES

All provinces and territories in Canada have a two-letter abbreviation code.

Several province names begin with N. Typing N will enter NB for New Brunswick. Clicking the list arrow again will enter NL; clicking again will enter NS and so on.

NOTES

All postal codes in Canada use the following pattern: Letter, Number, Letter, Number, Letter, Number. Any other sequence, as for other countries, will not be changed by the program, and you should enter the correct format.

PRO VERSION

pro You should select Non-Profit from the Industry Type drop-down list because you did not select it previously (there was no file conversion). Icon labels do not change when you select a different company type.

You can store seven years of company data.

NOTES

Companies may use a fiscal period shorter than one year for reporting purposes and close their books more frequently, but the most common period is one year.

NOTES

When we entered various dates, the program accepted dates between 1900 and 3000 without an error message. There appear to be no practical restrictions on the dates you can use.

Notice that the **default date format** for this file is day-month-year. We will enter these dates in text form and then change the date format for the file. By entering text with four digits for the year initially, we will ensure that we enter the date correctly.

Press *tab* to advance to the Fiscal Start field.

Type `oct 1 2014` **Press** *tab* **twice**.

Sage 50 entered 01/10/2014 as the fiscal start. The cursor is in the Fiscal End field.

Type `sep 30 2015` **Press** *tab* **twice**.

Sage 50 has entered 30/09/2015 as the fiscal end. The cursor is now in the Earliest Transaction field.

Type `jul 1 2015`

The session date and the latest transaction date will change automatically as you complete journal entries and advance the session date from the Home window. When the **latest transaction date** is later than the session date, it indicates there are postdated journal transactions.

You cannot change the earliest transaction date after finishing the history and making journal entries. The company name, address and fiscal end date can be edited at any time. Return to any field with errors to correct mistakes.

You will need to save the fiscal dates before completing the next step.

Click **OK**. If you change the industry type from this Information screen, you will see the following confirmation:

Click **Yes** to accept the changes.

Setting System Defaults

Click the **Settings icon** (Settings), or **choose** the **Setup menu** and **click Settings** to resume.

Click **System** in the list under Company to access the options:

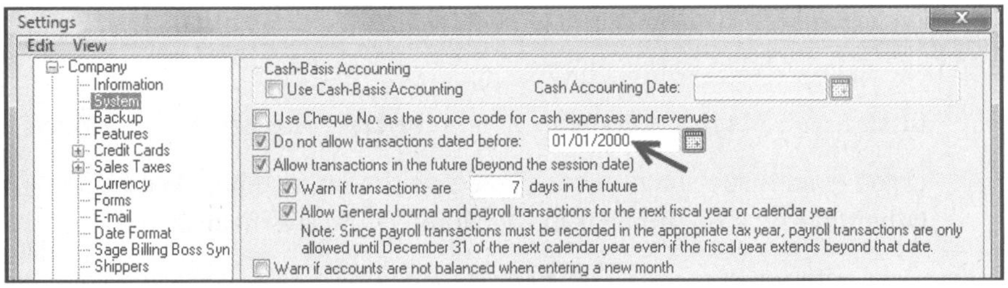

The Company System settings apply to all modules of the program.

This screen has several important settings. The first refers to whether the business is using **cash-basis accounting** instead of the default, **accrual-basis accounting**. The cash basis of accounting records revenues and expenses on the date the money is paid or received. In the accrual method, revenues and expenses are recorded on the transaction date (matching principle). To change to the cash-basis method, click the check box and enter the date on which the change is to take effect. This text uses the accrual basis. Do not change this setting.

The next option relates to the use of the **Cheque Number As The Source Code For Cash Expenses And Revenues** in account reconciliation. Since Toss for Tots uses only

NOTES
From the Fiscal End Date entry, 31/12/2000, you can tell that the date order is day, month, year. You cannot see the order from the Start and Earliest Transaction dates.

WARNING!
Type the date as text to avoid number confusion such as entering Jan 10 instead of Oct 1.
Type 2014 and 2015 (use four digits) for the year. If you type 14 and 15, Sage 50 may enter 1914 and 1915.

NOTES
When you view the Company Information again, the session and latest transaction dates will have been updated to match the new fiscal dates.

PRO VERSION
You will not see the warning about changing the industry type because the terminology does not change in the Pro version.

WARNING!
You must save the new fiscal dates before changing the Do Not Allow Transactions Before date.

PRO VERSION
The option to enter transactions in a later fiscal or calendar year is not available.

NOTES
Refer to Appendix O on the Student DVD for more information on accrual- and cash-basis accounting. Refer to Appendix H on the Student DVD for an exercise with keystrokes that uses cash-basis accounting in Sage 50.

PRO VERSION
You will see the terms Purchases and Sales instead of Expenses and Revenues.

WARNING!
The date you enter for Do Not Allow Transactions Dated Before must not be earlier than the Earliest Transaction Date on the Company Information screen.
If the check box is not checked, you can leave the date field blank. You can also enter the date later.
If you did not save the new fiscal dates, you will see an error message when you enter Jul 1 – the original fiscal year 2000 will restrict the date allowed.

the General Ledger, this option does not apply. When you are using the Payables and Receivables Ledgers, you should turn on the option.

The next option, **Do Not Allow Transactions Dated Before**, permits you to lock out transactions before the date you enter here to prevent posting incorrectly to an earlier date. Similarly, you should generally not **allow posting to future periods**, beyond the session date, unless you are entering a series of postdated transactions. You can add a warning for dates beyond a certain period as well. You can activate these features for specific transactions when needed by changing the settings so that you do not post with incorrect dates. We will restrict transactions before the earliest transaction date and not allow postdated transactions. Transactions before the earliest transaction date are not allowed after you finish the history.

Remember that the date format is still day-month-year.

Click **Do Not Allow Transactions Dated Before** to add the ✓.

Double-click the date **01/01/2000**.

Type `Jul 1` (Sage 50 will add the year from the fiscal date information.)

Click **Allow Transactions In The Future** to remove the ✓ and not allow postdating.

NOTES
Refer to page 104 for details on allowing transactions in a previous year.

Since Sage 50 allows journal entries before the company setup details are completed, you can add a reminder **warning** as you continue to work with an incomplete and **unbalanced account history**. If you choose to post journal entries before completing the history, you should turn on the warning.

Setting Backup Options

Click **Backup** in the list under Company:

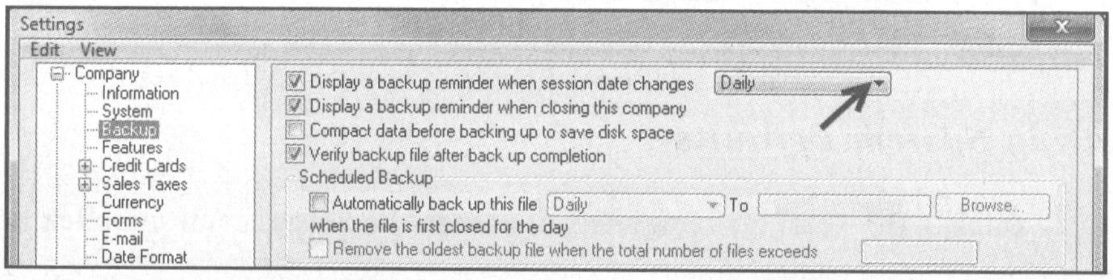

This screen has several options for backing up company files. You can select the **frequency** with which you **back up** your data. Since we usually advance the session date weekly, we will choose Weekly as the backup frequency as well. The program prompts you to back up according to this entry.

Click the **Display A Backup Reminder field list arrow** and **choose Weekly**.

If you want a specific number of days as the interval between backups, choose Other and type the number in the Number Of Days field that opens.

NOTES
Compacting the backup files will help prevent fragmentation of your data files on your hard drive.

The next option will show a **reminder** to back up the file each time you close the company file. Leave the option selected because you should back up data files regularly.

You can also choose to **compact** the backup files. You should **verify** the backup files regularly to ensure there are no errors that will prevent you from restoring the data later.

You can **schedule automatic backups** by choosing the frequency, the backup file location and the **number of old backup files** that should be saved.

Choosing Company Features

Click **Features** in the list below Company in the left-hand side panel:

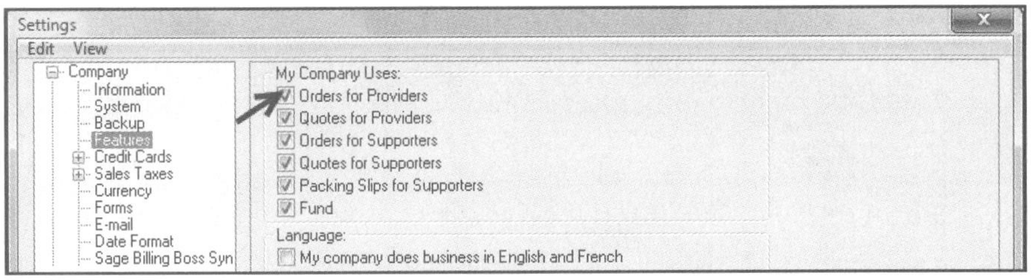

Most of these features (orders, quotes and packing slips) do not apply to General Ledger transactions. The final option refers to languages used. To create forms in both languages, you must choose the option to conduct business in French and English. The Settings option makes the language switch available for many name fields so you can enter names in both languages. The ability to work with the program in both languages is controlled from the View menu (see page 83), not from the Features setting.

Click **each line** to change all settings. This will remove all checkmarks and add one to **My Company Does Business In English And French**, the final option.

Credit cards, sales taxes, currency, e-mail and form numbers, such as for invoices and quotes, do not apply to the General Journal transactions entered by Toss for Tots. Toss for Tots does not use Shippers or the additional Names fields in the General Ledger, so you can skip these screens as well.

PRO VERSION

Packing slips are not available in the Pro version. The terms Vendors, Customers and Project replace Providers, Supporters and Fund.

Changing Date Formats

The date formats for the starter file are different from the formats we used for other files. To avoid entering incorrect dates, we will choose the same format that we used for our other data files. We need to change the default setting so that month appears first. You can choose any separator character you want.

Click **Date Format** in the list below Company in the left-hand side panel:

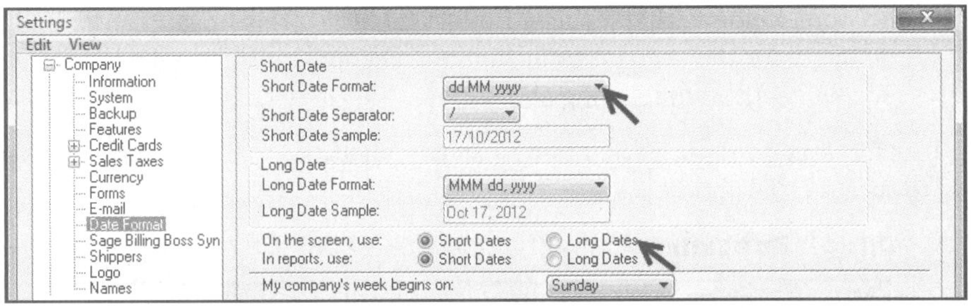

Choose **MM dd yyyy** from the Short Date Format drop-down list.

Choose another separator symbol from the Short Date Separator list, if you want.

On the screen we will show dates in the long form, text style, to make them as clear as possible. You can choose long or short dates for reports.

Click **Long Dates** beside the option for On The Screen, Use.

You can also enter the day that is normally the first day of the business week.

NOTES

The entry for Week Begins On is used for reports that have This Week To Date as an option for the date range.

Adding a Company Logo

Next we will add the company logo. This logo can be added to invoices or other company documents created in Sage 50.

NOTES
Company logo files are located in the SageData13\Logos folder. The default starting point for the Browse is the Forms folder in your Sage 50 program folder.

NOTES
You can click the ⊟ beside Company to close the expanded Company list.

CLASSIC VIEW
From the Home window you can access the General Settings window by clicking the Setup tool bar button and selecting Accounts. If the Chart of Accounts icon in the Home window is already selected, you will access the General Settings directly when you click the Setup tool.

NOTES
The budgeting feature is explained in the Village Galleries application, Chapter 14.
Departments are illustrated in Chapter 19.

PRO VERSION
Departments are not available in the Pro version.
In the Pro version, you cannot change the number of digits for account numbers.

NOTES
In Part Two of this text, we use four-digit account numbers so that the files can be used with the Pro or Premium versions. We introduce five-digit account numbers in Part Three, Chapter 19, for Premium users.

Click **Logo**:

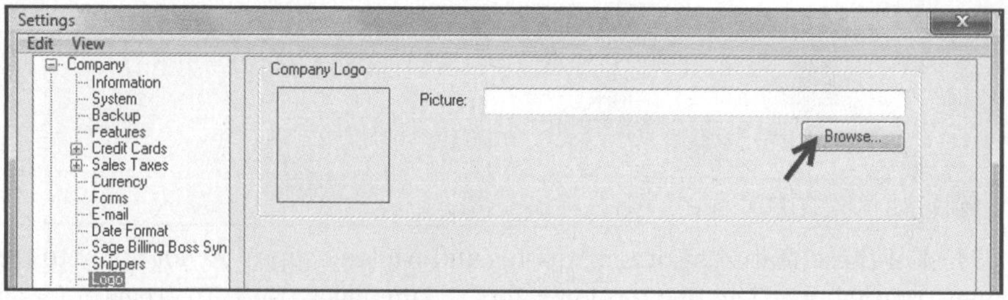

Click **Browse**. **Click Computer** in the left pane. **Double-click C:**. Then **double-click SageData13** and **Logos** to locate the folder with company logos.

Click **toss.bmp** (or **toss**) and **click Open** to return to the Logo Settings with the image and file name added:

Setting General Defaults

To change the settings for the General Ledger for Toss for Tots,

Click **General (Accounts)** in the list on the left:

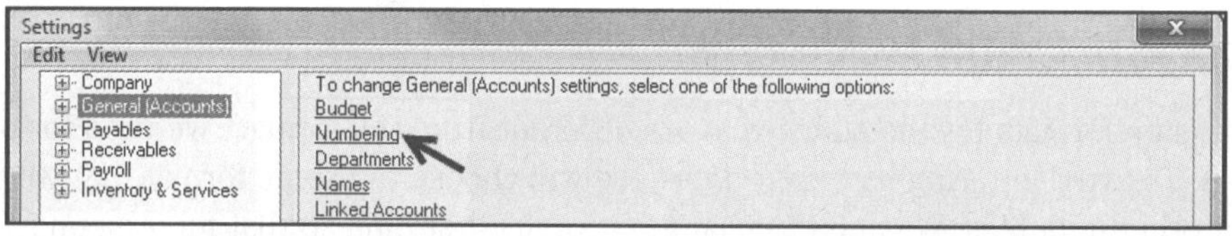

If you want Sage 50 to prepare budget reports, click **Budget** to open the Budget setup options and click Budget Revenue And Expense Accounts. Choose the budget period from the drop-down list. Each revenue and expense ledger account window will include a Budget tab. Click this tab and enter budget amounts for the account to include the account automatically in budget reports. You can activate budgeting at any time.

Toss for Tots does not have different **Departments** to track expenses, so we do not need to turn on this option.

Click **Numbering**:

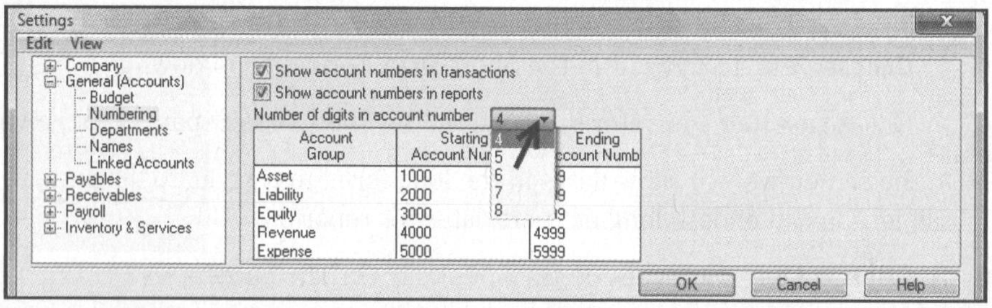

From the **Numbering** option, you can choose not to use account numbers in your reports and journal transactions when the account names are unique; that is, there is no duplication of names. We use account numbers in all the applications in this text.

You can also choose the **number of digits** for your account numbers. Each digit you add to create five- to eight-digit numbers will add an extra zero to the starting and ending number for the account group. For example, when you use six-digit numbers, the Asset accounts will range from 100 000 to 199 900, and the Liabilities accounts will range from 200 000 to 299 900. Using extra digits allows you to create more accounts.

We use four-digit account numbers in this text. You do not need to change the settings for the other ledgers — they are not used by Toss for Tots.

If you changed the number of digits, you will see this warning before you can make additional Settings changes:

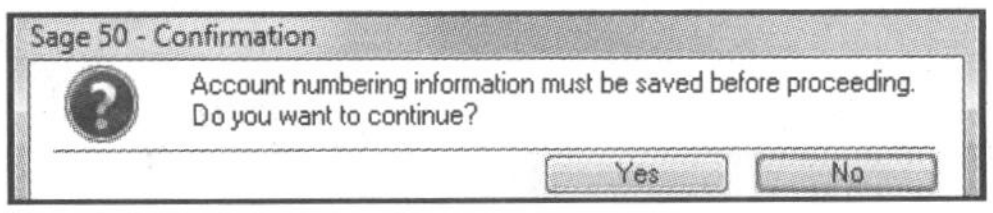

Click Yes to save the changes to account numbers if you see this message.

Click **OK** to save all the changes and return to the Home window.

Changing User Preference Settings

User preferences apply to individual users and indicate the way that person prefers to work with the data files. They do not affect the accounting processes. If you have multiple users who access the files, each user can set his or her own preferences.

Choose the **Setup menu**, then **click User Preferences** to see the options:

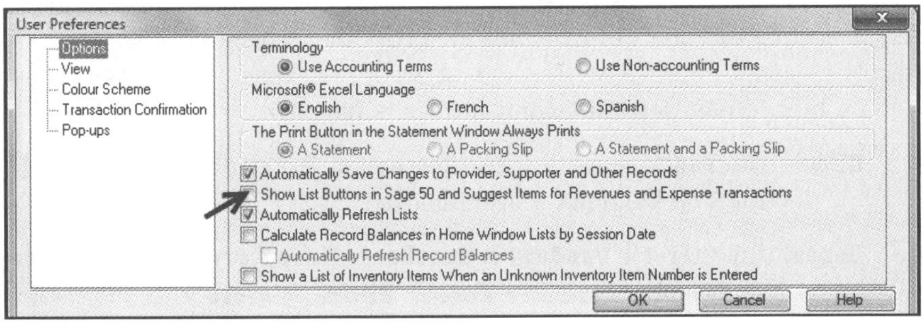

The first feature refers to the language used by the program. We use **accounting terms** throughout this workbook because most people who use accounting programs are familiar with that language. If you choose non-accounting terms, the Payables Ledger will be named Vendors and Purchases in menus and so on. To follow the instructions we provide, you should **Use Accounting Terms**. You can also choose the **language** of your **Excel** program — exported reports will use the language you choose here.

Some invoice windows include a **Print button**. If you print these invoices, you can set whether the invoice, packing slip or both will be printed as the default.

If you choose not to **automatically save changes** to ledger records when you close a record window, the program will prompt you to save if you close the ledger record after making changes and give you the option of always saving future changes automatically. **Including the list selection button** in all account fields to select account numbers, vendors, customers, tax codes, employees, inventory items and so on is the option we use in this text. The next feature allows the account **record balances** displayed in the Home windows (e.g., for customers) to be **calculated by session date** instead of by the latest transaction that may be later than the session date. The **refresh lists automatically** option applies when working in multi-user mode. You can select to show **inventory item lists** whenever a new item is entered in the item field. When you use the Project (Fund) feature, you can always **apply allocations** to the entire transaction. We turned off Fund in the Features Settings for this company (page 79), so you will not see this option. Inventory and allocations are covered in Chapters 10 and 13, respectively.

Click **Show List Buttons In Sage 50 And Suggest Items...**.

The remaining settings are correct for the screens and keystrokes we show in the text. They can be changed at any time by clicking the option.

NOTES
If you need to insert additional accounts, adding a digit to the account number creates room between adjacent account numbers.

PRO VERSION
You will not see the Automatically Refresh Lists option.
Packing slips are not available in the Pro version.

NOTES
Appendix B lists all equivalent accounting and non-accounting terms.

NOTES
The Excel language option will apply only if you have installed a non–English-language version of the Excel program.

NOTES
Many account input fields have list buttons or icons like the Account field that you saw in the General Journal in Chapter 3. Other fields have list arrows that provide a drop-down or pop-up list to select from.

NOTES
The Refresh Lists option applies only to the multi-user version of Sage 50 Premium.

Changing the View Settings

Several important display or appearance options are controlled from the View option.

Click **View**:

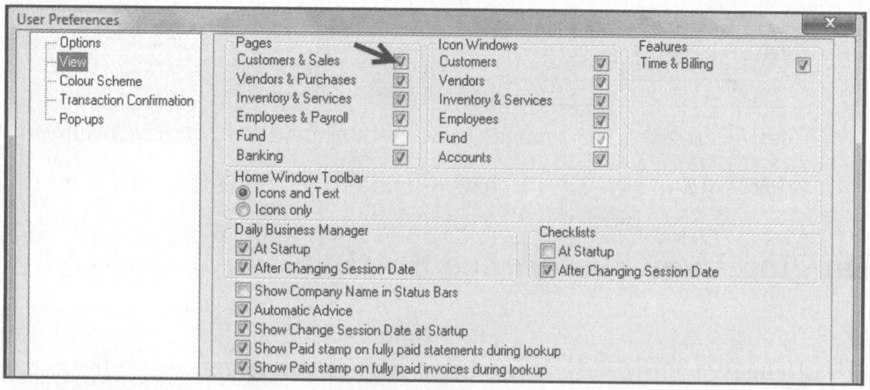

You can **hide**, that is, not display, the icons for **modules** or **pages** that you are not using. We must hide the modules that are not used before finishing the history.

The **Icon Windows** check boxes allow you to hide the accounts icon window for the ledgers. Selecting the Chart of Accounts icon (or other ledger icon) with this option on will display account information for the first account instead of the list of accounts. Icon windows can be hidden separately only if the module pages are not hidden.

Click the **Pages check box for Customers & Sales** to remove the ✓. The ✓ for Icon Windows is also removed.

Repeat this step for **Vendors & Purchases**, **Inventory & Services**, **Employees & Payroll Pages**. The **Time & Billing Feature** ✓ is automatically removed when you remove both Customers and Employees.

Do not remove the ✓ for **Banking**.

The next two options refer to the appearance of the **tool bar** in the Home window. You can display the tools with text or as icons only. The Classic view Home window tool bar never includes text. In our data files, we include the text with the icons.

Sage 50 has reminders about upcoming activities such as payments that are due, discounts available and recurring entries. The **Checklists** and the **Daily Business Manager** can remind you of these activities each time you start the program, each time you advance the session date or both. Toss for Tots does not use these lists.

Click **At Startup** and **click After Changing Session Date** for **Daily Business Manager** to **remove** the ✓s.

Click **After Changing Session Date** for **Checklists** to **remove** the ✓.

You can **Show Company Name In Status Bars** or omit this detail.

Automatic Advice shows advisory messages automatically while you are entering transactions, as, for example, when customers exceed credit limits or the chequing account is overdrawn. Clicking removes the ✓ and the feature. Leave Advice turned on.

We also select to **show the session date** each time we start a work session. If your company has several users who log on frequently during a single day, bypassing this step would be efficient. In that case, the system administrator would update the session date for all users at the start of each business day.

Showing the **Paid Stamp** on invoices and payments is another option. If you hide the Vendors & Customers pages, these options will be dimmed because they no longer apply.

From the **Colour Scheme** entry, you can choose backgrounds from a variety of colours and patterns for the different journal windows.

PRO VERSION
There is no Time & Billing feature in the Pro version, so you will not need to hide it. The term Project replaces Fund.

CLASSIC VIEW
You will see two lists: Modules and Icon Windows. Time & Billing is added to the Modules list.

NOTES
When you hide modules and icon windows, all information about icon positions is also removed. You will see the message about this when you display the records in the account windows by icon instead of by name.

WARNING!
If you do not hide the remaining modules, you will be unable to complete the final setup step of finishing the history because essential information for those modules is missing.

WARNING!
Do not hide the Banking page. If you hide this page, you will be unable to access the General Journal.

NOTES
Fund is already removed from the list of pages because we turned off the feature.

NOTES
You can access Checklists and the Daily Business Manager at any time from the Business Assistant menu, even if the automatic display for them is turned off. You can turn on the automatic display again at any time from this User Preferences View settings screen.

Confirming Posting of Transactions Settings

We will choose to have the program advise when transactions are successfully recorded.

Click **Transaction Confirmation**.

If you see a warning about losing icon position information (see margin Notes), click Yes to continue to the transaction confirmation window:

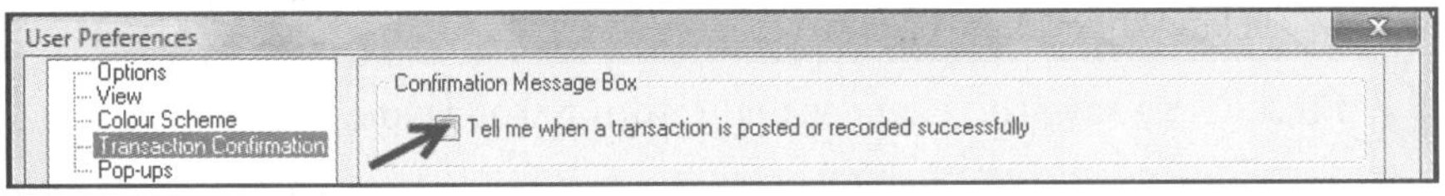

Click the **check box** beside Tell Me When A Transaction Is Posted Or Recorded Successfully to add a ✓ and turn on the confirmation.

Click **Pop-ups**:

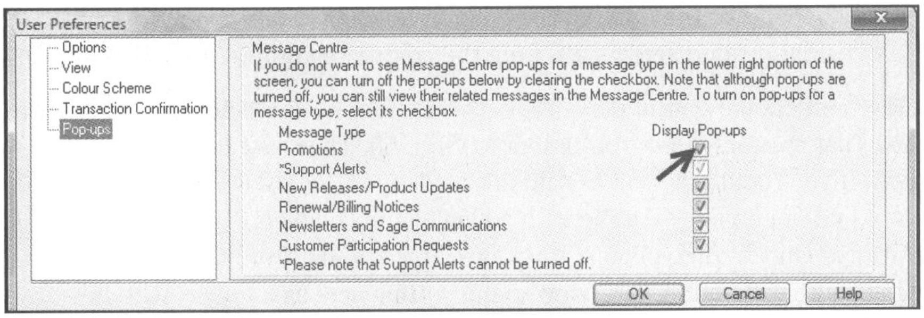

On this screen you control what kinds of messages you see. Clicking a check box will prevent that type of message from appearing for this data file.

Click the **messages** that you do not want to see to remove the ✓s.

Click **OK** to save the settings and return to the updated Home window:

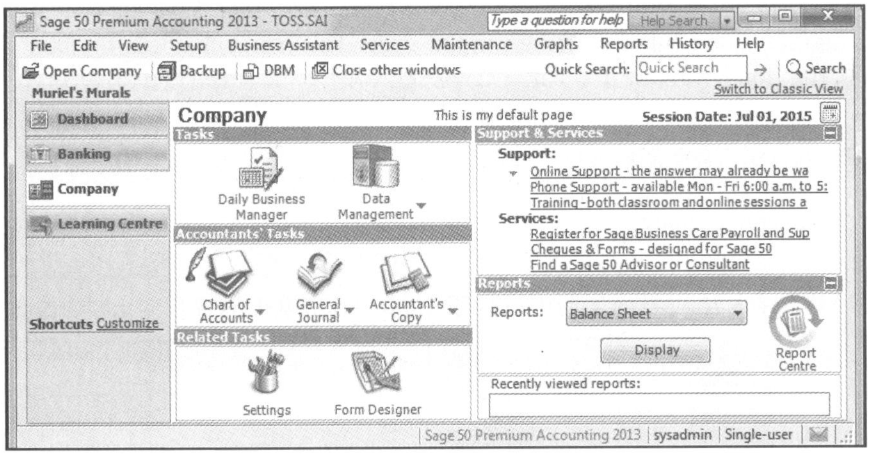

The unused modules (hidden pages) have been removed from the Modules pane list.

Changing View Menu Settings

The View menu controls some of the appearance options for the program:

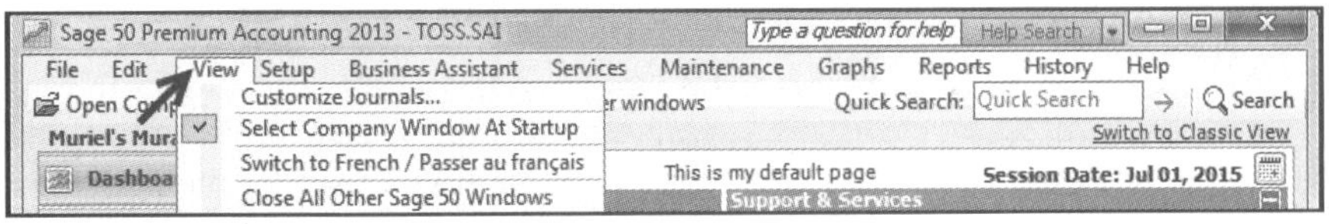

Each journal has optional fields that can be hidden if they are not required by the program and the business.

NOTES

Remember that these are user preferences – each user can change these settings for personal preferences. User setup is described in Chapter 16 and Appendix G.

NOTES

We have turned off pop-ups for the data files we provided on the Student DVD.

Support Alerts is dimmed – you cannot turn off the display of these messages.

NOTES

In Chapter 6, we customize journal columns and tabbing order.

NOTES

We have not hidden fields in any journals used in the applications in this text, except by turning off features, so you can see the full range of input options for each journal.

We show how to customize journals in Chapter 6 and invoices in Appendix F on the Student DVD.

NOTES

If you have the Select Company window hidden or deselected, you will start from the Open Company window each time you start Sage 50. You can turn on the selection again from the Home window View menu in any open data file.

You can also change the order in which journal fields are accessed from the *tab* key, that is, which field is next when you press *tab*. You can **customize all journals** from this menu or you can use the customize option within individual journals.

To customize a journal, choose the View menu and click Customize Journals. Click the journal you want. Click Columns or Tabbing Order and click the columns or details you want to change. Hidden fields may be restored at any time by clicking their names again.

Click OK to save the changes and return to the Home window.

The Customize Journal tool and View menu option in each journal provide the same options as the Home window View menu Customize Journals screen.

You can also customize the order and size of journal columns. To change the order, drag a column heading to the location you want. To change the column size, point to the edge of the column heading; when the pointer changes to a double-headed arrow, drag the column margin to its new size.

The next choice on the main View menu refers to the **Welcome and Select Company window** that appears when you first start Sage 50. There are advantages to showing this window. If you regularly use the same data file, you can bypass the Open Company file window, and open your data file with a single step by selecting Open The Last Company You Worked On. Similarly, you can restore a backup file from this window without first opening another data file. The View menu setting acts as a toggle switch, and you can change it at any time.

Sage 50 is a fully bilingual program. You can **switch the program language** (choose to work in French or in English) from the View menu with this toggle switch. When you are working in French, the View menu (now renamed *Vue*) option changes to *Passer A L'Anglais*/Switch To English.

The final View menu option allows you to **close all other Sage 50 windows** in a single step, leaving only the Home window open. This menu choice is the same as the one in the Home window tool bar.

Changing the Printer Defaults

PRO VERSION

You will not see the Time Slips entry.

WARNING!

You need to choose a printer for reports and for each form listed. The default may be incorrect if you have changed your computer setup after installing the program.

Printer settings may also be incorrect if you use a data file that was created on a different computer.

You may select a different printer for customized forms, or you may want to change the format of the printed reports. The following instructions should assist you.

Choose the **Setup menu** and **click Reports & Forms** to see the settings screen:

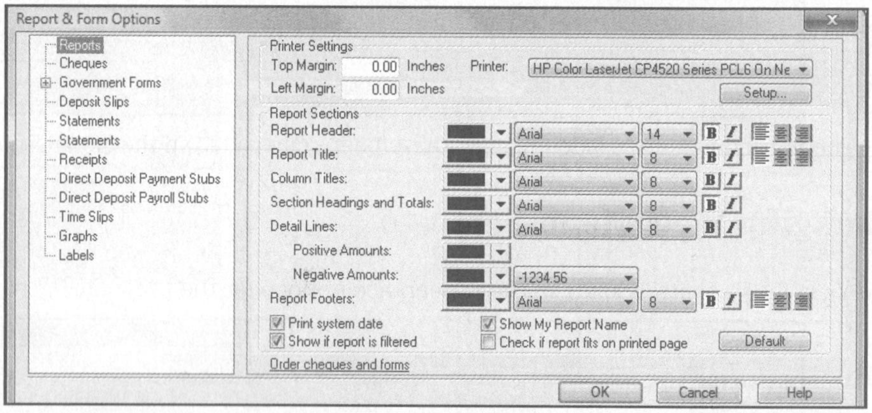

Printer selections are saved with each company file. If you use the file with another computer system or program installation, they may be incorrect. Sage 50 allows you to set up different printers and settings for reports, graphs, cheques, invoices, labels and so on. Many companies use different printers for their reports and preprinted forms and invoices. Even if you use one printer, you may want to adjust fonts, margins and form selections for each type of printed report or statement.

Choose the printer you will use for reports from the list provided by the arrow beside the field. All printers installed on your computer should be on the list. Change the page margins if necessary. For each part of the report, choose font, type size, colour and how to display positive and negative numbers by clicking the list arrows beside these fields. You can experiment to find the combination that will fit the reports neatly on the page. By default, reports include the computer system date and a message indicating whether filtering is applied.

To modify the printer setup for other outputs, click the relevant form in the list. You can modify printer setup information at any time by returning to this screen.

Additional printer settings may be available from the Setup button screen for print quality, paper source, paper size, two-sided printing, orientation and so on. The screens and options will vary from printer to printer.

Click **Cancel** to exit without making changes and return to the Home window, or click OK to leave each dialogue box and save the change.

You are now ready to make the necessary changes in the General Ledger.

> **WARNING!**
> You should view the additional printer control screens, but you do not need to change them. The printer control screens will vary from one printer to another. Usually the default settings are correct.
> Notice that the printer instructions are given as optional command statements.

Preparing the Ledgers

The third stage in setting up an accounting system involves preparing each ledger for operation. For Toss for Tots, this stage involves the following steps:

1. organizing all accounting reports and records (this step has been completed)
2. modifying some existing accounts (you will not need to delete any accounts)
3. creating new accounts
4. entering historical account balance information

Defining the Skeleton Starter Files

When you created the company files for Toss for Tots in stage one, Creating Company Files (page 70), the preset startup accounts were provided.

Print the **Chart of Accounts** for the current year, as shown here:

Toss for Tots
Chart of Accounts

No.	Description	Type	Account Class
Chart of Accounts - Current Year (2015)			
ASSET			
1000	CURRENT ASSETS	H	
1020	Bank	G	Asset
1200	Accounts Receivable	G	Asset
1390	TOTAL CURRENT ASSETS	T	
LIABILITY			
2000	CURRENT LIABILITIES	H	
2200	Accounts Payable	G	Liability
2690	TOTAL CURRENT LIABILITIES	T	
EQUITY			
3000	EARNINGS	H	
3560	Retained Earnings	G	Retained Earnings
3600	Current Earnings	X	Current Earnings
3690	TOTAL EARNINGS	T	
REVENUE			
4000	REVENUE	H	
4020	General Revenue	G	Revenue
4390	TOTAL REVENUE	T	
EXPENSE			
5000	EXPENSES	H	
5020	General Expense	G	Expense
5390	TOTAL EXPENSES	T	

Accounts are organized by **section**: Assets, Liabilities, Equity, Revenue and Expense. The chart also shows the **account type** — such as Heading (H), Subgroup total (S), Total (T), subgroup Account (A), Group account (G) and Current

> **NOTES**
> Print the Chart of Accounts before you begin and compare it to the Chart of Accounts for Toss for Tots. Choose the Reports menu in the Home window, then choose Lists and click Chart of Accounts. Refer to page 58 for help with displaying the Chart of Accounts if necessary.
> If you view Chart of Accounts from the Non-Profit template, you will see that it requires many more changes. To view its Chart of Accounts, you must create a new company using this template.

> **NOTES**
> Account classes will be explained in Chapter 7 when you set up the files for Air Care Services. For now you can accept the default class settings.

Earnings (X) — and the Account Class. Account type is a method of classifying and organizing accounts within a section or subsection of a report.

Initial account numbers for each account are also shown on the Chart of Accounts. We are using only four digits for account numbers, so the accounts in this chart follow the sectional boundaries we saw in Chapter 3, as follows:

- 1000–1999 Assets
- 2000–2999 Liabilities
- 3000–3999 Equity
- 4000–4999 Revenue
- 5000–5999 Expense

The Format of Financial Statements

When setting up the complete Chart of Accounts for Toss for Tots, it is important that you understand the composition and format of financial statements in Sage 50. The chart on the facing page summarizes the application of the following rules in Sage 50.

The Balance Sheet is divided into three **sections**, each with **headings**: Assets, Liabilities and Equity. The Income Statement is divided into two sections with headings: Revenue and Expense.

Each section of the financial statements can be subdivided into groups. Assets can be divided into groups such as CURRENT ASSETS, INVENTORY ASSETS and PLANT AND EQUIPMENT. Liabilities can be divided into groups titled CURRENT LIABILITIES and LONG TERM DEBT. Equity, Revenue and Expense sections can also be divided. Groups may be further divided by creating subgroups.

Sage 50 requires that all accounts, including group headings, subgroup totals and group totals, be assigned numbers even if you do not use account numbers in transactions or reports. This is different from manual accounting, in which numbers are assigned only to postable accounts. Predefined section headings and section totals (e.g., ASSETS, TOTAL ASSETS and LIABILITIES), however, are not assigned numbers by the program.

Financial Statement Sections

These four rules apply to financial statement sections in Sage 50:

1. Each of the five financial statement sections has a **section heading** and a **section total**. You cannot change the titles for these headings and totals.
2. A **section total** is the total of the individual group totals within that section. The program will calculate section totals automatically and print them in the financial statement reports. The five section totals are
   - TOTAL ASSETS
   - TOTAL LIABILITIES
   - TOTAL EQUITY
   - TOTAL REVENUE
   - TOTAL EXPENSE
3. The Liabilities and Equity section totals are also automatically added together. **LIABILITIES AND EQUITY** is the sum of TOTAL LIABILITIES and TOTAL EQUITY.
4. In the Income Statement, **NET INCOME**, the difference between TOTAL REVENUE and TOTAL EXPENSE, is automatically calculated and listed under TOTAL EXPENSE.

ORGANIZATION OF ACCOUNTS

BALANCE SHEET

Type	Number	Account Name	Amount	Amount
ASSETS [section heading]				
H	**1000**	**CURRENT ASSETS**		
A	1020	Bank: Toss for Tots	xxx	
A	1100	Cash on Hand	xxx	
S	1150	Total Cash		xxx
G	1200	Surprise Bag Supplies		xxx
G	1300	Food Supplies		xxx
		–		
		–		
T	**1390**	**TOTAL CURRENT ASSETS**		**xxx**
H	**1400**	**FIXED ASSETS**		
G	1420	Fax/Telephone		xxx
G	1450	Computer		xxx
	–			
T	**1590**	**TOTAL FIXED ASSETS**		**xxx**
TOTAL ASSETS [section total]				xxx
LIABILITIES [section heading]				
H	**2000**	**CURRENT LIABILITIES**		
G	2100	Bank Loan		xxx
G	2200	A/P – Designs U Wear		xxx
		–		
T	**2690**	**TOTAL CURRENT LIABILITIES**		**xxx**
TOTAL LIABILITIES [section total]				xxx
EQUITY [section heading]				
H	**3000**	**EQUITY**		
G	3560	Accumulated Surplus		xxx
X	3600	Net Income		xxx
		–		
T	**3690**	**TOTAL EQUITY**		**xxx**
TOTAL EQUITY [section total]				xxx
LIABILITIES & EQUITY				xxx

INCOME STATEMENT

Type	Number	Account Name	Amount	Amount
REVENUE [section heading]				
H	**4000**	**REVENUE**		
G	4020	Revenue: Registrations		xxx
G	4040	Revenue: Sponsors		xxx
		–		
		–		
T	**4390**	**TOTAL REVENUE**		**xxx**
TOTAL REVENUE [section total]				xxx
EXPENSE [section heading]				
H	**5000**	**ADMIN EXPENSES**		
G	5020	Court Rental Expense		xxx
G	5200	Office Supplies Used		xxx
		–		
		–		
T	**5440**	**TOTAL ADMIN EXPENSES**		**xxx**
H	**5450**	**MERCHANDISE & FOOD EXPENSES**		
G	5500	Cost of T-shirts		xxx
G	5520	Cost of Surprise Bags		xxx
		–		
T	**5690**	**TOTAL MERCHANDISE & FOOD EXPENSES**		**xxx**
TOTAL EXPENSE [section total]				xxx
NET INCOME				xxx

Type
H = Group **H**eading
T = Group **T**otal
G = Postable **G**roup Account
A = Postable Subgroup **A**ccount
S = Group **S**ubtotal
X = Current Earnings Account

Financial Statement Account Groups

Financial statement sections are further divided into account groups made up of different types of accounts. The following rules apply to account groups in Sage 50:

1. Each group must start with a **group Heading (H)**, which will be printed in boldface type. A heading is not considered a postable account, cannot be debited or credited through transaction entries and cannot have an amount assigned to it.

2. Each group must contain at least one **postable account** and can contain more. Postable accounts are those that can be debited or credited through journal transaction entries. Postable accounts may have an opening balance.

3. Postable accounts may be **subgroup Accounts (A)** or **Group accounts (G)**. Subgroup account balances appear in a separate column to the left of the group account balances, which are in the right column.

4. Postable subgroup accounts must be followed by a **Subgroup total (S)** account. A subgroup total is not a postable account and cannot be given an opening balance. The program automatically calculates a subgroup total by adding all preceding subgroup postable account balances that follow the last group, subgroup total or heading account. Subgroup total balances always appear in the right column. For

example, in the previous application, *GST Charged on Sales* and *GST Paid on Purchases* are subgroup accounts followed by the subgroup total *GST Owing (Refund)*. For Toss for Tots, the bank and cash accounts are subtotalled.

5. Each group must end with a **group Total (T)**. All amounts in the right-hand column, for postable and subgroup total accounts, are added together to form the group total. A group total is not a postable account. The program automatically calculates this total and prints it in boldface type.

The chart on the previous page summarizes the application of these rules.

The Current Earnings (X) Account

There are two linked accounts for the General Ledger — **Retained Earnings** and **Current Earnings**. Both accounts are required and appear in the EQUITY section of the Balance Sheet. You do not need to change the links for these accounts.

The Current Earnings account is the only **Type X** account in the Chart of Accounts. This account is calculated as follows:

Current Earnings = Total Revenue - Total Expense

Current Earnings is not a postable account, but it appears in the right-hand column with the group accounts. It cannot be removed, but its title and number can be modified (see Editing Accounts in the General Ledger, page 90). *Current Earnings* is updated from any transactions that change revenue and expense account balances. At the end of the fiscal period when closing routines are performed, the balance of this account is added to *Retained Earnings* (or its renamed account) and then reset to zero.

For Toss for Tots, a charitable organization, the *Retained Earnings* account will be renamed *Accumulated Surplus*. *Current Earnings* will be renamed *Net Income*.

Preparing the General Ledger

Compare the Skeleton Chart of Accounts you printed with the Toss for Tots Chart of Accounts, Balance Sheet and Income Statement provided in this application. You will see that some accounts are the same, and some accounts you need are not yet in the program. You have to customize the accounts for Toss for Tots.

NOTES
You will not need to delete any of the preset accounts for Toss for Tots.

Changing the Skeleton Accounts

The first step, that of identifying the changes needed in the Skeleton preset accounts to match the accounts needed for Toss for Tots, is a very important one. The changes that must be made to these preset accounts are outlined below:

1. Some starter accounts provided by the program require no changes. For the following accounts, the account title, the initial account number and the account type are the same as those in the financial statements:

CURRENT ASSETS	1000	Type H
TOTAL CURRENT ASSETS	1390	Type T
CURRENT LIABILITIES	2000	Type H
TOTAL CURRENT LIABILITIES	2690	Type T
REVENUE	4000	Type H
TOTAL REVENUE	4390	Type T

2. The following accounts have account titles or names that need to be changed. You must also change the account type for *Bank 1020*. (Account numbers are correct.)

FROM (SKELETON ACCOUNTS)			TO (TOSS FOR TOTS ACCOUNTS)
Account Name	Number	Type	Account Name (Type)
Bank	1020	Type G	Bank: Toss for Tots (Type A)
Accounts Receivable	1200	Type G	Surprise Bag Supplies
Accounts Payable	2200	Type G	A/P - Designs U Wear
EARNINGS	3000	Type H	EQUITY
Retained Earnings	3560	Type G	Accumulated Surplus
Current Earnings	3600	Type X	Net Income
TOTAL EARNINGS	3690	Type T	TOTAL EQUITY
General Revenue	4020	Type G	Revenue: Registrations
EXPENSES	5000	Type H	ADMIN EXPENSES
General Expense	5020	Type G	Court Rental Expense

3. The following account requires changes in both the account name and the number:

FROM (SKELETON ACCOUNTS)			TO (TOSS FOR TOTS ACCOUNTS)	
Account Name	Number	Type	Account Name	Number
TOTAL EXPENSES	5390	Type T	TOTAL ADMIN EXPENSES	5440

Creating the Chart of Accounts

After identifying the modifications that must be made to the Skeleton accounts, the next step is to identify the accounts that you need to create or add to the preset accounts. Again, you should refer to the company Chart of Accounts on page 67 to complete this step.

The chart that follows shows the accounts that you will need to create. The chart includes account names, account numbers, account types and the option to omit printing zero balances. It lists both postable (group and subgroup) and non-postable accounts (subgroup totals, group headings and group totals).

CHART OF ACCOUNTS TO BE CREATED

Account: *Number	*Name	Type	Omit
1100	Cash on Hand	A	No
1150	Total Cash	S	
1300	Food Supplies	G	Yes
1320	Office Supplies	G	Yes
1360	T-shirts	G	Yes
1400	FIXED ASSETS	H	
1420	Fax/Telephone	G	Yes
1450	Computer	G	No
1500	Digital Camera	G	No
1590	TOTAL FIXED ASSETS	T	
2100	Bank Loan	G	Yes
2300	A/P - Quiq Kopy	G	Yes
2350	A/P - Central College	G	Yes
2400	A/P - Snack City	G	Yes
2670	HST Paid on Purchases	G	Yes
4040	Revenue: Sponsors	G	No
4080	Revenue: Surprise Bags	G	No
4100	Revenue: Admissions	G	No ▶
▶4120	Revenue: Food Sales	G	No
5200	Office Supplies Used	G	Yes
5220	Non-refundable HST	G	Yes
5240	Postage Expense	G	Yes
5280	Printing & Copying	G	Yes
5300	Telephone Expense	G	Yes
5320	Publicity & Promotion	G	Yes
5400	Wages - Manager	G	Yes
5420	Miscellaneous Expenses	G	Yes
5450	MERCHANDISE & FOOD EXPENSES	H	
5500	Cost of T-shirts	G	Yes
5520	Cost of Surprise Bags	G	Yes
5550	Cost of Food	G	Yes
5690	TOTAL MERCHANDISE & FOOD EXPENSES	T	

Account Types: A = Subgroup Account S = Subgroup Total G = Group Account H = Heading T = Group Total
* Account number and account name are required fields

You are now ready to enter the account information into the Toss for Tots files.

Entering General Ledger Accounts

From the Chart of Accounts icon 

drop-down list, you can begin all ledger account record–related changes.

Click the **Chart of Accounts shortcuts list arrow** as shown:

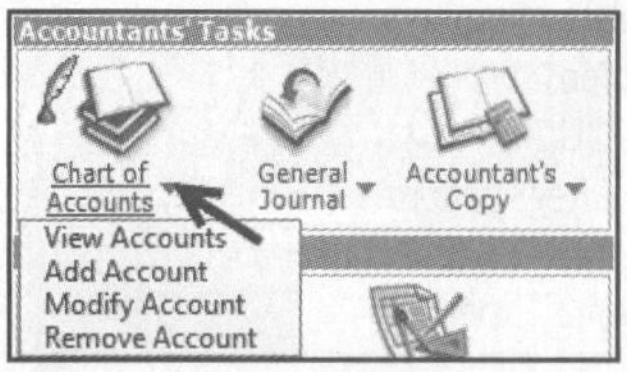

Editing Accounts in the General Ledger

We will change the first account that requires editing, *1020 Bank*. To modify accounts, use the Modify Account option.

Click **Modify Account** in the Chart of Accounts shortcuts list to open the Search window:

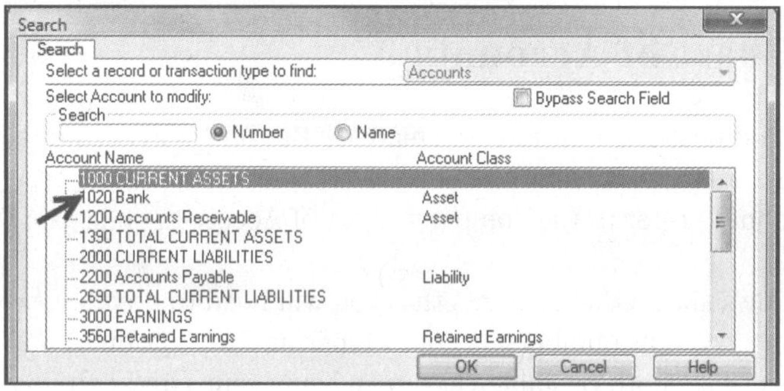

NOTES
You can advance to a later part of the account list by typing the first number in the Search field. You can also search by account name by choosing this option.

This Search screen is like the one in the General Journal that opens the Adjust Entry feature. Accounts is selected as the search field area.

Click **1020 Bank** to highlight or select it.

Click **OK** or double-click the account's name to open the account as shown:

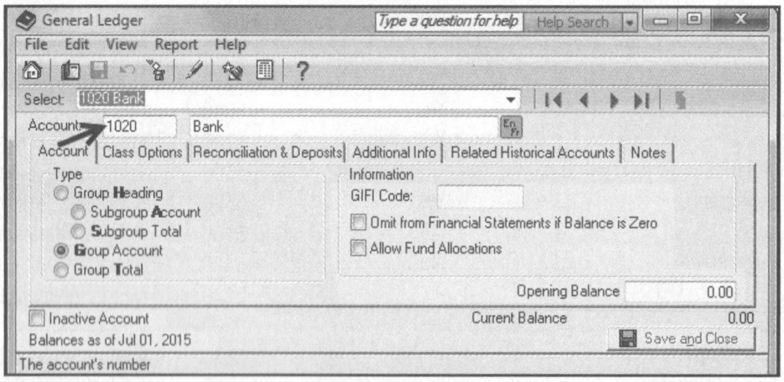

PRO VERSION
You will not see , the Refresh tool.

The Account information tab screen is displayed. We use this screen to edit the account name and type. For the bank account, the account number is correct.

Sometimes, it may be appropriate to print an account with a zero balance, although zero balance accounts usually do not need to be printed. In Sage 50, you have the option to omit accounts with zero balances from financial statements. You may select this option in the General Ledger or in the options windows for financial reports.

The balances of bank accounts should always be displayed, so do not select Omit From Financial Statements If Balance Is Zero.

NOTES
Initially the cursor is in the Select field. Pressing tab twice advances you to the Account number field and then the name field.

Press tab **twice** to advance to the name of the account and highlight it.

Type `Bank: Toss for Tots`

We are not using GIFI codes (Canada Revenue Agency's account numbering system for electronic report filing) or fund or project allocations, so we can leave these options unchanged. The current balance is displayed, but you cannot edit it. It is updated when you enter an opening balance and journal entries. The opening account balance will be added later (see Entering Historical Account Balances on page 94). There is no additional account information. We are not using Account Reconciliation, and we do not need to change the account class, so we can skip these tab screens. On the Related Historical Accounts tab screen, you can enter the relationship between different account numbers that are used for the same account in multiple fiscal periods. They do not apply here.

Click **Subgroup Account** to change the account type.

The bank and cash accounts together will be subtotalled. You can now advance to the next account for editing. There are different ways to do this.

Click the **Select field list arrow** to show the list of all accounts, as shown:

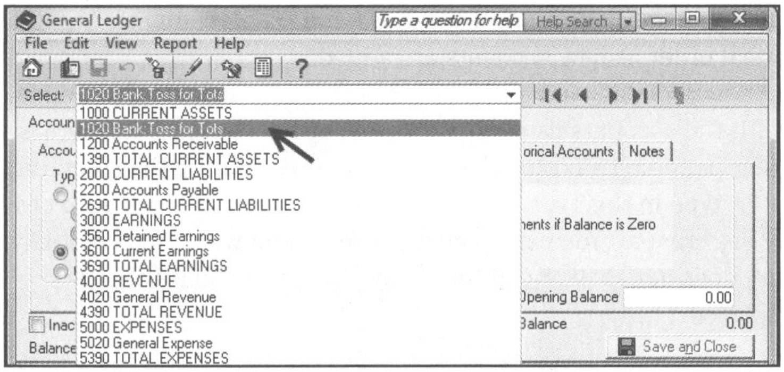

Click **1200 Accounts Receivable** to display the ledger record.

To open a different ledger record, you can also click the **Next Account tool** to open the ledger record for the next account in numerical sequence.

Or, you can close the bank account window to return to the Home window. Then click Modify Account in the Chart of Accounts shortcuts list again and select the next account to be changed.

Because you chose to save ledger record changes automatically (page 81) you do not need to save an account record (Save tool or File menu, Save) after each change.

Edit the **remaining accounts** shown on page 89 as required. You may choose to print zero balances or to omit them.

Close the **General Ledger window** to return to the Home window.

The Accounts Window

Click the **Chart of Accounts icon** in the Accountants' Tasks pane to open the Accounts window:

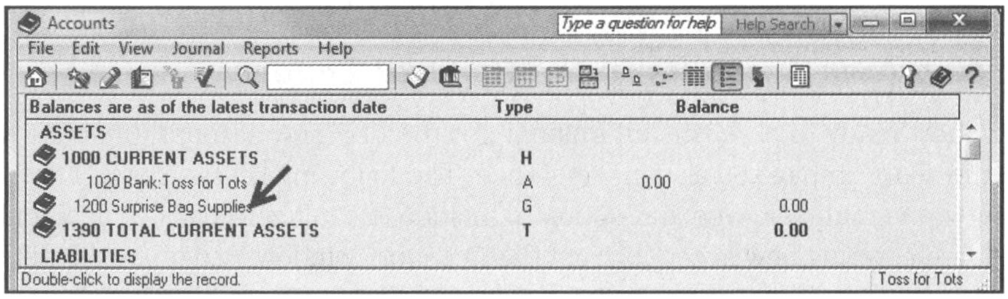

NOTES
GIFI codes and exporting GIFI reports are covered in Appendix K.
Information you enter on the Notes tab screen can be added to the financial statements (see page 54).

NOTES
Class Options are introduced in Chapter 7.

NOTES
To edit an account from the Accounts window, double-click the account you want to change, or click the account to select it and then either click the Edit tool or choose the File menu and click Open or press ctrl + O.

PRO VERSION
You will not see , the Refresh tool.

From this window, you can perform all ledger account–related activities as well. The tool buttons and menu options give access to the individual ledger records, and you can modify, delete, add records, display reports, access help and so on.

Click the Maximize button so that the Accounts window fills the screen. This will allow you to display more accounts and keep the Accounts window in view in the background while you are creating or editing accounts. To return the window to normal size, click , the Restore button.

Several tools control the appearance of the Accounts window. The preset accounts should be displayed in the **Type** format shown on page 91. You can also show the Accounts window in the large or small **Icon** format with icons representing each account. In the Icon view, you can rearrange icons by dragging so that frequently used accounts appear at the top for easier access. New accounts are automatically added at the bottom of the screen, but they can be moved to the desired location. In small icon viewing mode, more accounts can be displayed at the same time.

Another format is available with the **Name** view. Viewing accounts by name shows the account numbers, names and balances in debit and credit columns. Accounts remain in numerical order as new accounts are added.

For entering new accounts and editing a large number of existing accounts, it is easier to work with the accounts listed in numerical order. New accounts are inserted in their correct order, providing a better view of the progress during the setup phase. The addition of account type in the Type view is helpful for checking the logical order of accounts as they are created. You can change the Accounts window view at any time.

If your screen does not show the accounts by Type, you should change the way accounts are displayed.

Click the **Display By Type tool** or **choose** the **View menu** and **click Type**.

When others are using the same data file, you can click the **Refresh tool** to update your data file with changes that other users have made to accounts. In single-user mode, the tool is dimmed.

We can also check that the accounts are in proper sequence; that is, they follow the rules outlined on pages 86–88.

Click the **Check Validity Of Accounts tool** or **choose** the **File menu** and **click Check The Validity Of Accounts** to see the message:

NOTES
Only one error is listed, the first one encountered in checking the Chart of Accounts for validity of account order. After you correct the first error, the second error will be listed, if there is one.

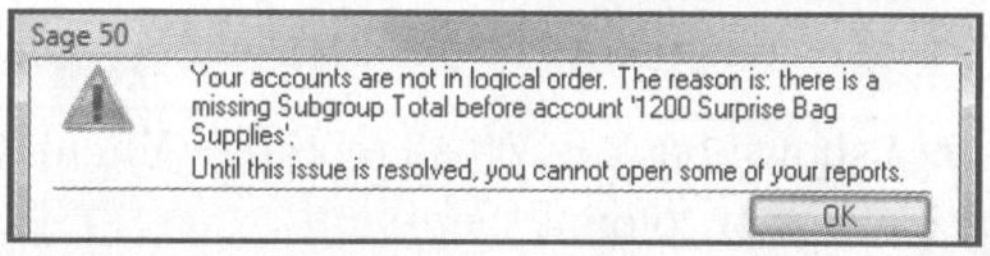

Without the second subgroup account and subgroup total, we have not followed the rules for Groups (page 87, rule 4). The accounts are not in logical order — a subtotal is missing. You can periodically check the validity of accounts while you are adding accounts to see whether you have made errors in your account type sequence that will prevent you from finishing the account history. When we add the remaining accounts, the accounts should be in logical order and the error will be corrected.

Click **OK** to return to the Accounts window.

Creating New Accounts in the General Ledger

You are now ready to enter the information for the first new account, *Cash on Hand*, using the chart on page 89 as your reference. The following keystrokes will enter the account name, number, type and option to include or omit zero balance accounts.

We are entering new accounts from the Accounts window, and it should still be open.

Click the **Create tool** on the Accounts window tool bar or **choose** the **File menu** and **click Create**.

You will display the new account window:

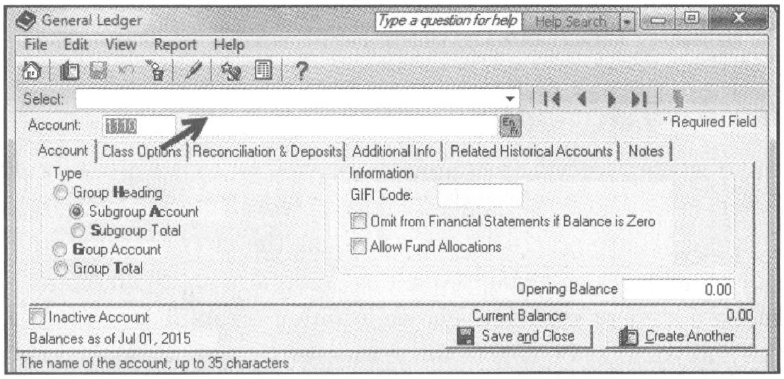

The tabs that appear in the ledger depend on the account section as defined by the account number. If no number is entered initially, only the tabs that apply to all accounts appear. We will create the first account that was not in the Skeleton Chart of Accounts, *Cash on Hand*. The account type is selected as the most likely option for logical account order. The default account type depends on the account record you used most recently. For example, group total accounts are often followed by a group account. The cursor is in the Account number field and the field is selected for editing. Sage 50 will not allow duplicate account numbers.

Two fields are required for accounts: the number and the name. An * appears beside a required field as long as it remains blank. Sage 50 may enter an account number and type that is the most likely next entry based on the previous selection. If an account number is entered as a default, as in the screen we show, the * will be removed. After the error message, account 1200 is selected in the Accounts window so that you can correct the error. Its preceding account is a Subgroup account, so another Subgroup account is expected. The account number will be selected for editing.

Type 1100

Press *tab* to advance to the Account name field.

Type Cash on Hand

Click **Subgroup Account** to change the account type if necessary.

Leave the option to Omit From Financial Statements turned off. Skip the GIFI field and the Fund (Project) Allocations check box.

Check your work. **Make** any necessary **corrections** by pressing *tab* to return to the incorrect field, typing the correct information and pressing *tab* if necessary.

When the information has been entered correctly, save your work.

Click **Create Another** [Create Another] to save the new account and to advance to another new account information window.

Both the number and name fields are now marked with an *.

Create the **remaining accounts** from page 89.

Subgroup totals, group headings and group totals — the non-postable accounts — will have the Balance fields removed when you choose these account types.

Click **Save And Close** [Save and Close] to save the final account.

NOTES

You can also press *ctrl* + N to open a new account ledger form from the Accounts window or from any account's General Ledger window.

NOTES

Depending on your previous step or cursor position, your initial account number and type may be different from the ones we show.

NOTES

When no number is entered, only the Account, Class Options and Additional Information tabs are shown. When you enter a 4000- or 5000-level account number, the Budget tab will be added. The Reconciliation & Deposits tab is included for all Balance Sheet accounts.

NOTES

Sage 50 enters an Account Class automatically (Class Options tab screen). For most accounts, the section heading is used (Assets, Liabilities, etc.). For Expense accounts, the default class is Cost of Goods Sold. This selection will not affect the financial statements for Toss for Tots so you can leave it. If you want, you can change the class on the Class Options screen by choosing Expense for these accounts.

Account class is introduced in Chapter 7.

Display or **print** the **Chart of Accounts** to check the accuracy of your work.

If you find mistakes, edit the account information as described in the Editing Accounts in the General Ledger section on page 90.

If you want to end your session, close the General Ledger window and close the Accounts window to return to the Home window.

Entering Historical Account Balances

WARNING!
Before you finish the history, the opening balance can be edited. The Current Balance has no data input field because you cannot edit it. Initially, it is the same as the opening balance but it changes when you add journal entries. Because you can enter journal transactions before finishing the history, this distinction is very important. The balance in the Accounts window is the current balance, which may not be the same as the opening balance.

After you finish the history, the opening balance field is removed.

Before completing this step, we will create one more account to use as a test account for our Trial Balance. If you close the General Ledger before entering all the account balances, or if the total debits and credits are not equal, the program forces the Trial Balance to balance by adding the required debit or credit amount to another account.

This automatic adjustment may compensate for other errors that you have made in entering amounts, and you may be able to finish the history with errors in opening balances. You cannot change these balances after finishing the history. To detect this problem, we will create a test account and put all the adjustments into it. If all the balances are entered correctly, the test account will have a zero balance and we can remove the account.

Create the new Group account **1005 Test Account**.

You are now ready to enter the opening historical account balances for all postable (type G or A) accounts. The opening balances for Toss for Tots can be found in the Trial Balance on page 69. Accounts with zero balances are not included in the Trial Balance. You should skip these accounts when entering account balances.

Click the **Select field** list arrow and **choose 1020 Bank: Toss for Tots**. The ledger window opens:

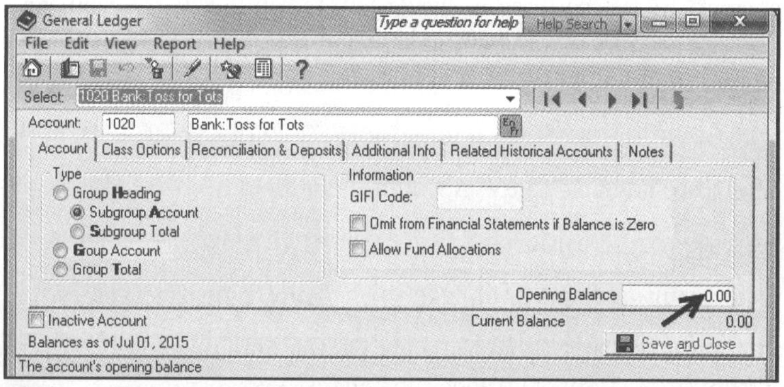

Click the **Opening Balance field** to highlight it.

Type 18550 **Press** *tab*.

The Current Balance is updated, but you cannot change it directly. Sage 50 updates this balance automatically from journal entries.

WARNING!
Remember to enter the amount for HST Paid on Purchases with a minus sign to create a debit entry.

Click the **Next tool** to advance to the next ledger account window.

Enter the **balances** for the remaining accounts in the Trial Balance on page 69.

Remember that *HST Paid on Purchases* has a debit balance (add a minus sign).

If you close the General Ledger window before entering all the account balances, you will see a screen like the following:

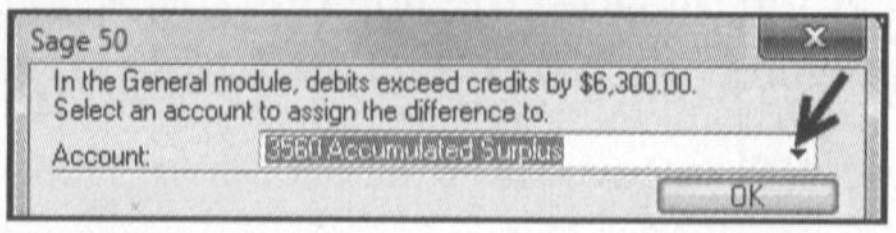

The message asks you to choose an account for the difference — an adjusting, balancing entry that will place the Trial Balance in balance. Choose *Test Account* from the drop-down list of accounts. You can choose any account from the drop-down list or accept the default. If you see this warning,

Choose **account 1005 Test Account** from the drop-down list. **Click OK**.

Close the **Ledger window** to return to the Accounts window after entering all the accounts and balances.

Display or **print** the **Chart of Accounts**, **Trial Balance**, **Balance Sheet** and **Income Statement** to check the accuracy of your work.

Choose the **Reports menu** in the Accounts window and **click Trial Balance** (or Balance Sheet or Income Statement).

Check all your **opening balances** carefully and **edit** any accounts with errors in **amounts** or **names** before finishing the history.

Close the **Accounts window** and any other open windows to return to the Home window.

Compare your reports with the information on pages 67–69 to be sure that all account numbers, names and balances are correct. The balance for *Test Account* should be zero. Make additional corrections if necessary.

NOTES
The default account for the balancing entry is the Retained Earning linked account – renamed Accumulated Surplus in our example.

Finishing the History

Making a Backup Copy

By having a backup copy of your files before finishing the history, you will be able to make changes easily, if you find an error, without having to repeat the entire setup from scratch. After the ledger history is finished, the program will not permit you to make certain changes, such as opening account balances and fiscal dates. You cannot change the account number for an account after making a journal entry to the account.

You should back up your unfinished open history files to a different folder so that they can be easily identified (e.g., NFTOSS).

Choose the **File menu** and **click Backup**, or **click** the **Backup tool**.

Create a **backup copy** by following the instructions. Refer to page 46 and page 248 if you need help.

WARNING!
Back up the not-finished Toss for Tots files before proceeding. See Chapter 3 if you need further assistance.

WARNING!
If an account was used in journal entries, you can change account numbers only after two fiscal periods have passed without additional transactions.

Finishing the General Ledger History

You should be in the Home window.

Choose the **History menu** and **click Finish Entering History**.

The following caution appears:

If you have not made a backup copy yet, click Backup and do so before proceeding. If you have made your backup copy, you should continue.

Click **Proceed**.

WARNING!
You can finish entering the history when the Trial Balance is in balance. Afterwards, you cannot change opening balances, even if they are incorrect. You will need to make adjusting entries. Sage 50 always keeps the Trial Balance balanced. Therefore, checking for a zero balance in the Test Account can stop you from proceeding with incorrect account balances.

> **NOTES**
> The first error on this screen states that accounts are not in logical order. The remaining messages refer to missing linked accounts for modules that are not used but are also not hidden.

If you see a different screen at this stage, like the following one, you have errors that must be corrected before you can continue:

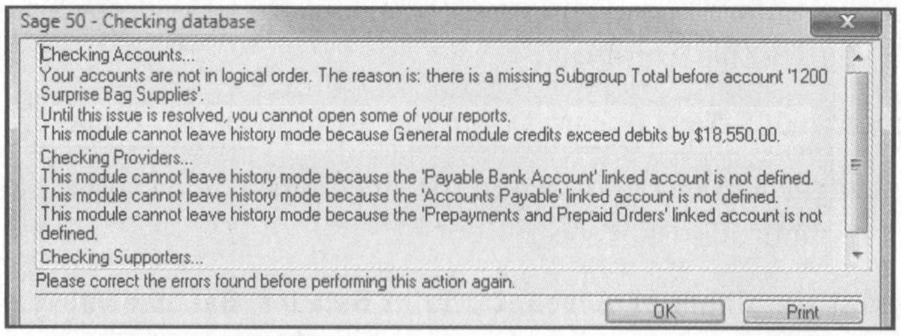

> **WARNING!**
> You can verify that the file is correct before making a backup – choose the Finish History option. If the option to proceed is available, click Backup on this screen or click Cancel, make the backup and then finish the history.

The message describes the mistakes you must correct. If your accounts are out of order, you cannot finish entering the history. If you did not hide the unused modules, you cannot finish entering the history because some essential linked accounts for these modules are not defined.

Read the error description carefully. Print the message for reference when you make corrections. Click OK to return to the Home window.

Make the necessary corrections. Remember to replace your previous unfinished history backup file. Then try again to finish the history.

> **NOTES**
> You can now unhide the unused modules, but you do not need to do so. If you want to set them up later, you must first unhide them, as we show in Chapter 9.

Notice that the open or not-finished history symbol , the quill pen, has been removed from the Chart of Accounts icon.

You can now exit the program or continue by entering the source documents. Remember to advance the Session Date. Enter all transactions for Toss for Tots in the General Journal.

SOURCE DOCUMENTS

SESSION DATE – JULY 7, 2015

> **NOTES**
> When you first change the session date or re-open the data file, you may see a wizard for updating the HST. If you see this, click I Have Already Updated My Tax Information and then click Finish. We have already entered the correct current tax settings.

1 **Purchase Invoice #QK-2252** **Dated July 2/15**
From Quiq Kopy, $200 plus $26 HST for photocopying registration and donation forms. Invoice total $226. Terms: net 25 days.

2 **Purchase Invoice #BC-10116** **Dated July 2/15**
From Bell Canada, $300 plus $39 HST for rental of cellular telephone equipment. Invoice total $339. Deposit required and balance due at end of month. Create new Group account 2140 A/P - Bell Canada.

3 **Payment Cheque #167** **Dated July 2/15**
To Bell Canada, $100 deposit on rental of telephone equipment. Reference invoice #BC-10116.

> **NOTES**
> In most businesses, the Cash on Hand balance is usually small and is used only for paying small amounts. In this application, we are using the Cash on Hand account to pay for any purchases that normally would require cash or credit card payments. The Event Manager receives cash advances to cover these costs.

4 **Memo #1** **Dated July 2/15**
From Event Manager: Give T-shirts to volunteers. Cost of T-shirts given out is $120. Reduce T-shirt asset account and increase Cost of T-shirts expense account.

5 **Memo #2** **Dated July 4/15**
From Event Manager: Issue cheque #168 for $3 500 to transfer funds to Cash on Hand for snack purchases for the tournament.

6 **Cash Purchase Invoice #SC-2168** **Dated July 4/15**

From Snack City, $3 000 plus $390 HST for drinks and snacks for participants and spectators. Invoice total $3 390 paid from Cash on Hand.

SESSION DATE – JULY 14, 2015

7 **Purchase Invoice #DW-9493** **Dated July 8/15**

From Designs U Wear, $1 100 plus $143 HST for T-shirts to sell to spectators at tournament. Invoice total $1 243. Terms: net 20 days.

8 **Cash Purchase Invoice #QAS-4632** **Dated July 10/15**

From Quarts Arts Supplies, $100 plus $13 HST for bristol board and paint supplies to make signs in gymnasiums. Invoice total $113. Paid from Cash on Hand. (Debit Office Supplies account.)

9

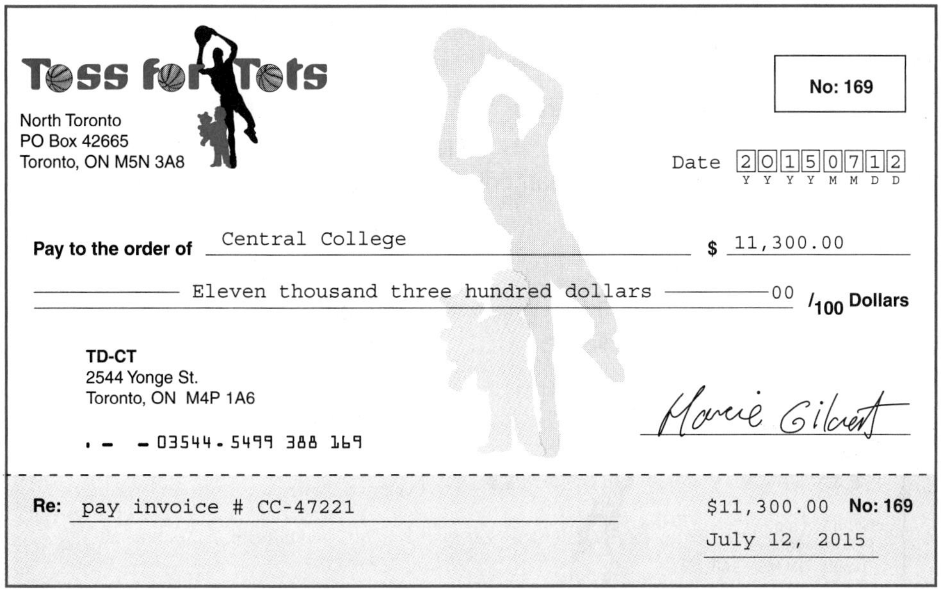

Toss for Tots
North Toronto
PO Box 42665
Toronto, ON M5N 3A8

No: 169

Date 20150712
YYYYMMDD

Pay to the order of Central College $ 11,300.00

Eleven thousand three hundred dollars 00 /100 Dollars

TD-CT
2544 Yonge St.
Toronto, ON M4P 1A6

Marie Gilbert

03544-5499 388 169

Re: pay invoice # CC-47221 $11,300.00 No: 169
July 12, 2015

10 **Funds Raised Form #FR-15-7** **Dated July 14/15**

Cash and cheques received on first two weekends of event. Create new revenue account 4160 Revenue: T-shirt Sales.

Participant registrations	$30 000
Sale of snack foods and drinks	3 500
Sale of T-shirts	1 000
Sale of surprise bags	560

Total $35 060 deposited in Bank: Toss for Tots.

SESSION DATE – JULY 21, 2015

11 **Purchase Invoice #QK-5306** **Dated July 17/15**

From Quiq Kopy, $500 plus $65 HST for printing cancer information leaflets for participants and spectators. Invoice total $565. Terms: net 25 days.

12 **Payment Cheque #170** **Dated July 18/15**

To Designs U Wear, $800 in payment of account. Reference invoice #DW-6299.

NOTES

Basic food and groceries are exempt from HST, but most snack foods are not.

13 **Funds Raised Form #FR-15-8** **Dated July 20/15**

Record $30 200 in pledges to sponsor participants from sponsor forms submitted. Create new asset account 1180 Donations Receivable. (Credit Revenue: Sponsors.)

NOTES
Charge pizza expense to Miscellaneous Expenses.

14 **Cash Purchase Invoice #PH-34982** **Dated July 20/15**

From Pizza House, $250 plus $32.50 HST for pizza and soft drinks for volunteers. Invoice total $282.50. Paid from Cash on Hand.

SESSION DATE – JULY 28, 2015

15 **Funds Raised Form #FR-15-09** **Dated July 26/15**

Record $80 500 in pledges to sponsor participants from sponsor forms submitted by participants. (Debit Donations Receivable.)

16 **Payment Cheque #171** **Dated July 26/15**

To Designs U Wear, $1 243 in payment of account. Reference invoice #DW-9493.

17 **Cash Purchase Invoice #PH-39168** **Dated July 27/15**

From Pizza House, $320 plus $41.60 HST for pizza and soft drinks for volunteers to celebrate successful tournament. Invoice total $361.60. Paid from Cash on Hand.

18 **Cheque #172** **Dated July 27/15**

To Sunni Husein, $1 000 for winning tournament. Create new Group account 5430 Tournament Prizes.

NOTES
Create new revenue account 4180 Revenue: Photos.

19

Toss for Tots

North Toronto
PO Box 42665
Toronto, ON M5N 3A8

FUNDS RAISED FORM: FR-15-10
Date: July 28, 2015
Comment: Cash & cheques received from third & fourth event weekends July 18-26

Description	Amount
T-shirt sales	$ 2 500
Admissions for spectators	11 160
Sale of snack foods and drinks	6 680
Surprise bag sales	1 750
Photo sales	3 900

Deposited to bank account July 28

Signature: *Marcie Gilcrest* **Total** $25 990

20 **Cheque #173** **Dated July 28/15**

To Marcie Gilcrest, manager, $2 000 for wages for one month.

SESSION DATE – JULY 31, 2015

21

Toss for Tots

North Toronto
PO Box 42665
Toronto, ON M5N 3A8

MEMO #3

Date: July 29, 2015
From: Marcie Gilcrest
Re: Adjustments required for event sales & supplies used

Cost of T-shirts sold	$1 670
Cost of food items sold	3 990
Cost of surprise bag items sold	500
Cost of office supplies used	300

Authorization: MG

22 **Payment Cheque #174** **Dated July 31/15**

To Quiq Kopy, $941 in full payment of account. Reference invoices #QK-5306, QK-2252 and previous balance owing.

23 **Payment Cheque #175** **Dated July 31/15**

To Bell Canada, $239 in full payment of account. Reference invoice #BC-10116 and cheque #167.

24 **Payment Cheque #176** **Dated July 31/15**

To Snack City, $900 in full payment of account. Reference invoice #SC-1005.

25 **Memo #4** **Dated July 31/15**

From Manager: Issue cheque #177 for $500 to transfer funds to Cash on Hand to purchase postage for mailing charitable donation receipts.

26 **Bank Debit Memo #TDCT-3881** **Dated July 31/15**

From TD Canada Trust, $21.50 in bank charges for cheques and statement preparation. Create new Group account 5010 Bank Charges.

27 **Memo #5** **Dated July 31/15**

From Event Manager: Apply for HST rebate of $1 812.07. Record this as the portion of HST Paid on Purchases as HST Refund Receivable, and $788.03 as the Non-refundable HST expense. Create new Group account 1190 HST Refund Receivable. (Refer to Accounting Procedures on page 69.)

28 **Funds Raised Form #FR-15-11** **Dated July 31/15**

Received $92 300 from sponsors for pledges previously recorded. Amount deposited in bank account. (Credit 1180 Donations Receivable.)

NOTES

Donated items are not included in these costs.

NOTES

The total amount of HST paid was $2 600.10. All purchases were taxed at the rate of 13 percent. Of this amount, $1 000.04 was the federal portion (50 percent rebate) and $1 600.06 was provincial (82 percent rebate).

KEYSTROKES FOR CLOSING

Ending a Fiscal Period

Sage 50 warns you as you approach the end of a fiscal period because important end-of-period adjusting entries are usually required.

Change the **session date** to **August 31**.

When you change the session date to August 31, you will see the following warning:

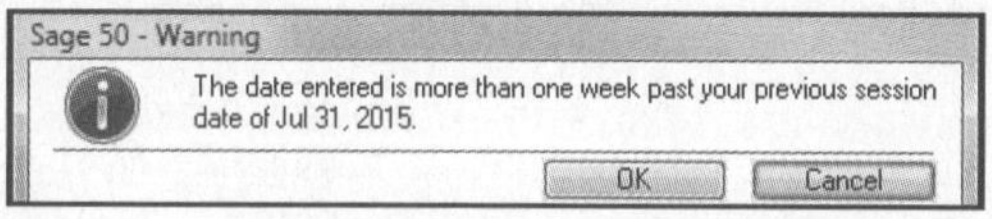

The date entered is more than one week past your previous session date of Jul 31, 2015.

Normally a business would advance the session date by a shorter period, so the warning helps you to avoid entering the wrong session date.

Click **OK** to confirm that you entered the date you intended.

You will see another message about preparing for year end. Sage 50 displays this message about one month before the end of the fiscal period:

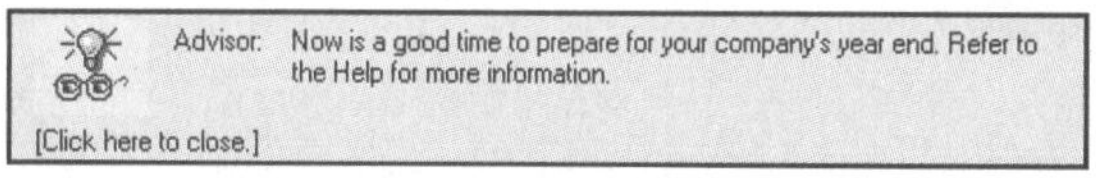

Advisor: Now is a good time to prepare for your company's year end. Refer to the Help for more information.
[Click here to close.]

Click to close the **Advisor**, **back up** your **data files** and **continue** with the **transactions** for August 31.

29 **Funds Received Form #FR-15-12** **Dated August 31/15**
Received $18 400 from sponsors for pledges previously recorded. Amount deposited in bank account.

30 **Cash Purchase Invoice #CP-2** **Dated August 31/15**
From Canada Post, $500 plus $65 HST for postage to mail receipts. Invoice total $565. Paid from Cash on Hand.

31 **Memo #6** **Dated August 31/15**
From Event Manager: Deposit $287.90, balance of Cash on Hand to bank.

32 **Bank Debit Memo #TDCT-5218** **Dated August 31/15**
From TD Canada Trust, withdraw $15 400 from chequing account to repay loan for $15 000 plus $400 interest. Create new Group account 5100 Interest Expense.

Closing Adjusting Entries

Change the **session date** to **September 30**.

When you advance the session date further to a date very close to the end of the fiscal period, September 30 in this case, you see the year-end Advisor message again.

Close the **Advisor window** and **back up** your **data files**.

Two source document entries — adjustments for the remaining supplies — provide the details for these year-end adjustments for Toss for Tots. For other businesses, adjusting entries include depreciation entries, inventory adjustments, adjustments for prepaid expenses that have expired, accrued wages and so on. Most adjusting entries do

NOTES
Adjusting entries always involve an Income Statement and a Balance Sheet account. For example, you might debit Expenses (Income Statement account) and credit Prepaid Expenses (asset account on the Balance Sheet), or debit Unearned Revenue and credit Customer Prepayments.

not have an external source document that reminds you to complete them, and most of them are General Journal entries.

Enter the **next two transactions** for September 30.

33

Toss for Tots
North Toronto
PO Box 42665
Toronto, ON M5N 3A8

MEMO #7

Date: September 30, 2015
From: Marcie Gilcrest
Re: Final account adjustments required to clear inventory of supplies (donated)

Cost of all remaining T-shirts donated to shelters	$110
Cost of all remaining food items donated to shelters	210
Cost of craft and office supplies not needed and donated to Campus Day Care Centre	280

Authorization: MG

34 **Cash Purchase Invoice #BC-32423** **Dated September 30/15**

From Bell Canada, $120 plus $15.60 HST for telephone service for two months. Invoice total $135.60 paid in full by cheque #178.

Starting a New Fiscal Period

Starting a new fiscal period is not a reversible step, so you should prepare a complete set of financial reports and make a backup of the data set as instructed in the next memo.

35 **Memo #8** **Dated September 30/15**

All accounts for the event are settled so the books can be closed. Make a backup of the data files. Start a new fiscal period to close the books.

Print all the **financial reports** for Toss for Tots for September 30, 2015.

Back up your **data files** with a file name to indicate it is the year-end copy.

There are two methods for beginning a new fiscal year. The first is the method we have been using to change the session date.

Choose the **Maintenance menu** and **click Change Session Date** or **click** the Change Date icon beside Session Date.

The first date of the new fiscal period is always on the drop-down list of dates in the Session Date window. The program will not accept any dates later than October 1, 2015.

Type October 1, 2015 or choose this date from the date field list or Calendar icon.

NOTES
You cannot start a new fiscal period in multi-user mode.

WARNING!
You should advance to the new fiscal period in two steps. First advance to the last day of the current fiscal period and then advance to the first day of the new fiscal period. This control feature prevents you from advancing by mistake and losing important data or forgetting year-end adjusting entries.

WARNING!
Initially, from the last day of the fiscal period, you cannot advance the session date past October 1, the first day of the new fiscal period.

NOTES

If the history is not finished when you choose to start a new fiscal year, the program will ask if you have finished entering the history and give you a chance to do so. You must finish the history before you can start a new fiscal period.

If you still have errors in your not-finished file, Sage 50 will list the errors that you must correct, as in the message on page 96, before you can finish the history and start a new fiscal period.

Click **OK**. Because this step is not reversible, you will see another warning:

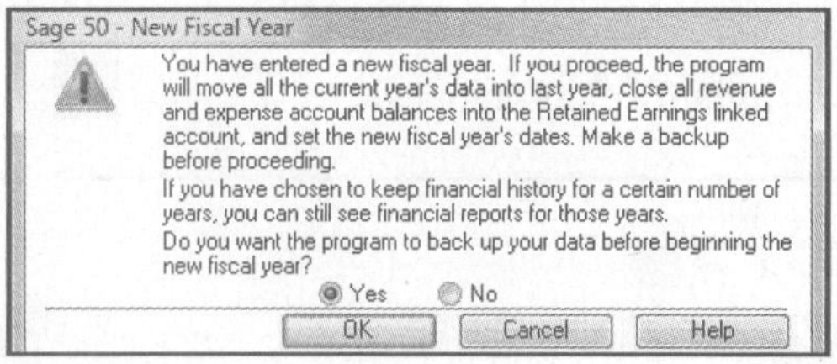

The expense and revenue amounts will be transferred to the capital account, but historical data will be saved in the data file.

Read the **warning** carefully.

The warning describes the changes about to take place in the data set. All revenue and expense accounts are reset to zero at the start of the new fiscal year. Their balances are closed out to the linked *Accumulated Surplus (Retained Earnings)* account, and the linked *Net Income (Current Earnings)* account is reset to zero to begin a new Income Statement. All previous-year entries that are not cleared are stored as data for the previous year. The program also updates the fiscal dates for the company by one year. The new fiscal end date becomes the final date allowed as a session date.

At this stage you can choose to back up the data files, continue with the date change or cancel the date change by clicking No.

Click **Cancel** to return to the Session Date window and then **click Cancel** again to close the Change Session Date screen. We will use the second menu option to change to a new fiscal year.

Choose the **Maintenance menu** and **click Start New Year**.

You may see a screen asking whether you want to start a new fiscal or calendar year:

NOTES

Because the start of the new fiscal year (October 1, 2015) precedes the date for the new calendar year (January 1, 2016), it is selected and the new Calendar Year option is dimmed.

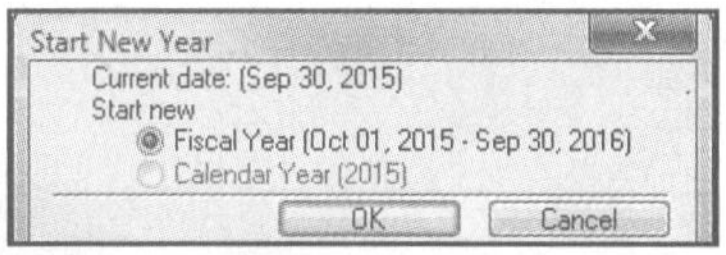

The default will be the period that starts next. Start New Fiscal Year is correctly selected.

Click **OK** to continue.

You will see a warning similar to the one on the previous page:

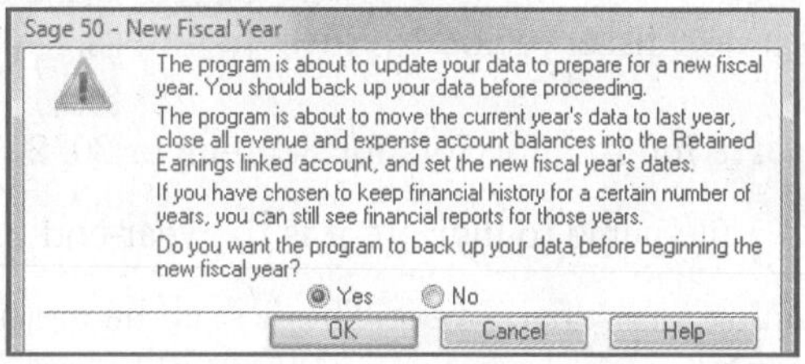

The default setting, again, is to make a backup before continuing. If you have not yet made a backup, do so now. If you do not want to begin a new year, you can click Cancel and the old dates will remain in effect.

Click **No** because you have already backed up your files.

Click **OK** to begin the new fiscal period.

You will see a confirmation that the new year has been started:

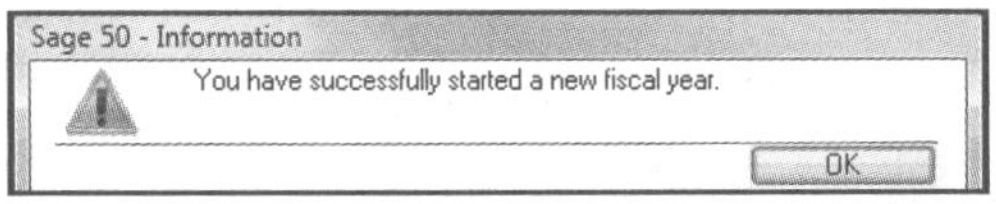

Click **OK** to close the message. You will now see another warning:

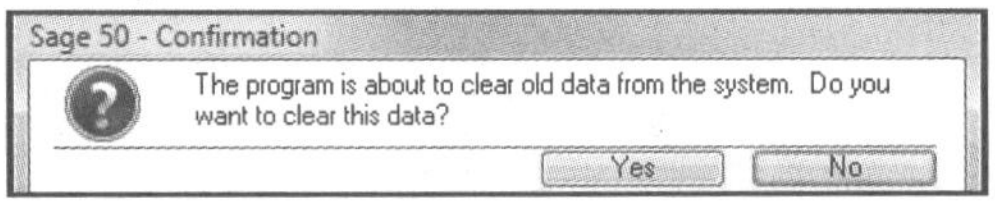

You have the option of retaining the old data or clearing it. Journal entries from the previous year are never cleared and Income Statement and Balance Sheet details for the previous year are also retained.

Click **Yes** because Toss for Tots has no other data. If in doubt, choose No.

Another message now appears:

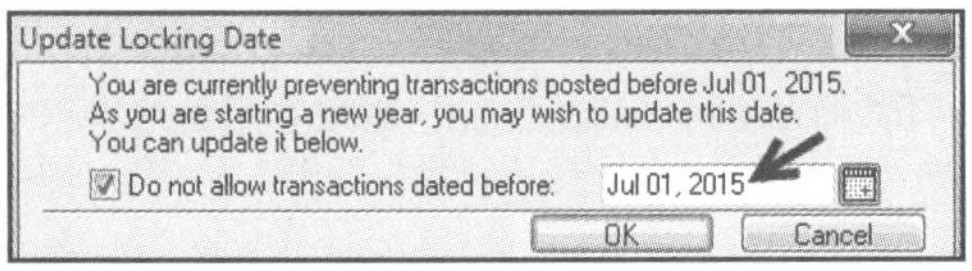

You must now change the earliest date for which you will allow transactions. We should not allow any transactions to the previous fiscal period so that the historical records cannot be altered in error.

Drag through **Jul 01, 2015**, the date entered.

Type 10/01

Click **OK** to continue. Close the message about payroll updates if it appears.

When you have more than one fiscal period, most financial reports offer comparisons with the previous year as an option. Journal reports and other reports are available for both periods — the Report On Fiscal Year field is available with Current Year and Previous Year options in a drop-down list.

Print the **Comparative Trial Balance** and **Balance Sheet** for September 30 and October 1.

Notice the changes in the capital accounts on the Balance Sheet. The *Net Income* balance for September 30 has been added to the *Accumulated Surplus* account to create the October 1 balance in the *Accumulated Surplus* account.

Print the **Comparative Income Statement for the previous year** (Oct. 1, 2014, to Sep. 30, 2015) and the **current fiscal year to date** (Oct. 1, 2015, to Oct. 1, 2015).

The Income Statement for the current year shows no income or revenue. All accounts have a zero balance because you have not recorded any transactions for the new fiscal year.

The files are now ready for transactions in the new fiscal period. When you check the Company Information, the fiscal dates are updated and you will see the additional information about last year's dates.

Choose the **Setup menu** and **click Settings**, or **click** the **Settings icon** [Settings].

NOTES

If you choose to clear old data, the program will clear the information you selected for the periods you entered in the Automatically Clear Data screen. See Chapter 15, page 617.

We describe how to clear data from company files in Chapter 15.

WARNING!

If you have cleared paid invoices, these details will be unavailable for reports. Comparative Income Statements and Balance Sheets are always available for the two fiscal periods.

> **NOTES**
> The program assumes a fiscal year of one year, so the fiscal end will be advanced by 12 months.

Click **Company** if necessary and then **click Information** to see the changes:

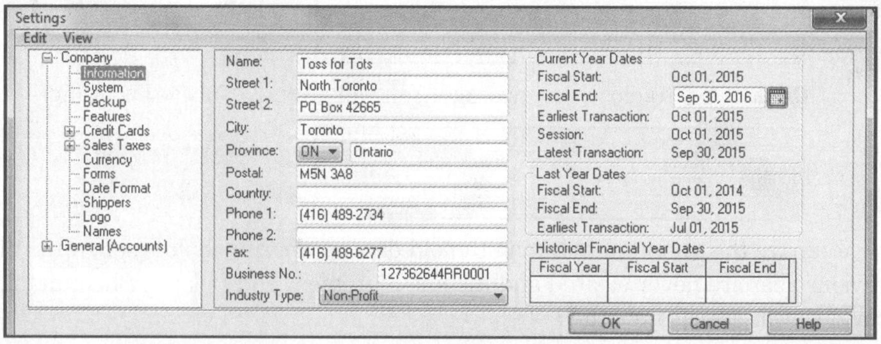

> **NOTES**
> After you start a new fiscal period, you cannot change the fiscal start date.

The new Fiscal Start is October 1, 2015, and the new Fiscal End is September 30, 2016. Sage 50 automatically updates the Fiscal End by 12 months, but you can edit this date if the fiscal period is shorter. In fact, this is the only date that you can edit after you have made journal entries to a data file. The Earliest Transaction Date has also been updated to October 1, 2015. The dates for the previous fiscal period (Last Year Dates) are provided for reference.

Click **Cancel** to close the Company Information window.

Entering Transactions for an Earlier Fiscal Period

> **NOTES**
> In Chapter 12, we show how to create a copy of your data for your accountant to update and how to import the transactions your accountant has completed for your company.

Sometimes not all the information required is available before the books are closed for the fiscal period. However, it may be necessary to close the books (start a new fiscal period) so that transactions in the new year may be entered. The details of the adjusting entries may be calculated by an accountant who does not have the information until after a business has started entering transactions for a new year. Sage 50 allows you to post transactions to the previous year (but not to future fiscal periods) so that the financial statements for both the previous year and the current year will be correct.

Enter **Memo #9**, the HST rebate receipt, with the **September 30** date, after starting the new fiscal period.

✓ 36

Memo #9 **Dated September 30/15**

Received cheque #488129 for $1 812.07 from the Receiver General for HST rebate. We closed the books before making the entry.

When you post the entry, you will see the following message:

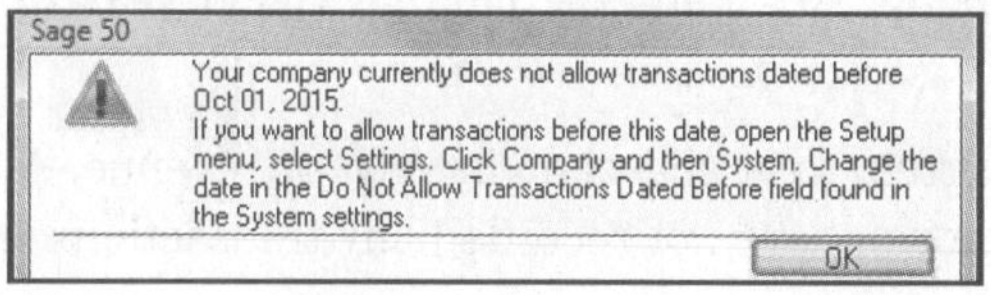

> **NOTES**
> Because the session date is Oct. 1, 2015, and we do not allow future-dated transactions, Oct. 1 is the only date allowed for journal entries until we advance the session date.

Before the program allows the entry, we must change the System Settings. We indicated that transactions earlier than Oct. 1, 2015, should not be allowed.

Click **OK** to close the message. **Close** the **journal** to discard the entry. **Click** **Yes** to confirm that you want to discard the entry.

Choose the **Setup menu** and **click Settings** or **click** the **Settings icon** .

Click **Company** if necessary and then **click System**.

This will access the settings field we need:

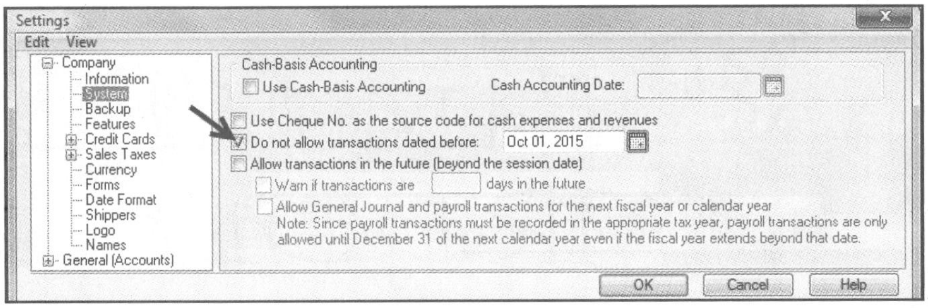

This is the same settings screen we saw earlier but now we must allow transactions in the previous period.

Click **Do Not Allow Transactions Dated Before** to **remove** the ✓.

Click **OK**.

Enter **Memo #9** again.

✓ 37

Memo #9 **Dated September 30/15**

Received cheque #488129 for $1 812.07 from the Receiver General for HST rebate. We closed the books before making the entry.

Review and then **post** it. This time you will see a different warning:

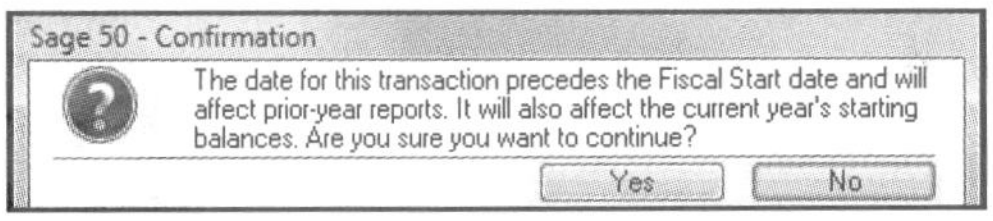

Because the transaction date is in a previous month or period, you are advised that prior period reports may be affected by the transaction. The warning gives you a chance to correct the date if it was incorrect. But we want to proceed. After completing the transaction, we will change the System Settings again to avoid mistakenly posting to the previous year.

Click **Yes** to continue with posting.

Close the **General Journal**.

Click the **Settings icon** 

or **choose** the **Setup menu**, then **choose** **Settings** and **click** **Company** and **System**.

Click **Do Not Allow Transactions Dated Before** to **add** the ✓.

Enter **Oct 1** as the date and **click** **OK**.

Finish your **session** by backing up and closing the files for Toss for Tots.

REVIEW

The Student DVD with Data Files includes Review Questions and Supplementary Cases for this chapter.

NOTES

The warnings in Sage 50 make it difficult to post to the wrong year by mistake.

NOTES

To display and print reports after starting a new fiscal period, you must choose Previous Year (2015) to view the transactions between July 1 and September 30.

CHAPTER FIVE

Chai Tea Room

OBJECTIVES

After completing this chapter, you should be able to

- ***open*** the General and Payables journals
- ***enter*** supplier- or vendor-related purchase transactions
- ***enter*** supplier-related payment transactions
- ***enter*** partial payments to suppliers
- ***enter*** payments to suppliers with early payment discounts
- ***enter*** cash purchase transactions
- ***enter*** sales taxes in the General Journal
- ***create*** shortcuts in the Home window
- ***store*** recurring purchase transactions
- ***add*** new supplier accounts
- ***edit*** supplier accounts
- ***edit*** and ***review*** transactions in the journals
- ***recall, use*** and ***edit*** stored purchase transactions
- ***adjust*** and ***reverse*** purchase invoices and payments after posting
- ***understand*** Payables Ledger linked accounts
- ***display*** and ***print*** payables transactions and reports
- ***graph*** payables reports

COMPANY INFORMATION

Company Profile

Chai Tea Room, located in Fredericton, New Brunswick, is owned by Sarah Quinte. Originally, Quinte wanted to name her business Quintessentials, but after an extended tour of the Far East, where she acquired a taste for exotic blends of tea, she chose the name Chai instead. Most Canadians are familiar with the name Chai, an East Indian word for tea that is often used for spiced Indian tea.

The downtown tea room, near the New Brunswick Parliament House, Art Gallery and other historic sites, with its scenic lookout over the Saint John River

NOTES
Chai Tea Room
125 King St.
Fredericton, NB E3B 2P4
Tel 1: (506) 454-6111
Tel 2: (800) 454-6000
Fax: (506) 454-6990
Business No.: 186 522 333

and railroad walking bridge, is very popular with professional women. Adjacent to a women's fitness and recreational centre, the tea room provides a comfortable atmosphere for customers to discuss finance, careers or social or political issues after working out. The tea room boasts refinements such as a fireplace, comfortable living-room–style cushioned sofas and chairs and personal care and service from the owner and staff.

Chai Tea Room, essentially a tea room serving specialty teas from all around the world, also provides light lunches and superb desserts. Coffees and other beverages — both alcoholic and non-alcoholic — are available too. Quinte sells gift sets as well: packaged variety teas and tea service sets consisting of teacups, teaspoons, a teapot and a tea cozy. The tea service set items can also be purchased separately.

Sarah Quinte manages the day-to-day activities of the store. An assistant manager and kitchen staff handle business during her absence. The payroll is managed by the bank for a small fee. She has set up accounts with regular vendors or suppliers, such as the suppliers of food and beverages, as well as the utility companies. Some of her suppliers offer discounts for early payment. Cleaning and maintenance of the premises is done professionally once a week by Sunbury Cleaning; they wash and wax the floors and steam clean the carpets and furniture. They also clean and check all equipment and complete minor repairs. On a day-to-day basis, the tea room staff do the regular cleaning.

Chai Tea Room does not pay HST (sales tax) on its food purchases, but its other purchases are subject to HST. Food consumed in restaurants is subject to HST, so HST at 13 percent is charged to customers on all food products consumed in the tea room and on the gift sets.

Quinte currently manages all the accounting records for the tea room and has just finished converting the manual records to Sage 50 using the following:

- Chart of Accounts
- Post-Closing Trial Balance
- Supplier Information
- Accounting Procedures

NOTES

HST, Harmonized Sales Tax, is charged instead of GST and PST in New Brunswick. HST at 13 percent includes both GST at 5 percent and PST at 8 percent. Refer to the Accounting Procedures on page 109 and Chapter 2 for further details.

CHART OF POSTABLE ACCOUNTS

CHAI TEA ROOM

ASSETS
1080 Chequing Bank Account
1300 Beverage Inventory
1320 Beer, Wine and Liquor
1340 Food Inventory
1360 Gift Set Inventory
1500 Cash Register and Computer
1520 Cutlery and Dishes
1540 Furniture and Fixtures
1560 Equipment
1580 Tea Room Premises ▶

▶LIABILITIES
2100 Bank Loan
2200 Accounts Payable
2650 HST Charged on Sales
2670 HST Paid on Purchases
2850 Mortgage Payable

EQUITY
3100 S. Quinte, Capital
3150 S. Quinte, Drawings
3600 Net Income ▶

▶REVENUE
4100 Customer Service and Sales

EXPENSE
5020 Advertising and Promotion
5040 Bank Charges
5060 Cleaning and Maintenance
5080 Cost of Goods Sold
5090 Purchase Discounts
5100 General Expense
5120 Hydro Expense ▶

▶5140 Interest Expense
5160 Licences and Permits
5180 Payroll Services
5220 Telephone Expense
5240 Wages

NOTES: The Chart of Accounts includes only postable accounts and the Net Income or Current Earnings account. Sage 50 uses the Net Income account for the Income Statement to calculate the difference between revenue and expenses before closing the books.

POST-CLOSING TRIAL BALANCE

CHAI TEA ROOM

August 1, 2015		Debits	Credits
1080	Chequing Bank Account	$ 11 155	
1300	Beverage Inventory	1 500	
1320	Beer, Wine and Liquor	2 500	
1340	Food Inventory	500	
1360	Gift Set Inventory	4 000	
1500	Cash Register and Computer	5 000	
1520	Cutlery and Dishes	5 000	
1540	Furniture and Fixtures	15 000	
1560	Equipment	25 000	
1580	Tea Room Premises	150 000	
2100	Bank Loan		$ 12 000
2200	Accounts Payable		2 945
2650	HST Charged on Sales		4 845
2670	HST Paid on Purchases	345	
2850	Mortgage Payable		120 000
3100	S. Quinte, Capital		80 210
		$220 000	$220 000

SUPPLIER INFORMATION

CHAI TEA ROOM

Supplier Name (Contact)	Address	Phone No. Fax No.	E-mail Web Site	Terms Tax ID
Atlantic Tea Company (Boise Chai)	20 Oceanview Dr. Halifax, NS B3K 2L2	Tel 1: (902) 777-2346 Tel 2: (888) 337-4599	bchai@atcc.com www.atcc.com	net 10 288 411 755
Bathurst Food Supplies (C. Ricotte)	56 Cheddar St. Oromocto, NB E2V 1M8	Tel: (506) 544-6292 Fax: (506) 544-5217	cricotte@bfoods.com www.bfoods.com	1/10, n/30 385 345 865
Fundy Gift House (Red Rose)	71 Ridge Way Hopewell Cape, NB E0A 1Y0	Tel: (506) 499-3481 Fax: (506) 499-3482	rrose@fundygifts.com www.fundygifts.com	net 30 124 653 779
Minto Beverages (Earl Gray)	910 Lemone Ave. Bathurst, NB E2A 4X3	Tel 1: (506) 622-3188 Tel 2: (800) 622-2881	eg@mintobev.com www.mintobev.com	net 30 901 200 862
Moncton Kitchenwares (Tiff Flaun)	4 Pottery Rd. Moncton, NB E1C 8J6	Tel: (506) 721-5121 Fax: (506) 721-5522	tflaun@monctonkitchens.com www.monctonkitchens.com	1/10, n/30 567 321 447
NB Gas (N. Bridge)	355 Pipeline Road Fredericton, NB E3A 5B1	Tel: (506) 454-8110	nbridge@naturalgas.com www.naturalgas.com	net 7
NB Hydro (N. Ergie)	83 Water Street Fredericton, NB E3B 2M6	Tel: (506) 455-5120	n.ergie@nbhydro.nb.ca www.nbhydro.nb.ca	net 7
NB Liquor Control Board (Darke Beere)	4 Spirits Rd. Fredericton, NB E3B 1C5	Tel: (506) 456-1182	dbeere@lcb.gov.nb.ca www.lcb.gov.nb.ca	net 1
NB Tel (Les Chatter)	2 Communicate Rd. Fredericton, NB E3A 2K4	Tel: (506) 456-2355	chatter@nbtel.ca www.nbtel.ca	net 7
Sunbury Cleaning Company (Dee Tergent)	49 Scrub St. Gagetown, NB E0G 1V0	Tel: (506) 454-6611 Fax: (506) 454-3216	dtergent@sunburyclean.com www.sunburyclean.com	1/30, n/60 481 532 556
Vermont Coffee Wholesalers (Java Jean)	60 Columbia Lane Saint John, NB E2M 6R9	Tel 1: (506) 366-1551 Tel 2: (877) 366-1500	java@vermontcoffee.com www.vermontcoffee.com	net 1 345 667 211

OUTSTANDING SUPPLIER INVOICES

CHAI TEA ROOM

Supplier Name	Terms	Date	Inv/Chq No.	Amount	Total
Bathurst Food Supplies	1/10, n/30	Jul. 26/15	BF-1044	$ 800	$ 800
Fundy Gift House	n/30	Jul. 6/15	FG-361	$ 920	$ 920
Moncton Kitchenwares	1/10 n/30	Jul. 25/15	MK-1341	$1 725	
		Jul. 25/15	Chq #167	500	
			Balance owing		$1 225
			Grand Total		$2 945

Accounting Procedures

The Harmonized Sales Tax (Provincial Sales Tax and Goods and Services Tax)

In New Brunswick, federal and provincial taxes are combined in the Harmonized Sales Tax, or HST, a single tax at the rate of 13 percent. The HST is applied to most goods and services. Like the GST, HST may be included in the price or added at the time of the sale. Chai Tea Room uses the regular method for calculating and remitting the HST. All items sold in the tea room have HST added to them. At the end of each quarter, the HST liability to the Receiver General is reduced by any HST paid to suppliers on purchases. Beverage and food supplies are zero rated for HST purposes. Chai's *HST Owing (Refund)* subgroup total account shows the amount of HST that is to be remitted to the Receiver General for Canada on the last day of each quarter. (For details please read Chapter 2 on the GST and HST.)

NOTES

Beverages and food items are zero rated goods; that is, the HST rate is 0 percent. Prepared food, as sold in restaurants, is taxed at 13 percent.

Most bank services and other financial institution services are exempt from HST charges. Bank payroll services are subject to HST charges.

Provincial sales tax is not levied as a separate tax in New Brunswick. It will be introduced in Chapter 6.

Open-Invoice Accounting for Payables

The open-invoice method of accounting for invoices allows a business to keep track of each individual invoice and partial payment made against the invoice. This is in contrast to methods that keep track only of the outstanding balance by combining all invoice balances owed to a supplier. Sage 50 uses the open-invoice method. Fully paid invoices can be cleared (removed) periodically; outstanding invoices cannot be cleared.

Discounts

When discounts for early payment are offered by suppliers, Chai takes advantage of them by paying invoices before the discount period ends. When the payment terms are set up correctly for the supplier and invoice, and dates are entered correctly, discounts are calculated automatically by Sage 50 and credited to *Purchase Discounts*, a contra-expense account that has a credit balance and reduces overall expenses.

NOTES

Discounts for early payment may be calculated on pretax amounts or on the full invoice amounts. This choice is entered in the ledger settings for the vendor or supplier.

Purchase of Inventory Items and Cost of Goods Sold

Inventory items purchased are recorded in the appropriate inventory or supplies asset account. Periodically, the food inventory on hand is counted to determine the value of items remaining and the cost price of inventory and food sold. The manager then issues a memo to reduce the inventory or supplies asset account and to charge the cost price to the corresponding expense account. For example, at the end of each month, the *Beverage Inventory* asset account (*1300*) is reduced (credited) and the *Cost of Goods Sold* expense account (*5080*) is increased (debited) by the cost price of the amount sold.

INSTRUCTIONS

1. **Enter** the **source documents for August** in Sage 50 using the Chart of Accounts, Trial Balance, Supplier Information and Accounting Procedures for Chai Tea Room. The procedures for entering each new type of transaction for this application are outlined step by step in the Keystrokes section with the source documents. These transactions are indicated with a ✓ in the upper part of the completion check box beside the source document. Source document numbers are included below or in the lower part of the check box.
2. **Print** the **reports and graphs** indicated on the printing form below after you have completed your entries. Instructions for reports begin on page 144.

REPORTS

Accounts
- ☐ Chart of Accounts
- ☐ Account List
- ☐ General Journal Entries

Financials
- ☑ Comparative Balance Sheet dates: Aug. 1 and Aug. 31 with difference in percentage
- ☑ Income Statement from Aug. 1 to Aug. 31
- ☑ Trial Balance date: Aug. 31
- ☐ All Journal Entries
- ☑ General Ledger accounts: 1340 4100 5080 from Aug. 1 to Aug. 31

Banking
- ☐ Cheque Log Report

Payables
- ☐ Supplier List
- ☑ Supplier Aged Detail for all suppliers Aug. 31
- ☐ Aged Overdue Payables
- ☑ Purchases Journal Entries: Aug. 1 to Aug. 31
- ☑ Payments Journal Entries: Aug. 1 to Aug. 31

Mailing Labels
- ☐ Labels

Management Reports
- ☐ Ledger

GRAPHS
- ☐ Payables by Aging Period
- ☑ Payables by Supplier
- ☐ Revenues by Account
- ☐ Expenses by Account
- ☑ Expenses and Net Profit as % of Revenue

KEYSTROKES

Opening Data Files

NOTES
If you are working from backup files, restore SageData13\chai1.CAB or chai1 to SageData13\Chai\chai. You should create the new folder. Refer to Chapter 1, page 22, if you need assistance with restoring files.

Open **SageData13\Chai\chai** to access the data files for Chai Tea Room. Refer to page 7 if you need assistance with opening data files.

You are prompted to enter the session date, which is August 7, 2015, for the first group of transactions in this application.

Type `Aug 7 15`

Click **OK** to enter the first session date for this application.

The Payables module appears. This is the default page for Chai Tea Room.

Accounting for Purchases

All supplier-related transactions can be entered from the Payables module window. Purchases from suppliers are entered in the Purchases Journal, accessed from the Invoices icon as shown here:

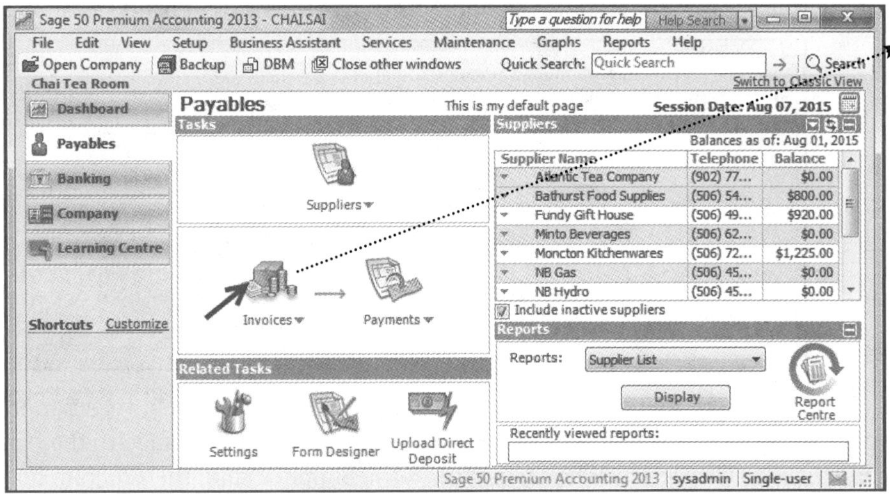

The first transaction is a normal purchase invoice.

✓ 1 **Purchase Invoice #FG-642** **Dated Aug. 1/15**

From Fundy Gift House, $800 plus $104 HST for eight tea service sets. Invoice total, $904. Terms: net 30.

Click the **Invoices icon** to open the Purchases Journal input form:

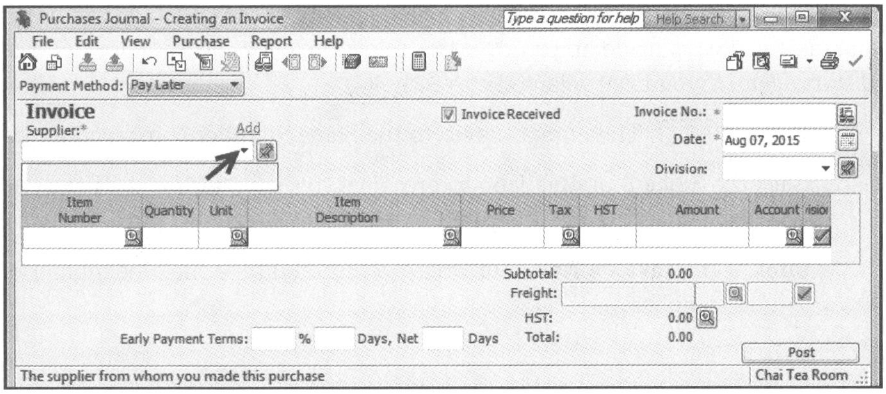

Move the mouse pointer across the various tool buttons and input fields and observe the labels and status bar messages.

Creating An Invoice is indicated in the title bar and the option to Pay Later is correct because this is a credit purchase. Payment methods include cheque, cash, direct deposits and credit cards (when these are set up).

Most tool buttons should already be familiar. Notice that the Calculator button appears again in the tool bar.

Several tool buttons have been added to the Purchases Journal window:

Look Up An Invoice, Look Up Previous and Next Invoice, Track Shipments, Printer Settings, Print Preview, E-mail and Print.

Each tool will be discussed when used. The column for projects is named Divisions for the food and beverage industry.

NOTES

Access to the Receivables, Payroll, Inventory and Division ledgers is hidden because these ledgers are not set up or ready to use.

PRO VERSION

The term Vendors will replace Suppliers for all icon labels and fields. Purchase Invoices is the label for the Purchases Journal icon.

Click the Purchase Invoices icon to open the journal.

CLASSIC VIEW

In the Classic view Home window, click the Purchases icon 

to open the Purchases Journal.

PRO VERSION

Project replaces the Division label.

The Refresh Lists tool applies to multi-user mode and does not appear in the Pro version.

NOTES

When the other features are not hidden, you will see a pull-down menu for Transaction types that includes quotes and purchase orders.

When payment is by cheque, a drop-down list of bank accounts is available. These topics are covered in later chapters.

WARNING!
You must click the list arrow to see the supplier list. Clicking the field will place an insertion point to prepare for typing a name.

Click the **Supplier** (or Vendor) **field list arrow** to expand the supplier list:

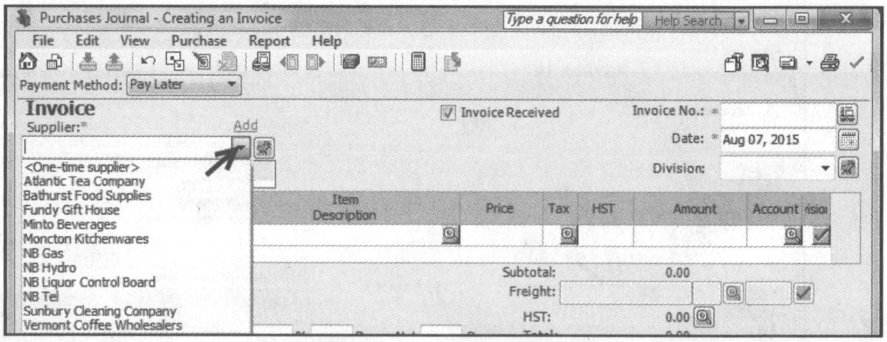

NOTES
When orders and quotes are used, fields for these features will be added to the journal.
Inventory is introduced in Chapter 10.

Whenever you see this arrow beside a field, you can make a selection from a drop-down list. Type the first letter of the supplier's name to advance to the names beginning with that letter. When you type in the Supplier field, the program fills in a name from the supplier list by trying to match the letters you type.

Click **Fundy Gift House**, the supplier for this purchase, to select and enter it.

Notice that the supplier's name and address have been added to your input form, making it easy to check whether you have selected the correct supplier. Many other details have also been added by default from the supplier's record. The tax code and the account number usually stay the same for a supplier so they are set up as defaults. The payment terms for the supplier are also included. Any of these details can be edited if required. If you have made an error in your selection, click the Supplier field list arrow and start again. If you have selected correctly,

NOTES
If you use the same supplier for consecutive purchases, preselecting the supplier can save data entry time. You can still select a different supplier from the list.

Press *tab*. The cursor moves to the Same Supplier (pin) icon.

Click the **Same Supplier** icon to preselect this supplier for the next purchase. When selected, the pin is pushed in. Click it again to turn off the selection.

Click the **Invoice No. field** where you should type the alphanumeric invoice number.

Type `FG-642`

Press *tab* to select the Invoice Lookup icon.

Press *tab* again to advance to the Date field.

Enter the date the transaction took place, August 1, 2015. The session date appears by default, in long (text) format according to the settings for the company file. It is highlighted, ready to be accepted or changed. You need to change the date.

NOTES
The year is automatically added when you enter the month and day in the Date field of the Purchases Journal.

Type `aug 1`

Many of the invoice fields (Item Number, Quantity, Unit, Item Description and unit Price) pertain mainly to inventory items. Because we are not using the Inventory Ledger for this application, you can skip the inventory-related fields. Any information you type in these fields does not appear in the journal report.

You can click the Item Description field and type a description. Or add the quantity (8) in the Quantity field and the unit price in the Price field.

Click the **Item Description field**.

Type `tea service sets`

To select a different tax code, or to see the codes set up and available,

Click the **Tax field List icon** to see the tax codes for Chai Tea Room:

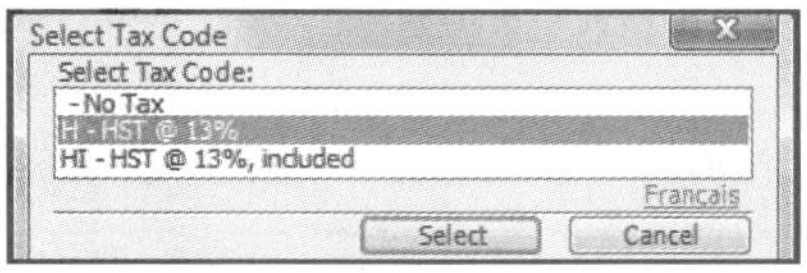

The selected tax code is H, that is, HST is charged on the purchase at 13 percent, and the tax is not included in the price. You can select a different code if needed, but in this case the tax code is correct.

Click **Cancel** so that the selection remains unchanged.

Click the **first line of the Amount field**, where you will enter the total amount for this purchase.

Type 800

Press *tab*.

The cursor moves to the Account field. The Account field for this purchase refers to the debit part of the journal entry, normally the acquisition of an asset or the incurring of an expense. It could also be used to decrease a liability or to decrease equity if the purchase were made for the owner's personal use. When you work in the subsidiary Payables journal, Sage 50 will automatically credit your *Accounts Payable* control account in the General Ledger for the purchase. In fact, you cannot access *Accounts Payable* directly when the Payables Ledger is set up and linked. If you click the Account List icon, you will see that this account is not included.

In this example, the business has acquired an asset, and the correct account, *Gift Set Inventory,* is entered as the default for this supplier.

To select a different account, click the List icon for the Account field, double-click the Account field or press *enter* to show the Select Account screen. You can also add a new account from the Select Account screen.

Press *tab* to advance the cursor to the next invoice line. You can now enter additional purchases from this supplier if there are any.

Sage 50 uses the tax code to calculate and enter the tax amount automatically in the HST field when you enter the amount for the purchase.

Your screen should now resemble the following:

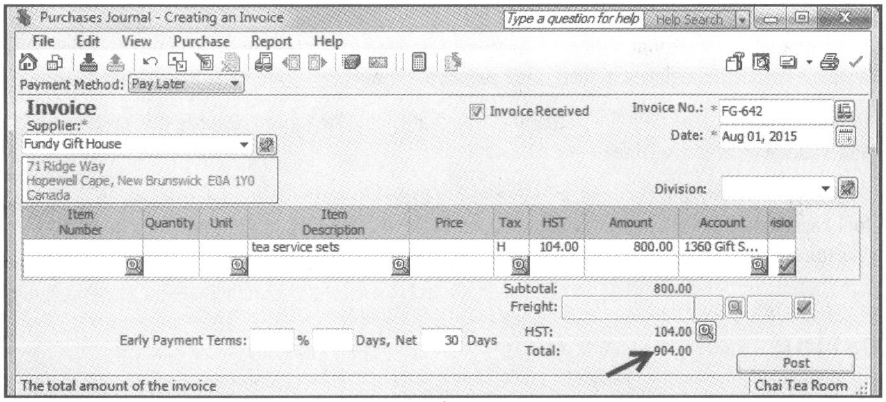

The payment terms have been set up as defaults for this supplier and are entered automatically. They can be edited if needed for specific purchases, but in this case they are correct. There is no discount and full payment is due in 30 days. The subtotal (amount owing before taxes) and the total amount are calculated and added automatically, so the entries for this transaction are complete and you are ready to review the transaction. By reviewing the journal entry, you can check for mistakes.

NOTES

For this application, the sales tax rate is set to 13 percent, the harmonized single tax rate for New Brunswick. For provinces that have a separate or no provincial sales tax, the rate is 5 percent and tax codes will display as GST @ 5%.

Since the provincial and federal retail sales taxes are harmonized, there is no separate amount for PST. When PST is applicable and is set up in the defaults for the company, the program will calculate PST as well, based on the tax rates and codes entered for PST.

NOTES

Typing negative amounts will generate a credit entry with a debit for Accounts Payable. This is similar to entering a negative amount in the General Journal to switch debits to credits and vice versa.

NOTES

The account name may not fit in the account column if the column is very narrow. To change the width of a column, point to the heading column margin. When the pointer changes to a double-sided arrow, drag the margin line to the new location. Make a journal window wider by dragging the side frame. You can also maximize a journal window to occupy the entire screen.

Reviewing the Purchases Journal Entry

> **NOTES**
> Pressing ctrl + J will also display the journal entry.

Choose the **Report menu** and **click Display Purchases Journal Entry**:

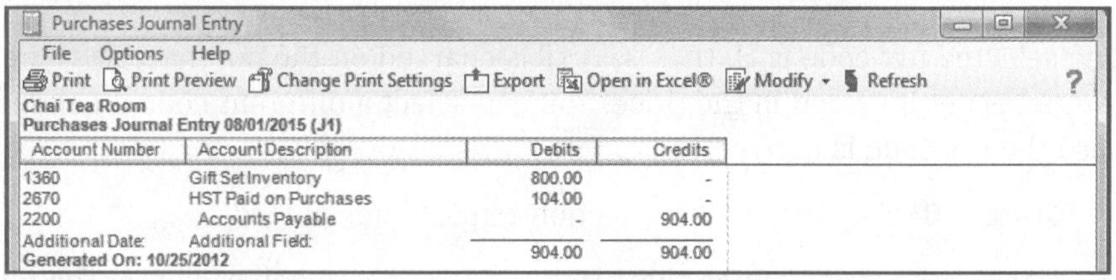

> **NOTES**
> Other linked accounts for the Payables Ledger include a bank account, a freight expense account and a purchase discounts account. Each linked account will be explained when it is used in this workbook.

Note that Sage 50 automatically updates the *Accounts Payable* control account because the Payables and General ledgers are linked or fully integrated. Even though you did not enter account *2200*, Sage 50 uses it because it is defined as the linked account to which all purchases should be credited. In fact, you cannot select *Accounts Payable* directly for posting when it is used as a linked account — it does not appear on the Select Account lists. *HST Paid on Purchases*, the linked tax account, is also automatically updated. Using the Purchases Journal instead of the General Journal to enter purchases is faster because you need to enter only half the journal entry. You should use this journal for purchases because the program credits the account of the selected supplier directly and prevents you from choosing an incorrect payables account. The automatic selection of tax codes and accounts and calculation of tax amounts also makes the transaction simpler to enter and increases accuracy.

Close the **display** to return to the Purchases Journal input screen.

> **NOTES**
> To correct a Purchases Journal entry after posting, refer to page 127 and Appendix C.

CORRECTING THE PURCHASES JOURNAL ENTRY BEFORE POSTING

Move to the field that has the error. **Press** tab to move forward through the fields or **press** shift and tab together to move back to a previous field. This will highlight the field information so you can change it. **Type** the **correct information** and **press** tab to enter it.

You can also use the mouse to **point** to a field and **drag through** the **incorrect information** to highlight it. **Type** the **correct information** and **press** tab to enter it.

If the supplier is incorrect, reselect from the supplier list by **clicking** the **Supplier field list arrow**. **Click** the name of the **correct supplier**.

Click an **incorrect amount** to highlight it. Then **type** the **correct amount** and **press** tab to enter the change.

To select a different account, **click** the **Account List icon** to display the list of accounts. **Click** the **correct account** number to highlight it, then **click Select** and **press** tab to enter the change.

To insert a line or remove a line, **click** the **line** that should be moved. **Choose** the **Edit menu** and **click Insert Line** or **Remove Line** to make the change.

To discard the entry and begin again, **click** (**Close**) to close the Journal or **click** (**Undo**) on the tool bar to open a blank journal window. When Sage 50 asks whether you want to discard the entry, **click Yes** to confirm your decision.

Posting

> **NOTES**
> You can press alt + P to post the journal entry.

When you are certain that you have entered all the information correctly, you must post the transaction to save it.

Click the **Post button** Post or **choose** the **Purchase menu** and **click Post** to save your transaction.

Click **OK** to confirm successful posting.

A new blank Purchases Journal form appears on the screen.

Storing a Recurring Journal Entry

The second transaction is the recurring purchase of food inventory. Businesses often have transactions that are repeated regularly. For example, loan payments, bank charges and rent payments usually occur on the same day each month; supplies may be ordered daily or weekly; insurance payments may occur less frequently but nonetheless regularly. Chai Tea Room is invoiced weekly for food supplies. By storing an entry and indicating the frequency, it can be recalled when it is needed without re-entering all the information.

✓ 2

Purchase Invoice #BF-1243 **Dated Aug. 1/15**

From Bathurst Food Supplies, $800 for pastries, breads, condiments and other foods. There is no HST on food products. Terms: 1/10, n/30. Store as a weekly recurring entry.

The Purchases Journal should still be open with payment method and date correct.

Choose **Bathurst Food Supplies** from the supplier list, or

Click the **Supplier field** and **type** `B`

Click the **Invoice field**.

Type `BF-1243`

Enter a **description** for the purchase.

The tax code is correct; no tax is charged on the purchase of food. The payment terms and account are also correct by default.

Click the **Amount field**, **type** `800` and **press** *tab* to complete the transaction.

Choose the **Report menu** and **click** **Display Purchases Journal Entry** to review the entry.

Close the **display** and **make corrections** if necessary.

Click the **Store tool** on the tool bar (or **choose** the **Purchase menu** and **click** **Store**) to open the following Store Recurring Transaction screen:

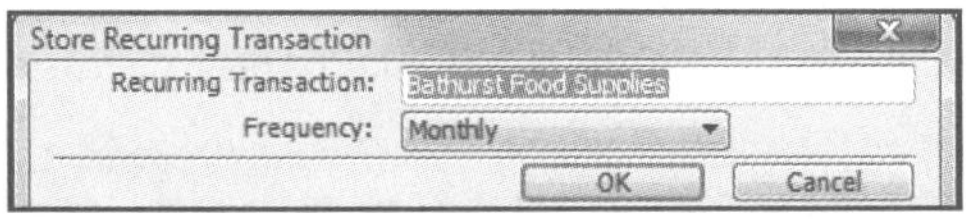

Sage 50 enters the supplier and Monthly as the default name and frequency for the entry. The cursor is in the name field. You can type another descriptive name to change it. Be sure to use one that you will recognize easily as belonging to this entry. The default frequency is incorrect since the invoices for food items are received weekly.

Click **Monthly** to display the list of choices for the recurring frequency:

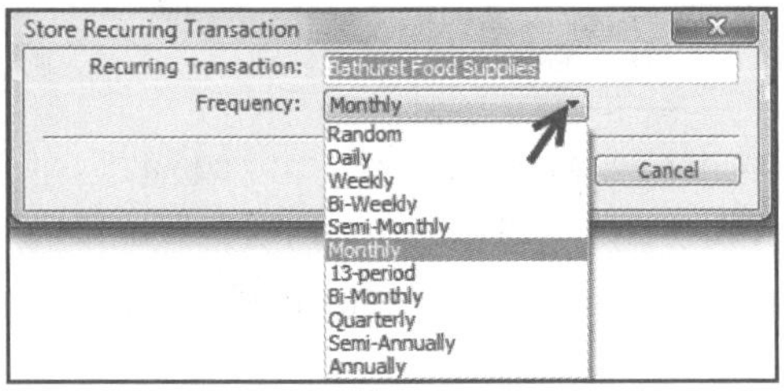

The frequency options are Random (for irregular purchases), Daily, Weekly, Bi-Weekly, Semi-Monthly, Monthly, 13-Period, Bi-Monthly, Quarterly, Semi-Annually and Annually.

NOTES

Typing the first letter of a supplier name in the Supplier field will add the first supplier name beginning with that letter. Since Bathurst Foods is the first supplier name starting with "B," it will be entered.

NOTES

The procedure for storing entries is the same for all journals when the option is available. Choose Store, assign a name to the entry, then choose a frequency and click OK to save it.

The shortcut for storing a transaction is *ctrl* + T.

NOTES

The recurring frequency options are: Daily, Weekly (52 times per year), Bi-Weekly (26 times per year, or every two weeks), Semi-Monthly (24 times per year), Monthly (12 times per year), 13-Period (13 times per year, or every four weeks), Bi-Monthly (six times per year, or every two months), Quarterly (four times per year, or every three months), Semi-Annually (twice per year, or every six months), Annually (once per year) and Random (irregular intervals using the session date when the entry is recalled).

Click **Weekly**.

Sage 50 will advance the default journal date when you recall the stored entry according to the frequency selected. The session date is entered if the Random frequency is chosen.

Click **OK** to return to the Purchases Journal window.

Notice that (the **Recall tool**) is now darkened and can be selected because you have stored a journal entry. The journal title bar label has also changed. It now shows Using Recurring Bathurst Food Supplies.

> **CORRECTING A STORED JOURNAL ENTRY**
>
> If you notice an error in the stored journal entry before posting, you must first **correct** the **journal entry** in the Purchases Journal window, then **click Store**. When asked to confirm that you want to overwrite or replace the previous version, **click Yes**.
>
> If you edit the journal entry after storing it and do not want to store the changed entry, Sage 50 will warn you that the entry has changed. **Click Yes** to proceed.

Posting

When you are sure that you have entered all the information correctly and you have stored the entry, you must post the transaction to save it.

Click the **Post button** Post or **choose** the **Purchase menu** and **click Post** to save your transaction. **Click OK** to confirm successful posting.

A new blank Purchases Journal form appears on the screen. The Recall tool is now available so we can recall the purchase we stored. Our next transaction is a payment, however, not a purchase.

Close the **Purchases Journal window** to return to the Payables window.

Accounting for Payments

Payments are made from the Payments Journal icon in the Tasks pane indicated by the arrow in the following screen:

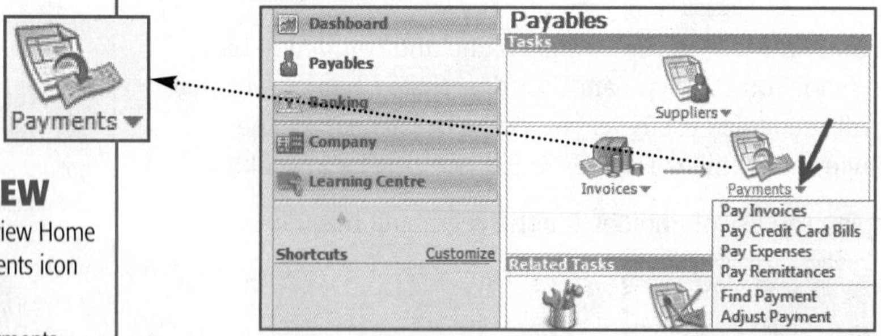

Click the **Payments icon list arrow**, as shown above, to see a list of shortcuts for different payment types.

When you click on one of these shortcuts, the journal will open with the correct type of transaction preselected.

Click **Pay Invoices** to open the Payments Journal:

CLASSIC VIEW
From the Classic view Home window, click the Payments icon to open the Payments Journal. Pay Invoices will be selected as the default type of transaction.

PRO VERSION
Choose Pay Purchase Invoices from the shortcuts list to open the Payments Journal.

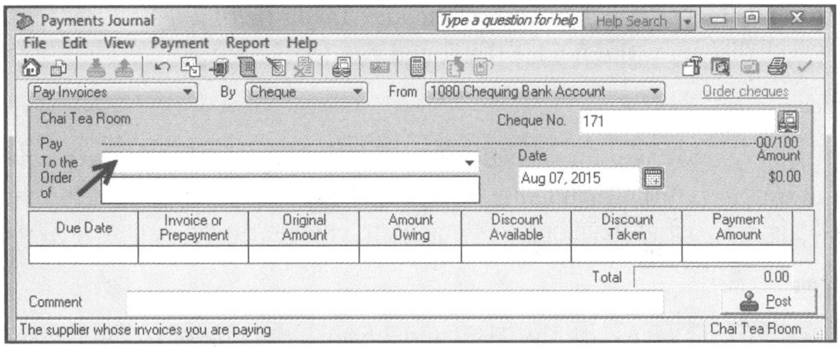

PRO VERSION

The Refresh tools do not appear in the Pro version. Pay Purchase Invoices appears as the transaction type.

Pay Invoices is selected as the type of payment in the Pay field because we made this selection in the Home window. Pay Invoices is also the default transaction type when you click the Payments icon. Cheque appears as the method of payment in the By field and *1080 Chequing Bank Account* is the account the payment is made from. These defaults are correct for the first payment.

NOTES

When more than one bank account is set up, you can select the bank from the drop-down list beside From. In Chapter 11, you will use these upper fields to work with multiple bank accounts.

✓ 3

Payment Cheque #171 **Dated Aug. 2/15**

To Fundy Gift House, $700 in payment of account. Reference invoice #FG-361.

Click the **To The Order Of** (Supplier) **field list arrow** to see the familiar list of suppliers displayed in alphabetic order.

Click **Fundy Gift House** (or **type** F) to choose and enter the supplier to whom the payment is made.

NOTES

You can type F in the Supplier field to enter Fundy Gift House because this is the only supplier beginning with "F."

The journal input form is updated with the supplier's name, address and outstanding invoice(s), making it easy to see whether you have selected correctly.

The updated journal is shown here:

NOTES

From the Pay drop-down list, you can select the other kinds of transactions for this journal, or you can choose the transaction type from the Payments icon shortcuts list in the Payables module window.

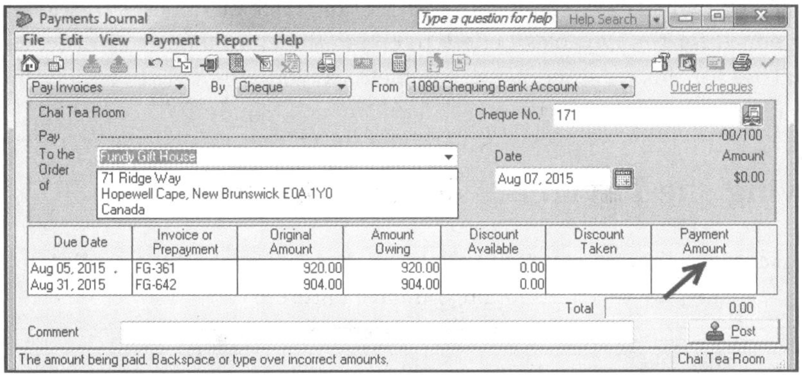

If you need to change the supplier, click the Supplier field list arrow again to select from the supplier list. The cheque number is entered in the Number field. The next cheque number appears according to the settings for the company. It is correct, so you can accept it. Normally the cheque number should be correct. It can be edited, if necessary, for reversing or correcting entries.

The default session date is entered and is incorrect; you must change it.

NOTES

Click (the Include Fully Paid Invoices tool) to display all paid and unpaid invoices for the selected supplier.

Click the **Calendar icon** for the Date field.

Click **2** in the August section. **Press** tab.

NOTES

The Lookup icon appears beside the cheque number and in the tool bar so you can look up previous payments.

The year will also be added correctly when you type the month and day in the Payments Journal Date field.

The cursor moves to the Due Date field for the first outstanding invoice. All outstanding invoices, including both the amount of the original invoice and the balance owing for the selected supplier, are listed on the screen.

Press tab to advance to the Discount Taken field. Since there is no discount, the field is blank and you can skip it.

Press tab again.

The amount outstanding for the selected invoice is highlighted as the payment amount. You can accept the highlighted amount, or type another amount for partial payments. This is a partial payment so we need to change the amount.

Type 700

Press tab to update the Total and advance the cursor to the Discount Taken field for the next invoice and complete the payment as shown:

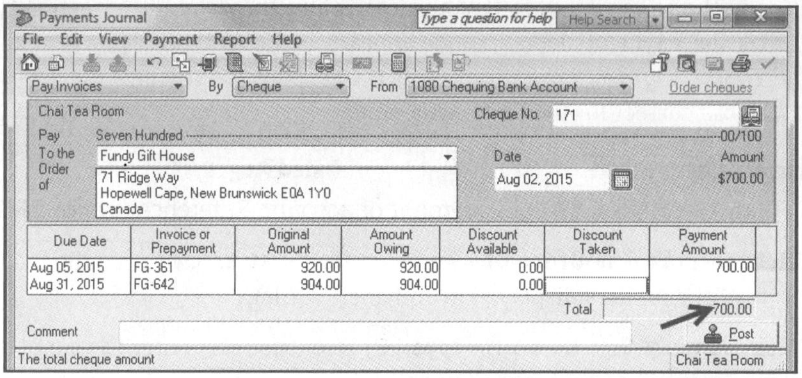

Notice that the upper cheque portion of the form is also complete. Notice too that there is no field for account numbers in the Payments Journal. You need to enter only the amount of the payment on the appropriate invoice line.

As you pay invoices in the subsidiary Payments Journal, you do not enter any accounts, so you cannot make an incorrect selection. Sage 50 chooses the default linked accounts defined for the Payables Ledger to create the journal entry.

The entries for this transaction are complete, so you are ready to review and post your transaction.

Reviewing the Payments Journal Entry

Choose the **Report menu** and **click Display Payments Journal Entry** to display the transaction you have entered:

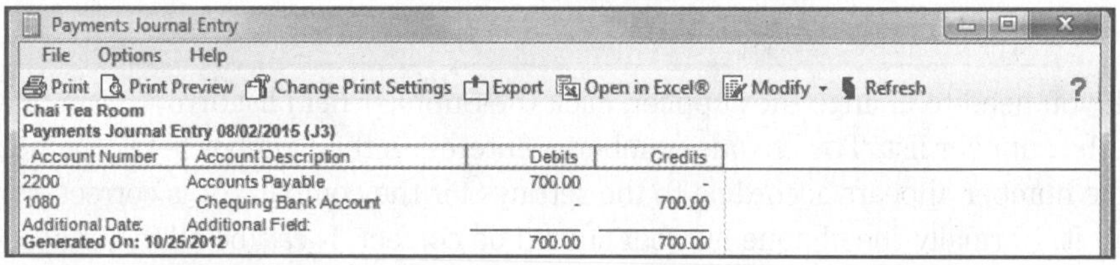

You can see that Sage 50 automatically creates a related journal entry when you complete a Payments Journal entry. The program updates *Accounts Payable* and *Chequing Bank Account* because the Payables and General ledgers are fully linked. *Chequing Bank Account* has been defined as the default Payables linked account to which payments are credited. The payment is also recorded to the supplier's account to reduce the balance owing.

Close the **display** to return to the Payments Journal input screen.

You can also print the cheque, but you must do so before posting. However, you should check that you have selected the correct printer and forms for printing cheques (see Chapter 4, page 84) and make corrections first, if necessary.

WARNING!
The amount for the next invoice should not be highlighted since this invoice is not being paid. If its amount is highlighted or entered, you must delete it by pressing del and then tab to correct the total cheque amount, as we show on page 130.

NOTES
The direct link between the Payments and Purchases journals for each supplier provides further reasons for using the Purchases Journal for purchases. Outstanding amounts (and discounts) are calculated and displayed automatically, and ledger account balances and supplier records are updated automatically.

CORRECTING THE PAYMENTS JOURNAL ENTRY BEFORE POSTING

Move to the field that has the error. **Press** *tab* to move forward through the fields or **press** *shift* and *tab* together to move back to a previous field. This will highlight the field information so you can change it. **Type** the **correct information** and **press** *tab* to enter it.

You can also use the mouse to **point** to a field and **drag through** the **incorrect information** to highlight it. **Type** the **correct information** and **press** *tab* to enter it.

If the supplier is incorrect, **click** to undo the entry or **reselect** from the **Supplier** list by **clicking** the **Supplier list arrow. Click** the name of the **correct supplier.** You will be asked to confirm that you want to discard the current transaction. **Click Yes** to discard the incorrect supplier entry and display the outstanding invoices for the correct supplier. **Re-enter** the **payment** information for this supplier.

Make **corrections**. **Click** the **Print tool** if you want to print the cheque.

Posting

When you are certain that you have entered all the information correctly, you must post the transaction to save it.

Click the **Post button** Post (or **choose** the **Payment menu** and **click** **Post**) to save your transaction and then **click OK** to confirm.

Entering Cash Purchases

The licence fees statement on August 2 is to be paid immediately on receipt of the invoice. Instead of recording the purchase and payment separately, you can record the payment with the purchase in the Payments Journal. This transaction also involves a company that is not listed as a supplier, so you must add the City Treasurer to the supplier list to record the transaction.

Suppliers can be added directly from the Payables Ledger or from the supplier field in the Purchases Journal or the Payments Journal. We will add the new supplier from the Payments Journal. The Payments Journal should still be open.

✓ 4

Cash Purchase Invoice #Fton-08 **Dated Aug. 2/15**

From City Treasurer (use Quick Add for the new supplier), $250 for August licensing fees. Paid by cheque #172.

The date and the cheque number are correct. The date is unchanged from the previous Payments Journal transaction. The next available cheque number is entered by default, and the bank account is selected for the payment. Cheque numbers are updated in sequence for both payment journal entries and cash purchases.

Click **Pay Invoices** to see the options for payment transactions:

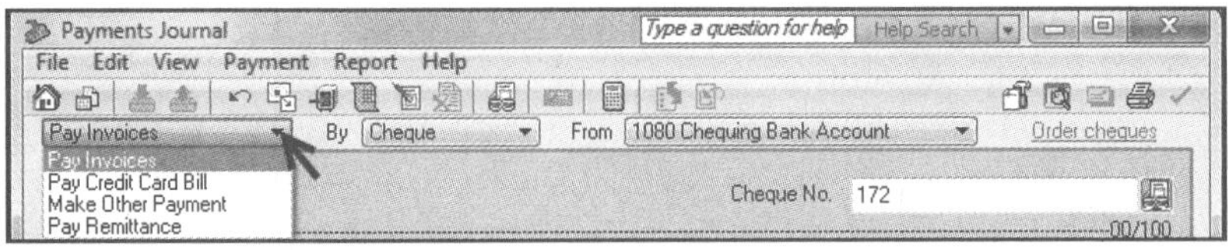

Click **Make Other Payment** from the drop-down list.

If you have closed the Payments Journal, you can open the form for cash purchases from the Home window. Click the Payments icon list arrow and click **Pay Expenses** (see page 116). In this case, you must enter August 2 as the date.

NOTES

You can correct payment amounts after posting by clicking the Adjust Payment tool. Select the payment to adjust, just as you select a purchase invoice or General Journal entry for editing. Make the correction and post the revised payment.

To correct a payment after posting, refer to page 137 and to the section on NSF cheques on page 176.

NOTES

When the batch printing option is selected in the settings for Forms, you can print cheques in batches after posting them. The Print Batches tool will be added to the tool bar. Batch printing is covered in Chapter 14.

To check printer settings, click , the Change The Default Printer Settings tool in the journal.

Turn on the printer and click , the Print tool.

PRO VERSION

Click Pay Purchase Invoices to see the payment options.

CLASSIC VIEW

From the Classic view Home window, click the Payments icon Payments to open the Payments Journal. Click Pay Invoices and then click Make Other Payment as the type of transaction.

> **WARNING!**
> If you have closed the Payments Journal, the session date will be displayed and you must change it to August 2.

Journal input fields are added to the payment form:

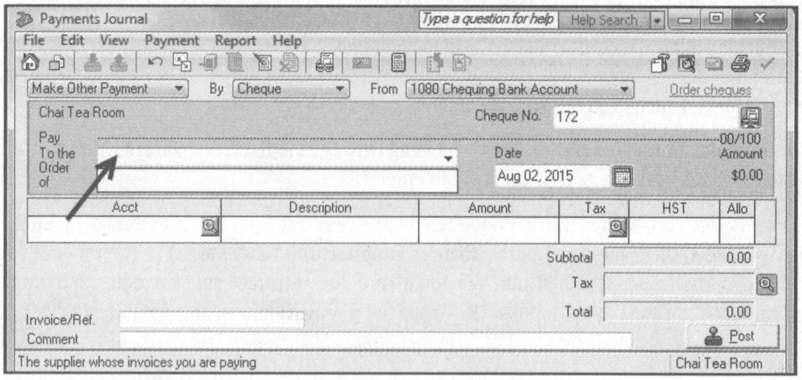

Click the **To The Order Of (Supplier) field** to move the cursor.

Type `City Treasurer` and then **press** *tab* to display the message:

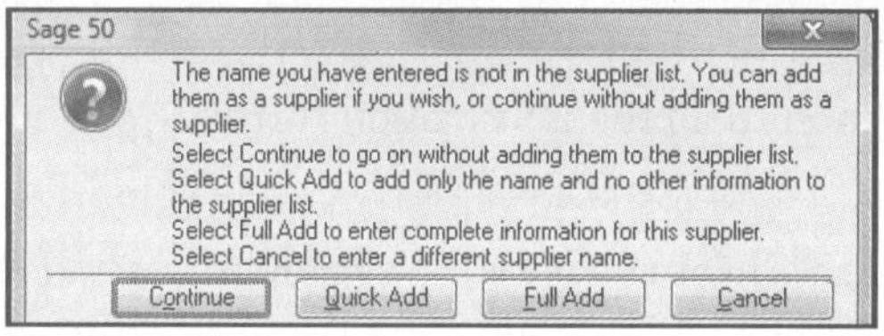

> **PRO VERSION**
> Remember that you will see the term Vendors instead of Suppliers in all journals.

The program recognizes that the name is new and gives you four options. **Continue** will add the name to the journal and the journal report and apply the default settings for the ledger. This option will not create a supplier record or include the name in the supplier list. **Quick Add** will create a partial record with only the supplier's name and will apply the default settings for the ledger. **Full Add** will open a new ledger record for the supplier and you can add complete details. **Cancel** will return you to the journal. You can then type or choose another name if the one you typed was incorrect.

If you are making a cash purchase and you will not be making additional purchases from this supplier, you can choose **One-Time Supplier** from the Supplier list. Type the supplier's name and address in the text box area below the To The Order Of field. The default settings for the ledger will apply to the invoice, but you can change them if needed. The transaction will be included in the GST/HST report, but the supplier's name will not appear in supplier lists or in the journal reports.

> **NOTES**
> The Continue option will add the supplier's name to journal entries for purchase invoices entered in the Purchases Journal, but not for Other Payments entered in the Payments Journal.
> If you create a partial supplier record with Quick Add, you can add more supplier details later by editing the record.

We want to add a partial record for the new supplier.

Click **Quick Add** to return to the Payments Journal.

The supplier's name is added to the journal. Because an account is not set up for the supplier, you must enter the asset or expense account that is debited for the transaction.

Click the **Account field List icon** to see the Select Account list.

Click **Suggested Accounts** to modify the list as shown:

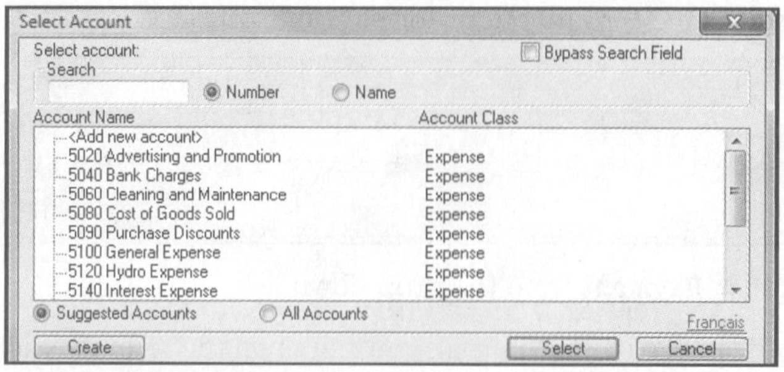

> **NOTES**
> If you scroll down the complete list of accounts, you will see that 2200 Accounts Payable is not included.

The list now shows only the expense accounts, the ones used most often for purchases. This list is easier to work with because it is shorter. When you enter sales in the Sales Journal, the suggested accounts will list only revenue accounts.

Scroll down and **click 5160 Licences and Permits**.

Click **Select** to add the account and advance to the Description field.

Type `August licensing fees`

Press *tab* to advance to the Amount field.

Type `250` **Press** *tab*.

Since no tax is charged on the fees, the default entry of No Tax is correct.

Click the **Invoice/Ref. field**.

Type `Fton-08` **Press** *tab* to advance to the Comment field.

The comment will become part of the journal record so you should include it.

Type `Fton-08, August licensing fees`

The subtotal and total amounts are entered automatically. Your completed payment form should now look like the one shown here, and you are ready to review it:

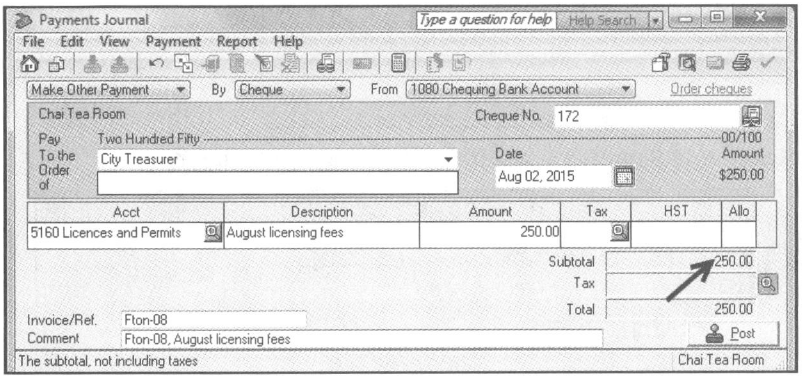

Choose the **Report menu** and **click Display Payments Journal Entry**. Your display should look like the following:

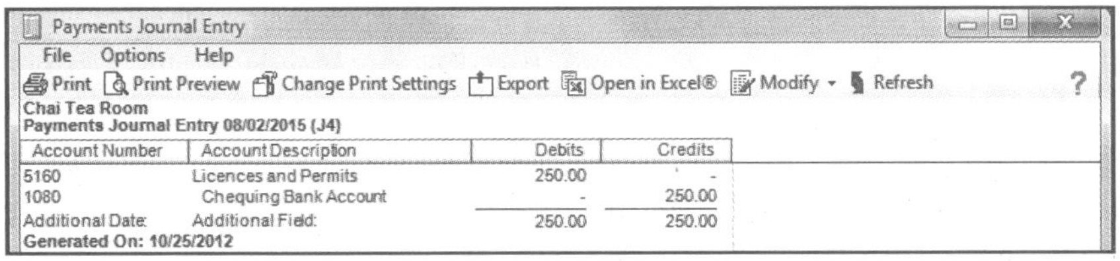

Chai Tea Room
Payments Journal Entry 08/02/2015 (J4)

Account Number	Account Description	Debits	Credits
5160	Licences and Permits	250.00	-
1080	Chequing Bank Account	-	250.00
Additional Date:	Additional Field:	250.00	250.00

Generated On: 10/25/2012

Notice that the program has automatically credited *Chequing Bank Account*, the Payables linked bank account, for the cash purchase instead of *Accounts Payable*.

Close the **display** when you have finished.

Make any **corrections** necessary. Double-click an incorrect entry and type the correct details.

Click the **Post button** Post to save the **entry** when you are certain that it is correct. **Click OK**.

Close the **Payments Journal**.

NOTES

You can use keyboard shortcuts to copy text. Click the text you want to copy and press *ctrl* + C. Then click the field you want the text copied to and press *ctrl* + V.

NOTES

If the purchase has taxes added, choose the tax code from the Tax field List icon selection list. Sometimes the tax code used for the previous supplier is entered and may be incorrect. If the tax code entered is incorrect, choose the correct code from the Tax field List icon selection list.

NOTES
Entering cash purchases in the Payments Journal as an Other Payment or in the Purchases Journal is a personal preference.

NOTES
All Campus Ads
✓ Terms: net 1
Expense account: 5020
Tax code: H - HST @ 13%

PRO VERSION
Click Add Vendor in the Vendors shortcuts list.

CLASSIC VIEW
From the Classic view Home window, click the Suppliers icon  to open the Suppliers window. Then click the Create tool , or choose the File menu and click Create, or press *ctrl* + N. Close the Suppliers window after saving the new record.

PRO VERSION
The Refresh tool does not appear in the Pro version.

NOTES
If you are missing any information for a supplier, you can leave the field blank and enter the details later by editing the record. See page 136.

Although the extra fields are not required, entering the details in the ledger record will speed up journal entry when you choose the supplier.

Adding a New Supplier Record

Cash purchases and new suppliers may be recorded in the Payments Journal or the Purchases Journal. We will record the next cash purchase in the Purchases Journal after we add a full record for the supplier. You can create a new supplier record on the fly, as in the previous transaction, by choosing Full Add, or you can open the Payables Ledger for a new supplier record from the Add Supplier option in the Suppliers shortcuts list. For this transaction, we will use the ledger option.

The next purchase is from a new supplier and requires a complete new record.

✓ 5

Memo #12 **Dated Aug. 3/15**

Add a new record for All Campus Ads (contact Pierre Fullovit)
Located at 447 Slick St., Fredericton, NB E3B 8J5
Tel: (506) 564-8907
E-mail: pfullovit@acads.ca

Click the **Suppliers icon shortcuts list arrow** as shown:

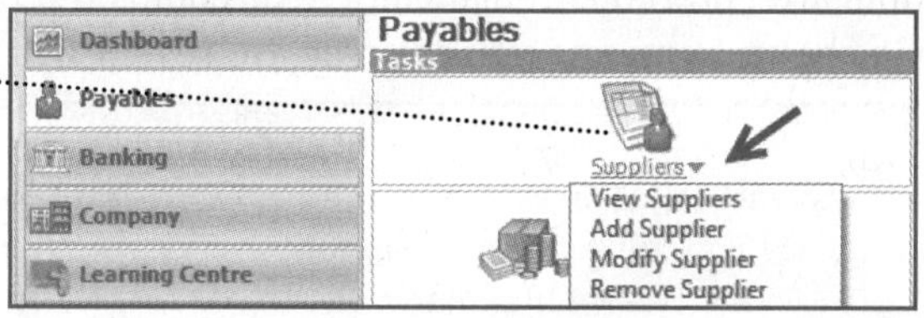

Click **Add Supplier** to open the Payables Ledger input form:

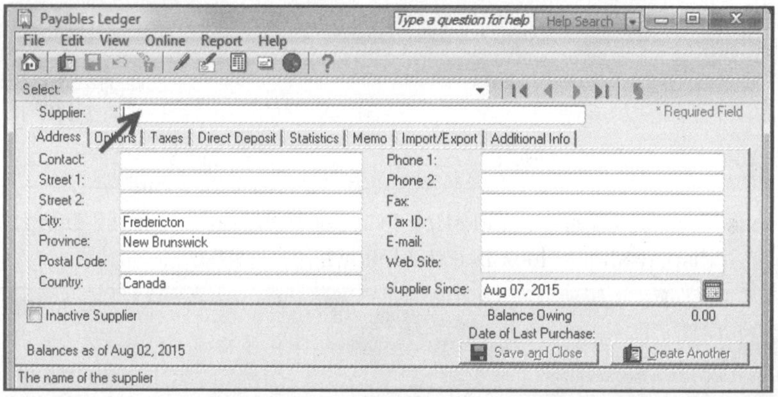

You are ready to enter the new supplier. The Supplier Address tab information screen appears first. Note that required fields have an * beside them as they do in the General Ledger. The supplier name is the only required field. As soon as you begin to type in the field, the * is removed.

Type `All Campus Ads` **Press** *tab*.

The cursor advances to the Contact field, where you enter the name of Chai Tea Room's contact person at All Campus Ads. This field can also be used to enter a third address line if two street lines are insufficient. This field or any other may be left blank by pressing *tab*.

Type `Pierre Fullovit`

Press *tab*. The cursor moves to the Street 1 field.

Type `447 Slick St.`

The Street 2 field can be used for a second address line, if there is one.

By default, the program has entered the city, province and country from the Payables Ledger Address settings. You can accept the defaults because they are correct.

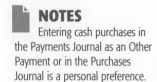

If the supplier is in a different city, province or country, type the correct information before continuing. Press tab to advance to a field and highlight the contents to prepare it for editing.

Click the **Postal Code field** to move the cursor.

When you enter a Canadian postal code, you do not need to use capital letters or leave a space within the postal code. The program makes these adjustments for you.

Type `e3b8j5` **Press** tab.

Notice that the format of the postal code has been corrected automatically. The cursor moves to the Country field and the entry is correct.

Press tab. The cursor moves to the Phone 1 field.

You do not need to insert a dash, space or bracket when you enter a telephone number. Telephone and fax numbers may be entered with or without the area code.

Type `5065648907` **Press** tab.

The format for the telephone number has been corrected automatically. The cursor advances to the Phone 2 field for the supplier's second phone number. We do not have additional phone or fax numbers at this time. They can be added later when they are obtained. The Tax ID number refers to the business's federal tax or GST registration number. Adding e-mail and Web site information allows you to send purchase orders by e-mail and connect to the supplier's Web site directly from Sage 50. Type e-mail and Web addresses just as you enter them in your Internet program.

Click the **E-mail field**. **Type** `pfullovit@acads.ca`

The date in the Supplier Since field is the session date or the date of the earliest transaction you enter for this supplier in Sage 50. You can enter a different date if this is appropriate. The Date Of Last Purchase is added automatically by the program based on the transactions you enter for the supplier.

Press tab **twice** to advance to the Supplier Since date field.

Type `Aug 3`

The last option concerns the supplier's status. You can make a supplier inactive and remove the name from the selection lists and reports. Suppliers that you will not use again can be made inactive.

Click the **Options tab** to open the next supplier information screen:

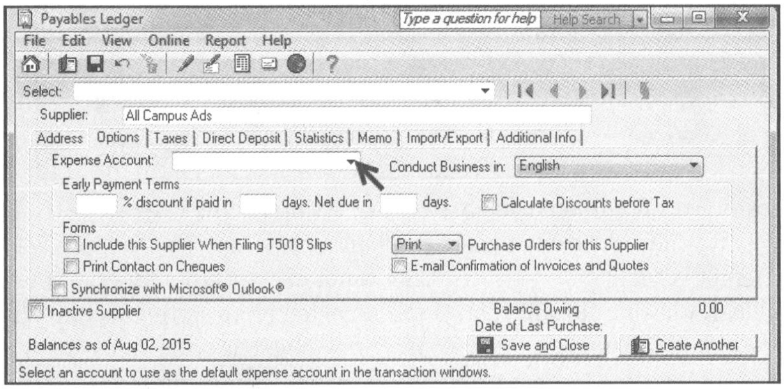

The Options screen has several important fields. In the first part of the Options screen, you can choose the default account and preferred language (English or French) for the supplier. Forms you send to that supplier will be in the selected language,

NOTES
Any account – except the type X account and Accounts Payable – can be used as the default expense account, including capital accounts. This allows you to set up the owner as a supplier and link the transactions to the Drawings account.

NOTES
If you need to create a new account for this supplier, type the new account number in the Expense Account field and press *tab*. Click Add to confirm that you want to create the account. The Add An Account wizard will open.

NOTES
Typing 0 (zero) in the Net Days field will leave the payment terms fields on the invoice blank. Therefore, we enter net 1 (one) when payment is due immediately.

PRO VERSION
The option to Synchronize With Microsoft Outlook is not available in the Pro version.

WARNING!
The tax exempt option Yes should be selected only if all purchases from the supplier are tax exempt because this setting prevents taxes from being calculated on any purchases from the supplier.

although your own screens will not change. You can also enter a default account for the supplier. Although the field is named Expense Account — usually an expense or asset account is the default — you may select any postable account. If you usually buy the same kinds of goods from a supplier, entering a default account saves time and prevents errors when completing journal entries. All Campus Ads provides promotional materials.

Click the **Expense Account list arrow** to see the accounts available.

Scroll down and **click 5020 Advertising and Promotion**.

In the **Early Payment Terms** section of the ledger, you can enter the discount for early settlement of accounts and the term for full payment. Discounts may be calculated on the amount before taxes or on the full invoice (after-tax) amount. Three fields are used to enter the discount. The first shows the discount rate as a percentage and the second holds the number of days over which the discount remains valid. In the final field, enter the number of days in which net payment is due. According to the source document, immediate payment is expected.

Click the **Net Due In ___ Days field** (Early Payment Terms section).

Type 1

The next fields appear as check boxes. There are no discounts from this supplier. Leave the check box for Calculate Discounts Before Tax blank.

Include This Supplier When Printing **T5018 Slips** applies to amounts paid to subcontractors for construction services and does not apply to Chai Tea Room. Selecting **Print Contact On Cheques** will add the name of the contact person to the cheque written to the supplier. If the Contact field contains address information, check this box; otherwise, leave it unchecked.

The next option allows you to choose **Print or E-mail Purchase Orders For This Supplier** as the default setting, but you can change the selection for individual purchase orders if necessary. If you usually e-mail the orders, you should check the **E-mail Confirmation Of Invoices And Quotes** option by clicking it.

If you want to synchronize lists in Sage 50 with Microsoft Outlook, click the **Synchronize With Microsoft Outlook** check box.

The next input screen defines the tax options for this supplier.

Click the **Taxes tab** to open the screen:

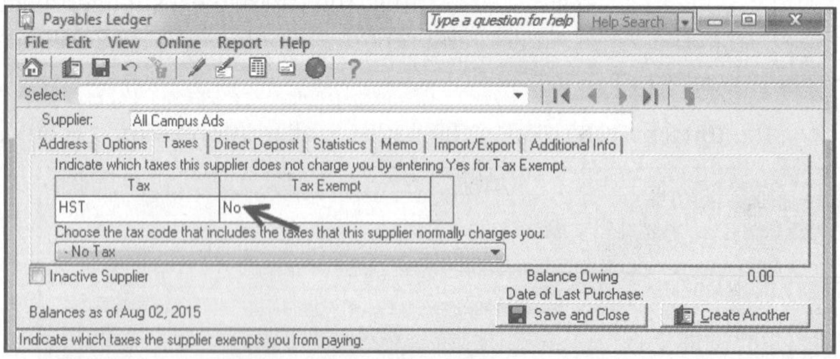

All the taxes Chai Tea Room usually pays are set up for the company and appear on the list. HST is the only applicable tax. The default option is to pay the tax — the option under Tax Exempt is set at No — that is, Chai is not exempt from taxes on purchases from this supplier. Clicking No will change the tax exemption setting to Yes. This change would be appropriate for suppliers that do not provide goods or services, such as the Receiver General. Refer to Chapter 2 for further information about taxes.

To enter a default tax code for purchases from the supplier, we can choose a code from the drop-down list in the next field. The default setting, No Tax, is incorrect.

Click **No Tax** to see the codes available:

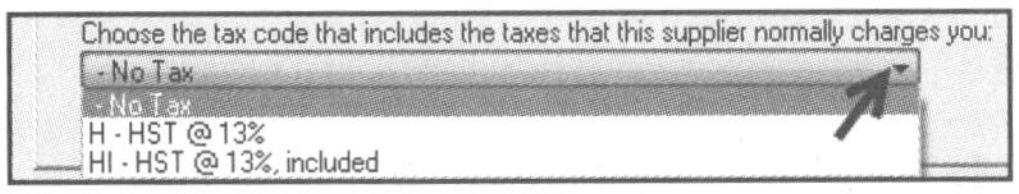

Three codes are defined for Chai Tea Room: **No Tax** for suppliers, such as Bathurst Foods, which do not charge any tax; **H** for suppliers of normal taxable goods or services when HST is not included in the price; and **HI** for suppliers of taxable goods such as gasoline or liquor when the tax is included in the purchase price.

All Campus Ads charges HST but does not include it in the price.

Click **H - HST @ 13%**.

The remaining input screens will be introduced in later applications. The **Direct Deposit** tab screen holds the details for automatic payments from your bank account, the **Statistics** tab screen stores cumulative historical transactions, the **Memo** tab screen allows you to add messages to the Daily Business Manager and the **Import/Export** tab allows you to specify corresponding inventory item codes for your business and your suppliers. The **Additional Info** tab screen has customizable fields for other information.

Check your work carefully before saving the information because the options you select will affect the invoices directly.

CORRECTING A NEW SUPPLIER ACCOUNT

Move to the field that has the error by **pressing** *tab* to move forward through the fields or **pressing** *shift* and *tab* together to move back to a previous field. **Type** the **correct information.**

You can also highlight the incorrect information by dragging the cursor through it. You can now type the correct information.

After a field has been corrected, **press** *tab* to enter the correction.

To open a different tab screen, **click** the **tab** you want.

When you are certain that all the information is correct,

Click **Save And Close**  to save the supplier information and return to the Home window.

Entering Vendor Records from the Purchases Journal

Click the Invoices icon  to open the journal and click the Suppliers field.

Type the new supplier's name in the Supplier field. Click the Add link (just above the Supplier field) to open a ledger record at the Address tab screen.

Or press *tab* after typing the name. The program recognizes the name as new:

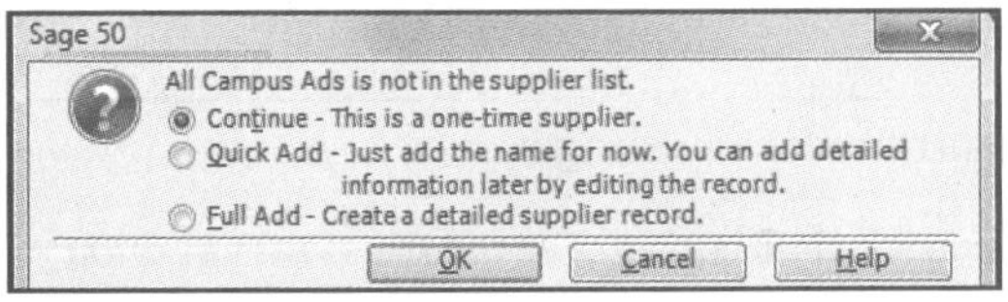

Click Full Add to open a Payables Ledger record at the Address tab screen. The new supplier name will be entered as you typed it in the Supplier field. Enter the remaining details for the supplier as described above. Click the Save And Close button to return to the invoice. The supplier's address, tax code and expense account will be added to the invoice form.

NOTES

When the tax exempt settings are No, you can change the tax codes in the journals and the tax calculations will be correct. If the tax exempt settings are Yes, you can change the codes but no taxes will be calculated.

NOTES

The Daily Business Manager is covered in Chapter 11 and the Import/Export options are explained in Appendix J on the Student DVD. Direct deposits are covered in Chapter 13.

The Additional Info tab fields are used for the Payroll Ledger in Chapter 9.

PRO VERSION

Click the Purchase Invoices icon.

CLASSIC VIEW

From the Classic view Home window, click the Purchases icon  to open the Purchases Journal.

NOTES

If you click Add before typing the name, add the name when the ledger record opens.

Entering Cash Purchases in the Purchases Journal

Open the **Purchases Journal**.

✓ 6

Cash Purchase Invoice #ACA-3492 **Dated Aug. 3/15**

From All Campus Ads, $200 plus $26 HST for advertising brochures. Terms: cash on receipt. Invoice total $226 paid in full by cheque #173.

> **NOTES**
> Remember that we use the term *cash purchase* for purchases with payment by cheque.

Choose All Campus Ads from the Supplier drop-down list. **Press** tab.

We can now enter the transaction details as we did for previous purchases. We need to change the payment method because this is a cash purchase.

Click **Pay Later** in the Payment Method field to see the payment options:

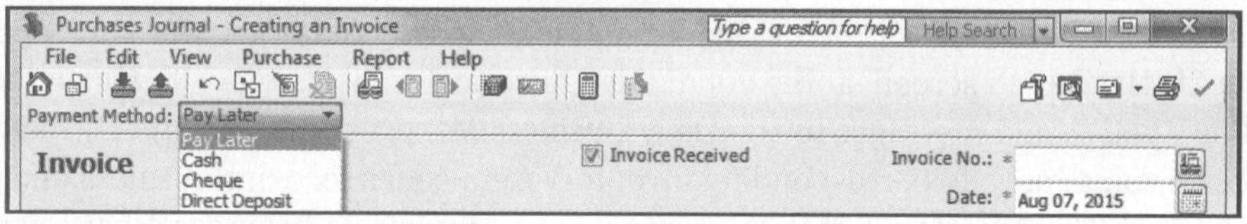

The payment options are the same as those in the Payments Journal for Other Payments, with the addition of Pay Later.

Click **Cheque**.

> **NOTES**
> The Net Days field is removed for the immediate payment, but discounts for early payment may still apply.

A cheque number field with the next cheque number is added in the upper right-hand corner of the invoice form. The cheque number is updated automatically. The account number and payment terms are added from the supplier record information we entered. You need to add the invoice number, transaction date and amount.

Click the **Invoice No. field** and **type** ACA-3492

Click the **Calendar icon** and **choose August 3**.

Click the **Amount field**.

Type 200 **Press** tab. Add a description to complete the invoice:

> **NOTES**
> Sometimes a business uses more than one bank account. If multiple accounts are set up, all bank accounts will be listed in the Paid From drop-down list. You can choose the appropriate bank account from the list for purchases by cheque and for payments. Credit cards, direct deposits and multiple bank accounts are used in later applications.

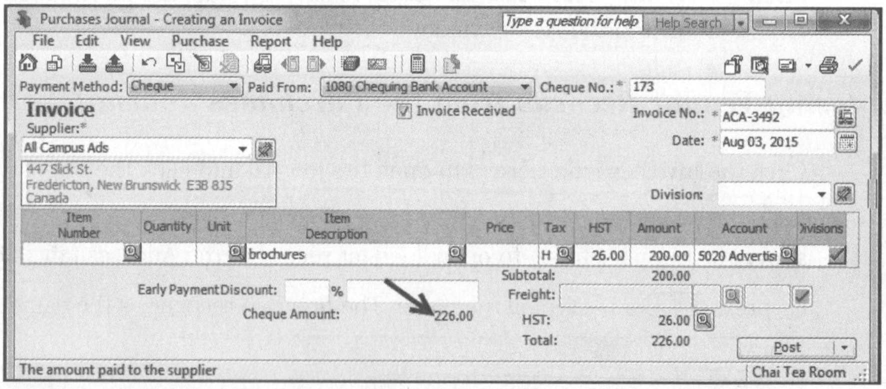

You should review the journal entry before posting it.

Choose the **Report menu** and **click Display Purchases Journal Entry**:

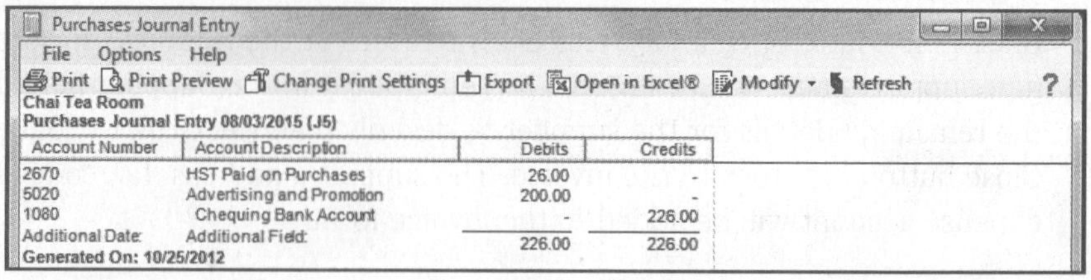

Chai Tea Room
Purchases Journal Entry 08/03/2015 (J5)

Account Number	Account Description	Debits	Credits
2670	HST Paid on Purchases	26.00	-
5020	Advertising and Promotion	200.00	-
1080	Chequing Bank Account	-	226.00
Additional Date:	Additional Field:	226.00	226.00

Generated On: 10/25/2012

This journal entry is the same as the one from the Payments Journal when we chose Make Other Payment. *Chequing Bank Account* is credited instead of *Accounts*

Payable. The supplier record is updated for the transaction by including both an invoice and a payment for the same date. Therefore, the method you choose for entering cash purchases — either in the Purchases Journal or as Other Payments in the Payments Journal — is a personal preference.

Close the **display**.

Check the **invoice** for errors and **make corrections** just as you would for regular purchases. When the information is correct,

Click **Post** [Post ▾] to save the transaction. **Click OK**.

NOTES
The Post button now includes a list arrow. From the drop-down list, you can select Print & Post instead of Post as your default. With this selection, you will print the cheque automatically when you enter the invoice.
This option is available only for cash purchases because they include cheques.

Adjusting a Posted Invoice

In the same way that you can correct or adjust a previously posted entry in the General Journal, you can edit a Purchases Journal invoice after posting. Sage 50 will create the necessary reversing entry when you post the revised invoice.

✓ 7 **Memo #13** **Dated Aug. 4/15**

From Owner: Adjust invoice #FG-642. The order received from Fundy Gift House was for 10 tea service sets for $900 plus $117 HST. The corrected invoice total is $1 017.

The Purchases Journal should still be open.

Click the **Adjust Invoice tool** or **choose** the **Purchase menu** and **click** **Adjust Invoice** to open the Search Purchase Invoices screen:

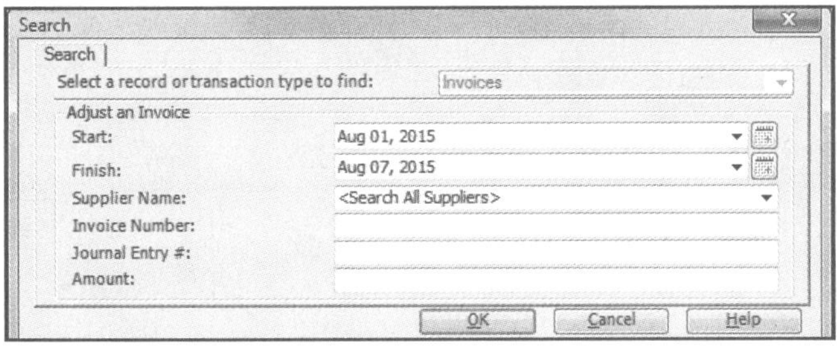

NOTES
You can also press ctrl + A to open the Adjust Invoice window from any journal. See Appendix B for a list of keyboard shortcuts.

NOTES
From the Home window, you can choose Adjust Invoice from the Invoices drop-down shortcuts list to open the Search window.

This is similar to the Search screen for the General Journal, but you have the additional option of searching for invoices by the name of the supplier. The program enters default start and finish dates. These dates can be edited like any other date fields or you can choose dates from the calendars. The default dates include all transactions for the journal, so we can accept them.

We will search all invoices by accepting the default to Search All Suppliers.

If you know the invoice, journal entry number or amount, you can enter this in the corresponding field and click OK to select the invoice directly.

Click **OK** to see the requested list of Purchases Journal invoices:

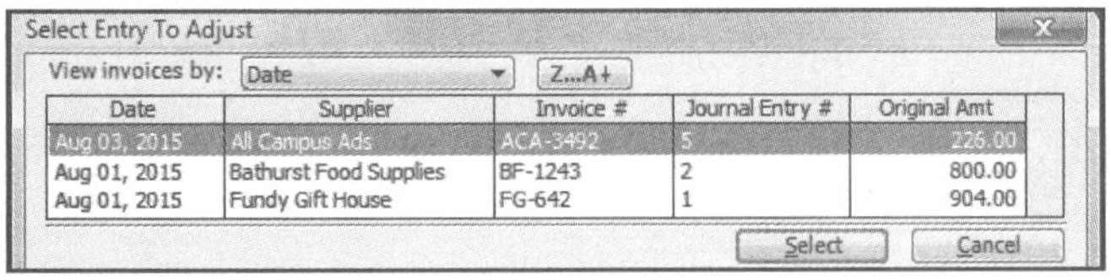

Select Entry To Adjust
View invoices by: Date
Z...A+
Date
Supplier
Invoice #
Journal Entry #
Original Amt
Aug 03, 2015 All Campus Ads ACA-3492 5 226.00
Aug 01, 2015 Bathurst Food Supplies BF-1243 2 800.00
Aug 01, 2015 Fundy Gift House FG-642 1 904.00
Select
Cancel

NOTES
Notice that the cash purchases entered in the Payments Journal are not included in this list. You can adjust these transactions from the Payments Journal after choosing Make Other Payment, or from the Payments icon Adjust Payment shortcut (see page 129).

Invoices are presented in order with the most recent one listed first and selected. The invoice that we need is Journal Entry #1, FG-642. You can change the order of the listed transactions by selecting from the **View Invoices By** drop-down list. You can list in order by date, supplier, invoice number, journal entry number or amount. And you can reverse the order of any list by clicking the [Z...A+] button.

Click **FG-642**. (Click anywhere on the line to highlight the invoice.)

Click **Select** or **double-click** the **entry** to recall the selected transaction:

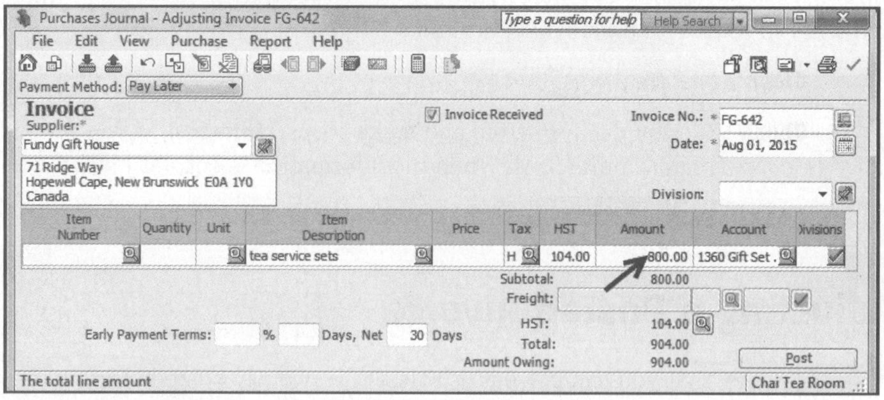

All fields are available for editing. We need to edit the amount.

Click **800.00** in the Amount field.

Type 900

Press tab to update the tax amount and totals.

You can add -R to the invoice number to indicate that this is the revised invoice.

Your completed entry should now resemble the following:

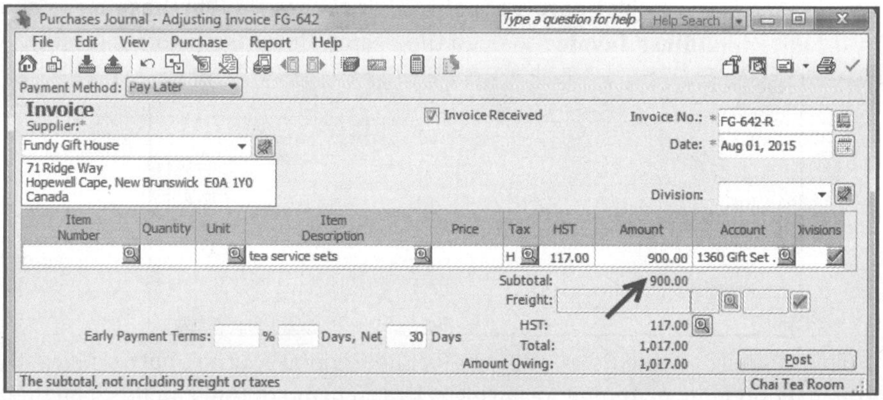

If you change the supplier, you will see a warning:

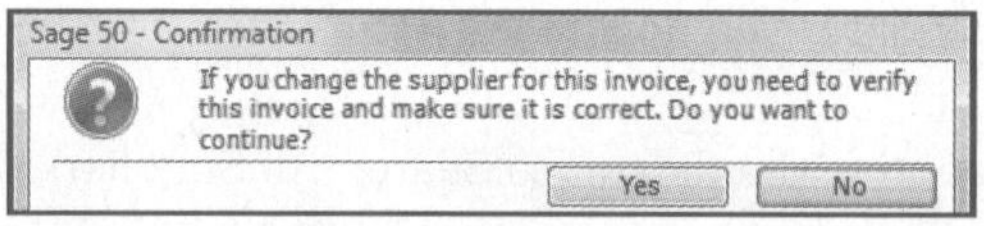

Before posting the revised transaction, review it for accuracy.

Choose the **Report menu** and **click Display Purchases Journal Entry**:

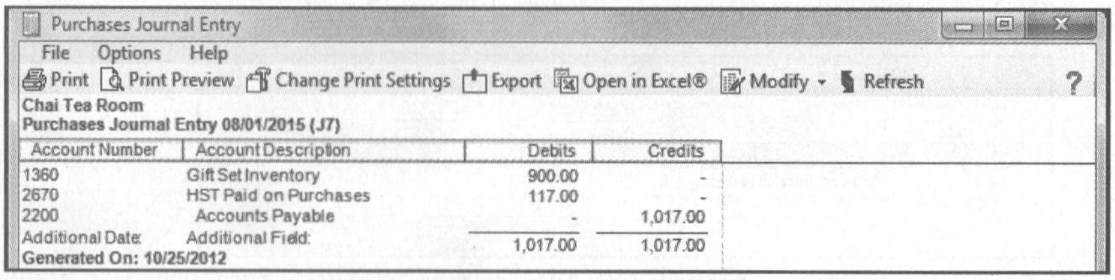

Chai Tea Room
Purchases Journal Entry 08/01/2015 (J7)

Account Number	Account Description	Debits	Credits
1360	Gift Set Inventory	900.00	-
2670	HST Paid on Purchases	117.00	-
2200	Accounts Payable	-	1,017.00
Additional Date:	Additional Field:	1,017.00	1,017.00

Generated On: 10/25/2012

Although only one journal entry is shown, three entries are connected with this transaction — J1, the first one that was incorrect, J6, the second one created by Sage 50 to reverse the incorrect entry and J7, the final correct one you see displayed. All use the original posting date unless you change the date for the adjustment. The previous transaction we posted was entry #5 (see page 126).

NOTES

The Post button for Pay Later invoices does not have a list arrow with the option to print.

You can still print the invoice from the File menu Print option or from the Print tool.

NOTES

When you change the supplier, the default settings for the previously selected supplier will still be used. Check your entry carefully before posting.

To change the supplier, it is easier and safer to reverse the invoice and then enter it correctly. Refer to page 139.

NOTES

If you edit the date, the final correct entry will be posted with the revised date. To see all three entries in the journal report, Corrections must be selected (see page 147).

Close the **report display** when you have finished and **make** additional **corrections** if necessary.

Click the **Post button**, **click OK** and **close** the **Purchases Journal**.

> NOTES
> The confirmation message shows that two journal entries were posted.

CORRECTING CASH PURCHASES AND PAYMENTS FROM THE PAYMENTS JOURNAL

Purchases entered as Other Payments in the Payments Journal do not appear on the Search Purchase Invoices list from the Purchases Journal. You can, however, adjust these other payments from the Payments Journal as follows:

- **Click** the Home window **Payments icon shortcuts list arrow**, and **click Adjust Payment**.
- **Select** your search parameters: the **date range**, **supplier** or **cheque number**. **Click OK**.
- **Click** the **cheque/invoice** you want to adjust. All cheques used to pay invoices and cash purchases will appear on this list.
- **Double-click** the **entry** or **click Select** to open the cheque.
- **Make** the **corrections**. **Review** your **entry** and **post** the revised transaction.
- If the **Payments Journal** is already open, **click Make Other Payment** from the transaction list if you want to adjust a cash purchase payment.
- **Click Pay Invoices** from the transaction list if you want to adjust a cheque used to pay invoices.
- **Click** the **Adjust Payment** or **Adjust Other Payment tool** or **choose** the **Payment menu** and **click Adjust Payment** or **Adjust Other Payment**.
- **Select** your search parameters. **Click OK** to open the list of cheques. Your list will include either payment or cash purchase (other payment) cheques, depending on the type of transaction you started from.
- **Make** the **corrections**. **Review** your **entry** and **post** the revised transaction.

Refer to page 137 for detailed instructions on correcting a payment cheque.

Entering Discounts for Early Payments

Entering discounts for early payments is very much like entering regular payments. The discounts show up automatically when the invoices and dates are correct.

✓ 8 **Payment Cheque #174** **Dated Aug. 4/15**

To Bathurst Food Supplies, $792 in payment of account, including $8 discount for early payment. Reference invoice #BF-1044.

Click the **Payments icon** to open the Payments Journal.

Choose Bathurst Food Supplies from the list to display the outstanding invoices:

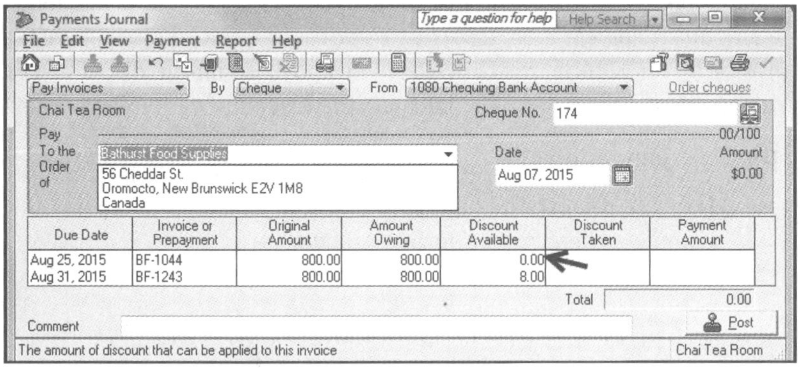

> NOTES
> The Payments Journal shows the due date for the invoice, the net 30 date that is 30 days after the invoice date of July 26 for invoice #BF-1044.

Initially, no discount is available for invoice #BF-1044 because the session date is beyond the discount period, that is, more than 10 days past the July 26 invoice date.

The discount shows for the second invoice because the session date lies within its 10-day discount period.

Enter **August 4** as the date of the payment. **Press** (tab).

Both discounts are now available because the payment date falls within the 10-day discount period for them:

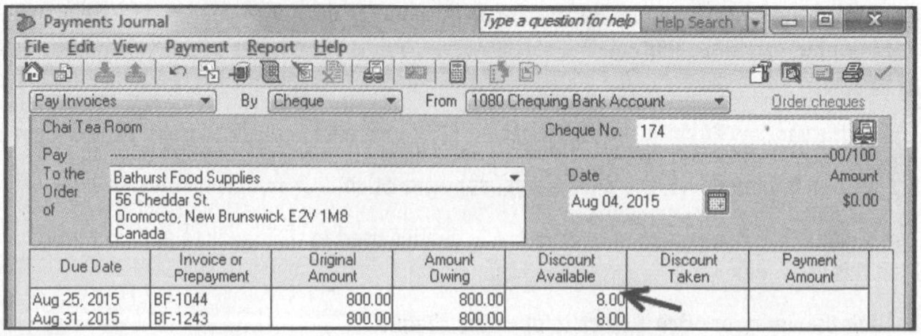

Press (tab) **twice** to advance to the Discount Taken field and enter the amount.

Press (tab) to advance to the Payment Amount field and accept the discount.

Notice that the discount has been subtracted from the invoice amount.

Press (tab) to accept the amount in the Payment Amount field and update the total and the cheque portion of the journal as shown:

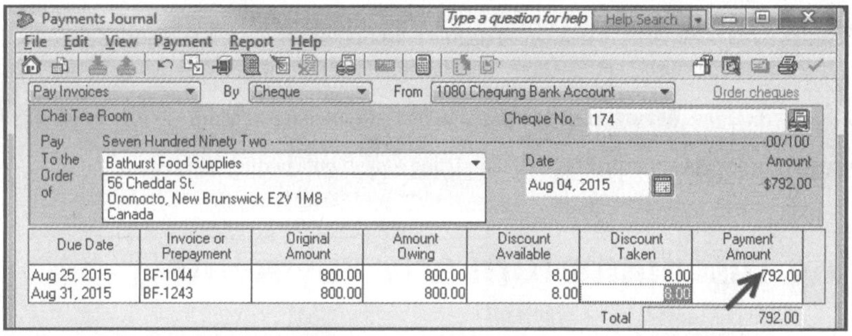

At this stage, a discount amount is entered for the second invoice, but this invoice is not being paid. Therefore you must delete this entry to avoid adding it to the invoice.

Press (ctrl) + **J** to see the payment as you have it entered so far:

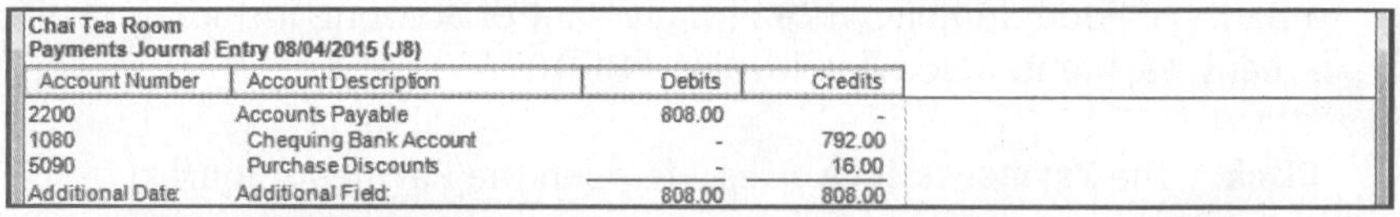
Chai Tea Room
Payments Journal Entry 08/04/2015 (J8)

Account Number	Account Description	Debits	Credits
2200	Accounts Payable	808.00	-
1080	Chequing Bank Account	-	792.00
5090	Purchase Discounts	-	16.00
Additional Date:	Additional Field:	808.00	808.00

WARNING!

If a second discount amount is displayed, you must delete it. It will be included in the journal entry even though the total payment and cheque amount appear correct. If you post at this stage, the discount will be accepted and included.

If you do not delete this second discount, your entry will be posted as shown. Both discount amounts are included — the *Purchase Discounts* amount is $16 instead of $8. The cheque amount is correct, but *Accounts Payable* is reduced by $808 instead of $800, the invoice amount. If the next invoice is not paid within the discount period, its balance owing would be shown as $792 because the discount was already taken.

Close the **journal display**.

Press (del) to remove the highlighted second discount taken amount and complete the payment form as shown:

WARNING!

Do not press (tab) after deleting the discount because this will add an amount paid for the second invoice. To be safe, you can click anywhere in the upper cheque portion of the form.

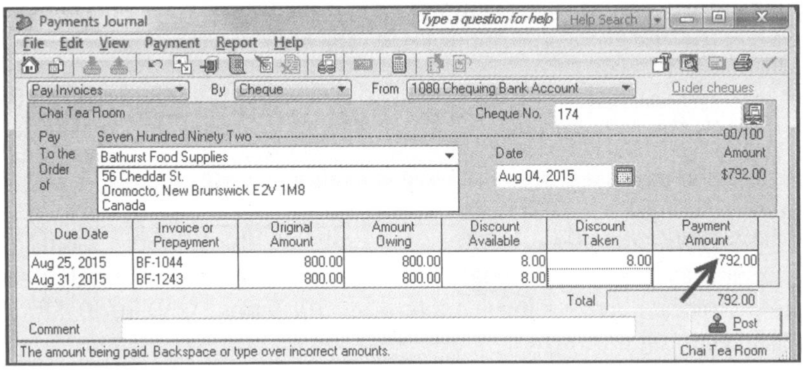

Choose the **Report menu** and **click Display Payments Journal Entry** to review the transaction before posting:

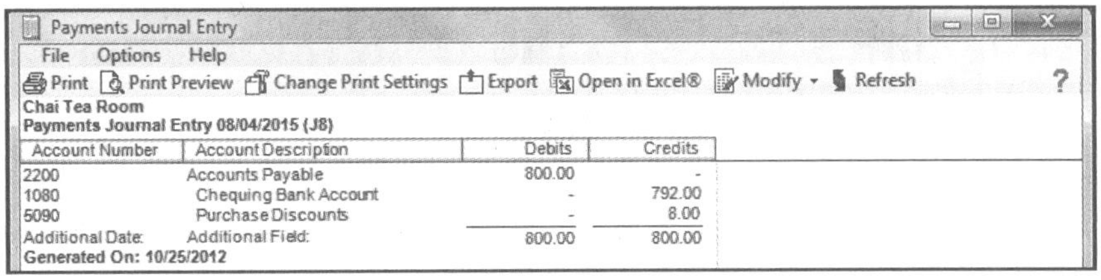

In the related journal entry, the program has now updated the General Ledger *Accounts Payable* control account for the full amount of the invoice and reduced the balance owing to the supplier by the same amount. The amount taken from *Chequing Bank Account* is the actual amount of the payment, taking the single discount amount into consideration. The discount amount is automatically debited to the linked *Purchase Discounts* account. *Purchase Discounts* is a contra-expense account. It has a credit balance, so it reduces total expense and increases income.

Close the **display** to return to the Payments Journal input screen and **correct** your **work** if necessary. (Refer to page 119 for assistance.)

Post the **transaction**. **Click OK**. **Close** the **Payments Journal**.

> **NOTES**
> If a second discount is not displayed, you can skip the step of deleting the discount amount.
> Notice that the status bar message advises you how to enter or change the amounts.

Using Continue to Enter New Suppliers

Sometimes you may want to include the name of a supplier in the journal record without creating a supplier record. In these situations, you can use the Continue feature. For the cheque to Tomailik, a cash purchase, we will use this approach.

✓ 9

Cash Purchase Invoice #BT-100 **Dated Aug. 7/15**

From Bette Tomailik (choose Continue for the new supplier), $50 as compensation to cover cost of dry cleaning for wine spilled by waiter. Issue cheque #175. Charge to General Expense account. No tax is applied on this transaction.

Click the **Invoices icon** 

to open the Purchases Journal.

Click the **Supplier field** and **type** `Bette Tomailik`

Press (tab) to open the message about a new supplier name:

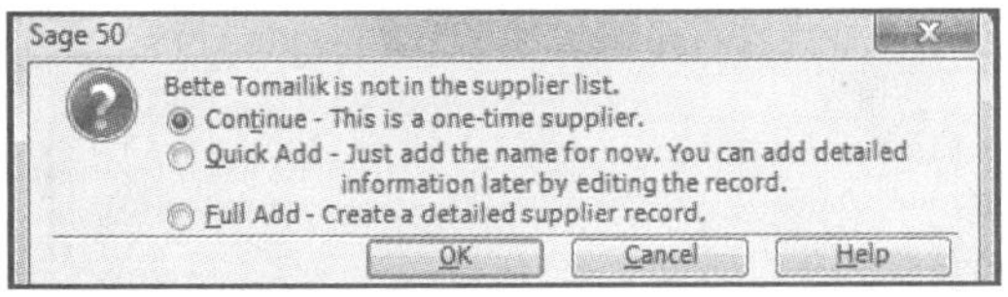

> **NOTES**
> When you choose One-Time Supplier, you can type the supplier's name in the Address field. The supplier's name will not be included in journal reports.

> **NOTES**
> Pay Later is not an option when you choose Continue or One-Time Supplier. Only immediate payment is allowed – Cash and Cheque. Cash is the default.

NOTES
When you choose Continue for a new supplier in the Make Other Payment journal, the name is not added to the journal entry.

WARNING!
Remember to change the payment method for the Sunbury Cleaning invoice to Pay Later and to store the entry before posting.

CLASSIC VIEW
Users who are more familiar with Sage 50 may prefer to work from the Classic view. You can access all journals and ledgers from a single Home window.

PRO VERSION
You will not see the entry for Time & Billing in the list of links.

Click **OK** to return to the journal. (Continue was already selected.) **Press** tab. Cash is the default payment method when you choose Continue.

Choose **Cheque** as the Payment Method and then **enter** the **remaining details** of the cash purchase as usual. **Review** and **post** the **transaction**.

Enter the **purchase** from **Sunbury Cleaning**.

10

Purchase Invoice #SC-701 **Dated Aug. 7/15**
From Sunbury Cleaning Company, $250 plus $32.50 HST for weekly cleaning of store premises. Purchase invoice total $282.50. Terms: 1/30, n/60. Store as a weekly recurring transaction.

Close the **Purchases Journal**.

Entering Sales Taxes in the General Journal

The sales summary on August 7 is entered in the General Journal because Chai does not use the Receivables Ledger. When you set up and link sales tax accounts, you can add General Journal sales tax entries to the tax reports. A Sales Taxes button becomes available when you use one of these linked tax accounts in the General Journal. Chai has two linked tax accounts, *HST Charged on Sales* and *HST Paid on Purchases*.

The General Journal is accessed from the Company module window that we used in the previous two chapters.

To open the Company module window, click Company in the list of modules in the upper left-hand Modules pane. Click the General Journal icon.

Instead, we will create a shortcut to open the General Journal.

Creating Shortcuts

Click **Customize** in the Shortcuts pane below the modules as shown:

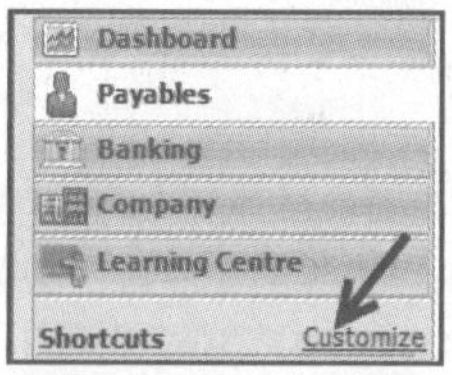

The Customize Shortcuts window opens:

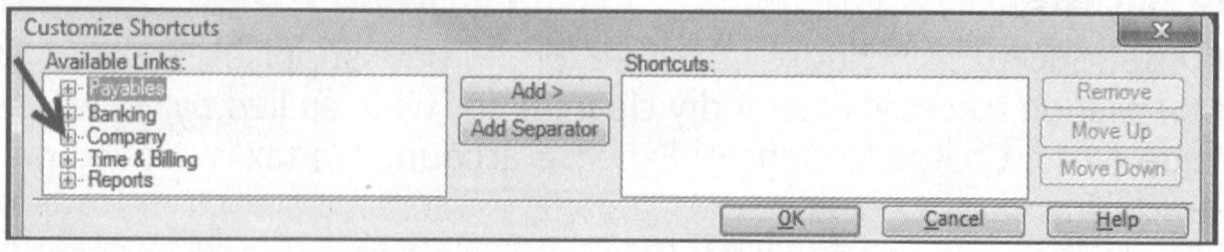

Click the ⊞ beside **Company** to expand the list of Company tasks:

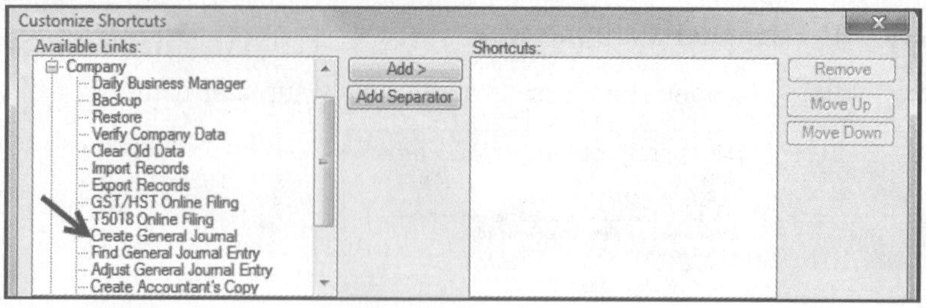

You can create up to 10 shortcuts for each user. The expanded list for each module shows the items for which you can create shortcuts. Once you create it, you can click the name in the Shortcuts pane to access that journal or task directly.

Click **Create General Journal** in the list of Company tasks.

Click **Add >** to move this task to the Shortcuts box as shown:

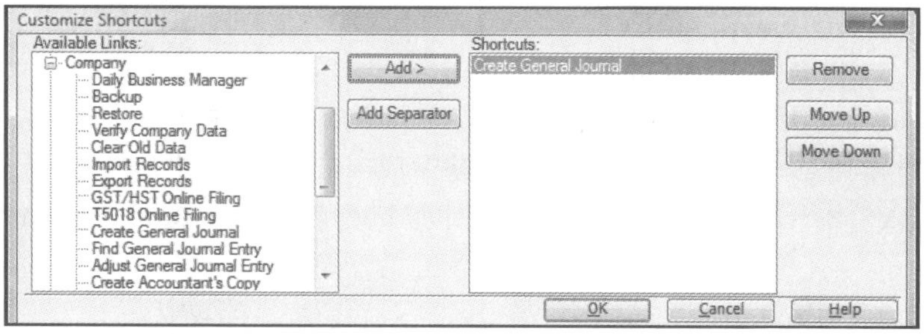

Click **OK** to return to the Home window. Create General Journal now appears in the Home window Shortcuts pane as shown:

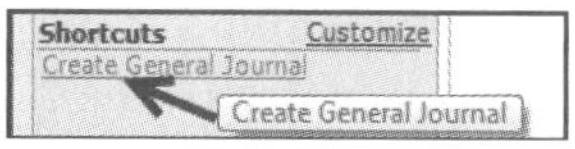

Click **Create General Journal** in the Shortcuts pane. The General Journal opens immediately. This shortcut will be available in all module Home windows.

> **NOTES**
> You can remove a shortcut if it is not needed. Just click Customize in the Home window. Click the shortcut in the Shortcuts pane and click Remove and OK.

✓ 11

Cash Sales Receipt #34 **Dated Aug. 7/15**

From tea room customers (tapes #5001–5380), $7 600 plus $988 HST for tea room sales and services. Total receipts $8 588 deposited in bank.

> **NOTES**
> Use the General Journal for sales in this application. We will introduce the Sales Journal in Chapter 6.

Enter the **Source** and **Comment** for the sale. The session date is correct.

Choose **Chequing Bank Account** as the account to be debited and **type** 8588 as the amount. **Enter** an appropriate **Comment** for the account.

Choose **HST Charged on Sales** as the account. Advance to the credit column.

Type 988 as the amount to be credited. **Press** *tab*. Your screen should now resemble the one shown here:

> **NOTES**
> Follow the keystroke instructions for the General Journal from the Muriel's Murals application starting on page 36.

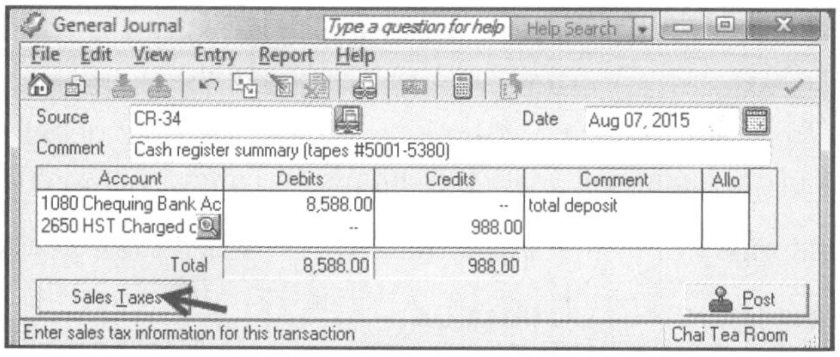

The Sales Taxes button became available as soon as you entered the tax amount.

Click the **Sales Taxes button** to open the tax detail screen:

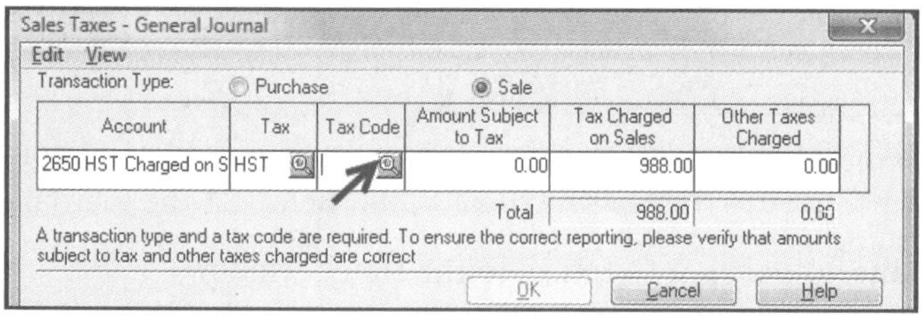

NOTES

HST Charged on Sales is the linked tax account for sales. When you enter HST Paid on Purchases as the account, Purchase will be selected as the default transaction type because this account is linked to the Payables module.

Because you entered *HST Charged on Sales* as the account, the transaction is recognized as a sale. You can change the transaction type if it is not correct. The account and tax amount are already entered on the form. We need to add the tax code.

Click the **List icon** in the Tax Code field to open the tax code list:

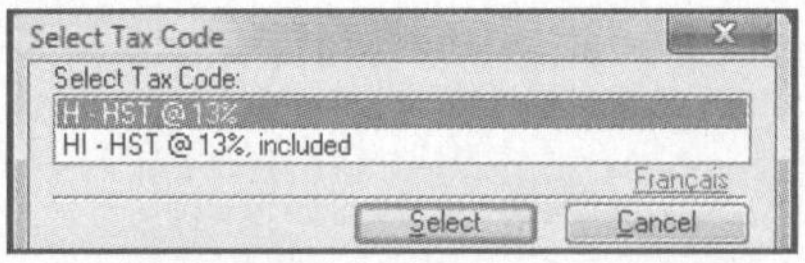

The same two HST codes we saw in the Purchases and Payments journals are available. Sales have HST at 13 percent added to the price, so the correct code is H.

Click **Select** because code H is already highlighted. You will return to the tax detail screen:

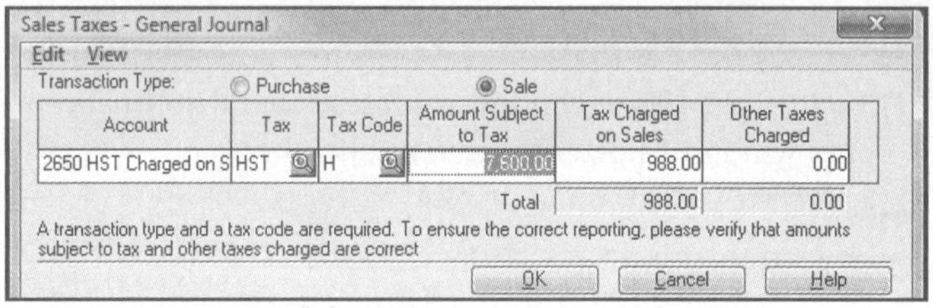

Because the tax amount was already entered, the sales amount — the Amount Subject To Tax — is calculated as soon as you select the tax code. The sales amount is correct so we can continue. If the amount is not correct because there are other taxes included, you can edit the default amount and enter an amount for Other Taxes Charged.

Click **OK**.

Enter a **Comment** for the tax line and then add the final account line — **choose** account **4100**, accept the amount and **add** an appropriate **comment** to complete your journal entry as shown here:

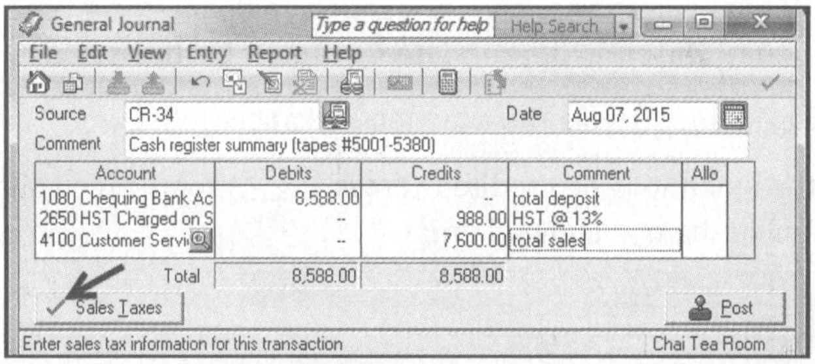

Notice that the Sales Taxes button has a ✓ on it to indicate that tax details have been added. Clicking the button again will show the details and allow you to edit them.

Review the **journal entry** and then **close** the **display**. When the entry is correct,

Click the **Post button** Post. **Click OK**.

If you forgot to enter the tax codes for *HST Charged on Sales*, you will see the warning message to confirm you do not want to add tax details:

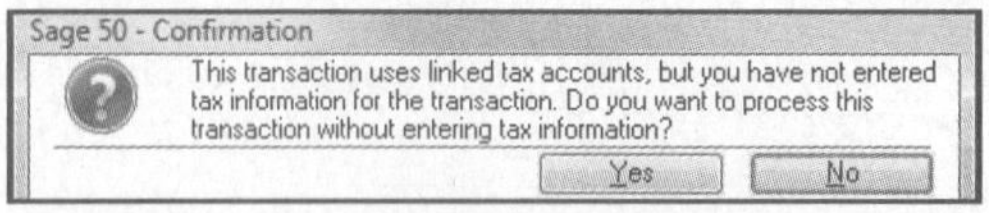

If you forgot to add the tax details, click No to cancel posting and open the Sales Taxes window. Add the missing details and then post the journal entry.

Close the **General Journal** to return to the Home window.

Advance the **session date** to **August 14**. **Back up** your **data file** when prompted.

Recalling a Stored Entry

The first journal entry for the August 14 session date is the recurring purchase from Bathurst Food Supplies. Since we have stored this purchase, we do not need to re-enter all the information.

✓ 12

Purchase Invoice #BF-2100 **Dated Aug. 8/15**

From Bathurst Food Supplies, $800 (no HST) for pastries, breads, condiments and other foods. Terms: 1/10, n/30. Recall stored entry.

Click the **Invoices icon** to open the Journal.

Click the **Recall tool** in the tool bar (or **choose** the **Purchase menu** and **click Recall**) to display the Recall Recurring Transaction dialogue box:

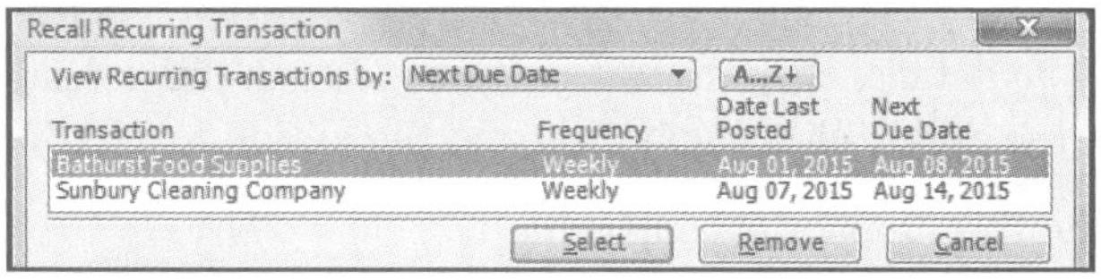

> **NOTES**
> You can press ctrl + R to recall a stored entry.

The stored entries are listed in order according to the next date that they will be repeated. If you want, you can display the stored entries in a different order.

Click the **View Recurring Transactions By list arrow** to see the options:

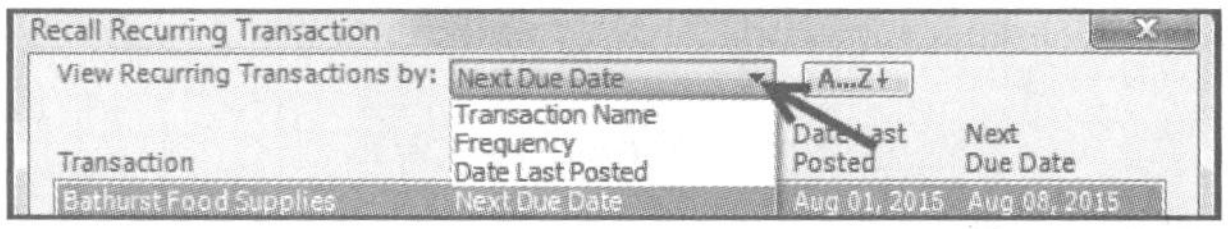

You can choose to view the stored entries in order by Transaction Name (which is the supplier's name if you did not change the default), by Frequency (how often the transaction is repeated), by the Date Last Posted or by the Next Due Date. If you have a large number of stored entries, it may be easier to find the one you need with a different order. You can also reverse the order for any of the order selections with the A...Z+ button. Since we have only two stored entries, the default order, Next Due Date, placed the one we want first. Do not change the default.

From the Recall Stored Entry dialogue box, you can remove an entry that is incorrect or no longer needed. Click an entry to select it. Click Remove and then click Yes to confirm that you want to delete the entry. (See page 444.)

Bathurst Food Supplies, the name of the entry we want to use, should be selected because it is the recurring entry that is due next.

Click **Bathurst Food Supplies** if it is not already selected.

Click **Select** or **press** enter to return to the Purchases Journal.

The entry we stored is displayed just as we entered it the first time, except that the date has been changed to one week past the previous posting date, as needed, and the Invoice field is blank so we can enter the new invoice number. Remember that Sage 50 does not accept duplicate invoice numbers.

Click the **Invoice No. field** to move the cursor.

Type `BF-2100` to complete the entry. You should review it before posting.

Choose the **Report menu** and **click Display Purchases Journal Entry**.

Close the **display** when finished and **make** any necessary **corrections**.

Click the **Post button** Post. **Click OK** and then **close** the **journal**.

Editing Supplier Information

The Home window Suppliers pane has the option to hide or display account phone numbers and balances. There may be times when it is appropriate to hide these details for security purposes.

> **PRO VERSION**
> Remember that the term Vendors will replace the term Suppliers.

Click the button above the Suppliers list to see the options:

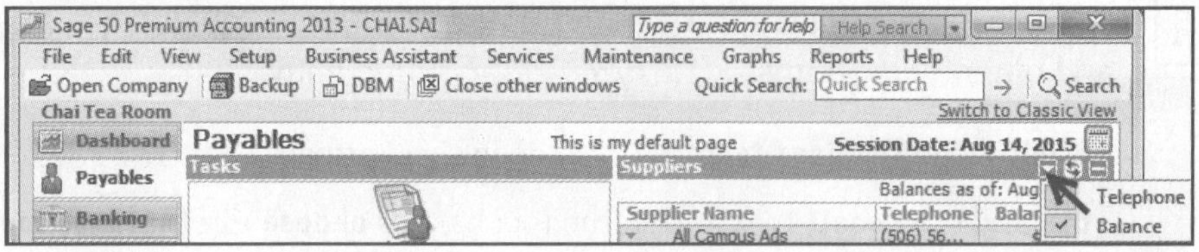

Checkmarks indicate that the information is displayed.

To hide the additional details, click the button and click the detail you want to hide. To restore the detail, click the button and the option to add the ✓.

To refresh or update the supplier balance amounts, click .

Click to hide the entire suppliers list. Click to restore the list.

> **NOTES**
> You can open the Suppliers window by clicking the Suppliers icon in the Home window in either the Classic or the Enhanced view. From the Suppliers window, double-click the supplier you want to open the record at the Address tab screen.

Sometimes a supplier record must be revised after it is saved because the initial information has changed or because information initially unavailable is now known. We need to edit the record for NB Gas to add the default expense account.

✓ 13

Memo #14 **Dated Aug. 9/15**

From Owner: Edit the supplier record for NB Gas to include the default expense account. Create a new Group account 5110 Heating Expense.

Supplier records are accessed from the Suppliers icon shortcuts list, the Suppliers list or the Suppliers window. The list arrow beside the supplier in the Suppliers list pane also has shortcuts for several tasks for the selected vendor. The journal or ledger will open with that supplier and task already selected. The drop-down shortcuts list with the Suppliers icon also has several options. As shown here, both provide access to supplier records:

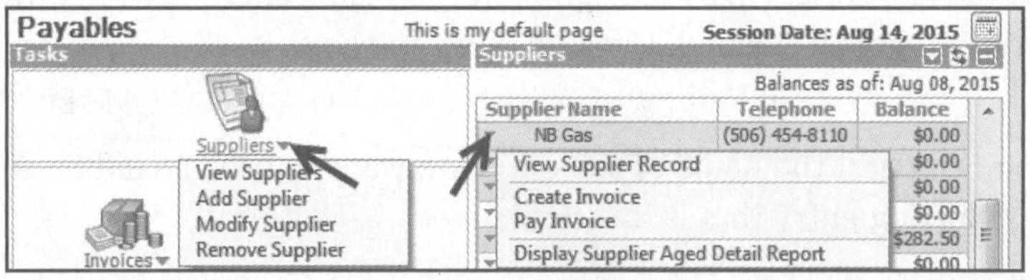

Click **NB Gas** in the Suppliers list (or click its list arrow and select View Supplier Record) to open the Address tab information screen. Or,

Click the **Suppliers icon shortcuts list arrow** and **click Modify Supplier** to open the Search Suppliers window:

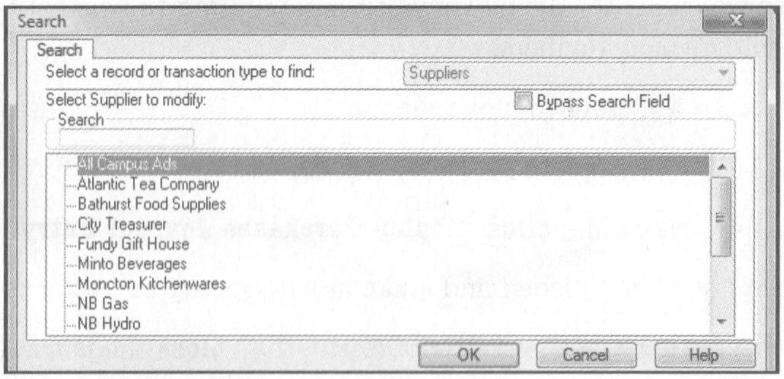

Each supplier on record is listed on the Search Suppliers selection window. Suppliers is entered as the search area. Notice that Bette Tomailik is not listed.

Double-click **NB Gas** to open the Address tab information screen.

Click the **Options tab** to access the Expense Account field:

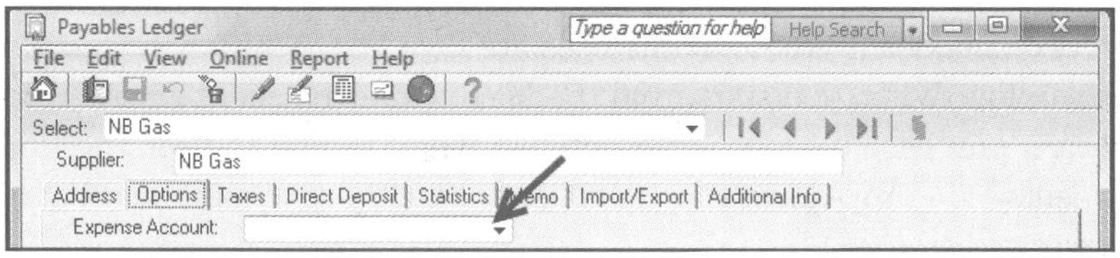

Click the **Expense Account field.**

You can choose an account from the list provided by the list arrow, type the account number or add a new account. We need to create an account.

Type 5110 **Press** *tab* and then **click Add** to start the Add Account wizard. **Enter Heating Expense** as the account name and accept the remaining default settings. **Click Finish** to return to the Ledger.

Click **Save And Close** [Save and Close] to close the Payables Ledger (supplier record) window to return to the Payables module window.

Click **Pay Expenses** from the Payments icon shortcuts list to open the Payments Journal or **click** the **Invoices icon**.

Enter the **cash purchase from NB Gas**; the account will appear automatically.

14 **Cash Purchase Invoice #NBG-559932** **Dated Aug. 9/15**

From NB Gas, $200 plus $26 HST for monthly supply of natural gas on equal billing method. Invoice total $226 paid in full by cheque #176. Because equal billing applies, store as a monthly recurring entry.

NOTES

Remember that although the field is named Expense Account, you can choose any postable account as the default for the supplier. You can also select a different account in the journal if necessary.

Adjusting a Posted Payment

Just as you can correct a purchase invoice after posting, you can correct a cheque that has been posted.

Choose **Pay Invoices** from the Payments transaction list in the Payments Journal. Open the Payments Journal first if necessary.

PRO VERSION

Choose Pay Purchase Invoices in the transaction list.

✓ 15 **Memo #15** **Dated Aug. 9/15**

From Owner: Adjust cheque #171 to Fundy Gift House. The cheque amount was $600 in partial payment of invoice #FG-361.

Click the **Adjust Payment tool** or **choose** the **Payment menu** and **click Adjust Payment** to open the Search screen for Adjust Payments:

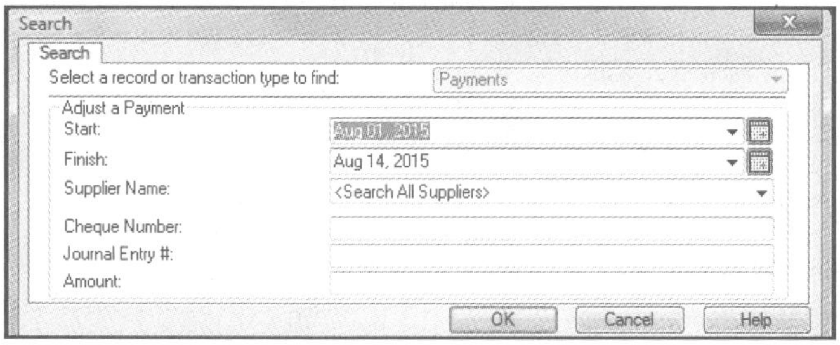

NOTES

Pressing *ctrl* + A will also open the Search window to begin the adjusting procedure.

Again we see the familiar Search window for the selected journal.

Click **OK** to see the list of cheques already posted for this date range:

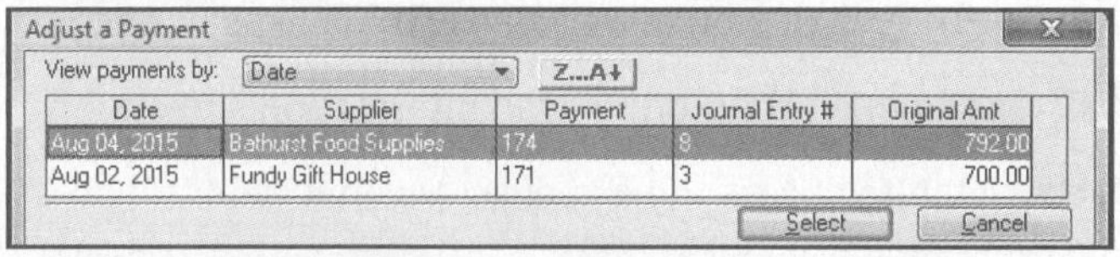

Only the two cheques used to pay invoices are listed because we started from the Pay Invoices window. When you start from the Make Other Payment window, you will see only the cash purchase payment transactions. When you begin from the Home window Payments icon drop-down shortcuts list, both Other Payment and Pay Invoice transactions will be listed.

Double-click **Fundy Gift House** to see the cheque we posted:

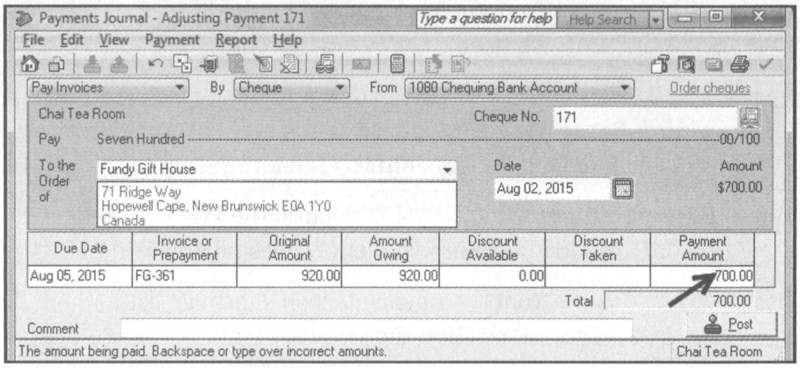

The cheque appears as it was completed. You can edit all the details.

Click **700.00** in the Payment Amount field.

Type `600`

Click the **Comment field**.

Type `previous chq amount incorrectly entered`

Check your **work** carefully. **Click** **Post** to save the changes:

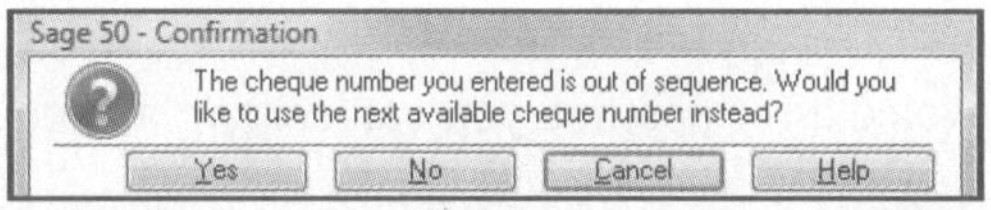

A message about the cheque number being out of sequence appears because we have already used this cheque number. The cheque number is correct so we should continue without changing it.

Click **No** to accept the number and continue.

Sage 50 will create an entry that reverses the original payment, and the original entry is also saved for a complete audit trail.

If you change a payment by selecting a different supplier, Sage 50 advises you that the original payment will be reversed and a new one created:

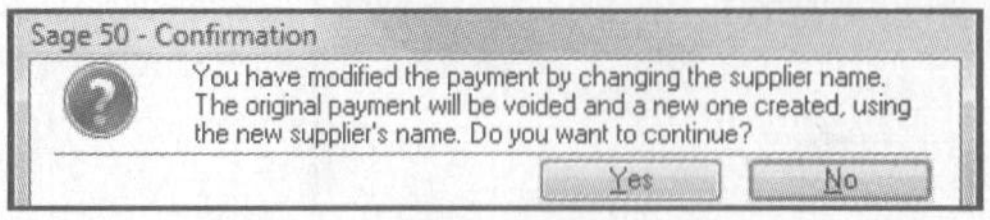

Click Yes to accept the changes or No to cancel the supplier change.

Enter the next group of three **transactions**.

NOTES

When you choose Adjust Payment from the Home window Payments icon shortcuts list, you will see the list of all cheques, those used to pay invoices and those for other payments.

NOTES

Notice that cash purchases entered in the Payments Journal are not included in this list. You can adjust these transactions from the Payments Journal after you select Make Other Payment (see page 129).

NOTES

If you cannot reprint the cheque using the same cheque number, you should click Yes to change the number.

NOTES

If you change the supplier for a cheque, Sage 50 will void the original cheque and create a new one for the revised supplier. You will be warned of this action so you can confirm the change or cancel it before it is made.

16 **Cash Purchase Invoice #NBH-45321** **Dated Aug. 9/15**

From NB Hydro, $120 plus $15.60 HST for one month of hydro service. Invoice total $135.60 paid in full by cheque #177.

17 **Payment Cheque #178** **Dated Aug. 10/15**

To Bathurst Food Supplies, $792 in payment of account, including $8 discount for early payment. Reference invoice #BF-1243.

WARNING!
Remember to delete the discount taken amount for the second invoice.

18 **Cash Purchase Invoice #SK-6110** **Dated Aug. 12/15**

From Moncton Kitchenwares, $180 plus $23.40 HST for pots, pans and kitchen utensils. Invoice total $203.40 paid in full by cheque #179.

Reversing a Posted Purchase Entry

The cash purchase for Moncton Kitchenwares selected an incorrect supplier. We will reverse this entry rather than adjust it because the default details such as account or payment terms may also be incorrect. These details do not change when you adjust the invoice by selecting a different supplier. Refer to the Confirmation message on page 128.

Any journal that has an Adjust option also has the option to reverse an entry. You can also use the Lookup feature to begin.

The journal you used to enter the purchase should still be open, either the Payments Journal with Make Other Payment selected or the Purchases Journal. In each case, you can follow the steps below.

✓ 19 **Memo #16** **Dated Aug. 12/15**

Cash Purchase Invoice #SK-6110 was entered for an incorrect supplier. The purchase was from Sweeney's Kitchenwares, a new supplier. Reverse the original entry.

Click the **Look Up Other Payment tool** in the Payments Journal with Make Other Payment selected, or the **Look Up An Invoice tool** in the Purchases Journal. Or

Click the **Adjust Other Payment (Adjust An Invoice) tool** to open the Search screen.

Click **OK** to see the list of cheques (or purchases) already posted.

Double-click **Moncton Kitchenwares** to see the cash purchase.

The Reverse tool in the tool bar is now available.

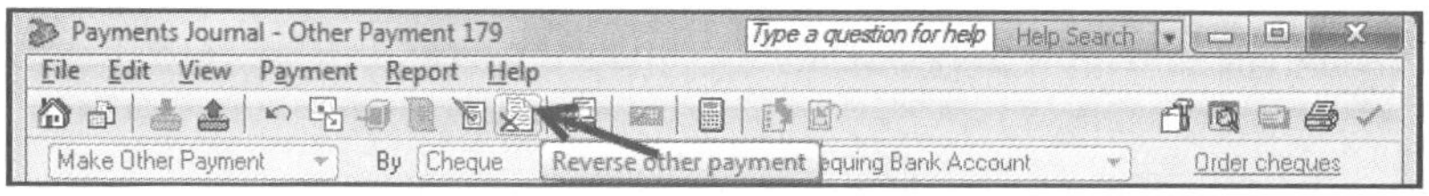

Click the **Reverse tool**, or **choose** the **Payment** (or **Purchase**) **menu** and **click** **Reverse Other Payment** (or **Invoice**) to see the confirmation:

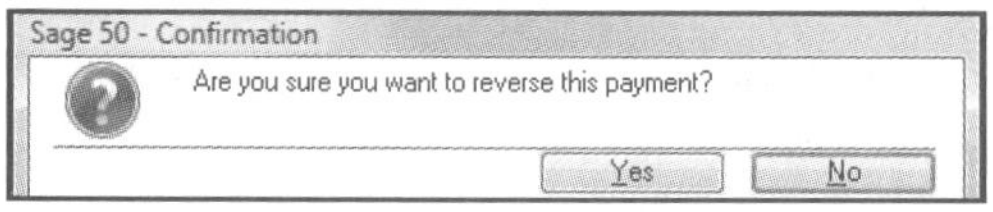

Click **Yes** to confirm.

NOTES
The Receipts Journal Report in Chapter 6, page 177, shows the two entries that result when you reverse a transaction.

NOTES
Sweeney's Kitchenwares
(contact Tracey Potts)
44 Panning Ave.
Grand Sault, NB E3Y 1E1
Tel: (800) 566-7521
Web: www.sweeneys.com
Terms: net 1
Expense account: 1560
Tax code: H - HST @ 13%

Sage 50 will create the entry that reverses the original one automatically. You can see both the original and the reversing entry in the journal report when you choose Show Corrections.

Click **OK**. Sage 50 confirms that the entry was successfully reversed.

Enter the **purchase** for the correct supplier this time.

20

Cash Purchase Invoice SK-6110 **Dated Aug. 12/15**

From Sweeney's Kitchenwares (use Full Add for the new supplier), for $180 plus $23.40 HST for pots, pans and kitchen utensils. Invoice total $203.40 paid in full by cheque #180.

Changing a Stored Entry

The next entry is the purchase from Sunbury Cleaning Company. Chai will be invoiced on a monthly basis and the rates have also increased. Therefore, we need to update the stored entry. If a change is for a single purchase and will not be repeated, edit the entry after recalling it but do not store the entry again.

✓ 21

Purchase Invoice #SC-1219 **Dated Aug. 14/15**

From Sunbury Cleaning Company, $1 200 plus $156 HST for one month of store cleaning services as per new contract. Purchase invoice total $1 356. Terms: 1/30, n/60. Recall the stored transaction. Edit the amount and store the revised transaction as a monthly recurring entry.

Click the **Invoices icon** in the Payables window to open the Journal.

Click the **Recall tool** on the tool bar, or **choose** the **Purchase menu** and **click Recall** to display the Recall Recurring Transaction dialogue box.

Double-click **Sunbury Cleaning Company**, the entry we want to use to display the purchase entry with the new date.

Click the **Invoice No. field** so you can add the invoice number.

Type SC-1219

Click **250.00**, the Amount, to highlight it so that you can edit it. Double-click if necessary to select the amount.

Type 1200

Press *tab* to enter the change.

Review the **journal entry** as usual to make sure that it is correct before proceeding.

Click the **Store button**, or **choose** the **Purchase menu** and **click Store**.

Choose **Monthly** as the new frequency and accept the name without change.

The following warning appears:

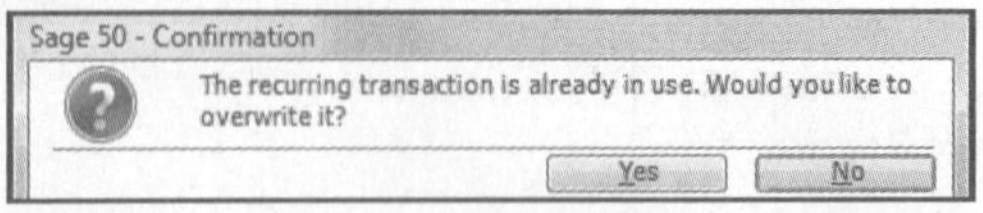

Click **Yes** to confirm that you want to replace the previous stored version and return to the Purchases Journal.

Click the **Post button** [Post] to save the entry. **Click OK** and **close** the **Journal**.

Enter the **remaining journal transactions** for August.

22

MINTO BEVERAGES
www.mintobev.com

910 Lemone Ave.
Bathurst, NB E2A 4X3
Phone: (506) 622-3188 Toll free: (800) 622-2881

Invoice: MB-6111
Delivery Date: Aug. 14, 2015
Sold to: Chai Tea Room
125 King St.
Fredericton, NB E3B 2P4
(506) 454-6111

Date	Description	Tax Code	Amount
Aug 14/15	Bottled spring water (20 cases)	1	200.00
Aug 14/15	Natural fruit beverages (10 cases)	1	400.00
	Thank you.		

Signature	Payment Terms: Net 30 days	HST	0.00
Sarah Pinto	Business No.: 901 200 862	TOTAL	600.00

23 **Bank Debit Memo #AT-53186** **Dated Aug. 14/15**

From Atlantic Trust, withdrawals from bank account for bi-weekly payroll:

Wages, including payroll taxes	$3 200.00
Payroll services	40.00
HST Paid on Purchases (payroll services)	5.20

24 **Cash Sales Receipt #35** **Dated Aug. 14/15**

From tea room customers (tapes #5381–5750), $7 400 plus $962 HST for tea room sales and services. Total receipts $8 362 deposited in bank.

SESSION DATE – AUGUST 21, 2015

25 **Purchase Invoice #BF-2987** **Dated Aug. 15/15**

From Bathurst Food Supplies, $800 weekly invoice for pastries, breads, condiments and other foods. Terms: 1/10, n/30. Recall the stored entry.

26 **Cash Purchase Invoice #VCW-345** **Dated Aug. 16/15**

From Vermont Coffee Wholesalers, $400 for specialty coffees. Invoice paid in full by cheque #181.

27 **Cash Purchase Invoice #NBLCB-776** **Dated Aug. 17/15**

From NB Liquor Control Board, $1 600 including HST and other taxes for beer, wine and liquor. Terms: COD. Invoice paid in full by cheque #182.

NOTES

Use the General Journal for the payroll transaction in this application.

Remember to enter the sales tax code for the purchase.

NOTES

You can press ctrl + R to recall a stored entry.

NOTES

Use HST code HI, taxes included, for purchases from the NB Liquor Control Board. This is the default tax code setting for this supplier.

28

Cash Purchase Invoice #Party **Dated Aug. 17/15**

From The Little Party Shop (choose Continue), $60 plus $7.80 HST for party favours and decorations to decorate tea room for special event (General Expense). Invoice total $67.80 paid in full by cheque #183.

29

NBTel

2 Communicate Rd.
Fredericton, NB
E3A 2K4
www.nbtel.ca
chatter@nbtel.ca

Account Number
506-454-6111

Account Address
Chai Tea Room
125 King St.
Fredericton, NB E3B 2P4

Account Inquiries: (506) 456-2355

Billing Date: August 18, 2015

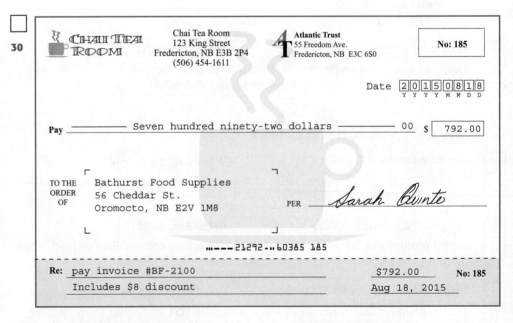

ACCOUNT SUMMARY

Current Charges	
Monthly Services (July 13–August 12)	60.00
Equipment Rentals	24.00
Chargeable Messages	16.00
	100.00
HST (93436 8699)	13.00
Total Current Charges	113.00
Previous Charges	
Amount of last bill	93.00
Payment Received July 19 – thank you	93.00
Adjustments	0.00
Balance Forward	0.00

Paid in full by cheque #184
Sarah Quinte 08/18/15

Invoice: NBT 557121	PLEASE PAY THIS AMOUNT UPON RECEIPT	$113.00

30

CHAI TEA ROOM

Chai Tea Room
123 King Street
Fredericton, NB E3B 2P4
(506) 454-1611

Atlantic Trust
55 Freedom Ave.
Fredericton, NB E3C 6S0

No: 185

Date 20150818
Y Y Y Y M M D D

Pay ——— Seven hundred ninety-two dollars ——— 00 $ 792.00

TO THE ORDER OF
Bathurst Food Supplies
56 Cheddar St.
Oromocto, NB E2V 1M8

PER *Sarah Quinte*

⑈--- 21292-⑆60385 185

Re: pay invoice #BF-2100 $792.00 **No: 185**
Includes $8 discount Aug 18, 2015

31

Cash Sales Receipt #36 **Dated Aug. 21/15**

From tea room customers (tapes #5751–6149), $7 750 plus $1 007.50 HST for tea room sales and services. Total receipts $8 757.50 deposited in bank.

SESSION DATE – AUGUST 28, 2015

32 **Purchase Invoice #BF-4633** **Dated Aug. 22/15**

From Bathurst Food Supplies, $1 700 for pastries, breads, condiments and other foods. Terms: 1/10, n/30. Recall stored entry. Change the amount and store the revised transaction as a bi-weekly recurring entry.

33 **Purchase Invoice #ATC-3468** **Dated Aug. 23/15**

From Atlantic Tea Co., $500 for a variety of herbal, black and green teas as specified on order form. Terms: net 10 days.

34 **Payment Cheque #186** **Dated Aug. 23/15**

To Bathurst Food Supplies, $792 in payment of account, including $8 discount for early payment. Reference invoice #BF-2987.

35 **Bank Debit Memo #AT-99553** **Dated Aug. 28/15**

From Atlantic Trust, withdrawals from bank account for bi-weekly payroll:

Wages, including payroll taxes	$3 200.00
Salaries	8 000.00
Payroll services	70.00
HST Paid on Purchases (payroll services)	9.10

Create new Group account 5250 Salaries.

36 **Cash Sales Receipt #37** **Dated Aug. 28/15**

From tea room customers (#6150–6499), $7 250 plus $942.50 HST for tea room sales and services. Total receipts $8 192.50 deposited in bank.

SESSION DATE – AUGUST 31, 2015

37 **Purchase Invoice #MK-8995** **Dated Aug. 31/15**

From Moncton Kitchenwares, $600 plus $78 HST for new gas burners for tea room kitchen. Invoice total $678. Terms: 1/10, n/30.

38 **Bank Debit Memo #AT-10023** **Dated Aug. 31/15**

From Atlantic Trust, withdrawals for bank charges and loan and mortgage payments:

Bank charges	$ 65
Mortgage payment (including $2 250 interest and $250 principal)	2 500
Loan payment (including $90 interest and $2 000 principal)	2 090

39 **Memo #17** **Dated Aug. 31/15**

From Owner: Make adjusting entries to reflect inventory used in the tea room during August. The end-of-month inventory count indicates the following inventory was used or sold:

Beverage inventory	$2 200
Beer, wine and liquor	1 700
Food inventory	3 100
Gift set inventory	1 000

All used inventory is charged to Cost of Goods Sold.

☐ 40

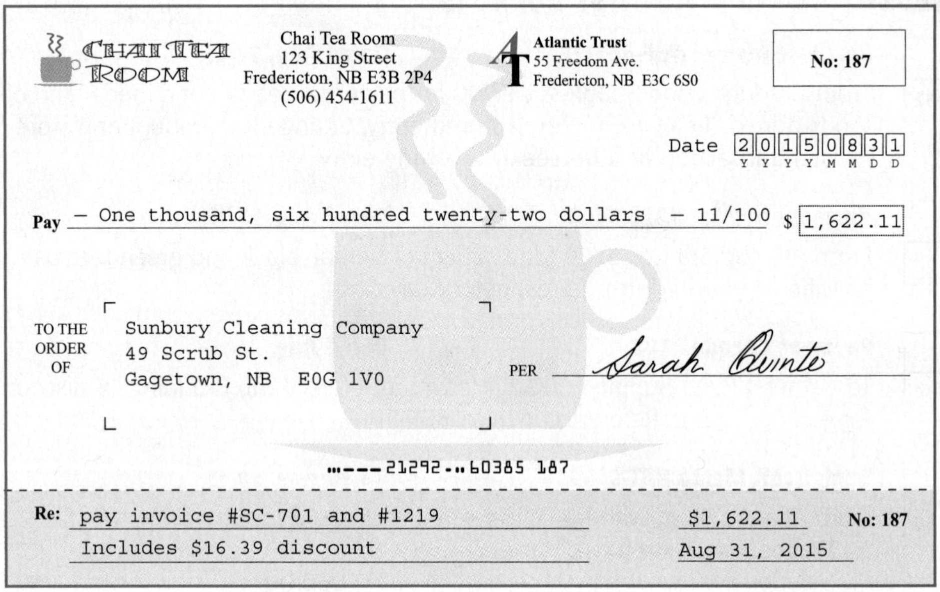
Chai Tea Room
Chai Tea Room
123 King Street
Fredericton, NB E3B 2P4
(506) 454-1611

Atlantic Trust
55 Freedom Ave.
Fredericton, NB E3C 6S0

No: 187

Date 20150831
YYYYMMDD

Pay — One thousand, six hundred twenty-two dollars — 11/100 $ 1,622.11

TO THE ORDER OF
Sunbury Cleaning Company
49 Scrub St.
Gagetown, NB E0G 1V0

PER Sarah Bunte

⑈---21292-⑈60385 187

Re: pay invoice #SC-701 and #1219 $1,622.11 No: 187
Includes $16.39 discount Aug 31, 2015

Displaying Supplier Reports

Like General Ledger reports, supplier-related reports can be displayed and printed from multiple starting points, including the Suppliers window.

Click the **Suppliers icon** to open the Suppliers window. The Reports menu in this window now lists only supplier reports. **Select** the **report** you want from this list to open the report options window.

Choose the **Reports menu** in the Home window, then **choose Payables** and **click** the **report** you want in order to see its options window.

Click the **Reports list arrow** in the Reports pane to see the list of supplier reports:

We will work from the Report Centre again so that we can see the report samples, descriptions and options.

Reporting from the Report Centre

Click the **Report Centre icon** in the Home window.

Click **Payables** in the Select A Report Type list to open the list of available supplier reports:

PRO VERSION
The term Vendor will replace Supplier in all report and graph names and fields.

NOTES
The Supplier Purchases Report deals mainly with inventory. It will be introduced in a later application.

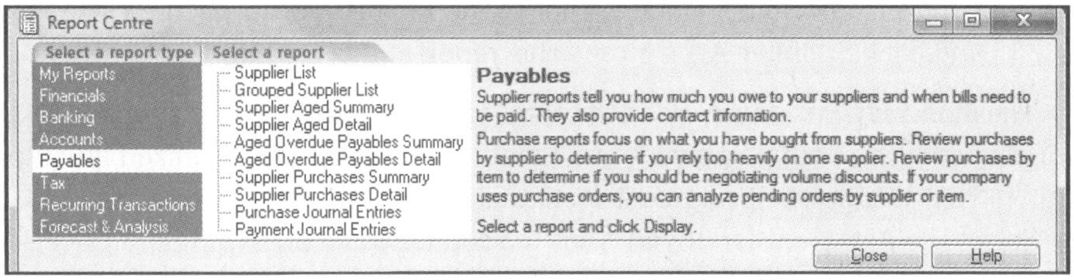

You should see a general description of the Payables module reports.

Displaying Supplier Lists

Click **Supplier List** in the Select A Report list to see the sample report and description.

Click **Modify This Report** to see the report options:

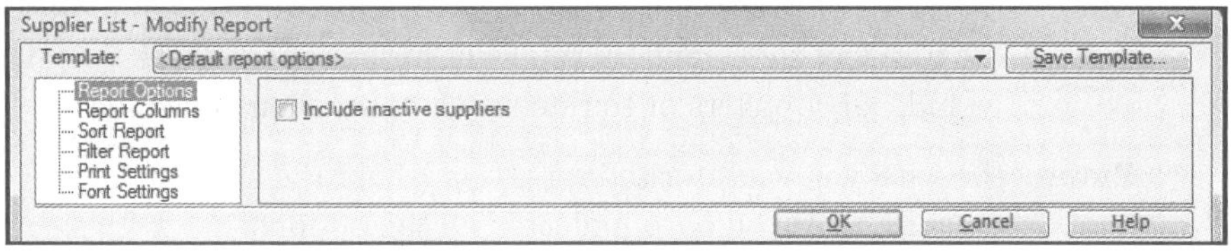

In any Home window, you can choose the Reports menu, then choose Lists and click Suppliers to see the report options.

By default, the supplier address tab details and balance owing are displayed. To select supplier details, you can choose the supplier record fields from the Report Columns screen. You can include suppliers marked as inactive if you want.

Click **OK** to see the report.

Close the **display** when you have finished viewing the report.

You will return to the starting point for the report.

If you want to organize the list of suppliers, you can group them automatically by a number of criteria with the **Grouped Supplier List**. Organizing the list may be helpful for assigning suppliers to different staff for phone calls.

Click Grouped Supplier List and then click Modify This Report. Click the Grouped By list arrow to see your options. Close the display when you have finished viewing the report.

Displaying Supplier Aged Reports

You can display Supplier Aged reports at any time.

Click **Supplier Aged Summary** in the Select A Report list to see the sample report and description.

Click **Modify This Report** to see the report options:

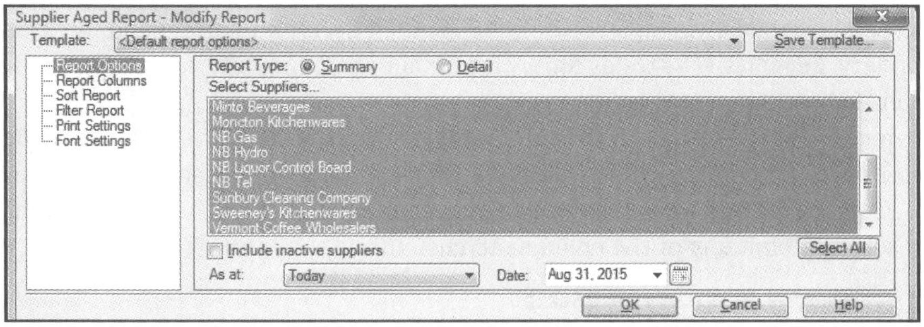

NOTES
The Report Centre can also be accessed from the Reports menu.

CLASSIC VIEW
Click the Report Centre icon in the My Business column or open the Report Centre from the Reports menu.

PRO VERSION
Forecast & Analysis reports and Grouped Lists are not available in the Pro version.

CLASSIC VIEW
From the Home window, right-click the Suppliers icon 

. (Clicking the left mouse button will open the ledger.) The Display tool label changes to the name of the report for the selected icon.

Click the Display tool  on the tool bar.

NOTES
You can drill down to the Supplier Aged Detail Report from the Supplier List.

NOTES
The Supplier Aged Summary and Detail reports are both available directly from the Report Centre.

NOTES
If you chose either One-Time Supplier or Continue for Bette Tomailik, she will not be included by name in the list of suppliers for reports and graphs. If you used Quick Add, her name will be included.

NOTES
From the Supplier Aged Detail Report, you can drill down to look up invoices and supplier ledgers. From the Summary Report, you can drill down to the Detail Report.

Or, from any Home window, choose the Reports menu, then choose Payables and click Supplier Aged to see this report options window.

The **Summary** option provides the total balance owing to each supplier. It displays an alphabetic list of suppliers with outstanding total balances organized into aged columns. By default, the program selects this option.

Select the **Detail** option if you want to see individual outstanding invoices and payments made to suppliers. This more descriptive report is also aged. Management can use it to make payment decisions. With the Detail option, you can also add supplier payment terms by clicking **Include Terms**.

You can sort and filter the reports by supplier name or balance owing (or by aging period for the summary report). You can select or omit any columns to customize reports.

Click **Detail** if you want the Detail Report.

Click the **name** or **press** and **hold** ctrl and **click** the **names** in the Suppliers list to select the suppliers you want in the report. **Click Select All** to include all suppliers or to remove all when all are selected.

Enter the **date** you want for the report or accept the session date given by default. After you have indicated all the options,

Click **OK** to see the report.

Close the **displayed report** when you have finished.

Displaying Aged Overdue Payables Reports

You can display Aged Overdue Payables reports at any time.

NOTES
You can drill down to look up invoices and to the Supplier Aged Report from the Aged Overdue Payables Report. From the Summary Report, you can drill down to the Detail Report.

Click **Aged Overdue Payables Summary** in the Select A Report list to see the sample report and description.

Click **Modify This Report** to see the report options:

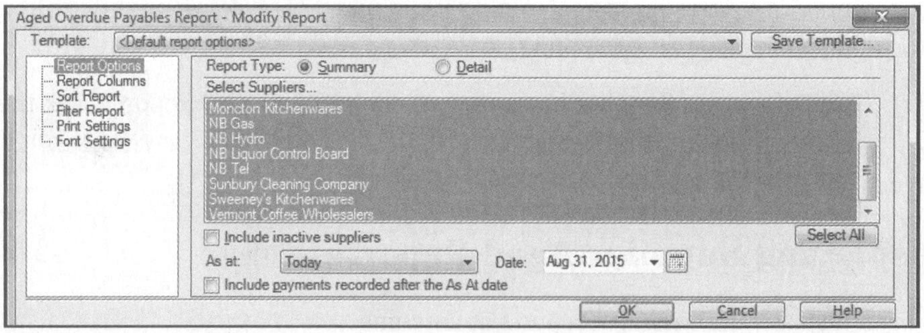

From the Home window, choose the Reports menu, then choose Payables and click Aged Overdue Payables to see the report options.

The Aged Overdue Payables Report includes the same information as the Supplier Aged Report but it adds a column for the invoice amounts that are overdue. Supplier name and balance owing may be selected as the criteria for sorting and filtering. The **Summary Report** shows totals for each supplier while the **Detail Report** includes details for each invoice.

You also have the option to **Include Payments Recorded After The As At Date** to omit from the report overdue invoices for which you have remitted postdated cheques.

You can sort and filter the reports by supplier name or by the balance owing. You can select or omit any of the columns to customize the report.

Choose **Summary** or **Detail**.

Press and **hold** ctrl and then **click** the **names** in the Suppliers list to select the suppliers that you want to see in the report. **Click Select All** to include all suppliers or to remove all when all are selected.

Enter the **date** you want for the report, or accept the session date given by default. After you have indicated all the options,

Click **OK** to see the report. One invoice from Moncton Kitchenwares and the balance on the first invoice from Fundy Gift House are overdue.

Close the **displayed report** when you have finished.

Displaying the Purchases Journal

Click **Purchase Journal Entries** in the Select A Report list to see the sample report and description.

Click **Modify This Report** to see the report options:

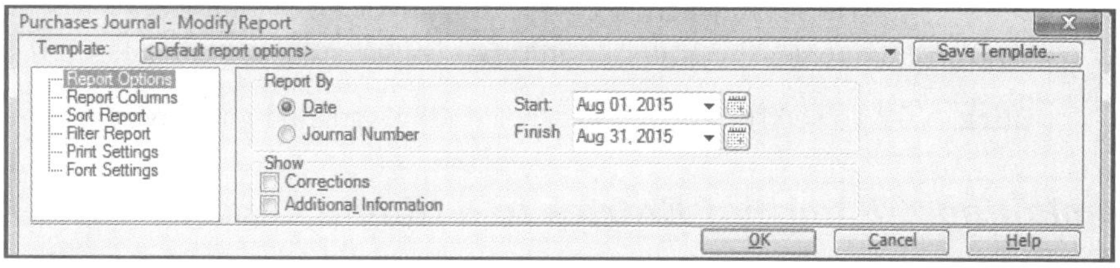

Or choose the Reports menu, then choose Journal Entries and click Purchases.

Entries for the Purchases Journal can be selected by posting date or by journal entry number. By default, the Date option is selected, and the first transaction date and session date are the default dates for the report. All journal reports may be sorted and filtered by date, journal number, source or comment. You can choose the account name and number, and debits and credits columns to customize the report column settings. Correcting or adjusting entries may be included or omitted from the report.

Type the **beginning date** for the transactions you want.

Press tab **twice**.

Type the **ending date** for your transaction period.

Click **Corrections** so that adjusting and reversing entries are included.

Click **OK** to see the report.

Close the **display** when you have finished.

Displaying the Payments Journal

Click **Payment Journal Entries** in the Select A Report list to see the sample report and description.

Click **Modify This Report** to see the report options:

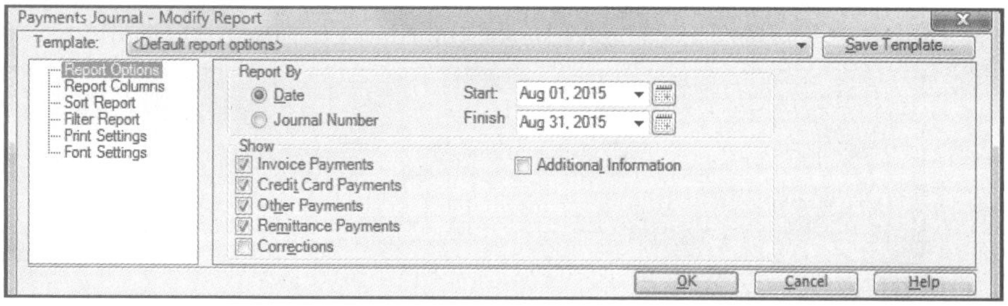

CLASSIC VIEW

From the Home window, right-click the Purchases icon  to select it. Click  (the Display tool on the tool bar).

If no icons are selected in the Home window, Purchases and Payments Journal reports are available from the Select Report list when you click the Display tool.

NOTES

The dates August 1 and August 31 are available from drop-down lists for both date fields.

NOTES

If you omit corrections, the journal reports will appear to be out of sequence because the journal entry numbers for the incorrect transactions and their reversing entries will be omitted from the report.

CLASSIC VIEW

From the Home window, right-click the Payments icon  to select it. Click  (the Display tool).

NOTES

You can drill down to the Supplier Aged Report and to the General Ledger Report from the Purchases Journal or the Payments Journal Report.

Or choose the Reports menu, then choose Journal Entries and click Payments to see the report options.

For the Payments Journal, like other journal reports, you can select the transactions by posting date — the default setting — or by journal entry number. In addition, you can choose the type of payment for the report — invoice payments, credit card payments, other payments (cash purchases) and remittance payments. All types are selected initially and clicking any one will remove it from the report. Corrections or adjustments may be included or omitted. Clicking will change your selections.

Type the **beginning date** for the transactions you want.

Press *tab* **twice**.

Type the **ending date** for your transaction period.

Click **Corrections**.

Click **Credit Card Payments** and **Remittance Payments** because we did not use these transaction types. Only Invoice Payments and Other Payments, the transaction types we entered, will be included.

Click **OK** to see the report. **Close** the **display** when you have finished.

NOTES
Including the types of transactions for which you have no entries does not result in an error message and will not change the report.

Displaying All Journal Entries in a Single Report

To view the entries for all journals in a single report from a Home window, choose the Reports menu, then choose Journal Entries and click All.

From the Report Centre, click Financials in the Select A Report Type list and then click All Journal Entries in the Select A Report list. Click Display or choose Modify This Report if you want to change the default options.

Displaying Cheque Log Reports

If you regularly print cheques through Sage 50 from the Payables journals or the Payroll journals, you can display and print a summary of these printed cheques in the Cheque Log Report.

Click **Banking** in the Select A Report Type list to see the general description of banking reports and the list of available reports:

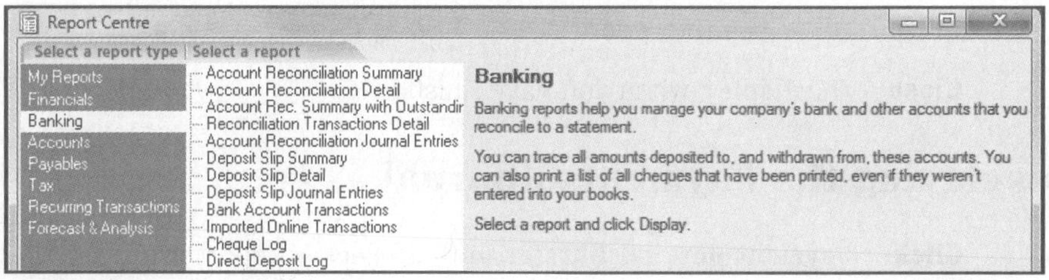

Click **Cheque Log** in the Select A Report list to see the sample report and description.

Click **Modify This Report** to see the report options:

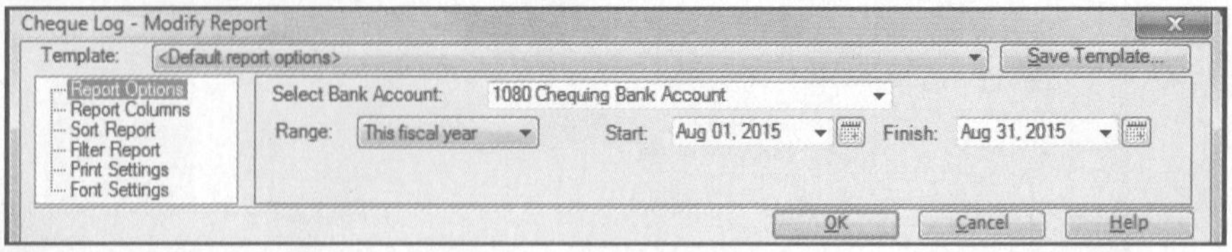

PRO VERSION
The Bank Account Transactions Report is not available in the Pro version.

From any Home window, choose the Reports menu, then choose Banking and click Cheque Log to open the report options window.

The report will include details for all cheques that you entered, including whether or not the journal entry was posted and the number of times the cheque was printed. If you do not print cheques through the program, these payments are listed with a 0 (zero) for the number of times printed. Adjusted cheques are identified as Reversed.

To customize the report, you can choose any of the column headings to sort or filter the report and you can choose to include or omit any of these columns.

NOTES
No drill down reports are available from the Cheque Log report, but you can sort or filter on any of the information in the report.

Choose the **bank account** from the Select Bank Account drop-down list.

Enter the **Start** and **Finish dates** for the report.

Click **OK** to see the report.

Close the **display** when you have finished.

Recurring Transactions Report

If you have stored transactions, you can generate a report of these transactions.

Click **Recurring Transactions** in the Select A Report Type list to see the general description of the report type and the list of available reports:

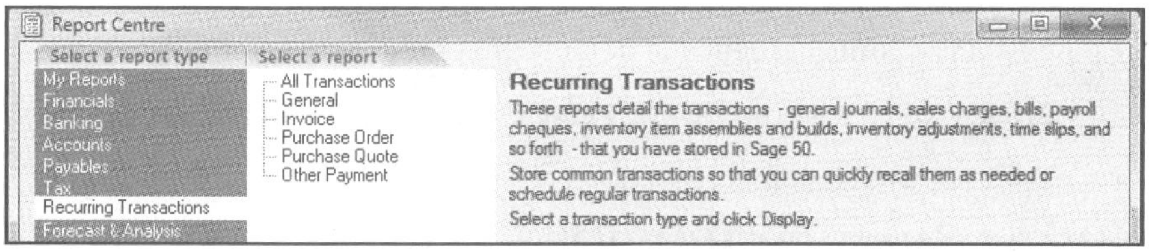

NOTES
Journals for hidden modules are not listed. When you use them and they allow recurring entries, they will be added to this list.

The list now shows the different types of transactions that can be stored.

Click **All Transactions** in the Select A Report list to see the sample report and description.

Click **Modify This Report** to see the report options:

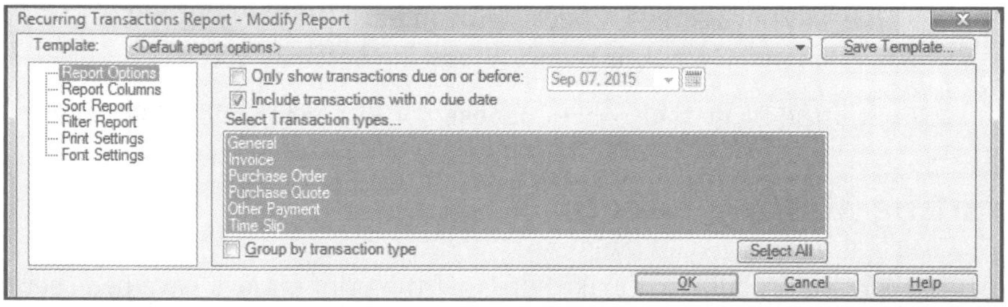

PRO VERSION
You will not see the entry for Time Slip.

Again, the list shows the different types of transactions that can be stored, and all are selected initially. Transactions without due dates are also included by default. You can restrict the report to include only those entries that are due within a specific time period by selecting **Only Show Transactions Due On Or Before**. The default date for this option is one week past the session date, but you can enter any date you want. You can **Group** the report **By Transaction Type**, or accept the default to show entries in order by the due date.

NOTES
When you choose Random as the frequency for recurring transactions, they do not include a due date.

You can sort and filter this report by type of transaction, description, frequency, the date the entry was last processed or posted or by the due date.

Choose the **options** you want and **click OK**.

Double-click an **entry** in the report to recall it for the next due date.

Close the **Report Centre** when you have finished.

Displaying Management Reports

CLASSIC VIEW
You can also access Management Reports from the Advice tool in the Classic view Home window tool bar.

NOTES
The Crystal Reports Print Manager is needed to view Management Reports. The Crystal Reports program is required to modify these reports.

Management reports are available for each ledger. They can be displayed only from the Home window and they will not be added to the Recently Viewed Reports pane.

Choose the **Reports menu**, then **choose Management Reports** and **click Payables** to open the report options window:

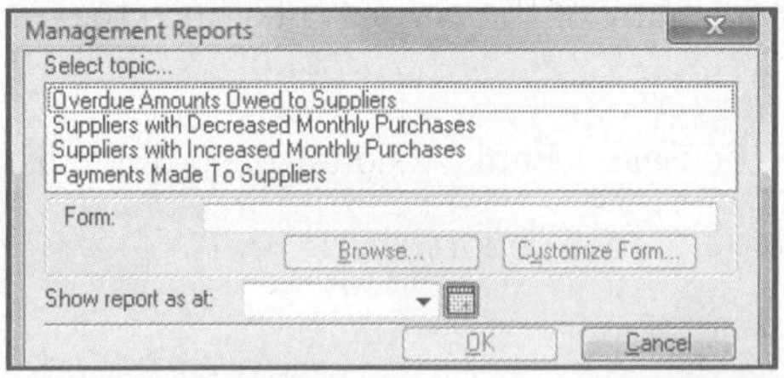

WARNING!
Always check that the file location for the Form used for the report is correct for your program setup. The file named in the Form field should be in the Forms folder, a subfolder of your Sage 50 Premium Accounting 2013 folder.

Sometimes management reports can reveal patterns in the business more clearly than the regular financial reports. For example, the report for overdue accounts lists invoices that are outstanding, with supplier contact and invoice details and the number of days remaining until payment is due. The reports for increased or decreased monthly purchases show changes in purchase patterns over the previous year that an aged detail report may not.

When you click a topic, the appropriate form will be selected from those installed with the program. Unless you have the programs required to customize forms, accept the default. If appropriate, enter a date for the report.

Click **OK** to see the report. **Print** the **report** and then **close** the **display**.

NOTES
In the management report for overdue payments, negative numbers indicate the number of days until payment is due (current invoices) and positive numbers show the number of days that the payment is overdue.

Printing Supplier Reports

Before printing supplier reports, make sure that you set the print options.

WARNING!
When you click the Print tool, printing will begin immediately with your current settings. Choosing Print from the File menu in the report will open the Print options screen and you can check and modify your printer selection and settings.

Display the **report** you want to print.

Click the **Change Print Settings tool** to open the Reports & Forms Settings screen. Check that you have the correct printer and form files selected for your report. **Close** the **Settings screen**.

Click the **Print tool** or **choose** the **File menu** and **click Print**.

Printing Mailing Labels

To print labels, you should first make sure that the print options have been set correctly and that your printer is turned on and has the correct labels paper. To set the program to use your printing labels,

Choose the Setup menu in the Home window and click Reports & Forms.
Click Labels in the list under Reports. Choose your printer.
Enter the appropriate margins, size and number across the page for your labels.
Click OK to return to the Home window.

WARNING!
You cannot display labels, so you should check the printer settings first.

Choose the **Reports menu** in the Home window, then **choose Mailing Labels** and **click Suppliers**:

NOTES
For practice, you can print the labels on plain paper.

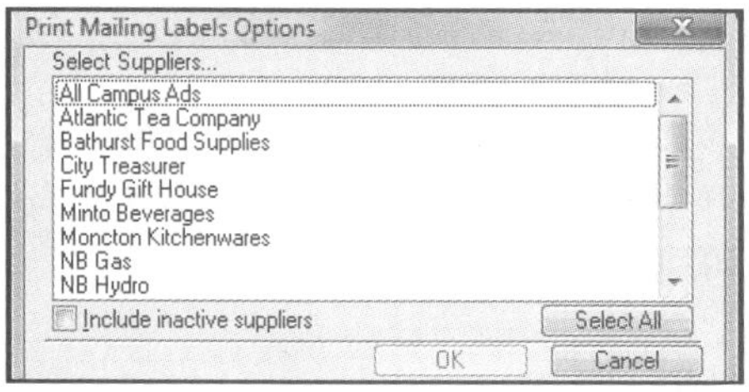

Press and **hold** ctrl and then **click** the **names** of the suppliers for whom you want labels, or **click Select All** to include all suppliers.

Click **OK** to print the labels. Printing will begin immediately.

Printing T5018 Slips

You can also print T5018 slips if you have suppliers with this option checked in the ledger records.

Choose the **Reports menu** in the Home window, then **choose Payables** and **click Print T5018 Slips**. **Select** the **suppliers** you want for the report, select other options you want and **click OK.**

NOTES
T5018 slips are compulsory for construction companies that pay subcontractors for construction services. The reports record the amounts paid and can be filed with the CRA electronically.

Graphing Supplier Reports

Payables by Aging Period Charts

Choose the **Graphs menu** in the Home window, then **click Payables By Aging Period** to display the date entry screen:

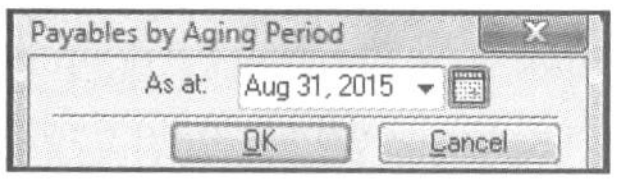

Type the **date** for the graph or accept the default session date.

Click **OK** to display the pie chart:

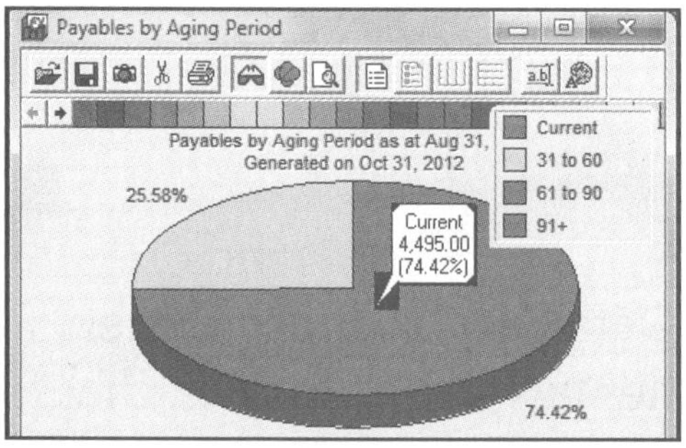

Your graph provides a quick visual reference of amounts due to all suppliers combined in each of the aging periods selected in the company setup options. Most of the payments due are current, but about 25 percent are overdue (over 31 days) — the amounts owing to Moncton Kitchenwares and Fundy Gift House.

Double-click a portion of a graph to see the aging period, the dollar amount and the percentage of the total. Double-click the legend to make it larger and add the aging periods if they are not included already. Double-click the expanded legend to reduce it.

Close the **graph** when you have finished.

NOTES
The tool bar options and the control of the colour and the legend are the same for all graphs. Refer to page 63 for a review of these features.

Payables by Supplier Charts

Choose the **Graphs menu** in the Home window, then **click Payables By Supplier** to display the pie chart options:

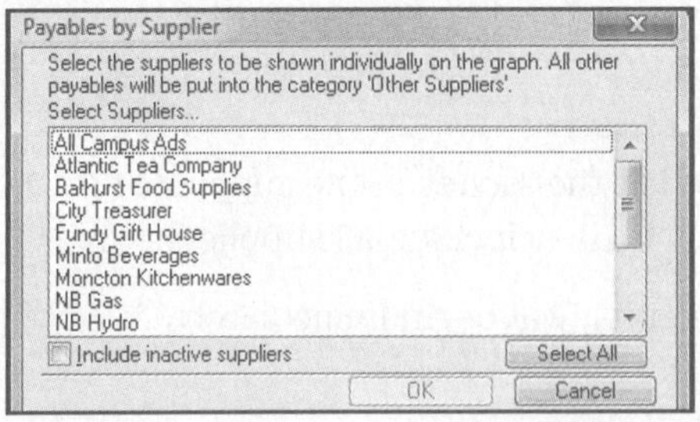

Press and **hold** ctrl and then **click** the **names** of the suppliers to include in your pie chart, or **click Select All** to include all the suppliers.

Click **OK** to display the pie chart:

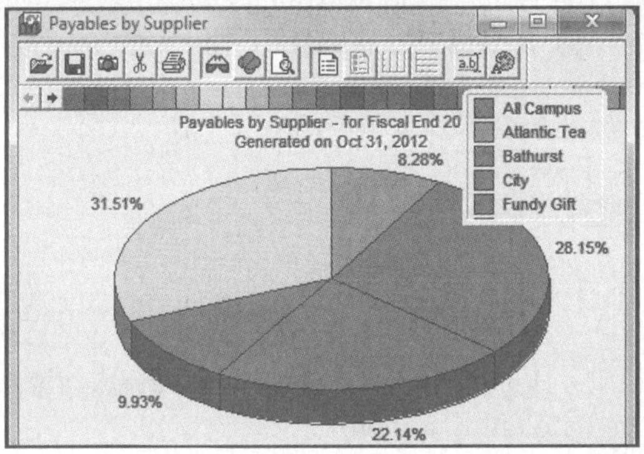

The graph shows the proportion of the total payables that is owed to each selected supplier. Amounts for suppliers not selected will be combined into a single category labelled Other. The tool bar options and the control of the colour and the legend are the same as for the other graphs.

Close the **graph** when you have finished.

Close the **data file** to finish your Sage 50 session.

R E V I E W

The Student DVD with Data Files includes Review Questions and Supplementary Cases for this chapter.

CHAPTER SIX

Phoebe's Photo Studio

OBJECTIVES

After completing this chapter, you should be able to

- ***enter*** transactions in the General, Payables and Receivables journals
- ***enter*** and ***post*** cash, credit card and account sale transactions
- ***enter*** and ***post*** customer payment transactions
- ***customize*** journals and ***preview*** invoices
- ***enter*** transactions including GST and PST
- ***store*** and ***recall*** recurring entries
- ***enter*** customer discounts and partial payments
- ***add*** and ***edit*** customer accounts
- ***reverse*** receipts to enter NSF cheques from customers
- ***edit*** and ***review*** customer-related transactions
- ***create*** shortcuts for General and Payables transactions
- ***display***, ***print*** and ***graph*** customer reports
- ***understand*** linked accounts for the Receivables Ledger

COMPANY INFORMATION

Company Profile

NOTES
Phoebe's Photo Studio
100 Light St., Suite 202
Winnipeg, MB R2T 7G4
Tel 1: (204) 649-3358
Tel 2: (888) 649-3358
Fax: (204) 642-4967
Business No.: 296 654 590

Phoebe's Photo Studio has its main portrait studio in Winnipeg, Manitoba. Here Phoebe Maniwake takes individual and family portraits and develops and prints the black and white photographs. She also has a summer residence outside of Riverton, Manitoba, on Lake Winnipeg that allows her easier access to the northern parts of the province as well as the Hecla / Grindstone Provincial Park where she composes her nature photographs for sale in galleries across Canada.

After completing an art program at the Ontario College of Art, Maniwake opened her studio in Winnipeg, her home town, and has now had the studio for several years. In the summers she also accompanies Arctic cruises and other tours to photograph cruise passengers on location, as well as to take more of her own northern landscape photos. Revenue comes from these three sources: portraits (including students and weddings), photographing tour clients and art gallery sales. Sometimes she brings in a student for the summer as an assistant/apprentice to accompany her on her personal photo tours.

Most regular customers — families, galleries, cruise lines — have accounts with Phoebe's Photo Studio and receive a 2 percent discount if they pay within 10 days. They are asked to settle their accounts in 30 days, paying by cash or by cheque. PST and GST apply to all work completed by Phoebe's Photo Studio.

Accounts have been set up with a local photographic supplies store, a camera sales and repair store and some other regular suppliers.

After remitting all taxes before the end of June 2015, Maniwake converted the accounts for Phoebe's Photo Studio using the following information:

- Chart of Accounts
- Post-Closing Trial Balance
- Supplier Information
- Customer Information
- Accounting Procedures

CHART OF POSTABLE ACCOUNTS

PHOEBE'S PHOTO STUDIO

ASSETS
1080 Chequing Account
1100 Credit Card Bank Account
1200 Accounts Receivable
1300 Darkroom Supplies
1310 Photo Paper
1320 Framing Supplies
1340 Other Supplies
1440 Computers and Software
1460 Development Equipment
1480 Camera Accessories
1500 Digital SLR Camera ▶

▶1550 Van
1580 Studios

LIABILITIES
2100 Bank Loan
2200 Accounts Payable
2640 PST Payable
2650 GST Charged on Services
2670 GST Paid on Purchases
2850 Mortgage Payable ▶

EQUITY
3560 P. Maniwake, Capital ▶

▶3600 Net Income

REVENUE
4100 Revenue from Tours
4140 Revenue from Portraits
4180 Sales Discounts

EXPENSE
5100 Advertising & Promotion
5120 Bank Charges & Card Fees
5130 Interest Expense
5140 Hydro Expense
5150 Framing Supplies Used ▶

▶5160 Photo Supplies Used
5170 Other Supplies Used
5190 Postage Expenses
5200 Purchase Discounts
5220 Telephone Expenses
5240 Travel Expenses
5260 Vehicle Expenses
5300 Wages
5310 Payroll Service Charges

NOTES: The Chart of Accounts includes only postable accounts and the Net Income or Current Earnings account.

POST-CLOSING TRIAL BALANCE

PHOEBE'S PHOTO STUDIO

June 30, 2015		Debits	Credits
1080	Chequing Account	$ 48 486	
1100	Credit Card Bank Account	2 900	
1200	Accounts Receivable	7 989	
1300	Darkroom Supplies	420	
1310	Photo Paper	2 620	
1320	Framing Supplies	1 380	
1340	Other Supplies	240	
1440	Computers and Software	14 900	
1460	Development Equipment	5 600	
1480	Camera Accessories	6 320	
1500	Digital SLR Cameras	7 370	
1550	Van	21 900	
1580	Studios	320 000	
2100	Bank Loan		$ 10 000
2200	Accounts Payable		5 840
2850	Mortgage Payable		180 000
3560	P. Maniwake, Capital		244 285
		$440 125	$440 125

SUPPLIER INFORMATION

PHOEBE'S PHOTO STUDIO

Supplier Name (Contact)	Address	Phone No. Fax No.	E-mail Web Site	Terms Tax ID
Calm Air (Arie Fliegel)	50 Jett Ave. Winnipeg, Manitoba R2P 1S7	Tel: (800) 839-2256 Fax: (204) 476-5110	af@calmair.com www.calmair.com	1/15, n/30 566 478 913
Lumber Shed (C. Woods)	91 Walnut St. Winnipeg, Manitoba R3P 8V3	Tel: (204) 382-7845 Fax: (204) 383-2489	cwoods@lumbershed.com www.lumbershed.com	1/5, n/30 571 277 631
Manitoba Hydro (Mannie Ergs)	1 Watts Rd. Winnipeg, Manitoba R6G 2C1	Tel: (204) 435-2633	m.ergs@mnhydro.man.ca www.mnhydro.man.ca	net 1
Manitoba Telephone (Chata Lot)	11 Vocal Channel Winnipeg, Manitoba R3E 6R4	Tel: (204) 488-8532	www.manitobatel.ca	net 1
Riverton Garage (Karl Fixe)	6 Ford St. Riverton, Manitoba R0C 2R0	Tel: (204) 378-1297 Fax: (204) 378-6388	Karl@rivercars.com www.rivercars.com	net 30 344 566 872
Starlight Photo Solutions (Star Lightman)	300 Aurora St. Winnipeg, Manitoba R3P 4D5	Tel: (204) 577-1369 Fax: (204) 577-2229	star@sps.com www.sps.com	2/10, n/30 610 728 365
UPS Delivery (Yvette Panier)	8 Carrier Ave. Winnipeg, Manitoba R2C 6A1	Tel 1: (204) 698-2357 Tel 2: (800) 477-1UPS Fax: (204) 698-6102	www.ups.com	net 1 498 458 561
Web Exposure (B. Online)	72 Memorial Cres. Brandon, Manitoba R7A 3G5	Tel: (204) 469-8080 Fax: (204) 469-4987	online@webexposure.com www.webexposure.com	net 15 385 416 822

OUTSTANDING SUPPLIER INVOICES

PHOEBE'S PHOTO STUDIO

Supplier Name	Terms	Date	Invoice No.	Amount	Total
Calm Air	1/15, n/30	Jun. 26/15	CA-224	$3 900	$3 900
Lumber Shed	1/5, n/30	Jun. 21/15	LS-894	$1 050	$1 050
Riverton Garage	net 30	Jun. 16/15	RG-1904	$890	$890
			Grand Total		$5 840

CUSTOMER INFORMATION

PHOEBE'S PHOTO STUDIO

Customer Name (Contact)	Address	Phone No. Fax No.	E-mail Web Site	Terms Credit Limit
Borealis Delights (J. Franklin)	4 Lighter Way Winnipeg, Manitoba R4A 1E1	Tel 1: (204) 476-4669	franklin@borealis.com www.borealis.com	2/10, n/30 $15 000
Brandon Art Gallery (Art North)	49 Viewer St. Brandon, Manitoba R7B 2T5	Tel 1: (204) 823-5100 Tel 2: (204) 826-1297 Fax: (204) 826-2196	AN@bag.com www.bag.com	2/10, n/30 $10 000
Geraldine Reuben (G. Reuben)	4 Chapel Lane Winnipeg, Manitoba R4A 1E1	Tel: (204) 476-4669	GReuben@yahoo.com www.weddings.com\GR	2/10, n/30 $10 000
Kandinski Party (Sophia Kandinski)	77 Memory Lane Winnipeg, Manitoba R3G 5D2	Tel: (204) 326-7528 Fax: (204) 326-7436	skandinski@gmail.com www.kandinskis.com	2/10, n/30 $5 000

Customer Name (Contact)	Address	Phone No. Fax No.	E-mail Web Site	Terms Credit Limit
Polar Discoveries (Robert Peary)	4 Exploration Ave. Churchill, Manitoba R0B 0E0	Tel: (204) 624-7900 Fax: (204) 624-7556	peary@polartours.com www.polartours.com	2/10, n/30 $15 000
Young'uns Preschool (Ella Little)	588 Totts Cres. Winnipeg, Manitoba R3P 4C2	Tel: (204) 369-4545 Fax: (204) 369-8765	ella@YPS.com www.YPS.com	2/10, n/30 $8 000

OUTSTANDING CUSTOMER INVOICES

PHOEBE'S PHOTO STUDIO

Customer Name	Terms	Date	Inv/Chq No.	Amount	Total
Geraldine Reuben	1/10, n/30	Jun. 25/15	PS-377	$2 260	
		Jun. 25/15	Chq #266	1 460	
		Jun. 27/15	PS-381	1 695	
			Balance owing		$2 495
Young'uns Preschool	1/10, n/30	Jun. 28/15	PS-383	$4 294	
		Jun. 30/15	PS-387	1 200	
			Balance owing		$5 494
			Grand Total		$7 989

Accounting Procedures

NOTES

For the service business, the terms Revenues Journal and Client replace Sales Journal and Customer. These terms will be used interchangeably in this chapter.

Open-Invoice Accounting for Receivables

The open-invoice method of accounting for invoices issued by a business allows the business to keep track of each individual invoice and of any partial payments made against it. In contrast, other methods keep track only of the outstanding balance by combining all invoice balances owed by a customer. Sage 50 uses the open-invoice method. Fully paid invoices can be removed (cleared) periodically.

Discounts for Early Payments

Phoebe's Photo Studio offers discounts to regular customers if they pay their accounts within 10 days. Full payment is expected in 30 days. Customers who pay by credit card do not receive discounts. No discounts are allowed on partial payments.

Some suppliers with whom Phoebe's Photo Studio has accounts set up also offer discounts for early payments.

NSF Cheques

If a cheque is deposited from an account that does not have enough money to cover it, the bank may return it to the depositor as NSF (non-sufficient funds). The NSF cheque from a customer requires a reversing entry in the Receipts Journal. Sage 50 can complete these reversals automatically (see Keystrokes, page 176). In most companies, the accounting department notifies the customer who wrote the NSF cheque to explain that the debt remains unpaid. Many companies charge an additional fee to the customer to recover their bank charges for the NSF cheque. A separate sales invoice should be prepared for the additional charge. NSF cheques to suppliers are handled in the same way, through reversing entries in the Payments Journal.

Taxes (GST and PST)

Phoebe's Photo Studio is a service business using the regular method of calculating GST. GST, at the rate of 5 percent, charged and collected from customers will be recorded as a liability in *GST Charged on Services*. GST paid to suppliers will be recorded in *GST Paid on Purchases* as a decrease in tax liability. The balance owing, the difference between the GST charged and GST paid, or the request for a refund will be remitted to the Receiver General for Canada quarterly.

Phoebe's Photo Studio charges customers 7 percent PST on all sales and pays PST on some goods. The Studio is exempt from PST for purchases of items used in preparing photos, such as framing supplies, photo paper and developing chemicals because the customer pays PST on the products that use these components.

Cash and Credit Card Sales of Services

Cash and credit card transactions are a normal occurrence in most businesses. Sage 50 has payment options to handle these transactions. When you make the correct Payment Method or Paid By selection, the program will debit *Chequing Account* or *Credit Card Bank Account* instead of the *Accounts Receivable* control account (see Keystrokes, page 169 and page 180).

NOTES

In July, 2013, Manitoba changed its provincial tax rate to 8 percent. This change was announced too late to be incorporated into the current text.

INSTRUCTIONS

1. **Record entries for the source documents** in Sage 50 using all the information provided for Phoebe's Photo Studio. The procedures for entering each new type of transaction in this application are outlined step by step in the Keystrokes section with the source documents. These transactions are indicated with a ✓ in the upper part of the completion check box beside the source document. Source document numbers are included below or in the lower part of the check box.
2. **Print** the **reports and graphs** indicated on the following printing form after you have finished making your entries. Instructions for reports begin on page 189.

REPORTS

Accounts
- ☐ Chart of Accounts
- ☐ Account List
- ☐ General Journal Entries

Financials
- ☑ Balance Sheet: July 31
- ☑ Income Statement from July 1 to July 31
- ☑ Trial Balance date: July 31
- ☑ All Journal Entries: July 1 to July 31
- ☑ General Ledger accounts: 1300 4120 4140 from July 1 to July 31
- ☐ Statement of Cash Flows
- ☑ Cash Flow Projection Detail Report for account 1080 for 30 days

Taxes
- ☑ GST Report July 31
- ☑ PST Report July 31

Banking
- ☐ Cheque Log Report

Payables
- ☐ Supplier List
- ☐ Supplier Aged
- ☐ Aged Overdue Payables
- ☐ Purchases Journal Entries
- ☐ Payments Journal Entries

Receivables
- ☐ Client List
- ☑ Client Aged Detail for all customers
- ☐ Aged Overdue Receivables
- ☑ Revenues Journal Entries: July 1 to July 31
- ☑ Receipts Journal Entries: July 1 to July 31
- ☐ Client Statements

Mailing Labels
- ☐ Labels

Management Reports
- ☐ Ledger

GRAPHS
- ☐ Payables by Aging Period
- ☐ Payables by Supplier
- ☐ Receivables by Aging Period
- ☐ Receivables by Client
- ☑ Revenues vs Receivables
- ☑ Receivables Due vs Payables Due
- ☑ Revenues by Account
- ☐ Expenses by Account
- ☑ Expenses and Net Profit as % of Revenue

KEYSTROKES

Opening Data Files

NOTES
If you are using backup files, restore SageData13\photo1.CAB or photo1 to SageData13\Photo\photo. Refer to the instructions for restoring data files in Chapter 1, page 22, if you need assistance.

Open the data file **SageData13\Photo\photo** to access the data files for Phoebe's Photo Studio.

Type `July 8 2015` to enter the first session date.

Click **OK** to see the following warning statement:

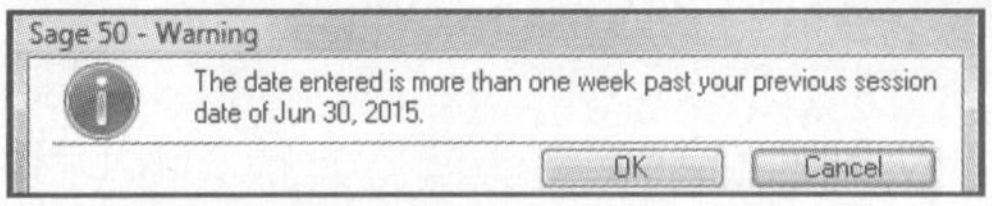

This warning appears whenever you advance the session date by more than one week. Normally a business would update its accounting records more frequently. If you have entered the correct date,

Click **OK** to accept the date entered and display the Home window.

The Payroll, Inventory and Project ledger names do not appear in the Modules pane list. These ledgers are hidden because they are not set up.

Accounting for Sales

Sales are entered in the Revenues Journal indicated by the Client Invoices icon in the Receivables module Home window:

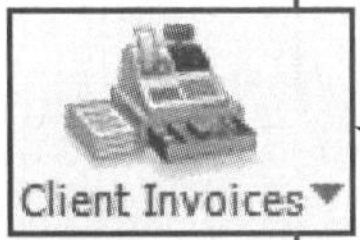

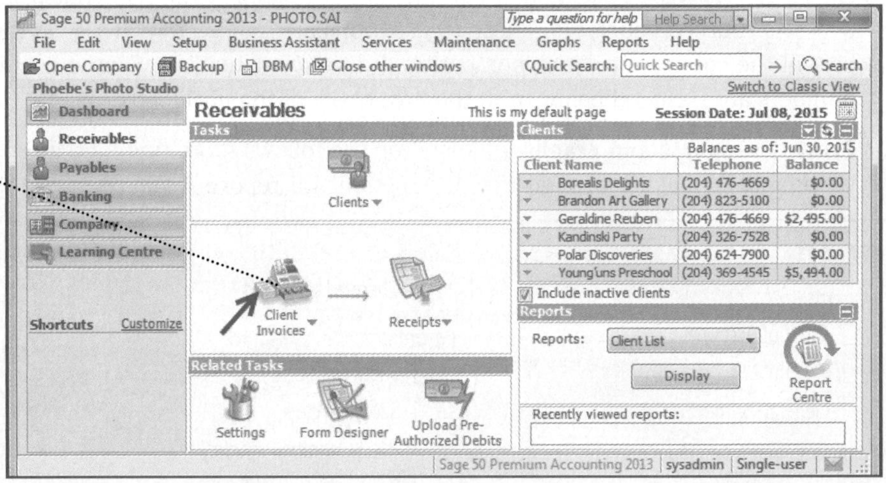

PRO VERSION
Icon labels are the same for all company types.
Click the Sales Invoices icon  to open the Sales Journal. In the Pro version Classic view, this icon is labelled Sales.

You can enter sales from the Client Invoices icon in the Receivables window. The Client Invoices label is used for service companies. For other company types, the label for this icon may be Sales, Invoices, Sales Invoices, Customer Invoices, Bills, Statements or Charges. The icon itself does not change.

Customer balances are shown as at the date of the latest transaction.

WARNING!
Do not include PS- in the sales invoice number in the journal. The numeric portion will then be correctly updated by the program.
If you want to include PS- in the journal entries, you must update the invoice number for each invoice.

✓ 1 **Sales Invoice #PS-391** **Dated July 1/15**

To Brandon Art Gallery, $4 200 plus $210 GST and $294 PST for sale of three framed original photographic prints. Invoice total, $4 704. Terms: 2/10, n/30. Create new Group account 4120 Revenue from Gallery Sales. Customize the sales invoice by removing the columns not used by Phoebe's Photo Studio.

Click the **Client Invoices icon** to open the Revenues Journal input form:

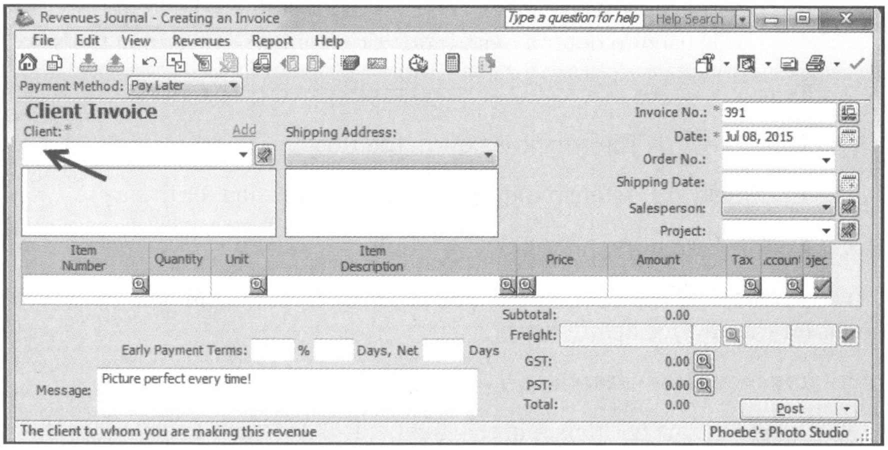

Most tool bar buttons in the Revenues Journal are familiar from other journals — Home window, Daily Business Manager, Store, Recall, Undo, Customize Journal, Calculator and Allocate. Print and E-mail buttons allow you to print or e-mail the invoice before posting to provide a customer or store copy of the sales invoice. You can also use tool buttons to preview an invoice, change print settings and adjust or reverse a posted invoice. The tools for Invoice Lookup, Additional Information, Track Shipments and Add Time Slip Activities will be explained in later applications.

Pay Later is correctly selected as the payment option for this regular sale.

Click the **Client field list arrow** to obtain the list of customers as shown on the following screen:

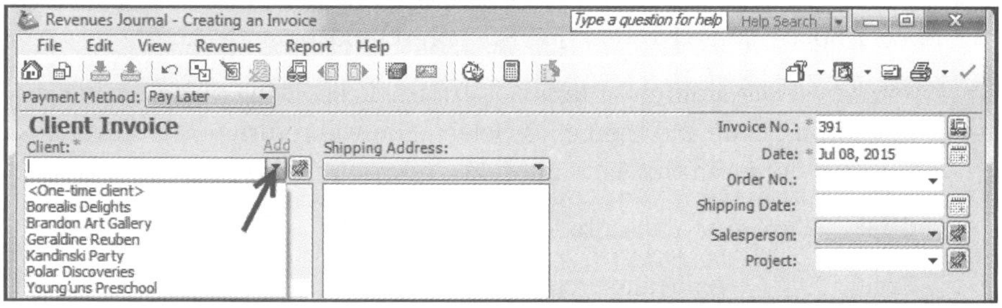

Click **Brandon Art Gallery**, the customer in the first source document, to select and enter it.

Notice that the customer's name and address have been added to your input form. If you have made an error in your selection, click the client list arrow and start again. By default, the Client and the Shipping Address fields are completed from the customer's ledger record. You can edit the shipping address if necessary. If you have selected the correct customer, you can skip over the shipping information.

The invoice number, 391, the numeric portion, is entered and correct. It is updated automatically by the program. The payment terms and tax code for the customer have also been entered. The default revenue account for the Receivables module is entered as the default. We need to change it — and create a new account — for this customer.

The session date appears by default so you need to change it as well. Enter the date on which the transaction took place, July 1, 2015.

Click the **Date field Calendar icon**.

Click **1**.

If you want, you can enter a quantity (three for the number of prints) and $1 400 as the price per unit in the Price field and let the program calculate the amount by multiplying the two together. You can use this method if you are selling more than one item that is not an inventory item.

CLASSIC VIEW

Click the Revenues icon

to open the Revenues Journal.

PRO VERSION

The term Sales Journal replaces Revenues Journal in the journal title bar and Customer replaces Client in all fields.

The Time Slips and Refresh tools and the Order No. and Shipping Date fields do not appear in the Pro version.

WARNING!

You must click the list arrow to see the customer list. Clicking the field will place an insertion point to prepare for typing a name.

NOTES

The year is added correctly in the Revenues Journal when you type the month and day.

NOTES

When you use the long date format, the parts of the date appear as separate words. Double-clicking the date will select only one part of the date, either the month, the day or the year.

Remember that you can always choose the date from the pop-up calendar in the Date field.

NOTES

You can also press tab repeatedly to move to any field you need.

Click the **Item Description field** on the first line. The Item Description field is used to enter a description or comment concerning the sale.

Type `three framed original photo prints`

Press tab. The cursor is now in the Price field.

The Price field also refers to unit prices; it is not needed for this sale.

Press tab.

NOTES

Entering a negative amount in the Amount field will generate a debit entry for the sale with a credit to Accounts Receivable.

This is similar to replacing credit amounts with debit amounts in the Purchases Journal when you type a negative number, and to switching between debits and credits in the General Journal by adding the minus sign to amounts.

The cursor should now be positioned in the Amount field, where you will enter the amount for this invoice before taxes.

Type `4200` **Press** tab.

The cursor is now positioned in the Tax field. The default tax code for the customer, GP, is entered from the customer record details in the data files and it is correct. Customers pay both GST and PST on services. The invoice subtotal and total have been updated.

Press enter to see the tax code descriptions set up for Phoebe's Photo Studio:

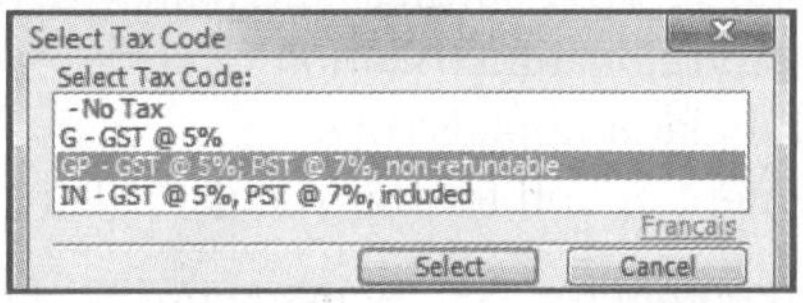

NOTES

PST is usually charged on services that are applied to goods that are themselves taxable for PST.

The tax code options are: charge **No Tax** on the sale; code **G**, charge GST only; code **GP**, charge both GST and PST; and code **IN**, both GST and PST are charged and included in the price. Notice that PST is described as non-refundable.

You can select a different tax code from this list if the default is incorrect. Click the correct code and then click Select. You will return to the Revenues Journal with the cursor in the Account field.

NOTES

When you select a tax code from the selection list, the cursor advances to the next invoice field. When you choose Cancel, the cursor does not move to the next field.

Click **Cancel** to return to the journal.

Press tab to advance to the Account field.

The Account field in a sales invoice refers to the credit portion of the journal entry, usually a revenue account. Again, you cannot access *Accounts Receivable*, the linked account, directly. The software will automatically debit the *Accounts Receivable* control account in the General Ledger when you enter positive amounts.

NOTES

You can choose any postable account as the default revenue account for customers, just as you can use any account as the default expense account for suppliers.

You may set up a default revenue account for customers, just as you set up default expense accounts for suppliers. For Phoebe's Photo Studio's customers, more than one revenue account applies. We have entered 4100 as the default account for the module, but it is not correct for this sale. In the Account field, you can choose an account from the list of accounts or create a new account, just as you can in any other account field. We need to create a new revenue account for this sale.

NOTES

Because Add An Account is already selected, pressing enter will choose it.

Type `4120` **Press** enter.

Press enter to open the Add An Account wizard (Add An Account is selected).

Press tab.

Type `Revenue from Gallery Sales` as the **account name** and **accept** the remaining **defaults**. **Click Finish** to return to the journal.

The new account number is added to the journal.

Press tab to advance the cursor to line 2 in the Item field, ready for additional sale items if necessary.

The Message field can be used in two ways: you can set up a default comment for the business that appears on all invoices, or you can enter a comment at the time of the sale. You can add to or change a default comment if you want. The default comment is entered for Phoebe's Photo Studio.

The payment terms have been set up as defaults for customers as 2 percent discount in 10 days with net payment due in 30 days. You can change terms for individual customers or sales invoices.

Click the **List icon beside the GST** or the **PST amount field** to see the detailed summary of taxes included in the sale:

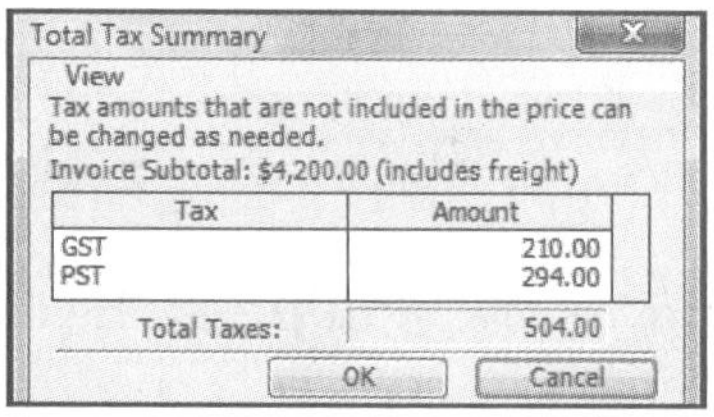

Close the **Tax Summary window** to return to the invoice.

The transaction is now complete, and your invoice should resemble the following:

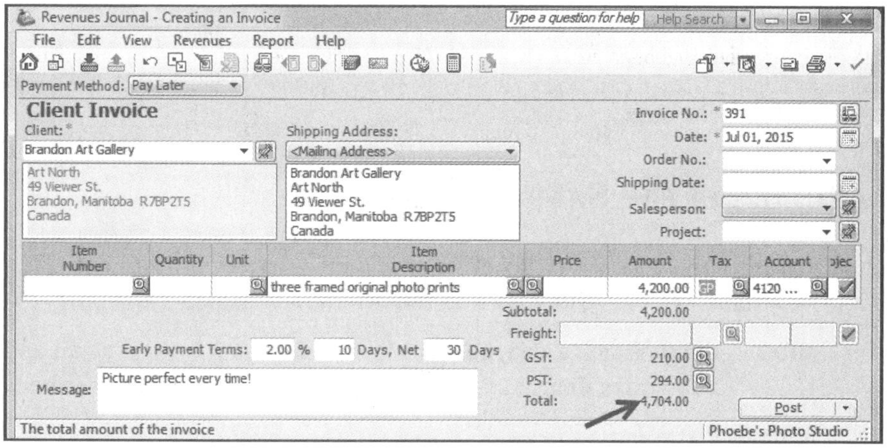

Before storing, posting or printing a revenues journal entry, review it carefully.

Reviewing the Revenues Journal Entry

Choose the **Report menu** and **click Display Revenues Journal Entry** to display the transaction:

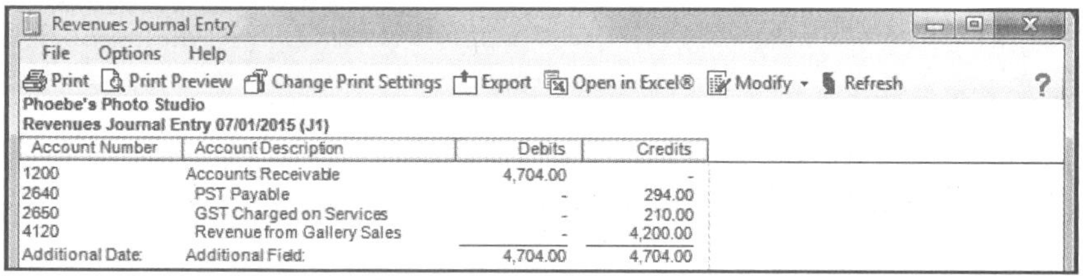

Revenues Journal Entry

Phoebe's Photo Studio
Revenues Journal Entry 07/01/2015 (J1)

Account Number	Account Description	Debits	Credits
1200	Accounts Receivable	4,704.00	-
2640	PST Payable	-	294.00
2650	GST Charged on Services	-	210.00
4120	Revenue from Gallery Sales	-	4,200.00
Additional Date:	Additional Field:	4,704.00	4,704.00

Review the **journal entry** to check for mistakes.

You can see that *Accounts Receivable*, the control account, has been updated automatically by Sage 50 because the Receivables and General ledgers are fully integrated. All credit sales are debited to *Accounts Receivable*, the default linked account for the Receivables Ledger. *GST Charged on Services* has also been updated correctly because of the tax code you entered and because *GST Charged on Services* was defined as the GST linked account for sales. Similarly, *PST Payable* is defined as the linked account for PST collected from customers and it too is updated correctly

NOTES
Payment terms can be modified for individual customers in the Receivables Ledger. You can also edit the terms for individual sales in the Revenues Journal.

NOTES
If necessary, such as for rounding errors, or to separate tax amounts that are combined, you can edit the tax amounts on the Tax Summary screen.

NOTES
You can also press ctrl + J to open the journal display.

NOTES
Using the Revenues Journal for sales instead of the General Journal is recommended because the accounts, tax codes and payment terms can be set up automatically for the business or linked to individual customers. Preset linked accounts ensure that tax amounts are calculated and updated correctly. Outstanding amounts are directly connected with the correct customer and ledger records are updated.

NOTES
Other Receivables Ledger linked accounts will be used and explained later. These are the Receivables bank account, freight revenue account and sales discount account.

because of the tax code. You did not need to enter any of these accounts or amounts directly in the Revenues Journal. The balance owing by this customer is also directly updated as a result of the linked *Accounts Receivable* account and journal entry.

Close the **display** to return to the Revenues Journal input screen.

CORRECTING THE REVENUES JOURNAL ENTRY BEFORE POSTING

Move to the field that has the error. **Press** tab to move forward through the fields or **press** shift and tab together to move back to a previous field. This will highlight the field information so you can change it. **Type** the **correct information** and **press** tab to enter it.

You can also use the mouse to **point** to a field and **drag through** the **incorrect information** to highlight it. **Type** the **correct information** and **press** tab to enter it.

If the customer is incorrect, **reselect** from the **Client** list by **clicking** the **Client list arrow**. **Click** the name of the **correct client**.

Click an **incorrect amount** or description to highlight it. Then **type** the **correct information** and **press** tab to enter the change.

To correct an account number or tax code, **click** the **Account List icon** to display the selection list. **Click** the **correct entry** to highlight it, then **click Select** and **press** tab to enter the change.

To insert a line or remove a line, **click** the **line** that you need to move. **Choose** the **Edit menu** and **click Insert Line** and **type** the new line or **click Remove Line** to delete a line.

To discard the entry and begin again, **click** (**Close**) to close the journal or **click** (**Undo**) on the tool bar to open a blank journal window. When Sage 50 asks whether you want to discard the entry, **click Yes** to confirm your decision.

NOTES
To correct Revenues Journal entries after posting, refer to page 182 and Appendix C.

Customizing the Sales Invoice

The sales invoice includes a number of fields/columns that we do not need. Before saving the invoice, we will customize it to remove the unnecessary columns.

Click the **Customize Journal tool** or **choose** the **View menu** and **click Customize Journal** to open the Settings options for Client Invoices:

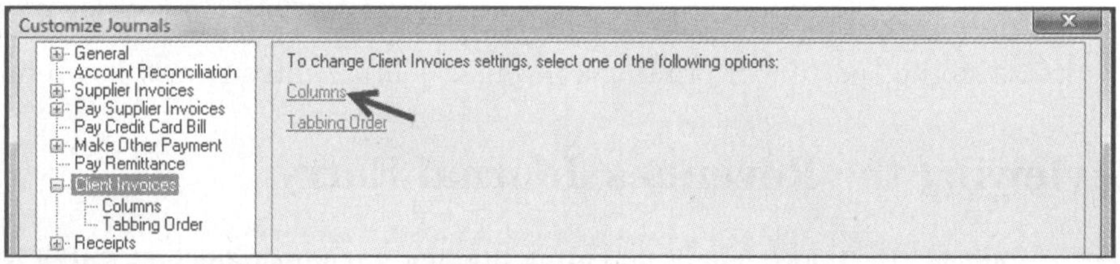

We can modify the selection of columns and the order in which the tab key advances you from one part of the invoice to another. For the Client Invoices (Sales Invoices), we will modify the column selections. For Receipts, we will modify the tabbing order.

NOTES
When Orders and Quotes are used (Company Settings, Features), they will appear on the list as well. You can customize orders and quotes differently from invoices in the Premium version.

Click **Columns** to open the column selection window:

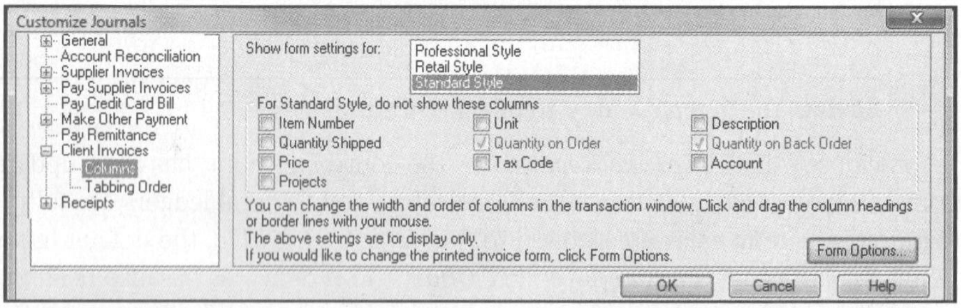

PRO VERSION
Different invoice styles are not available in the Pro version. The Standard Style is the only one used. Form Options for printed invoices cannot be accessed from this window.
You cannot customize orders and quotes separately from invoices.

The Premium version has three predefined invoice styles for different business types built in. Each style displays a different combination of columns. The Standard Style, the default, includes all columns. The Standard and Retail styles include columns for inventory and orders while the Professional style does not. The Tax Code, Account, Description and Projects columns are common to all styles.

We can remove or hide most of the fields to match the Professional Style (refer to sidebar Warning). The columns we can remove are listed under the **For Standard Style, Do Not Show These Columns** heading. We can remove additional columns by clicking check boxes to add ✓s. The **Form Options** button accesses printer setup options for the forms. Modifying printed forms is covered in Appendix F on the Student DVD.

> **WARNING!**
> When we tested these styles, they did not change the invoice as required, so we started by modifying the Standard Style.

Click the **check boxes** for **Item Number**, **Quantity Shipped**, **Price**, **Unit** and **Projects**.

Click **OK** to return to the modified journal:

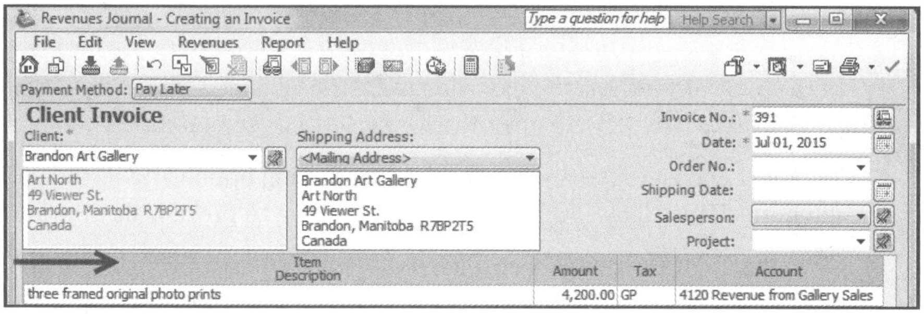

You can adjust the column spacing by dragging the column headings to change the size of columns and display all the information in all fields. We have resized the columns for this screenshot.

> **NOTES**
> You can customize journals by dragging the column headings to remove or change the size of columns.

Point to the column heading margin. When the arrow changes to ⇔ (a double-headed arrow), drag the margin to its new location or size. Dragging the right column margin to the left until it overlaps the next column will remove that column. You can restore missing columns from the Customize Journal window.

Now when we press the *tab* key for the invoice details, the cursor will advance to the next field, and it will be one we use for the sale.

Previewing Invoices

Before printing and posting the invoice, you can preview it from the Preview tool. You can preview the invoice or, if you have the packing slip details, you can preview the packing slip (an invoice with shipping and item details and without prices).

Click the **list arrow** beside the Preview tool to see preview options:

> **PRO VERSION**
> The Pro version does not have packing slips, so the Preview tool has no list arrow with options. The tool allows only previewing of invoices.

Click **Print Preview For Invoice** or **choose** the **File menu**, **Invoices** and **click Print Preview.**

The form settings for the invoice must be correct. If your invoice form is not in the location indicated on the Report & Form Options page, you will see this message when you attempt to preview or print an invoice:

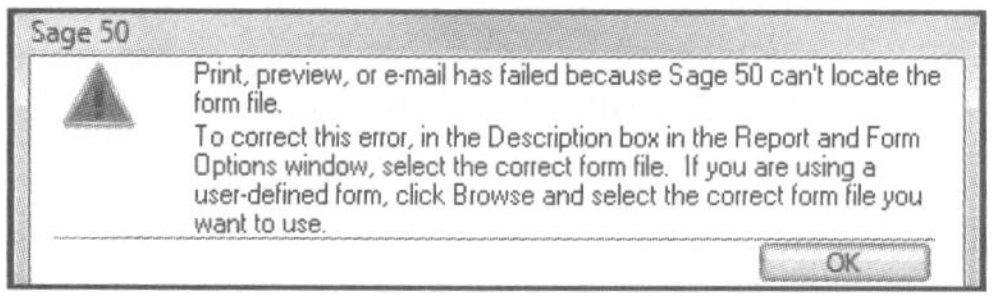

> **WARNING!**
> The file locations in the Form fields (for Printer and E-mail) must be correct for your setup or you will receive an error message. You can click Browse and locate the Forms folder inside the Sage 50 Premium Accounting 2013 folder.

Click OK to open the Report & Form Options window:

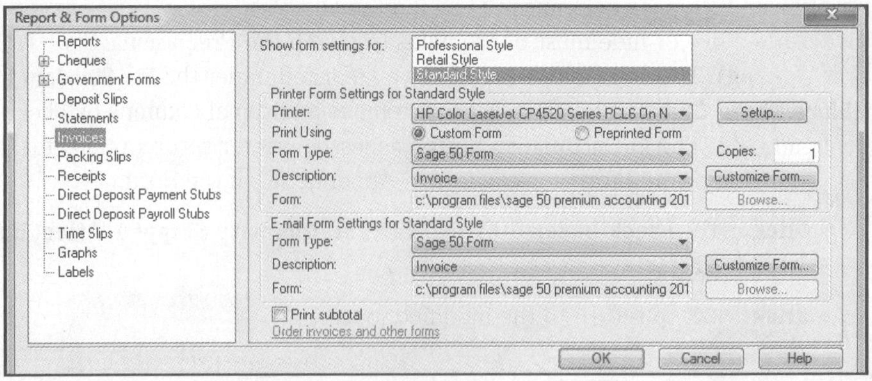

In the journal window, you can click [icon], the Change The Default Printer Settings tool, any time to open the forms settings screen for customer invoices.

You must choose Custom Form as the Print Using option and Sage 50 Form as the Form Type. Click OK. You should now be able to preview the invoice.

Click the Print Preview For Invoice tool to see a copy of your invoice:

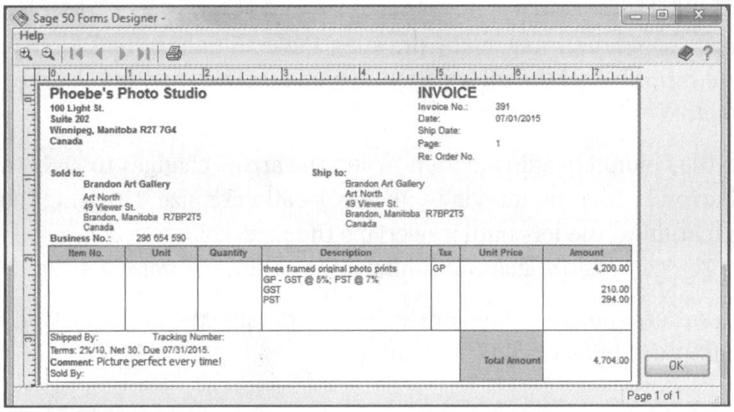

You can now print the invoice if you want by clicking the Print tool [icon] in the Preview window or clicking OK, returning to the Invoice and choosing the File menu and clicking Print or by clicking the Print tool in the journal window.

NOTES
Customizing the journal does not change the printed invoice. Refer to Appendix F on the Student DVD to learn how to customize printed invoices and other forms.

NOTES
You need the Crystal Report Writer program to view and customize Custom Crystal Forms – the other option on the Form Type drop-down list.

Posting

When you are certain that you have entered the transaction correctly, you must post it.

Notice that the Post button has a list arrow with two options:

If you regularly print invoices when you enter them, as for point-of-sale transactions, you can click Print & Post on this button (add a ✓). Printing and posting will become the default selection and the button label changes to reflect this choice:

Previewing invoices is always recommended before printing. Because we do not want to print all invoices, we will accept the initial default setting to Post.

Click the **Post button** [Post]. **Click OK** to confirm successful posting. A new blank Revenues Journal form appears on the screen.

NOTES
If invoices are printed as a batch or when you are learning the program, you should use Post as the default selection.
Batch printing of invoices and other forms is covered in Chapter 14.

NOTES
You can also choose the Revenues menu and click Post or press alt + P to save your transaction.

Close the **Revenues Journal** because the next transaction is a receipt.

Notice that the balance for Brandon Art Gallery in the Clients list has been updated.

Accounting for Receipts

Receipts from customers are entered in much the same way as payments to suppliers. After you choose the customer, outstanding invoices appear automatically and you can enter the payment amounts without entering any accounts. Phoebe's Photo Studio offers early payment discounts as an incentive to customers to pay their accounts promptly.

Receipts are entered in the Receipts Journal indicated by the arrow:

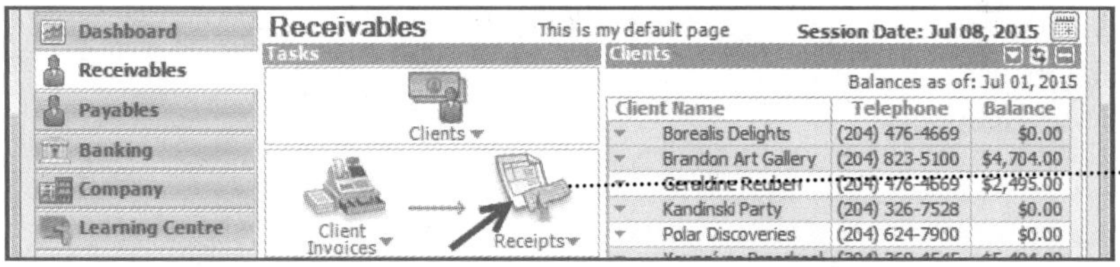

NOTES

A discount of 2 percent for paying within 10 days is comparable to an interest penalty of 36 percent per year – it costs the customer 2 percent to borrow the money for the extra 20 days.

✓ 2

Cash Receipt #41 **Dated July 2/15**

From Geraldine Reuben, cheque #302 for $1 754.80, including $754.80 in full payment of invoice #PS-377 and $1 000 in partial payment of invoice #PS-381, and allowing $45.20 discount for early payment. Customize the journal by changing the tabbing order.

CLASSIC VIEW

The Receipts icon is located below the Revenues icon. It has no shortcuts list arrow.

Click the **Receipts icon** to open the Receipts Journal:

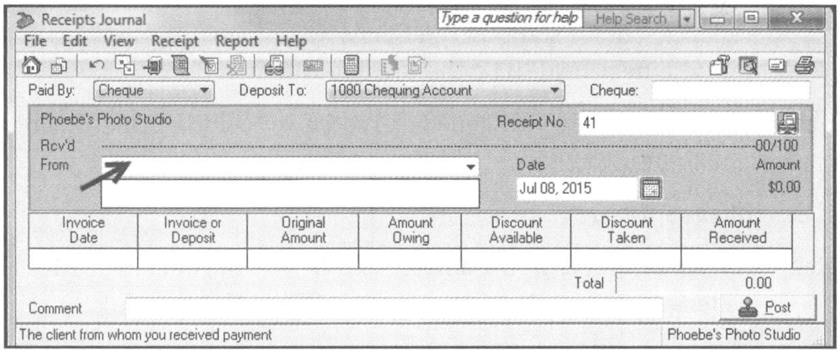

PRO VERSION

The Refresh tools do not appear in the Pro version; Invoice replaces Client Invoice in the journal column headings.

As with the Sales Invoice, you can customize the journal by removing fields and changing the tabbing order.

Click the **Customize Journal tool** or **choose** the **View menu** and **click Customize Journal**:

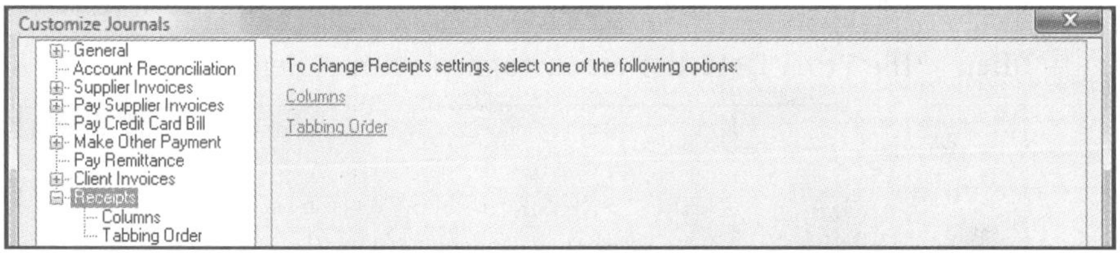

NOTES

Two tools, and , will refresh the journal with changes made by other users, such as the addition of new invoices. The list of outstanding invoices and the invoices themselves can be updated.

Click **Columns** to open the customization options for columns.

When they are not needed, you can remove the Invoice Date and the two Discount columns. Phoebe's Photo Studio offers customer discounts so we must include these columns.

Click **Tabbing Order** in the list under Receipts to continue:

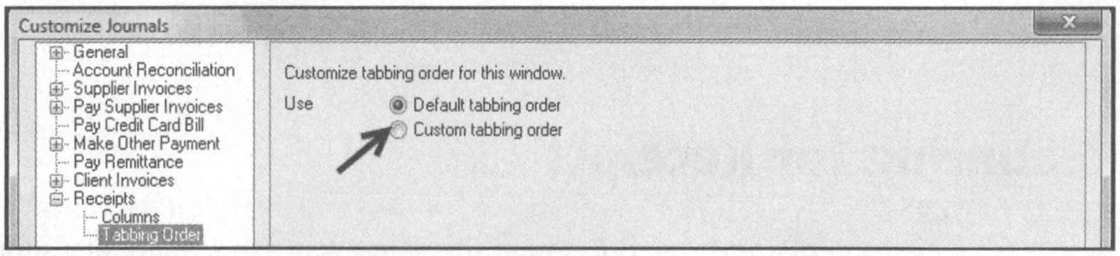

You can choose the default tabbing order or you can change the order.

Click **Custom Tabbing Order** to continue:

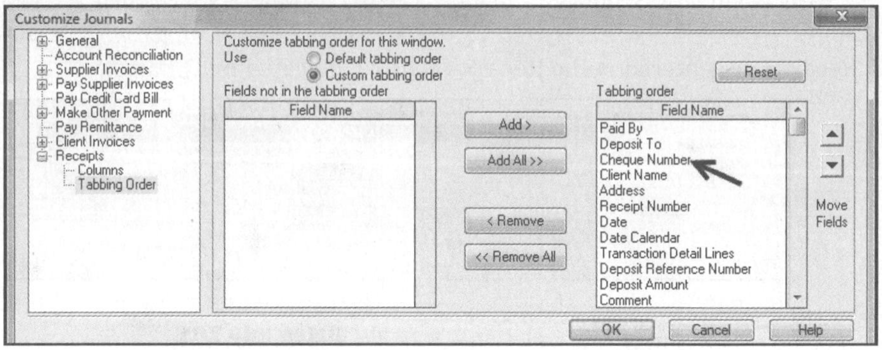

We will change the order so that after choosing the customer, the cursor will move to the cheque number field. This field is in the upper right-hand corner. With the default tabbing order, the cursor reaches this field last, making it easy to forget to enter the number. The cheque number is not a required field, so the program does not warn you if you omit the number.

Notice that Cheque Number appears before Client Name. However, when you open the Receipts Journal, the cursor starts in the Client Name field, so the Cheque Number field is last. We want the next field to be the Cheque Number.

NOTES

You can customize the order further by making the date field follow the cheque number and so on.

You can also choose to remove other fields that are not used. To access a skipped field after you remove it from the tabbing order, you can click the field.

To move a field, select it and then click the Move Fields Up and Down arrows beside the list until you have the order you want.

Click **Cheque Number**.

Click the **Move Fields Down button** beside the Tabbing Order list. This will place Cheque Number after the Client Name.

Click **Address** in the Tabbing Order column. **Click Remove** to skip all the address field lines when you press Tab.

Removing fields from the tabbing order does not remove them from the journal, just from the tabbing sequence.

Click **OK** to return to the form. You can now enter the receipt.

Click the **From field list arrow** to display the Client list:

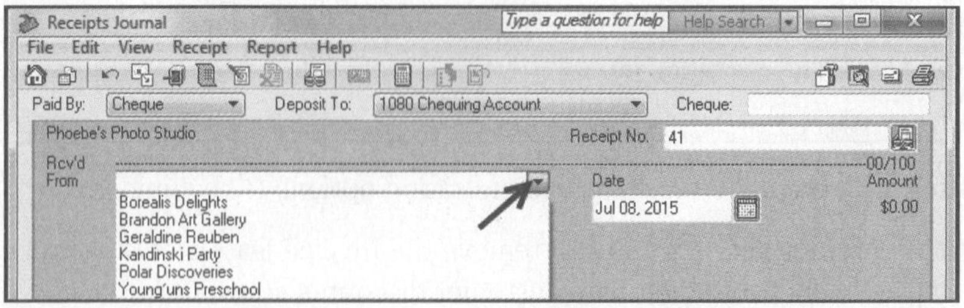

Click **Geraldine Reuben** to choose this customer:

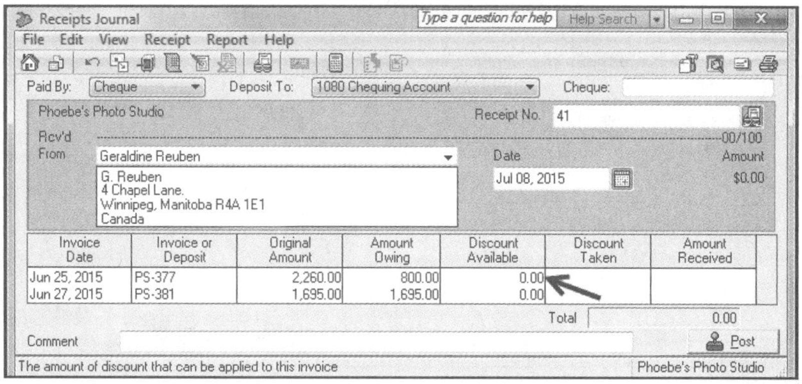

The customer's name and address have been added to your input form, together with all outstanding invoices for the customer. Notice that no discount appears in the Discount Available fields because the session date is past the 10-day discount period.

As with payments to suppliers, you cannot enter account numbers in the Receipts Journal. You need to enter only the amount paid on the appropriate invoice line. The program automatically creates the journal entry.

Phoebe's Photo Studio has a single bank account so it is correctly selected in the Deposit To field. If you have chosen the wrong customer, display the list again and click the correct customer. If you have selected correctly,

Press *tab* to move to the **Cheque field**.

Type 302

The Receipt No. field records the receipt number, which increases automatically. From the Lookup icon beside the Receipt No. field, you can look up previously posted receipts.

We need to replace the session date with the date for this transaction.

Choose July 2 from the Date field pop-up calendar. **Press** *tab* to move the cursor to the Invoice Date field. The discounts are now available:

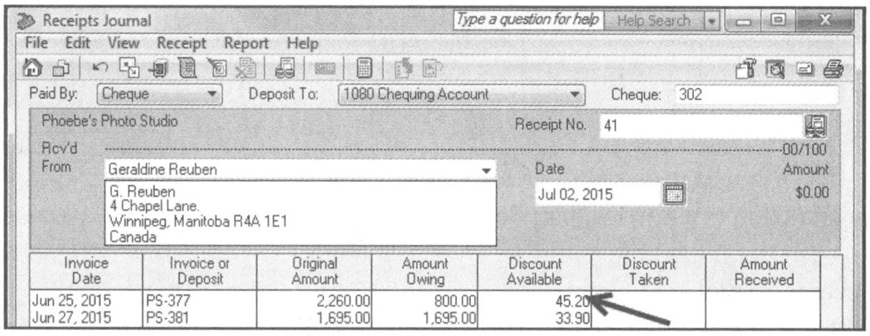

Notice that the discount is 2 percent of the original amount, not the amount owing. Until the discount period has passed, the full discount remains available.

Press *tab* to advance to the Discount Taken field.

Discount amounts can be changed or deleted. We will accept this discount.

Press *tab* to advance to the Amount Received field.

By default, the amount owing on the first invoice is shown and highlighted. All outstanding invoices are listed on the screen. For this invoice, the full amount is being paid so you can accept the default. Notice that the discount has been subtracted from the amount owing.

Press *tab* to accept the discounted amount in the Amount Received field.

NOTES
Sage 50 allows you to set up more than one bank account. When more than one bank account is set up, choose the account from the Deposit To drop-down list.

NOTES
You can use the Lookup button to review a receipt or to reverse it (see page 176).

NOTES
The year is added correctly in the Receipts Journal when you type the month and day.

NOTES
For other company types, the Invoice Date column may be labelled Statement Date, Bill Date and so on.

NOTES
You can accept a highlighted amount or type an exact amount for a partial payment.

The cursor will advance to the Discount Taken field for the next invoice:

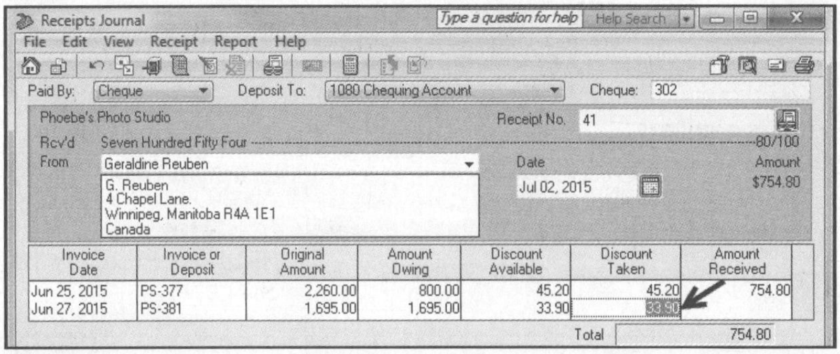

Because the payment for this invoice is only a partial payment, we need to remove the discount.

Press del to remove the discount for the second invoice.

Press tab to advance to the Amount Received field.

This time the full invoice amount is entered because the discount has been changed to zero. However, the full amount is not being paid, so we must edit the amount. To replace the highlighted default amount,

Type 1000

Press tab to enter the new amount and complete the invoice as shown:

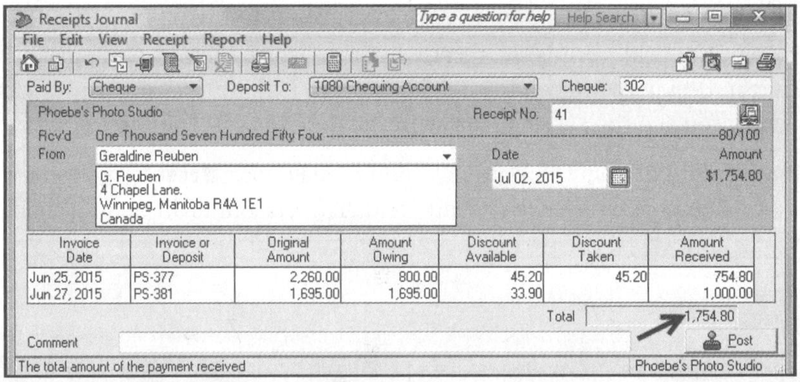

Notice that the upper cheque portion of the form has also been completed. In making Receipts Journal entries, you do not need to enter any accounts because Sage 50 chooses the linked bank and receivable accounts defined for the Receivables Ledger to create the journal entry.

You have made all the entries for this transaction, so you are ready to review before posting your transaction.

Reviewing the Receipts Journal Entry

Choose the **Report menu** and **click Display Receipts Journal Entry**:

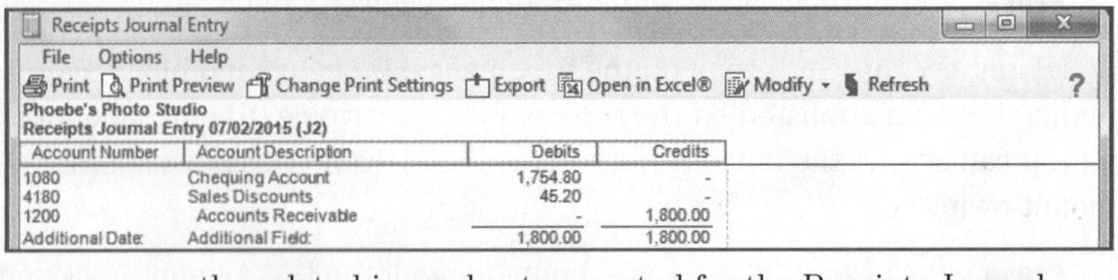
Receipts Journal Entry

File Options Help

Print | Print Preview | Change Print Settings | Export | Open in Excel® | Modify | Refresh

Phoebe's Photo Studio

Receipts Journal Entry 07/02/2015 (J2)

Account Number	Account Description	Debits	Credits
1080	Chequing Account	1,754.80	-
4180	Sales Discounts	45.20	-
1200	Accounts Receivable	-	1,800.00
Additional Date:	Additional Field:	1,800.00	1,800.00

Here you can see the related journal entry created for the Receipts Journal transaction. Sage 50 updates the General Ledger *Accounts Receivable* control account and *Chequing Account* because the Receivables and General ledgers are fully

WARNING!

When an invoice or discount amount is highlighted and it is not being included, press del to remove the amount from the total, and press tab to advance to the Amount Received field.

Refer to the Payment transaction on page 130 to see the error from not removing the second discount. Even though the cheque total appears correct on the screen, the posted entry will be incorrect.

NOTES

The direct link between sales and payments for a customer provides another reason for using the Receivables Ledger for sales entries instead of the General Ledger. In addition, discounts are calculated automatically and you cannot select incorrect accounts.

integrated. Phoebe's Photo Studio uses *Chequing Account* as its single default linked bank account for the Receivables Ledger as well as for the Payables Ledger. *Accounts Receivable* and the customer's balance owing are reduced by the full amount of the payment plus the amount of the discount taken ($1 800). The discount amount is automatically debited to the linked *Sales Discounts* account. *Sales Discounts* is a contra-revenue account. It has a debit balance and reduces total revenue.

Close the **display** to return to the Receipts Journal input screen.

CORRECTING THE RECEIPTS JOURNAL ENTRY BEFORE POSTING

Move to the field with the error. **Press** tab to move forward or shift and tab together to move back to a previous field. This will highlight the field contents. **Type** the **correct information** and **press** tab to enter it.

You can also use the mouse to **point** to a field and **drag through** the **incorrect information** to highlight it. **Type** the **correct information** and **press** tab to enter it.

If the customer is incorrect, **reselect** from the **Client** list by **clicking** the **Client list arrow**. **Click** the name of the correct **client**. To confirm that you want to discard the current transaction, **click Yes** to display the outstanding invoices for the correct customer. **Type** the **correct** receipt **information**.

You can also discard the entry and begin again. **Click** [X] or [↶] and then **click Yes** to confirm.

Posting

When you are certain that you have entered all the information correctly, you must post the transaction to save it.

Click the **Post button** Post or **choose** the **Receipt menu** and **click Post** to save your transaction. **Click OK**.

Close the **Receipts Journal**.

Entering Cash Sales

For the next sale, the customer made an immediate payment by cheque. We use the term cash sale for all sales when immediate payment is made by cash or cheque.

✓ 3

Cash Sales Invoice #PS-392 **Dated July 3/15**

To Kandinski Party, $1 800 plus $90 GST and $126 PST for family portrait photo package before wedding. Terms: 2 percent discount ($40.32) with cash received on completion of work. Received cheque #569 for $1 975.68 in full payment.

Click the **Client Invoices icon** Client Invoices to open the Revenues Journal. Notice that the invoice number has been updated to 392.

Click the **Payment Method list arrow** to view the payment options — Pay Later, Cash, Cheque, Pre-Authorized Debit and Credit Card:

PRO VERSION
Click the Sales Invoices icon Sales Invoices to open the Sales Journal.

NOTES
Pre-Authorized Debits (PAD) are covered in Chapter 13.

NOTES
When you choose Cash as the payment method, the cheque number field is not included. For Pre-Authorized Debits, the Cheque No. field becomes the PAD No. field.

Click **Cheque** as the method of payment to modify the invoice screen.

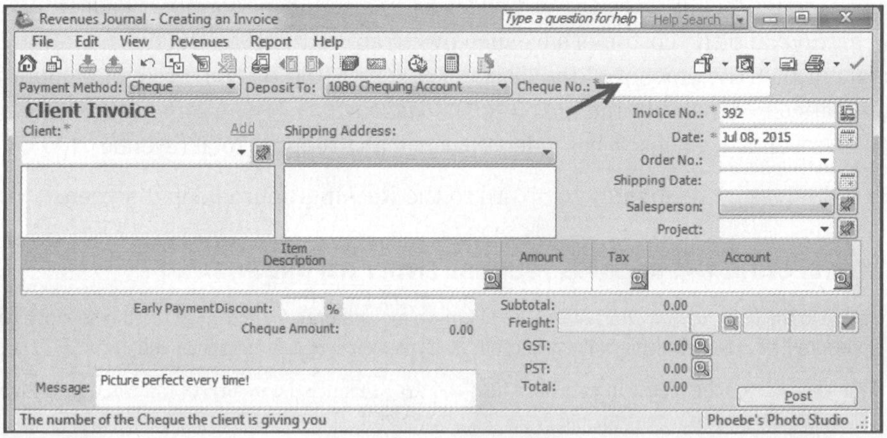

As shown here, when you choose Cheque as the method of payment, a cheque number field is added in the upper right-hand corner of the invoice so that you can add the customer's cheque number. The Deposit To bank account field is also added. In the payment terms section, the Net Days field has been removed and a Cheque Amount field has been added.

Press *tab* **twice** to advance to the Cheque No. field.

Type `569` **Press** *tab* to advance to the Client field.

Type `K`

Kandinski Party is added to the Client field because it is the first customer entry beginning with K. The rest of the name is still highlighted in case you want to continue typing another name.

Enter **July 3** in the Date field as the transaction date.

Enter a **description**. **Press** *tab* to advance to the Amount field.

Type `1800`

Double-click the **Account field**.

Notice that the cheque amount below the terms has been updated.

Click **Suggested Accounts** below the account list to modify the list:

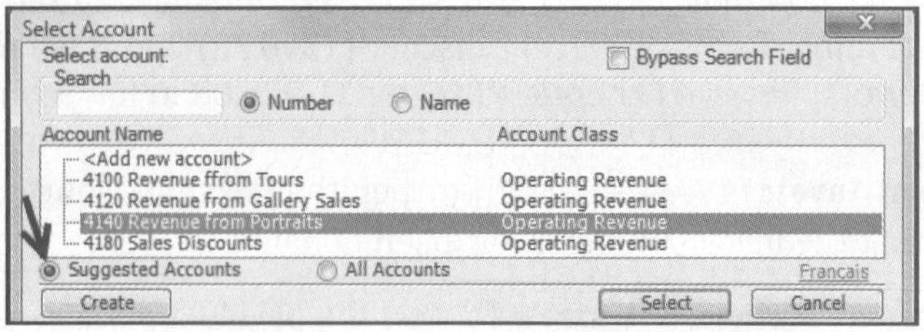

NOTES
When you open the Purchases Journal, the list of suggested accounts will show only the Expense accounts. You will need to choose All Accounts to include Asset accounts in the list.

The list of suggested accounts now includes only Revenue accounts because we are in the Revenues Journal. This shorter list makes it easier to select the correct account. For purchases, only expense accounts will be listed. You can switch back to the complete account list at any time by selecting **All Accounts**. The Suggested Accounts button remains selected when we close the journal until we change the selection again.

In this case, however, the default account for the customer is correct and may still be selected.

Click **4140 Revenue from Portraits**. **Press** *enter*.

Click the **Message field**. **Type** `Thank you` to complete the sales entry:

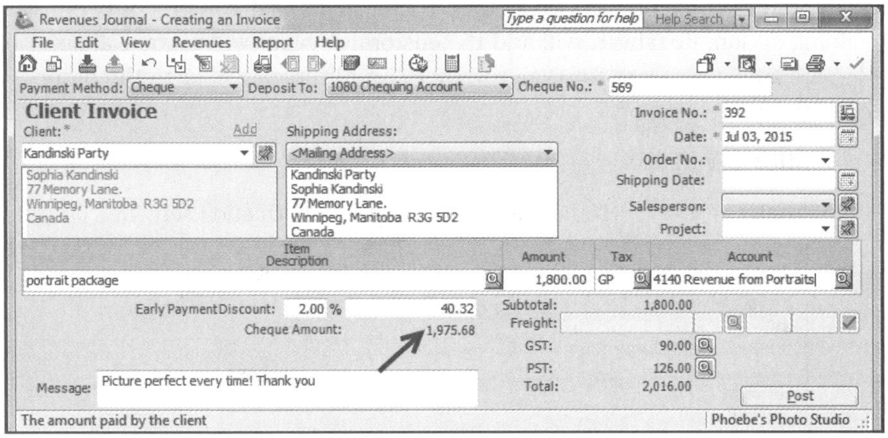

As usual, you should review the entry.

Choose the **Report menu** and **click Display Revenues Journal Entry**:

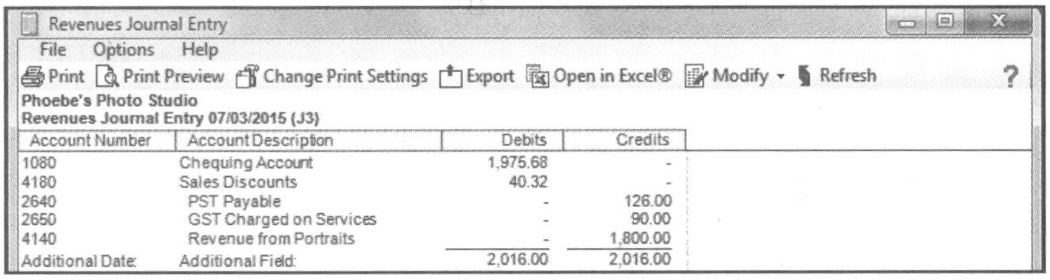

Account Number	Account Description	Debits	Credits
1080	Chequing Account	1,975.68	-
4180	Sales Discounts	40.32	-
2640	PST Payable	-	126.00
2650	GST Charged on Services	-	90.00
4140	Revenue from Portraits	-	1,800.00
Additional Date:	Additional Field:	2,016.00	2,016.00

Notice that *Chequing Account* is debited automatically instead of *Accounts Receivable* because we selected Cheque as the method of payment.

Close the **display** when you have finished. **Make corrections** if necessary.

Click **Post** [Post] to save the entry. **Click OK**. Leave the journal open.

Adding a New Customer

The next sale is to a new customer who should be added to your files. We will add the customer directly from the Revenues Journal.

✓ 4 **Sales Invoice #PS-393** **Dated July 3/15**

To Marci Litman (use Full Add for the new customer), $2 100 plus $105 GST and $147 PST for modelling portfolio. Invoice total $2 352. Terms: 2/10, n/30.

Click the **Payment Method field** and **choose Pay Later**. The date is correct.

Click the **Client field**.

Type `Marci Litman`

Press *tab* to display the notice that you have typed a name that is not on the list. This notice provides the option to add a ledger record:

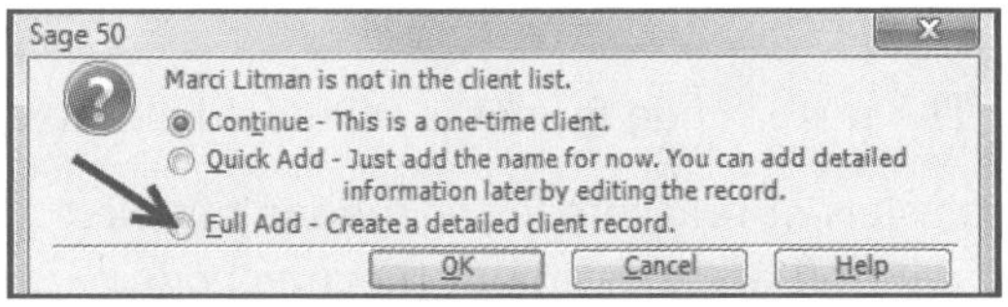

The options are the same as for new suppliers. If you typed an incorrect name, click **Cancel** to return to the journal and start again. If you typed the name correctly, you can choose to add the customer's name only — **Quick Add** — or to add a full customer record with the **Full Add** option. If you need to change any defaults, you must choose

NOTES

Marci Litman
✓ (contact Marci)
36 Runway Alley, Apt. 201
Oakbank, MB R0E 1J0
Tel 1: (204) 538-2436
Mobile: (204) 638-2436
E-mail: marci@hotmail.com
Web: www.marci.com
Terms: 2/10, n/30
Revenue account: 4140
Tax code: GP
Credit limit: $3 000

the Full Add option. You can still skip customer fields that you do not need. The remaining option, **Continue**, will add the customer's name to the journal entry but will not create a ledger record for the customer or add the customer to the other Receivables Ledger reports.

Click **Full Add**.

Click **OK** to open the customer's Address information screen:

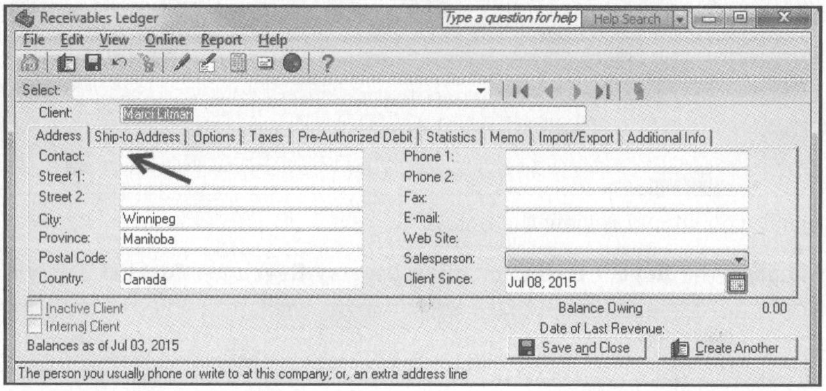

Clicking Add above the Client field opens this ledger form directly from the journal at the Address tab screen.

PRO VERSION
Remember that you will see the term Customer instead of Client. The Internal Client option and the Refresh tool do not apply to the Pro version.

You are ready to enter your new customer. The Client field is completed with the new name highlighted for editing if necessary. The Client name is the only required field for new customer records. Because it is already entered, the * reminder symbol for required fields has been removed.

The field we need next is the Contact field. Enter the name of the particular individual Phoebe's Photo Studio normally deals with.

Click the **Contact field**.

Type `Marci`

Press *tab* to move the cursor to the Street 1 field.

Type `36 Runway Alley` **Press** *tab*.

Type `Apt. 201` **Press** *tab* to move to and select the City field.

Notice that the city, province and country in which Phoebe's Photo Studio is located have been entered by default from the Address Settings. The province is correct but you must change the city.

Type `Oakbank`

Click the **Postal Code field**.

You do not need to use capital letters or to leave a space within Canadian postal codes. The program will make these adjustments.

Type `r0e1j0`

Click the **Phone 1 field**. The postal code format is corrected automatically.

You do not need to add spaces, dashes or brackets for telephone numbers. Telephone and fax numbers may be entered with or without the area code.

Type `2045382436` **Press** *tab*. Enter the mobile number as Phone 2.

Type `2046382436` **Press** *tab* to move to the Fax field.

Press *tab* to skip the fax field and advance to the E-mail field.

Notice that the format for telephone and fax numbers is corrected automatically.

E-mail and Web addresses are typed exactly as you would type them in your regular Internet and e-mail access programs. You can also add these details later when you actually want to use them. When you click the Web or E-mail tools, you will be prompted to enter the addresses if they are not part of the customer's record already.

Type `marci@hotmail.com` **Press** *tab*.

Type `www.marci.com`

When salespersons are set up, you can choose the name of the regular sales contact person for a customer from the drop-down list in the **Salesperson** field. Phoebe's Photo Studio does not have salespersons set up. Salespersons are covered in Chapter 9.

Litman is making her first purchase on July 3, but the session date is entered as the default date in the **Client Since** field.

Choose **July 3** from the Client Since field calendar icon.

The **Internal Client** option applies when one department supplies services to another and charges for these services. The option is available when time and billing is used. If the customer no longer buys from the company, but you still want to keep the record on file, mark the customer as **Inactive**. The **Balance Owing** and **Date Of Last Sale** will be entered automatically by the program based on the customer's transactions.

PRO VERSION
The Pro version does not have an Internal Client option.

Click the **Ship-To Address tab**.

Click the **Address Name list arrow** to see the predefined names:

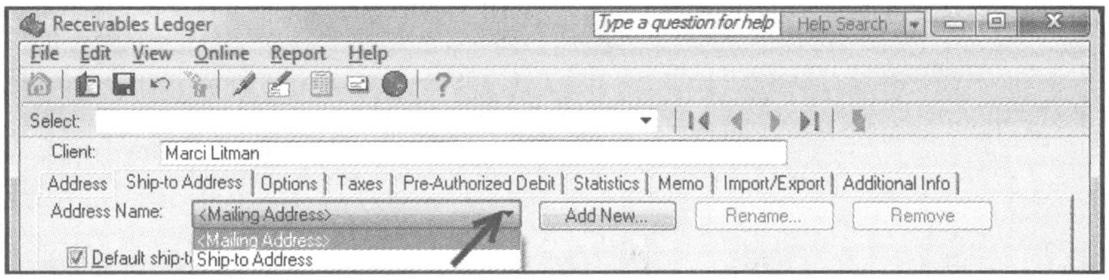

You can enter multiple customer addresses and apply your own labels for these addresses. For example, you may have separate summer and winter addresses for residential customers or different store locations for wholesale customers. The billing address may be different from the location where a service is provided or products are delivered. The mailing address is provided as the default ship-to address, as indicated by the ✓ for Default Ship-To Address and its entry in the Address Name field. The address information is dimmed because you cannot remove the mailing address on this screen. You can enter complete address and contact information for the shipping address, add new address labels and information for them, edit the labels and remove address names and labels that are not needed.

PRO VERSION
The Pro version allows only one additional address – the shipping address. You cannot edit the name of this second address. If the mailing address is different from the shipping address, click the Same As Mailing Address check box to remove the ✓ and then enter or edit the address fields.

Click **Ship-To Address** (or another address name) in the drop-down list.

This will remove the Default Ship-To Address ✓ and open the address fields for editing:

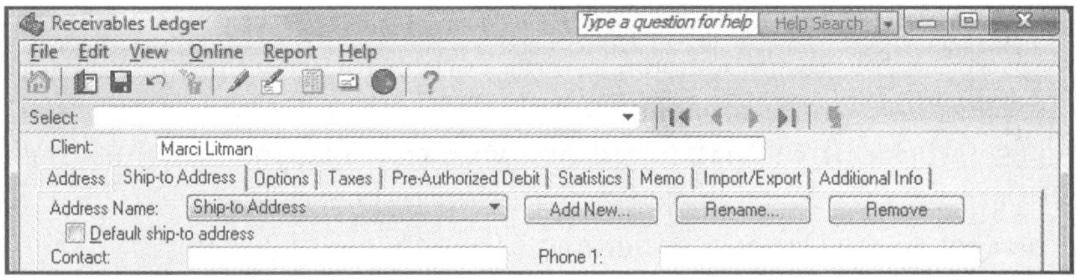

All the fields are now open for editing. You can make any address the Default Ship-To Address by clicking the check box when this label's information is displayed.

The shipping address is the same as the mailing address for this customer, so we can remove the ship-to address name for this customer.

Click **Remove** to see the confirmation warning message:

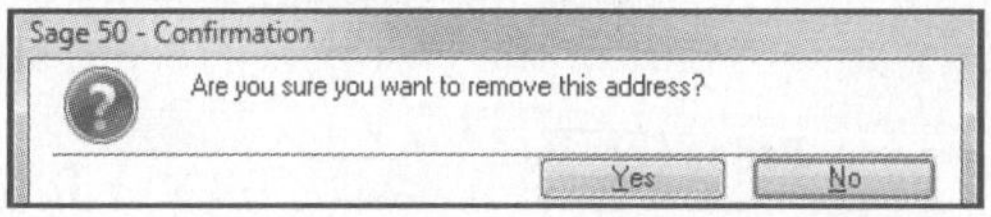

NOTES
You can add back an address name that you removed by clicking Add New and re-entering its name.

Click **Yes** to confirm the removal.

Click **Add New** to open the name field to add a new address:

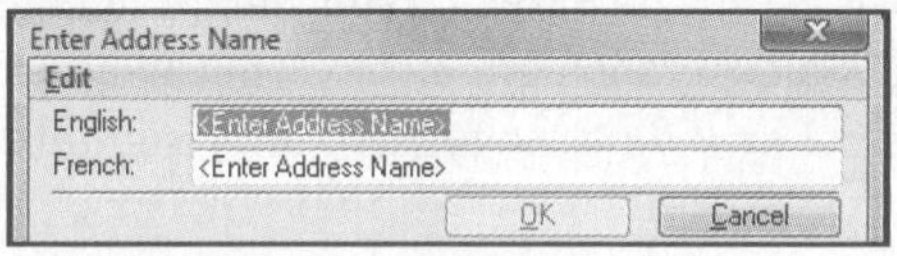

Type a new name and then click OK to have the new name appear in the drop-down list. Then you can select it to add the address details.

Click **Cancel** to return to the Ship-To Address tab screen.

Click the **Options tab**:

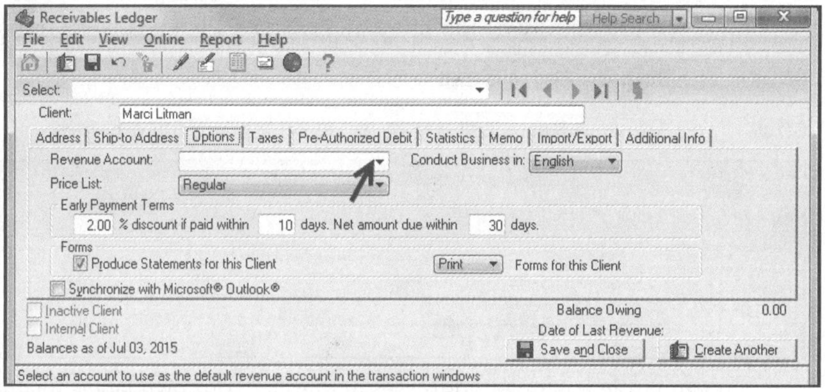

The first option is to add a default revenue account for the customer.

Click the **Revenue Account list arrow**.

Click **4140**.

The Options tab screen contains payment terms details. The default terms are entered from the ledger settings. The **Price List** — Regular, Preferred or Web Price — refers to the prices customers pay for inventory items and will be introduced in Chapter 10. For Phoebe's Photo Studio, all customers pay Regular prices. You can select French or English as the customer's preferred **language for conducting business**. Sales invoices and other forms you prepare for customers will be printed in the language you select here. Your own program screens will not change.

The payment terms for Marci Litman are the same as those for other customers and are entered by default.

PRO VERSION
The option to Synchronize With Microsoft Outlook is not available in the Pro version.

You may also choose to **Produce Statements For This Client**, and you may print or e-mail invoices and quotes. You should use the correct forms, but you can also print statements on ordinary printer paper.

If you use **Microsoft Outlook** to organize your contacts, you can synchronize the address list in Sage 50 with Outlook.

You can change the Options tab settings at any time.

Click the **Taxes tab**:

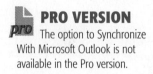

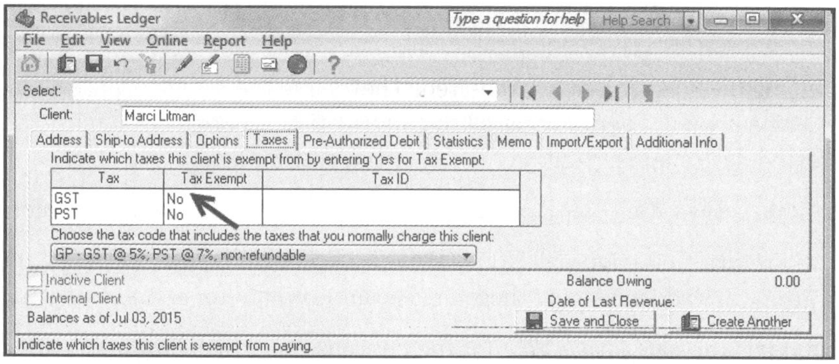

The customer is correctly described as not **Tax Exempt** for PST and GST by default, allowing accurate tax calculations for sales transactions to be included in Tax reports. The default tax code taken from the ledger settings is also correct.

Click **GP - GST @ 5%; PST @ 7%, non-refundable** to see the codes available. Do not change the tax code for this customer.

Click the **Pre-Authorized Debit tab**:

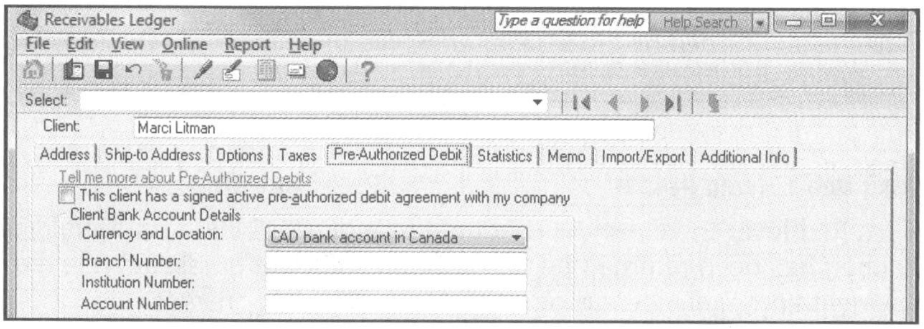

If your customer allows direct payment from its bank account, you must enter the bank account information on this screen.

Click the **Statistics tab** to open the next screen we need:

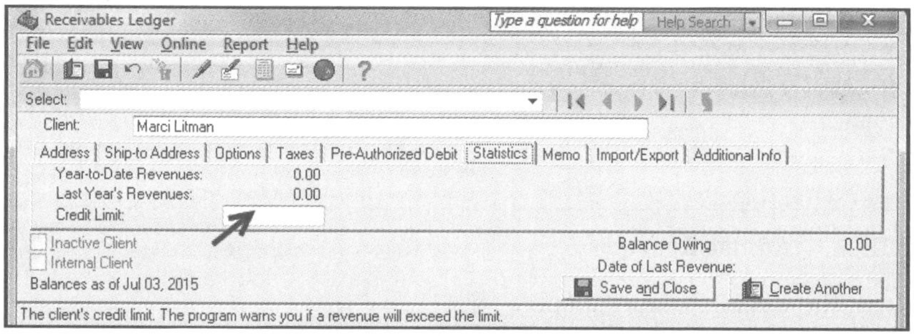

The Statistics screen has a summary of the sales to the customer for the current year and the previous year. These fields are updated from sales transactions.

In the **Credit Limit** field, you can enter the customer's credit limit to help minimize bad debts. When a customer exceeds the credit limit, the program will warn you before you can post the sale with this message:

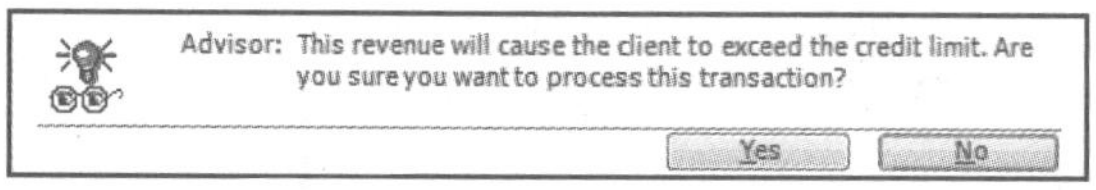

You can click Yes to accept the over-the-limit sale, or No to return to the invoice and ask for a deposit to avoid exceeding the credit limit. Customers who have previously defaulted on making their payments can be placed on a cash-only basis by setting their credit limits at zero. Phoebe's Photo Studio is analyzing customer payment trends at present and will set Litman's limit at $3 000 on a trial basis.

Click the **Credit Limit field** to position the cursor and **type** 3000

WARNING!

Unless you have indicated that the customer is not exempt from taxes, the taxes will not be calculated in the Revenues Journal for that customer, even if you select the correct tax code in the journal.

NOTES

You must have a signed agreement from your customer allowing the pre-authorized debit. Then click the check box on this tab screen and enter the customer's banking details. Usually the customer provides a void cheque for the bank account details.

Pre-authorized debits are covered in Chapter 13.

NOTES

Sage 50 adds the total amount from the current sale to the balance owing to assess whether the customer has exceeded the credit limit.

NOTES

Customers should be notified of credit policy changes.

Saving a New Customer Account

The remaining tab screens are not required. They serve the same purpose as they do for suppliers. When you are certain that all the information is correct, you must save the newly created customer account and add it to the current list.

Click **Save And Close** [Save and Close] to save the new customer information.

You will return to the journal. Notice that the tax code, revenue account and payment terms are added. Any of these fields can be edited for an individual invoice.

Enter the **sale** (page 171) for the new customer by following the procedures outlined earlier.

Review the **journal entry**. **Close** the **display** and **make corrections**.

Click **Post** [Post]. **Click OK** and then **close** the **Revenues Journal**.

Reversing a Receipt (NSF Cheques)

When a cheque is returned by the bank as NSF, you need to record the fact that the invoice is still outstanding. You can do this in the Receipts Journal by reversing the cheque.

✓ 5

Bank Debit Memo #14321 **Dated July 4/15**

From Red River Credit Union, cheque #302 for $1 754.80 from Geraldine Reuben has been returned because of non-sufficient funds. Reverse the payment and notify the customer of the outstanding charges.

Click the **Receipts icon shortcuts list arrow** [Receipts▾] as shown:

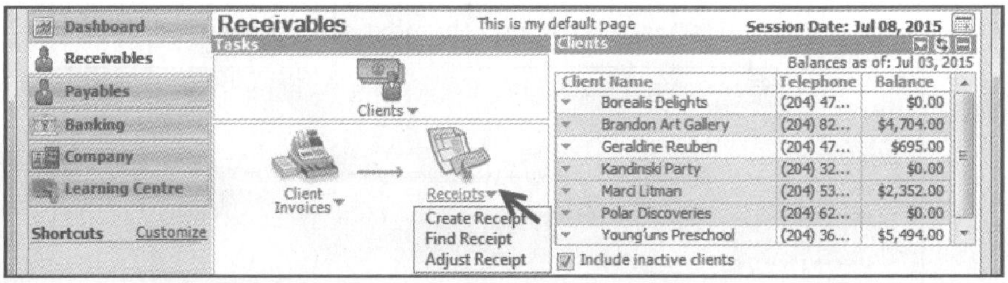

Click **Adjust Receipt.**

Or, with the Receipts Journal open,

Click the **Adjust Receipt tool**, or **press** ctrl + **A**, or **choose** the **Receipt menu** and **click Adjust Receipt**.

You can also **click** the **Lookup tool**, or **press** ctrl + **L**, or **choose** the **Receipt menu** and **click Look Up Receipt**.

The familiar Search screen opens with Receipts as the search area:

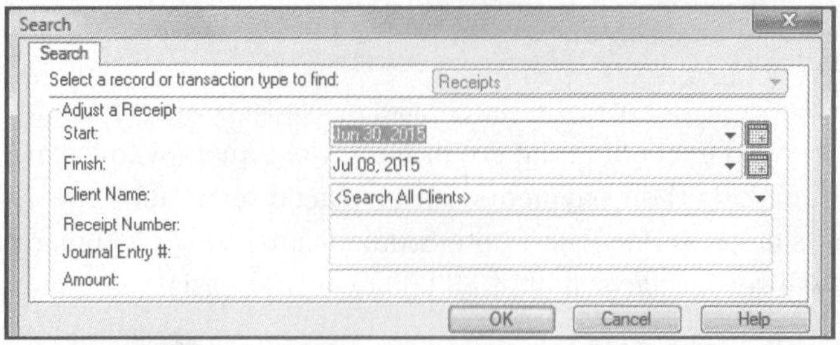

NOTES

The Home window Clients list pane shows the balances as at July 3, the latest transaction date, and not at the session date. This selection is a user preference.

NOTES

The Lookup and Adjust tools both open the Search window. The Reverse tool and menu option are available from the journal windows provided by both.

Find Receipt in the Receipts icon shortcuts list also opens the Search window.

From Lookup and Find Receipt, the search parameters will show Receipt Lookup as the heading.

NOTES

If you recorded a receipt incorrectly, and do not need to reverse it, you can choose the Adjust Receipt tool to access the posted receipt and make the correction, just as you do for sales (page 182) or for payments (page 137).

Click **OK** to see all the receipts we have entered:

The single cheque from Geraldine Reuben we have entered is selected.

Press *enter* or **click Select** to open the cheque we entered:

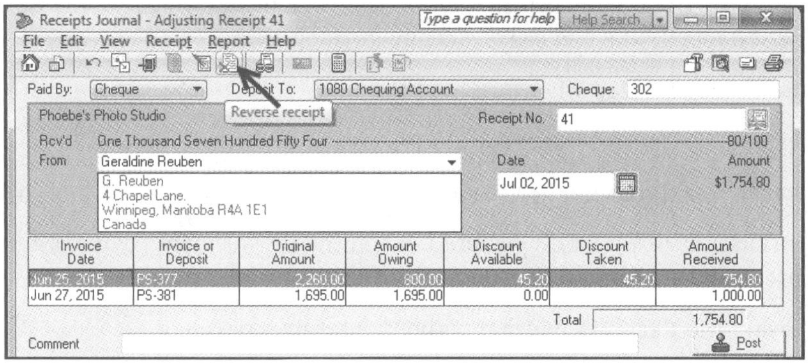

At this stage you can adjust the cheque by editing incorrectly entered information, just as you can edit a purchase invoice or payment cheque.

We need to reverse the cheque because it has been returned as NSF.

Click the **Reverse Receipt tool** or **choose** the **Receipt menu** and **click Reverse Receipt** to see the confirmation message:

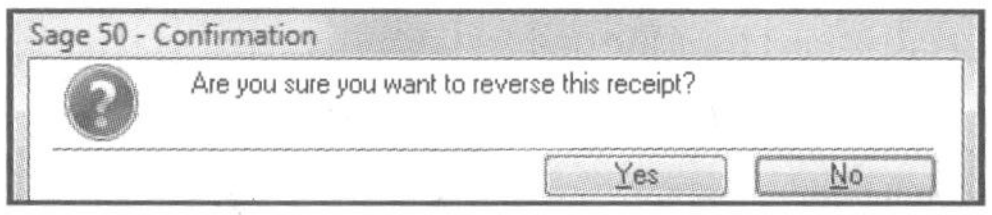

Click **Yes** to confirm the reversal. **Click OK** when Sage 50 confirms the successful reversal. A blank Receipts Journal form opens.

We will look at the journal report generated by reversing this receipt.

Minimize the **Receipts Journal** (**click**) to return to the Home window.

Choose the **Reports menu**, then **choose Journal Entries** and **click Receipts** to open the report options window:

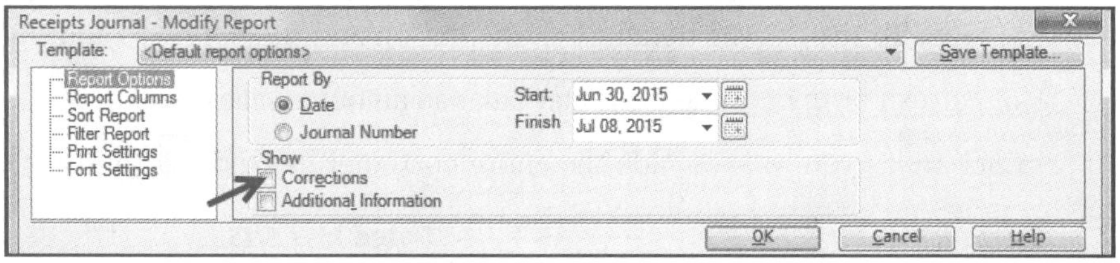

By default, corrections are not included in reports. In order to see adjustments, we must include them. The remaining defaults are correct.

Click **Corrections** under the Show heading. **Click OK**:

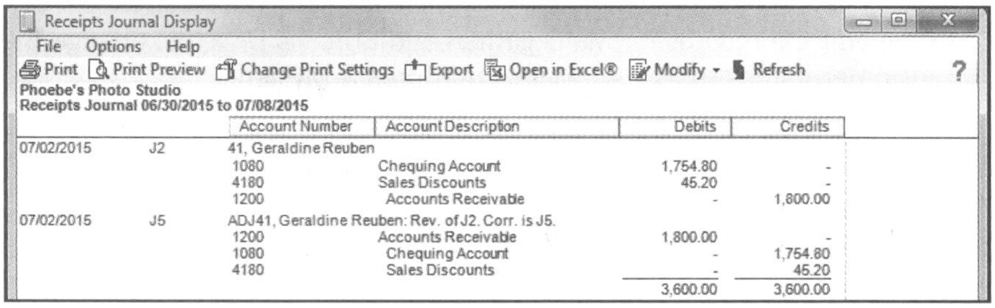

NOTES

In Chapter 15, you will see that you cannot reverse the receipt if the cheque is not deposited directly to the bank account when you enter the receipt (that is, the bank deposit is recorded later as a separate transaction). Instead, you must enter a negative receipt.

NOTES

If you started from the Lookup window, you can click the Adjust Receipt tool if you need to open the fields for editing.

NOTES

If you change the customer when adjusting a receipt, the program will reverse the original receipt when you click Yes to confirm this action.

CLASSIC VIEW

From the Home window, right-click the Receipts icon . Click the Display tool to see the Receipts Journal report options.

NOTES

You can also click the Report Centre icon. Then click Receivables, Receipts Journal Entries and Modify This Report to open the report options.

WARNING!

If you display the Journal Report from the Home window Reports pane list of reports, you will use the default settings, which do not show corrections. You will see the message that there is no data because there are no other Receipts Journal entries.

You can see that the two entries cancel each other — all amounts were reversed, including the discount. The debits to *Chequing Account* and *Sales Discounts* were entered as credits in the reversing entry, and the credit to *Accounts Receivable* was entered as a debit. Sage 50 created the reversing entry automatically when we reversed the receipt, adding ADJ to the receipt number so that you can link the two transactions.

When you adjust a receipt and post the corrected entry, Sage 50 will create the intermediate reversing entry automatically. Three entries result — the original incorrect one, the reversing entry and the final corrected version, just as they do when you make adjustments in the General, Purchases and Payments journals. By including Corrections in the Journal Reports, you can see the complete audit trail.

NOTES
To restore the Receipts Journal, point to the Sage 50 icon or name on the Windows task bar. You should see pop-ups for both the Home window and the Receipts Journal (Windows 7). Click the Receipts Journal image (or its name on the task bar).

Close the **display** when you have finished.

Restore the **Receipts Journal**.

Choose **Geraldine Reuben** from the Client list.

Both invoices have been fully restored. When the replacement payment is received, you can enter it in the usual way.

Close the **Receipts Journal** without entering a payment.

Editing Customer Information

You can change customer information and you can change the way the Home window displays Clients pane details, just as you can modify the Suppliers pane.

When you click the button above the Clients list, you can see that the telephone number and balance owing can be removed from the Home window.

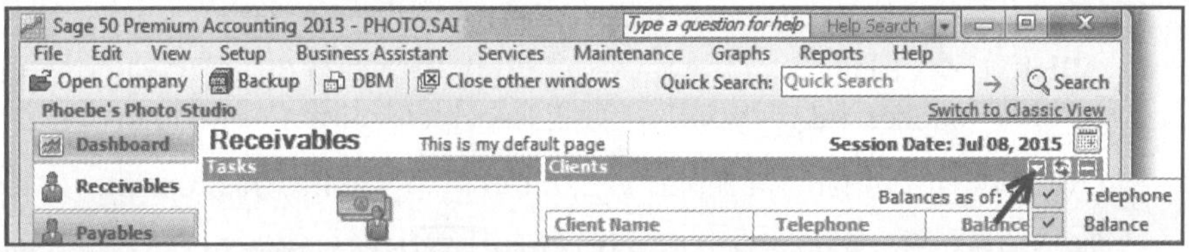

The ✓ indicates that information is displayed. When the computer is in a public area, you should hide the extra information.

To hide the additional details, click the button and click the detail you want to hide. To restore the detail, click the button and the option to add the ✓.

To refresh or update the customer balance amounts, click .

Click if you want to hide the entire customer list and to restore the list.

✓ 6

Memo #1 **Dated July 5/15**

From Owner: Edit the ledger record for Geraldine Reuben to change the payment terms to net 1. Certified cheques will be requested in the future. Set her credit limit to zero. Edit the customer's name as well – the last name should be first to keep the records in correct alphabetical order.

Then edit the records for Marci Litman and Borealis Delights. Change these customer names to Litman, Marci and Borealis Mysteries.

Most fields in the customer record can be changed at any time. Only the current balance owing, which is updated from sale and payment transactions, cannot be changed.

Click the **Clients icon shortcuts list arrow** as shown:

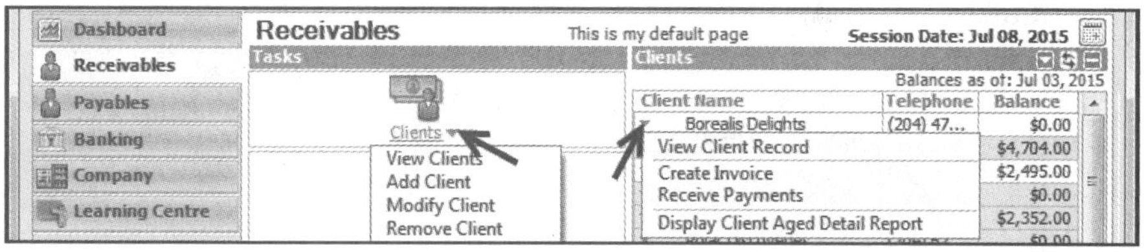

From the Clients shortcuts list, you can choose Modify Client. When the Search screen opens, you can select the customer.

You can click the customer's name in the right-hand Clients pane, or you can click the list arrow beside the customer's name and click View Client Record to open a record for a customer directly.

We will use a third option — to work from the Clients window.

Click the **Clients icon** to open the Clients window:

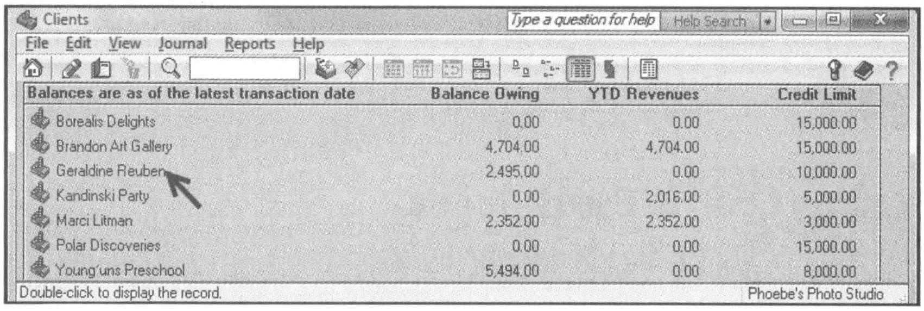

Click **Geraldine Reuben** to select her.

Click the **Edit tool** or **choose** the **File menu** and **click Open** or **double-click Geraldine Reuben**.

The Receivables Ledger record for Geraldine Reuben opens at the Address screen.

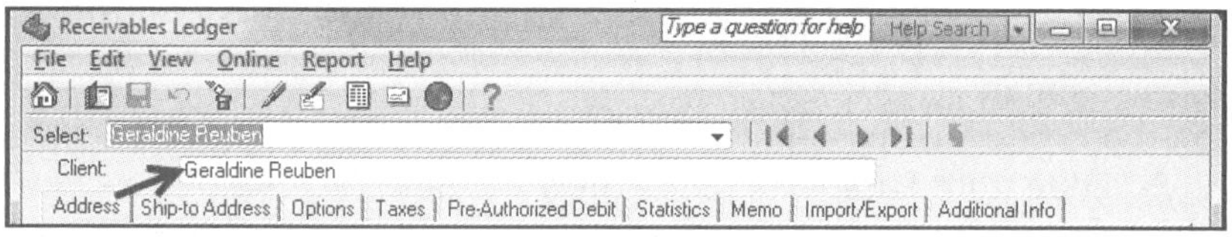

Double-click Geraldine Reuben in the Client name field to highlight the name.

Type `Reuben, Geraldine`

Next, we need to modify the Terms, which appear on the Options tab.

Click the **Options tab** to access the payment terms information:

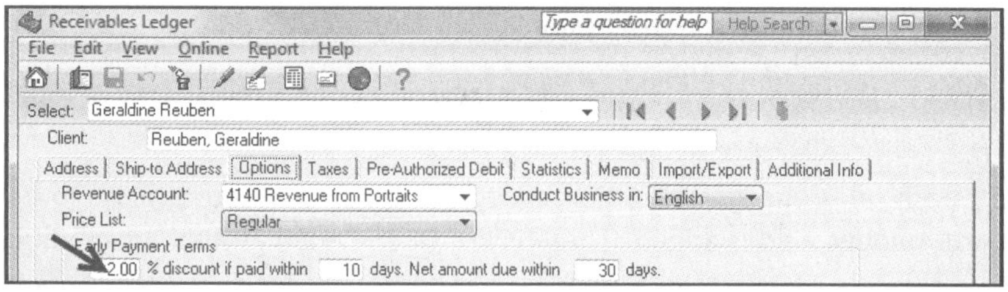

Click **2.00** in the % Discount field of the Early Payment Terms section.

Press *del* to remove the entry. **Press** *tab* to advance to the Days field.

Press *del*. **Press** *tab* to advance to the Net Days field. **Type** 1

NOTES

Typing zero (0) in the Net Days field will leave the field blank in the ledger and the journal.

Click the **Statistics tab**:

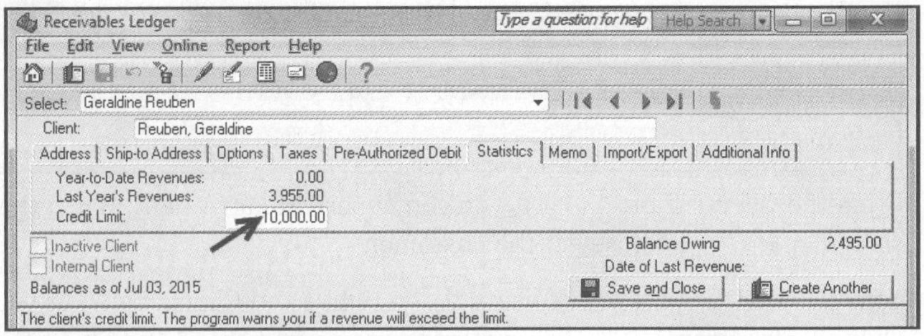

Click the **Credit Limit field** and **type** 0

To modify other customer records, click Next or Previous to move to a different record or choose the customer you need from the Select drop-down list. The Statistics tab screen will remain selected.

Click the **Address tab** and **edit** the other two **customer names**.

Close the **Receivables Ledger** and **close** the **Clients window**.

NOTES
The transaction fee varies from one card company to another, as well as from one retail customer to another and may range from 2 to 4 percent. Stores that have a larger volume of credit card sales usually pay lower transaction fees.

Entering Credit Card Sales

Most businesses accept credit cards from customers in lieu of cash and cheques. Customers expect this convenience, and although businesses benefit by avoiding NSF cheques, they do incur a cost for this service. Credit card companies charge the business a transaction fee: a percentage of each sale is withheld by the card company.

Credit card sales are entered like other sales, by selecting the correct payment method and then entering the invoice details.

NOTES
Choose One-Time Client and type Sales Summary in the Address field.
Use tax code GP for the Cash Sales.
When you recall the entry, you can edit amounts and, if necessary, the accounts. Refer to page 185.

✓ 7

Credit Card Sales Invoice #PS-394 **Dated July 5/15**

Sales Summary
To various one-time customers

Revenue from Passport Photos (new account)	$ 240.00
Revenue from Portraits	1 600.00
GST charged	92.00
PST charged	128.80
Total deposited to credit card bank account	$2 060.80

Create new Group account: 4160 Revenue from Passport Photos.
Store the sale as a weekly recurring transaction.

PRO VERSION
Click the Sales Invoices icon

to open the Sales Journal. Then click One-Time Customer.

Click the **Client Invoices icon**

.

Click the **Payment Method list arrow** and **click Credit Card** to modify the invoice.

As for cash sales, the Net Days field for early payment discounts is removed and a Credit Card Amount field is added. There is no cheque number field for credit cards.

NOTES
Close the message about credit card processing if it opens. Credit card processing is covered in Chapter 13.

Choose **One-Time Client** from the Client drop-down list.

Type `Sales Summary` in the Address text box.

Enter **July 5** as the transaction date.

Click the **Item Description field** and **type** the **description** for the first sale item.

Press tab and **type** `240`

Press *tab* **twice** and **enter 4160** as the account. **Press** *tab* to start the Add An Account wizard. Enter the account name and finish adding the account.

Enter the **second invoice line details** for the portrait revenue work. **Change** the **default account**. This step will complete the invoice as shown:

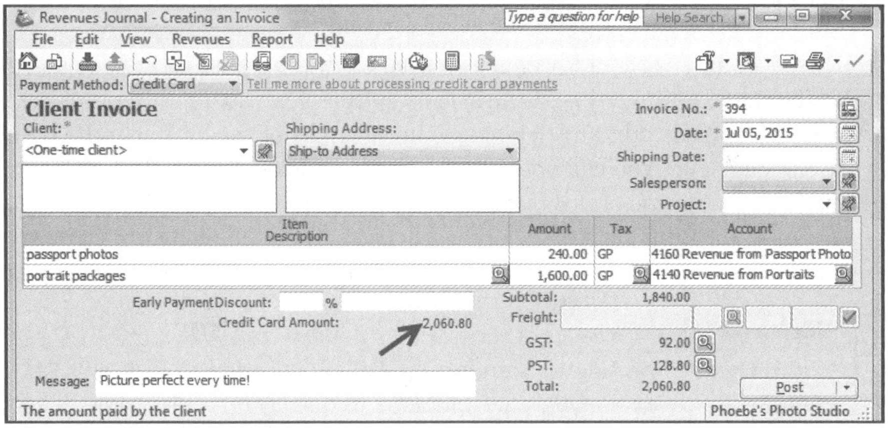

As usual, we will review the journal entry before posting.

Choose the **Report menu** and **click Display Revenues Journal Entry**:

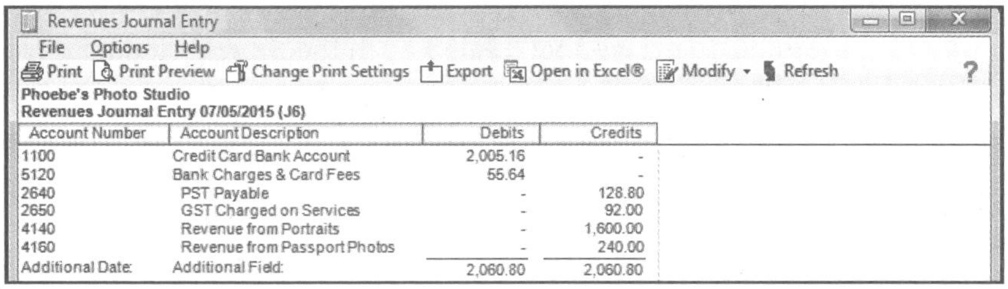
Revenues Journal Entry

File Options Help

Print | Print Preview | Change Print Settings | Export | Open in Excel® | Modify | Refresh

Phoebe's Photo Studio
Revenues Journal Entry 07/05/2015 (J6)

Account Number	Account Description	Debits	Credits
1100	Credit Card Bank Account	2,005.16	-
5120	Bank Charges & Card Fees	55.64	-
2640	PST Payable	-	128.80
2650	GST Charged on Services	-	92.00
4140	Revenue from Portraits	-	1,600.00
4160	Revenue from Passport Photos	-	240.00
Additional Date:	Additional Field:	2,060.80	2,060.80

This entry differs somewhat from the standard cash sale entry. Instead of *Chequing Account*, the linked *Credit Card Bank Account* is debited for the amount of the deposit, but this is less than the total amount of the sale. The deposit is reduced by the transaction fee that is charged to the linked expense account *Bank Charges & Card Fees*. In this case, the credit card company withholds 2.7 percent of each transaction as the fee for using the card. This fee includes the cost to the credit card company for collecting from customers and assuming the risk of non-payment from customers.

Close the **display** and **make corrections** to the invoice if necessary.

Before posting the transaction, we will store it so that we will not need to re-enter all the details the next time we enter the sales summary transaction.

Storing a Recurring Sales Entry

Completing and storing a recurring entry in the Revenues Journal is similar to storing a General or Purchases Journal entry.

Click the **Store tool** or **choose** the **Sales menu** and **click Store**.

The familiar Store Recurring Transaction window appears with the customer name as the entry name and the default frequency, Monthly, selected. If you want, you can change the entry name to Sales Summary.

Click Monthly to display the frequency options. **Click Weekly** as the frequency.

Click **OK** to save the entry and return to the Revenues Journal. The Recall button will be available.

Click **Post** [Post] to save the journal entry. **Click OK**.

Adjusting a Posted Revenues Journal Entry

If you discover an error in a Revenues Journal entry after posting it, you can adjust or correct the posted transaction in the same way that you can adjust a purchase invoice after posting. You can edit any field in the invoice except the customer. If you need to change the customer, you can open the Adjust (or Lookup) window and click the Reverse tool, just as you do for purchases or receipts.

The entry for Brandon Art Gallery was missing the second invoice line to record the revenue from copyright permissions. The Revenues Journal should still be open.

✓ 8

Memo #2 **Dated July 5/15**

From Owner: The sale to Brandon Art Gallery included $2 000 plus $100 GST and $140 PST for copyright permissions to display artwork on the gallery Web site. The revised and correct invoice total is $6 944. Adjust the posted entry (reference invoice #PS-391). Create new Group revenue account: 4170 Revenue from Copyrights.

Click the **Adjust Invoice tool** to open the Search window:

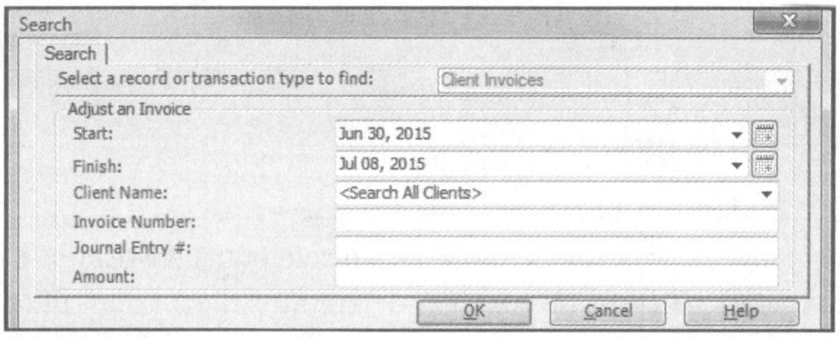

The default date and customer selections will include all invoices.

Click **OK** to open the Select Entry To Adjust screen:

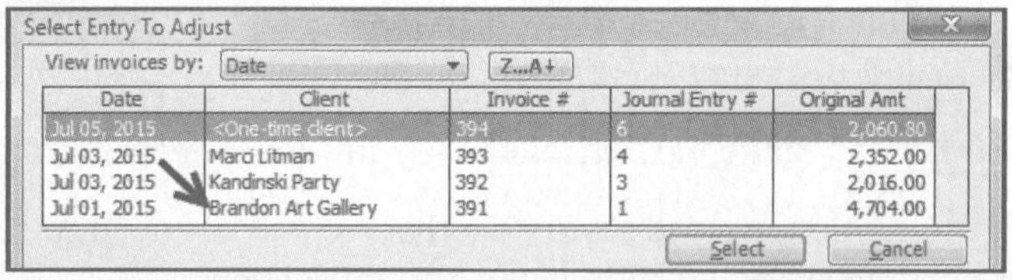

All Revenues Journal entries for the selected customers and within the selected date range are listed. You can **view** the list of transactions in order by date, the default selection, or by customer, invoice number, journal entry number or amount. For each view, you can switch between descending and ascending order with the [Z...A+] **button**.

Journal Entry #1 for Brandon Art Gallery is the one we need to edit.

Click **Brandon Art Gallery**.

To choose an invoice for adjusting, you can click on any part of the line for that invoice to highlight it then click Select, or you can double-click the entry to open the journal immediately.

Click **Select** to open the invoice. It is ready for editing:

NOTES

Just as you can choose a specific supplier for purchase invoice adjustments, you can choose a specific customer and click OK to see a reduced list of invoices for the selected customer. You can also enter a specific invoice number or journal entry number and click OK to access the invoice directly.

NOTES

If the invoice has already been paid, the program will ask if you want to create a credit note for the customer – a negative invoice. The default source for this invoice will be CN plus the original invoice number, e.g., CN-391, but you can enter a different reference number if you want.

This credit amount can be applied (paid) to other outstanding invoices for the customer.

Credit notes are demonstrated in Chapter 10.

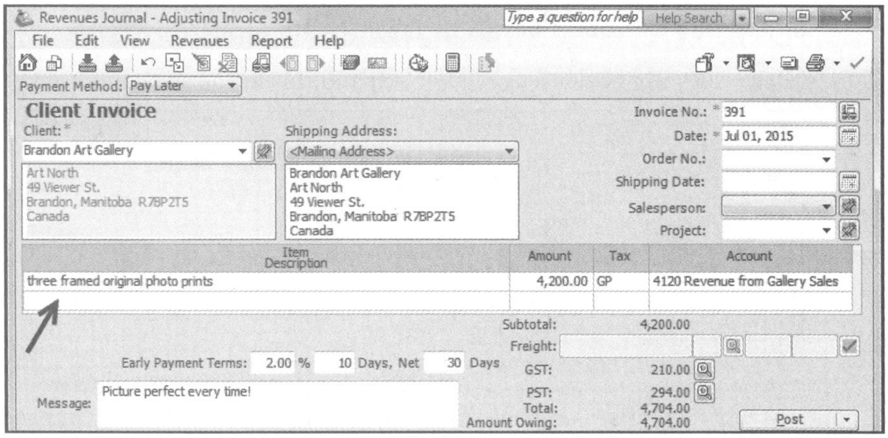

Click the **Item Description field** on the second line, below the first description.

Type `copyright permissions` **Press** (tab) to advance to the Amount field.

Type `2000` **Press** (tab).

The tax code and revenue account from the previous line should be entered. You can select or change them if needed. Click the Tax field List icon to open the Tax Code screen and change the selection. We need to change the account.

Click the **Account field**. **Type** `4170`

Press (tab). **Create** the **new revenue account** when prompted.

Click the **Message field** and **type** `Revised invoice`

As with other adjustments in other journals, this adjustment creates a reversing entry (J7) in addition to the corrected journal entry (J8). You will see all three transactions in the journal reports when you include corrections. You can preview the invoice to ensure that you made the changes correctly.

If you change the customer for an invoice, Sage 50 warns that the name will be changed, but the remaining information (terms, tax codes and so on) will not. If you need to change the customer for a posted invoice, you should reverse the original entry and then create a new invoice for the correct customer. This ensures that the correct customer's settings will apply to the sale.

Review the **entry**. **Close** the **display**. **Make** **corrections** if necessary.

Post the **transaction** and then **close** the **Revenues Journal**.

Adding Shortcuts for Other Transactions

Just as we added a shortcut for General Journal entries in Chapter 5, we can add shortcuts for the Payables journals and tasks we will use for Phoebe's Photo Studio. Refer to page 132 if you need help.

✓ 9

Memo #3 **Dated July 5/15**

Create shortcuts for tasks and transactions in other modules.

Click **Customize beside Shortcuts** in the Home window.

Click the ⊞ **beside Company** to expand the list.

Click **Create General Journal** and then **click Add**.

NOTES

You can change the invoice number if you want to make the audit trail clearer. For example, you can enter 391-R as the invoice number to identify it as a revised invoice.

If you change the date, only the corrected entry will have the revised date. Remember that changing the date will affect the discount period as well.

NOTES

To reverse a sale, open the Adjusting Client Invoice (Sale) window and click the Reverse tool. Click Yes to confirm that you want to reverse the sale.

NOTES

Refer to page 163 and Appendix F on the Student DVD for more detail on previewing and printing invoices.

NOTES

The transaction confirmation message tells you that two entries were posted for the adjustment.

NOTES
Collapsing a list after finishing with it makes it easier to advance to the next ledger heading. Alternatively, you can scroll down the list.

PRO VERSION
pro Add shortcuts for Create General Journal, Create Purchase Invoice, Pay Purchase Invoices, Pay Expenses, View Vendors and View Accounts.

NOTES
You can add more shortcuts if you want. The maximum number is 10 for each user.

NOTES
The View Accounts icon opens the Accounts window.

NOTES
PST paid on purchases is included with the expense or asset part of the purchase because this tax is not refundable.

Click the ⊟ **beside Company** to collapse this list.

Click the ⊞ **beside Payables** to expand this list as shown:

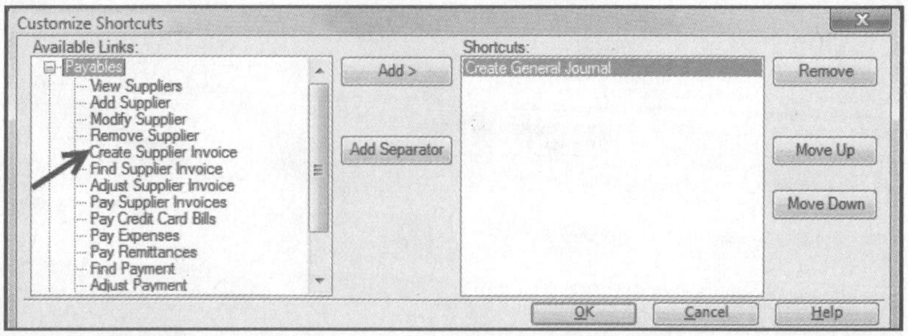

All transactions that are available from the Invoices, Payments and Suppliers drop-down lists can be added as Home window shortcuts. We will add shortcuts for the types of Payables transactions we use most frequently: creating and paying invoices and making other cash purchases (expenses). We will also add a shortcut to View Suppliers so that we can edit supplier records.

Click **Create Supplier Invoice** and then **click Add**.

Click **Pay Supplier Invoice** and then **click Add**.

Click **Pay Expenses** and then **click Add**.

Click **View Suppliers** and then **click Add**.

Click the ⊞ **beside Banking** to expand the list.

Click **View Accounts** and then **click Add**.

Click **OK** to return to the Home window with your shortcuts added:

These six tasks/windows are now available from any module Home window by clicking the shortcut.

Enter the **transactions** until the sales summary on July 12.

10 **Payment Cheque #451** **Dated July 6/15**
To Calm Air, $3 861 in payment of account, including $39 discount for early payment. Reference invoice #CA-224.

11 **Purchase Invoice #RG-3160** **Dated July 6/15**
From Riverton Garage, $80 for gasoline, including taxes (use tax code IN) for gasoline for van. Terms: net 30.

12 **Purchase Invoice #CA-392** **Dated July 6/15**
From Calm Air, $1 215 plus $60.75 GST. Invoice total $1 275.75 for return flight to Churchill. Terms: 1/15, n/30. Store as a bi-weekly recurring transaction.

13 **Sales Invoice #PS-395** **Dated July 7/15**
To Polar Discoveries, $2 270 plus $113.50 GST and $158.90 PST for tour customer photographs. Invoice total $2 542.40. Terms: 2/10, n/30.

14 **Payment Cheque #452** **Dated July 7/15**
To Lumber Shed, $1 050 in payment of account. Reference invoice #LS-894. The discount period has expired.

15 **Payment Cheque #453** **Dated July 7/15**
To Riverton Garage, $890 in payment of account. Reference invoice #RG-1904.

16 **Purchase Invoice #SPS-4668** **Dated July 8/15**
From Starlight Photo Solutions, $1 820 plus $91 GST for rolls of large photo paper for gallery prints. Invoice total $1 911. Terms: 2/10, n/30.

17 **Sales Invoice #PS-396** **Dated July 8/15**
To Calm Air (use Full Add for the new customer), $1 900 plus $95 GST and $133 PST for permission to use photographs on Web site. Invoice total $2 128. Terms: 2/10, n/30.

NOTES

Calm Air
(contact Arie Fliegel)
50 Jett Ave.
Winnipeg, MB R2P 1S7
Tel 1: (800) 839-2256
Fax: (204) 476-5110
E-mail: af@calmair.com
Web site: www.calmair.com
Revenue account: 4170
Terms: 2/10, n/30
Tax code: GP
Credit limit: $8 000

SESSION DATE – JULY 15, 2015

18 **Cash Receipt #42** **Dated July 9/15**
From Litman, Marci, cheque #29 for $2 304.96, including $47.04 discount for early payment of invoice #PS-393.

19 **Sales Invoice #PS-397** **Dated July 9/15**
To Kandinski Party, $4 600 plus $230 GST and $322 PST for wedding photo package with DVD. Invoice total $5 152. Terms: 2/10, n/30. Create new revenue account: 4150 Revenue from Weddings. Allow the customer to exceed the credit limit.

20 **Cash Receipt #43** **Dated July 10/15**
From Brandon Art Gallery, cheque #28874 for $6 805.12 in full payment of invoice #PS-391 with $138.88 discount for early payment.

21 **Cash Receipt #44** **Dated July 11/15**
From Reuben, Geraldine, certified cheque #302 for $2 495 in full payment of account to replace NSF cheque. Reference invoices #PS-377 and #PS-381.

Recalling a Stored Sales Entry

The procedures for recalling and changing a stored entry are the same for all journals.

NOTES

Remember to change the amounts when you recall the sales summary.

NOTES

You can store the changed sales summary if you want. In this case, you should confirm that you are replacing the previous stored transaction.

✓ 22 **Credit Card Sales Invoice #PS-398** **Dated July 12/15**
Sales Summary
To various one-time customers

Passport photos	$ 130.00
Portraits	1 200.00
GST charged	66.50
PST charged	93.10
Total deposited to credit card bank account	$1 489.60

Click the **Client Invoices** (Sales or Sales Invoices) **icon** 

to open the Revenues Journal.

Click the **Recall tool**  or **choose** the **Revenues menu** and **click Recall** to display the Recall Recurring Transaction window.

Click the **transaction** you want to use. **Click Select** to display a copy of the entry previously posted.

Edit the **amounts** or the **accounts** as needed.

The default date is entered according to the frequency selected. The payment method is still selected as Credit Card. The invoice number is updated automatically so the entry is complete.

Review the **entry** to be certain that it is correct. **Click** Post to save it.

When you make changes to a stored entry, Sage 50 warns that posting the entry may affect the next due date. This warning appears if you have made any changes to the entry before posting, although the message mentions only the date.

Click **Yes** to accept the change and post. **Click** **OK** to confirm posting.

Enter the **remaining transactions** for July.

23 **Bank Debit Memo #29321** **Dated July 15/15**

From Red River Credit Union, cheque #29 for $2 304.96 from Litman has been returned because of non-sufficient funds. Reverse the payment and notify the customer of the outstanding charges. Edit the customer's terms to net 1 and change her credit limit to zero.

24 **Cash Purchase Invoice #UPS-6101** **Dated July 15/15**

From UPS Delivery, $380 for courier delivery of photographs to clients plus $19 GST. Invoice total, $399. Issued cheque #454 in full payment.

25 **Purchase Invoice #CA-487** **Dated July 15/15**

From Calm Air, $1 215 plus $60.75 GST. Invoice total $1 275.75 for return flight to Churchill. Terms: 1/15, n/30. Recall the stored entry, edit the date and then store it as a weekly recurring transaction. Replace the previous stored transaction.

SESSION DATE – JULY 22, 2015

26

Phoebe's Photo Studio
phoebephoto.com
100 Light Street, Suite 202
Winnipeg, MB R2T 7G4
Phone: (204) 649-3358 Toll free: (888) 649-3358 Fax: (204) 642-4967

Invoice: PS-399
Date: July 16, 2015
Sold to: Borealis Mysteries (J. Franklin)
4 Lighter Way
Winnipeg, MB R4A 1E1

Description	Tax Code	Amount
Photographs of tour customers	GP	1 140.00

bi-weekly recurring sale:

Picture perfect every time!	Payment Terms: 2/10, net 30	Customer Initials	GST	57.00
			PST	79.80
	GST #296 654 590	JF	TOTAL	1 276.80

27 **Payment Cheque #455** **Dated July 18/15**

To Starlight Photo Solutions, $1 872.78 in payment of account, including $38.22 discount for early payment. Reference invoice #SPS-4668.

28

Phoebe's Photo Studio
www.phoebestudio.com

100 Light Street, Suite 202
Winnipeg, MB R2T 7G4
Phone: (204) 649-3358 Toll free: (888) 649-3358 Fax: (204) 642-4967

Invoice: PS-400
Date: July 19, 2015
Sold to: Sales Summary

Description	Tax Code	Amount
Passport photos	GP	180.00
Portrait packages	GP	1 400.00

Deposited to credit card bank account
July 19/15

Picture perfect every time!

Payment Terms: Credit Card	Customer Initials	GST	79.00
		PST	110.60
Business No.: 296 654 590		TOTAL	1 769.60

> **NOTES**
> Remember to change the amounts if you recall the sales summary.

29 **Purchase Invoice #WE-56691** **Dated July 19/15**

From Web Exposures, $3 100 plus $155 GST and $217 PST for redesigning Web site with updated text and photos. Invoice total, $3 472. Terms: net 15.

30 **Cash Purchase Invoice #SBD-4821** **Dated July 20/15**

From Staples Business Depot (use Full Add for the new supplier), $60 plus $3.00 GST and $4.20 PST for stationery and office supplies. Invoice total, $67.20. Paid by cheque #456.

> **NOTES**
> Staples Business Depot
> Expense account: 1340
> Tax code: GP
> Leave the remaining fields blank.

31 **Payment Cheque #457** **Dated July 20/15**

To Calm Air, $1 262.99 in payment of account, including $12.76 discount for early payment. Reference invoice #CA-392.

32 **Sales Invoice #PS-401** **Dated July 21/15**

To Polar Discoveries, $2 270 plus $113.50 GST and $158.90 PST for tour customer photographs. Invoice total $2 542.40. Terms: 2/10, n/30.

33 **Purchase Invoice #CA-598** **Dated July 22/15**

From Calm Air, $1 215 plus $60.75 GST. Invoice total $1 275.75 for return flight to Churchill. Terms: 1/15, n/30. Recall the stored entry.

34 **Purchase Invoice #RG-5619** **Dated July 22/15**

From Riverton Garage, $85 including taxes for gasoline. Terms: net 30.

35

Borealis Mysteries
4 Lighter Way
Winnipeg, MB R4A 1E1

No: 18963

Date 2 0 1 5 0 7 2 2
Y Y Y Y M M D D

Pay to the order of Phoebe's Photo Studio $ 1251.26

— One thousand two hundred fifty-one dollars — 26 /100 Dollars

RR Red River Credit Union
389 Prairie Blvd.
Winnipeg MB R2P 1B6

Signature

⑈---92999-⑈16883 18963

Re: pay invoice #PS-399 $1251.26 No: 18963
includes $25.54 discount (receipt #45) July 22, 2015

SESSION DATE – JULY 31, 2015

NOTES
Change the default account to 1300 for the developing solutions and apply tax code GP for the repair expenses.

36 **Purchase Invoice #SPS-5936** **Dated July 25/15**

From Starlight Photo Solutions, $310 plus $15.50 GST for developing solutions and $420 plus $21 GST and $29.40 PST for camera repairs. Invoice total, $795.90. Terms: 2/10, n/30. Create new Group expense account: 5180 Repair Expenses.

37

Calm Air
50 Jett Ave.
Winnipeg, MB R2P 1S7
Tel: (800) 839-2256

RR Red River Credit Union
389 Prairie Blvd.
Winnipeg MN R2P 1B6

No: 2910

Date 2 0 1 5 0 7 2 6
Y Y Y Y M M D D

Pay — Two thousand one hundred twenty-eight dollars — 00 $ 2,128.00

TO THE ORDER OF Phoebe's Photo Studio
100 Light St. Suite 202
Winnipeg, MB R2T 7G4

PER

⑈---92999-⑈46771 2910

Re: pay invoice #PS-396 $2 128 No: 2910
(receipt #46) July 26, 2015

38 **Payment Cheque #458** **Dated July 26/15**

To Starlight Photo Solutions, $400 in partial payment of account. No discount is allowed on the partial payment. Reference invoice #SPS-5936.

39 **Cash Purchase Invoice #MT-421576** **Dated July 26/15**

From Manitoba Telephone, $190 plus $9.50 GST and $13.30 PST for telephone and Internet service. Invoice total, $212.80. Paid by cheque #459.

40 **Cash Purchase Invoice #MH-66832** **Dated July 26/15**

From Manitoba Hydro, $180 plus $9 GST hydro for two studios. Invoice total, $189. Paid by cheque #460.

41 **Credit Card Sales Invoice #PS-402** **Dated July 26/15**

Sales Summary
To various one-time customers

Passport photos	$ 130.00
Portraits	1 200.00
GST charged	66.50
PST charged	93.10
Total deposited to credit card bank account	$1 489.60

42 **Purchase Invoice #CA-622** **Dated July 29/15**

From Calm Air, $1 215 plus $60.75 GST. Invoice total $1 275.75 for return flight to Churchill. Terms: 1/15, n/30. Recall the stored entry.

43 **Cash Receipt #47** **Dated July 29/15**

From Polar Discoveries, cheque #43692 for $1 200 in partial payment of invoice #PS-395.

44 **Sales Invoice #PS-403** **Dated July 30/15**

To Borealis Mysteries, $1 800 plus $90 GST and $126 PST for tour customer photographs. Invoice total $2 016. Terms: 2/10, n/30. Recall the stored entry and edit the amount.

45 **Bank Credit Memo #55131** **Dated July 30/15**

From Red River Credit Union, $4 000 six-month loan at 7% interest for new dichroic enlarger approved and deposited to bank account.

46 **Bank Debit Memo #61821** **Dated July 30/15**

From Red River Credit Union, pre-authorized monthly payroll for assistant.

Wages and payroll expenses	$3 000.00
Payroll services fee	70.00
GST paid on payroll service	3.50
Total withdrawal	$3 073.50

47 **Memo #4** **Dated July 31/15**

From Owner: Create new Group expense account for supplies used during the month: 5145 Darkroom Supplies Used. Enter adjustments for supplies used:

Framing supplies	$510
Photo paper & supplies	480
Darkroom supplies	290
Office & other supplies	140

48 **Bank Debit Memo #62002** **Dated July 31/15**

From Red River Credit Union, pre-authorized withdrawals for service charges, mortgage and loan payments.

Bank charges, including NSF cheques	$ 135
Interest expense	1 120
Loan principal repayment	1 040
Mortgage principal repayment	920

NOTES
Remember to change the amounts when you recall the sales summary.

Displaying Client/Customer Reports

Client (or customer) reports can be accessed at any time from the Home or the Clients window, or from the Report Centre.

Click the Clients icon to open the Clients window.

PRO VERSION
Click Customers, the Customers icon.

NOTES
Management reports and graphs are not available from the Clients window or from the Report Centre. You can access these from the Home window.

The Clients window Reports menu now contains only client reports. Select the report you want from this list and follow the instructions below to choose report options. You can also obtain all client (customer) reports from the Home window Reports menu.

In the Receivables module Home window, the Reports pane includes all the customer reports in the drop-down list. Opening the reports from this list will display them immediately with the default settings. This report list is shown here:

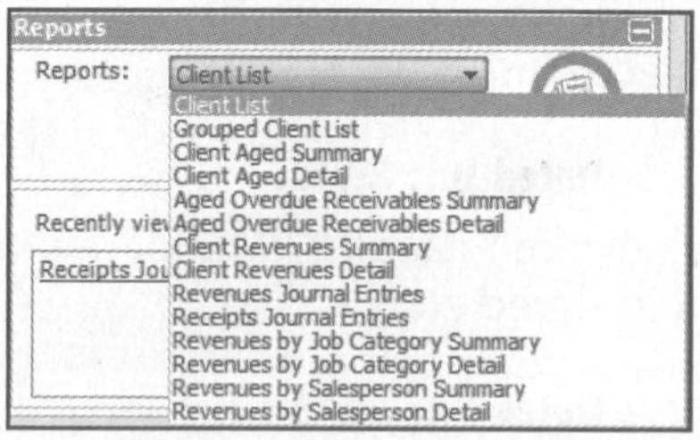

We will continue to work from the Report Centre, so we can see the sample reports, descriptions and report options.

Click the **Report Centre icon**  in the Home window.

The Receivables reports are listed because we started from the Receivables window. The sample and description for Client List, the first report, is displayed:

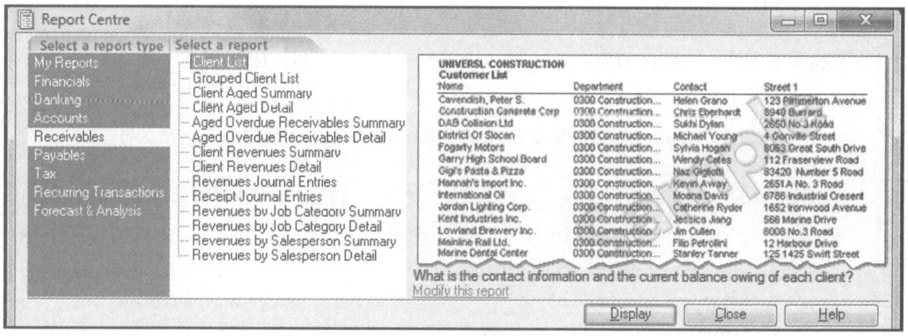

If you click Receivables in the Select A Report Type list, you will see the general description for Receivables reports.

PRO VERSION
Grouped Client List, Time & Billing and Forecast & Analysis reports are not available in the Pro version.

NOTES
Forecast & Analysis reports use data for multiple fiscal periods. They are covered briefly in Chapter 10.

Displaying Client/Customer Lists

Click **Client List** in the Select A Report list to open the sample report and its description.

Click **Modify This Report** to open the report options:

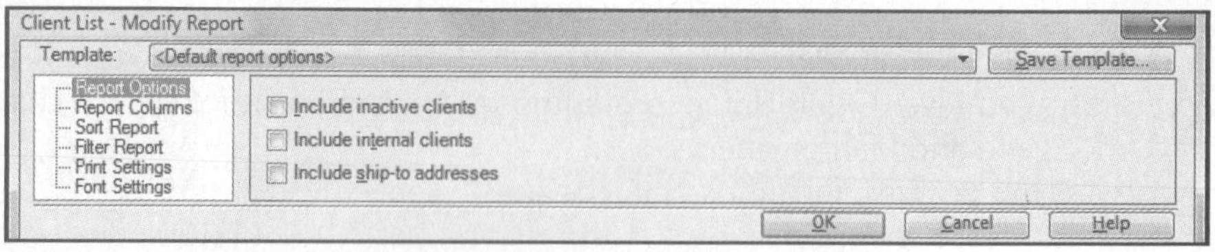

Or choose the Reports menu, then choose Lists and Clients.

PRO VERSION
Remember that you will see the terms Customer and Sales instead of Client and Revenues.
The options to Include Internal Clients and Ship-To Addresses are not available.

CLASSIC VIEW
From the Home window, right-click the Clients icon  . Click the Display tool .

NOTES
You can drill down to the Client Aged Report from the Client List.

You can include or omit inactive and internal customers, and shipping addresses. You can sort and filter Client Lists by any of the fields selected for the report. You can select customer record fields by customizing the Report Columns. You can also sort the columns directly in the report. For example, if you want to list customers in order according to the amount they owe, with the largest balance reported first, click the Balance column heading to sort the report by balance. Then click the heading again to reverse the order.

Click **OK**. **Close** the **display** when you have finished viewing it.

Displaying Grouped Client Lists

Click **Grouped Client List** in the Select A Report list to open the sample report and its description.

Click **Modify This Report** to open the report options.

Click the **list arrow for the Group By field**:

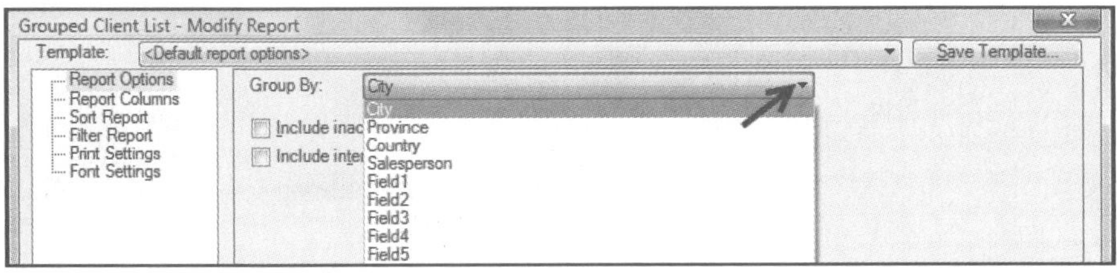

The criteria you can use to group the customers are displayed.

Choose the **grouping criterion** you want. **Click OK** to display the report.

Close the **display** when you have finished viewing it.

NOTES
You could use the Grouped Client List to prepare customer contact lists for salespersons in different regions.
Field1, Field2 and so on are extra fields you define for the company that appear on the Additional Information tab screens of customer records.

Displaying Client Aged Reports

Click **Client Aged Summary** in the Select A Report list to open the sample report and its description.

Click **Modify This Report** to open the report options:

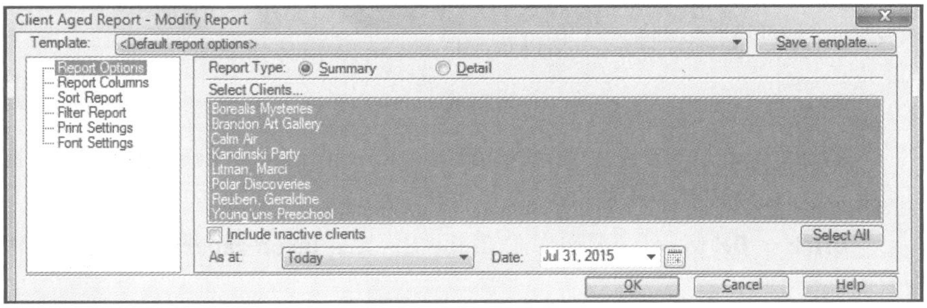

Or choose the Reports menu, then choose Receivables and Client Aged.

NOTES
You can drill down to look up invoices and to the Client Ledger from the Client Aged Detail Report. From the Summary Report you can drill down to the Detail Report.

New customers you entered using Quick Add will appear on the list of customers in the report options windows. Sales for one-time customers and customers for whom you chose the Continue option will not appear because these cash transactions did not create a ledger record or an entry for *Accounts Receivable*.

The **Summary** option will display an alphabetic list of the selected customers with outstanding total balances owing, organized into the aging periods columns set up for the company. The **Detail** option shows all the invoices and payments made by customers and the balance owing. This more descriptive report is also aged and can be used to make credit decisions. You can add payment terms to the Detail Report. You can customize the Client Aged and Aged Overdue reports (that is, choose any columns in the report, and sort and filter by name and balance owing.)

NOTES
The Client Aged and Aged Overdue Detail Reports are also available directly from the Select A Report list for Receivables in the Report Centre.

Click **Detail** to include details for individual transactions.

Enter the **date** for the report or accept the default session date.

Press and **hold** ctrl and **click** the **client names**. **Click Select All** to include all customers, or remove them when they are all selected.

Click **OK** to see the report. **Close** the **displayed report** when finished.

Displaying Aged Overdue Receivables Reports

Click **Aged Overdue Receivables Summary** in the Select A Report list to open the sample report and its description.

Click **Modify This Report** to open the report options:

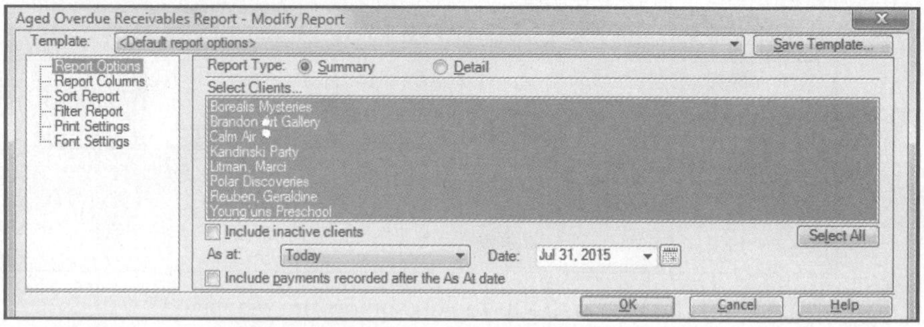

From the Home window, choose the Reports menu, then choose Receivables and click Aged Overdue Receivables to see the options.

Enter the **date** for the report, or accept the default session date.

NOTES
You can drill down to look up invoices and to the Client Aged Report from the Aged Overdue Receivables Detail Report. From the Summary Report you can drill down to the Detail Report.

The **Summary** option will display an alphabetic list of the selected customers with outstanding total balances owing, organized into aging periods, with an additional column for the overdue amount. Individual invoices, due dates, payments, overdue amounts and the balance owing for the selected customers are added when you choose the **Detail** Report. Selecting **Include Payments Recorded After The As At Date** will add postdated receipts to the report.

NOTES
You can use name and balance owing as the criteria for sorting and filtering the Aged Overdue Receivables reports and you can choose any of the columns in the report.

Click **Detail** if you want to include the invoice details.

Enter the **date** for the report, or accept the default session date.

Press and **hold** ctrl and **click** the appropriate **names** in the client list. **Click** **Select All** to include all customers or remove them all.

Click **OK** to see the report. **Close** the **displayed report** when finished.

Displaying the Client Revenues Report

PRO VERSION
Click Customer Sales Summary to see this report.

Click **Client Revenues Summary** in the Select A Report list to open the sample report and its description.

Click **Modify This Report** to open the report options:

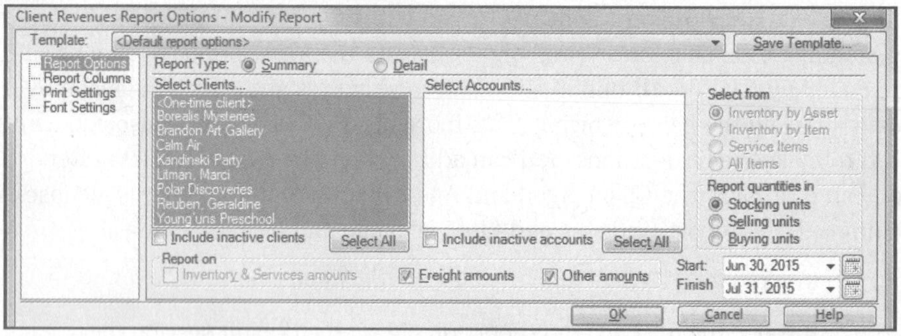

From the Home window, choose the Reports menu, then choose Receivables and click Client Revenues to see the options.

NOTES
You can drill down to the Journal Report and the Client Aged Report and look up the invoice from the Client Sales Detail Report. From the Summary Report you can drill down to the Detail Report.

In this report, you can display the total number of transactions and the total sales for each customer (in the **Summary** Report) or the individual sales invoice amounts (in the **Detail** Report). The Detail Report also includes journal details (date, source, journal entry number and revenue amounts) for each transaction. Only the Other Amounts and Freight Amounts are available when the inventory module is not set up. When inventory items are set up, you can display the sales for these items as well. This report will be discussed further when inventory is introduced in Chapter 10. The earliest transaction and session date provide the default date range.

You can select the customers to include and the date range for the report.

Press and **hold** ctrl and **click** the appropriate **names** in the customer list. **Click** **Select All** to include all customers or remove the entire selection.

Enter the **Start** and **Finish dates** for the report.

Click **OK** to see the report. **Close** the **displayed report** when finished.

Displaying the Revenues (Sales) Journal

Click **Revenues Journal Entries** in the Select A Report list to open the sample report.

Click **Modify This Report** to open the report options:

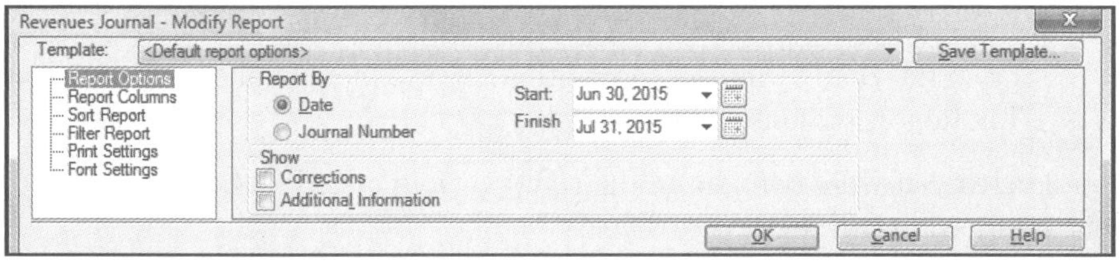

From the Home window, choose the Reports menu, then choose Journal Entries and click Revenues (Sales) to see the report options.

You can select Revenues Journal entries by posting date or by journal entry number. We use the default setting, By Date, for all reports in this workbook, so leave the selection unchanged. You can include corrections (adjusting and reversing entries) or omit them.

You can sort and filter journal reports by Date, Journal No., Source and Comment. You can choose account, description, debits and credits columns for the reports.

Enter the **beginning date** for the journal transactions you want. Or choose a date from the list arrow selections.

Press tab **twice**. **Enter** the **ending date** for the transaction period.

Click **Corrections** to provide a complete audit trail.

Click **OK** to view the report. **Close** the **display** when you have finished.

Displaying the Receipts Journal

The Receipts Journal was covered earlier in this chapter. Refer to page 177.

Displaying Tax Reports

The next three reports are general financial reports that include customer information. Because they are accessed from the Report Centre, they are included before the final customer reports and graphs that are accessed from the Home window Reports menu.

NOTES

Each sales invoice line is counted as one transaction for this report. For Brandon Art Gallery, four transactions are counted, the final two invoice lines, the original one we adjusted and its reversing entry.

PRO VERSION

Click Sales Journal Entries to see the report.

CLASSIC VIEW

From the Home window, right-click the Revenues icon 

.

Click the Display tool .

Revenues and Receipts Journal reports are also available from the Select A Report list when you click the Display tool button if no icon is selected in the Home window.

NOTES

You can drill down to an invoice, to the Client Aged Report and to the General Ledger Report from the Revenues and the Receipts journal reports.

NOTES

To include all journal entries in a single report, choose the Reports menu, then choose Journals and click All. Enter June 30 and July 31 in the Start and Finish date fields if these are not the default entries.

From the Report Centre, you can choose Financials and then All Journal Entries to include all transactions in a single report.

Tax reports show the taxable purchases and sales with and without tax amounts included, the taxes paid or charged on each transaction and the totals.

Click **Tax** in the Select A Report Type list to open the list of tax reports:

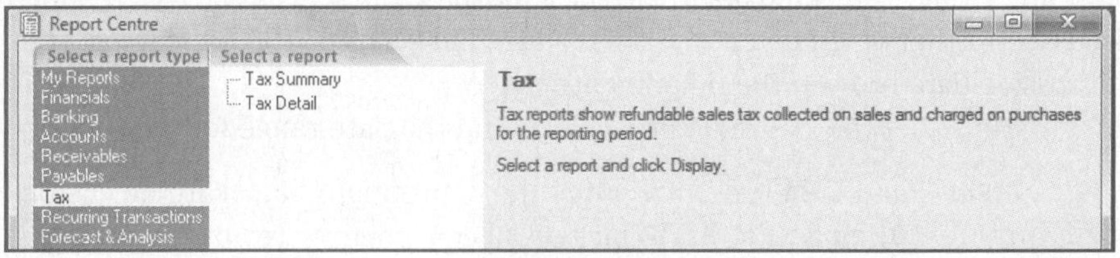

Click **Tax Summary** to display a sample report and description.

Click **Modify This Report** to display the Tax Report options window:

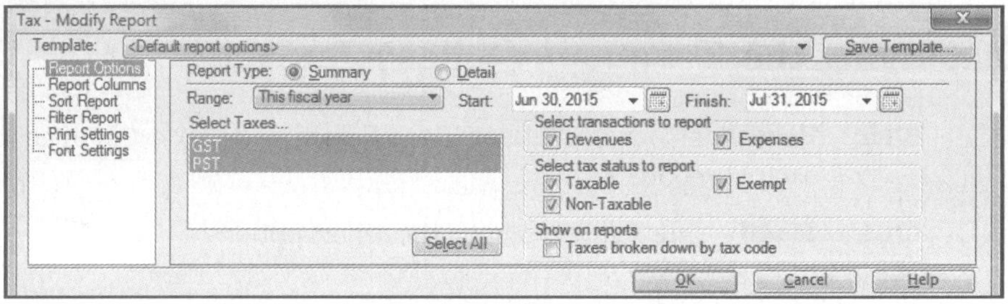

From the Home window, choose the Reports menu and click Tax to display the Tax Report options window.

PRO VERSION
The terms Sales and Purchases replace Revenues and Expenses.

All taxes that were defined for the company and included the option to report on them are listed in the Select Taxes field.

The earliest transaction and the session date are entered as the default date range for the report. You can include either transactions for revenues or expenses (sales or purchases) that include tax or for both. Both purchases and sales are reported by default for all taxes. In addition, the report can include taxable, exempt and non-taxable transactions. By default all are selected. You can also organize the report by tax codes.

NOTES
You can sort and filter tax reports by taxable purchases/sales excluding or including taxes, taxes paid/charged, other taxes paid/charged and total purchases/sales including taxes.

The **Summary** Report has only the totals for each category selected while the **Detail** Report lists individual transactions for each category. You can include the total tax amounts for each tax code as well.

Click **Detail** to select the more detailed level for the report.

Enter or **choose** the **dates** for which you want the report to start and finish.

Click a **tax name** in the Select Tax list to change the selection.

Click the **transactions** (Revenues or Expenses) to remove a ✓ or to add one if it is not there to include the transaction in the report.

Click a **transaction tax status** (Taxable, Exempt or Non-Taxable) to remove a ✓ or to add one if it is not there.

Once you have selected the options you want,

Click **OK** to view the report. **Close** the **display** when you have finished.

Displaying Cash Flow Reports

Displaying the Statement of Cash Flows

The Statement of Cash Flows summarizes sources (income, investments, etc.) and uses (purchase of assets, etc.) of cash and changes in liabilities during the designated period.

Click **Financials** in the Select A Report Type list to open the list of reports:

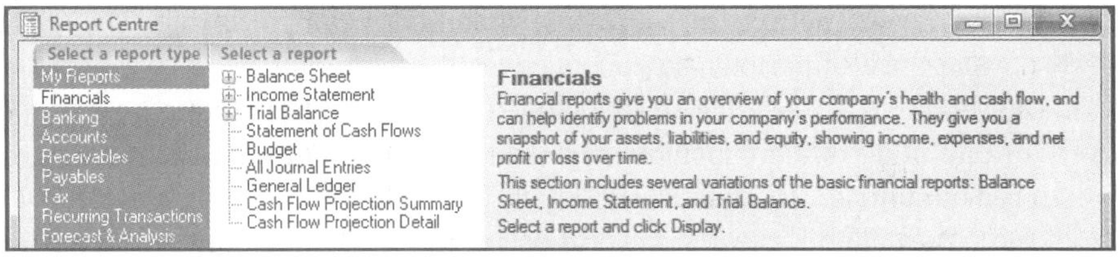

Click **Statement Of Cash Flows** to display a sample report and description.

Click **Modify This Report** to display the Modify Report window:

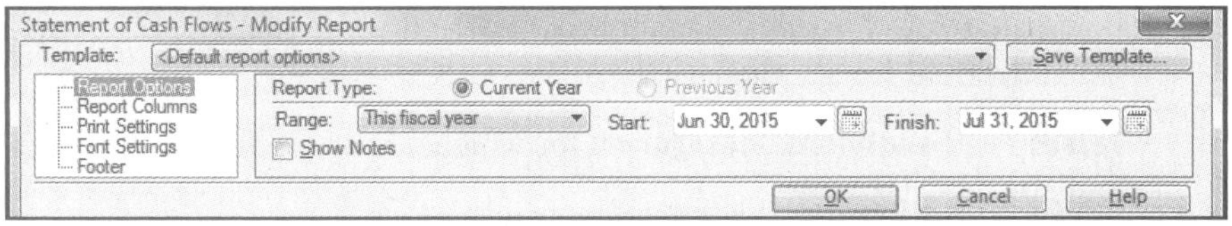

From the Home window, choose the Reports menu, then choose Financials and click Statement Of Cash Flows to see the report options.

Enter the **Start** and **Finish dates** for the report. The fiscal start and session dates are the defaults.

Click **OK** to view the report.

By organizing the transactions involving cash, net changes in cash positions, as well as changes in liabilities, the statement allows the owner to judge how efficiently cash is being used for the business. The owner can also see potential problems resulting from increases in liabilities or decreases in the collection of receivables.

Close the **display** when you have finished.

NOTES
You cannot sort or filter the Statement of Cash Flows or the Cash Flow Projection Report, but you can choose report columns.

Displaying Cash Flow Projection Reports

Cash Flow Projection reports predict the flow of cash in and out of an account — usually a bank account — over a specific future period based on current information.

Click **Cash Flow Projection Summary** to display a sample report and description. **Click** **Modify This Report** to display report options:

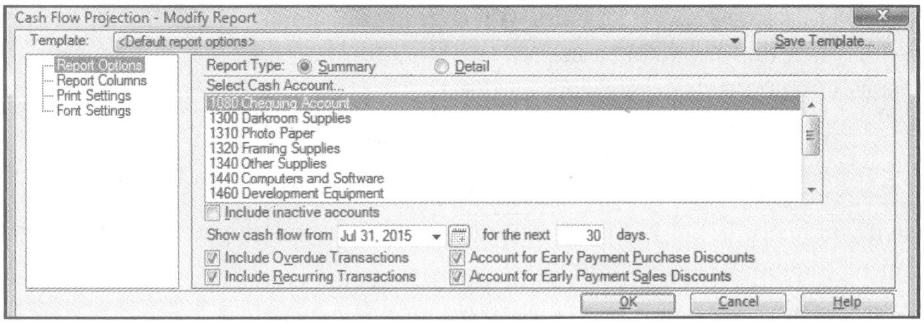

From the Home window, choose the Reports menu, then choose Financials and click Cash Flow Projection to see the report options.

Click **1080 Chequing Account** or the account for which you want the report.

Click the **Date field**. **Type** the **date** at which you want the projection to start.

Press tab **twice** to advance past the Calendar icon.

Enter the **number of days** in the future for which the report should project the cash flow.

Usually, you will include only the number of days for which you have reasonable information, such as the number of days in which net payment is due. The session date and 30 days are useful periods, so you can accept the defaults.

In the report, you may choose to include discounts in the amounts you expect to receive or pay, and you may include overdue transactions or omit them if you expect them to remain unpaid. By default, all details are included. Clicking a detail will remove it from the report. The Projection Report assumes overdue amounts will be paid and all other amounts will be paid on the invoice due date.

NOTES
You might want to compare projection reports prepared with and without some of these extra details.

The report projects the account balance based on receivables and payables due and recurring transactions coming due within the time frame specified. The **Summary** Report shows the totals for the specified report period while the **Detail** Report shows, by date, the individual transactions that are expected.

Select the **additional categories** for which you want details.

Click **Detail** to include individual transactions.

Click **OK** to view the report.

Close the **display**. **Close** the **Report Centre** to return to the Home window.

Displaying Management Reports

CLASSIC VIEW
You can also access Management Reports in the Home window from the Advice tool.

Management reports are displayed from the Home window Reports menu.

Choose the **Reports menu**, then **choose** **Management Reports** and **click** **Receivables** to see the reports and options:

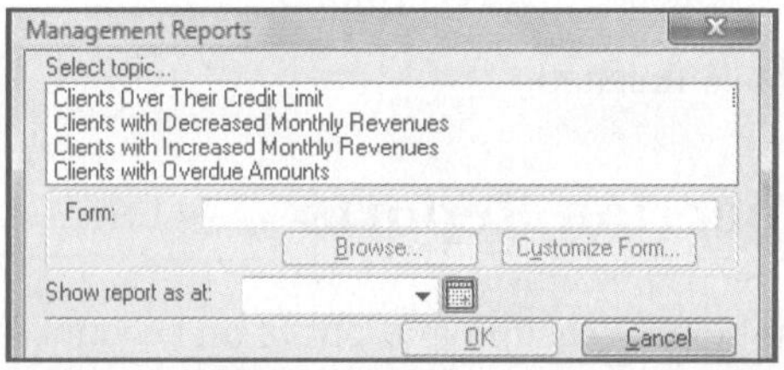

WARNING!
If a form appears in the Form field, check that its location is correct for your program installation. It should be located in the Forms folder, in your Sage 50 Premium Accounting 2013 folder.

You can produce four different reports for the Receivables Ledger: a list of all customers who have exceeded their credit limits, sales amounts for customers who have decreased their purchases since the previous year, amounts for customers who have increased purchases and customers with overdue payments. The Overdue Amounts Report is helpful for making a list of customers to remind about settling their accounts because it includes customer contact details.

NOTES
The report for overdue accounts shows that one customer payment is overdue – the one for Young-uns Preschool (Terms: 2/10, net 30).
Two customers have exceeded their credit limit – Kandinski Party ($5 000 limit) and Litman, Marci ($0 limit).

Click the **topic** for the report.

The program will add a date, if appropriate, and a form for the report. Change the date if you need to, but leave the default report form unless you have the programs required to modify these forms.

Click **OK** to display the report and print it if you want. **Close** the **display**.

Printing Client Reports

Display the **report** you want to print.

Click the **Change Print Settings tool** to check that you have the correct printer selected. **Click OK** to return to the report.

Click the **Print tool** or **choose** the **File menu** in the report window, and then **click Print**.

Close the **display** when you have finished.

Printing Client Statements

You can e-mail all customer statements or print them, or you can choose e-mail and print on a customer-by-customer basis according to the setting (preference) in the customer's ledger record Options tab screen (see page 174).

Choose the **Reports menu** in the Home window, then **choose Receivables** and **click Client Statements**.

You will see the following customer list with statement options:

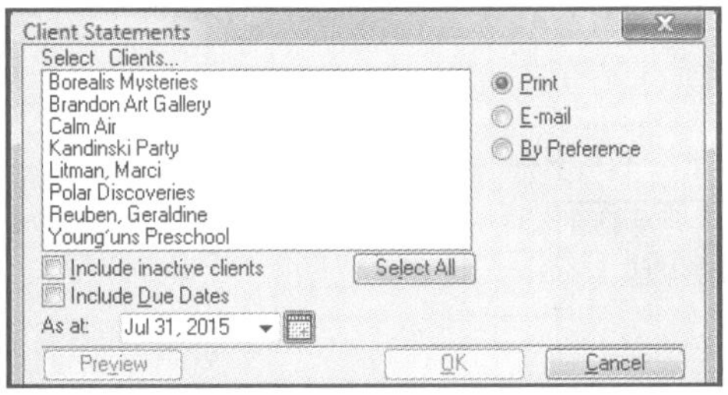

You should preview statements before printing them.

Press and **hold** ctrl and **click** the **clients** for whom you want to print statements, or **click Select All** to include all clients.

Enter the **date** for the statements.

Click **Include Due Dates** if you want to add the payment due dates for invoices, and **click Preview**.

Click **OK** to close the preview and return to the options screen.

Click **OK** again to print the statements.

Printing Client Mailing Labels

You should turn on the printer, insert labels paper and set the program for printing labels before choosing the options for the labels because printing begins immediately.

Choose the Setup menu in the Home window and click Reports & Forms. Click Labels. Enter the details for the labels. Click OK.

Choose the **Reports menu** in the Home window, then **choose Mailing Labels** and **click Clients**.

NOTES

Refer to Chapter 4, page 84, for details on setting up printers for different forms, reports and labels.

WARNING!

When you print from the Print tool, printing will start immediately. If you want to check your printer selection and settings, choose Print from the report's File menu.

WARNING!

Be sure your printer is set up with the correct forms before you begin because statements are printed immediately when you click OK after selecting your options or previewing the statements.

NOTES

You can customize customer statements, but not mailing labels.

Customizing statements is similar to customizing invoices. Refer to Appendix F on the Student DVD for assistance with previewing and customizing forms.

NOTES

To preview statements, you must select Custom Form. Choose the Setup menu and click Reports & Forms. Click Statements. Choose Custom Form and then Sage 50 Form. If you also want to customize the statements, choose User Defined Form in the Printed Form Description field. Click the Customize button to open the Form Designer. Save the new form when finished.

PRO VERSION
Your only options are to print mailing addresses or shipping addresses.

You will see the following options:

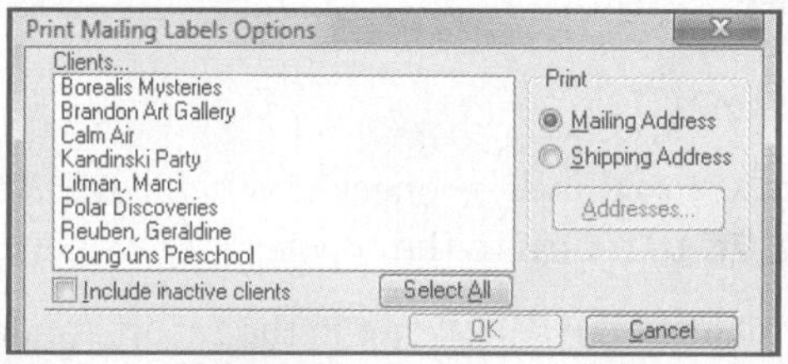

You can print labels for business mailing addresses, for shipping addresses or for any address list you created.

Press and **hold** ctrl and **click** the **clients** for whom you want to print the labels, or **click Select All** to include all customers. **Click OK**.

Graphing Client Reports

Receivables by Aging Period Graph

NOTES
The customer-related graphs are available only from the Home window Graphs menu. You cannot view them from the Clients window or from the Report Centre.

Choose the **Graphs menu** in the Home window and **click Receivables By Aging Period** to see the options screen:

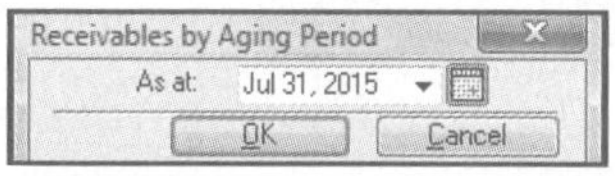

Enter a **date** for the graph and **click OK**.

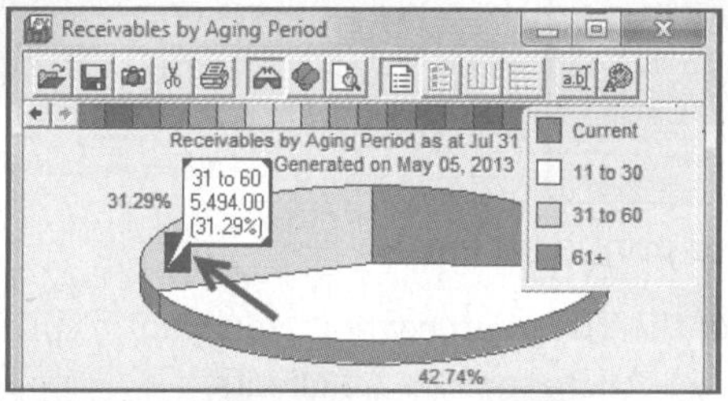

NOTES
One customer account is currently overdue by more than 30 days. Two more customers have passed the 10-day discount window.

The pie chart shows the total receivables divided according to the aging intervals set up in the company defaults. The chart is the customer equivalent of the Payables By Aging Period graph and shows the timeliness of account collections.

Double-click a portion of a graph to see the aging period, the dollar amount and the percentage of the total. Double-click the legend to make it larger. Double-click the expanded legend to reduce it.

NOTES
You have the same tool bar options and colour and legend control choices that you have for the other graphs. Refer to page 63 for a review of these features if you need further assistance.

Close the **graph** when you have finished.

Receivables by Client Graph

Choose the **Graphs menu** in the Home window and **click Receivables By Client**:

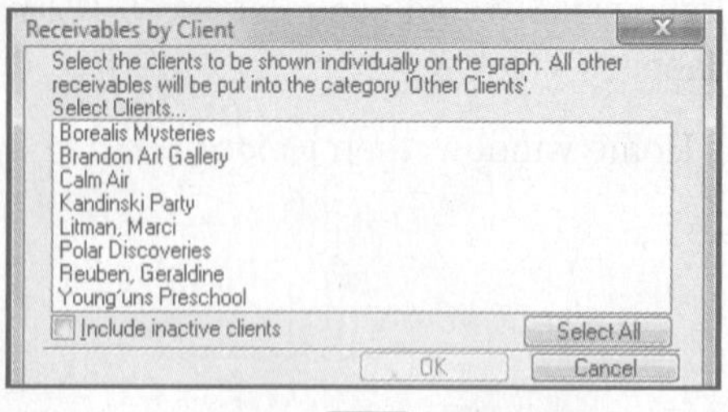

Press and **hold** ctrl and **click** the individual **clients** you want on the chart, or **click Select All** to include all customers. **Click OK**:

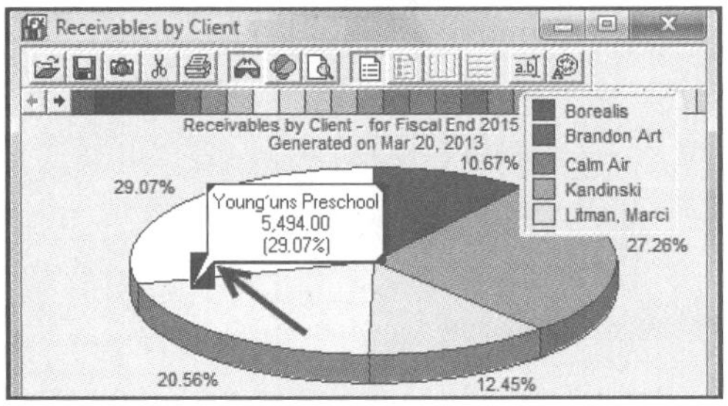

The pie chart graph shows the amount owed by each customer, represented by different colours, as a proportion of the total receivables.

> **NOTES**
> The options for displaying, editing, printing and exporting the graph are the same for all graphs.

Double-click a portion of a graph to see the customer, the dollar amount and the percentage of the total. Double-click the legend to make it larger and add the customer names. Double-click the expanded legend to reduce it.

Close the **graph** when you have finished.

Revenues vs Receivables Graph

Choose the **Graphs menu** and **click Revenues Vs Receivables** to see the options:

Press and **hold** ctrl and **click** the **revenue accounts** that you want in the graph. **Click Select All** to include all revenue accounts.

Click **OK** to display the following bar chart for the end of July:

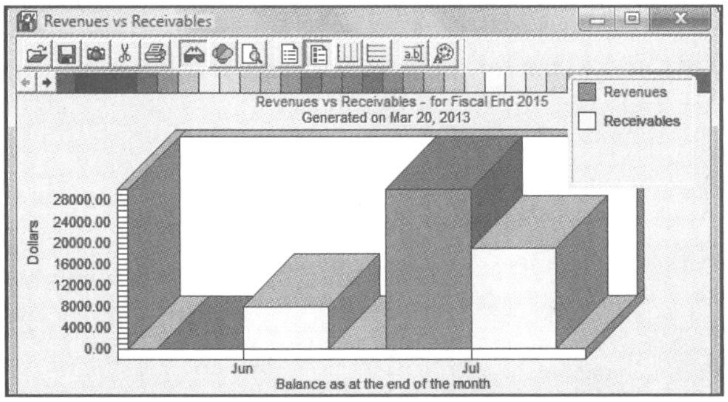

> **NOTES**
> The sales for June show as zero because we have not entered any transactions for June. The June receivables balance was the historical amount outstanding when we set up the data file.

> **NOTES**
> Although this is not a pie chart, you have the same options for exporting, copying, changing the display and so on that you do for other graphs.

The graph indicates cash flow by showing the amount of sales not yet collected.

Double-click a portion of the chart to see the period (month), the category (Revenues or Receivables) and the dollar amount.

Close the **graph** when you have finished.

Receivables Due vs Payables Due Graph

Choose the **Graphs menu** and **click Receivables Due Vs Payables Due**:

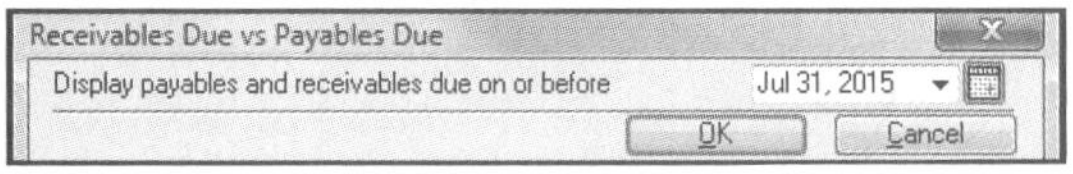

All receivables and payables due by the date displayed will be included. The session date is the default.

Enter the **date** that you want for the graph. **Click OK** to display the bar chart:

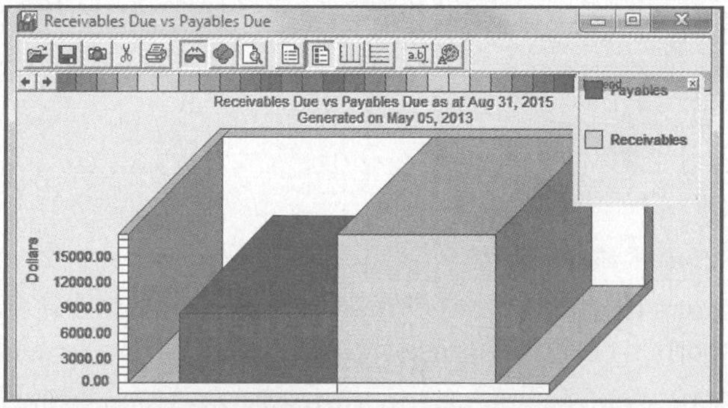

NOTES
For the Receivables Due vs Payables Due bar chart, you have the same options for exporting, copying, changing the display and so on that you do for other graphs.

NOTES
We entered August 31 as the date for this chart because no payments were due by July 31.

The graph shows the total amounts for receivables and payables due by August 31, one month beyond the session date, providing another indicator of cash flow.

Double-click a portion of the graph to see the period, the category (Payables or Receivables) and the dollar amount.

Close the **graph** when you have finished.

Revenues by Account Graph

Choose the **Graphs menu** and **click Revenues by Account**:

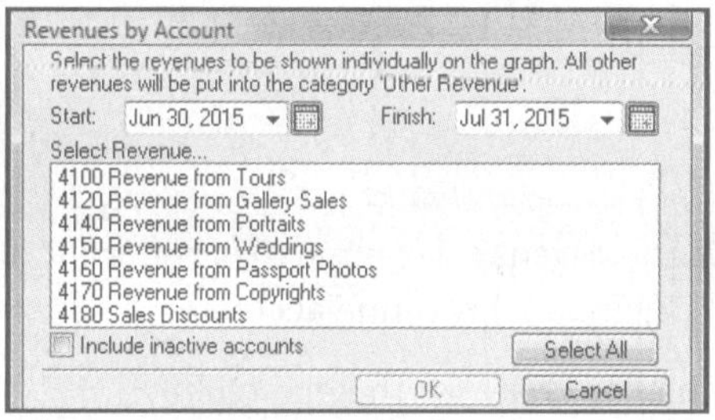

All revenue accounts are listed.

Select the **accounts** and **dates** for the graph. **Click OK** to display the pie chart:

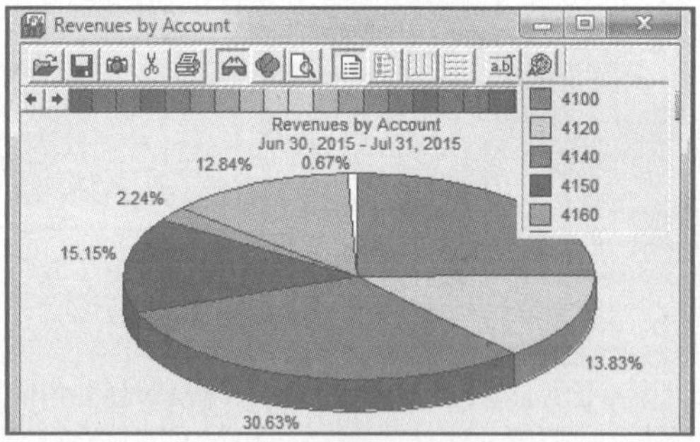

The pie chart graph shows the revenue from each account, represented by different colours, as a proportion of the total revenue.

Double-click a portion of the graph to see the account name, revenue amount and its percentage of the total revenue.

Close the **graph** when you have finished.

R E V I E W

The Student DVD with Data Files includes Review Questions and Supplementary Cases for this chapter.

CHAPTER SEVEN

AirCare Services

OBJECTIVES

After completing this chapter, you should be able to

- ***plan*** and ***design*** an accounting system for a small business
- ***prepare*** procedures for converting from a manual system
- ***understand*** the objectives of a computerized system
- ***create*** company files
- ***create*** and ***understand*** linked accounts
- ***set up*** accounts in the General, Payables and Receivables ledgers
- ***enter*** historical information for suppliers and customers
- ***correct*** historical transactions after recording them
- ***set up*** credit cards for receipts and payments
- ***set up*** sales taxes and tax codes
- ***finish*** entering history after entering journal transactions
- ***enter*** postdated transactions

COMPANY INFORMATION

Company Profile

NOTES
Air Care Services
100 Belair Avenue, Unit 25
Regina, SK S4T 4U2
Tel 1: (306) 456-1299
Tel 2: (888) 455-7194
Fax: (306) 456-3188
Business No.: 533 766 455

Air Care Services, located in sunny Regina, Saskatchewan, has been operating successfully for the past 15 years under the ownership and management of Simon Arturro. After his mechanical engineering education and several years' experience with heating installations, he became a certified installer of solar electrical panels. As more consumers are eager to rely less on fossil fuels as their source of power, the demand for solar energy is steadily increasing. Arturro has two assistants: a certified electrician and an assistant installer.

Revenue comes from four sources: installation of new units, repairs, service contracts and subcontracting. Most jobs are new installations, either for individual customers or subcontracts for building projects. Small and medium-sized home roof installation jobs are usually finished in two to four days. Repair work, outside of the service contracts, may include removing and replacing the panels when customers are replacing a roof. Arturro also offers annual service contracts that provide free labour for existing installations.

Some customers — homeowners, owners of office buildings and builders — have accounts with Air Care and receive a 1 percent discount if they pay within 10 days. They are asked to settle their accounts in 30 days, paying by cash or by cheque. PST and GST apply to all work completed by Air Care.

Accounts have been set up with a local hardware store, with suppliers of solar panels and inverters (units that convert the solar DC power to AC), and other regular suppliers.

After remitting all taxes before the end of March 2015, Arturro converted the accounts for Air Care using the following information:

- Business Information
- Chart of Accounts
- Income Statement
- Balance Sheet
- Trial Balance
- Supplier Information
- Customer Information
- Accounting Procedures

BUSINESS INFORMATION

AIR CARE SERVICES

COMPANY INFORMATION

Address: 100 Belair Avenue, Unit 25
Regina, Saskatchewan S4T 4U2
Telephone 1: (306) 456-1299
Telephone 2: (888) 455-7194
Fax: (306) 456-3188
Business No.: 533 766 455 RT0001
Fiscal Start: Jan. 1, 2015
Fiscal End: June 30, 2015
Earliest Transaction: March 31, 2015
Company Type: Construction/Contractor

REPORTS & FORMS

Choose settings for your printer and forms

USER PREFERENCES

Options
Use Accounting Terms
Automatically Save Changes to Records
Show List Buttons
Calculate Record Balances in Home Window by Session Date

View Settings
Hide: Inventory & Services, Employees & Payroll, Job Sites, Time & Billing
Daily Business Manager: turn off
Checklists: turn off
Show Session Date at Startup

Transaction Confirmation: turned on

Pop-Ups: your preferences

COMPANY SETTINGS

System
Do not allow dates before March 31, 2015
Allow Future Transactions
Warn if more than 7 days in future
Warn if Accounts Not Balanced

Backup
Backup Weekly; Display reminders
Turn off scheduled backup

Features
Do not use orders, quotes, packing slips & projects
Use both French and English

Credit Card Information
Card Used: Visa
Payable Account: 2160
Expense Account: 5020
Card Accepted: Visa
Discount Fee: 2.9%
Expense Account: 5020
Asset Account: 1070
Card Accepted: MasterCard
Discount Fee: 2.7%
Expense Account: 5020
Asset Account: 1080

Sales Taxes
Taxes: GST; PST
Codes: G - GST @ 5%;
GP - GST @ 5%, PST @ 5%, non-refundable

Forms Settings (Next Number)
Sales Invoices No. 710
Receipts No. 20

Date Format:
Short date format: mm/dd/yyyy
Use long dates on the screen

Logo: SageData13\Logos\aircare.bmp

GENERAL SETTINGS: No changes

PAYABLES SETTINGS

Address: Regina, Saskatchewan, Canada
Options
Aging Periods: 10, 30, 60 days
Discounts before Tax: Yes

RECEIVABLES SETTINGS

Address: Regina, Saskatchewan, Canada
Options
Aging Periods: 10, 30, 60 days
Interest Charges: 1.5% after 30 days
Statements Include Invoices for 31 days
New Customer Tax Code: GP

Discounts
Payment Terms: 1/10, n/30 after tax
Discounts before Tax: No
Line Discounts: No

Comments
Sales Invoice: Interest @ 1.5% per month charged on accounts over 30 days.

BANK ACCOUNTS: NEXT CHEQUE NO.

Bank: Chequing 101

CHART OF ACCOUNTS

AIR CARE SERVICES

ASSETS
1000 CURRENT ASSETS [H]
1010 Test Balance Account
1060 Bank: Chequing [A]
1070 Bank: Visa [A]
1080 Bank: MasterCard [A]
1100 Net Bank [S]
1200 Accounts Receivable
1210 Prepaid Insurance
1300 Solar Panels
1310 Inverters
1320 Electrical Supplies
1340 Office Supplies
1390 TOTAL CURRENT ASSETS [T]

1400 SHOP & EQUIPMENT [H]
1440 Computer System
1460 Service Equipment
1480 Tools
1500 Van ▶

▶1550 Shop
1590 TOTAL SHOP & EQUIPMENT [T]

LIABILITIES
2000 CURRENT LIABILITIES [H]
2100 Bank Loan
2160 Credit Card Payable
2200 Accounts Payable
2640 PST Payable
2650 GST Charged on Sales [A]
2670 GST Paid on Purchases [A]
2750 GST Owing (Refund) [S]
2790 TOTAL CURRENT LIABILITIES [T]

2800 LONG TERM LIABILITIES [H]
2850 Mortgage Payable
2890 TOTAL LONG TERM LIABILITIES [T] ▶

▶**EQUITY**
3000 OWNER'S EQUITY [H]
3560 S. Arturro, Capital
3650 Net Income [X]
3690 UPDATED CAPITAL [T]

REVENUE
4000 GENERAL REVENUE [H]
4100 Installation Revenue
4140 Service Contract Revenue
4160 Subcontracting Revenue
4180 Sales Discounts
4200 Interest Revenue
4290 TOTAL REVENUE [T]

EXPENSE
5000 OPERATING EXPENSES [H]
5010 Bank Charges
5020 Credit Card Fees ▶

▶5040 Purchase Discounts
5060 Hydro Expense
5070 Maintenance Services
5110 Computer Supplies Used
5120 Office Supplies Used
5150 Solar Panels Used
5160 Inverters Used
5180 Insurance Expense
5190 Telephone Expense
5200 Loan Interest Expense
5210 Mortgage Interest Expense
5290 TOTAL OPERATING EXPENSES [T]

5300 PAYROLL EXPENSES [H]
5320 Wages
5340 Payroll Service Charges
5390 TOTAL PAYROLL EXPENSES [T]

NOTES: The Chart of Accounts includes all accounts. Account types are marked for all subgroup Accounts [A], Subgroup totals [S], Heading accounts [H], Total accounts [T] and the type X account. All other unmarked accounts are postable Group accounts.

INCOME STATEMENT

AIR CARE SERVICES

January 1 to March 31, 2015

Revenue		
4000	GENERAL REVENUE	
4100	Installation Revenue	$ 82 500
4140	Service Contract Revenue	9 900
4160	Subcontracting Revenue	21 000
4180	Sales Discounts	−800
4200	Interest Revenue	525
4290	TOTAL REVENUE	$113 125
TOTAL REVENUE		$113 125 ▶

▶ Expenses		
5000	OPERATING EXPENSES	
5010	Bank Charges	$ 225
5020	Credit Card Fees	590
5040	Purchase Discounts	−300
5060	Hydro Expense	750
5070	Maintenance Services	1 365
5110	Computer Supplies Used	1 200
5120	Office Supplies Used	1 150
5150	Solar Panels Used	36 000
5160	Inverters Used	16 000
5180	Insurance Expense	3 600
5190	Telephone Expense	400
5200	Loan Interest Expense	625
5210	Mortgage Interest Expense	2 400
5290	TOTAL OPERATING EXPENSES	$64 005
5300	PAYROLL EXPENSES [H]	
5320	Wages	12 000
5340	Payroll Service Charges	330
5390	TOTAL PAYROLL EXPENSES	$12 330
TOTAL EXPENSE		$76 335
NET INCOME (LOSS)		$36 790

BALANCE SHEET

AIR CARE SERVICES

March 31, 2015

Assets			
1000	CURRENT ASSETS		
1060	Bank: Chequing	$ 34 660	
1070	Bank: Visa	1 950	
1080	Bank: MasterCard	1 060	
1100	Net Bank		$ 37 670
1200	Accounts Receivable		24 200
1210	Prepaid Insurance		3 800
1300	Solar Panels		28 280
1310	Inverters		33 420
1320	Electrical Supplies		6 100
1340	Office Supplies		400
1390	TOTAL CURRENT ASSETS		$ 133 870
1400	OFFICE & EQUIPMENT		
1440	Computer System		10 500
1460	Service Equipment		10 000
1480	Tools		3 000
1500	Van		31 000
1550	Shop		110 000
1590	TOTAL SHOP & EQUIPMENT		$164 500
TOTAL ASSETS			$298 370 ▶

▶ Liabilities			
2000	CURRENT LIABILITIES		
2100	Bank Loan		$ 25 000
2160	Credit Card Payable		1 010
2200	Accounts Payable		20 100
2640	PST Payable		1 530
2650	GST Charged on Sales	$1 530	
2670	GST Paid on Purchases	−840	
2750	GST Owing (Refund)		690
2790	TOTAL CURRENT LIABILITIES		$ 48 330
2800	LONG TERM LIABILITIES		
2850	Mortgage Payable		80 000
2890	TOTAL LONG TERM LIABILITIES		$ 80 000
TOTAL LIABILITIES			$ 128 330
Equity			
3000	OWNER'S EQUITY		
3560	S. Arturro, Capital		$ 133 250
3650	Net Income		36 790
3690	UPDATED CAPITAL		$ 170 040
TOTAL EQUITY			$ 170 040
LIABILITIES AND EQUITY			$298 370

TRIAL BALANCE

AIR CARE SERVICES

March 31, 2015

		Debit	Credit
1060	Bank: Chequing	$ 34 660	
1070	Bank: Visa	1 950	
1080	Bank: MasterCard	1 060	
1200	Accounts Receivable	24 200	
1210	Prepaid Insurance	3 800	
1300	Solar Panels	28 280	
1310	Inverters	33 420	
1320	Electrical Supplies	6 100	
1340	Office Supplies	400	
1440	Computer System	10 500	
1460	Service Equipment	10 000	
1480	Tools	3 000	
1500	Van	31 000	
1550	Shop	110 000	
2100	Bank Loan		$ 25 000
2160	Credit Card Payable		1 010
2200	Accounts Payable		20 100
2640	PST Payable		1 530
2650	GST Charged on Sales		1 530
2670	GST Paid on Purchases	840	
2850	Mortgage Payable		80 000 ▶

		Debit	Credit
▶ 3560	S. Arturro, Capital		$133 250
4100	Installation Revenue		82 500
4140	Service Contract Revenue		9 900
4160	Subcontracting Revenue		21 000
4180	Sales Discounts	$ 800	
4200	Interest Revenue		525
5010	Bank Charges	225	
5020	Credit Card Fees	590	
5040	Purchase Discounts		300
5060	Hydro Expense	750	
5070	Maintenance Services	1 365	
5110	Computer Supplies Used	1 200	
5120	Office Supplies Used	1 150	
5150	Solar Panels Used	36 000	
5160	Inverters Used	16 000	
5180	Insurance Expense	3 600	
5190	Telephone Expense	400	
5200	Loan Interest Expense	625	
5210	Mortgage Interest Expense	2 400	
5320	Wages	12 000	
5340	Payroll Service Charges	330	
		$376 645	$376 645

SUPPLIER INFORMATION

AIR CARE SERVICES

Supplier Name (Contact)	Address	Phone No. Fax No.	E-mail Web Site Tax ID	Terms Account	YTD Purchases (YTD Payments) Tax Code
Beausejour Electrical Products (Janine Beausejour)	50 Shockley Rd., Unit 18 Regina, Saskatchewan S4F 2T2	Tel: (306) 476-5282 Tel 2: (306) 476-3997 Fax: (306) 476-5110	jb@beausejour.com www.beausejour.com 444 276 534	1/10, n30 (before tax) 1320	$2 100 ($2 100) G
Green Earth Products Inc. (Ezra Green)	2 Greening St. Regina, Saskatchewan S4F 9J9	Tel: (306) 475-6432 Fax: (306) 475-8600	egreen@greenearth.com www.greenearth.com 177 235 441	1/10, n/30 (before tax) 1310	G
Killarney Solar Equipment (Kieper Warme)	91 Radiation St. Regina, Saskatchewan S4B 4F4	Tel: (306) 363-0210 Fax: (306) 363-2000	kw@heatexchange.com www.heatexchange.com 571 277 631	1/5, n/30 (before tax) 1300	G
Receiver General for Canada	Sudbury Tax Services Office PO Box 20004 Sudbury, Ontario P3A 6B4	Tel 1: (800) 561-7761 Tel 2: (800) 959-2221	www.cra-arc.gc.ca	net 1	($790) No tax
Saskatchewan Energy Corp. (Kira Strong)	50 Watts Rd. Regina, Saskatchewan S4G 5K8	Tel 1: (306) 755-6000 Tel 2: (306) 755-3997 Fax: (306) 754-7201	accounts@seg.ca www.seg.ca 459 021 643	net 10 5060	$802 ($802) G
Saskatel (Sotto Voce)	4 Speakers Corners Regina, Saskatchewan S4L 4G2	Tel 1: (306) 361-3255	accounts@saskatel.ca www.saskatel.ca 492 304 590	net 10 5190	$630 ($630) GP
Starbuck Advertising Agency (Pam Fletts)	300 Flyer St. Suite 800 Regina, Saskatchewan S4B 1C6	Tel 1: (306) 361-1727 Fax: (306) 361-8229	pfletts@saa.com www.saa.com 610 728 365	net 10	$1 200 ($1 200) GP
Wheatfields Hardware (Nutley Bolter)	72 Hammer St. Regina, Saskatchewan S4P 1B8	Tel 1: (306) 369-0808 Tel 2: (306) 369-6222	nbolter@yahoo.com 385 416 822	net 15 1480	$980 ($980) GP
Willow Garage (Axel Rodd)	699 Willow St. Regina, Saskatchewan S4P 1B3	Tel 1: (306) 368-6444 Tel 2: (306) 368-6000	axel@wefixcars.com www.wefixcars.com 129 732 010	net 30	$420 ($420) GP

OUTSTANDING SUPPLIER INVOICES

AIR CARE SERVICES

Supplier Name	Terms	Date	Inv/Chq No.	Amount	Tax	Total
Beausejour Electrical Products	1/10, n/30 (before tax)	Mar. 26/15	B-894	$10 000	$500	$10 500
		Mar. 26/15	Chq 94			4 500
	1/10, n/30 (before tax)	Mar. 28/15	B-921	2 000	100	2 100
			Balance owing			$ 8 100
Killarney Solar Equipment	1/5, n/30 (before tax)	Mar. 25/15	KS-1031	$20 000	1 000	$21 000
		Mar. 28/15	Chq 96			5 200
		Mar. 31/15	Chq 98			9 900
			Balance owing			$ 5 900
				Grand Total		$14 000

CUSTOMER INFORMATION

AIR CARE SERVICES

Customer Name (Contact)	Address	Phone No. Fax No.	E-mail Web Site	Terms Revenue Acct Tax Code	YTD Sales (Credit Limit) Customer Since
Grande Pointe Towers (Sophie Grande)	77 LaPointe Cr. White City Saskatchewan S0G 5B0	Tel 1: (306) 322-7500 Fax: (306) 322-7436	sgrande@GPTowers.com www.GPTowers.com	1/10, n/30 (after tax) 4100 GP	$11 000 ($20 000) Jan. 1/15
Midwest Funeral Home (N. Mourning)	8 Quiet St. Regina, Saskatchewan S4B 1E1	Tel: (306) 763-WAKE or (306) 763-9253 Fax: (306) 762-9301	nm@midwestfh.com www.midwestfh.com	1/10, n/30 (after tax) 4140 GP	($10 000) Aug. 1/13
Oak Bluff Banquet Hall (Ann Oakley)	4 Celebration Ave. Regina, Saskatchewan S4V 3H7	Tel: (306) 622-7391 Fax: (306) 622-7900	annie@OBBH.com www.OBBH.com	1/10, n/30 (after tax) 4160 GP	($20 000) Mar. 1/15
Passions Dept Store (Mann E. Kinn)	44 Highlife Ave. Regina, Saskatchewan S4L 2K0	Tel: (306) 762-8662 Fax: (306) 763-9115	www.passions.com	1/10, n/30 (after tax) 4100 GP	$6 300 ($15 000) Jan. 1/10
Regina School Board (Ed Ducate)	49 Trainer St. Regina, Saskatchewan S4C 4B6	Tel 1: (306) 466-5000 Tel 2: (306) 466-1123 Fax: (306) 466-2000	edd@rdsb.ca www.rdsb.ca	1/10, n/30 (after tax) 4100 GP	$8 400 ($15 000) Mar. 1/15
Selkirk Community Centre (Elsa Peeples)	588 Populous St. Regina, Saskatchewan S4CT 8N1	Tel: (306) 368-4575 Fax: (306) 368-2198	elsas@selkirk.com www.selkirk.com	1/10, n/30 (after tax) 4100 GP	($20 000) Jul. 1/12

OUTSTANDING CUSTOMER INVOICES

AIR CARE SERVICES

Customer Name	Terms	Date	Inv/Chq No.	Amount	Total
Grande Pointe Towers	1/10, n/30 (after tax)	Mar. 24/15	699	$4 400	
		Mar. 28/15	Chq 4896	2 400	
	1/10, n/30 (after tax)	Mar. 28/15	703	2 200	
			Balance owing		$4 200
Regina School Board	1/10, n/30 (after tax)	Mar. 28/15	701	$22 000	
		Mar. 28/15	Chq 10367	2 000	
			Balance owing		$20 000
				Grand Total	$24 400

Accounting Procedures

Open-Invoice Accounting for Payables and Receivables

The open-invoice method of accounting for invoices allows the business to keep track of each individual invoice and any partial payments made against it. This method is in contrast to methods that keep track of only the outstanding balance by combining all invoice balances owed to a supplier or by a customer. Sage 50 uses the open-invoice method. When invoices are fully paid, they should be removed periodically after statements are received from the supplier or sent to the customers.

GST and PST

Air Care Services is a contractor business using the regular method of calculating GST. GST, at the rate of 5 percent, charged and collected from customers will be recorded as a liability in *GST Charged on Sales*. GST paid to suppliers will be recorded in *GST Paid on Purchases* as a decrease in tax liability. The balance owing, the difference between the GST charged and GST paid, or the request for a refund will be remitted to the Receiver General for Canada quarterly.

Air Care charges customers 5 percent PST on all sales and pays PST on some goods. Air Care is exempt from PST for purchases of items that are sold or used in the installation work because the customer pays PST on the sales using these products.

NOTES
Most bank services and other financial institution services are exempt from GST collection.

Sales of Services

Accounts are set up for several customers. Other customers pay for their purchases immediately by cash, cheque or credit card. Separate bank accounts are set up for credit card deposits. You can enter transactions for cash and credit card customers by choosing One-Time Customer and typing the name of the customer in the Address field or by typing the customer's name in the Name field and choosing the Quick Add or Continue option.

For cash sales, the program will debit *Bank: Chequing* (or *Bank: Visa* or *MasterCard* for credit card payments) instead of the *Accounts Receivable* control account.

NOTES
The terms Invoice and Bill are interchangeable. The Premium version uses Bill for the construction/contracting business and the Pro version uses Sales Invoice.

Purchases

Most regular suppliers have given Air Care credit terms, including some discounts for early payment. Some purchases are accompanied by immediate payment, usually by cheque or credit card. Cheque payments are preferred because the cancelled cheques become part of the business records. Enter the cash transaction for purchases from new suppliers in the Payments Journal as an Other Payment or in the Purchases Journal. Choose the appropriate Payment Method; choose One-Time Supplier from the Supplier list and type the supplier's name in the Address field. You can also type the name in the Supplier field and choose Quick Add or Continue.

For cash purchases paid by cash or cheque, the program will credit *Bank: Chequing* instead of the *Accounts Payable* control account. For credit card purchases, *Credit Card Payable* is credited. All other accounts for this transaction will be appropriately debited and credited.

PRO VERSION
When we use the term Supplier for the Premium version, Pro version users should substitute the term Vendor.

Discounts

Air Care Services offers a 1 percent discount to account customers if they settle their accounts within ten days. Full payment is requested within 30 days. These payment terms are set up as defaults. When the receipt is entered, if the discount is still available, the program will show the amount of the discount and the net amount owing automatically. Discounts are not allowed on partial payments or on cash purchases paid by cheque or credit card. All customer sales discounts are calculated on after-tax amounts.

Some suppliers also offer discounts, calculated on the amounts before taxes, for early settlement of accounts. Again, when the terms are entered for the supplier and full payment is made before the discount period expires, the program will display the pretax discount as available and automatically calculate a net balance owing. Payment terms vary from supplier to supplier.

INSTRUCTIONS

NOTES

Source documents begin on page 252 after the setup instructions.

1. **Set up** the **company accounts** using the Business Information, Chart of Accounts, Balance Sheet, Income Statement, Trial Balance and Supplier and Customer Information provided for March 31, 2015. Detailed instructions to assist you in setting up the company accounts follow.
2. **Enter** the **transactions** beginning on page 252 in Sage 50 using the Chart of Accounts, Supplier Information, Customer Information and Accounting Procedures.
2. **Print** the **reports and graphs** indicated on the following printing form after you have completed your entries:

REPORTS

Accounts
- ☐ Chart of Accounts
- ☐ Account List
- ☐ General Journal Entries

Financials
- ☑ Comparative Balance Sheet: April 1 and April 30, difference in percentage
- ☑ Income Statement: January 1 to May 1
- ☑ Trial Balance: May 1
- ☑ All Journal Entries: April 1 to June 11
- ☑ General Ledger accounts: 1060 4040 4100 from April 1 to May 1
- ☑ Cash Flow Projection Detail Report for account 1060 for 30 days
- ☐ Statement of Cash Flows

Tax
- ☑ GST Report April 1 to May 1

Banking
- ☐ Cheque Log Report

Payables
- ☐ Supplier List
- ☐ Supplier Aged
- ☑ Aged Overdue Payables: May 1
- ☐ Expenses Journal Entries
- ☐ Payments Journal Entries

Receivables
- ☐ Customer List
- ☐ Customer Aged
- ☑ Aged Overdue Receivables: May 1
- ☐ Sales Journal Entries
- ☐ Receipts Journal Entries
- ☐ Customer Statements

Mailing Labels
- ☐ Labels

Management Reports
- ☐ Ledger

GRAPHS
- ☐ Payables by Aging Period
- ☐ Payables by Supplier
- ☐ Receivables by Aging Period
- ☐ Receivables by Customer
- ☐ Sales vs Receivables
- ☐ Receivables Due vs Payables Due
- ☐ Sales by Account
- ☐ Expenses by Account
- ☑ Expenses and Net Profit as % of Revenue

KEYSTROKES FOR SETUP

Creating Company Files

For Air Care Services, we will create the company files from scratch rather than use one of the starter files. Once we create the files and define the defaults, we will add the accounts, define linked accounts for the General, Payables and Receivables ledgers and create supplier and customer records.

Start the **Sage 50 program.**

You should see the familiar Sage 50, Welcome and Select Company window:

Click **Create A New Company**. **Click OK**.

You will see the Setup wizard introduction screen:

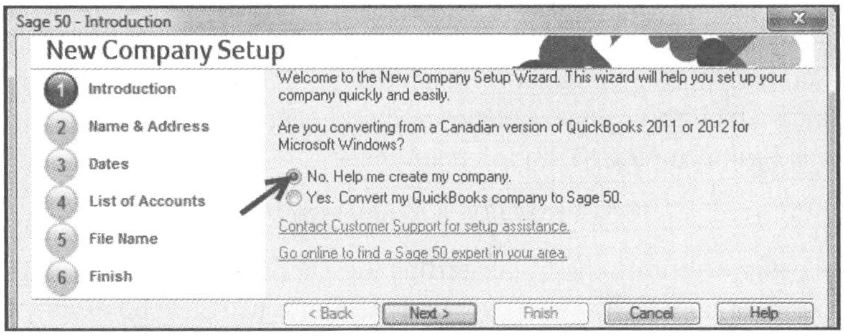

This screen introduces the Setup wizard and some support options.

Click **Next** to continue:

You must now enter company information for the business. The cursor is in the Name field. Alberta and its two-letter abbreviation — the first entry in the province list — are entered as defaults. Use the Business Information on page 202 to enter the company name and address details.

Type `Air Care Services` **Press** *tab* to enter the name.

Type `100 Belair Avenue` **Press** *tab* to enter the street address.

Type `Unit 25` **Press** *tab* to complete the address.

Type `Regina` **Press** *tab* and **Type** `S` **Click** the **Postal Code field**. SK and Saskatchewan are entered automatically as this is the only province name beginning with S.

Type `s4t4u2` **Press** *tab* to enter the postal code.

Type `Canada` **Press** *tab* to enter the country.

Type `3064561299` **Press** *tab* to enter the phone number.

Type `8884557194` to enter Phone 2 field and move to the Fax field.

Type `3064563188`

NOTES
Another setup option is to convert data files that were created with the QuickBooks program to Sage 50 data files.

NOTES
Remember that you can personalize the data file by adding your own name to the company name.

NOTES

We will set the date format with the Company settings. The initial date format for your new file is determined by your computer system settings, so your screen may show DD-MM-YYYY or MM-DD-YYYY. The author's computer had MM-DD-YYYY as the setting, so this format is shown initially for dates.

The Calendar icon shows the current month for your computer system. It is easier to type in the dates than it is to scroll through several months to find the one you need.

Typing the date in text format ensures that you will enter it correctly. You should type a four-digit year the first time you enter a date in the year 2000 or later to be certain that the year will be 2015 and not 1915.

NOTES

To find out if you need to enter four digits for the year, try typing a date such as 6-5-15.

NOTES

The Earliest Transaction date is also the initial date before which you do not allow transactions.

Click **Next** to open the company fiscal dates screen:

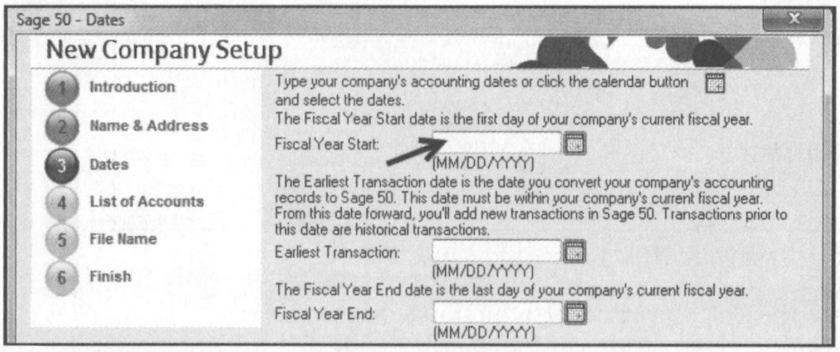

These company fiscal dates are like the ones you entered for Toss for Tots (Chapter 4) as part of the Company Information setup. The cursor is in the Fiscal Year Start field. This is the date on which the business begins its fiscal year. For Air Care Services, the fiscal start date is the beginning of the calendar year.

Type `jan 1 2015` **Press** *tab* to advance to the calendar.

Initially the program enters the fiscal start as the **earliest transaction date**. You need to enter the date on which the business is starting to use Sage 50 as its computerized accounting system — the earliest date for posting journal entries and the latest date for historical information. Air Care is converting its records on March 31.

Press *tab* to advance to the Earliest Transaction date field.

Type `mar 31 2015`

Press *tab* **twice** to advance to the Fiscal Year End field — the date Air Care Services ends its fiscal period. The end of the year is the default fiscal end date. Air Care Services's fiscal period is six months.

Type `jun 30 2015` **Click Next** to continue:

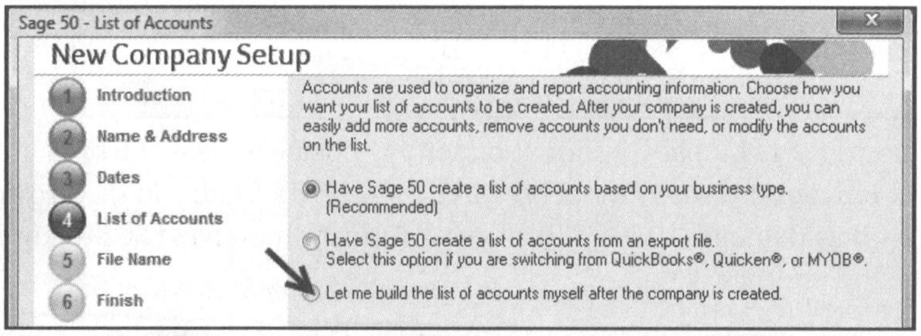

You can let Sage 50 create a set of accounts that are suitable for the business type you selected, start from scratch to create the accounts or copy data exported from another program. The set of accounts created by the program will include many accounts not required for Air Care Services. Because our setup is relatively small and we want to show all the stages of the setup, we will create the accounts ourselves. This approach allows us to show all the options available for each stage.

Click **Let Me Build The List Of Accounts Myself After The Company Is Created**. **Click Next**:

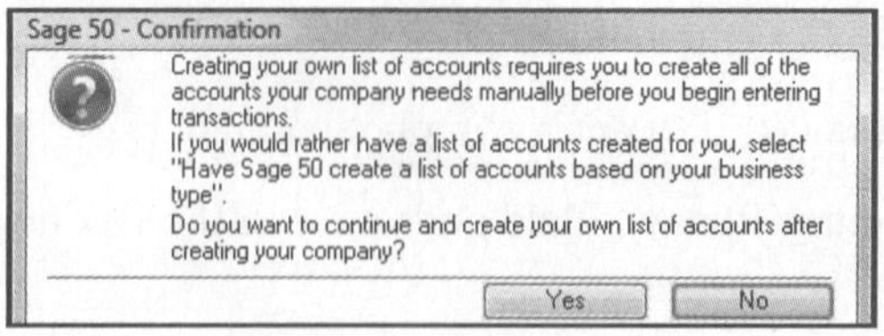

This message confirms your selection to create all the accounts on your own.

Click **Yes** to continue to the industry type selection list:

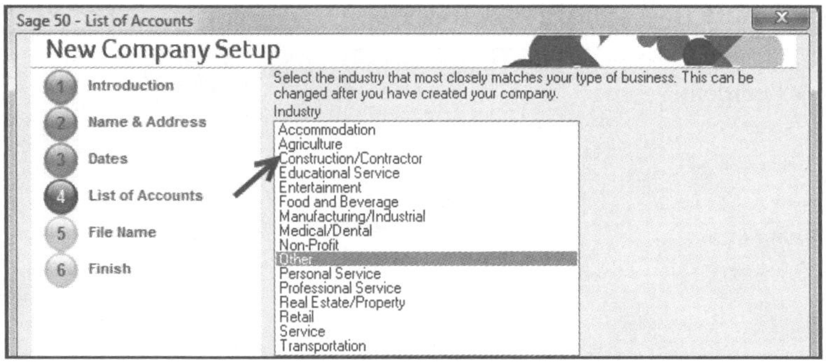

At this stage you should choose the type of business that best describes your company. This selection will determine some of the default settings and icon labels. Air Care Services is a construction/contractor business.

Click **Construction/Contractor** as the Industry type.

Click **Next** to open the File Name screen:

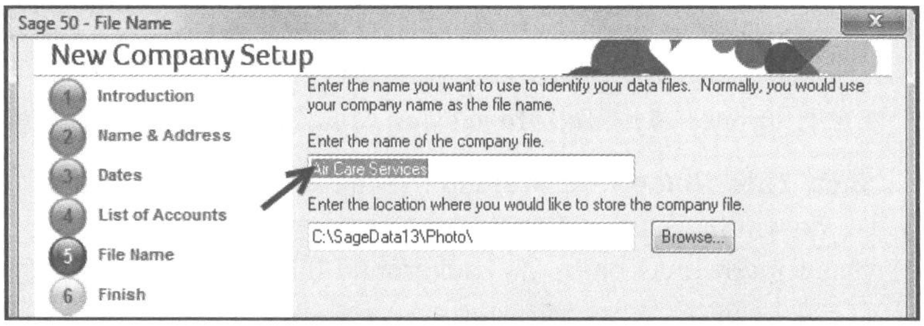

Now you must choose a file name and folder to store the new data set. The company name is entered as the default name for the data file, and it is selected.

Type `aircare` **Press** *tab* to advance to the location field.

The last folder you used will be the default selection — that is, Photo, if you last worked with the Phoebe's Photo Studio data set. Change folders if necessary to access the one with your other data files. If you have already created the folder you want to use,

Click **Browse** to open the Browse For Folder screen to select a folder. Otherwise,

Drag through **Photo** in the folder name or the last folder in the location field.

Type `Aircare\` to replace Photo\ or the last folder in the location.

Click **Next** to see the confirmation message:

Sage 50 asks if you want to create the new folder.

Click **Yes** to create the new folder and file:

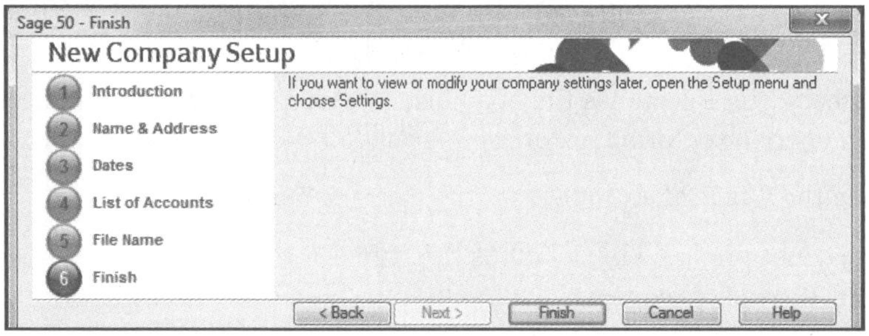

This screen reminds you that you can change this information from the Setup menu.

PRO VERSION

Remember that icon labels are the same for all company types – Customer and Vendor are the terms used throughout the Receivables and Payables modules, respectively.

NOTES

Sage 50 will automatically add the correct file extension. You do not need to type it when you are creating a new data set.

Click **Finish** to see the final Setup screen:

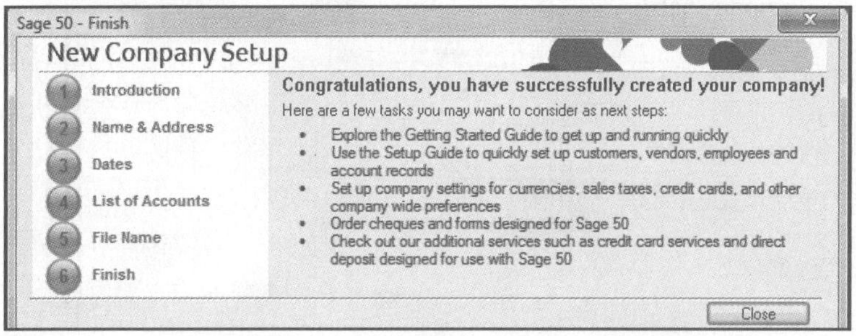

Wait for Sage 50 to finish creating the database for your new company files.

Click **Close** to complete the file creation stage. The HST Update wizard opens:

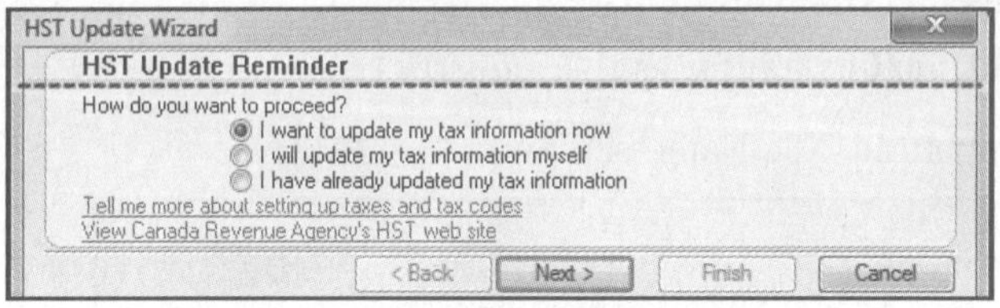

Click **I Will Update My Tax Information Myself** and then **click Finish**.

Click **Show This Window On Startup** to remove the ✓ in the Getting Started Guide window so that it will not open each time you start the program. This window may be in the background initially.

Click **Close** to display the Receivables module Home window:

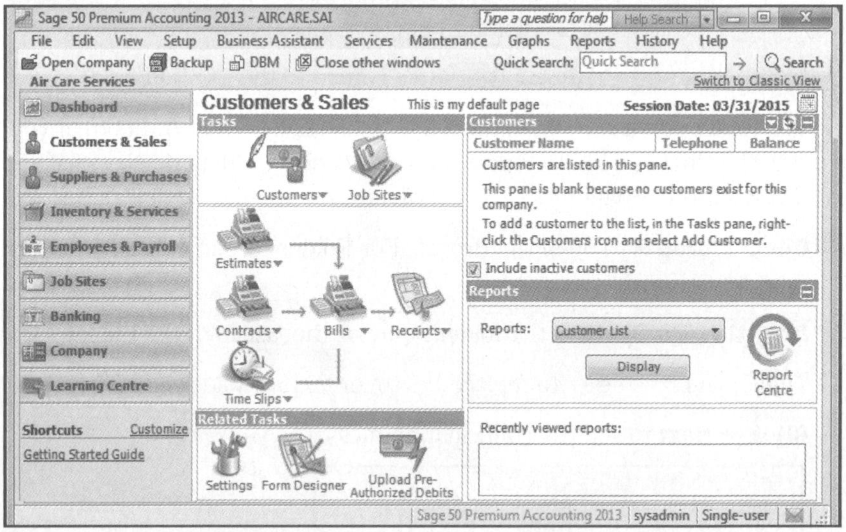

The Home window is now open with the name Aircare in the title bar. One shortcut, for the Getting Started Guide, is added by default. However, non-accounting terms are selected, so the module names are different from the ones in previous applications. Customers & Sales replaces Receivables, and Suppliers & Purchases replaces Payables. We will change these terms as part of the setup.

The Customers ledger icon has the open history quill pen icon because the ledgers are still open for entering historical information. No ledgers are hidden.

Display the **Chart of Accounts** for the Current Year.

The only account provided by default is the type X account, the General Ledger linked account, *Current Earnings*.

Close the **Chart of Accounts**.

NOTES

If you see a message about the payroll plan or any other Advisor messages, you can close these messages.

The tax update wizard was added for the 2011 version because the HST changed in 2010.

The Getting Started window may be hidden by the Home window initially. Click the Sage 50 icon in the task bar and then click the window you want to display.

NOTES

The session date you see initially will depend on the date settings in your own computer system. You may see the day, month or year first, and the year may have two or four digits.

PRO VERSION

The Sales Invoices icon replaces Bills, and Job Sites are named Projects. You will not see icons for Estimates, Contracts and Time Slips.

In the Modules pane, you will see Vendors & Purchases.

NOTES

The list of equivalent accounting and non-accounting terms is shown in Appendix B.

NOTES

Update your backup copy frequently as you work through the setup. Until you change the backup settings (page 214), the file will be backed up automatically when you close program.

NOTES

You may want to refer to the keystrokes in Chapter 4 to assist you in completing the setup and to the keystrokes in other chapters to assist you with the transactions for this application.

Preparing the System

The next step is to enter the company information that customizes the files for Air Care Services. You begin by preparing the system and changing the defaults. Use the Business Information on page 202 to enter defaults for Air Care Services.

You should change the user preference and reports and forms defaults to suit your own work environment.

PRO VERSION
The Automatically Refresh Lists option does not apply for the single-user Pro version.

Changing User Preferences

Choose the **Setup menu**, then **click User Preferences**.

If you are working in multi-user mode, decide whether you want to refresh lists automatically so that changes other users make affect your file immediately. The option to Show List Buttons is already selected.

Choose **Use Accounting Terms** so that your on-screen terms will match the ones used in this workbook.

Choose **Automatically Save Changes To Supplier, Customer And Other Records**.

Choose **Calculate Record Balances In The Home Window By Session Date**, instead of the default — balances based on the latest transactions.

NOTES
When you automatically save changes to records, you will not be prompted to save information each time you close a ledger after making a change.
When you display record balances by the session date, they will not include postdated transactions. You can automatically refresh these amounts or refresh them yourself by clicking the Refresh tool.

Click **View**.

Click **Inventory & Services**, **Employees & Payroll** and **Time & Billing** to hide the unused modules and features. You can hide Job Sites if you want, but you do not need to.

PRO VERSION
The Time & Billing module is not available in Pro, so you do not need to hide it.
You will click Project instead of Job Site.

Click **After Changing Session Date** to remove the ✓ for **Daily Business Manager** and **Checklists**.

Choose **Show Change Session Date At Startup**.

Click **Transaction Confirmation**. **Confirm** that the **Confirmation Message Box** is checked to activate this option.

NOTES
The option to show inventory lists does not apply to Air Care. You can remove this checkmark if you want.

Click **Pop-ups**. Choose the messages you want to display and hide.

Click **OK** to save the preference changes and return to the Home window.

You should now see the familiar accounting term labels for the modules. At this stage your Home window should look like the following, with hidden modules removed:

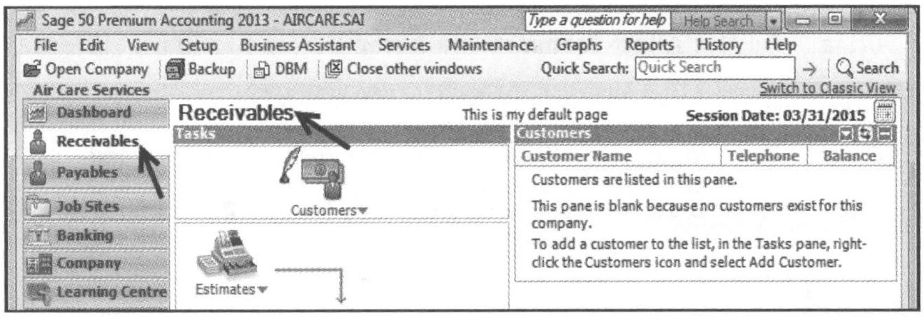

NOTES
The session date is still set at the default format, based on your computer system settings. We will change this when we customize the Company Settings (Date Format options).

Changing Company Default Settings

Many of the next steps for setting up company defaults and entering General Ledger accounts can be completed directly from the Company module Home window. We will start from that point.

WARNING!
You cannot complete many of the setup steps in multi-user mode.

Click **Company** in the Modules list to change the Home window.

You should now see the company window that we used for Muriel's Murals and Toss for Tots. You can open the Company Settings screen from the Settings icon, and you are able to create ledger accounts by clicking on the Chart of Accounts icon.

If you need help entering company settings, refer to page 74.

Changing Company Information

CLASSIC VIEW

The Setup tool is available. Clicking it when a ledger icon is selected will display the settings for that ledger.

If you click the Setup tool when no ledger or journal icon is selected, you must select a ledger from the list.

Click the **Settings icon** in the Related Tasks pane.

Click **Information** to display the Company Information screen.

From any Home window, you can also choose the Setup menu, then click Settings, Company and Information.

Most of the fields on this screen are complete from the information we entered to create the company files. You can edit the information if you made a mistake. We still need to add the business number.

Notice that the earliest transaction date appears as the session date on the Company Information screen. If there are any postdated transactions in the file, the Latest Transaction Date will be later than the session date.

You can return to the Company Information screen at any time to make changes. The program will set up defaults for the session date based on this information.

Click the **Business Number field**.

Type 533 766 455 RT0001

NOTES

The RT extension for the business number indicates the area of the business for reporting to the Canada Revenue Agency. For example, registered charity and payroll GST reports have different extensions than income tax.

Changing System Defaults

Click **System** in the list of company options on the left.

Most of the default System Settings are correct. Air Care uses the accrual basis of accounting, so Use Cash-Basis Accounting should remain unchecked. The option to Use Cheque No. as the source code can remain selected. This setting will include the cheque number in reports.

Initially, we will not allow any transactions before March 31, the earliest transaction date. We want to allow posting to future transactions but receive a warning if the dates are more than seven days in the future. Since you can enter transactions before completing the history, you should activate the warning about unbalanced accounts to prevent mistakes. The warning makes you aware of errors or omissions before you proceed too far with transactions.

NOTES

If you click the calendar for the prior transactions field, you will see that the program does not allow you to see a month before March. Entering a date prior to March 31 will generate an error with the advice that the date must be between March 31 (the earliest transaction date) and June 30 (the fiscal end date).

Click **Do Not Allow Transactions Dated Before** to add a ✓. **Press** tab.

Type 3-31-15 (This date entry is not ambiguous.)

Enter **7** as the number of days in future before you are warned.

Click **Warn If Accounts Are Not Balanced When Entering A New Month**.

Changing the Backup Options

We will back up the files on a weekly basis and leave on the reminder to back up each time we close the data file.

Click **Backup** in the list on the left. **Choose** **Weekly** as the frequency for Backup Reminders.

Click **Automatically Back Up This File** to remove the ✓.

NOTES

If you choose to back up your file automatically, leave the option checked and choose the backup frequency, the backup file location and the number of backup files you want to keep.

Changing the Features Selections

Customizing the icons and features that appear can simplify journal entries.

Click **Features** in the list on the left.

Click **each feature** and the **language setting** to change the status.

This removes the unused features and makes bilingual data entry and forms available.

Since we need to choose linked accounts when we set up credit cards and sales taxes, we will create accounts before entering these settings. Since Air Care does not use other currencies, we can skip this setup screen.

Changing Forms Default Settings

Click **Forms** to display the Settings for Forms:

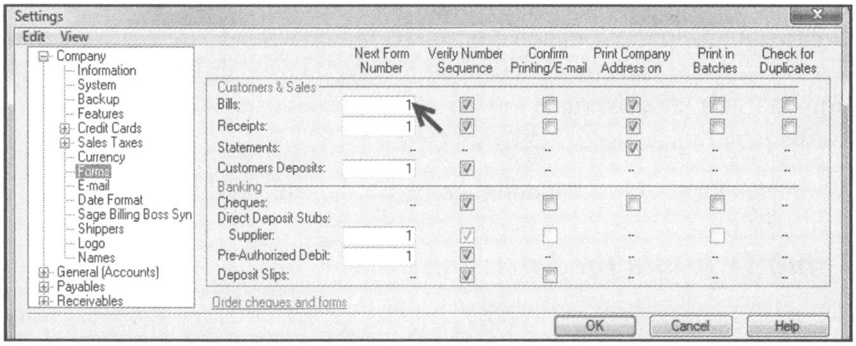

The Forms screen allows us to set up the automatic numbering sequences for business forms and to include warnings if the number you entered is a duplicate or out of sequence. You can set up the numbering sequence for all business forms that are generated internally or within the company.

We can skip the forms that Air Care does not use — for customer deposits, direct payments and pre-authorized debits. Cheque and bank deposit sequence numbers are added separately in the reports and forms settings for each bank account (see page 221).

Click the **Bills Next Form Number field**.

Type `710`

Click the **Receipts Next Form Number field**. **Type** `20`

The five column checklists on the Forms Settings screen allow you to **verify number sequences** and add reminders if you print bills or invoices, quotes, purchase orders and so forth. Verifying sequence numbers will warn you if you skip or duplicate a number and give you a chance to make a correction if necessary before posting. Choosing to **confirm** will set up the program to remind you to print or e-mail the form if you try to post before printing since posting removes the form from the screen. You should add the confirmation if you print or e-mail these forms regularly.

The third column allows you to add the **company address** to various forms. If you use preprinted forms that already include the address, remove the checkmarks to avoid double printing this information. If you have generic blank forms, leave the checkmarks so that the address is included. The next column refers to **batch printing**. If you want to print the forms on the list in batches (for example, print all the invoices for the day at the end of each day) you should check this option. The final column allows the program to check for duplicate bill and receipt numbers. We should check for these duplicates.

Click the **check box for Bills** and the **check box for Receipts** in the Check For Duplicates column.

Click to add a ✓ to any check box and click again to remove a ✓.

PRO VERSION

Click My Company Does Business In English And French. The other features are already deselected.

Packing slips are not available in the Pro version.

NOTES

Form Numbers are hidden for features in the modules that are not used. For Payroll, the Direct Deposit Stubs are numbered, and for Time & Billing, the time slips are numbered.

The Sage Billing Boss program is no longer available.

PRO VERSION

Invoice will replace the term Bill throughout the program.

NOTES

The additional options in the columns also apply to cheques, deposit slips and pre-authorized debits, even though we do not have sequence numbers for cheques on the Forms Settings screen. These should be set correctly for your own setup.

NOTES

Batch printing is covered in Chapter 14.

NOTES

E-mailing invoices and orders is covered in Chapter 12 and in Appendix J on the Student DVD.

Entering Default Comments for E-mail

The next step is to add a default message to e-mail communications.

Click **E-mail** in the list of Company options to open the next Settings screen:

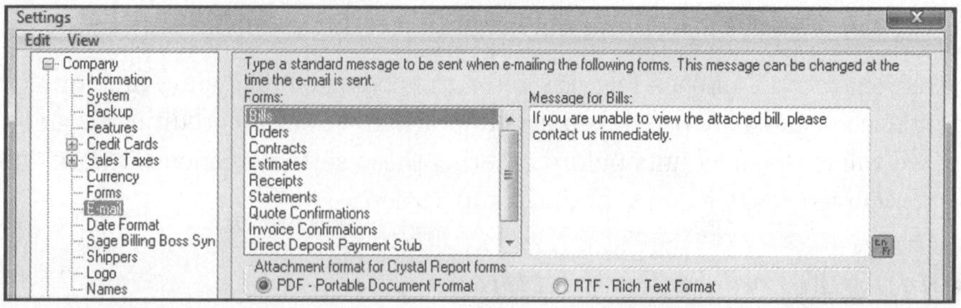

The left-hand list box contains the forms that you can e-mail to suppliers or customers. The right-hand box contains the message that will be added to the selected e-mail. You could add the company phone and fax numbers to the message so that the customer or supplier can contact you more easily. You can also select PDF or RTF as the format for the file you e-mail to your customers and suppliers. You do not need to change the default messages or formats for Air Care.

Click a form to select it and then type a message in the box beside it.

Entering Defaults for Date Formats

WARNING!

If your screen shows a different Short Date Format, you must change this to match the date formats used in the text.

Select MM dd yyyy from the Short Date Format drop-down list.

The default date formats use the short form on-screen. We want to use the long form so that the date will always be clear. Sunday is correct as the first day of the week.

Click **Date Format** in the list of Company options:

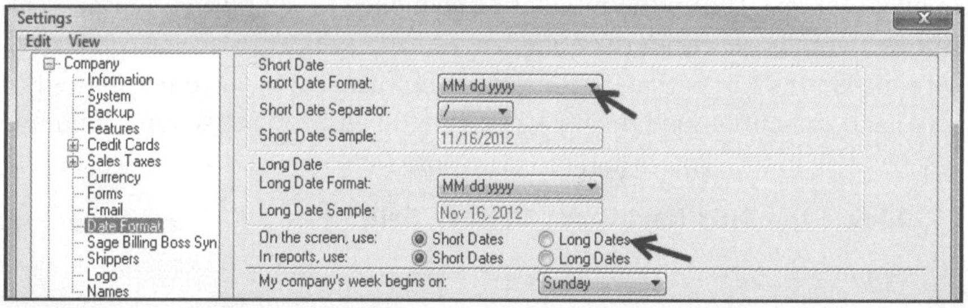

Click **Long Dates** beside On The Screen, Use to change the selection. **Choose** **MM dd yyyy** from the Short Date Format drop-down list if necessary.

Adding a Company Logo

We still need to add the company logo. The logo is located in the SageData13\Logos folder (or the folder you chose) where you installed the other data files.

Click **Logo** in the list on the left:

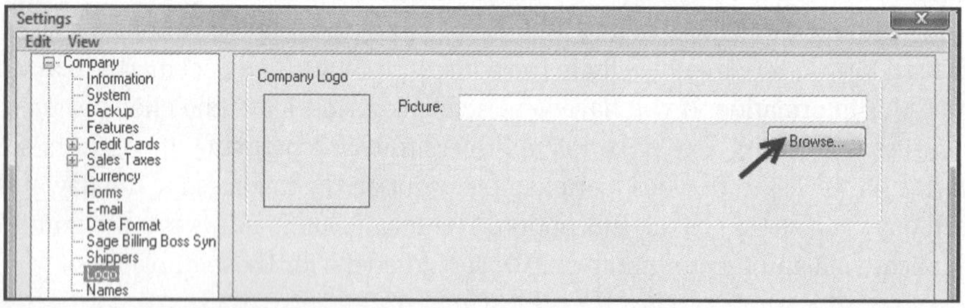

Click **Browse**. **Click Computer** in the left-hand pane. **Double-click C:**, **SageData13**, **Logos** and then **click aircare**.

Click the **Open button** to add the image and file name as shown:

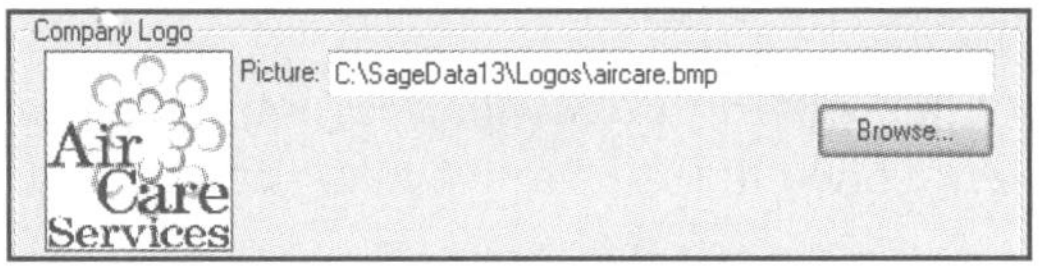

Check the **information** you have just entered and **make** any necessary **corrections**, including corrections to the fiscal dates.

Click **OK** to save the new information and return to the Home window.

> **NOTES**
> The Forms folder in the Sage 50 Program folder is the default location for the logo when you click Browse.
> If you are showing file extensions, the picture file will be named aircare.bmp.

Changing the Printer Defaults

Choose the **Setup menu** and **click Reports & Forms**.

The printer setting options for reports are given. Notice that the defaults include adding the computer system (calendar) date to reports and information about whether the report is filtered. You can check to see if the report fits on the page to improve the appearance of your printed reports, and you can change Reports & Forms settings any time. When the settings are correct,

Click **OK** to save the new information, or click Cancel if you have not made any changes, and return to the Home window.

> **WARNING!**
> Verify that the Form locations for the forms are valid for your program setup. If they are not, you will see an error message when you try to close the Reports & Forms window. The default folder is Sage 50 Premium Accounting 2013.

> **NOTES**
> Refer to Appendix E on the Student DVD for more information about printing options and customizing reports.

Preparing the Ledgers

Before entering the remaining settings, we should create the Chart of Accounts because many of the settings require us to enter default or linked accounts.

The next stage in setting up an accounting system involves preparing each ledger, beginning with the General Ledger. This stage involves the following steps:

1. organizing all accounting reports and records (this step has been completed)
2. modifying the *Current Earnings* account
3. creating new accounts
4. setting up credit cards, taxes and other features
5. defining linked accounts for the ledgers
6. entering supplier and customer information
7. adding historical account balances, invoices and payments

> **NOTES**
> Although you can create new accounts as you need them in any Account field, creating them all at the beginning allows you to check them more easily for accuracy and type. In the same way, it is safer to add all the opening balances at the start rather than one at a time to check that the Trial Balance is correct.

Preparing the General Ledger

Accounts are organized by section, including Assets, Liabilities, Equity, Revenue and Expense. **Account type** — such as **Heading** (H), **Subgroup total** (S), **Total** (T), **subgroup Account** (A), **Group account** (G) and **Current Earnings** (X) — is a method of classifying and organizing accounts within a section or subsection of a report.

The accounts follow the same pattern described previously:

- 1000–1999 Assets
- 2000–2999 Liabilities
- 3000–3999 Equity
- 4000–4999 Revenue
- 5000–5999 Expense

Use the Chart of Accounts, Income Statement and Balance Sheet on pages 203–204 to enter all the accounts you need to create. Remember to include all group headings, totals and subgroup totals in addition to the postable group and subgroup accounts.

> **NOTES**
> If necessary, refer to the Toss for Tots application, pages 86–88, for a review of the financial statement formats, the organization of accounts and the Current Earnings account.

> **NOTES**
> We are not using expanded account numbering so that the instructions will be the same for Premium and Pro version users in all chapters in Part Two.

Modifying Accounts in the General Ledger

The following keystrokes will modify the *Current Earnings* account in the General Ledger to match the account number defined in the Chart of Accounts.

In the Home window,

Click the **Chart Of Accounts icon** in the Accountants' Tasks pane to open the Accounts window.

> **NOTES**
> If necessary, change the view by choosing the Accounts window View menu and clicking Type.

The accounts should be displayed in Type view — in numerical order, with names, account types and balances. There is only one predefined account.

Double-click **3600 Current Earnings** to display its ledger record.

You can also open the ledger by clicking the account to select it. Then click the Edit tool button or choose the File menu and click Open.

Press *tab* to select the Account number field.

Type `3650` **Press** *tab* and **type** `Net Income`

The account types are dimmed because the *Current Earnings* account type must remain as type X. Only the account number and account name can be edited. You cannot enter a balance because the program automatically calculates the amount as the net difference between the total revenue and expense account balances for the fiscal period.

Click **Save And Close** Save and Close.

> **NOTES**
> You can also close the ledger window directly to save the changes. If you did not choose to save changes automatically (page 213), you will be asked if you want to save the changes and if you want to always save changes without asking. Choose to save changes without asking.

Close the Accounts window to return to the Home window unless you want to continue to the next step, which also involves working in the General Ledger.

Creating New Accounts in the General Ledger

We will enter account balances later as a separate step so that you can enter all balances in a single session. This may help you avoid leaving the data file with an incorrect Trial Balance.

> **NOTES**
> Refer to page 92 for assistance with creating new account records and page 94 for assistance with entering historical account balances.

Open the **Accounts window** or any **account ledger window**, if necessary.

Click the **Create tool** in the Accounts window or **choose** the **File menu** and **click** **Create**.

> **NOTES**
> Pressing *ctrl* + N or choosing Add Account from the Home window Chart of Accounts icon shortcuts list will also open a new ledger record form.

Enter **account information** for all accounts from the Chart of Accounts on page 203. Remember, you cannot use duplicate account numbers.

Type the **account number** and **press** *tab*.

Type the **account name** or title.

Click the **account Type** for the account.

If this is a postable account, indicate whether you want to omit the account from financial statements if its balance is zero. You do not need to change the default setting for Allow Project Allocations. The option will be checked when you enter 4000- and 5000-level accounts.

> **NOTES**
> The project allocation option will not apply until you choose to use projects. The default settings will then be appropriate.

Skip the **Opening Balance field** for now. We will enter all account balances in the next stage.

When all the information is entered correctly, you must save your account.

Click **Create Another** Create Another to save the new account and advance to a new blank ledger account window.

Create the **remaining accounts** from the Chart of Accounts.

Click **Save And Close** [Save and Close] to close the General Ledger account window after entering the last account.

Display or **print** your updated **Chart of Accounts** to check for account type errors as well as incorrect numbers and misspelled names. **Make corrections**.

Click the **Check The Validity Of Accounts tool** for descriptions of errors in account type. **Make** the **corrections** required.

Check the **validity** again and repeat the process until you see the message that the accounts are in logical order.

WARNING!
Remember that Net Bank and GST Owing (Refund) are subgroup totals, following the subgroup bank and GST accounts, respectively.

Entering Opening Account Balances

The opening historical balances for Air Care Services can be found in the Trial Balance dated March 31, 2015, on page 204. Headings, totals and subgroup totals — the non-postable accounts — have no balances and the Balance field is removed.

Use the *Test Balance Account* for any adjustments that would leave the Trial Balance in a forced balance position before you are finished or if one of the remaining balances is incorrect. After entering all balances, the *Test Balance Account* should have a zero balance, and you can remove it.

The Accounts window should be open.

Open the **General Ledger** account information window for the first account that has a balance, **1060 Bank: Chequing**.

Click the **Opening Balance field** to highlight its contents.

Type the **balance**.

Balances for accounts that decrease the total in a group or section (i.e., *GST Paid on Purchases*, *Sales Discounts* and *Purchase Discounts*) must be entered as negative numbers. The balances for these accounts have a (–) minus sign in the Balance Sheet or Income Statement. Balances for Drawings accounts would also be entered as negative amounts.

Correct the **information** if necessary by repeating the above steps.

Click the **Next button** in the Ledger window to advance to the next account ledger record.

Enter the **remaining account balances** in the Trial Balance by repeating the above procedures.

Close the **General Ledger window** to return to the Accounts window. You can check your work from the Trial Balance.

Choose the **Reports menu** and **click Trial Balance** to display the Trial Balance. **Print** the **report**.

Close the **display**. **Correct** the account **balances** if necessary. Open the ledger window, click the amount and type the correction.

Close the **Accounts window** if you want to save your work and finish your session.

NOTES
To remove the Test Balance Account, click its icon or name in the Accounts window and click the Remove tool or choose the File menu and click Remove. Check that you have selected the right account. Click Yes to confirm that you want to remove the account.

If the Test Balance Account balance is not zero, you cannot remove the account.

Entering the Account Class: Bank Accounts

Before setting up the Payables and Receivables ledgers, we must change the account class for bank accounts and some other accounts. **Account class** is another way of organizing accounts into related groups. Each section may be divided into various classes. For example, assets may be subdivided into bank accounts, credit card accounts, receivables, inventory and so on. When you create a new account, the program assigns a default class (Asset, Liability, Equity, Operating Revenue or Cost of Goods Sold) according to the first digit of the account number. For most accounts, you can accept this setting and the program will prompt you to change the class for special purpose accounts as needed. Bank accounts are not automatically reassigned by the program. You should also change the class for expense accounts by choosing either Expense or Operating Expense as the account class. Air Care does not sell merchandise and has no Cost of Goods Sold accounts.

Chequing bank accounts have additional information that must be entered in the ledger and therefore require that you change the class. You cannot select bank accounts for payments and receipts unless the **Bank** or **Cash class** is assigned. Bank class accounts must also be defined as such before you can select them as the default linked accounts for the Payables, Receivables and Payroll ledgers. The chequing account *Bank: Chequing* must be defined as a Bank class account.

NOTES
The available account classes vary for different account sections. For example, you cannot assign the Bank class to an expense account. You can assign the Bank class to liability accounts. This allows you to set up a line of credit as an account that you can choose to pay for purchases and update cheque numbers automatically.

Click the **Chart of Accounts icon** 

.

Double-click **1060 Bank: Chequing** to open its ledger window.

Click the **Class Options tab** to see the current class setting — Asset:

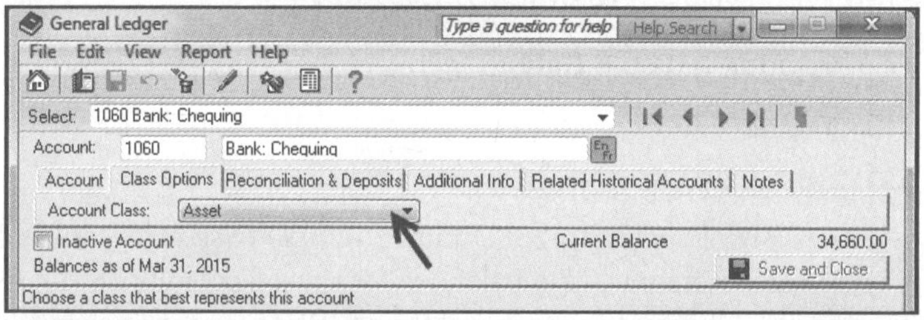

Click the **Account Class list arrow** to see the asset account class options.

Click **Bank** from the list to open the bank-related fields:

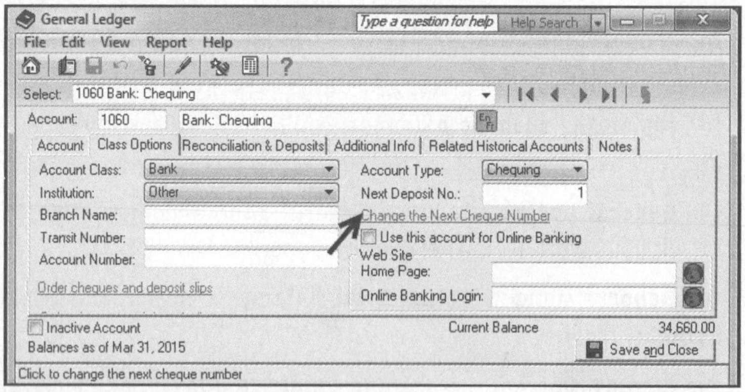

This screen allows you to define the type of bank account, and Chequing, the default, is correct. You can also enter a starting number for the deposit slip sequence and identify the bank for online banking access. We are not using deposit slips in this exercise, so you can skip this field. When different currencies are used, the currency for the bank account is also identified on the Class Options tab screen.

NOTES
Deposit slips are used in Chapter 15 together with account reconciliation. Online banking is introduced in Appendix I on the Student DVD.

Click **Change The Next Cheque Number** to open the cheque Form settings:

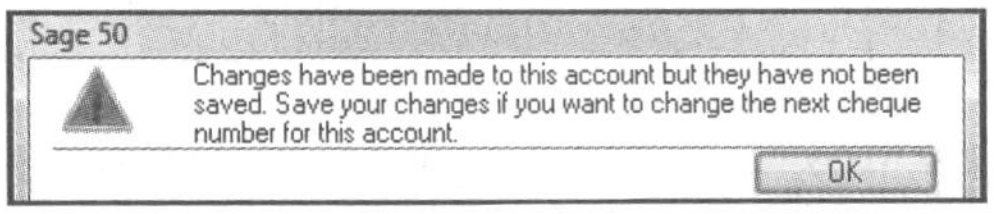

Before entering the cheque number, we need to save the account class change.

Click **OK** to return to the ledger window.

Click the **Save tool** or **choose** the **File menu** and **click Save**.

Click **Change The Next Cheque Number** to open the cheque Form settings:

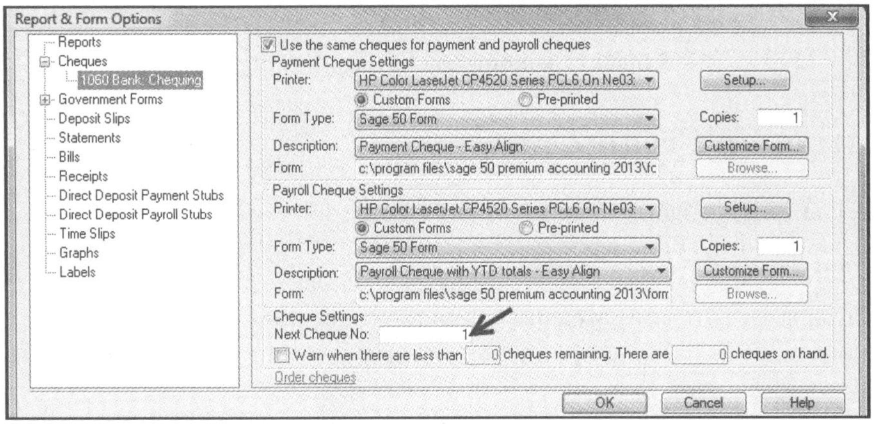

We need to enter only the cheque number. We do not need to change the printer settings for the cheques.

Click the **Next Cheque No. field** near the bottom of the form.

Type 101

Click **OK** to return to the account ledger window at the Class Options tab.

Defining the Class for Credit Card Accounts

Although credit card accounts are bank accounts, they are used as credit card linked accounts and are assigned the Credit Card class. Before setting up the cards with their linked accounts, we must change the account class for the accounts we need. We will change the linked asset accounts to the Credit Card Receivable class and the payable account to the Credit Card Payable class. If you also write cheques from or deposit customer cash or cheques to these accounts, you should use the Bank class so they will be available in the bank account fields in the journals.

Click the **Next button** to advance to account 1070 Bank: Visa.

Choose **Credit Card Receivable** from the Account Class list to change the class.

Click the **Next button** to open the ledger for 1080 Bank: MasterCard.

Choose **Credit Card Receivable** from the Account Class list.

Click the **Select field list arrow** to see the list of accounts.

Click **2160 Credit Card Payable** to open this account ledger.

Choose **Credit Card Payable** from the Account Class list.

Defining the Class for Expense Accounts

Expense accounts are defined as Cost of Goods Sold by default when you create them from the General Ledger new account window. These account classes should be changed unless they refer to inventory cost accounts. When you create expense

NOTES

Until you have saved the record or closed the ledger, the account class change has not been recorded. The cheque numbering fields for the account will not be available.

WARNING!

To avoid an error message, the Form fields must contain valid file locations. The forms you need are in the Forms folder inside the Sage 50 Premium Accounting 2013 program folder.

NOTES
You can assign the Payroll Expense class to the two payroll accounts.

accounts from an Account field using the Add An Account wizard, the default account class is Operating Expense, so you do not need to change it.

To create the Gross Margin Income Statement Report that applies when inventory is sold, you must correctly separate the Cost of Goods Sold accounts from other expenses.

Choose **account 5010** from the Select Account list to open the ledger.

Choose **Operating Expense** (or **Expense**) from the Account Class list.

Click the **Next button** . **Change** the **class** for all Group expense accounts.

Click **Save And Close** to close the Ledger window.

Close the **Accounts window** to return to the Home window.

Setting Up Credit Cards

Now that all the ledger accounts have been created, we can enter the remaining company and ledger settings.

Since Air Care accepts credit card payments from customers and uses credit cards in payment for purchases, we must set up the credit cards by naming them and identifying the linked accounts for deposits, payments and fees associated with the cards.

Air Care accepts Visa and MasterCard for sales, and uses Visa for credit card payments. You should be in the Company module Home window.

Entering the Credit Cards

Click the **Settings icon** to open the Company Settings options list.

Click **Credit Cards** (**click Company** first if necessary):

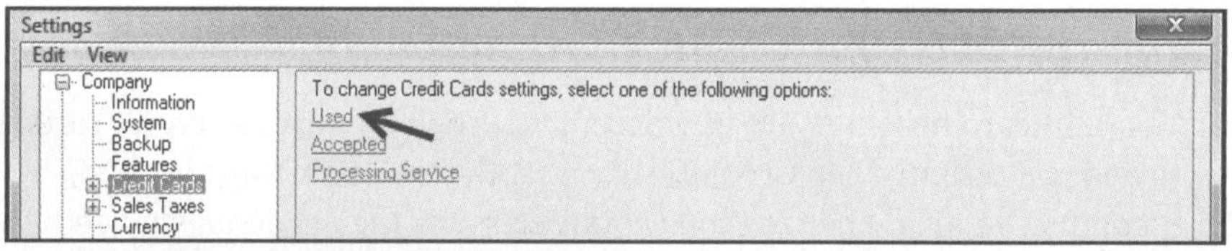

NOTES
You may see a message about credit card processing services, a fee-based service offered by Sage. Read and then close this message.
Information about this online service is also available from the Sales Journal when you choose a credit card for payment.

NOTES
The setup and use of Credit Card Processing Services is introduced in Chapter 13.

You can set up **Credit Cards Used** to make purchases from suppliers and **Credit Cards Accepted** to enter receipts from customers.

Click **Used** to open the screen for the cards that the business uses:

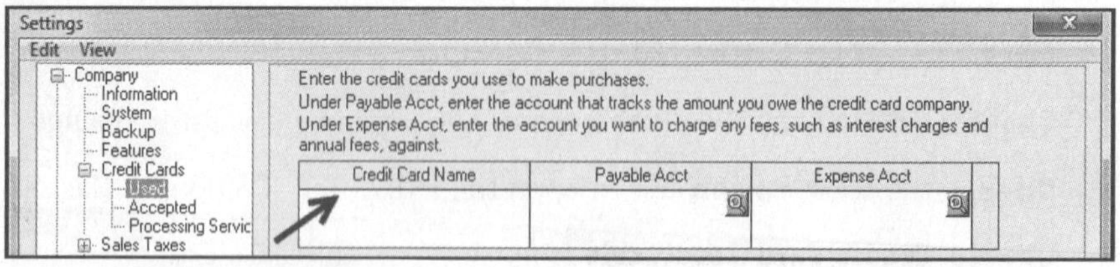

Each card named on this screen will appear in the Purchases and Payments journals in the Payment Method list. There is no discount fee associated with individual purchases, although there may be an annual or monthly fee attached to the card. Each card is listed on a separate line with its associated linked accounts.

Click the **Credit Card Name field** or **press** tab.

Type `Visa` **Press** tab.

The cursor moves to the **Payable Acct** field. This account is the liability account that records the balance owing to the card company.

Click the **Account List icon** to see the list of available accounts.

Click **2160**, the liability account for the card.

Click **Select** to add the account and move to the Expense Acct field.

The **Expense Account** records any monthly or annual fees paid to the card company for the privilege of using the card and interest charges on cash advances or overdue amounts. Not all cards have user fees, but all cards charge interest on cash advances and balances not paid by the due date. These additional fees are added to this linked expense account for credit card payment transactions in the Payments Journal (see Chapter 12). Air Care uses one expense account for all credit card–related expenses.

Click the **Account List icon** to see the account list.

Double-click **5020**.

Cards accepted in payment from customers are set up in the same way. The business may use and accept the same cards or different cards.

Click **Accepted** in the Company list under Credit Cards.

If you did not change the account class correctly, you will see the following warning message about incorrect account classes:

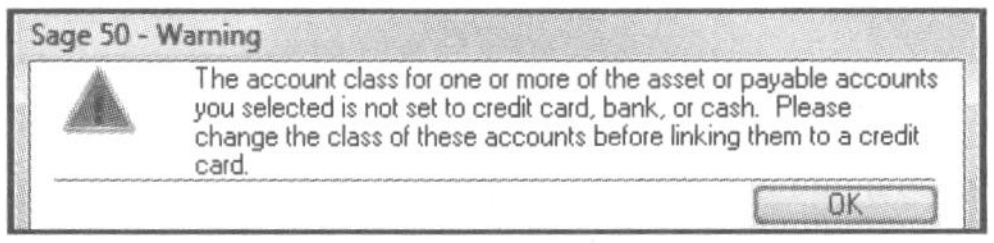

Click OK. Click Cancel to close the Credit Card Information window. Make the necessary account class changes and re-enter the credit card details.

The cards customers can use to make payments are entered on this screen:

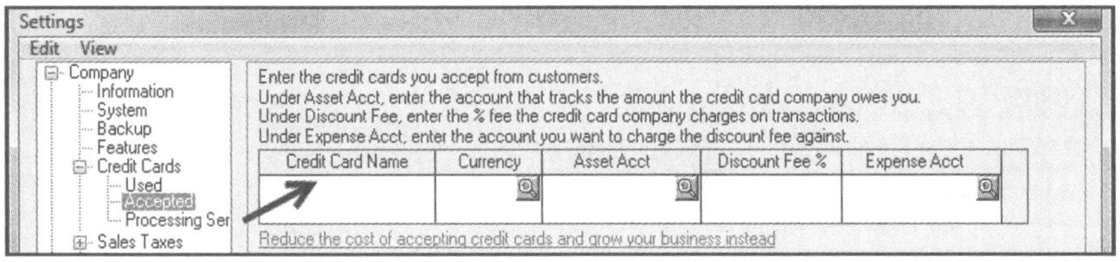

All the cards you name here will appear in the Payment Method list for Sales Invoices. Each card accepted should be listed on a separate line.

Click the **Credit Card Name field** or **press** tab.

Type Visa **Press** tab. The cursor advances to the **Currency** field.

Click the **List icon** to see the options:

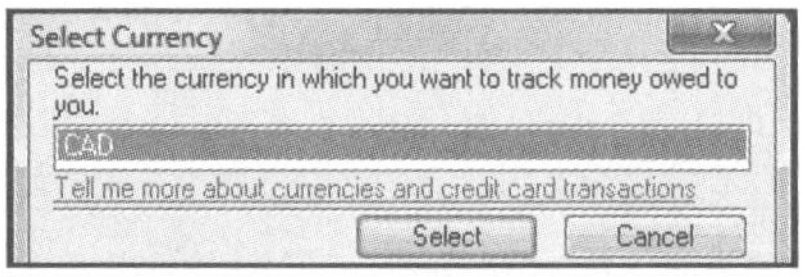

You can choose the currency of this credit card. Air Care has only Canadian customers, so CAD is preselected. Credit cards in other currencies must be connected to Credit Card Receivable or Bank class accounts with those currencies.

Click **Select** or **press** enter to continue. **Press** tab.

The cursor is in the **Asset Acct** field, the linked account for deposits from the card company. Normally a bank account is set up for credit card deposits.

Click the **Account List icon** to see the accounts available for linking.

WARNING!

You must choose a Bank, Cash or Credit Card Payable class account as the linked Payable account for credit cards used.

NOTES

You can add a new account at this stage if necessary. Type the new account number and press tab. Click Add to start the Add An Account wizard. Remember to choose the correct Account Class – Credit Card Payable – (on the fifth wizard screen) when using the wizard. Additional screens related to bank account settings are added to the wizard when you select the correct Account Class. You do not need to enter information on these screens.

NOTES

Return to the section Defining the Class for Credit Card Accounts (page 221) if you need assistance with this step.

PRO VERSION

The Currency option for credit cards is not available in the Pro version. You will advance to the Asset account field after the Name.

WARNING!

You must choose either a Credit Card, Cash or Bank class account as the linked asset account for cards accepted. Although other accounts are displayed, choosing them will give you an error message.

NOTES

Debit card transactions are set up as credit cards, but the discount fee is entered as 0.0 percent.

If you do not know the discount fee or you have cards with different rates, leave the field blank and enter the charges when you reconcile the accounts.

NOTES

Remember that if you use the Add An Account wizard to create the new bank accounts, you must indicate that the accounts are part of a subtotal (on the fourth wizard screen) and select Credit Card Receivable as the Account Class on the fifth wizard screen. You do not need to enter information on the additional bank-related screens.

NOTES

Other taxes and tax codes can be added later if needed. The details for each tax and code can be modified if the tax legislation changes, as it has several times in recent years.

Click **1070 Bank: Visa** to choose the account.

Click **Select** to add the account and advance to the next field.

The cursor advances to the **Discount Fee %** field. The discount fee is the amount that the card company withholds as a merchant transaction fee for use of the card. This expense is withheld from the total invoice amount that the card company deposits to the business bank account for each sale. Fees vary from one credit card company to another and also for the type of business. For example, high-volume businesses pay a lower percentage than businesses with a smaller volume of sales.

Type 2.9 **Press** tab.

The cursor advances to the **Expense Acct** field. This is the linked account that will be debited automatically for the discount fee for a credit card sale. The expense amount or fee is the total invoice amount times the discount fee percentage.

Click the **Account List icon** to see the accounts available for linking.

Click **5020** to choose the account.

Click **Select** to add the account to the Card Information screen.

Enter **MasterCard** in the Name field. **Choose** Asset Account **1080**, **enter 2.7** in the Discount Fee % field and **choose** Expense Account **5020**.

You can enter information for additional credit cards the same way.

Setting Up Sales Taxes

Setting up sales taxes before entering supplier and customer records will allow us to choose default tax codes for customers and suppliers for automatic entry in journals.

Click **Sales Taxes** to see the options for sales tax settings:

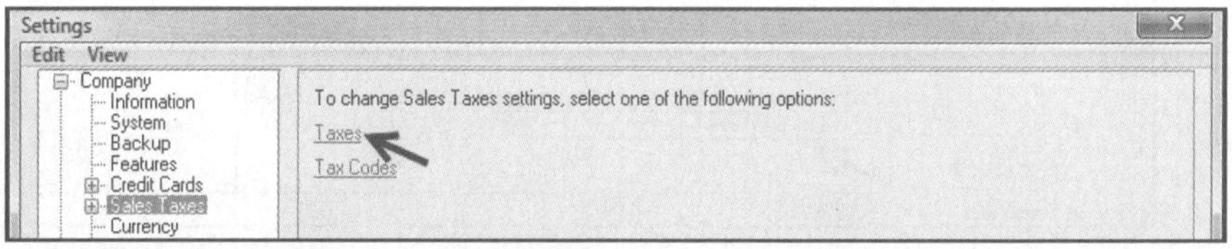

To set up sales taxes, we must identify the taxes that are charged and paid, and then define the codes that will be displayed in the journals.

Click **Taxes**:

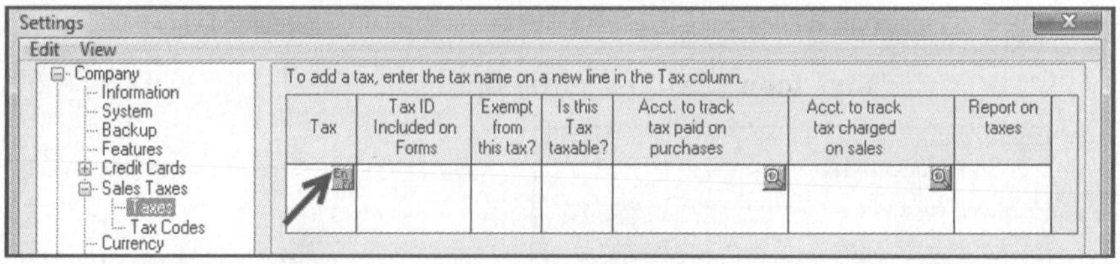

Sage 50 has no preset tax information. You can customize the taxes to suit any business by entering all the taxes applied and paid by a business and by creating as many tax codes as needed to account for all the possible combinations of taxes. Taxes can be added later or edited if needed. Air Care has two taxes: GST and PST and reports on both. Because PST is not refundable, PST paid is not tracked in a separate account.

Click the **Tax field** or **press** tab so you can enter the name of the tax.

Type GST and **press** tab to advance to the Tax ID field.

The tax number should be included on invoices, so you should enter it in this field. For GST, this is the business number. For PST, it is the provincial registration number that indicates the supplier is licensed to charge PST. GST numbers are normally included on forms because GST is refundable. PST numbers are not normally included on invoices.

Type 233 281 244 RT0001 **Press** *tab*.

The cursor moves to the **Exempt From This Tax?** column. Choose Yes only if your business — Air Care in this case — does not pay the tax. Air Care Services pays GST, so the default selection No is correct. The next field, **Is This Tax Taxable?** asks if another tax includes this tax in its base calculation. Currently no provinces apply this method of tax calculation. For Saskatchewan, where Air Care is located, the correct answer is No.

The next two fields define the linked accounts that **track the taxes paid** and the **taxes charged**. The taxes paid account records the total of the amounts entered in the GST field in the Purchases Journal whenever a purchase is made. Although you may choose an asset or a liability account, we use liability accounts because there is normally a balance owing to the Receiver General. If the tax is not refundable, such as PST paid, you should leave the account field for tracking taxes paid blank.

Click the **List icon for Acct. To Track Tax Paid On Purchases**.

Double-click 2670 GST Paid on Purchases.

The cursor advances to the field for the Account To Track Tax Charged On Sales. This account records the total of the amounts entered in the GST field in the Sales Journal whenever a sale is made. You may use an asset or a liability account.

Choose 2650 GST Charged on Sales from the List icon list of accounts.

The cursor advances to the **Report On Taxes** field. To generate tax reports from Sage 50, you should choose Yes. The Yes and No entries on the tax screens act as toggle switches. Clicking will change the entry from one to the other, and you can change these entries at any time.

Click **No** to change the default entry to Yes.

Press *tab* to advance to the next line and **type** PST

Click the **List icon for Acct. To Track Tax Charged On Sales**.

Choose 2640 PST Charged on Sales. **Press** *tab*.

Click **No** to change the default entry to Yes for reporting.

Click **Tax Codes** to open the next information screen:

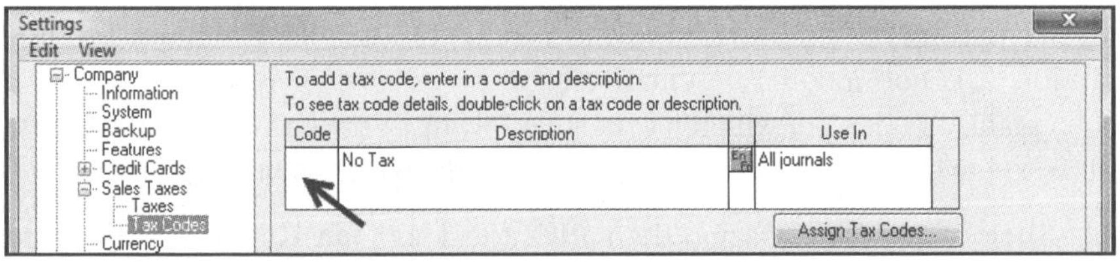

On this screen, you can create the tax codes required for all the different rates and combinations of taxes that apply to a business. No codes are entered initially, so the only entry is the blank code used when **No Tax** is applied. If you want to change or assign tax codes for all suppliers and customers, use the **Assign Tax Codes** feature.

Click the **Code column** below the blank on the first line.

Type G **Press** *tab* to move to the Description field.

NOTES

PST registration is required for businesses that charge PST on sales and do not pay PST on purchases of merchandise that they sell to customers (only the final customer pays PST).

NOTES

Sales tax amounts entered in the General Journal are also tracked in these linked accounts.

NOTES

By using liability accounts for both taxes paid and taxes charged, we can show the subtotal (GST Owing) in the Balance Sheet.

NOTES

After creating all tax codes and all supplier and customer records, you can update all tax information from the Assign Tax Codes window. We show this approach in Chapter 16.

NOTES

If at any time the tax regulations change, you can return to this screen and change the settings. For example, in 2010, BC applied the 12 percent HST to replace the separate GST and PST, and reversed this decision for 2013. The federal government has changed the GST rate twice in recent years. To make these changes in the data files, just edit the Rate in the Tax Code Details screen and the Description in the Tax Code screen. The description is not automatically updated when you change the tax rate. New tax codes may be needed as well.

Press *enter* or **double-click** to open the Tax Code Details screen:

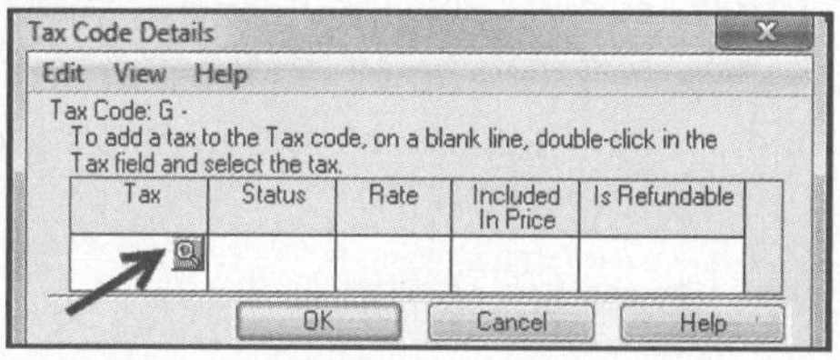

On this screen, you define how the tax is calculated and reported.

Click the **Tax field List icon** to see the list of taxes entered:

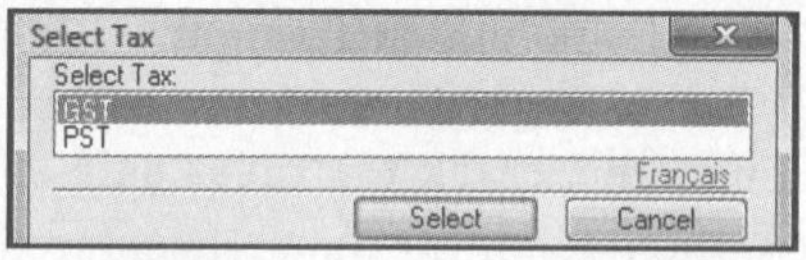

Both taxes we named are listed here. At this stage, you are asked to choose the taxes that should be applied (charged or paid) when this code is used in a journal entry.

Click **Select**, because GST is already selected, and return to the Details.

Defaults are entered for the remaining fields. The tax **Status** is Taxable, and this is correct — tax is calculated and charged. Other status options and their explanations can be viewed by clicking the List icon. The Non-Taxable Status is used for items that are not taxed but for which the amounts are still included in reports to the Receiver General. Similarly, the Exempt Status is used for items that are exempt from the tax but the amounts are still included in the tax reports filed. For example, although food is zero rated (no tax is charged), suppliers may still claim a GST refund and must report their sales amounts.

The remaining fields are straightforward. **Rate** is the percentage rate for the tax. Taxes may be **included** in the sales and purchase prices or not included. If some suppliers include the tax and others do not, create two separate tax codes. And finally, is the tax **refundable** — that is, are the taxes paid on purchases refunded? GST is not included for any of Air Care's suppliers' or customers' prices and GST is refundable. Non-refundable taxes, like PST, are automatically added to the asset or expense amount for the purchase.

Click the **Rate field**. **Type** 5

Click **No** in the Is Refundable column to change the entry to Yes.

Click **OK** to return to the Tax Codes screen for additional codes.

The description GST @ 5% appears beside the code G. You can edit the description if you want. If the tax were not refundable, non-refundable would be added to the description automatically. However, if you change the details, you must also update the description. It is not updated automatically.

You can also choose in which journals you want to have the tax codes appear. The default is to have the codes available in all journals, which is usually the correct choice.

Click **All Journals** and then **click** the **List icon** to see the options:

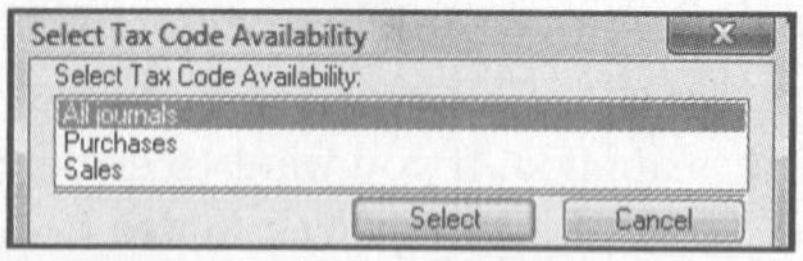

You can choose to have the tax codes available for all revenues, all expenses, or for all transactions (Purchases Journal, Sales Journal and General Journal). The default selection, All Journals, is correct.

Click **Cancel** or **Select** to return to the Tax Codes screen.

NOTES

For charities eligible for a 50 percent refund of the GST they pay, you can set up two taxes: one for the refundable portion and one for the non-refundable portion. Then create a tax code that uses both the refundable tax at 2.4999 percent and the non-refundable tax at 2.5001 percent. (The extra decimals will ensure that you avoid rounding errors resulting in overclaiming refunds.) For the non-refundable tax, you do not need to track taxes paid. They will then be added to the asset or expense portion of the entry, just like non-refundable PST.

NOTES

Charities that do not charge GST but are eligible for GST refunds may choose to show tax codes only in the Purchases Journal.

Click the **Code field below G**. **Type** GP **Press** (tab) and then **press** (enter).

Select **GST** as the first tax for this code. **Click** the **Rate field**. **Type** 5

Click **No** in the Is Refundable column to change the entry to Yes.

Press (tab). **Select** or **type PST** as the second tax for this code.

Click the **Rate field**. **Type** 5 **Click OK** to return to the Settings screen. (PST is not refundable, so the default selection, No, is correct.)

Click the ⊟ **beside Company** to reduce the Settings list.

Linked Accounts

Linked accounts are accounts in the General Ledger that are affected by entries in journals for the other ledgers. We have seen some of these linked accounts at work in journal entries in previous chapters. For example, an entry to record a credit sale in the Sales Journal will cause automatic changes in several General Ledger accounts. In the General Ledger, the *Accounts Receivable* [+], *Revenue from Sales* [+], *GST Charged on Services* [+] and *PST Payable* [+] accounts will all be affected by the sale. The type of change, increase [+] or decrease [–], is indicated in the brackets. The program must know which account numbers to use for posting journal entries in any of the journals. Often you do not enter account numbers for linked accounts in the journals. It is this interconnection of accounts between ledgers that makes Sage 50 fully integrated.

Since only *Current Earnings*, the General linked account for Current Earnings, is defined, we must identify the remaining linked accounts for the General, Payables and Receivables ledgers. Air Care does not use the Payroll or Inventory ledgers and you do not need to define linked accounts for them. Linked accounts are entered from the Settings screens for the ledgers, so we will enter them with other default ledger settings.

Changing Ledger Settings and Linked Accounts

Changing General Ledger Settings and Linked Accounts

Click **General (Accounts)** in the list on the left:

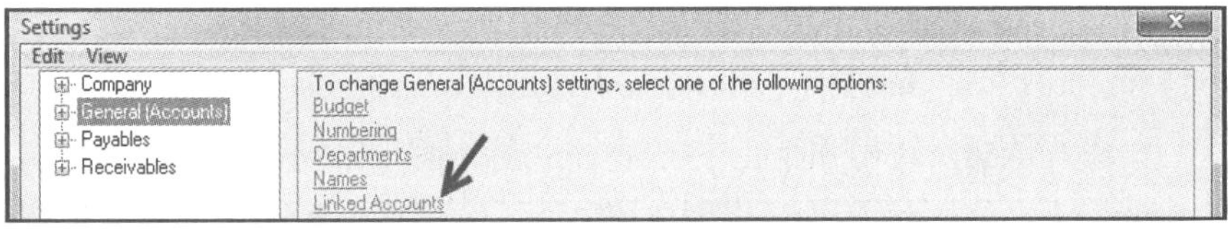

The General Ledger settings are correct for Air Care Services. The budget feature, departmental accounting and expanded account numbers are not used.

We need to add linked accounts.

Defining the General Linked Accounts

Click **Linked Accounts** to display the General Linked Accounts window:

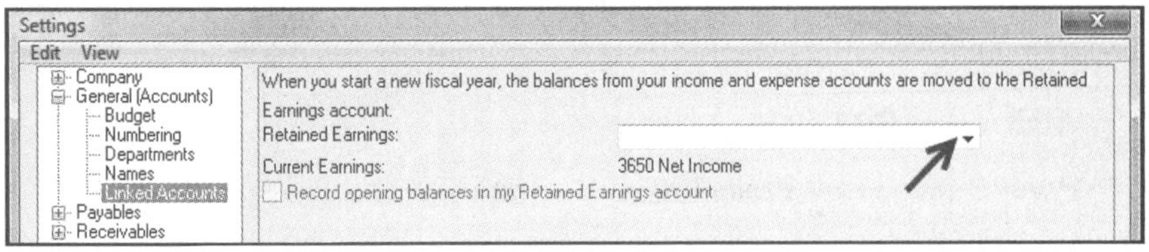

Press (tab) to place the cursor in the Retained Earnings field.

WARNING!
You must define essential linked accounts before you can finish the history for a company and before you can enter sales and purchase transactions.

CLASSIC VIEW
The Setup tool can be used to enter linked accounts. Select (right-click) a journal icon and click the Setup tool to see the Linked Accounts window for that ledger. If no icon is selected, choose the journal name from the Select Setup list to display the linked accounts for the ledger. If a ledger icon is selected, clicking the Setup tool displays ledger settings.

PRO VERSION
Departmental Accounting and expanded Numbering are not included in the Pro version, so you will not see entries for them.

NOTES
Names are used to add labels for the additional fields in each ledger. Additional fields for the Payroll Ledger are named and used in Chapter 9 (see pages 320 and 337).

CLASSIC VIEW
In the Home window, right-click the General Journal icon (General Journal). Click the Setup tool to open the General Linked Accounts screen.

Do not click (i.e., click the left mouse button) the journal icons because you want to select the icon without opening the journal. Right-clicking will select the icon.

WARNING!
Sage 50 will not allow you to remove accounts if they are being used as linked accounts. First you must remove the account in the Linked Accounts screen. Then you can remove the account in the General Ledger.

The Retained Earnings account is the capital (equity) account to which expense and revenue accounts are closed at the end of the fiscal period. You must choose a capital (3000-range) account.

Click the **list arrow** beside the field. All postable capital accounts are listed.

Click **3560 S. Arturro, Capital.**

You can also type account numbers directly in the linked account fields. Then press *tab* to complete the entry and advance to the next field. If you type a new account number, you can create the new account.

The Current Earnings account is predefined — the single type X account is always used. This linked setup cannot be changed, although you can modify the account number and account name.

The final option, to **Record Opening Balances In My Retained Earnings Account**, will automatically use the Retained Earnings linked account for amounts that will balance the Trial Balance when you close the ledger. To use this option, you must enter the linked accounts before adding the historical account opening balances. We have already added the opening balances. Instead of showing the select account window from which we selected *Test Balance* (see page 94), choosing this option will display the following message when you have a discrepancy:

NOTES
You can click the ⊟ beside entries for the other modules to reduce the Settings list.

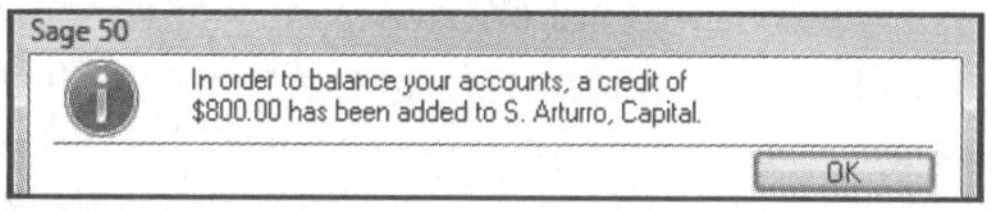

Click OK to confirm and to update the Retained Earnings opening balance.

Payables Default Settings

Click **Payables** in the list on the left to expand the options list:

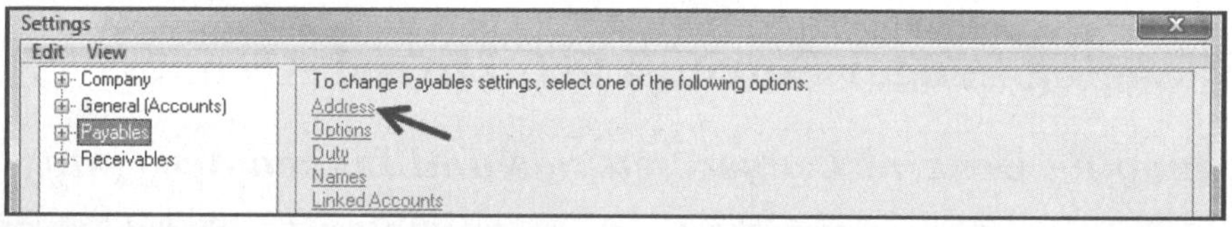

CLASSIC VIEW
In the Home window, you can right-click the Suppliers icon. Click the Setup tool to open the Payables Ledger Settings screen.

The Payables Ledger has Address settings, general Options, settings for imports (Duty), Names for icons and additional ledger fields, and Linked Accounts. Air Care does not import items that have duty applied and does not use the additional fields.

Click **Address** to display the default address fields for the suppliers:

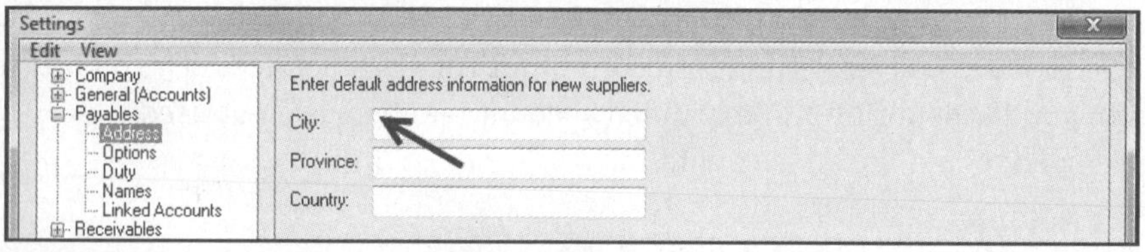

PRO VERSION
The term Vendor will replace Supplier on all Settings screens.

The information you enter here will be used in the ledger records as the defaults when you add suppliers. If most suppliers are in the same location, entering these locations here will save data entry time later. Most of the suppliers for Air Care are located in Regina, Saskatchewan.

NOTES
If all suppliers are in the same province but not in the same city, you can complete the Province field and leave the City field blank.

Click the **City field**.

Type `Regina` **Press** *tab* to advance to the Province field.

Type `Saskatchewan` **Press** *tab* to advance to the Country field.

Type `Canada`

Click **Options** to display the default settings for the Payables Ledger:

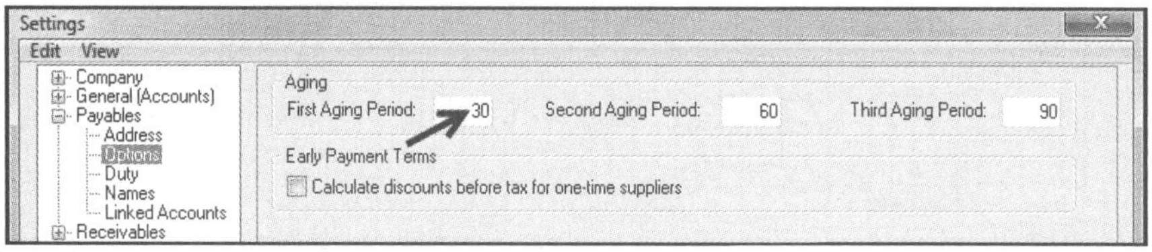

The option for the **aging** of accounts in the Payables Ledger is preset at 30, 60 and 90 days. We will change these options for Air Care to reflect the payment and discount terms most commonly used by Air Care's suppliers.

Double-click **30** in the First Aging Period field.

Type 10 **Press** *tab* to advance to the Second Aging Period field.

Type 30 **Press** *tab* to advance to the Third Aging Period field.

Type 60

NOTES
Usually, clicking a number in a field will select the entire number. Sometimes, however, depending on exactly where you click, only part of the number is selected or an insertion point is added. Double-clicking will always select the entire number in the field so that you can edit it.

The second option determines how discounts are calculated. If the discount is taken only on pretax subtotals, the discount is calculated before taxes. If the discount is applied to the entire invoice amount, including taxes, the discount is not calculated before taxes. Air Care's suppliers calculate discounts before taxes, so you must change the setting.

Click **Calculate Discounts Before Tax For One-Time Suppliers**.

NOTES
We will add discount terms to individual supplier records when we set up the Payables Ledger.

Changing Payables Terminology

Sage 50 has a set of default terms that it uses, based on the type of company you define. These are the terms we saw that changed for different company types in previous chapters. If you want, you can modify the default selections.

PRO VERSION
The Names screen includes only the Additional Information fields. You cannot change the terminology in the Pro version.

Click **Names** under Payables to display the Names and Terminology window:

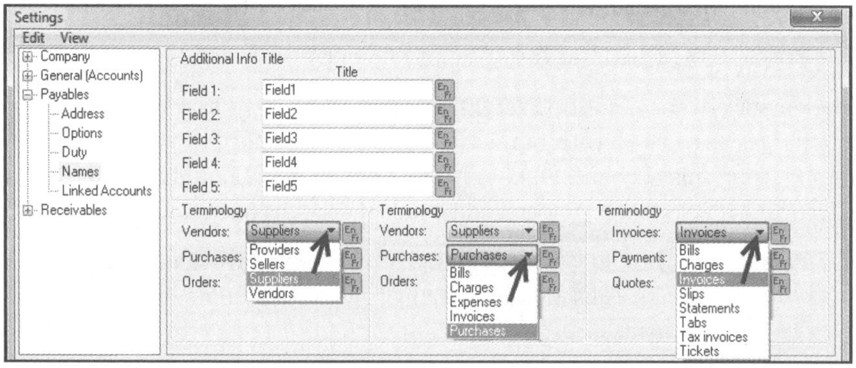

The Names window includes fields for five **Additional Information** names for the Payables Ledger. These will appear on the Additional Information tab screen for ledger records and you have the option to include them in journal windows.

The second part of the screen has the terms used for icons and fields throughout the program. The drop-down lists for the three names you can change — the names for Vendors, Purchases and Invoices — are shown together in the screen above. You cannot modify the Payments label. The names you select will apply to icons, fields and reports.

If you want to use different names, click the field for the name you want and select a different name from the drop-down list.

Defining the Payables Linked Accounts

We will enter the Payables Ledger linked accounts next.

CLASSIC VIEW

In the Home window, you can right-click the Purchases Journal or Payments Journal icon  or .

Click the Setup tool  to open the Payables Linked Accounts screen.

Click **Linked Accounts** under Payables to display the Linked Accounts window:

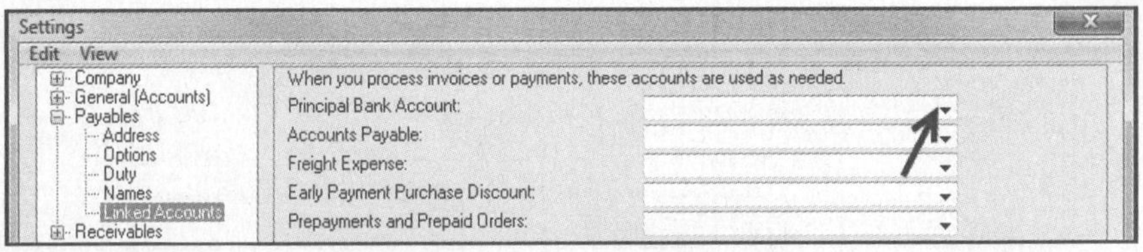

We need to identify the default General Ledger bank account used to make payments to suppliers. This is an essential linked account; it is required before you can finish the history for the company data file. Cash transactions in the Payments Journal will be posted to the bank account you select in the journal window. All Bank and Cash class accounts are available in the journals, and the **principal bank account** defined here will be selected as the default.

You can see the accounts available for linking by clicking the drop-down list arrow for any linked account field. Only Bank class (or Cash) accounts may be used in the bank fields. That is why we needed to define the Bank class accounts first.

When additional currencies are used, fields will be available for linked bank accounts for those currencies as well. Because we have not set up foreign currencies, their linked bank account fields are omitted. The chequing account is Air Care's principal bank account for supplier transactions.

Click the **Principal Bank Account field list arrow**.

Click **1060 Bank: Chequing** and **press** *tab*.

The cursor advances to the **Accounts Payable** field. This control account is also required and is used to record the amounts owing to suppliers whenever a credit (Pay Later) Purchases Journal entry or invoice payment is completed. The balance in this account reflects the total owing to all suppliers, which must match the opening General Ledger balance for *Accounts Payable*. You must use a liability account in this field.

Select **2200 Accounts Payable** from the Account list.

Press *tab* to enter the account number.

The cursor advances to the **Freight Expense** field, used to record the delivery or freight charges associated with purchases. Only freight charged by the supplier should be entered using this account. Since Air Care's suppliers do not charge for delivery, you should leave this field blank. You can add a linked account for freight later if you need it.

Press *tab* to advance to the **Early Payment Purchase Discount** field. This account is used to record any supplier discounts taken for early payments.

Choose **5040 Purchase Discounts** from the drop-down list.

Press *tab* to advance to the **Prepayments And Prepaid Orders** field.

NOTES

The linked account for prepayments is also a required linked account. Because we are not using the feature, we can enter Accounts Payable.

Air Care's suppliers do not request prepayments at this time, but you cannot leave this field blank.

Choose **2200 Accounts Payable** from the drop-down list.

Check the linked accounts carefully. To **delete a linked account**, click it to highlight it and press *del*. You must complete this step of deleting the linked account before you can remove the account in the General Ledger from the Accounts window.

To select a different account, highlight the one that is incorrect and type the correct number, or select an account from the drop-down list.

Receivables Default Settings

Click **Receivables** to display the Receivables Ledger choices:

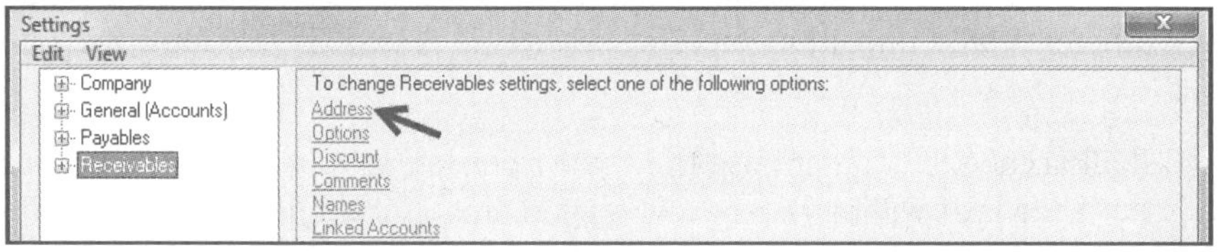

The Receivables Ledger has Address, general Options, Discount and Comments settings, Names for icons and additional ledger fields, and Linked Accounts.

Click **Address** to display the default address fields for the customers:

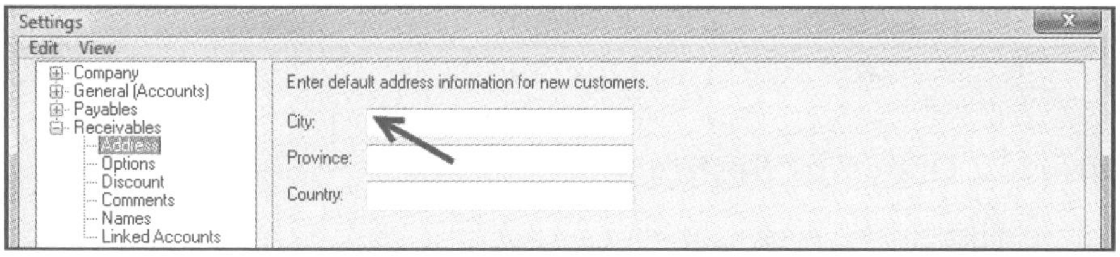

Just as you entered default address information for suppliers, the information you enter here will be used in the ledger records as the defaults when you add customers. Most of Air Care's customers are also located in Regina.

Click the **City field**. **Type** `Regina` **Press** *tab*.

Type `Saskatchewan` **Press** *tab* to advance to the Country field.

Type `Canada`

Click **Options** to display the default settings for the Receivables Ledger:

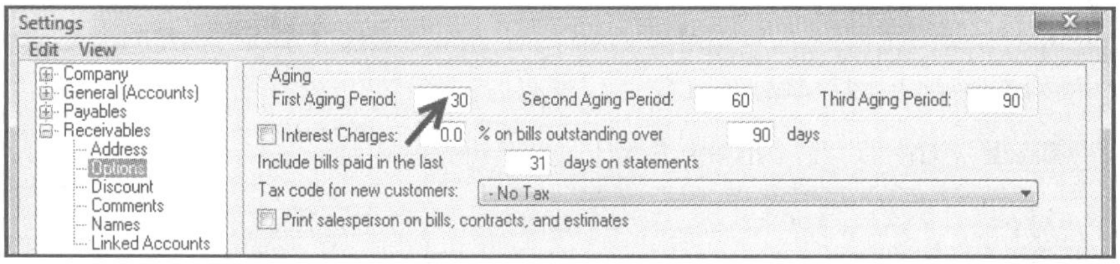

Air Care Services offers a 1 percent discount if customers pay within 10 days and expects full payment within 30 days. After 30 days, customers are charged 1.5 percent interest per month on the overdue accounts. Therefore, the **aging periods** 10, 30 and 60 days will be used, and we must change the default settings.

Press *tab*, or **double-click** **30** in the First Aging Period field.

Type `10` **Press** *tab* to advance to the Second Aging Period field.

Type `30` **Press** *tab* to advance to the Third Aging Period field.

Type `60`

Click **Interest Charges** to add a ✓ and select this feature.

When interest charges are applied on overdue invoices, Sage 50 calculates interest charges and prints them on the customer statements and management reports. However, the program does not create an invoice for the interest. You must create a Sales Journal entry for the amount of interest charged.

Press *tab* to advance to and select the contents of the Interest Rate field.

Type `1.5` **Press** *tab* to advance to and select the Days field for editing.

Type `30`

NOTES
You can click the ⊟ beside Payables to reduce the Settings list.

CLASSIC VIEW
In the Home window, you can right-click the Customers icon. Click (the Setup tool) to open the Receivables Ledger Settings screen.

NOTES
You can use customer statements to find the interest amount that you will enter on the invoice.

The next option relates to printing historical information on invoices. The maximum setting is 999 days. For Air Care Services, customer statements are sent every month, so the period should be 31 days. Any invoices paid in the past 31 days will be included in the statements, and unpaid invoices are always included. The default setting is correct.

If all or most customers use the same sales tax code, you can choose a **default tax code** that will be entered when you create new customers or when you choose One-Time Customer or Quick Add in a sales invoice.

Click the **Tax Code For New Customers list arrow**.

Click **GP - GST @ 5%; PST @ 5%** as the default tax code.

When salespersons are set up, you can **print** the name of the **salesperson** on invoices, orders and quotes. Air Care does not have sales staff.

Entering Discount Settings

Next we must enter the payment terms for account customers.

Click **Discount** in the list under Receivables on the left:

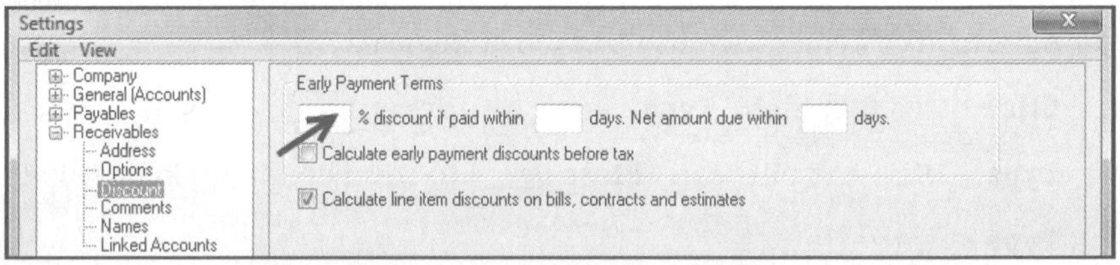

PRO VERSION
Line discounts are not available in the Pro version.

For all account customers, the payment terms are 1 percent discount if the account is paid in the first 10 days and net payment is due in 30 days. All customer discounts are calculated on after-tax amounts, so the **Calculate Early Payment Discounts Before Tax** selection is correctly turned off.

Click the **% field** in the first Early Payment Terms field to advance the cursor.

Type 1.0 **Press** *tab* to advance to the Days field.

Type 10 **Press** *tab* to advance to the Net Days field.

Type 30

Sage 50 adds the payment terms you just entered as a default for all customers. Individual customer records or invoices can still be modified if needed.

Air Care does not use the remaining discount option — to apply discounts to individual lines on an invoice. A % Discount column will be added to the invoice form when you use this feature.

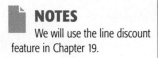

NOTES
We will use the line discount feature in Chapter 19.

Click **Calculate Line Item Discounts On Bills, Contracts And Estimates** to remove the ✓. You will see a warning:

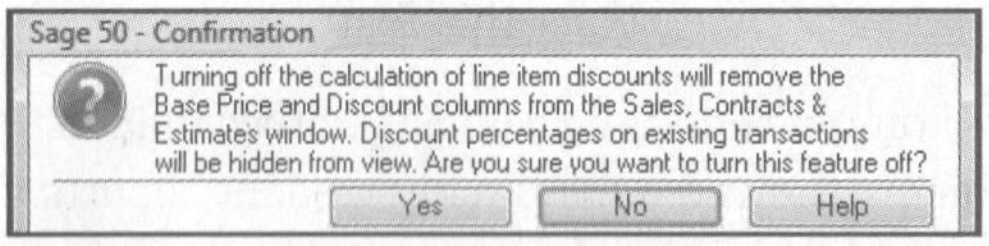

Click **Yes** to confirm the removal of line discounts.

If you later change the default customer payment terms, you will see a message asking whether you want to update all customer terms to match the new terms.

Entering Default Comments

Sage 50 allows you to add a default comment to the Message field on all customer forms. You can change the default message any time you want, and you can edit it for a particular form when you are completing the invoice, quote or order confirmation.

Click **Comments** under Receivables to open the screen for default comments:

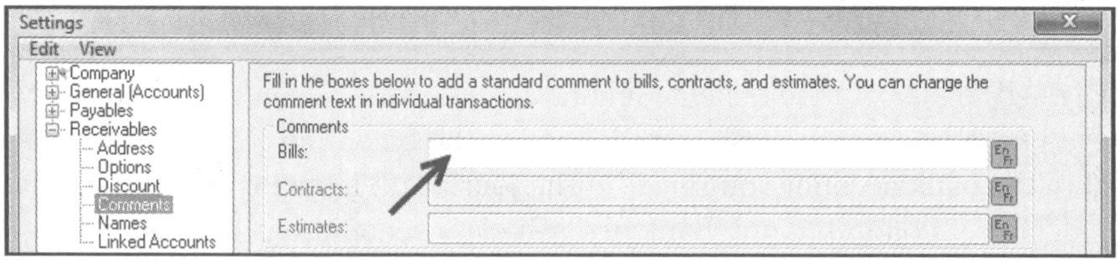

We want to add a comment that will appear on every customer invoice. The comment may include payment terms, company motto, notice of an upcoming sale or a warning about interest charges.

Click the **Bills (Invoices) field** to move the cursor.

Type `Interest @ 1.5% per month charged on accounts over 30 days.`

You can enter the same comment for all sales forms (invoices, orders and quotes), or you can add a unique comment for each. The comment fields for quotes and orders are dimmed because Air Care does not use these features.

Changing Receivables Terminology

The terms for the Receivables Ledger can also be customized.

Click **Names** under Receivables to display the Names and Terminology window:

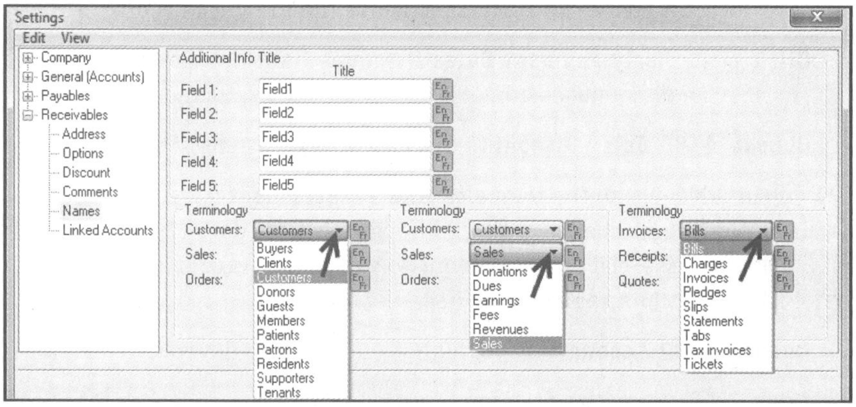

For Receivables, you can also name five additional fields to appear in ledger records and, if you choose, in journal windows.

The second part of the screen shows the industry-specific terms used. The drop-down lists for the names you can change — Customers, Sales and Bills — are shown together in the screen above. You cannot modify the Receipts label. The names you select will apply to icons, fields and reports.

If you want to use different names, click the field for the name you want and select a different name from the drop-down list.

Defining the Receivables Linked Accounts

The Receivables Ledger linked accounts parallel those for the Payables Ledger.

PRO VERSION
The field label Sales Invoices replaces Bills in the Pro version. Orders and Quotes will replace Contracts and Estimates.

NOTES
Contracts and Estimates are the terms used for Orders and Quotes for a contractor business.

PRO VERSION
The Names screen includes only the Additional Information fields. You cannot change the terminology in the Pro version.

CLASSIC VIEW
In the Home window, you can right-click Sales Journal or Receipts Journal icon,

or

.

Click the Setup tool  to open the Receivables Linked Accounts screen.

Click **Linked Accounts** under Receivables:

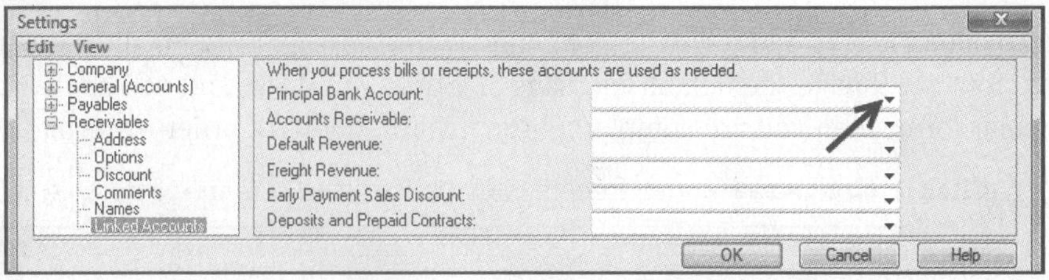

NOTES
The linked accounts for Principal Bank, Accounts Receivable and Deposits are all essential linked accounts.

NOTES
When additional currencies are used, fields will be available for linked bank accounts for them as well. You can choose a separate linked account for each currency, or you can use the Canadian dollar account for more than one currency. Because we have not set up foreign currencies, their linked bank account fields are omitted.

We need to identify the default General Ledger bank account used to receive payments from customers. Cash transactions in the Sales and Receipts journals will be posted to the bank account you select in the journals. The **principal bank account** will be the default account, but any Bank or Cash class account can be selected.

Air Care uses *Bank: Chequing* as the principal bank account for customer transactions. Although most linked accounts may be used only once, one bank account can be linked to the Payables, Receivables and Payroll ledgers.

Click the **Principal Bank Account field list arrow**.

Click **1060 Bank: Chequing** and **press** tab.

The cursor advances to the **Accounts Receivable** field. This control account records the amounts owed to Air Care by customers whenever a credit (Pay Later) Sales Journal invoice or receipt is entered. The General Ledger balance for *Accounts Receivable* reflects and must match the total owed by all customers. You must use an asset account in this field.

WARNING!
You may prefer to leave the Default Revenue Account field blank. If you enter 4100 Installation Revenue as the default revenue account, you must remember to change the account for journal entries that require a different revenue account.

Select **1200 Accounts Receivable** from the drop-down list. **Press** tab.

Click the **Default Revenue list arrow** and **choose 4100 Installation Revenue**.

Air Care does not charge for deliveries. Leave the Freight Revenue field blank.

Click the **Early Payment Sales Discount field list arrow**. This field records the discounts customers receive for early settlement of their accounts.

Choose **4180 Sales Discounts** from the drop-down list. **Press** tab.

The cursor advances to the **Deposits And Prepaid Contracts** (Orders) field. This account is linked to customer deposits. Although Air Care does not request customer deposits, this is an essential linked account so we cannot leave this field blank. Because we do not use it, we can use *Accounts Receivable*.

Choose **1200 Accounts Receivable** from the drop-down list.

Click **OK** to see the program's message about class changes for account 3560:

NOTES
You must choose Yes to confirm the account class changes and to continue. If you choose No, you will return to the Linked Accounts screen.

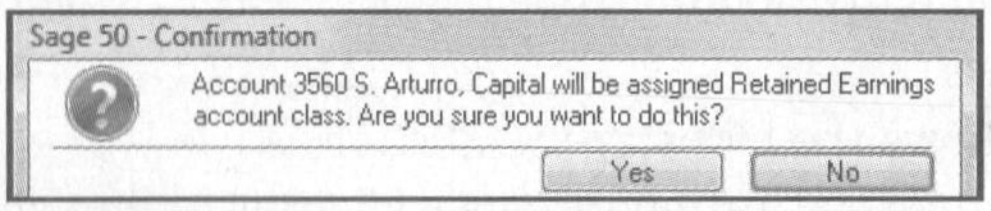

Many linked accounts must have a specific account class to be used as linked accounts. Normally, you can allow the program to assign and change the account class definitions. The exceptions are the credit card and Bank class accounts, which you must define before you can use them as linked bank accounts.

Click **Yes** to accept the change and save the linked account setting. You will see a second confirmation message for account 2200:

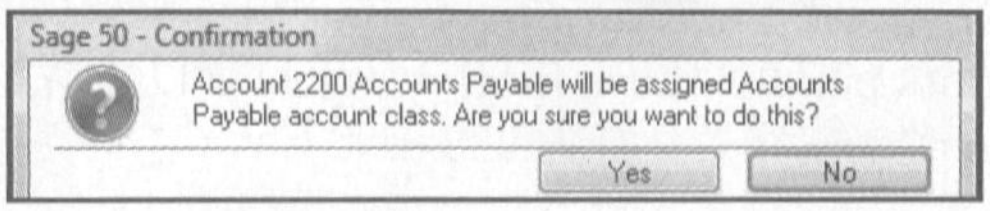

Click **Yes** to accept the class change and save the linked accounts. You will see the final message about the account class change for account 1200:

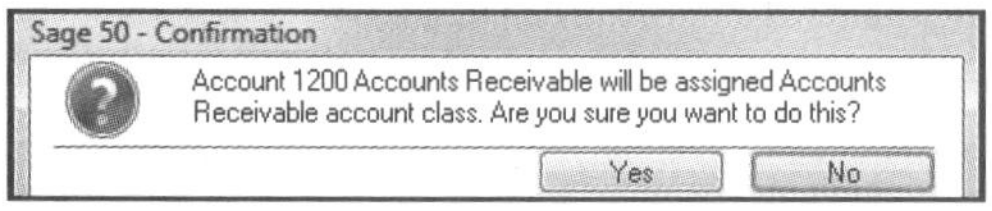

Click **Yes** to accept the change and return to the Home window.

This may be a good time to take a break.

Entering Suppliers in the Payables Ledger

Use the Supplier Information for Air Care Services on page 205 to enter supplier details and historical invoices. The following keystrokes will enter the information for Beausejour Electrical Products, the first supplier on Air Care Services' list.

You can open the ledger screen from the Payables module window Suppliers icon or from its shortcuts list. First we must open the Payables module window.

Click **Payables** in the Modules pane to open the window we need.

Click the **Suppliers shortcuts list arrow** as shown and **choose View Suppliers**:

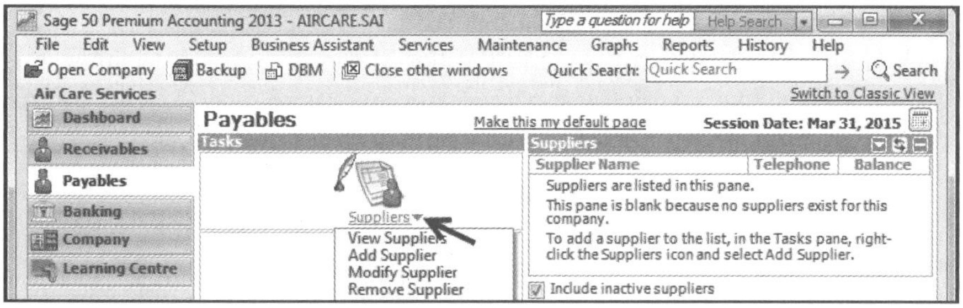

Or **click** the **Suppliers icon**  in the window:

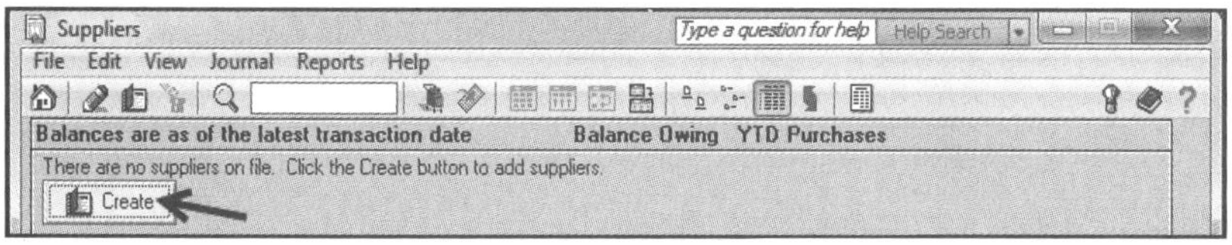

The Suppliers window is empty because no suppliers are on file. Once we add the supplier accounts, this window will contain a listing for each supplier that you can use to access the supplier's ledger record. The suppliers may be displayed in icon form or by name with balances and year-to-date amounts. The default is the listing by name.

Click the **Create button**  or the **Create tool**  in the Suppliers window, or **choose** the **File menu** and **click Create**:

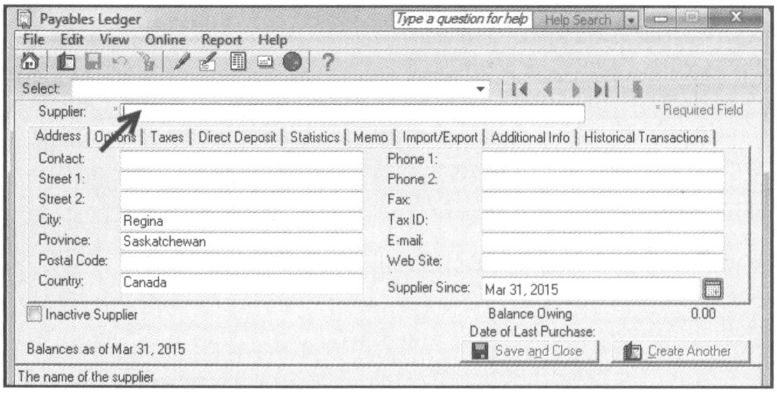

NOTES

If you click Add Supplier on the shortcuts list, you will open the New Supplier ledger window immediately.

PRO VERSION

pro Click the Vendors icon to open the Vendors window.

NOTES

If you prefer to list the suppliers by icon in the Suppliers window, choose the View menu and click Icon or click the Display By Icon tool. New suppliers will be added at the end of the display, but you can drag icons to any position you want so that frequently used icons appear together at the top of the window.

If you display the suppliers by icon, you can restore the alphabetic order for the icons by choosing the View menu and clicking Re-sort Icons.

NOTES

Pressing *ctrl* + N in the Suppliers window or in a ledger record window will also open a new supplier ledger record form.

NOTES

If you choose to skip the Suppliers icon window from the Home window Setup menu (User Preferences, View), you will see this Payables Ledger (supplier) Address tab window immediately when you click the Suppliers icon.

> **NOTES**
> You may skip any of the address tab fields, except the name, if the information is missing for the supplier. Just click the next field for which you have information to move the cursor. To edit any field, drag to highlight the contents and type the correct information.

> **NOTES**
> Remember that the postal code sequence for Canada is letter, number, letter, number, letter and number.

The supplier Address tab screen opens. Most of the supplier input screens should be familiar from entering records for new suppliers in previous chapters. The cursor is in the Supplier name field, the only required field for the record.

Type Beausejour Electrical Products **Press** *tab*.

The cursor advances to the Contact field. Here you should enter the name of the person (or department) at Beausejour Electrical Products with whom Air Care Services will be dealing. This information enables a company to make professional and effective inquiries. For a small business, the owner's name may appear in this field.

Type Janine Beausejour **Press** *tab* to advance to the Street 1 field.

Type 50 Shockley Rd. **Press** *tab* to move to the Street 2 field.

Type Unit 18

The program uses the Payables Address Settings as the defaults for City, Province and Country fields. In this case, they are correct.

Click the **Postal Code field**.

Type s4f2t2

Click the **Phone 1 field**.

The program corrects the format of the postal code. (Only Canadian postal codes are reformatted — those with the specific letter and number sequence.) You can enter phone and fax numbers with or without the area code.

Type 3064765282 **Press** *tab* to advance to the Phone 2 field.

Type 3064763997 **Press** *tab* to advance to the Fax field.

Type 3064765110 **Press** *tab* to advance to the Tax ID field.

The program corrects the format of the phone numbers. The Tax ID field allows you to enter the supplier's tax ID or business number. The following two fields contain the e-mail and Web site addresses for the supplier. Enter them just as you would type them in your e-mail and Internet programs.

Type 444 276 534 **Press** *tab*.

Type jb@beausejour.com **Press** *tab*.

Type www.beausejour.com **Press** *tab*.

The cursor moves to the Supplier Since field. The program has entered the session date as the default, but we should change it to reflect the company's actual transaction history. All suppliers have been used by Air Care since 2010.

Type Jan 1 2010

Notice that the supplier's account balance appears at the bottom of the ledger. A supplier may be marked as Inactive if there are currently no transactions. You have the option to include or omit inactive suppliers from reports. All Air Care's suppliers are active.

The remaining supplier details are entered from the other tab screens.

Click the **Options tab** to open the next screen:

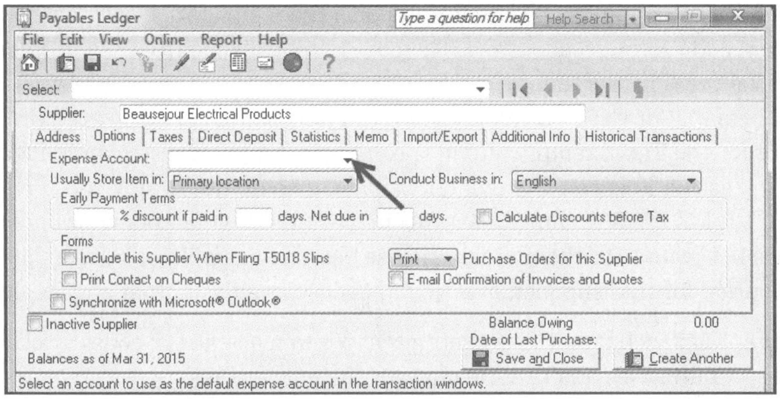

The supplier's name appears on each tab screen for reference. We want to enter the default expense account so that it will automatically appear in journal entries.

Click the **Expense Account list arrow**. All postable accounts are listed.

Click **1320 Electrical Supplies**.

When you use multiple currencies, they can also be linked to suppliers on the Options tab screen. The **Usually Store Item In** field refers to locations. When multiple locations are used for storage, you can link the supplier to the location. Air Care has only one location.

Regardless of the language you use to work in Sage 50, you can choose a language for the supplier so that all Sage 50 forms you send to this supplier will be in the language selected on the Options tab screen.

If the supplier offers a discount for early payment or has a term for the net amount, enter these details in this screen. The terms with Beausejour are 1/10, net 30.

Click the **% Discount field** (the first Early Payment Terms field).

Type 1 **Press** *tab* to advance to the If Paid In Days field.

Type 10 **Press** *tab* to advance to the Net Due In Days field.

Type 30

Click the **Calculate Discounts Before Tax check box** to select this option.

Do not turn on the option to **Print Contact On Cheques** because the Contact field does not contain address information.

If you e-mail purchase orders to a supplier, choose this option from the drop-down list to replace the default option to print purchase orders. Click **E-mail Confirmation** if you e-mail purchase orders to be certain that the order is sent. Even if you choose Print as the default, you can still e-mail the order from the Purchases Journal.

Click the **Taxes tab** to access the next input screen:

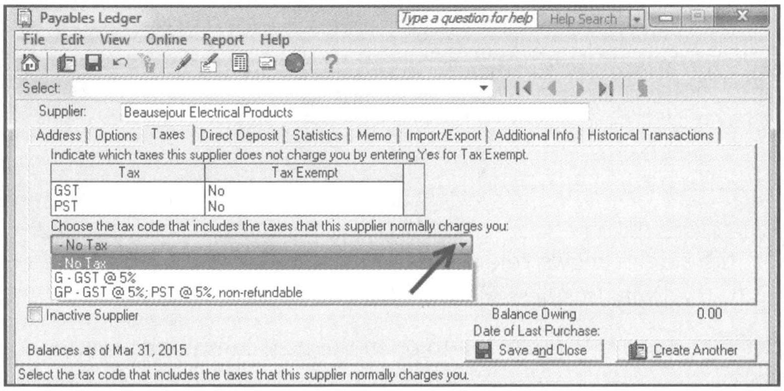

NOTES

If you have not yet created the account you want to use as the default account, type the new account number in the Expense Account field and press *tab* to start the Add An Account wizard. Choose Add when asked if you want to create the account.

PRO VERSION

You will not see the Usually Store Item In Location field or the option to Synchronize With Microsoft Outlook.

NOTES

T5018 slips are submitted to the CRA by construction companies when they make payments to subcontractors.

Multiple inventory locations are used in Chapter 18.

NOTES

Remember that all supplier discounts are calculated on before-tax amounts.

NOTES

For suppliers who request payment on receipt, enter 1 in the Net Days field. When you enter zero in the Net Days field, the Terms fields remain blank and invoices will not show as overdue. Payment terms may be changed in the journal for individual invoices.

NOTES

When PST applies, businesses that sell inventory or other products do not pay PST on the products they purchase for sale or use to make the products they sell. Thus they are exempt from paying PST. If, however, the supplier charges for shipping – and shipping charges are subject to PST charges – you must choose No in the Exempt column for PST so that taxes can be calculated correctly for the shipping charges.

This screen allows you to indicate which taxes the supplier normally charges and the default tax code for journal entries. The codes are available from the drop-down list as shown in the previous screen.

All suppliers for Air Care Services, except the Receiver General, charge GST, so the correct entry for the Tax Exempt column is No. Some suppliers also charge PST. Suppliers such as the Receiver General for Canada, who do not supply goods or services eligible for input tax credits, should have Yes in the Tax Exempt column to indicate that Air Care does not pay tax to them. If you choose Yes, the tax will not be calculated in the Purchases Journal for that supplier, even if you choose a tax code that applies the tax.

Leave all **Tax Exempt** entry settings at **No** to make all tax codes available for purchases. Clicking No changes the entry to Yes.

Click the **list arrow beside No Tax** to choose a default tax code.

Click **G - GST @ 5%** to select the code.

Click the **Direct Deposit tab** to open the next information screen:

NOTES

Direct Deposit is covered in Chapter 13.

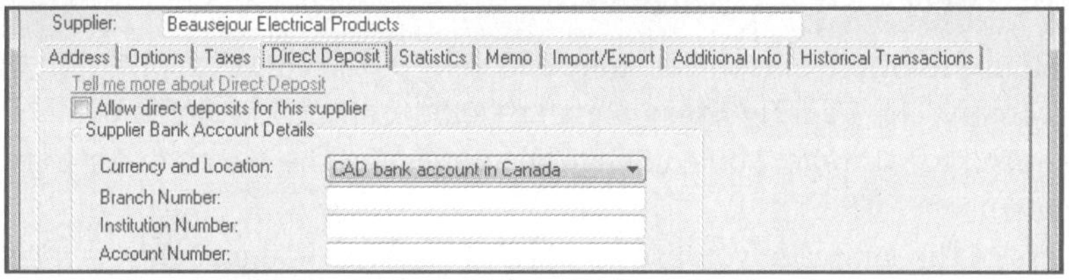

The Direct Deposit fields record your bank account details for automatic withdrawals you allow this supplier to make.

Click the **Statistics tab** to open the next information screen:

NOTES

When the supplier uses a foreign currency, the statistics summary information is presented for both currencies.

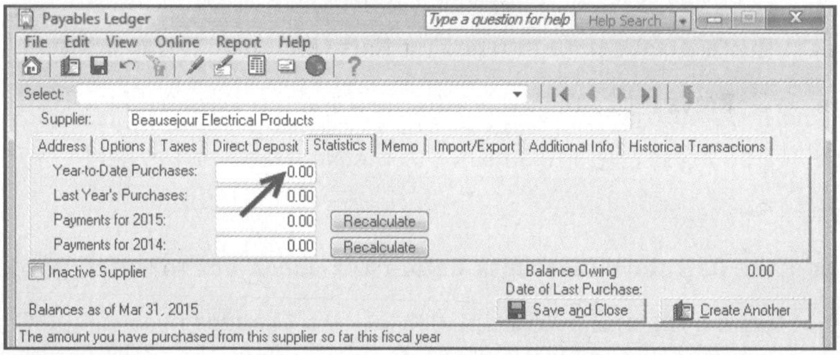

The Statistics fields record the historical purchase and payment totals for two years and are updated automatically from journal entries.

Click the **Year-To-Date Purchases field**.

Type 2100

Click the **Payments For 2015 field**.

Type 2100

Click the **Memo tab** to advance to the next screen:

NOTES

The message in the memo may be up to 255 characters in length.

The Daily Business Manager is used in Chapter 11.

The Import/Export feature is described in Appendix J on the Student DVD.

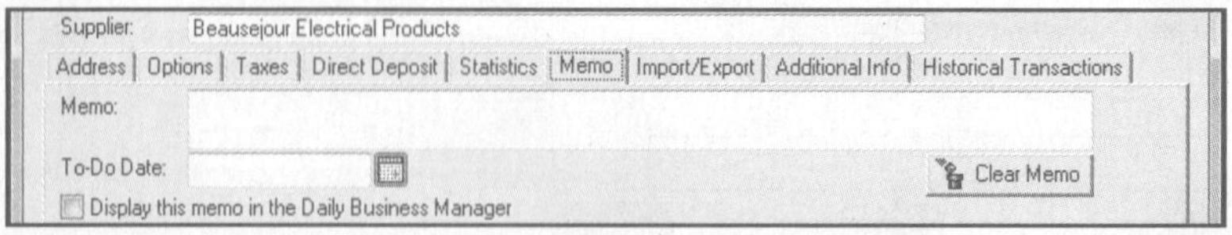

The Memo tab screen allows you to enter a message related to the supplier that may be added to the Daily Business Manager lists, the automatic reminder system.

Click the **Import/Export tab** to open the next information screen:

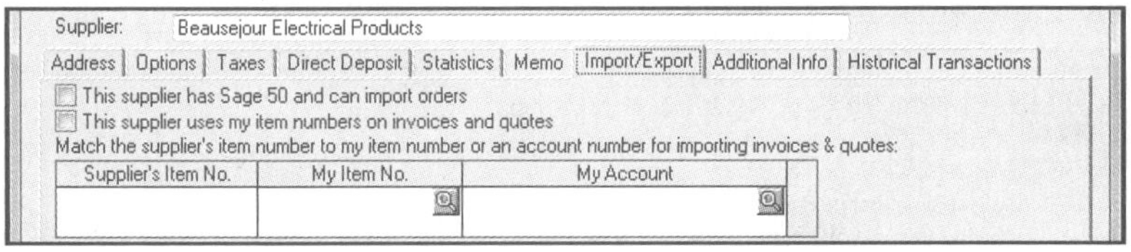

The Import/Export screen refers to inventory items. If the supplier also uses Sage 50, you can match the supplier's inventory item codes to your own for electronic transfers of information.

Click the **Additional Info tab**:

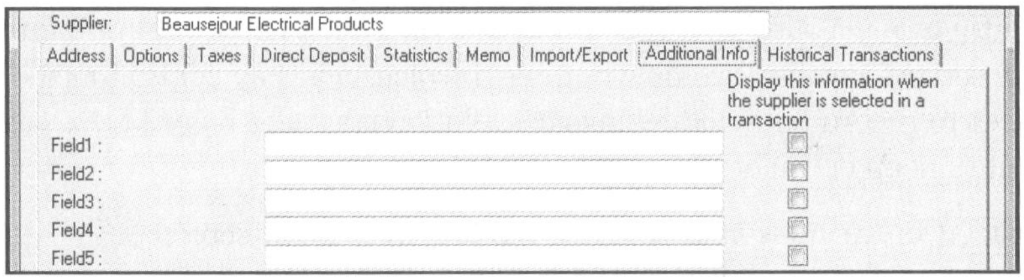

You can customize the records for any ledger by adding up to five fields. The customized names you added from the Names Settings option for the ledger will appear on this Additional Info screen. This additional information can be included in journal transaction windows and in Supplier List reports. Air Care Services does not use any additional fields, so we are ready to enter the supplier's historical transactions.

NOTES
The field names on this tab screen are taken from the Names settings for the ledger (see page 229).
We will customize Payroll Ledger records by adding fields in Chapter 9.

Correct any **errors** by returning to the field with the mistake. **Highlight** the **errors**, **enter** the **correct information** and then save the record.

WARNING!
Remember to click Calculate Discounts Before Tax for all suppliers who offer discounts.

If there are **no historical invoices**, proceed to the final step of saving the supplier record. Click Create Another  and then click the Address tab to prepare for entering the next supplier.

For all suppliers, the date for **Supplier Since** is **January 1, 2010**.

Entering Historical Supplier Information

You can enter all the historical invoices and payments for the fiscal year to date, but you must enter all outstanding invoices and partial payments toward them. Beausejour Electrical Products has outstanding invoices, so we must enter historical transaction details. The following keystrokes will enter the historical information from page 205 for Beausejour Electrical Products.

You can also enter and save other ledger details for all suppliers and then open the ledger to add historical information by clicking the Historical Transactions tab. Open the ledger for any supplier by double-clicking the supplier's name in the Suppliers window.

Click the **Historical Transactions tab**:

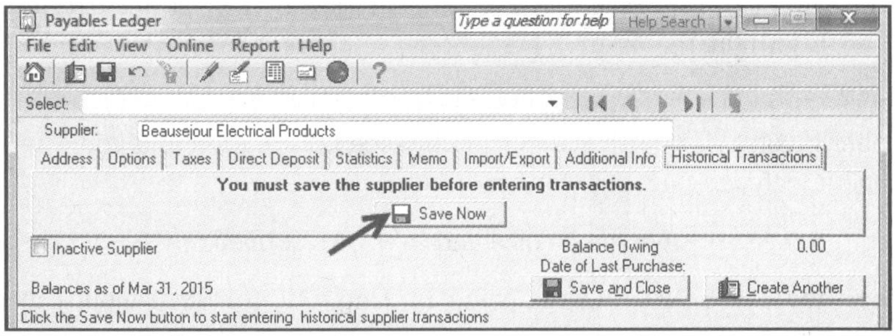

You must save or create the supplier record before adding historical invoices.

NOTES
If you have already created and saved the record, you will not see the Save Now option on the Historical Transactions tab screen. Instead, you will see the next screen asking you to choose Invoices or Payments.

Click the **Save Now button** to modify the ledger screen:

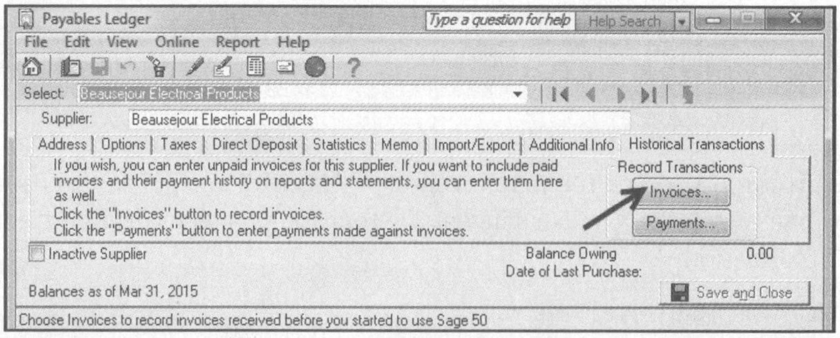

WARNING! Enter invoice details carefully. To correct a historical invoice amount, you must pay the invoice and clear the paid transactions (Maintenance menu). Then reset the historical payments for the year to zero (Payables Ledger, Statistics tab screen) and re-enter the outstanding invoices. Refer to page 250.

The Create Another button has been removed and the Save And Close button is dimmed. The screen now has two new buttons: Invoices and Payments. You should select **Invoices** to record outstanding invoices and **Payments** to record prior payments that you want to keep on record after entering invoices.

Click the **Invoices button** to see the following input screen:

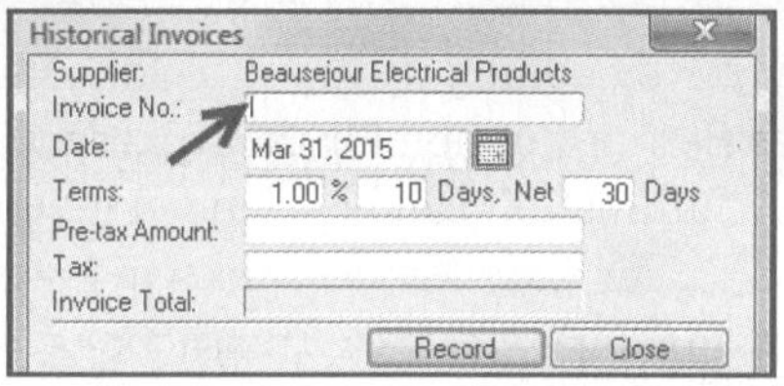

The cursor is in the Invoice No. field so you can enter the first invoice number.

Type `B-894` **Press** *tab* to advance to the Date field.

Enter the invoice date to replace the default earliest transaction date. The invoice date must not be later than the earliest transaction date — the date of the first journal transaction after the historical data in the setup.

Type `03-26-15`

The Terms are entered from the Supplier record and are correct, although they can be edited if necessary. You should enter the amount for the first invoice. The amount is divided into pretax and tax amounts so that Sage 50 can correctly calculate the discount on the before-tax amount. When the option to calculate discounts before tax is not selected, a single amount field appears on the invoice for the full amount of the invoice with taxes included — as on page 246 for customers.

Click the **Pre-tax Amount field** to advance the cursor.

Type `10000` **Press** *tab* to advance to the Tax amount field.

Type `500` **Press** *tab* to update the Invoice Total.

The totals of all outstanding invoice and payment amounts must match the opening balance in the *Accounts Payable* control account in the General Ledger.

Correct any **errors**. **Press** *tab* to return to the field with the error and **highlight** the **error**. Then **enter** the **correct information**.

Be sure that all the information is entered correctly before you save your supplier invoice. If you save incorrect invoice information and you want to change it, refer to page 250 for assistance.

WARNING! You must choose Record to save each invoice and payment and then Close the invoice form. If you close the input screen before selecting Record, the information is not saved.

Click **Record** to save the invoice and to display a blank invoice for the supplier.

Enter **invoice B-921** (not the payment, Chq #94) for Beausejour Electrical Products by repeating the steps above. **Click Record**.

When you have recorded all outstanding invoices for a supplier,

Click **Close** to return to the ledger.

The two invoices have been added to the Balance Owing field at the bottom of the ledger screen. Now you can enter historical payment information for this supplier.

Click the **Payments button** to display the payments form:

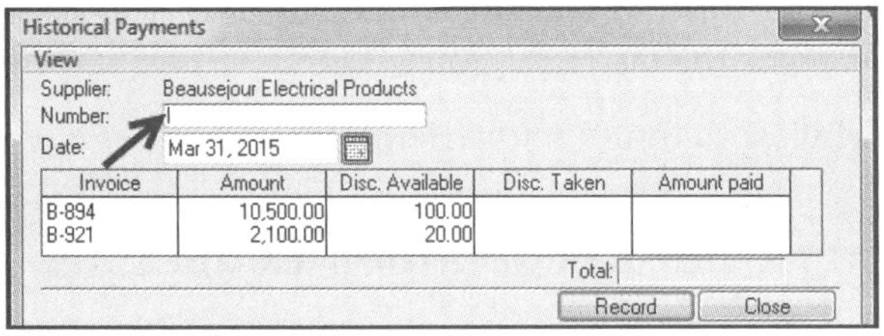

All outstanding invoices that you entered are displayed. Notice that the discount amounts are 2 percent of the pretax amounts. Entering historical payments is very much like entering current payments in the Payments Journal. You should make separate payment entries for each cheque.

Click the Number field if necessary to move the cursor to the cheque number field.

Type 94 **Press** tab to advance to the Date field.

Enter the cheque date for the first payment toward invoice #B-894 to replace the default earliest transaction date.

Type 3-26

Click the **Amount Paid column** on the line for Invoice #B-894.

Because the full amount is not being paid, the discount does not apply. The full amount of the discount will remain available until the 10 days have passed. If the balance is paid within that time, the full discount will be taken.

The full invoice amount, displayed as the default, is highlighted so you can edit it.

Type 4500 **Press** tab. **Press** del to delete the Disc. Taken amount.

Check the **information** carefully and **make corrections** before you proceed.

Click **Record** to save the information and display another payment form for this supplier in case there are additional payments to record.

The amount owing for invoice #B-894 has been updated to include the payment you entered, but the full discount amount remains available.

Repeat these procedures to enter any other payments to this supplier.

When you have recorded all outstanding payments to a supplier,

Click **Close** to return to the supplier information form.

When you click the Statistics tab, you will see that the invoices and payment you entered have been included to increase the totals for 2015.

Click the **Create tool** or **press** ctrl + **N** to enter the next supplier.

Click the **Address tab** to prepare for entering the next supplier record.

When you return to the Suppliers window, you will see that Sage 50 has created a Supplier icon and listing for Beausejour Electrical Products. The default view for suppliers is to list them alphabetically by name with the balance owing and year-to-date purchases. The Create button has been removed. The Create tool is still available.

NOTES
The View menu has the option to refresh the invoices from information added by other users. It applies only to the multi-user mode and is not available in the Pro version.

NOTES
The discount amounts based on pretax amounts are $100 (1 percent of $10 000) and $20 (1 percent of $2 000).

NOTES
Clicking the Amount Paid field directly ensures the discount amount is not entered.

WARNING!
When an amount appears in the Disc. Taken field, you must delete it before recording the payment. Otherwise, the balance owing to the supplier will be incorrect. The total owing to vendors will not match the Accounts Payable General Ledger balance and you will be unable to finish the history.

NOTES
If you display suppliers by icon, you can restore the alphabetic order for icons by choosing the View menu and then Re-sort Icons.

NOTES
Even though the historical invoices and payments were entered correctly, you will notice that there is an outstanding historical difference. This is addressed on page 250.

Enter the **remaining suppliers** and historical transactions on page 205.

Click **Save And Close** [Save and Close] to close the Supplier Ledger after entering the last supplier record that has no historical transactions.

Display or **print** your **Supplier List** to check the address details from the Reports menu in the Suppliers window.

Display or **print** a **Supplier Aged Detail Report**. Include terms and historical differences to check the historical transactions.

Close the **Suppliers window** to return to the Home window.

Entering Customers in the Receivables Ledger

Use the Customer Information chart for Air Care Services on page 206 to complete this step. The following keystrokes will enter the information for Grande Pointe Towers, the first customer on the list for Air Care Services. You should open the Receivables window.

Click **Receivables** in the Modules pane list to open the window we need.

Click the **Customers icon** [Customers] to display the Customers window. The Customers window is empty because there are no customers on file yet.

Click the **Create button** [Create] or **tool** in the Customers window, or **choose** the **File menu** and **click Create**.

You will open the Receivables Ledger new customer Address tab screen:

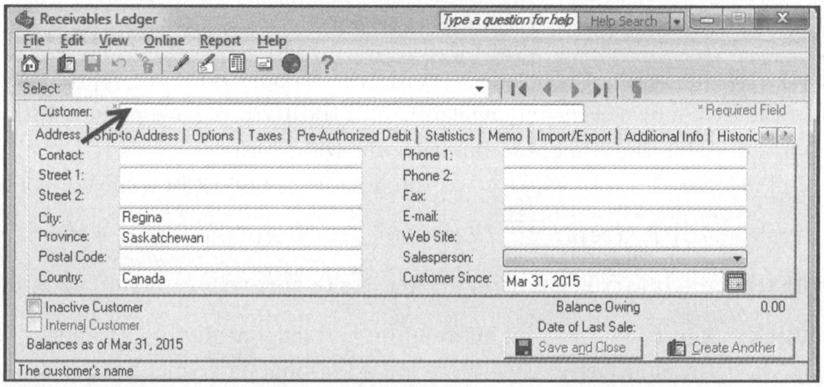

NOTES
If you choose not to view the Customers icon window from the Home window Setup menu (User Preferences, View), you will see this Receivables Ledger window immediately when you click the Customers icon.

PRO VERSION
The option to define Internal Customers does not appear in the Pro version.

The customer information screen opens at the Address tab screen. The cursor is in the Customer field, the only required field. The default Province and Country entered from the module's Address settings are correct, but we need to change the city name.

You may skip any of the address tab fields if information is missing. Just click the next field for which you have information to move the cursor.

Type `Grande Pointe Towers` **Press** *tab*.

Air Care's primary contact about a sale should be entered in the Contact field.

Type `Sophie Grande` **Press** *tab* to advance to the Street 1 field.

Type `77 LaPointe Cr.` **Press** *tab* to move to the Street 2 field.

Press *tab* to advance to the City field. We need to replace the default entry.

Type `White City`

Click the **Postal Code field**.

NOTES
The Internal Customers option works with the Time & Billing feature and is used to identify other departments within the company that use your services. The time and cost for these internal services can be tracked. Time and billing is covered in Chapter 18.

Type s0g5b0

Click the **Phone 1 field**. The postal code format is corrected.

Type 3067227500 **Press** tab. The format is corrected automatically.

Click the **Fax field**.

Type 3063227436 **Press** tab to advance to the E-mail field.

Type sgrande@GPTowers.com **Press** tab.

Type www.GPTowers.com to enter the Web site.

Press tab **twice** to move to the Customer Since date field.

Type Jan 1 15

The current balance is noted at the bottom of the Ledger window. Like suppliers and accounts, customers may be marked as inactive and omitted from reports if they have not bought merchandise or services for some time.

Click the **Ship-To Address tab**:

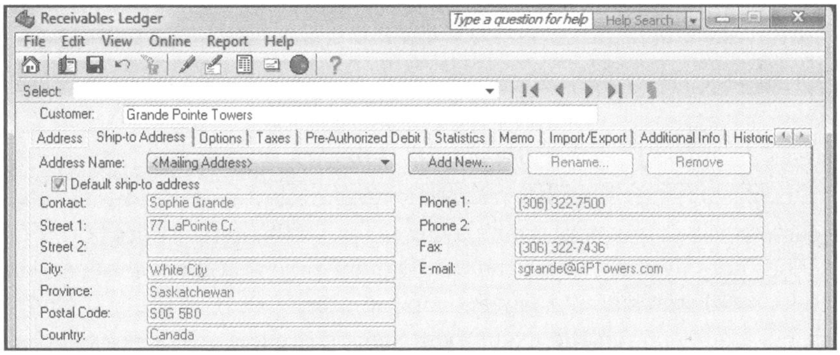

The Ship-To Address screen allows you to enter multiple addresses for customers who want merchandise to be shipped to different addresses. You can apply labels to each address. The default setting is to use the mailing address as the shipping address.

Click the **Options tab** to see the customer's payment and invoice options:

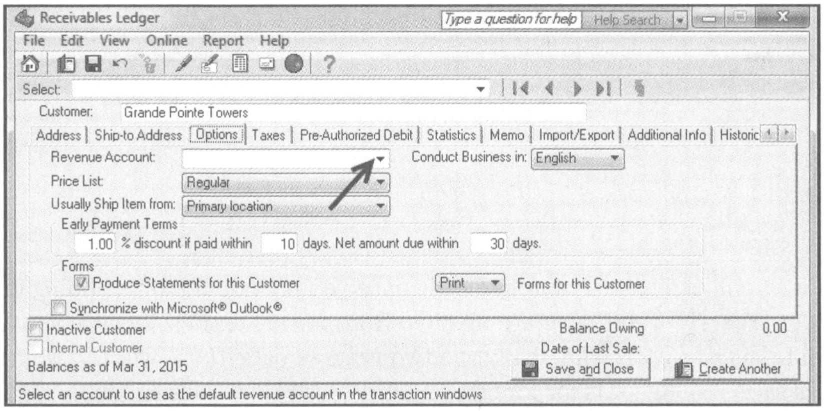

All the default settings are correct. You can select English or French as the customer's language — all forms you send to the customer will be prepared in the selected language. The **Price List** field applies to inventory and services prices that can be set at different rates for different customers. Air Care supplies customized services and does not use the Inventory module. The payment terms are entered automatically from the Receivables Settings. Terms can be edited if necessary for individual customers and invoices in the Sales Journal. Air Care charges interest on overdue accounts, so we need to be able to **produce statements**.

NOTES

Remember that the postal code sequence for Canada is letter, number, letter, number, letter and number.

PRO VERSION

The Pro version does not allow multiple addresses. Only one mailing and one shipping address can be entered. Click Same As Mailing Address to remove the ✓ if you need to change the mailing address.

NOTES

As soon as you choose another address in the Address Name field, the address fields will open. Refer to Chapter 6 for more information on shipping addresses.

NOTES

The option to calculate discounts before or after tax is selected for the Receivables Ledger as a whole (see page 232). You cannot change the setting for individual customers.

PRO VERSION

You will not see the options for inventory location (Usually Ship Item From) or Synchronize With Microsoft Outlook.

When a business sells inventory from more than one location, you can link a customer to one of these locations with the entry in the **Usually Ship Item From** location field. Air Care has only one location. The customer's currency is also defined on the Options tab screen when a business uses more than one currency.

You need to add only a default revenue account for the customer. Although there are three revenue accounts that apply to customers, most customers use Air Care's installation services, so we can choose this as the default. Remember that you can choose a different account in the Sales Journal for any invoice. You may prefer to omit the default Revenue Account to avoid using an incorrect revenue account for sales.

NOTES
If you do not add a default revenue account for a customer, the default linked revenue account for the ledger will be entered in the journal.

Click the **Revenue Account field list arrow**.

Click **4100 Installation Revenue**.

Click the **Taxes tab**:

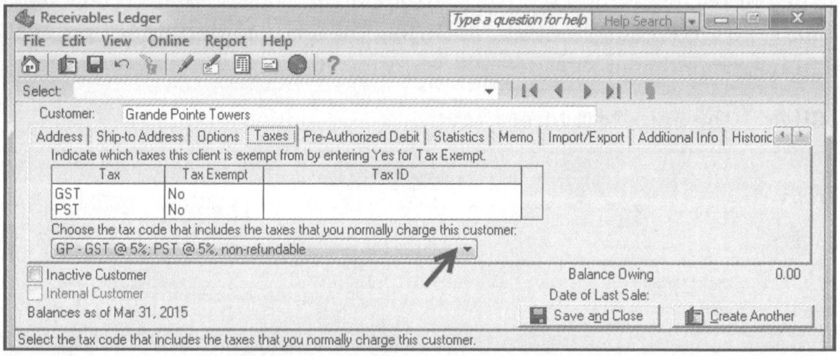

NOTES
The PST Tax ID number for retailers identifies that they can collect PST from their customers and be exempted from paying the tax on purchases of the items they sell.

NOTES
You can change the default tax code for individual customers if necessary by choosing a different code from the Tax Code list. You can also change the code for individual invoices or amounts on the invoice.

The customer is not exempt from paying taxes, so the defaults are correct. If the customer does not pay a tax, enter the tax ID number so that it appears on invoices. For example, retail stores do not pay PST on inventory that they will sell. They must have a tax number to permit the exemption. Some customers are also exempt from GST payments. Taxes will be calculated only if the customer is marked as not tax exempt. The default tax code, GP - GST @ 5%, PST @ 5%, non-refundable, should be entered.

Click the **Statistics tab** to view the next set of customer details:

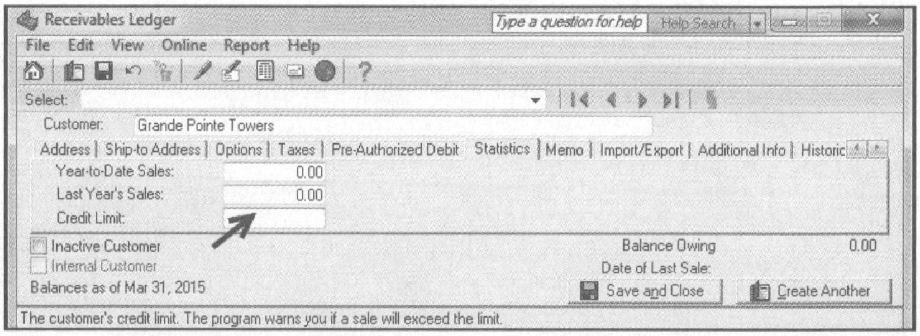

Balances will be included automatically once you provide the outstanding invoice information. **Year-To-Date Sales** are updated from journal entries, but you can add a historical balance as well. When you have two years of data, there will be an amount for last year's sales too. Records for foreign customers will have sales summary amounts and balances in both currencies.

The **Credit Limit** is the amount that the customer can purchase on account before payments are required. If the customer goes beyond this credit limit, the program will issue a warning when you attempt to post the invoice.

Click the **Year-To-Date Sales field**.

Type 11000 **Press** tab **twice** to advance to the Credit Limit field.

Type 20000

The **Memo tab** screen for customers is just like the Memo tab screen for suppliers. It allows you to enter messages related to the customer. If you enter a reminder date, the program can display the message in the Daily Business Manager on the date you provide. If the customer also uses Sage 50, you can match the customer's inventory codes to your own on the **Import/Export tab** screen to allow for electronic data transfers. The **Additional Info tab** screen allows you to enter details for the custom-defined fields you created for customers, similar to the Additional Info tab fields for suppliers. The **Pre-Authorized Debit** tab holds the customer's bank account information when you are authorized to make automatic withdrawals.

NOTES
The Daily Business Manager is covered in Chapter 11.

NOTES
The Additional Information field labels are defined on the Receivables Names Settings screen (see page 233).
Pre-Authorized Debits are covered in Chapter 13.

Correct errors by returning to the field with the error. **Click** the appropriate **tab**, **highlight** the **error** and **enter** the **correct information**. You can correct address and options details any time.

If there are no historical invoices, proceed to the final step of saving the customer record (page 247). Click Create Another [Create Another] and then click the Address tab to prepare for entering the next customer. Sage 50 has created a listing for the customer in the Customers window.

Entering Historical Customer Information

As for suppliers, you can enter all historical invoices and payments for the year to date, but you must enter outstanding invoice amounts. The following keystrokes will enter historical information for Grande Pointe Towers from page 206.

Click the **Historical Transactions tab**:

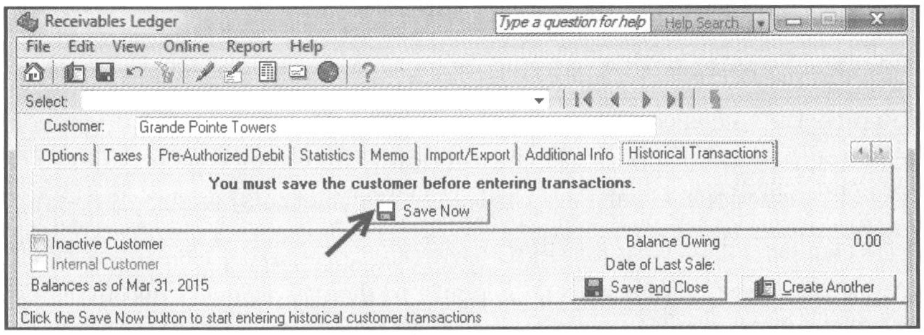

NOTES
If you have already saved (created) the record, you will not see the Save Now option on the Historical Transactions tab screen. Instead, you will see the next screen asking you to choose Bills or Payments.

You must save or create the customer record before adding historical invoices.

Click the **Save Now button** to access the invoice and payment buttons:

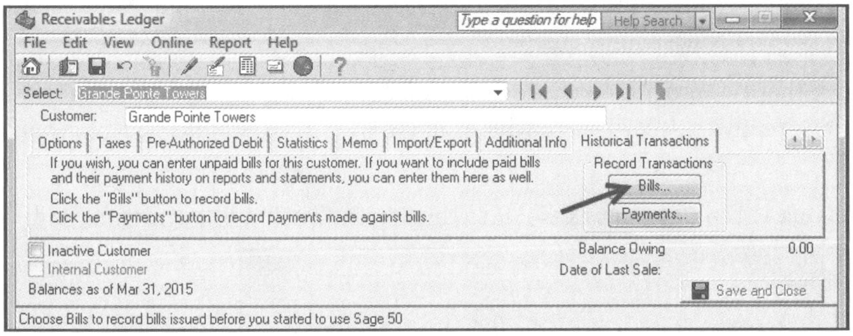

PRO VERSION
Invoices replaces Bills on the Historical Transactions tab screen and the Historical Bills screen on the next page.

Again, the Create Another button has been removed and the Save And Close button is dimmed because you have already saved the record.

If you prefer, you can enter address, options and credit limit details for all customers before adding historical bills and payments. You can open a customer ledger record by double-clicking the customer's name in the Customers window. Then click the Historical Transactions tab.

WARNING!
Enter invoice details carefully. To correct a historical invoice amount, you must pay the invoice and then clear paid transactions (Maintenance menu). Then re-enter the outstanding invoices. See page 250.

Just as in the Payables Ledger, you enter invoices and payments separately. You can use the Payments option to record any payments against previous invoices that you want to keep on record. The totals of all outstanding invoices, after payments, must match the opening balance in the *Accounts Receivable* control account in the General Ledger.

Click the **Bills button** to display the following input form:

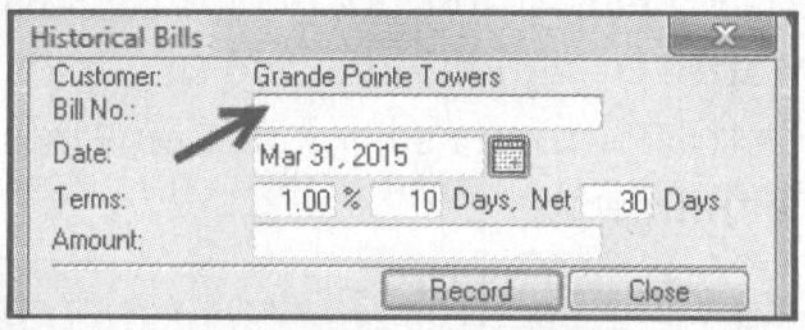

There is a single Amount field because customer discounts are calculated on after-tax amounts. When discounts are calculated before tax, there is an additional input field so that the sale and the tax amounts can be entered separately, as we saw in the Payables Historical Invoices screen. The earliest transaction date is the default invoice date. The cursor is in the Bill No. field so you can enter the first invoice number.

Type `699` **Press** *tab* to advance to the Date field.

Type `mar 24`

Because the payment terms are correctly entered, we can skip them. Discounts are calculated after taxes, so only the single after-tax amount is needed.

NOTES
This invoice amount will be added to the Year-To-Date Sales amount on the Statistics tab screen.

Click the **Amount field**.

Type `4400`

Correct **errors** by returning to the field with the error, **highlighting** the **error** and **entering** the **correct information**.

Check the **information** carefully before saving the invoice.

Incorrect invoices can be changed only by paying the outstanding invoices, clearing paid transactions (Home window, Maintenance menu, Clear Data, Clear Paid Transactions, Clear Paid Customer Transactions) and then re-entering the invoices (see page 250).

NOTES
You must click Record for each invoice you enter to save it. Clicking Close will discard the entry.

Click **Record** to save the invoice and to display a new blank invoice form for this customer.

Repeat these **procedures** to enter the second invoice for this customer.

Click **Close** to return to the Historical Transactions window after entering all invoices for a customer.

Notice that the program has added the customer's balance to the Ledger window. You are now ready to record the payment made by Grande Pointe Towers against this invoice.

Click the **Payments button** to display the customer payments form:

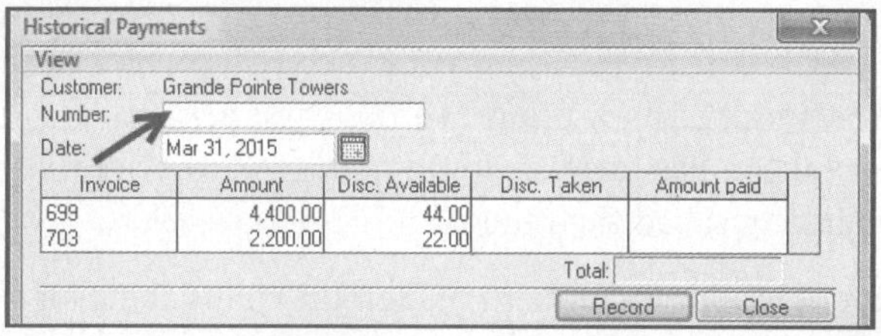

All outstanding invoices that you entered are displayed. Entering historical customer payments is much like entering current receipts in the Receipts Journal. As usual, the earliest transaction date is the default. The default March 31 transaction date is less than 10 days after the invoice date, so the discount is still available. The discount amount — $44.00— is 1 percent of the total after-tax invoice amount.

Click the Number field to move the cursor to the cheque number field if necessary.

Type 4896 **Press** *tab* to advance to the Date field.

Type 03-28

Discounts can be taken only when the full payment is made before the due date, so we must skip the Discount fields. The full discount remains available until the discount period has ended.

Click the **Amount Paid column** on the line for invoice #699.

The full invoice amount is displayed as the default and highlighted so you can edit it.

Type 2400 **Press** *tab*. **Press** *del* to remove the discount amount.

Check your **information** carefully before you proceed and **make corrections** if necessary.

Click **Record** to save the information and to display another payment form for this customer in case there are additional payments to record.

Notice that the full discount remains available after the payment — its amount is not reduced, although the balance owing has been reduced.

Repeat these procedures to enter other payments by this customer if there are any.

When you have recorded all outstanding payments by a customer,

Click **Close** to return to the customer information form.

Notice that the balance owing in the ledger has been updated to $4 200 to include the payment entry just completed.

Click the **Address tab** to prepare for entering the next customer.

Click the **Create tool** to open another new customer input screen.

WARNING!

If an amount appears in the Disc. Taken field, delete it before recording the payment. If you do not, you cannot finish the history because the ledgers are not balanced.

Saving a Customer Record without Historical Information

When all the information is entered correctly, you must save the customer information. If you have not added historical information,

Click **Create Another** [Create Another] to save the information and advance to the next new customer input screen.

Click the **Address tab** to prepare for entering the next customer.

Repeat these **procedures** to enter the remaining customers and historical transactions on page 206. After entering the last customer,

Click **Save And Close** [Save and Close] to close the Customer Ledger window.

Display or **print** the **Customer List** from the Customers window Reports menu to check the accuracy of your address information.

Display or **print** a **Customer Aged Detail Report** including terms and historical differences to check the historical information.

Close the **Customers icon window** to return to the Home window.

Preparing for Journal Entries

The last stage in setting up the accounting system involves closing off the historical entries. This step indicates that all historical data have been entered and cannot be changed. You can proceed with journalizing before finishing the history, but you must finish the history before beginning a new fiscal period. Finishing history involves changing the status of each ledger from an open to a finished history state. In the open history state the ledgers are not integrated, so you can add or change historical information in one ledger without affecting any other ledger. It is easier to correct mistakes.

Making a Backup of the Company Files

WARNING!
Make a backup copy before proceeding. If you finish entering history and discover an incorrect amount, you can correct the error without re-entering all the information.

WARNING!
You cannot use Save As with CDs or DVDs in Sage 50. You can use Backup and Save A Copy to make CD backups.

Refer to page 20 for more information on backup methods and storage media.

To make a backup of the not-finished files, you can use Save A Copy from the File menu or use the Backup command. Both methods allow you to keep working in your original working data file.

Choose the **File menu** and **click Backup** or **click** the **Backup tool**:

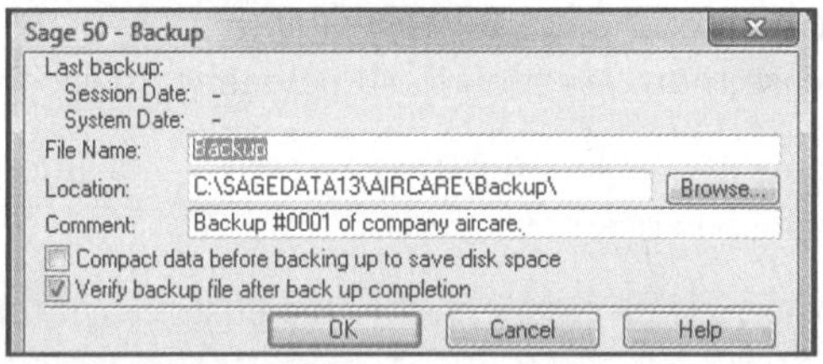

On this backup screen, you should enter the name and location of the new backup.

Click Browse.

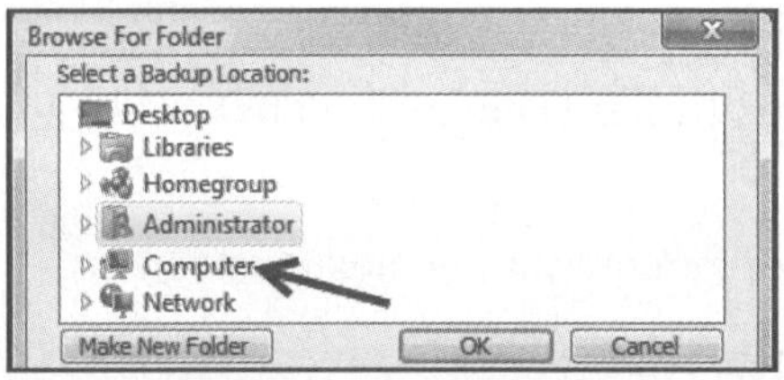

NOTES
Substitute the appropriate drive and folders for the location of your files.

Click **Computer**, then **click C:**. **Scroll down** and **click SageData13** to locate and select the SageData13 folder that contains your other data files.

Click the **Make New Folder button** and **type** NF-AIR to replace New Folder — the selected name. **Click OK** to return to the Backup screen.

Double-click **Backup** in the File Name field. **Type** nf-aircare

Click **OK** to begin backing up the data file.

The "NF" designates files as not finished or open to distinguish them from the ones you will work with to enter journal transactions. Continue by following the backup instructions on-screen. You can use another name and location for your backup if you want. This will create a backup copy of the files for Air Care Services.

Click **OK** when the backup is complete.

Working with Unfinished History

WARNING!
Read this section carefully before proceeding.

Sage 50 allows you to enter current journal transactions before the history is finished and balanced. In this way, you can keep the journal records current and enter the historical details later when there is time available to do so, or the setup may be completed later by a different individual.

There are, however, a number of elements that you must complete before you can make journal entries. You must create the General Ledger accounts and define the essential linked accounts before you can use the journals. You must enter historical customer and supplier invoices before you can enter payments for them, and invoices must have the correct payment terms and dates. Automatic payroll tax calculations are also unavailable until the history is finished.

You do not need to enter General Ledger opening account balances. These balances may be added later in the Opening Balance field on the Account tab screen. The General Ledger also shows the current balance, which changes as you post new journal entries. However, without the opening balances, the current balance is not correct and you cannot generate accurate reports. The Trial Balance and the Accounts window display only current balances, making it more difficult to trace the correct historical amounts.

Some errors may be corrected at any time. For example, after entering journal transactions and after finishing the history, you can correct account, supplier and customer names and address details, but you cannot change historical amounts because their dates precede the earliest transaction date.

From a control point of view, it is preferable to enter all historical information first so that you do not confuse the historical and current data or work with accounts that are not correct in some way. You cannot change account numbers after the accounts are used in journal entries, so some corrections may be difficult to make later. After you start journalizing, the balances for *Accounts Receivable* and *Accounts Payable* reflect all the entries made to date. There may be mistakes in current journal entries as well as in the history, making it more difficult to find the historical errors later.

There are a number of checks that you can perform to increase the accuracy of your work. You should compare your reports carefully with the financial reports for your company — the charts given at the beginning of this application — and make corrections. Pay particular attention to correct account numbers and historical invoices. Printing Supplier and Customer Aged Detail reports with historical differences and payment terms can reveal errors in invoices or payments. The Accounts window has an option to check the validity of accounts from the File menu or the tool button. The Home window Maintenance menu has an option to **check data integrity** that looks for differences in balances between the subsidiary ledgers and the corresponding General Ledger control accounts. All these checks help point to mistakes that should be corrected before proceeding.

Choose the **Maintenance menu** and **click Check Data Integrity**:

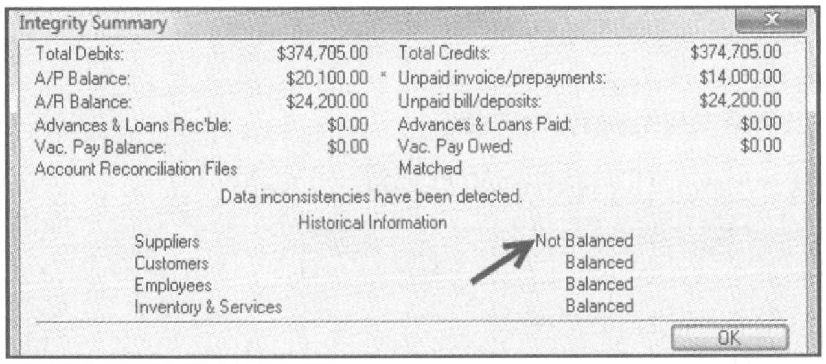

Click **OK** to return to the Home window.

Both the Data Integrity check and the error summary (see page 250) that opens when we attempt to finish the history show that the supplier history is not correct — the A/P Balance does not match the Unpaid Invoices amount. This error will prevent us from finishing the history.

NOTES
You can create new accounts "on the fly" while making journal entries by using the Add An Account wizard. You will also be prompted to add the essential linked accounts when you try to open the journals. Some linked accounts, such as Sales Discounts, are not essential and you can access the journals without them. However, the journal entry will not be correct without the linked account, so there are some accounts that you must create before you can use the journals.

WARNING!
Make sure that the Test Account balance is zero. An error in this amount will not prevent you from finishing the history.

NOTES
If you printed the Supplier Aged Detail Report with historical difference, you would also see that the supplier history was not correct.

NOTES
Notice that the unused, hidden ledgers are balanced. If you view these ledgers and finish the history, you will be unable to add historical information for them later.

If you finish the history when the unused ledgers are hidden, they remain in the unfinished state and you can add historical information later. (See Chapter 9.)

> **NOTES**
> You could hide the Payables module now (Settings menu, User Preferences, View settings) and finish the history for the other two modules. Then view the Payables module again to complete the journal entries. After entering the missing historical invoices, you can finish the history for the Payables module.
> We use this approach when we add the Payroll module in Chapter 9.

Choose the **History menu** and **click Finish Entering History**:

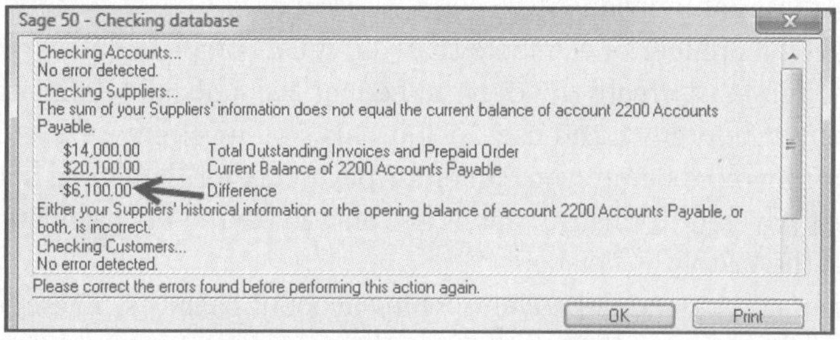

When all your essential linked accounts are defined and all historical amounts balance, you will see the warning that this step cannot be reversed, as in Chapter 4, page 95. Otherwise, Sage 50 warns about errors that prevent you from finishing the history. For example, the accounts may be out of order if a subgroup total is missing after a set of subgroup accounts, or the Receivables Ledger balances may not equal the *Accounts Receivable* control account balance. If you have omitted an essential linked account, that information will also be included on this screen.

In this case, we see the message that the Suppliers or Accounts Payable history is not balanced, the same information we had in the Data Integrity Check. Since the Trial Balance is correct, we may be missing a historical Payables Ledger invoice.

Click **Print** to print the message for reference to help you correct mistakes.

Click **OK** to return to the Home window.

We can proceed with entering the source documents. When the missing invoice surfaces, we can enter it and finish the history. You can proceed with journal entries until you start the next fiscal period. At that point, you must finish the history.

Correcting Historical Invoices

In reviewing all the records for the year to date, Air Care discovered part of the discrepancy between the *Accounts Payable* balance and the supplier ledger balances. Invoice #B-921 from Beausejour Electrical Products was incorrectly entered. The correct amount was $4 000 plus $200 tax, and the amount for cheque #94 was $3 800. We will correct these errors before making journal entries. The first step is to pay the invoices already entered.

> **NOTES**
> You must pay the invoices before you can clear them. You also cannot use the same invoice numbers if you have not cleared the incorrect entries.

Click **Payables** in the Home window Modules pane list.

Click **Beausejour Electrical Products** in the Suppliers list pane to open the ledger.

Click the **Historical Transactions tab**.

Click **Payments** to open the Historical Payments form:

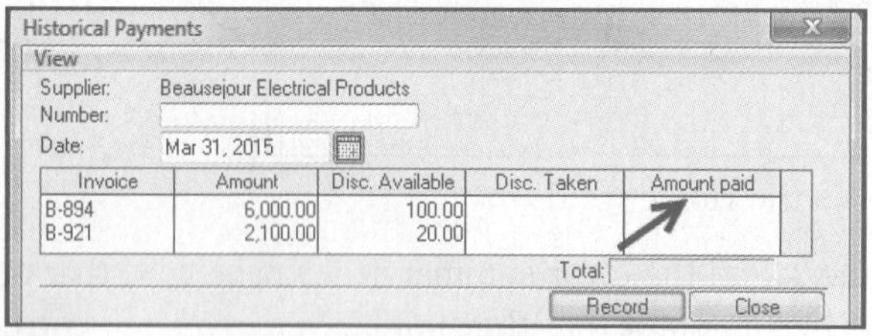

> **WARNING!**
> Be certain that the Discount Taken amounts are not selected and included in the amounts paid.

Type 95 in the Number field.

Type 3-28 in the Date field.

Click the **Amount Paid column for Invoice B-894**.

Click the **Amount Paid column for Invoice B-921** and **press** tab to update the total.

Click **Record** and then **click Close**.

Click the **Statistics tab**.

Delete the **year-to-date** expense and payment **amounts** to restore the balance amounts to zero. **Close** the **supplier ledger record**.

Next we must clear the paid transactions for Beausejour. This step will remove invoices and payments from the records, allow us to reuse the invoice numbers and provide accurate reports.

Choose the **Maintenance menu** and then **choose Clear Data** and **Clear Paid Transactions**. **Click Clear Paid Supplier Transactions** as shown:

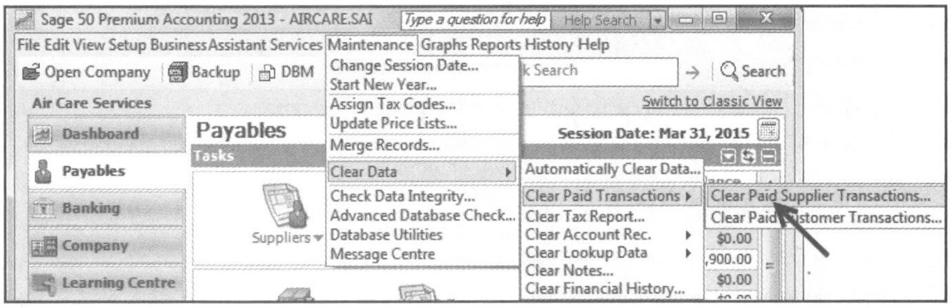

You will see the list of suppliers:

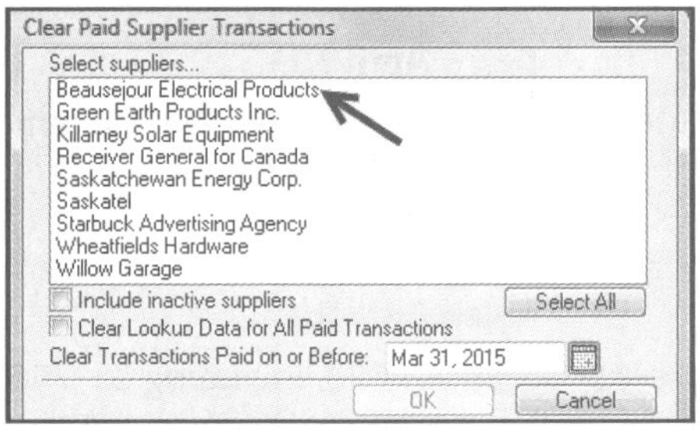

Click **Beausejour Electrical Products** to select the supplier.

Accept the **default date** and the other **settings** and **click OK**:

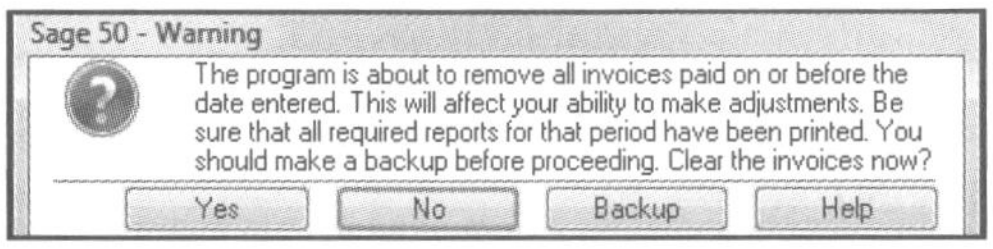

Sage 50 warns that cleared invoices cannot be adjusted or included in reports.

Click **Yes** to confirm that you want to clear the data.

Click **Beausejour Electrical Products** in the Home window Suppliers list pane.

Click the **Statistics tab**. **Enter $2 100** as the YTD Purchases and Payments.

Click the **Historical Transactions tab**.

Supplier Name	Terms	Date	Inv/Chq No.	Amount	Tax	Total
Beausejour Electrical Products	1/10, n/30 (before tax)	Mar. 26/15	B-894	$10 000	$500	$10 500
		Mar. 26/15	Chq 94			3 800
	1/10, n/30 (before tax)	Mar. 28/15	B-921	4 000	200	4 200
			Balance owing			$ 10 900

Enter the **correct invoices** and **payments** shown below:

Close the **supplier ledger record**.

PRO VERSION

Choose Clear Paid Vendor Transactions.

NOTES

If you do not clear the transactions, they will be stored for the supplier and will be included in the Aged Detail Report. By clearing them, you can also use the original invoice and cheque numbers. Duplicate numbers are not allowed, but if they are cleared the numbers are not stored.

NOTES

You must pay and clear all invoices and then re-enter all invoices. Otherwise, the errors will be included in the aged reports and the historical amounts on the Statistics tab screen will be incorrect.

Advance the **session date** to **April 7** to prepare for the journal entries.

When we change the session date to April 7, the program will show a warning because we are entering a new month and we turned on the warning (page 214):

> **NOTES**
> You will see this reminder again when you advance the session date to May 1.

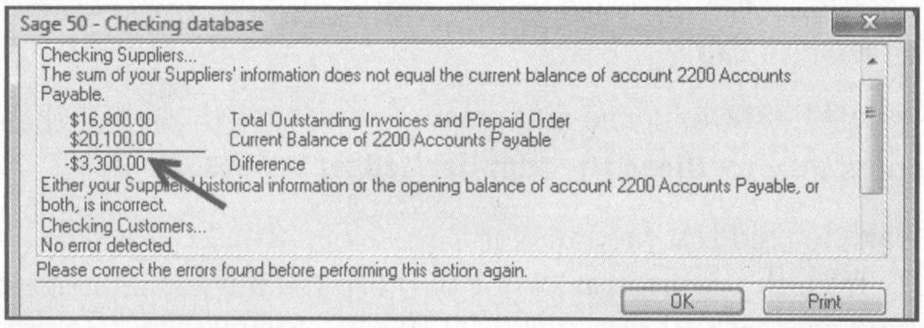

There are still invoices outstanding. They will be entered in Memo #8 on May 1.

Back up your **file** again. You can now exit the program or continue by entering the transactions that follow.

> **WARNING!**
> Be sure to select the correct revenue account for sales. You may need to change the default selection.

> **NOTES**
> You can also add shortcuts for View Suppliers and View Accounts shortcut (Banking module). Refer to pages 132 and 183 if you need assistance with creating shortcuts.

> **NOTES**
> You will see a screen with the Opening Balance field when you create new accounts because the history is not finished. Leave this field blank.

> **NOTES**
> You can customize the sales invoice by removing the columns that are not used by Air Care Services – Item Number, Quantity, Unit, Price and Job Sites – and the purchase invoice by removing the columns that are not used by Air Care Services – Item Number, Quantity, Unit, Price and Job Sites.

SOURCE DOCUMENTS

SESSION DATE – APRIL 7, 2015

1 **Memo #1** — **Dated Apr. 1/15**
Create shortcuts for General Journal entries, purchase invoices, pay expenses (other payments), invoice payments, the journals used in this chapter.

2 **Sales Invoice #710** — **Dated April 1/15**
To Selkirk Community Centre, $1 800 plus $90 GST and $90 PST for removing and reapplying solar panels for roof replacement. Invoice total, $1 980. Terms: 1/10, n/30. Create new Group account 4120 Repairs Revenue.

3 **Cash Receipt #20** — **Dated April 2/15**
From Grande Pointe Towers, cheque #5033 for $2 456, including $1 956 in full payment of invoice #699 and $500 in partial payment of invoice #703, and allowing $44 discount for early payment. Customize the journal by changing the tabbing order so that the cheque number follows the customer number.

4 **Purchase Invoice #WH-42001** — **Dated April 3/15**
From Wheatfields Hardware, $1 500 plus $75 GST and $75 PST for new ladders and other tools. Invoice total $1 650. Terms: net 15.

5 **Payment Cheque #101** — **Dated April 4/15**
To Beausejour Electrical Products, $10 760 in payment of account, including $140 discount for early payment. Reference invoices #B-894 and #B-921.

6 **Payment Cheque #102** — **Dated April 5/15**
To Killarney Solar Equipment, $5 900 in payment of invoice #KS-1031.

> **NOTES**
> Allow Selkirk Community Centre to exceed the credit limit.

7 **Sales Invoice #711** — **Dated April 5/15**
To Selkirk Community Centre, $18 000 plus $900 GST and $900 PST for installing additional solar panels. Invoice total, $19 800 Terms: 1/10, n/30.

> **NOTES**
> Add the description GST @ 5% included; PST @ 5% included, non-refundable.

8 **Memo #2** — **Dated Apr. 6/15**
Create new tax code IN using taxes GST at the rate of 5% and PST at the rate of 5%. GST is included and refundable; PST is included, and not refundable. The description is not included so you must add it.

9 **Memo #3** **Dated Apr. 6/15**

Edit the supplier record for Willow Garage. Add IN as the default tax code and create 5220 Vehicle Expenses, a new Group expense account as the default expense account for the supplier.

10 **Purchase Invoice #W-1993** **Dated April 6/15**

From Willow Garage, $120 including taxes (tax code IN), for gasoline for van. Store the transaction as a bi-weekly recurring entry. Terms: net 30.

11 **Cash Receipt #21** **Dated April 7/15**

From Regina School Board, cheque #12488 for $19 780 including $220 discount for early payment. Reference invoice #701.

12 **Sales Invoice #712** **Dated April 7/15**

To Hazel Estates (use Full Add for the new customer), $1 200 plus $60 GST and $60 PST for a one-year service contract. Invoice total $1 320. Terms: 1/10, n/30.

13 **Visa Sales Invoice #713** **Dated April 7/15**

Sales Summary
To various one-time customers

Repairs Revenue	$3 600
Service Contract Revenue	2 800
GST charged	320
PST charged	320
Total deposited to Visa Bank Account	$7 040

NOTES

Hazel Estates
(contact Joelle Beausoleil)
488 Sunshine St., Ste 1200
Moose Jaw, SK S4G 5H3
Tel 1: (306) 367-7711
Tel 2: (877) 367-9770
Fax: (306) 369-2791
E-mail: JB@hazelestates.com
Web: www.hazelestates.com
Terms: 1/10, n/30
Revenue account: 4140
Tax code: GP
Credit limit: $10 000

SESSION DATE – APRIL 14, 2015

14 **Bank Debit Memo #14321** **Dated April 8/15**

From Flatlands Credit Union, cheque #5033 for $2 456 from Grand Pointe Towers has been returned because of non-sufficient funds. Reverse the payment and notify the customer of the outstanding charges.

15 **Memo #4** **Dated April 8/15**

From Owner: Change the payment terms for Grande Pointe Towers to net 1. Certified cheques will be requested in the future. Set the credit limit to zero.

16 **Memo #5** **Dated April 8/15**

From Owner: The work done for Hazel Estates included $1 600 plus $80 GST and $80 PST for replacement of damaged microinverters. The revised and correct invoice total is $3 080. Adjust invoice #712 to add the extra amount.

17 **MasterCard Sales Invoice #714** **Dated April 9/15**

To Vinod Residence (use Full Add for the new customer), $600 plus $30 GST and $30 PST for repairs. Invoice total $660 paid in full by MasterCard.

18 **Cash Receipt #22** **Dated April 10/15**

From Selkirk Community Centre, cheque #533 for $7 960.20, including $1 960.20 in full payment of invoice #710 with $19.80 discount for early payment, and $6 000 in partial payment of invoice #711.

19 **Purchase Invoice #GE-2579** **Dated April 10/15**

From Green Earth Products Inc., $14 000 plus $700 GST for microinverters. Invoice total $14 700. Terms: 1/10, n/30. Store as a bi-weekly recurring entry.

NOTES

Vinod Residence
(contact Viran Vinod)
56 House St.
Regina, SK S4P 8K1
Tel: (306) 761-8114
E-mail: v.vinod@interlog.com
Terms: net 1
Revenue account: 4120
Tax code: GP
Credit limit: $2 000

NOTES
Use Full Add for the new supplier if you want to add the default expense account (Insurance Expense). GST is not charged on insurance, so you do not need to add a tax code.

NOTES
Add B and C to the original purchase invoice numbers for the postdated payment entries.

20 **Cash Purchase Invoice #WI-6913** **Dated Apr. 11/14**
From Westrock Insurance (use Quick Add), $185 per month for a one-year car insurance policy with $2 000 000 liability coverage and $4 000 deductible. Terms: first month payable in advance on acceptance of quote followed by monthly instalments at the end of each month. Pay first month's premium of $185 in advance. Issue cheque #103. Store as a recurring monthly transaction.

21 **Memo #6** **Dated Apr. 11/14**
Recall the stored entry for car insurance from Westrock Insurance to pay next month's premium of $185. Issue cheque #104 postdated for May 11. After posting, recall the entry again to pay the premium due June 11 with cheque #105.

22 **Payment Cheque #106** **Dated April 14/15**
To Green Earth Products Inc., $14 560 in payment of account, including $140 discount for early payment. Reference invoice #GE-2579.

23 **Cash Receipt #23** **Dated April 14/15**
From Selkirk Community Centre, cheque #586 for $13 602 in payment of account, including $198 discount for early payment. Reference invoice #711.

SESSION DATE – APRIL 21, 2015

24 **Bank Debit Memo #35589** **Dated April 15/15**
From Flatlands Credit Union, cheque #12488 for $19 780 from Regina School Board has been returned because of non-sufficient funds. Reverse the payment and notify the customer of the outstanding charges.

25 **Cash Purchase Invoice #SAA-1098** **Dated April 15/15**
From Starbuck Advertising Agency, $1 100 plus $55 GST and $55 PST for flyers on clean energy alternatives. Create new Group expense account: 5230 Promotion Expenses. Invoice total, $1 210. Paid by cheque #107.

26 **Cash Receipt #24** **Dated April 15/15**
From Hazel Estates, cheque #230 for $3 049.20 in full payment of account, including $30.80 discount for early payment. Reference invoice #712.

27 **Cash Purchase Invoice #FX-3467** **Dated April 16/15**
From FedEx (use Quick Add for the new supplier), $120 for special delivery of solar panels plus $6 GST. Invoice total, $126. Issued cheque #108 in full payment. Create new Group account 5240 Delivery Expenses.

28 **Payment Cheque #109** **Dated April 16/15**
To Wheatfields Hardware, $1 650 in payment of account. Reference invoice #WH-42001.

29 **Cash Purchase Invoice #SEC-44371** **Dated April 19/15**
From Saskatchewan Energy Corp., $200 plus $10 GST for two months of hydro service. Invoice total, $210. Paid by cheque #110.

30 **Cash Purchase Invoice #SKT-36128** **Dated April 19/15**
From Saskatel, $330 plus $16.50 GST and $16.50 PST for telephone, cellular and Internet service. Invoice total, $363. Paid by cheque #111.

31

AirCare Services
www.aircare.com
clean energy for a better future
100 Belair Avenue, Unit 25
Regina, SK S4T 4U2
Phone: (306) 456-1299 Toll free: (888) 455-7194 Fax: (306) 456-3188

Invoice: 715
Date: April 19, 2015
Sold to: Oak Bluff Banquet Hall
(Ann Oakley)
4 Celebration Ave.
Regina, SK S4V 3H7

Description	Tax Code	Amount
Installation of additional solar panels	GP	20 000.00
Adjustments to older solar panels	GP	2 000.00

Authorization to exceed credit limit: Simon Antonio

Interest at 1.5% charged on accounts over 30 days.	Payment Terms: 1/10, net 30	Customer Initials	GST	1 100.00
		AO	PST	1 100.00
	GST #533 766 455		TOTAL	24 200.00

32

AirCare Services
www.aircare.com
clean energy for a better future
100 Belair Avenue, Unit 25
Regina, SK S4T 4U2
Phone: (306) 456-1299 Toll free: (888) 455-7194 Fax: (306) 456-3188

Invoice: 716
Date: April 21, 2015
Sold to: Sales Summary

Description	Tax Code	Amount
Installation upgrades	GP	6 000.00
Service Contracts	GP	900.00

Deposited to Visa bank account
April 19/15 Simon Antonio

Thank you.	Payment Terms: Visa Credit Card	Customer Initials	GST	345.00
			PST	345.00
	Business No.: 533 766 455		TOTAL	7 590.00

NOTES
Remember to change the default revenue account for invoices as required.

SESSION DATE – APRIL 30, 2015

NOTES
Change the transaction date for the recurring entry.

33 **Purchase Invoice #W-3466** **Dated April 22/15**
From Willow Garage, $120 including taxes (use tax code IN) for gasoline for van. Terms: net 30. Recall stored entry.

34 **Purchase Invoice #GE-4906** **Dated April 24/15**
From Green Earth Products Inc., $14 000 plus $700 GST for microinverters. Invoice total $14 700. Terms: 1/10, n/30. Recall stored entry.

35 **Purchase Invoice #KE-1679** **Dated April 25/15**
From Killarney Solar Equipment, $30 000 plus $1 500 GST for solar panels. Invoice total, $31 500. Terms: 1/5, n/30.

NOTES
Close the Advisor message for Grande Pointe Towers about the customer often paying late.

36 **Sales Invoice #717** **Dated April 25/15**
To Grande Pointe Towers, $24 000 for new subcontracting job, plus $1 200 GST and $1 200 PST. Invoice total, $26 400. Terms: net 1.

37

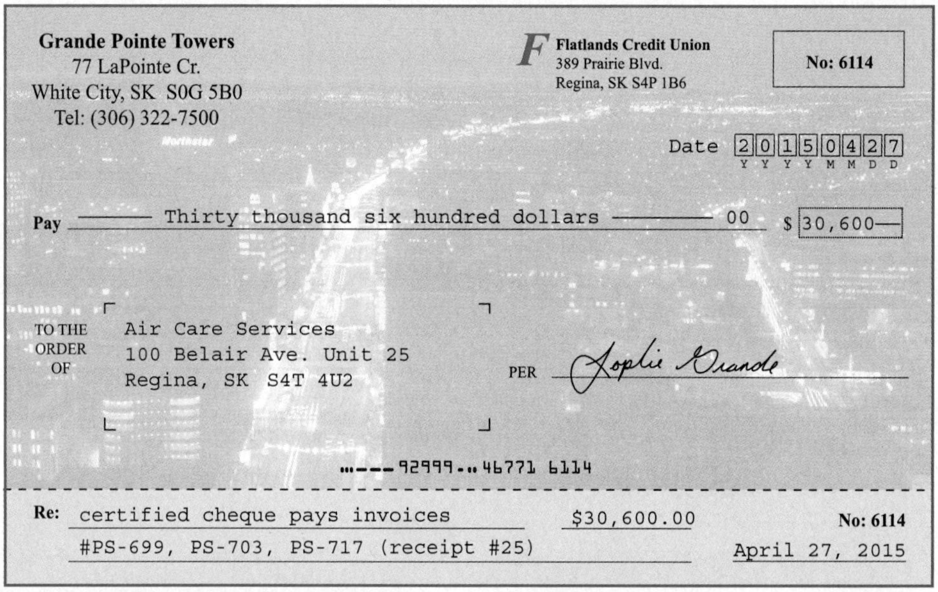
Grande Pointe Towers
77 LaPointe Cr.
White City, SK S0G 5B0
Tel: (306) 322-7500

Flatlands Credit Union
389 Prairie Blvd.
Regina, SK S4P 1B6

No: 6114

Date 20150427
Y Y Y Y M M D D

Pay ——— Thirty thousand six hundred dollars ——— 00 $ 30,600—

TO THE ORDER OF
Air Care Services
100 Belair Ave. Unit 25
Regina, SK S4T 4U2

PER Sophie Grande

---92999-- 46771 6114

Re: certified cheque pays invoices $30,600.00 **No: 6114**
#PS-699, PS-703, PS-717 (receipt #25) April 27, 2015

38 **Bank Debit Memo #55131** **Dated April 30/15**
From Flatlands Credit Union, pre-authorized monthly payroll for employees.

Wages and payroll expenses	$7 000
Payroll services fee	100
GST paid on payroll service	5
Total withdrawal	$7 105

39 **Bank Debit Memo #56159** **Dated April 30/15**
From Flatlands Credit Union, pre-authorized withdrawals for service charges, mortgage and loan payments.

Bank charges, including NSF cheques	$ 120
Loan interest	125
Mortgage interest	775
Loan principal repayment	1 000
Mortgage principal repayment	800

40

AirCare Services

MEMO #7

www.aircare.com
clean energy for a better future
125 Belair Ave., Unit 25, Regina, SK S4T 4U2
Tel: (306) 456-1299 (888) 455-7194 Fax: (306) 456-3188

Date: April 30, 2015
From: Simon Arturro
Re: End of month adjustments needed

Supplies used in April:	Solar Panels	$29 000
	Inverters	24 200
	Electrical Supplies	2 550
	Office Supplies	150

New expense account required: 5170 Electrical Parts Used.

Authorization *SA April 30*

SESSION DATE – MAY 1, 2015

41

Memo #8 **Dated May 1/15**

From Owner: Received monthly statements showing missing historical information. The statement from Wheatfields Hardware included an overdue amount of $1 100 from invoice #WH-20001 dated March 24, 2015. The statement from Starbucks Advertising Agency included an overdue amount of $2 200 from invoice #SAA-987 dated March 14, 2015.

Add the historical invoices for these two transactions in the supplier ledger records as historical transactions. You can open the Payables module window or use the View Suppliers shortcut to access the records for these suppliers.

Pay these two invoices in the Payments Journal as current transactions dated May 1 using cheques #112 and #113.

42

Memo #9 **Dated May 1/15**

Check the data integrity (Maintenance menu) after entering the historical invoices. Make a backup copy of the data files and finish entering the history. Choose the History menu in the Home window and click Finish Entering History.

43

Memo #10 **Dated May 1/15**

From Owner: Print or preview customer statements. One invoice for Regina School Board is overdue. Complete sales invoice #718 for Regina School Board for $300, the interest charges on the overdue amount. Terms: net 15 days. Use the No Tax code for the interest charges and choose Interest Revenue as the account. Remember to remove the discount.

WARNING!
You must enter these outstanding invoices as historical invoices and the payments as current payments or you will be unable to finish the history.

NOTES
Refer to page 239 if you need help with adding historical invoices.

REVIEW

The Student DVD with Data Files includes Review Questions and Supplementary Cases for this chapter.

CHAPTER EIGHT

HELENA'S ACADEMY

OBJECTIVES

After completing this chapter, you should be able to

- ***open*** the Payroll Journal
- ***enter*** employee-related payroll transactions
- ***understand*** automatic payroll deductions
- ***understand*** Payroll Ledger linked accounts
- ***edit*** and ***review*** payroll transactions
- ***adjust*** Payroll Journal invoices after posting
- ***enter*** employee benefits and entitlements
- ***complete*** payroll runs for a group of employees
- ***release*** vacation pay to employees
- ***remit*** payroll taxes
- ***display*** and ***print*** payroll reports
- ***prepare*** Record of Employment and T4 slips

COMPANY INFORMATION

Company Profile

NOTES

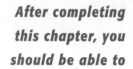

Helena's Academy
250 Satchel Lane
Edmonton, AB T7F 3B2
Tel: (780) 633-8201
Fax: (780) 633-8396
Business No.: 189 245 053

Helena's Academy was opened in Edmonton, Alberta, in 2002 by Helena Teutor as a small private junior elementary school. The school has maintained its small size in order to offer individualized programming with high academic standards for students with artistic interests and abilities. Helena works as principal and also teaches the upper grades. Two other teachers handle the kindergarten and junior primary grades. Although all teachers have a background in fine arts and are trained music teachers, an additional half-time art and music specialist rotates among all the classes. A full-time office administrator, caretaker and classroom assistant make up the rest of the staff. The classroom assistant also runs the after-school program.

Parents pay tuition fees in two instalments, one before the start of the school year in August and the second at the beginning of January. They pay additional fees to participate in the after-school programs. Three teachers offer private half-hour weekly music lessons that parents also pay for separately.

All classes are split-grade classes, an arrangement required by the small school enrolment, but desired because of the opportunities for students to help each other. Older students in each class, even in kindergarten, are expected to help their younger classmates. All parents are also required to volunteer in the classroom and library, and the kindergarten parents provide the healthy daily snacks for the kindergarten classes. The volunteer expectations are viewed favourably by the families at the school because they enable parents to understand and reinforce the learning philosophy of the school.

The school closes for the month of July each year, but all teachers and staff return to work in August to plan their programs for the coming year. The caretaker uses this month before students return to catch up on repairs and maintenance.

Individual client accounts are not set up for this exercise and tuition fees for the first semester have been paid. Fees for the after-school program and private lessons are paid on the first of each month. No taxes are charged on any of the school's fees, and as an educational institution providing only tax-exempt services, the academy is not eligible for GST refunds on the taxes it pays. The school has accounts set up with a few regular suppliers, and some of these offer discounts.

On October 1, 2015, Helena's Academy converted its accounts, using the following information:

- Chart of Accounts
- Trial Balance
- Supplier Information
- Client Information
- Employee Profiles and Information Sheet
- Accounting Procedures

CHART OF POSTABLE ACCOUNTS

HELENA'S ACADEMY

ASSETS
1080 Bank: Chequing Account
1090 Bank: Savings Account
1100 Investments: Restricted Use Funds
1200 Fees Receivable
1240 Advances & Loans Receivable
1260 Prepaid Taxes
1280 Office Supplies
1300 Arts Supplies
1320 Library Material
1340 Textbooks
1520 Classroom Computers
1540 Office Equipment
1560 Furniture
1580 School Vehicle
1620 School Premises ▶

▶LIABILITIES
2100 Bank Loan
2200 Accounts Payable
2300 Vacation Payable
2310 EI Payable
2320 CPP Payable
2330 Income Tax Payable
2400 RRSP Payable
2410 Family Support Payable
2430 Medical Payable - Employee
2440 Medical Payable - Employer
2460 WCB Payable
2920 Mortgage Payable

EQUITY
3560 Academy, Invested Capital
3580 Retained Surplus
3600 Net Income ▶

▶REVENUE
4020 Revenue from School Fees
4040 Revenue from Lessons
4060 Revenue from Programs
4100 Revenue from Interest

EXPENSE
5020 Purchase Discounts
5040 Bank Charges
5060 Hydro Expenses
5080 Insurance Expense
5100 Office Supplies Used
5110 Textbook Expenses
5120 Art Supplies Used
5140 Interest Expense
5180 Promotional Expenses
5190 Property Taxes
5200 Telephone Expenses ▶

▶5210 Vehicle Expenses
5250 Wages: Teaching Staff
5260 Wages: Support Staff
5280 Wages: Music Lessons
5310 EI Expense
5320 CPP Expense
5330 WCB Expense
5380 Tuition Fees Expense
5400 Medical Premium Expense

NOTES: The Chart of Accounts includes only postable accounts and Net Income.

TRIAL BALANCE

HELENA'S ACADEMY

October 1, 2015

		Debits	Credits
1080	Bank: Chequing Account	$ 120 000.00	
1090	Bank: Savings Account	160 000.00	
1100	Investments: Restricted Use Funds	540 000.00	
1260	Prepaid Taxes	2 700.00	
1280	Office Supplies	4 100.00	
1300	Arts Supplies	3 850.00	
1320	Library Material	14 500.00	
1340	Textbooks	5 300.00	
1520	Classroom Computers	6 800.00	
1540	Office Equipment	4 900.00	
1560	Furniture	16 000.00	
1580	School Vehicle	23 000.00	
1620	School Premises	840 000.00	
2100	Bank Loan		$ 65 000.00
2200	Accounts Payable		1 880.00
2300	Vacation Payable		3 841.68
2310	EI Payable		869.33
2320	CPP Payable		2 433.02
2330	Income Tax Payable		5 892.00
2400	RRSP Payable		300.00
2410	Family Support Payable		1 000.00
2430	Medical Payable - Employee		484.00
2440	Medical Payable - Employer		484.00
2460	WCB Payable		392.30
2920	Mortgage Payable		420 000.00 ▶
▶ 3560	Academy, Invested Capital		585 000.00
3580	Retained Surplus		57 665.79
4020	Revenue from School Fees		680 000.00
4040	Revenue from Lessons		500.00
4060	Revenue from Programs		3 000.00
4100	Revenue from Interest		2 150.00
5040	Bank Charges	66.00	
5060	Hydro Expenses	1 220.00	
5080	Insurance Expense	3 680.00	
5100	Office Supplies Used	240.00	
5110	Textbook Expenses	800.00	
5120	Art Supplies Used	280.00	
5140	Interest Expense	4 600.00	
5180	Promotional Expenses	2 800.00	
5190	Property Taxes	1 800.00	
5200	Telephone Expenses	350.00	
5210	Vehicle Expenses	600.00	
5250	Wages: Teaching Staff	35 956.40	
5260	Wages: Support Staff	29 370.48	
5280	Wages: Music Lessons	1 680.00	
5310	EI Expense	1 244.72	
5320	CPP Expense	2 707.84	
5330	WCB Expense	762.68	
5380	Tuition Fees Expense	660.00	
5400	Medical Premium Expense	924.00	
		$1 830 892.12	$1 830 892.12

SUPPLIER INFORMATION

HELENA'S ACADEMY

Supplier Name (Contact)	Address	Phone No. Fax No.	E-mail Web Site	Terms Tax ID
Aspen Life Financial (A.M. Weller)	280 Wellness Blvd. Edmonton, AB T6G 2B7	Tel: (780) 327-7164 Fax: (780) 327-8109	www.aspenlife.com	net 1
Alberta Workers' Compensation Board	55 Payout Cr. Edmonton, AB T5J 2S5	Tel: (780) 498-3999 Fax: (780) 498-7999	www.wcb.ab.ca	net 1
Energy Supply Services (N.U. Cleer)	690 Service Ave. Edmonton, AB T6T 4G4	Tel: (780) 456-3293 Fax: (780) 456-1229	nucleer@ess.ca www.ess.ca	net 1
Loomis Art Supplies (Dee Ziner)	64 Canvas St. Edmonton, AB T5Z 2S4	Tel: (780) 462-1706 Fax: (780) 452-1700	dz@loomis.com www.loomis.com	1/10, n/30 186 519 184
Maintenance Enforcement Program (Al I. Mony)	43 Brownlee St. Edmonton, AB T5J 3W7	Tel: (780) 422-5555 Fax: (780) 401-7575	alberta.mep@gov.ab.ca www.justice.gov.ab.ca/mep	net 1
Receiver General for Canada	56 Heron Rd. Ottawa, Ontario K3A 6B4	Tel 1: (800) 561-7761 Tel 2: (800) 959-2221	www.cra-arc.gc.ca	net 1
Rocky Mountain Trust (Rocky)	59 High St. Edmonton, AB T4P 1M3	Tel: (780) 388-1825 Fax: (780) 388-2663	www.rockymtntrust.ca	net 1
Telus Alberta (Toks Lotts)	499 Cellular Rd. Edmonton, AB T8F 2B5	Tel: (780) 348-5999	www.telus.com	net 1

OUTSTANDING SUPPLIER INVOICES

HELENA'S ACADEMY

Supplier Name	Terms	Date	Invoice No.	Amount	Total
Loomis Art Supplies	1/10, n/30	Sep. 29/15	LT-438	$1 880	$1 880

CLIENT INFORMATION

HELENA'S ACADEMY

Client Name	Address
Parents of Students	Edmonton

(individual client records are not set up for this application)

EMPLOYEE INFORMATION SHEET

HELENA'S ACADEMY

	Helena Teutor	Marina Booker	Lars Teicher	Arte Tiste	Neela Nerture	Morty Filer	Jerome Handie
Position	Principal	Teacher	Teacher	Specialist	Assistant	Office Admin	Caretaker
Social Insurance No.	699 344 578	277 639 118	403 401 599	513 288 191	129 495 768	374 588 127	813 402 302
Address	21 Socratic Blvd. Edmonton, AB T5H 2L2	49 Dewey Pl. Edmonton, AB T6K 4K2	15 Practicum St. Edmonton, AB T5B 4C1	2 Creative Way Edmonton, AB T6H 1X3	93 Formula Cr. Edmonton, AB T5E 2L2	10 Basics Lane Edmonton, AB T5A 4K2	4 Repairal Cr. Edmonton, AB T5B 4C1
Telephone	(780) 466-7736	(780) 436-9015	(780) 463-4870	(780) 429-5656	(780) 488-8554	(780) 440-3301	(780) 461-1328
Date of Birth (mm-dd-yy)	7-28-72	9-14-84	10-5-85	7-18-82	5-19-80	4-3-77	3-3-74
Federal (Alberta) Tax Exemption – TD1							
Basic Personal	$11 038 (17 593)	$11 038 (17 593)	$11 038 (17 593)	$11 038 (17 593)	$11 038 (17 593)	$11 038 (17 593)	$11 038 (17 593)
Other Indexed	–	$13 272 (17 593)	–	$17 568 (27 777)	$13 272 (17 593)	$11 038 (17 593)	–
Other Non-indexed	–	$2 960 (3 220)	–	–	–	$6 020 (6 540)	–
Total Exemptions	$11 038 (17 593)	$27 270 (38 406)	$11 038 (17 593)	$28 606 (45 370)	$24 310 (35 186)	$28 096 (41 726)	$11 038 (17 593)
Employee Earnings							
Regular Wage Rate	–	–	–	$40.00	$26.00	$28.00	$28.00
Overtime Wage Rate	–	–	–	–	$39.00	$42.00	$42.00
Regular Salary	$5 500	$4 600	$4 200	–	–	–	–
Pay Period	monthly	monthly	monthly	semi-monthly	semi-monthly	semi-monthly	semi-monthly
Hours per Period	160	160	160	40	82.5	82.5	82.5
Lessons (#/period)	–	$30.00 (16)	$30.00 (12)	$30.00 (22)	–	–	–
Vacation	4 weeks	4 weeks	4 weeks	6% retained	6% retained	6% retained	6% retained
Vacation Pay Owed	–	–	–	$2 179.20	$533.52	$564.48	$564.48
WCB Rate	0.89	0.89	0.89	0.89	1.15	0.89	2.44
Employee Deductions							
Medical	$44.00	$88.00	$44.00	$44.00	$44.00	$44.00	$22.00
RRSP	$100.00	$50	$50	–	$25.00	–	$25.00
Family Support	–	–	$500.00	–	–	–	$250.00
Additional Tax			$200.00				
EI, CPP & Income Tax Calculations are built into Sage 50							
Direct Deposit	No	Yes	Yes	No	Yes	No	Yes

NOTES: Medical premiums are deducted every pay period. The amounts are adjusted for the monthly rates.

Employee Profiles and TD1 Information

Employee Benefits and Entitlements All employees are entitled to 10 days per year as sick leave. If the days are not needed, employees can carry these days forward to a new year, to a maximum of 90 days. Currently, all employees have some unused sick leave days accrued from previous years. Most employees take their vacations in July when the school is closed, with salaried employees receiving their regular salary and the full-time hourly workers receiving the retained vacation pay at the end of June with their regular paycheque. Vacation pay cannot be accumulated or carried forward beyond the calendar year. Tiste has not yet collected any vacation pay this year.

In keeping with the educational goals, the Academy encourages all employees to continue their education by paying part of their tuition fees for college or university programs. Booker and Filer are currently taking courses and receiving the tuition fee benefit. A second benefit applies to all employees — the Academy pays 50 percent of the medical premiums for an extended health care insurance plan. Both benefits are taxable income for the employee and expenses for Helena's Academy.

NOTES
In January 2009, the province of Alberta eliminated the provincial medical plan premiums. Private health care plans usually cover the costs of services not included in the provincial plan, such as prescription drugs, dental care or semi-private hospital rooms.

Music Lessons Booker, Teicher and Tiste give private music lessons at lunchtime and after school. Parents pay the school $35 per half-hour lesson and the school pays the teachers. These fees are set up on a "piece rate" basis at $30 per lesson for teachers and added to each paycheque.

Employer Expenses In addition to the expenses for the tuition fees and medical premium benefits, Helena's Academy pays the compulsory CPP, EI and WCB.

Helena Teutor As the principal and founder of the school, Teutor frequently speaks to parent groups in order to promote the school. She also teaches the senior class of grade 4, 5 and 6 students and hires new staff when needed. She is married and has no children. Since her husband is also fully employed, she uses the single federal and provincial tax claim and medical premium amounts. At the end of each month, she receives her salary of $5 500 per month by cheque. She makes monthly contributions to her RRSP plan as well.

NOTES
The Academy pays Booker's tuition fees at the rate of $120 per pay period until the full amount is paid.

Marina Booker is the regular teacher for the primary class of grade 1, 2 and 3 students. She supplements her monthly salary of $4 600 with income from private music lessons offered through the school. For each half-hour lesson taught in the previous month, she earns $30. Booker is married with one child and claims the basic, spousal and child amounts for income tax purposes. She also has a claim for her RRSP contributions and her tuition fees of $2 400 for a four-month university course and the $140 per month federal ($205 provincial) education deduction for the part-time course. She pays medical premiums at the family rate. Her pay is deposited directly to her bank account every month.

Lars Teicher teaches the two junior and senior kindergarten classes. He too supplements his monthly salary of $4 200 with income from private music lessons at $30 per lesson. Teicher is separated from his wife and is required to make family support payments. For this, $500 is deducted from each paycheque. As a single employee, he claims only the basic federal and provincial amounts for income tax purposes, but he does have an additional deduction for his RRSP contributions. He also pays the single rate toward the provincial medical plan. He too has his paycheque deposited directly to his bank account.

Arte Tiste is the half-time art teacher who works four hours in the school every afternoon, dividing his time among the three classes but concentrating on the senior class. He spends the mornings painting in his home art studio. Although he is single, he can claim the spousal equivalent plus caregiver amounts because he looks after his infirm brother. These claims significantly reduce the income tax he pays on his wages of $40 per hour. He teaches music lessons after school at the per-lesson rate of $30. His medical premium is deducted from his semi-monthly paycheque at the family rate to cover himself and his brother. His 6 percent vacation pay is retained. Instead of receiving his vacation pay in June like the other hourly workers, Tiste takes his vacation pay sometime in the fall to pay for his December travels. Because Tiste has additional income from the sale of his paintings, he has elected to pay additional federal taxes in each pay period instead of making extra quarterly tax remittances on this extra income. Tiste is paid by cheque twice each month.

Neela Nerture works full-time in the school as a classroom assistant and also runs the after-school program for children who require daycare. She divides her time among the three classes as needed by the teachers and program schedules. Nerture is married and fully supports her child and her husband while he is finishing his studies. Therefore, she pays the family medical premiums and has the basic, spousal and child claim amounts for income taxes. She is paid twice a month at the hourly rate of $26 per hour. When she works more than 7.5 hours in a day, she earns $39 per hour for the extra time. Overtime is often required for extended daycare and can be charged back to the parents. This extra charge encourages parents to pick up their children on time. On top of her pay, she earns 6 percent vacation pay that is retained until the end of June. Nerture has her paycheques deposited directly to her bank account.

NOTES
Because hourly employees are paid twice a month, the hours worked in the pay period vary. The number of regular hours may be either 75 (10 days) or 82.5 hours (11 days), based on working 7.5 hours per day. Occasionally a half-month period has 12 working days for a total of 90 regular hours.

Morty Filer runs the school office, handling the routine phone calls to and from parents, arranging lessons, scheduling parent volunteers, collecting fees and doing the bookkeeping. For these duties he earns $28 per hour for the first 7.5 hours each day in each half-month pay period and is paid by cheque. For additional hours, he earns $42 per hour. The 6 percent vacation pay he earns on his regular and overtime wages is retained until the end of June. Filer supports his wife and claims both the basic and spousal federal and provincial amounts for tax purposes. His medical premium is at the family rate. He has an additional claim for his university tuition of $4 900 and the $140 per month federal education deduction ($205 provincial) for the eight-month school year.

NOTES
The Academy pays Filer's tuition at the rate of $125 per pay until the full amount is paid.

Jerome Handie is the caretaker for the school and grounds. He works year-round, except for his vacation time in July, cleaning the school's rooms and providing general maintenance. During August, he paints the classrooms and steam-cleans all carpets. From each semi-monthly paycheque that is deposited to his bank account, $250 is withheld to support his ex-wife and two children. He claims only the basic federal and provincial amounts for tax purposes, and the single medical premium. He also makes contributions to his RRSP program with regular payroll deductions. His hourly pay rate is $28 for the first 7.5 hours per day and $42 per hour for any additional time. His vacation pay is calculated and retained at the rate of 6 percent.

Accounting Procedures

Taxes: GST and PST

As an educational institution that offers only tax-exempt services, Helena's Academy is not eligible for any refunds on the GST it pays for products and services. Therefore, no sales taxes are set up in this application and the prices in the source documents include all taxes. Provincial sales tax is not charged in Alberta.

NOTES
The sales tax amounts are included with the asset or expense portion of the purchase.

Discounts

Some suppliers offer discounts on after-tax purchase amounts. These discount terms are set up in the supplier records so that Sage 50 will automatically calculate the

NOTES
For an educational service company, the Customers icon is labelled Clients, Sales Invoices are labelled as Statements and Sales or Revenues are renamed Fees.

PRO VERSION
In the Pro version, Customer replaces the term Client, Vendor replaces the term Supplier, Sales Invoices replaces the icon label Statements and Sales Journal replaces the term Fees Journal.

discount when full payment is made within the discount period. No discounts are offered on school fees.

Direct Payroll Deposits

The Academy allows employees to have their regular pay deposited directly to their bank accounts or to be paid by cheque. Four employees have selected direct payroll deposits.

Payroll Remittances

Some suppliers are identified as payroll authorities with the following remittances: EI, CPP and income tax are remitted to the Receiver General for Canada; medical premiums are remitted to Aspen Life Financial; Workers' Compensation Board (WCB) premiums are remitted to Alberta Workers' Compensation Board; RRSP contributions are remitted to Rocky Mountain Trust; family support payments are remitted to Maintenance Enforcement Program. All payments are remitted monthly for the pay period ending the previous month.

Tuition fees are reimbursed directly to the employee on their regular payroll cheques.

INSTRUCTIONS

1. **Enter** the **transactions** in Sage 50 using the Chart of Accounts and Supplier, Client and Employee Information. The procedures for entering new transactions for this application are outlined step by step in the Keystrokes section with the source documents.
2. **Print** the **reports and graphs** marked on the following printing form after you have finished making your entries.

REPORTS

Accounts
- ☐ Chart of Accounts
- ☐ Account List
- ☐ General Journal Entries

Financials
- ☑ Balance Sheet: Dec. 31
- ☑ Income Statement: Aug. 1 to Dec. 31
- ☑ Trial Balance date: Dec. 31
- ☑ All Journal Entries: Oct. 1 to Dec. 31
- ☑ General Ledger accounts: Oct. 1 to Dec. 31 5250 5260 5280
- ☐ Statement of Cash Flows
- ☑ Cash Flow Projection Detail Report: for 1080 for next 30 days

Banking
- ☐ Cheque Log Report

Payables
- ☐ Supplier List
- ☐ Supplier Aged
- ☐ Aged Overdue Payables
- ☐ Purchases Journal Entries
- ☐ Payments Journal Entries

Receivables
- ☐ Client List
- ☐ Client Aged
- ☐ Aged Overdue Receivables
- ☐ Fees Journal Entries
- ☐ Receipts Journal Entries
- ☐ Client Statements

Employees & Payroll
- ☐ Employee List
- ☑ Summary for all employees
- ☐ Deductions & Expenses
- ☑ Remittances Summary Report: for all payroll authorities Dec. 31
- ☑ Payroll Journal Entries: Oct. 1 to Dec. 31
- ☑ T4 Slip for Tiste
- ☑ Record of Employment for Tiste
- ☑ Year End Review (PIER) for all employees

Mailing Labels
- ☐ Labels

Management Reports
- ☐ Ledger

GRAPHS
- ☐ Payables by Aging Period
- ☐ Payables by Supplier
- ☐ Receivables by Aging Period
- ☐ Receivables by Client
- ☐ Fees vs Receivables
- ☐ Receivables Due vs Payables Due
- ☐ Revenues by Account
- ☐ Expenses by Account
- ☐ Expenses and Net Profit as % of Revenue

KEYSTROKES

Open **SageData13\Helena\helena.SAI** for Helena's Academy. **Enter** **October 15** as the session date.

The Employees & Payroll module window opens. This is the default Home window for Helena's Academy.

Create **shortcuts** for **Create General Journal** (Company), **Create Statement** (Receivables) and **Pay Expenses** or **Pay Invoices** (Payables).

Enter the **cash sale** and the **cash purchase** and **payment transactions**.

Transaction confirmation is turned on, so you should click OK after posting each transaction. We will not repeat this instruction.

1 **Cash Sales Invoice #1036** **Dated Oct. 1/15**

To parents of students, $3 200 total monthly fees for after-school programs and $2 130 total monthly fees for individual music lessons. Deposited $5 330 to chequing account.

2 **Cash Purchase Invoice #GL-38827** **Dated Oct. 2/15**

From Global Liability Inc. (use Full Add for new supplier), $1 800 for monthly premium on a one-year insurance policy for school and staff. Paid by cheque #211. Store as a recurring monthly entry.

3 **Payment Cheque #212** **Dated Oct. 5/15**

To Loomis Art Supplies, $1 861.20 in payment of account, including $18.80 discount for early payment. Reference invoice #LT-438.

Entering Payroll Transactions

Payroll transactions may be entered in the Payroll Journal or in the Payroll Run Journal. We will show both methods. If you are preparing paycheques for more than one employee, the Payroll Run Journal is usually faster.

Individual paycheques are entered in the Payroll Journal indicated by the arrow on the Paycheques icon on the following screen:

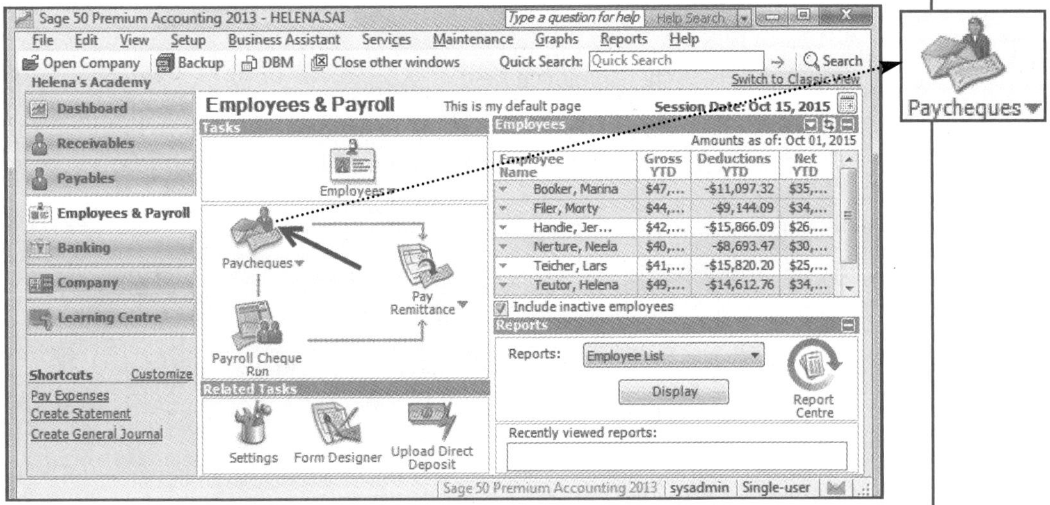

> **NOTES**
> If you are using the backup files, restore helena1.CAB or helena1 to SageData13\Helena\helena.

> **NOTES**
> If you choose not to create shortcuts, you can change modules each time you need to access a journal in a different module.

> **NOTES**
> Global Liability Inc.
> Terms: net 1
> Expense account: 5080

> **NOTES**
> Remember that you must have a valid and active Payroll ID code from Sage to use the payroll features if you are not using the Student version.
> Choose the Services menu in the Home window and click Sage Business Care for more information.

PRO VERSION
The Refresh and Time Slips tools do not appear in the Pro version.

NOTES
The Payroll Journal has a link below the tool bar to switch to the Payroll Run Journal to Pay Multiple Employees. The Payroll Run Journal is introduced on page 284.

Click the **Paycheques icon** to open and display the Payroll Journal:

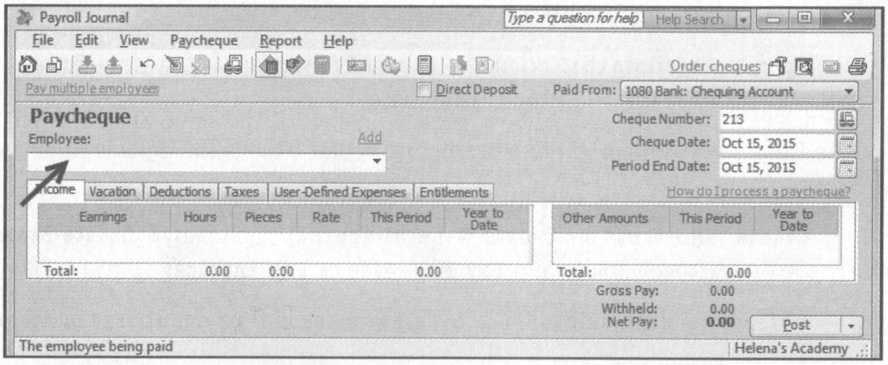

The Calculate Taxes Automatically, , Enter Taxes Manually and Recalculate Taxes tools apply specifically to the Payroll Journal.

The Time Slips tool is dimmed — it is used to add information from time slips for the employee and will be covered in Chapter 18. The remaining tools — Home window, Daily Business Manager, Store, Recall, Undo, Adjust Paycheque, Reverse Paycheque, Enter Additional Information, Windows Calculator and Refresh — serve the same purpose as they do in other journals. You can also change report form options, preview and e-mail the paycheque before printing. Adjust and Reverse Paycheque are the Payroll equivalent of these tools in other Journals.

Four hourly paid employees are paid on the first payroll date. Filer is first.

NOTES
The pay period for hourly paid employees included 11 days and 7.5 hours per day.

NOTES
Use the bookmark attached to the back cover to mark the page with the source document.

✓ 4 **Employee Time Summary Sheet #19** **Dated Oct. 15/15**

For the pay period ending October 15, 2015

Name of Employee	Regular Hours	Overtime Hours	Lessons	Tuition	Advance (Repaid)	Loan (Repaid)	Sick Days	Direct Deposit
Filer, Morty	82.5	4	–	$125	$200	–	–	No
Handie, Jerome	82.5	2	–	–	–	–	1	Yes
Nerture, Neela	82.5	–	–	–	–	–	–	Yes
Tiste, Arte	44.0	–	20	–	–	–	–	No

a. Using Employee Time Summary Sheet #19 and the Employee Information Sheet, complete payroll for hourly paid employees. Handie has taken one sick day.
b. Issue $200 advance to Morty Filer and recover $50 from each of the following four paycheques.
c. Issue cheques #213 and #214 and Direct Deposit (DD) slips #55 and #56.

The cursor is in the Employee field.

NOTES
You can add new employees from the Payroll Journal. Type the new name in the Name field. Press *tab* and click Add. Or click the Add link above the Employee field. There is no Quick Add option for employees because additional details are required for income tax purposes.

Click the **Employee field list arrow** to see the employee list:

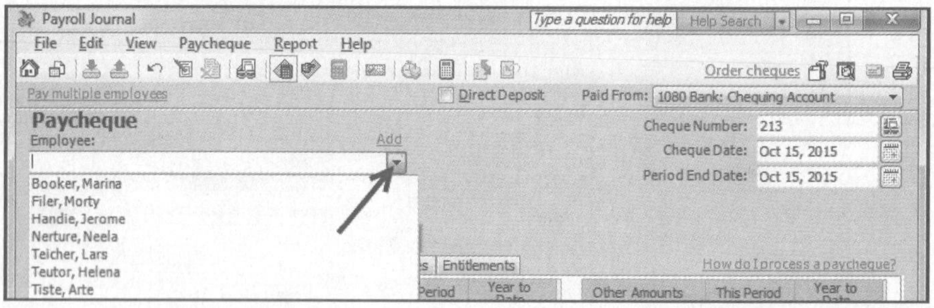

Click **Filer, Morty** to select this employee and add his name to the form. If you have not chosen correctly, return to the employee list and select again.

Press *tab* to add the payroll details for the selected employee:

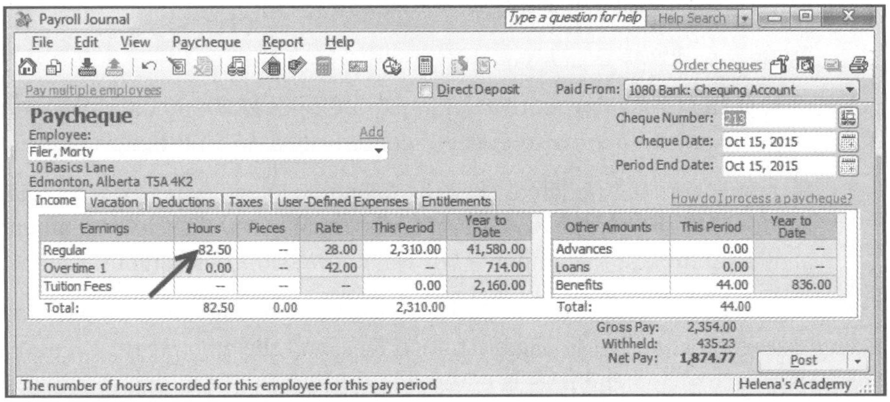

Most of the payroll form is completed automatically based on the ledger details for the employee. The cursor is now in the Cheque Number field. The employee's address has been added. The cheque number, 213, should be correct because we have set up automatic numbering. If the number is incorrect, you can change it.

There are two date fields. In the **Cheque Date** field, you should enter the date of payment. As usual, the session date, October 15, has been entered by default. Since this session date is correct, you should accept it. The **Period End Date** field refers to the last day of the pay period for the employee. It may be later or earlier than the cheque date. In this case, the session date is also the same as the pay period ending date, so you can accept the default date again.

The Payroll Journal information has several tabs. The Income tab screen has all the sources of income for the employee divided into two categories: Earnings and Other Amounts. **Earnings** include the regular income sources such as Regular and Overtime wages for the hourly paid employees and tuition fees repaid. Employee records are set up so that only their own sources of income appear on the form. The **Other Amounts** pane has all the other sources of income, including payroll advances, loans and taxable benefits. Year-to-date amounts are added for all fields.

The **Regular Hours** field contains the number of hours an employee has worked for the regular pay rate during the pay period. You can edit the default entry. The **Overtime** field contains the number of overtime hours an employee has worked during the pay period. No default number of overtime hours is entered because the time varies. If there are different overtime rates, you can set up a second overtime field and rate or create additional incomes. For example, employees may be paid more for overtime work on Sundays or holidays than in the evenings. You can define 20 different sources of income.

The **Gross Pay** amount (the pay rate times hours worked plus benefits) is calculated and added to the bottom portion of the journal window. The total amount **Withheld** for taxes and other deductions and the **Net Pay** also appear at the bottom of the journal.

For salaried employees, the Salary field will replace the Regular and Overtime fields and salary amounts are entered automatically from the employee record.

Click the **Taxes tab**. Tax amounts are calculated automatically:

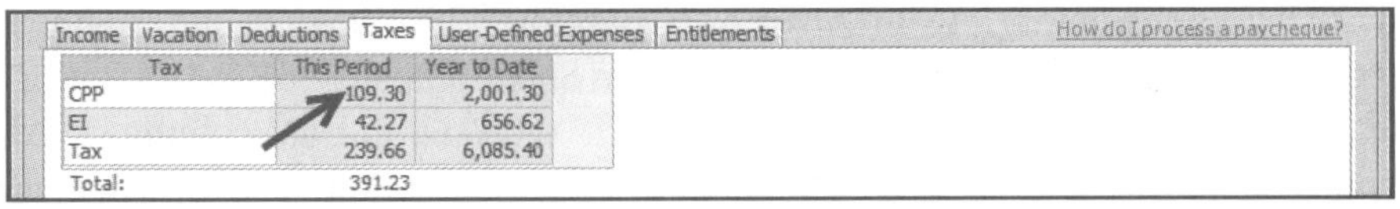
Income
Vacation
Deductions
Taxes
User-Defined Expenses
Entitlements
How do I process a paycheque?
Tax | This Period | Year to Date
CPP | 109.30 | 2,001.30
EI | 42.27 | 656.62
Tax | 239.66 | 6,085.40
Total: | 391.23

Because we have chosen to let the program complete the tax calculations, the tax fields are not available for editing.

If you need to edit the tax amounts, click the **Enter Taxes Manually tool**  to open the tax fields for editing.

Click the **Income tab** to continue with the payroll entry.

NOTES

Year To Date amounts in payroll are always based on the calendar year, not on the fiscal year as in other modules.

NOTES

Helena's Academy uses a single chequing account for Payables and Payroll cheques, so there is a single sequence of cheque numbers.

NOTES

The period end date is usually earlier than the cheque date for hourly paid employees who must complete the hours and have this summary submitted to the payroll department before a cheque is prepared.

For salaried workers, the period end date may be later than the cheque date because they are paid at the same rate each period.

NOTES

If sales commissions are paid to employees, they must be calculated separately and added manually.

Click the **Overtime 1 Hours field** to continue.

Type 4 **Press** tab.

Notice that the Gross Pay and Vacation pay are updated to include the additional pay. Year-to-date amounts are also updated continually as you add information.

> **NOTES**
> To verify that tax amounts have also changed, click the Taxes tab. Click the Income tab again to continue with the payroll entry, and click the Tuition Fees This Period field to position the cursor.

If amounts are not updated, click the **Calculate Taxes Automatically tool** on the tool bar. The option to enter taxes manually may be selected, an option that allows you to edit tax amounts but will not update these amounts automatically.

The cursor has advanced to the **Tuition Fees This Period** amount field. Helena's Academy pays a portion of the eligible tuition fees, and the amount refunded to employees — a taxable benefit — is entered in this income field. Because the amount is paid directly to the employee, and it is taxable, it is set up as an income amount. Filer is currently taking a course and will receive $125 per pay period as the refund for his tuition until the entire amount has been repaid.

> **NOTES**
> The tuition fee benefit could also be set up in the employee ledger so that it is added automatically until the entire amount is paid. Then you would remove it from the ledger. Instead, we will edit the amount in the journal.

Type 125 **Press** tab to enter the amount paid for tuition fees.

The cursor now moves to the amount for Advances in the Other Amounts pane. The **Advances This Period** field is used to enter amounts advanced to an employee in addition to his or her normal pay from wages or salary. Advances are approved by management for emergencies or other personal reasons. An advance offered to an employee is shown as a positive amount. An advance recovered is indicated as a negative amount in this same field. An advance of $200 for Morty Filer has been approved. Advanced amounts are taxable in the period received. Advance amounts owing will appear in the Year To Date column for Advances.

> **NOTES**
> By dividing the tuition fee benefit among several pay periods, the income tax burden will also be spread out over several paycheques.

> **NOTES**
> Advances not repaid before the end of the year are converted to payroll loans automatically by Sage 50. Preferred interest rate amounts are taxable benefits.

Type 200 **Press** tab.

The **Benefits** field under Other Amounts is used to enter the total amount of taxable benefits a business offers to its employees, such as health insurance or dental plans when the payments are made to a third party. Half of Filer's medical premium is paid by Helena's Academy. Benefit amounts are included in the gross income to arrive at the amount of income tax and then subtracted again to determine the net pay amount.

> **NOTES**
> Benefits are not paid in cash to the employee. They are added to gross pay to determine income tax and then subtracted again to determine the net pay.
> You can see the tax implications of benefits by deleting the amount and then re-entering it while observing the changes in gross pay and amounts withheld.
> Premiums paid to private health care providers are not usually taxable benefits for employees, but we want to show the tax effect of benefits.

Click the **Vacation tab**:

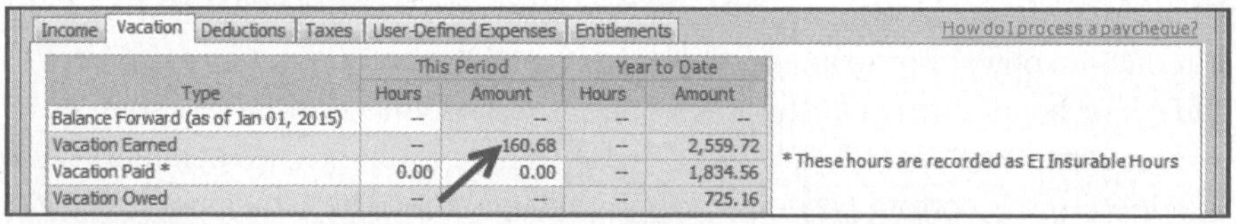

The **Vacation tab screen** has the employee amounts for this period based on the income and the year-to-date amounts. Sage 50 automatically calculates an amount in the **Vacation Earned This Period Amount** field and displays it as a default. Filer's default amount, calculated at the vacation pay rate of 6 percent, will be retained by the business — accrued in the *Vacation Payable* account — until he takes a vacation in July or leaves the employ of the Academy. Therefore, the Vacation Paid amount on this cheque is zero. (See the Employee Information Sheet on page 261 for each employee's vacation pay rate.) The Vacation Paid amount in the Year To Date column shows the amount of vacation pay that has been paid to the employee already this calendar year.

> **NOTES**
> Salaried employees receive their regular pay during their vacations instead of receiving vacation pay. They receive vacation days as an entitlement.

The total accumulated vacation pay owing (withheld since vacation pay was last paid and including this pay) shows as the Year To Date amount for the Vacation Owed. This amount appears in the **Vacation Paid This Period** field when you release the accumulated vacation pay retained for an employee. The amount retained and available for release appears as a default when you turn off the option to retain vacation in the Employee Ledger (see page 278).

Click the **Deductions tab**:

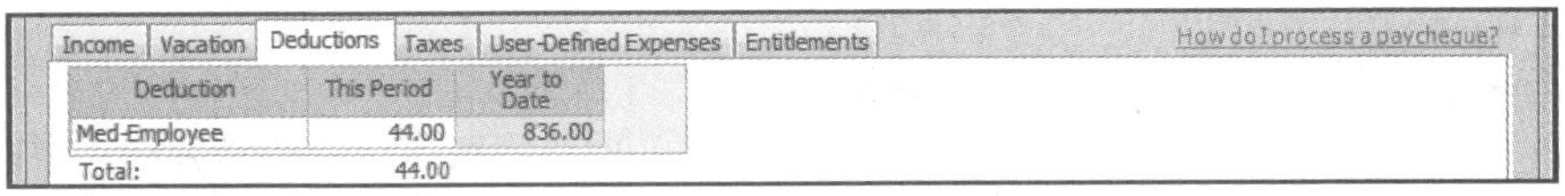

The **Deductions tab screen** has the employee medical deduction entered automatically from the amounts stored in the ledger record. For other employees, the RRSP contributions and/or family support payments also appear on this screen. These amounts can be edited.

Click the **User-Defined Expenses tab**:

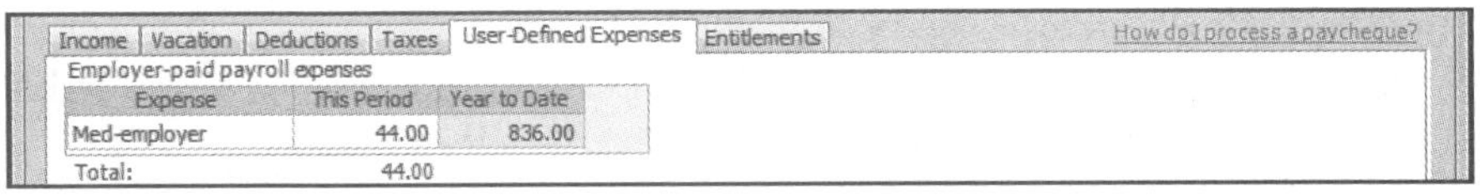

The employer contribution to medical premiums (an employer expense) is also set up as an automatic entry that appears on the User-Defined Expenses tab screen.

We will use the Entitlements tab screen for Handie's payroll entry.

Click the **Income tab** to continue:

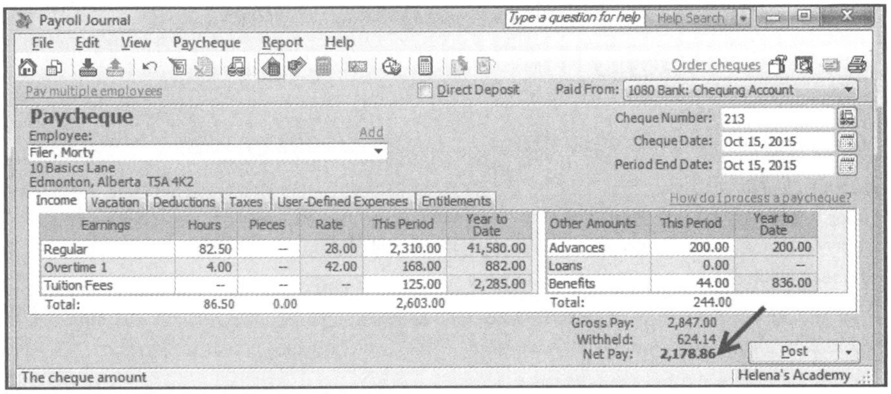

You have now entered all the information for Filer so you should review the completed transaction before posting.

Reviewing the Payroll Journal Transaction

Choose the **Report menu** and **click Display Payroll Journal Entry**. The transaction you have just completed appears as follows:

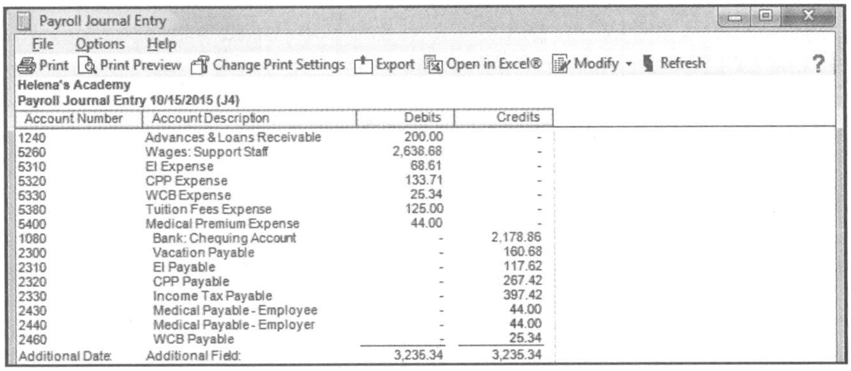
Payroll Journal Entry

File Options Help

Print | Print Preview | Change Print Settings | Export | Open in Excel® | Modify | Refresh

Helena's Academy
Payroll Journal Entry 10/15/2015 (J4)

Account Number	Account Description	Debits	Credits
1240	Advances & Loans Receivable	200.00	-
5260	Wages: Support Staff	2,638.68	-
5310	EI Expense	68.61	-
5320	CPP Expense	133.71	-
5330	WCB Expense	25.34	-
5380	Tuition Fees Expense	125.00	-
5400	Medical Premium Expense	44.00	-
1080	Bank: Chequing Account	-	2,178.86
2300	Vacation Payable	-	160.68
2310	EI Payable	-	117.62
2320	CPP Payable	-	267.42
2330	Income Tax Payable	-	397.42
2430	Medical Payable - Employee	-	44.00
2440	Medical Payable - Employer	-	44.00
2460	WCB Payable	-	25.34
Additional Date:	Additional Field:	3,235.34	3,235.34

Notice that all the relevant wage expense accounts have been debited. The hourly wages and tuition fee benefit are tracked in separate wage expense accounts. The expense for vacation pay is added to the wages expense account. In addition, all the wage-related liability accounts and *Bank: Chequing Account* have been updated automatically because the Payroll Ledger is linked to the General Ledger. All accounts in

NOTES

If the amount of a deduction or user-defined expense is incorrect, and it is not a one-time change, you should edit the employee ledger record. The next time you open the Payroll Journal for the employee, the edited amount will be entered.

NOTES

If the User-Defined Expenses amount is omitted from the record, it can be entered in the paycheques journal as needed.

NOTES

If you are using a later version of the Sage 50 program than 2013 Release 1, your tax amounts and total amount withheld may be different from those shown because different tax tables are used. Your Gross Pay and Vacation amounts should always be the same as the ones we show.

The tax tables for version 2013 Release 1 cover the period from January to December 2012, as indicated in the confirmation note on page 271. The rates in the 2013 tax tables may be different.

the journal entry have been defined as linked accounts for the Payroll Ledger, so you do not enter any account numbers directly.

Sage 50 uses the Canada Revenue Agency tax formulas to calculate the deduction amounts for CPP, EI and income tax. These formulas are updated every six months. The remaining deductions are determined from Employee Ledger entries. These rates can be modified for individual employees in their ledger records.

Payroll expense accounts reflect the employer's share of payroll tax obligations. The liabilities reflect the amounts that the owner must remit to the appropriate agencies and include both the employer's share of these tax liabilities and the employee's share (deductions withheld). For example, CPP contributions by the employee are matched by the employer. Therefore, the *CPP Expense* (employer's share) is one-half of the *CPP Payable* amount (employee plus employer's share). WCB is paid entirely by the employer, so the expense amount is the same as the liability amount. Medical contributions by employer and employee are equal, but they are represented in different accounts — the employer's share is shown in expense and payable accounts, *Medical Premium Expense* and *Medical Payable - Employer*, while the employee's share appears only in the payable account, *Medical Payable - Employee*. For EI, the employer's share is 1.4 times the employee's share. Vacation pay is part of the Wages expense. The tuition benefit is entered as a debit to *Tuition Fees Expense*.

NOTES

Both the employer's and the employee's share of the medical premiums are payable to Aspen Life Financial.

The province of Alberta has eliminated the personal medical premiums for the provincial health plan.

Close the **display** to return to the Payroll Journal input screen.

NOTES

Correcting payroll journal entries after posting is covered on page 274.

CORRECTING THE PAYROLL JOURNAL ENTRY BEFORE POSTING

Move the cursor to the field that contains the error. If you need to change screens to access the field you want, **click** the appropriate **tab**. **Press** tab to move forward through the fields or **press** shift and tab together to move back to a previous field. This will highlight the field information so that you can change it. **Type** the **correct information** and **press** tab to enter it.

You can also use the mouse to **point** to a field and **drag through** the **incorrect information** to highlight it. You can highlight a single number or letter or the entire field. **Type** the **correct information** and **press** tab to enter it.

Click an **incorrect amount** to highlight it. **Type** the **correct amount** and **press** tab.

You can discard the entry by **clicking** (**Close**) or (**Undo**) or by returning to the Employee list and **clicking** a **different employee** name. **Click** the name of the **correct employee** and **press** tab. When prompted, confirm that you want to discard the incorrect entry. **Click Yes**, and start again.

NOTES

If you see an error message about a missing file or form when you preview the cheque, click OK. In the Journal, click the Change The Default Printer Settings tool to access the form settings. Choose Custom Form and Sage 50 Form. In the Description fields, choose the generic forms Payment Cheque for payments and Payroll Cheque With YTD Totals for paycheques. If you are previewing direct deposit stubs, choose Direct Deposit Stubs as the description. Locate the files you need in the Forms folder in the Sage 50 Premium Accounting 2013 folder. Click OK.

You should now be able to preview the payment.

You can preview the paycheque before printing it if you want. You can also modify the reports and forms settings from the journal. Tool buttons are included for both these functions. You must have selected Custom Form and Sage 50 Form as the Form Type in the Reports and Forms settings screen to preview the cheque. The default form locations (file name references) should be correct (see margin Notes). They may refer to incorrect file locations because these settings are saved with the data file that was created with different default settings.

Click the **Print Preview tool** (see margin Notes). You will see a warning about advances and taxes:

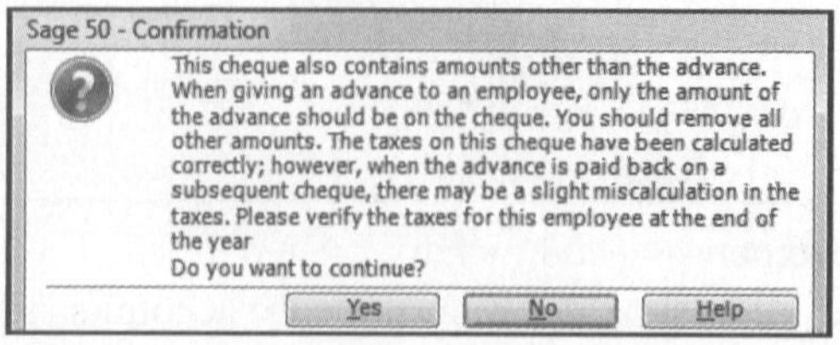

The warning advises that payroll advances are usually issued in a separate cheque. We showed the advanced amount with the cheque to familiarize you with Sage 50 warning messages.

Click **Yes** to continue. You will now see a warning about payroll formula dates:

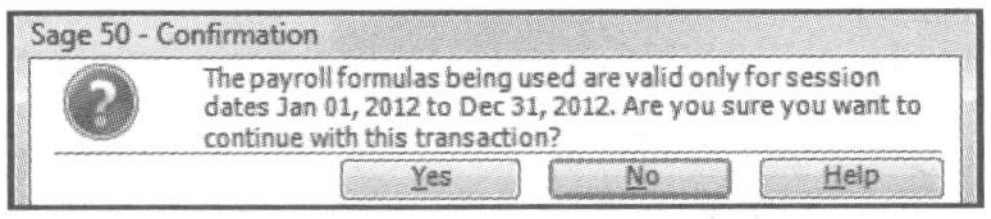

The caution is displayed whenever the dates of the transaction are different from the dates of the tax tables in your Sage 50 program.

Click **Yes** to continue to the preview. At this point, you have not yet posted the transaction, so you can still make changes if needed.

The preview shows the cheque and cheque stub with payroll summary details for the current period and the year to date.

Click **OK** to close the preview when finished to return to the journal.

Posting

When all the information in your journal entry is correct,

Click **Post** [Post ▾]. The Post button includes the option to print and post, which may be selected as the default setting. A blank Payroll Journal input screen appears.

Entering Payroll Entitlements

Choose **Handie, Jerome** from the employee list. **Press** *tab*:

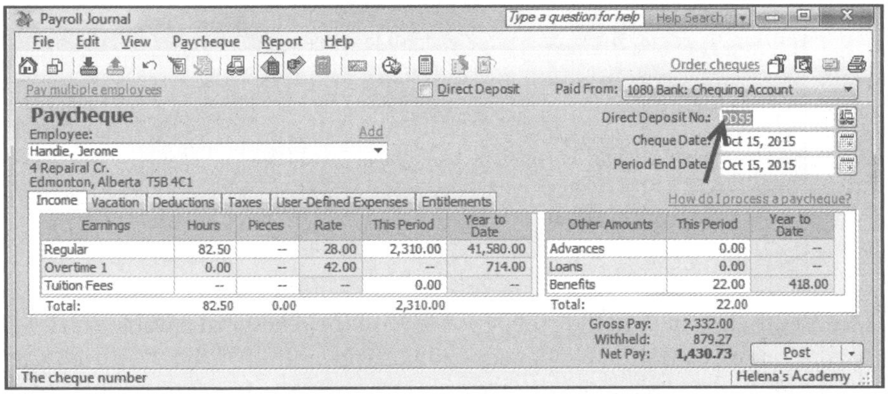

Handie's payroll details are added to the form. You will notice that instead of a cheque number, the entry DD55 appears on the form because the check box for **Direct Deposit** is selected. Handie has chosen to have his pay deposited directly to his bank account. The bank account deposit details are added to the employee's ledger record.

Handie has overtime hours for this pay period.

Click **0.00** in the **Hours field** beside Overtime 1.

Type 2

Click the **Deductions tab** to open these fields.

Handie has two deductions in addition to the medical premium: one for his RRSP contribution and one for his family support payment.

Jerome Handie has taken a sick leave day during the two-week period. We add this information on the Entitlements tab screen.

NOTES

A real business should work only with the current payroll tax tables. Sage provides payroll updates every six months when you sign up for the payroll service. We cannot change the source dates in the text after publishing, and using fixed dates and program (tax table) versions ensures that you can obtain the same results we show.

You cannot update payroll tax tables in the Student version.

NOTES

Payroll Journal entries may be stored as recurring entries before posting. Follow the same steps as you do for recurring sales or purchases.

NOTES

We have turned on the option to confirm successful posting of transactions, so you should click OK each time you see this message.

NOTES

Refer to the Employee Time Summary on page 266 for Handie's payroll details.

Uploading direct deposits is covered in Chapter 13.

NOTES

For every 20 days of work, the employee is entitled to one day of sick leave (the rate is 5 percent).

For some entitlements, employers may require the employee to work a minimum number of months before taking any time off.

The total number of days accrued also appears in the journal and is printed on the cheque stub.

Click the **Entitlements tab** to open these fields:

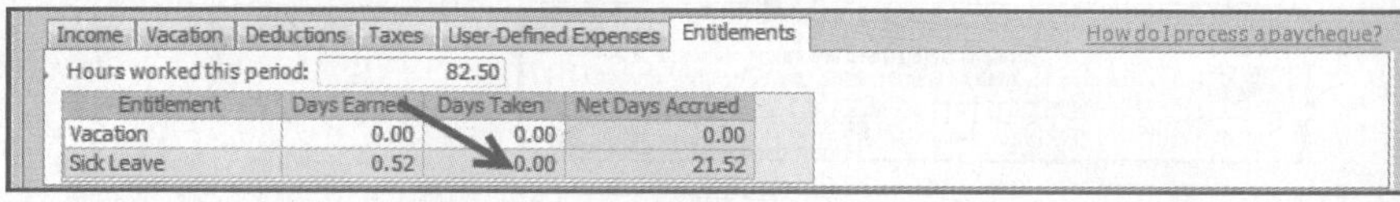

Entitlement	Days Earned	Days Taken	Net Days Accrued
Vacation	0.00	0.00	0.00
Sick Leave	0.52	0.00	21.52

Two entitlements are defined for Helena's Academy: vacation days (only for salaried employees) and sick leave days for all full-time employees. The amounts entered in the Days Earned fields show only the number of days earned for this pay period — two weeks. Sick leave is accrued at the rate of 5 percent per hour worked. The total number of days accrued from prior work periods is recorded and updated in the ledger record and on the employee's cheque stub. If the number of days taken exceeds the number of days accrued, you will see a warning message that asks you if a negative balance is allowed.

Handie has taken one day of sick leave in this pay period.

Click the **Days Taken column beside Sick Leave**.

Type 1 **Press** *tab* to save the entry and update the Net Days Accrued:

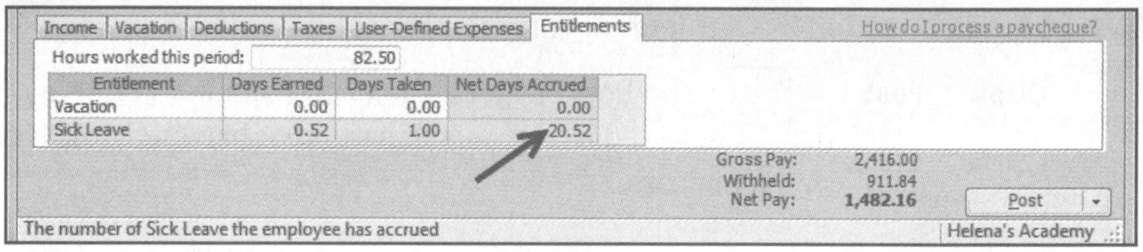

Entitlement	Days Earned	Days Taken	Net Days Accrued
Vacation	0.00	0.00	0.00
Sick Leave	0.52	1.00	20.52

Entitlements do not affect gross pay, net pay or taxes. You are now ready to review the journal entry.

Choose the **Report menu** and **click Display Payroll Journal Entry**:

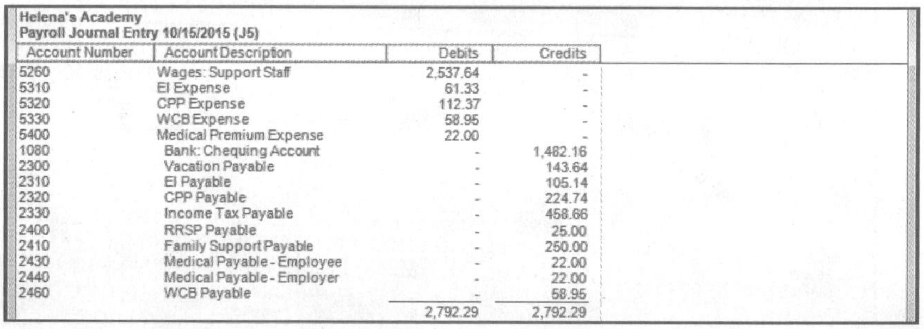

Helena's Academy
Payroll Journal Entry 10/15/2015 (J5)

Account Number	Account Description	Debits	Credits
5260	Wages: Support Staff	2,537.64	-
5310	EI Expense	61.33	-
5320	CPP Expense	112.37	-
5330	WCB Expense	58.95	-
5400	Medical Premium Expense	22.00	-
1080	Bank: Chequing Account	-	1,482.16
2300	Vacation Payable	-	143.64
2310	EI Payable	-	105.14
2320	CPP Payable	-	224.74
2330	Income Tax Payable	-	458.66
2400	RRSP Payable	-	25.00
2410	Family Support Payable	-	250.00
2430	Medical Payable - Employee	-	22.00
2440	Medical Payable - Employer	-	22.00
2460	WCB Payable	-	58.95
		2,792.29	2,792.29

This entry is similar to the previous one, with the additional payable entries for RRSP and family support. Entitlements taken do not appear in the payroll journal entry, but the days accrued are recorded on the cheque stub and in the employee's ledger record.

Close the **journal entry display** to return to the journal.

Make **corrections** to the journal entry if necessary.

Click **Post** to save your work.

Click **Yes** to bypass the warning about payroll dates. **Click** the **Income tab**.

Select **Nerture, Neela** for the next payroll transaction. **Press** *tab*.

Nerture has no additional income, deductions or entitlements, so you can accept all the default amounts.

Click **Post**. **Click Yes** to bypass the warning about payroll dates.

Select **Tiste, Arte** for the next payroll transaction.

Press *tab* to add his default payroll amounts:

NOTES

To preview a direct deposit stub, click the Preview tool. The deposit stub has the message "non-negotiable" added.

If you see an error message about missing forms, click OK. In the Journal, click the Change The Default Printer Settings tool to access the form settings. Choose Custom Form and Sage 50 Form. In the Description fields, choose the generic form Direct Deposit Stubs as the description. Locate the files you need in the Forms folder in the Sage 50 Premium Accounting 2013 folder. Click OK.

You should now be able to preview the payment.

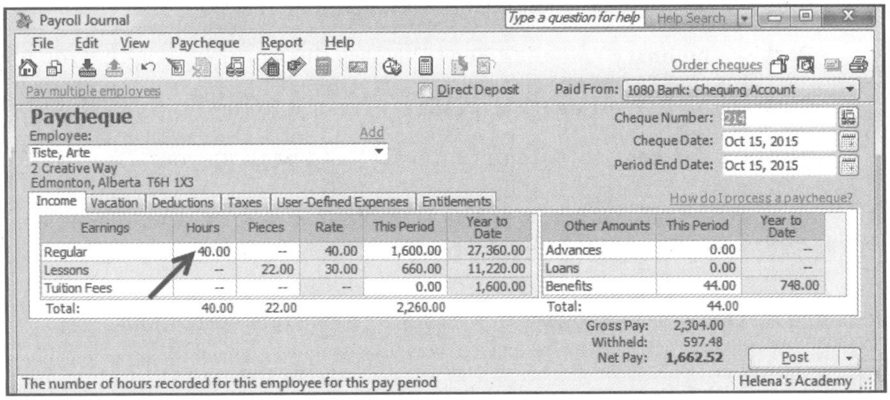

Tiste has 40 entered as the regular number of hours per period. Because this half month has 11 days and he works 4 hours per day, we need to change the hours. Tiste does not receive overtime pay.

Click **40.00** in the Hours field for Regular.

Type 44 **Press** tab to update the gross pay and taxes.

Lesson rates and a default number of lessons per period are entered in each teacher's ledger record. Sage 50 calculates the total dollar amount by multiplying the per lesson piece rate times the number of lessons. You can define a different rate for each employee. If different rates are paid for different kinds of work, you can define additional piece rate fields. Tiste has given 20 individual lessons in the past two weeks, so we need to change the default entry, 22.00. This number should be highlighted.

Type 20 **Press** tab to enter the number of lessons for This Period and complete the entry as shown:

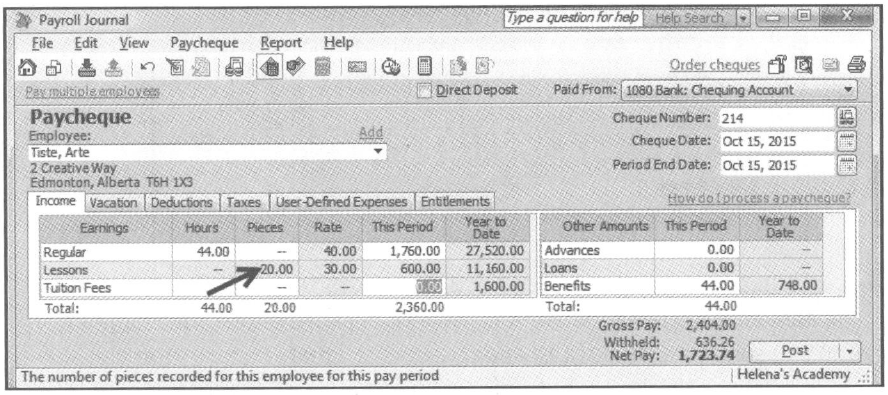

Press ctrl + **J** to open the journal entry display:

Helena's Academy
Payroll Journal Entry 10/15/2015 (J7)

Account Number	Account Description	Debits	Credits
5250	Wages: Teaching Staff	2,501.60	-
5310	EI Expense	60.47	-
5320	CPP Expense	111.78	-
5330	WCB Expense	21.39	-
5400	Medical Premium Expense	44.00	-
1080	Bank: Chequing Account	-	1,723.74
2300	Vacation Payable	-	141.60
2310	EI Payable	-	103.66
2320	CPP Payable	-	223.56
2330	Income Tax Payable	-	437.29
2430	Medical Payable - Employee	-	44.00
2440	Medical Payable - Employer	-	44.00
2460	WCB Payable	-	21.39
		2,739.24	2,739.24

Again, we see a similar journal entry. For each employee, you can choose one account for all sources of income, or you can choose the separate default linked accounts for each income. For Tiste, a teacher, we have linked his hourly wages to *Wages: Teaching Staff* rather than to the *Wages: Support Staff* account used for other hourly employees. Therefore, his wages for lessons are included with the expense for teaching wages. For salaried teachers, lesson wages are linked to a separate expense account.

NOTES

The Post button has a list arrow that provides the option to select Print & Post as the default setting. With this selection, you will automatically print the paycheque when you post the entry.

NOTES

The $200 additional federal tax amount Tiste has deducted is not shown separately in the journal or in the report. It is combined with regular income tax as a single entry for Income Tax Payable.

Close the **display** when finished and make corrections if necessary.

Post the **entry** and **click Yes** to bypass the warning about payroll formulas.

Close the **Payroll Journal window** to return to the Home window.

Advance the **session date** to October 31 and **back up** your **data file.**

Adjusting Payroll Entries

The memo on October 17 shows the need for a paycheque correction:

✓ 5

Memo #1 **Dated Oct. 17/15**

From Manager: Morty Filer returned his paycheque for adjustment. He worked 6 hours of overtime during the week but was paid for only 4 hours. Adjust his paycheque and re-issue cheque #213 to make the correction.

Sage 50 does not require reversing and correcting entries for these situations. Instead, you can complete a paycheque adjustment in the Payroll Journal, as you do in the other journals. You can access the Adjust Paycheque screen in different ways.

NOTES
You can look up Payroll Journal entries in the same way you can look up transactions in other journals.

Click the **Paycheques icon shortcuts list arrow** and **click Adjust Paycheque**. Or,

Click the **Paycheques icon**. **Click** the **Adjust Paycheque tool** or **choose** the **Paycheque menu** and **click Adjust Paycheque.**

NOTES
In the Payroll Journal, pressing ctrl + A also opens the Adjust entry search screen, as it does in the other journals.

These methods will open the familiar Search window:

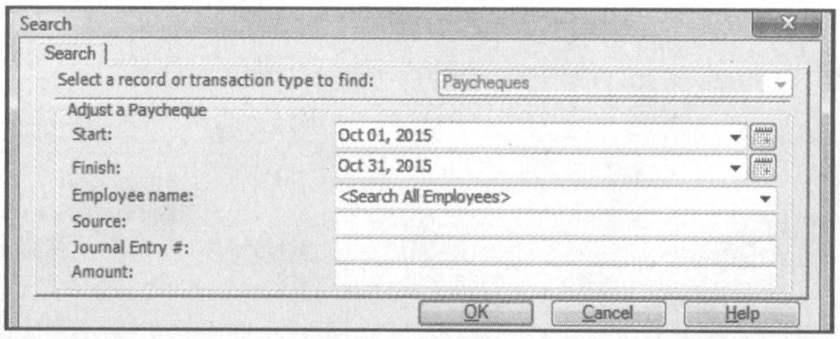

Paycheques is selected as the search area because of our starting point.

You can select beginning and ending dates to create the list. You can also enter the source (cheque or direct deposit number), journal entry number or amount and click OK to access the paycheque immediately.

The default dates are the earliest transaction date and the session date for the data file. We can accept the default dates to have all payroll transactions listed.

Click **OK** to access the list of posted payroll entries:

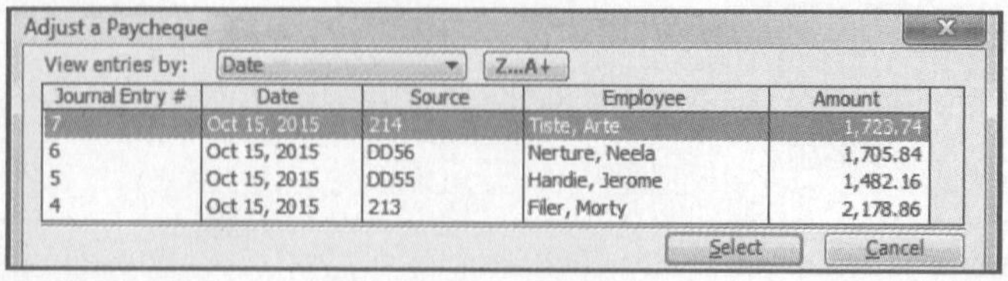

NOTES
Your journal entry numbers may be different if you have made other correcting or adjusting entries.

Click **Journal Entry #4 Filer, Morty** to select Filer's journal entry.

Click **Select** to display the entry that was posted.

First, Sage 50 reminds you about recalculating taxes:

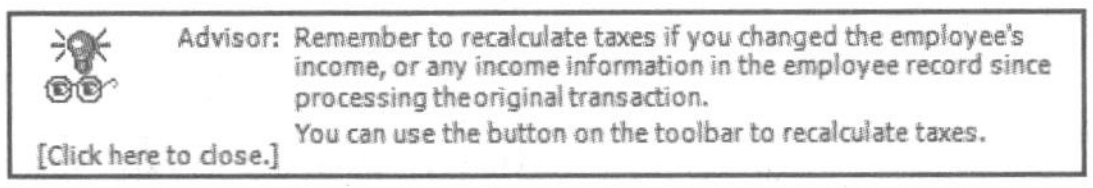
Advisor: Remember to recalculate taxes if you changed the employee's income, or any income information in the employee record since processing the original transaction.
You can use the button on the toolbar to recalculate taxes.
[Click here to close.]

The program is advising you that the tax recalculation will not be automatic if you change an amount on the payroll entry.

Click the **Advisor icon** to close the warning and display the journal:

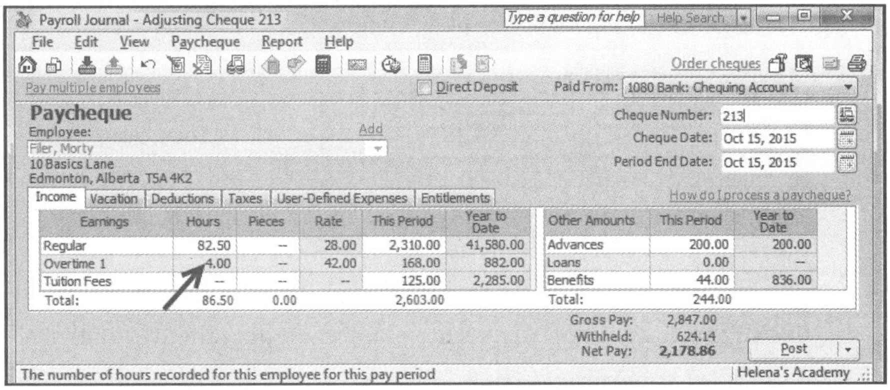

This is a duplicate of the payroll entry. All fields can be edited except the employee name. If you change the date for the new cheque to October 17, the reversing entry will retain the original posting date. Normally you would prepare a new cheque. However, Filer has returned the cheque so we can use the same number. We need to change the number of overtime hours.

Click **4.00** in the **Hours column for Overtime 1** to select the current entry.

Type 6 **Press** tab to enter the change and update the gross pay.

The Vacation pay and Withheld amounts have not been updated for the new amount of gross pay. Compare the Vacation tab screen amounts below with those in the journal screen display on page 268.

Click the **Taxes tab**. Tax amounts have not changed and they can be edited:

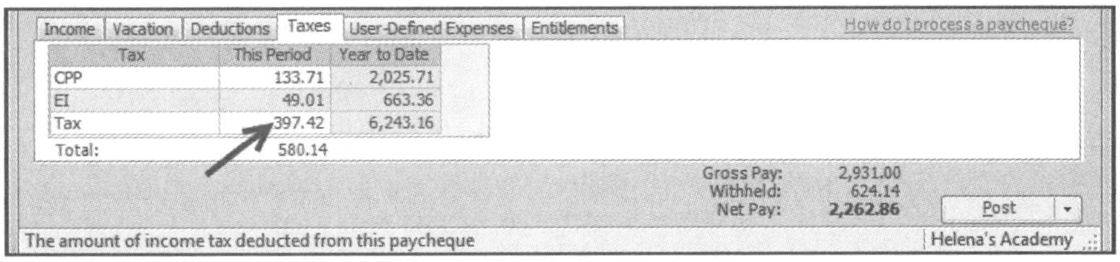

Click the **Recalculate Taxes button** on the Payroll Journal tool bar or **choose** the **Paycheque menu** and **click Recalculate Taxes**:

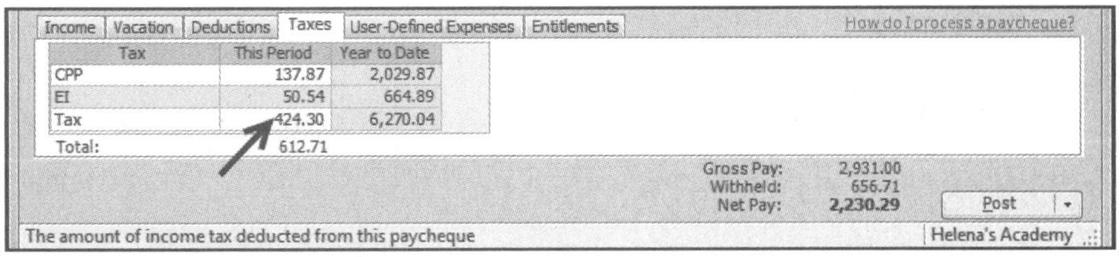

All the tax deduction and vacation pay amounts are updated for the extra overtime hours worked.

Click the **Vacation tab** to see that the Vacation amount has increased from $160.68 to $165.72.

Review the Payroll Journal **entry**. **Close** the **display** when you have finished. **Make corrections** if necessary.

NOTES
If you need to change the employee or to reverse a cheque for other reasons, you can reverse the payroll transaction. See page 276.

NOTES
The total amount Withheld is still $624.14 and the Vacation Accrued is still $160.68.

WARNING!
Do not confuse the Recalculate Taxes tool with the Windows Calculator tool. The Calculator tool is the last one on the left-hand side of the tool bar before the Refresh tools.

NOTES

When you review the adjusted entry, you will see that the entry is J9. The reversing entry that you do not see at this stage is J8.

Click the **Post button** to save the adjustment.

Sage 50 displays the following warning when you do not recalculate the taxes:

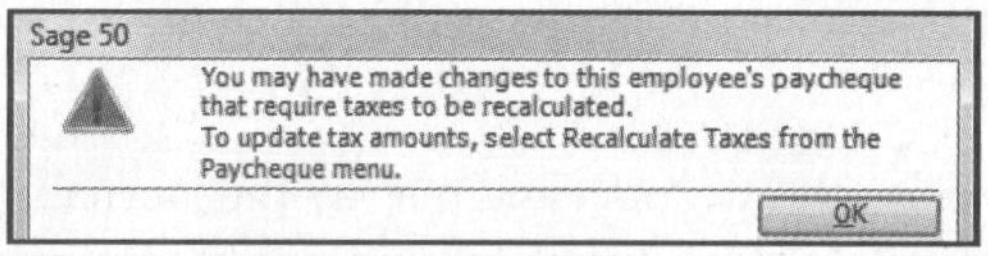

Sage 50 displays the following warning when you do not change the cheque number:

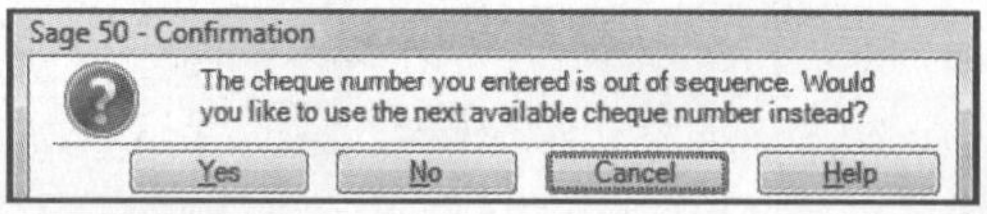

NOTES

The program provides a warning about the cheque sequence because we selected to verify number sequences in the Forms Settings window (see page 215).

Read the question in the warning carefully. To change the cheque number to the next number in the automatic sequence, click Yes. In this case, you can use the duplicate cheque number because Filer returned the original cheque.

Click **No** to continue. **Click OK** to confirm posting the two journal entries.

Close the **Payroll Journal** to return to the Home window.

When you display the Payroll Journal and include corrections, you will see three journal entries for Filer: the original entry (J4), the reversing adjusting entry (J8) and the final correct entry (J9).

All three journal entries are posted with the original date, unless you changed it.

Reversing a Paycheque

NOTES

The procedure for reversing a transaction is the same in all journals when the option is available.

You can also click , the Lookup tool, to view a payroll transaction and then click the Reverse tool .

You should reverse an entry to correct it when you have selected the wrong employee or because you need to delete it. The Reverse tool performs this in a single step.

Open the Payroll Journal.

Click the Adjust Paycheque tool or press ctrl + A.

Define your search parameters and click OK to access the list of posted entries.

Double-click the entry you want to reverse to open the journal entry.

Click the Reverse Paycheque tool or choose the Paycheque menu and click Reverse Paycheque.

Click Yes to confirm that the entry will be reversed.

Sage 50 saves both the original and the reversing entry. When you show corrections for journal reports, you have a complete audit trail.

Releasing Vacation Pay

Tiste needs to receive his retained vacation amount to pay for his booked vacation.

✓ 6

Memo #2 **Dated Oct. 17/15**

Tiste has booked his vacation and will receive his retained vacation pay to pay for the holiday. Release the accrued retained vacation pay for Arte Tiste and issue cheque #215.

Before releasing the vacation pay, you must change the setting in the employee ledger so that the vacation pay is not retained. There are several ways to open the employee record.

Click **Modify Employee** in the Employees shortcuts list as shown:

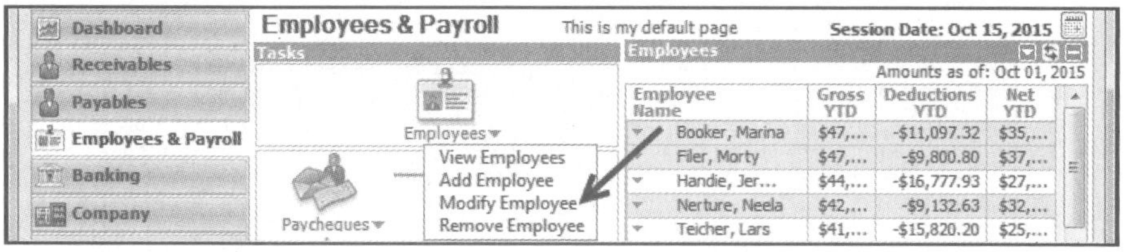

The Search window for employees will open for you to select the employee:

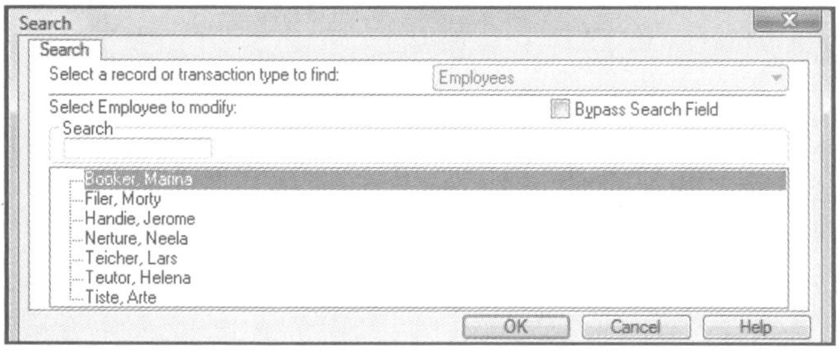

Click **Cancel**. (Double-clicking an employee name opens the record.)

Click the **Employees icon**  to open the Employees window:

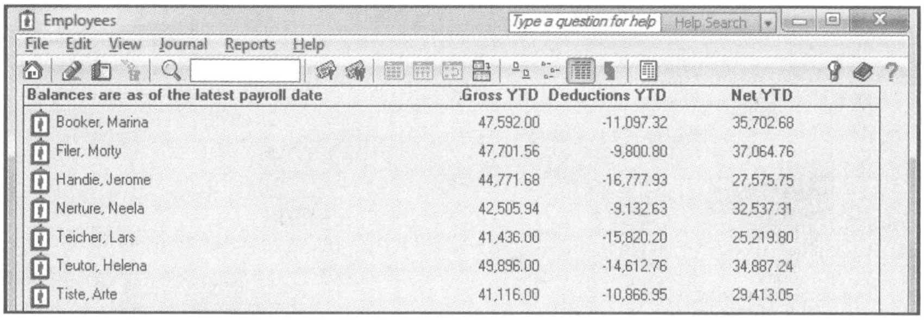

Double-click the listing for **Arte Tiste**.

However, the most direct way to open the record is from the Home window Employees pane list. Click Tiste, Arte or click the shortcuts list arrow beside his name and choose View Employee Record as shown:

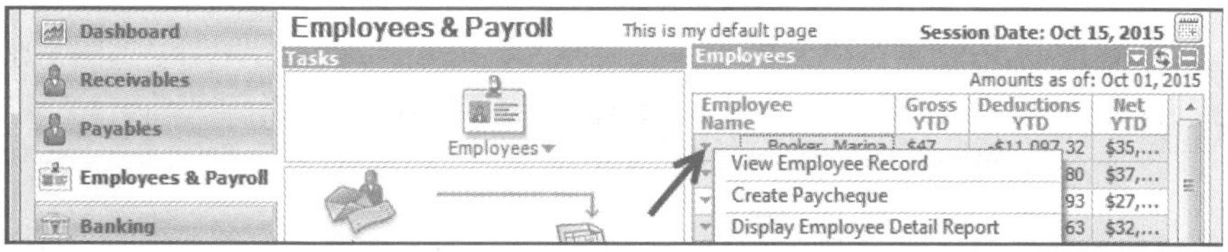

The ledger record opens with the Personal tab screen:

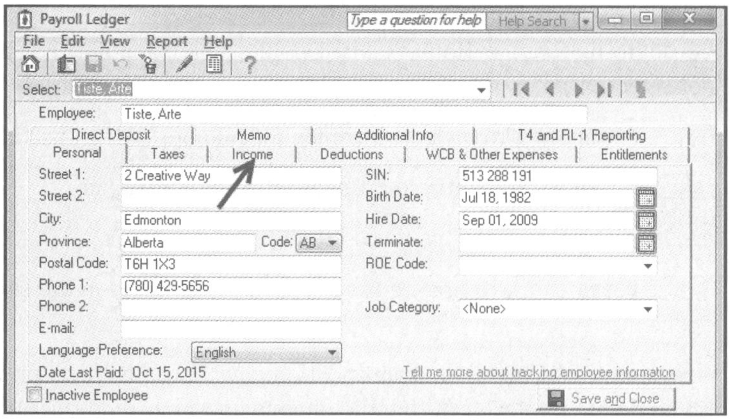

CLASSIC VIEW

Click the Employees icon  to open the Employees window. Then double-click the entry for Tiste to open his record. Or click Tiste to select the employee and then click the Edit tool or choose the File menu and click Open to open his ledger record.

NOTES

You can hide the year-to-date details for employees from the Employees list pane, just as you can hide details for vendors and customers. Click the list arrow button to show the details you can hide.

NOTES

Clicking View Employees in the Employees icon shortcuts list will also open the Employees window.

NOTES

In the Employees window, if Tiste is selected, you can click the Payroll Journal icon  or choose the Journal menu and click Payroll Journal to access the journal with Tiste already selected.

NOTES

From the Employee list shortcuts list arrow you can complete other tasks directly for the selected employee – create a paycheque or display the detail report.

Click the **Income tab** to access the vacation pay settings:

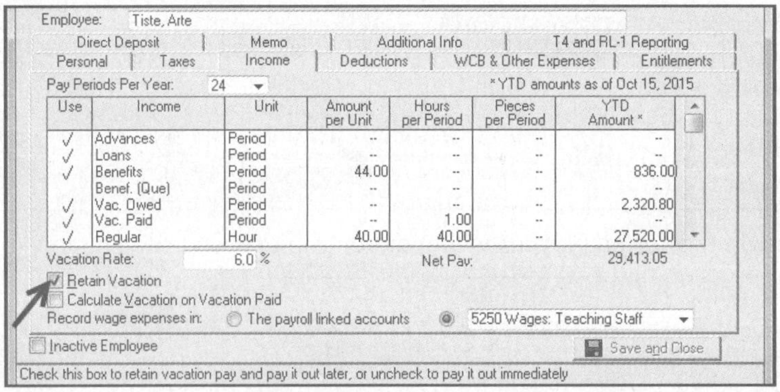

Click **Retain Vacation** near the bottom of the screen to remove the ✓.

Close the **Ledger window** to return to your starting point. Close the Employees window if it is open.

Click the **Paycheques icon** .

Choose **Tiste** from the employee list and **press** *tab* to continue.

Click the **Vacation tab**:

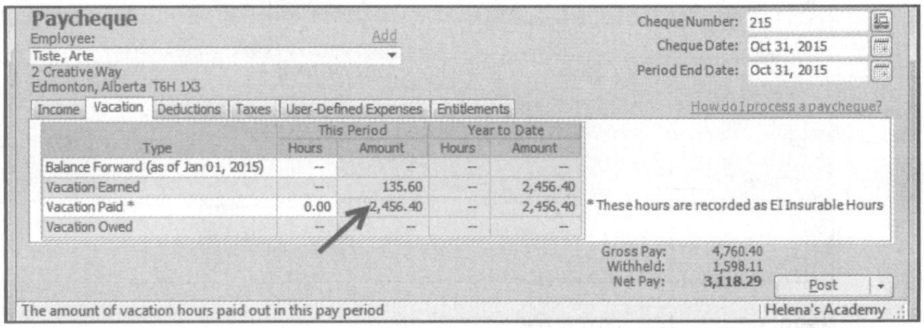

> **NOTES**
>
> The ✓s in the Use column show which items will appear in the journal for this employee. There is no ✓ for Overtime 1, so Overtime does not appear in the journal's Earnings column for Tiste (see the Payroll Journal screen for Tiste on this page).

> **NOTES**
>
> The Vacation Earned Amount ($135.60) is the vacation pay on the wages for this pay period and is included in the Vacation Paid Amount.
>
> When you remove the regular hours and number of lessons, the earned amount is reduced to zero and the vacation paid is also reduced by $135.60.
>
> Employers should always check whether provincial regulations require them to add Insurable Hours for vacation paid.

The accumulated vacation pay now appears in the Vacation Paid This Period Amount field. However, amounts for regular wages and benefits are also included in the cheque so we must edit the default entries. No regular hours should be included and benefits and optional deductions do not apply to vacation pay.

Click the **Income tab**:

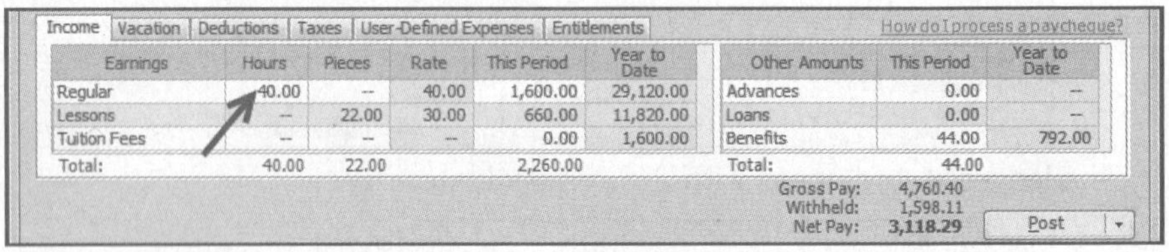
Income | Vacation | Deductions | Taxes | User-Defined Expenses | Entitlements
How do I process a paycheque?
Earnings | Hours | Pieces | Rate | This Period | Year to Date
Regular | 40.00 | 40.00 | 1,600.00 | 29,120.00
Lessons | 22.00 | 30.00 | 660.00 | 11,820.00
Tuition Fees | 0.00 | 1,600.00
Total: | 40.00 | 22.00 | 2,260.00
Other Amounts | This Period | Year to Date
Advances | 0.00
Loans | 0.00
Benefits | 44.00 | 792.00
Total: | 44.00
Gross Pay: 4,760.40
Withheld: 1,598.11
Net Pay: 3,118.29
Post

Click **40.00** in the Regular Hours field. (Double-click if the entire amount is not selected.)

Press *del*. **Press** *tab* to select the entry for number of lessons (Pieces).

Press *del* to remove the entry and update the amounts again.

Click **44.00** in the Benefits This Period field.

Press *del*. **Press** *tab* to update the amounts. The Vacation tab screen opens.

Since deductions should not be taken from vacation pay, Tiste's medical premium amount should also be deleted before printing the cheque and recording the entry. This is a one-time change, and it should be made directly in the journal.

Click the **Deductions tab** to open this screen:

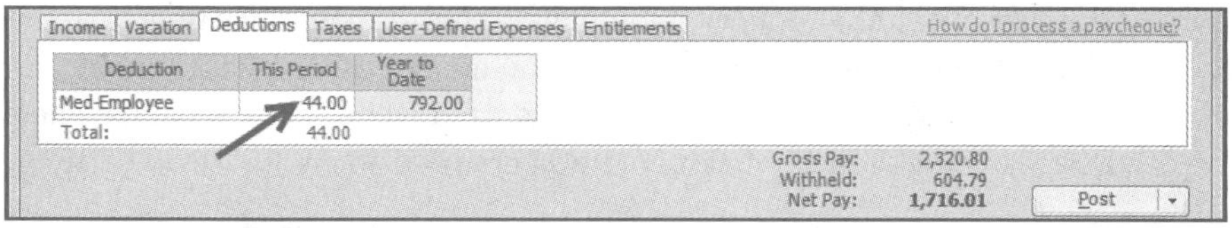

Click the **Med-Employee This Period field entry** to select it.

Press *del* to remove the amount. **Press** *tab* to update the net pay. The Taxes tab screen opens.

Click the **User-Defined Expenses tab**:

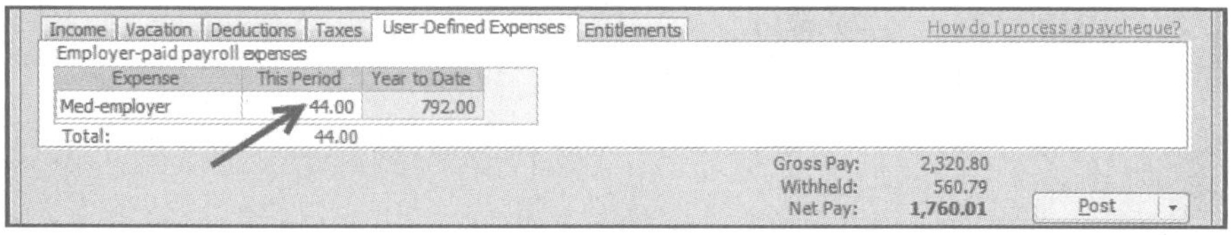

Click the **Med-Employer This Period field entry** to select it.

Press *del* to remove the amount. **Press** *tab* to update the journal and open the Entitlements tab screen:

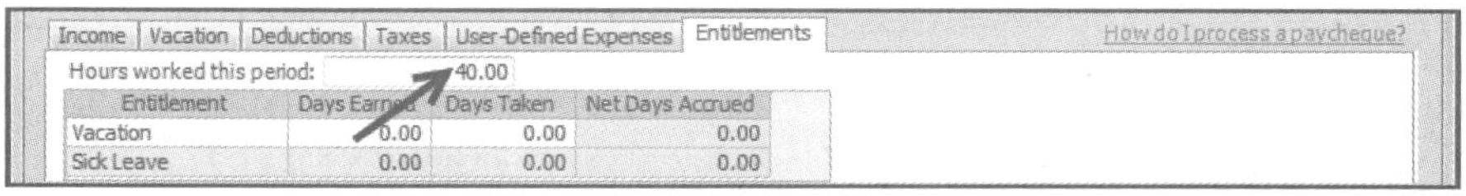

Click **40.00** in the Hours Worked field. **Press** *del* to remove the entry.

For employees with entitlements, this will reduce the Days Earned amounts to zero. We still need to change the dates for the paycheque.

Enter **Oct 17** as the cheque date and **Oct 15** as the Period Ending date.

Click the **Vacation tab** to show the completed journal entry, ready for review:

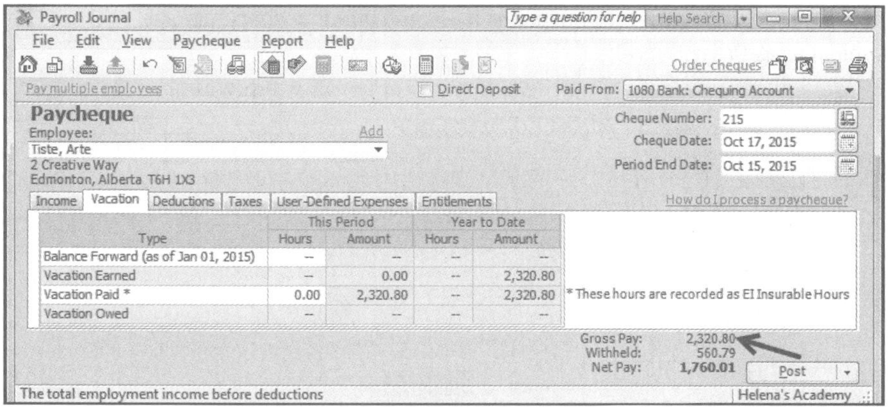

The gross pay amount now matches the vacation paid amount.

Choose the **Report menu** and **click** **Display Payroll Journal Entry**:

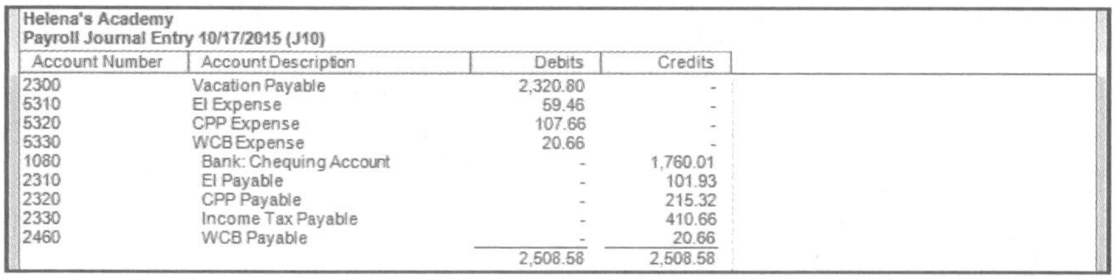
Helena's Academy
Payroll Journal Entry 10/17/2015 (J10)

Account Number	Account Description	Debits	Credits
2300	Vacation Payable	2,320.80	-
5310	EI Expense	59.46	-
5320	CPP Expense	107.66	-
5330	WCB Expense	20.66	-
1080	Bank: Chequing Account	-	1,760.01
2310	EI Payable	-	101.93
2320	CPP Payable	-	215.32
2330	Income Tax Payable	-	410.66
2460	WCB Payable	-	20.66
		2,508.58	2,508.58

NOTES

Tiste, a part-time employee, does not receive entitlements – his entries for days earned are blank. For other employees, delete the number of hours in the Entitlements tab screen because entitlements are not earned on vacation pay.

NOTES

The additional tax amount is still included for this payment. To remove it, you would need to choose Enter Taxes Manually and then edit the income tax amount, or make a temporary change to the entry in the employee's ledger record.

The released vacation pay shows as a debit (decrease) to *Vacation Payable*. Payroll taxes are charged on the vacation pay, as they are on other wages, because taxes were not paid on the retained vacation pay. The employer's expense for vacation pay, a debit to the wages expense account, was recognized when the original paycheque was prepared. At that time *Vacation Payable* was credited to create the liability.

Close the **display** to return to the journal and **make corrections** if necessary.

Click **Post** . **Click Yes** to skip the payroll formula warning.

Close the **Payroll Journal**.

Open the **Ledger** for **Tiste** and **click** the **Income tab**.

Click **Retain Vacation** so that his future paycheques will be entered correctly with vacation pay retained.

Close the **Ledger window** and the **Employees window** if it is open.

Making Payroll Tax Remittances

Sage 50 tracks payroll remittances when the suppliers are linked to payroll taxes. Helena's Academy has five suppliers for whom remittances are due.

✓ 7

Memo #3 **Dated Oct. 17/15**

Make payroll remittances for the pay period ending October 1.
- Receiver General for Canada: EI, CPP and income tax
- Aspen Life Financial: Medical premiums from employee and employer
- Alberta Workers' Compensation Board: WCB
- Rocky Mountain Trust: RRSP
- Maintenance Enforcement Program: Family support payments

Issue cheques #216 to #220.

Taxes are remitted from the Payments Journal. You can open this journal from the Payables module Payments Journal or its Home window shortcuts list, or from the Employees & Payroll module.

We will demonstrate the access from the Payroll window first.

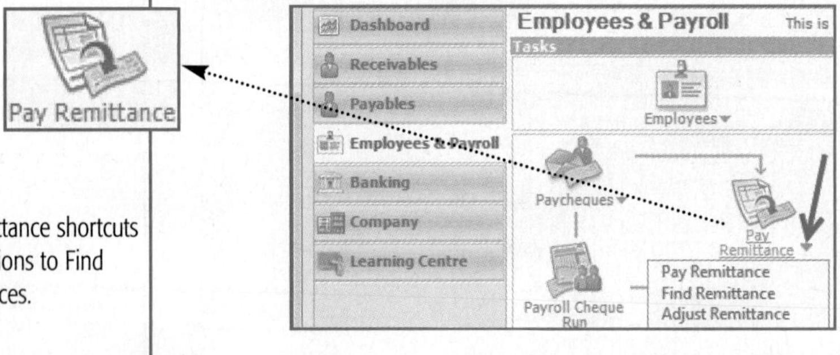

NOTES
The Pay Remittance shortcuts list includes the options to Find and Adjust remittances.

Click the **Pay Remittance icon** to open the Payments Journal form we need.

Click the **To The Order Of list arrow** to see the remittance suppliers:

CLASSIC VIEW
Click the Payments icon  to open the Payments Journal. Then select Pay Remittance from the Pay transaction list to open the journal form we need.

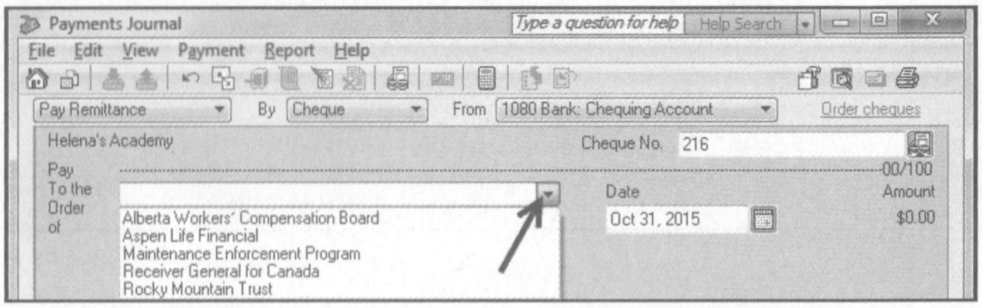

The five suppliers who collect payroll deductions and taxes are listed. The first remittance will be to the Receiver General for EI, CPP and income tax.

Click **Receiver General for Canada** to select the supplier.

The Payments Journal is updated with the taxes collected for this supplier:

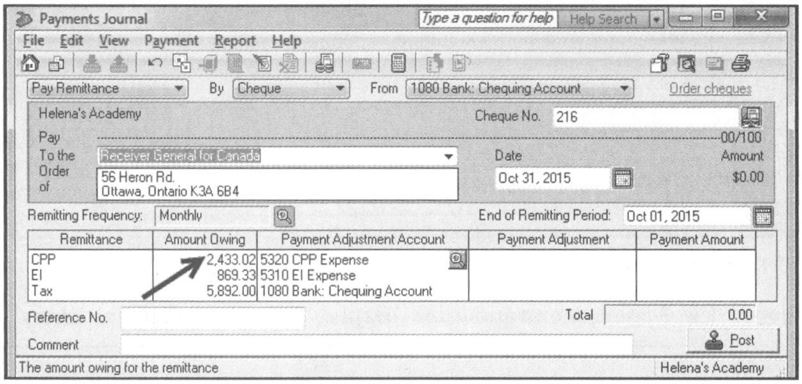

Three taxes are remitted to the Receiver General for Canada. The balances are the amounts in the General Ledger linked accounts as at the remittance period end date, October 1. For Helena's Academy, taxes were not remitted immediately before the files were converted to Sage 50 and the payroll tax liability accounts have outstanding balances. You can see that these balances match the amounts in the Trial Balance for October 1 on page 260. The remitting period and the next payment due date are entered as Payroll Ledger settings.

NOTES
Accept the default amounts in your data file, unless you know that you have made an error in the paycheque. In that case, you should correct the paycheque first.

The Remittance journal has two date fields: one for the date of the cheque and a second below the cheque section for the payroll period covered by the remittance. The session date is the default cheque date. The **End Of Remitting Period date** is entered as a Payroll setting. When you change the End Of Remitting Period date, the amounts will be updated to show the General Ledger amounts at that date. Remittances are usually due one month after the pay period they cover, so we are paying the taxes that were withheld to the end of September. The ending date is updated according to the frequency of payment entered as a Payroll Remittance setting.

NOTES
In Chapter 9, we show how to enter the Payroll Ledger settings.

NOTES
Because the earliest transaction date allowed is October 1, we have not entered September 30 as the date for the end of the remitting period. The amounts for October 1 are the same as the amounts for September 30.

The Payment Adjustment field should be used for any tax expenses that are not already included in the payable account balances. Separate linked accounts may be used for these adjustments. A positive entry will increase the tax expense and the total amount submitted. Negative adjustment amounts will decrease the tax expense amount and the total amount submitted.

The full amount is being paid for each tax.

Click the **Payment Amount column for CPP** to enter the amount owing as the payment amount.

Press ↓ to enter the payment amount for EI.

Press ↓ to enter the payment amount for Tax.

Press *tab* to accept the final payment, update the cheque amount and advance to the Reference No. field.

Type `Memo 3A` **Press** *tab* to advance to the comment field.

Type `Payroll Tax remittance for September`

NOTES
The Reference No. is added for the Remittance Journal report, so you do not need to repeat it in the Comment as we did for Other Payment entries in this journal.

Enter **Oct 17** as the Cheque Date to complete the form:

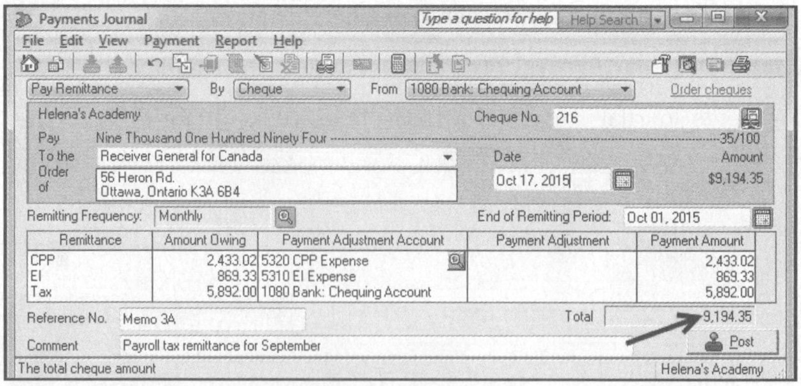

We can now review the journal entry.

Choose the **Report menu** and **click** **Display Payments Journal Entry**:

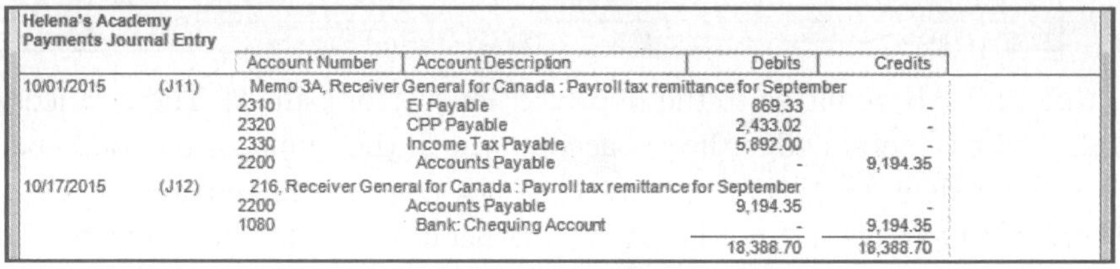
Helena's Academy
Payments Journal Entry

		Account Number	Account Description	Debits	Credits
10/01/2015	(J11)	Memo 3A, Receiver General for Canada : Payroll tax remittance for September			
		2310	EI Payable	869.33	-
		2320	CPP Payable	2,433.02	-
		2330	Income Tax Payable	5,892.00	-
		2200	Accounts Payable	-	9,194.35
10/17/2015	(J12)	216, Receiver General for Canada : Payroll tax remittance for September			
		2200	Accounts Payable	9,194.35	-
		1080	Bank: Chequing Account	-	9,194.35
				18,388.70	18,388.70

NOTES

Amounts entered in the Payment Adjustment field affect the balances in the linked adjustment accounts and not the liability account balances. For Helena's Academy, we are using the related expense account for adjustments to the employer's liability amounts and the Bank account for adjustments to employee deductions.

You must identify a linked account if you enter a payment adjustment.

The remittance creates two journal entries. The three liability accounts have been debited to reduce the liability, and *Accounts Payable* is credited with Oct. 1 as the effective date. If you had entered adjustments, those amounts would be debited (for positive adjustments) to the corresponding linked account. The second entry recognizes the payment on the cheque date, Oct. 17 — it clears the *Accounts Payable* balance with a credit entry to the Bank account.

Close the **display** when finished.

NOTES

You can adjust and reverse remittance payments just as you can other payments when the Remittance Payment Journal is open, but not when another type of payment transaction is selected.

From the Payments icon shortcuts list in the Payables window, the option to Find Payment will show all payment entries. Select the remittance to view the transaction you want and then click the Adjust or Reverse tool from the lookup window.

CORRECTING THE PAYROLL REMITTANCE

Move the cursor to the field that contains the error. **Double-click** or **drag through** the **incorrect information** to highlight it. **Type** the **correct information** and **press** (tab) to enter it. **Enter** a different **remittance end period date** if this is appropriate to enter the amounts owing for that date.

You can discard the entry by **clicking** [X] **(Close)** or [↶] **(Undo)** or by returning to the Supplier list and **clicking** a **different supplier** name. **Click** the name of the **correct remittance supplier** and **press** (tab). When prompted, confirm that you want to discard the incorrect entry. **Click** **Yes**, and start again.

You can adjust a remittance **after posting** as you can other payments. **Choose** **Adjust Remittance** from the Pay Remittances icon shortcuts list. Or open the Pay Remittance journal and **click** the **Adjust Remittance tool** or **choose** the **Payment menu** and **choose** **Adjust Remittance**. **Enter** the search **criteria** you want to show the list of payments. Only remittances appear on this list. **Select** the **remittance** that requires correction and **make** the **changes** you need. **Post** the revised correction after reviewing it.

From the journal Report menu you can also display the Remittance Report, the same report that you get from the Home window Reports menu or Report Centre. If you display this report before posting the payment, the payment amount will still be zero. First, we must make corrections and post the payment.

Make **corrections** if necessary and then **post** the **payment**.

Choose the **Report menu** and **click** **Display Remittance Report**:

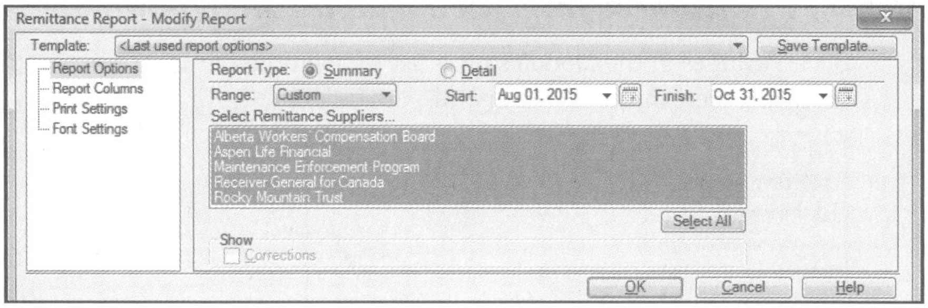

You can display a **Summary Report** with total amounts for each tax, or a **Detail Report** with a line entry for each tax for each payroll transaction in the report period. You can prepare the report for one or more payroll authorities, and you can choose a remittance period for the report. We can accept the default dates — we want the report for October. Only one remittance was posted so we will view the Summary Report for the Receiver General to see the remittance we just completed.

Click **Receiver General For Canada** and then **click OK** to see the report:

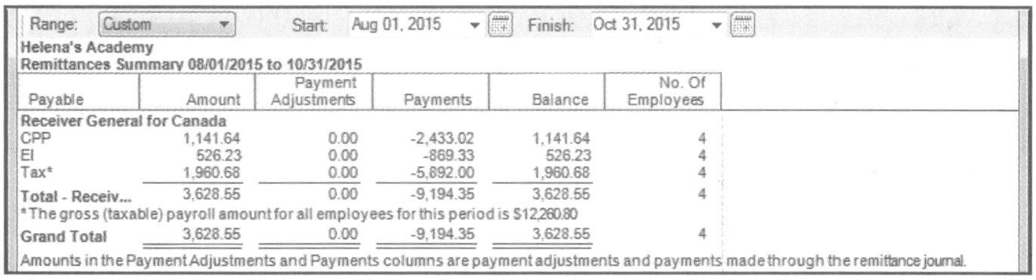
Range: Custom Start: Aug 01, 2015 Finish: Oct 31, 2015

Helena's Academy
Remittances Summary 08/01/2015 to 10/31/2015

Payable	Amount	Payment Adjustments	Payments	Balance	No. Of Employees
Receiver General for Canada					
CPP	1,141.64	0.00	-2,433.02	1,141.64	4
EI	526.23	0.00	-869.33	526.23	4
Tax*	1,960.68	0.00	-5,892.00	1,960.68	4
Total - Receiv...	3,628.55	0.00	-9,194.35	3,628.55	4
*The gross (taxable) payroll amount for all employees for this period is $12,260.80					
Grand Total	3,628.55	0.00	-9,194.35	3,628.55	4

Amounts in the Payment Adjustments and Payments columns are payment adjustments and payments made through the remittance journal.

The report shows the total of Payroll Journal entry amounts for all tax, adjustments, payments and final balances. The new balances are the total amounts for the October paycheques for the four employees and the vacation pay for Tiste.

Close the **report** when finished to return to the Payments Journal.

Choose **Aspen Life Financial** as the supplier for the next remittance.

Pay the **two Medical premium amounts**. The dates Oct. 1 and Oct. 17 should be correct from the previous remittance.

Enter **Memo 3B** in the Reference field and **enter** an appropriate **comment**.

Review and then **post** the **payment**.

Choose **Alberta Workers' Compensation Board** as the supplier.

Pay the **WCB amount**.

Enter **Memo 3C** in the Reference field and **enter** an appropriate **comment**.

Review and then **post** the **payment**.

Choose **Rocky Mountain Trust** as the supplier for the next remittance.

Pay the **RRSP contributions** withheld.

Enter **Memo 3D** in the Reference field and **enter** an appropriate **comment**.

Review and then **post** the **payment**.

Choose **Maintenance Enforcement Program** as the supplier.

Pay the **Family Support payments** withheld.

Enter **Memo 3E** in the Reference field and **enter** an appropriate **comment**.

Review and then **post** the **payment**. **Close** the **Payments Journal**.

NOTES

The Amount column entries in the report reflect only the amounts from Payroll Journal entries for the four paycheques on Oct. 15 and Tiste's vacation pay. They do not include the opening balance forward amounts.

The note reminds us that the report accounts only for transactions completed with the Pay Remittance feature.

NOTES

If you choose Receiver General For Canada again as the supplier, you will see that the remitting period date has been advanced by one month and the current account balances are displayed.

NOTES

The Medical liability has two entries, one for the employee's share and one for the employer's share.

Entering Remittances from the Payables Module Window

Click Payables in the Modules pane list to open the Payables window. Click the Payments icon shortcuts list arrow:

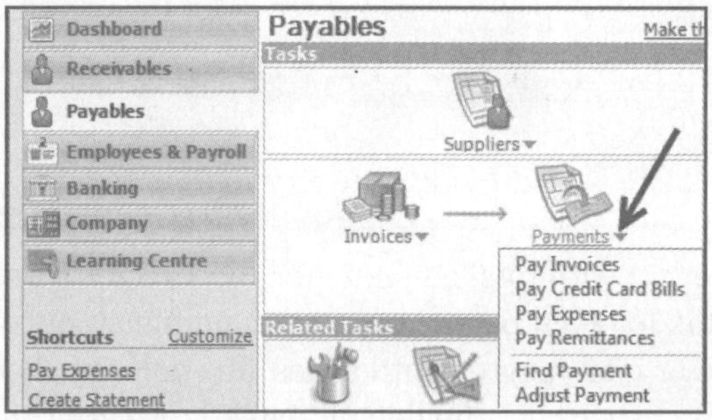

The shortcuts include Pay Remittances. Click Pay Remittances to modify the Payments Journal.

You can also click the Payments icon  to open the Payments Journal. Once the Journal is open, click Pay Invoices to see the payment types:

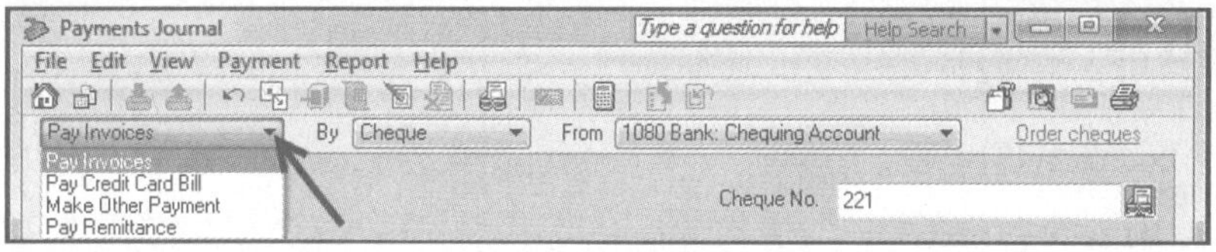

Click Pay Remittance to modify the Payments Journal. Choose the remittance supplier and continue with the remittance entry as outlined above.

Enter the **next two cash purchase transactions** and then close the journal.

8

Cash Purchase Invoice #ESS-4689 **Dated Oct. 18/15**

From Energy Supply Services, $810 including taxes for heat and hydro on equal monthly billing plan. Store as a recurring monthly entry. Paid by cheque #221.

9

Cash Purchase #TA-113368 **Dated Oct. 20/15**

From Telus Alberta, $220 including all taxes for one month of telephone services. Invoice total paid in full with cheque #222.

Completing a Payroll Cheque Run

When several employees are paid at the same time, you can complete a payroll cheque run to prepare all the cheques and journal entries in a single transaction.

Click **Employees & Payroll** in the Modules list to return to the default page.

The Payroll Run Journal, shown with the pointer in the following screen, is used to pay multiple employees:

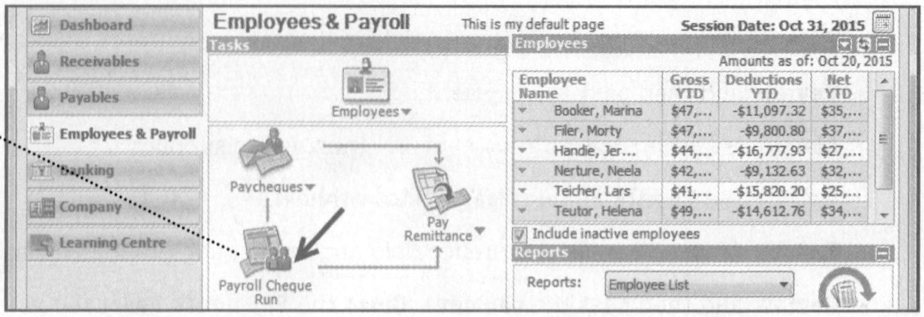

NOTES

The Payroll Cheque Run icon does not have a shortcuts list.

Notice that the details in the Home window Employees list have been updated. You can hide these year-to-date details for employees as you do for vendors and customers from the Employees list pane arrow button:

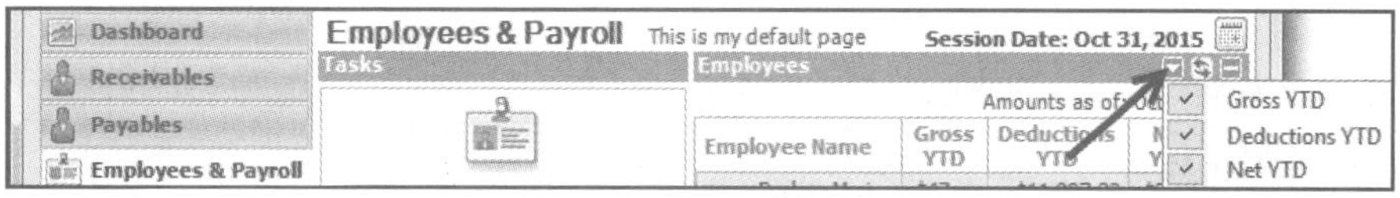

Click the **Payroll Cheque Run icon** to open the Payroll Run Journal:

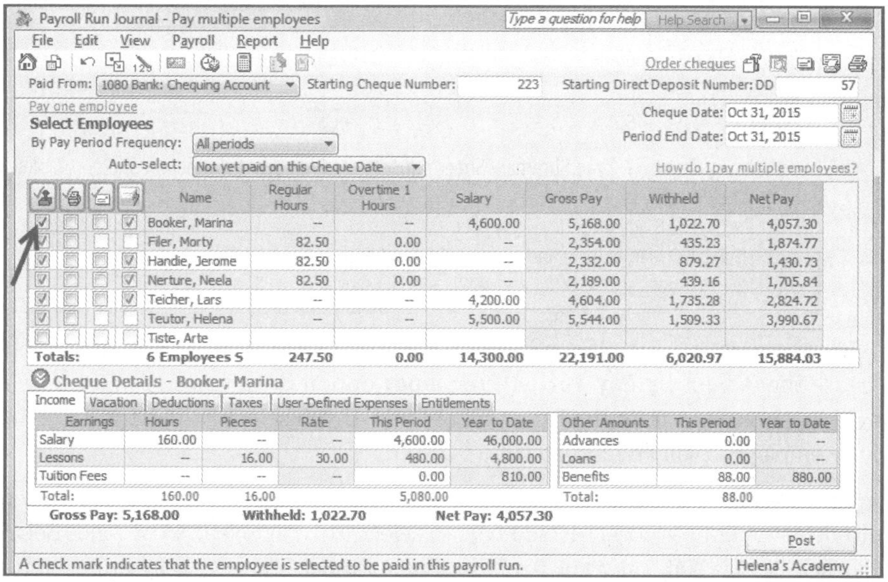

From this screen, you can pay all employees, and you can enter or edit any details that you can enter or edit in the Payroll Journal. Employees are listed in alphabetic order and checkmarks indicate who will be paid in this payroll run and who has selected direct deposits instead of cheques. The upper journal pane lists all active employees with summary information for each. You can edit three details directly in the summary pane without opening the cheque details — the number of regular and overtime hours for hourly paid employees and salary amounts for salaried employees. This offers a quick way to complete simple payroll runs.

You cannot change the Gross Pay, Net Pay or Withheld amounts. Sage 50 calculates these from the details you enter.

The lower pane shows the cheque details for the selected employee with tabs that mirror the tabs in the Payroll Journal. Because Booker is selected, her cheque details are shown initially. To change details not shown in the summary pane — the other details that are available in the Payroll Journal — you can access fields by selecting an employee and the appropriate tab screen.

The summary on the following page shows that all employees are being paid on October 31.

PRO VERSION

pro

The Refresh tool applies to multi-user operation of the program. It does not apply in the single-user Pro version. The Time Slips tool also does not appear in the Pro version.

NOTES

The Payroll Run Journal has a link below the tool bar to switch to the Payroll Journal if you want to Pay One Employee.

You must use the Payroll Journal to edit tax amounts or previous payroll entries.

NOTES

You cannot adjust or reverse paycheques from the Payroll Run Journal – Adjust and Reverse entry tools are not included in the tool bar. However, paycheques prepared here can be adjusted in the Paycheques Journal. See page 294.

The Manually Calculate Taxes tool is also omitted from the tool bar. Taxes cannot be changed in the Payroll Run Journal.

> **NOTES**
> The October 31 paycheque included 11 days for hourly paid employees – 82.5 regular hours.

✓ 10

Employee Time Summary Sheet #20 **Dated Oct. 31/15**

For the pay period ending October 31, 2015

Name of Employee	Regular Hours	Overtime Hours	Lessons	Tuition	Advance (Repaid)	Loan (Repaid)	Sick Days	Direct Deposit
Filer, Morty	82.5	2	–	$125.00	($50)	–	–	No
Handie, Jerome	82.5	2	–	–	–	–	–	Yes
Nerture, Neela	82.5	–	–	–	–	–	–	Yes
Tiste, Arte	44.0	–	22	–	–	$100	–	No
Booker, Marina	160	–	16	$120.00	–	–	1	Yes
Teicher, Lars	160	–	12	–	–	–	–	Yes
Teutor, Helena	160	–	–	–	–	–	–	No

a. Using Employee Time Summary Sheet #20 and the Employee Information Sheet, complete payroll for all employees.
b. Recover $50 advanced to Morty Filer.
c. Issue $100 loan to Tiste and recover $25 from each of the next four paycheques.
d. Issue cheques #223, #224 and #225 and DD slips #57, #58, #59 and #60.

The program selects all employees for inclusion if their pay cycle has ended because the default **By Pay Period Frequency** option is All Periods. You can select any single pay frequency from the list, or all of them. If you select 24 periods, only the four hourly employees will be marked with a ✓.

Initially, all employees have a ✓ in the **Post column** except Tiste. From the Auto-Select options you can decide how to select the employees to be paid. Because the initial selection is **Not Yet Paid On This Cheque Date**, Tiste is excluded — he received his vacation pay after October 15.

Click the **Auto-Select list arrow**:

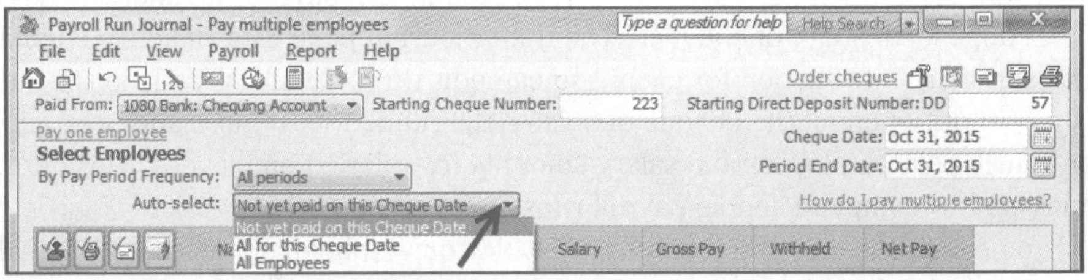

You can select all employees, all employees who should be paid on this date or all employees not yet paid for this cheque date.

Click **All For This Cheque Date**. Tiste is now marked for payment too.

The form also includes deposit information in the **Direct Deposit column**. A ✓ in this column indicates that the pay will be deposited to the employee's bank account. Both the next Cheque and Direct Deposit Numbers are on the form.

For direct deposit employees, you can check the **E-mail column** if you e-mail the cheque stubs to them. This check box is dimmed for employees paid by cheque.

The cheque date, pay period end date and initial cheque and deposit numbers can all be edited if necessary.

> **PRO VERSION**
> The cheque date cannot be later than the session date.

You can remove an employee from the payroll run by clicking the ✓ in the Post column to remove it. You can change the direct deposit status for an employee by clicking the ✓ in the Direct Deposit column to remove it. A cheque will then be created instead.

Click **Filer** to select this employee. His income details are shown:

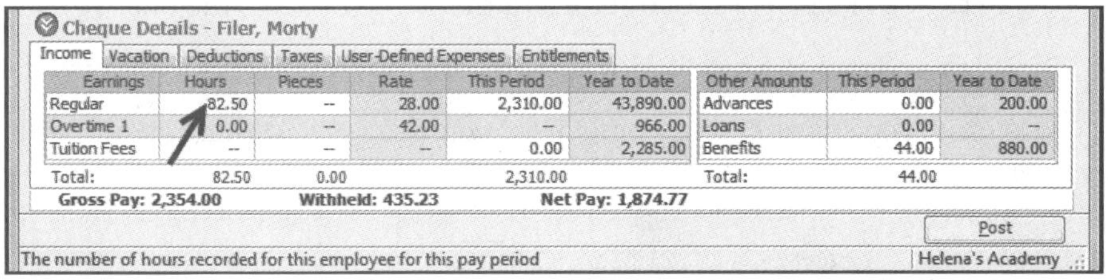
Cheque Details - Filer, Morty

Income | Vacation | Deductions | Taxes | User-Defined Expenses | Entitlements

Earnings	Hours	Pieces	Rate	This Period	Year to Date	Other Amounts	This Period	Year to Date
Regular	82.50	--	28.00	2,310.00	43,890.00	Advances	0.00	200.00
Overtime 1	0.00	--	42.00	--	966.00	Loans	0.00	--
Tuition Fees	--	--	--	0.00	2,285.00	Benefits	44.00	880.00
Total:	82.50	0.00		2,310.00		Total:	44.00	

Gross Pay: 2,354.00 Withheld: 435.23 Net Pay: 1,874.77

Post

The number of hours recorded for this employee for this pay period | Helena's Academy

This screen is just like Filer's Income tab screen in the Payroll Journal as shown on page 267, and we can enter or edit all the amounts in the same way as in that journal. For Filer, we need to add the overtime hours, the tuition fee amount and the advances repayment. All these details are entered in the Income tab screen.

Click **0.00** in the **Hours column beside Overtime 1**. **Type** 2

Press *tab* to select the Tuition Fees amount.

Type 125 **Press** *tab* to select the Advances amount.

By default, –200.00, the entire amount owing, is entered. Filer is repaying $50 each pay period so we must change the amount.

Type -50

Click the **Vacation tab**:

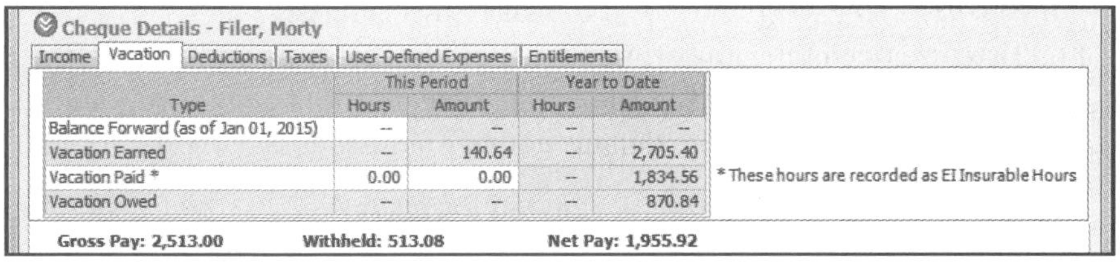
Cheque Details - Filer, Morty

Income | Vacation | Deductions | Taxes | User-Defined Expenses | Entitlements

Type	This Period Hours	This Period Amount	Year to Date Hours	Year to Date Amount
Balance Forward (as of Jan 01, 2015)	--	--	--	--
Vacation Earned	--	140.64	--	2,705.40
Vacation Paid *	0.00	0.00	--	1,834.56
Vacation Owed	--	--	--	870.84

* These hours are recorded as EI Insurable Hours

Gross Pay: 2,513.00 Withheld: 513.08 Net Pay: 1,955.92

Vacation amounts are calculated and updated automatically.

Click the **Deductions tab**:

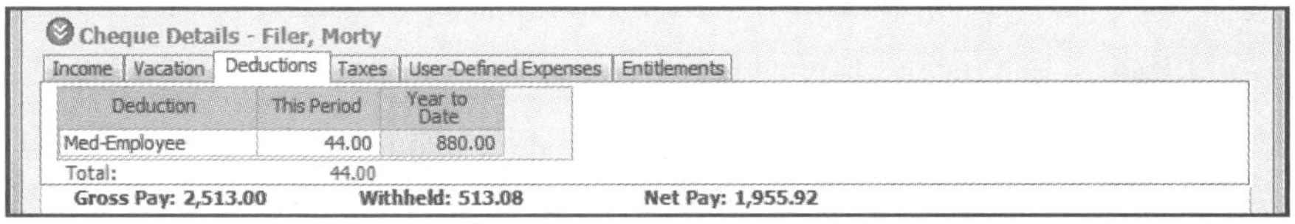
Cheque Details - Filer, Morty

Income | Vacation | Deductions | Taxes | User-Defined Expenses | Entitlements

Deduction	This Period	Year to Date
Med-Employee	44.00	880.00
Total:	44.00	

Gross Pay: 2,513.00 Withheld: 513.08 Net Pay: 1,955.92

We do not need to change these amounts, but you can see that the deduction amounts are available for editing.

Click the **Taxes tab**:

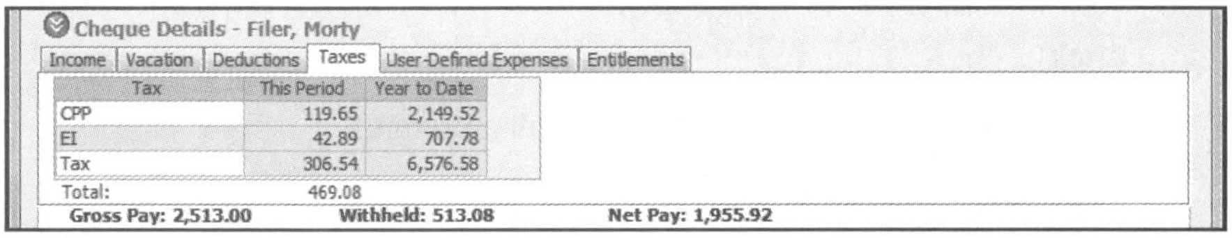
Cheque Details - Filer, Morty

Income | Vacation | Deductions | Taxes | User-Defined Expenses | Entitlements

Tax	This Period	Year to Date
CPP	119.65	2,149.52
EI	42.89	707.78
Tax	306.54	6,576.58
Total:	469.08	

Gross Pay: 2,513.00 Withheld: 513.08 Net Pay: 1,955.92

Taxes cannot be edited in the Payroll Run Journal. If you need to change tax amounts, you must use the Payroll Journal and choose to calculate taxes manually.

Click the **User-Defined Expenses tab**:

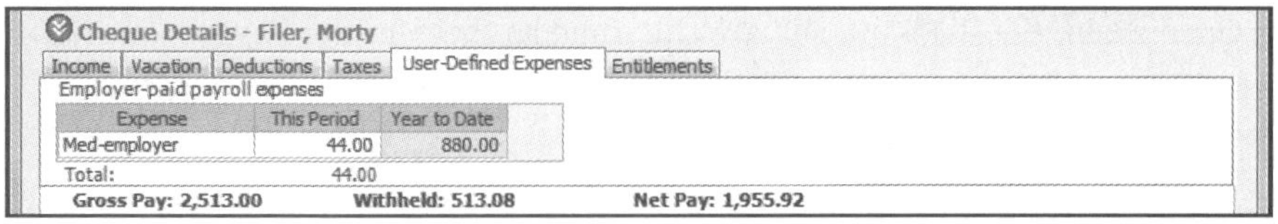
Cheque Details - Filer, Morty

Income | Vacation | Deductions | Taxes | User-Defined Expenses | Entitlements

Employer-paid payroll expenses

Expense	This Period	Year to Date
Med-employer	44.00	880.00
Total:	44.00	

Gross Pay: 2,513.00 Withheld: 513.08 Net Pay: 1,955.92

The employer's expense for the medical premium is included here and can be edited if required. Entitlements can also be edited, as we will see for Booker.

NOTES

Clicking the employee name will open the tab screen for that employee directly. Then you can change to any other tab screen if you want.

WARNING!

Remember to enter a negative number for advances that are repaid.

Each time you enter a partial repayment for an advance, Sage 50 will show the warning on pages 270 and 288. Click Yes.

Click the **Income tab** to return to this screen — it is the one we use most.

Click **Handie** to select him and prepare for entering his additional details.

As soon as you select another employee, you will see a warning about partial payments of advances:

NOTES
We chose the partial repayment method so that you can see the various warning and confirmation messages in Sage 50.

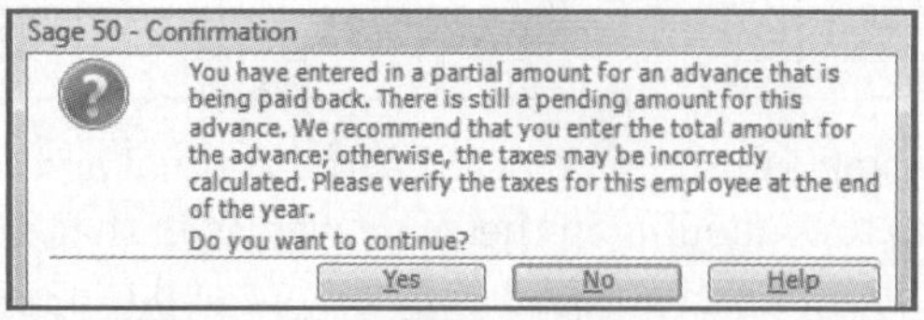

The warning advises that the entire amount of an advance should be repaid at one time to facilitate the calculation of taxes.

Click **Yes** to continue.

We need to update the number of overtime hours for Handie. We can change this in the upper summary pane. Handie is already selected.

Press *tab* to highlight his number of Regular Hours.

Press *tab* to select the Overtime Hours entry for Handie.

Type 2 to enter the Overtime hours. **Press** *tab* to update all amounts.

For Nerture's pay, we do not need to make any changes.

For Tiste, we need to change the number of regular hours and include the loan. We can change the number of hours in the upper pane, but we need to work in the Cheque Details pane to add the loan. The default number of lessons is correct.

Click **Tiste** to open the Income tab Earnings fields in the Cheque Details.

Click **0.00 beside Loans** in the This Period column of the Cheque Details pane.

Type 100 **Press** *tab* to update all amounts.

Click **Booker** to prepare for entering the additional details for her.

The Income tab should still be open. Income details for Booker are shown in the journal screen on page 285.

Booker is a salaried employee who also teaches music lessons after school. Her regular salary is entered as the default, but the amount can be edited if necessary in the Cheque Details pane or in the summary pane. We need to add her tuition fees benefit and enter one day of sick leave.

Click **0.00** in the Tuition Fees This Period column.

Type 120 **Press** *tab* to update all amounts.

Click the **Entitlements tab** to open the entitlements fields:

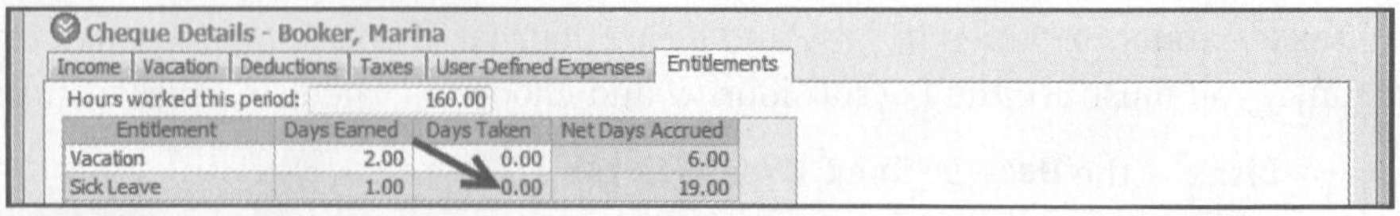

NOTES
Remember that the entry for Days Earned reflects only the amount earned for this pay period based on the number of hours worked in this pay period.

Once again, the fields we see are the same as those in the Payroll Journal Entitlements tab screen (see page 272).

Click the **Days Taken field beside Sick Leave**.

Type 1 **Press** *tab* to update the form, reducing the number of Net Days Accrued to 18.

No changes are required for Teicher or Teutor's salaried paycheques, so the transaction is complete and should look like the one we show here:

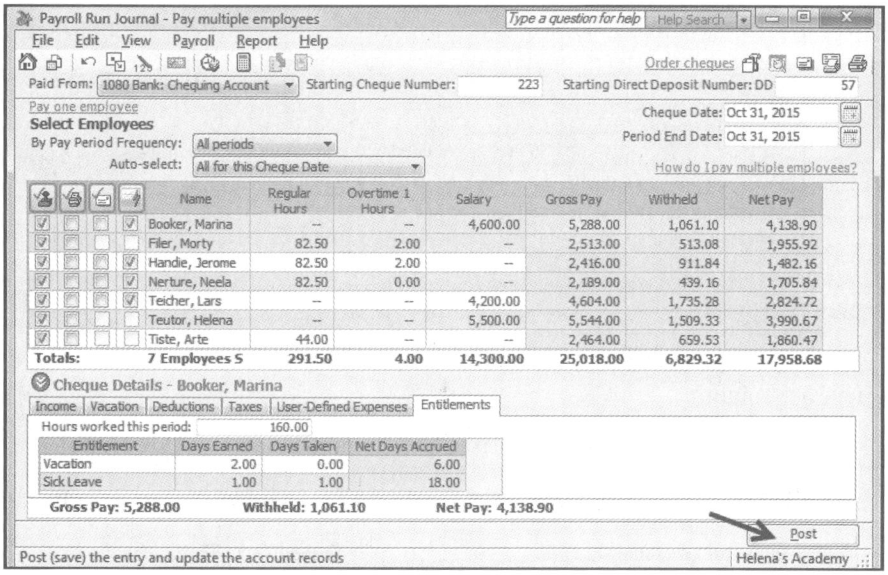

You are now ready to review the journal entry.

Choose the **Report menu** and **click Display Payroll Journal Entry** to review the journal entry.

There are seven journal entries, one for each employee in the payroll run.

Close the **display** when finished.

You can print paycheques from the Payroll Run Journal, but you cannot preview them. You can modify the reports and forms setting from the journal by using the tool button.

Turn on your **printer**.

Choose the **Report menu** and **click Print Payroll Cheque Run Summary** to provide a printed record of the payroll run transactions paid by cheque or **click Print Direct Deposit Stub Summary** to provide a printed record of the payroll run transactions paid by direct deposit. You cannot display these summaries.

Click **Post** [Post] to save the transaction. **Click Yes** to bypass the warning about payroll formula dates.

The confirmation message advises that seven journal entries were posted. The Payroll Run Journal remains open with the direct deposit and cheque numbers updated after the payroll run cheques and direct deposits. All employees are still selected with pay amounts because of the Auto-Select entry.

Choose **Not Yet Paid On This Cheque Date** from the Auto-Select list.

NOTES

To print paycheques and deposit slip stubs from the Payroll Run Journal, click the Print check box in the second column beside the employee's name. Then click the Print tool, press ctrl + P or choose the File menu and click Print Payroll Cheques.

The updated form is displayed :

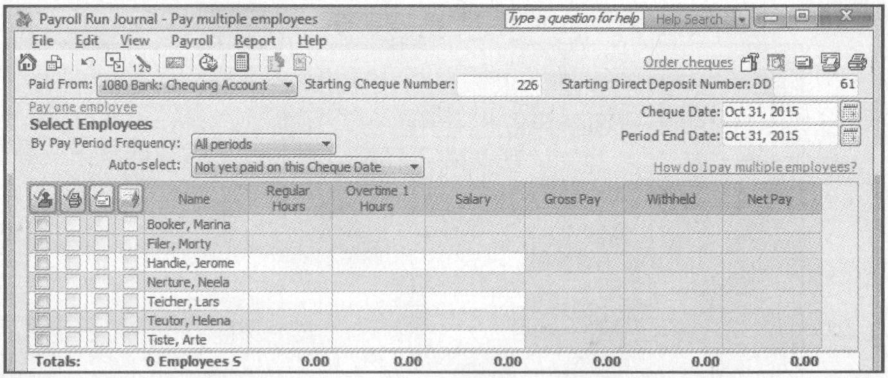

Now, no employees are selected because they have all been paid. There are no ✓s in the Post column.

Close the **Journal** to return to the Home window.

Enter the following **source documents** for October 31 and November 15.

11

Bank Debit Memo #277581 **Dated Oct. 31/15**

From Scholar Heights Bank, $4 235 was withdrawn from chequing account for the following pre-authorized transactions:

Bank Charges	$ 35
Interest on Bank Loan	320
Reduction of Principal on Bank Loan	880
Interest on Mortgage	2 500
Reduction of Principal on Mortgage	500

Store as a recurring monthly entry.

12

Bank Credit Memo #467116 **Dated Oct. 31/15**

From Scholar Heights Bank, $1 890 interest on investments and bank account was deposited to chequing account. Store as a recurring monthly entry.

NOTES
Remember that when you store adjusting entries, you must edit the source and amounts when you recall the transaction.

13

Memo #4 **Dated Oct. 31/15**

Complete end-of-month adjusting entries for the following:

Office supplies used	$180
Art supplies used	335
Textbooks damaged	185
Prepaid property taxes	900

You can store this as a recurring monthly entry if you want.

SESSION DATE – NOVEMBER 15, 2015

14

Cash Sales Invoice #1037 **Dated Nov. 1/15**

To parents of students, $3 200 total monthly fees for after-school programs, and $2 280 total monthly fees for individual music lessons. Deposited $5 480 to chequing account.

15

Cash Purchase Invoice #GL-38827-B **Dated Nov. 2/15**

To Global Liability Inc., $1 800 for monthly insurance premium as stated on policy #GL-38827. Paid by cheque #226. Recall stored entry.

16

Cash Purchase Invoice #ES-1446 **Dated Nov. 15/15**

From Engine Services (use Quick Add), $220 including taxes for gasoline, tire repairs, oil change and lubrication on school vehicle. Invoice total paid in full with cheque #227.

☐ 17

HELENA'S ACADEMY

Aim higher!

Employee Time Summary Sheet
Business No.: 189 245 053 RP 0001

#21
Cheque Date: November 15, 2015 Last day of pay period end: November 15, 2015

Employee SIN	M. Filer 374 588 127	J. Handie 813 402 302	N. Nerture 129 495 768	A. Tiste 513 288 191	H. Teutor 699 344 578	M. Booker 277 639 118	L. Teicher 403 401 599

Nov 2-6	37.5	39.5	37.5	20			
Nov 9-13	37.5	39.5	37.5	20			

Reg. hrs	75.0	75.0	75.0	40			
Overtime	--	4	--	--			
Lessons	--	--	--	22			
Tuition	125.00	--	--	--			
Loan	--	--	--	-25.00			
Advance	-50.00	--	--	--			
Sick leave	--	--	1	--			
Chq/DD #	Chq 228	DD61	DD62	Chq 229			

Payroll Prepared by: Morty Filer Nov 15/15

When you open the Payroll Run Journal for the November 15 pay period, the four hourly paid employees will be selected, as shown:

Pay one employee
Select Employees
By Pay Period Frequency: All periods
Auto-select: Not yet paid on this Cheque Date
Cheque Date: Nov 15, 2015
Period End Date: Nov 15, 2015
How do I pay multiple employees?

				Name	Regular Hours	Overtime 1 Hours	Salary	Gross Pay	Withheld	Net Pay
☐	☐	☐	☐	Booker, Marina						
☑	☐	☐	☐	Filer, Morty	82.50	0.00	--	2,354.00	435.23	1,874.77
☑	☐	☐	☑	Handie, Jerome	82.50	0.00	--	2,332.00	879.27	1,430.73
☑	☐	☐	☑	Nerture, Neela	82.50	0.00	--	2,189.00	439.16	1,705.84
☐	☐	☐	☐	Teicher, Lars						
☐	☐	☐	☐	Teutor, Helena						
☑	☐	☐	☐	Tiste, Arte	40.00	--	--	2,304.00	597.48	1,662.52
Totals:				4 Employees 5	287.50	0.00	0.00	6,875.00	1,753.66	5,011.34

The salaried employees are not due to be paid until November 30 and are not selected.

Advance the **session date** to **November 30**; **make** a **backup**. **Continue** entering **transactions** up to the payroll adjustment for Dec. 17.

☐ 18

Memo #5 **Dated Nov. 17/15**

Make payroll remittances for the pay period ending October 31.
Receiver General for Canada: CPP, EI and income tax
Aspen Life Financial: Medical premiums from employee and employer
Alberta Workers' Compensation Board: WCB
Rocky Mountain Trust: RRSP
Maintenance Enforcement Program: Family support payments
Issue cheques #230 to #234.

☐ 19

Cash Purchase Invoice #ESS-5568 **Dated Nov. 18/15**

From Energy Supply Services, $810 including taxes for heat and hydro on equal monthly billing plan. Recall the stored entry. Paid by cheque #235.

WARNING!

Remember to change the number of regular hours from 82.5 to 75 for Income (Regular Hours) and Entitlements. This pay period included 10 days for hourly paid employees.

NOTES

Type –50 in the Advances This Period field for Filer and –25 in the Loans This Period field for Tiste to recover these amounts.

NOTES

You can change the number of hours directly on the Payroll Run Journal summary screen by typing 75 in the Hours column to replace 82.5.

NOTES

Tiste's amounts are not included in the totals. If you choose 24 as the Pay Period Frequency, his amounts will be added. You can also click his selection box and then click it again to add his amounts. His name is selected, so you can enter his payroll details.

NOTES

You will see the warning about the partial repayment of Filer's advance amount again.

NOTES

The default date entry for the End Of Remitting Period is November 1, one month past the previous October 1 remittance. If you enter October 31 instead, you will see the message that the date precedes the current period because October 31 is in the previous month. You can click Yes to confirm that this is correct or you can accept November 1 as the remittance period ending date.

20

Cash Purchase #TA-193245 **Dated Nov. 20/15**

From Telus Alberta, $165 including all taxes for one month of telephone services. Invoice total paid in full with cheque #236.

21

HELENA'S ACADEMY

Aim higher!

Employee Time Summary Sheet
Business No.: 189 245 053 RP 0001

#22
Cheque Date: November 30, 2015

Last day of pay period end: November 30, 2015

Employee	M. Filer	J. Handie	N. Nerture	A. Tiste	H. Teutor	M. Booker	L. Teicher
SIN	374 588 127	813 402 302	129 495 768	513 288 191	699 344 578	277 639 118	403 401 599
Nov 2-6	pd	pd	pd	pd	➸	➸	➸
Nov 9-13	pd	pd	pd	pd	➸	➸	➸
Nov 16-20	37.5	39.5	41.5	20	➸	➸	➸
Nov 23-27	37.5	37.5	39.5	20	➸	➸	➸
Nov 30	7.5	7.5	7.5	4	➸	➸	➸
Reg. hrs	82.5	82.5	82.5	44	160	160	160
Overtime	--	2	6	--	--	--	--
Lessons	--	--	--	22	--	16	12
Tuition	125.00	--	--	--	--	120.00	--
Advance	-50.00	--	--	--	--	--	--
Loan	--	--	--	-25.00	--	--	--
Sick leave	--	--	1	--	--	--	--
Chq/DD #	Chq 237	DD64	DD65	Chq 239	Chq 238	DD63	DD66

Payroll Prepared by: Morty Filer Nov 30/15

NOTES

Type –50 in the Advances This Period field for Filer and –25 in the Loans This Period field for Tiste to recover these amounts.

The November 30 pay period included 11 days for hourly workers.

22

Bank Debit Memo #422344 **Dated Nov. 30/15**

From Scholar Heights Bank, $4 235 was withdrawn from chequing account for the following pre-authorized transactions. Recall the stored entry.

Bank Charges	$ 35
Interest on Bank Loan	320
Reduction of Principal on Bank Loan	880
Interest on Mortgage	2 500
Reduction of Principal on Mortgage	500

23

Bank Credit Memo #64567 **Dated Nov. 30/15**

From Scholar Heights Bank, $1 890 interest on investments and bank account was deposited to chequing account. Recall the stored entry.

24

Memo #6 **Dated Nov. 30/15**

Complete end-of-month adjusting entries for the following:

Office supplies used	$275
Art supplies used	180
Textbooks damaged	110
Prepaid property taxes	900

SESSION DATE – DECEMBER 15, 2015

When you approach the end of a calendar year, you will see the year-end advisor message — it may include information about renewing the payroll plan:

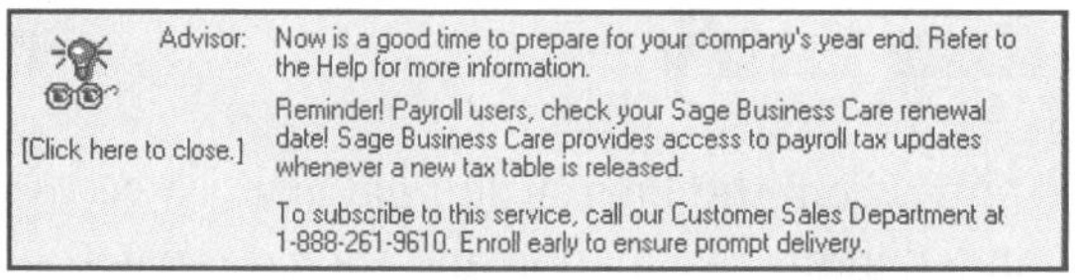
Advisor:
[Click here to close.]
Now is a good time to prepare for your company's year end. Refer to the Help for more information.
Reminder! Payroll users, check your Sage Business Care renewal date! Sage Business Care provides access to payroll tax updates whenever a new tax table is released.
To subscribe to this service, call our Customer Sales Department at 1-888-261-9610. Enroll early to ensure prompt delivery.

Payroll taxes are updated every six months and these updates should be downloaded regularly in an active business.

25 **Cash Sales Invoice #1038** **Dated Dec. 1/15**

To parents of students, $2 400 total monthly fees for after-school programs, and $1 580 total monthly fees for individual music lessons. Deposited $3 980 to chequing account.

26 **Cash Purchase Invoice #GL-38827-C** **Dated Dec. 2/15**

To Global Liability Inc., $1 800 for monthly insurance premium as stated on policy #GL-38827. Paid by cheque #240. Recall the stored entry.

27

HELENA'S ACADEMY

Aim higher!

Employee Time Summary Sheet
Business No.: 189 245 053 RP 0001

#23
Cheque Date: December 15, 2015 Last day of pay period end: December 15, 2015

Employee	M. Filer	J. Handie	N. Nerture	A. Tiste	H. Teutor	M. Booker	L. Teicher
SIN	374 588 127	813 402 302	129 495 768	513 288 191	699 344 578	277 639 118	403 401 599
Dec 1-4	28.0	29.0	28.0	16			
Dec 7-11	37.5	38.5	41.5	20			
Dec 14-15	15.0	15.0	16.0	8			

Reg. hrs	82.5	82.5	82.5	44			
Overtime	--	2	5	--			
Lessons	--	--	--	22			
Tuition	125.00	--	--	--			
Loan	--	--	--	-25.00			
Advance	-50.00	--	--	--			
Sick leave	--	--	--	--			
Chq/DD #	Chq 241	DD67	DD68	Chq 242			

Payroll Prepared by: Morty Filer Dec 15/15

NOTES

Type –50 in the Advances This Period field for Filer and –25 in the Loans This Period for Tiste to recover these amounts.

The December 15 pay period includes 11 days for hourly paid employees.

SESSION DATE – DECEMBER 31, 2015

28 **Memo #7** **Dated Dec. 17/15**

Make payroll remittances for the pay period ending November 30.

Receiver General for Canada: CPP, EI and income tax
Aspen Life Financial: Medical premiums from employee and employer
Alberta Workers' Compensation Board: WCB
Rocky Mountain Trust: RRSP
Maintenance Enforcement Program: Family support payments

Issue cheques #243 to #247.

Adjusting a Payroll Run Entry

We can adjust a Payroll Run Journal entry from the Payroll Journal, just as we edited the transaction for Filer. Tiste has handed in his resignation and should repay the remainder of his loan. As described in the Memo #8, Tiste should also receive his final vacation pay.

☐ 29

HELENA'S ACADEMY — Aim higher!

MEMO #8

From the desk of Morty Filer
Dated: Dec. 17, 2015

RE: Payroll Adjustment required for Arte Tiste and vacation pay

Adjust the Dec. 15 paycheque for Tiste —
Tiste is leaving the Academy and should have the full loan recovered from his paycheque. (Increase the loan recovered to $50.)
Tiste also requires his accrued vacation pay as a separate cheque.

Paycheque (cheque #248) released *Dec 17 Morty Filer*

First, we will change his retained vacation pay option as we did before. Refer to page 276 if you need assistance.

Click **Tiste, Arte** in the Employees List pane in the Home window to open his ledger record.

Click the **Income tab**.

Click the ✓ **for Retain Vacation** to change the setting.

Close the **ledger record**.

Click the **Paycheques icon**.

Click the **Adjust Paycheque tool** or **press** ctrl + **A**.

Click **OK** to see the list of posted payroll entries. Notice that all the entries from both payroll journals are included.

Double-click the **Dec. 15 entry for Tiste**. You will see the following warning:

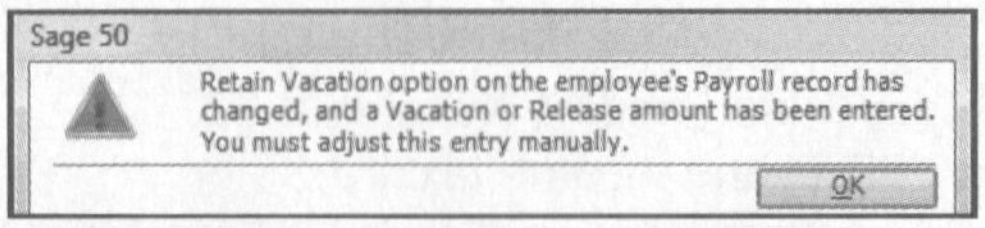

We cannot add vacation pay as a paycheque adjustment unless we enter all the amounts and taxes manually. Instead, we will prepare a separate paycheque for the vacation pay amount after making the adjustment.

Click **OK** to close the message. **Close** the **Paycheques Journal**.

NOTES
You do not need to close the Paycheques Journal to open the ledger window, but you cannot edit the ledger for Tiste while he is selected in the journal.

Click **Tiste, Arte** in the Employees List pane of the Home window to open his ledger record. **Click** the **Income tab**. **Click** **Retain Vacation** to change the option again so that his vacation pay is retained.

Close the **ledger record**.

Click the **Paycheques icon** to open the Payroll Journal.

Click the **Adjust Paycheque tool**, or **choose** **Adjust Paycheque** from the Paycheques icon shortcuts list.

Click **OK** to access the list of posted payroll entries.

Double-click the **Dec. 15 entry for Tiste**.

Click the **Advisor icon** to close the warning and display the paycheque:

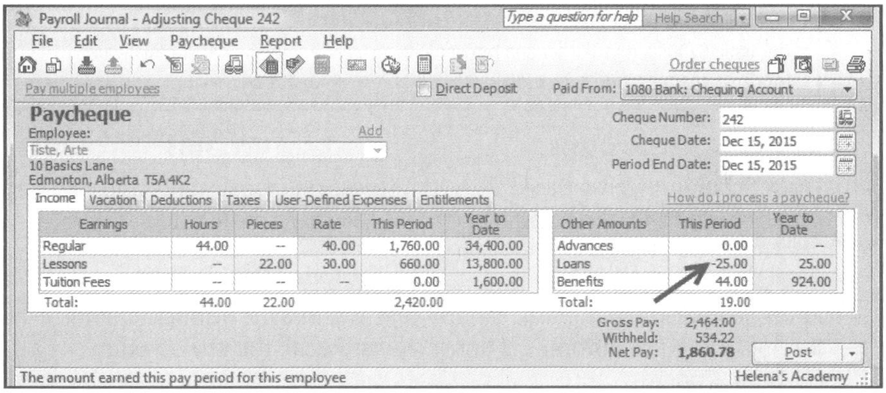

Click **-25** in the **This Period field for Loans** to select the current entry.

Type -50 **Press** tab to enter the change and update the gross pay. The Year To Date amount for Loans is reduced to zero.

Click the **Recalculate Taxes tool** on the Payroll Journal tool bar or **choose** the **Paycheque menu** and **click** **Recalculate Taxes**.

Review the Payroll Journal **entry**. **Close** the **display** when you have finished. **Make** **corrections** if necessary.

Click Post to save the adjustment.

Click **No** to bypass the cheque number warning.

Change the **Retain Vacation** settings for Tiste so you can issue the vacation pay.

Release the **remaining accrued vacation for Tiste**. Remember to delete all amounts that do not apply. Refer to page 278.

Close the **Paycheques Journal**. **Enter** the **next group of transactions**.

NOTES

Although this correction does not affect tax amounts, you must recalculate to post the entry. You cannot bypass the warning message advising you to recalculate.

30 **Cash Purchase Invoice #ESS-7889** **Dated Dec. 18/15**

From Energy Supply Services, $810 including taxes for heat and hydro on equal monthly billing plan. Recall the stored entry. Paid by cheque #249.

31 **Cash Purchase #TA-266778** **Dated Dec. 20/15**

From Telus Alberta, $170 including all taxes for one month of telephone services. Invoice total paid in full with cheque #250.

NOTES
Remember to remove Tiste from the list of employees paid in this pay period.

NOTES
Because of the additional holiday time provided, the pay period for hourly paid employees is prepared for 11 days (this period actually included 12 weekdays).

32

Employee Time Summary Sheet #24 **Dated Dec. 31/15**

For the pay period ending December 31, 2015

Name of Employee	Regular Hours	Overtime Hours	Lessons	Tuition	Advance (Repaid)	Loan (Repaid)	Sick Days	Direct Deposit
Filer, Morty	82.5	–	–	$125.00	–	–	–	No
Handie, Jerome	82.5	4	–	–	–	–	–	Yes
Nerture, Neela	82.5	–	–	–	–	–	1	Yes
Booker, Marina	160	–	10	$120.00	–	–	–	Yes
Teicher, Lars	160	–	8	–	–	$200	–	Yes
Teutor, Helena	160	–	–	–	–	–	–	No

a. Using Employee Time Summary Sheet #24 and the Employee Information Sheet, complete payroll for all employees. Hourly paid employees are paid for their regular hours during the Christmas holiday break.
b. Issue $200 loan to Teicher and recover $50 from each of the next four paycheques.
c. Issue cheques #251 and #252 and DD slips #69, #70, #71 and #72.

33

Bank Credit Memo #69886 **Dated Dec. 31/15**

From Scholar Heights Bank, $1 890 interest on investments and bank account was deposited to chequing account. Recall the stored entry.

34

Bank Debit Memo #532281 **Dated Dec. 31/15**

From Scholar Heights Bank, $4 235 was withdrawn from chequing account for the following pre-authorized transactions. Recall the stored entry.

Bank Charges	$ 35
Interest on Bank Loan	320
Reduction of Principal on Bank Loan	880
Interest on Mortgage	2 500
Reduction of Principal on Mortgage	500

35

Memo #9 **Dated Dec. 31/15**

Complete end-of-month adjusting entries for the following:

Office supplies used	$230
Art supplies used	250
Textbooks damaged	350
Prepaid property taxes	900

36

Cash Sales Invoice #1039 **Dated Dec. 31/15**

Received $300 000 instalment payment toward school fees for the next semester. Total cash deposited to bank account.

Entering Paycheques in a Future Year

PRO VERSION
pro This feature is not available in the Pro version. Instead, you can start a new calendar year, advance the session date and complete the payroll run.

Sometimes you will need to prepare payroll transactions in advance, such as when the payroll preparation date falls during a holiday period. When that date also falls in a future calendar year, you need to separate the year-to-date amounts for the two years for income tax reporting purposes.

Sage 50 allows you to enter payroll entries for a later year and tracks these separate amounts for each employee. Current year reports are not affected. Permission to complete these entries is controlled from the Company System Settings screen as shown here:

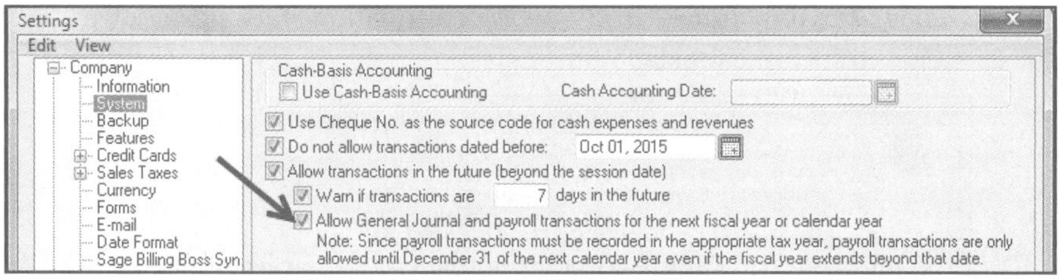

Filer may not have time to complete the first payroll entry in early January because the beginning of term is a very busy time. He can create these cheques in December.

✓ 37

Employee Time Summary Sheet #25 Dated Jan. 15/16

For the pay period ending January 15, 2016

Name of Employee	Regular Hours	Overtime Hours	Lessons	Tuition	Advance (Repaid)	Loan (Repaid)	Sick Days	Direct Deposit
Filer, Morty	82.5	–	–	$125	–	–	–	No
Handie, Jerome	82.5	–	–	–	–	–	–	Yes
Nerture, Neela	82.5	–	–	–	–	–	–	Yes

a. Using Employee Time Summary Sheet #25 and the Employee Information Sheet, complete payroll for hourly paid employees. (Adjustments for overtime hours worked will be made on the following paycheque.)
b. Issue cheque #253 and Direct Deposit (DD) slips #73 and #74.

Open the **Payroll Run Journal**.

Enter **Jan 15, 2016** as the **Cheque Date** and as the **Period End Date**.

Your journal should look like the following:

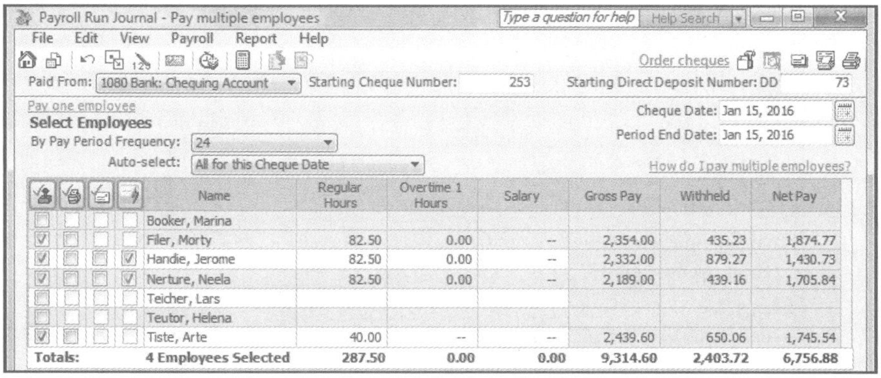

Payroll Run Journal - Pay multiple employees
File Edit View Payroll Report Help
Order cheques
Paid From: 1080 Bank: Chequing Account
Starting Cheque Number: 253
Starting Direct Deposit Number: DD 73
Pay one employee
Select Employees
By Pay Period Frequency: 24
Auto-select: All for this Cheque Date
Cheque Date: Jan 15, 2016
Period End Date: Jan 15, 2016
How do I pay multiple employees?
Name | Regular Hours | Overtime 1 Hours | Salary | Gross Pay | Withheld | Net Pay
Booker, Marina
Filer, Morty | 82.50 | 0.00 | -- | 2,354.00 | 435.23 | 1,874.77
Handie, Jerome | 82.50 | 0.00 | -- | 2,332.00 | 879.27 | 1,430.73
Nerture, Neela | 82.50 | 0.00 | -- | 2,189.00 | 439.16 | 1,705.84
Teicher, Lars
Teutor, Helena
Tiste, Arte | 40.00 | -- | -- | 2,439.60 | 650.06 | 1,745.54
Totals: | 4 Employees Selected | 287.50 | 0.00 | 0.00 | 9,314.60 | 2,403.72 | 6,756.88

All hourly paid employees are selected, but Tiste has resigned and should not be paid.

Click the **Post column** for **Tiste** so that he will not be paid in January.

Click **Filer's name** and **enter 125** as his tuition amount for this period to complete the entry.

Review your **entry** and **make corrections** if needed.

Click **Post** to see the following confirmation warning:

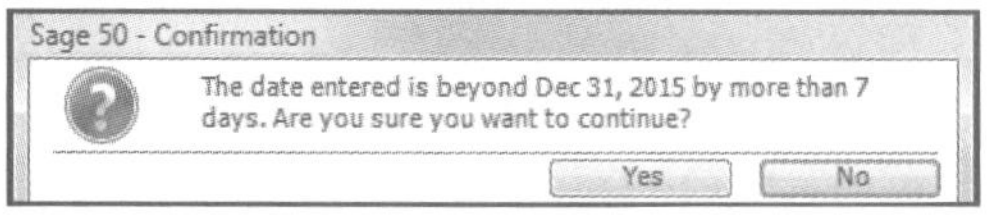

Our Company System Settings allow future dates but warn if these are more than seven days in the future (see the screenshot at the top of this page).

NOTES

The option to post transactions to the next fiscal or calendar year applies only to Payroll and General Journal entries.

WARNING!

You must add the year for these pay dates. If you do not, 2015 will be the default entry and this date is not allowed – it is earlier than October 1, 2015, the Earliest Transaction Date allowed in the Company Settings (see the screenshot at the top of this page).

Click **Yes** to continue to the next confirmation warning about using a date in a future calendar year:

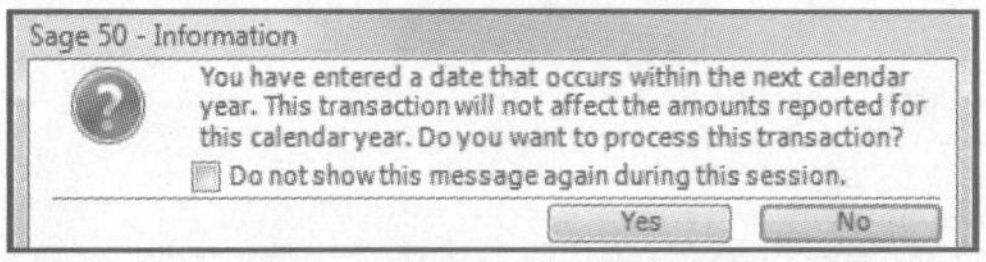

Read the message carefully — it advises that prior year amounts (those for 2015) will not be affected by this entry.

Click **Yes** to continue and save the payroll entry. **Close** the **journal**.

Terminating an Employee

NOTES
From the Report Centre, you can print only the reports that you can display. For reports that are only printed, you must start from the Employees window or from the Reports menu.

When an employee leaves the company, his or her ledger record should be updated with the date of termination and the reason for leaving. Then a record of employment can be issued that indicates the number of hours worked and the total income. This form is used to determine eligibility for Employment Insurance.

Tiste will be going back to school full time in January and he has received his last paycheque, so we should modify his record. We will work from the Employees window so that we can also print reports.

✓ 38

Memo #10 **Dated Dec. 31/15**
Prepare a Record of Employment and T4 slip for Tiste.

Click the **Employees icon** 

to open the Employees window.

Double-click **Tiste, Arte** to open his ledger record at the Personal tab screen:

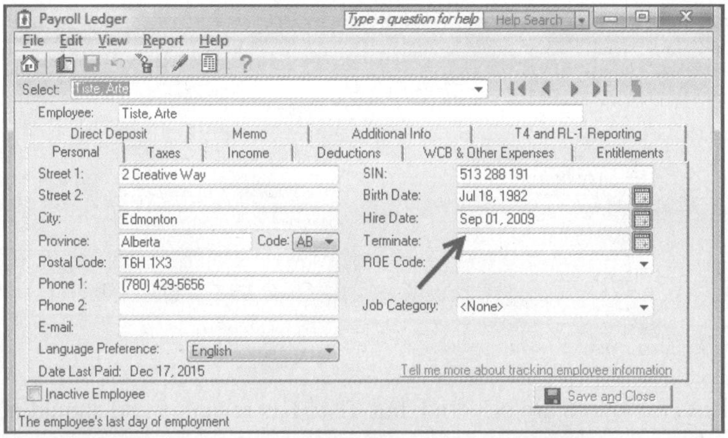

We need to enter the Terminate date and the ROE (Record of Employment) Code.

Click the **Terminate field**. **Type** `12 15`

Click the **ROE Code list arrow** to see the codes available:

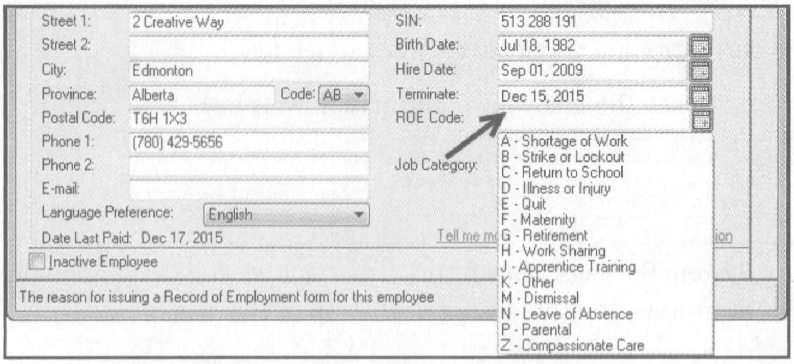

Click **C - Return To School**.

Click **Save And Close** to open the following message:

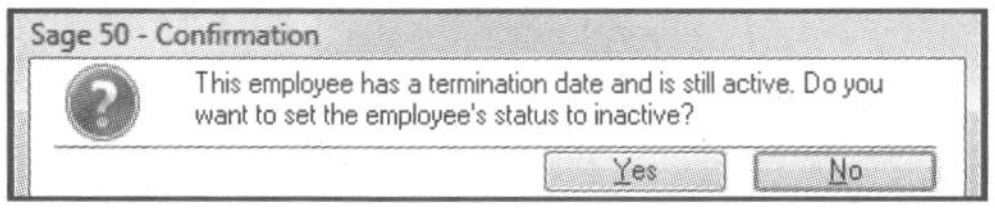

Normally, an employee's status is changed to inactive when he or she has left the company. In this way, the employee's name will no longer appear in employee lists for reports or journals. Data for the inactive employees can still be included in any reports by choosing to include inactive employees.

Click **Yes** to change the status and close the ledger.

We will now be able to print a Record of Employment for Tiste. We will print this report from the Employees window.

Printing Payroll Reports

You can access payroll reports from the Reports menu in the Employees window and from the Home window. In addition, most payroll reports can also be accessed from the Report Centre. Some payroll reports cannot be displayed; they are printed directly.

The Employees window should be open.

Printing Record of Employment Reports

The Record of Employment Report provides information about employees who have terminated their employment to determine their eligibility for Employment Insurance benefits. The report includes the length of employment, earnings, total number of hours worked and the reason (code) for termination. You can print the report only for employees who have been terminated, and you must have the correct preprinted forms.

Reports are remitted directly to Service Canada. Employees may view their ROE on the Service Canada Web site or request a copy from the employer.

Choose the **Reports menu**, and **click Print Record Of Employment**:

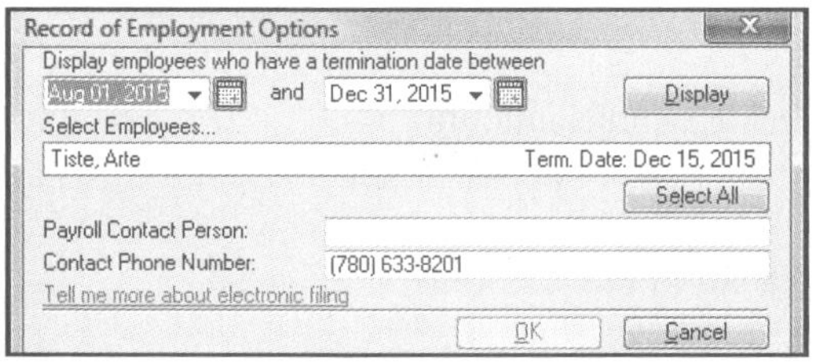

From the Home window, choose the Reports menu, then choose Payroll and click Print Record Of Employment.

Tiste is the only employee listed in this option window because he is the only one with a termination date. The date range includes the fiscal year to date. If you have data for a different time period, you can change these dates and then click Display to update the list of employees. For this report, you need to provide the name and telephone number to contact about the company payroll.

Click **Tiste, Arte** to select the employee for the report.

If there are more employees with termination dates, you can click Select All to create reports for all the listed employees.

Click the **Payroll Contact Person field**. **Type** `Morty Filer`

NOTES

You cannot access the Record of Employment from the Report Centre.

Submitting ROE reports to Service Canada electronically from the program is covered in Appendix K.

Service Canada is the branch of the federal government that deals with Employment Insurance and pensions.

Click **OK** to continue:

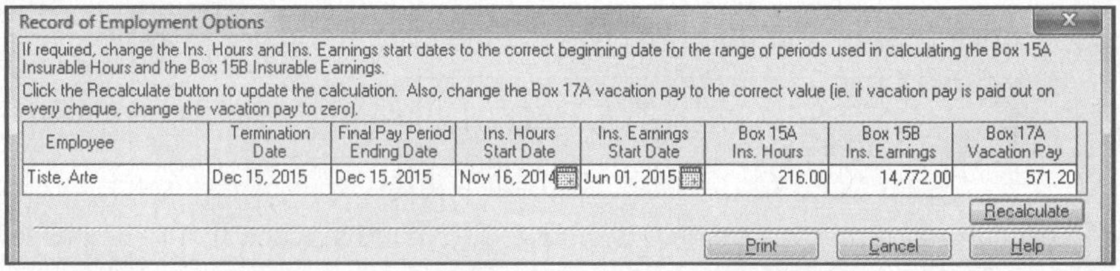

You now have the summary details for the selected employee. They include only the amounts entered in the payroll journals; they do not include the year-to-date opening balance amounts. You can edit the fields in this window. If you have payroll data for a longer period, you can enter those dates and recalculate the amounts. However, only the three months of payroll data we entered in Sage 50 are tracked in this form, so we must update the details.

The year-to-date insurable earnings amount is tracked in the employee ledger on the T4 and RL-1 Reporting tab screen as shown here:

NOTES
You cannot view the employee's ledger record while the Record of Employment report or its options window is open.

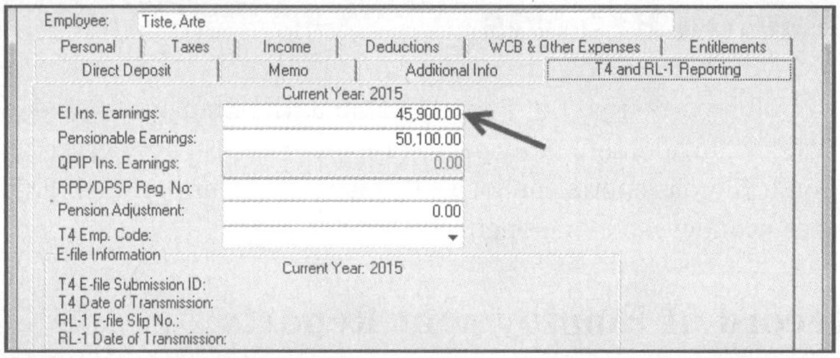

We can see that Tiste has $45 900 in EI insurable earnings this year (the maximum amount for 2012). He has also worked additional hours before October — 20 hours per week for 34 weeks, or 680 hours, so his total number of hours is 896 (680 + 216). And finally, he has received all his vacation pay, so this amount should be changed to zero. You can also edit the start dates for EI insurable hours and earnings.

NOTES
Because our tax tables apply to 2012, the maximum amounts for Pensionable Earnings and EI Insurable Earnings also will apply.
For 2013, the maximum amounts increased to $47 400 and $51 100, respectively.
Once an employee earns the maximum amounts, no further pay amounts are added and no further CPP or EI will be deducted.

Enter **Jan 1** in the Ins. Hours Start Date field and also in the Ins. Earnings Start Date field.

Click **216.00** in the Box 15A Ins. Hours field.

Type 896

Press tab to select the Ins. Earnings amount.

Type 45900

Press tab to select the Vacation Pay amount.

Press del. Check your entries.

Click **Print** to see an additional warning:

NOTES
For practice, you can print the ROE on plain paper, but you will not see any labels for the details on the report.

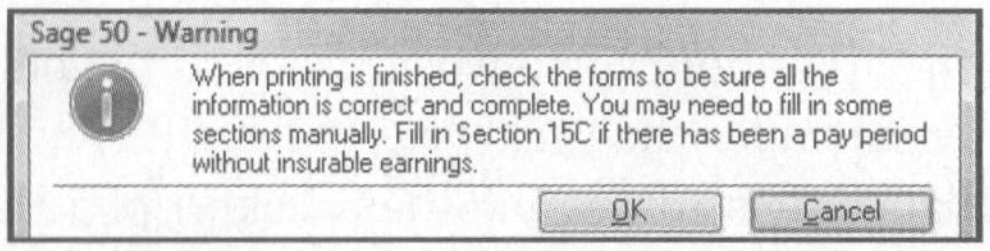

You may need to add missing details on the form manually if the final printed form is not complete.

Click **OK** to begin printing. **Close** the **Employees window**.

Printing T4s

T4 Slips and Relevé 1 Slips are also not available for display but they can be printed. Relevé 1 slips are used only in Quebec, and the Print Relevé 1 Slips Report options screen will list only employees for whom Quebec is the province of taxation. Relevé 1 options are similar to those for T4 slips. You can print T4 slips, which are compulsory for employees filing income tax returns, using either the tax statement forms from the Canada Revenue Agency (CRA) or plain paper. You should retain payroll information for employees who leave during the year so that you can prepare T4 slips to mail to them.

Before printing T4s, you should check your printer and forms selections.

Choose the **Setup menu**, then **choose Reports & Forms** and **click Government Forms** and **click Federal Payroll** to display the following options:

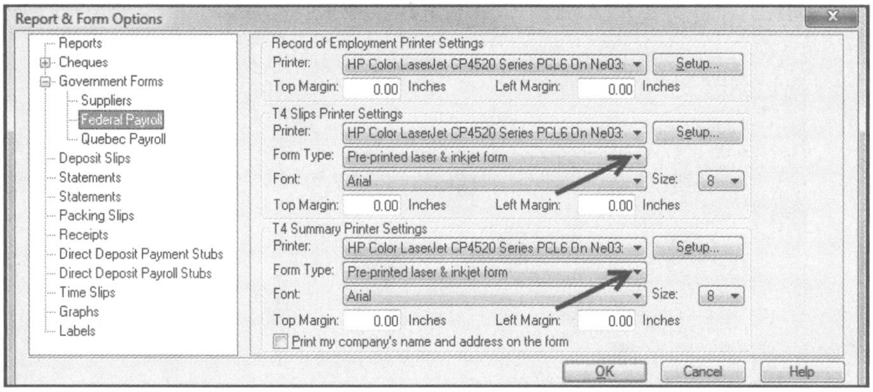

Select **Plain Paper** as the Form Type for T4 Slips and T4 Summary.

Click **OK** to save the selections and return to the Home window.

Choose the **Reports menu**, then **choose Payroll** and **click Print T4 Slips And Summary** (or Print Relevé 1 Slips) to display the following options:

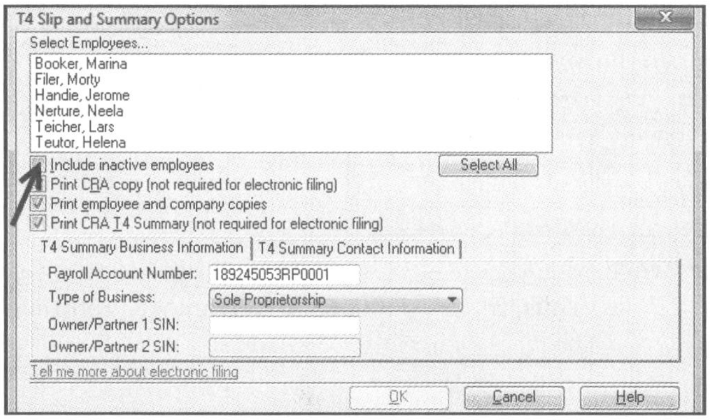

You need to select the employees in order to prepare their T4 slips. Inactive employees are not listed by default. You can print copies of the T4s for the employees and the company and for the Canada Revenue Agency (CRA). You can also print the summary for the CRA. All are selected as the default.

To submit the report, you must include the type of business, business payroll account number (the business number with an RP code extension), the social insurance numbers (SIN) of the owners/partners, the name of the person who can be contacted about the form and the phone number and position of that individual. The Payroll Account Number should be entered from the Company Settings Information window.

Click **Include Inactive Employees** to add Tiste to the list.

Click **Tiste, Arte**.

NOTES
You cannot access the T4 Slips from the Report Centre.
Submitting T4s electronically to the Canada Revenue Agency is covered in Appendix K.

NOTES
You can also print T4s and Summary from the Employees window. Choose the Reports menu and click Print T4s and Summary to open the options window.

NOTES
If you file T4 reports electronically, you do not need to print copies for the Canada Revenue Agency.

Press and hold *ctrl* and click the names of the employees for whom you want the report printed or click Select All to prepare T4s for all employees.

Select the **Type Of Business**. **Click** the **Type** that applies: sole proprietorship, partnership or private company.

> **NOTES**
> The payroll account number and the social insurance number (SIN) must be valid numbers and you cannot leave these fields blank.

Enter **189245053RP0001** (without spaces) in the Payroll Account Number field if it is not entered automatically.

Enter the **Social Insurance Number** of the owners or partners. You can enter Teutor's Social Insurance Number (from page 261) as the owner's SIN.

> **NOTES**
> Teutor's Social Insurance No. is 699 344 578.

On the second tab screen, you must enter the contact details for the person completing the forms.

Click the **T4 Summary Contact Information tab** to open the contact fields:

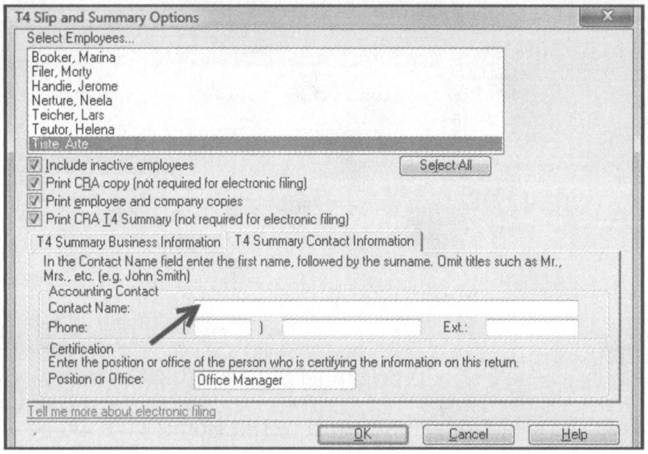

> **NOTES**
> Morty Filer is the Office Manager. His work phone number is (780) 633-8201.

Enter the **contact details** for the person completing the forms: name, phone number and position in the company. You can use Morty Filer's name with the school phone number (see page 258).

Click **OK** to open the warning:

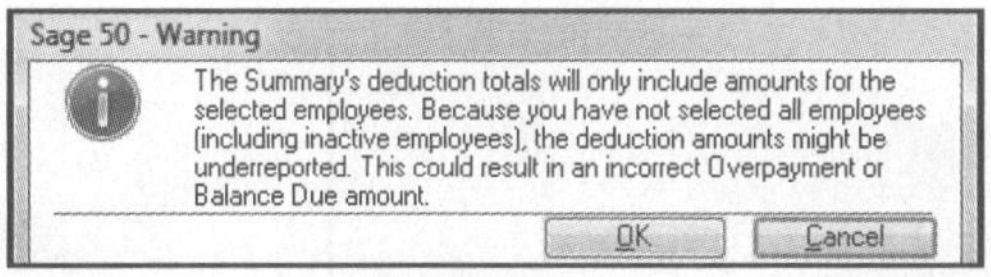

The warning appears when you do not select all employees because the remittance amounts apply to all employees. Thus, reported amounts for employer contributions may be incorrect.

Click **OK** to open the T4 Box Options screen:

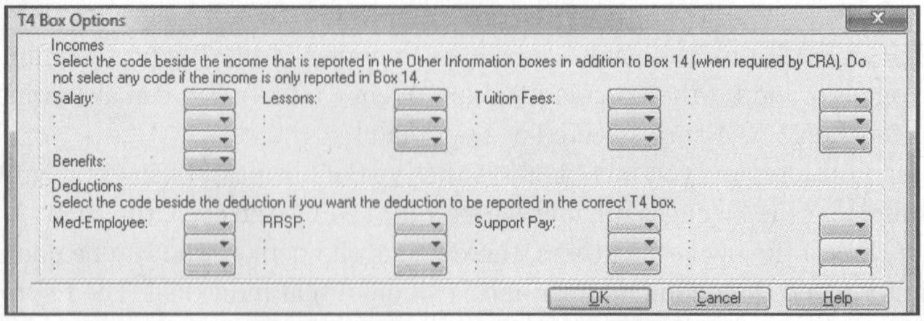

> **NOTES**
> The printed T4 slips will also include descriptions of the purpose of each box on the form. This information is used by the employee to complete the income tax return and can serve as a guide for employers preparing the T4s.

Each box on the T4 slip is numbered and can be designated for a specific deduction or income. You can choose a form box number for these amounts if they are related to income tax and should be included on the T4s. Each item has a list of box numbers that you can select. Income and tax items that are standard for T4s are not listed because their boxes are already assigned. If you do not change the box selections, the income amounts are all combined and the deductions listed are not reported. You can check with the CRA to see what each box number is used for. The defaults are correct for Tiste.

Choose appropriate **box numbers** for the items that should appear on the T4.

Click **OK** to begin printing.

After the T4s are printed, the T4 Summary report is displayed:

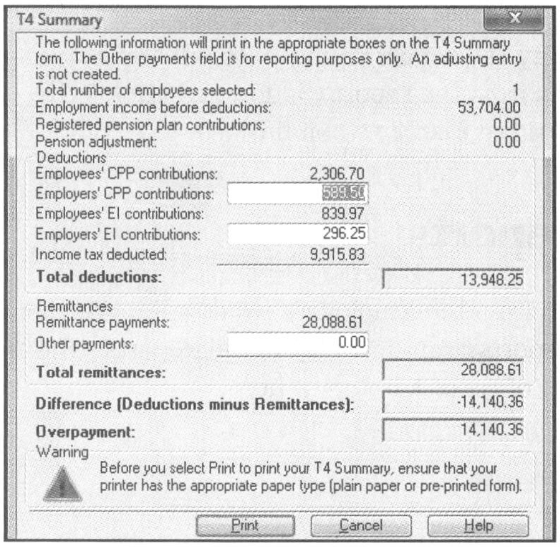

The amounts are only those for Tiste because he was the only employee selected. These amounts do not include the year-to-date remittances made before Sage 50 was used for payroll. The remittance amounts shown are those for all employees for three months. The employee contribution amounts are the year-to-date totals for the individual, and the employer contribution amounts are those related to this employee for three months. The employer contribution and remittance year-to-date totals are not included in the payroll history when you do not set up the program at the start of the calendar year. You should edit the amounts.

Click **Print** to continue when the amounts are correct.

After printing, you should see a summary of the items printed:

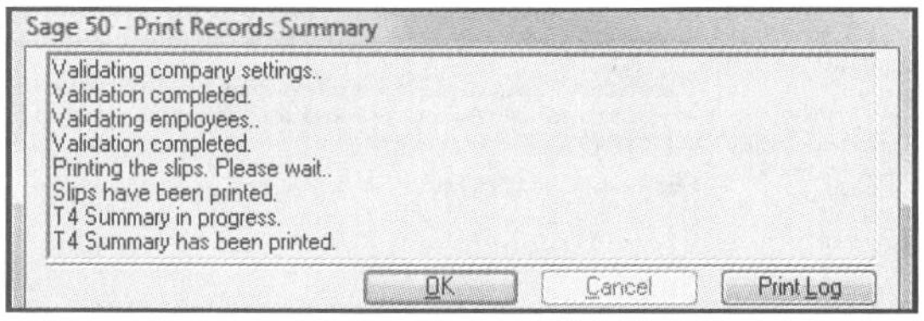

Click **Print Log** to print this summary or **click OK** to close the summary.

Printing Employee Mailing Labels

We will continue with the payroll reports that are not available from the Report Centre. You can print labels for employees (like labels for suppliers and clients).

Set up the **printer** for printing labels (Setup menu, Reports and Forms, Labels) before starting.

Choose the **Reports menu**, then **choose Mailing Labels** and **click Employees**.

NOTES

Total income includes vacation pay paid and benefits.

Employee year-to-date historical amounts are entered in the ledger record when you set up the payroll module. However, year-to-date employer amounts are not included as part of the setup, so these amounts may be incomplete.

If you have entered all payroll transactions for the entire year, the amounts on the summary should be correct.

You can edit the employer payment amounts for CPP and EI.

> **NOTES**
> You cannot display mailing labels.
> You can include or omit inactive employees.

> **NOTES**
> Remember to check that you have selected the correct printer for your setup. If you click the Print tool, printing will start immediately and you cannot change the selected printer.

> **PRO VERSION**
> The Pro version does not have Grouped Lists.

> **NOTES**
> The Job Category Report will be covered in Chapter 9.

> **CLASSIC VIEW**
> From the Home window, right-click the Employees icon . Click the Display tool  to open the Modify Report window.

> **NOTES**
> To access Employee Lists from the Home window, choose the Reports menu, then choose Lists and click Employees to see the report options.

You will display the list of employee names:

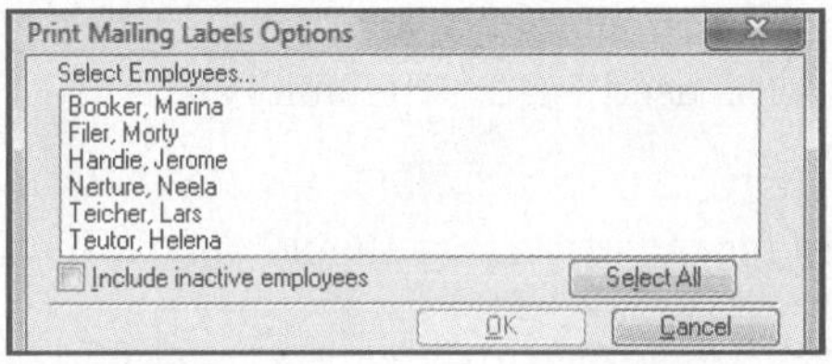

Press and **hold** ctrl and **click** the **employees' names** or **click Select All**. **Click OK** to start printing.

To print other reports, **display** the **report** you want to print as instructed below. **Choose** the **File menu** from the report window and **click Print**. **Choose** your **printer**. **Click OK**. **Close** the **display** when finished.

Displaying Payroll Reports

Most payroll reports can be accessed from the Employees window Reports menu, the Home window Reports menu, the Reports drop-down list in the Reports pane or the Report Centre. The Reports pane list of reports is shown here:

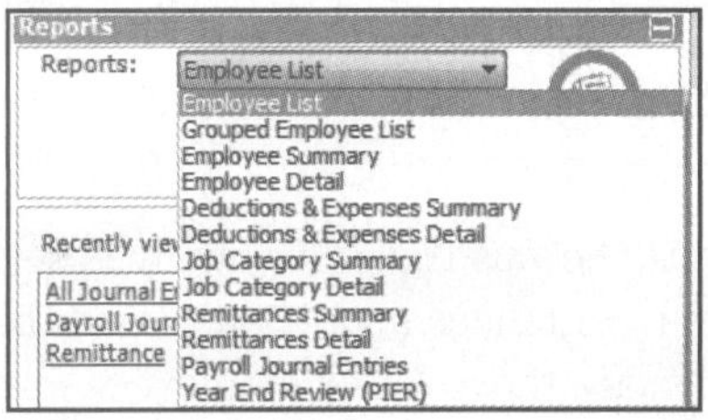

As usual, we will work from the Report Centre so that you can see sample reports and the report description and purpose.

Click the **Report Centre icon**  in the Reports pane.

Click **Employees & Payroll** in the Select A Report Type list to see the general description of payroll reports:

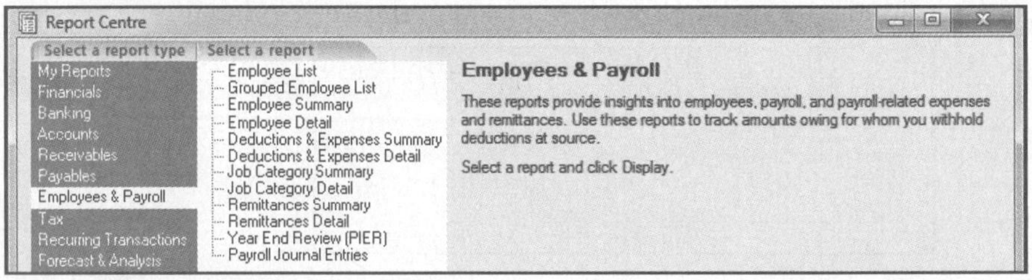

Displaying Employee Lists

Lists of employees are available, just like lists for other ledgers.

Click **Employee List** in the Select A Report list.

Click **Modify This Report** to see the report options:

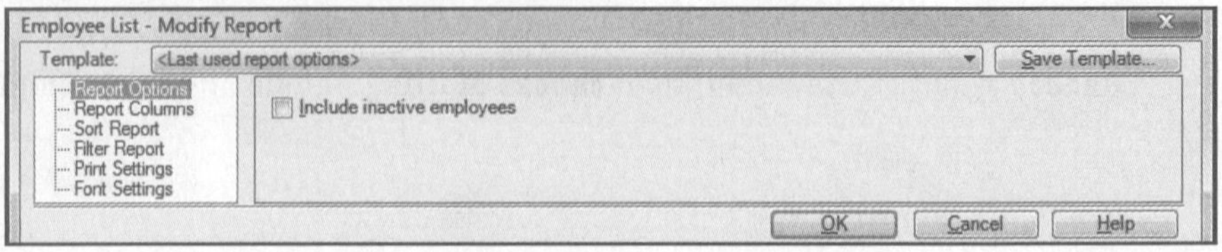

To select employee fields, you can customize the Report Columns. Choose Custom Report Column Settings and select the ones you want.

The report will display a list of all current employees, together with data for all the details you chose. The default report shows the address, phone number and date of hire.

Close the **display** when you have finished.

Displaying Employee Reports

Click **Employee Summary** in the Select A Report list.

Click **Modify This Report** to see the report options:

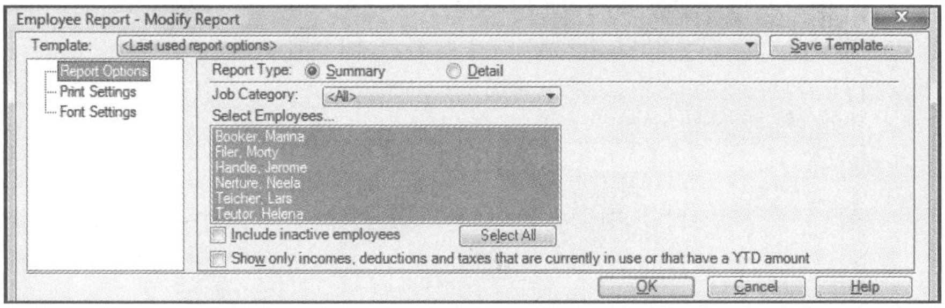

Or choose the Reports menu, then choose Payroll and click Employee.

The **Summary** report has accumulated totals for each selected employee for all incomes, deductions and payments, which are updated each pay period. Summary reports are available only for the session date.

You can include or omit inactive employees from the report. You can also omit details that have no amounts or have not been used.

If you use job categories, you can prepare a report for a specific category by choosing it from the drop-down list of categories.

You cannot customize the Employee Summary Report. You can use the **Detail** report to see individual amounts for each paycheque. To prepare a report for specific deductions or payments, you can customize the column selection for the Detail Report.

Click **Include Inactive Employees** if you want to report on them as well.

Press and **hold** *ctrl* and **click** the **employees** you want in the report, or **click Select All** to include all employees in the report.

Click **Show Only Incomes, Deductions And Taxes That Are Currently In Use Or That Have A YTD Amount** to omit fields with no entries.

Click **Detail** to include individual transaction details.

Enter the **Start** and **Finish dates** for the Detail Report.

Click **Report Columns** in the left-hand pane. **Click Custom Report Column Settings**:

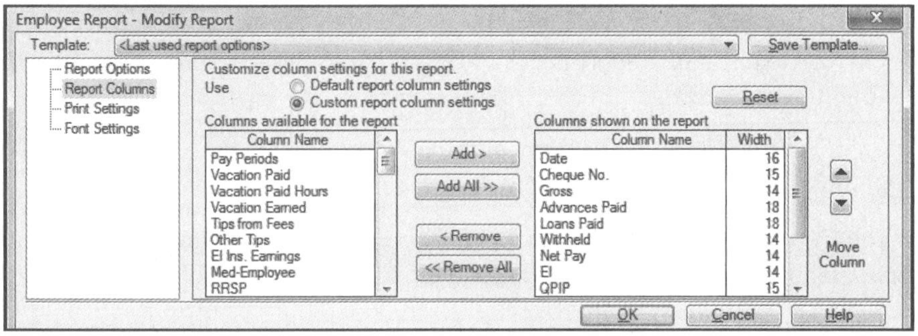

NOTES
You can drill down to the Employee Detail Report from the Employee List.
You can sort and filter the list by the fields available for the employee list.

NOTES
The Grouped Employee List allows you to sort the employees into categories according to a number of criteria, such as the city they live in.

NOTES
The Summary Report also shows the tax claim amounts and rates of pay for each employee.

NOTES
Sorting and filtering are not available for the Employee Summary Report.
You can drill down to the Detail Report from the Summary Report. From the Detail Report you can look up the Payroll Journal entry and open the Employee Ledger.

This window shows the information that is included by default and the details that you can add to the report. The amount for each detail you choose will be listed for each payroll period in the selected date range for the selected employees, together with the totals for the period selected. The calendar year provides the default dates for the Detail Report.

Select the **columns** you want to include or remove.

Click **OK** to see the report. **Close** the **display** when you have finished.

Displaying Deductions and Expenses Reports

Click **Deductions & Expenses Summary** in the Select A Report list.

Click **Modify This Report** to see the report options:

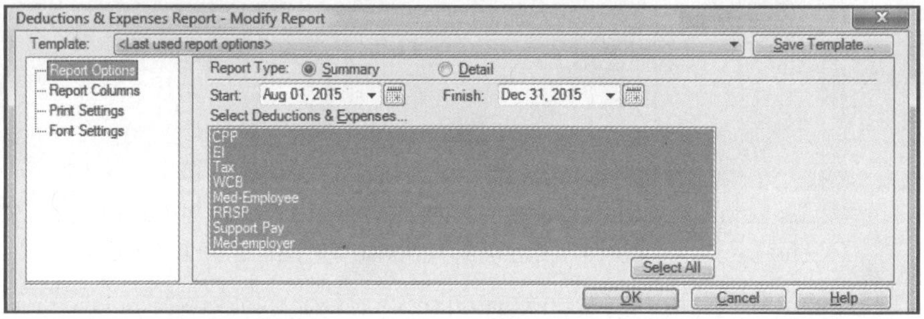

From the Home window, choose the Reports menu, then choose Payroll and click Deductions & Expenses.

NOTES
From the Summary Deductions and Expenses Report you can drill down to the Detail Report. From the Detail Report you can drill down to the Employee Detail Report and look up the paycheque.

This report provides details for all payroll deductions and expenses. Only amounts entered in the Payroll journals in Sage 50 will be included in this report. Prior historical balance amounts for the year to date from the employee records will not be shown. The **Summary Report** shows the total amounts and the number of employees the deduction or expense applied to for each payroll item in the selected date range. The **Detail Report** shows individual entries for each selected item, including the date, cheque or deposit number, employee, job category, amount, period totals and number of employees.

You can customize the report by selecting the columns you want to include.

Initially, the selection list shows only deductions. Select the details you want in the report and the date range for the report. The earliest transaction and session dates are the default selections.

Press and **hold** *ctrl* and **click** the **deductions** and **expenses** you want in the report, or **click Select All** to include all details in the report.

Enter the **Start** and **Finish dates** for the report.

Click **OK** to see the report and **close** the **display** when you have finished.

Displaying Payroll Remittance Reports

NOTES
From the Remittance Summary Report, you can drill down to the Detail Report. From the Detail Report, you can drill down to the Supplier Ledger, the Employee Detail Report, the journal entry and look up the entry in the Paycheques Journal.

The Payroll Remittance Report is described on pages 282–283. To access this report from the Report Centre,

Click Remittances Summary in the Select A Report list. Click Modify This Report to see the report options and click OK to display the report.

The Payroll Remittance Journal Entries are included with the Payments Journal Entries Report (see the Payments Journal Modify Report screen on page 147).

To access this report from the Report Centre,

Click Payables in the Select A Report Type list. Click Payment Journal Entries and Modify This Report to see the options. Click OK to display the report.

Remittance Payments should have a ✓ in the check box as the default selection.

Displaying the Payroll Journal

The Payroll Journal Report includes all transactions from the Payroll Journal and the Payroll Run Journal. Return to the Employees & Payroll report list if necessary.

Click **Payroll Journal Entries** in the Select A Report list (in the Employees & Payroll group of reports).

Click **Modify This Report** to see the report options:

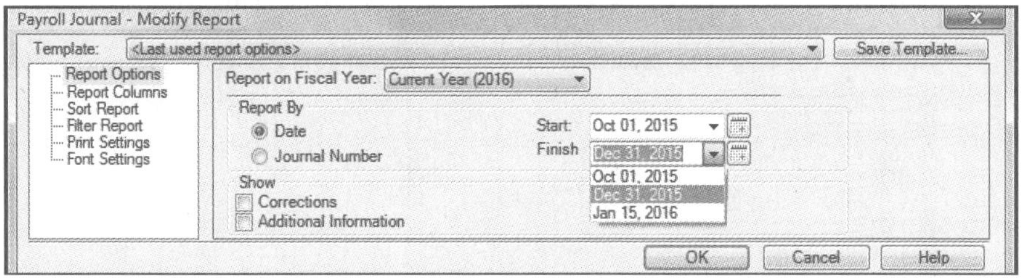

Or choose the Reports menu, then choose Journal Entries and click Payroll to display the Options window.

The usual sort and filter journal options are available for the Payroll Journal Report, and the Date option we use for selecting transactions is the default. Your earliest transaction and session dates appear as the default Start and Finish dates.

Type the **beginning** and **ending dates** for the report.

Click **Corrections** to include the original and reversing entries for the paycheques you adjusted or reversed.

Click **OK**. **Close** the **display** when you have finished.

Displaying Year End Review (PIER) Reports

The PIER (Pensionable and Insurable Earnings Review) report shows the total amounts contributed in the year to date for EI and CPP. Based on the Insurable Earnings amount for each employee (also in the report), the program determines whether the employee has contributed the correct amounts and displays the amount of under- or overcontributions.

Click **Year End Review (PIER)** in the Select A Report list.

Click **Modify This Report** to see the report options:

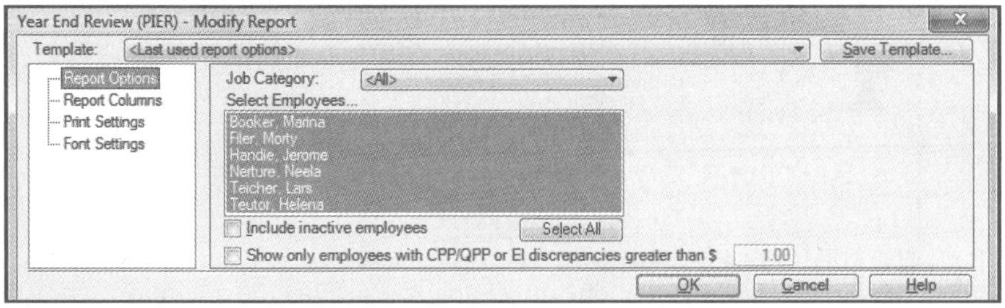

From the Home window, choose the Reports menu, then choose Payroll and click Year End Review (PIER) to display the report options.

CLASSIC VIEW

From the Home window, right-click either the Paycheques or the Payroll Cheque Run icon,

or

. Then click the Display tool  to open the Modify Report window for the Payroll Journal Report.

NOTES

You can drill down to the Employee Detail Report and the General Ledger Report from the Payroll Journal.

NOTES

January 15 will be included in the drop-down lists in the date fields.

NOTES

Remember that you can see the journal entries for all journals in a single report. From the Report Centre, choose the Financials list of reports and then click All Journal Entries. From the Home window, choose the Reports menu, then choose Journal Entries and click All. You will open the report options window.

NOTES

The PIER report for Helena's Academy shows that all the employees have paid the maximum amounts for CPP and EI.

NOTES

You cannot sort or filter the PIER report.

You can modify this report by selecting the report columns, removing any of the default information or adding the amounts for expected EI and CPP deductions and the number of paycheques and pay periods.

You can define the minimum discrepancy that should be included and then show the report only for those employees who have a discrepancy of this amount or more. The default amount is $1.00.

Click **Include Inactive Employees** to add these employees to the list.

Click the **name** of the employee you want the report for, **press** and **hold** ctrl and **click additional names**, or **click Select All** to include all employees in the report.

Click **OK** to display the report. **Close** the **display** when you have finished.

Close the **Report Centre** to return to the Home window.

Management Reports for Payroll

Management reports can be displayed only from the Home window Reports menu.

CLASSIC VIEW

You can also access Management Reports from the Advice tool in the Classic view Home window tool bar.

Choose the **Reports menu**, then **choose Management Reports** and **click Payroll**:

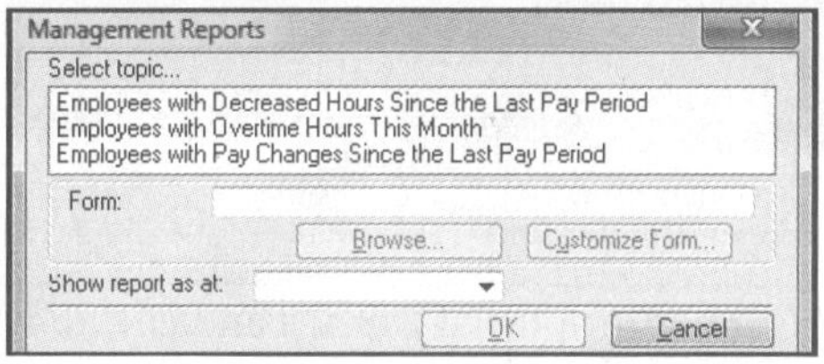

NOTES

You should verify that the form location for the Management Reports is correct for your program setup.

Click the **topic** you want to see. For the report on Employees With Overtime Hours This Month,

Choose a **month** from the list for Show Report As At. Choose a form, if appropriate.

Click **OK** to see the report. **Close** the **display** when you have finished.

Starting a New Calendar Year

When you are ready to advance to the next session date at the end of December, you must start a new year.

Close **all other windows** except the Home window.

Choose the **Maintenance menu** and **click Start New Year**:

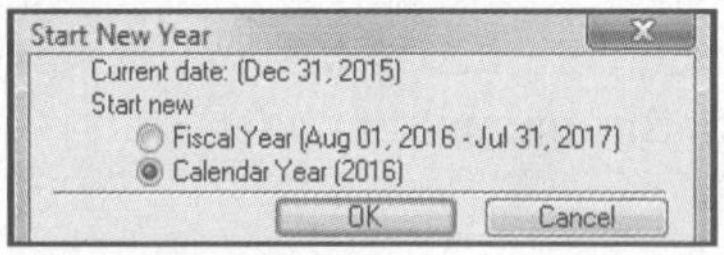

Because the fiscal period ends in August, the new calendar year comes first and you will see this as the default option.

Click **OK** to continue to the next information screen:

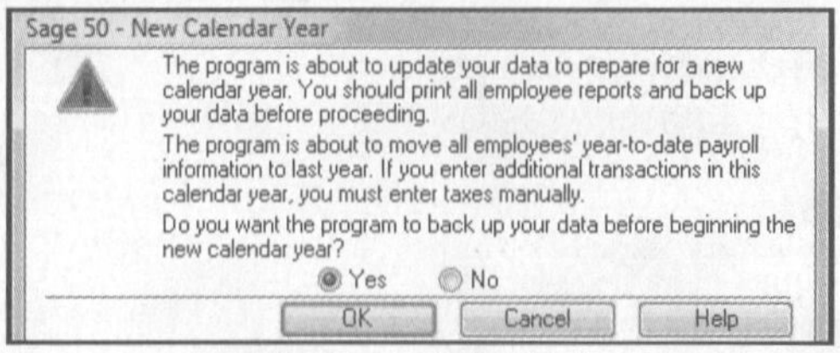

This message advises you about the changes that Sage 50 will make when you start the new year. Because this step is not reversible, you should have an end-of-year backup. This is the default selection.

Click **OK** to proceed with the backup.

After the backup has been completed, you will see the confirmation message that the date has been changed.

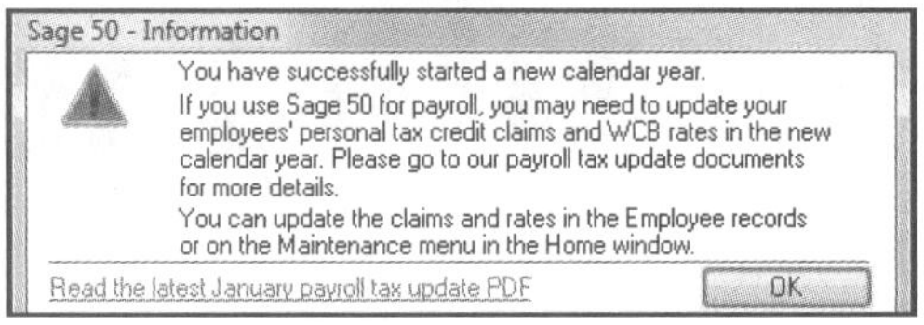

Click **OK** to proceed to the locking date screen:

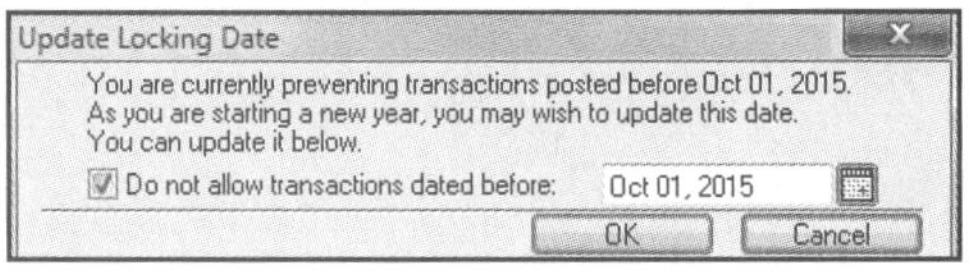

Enter **Jan 1 2016** as the new date on this screen.

Click **OK** to return to the Home window.

Click the **Refresh tool** above the Employees list pane to update the amounts to include the latest transaction entries:

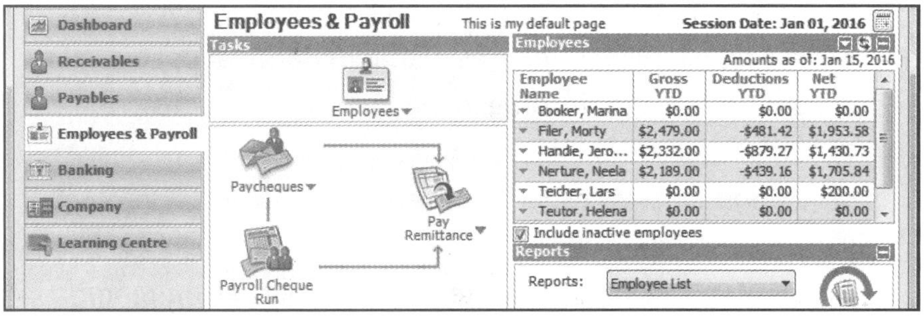

The new year-to-date amounts show the balances as at January 15 for the hourly paid employees. Teicher's loan amount, carried forward from his December 31 paycheque, is also included.

If you have not entered any payroll transactions yet when you start the new calendar year, the amounts in the Employees list pane will be zero except for Teicher's loan amount.

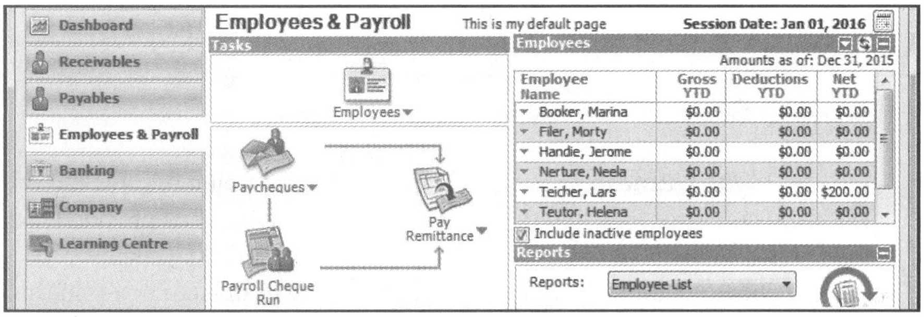

NOTES

Showing balances as at the session date, which is January 1 (a User Preference View setting), will also show zero amounts in the Employees pane.

REVIEW

The Student DVD with Data Files includes Review Questions and Supplementary Cases for this chapter.

CHAPTER NINE

Lime Light Laundry

Laundry Services • Pickup & Deliver

OBJECTIVES

After completing this chapter, you should be able to

- ***add*** the Payroll Ledger to a company data file
- ***enter*** Payroll Ledger settings
- ***enter*** Payroll Ledger linked accounts
- ***create*** employee ledger records
- ***enter*** employee historical information
- ***set up*** payroll remittances with remittance suppliers
- ***set up*** taxes for income, benefits and deductions
- ***create*** job categories
- ***assign*** employees to job categories
- ***enter*** salespersons on invoices
- ***display*** and ***print*** job category and salesperson reports

COMPANY INFORMATION

Company Profile

NOTES
Lime Light Laundry
25 Snow White Lane
Vancouver, BC V8G 3B2
Tel: (604) 633-8201
Fax: (604) 633-8396
Business No.: 324 732 911

Lime Light Laundry started in Vancouver, British Columbia, in 1996 with a single employee assisting the owner, Charles Chaplin. They provided laundry services to one hotel as a regular client and to a few individual clients. Now Lime Light provides complete laundry services for a number of large hotels in the Vancouver area and has seven full-time employees. Chaplin himself is no longer involved in daily business operations, and the laundry serves only hotels and no individual clients. Chaplin's goal as an entrepreneur is business growth. In fact, two employees have recently been hired. Chaplin is negotiating new contracts with a major hotel chain and considering expansion into adjacent premises that are for sale.

Lime Light's business success has enabled it to establish favourable account terms with regular suppliers, including some discounts for early payment. The discount terms for clients also encourage timely payment of accounts. All discounts are calculated on after-tax amounts. Because there are no individual clients, only hotels, Lime Light does not accept credit card payments. Similarly, most regular suppliers do not accept credit cards and Chaplin does not use them in his business.

All laundry services provided by Lime Light are subject to 5 percent GST. Lime Light pays the 5 percent GST and 7 percent PST on most purchases.

On January 31, 2015, Chaplin closed his books so he could begin using the payroll feature in Sage 50. The following information summarizes his data:

- Chart of Accounts
- Post-Closing Trial Balance
- Supplier Information
- Client Information
- Employee Profiles and Information Sheet
- Accounting Procedures

PRO VERSION
The terms Vendor and Customer will replace Supplier and Client. Sales and Purchases replace the terms Revenues and Expenses in the program for journals and reports.

CHART OF POSTABLE ACCOUNTS

LIME LIGHT LAUNDRY

ASSETS
1080 Bank: Chequing
1200 Accounts Receivable
1240 Advances & Loans Receivable
1260 Prepaid Insurance
1280 Cleaning Supplies
1320 Packaging Supplies
1520 Computer System
1540 Delivery Vehicle
1560 Laundry and Cleaning Equipment
1580 Pressing Equipment
1600 Railings and Belts
1620 Laundry Premises ▶

▶LIABILITIES
2100 Bank Loan
2200 Accounts Payable
2250 Accrued Wages
2300 Vacation Payable
2310 EI Payable
2320 CPP Payable
2330 Income Tax Payable
2400 MSP Payable - Employee
2410 RRSP Payable
2420 Travel Allowances Payable
2430 Tuition Fees Payable
2440 MSP Payable - Employer
2460 WCB Payable
2650 GST Charged on Services ▶

▶2670 GST Paid on Purchases
2920 Mortgage Payable

EQUITY
3560 C. Chaplin, Capital
3600 Current Earnings

REVENUE
4020 Revenue from Services
4040 Sales Discounts

EXPENSE
5020 Advertising Expenses
5040 Bank Charges
5060 Hydro Expenses
5080 Insurance Expense ▶

▶5100 Cleaning Supplies Used
5140 Packaging Supplies Used
5150 Purchase Discounts
5160 Telephone Expenses
5180 Vehicle Expenses
5300 Wages: General
5305 Wages: Cleaning Staff
5310 EI Expense
5320 CPP Expense
5330 WCB Expense
5340 Commissions
5350 Piece Rate Bonuses
5360 Travel Allowances
5380 Tuition Fees Expense
5400 MSP Premium Expense

NOTES: The Chart of Accounts includes only postable accounts and Current Earnings.

POST-CLOSING TRIAL BALANCE

LIME LIGHT LAUNDRY

February 1, 2015

		Debits	Credits
1080	Bank: Chequing	$ 53 140.30	
1200	Accounts Receivable	4 305.00	
1240	Advances & Loans Receivable	200.00	
1260	Prepaid Insurance	2 200.00	
1280	Cleaning Supplies	2 000.00	
1320	Packaging Supplies	1 200.00	
1520	Computer System	3 800.00	
1540	Delivery Vehicle	35 000.00	
1560	Laundry and Cleaning Equipment	15 000.00	
1580	Pressing Equipment	25 000.00	
1600	Railings and Belts	10 000.00	
1620	Laundry Premises	250 000.00	
2100	Bank Loan		$12 000.00
2200	Accounts Payable		5 040.00 ▶
▶ 2250	Accrued Wages		1 150.00
2300	Vacation Payable		1 098.00
2310	EI Payable		1 056.86
2320	CPP Payable		2 299.80
2330	Income Tax Payable		3 019.87
2400	MSP Payable - Employee		321.20
2410	RRSP Payable		200.00
2430	Tuition Fees Payable	425.00	
2440	MSP Payable - Employer		321.20
2460	WCB Payable		977.30
2650	GST Charged on Services		2 765.00
2670	GST Paid on Purchases	915.00	
2920	Mortgage Payable		200 000.00
3560	C. Chaplin, Capital		172 936.07
		$403 185.30	$403 185.30

SUPPLIER INFORMATION

LIME LIGHT LAUNDRY

Supplier Name (Contact)	Address	Phone No. Fax No.	E-mail Web Site	Terms Tax ID
BC Energy Group (Sol R. Heater)	33 Windmill Rd. Vancouver, BC V8K 3C3	Tel: (604) 388-1298	srh@bceg.ca www.bceg.ca	net 1
BC Minister of Finance (M.T. Handed)	7 Fiscal Way Victoria, BC V8V 2K4	Tel: (250) 887-3488 Fax: (250) 887-8109	www.fin.gov.bc.ca	net 1
BC Telephone (Kommue Nicate)	91 Cellular Way Vancouver, BC V8G 8B5	Tel: (604) 348-2355	www.bell.ca	net 1
BC Workers' Compensation Board (N. Jured)	55 Accidental Cr. Victoria, BC V8W 3X6	Tel: (250) 887-7199 Fax: (250) 887-9211	www.worksafebc.com	net 1
Ferndale Paper Products (T. Issue)	43 Ferndale Ave. Vancouver, BC V8F 2S6	Tel: (604) 466-3929 Fax: (604) 466-3935	tissue@ferndalepaper.com www.ferndalepaper.com	1/10, n/30 (after tax) 445 668 714
Langley Service Centre (Otto Fixer)	64 Mechanic St. Langley, BC V2Z 2S4	Tel: (778) 556-7106 Fax: (778) 556-7188	otto@lss.com www.lss.com	net 1 672 910 186
Pacific Laundry Suppliers (Al Washindon)	29 Spotless Dr. Vancouver, BC V8K 1N6	Tel: (604) 782-1618 Fax: (604) 781-5127	aw@pacificlaundry.com www.pacificlaundry.com	net 30 129 554 377
Receiver General for Canada	PO Box 20004 Sudbury, Ontario P3A 6B4	Tel 1: (800) 561-7761 Tel 2: (800) 959-2221	www.cra-arc.gc.ca	net 1
Richmond Equipment Co. (N.U. Dryer)	78 Richmond St. Richmond, BC V7C 3V2	Tel: (778) 699-3601 Fax: (778) 699-1577	Dryer@REC.com www.REC.com	1/10, n/30 (after tax) 366 455 281
Surrey Printers (H.P.L. Jett)	690 Surrey Ave. Surrey, BC V3H 6T1	Tel: (778) 286-9193 Fax: (778) 286-9100	jett@surreyprinters.com www.surreyprinters.com	net 1 125 481 262
Victoria Trust (Victoria Royale)	59 Queen St. Vancouver, BC V8U 1M6	Tel: (604) 388-1825 Fax: (604) 388-2663	www.victoriatrust.ca	net 1

OUTSTANDING SUPPLIER INVOICES

LIME LIGHT LAUNDRY

Supplier Name	Terms	Date	Invoice No.	Amount	Total
Ferndale Paper Products	1/10, n/30	Jan. 29/15	FP-901	$560	$560
Pacific Laundry Suppliers	net 30	Jan. 3/15	PL-644	$1 120	$1 120
Richmond Equipment Co.	1/10, n/30	Jan. 27/15	RE-4111	$3 360	$3 360
			Grand Total		$5 040

CLIENT INFORMATION

LIME LIGHT LAUNDRY

Client Name (Contact)	Address	Phone No. Fax No.	E-mail Web Site	Terms Credit Limit
Capilano Centre Hotel (Lotte Reste)	3 Stopover Cr. North Vancouver, BC V7H 5D3	Tel 1: (604) 587-2563 Tel 2: (888) 587-3882	lreste@cch.com www.cch.com	1/15, n/30 (after tax) $5 000
Coquitlam Motel (B. & B. Roadside)	56 Sliepers Rd. Vancouver, BC V8K 6F3	Tel 1: (604) 366-7155 Tel 2: (800) 366-9175	bbr@coquitlammotel.com www.coquitlammotel.com	1/15, n/30 (after tax) $5 000

CLIENT INFORMATION CONTINUED

Client Name (Contact)	Address	Phone No. Fax No.	E-mail Web Site	Terms Credit Limit
Delta Hotel (A. Good-Knight)	86 Holiday St. Richmond, BC V7R 4D9	Tel: (778) 782-5431 Fax: (778) 781-7528	goodknight@deltahotel.com www.deltahotel.com	1/15, n/30 (after tax) $5 000
Kingsway Inn (Abel Traveller)	77 Roomie Dr. Vancouver, BC V8E 2W2	Tel: (604) 566-7188 Fax: (604) 565-4281	at@kingsway.com www.kingsway.com	1/15, n/30 (after tax) $5 000
Port Moody Resort (Kat Napper)	425 Vacation Ave. Port Moody, BC V3H 4S3	Tel: (778) 369-5826 Fax: (778) 369-7993	knapper@pmresort.com www.pmresort.com	1/15, n/30 (after tax) $5 000

OUTSTANDING CLIENT INVOICES

LIME LIGHT LAUNDRY

Client Name	Terms	Date	Invoice No.	Amount	Total
Delta Hotel	1/15, n/30	Jan. 28/15	69	$2 940	$2 940
Kingsway Inn	1/15, n/30	Jan. 30/15	72	$1 365	$1 365
			Grand Total		$4 305

EMPLOYEE INFORMATION SHEET

LIME LIGHT LAUNDRY

	Clyne Fretton	Mouver Durtee	Soffte Landings	Iean Sissler	Claire Brumes	S. Pott Tran	Cryper Houseman
Position	Senior Cleaner	Cleaner	Senior Presser	Presser	Manager	Delivery	Maintenance
Social Insurance No.	218 738 631	552 846 826	422 946 541	931 771 620	726 911 134	638 912 634	822 546 859
Address	21 Spotter St. Vancouver, BC V3K 4K2	34 Wash Ave. Vancouver, BC V9B 4C1	92 Flat St. Vancouver, BC V8U 1X3	63 Iron Blvd., #2 Vancouver, BC V7N 2L2	11 Sweeper St. Vancouver, BC V7N 2L2	2 Kerry St. Richmond, BC V8K 4K2	4 Fixall Cr. Vancouver, BC V9B 4C1
Telephone	(604) 693-7595	(778) 381-8138	(604) 488-6353	(604) 389-2291	(604) 829-6291	(778) 693-7995	(778) 381-2238
Date of Birth (mm-dd-yy)	8-15-84	11-3-81	8-6-71	7-31-78	7-31-78	8-15-84	11-3-81
Date of Hire (mm-dd-yy)	2-7-09	12-4-14	4-6-09	11-6-14	1-1-10	8-5-10	6-6-06
Federal (BC) Tax Exemption – TD1							
Basic Personal	$11 038 (10 276)	$11 038 (10 276)	$11 038 (10 276)	$11 038 (10 276)	$11 038 (10 276)	$11 038 (10 276)	$11 038 (10 276)
Other Indexed	$15 506 (8 860)	–	$22 382 (17 595)	–	–	$13 272 (8 860)	$11 038 (8 860)
Non-Indexed		–	–	$3 670 (3 030)	–	–	–
Total Exemptions	$26 544 (19 136)	$11 038 (10 276)	$33 420 (27 871)	$14 708 (13 306)	$11 038 (10 276)	$24 310 (19 136)	$22 076 (19 136)
Additional Fed Taxes	$100	–	–	–	–	–	–
Employee Taxes							
Historical Income Tax	$613.84	$380.32	$77.55	$314.55	$819.07	$397.28	$417.26
Historical EI	$64.95	$52.20	$55.57	$50.66	$83.48	$64.08	$69.42
Historical CPP	$170.22	$133.26	$143.86	$133.96	$219.30	$167.52	$181.78
Deduct EI; EI Rate	Yes; 1.4	Yes; 1.4	Yes; 1.4	Yes; 1.4	Yes; 1.4	Yes; 1.4	Yes; 1.4
Deduct CPP	Yes	Yes	Yes	Yes	Yes	Yes	Yes
Employee Income							
Loans: Hist Amt	$200.00	(use) ✓	(use) ✓	(use) ✓	(use) ✓	(use) ✓	(use) ✓
Benefits Per Period	$30.69	$ 7.62	$27.81	$ 7.62	$60.25	$30.69	$66.50
Benefits: Hist Amt	$61.38	$30.48	$55.62	$150.48	$60.25	$61.38	$66.50
Vacation Pay Owed	$464.98	$170.06	$295.76	$167.20	–	–	–
Vacation Paid	–	–	–	–	–	–	–

EMPLOYEE INFORMATION SHEET CONTINUED

	Clyne Fretton	Mouver Durtee	Soffte Landings	Iean Sissler	Claire Brumes	S. Pott Tran	Cryper Houseman
Employee Income Continued							
Regular Wage Rate	$20.00	$16.00	$18.00	$16.00	(do not use)	(do not use)	(do not use)
(Hours per Period)	(80 hours)	(40 hours)	(80 hours)	(40 hours)	–	–	–
Reg. Wages: Hist Amt	$3 200.00	$2 560.00	$2 880.00	$2 560.00	–	–	–
Overtime 1 Rate	$30.00	$24.00	$27.00	$24.00	(do not use)	(do not use)	(do not use)
Overtime 1: Hist Amt	$60.00	$192.00	$54.00	$96.00	–	–	–
Salary	(do not use)	(do not use)	(do not use)	(do not use)	$4 300.00	$1 800.00	$3 900.00
(Hours per Period)	–	–	–	–	(150 hours)	(80 hours)	(150 hours)
Salary: Hist Amt	—	–	–		$4 300	$3 600	$3 900
Commission	(do not use)	(do not use)	(do not use)	(do not use)	1% net sales	(do not use)	(do not use)
Commission: Hist Amt	–	–	–	–	$390.00	–	–
Piece Rate/Set	$0.10	$0.10	$0.10	$0.10	(do not use)	(do not use)	(do not use)
Piece Rate: Hist Amt	$189.00	$180.00	$188.00	$190.00	–	–	–
Pay Periods	26 (bi-weekly)	52 (weekly)	26 (bi-weekly)	52 (weekly)	12 (monthly)	26 (bi-weekly)	12 (monthly)
Vacation Rate	6% retained	4% retained	6% retained	4% retained	0% (3 weeks)	0% (3 weeks)	0% (3 weeks)
Record Wage Exp in	Linked Accts	Linked Accts	Linked Accts	Linked Accts	Linked Accts	Linked Accts	Linked Accts
Employee Deductions							
RRSP	(use) ✓	(use) ✓	(use) ✓	$25.00	$50.00	(use) ✓	$50.00
RRSP: Hist Amt	–	–	–	$100.00	$50.00	–	$50.00
MSP-Employee	$30.69	$ 7.61	$27.81	$ 7.61	$60.25	$30.69	$66.50
MSP-Hist Amt	$61.38	$30.44	$55.62	$30.44	$60.25	$61.38	$66.50
WCB and Other Expenses							
WCB Rate	3.77	3.77	3.77	3.77	3.77	5.01	3.77
Travel Allow	–	–	–	–	$300.00	–	–
Travel Allow: Hist Amt	–	–	–	–	$300.00	–	–
Tuition Fee	–	–	–	$30.00	–	–	–
Tuition Fee: Hist Amt	–	–	–	$120.00	–	–	–
MSP-Employer	$30.69	$ 7.62	$27.81	$ 7.62	$60.25	$30.69	$66.50
MSP-Employer: Hist Amt	$61.38	$30.48	$55.62	$30.48	$60.25	$61.38	$66.50
Entitlements: Rate, Maximum Days, Clear? (Historical Amount)							
Vacation: Rate, Max	–	–	–	–	8%, 25 days	8%, 25 days	8%, 25 days
Clear? (Days Accrued)	–	–	–	–	No (10 days)	No (5 days)	No (15 days)
Sick Leave: Rate, Max	5%, 20 days	5%, 20 days	5%, 20 days	5%, 20 days	5%, 20 days	5%, 20 days	5%, 20 days
Clear? (Days Accrued)	No (7 days)	No (5 days)	No (9 days)	No (8 days)	No (8 days)	No (8 days)	No (10 days)
Personal Days: Rate, Max	2.5%, 10 days	2.5%, 10 days	2.5%, 10 days	2.5%, 10 days	2.5%, 10 days	2.5%, 10 days	2.5%, 10 days
Clear? (Days Accrued)	No (3 days)	No (4 days)	No (1 day)	No (2 days)	No (3 days)	No (2 days)	No (2 days)
Direct Deposit							
Yes/No	Yes	No	No	Yes	Yes	No	Yes
Branch No., Institution No.	49921, 300	–	–	06722, 180	30099, 103	–	12084, 285
Account No.	2883912	–	–	4556221	2009123	–	2399012
Percent	100%	–	–	100%	100%	–	100%
Additional Information							
Emergency Contact	Aidan Fretton	Alex Durtee	Petra Landings	Kierin Safta	Jay Brumes	Sima Tran	Pedro Perez
Contact Number	(604) 497-1469	(778) 477-4573	(604) 488-6353	(604) 364-1892	(604) 899-2197	(778) 693-7995	(778) 447-5602
T4 and RL-1 Reporting							
EI Insurable Earnings	$3 449.00	$2 932.00	$3 122.00	$2 846.00	$4 690.00	$3 600.00	$3 900.00
Pensionable Earnings	$3 510.38	$2 962.48	$3 177.62	$2 996.48	$4 750.25	$3 661.38	$3 966.50
Withheld	$910.39	$596.22	$332.60	$629.61	$1 232.10	$690.26	$784.96
Net Pay	$2 738.61	$2 335.78	$2 789.40	$2 216.39	$3 457.90	$2 909.74	$3 115.04

EI, CPP & Income Tax Calculations are built into Sage 50

NOTES: Medical (MSP) premiums are deducted every pay period. The amounts are adjusted for the monthly rates.

Employee Profiles and TD1 Information

Employee Benefits and Entitlements All employees are entitled to 10 days per year as sick leave and five days' leave for personal reasons. If the days are not needed, employees can carry these days forward to a new year, to a maximum of 20 and 10 days, respectively. Currently, all employees have some unused sick leave and personal leave days accrued from the previous year. Salaried employees are allowed to carry forward two of their three weeks' vacation entitlement. That is, they are allowed to accumulate a maximum of 25 unused vacation days at any one time.

To encourage personal development, Lime Light pays 50 percent of the tuition fees for any employee enrolled in college or university programs. Currently, only Iean Sissler is taking courses and receiving the tuition fee benefit. This taxable benefit for Sissler is considered an expense for Lime Light Laundry. A second benefit applies to all employees — Lime Light Laundry pays 50 percent of the provincial medical premiums.

NOTES
Taxable benefits are not paid in cash to the employee. However, they are added to gross pay to determine income tax and then subtracted again to determine the net pay.
The medical premiums are paid for a government-sponsored plan and, therefore, are taxable benefits.

Piece Rate Bonuses Lime Light Laundry records the number of sheet sets in excess of the first 500 sets each week and pays the cleaning staff — the cleaners and pressers — a piece rate bonus of 10 cents per extra set. This bonus is added to each paycheque.

Employer Expenses Lime Light Laundry currently has three employer payroll expenses beyond the compulsory CPP, EI and WCB: 50 percent of the employee's medical premiums for the BC Medical Services Plan (MSP), 50 percent of eligible tuition fees and a travel allowance for Brumes as compensation for using her car for business travel.

Claire Brumes As the manager of the laundry, Brumes negotiates deals with clients, schedules work, hires new staff and discusses problems with the owner, who does not participate in the day-to-day affairs of the business. She is married and has no children. Since her husband is also fully employed, she uses the single federal and provincial tax claim amounts, but she pays the medical premiums for a couple. At the end of each month, her salary of $4 300 per month plus a commission of 1 percent of revenue from services, net of taxes, is deposited to her account. She is recorded as salesperson for all sales for the purpose of calculating her commission. In addition, she receives $300 per month in a separate cheque as a travel allowance to cover the expense of her regular client visits and business promotion. This amount is an employer expense, not an employee benefit. She makes monthly contributions to her RRSP plan as well. In lieu of vacation pay, she is entitled to take three weeks of paid vacation each year.

Clyne Fretton As the senior cleaner, Fretton performs regular laundry duties, such as cleaning the incoming bed sheets and table linens. She has several years of experience with Lime Light and is helping to train Durtee, the junior cleaner who was recently hired. Her regular pay of $20 per hour is supplemented by the piece rate bonus and by overtime wages at the rate of $30 per hour when she works more than 40 hours per week. In addition, she receives vacation pay at the rate of 6 percent of her total wages, equivalent to about three weeks of pay, but this amount is retained until she chooses to take a vacation. Because she supports her husband and two children under 12, she claims the spousal and child claim amounts for income tax purposes and she also pays medical premiums at the family rate. To offset the tax from her additional income, she chooses to have an additional $100 in taxes withheld each pay period. She has received a loan of $200 which she will repay over the next four pay periods. She has her pay deposited directly to her bank account every two weeks.

NOTES
Federal claims allow a claim amount for eligible children; provincial claims to not.

Mouver Durtee is the second and junior cleaner. For sharing all the cleaning duties with Fretton, he earns $16 per hour, $24 per hour overtime when he works more than 40 hours in a week and the piece rate bonus. He is paid weekly by cheque and his 4 percent vacation pay is retained. As a single self-supporting person, Durtee claims the basic single amount for income tax and pays single medical premiums.

Soffte Landings is the senior presser. She operates the clothes pressing equipment, assisted by Sissler. Landings is single but supports her invalid aged mother so she is able to claim the spousal equivalent TD1 amount, the caregiver amounts and her mother's age amount. These claims significantly reduce the income tax she pays on her wages of $18 per hour, $27 for overtime hours and piece rate bonus. Her medical premium for two people is deducted from her bi-weekly paycheque at the family rate to cover herself and her mother. Her 6 percent vacation pay is retained.

Iean Sissler assists Landings with operating the equipment to press the laundry. She is single with no dependants, so she pays single medical premiums and has only the basic single TD1 claim amounts, plus her tuition of $2 050 and the education allowances ($140 per month federal and $60 provincial). From her weekly deposited pay, she contributes $50 to an RRSP program. Her pay, at $16 per hour and $24 for overtime hours with 4 percent vacation pay, is less than Landings' pay because she has less experience. She also receives the piece rate bonus. Sissler is enrolled in a business program at the local community college. She pays 50 percent of her tuition herself and Lime Light Laundry pays an equal amount. This taxable benefit, entered on Sissler's paycheque at the rate of $30 per week, has already been paid for one month.

S. Pott Tran Tran's main responsibility with Lime Light is delivery. He picks up the dirty laundry from hotels throughout the city and drops off the clean linens. Tran is married and fully supports his wife and one child, so he pays the family medical premiums and has the basic, spousal and child tax claim amounts. He is paid his bi-weekly salary of $1 800 by cheque, and he can take three weeks of vacation yearly.

Cryper Houseman is responsible for general maintenance at Lime Light — he keeps the machines running and cleans the premises. As a single parent who supports two children, he pays the family medical premium. For income tax purposes, he claims the spousal amount and the amount for one child. He has worked for Lime Light since the business started. At the end of each month, Houseman has his monthly salary of $3 900 deposited to his bank account. He also makes contributions to his RRSP program with regular payroll deductions. As a salaried employee, he is entitled to take three weeks of paid vacation per year.

Accounting Procedures

Taxes: GST and PST

The provincial and federal sales taxes are separate in British Columbia at the rate of 5 percent GST and 7 percent PST. PST is not applied to the services that Lime Light Laundry offers — only GST applies to this service. Lime Light Laundry uses the regular method for remitting the GST. It records the GST collected from clients as a liability in *GST Charged on Services*. GST paid to suppliers is recorded in *GST Paid on Purchases* as a decrease in the liability to the Canada Revenue Agency. The GST quarterly refund or remittance is calculated automatically in the *GST Owing (Refund)* subgroup total account. Lime Light files for a refund or remits the balance owing to the Receiver General for Canada by the last day of the month for the previous quarter.

Tax codes are set up in the defaults for the company so that Sage 50 will automatically calculate the tax when it applies.

NOTES

Acting on referendum results, BC reverted to separate application of GST and PST as it was administerd before harmonization in 2010. This change took effect in 2013.

PST paid on purchases is not refundable – the amount paid is automatically included in the asset or expense portion of the purchase.

Discounts

All clients are offered a discount of 1 percent on the after-tax amount of the sale if they pay their accounts in full within 15 days. Full payment is requested in 30 days. Discount terms are set up as the default in the client records. Some suppliers also offer discounts on after-tax purchase amounts. These discount terms are set up in the supplier records so that Sage 50 will automatically calculate the discount when full payment is made within the discount period.

Direct Payroll Deposits

Chaplin allows employees to have their regular pay deposited directly to their bank accounts or to be paid by cheque. Four employees have selected direct payroll deposits.

Payroll Remittances

Four suppliers are identified as payroll authorities with the following remittances: EI, CPP and income tax are remitted to the Receiver General for Canada; medical premiums are remitted to the BC Minister of Finance; Workers' Compensation Board premiums are remitted to the BC Workers' Compensation Board; and RRSP contributions are remitted to Victoria Trust.

INSTRUCTIONS

1. **Set up** the **Payroll Ledger** using the employee information, employee profiles and TD1 information. Detailed keystroke instructions for setting up payroll follow.
2. **Enter** the **transactions** in Sage 50 using the Chart of Accounts and Supplier, Client and Employee Information. The first source document is on page 342.
3. **Print** the **reports and graphs** marked on the following printing form after you have finished making your entries.

REPORTS

Accounts
- ☐ Chart of Accounts
- ☐ Account List
- ☐ General Journal Entries

Financials
- ☑ Comparative Balance Sheet: Feb. 1 and Feb. 28 with difference in percentage
- ☑ Income Statement: Feb. 1 to Feb. 28
- ☑ Trial Balance date: Feb. 28
- ☑ All Journal Entries: Feb. 1 to Feb. 28
- ☑ General Ledger accounts: Feb. 1 to Feb. 28 4020 5300 5305 5350
- ☐ Statement of Cash Flows
- ☑ Cash Flow Projection Detail Report: for 1080 for next 30 days

Tax
- ☐ GST Report

Banking
- ☐ Cheque Log Report

Payables
- ☐ Supplier List
- ☐ Supplier Aged
- ☐ Aged Overdue Payables
- ☐ Expenses Journal Entries
- ☐ Payments Journal Entries

Receivables
- ☐ Client List
- ☐ Client Aged
- ☐ Aged Overdue Receivables
- ☐ Revenues Journal Entries
- ☐ Receipts Journal Entries
- ☑ Revenues by Salesperson Feb. 1 to Feb. 28
- ☐ Revenues by Job Category
- ☐ Client Statements

Employees & Payroll
- ☐ Employee List
- ☑ Summary for all employees
- ☐ Deductions & Expense
- ☐ Job Category
- ☐ Remittances
- ☑ Payroll Journal Entries: Feb. 1 to Feb. 28
- ☐ T4 Slips
- ☐ Record of Employment
- ☐ Year End Review (PIER)

Mailing Labels
- ☐ Labels

Management Reports
- ☐ Ledger

GRAPHS

- ☐ Payables by Aging Period
- ☐ Payables by Supplier
- ☐ Receivables by Aging Period
- ☐ Receivables by Client
- ☐ Revenues vs Receivables
- ☐ Receivables Due vs Payables Due
- ☐ Revenues by Account
- ☐ Expenses by Account
- ☑ Expenses and Net Profit as % of Revenue

PAYROLL SETUP KEYSTROKES

Adding the Payroll Module

Open **SageData13\Limelite\limelite** to access the data file for **Lime Light**.
Accept Feb. 1 as the **session date**.

The Payroll module is hidden because it was not used. Before we can set it up, we need to unhide it. We will then work from this module to enter settings and employees.

Choose the **Setup menu** and **click User Preferences** to open the Options screen.

Click **View** to access the screen we need:

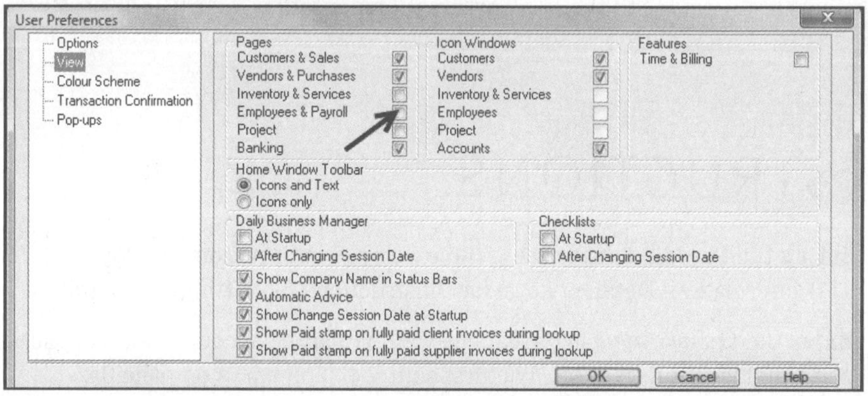

Click the **Pages check box for Employees & Payroll** to add ✓s for Pages and Icon Windows.

Click **OK** to save the settings and return to the Home window.

Click **Employees & Payroll** in the Modules pane list:

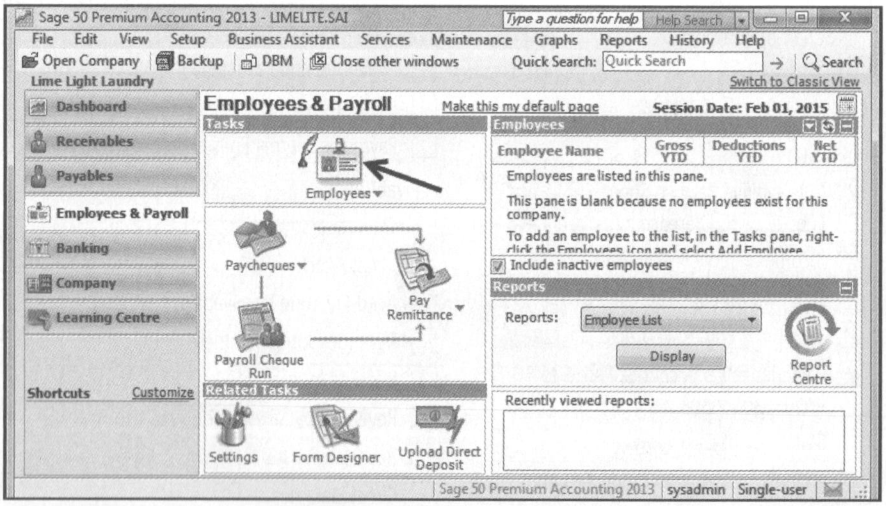

The Payroll Ledger and its icons have been added. The Employees icon has the not-finished symbol to indicate that the module history is not finished. If you try to finish the Payroll history now, you will see an error message about several missing linked accounts.

From the Employees & Payroll window we can enter ledger settings and records.

NOTES
Remember that you must have a valid and active Payroll ID code from Sage in order to use the payroll features for non-Student versions of the program.
Choose the Services menu and click Sage Business Care for more information.

NOTES
If you are using the backup installation set or the Pro version, restore SageData13\limelite1.CAB or limelite1 to SageData13\Limelite\limelite to open the data file for Lime Light.

CLASSIC VIEW
The User Preferences View screen has two columns: one for Modules that includes Time & Billing and one for the Icon Windows.

PRO VERSION
The Pro version does not have the Time & Billing feature.

NOTES
Clicking the Pages check box will add the ✓s for viewing both the Module and Icon Windows. Then you can remove the ✓ for the Icon Window if you want.

NOTES
You can make Employees & Payroll your default home page while you are completing the payroll setup. When you close the file and re-open it, you will open this page to continue the setup.

NOTES
If you open the Payroll Journal now, you will display the message that essential linked accounts are missing. Clicking OK will then open the Linked Accounts Settings screen.

Setting Up the Payroll Ledger

Before you can enter payroll journal transactions, you must set up the payroll module. This involves the same steps as setting up other ledgers:

1. Change the settings for the ledger.
2. Create employee ledger records.
3. Add historical employee data.
4. Back up the data file and finish the history.

Changing Payroll Ledger Settings

Click the **Settings icon** Settings to open the Payroll Settings screen:

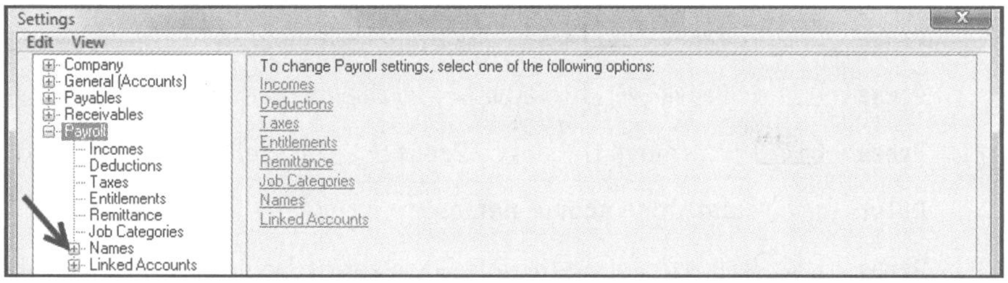

You can also choose the Setup menu and click Settings. Click Payroll if necessary.

Because the Employees & Payroll module window is open, the Settings window opens with the Payroll Settings list. For payroll, we need to define the types of income paid to employees; the payroll deductions; payroll taxes; employee entitlements; remittances; job categories; names for income; deductions and additional fields; and linked accounts for all these functions. We will begin by entering names and deleting the ones we do not need. The reduced list will be easier to work with.

Click the ⊞ **beside Names** and the ⊞ **beside Linked Accounts**.

This will expand the list, making the links to all the Payroll settings available.

Changing Payroll Names

Click **Income & Deductions** under the Names subheading:

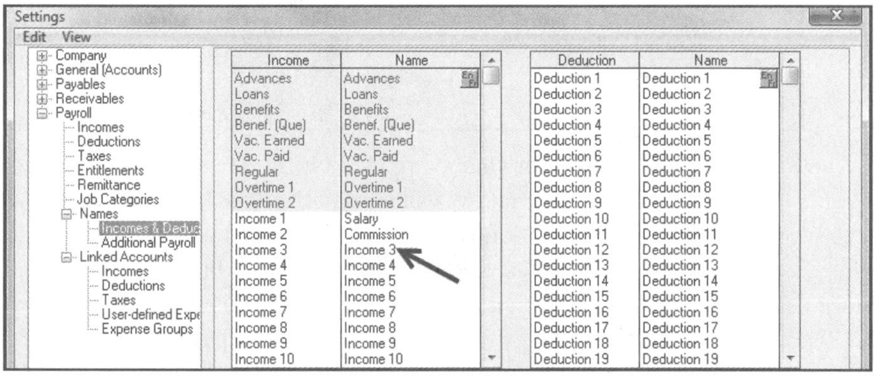

The first screen we need to modify has all the names for incomes and deductions used. Many of the standard income types are mandatory and cannot be changed. These fields are shown on a shaded background. Some of the other default names are also correct, so you do not need to redefine them. You can leave Income 1 and Income 2, labelled "Salary" and "Commission," unchanged because Lime Light Laundry has salaried employees and pays a sales commission to Brumes. There is allowance for

CLASSIC VIEW
From the Home window, right-click the Employees icon Employees. Then click the Setup tool. You can also click the Setup tool and select Employees from the drop-down list.

NOTES
In any module window, click the Settings icon and then click Payroll to open the Payroll Settings screen.

NOTES
By modifying the names first, only the ones we need to set up will appear on later screens.

NOTES
You can enter names for any of these fields later if you need to add more incomes or deductions.

PRO VERSION
You will not see the Expense Groups entry under Linked Accounts.

NOTES
Lime Light Laundry does not use Expense Groups (under Linked Accounts).

NOTES
We are not setting up travel allowances as income because separate cheques are issued for this. If it were set up as income (reimbursement), it would be added to the paycheque as non-taxable income.

NOTES
If clicking does not highlight the field contents, drag through an entry to select it. Double-clicking will open the English/French names screen.

WARNING!
If you later change the province in the Company Information screen, the WCB name entered for Worker's Comp. will not change automatically. You must enter the correction manually by choosing from the drop-down list.

NOTES
The Worker's Comp. drop-down list has several other employer expenses that may apply to all employees.
You may use up to 20 characters to name the additional fields and user-defined expenses.

20 different kinds of income in addition to the compulsory fields and 20 different payroll deductions. Each income and deduction label may have up to 12 characters.

Lime Light uses an additional income field for the piece rate bonus that is based on the number of sets of bedding the employees launder. The travel allowance for Brumes will be set up as a user-defined expense. The remaining income fields are not used.

Lime Light also has two payroll deductions at this time: RRSP, the Registered Retirement Savings Plan, and the employee share of provincial medical plan premiums (MSP-Employee). The remaining deduction fields are not used.

Click **Income 3 in the Name column** to highlight the contents.

Type Piece Rate **Press** tab to advance to the Income 4 field.

Click the **En/Fr language icon** to open the extra fields if you want to enter labels or names in both French and English.

Press del. **Press** tab to advance to the Income 5 field.

Press del. **Press** tab to advance to the Income 6 field.

Press del to remove the entry. **Press** tab to select the next field.

Delete the **remaining Income names** until they are all removed.

Press tab after deleting Income 20 to select Deduction 1 in the Name column. **Click** tab again if you are in the Deduction column.

Type RRSP **Press** tab to advance to the second deduction Name field.

Type MSP-Employee **Press** tab to highlight the next field.

Delete the **remaining deductions** because Lime Light Laundry does not have other payroll deductions.

Click **Additional Payroll** under the Names subheading:

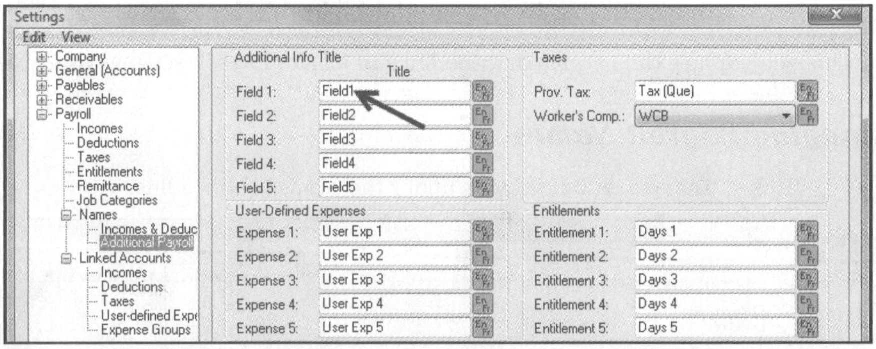

The Prov. Tax field is used for Quebec payroll taxes. Since we will not enter linked accounts for Quebec taxes, the program will automatically skip the related payroll fields. WCB (Workers' Compensation Board) is entered as the name for Workers' Compensation because we selected British Columbia as the business province.

We can also name the additional ledger fields, the additional payroll expenses for Lime Light and the entitlements for employees. Lime Light pays 50 percent of the employees' provincial health care plan medical premiums and eligible tuition fees. It also pays a travel allowance to Brumes and offers sick leave and personal leave days for all employees as well as vacation days for salaried employees. First, we will name the ledger fields. We will use these fields to store the name and phone number of each employee's emergency contact.

Double-click **Field1** or **press** tab.

Type Emergency Contact

Press tab **twice** to skip the language label icon and highlight the next field.

Type `Contact Number`

Press tab **twice**. **Press** del to delete the name for Field3.

Delete the **names** for Field4 and Field5.

> **NOTES**
> When you are not using both French and English (Company Settings, Features options) you will press tab once after each entry.

Benefits and expenses can be handled in different ways.

The medical premium payment is a taxable benefit for employees. It is also entered as a user-defined expense because the premiums are paid to a third party rather than to the employee. Tuition, the other taxable benefit and user-defined expense, is also paid to a third party — the educational institution. Benefits paid directly to the employee on the payroll cheque should be set up as income. Reimbursements for expenses may be entered as non-taxable income or as user-defined expenses. If we repay the expenses on the payroll cheque, we define them as reimbursements — an income type that is not taxable — and link them to an expense account. If we enter them as user-defined expenses, we create both a linked payable and expense account and issue a separate payment to the employee. Brumes' travel allowance is set up as a user-defined expense.

> **NOTES**
> For Lime Light Laundry, we use the generic Benefits field to enter all employee benefits.

> **NOTES**
> In Chapter 16, we create Travel Expenses as income (reimbursement type) that is added to the paycheque. Here it is a user-defined expense and we issue separate cheques to the employee for it.

Drag through **User Exp 1**, the Expense 1 field, to highlight the contents.

Type `Travel Allow` **Press** tab **twice** to skip the language button and select the next expense name.

Type `Tuition Fees` **Press** tab **twice**.

Type `MSP-Employer` **Press** tab **twice**.

Press del. **Press** tab **twice** to select the final expense. **Press** del.

Drag through **Days 1**, the Entitlement 1 field, to highlight the contents.

Type `Vacation` **Press** tab **twice** to select the next entitlement name.

Type `Sick Leave` **Press** tab **twice**.

Type `PersonalDays` **Press** tab **twice**.

Press del. **Press** tab **twice** to select the final name. **Press** del.

> **NOTES**
> You can use up to 12 characters for User-Defined Expense and Entitlement names including spaces – that is why we omitted the space for the Personal Days entitlement name.

Setting Defaults for Payroll

Click **Incomes** under the Payroll heading to display the income setup:

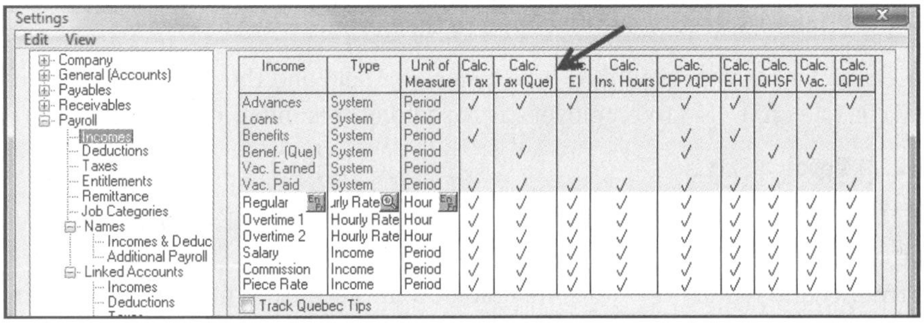

Income	Type	Unit of Measure	Calc. Tax	Calc. Tax (Que)	Calc. EI	Calc. Ins. Hours	Calc. CPP/QPP	Calc. EHT	Calc. QHSF	Calc. Vac.	Calc. QPIP
Advances	System	Period	✓	✓	✓		✓	✓	✓	✓	✓
Loans	System	Period									
Benefits	System	Period	✓				✓	✓			
Benef. (Que)	System	Period		✓			✓		✓	✓	
Vac. Earned	System	Period									
Vac. Paid	System	Period	✓	✓	✓	✓	✓	✓	✓		✓
Regular	Hourly Rate	Hour	✓	✓	✓	✓	✓	✓	✓	✓	✓
Overtime 1	Hourly Rate	Hour	✓	✓	✓	✓	✓	✓	✓	✓	✓
Overtime 2	Hourly Rate	Hour	✓	✓	✓	✓	✓	✓	✓	✓	✓
Salary	Income	Period	✓	✓	✓	✓	✓	✓	✓	✓	✓
Commission	Income	Period	✓	✓	✓	✓	✓	✓	✓	✓	✓
Piece Rate	Income	Period	✓	✓	✓	✓	✓	✓	✓	✓	✓

> **NOTES**
> The incomes with shaded background are defined by the program and cannot be changed – System is entered under the heading Type.

At this stage, we will change the tax settings for Incomes and Deductions.

We will first modify this screen by hiding the columns that do not apply to British Columbia so that only the columns we need are on-screen at the same time.

Point to the **right-hand column heading margin for Calc. Tax (Que.)** until the pointer changes to a two-sided arrow ↔.

Drag the **margin to the left** until the column is hidden.

Point to the **right-hand column heading margin for Calc. EHT** until the pointer changes to a two-sided arrow. **Drag** the **margin to the left**.

Remove the **columns for Calc. QHSF** and **Calc. QPIP** in the same way.

Notice that only the income names you did not delete (page 320) appear on this screen. For each type of income you must indicate what taxes are applied and whether vacation pay is calculated on the income. Most of the information is correct. Regular and overtime hours are paid on an hourly basis, while salary and commissions are paid at designated income amounts per period. All taxes apply to these types of income in British Columbia, so these default settings are correct. Vacation pay, however, is paid only to the hourly paid employees, so some checkmarks should be removed. In addition, we should designate the type of income for Piece Rate, the income we added, and the taxes that apply to it. Choosing the type of income will change the defaults that are applied.

Click **Piece Rate** to place the cursor on the correct line.

Press tab to move to the Type column. A List icon is added.

Click the **List icon** to see the types we can select:

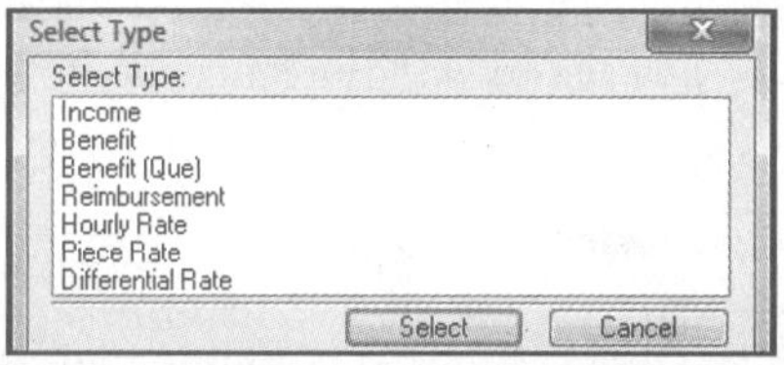

By default, all new income entries are assigned to the **Income** type. This assignment is correct for Salary. Taxable benefits paid to a third party should be classified as **Benefits** (see Warning note). The benefit amount is added to income to determine taxes and then subtracted again to calculate the net pay amount. Taxable benefits paid directly to the employee instead of a third party should also be classified as Income. If a benefit is added to net pay, it should be classified as an Income. Tuition is not paid to the employee, so it is a benefit.

Reimbursements are not taxable — the employee is being repaid for company-related expenditures. The **Piece Rate** type calculates pay based on the number of units. **Differential Rates** apply to different hourly rates paid at different times and are not used by Lime Light.

Click **Piece Rate** to select this type for Piece Rate.

Click **Select** to add the Type to the Settings screen. **Press** tab.

The cursor advances to the Unit of Measure field and the entry has changed to Item. The amount paid to employees is based on the number of sheet sets laundered.

Type `Sets`

Notice that the Insurable Hours checkmark was removed as soon as we changed the type.

We need to modify the other Insurable Hours settings. The number of hours worked determines eligibility for Employment Insurance benefits. Regular, overtime and salary paid hours are entered but commissions are not — no time can be reasonably attached to commissions, so they are not counted. The checkmark for it should be removed. The ✓ for Piece Rate was automatically removed when we changed the income type.

Click **Commission** to select this income line.

Press tab **repeatedly** until the cursor is in the **Calc. Ins. Hours field**.

NOTES

When you close and re-open the Payroll Settings screen, the hidden and resized columns will be restored – the column changes you made are not saved.

QHSF is the provincial health services plan for Quebec.

QPIP (Quebec Parental Insurance Plan) provides parental leave benefits to EI insurable employees. Both employers and employees pay into the plan.

EHT (Employer Health Tax) applies only in Ontario.

NOTES

An alternative approach for tuition fees is to set them up as a taxable income (on which vacation pay is not calculated) and add the amount to the employee's paycheque. You would use this method when the employee pays the tuition and is repaid (as in Helena's Academy, Chapter 8, and VeloCity, Chapter 16). Tuition is not a reimbursement type of income because it is taxable.

WARNING!

If you choose Benefit from this Select Type list of income categories, the expense amount for it will not be reported in the journal entry – as if it happens behind the scenes and requires a separate journal entry.

NOTES

When you select Reimbursement as the type, all taxes are removed because this type of payment is not taxable.

Click to remove the ✓, or **press** the **space bar**.

We also need to modify the entries for vacation pay. In British Columbia, vacation pay is calculated on all performance-based wages. This includes the regular wages, overtime wages and piece rate pay. We need to remove the remaining ✓s. Salaried workers receive paid time off rather than a percentage of their wages as vacation pay. We do not need to remove the ✓ for Overtime 2. If it is used later, vacation pay will be calculated on it as well.

Click **Salary** in the Income column.

Press tab **repeatedly** until the cursor is in the **Calc. Vac. column**.

Click to remove the ✓, or **press** the **space bar**.

Press ↓ to place the cursor in the **Calc. Vac. field for Commission**.

Click to remove the ✓, or **press** the **space bar** and complete the Settings screen as shown:

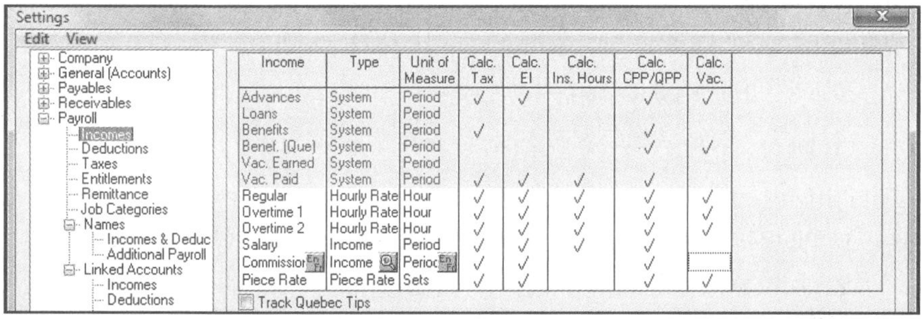

Income	Type	Unit of Measure	Calc. Tax	Calc. EI	Calc. Ins. Hours	Calc. CPP/QPP	Calc. Vac.
Advances	System	Period	✓	✓		✓	✓
Loans	System	Period					
Benefits	System	Period	✓			✓	
Benef. (Que)	System	Period				✓	✓
Vac. Earned	System	Period					
Vac. Paid	System	Period	✓	✓	✓	✓	
Regular	Hourly Rate	Hour	✓	✓	✓	✓	✓
Overtime 1	Hourly Rate	Hour	✓	✓	✓	✓	✓
Overtime 2	Hourly Rate	Hour	✓	✓	✓	✓	✓
Salary	Income	Period	✓	✓	✓	✓	
Commission	Income	Period	✓	✓		✓	
Piece Rate	Piece Rate	Sets	✓	✓		✓	✓

Click **Deductions** under the Payroll heading:

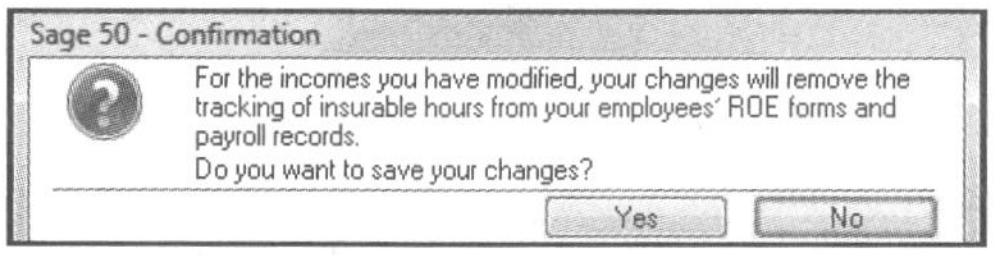

You are warned that the changes will affect the insurable earnings amounts reported on the Record of Employment. The changes are correct so you should continue.

Click **Yes** to continue to the Deductions settings:

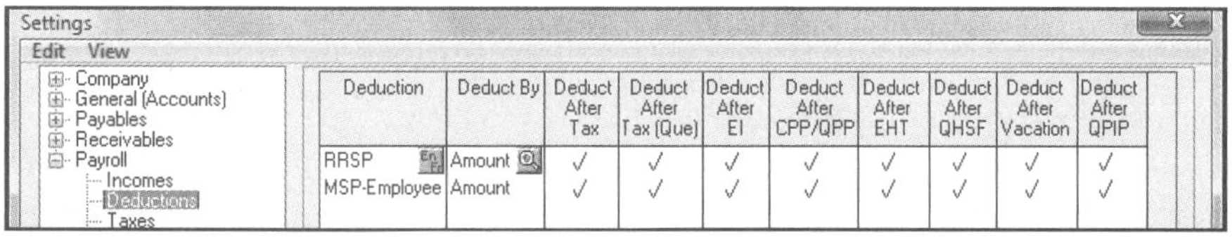

Deduction	Deduct By	Deduct After Tax	Deduct After Tax (Que)	Deduct After EI	Deduct After CPP/QPP	Deduct After EHT	Deduct After QHSF	Deduct After Vacation	Deduct After QPIP
RRSP	Amount	✓	✓	✓	✓	✓	✓	✓	✓
MSP-Employee	Amount	✓	✓	✓	✓	✓	✓	✓	✓

Only the two deduction names you entered earlier appear on this screen. You can calculate deductions as a percentage of the gross pay or as a fixed amount. Some deductions, like union dues, are usually calculated as a percentage of income. The Amount settings are correct for Lime Light Laundry.

All deductions are set by default to be calculated after all taxes (Deduct After Tax is checked). For MSP-Employee, this is correct — it is subtracted from income after income tax and other payroll taxes have been deducted. However, RRSP contributions qualify as tax deductions and will be subtracted from gross income before income tax is calculated, but not before EI, CPP and so on, so you must change only this setting.

Click the **Deduct After Tax column** for RRSP to remove only the one ✓ and change the setting to before tax.

The remaining settings are correct. RRSP is deducted after the other payroll taxes and vacation pay because these deductions are based on gross wages.

NOTES

Vacation pay is also paid for statutory holidays. Lime Light pays workers their regular pay for these days, as if they had worked. For occasional workers, this pay may be calculated as a percentage of wages.

In Quebec, vacation pay is also paid on benefits.

NOTES

Vacation pay is calculated on all wages. This calculation includes the piece rate pay – number of sheet sets – because it is a performance-based wage or income. Vacation pay is not applied to benefits.

The regulations governing vacation pay are set provincially.

NOTES

Although checkmarks will remain for the columns we hid, the fields for them will be skipped in ledger screens and journals because we will not enter linked accounts for them.

NOTES

You can modify the Deductions screen as you modified the Incomes Settings screen so that only the columns you need are on-screen. You can remove the Deduct After Tax (Que.), EHT, QHSF and QPIP columns.

Click **Taxes** under the Payroll heading:

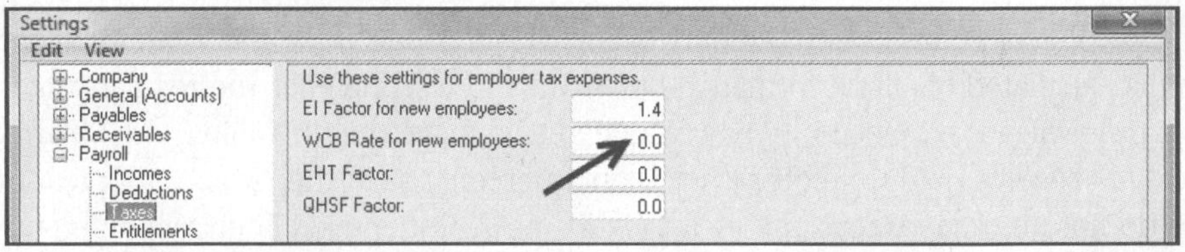

This next group of fields refers to the rate at which employer tax obligations are calculated. The factor for Employment Insurance (**EI Factor**) is correct at 1.4. The employer's contribution is set at 1.4 times the employee's contribution. In the next field, you can set the employer's rate for **WCB** (Workers' Compensation Board) premiums. On this screen, you can enter 3.77, the rate that applies to most Lime Light employees. You can modify rates for individual employees in the ledger records, as we will do for Tran.

The next field, **EHT Factor**, shows the percentage of payroll costs that the employer contributes to the provincial health plan in Ontario. The rate is based on the total payroll costs per year. It does not apply to BC employees.

The **QHSF Factor** (Quebec Health Services Fund) applies to payroll in Quebec, so we do not need to enter it. QHSF is similar to EHT.

NOTES
The WCB rate is based on the injury history and risk factors for the job and for the industry. Tran's rate is higher than the others' because his work – driving a delivery truck – is considered more dangerous.

NOTES
EHT applies to payroll in Ontario. The factor or rate ranges from 0.98 to 1.95 depending on the total payroll amount.
QHSF is used for Village Galleries in Chapter 14.

Click the **WCB Rate field**.

Type 3.77

The Quebec tax fields will not be available for employees because we will not enter linked accounts for them. They do not apply to employees in British Columbia.

Click **Entitlements** under the Payroll heading:

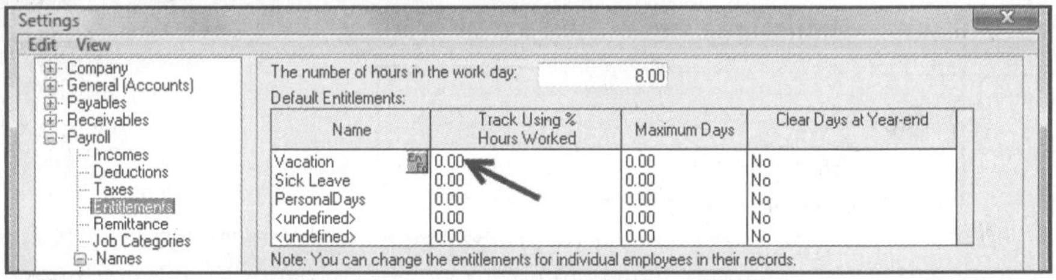

On this screen you can enter the rules for entitlements that apply to all or most employees. When we enter the rules here, they will be added to each employee's record. You can change entitlement amounts for individual employees in their ledger records.

Entitlements may be given directly or may be linked to the number of hours worked. For example, usually employees are not entitled to take vacation time until they have worked for a certain period of time. Or they may not be allowed to take paid sick leave immediately after being hired. You can use the **Track Using % Hours Worked** to determine how quickly vacation or sick days accumulate. For example, 5 percent of hours worked yields about one day per month. Thus, you would enter 5 percent if the employee is entitled to 12 days of leave per year. You can also indicate the **Maximum** number of **Days** per year that an employee can take or accumulate. And finally, you must indicate whether the unused days are **cleared at the end of a year** or can be carried forward. If the days earned, but not used, at the end of a year are carried forward, then the Maximum will still place a limit on the number of days available. When the maximum number of days has been reached, no additional days will accrue — the entry in the Days Earned field on the journal Entitlements tab screen will be zero — until the employee takes time off and the days accrued drops below the maximum again. The number of days of entitlement is based on an eight-hour day as the default, but this can be changed.

NOTES
You can also apply entitlements as a fixed amount per year by omitting the tracking percentage, entering a maximum and then entering the balance for the employee in the ledger.

Lime Light Laundry gives salaried workers three weeks of vacation (tracked at 8 percent) and allows a maximum of 25 days. Sick leave at 10 days per year is earned at the rate of 5 percent to a maximum of 20 days. Personal leave days (5 days) accrue at the rate of 2.5 percent to a maximum of 10 days. None are cleared at year-end.

Lime Light Laundry allows two weeks of vacation time and sick leave and one week of personal days to be carried over to the following year.

Click the **Track Using % Hours Worked field for Vacation**.

Type 8 **Press** tab to advance to the Maximum Days field.

Type 25 **Press** tab.

Click the **Track Using % Hours Worked field for Sick Leave**.

Type 5 **Press** tab to advance to the Maximum Days field.

Type 20 **Press** tab.

Click the **Track Using % Hours Worked field for PersonalDays**.

Type 2.5 **Press** tab to advance to the Maximum Days field.

Type 10 **Press** tab.

Until we identify linked accounts we cannot set up Remittances. To set up Job Categories, we must first create employee records. Therefore, we will add Payroll Remittance and Job Category settings later.

Identifying the Payroll Linked Accounts

There are many linked accounts for payroll because each type of income, tax, deduction and expense that is used must be linked to a General Ledger account. You do not need to create any of these accounts; they are already in the Chart of Accounts. The following **linked accounts** are used by Lime Light Laundry for the Payroll Ledger.

PAYROLL LINKED ACCOUNTS

Income

Principal Bank	1080	Bank: Chequing			
Vacation Owed	2300	Vacation Payable	Advances & Loans	1240	Advances & Loans Receivable
Vac. Earned	5305	Wages: Cleaning Staff	Salary	5300	Wages: General
Regular	5305	Wages: Cleaning Staff	Commission	5340	Commissions
Overtime 1	5305	Wages: Cleaning Staff	Piece Rate	5350	Piece Rate Bonuses
Not used	Overtime 2				

Deductions

	Deduction		Payment Adjustment	
RRSP:	2410	RRSP Payable	2410	RRSP Payable
MSP-Employee:	2400	MSP Payable - Employee	2400	MSP Payable - Employee

Taxes

Payables			Expenses			Payment Adjustment		
EI	2310	EI Payable	EI	5310	EI Expense	EI	5310	EI Expense
CPP	2320	CPP Payable	CPP	5320	CPP Expense	CPP	5320	CPP Expense
Tax	2330	Income Tax Payable				Tax	1080	Bank: Chequing
WCB	2460	WCB Payable	WCB	5330	WCB Expense	WCB	5330	WCB Expense

Not used

EHT, Tax (Que.), QPP, QHSF, QPIP	EHT, QPP, QHSF, QPIP	EHT, Tax (Que.), QPP, QHSF, QPIP

User-Defined Expenses

Payables			Expenses		
Travel Allow	2420	Travel Allowances Payable	Travel Allow	5360	Travel Allowances
Tuition Fees	2430	Tuition Fees Payable	Tuition Fees	5380	Tuition Fees Expense
MSP-Employer	2440	MSP Payable - Employer	MSP-Employer	5400	MSP Premium Expense

Payment Adjustments

Travel Allow	5360	Travel Allowances
Tuition Fees	5380	Tuition Fees Expense
MSP-Employer	5400	MSP Premium Expense

NOTES

Three weeks' vacation is equivalent to about 6 percent when paid as a percentage of wages. When tracked as a percentage of hours worked, 8 percent will yield about three weeks of time off.

CLASSIC VIEW

You can access the Payroll Ledger linked accounts by right-clicking the Paycheques or the Payroll Cheque Run Journal icon in the Home window to select it.

Click the Setup tool or choose the Setup menu, then click Settings, Payroll, Linked Accounts and Income.

If no Home window icon is selected, you can use the Setup tool pop-up list, choose Payroll and click Select.

NOTES

You can also access the Payroll Linked Accounts screens from the Setup menu (and from the Paycheques Journal at this stage). Choose Settings and click Payroll and Linked Accounts or open the journal and click OK in response to the warning about missing essential linked accounts.

NOTES
The deleted income and deduction names do not appear on the screens for linked accounts. Deleting the unused names also simplifies the data entry for linked accounts.

NOTES
All the accounts you will need for this stage are already in the Chart of Accounts.
However, you can add accounts from the Linked Accounts windows. Type a new number, press *enter* and choose to add the account.

Click **Incomes** under the Linked Accounts subheading:

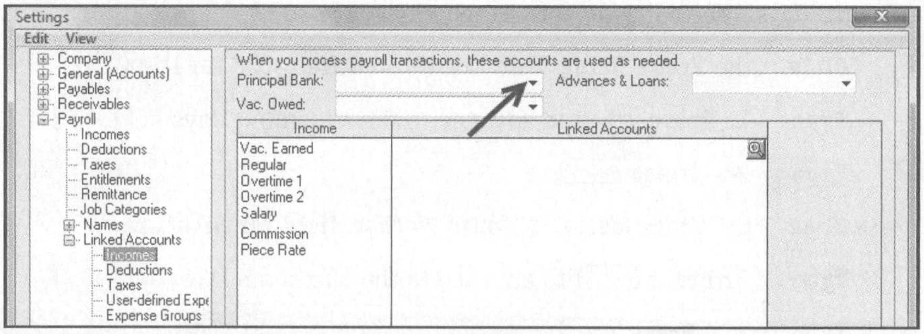

The linked accounts for all types of income appear together on this first screen. You must identify a wage account for each type of employee payment used by the company, even if the same account is used for all of them. Once the Payroll bank account is identified as the same one used for Payables, the program will apply a single sequence of cheque numbers for all cheques prepared from the Payables and Payroll journals.

Accounts you can use for more than one link will be available in the drop-down list. Otherwise, once an account is selected as a linked account, it is removed from the list.

To enter accounts, you can **type** the **account number** or **select** the **account** from the drop-down list and **press** *tab* to advance to the next linked account field, just as you did to enter the linked accounts for Air Care.

Choose **1080 Bank: Chequing** for the Principal Bank field.

Choose **2300 Vacation Payable** for the Vacation field.

Choose **1240 Advances & Loans Receivable** for the Advances & Loans field.

Choose **5305 Wages: Cleaning Staff** for Vacation Earned, Regular and Overtime 1. Do not enter an account for Overtime 2.

Choose **5300 Wages: General** for Salary.

Choose **5340 Commissions** for Commission.

Choose **5350 Piece Rate Bonuses** for Piece Rate.

WARNING!
Do not enter linked accounts for Overtime 2 and other unused incomes. In this way, the program will skip these fields in the employee records.

Click **Deductions** under Linked Accounts to see the next set of accounts:

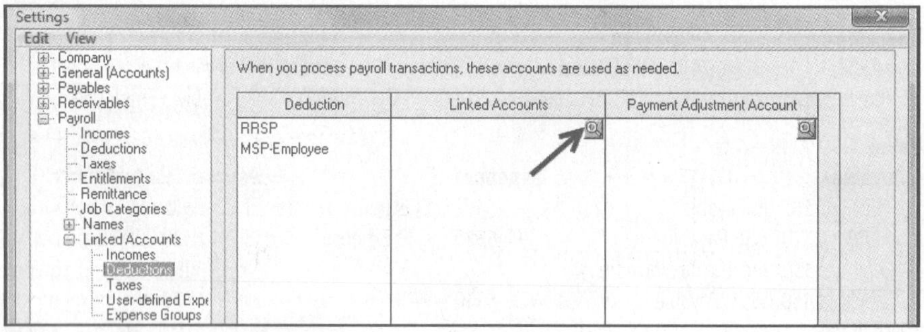

NOTES
Payment Adjustment accounts are not essential, unless you need to use them.

The names here are the ones you entered in the Names: Incomes & Deductions screen. If you deleted a name, it will not appear here.

Enter the **Deductions** and **Payment Adjustment linked accounts** for **RRSP** and **MSP-Employee** from the chart on page 325.

Click **Taxes** under Linked Accounts to see the next set of linked accounts:

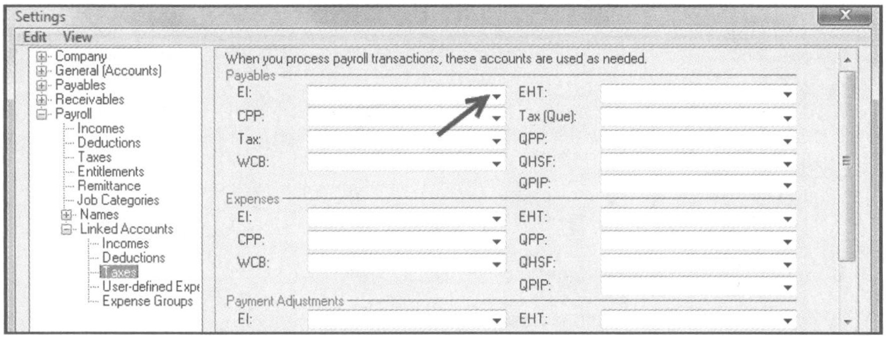

When the employer pays the tax, linked payable and expense accounts are needed. Only the employee pays the income tax, so only the payable linked account is needed. This tax does not create an employer expense. For EI and CPP, employee contributions are added to those of the employer to calculate the total amount payable.

WARNING!
Do not enter linked accounts for the unused taxes. In this way, the program will skip these fields in the employee records.

Enter the **linked Payables accounts** for **EI**, **CPP**, **Tax** and **WCB** in the Payables section. **Enter** the **linked accounts** for **EI**, **CPP** and **WCB** in the **Expenses** section and for the related **Payment Adjustments** accounts from the chart on page 325.

Click **User-Defined Expenses** under the Linked Accounts subheading to see the final Payroll accounts:

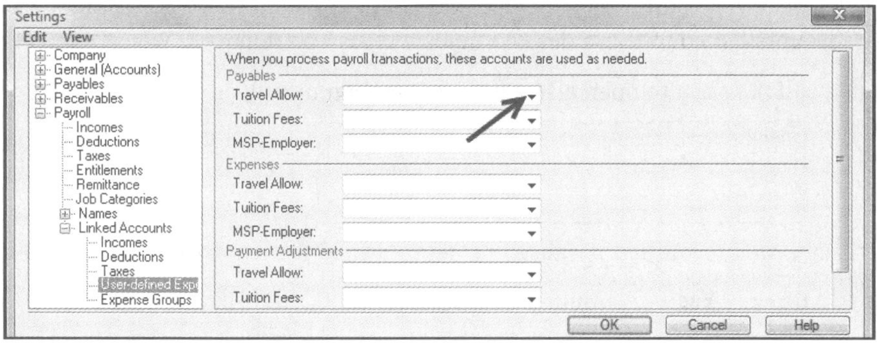

Enter the **linked Payable accounts**, the **linked Expenses accounts** and the **linked Payment Adjustments accounts** for **Travel Allow**, **Tuition Fees** and **MSP-Employer**. Refer to the chart on page 325.

Check the **linked** payroll **accounts** against the chart on page 325 before proceeding. Click each heading under Linked Accounts to see the different screens.

Changing Payroll Form Settings

Before closing the setting screens, we still need to enter the form number to set up the automatic numbering of direct deposit slips. This number is entered with the other automatic numbering sequences as part of the Company Settings.

PRO VERSION
You will not see the entry for Packing Slips.

Click **Company** and then **click Forms** to see the number setup screen:

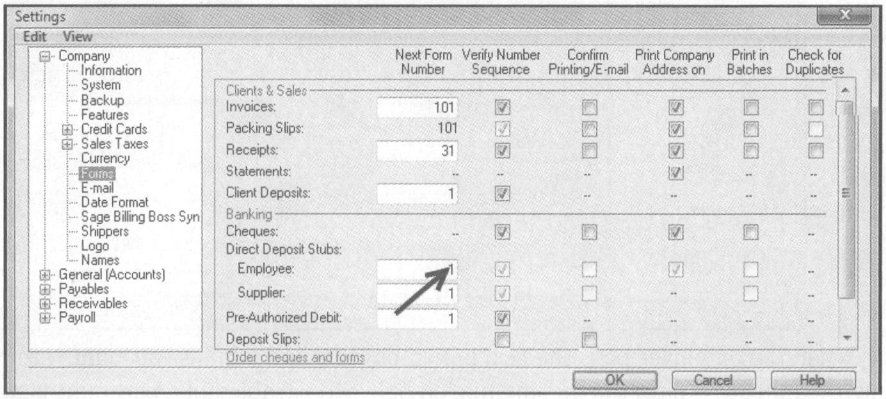

Click the **Direct Deposit Stubs Next Form Number field** for **Employees**.

Type 48

Click the **Check For Duplicates check boxes** if these are not yet checked.

Click **OK** to save the Settings changes:

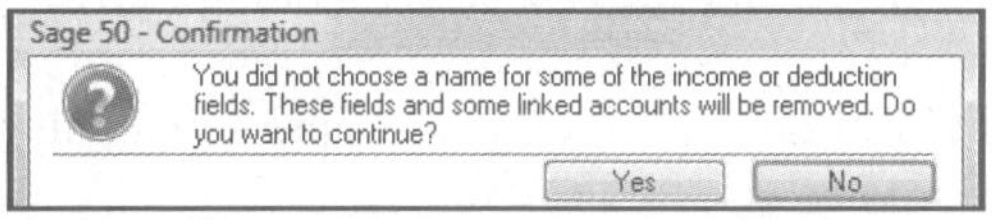

Because we deleted some income and deduction names, we are being warned that any accounts linked to these deleted fields will also be removed. We can proceed.

NOTES
You are still unable to finish the Payroll history now (History menu). Although we have entered linked accounts, the ledger is unbalanced because the Advances & Loans Receivable and Vacation Payable ledger account balances do not match these amounts in the employee records.

Click **Yes** to open a second confirmation message:

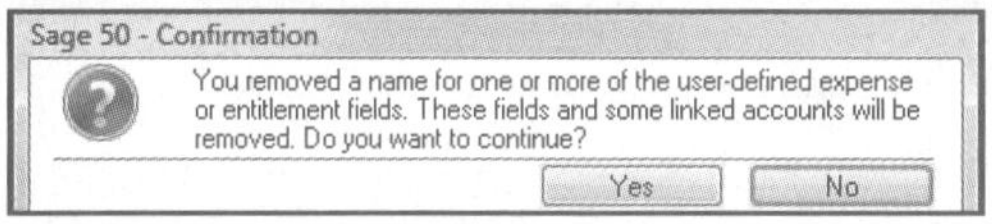

Again, we are warned because of the other field names we deleted.

Click **Yes** to continue and return to the Payroll Home window.

Entering Employee Ledger Records

Use the Lime Light Laundry Employee Information Sheet, Employee Profiles and Additional Payroll Information on pages 313–316 to create the employee records and add historical information.

We will enter the information for Lime Light Laundry employee Clyne Fretton.

Click the **Employees icon**  in the Home window.

The Employees icon window opens:

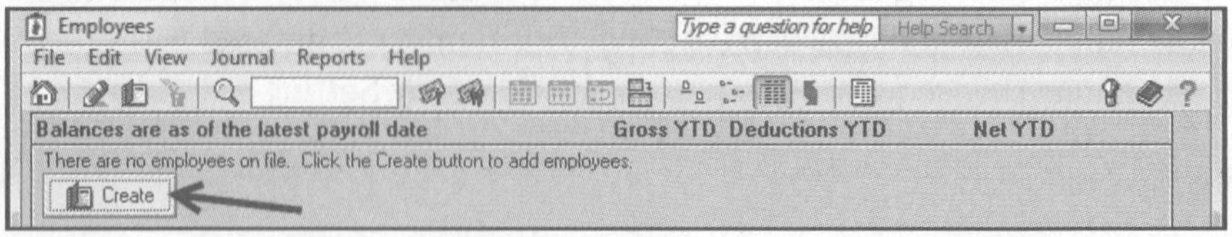

The Employees icon window is blank because no employees are on file at this stage.

Click the **Create button**  or **choose** the **File menu** and **click Create**.

You can also click the Employees icon shortcuts list, as shown below, and choose Add Employee to bypass the Employees window and open the new employee ledger window:

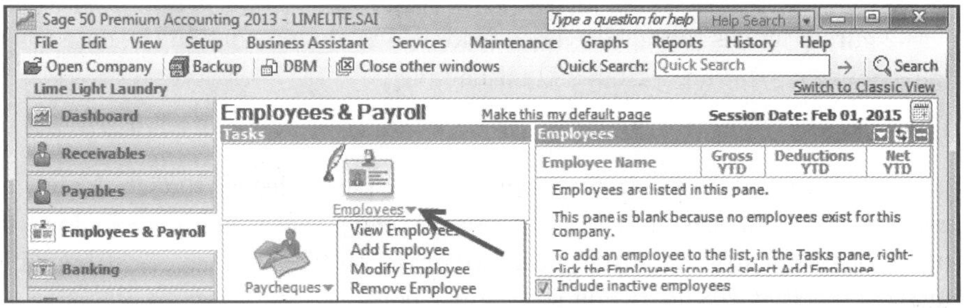

Entering Personal Details

The Payroll Ledger new employee information form will open so you can begin to enter the employee record. There are several required fields in the employee ledger records because this information links to government income tax tables and rules.

The opening Personal information page holds the personal details for the employee:

NOTES

If you hide the Employees icon window (Setup menu, User Preferences, View screen) you will see the Payroll Ledger window immediately when you click the Employees icon.

You will also skip the Employees window if you use the Add Employee shortcut.

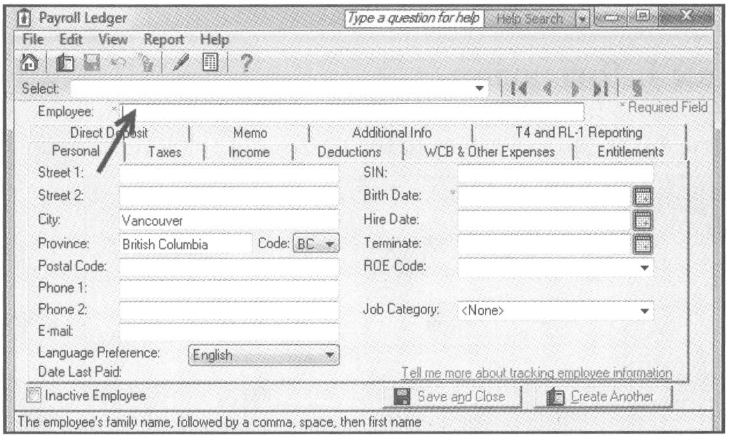

NOTES

The Set Field Names tool in the ledger window will open the Payroll Settings Additional Names screen.

The Payroll Ledger has a large number of tabs for the different kinds of payroll information and many required fields, those marked with *. The cursor is in the Employee field, ready for you to enter information. If you enter the surname first, your employee lists will be in correct alphabetic order. You can change this information at any time.

Type `Fretton, Clyne` **Press** *tab*.

The cursor advances to the Street 1 field.

Type `21 Spotter St.`

The default city, province and province code, those for the business, are correct.

NOTES

As in other ledgers, required fields that you cannot leave blank are marked with *.

On the Personal tab screen, the employee name and the date of birth are essential. All other fields can be completed later.

Click the **Postal Code field**.

Type `v3k4k2` **Press** *tab*.

The program corrects the postal code format and advances the cursor to the Phone 1 field.

Type `6046937595` **Press** *tab* to see the corrected phone number format.

The default **Language Preference** is correctly set as English.

Click the **Social Insurance Number (SIN) field**. You must use a valid SIN.

Type `218738631` **Press** *tab*.

NOTES

The program will allow you to omit the Social Insurance Number, but you must enter the employee's date of birth. The SIN can be added later and is required for the Record of Employment. The date of birth is required because it determines whether CPP will be deducted.

The cursor advances to the Birth Date field. Enter the month, day and year using any accepted date format.

Type 8-15-84 **Press** tab **twice**.

The cursor moves to the Hire Date field, which should contain the date when the employee began working for Lime Light Laundry.

Type 2-7-09 **Press** tab.

The next two fields will be used when the employee leaves the job — the date of termination and the reason for leaving that you can select from the drop-down list. The final option designates employees as active or inactive. All employees at Lime Light Laundry are active, so the default selection is correct.

Job Categories are used to identify salespersons who can be linked to specific sales so that their sales revenue is tracked and used to calculate commissions. The employee's Job Category can be selected here from the drop-down list if categories are already set up, or you can place employees in categories later from the Payroll Settings screen. We will create categories later and assign employees to them at that stage.

When you use Sage 50 to pay employees, the Date Last Paid will be entered automatically by the program.

The remaining details for the employee are entered on the other tab screens.

NOTES

The termination date and reason for leaving a job will determine the employee's eligibility to collect Employment Insurance. Refer to page 298.

Entering Tax Information

Click the **Taxes tab** to advance to the next set of employee details:

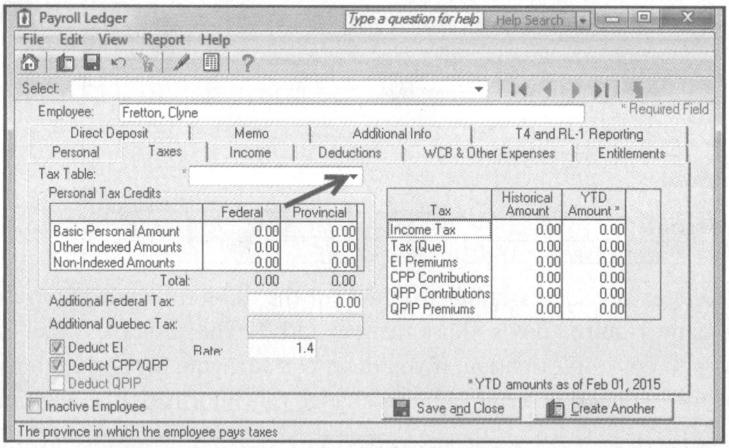

NOTES

You should drag the column margins so that all amounts and headings are on-screen. The YTD column may be hidden initially.

This screen allows you to enter income tax–related information. The **Personal Tax Credits** you enter are divided between **federal** and **provincial** and then again among the **basic** amount, the total of all other amounts that are **indexed** and the total of amounts that are **non-indexed**. Provincial personal income taxes are not linked to the rates for federal income taxes, so separate claim amounts are needed. Sage 50 will enter the total claim amount. The total is used to calculate income taxes for each paycheque. Historical tax amounts for the year to date are also entered on this screen.

Click the **Tax Table list arrow**. A list of provinces and territories appears on the screen. This is a required field.

Click **British Columbia**, the province of taxation for Lime Light Laundry for income tax purposes.

Press tab to advance to the **Basic Personal Amount** label.

Press tab again for the **Federal amounts** field, which holds the basic claim amount.

NOTES

The Tax Table (Province) is the only required field on this screen. Taxes will be based on the minimum basic claim amounts if no claim amounts are entered. Tax Table is a required field because different provinces have different income tax rates.

Type 11038 **Press** *tab* to advance to the field for the Provincial Basic Personal Amount.

Type 10276 **Press** *tab* to advance to the field for Other Federal Indexed Amounts. For Fretton, this is her amount for a spouse and two children.

Type 15506 **Press** *tab* to advance to the field for Other Provincial Indexed Amounts.

Type 8860 **Press** *tab* to advance to the field for Federal Non-Indexed Amounts. Fretton has no claim amounts that are not indexed.

For **Sissler**, enter **3670** in this field.

Press *tab* again to move to the Provincial Non-Indexed Amounts field.

For **Sissler**, enter **3030** in this field.

Press *tab*. The cursor advances to the **Additional Federal Tax** field.

When an employee has chosen to have additional federal income tax deducted from each paycheque, you enter the amount of the deduction in the **Additional Federal Tax** field. Employees might make this choice if they receive regular additional income from which no tax is deducted. By making this choice, they avoid paying a large amount of tax at the end of the year and possible interest penalties. Fretton is the only employee with other income who chooses to have additional taxes withheld.

Type 100

If an employee is insurable by EI, you must leave the box for **Deduct EI** checked. The default EI contribution factor, 1.4, for Lime Light Laundry is correct. We entered it in the Payroll Taxes Settings window (page 324.)

All employees at Lime Light make CPP contributions, so this check box should remain selected. Employees under 18 or over 70 years of age do not contribute to CPP, so clicking the **Deduct CPP/QPP** option for these employees (to remove the ✓) will ensure that CPP is not deducted from their paycheques. Employees over 65 years may choose not to pay CPP premiums when they collect the pension.

We will enter the historical income tax amounts next. You can drag the column margins so that all amounts and headings are on-screen.

Click the **Historical Amount field** for **Income Tax**.

Type 613.84 **Press** *tab* to advance to the EI Premiums Historical Amount field, where you should enter the amount of EI paid to date.

Type 64.95 **Press** *tab* to move to the CPP Contributions Historical Amount field.

Type 170.22

Entering Income Amounts

We defined all the types of income for Lime Light Laundry when we set up Names (see page 319). All the details you need to complete the Income tab chart are on pages 313–314. The following list summarizes the types of income used by each employee. Not all will be used on all paycheques.

- Advances, Loans and Benefits: all employees (see margin Notes on next page)
- Vac. Owed and Vac. Paid: all hourly paid employees (see margin Notes on next page)
- Regular: four hourly paid employees — Fretton, Durtee, Landings, Sissler

NOTES
When you subscribe to the payroll services plan, you can update the tax claim amounts with the aid of a tax wizard. Only the indexed amounts will be updated.

NOTES
Sissler is the only employee with amounts that are not indexed – her education amounts. Governments raise indexed claim amounts based on inflation and budget decisions.

Sissler's claim has $3 670 federal and $3 030 provincial for tuition and education deductions. These amounts are not subject to indexing.

WARNING!
Enter employee historical payroll details carefully. You will be unable to edit these fields after finishing the history.

They must also be correct because they are used to create T4s for tax reporting.

NOTES
All employees under the age of 65 must pay CPP premiums if they are employed. They may collect CPP as early as 60 years, with a reduction for taking the pension early, or after 65 with increased payouts for the delay in collecting.

NOTES
These historical details are needed because there are yearly maximum amounts for CPP and EI contributions. Totals for optional deductions are also retained in the employee record.

NOTES
The program skips the Quebec tax fields because British Columbia was selected as the province of taxation and no linked accounts were entered for the Quebec taxes.

> **NOTES**
> In the chart on pages 313–314, the incomes that are used by an employee have a ✓ or an amount in the employee's column.

> **NOTES**
> Checkmarks are added by default for all incomes, deductions and expenses that have linked accounts entered for them.
> The checkmarks for Advances, Loans, Benefits, Vacation Owed and Vacation Paid cannot be removed.

> **NOTES**
> If calculating vacation on vacation paid is required by legislation, you should click the check box for this option.

- Overtime 1: four hourly paid employees — Fretton, Durtee, Landings, Sissler
- Piece Rate: four hourly paid employees — Fretton, Durtee, Landings, Sissler
- Salary: three salaried employees — Brumes, Tran, Houseman
- Commission: Brumes

Click the **Income tab** to open the next screen of employee details:

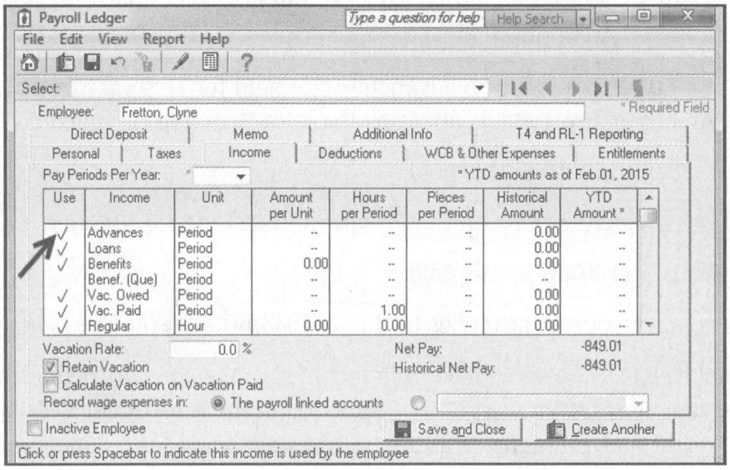

On the Income chart you can indicate the types of income that each employee receives (the **Use** column), the usual rate of pay for that type of income (**Amount Per Unit**), the usual number of hours worked (**Hours Per Period**), the usual number of units for a piece rate pay base (**Pieces Per Period**) and the amounts received this year before the earliest transaction date or the date used for the first paycheque (**Historical Amount**). The **Year-To-Date (YTD) Amount** is added automatically by the program based on the historical amounts you enter and the paycheques entered in the program.

Checkmarks must be entered in the Use column to make the fields available in the payroll journals, even if they will not be used on all paycheques.

> **NOTES**
> Because advances are taxable, Lime Light Laundry issues short-term loans to employees instead.

We need to add the historical loans, benefits and vacation amounts for Fretton. Fretton has $200 in loans not yet repaid, and she has not received all the vacation pay she earned last year. The total of the advances/loans and vacation owed amounts for all employees must match the opening General Ledger balances for the corresponding linked accounts.

> **WARNING!**
> The totals for all employees for advances and loans paid and vacation pay owing must match the corresponding General Ledger linked account balances before you can finish entering the history. These are the two control accounts for the Payroll Ledger.

No employees have received vacation pay this year. If they had, you would enter the amount in the **Vac. Paid Historical Amount** field. Vacation pay not yet received is entered in the **Vac. Owed Historical Amount** field. Any loans paid to the employees and not yet repaid are recorded in the **Loans Historical Amount** field. There is no record of loan amounts recovered.

Click the **Historical Amount column beside Loans** to move the cursor.

Type `200` **Press** *tab* to move to the Benefits Amount Per Unit column.

The provincial medical premiums paid by the employer are employee benefits.

> **NOTES**
> Sissler's Benefit Amount Per Unit includes only the medical premium. The historical amount includes the medical benefit and tuition fees already paid.

Type `30.69` **Press** *tab* to move to the Historical Amount for Benefits.

Type `61.38` **Press** *tab* to advance to the Vac. Owed Historical Amount.

Type `464.98` **Press** *tab* to advance to the Historical Vac. Paid Amount.

Press *tab* again to advance to the **Use column for Regular**.

> **WARNING!**
> Do not click the Use column beside Regular for hourly paid employees as that will remove the checkmark.

Press *tab* to advance to the Amount Per Unit field where we need to enter the regular hourly wage rate for Fretton.

Type `20` **Press** *tab* to advance to the Hours Per Period field.

Bi-weekly paid employees usually work 80 hours per period. You can change the amount in the Payroll journals. Salaried workers normally work 150 hours each month.

Type 80 **Press** tab to advance to the Historical Amount field.

Historical income and deduction amounts for the year to date are necessary so that taxes and deductions can be calculated correctly and T4 statements will be accurate.

Type 3200 **Press** tab.

> **NOTES**
> When an amount varies from one pay to another, you should leave its Amount Per Unit field blank in the ledger and enter the amount in the journal.

This amount is entered automatically in the YTD column and the cursor advances to the Use column for Overtime 1.

Press tab so you can enter the overtime hourly rate.

Type 30

Press tab **twice** to advance to the Historical Amount field. There is no regular number of overtime hours.

Type 60 **Press** tab to advance to the Overtime 2 Use column.

> **NOTES**
> No linked account was entered for Overtime 2, so no checkmark appears beside it.

The next three income types do not apply to Fretton so they should not be checked. The next income that applies is Piece Rate, the piece rate method of pay. We need to enter the rate or amount per unit (set) and the historical amount. There is no fixed number of pieces per period.

If no linked account is entered for an income, the Use column will be blank.

Click the **Use column beside Salary** to remove the ✓.

Click the **Use column beside Commission** to remove the ✓.

Click **Piece Rate** in the Income column to select the line. Do not click the Use column. **Press** tab.

Type 0.10 to enter the amount received for each set. **Press** tab **twice**.

Type 189 to enter the historical amount.

> **NOTES**
> Pressing the space bar when you are in the Use column will also add a ✓ or remove one if it is there.
> Pressing ↓ will move you to the next line in the same column.

For **Tran** and **Houseman**, click the Use column for Regular, Overtime 1, Commission and Piece Rate to remove the ✓. Enter the monthly salary and press tab. Enter 150 as the number of hours worked in the pay period for Houseman and 80 for Tran. Press tab and enter the historical amount. You cannot remove the ✓ for Vac. Owed and Vac. Paid, even if they are not used.

For **Brumes**, repeat these steps but leave Commission checked and enter $390 as the historical amount.

> **NOTES**
> Remember that commissions must be calculated manually and entered in the Payroll journals. The Commission field in the Payroll Ledger allows only a fixed amount, not a percentage of sales, as the entry.

Pay Periods Per Year refers to the number of times the employee is paid, or the pay cycle. This is a required field. Fretton is paid every two weeks, 26 times per year.

Click the **list arrow** beside the field for **Pay Periods Per Year**:

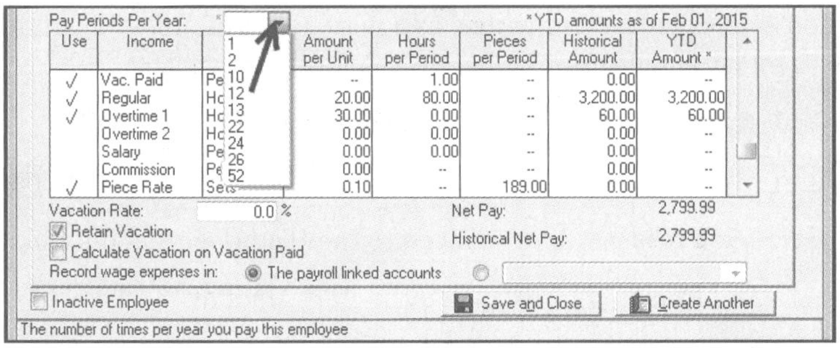

Click **26**.

> **NOTES**
> Employees may be paid yearly (1), semi-annually (2), monthly for 10 months (10), monthly (12), every four weeks (13), every two weeks for a 10-month year (22), twice a month (24), every two weeks (26) or weekly (52).

Retaining Vacation pay is normal for full-time hourly paid employees. Part-time and casual workers often receive their vacation pay with each paycheque because their work schedule is irregular. You will turn the option to retain vacation off when an employee receives the vacation pay, either when taking a vacation or when leaving the company (see page 276). If the employee is salaried and does not receive vacation pay, the option should also be turned off. For employees who receive vacation pay, leave the option to Retain Vacation checked and type the vacation pay rate in the % field.

Double-click the **% field beside Vacation Rate**.

Type 6

For **Brumes**, **Tran** and **Houseman**, click Retain Vacation to remove the ✓.

NOTES
When you select a specific account, all payroll expenses for that employee will be linked to the same account – the one you identify in this field. If you want to use different accounts for different wage expenses, you must use the linked accounts.

Employee wages may be linked to their separate default expense accounts or they can all be linked to the single expense account that you select from the drop-down list. Wage expenses for all Lime Light Laundry employees are linked to the default accounts entered on pages 325–326, so the default selection is correct.

Entering Payroll Deduction Amounts

The next step is to enter current and historical details for deductions, just as we did for income. You must indicate which deductions apply to the employee (Use column), the amount normally deducted and the historical amount — the amount deducted to date this year.

Click the **Deductions tab** to open the screen for payroll deductions:

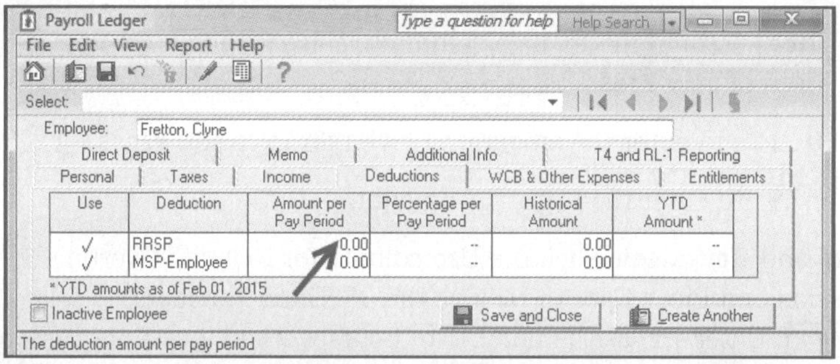

Both deductions are selected in the Use column (a ✓ is entered).

By entering deduction amounts here, they will be included automatically on the Payroll Journal input forms. Otherwise, you must enter them manually in the journal for each pay period. Not all employees make RRSP contributions at this time, but they have done so in the past, so we will leave this field available. When you enter the amounts here, the deductions are automatically added in the journal, but changes can still be made in the journals. You should make permanent changes by editing the employee ledger record. Fretton does not currently have RRSP contributions withheld from her pay.

NOTES
For one-time changes, you can edit deduction amounts in the payroll journals on the Deductions tab screen.

NOTES
If the employee's ledger record Use column does not have a ✓, that field will be removed from the payroll journal for the employee.

If you choose to calculate deductions as a percentage of gross pay in the Payroll Settings, the Percentage Per Pay Period fields will be available.

Click **MSP-Employee** in the Deduction column to select the line.

Press (tab). You should enter the amount that is withheld in each pay period.

Type 30.69 **Press** (tab) to advance to the Historical Amount field.

Type 61.38 **Press** (tab) to update the YTD Amount.

The remaining deductions are not used by Lime Light Laundry. The names were deleted so they do not appear on the chart.

Entering WCB and Other Expenses

In other provinces, the tab label will be changed to match the name used for WCB in that province. Ontario uses the name WSIB — Workplace Safety and Insurance Board — instead of WCB, so the tab label will be WSIB & Other Expenses.

Click the **WCB & Other Expenses tab**:

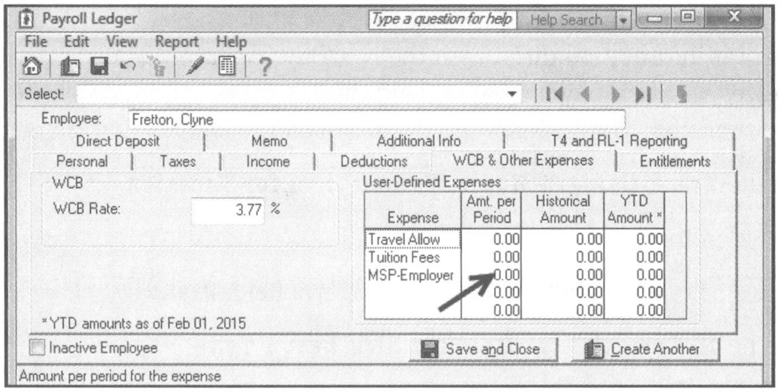

The user-defined expenses we created in the Additional Payroll Names screen (page 320) and the default WCB rate (page 324) are entered on this screen. The default WCB rate is entered from our setup information, but you can enter a different rate for an individual employee in this field. The rate is correct for Fretton.

For **Tran**, enter **5.01** as the WCB rate.

Other user-defined expenses are also added on this screen. Lime Light Laundry has three user-defined expenses, but only MSP-Employer applies to Fretton now.

Click the **MSP-Employer Amt. Per Period**. Enter the amount that the employer contributes in each pay period.

Type `30.69` **Press** *tab* to advance to the Historical Amount field.

Type `61.38`

For **Sissler**, enter **30** as the Tuition Fees Amt. Per Period and **120** as the Historical Amount.

For **Brumes**, enter **300** as the Travel Allow Amt. Per Period and **300** as the Historical Amount.

The remaining expenses are not used by Lime Light Laundry.

Entering Entitlements

Click the **Entitlements tab**:

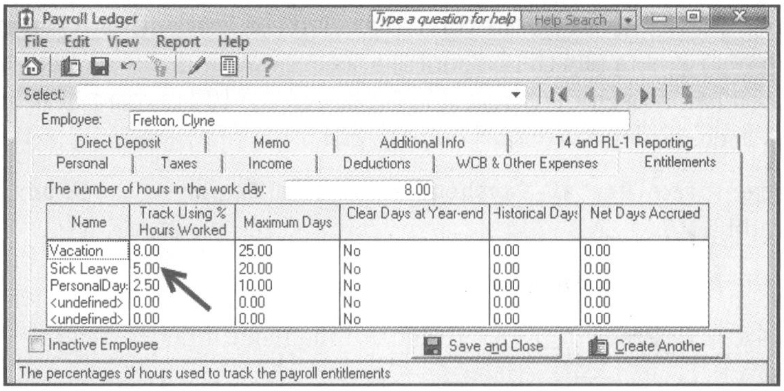

NOTES
You should drag the column margins so that all amounts and headings are on-screen. The YTD column may be hidden initially.

NOTES
Tran's WCB rate is different because his job is in a different rate class. Both Houseman and Brumes help out with laundry work as needed, so they share the same rate as the other cleaning staff.

NOTES
The employer expense for Sissler's tuition benefit is set up to be entered automatically. The benefit amount will be added in the Payroll Journal.

NOTES
You should drag the column margins so that you can see all the columns and amounts on-screen.

We entered the default rates and amounts for entitlements as Payroll Settings (page 324), but they can be modified in the ledger records for individual employees.

We must also enter the historical information for entitlements. The number of **Historical Days** will include any days carried forward from the previous periods. The number of days accrued cannot be greater than the maximum number of days defined for the entitlement for an employee. The number of **Net Days Accrued**, the amount unused and available for carrying forward, is updated automatically from the historical information and current payroll journal entries.

You cannot enter information directly in the Net Days Accrued field.

Fretton receives vacation pay instead of paid time off so the vacation entitlements details should be removed. The defaults for sick leave and personal days are correct.

NOTES
If employees take days before the sufficient number of hours worked have been accrued, the program will warn you. Then you can allow the entry for entitlements or not. This permission is similar to allowing clients to exceed their credit limits.

Click the **Track Using % Hours Worked field for Vacation**.

Press del to remove the entry 8.00.

Press tab to advance to the Maximum Days field. **Press** del.

Click the **Historical Days field for Sick Leave**. **Type** 7

Press ↓ to advance to the Historical Days field for PersonalDays. The number of days is added to the Net Days Accrued.

Type 3 **Press** tab to enter the amount.

For Brumes, Tran and Houseman, the default entries for tracking and maximum days are correct, but you must enter the Historical Days for each entitlement.

NOTES
Third parties, such as Beanstream and Sage Payment Solutions, provide the service of transferring the payroll deposits to the employees' bank accounts.
Direct deposits will be covered in Chapter 13.

Entering Direct Deposit Information

Click the **Direct Deposit tab**:

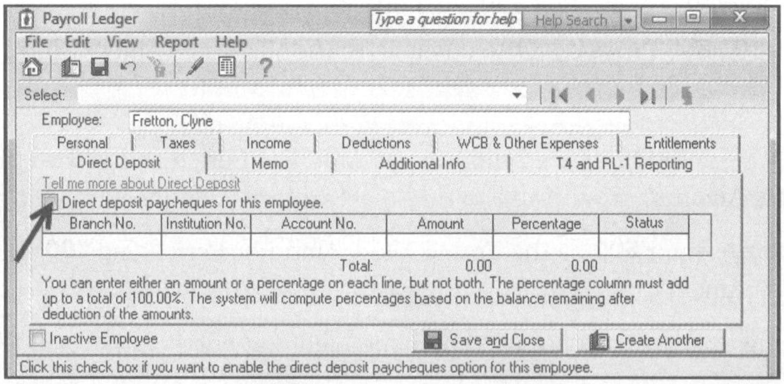

NOTES
All banks in Canada are assigned a three-digit bank or institution number and each branch has a unique five-digit transit number. You must enter the correct number of digits for these.
Account numbers may vary from five to twelve digits.

Four employees have elected to have their paycheques deposited directly to their bank accounts. On this screen, we need to enter the bank account details. For each employee who has selected the Direct Deposit option, you must turn on the selection in the **Direct Deposit Paycheques For This Employee** check box. Then you must add the five-digit Transit or **Branch Number**, the three-digit Bank or **Institution Number**, the bank **Account Number** and finally the amount that is deposited, or the percentage of the cheque. Fretton has chosen the direct deposit option for 100 percent of her net pay. Refer to the bank account deposit details on page 314.

NOTES
The paycheque deposit may be split among more than one bank account by entering different percentages for the accounts or by entering an amount for each bank account.
To delete bank account details, click the employee's Direct Deposit tab. Click Active in the Status column to change the entry to Inactive and then delete the bank information. Click the check box for Direct Deposit Paycheques to remove the ✓.

Click the **Direct Deposit Paycheques For This Employee check box** to add a ✓.

Click the **Branch No. field**.

Type 49921 **Press** tab to advance to the Institution No. field.

Type 300 **Press** tab to advance to the Account No. field.

Type 2883912 **Press** *tab* **twice** to advance to the Percentage field.

Type 100

Click the **Memo tab**:

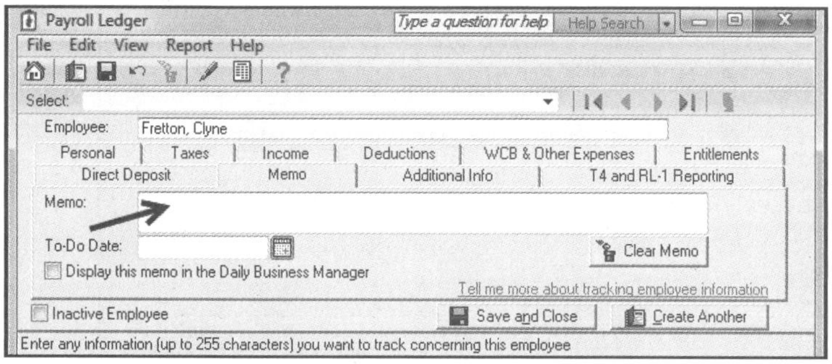

The Memo tab will not be used at this time. You could enter a note with a reminder date to appear in the Daily Business Manager; for example, a reminder to issue vacation paycheques on a specific date, to recover advances and loans or to celebrate a birthday.

NOTES
The Daily Business Manager is covered in Chapter 11.

Entering Additional Information

Lime Light Laundry enters emergency contacts for each employee.

NOTES
Additional information for other ledgers may also be displayed or hidden in journal transactions.

Click the **Additional Info tab** to access the additional fields:

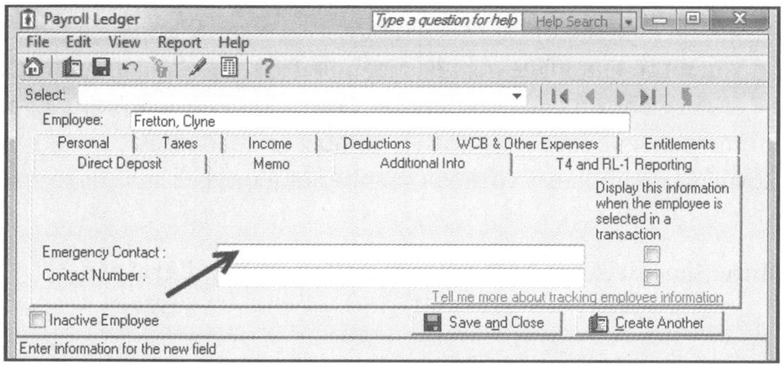

You can indicate whether you want to display any of the additional information when the employee is selected in a transaction. We do not need to display the contact information in the Payroll Journal. Enter the contact information from page 314.

Click the **Emergency Contact field**.

Type Aidan Fretton **Press** *tab* **twice**.

Type (604) 497-1469 to enter the contact's phone number.

WARNING!
The Contact Number field is not predefined as a telephone number. The format will not be corrected automatically by the program.

Entering T4 and RL-1 Reporting Amounts

The next information screen allows you to enter the year-to-date EI insurable and pensionable earnings. By adding the historical amounts, the T4 slips prepared for income taxes at the end of the year and the Record of Employment termination reports will also be correct. Refer to the T4 historical information on page 314.

> **NOTES**
> The EI Insurable amount is the total of gross wages, including overtime wages and vacation pay. If EI is calculated on the income, the income is added to EI Insurable Earnings.
> For pensionable earnings, benefits are added to EI insurable amounts.

Click the **T4 and RL-1 Reporting tab** to open the final screen:

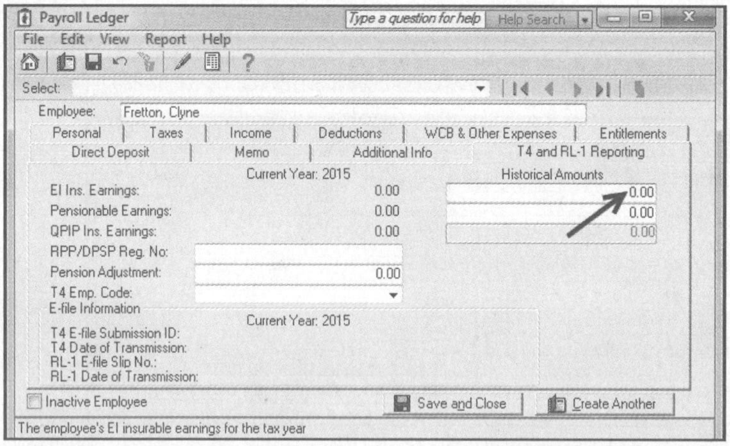

In the **Historical Amounts field for EI Ins. Earnings**, you should enter the total earned income received to date that is EI insurable. The program will update this total every time you make payroll entries until the maximum salary on which EI is calculated has been reached. At that time, no further EI premiums will be deducted.

Pensionable Earnings — the total of all income plus benefits — are also tracked by the program. This amount determines the total income that is eligible for the Canada Pension Plan. Again, when the maximum is reached, no further CPP deductions are made. The **Pension Adjustment** amount is used when the employee has a workplace pension program that will affect the allowable contributions for personal registered pension plans and will be linked with the Canada Pension Plan. Workplace pension income is reduced when the employee also has income from the Canada Pension Plan. Since Lime Light Laundry has no company pension plan, the Pension Adjustment amount is zero and no pension plan registration number is needed.

> **NOTES**
> The T4 Employee Code is required only for the types of employment in the drop-down list for the field. No employees with Lime Light are in these positions.

The T4 Employee Code applies to a small number of job types that have special income tax rules.

Double-click the **Historical Amounts field for EI Ins. Earnings**.

Type 3449

Double-click the **Historical Amounts field for Pensionable Earnings**.

Type 3510.38

Correct any employee information **errors** by returning to the field with the error. **Highlight** the **error** and **enter** the **correct information**. **Click each tab** in turn so that you can check all the information.

When all the information is entered correctly, you must save the employee record.

Click **Create Another** 

. Changes are saved automatically.

A new blank employee information form opens.

Click the **Personal tab** so that you can enter address information.

Repeat these procedures to **enter** other employee **records** using the information on pages 313–316.

Click **Save And Close** 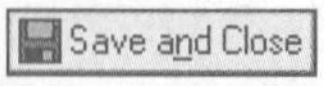

after entering the last record to save the record and close the Payroll Ledger.

Do not finish the **history** if you are prompted to do so at this stage.

> **WARNING!**
> When you close the payroll ledger after entering the last hourly employee, or after all employees, you may see the message that the payroll history is balanced, asking if you want to finish the history now. Choose No. Do not finish the history until you have printed your reports to check all the historical and current amounts and made a backup.

Only the *Advances & Loans Receivable* and *Vacation Payable* amounts must match before you can finish the history. Other amounts that are not verified may be incorrect and you will be unable to change them after finishing the history.

Close the **Employees window** to return to the Home window.

Display or **print** the **Employee List** and the **Employee Summary Report** to check the accuracy of your work.

NOTES
If you started from the Add Employee shortcut, you will return directly to the Payroll Home window.

Setting Up Payroll Remittances

Because we have entered all other payroll settings and records, we can modify the final settings — for payroll remittances and job categories. Supplier records are also required for this step, but they had already been entered. Entering remittance settings involves two steps: linking the suppliers who receive payroll remittance amounts to the taxes or deductions they receive and entering payment frequency and next remittance dates.

NOTES
Remember that you must have a valid and current payroll service plan with Sage to ensure the payroll tax tables you use are current and that tax amounts will be correctly calculated.

Linking Remittances to Suppliers

The chart below identifies remittance suppliers, the liability linked to each supplier, the remitting period frequency and the ending payroll date for the next remittance period.

PAYROLL SUPPLIERS

Supplier	Payroll Liability	Remitting Frequency	Next Remittance Period End Date
BC Minister of Finance	MSP-Employee	Monthly	Feb. 28, 2015
	MSP-Employer	Monthly	Feb. 28, 2015
BC Workers' Compensation Board	WCB	Monthly	Feb. 28, 2015
Receiver General for Canada	EI	Monthly	Feb. 28, 2015
	CPP	Monthly	Feb. 28, 2015
	Tax	Monthly	Feb. 28, 2015
Victoria Trust	RRSP	Monthly	Feb. 28, 2015

NOTES
We will not enter remittance suppliers for tuition or for travel allowance. Tuition may be paid to different institutions and the travel allowance is paid to the employee.

Click the **Settings icon** to open the Payroll Settings screen.

Click **Remittance** to open the screen we need:

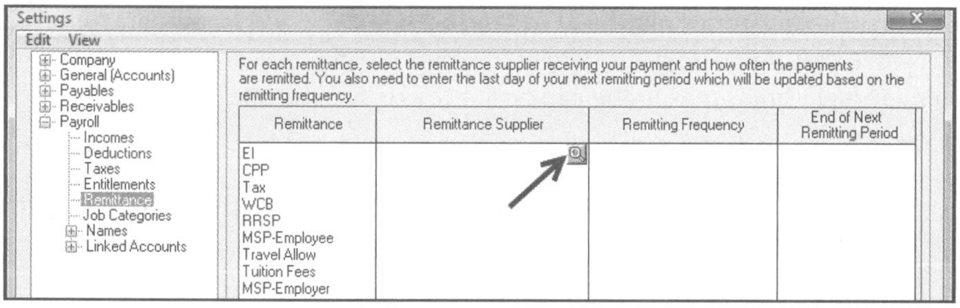

All the payroll items that are linked to liability (remittance) accounts are listed: taxes, deductions and user-defined expenses. For each liability, we can select a supplier and payment frequency from lists and then enter the last date of the pay period covered by the next remittance payment.

Click the **List icon** in the Remittance Supplier column on the line for EI.

NOTES

You can also double-click the supplier's name to add it to the Settings screen.

If you type the first few letters of the name and then press *tab*, the Select Supplier list will have the supplier you need selected. Press *enter* to add the name to the Settings screen.

When you choose Receiver General for CPP and Income Tax, the frequency and date will be entered automatically from the one for EI. When you choose the BC Minister of Finance for MSP-Employer, the entries from MSP-Employee will be added automatically.

The selection list opens with all suppliers included:

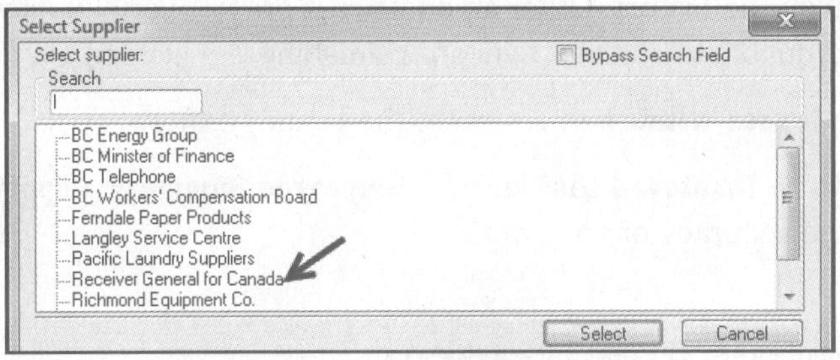

Click **Receiver General for Canada**.

Click **Select** or **press** *enter* to return to the Remittance Settings screen.

The cursor advances to the Remittance Frequency field for EI. The frequency for all remittances is Monthly. The next remittance for all liabilities will be made on February 28.

Click the **List icon** in the Remitting Frequency field. **Double-click** **Monthly**. **Press** *tab* to advance to the End Of Next Remitting Period field.

Type `2 28` **Press** *tab*.

Enter the remaining **suppliers**, **periods** and **dates** from page 339.

Entering Job Categories

Job categories can be used to identify salespersons and to organize reports.

PRO VERSION

The column for Submit Time Slips is not available in the Pro version. It applies to Time & Billing, a Premium feature.

Click **Job Categories**:

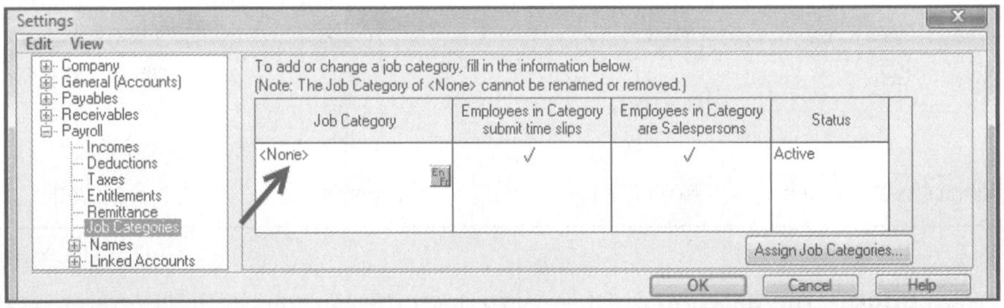

On the Job Categories screen, you enter the names of the categories and indicate whether the employees in each category submit time slips and whether they are salespersons. Categories may be active or inactive. We need a new category called Sales.

Notice that if you do not create categories, all employees can be selected in the Sales Journal. Employees in the category <None> are salespersons.

Click the **Job Category field below <None>**.

Type `Sales` **Press** *tab* to add checkmarks to the next two columns and set the status to Active.

Click the **Job Category field below Sales**.

Type `Other` **Press** *tab* to add the checkmarks.

The Other category does not apply to sales or time slips so we need to change the settings. Employees in the Other category should not appear in the Salesperson field on sales invoices. We will remove the ✓s for them.

Click the ✓ in the column Employees In Category Submit Time Slips.

Click the ✓ in the column Employees In Category Are Salespersons.

Click **Sales** in the Job Category list.

Click **Assign Job Categories** to change the screen:

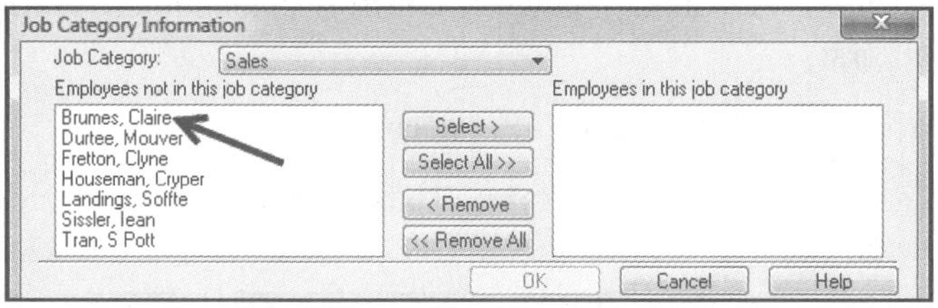

The screen is updated with employee names. Initially all are Employees Not In This Job Category.

You can add employee names to the category by choosing an employee and clicking **Select** or by choosing **Select All**. Once employees are in a category (the column on the right), you can remove them by selecting an employee and clicking **Remove** or clicking **Remove All** to move all names at the same time.

Click **Brumes** and then **click Select** to place her in the Sales category.

Click the **Job Category drop-down list** as shown and **click Other**:

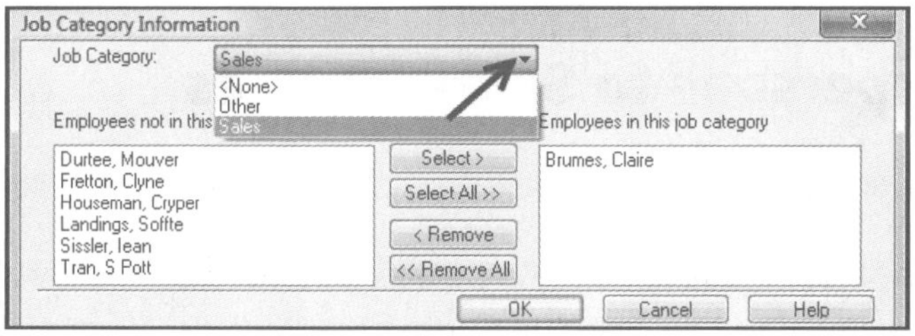

Notice that <None> is one of the category list choices. Brumes appears on the In This Category list for the Sales Category.

Press *tab* to add the employee names. Again, all employees are listed as Not In This Category.

Click **Select All** to place all names on the Employees In This Job Category list. Now we need to remove Brumes' name from this list.

Click **Brumes** and then **click Remove** to remove her from the Other category.

Click **OK** to save the information and return to the Settings screen. **Click OK** to save the settings and close the Settings screen.

Finishing Payroll History

Once the setup is complete, we can back up the data file and finish the payroll history. Like the other modules, you can use the payroll journals before finishing the history. However, the automatic payroll calculation feature will be turned off and you cannot use the Payroll Cheque Run Journal. Therefore, we should finish the history first. We can also check the data integrity as we did for Air Care to see if there are any data inconsistencies that we need to correct.

Choose the **Maintenance menu** and **click Check Data Integrity**.

Two control accounts are used for the Payroll Ledger — *Advances & Loans Receivable* and *Vacation Payable*. The General Ledger account balance for these must equal the total advances and loans paid and the total vacation owed to all employees. The Historical Information entry for **Employees** should be **Balanced**.

Click **OK** to close the Data Integrity window.

WARNING!

If the payroll history is not finished, you must calculate and enter taxes manually. You will also be unable to use the Payroll Run Journal.

NOTES

These two payroll control accounts are like Accounts Payable and Accounts Receivable in that historical amounts must match the General Ledger account balances.

If corrections are necessary, compare your amounts with the ones on pages 313–314 and modify the employee ledger records.

Once we finish the history, we cannot change any historical amounts. Therefore, we should prepare a backup first.

Back up the **data file**. Refer to page 248 if necessary.

Choose the **History menu** and **click Enter Historical Information** and **Payroll** as shown:

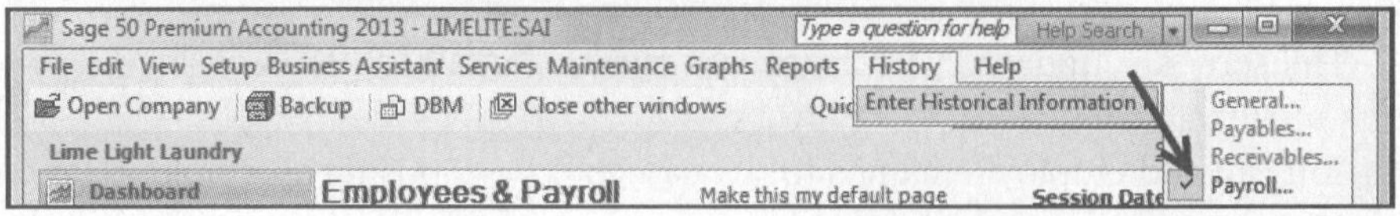

NOTES
The remaining modules on the Finish History menu are not available (do not have a ✓) because the history for them is already finished.

When we added the Payroll module, the History menu became available again, but only for this module — the other modules have the ✓ removed because the history for them is finished. When you finish the Payroll history, the Home window has all modules in the finished history state. The History menu has been removed from the Home window. You are now ready to enter transactions.

Adding Salespersons to Sales Invoices

The first transaction adds the salesperson to an invoice, applying the job category we set up to track sales for commissions.

When employees receive sales commissions, you can add the salesperson's name to the sales invoice. You can then use the Sales By Salesperson Report to determine the sales revenue amount for calculating the commission. After creating job categories, we indicated for each category whether its employees were salespersons and then identified the employees in the category.

Advance the session date to **February 7**.

Click **Receivables** in the Modules pane list.

NOTES
Enter Brumes as the salesperson for all sales, either in the journal (see page 343) or by adding her to the client records (also shown on page 343).

✓ 1

Sales Invoice #101 **Dated Feb. 2/15**
To Capilano Centre Hotel, $2 900 plus $145 GST for weekly contracted linen laundry service. Invoice total $3 045. Terms: 1/15, n/30. Enter Brumes as the salesperson. Store as a recurring weekly transaction.

PRO VERSION
Click the Sales Invoices icon to open the Sales Journal.

Click the **Client Invoices icon** to open the Revenues (Sales) Journal.

Choose **Capilano Centre Hotel** as the client.

Enter **Feb 2, 2015** as the invoice date.

Enter a **description** for the sale.

Enter **2900** as the invoice amount.

Click the **Salesperson list arrow** to see the list of salespersons as shown:

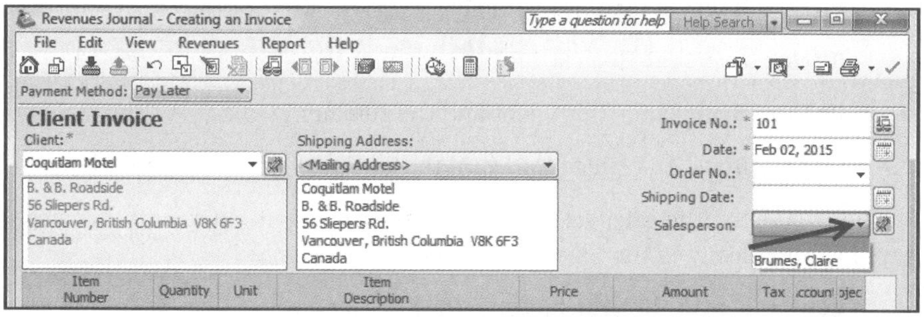

Brumes is the only employee responsible for sales at Lime Light Laundry, so she is the only employee we placed in the Sales job category. Therefore, Brumes is the only name listed. All other employees are in the second category labelled "Other," which does not have any salespersons.

Click **Brumes** to add her name to the invoice.

Click the **Use The Same Salesperson pin icon** .

This will lock in the salesperson's name on the invoice form until we close the journal. The pin has changed position — it now looks like it has been pushed in:

If you leave the journal open in the background, the salesperson remains selected. If you close the journal, you must reselect the salesperson for each invoice. You must close the journal before advancing the session date.

Review the **journal display**. The salesperson is not added to the journal report.

Close the **display** when finished.

Check your **work** and **make corrections** if necessary.

Store the **transaction** to recur **weekly**. Brumes will be entered as the salesperson in the stored transaction.

Post the **invoice** and **minimize** (or close) the **Sales Journal**.

> **NOTES**
> The Use The Same Salesperson pin icon is the same as the Use The Same Client Next Time tool and it works the same way.

Adding Salespersons to Client Records

Because Brumes is the only salesperson, we can add her name to all client records. By changing the ledger records, Brumes will be entered in the Sales Journal automatically for these clients. For new clients, you can create a full record and add the salesperson or add the name in the journal.

Click **Capilano Centre Hotel** in the Clients pane list of clients to open the ledger. **Click** the **Salesperson field list arrow** as shown:

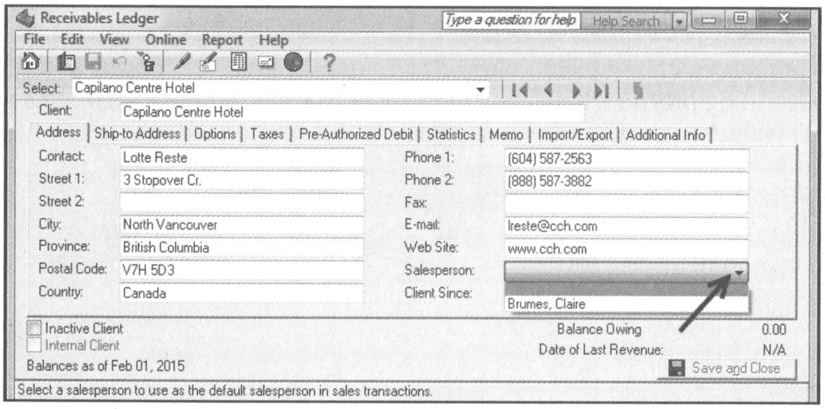

> **NOTES**
> You can still select a different salesperson in the journal if the default selection is incorrect for an individual sale.

Click **Brumes** to add her name.

Click the **Next Record tool** to open the next client's record.

Choose **Brumes** for this client and the remaining ones.

Click **Save And Close** to return to the Home window.

When you open the sales journal and choose any client on record, Brumes will be entered automatically in the Salesperson field.

Continue with the **transactions** for February.

2 **Memo #1** **Dated Feb. 2/15**

Add shortcuts for entries in other journals.

3 **Memo #2** **Dated Feb. 2/15**

Complete an adjusting entry to reverse the year-end accrued wages entry for $1 150. (Debit 2250 Accrued Wages and credit 5305 Wages: Cleaning Staff.)

4 **Cash Purchase Invoice #LS-504** **Dated Feb. 2/15**

From Langley Service Centre, $400 plus $20 GST and $28 PST for maintenance service and repairs to delivery truck. Invoice total $448. Paid by cheque #74.

5 **Purchase Invoice #FP-1297** **Dated Feb. 2/15**

From Ferndale Paper Products, $200 plus $10 GST and $14 PST for bags and wrapping paper for clean laundry. Invoice total $224. Terms: 1/10, n/30. Store as a bi-weekly recurring entry.

6 **Cash Receipt #31** **Dated Feb. 3/15**

From Delta Hotel, cheque #4123 for $2 910.60 in payment of account, including $29.40 discount for early payment. Reference invoice #69.

7 **Payment Cheque #75** **Dated Feb. 5/15**

To Ferndale Paper Products, $554.40 in payment of account, including $5.60 discount for early payment. Reference invoice #FP-901.

8 **Sales Invoice #102** **Dated Feb. 6/15**

To Coquitlam Motel, $3 400 plus $170 GST for contracted laundry services. Invoice total $3 570. Terms: 1/15, n/30. Enter Brumes as the salesperson if her name is not added automatically. Store as a recurring bi-weekly transaction.

9 **Purchase Invoice #PL-903** **Dated Feb. 6/15**

From Pacific Laundry Suppliers, $300 plus $15 GST and $21 PST for regular supply of cleaning products. Invoice total $336. Terms: net 30. Store as a bi-weekly recurring transaction.

10 **Cash Purchase Invoice #SP-2991** **Dated Feb. 7/15**

From Surrey Printers, $600 plus $30 GST and $42 PST for copying and mailing advertising brochures outlining new prices to clients. Invoice total $672 paid in full with cheque #76.

11 **Sales Invoice #103** **Dated Feb. 7/15**

To Port Moody Resort, $5 200 plus $260 GST for contracted laundry services for one month. Invoice total $5 460. Terms: 1/15, n/30. Enter Brumes as the salesperson. Store as a monthly recurring transaction.

NOTES

You will need shortcuts for Create General Journal (Company), Create Supplier Invoice and Pay Supplier Invoices (Payables), Payroll Cheque Run and Create Paycheque (Employees & Payroll).

You can Pay Remittances and Make Other Payments from the Pay Supplier Invoices transaction drop-down list. You can adjust paycheques from the Payroll Journal.

PRO VERSION

Purchase will replace Supplier for the shortcut labels.

WARNING!

Remember not to include the discount for the second invoice in payments and receipts.

12 **Payment Cheque #77** **Dated Feb. 7/15**

To Pacific Laundry Suppliers, $1 120 in payment of invoice #PL-644.

13

Lime Light Laundry
Laundry Services • Pickup & Deliver

Lime Light Laundry
Employee Time Summary Sheet #5

Cheque Date: Feb 7, 2015 Pay period end: Feb 7, 2015

Employee	M. Durtee	I. Sissler	C. Fretton	S. Landings	S. Pott Tran	C. Houseman	C. Brumes
SIN	552 846 826	931 771 620	218 738 631	422 946 541	638 912 634	822 546 859	726 911 134
Week 1	40	40					
——							
Regular hrs	40	40					
Overtime hrs	2	—					
#sheet sets	480	395					
Benefits	7.62	37.62					
Loan	100.00*	—					
Sick leave days	—	—					
Personal days	—	1**					
Chq/DD #	Chq 78	DD48					

* to be repaid at $25 per pay
** personal day to enroll in university course

Completed by: *Brumes 2/7/15*

NOTES
You can use the Paycheques or the Payroll Cheque Run Journal to complete the payroll transactions.

WARNING!
Remember to edit the benefit amount for Sissler so that the tuition amount is included – type 37.62 in the Benefits This Period field.

Or, you can edit her ledger record and enter 37.62 as the Amount Per Period for Benefits.

SESSION DATE – FEBRUARY 14, 2015

14

Lime Light Laundry
Laundry Services • Pickup & Deliver

Memo #3
From Manager's Desk

Dated Feb. 9/15

Corrected Feb 7 paycheque for Mouver Durtee to include 6 hours of overtime.
He was paid for only 2 hours.
Re-issued cheque #78 -- original cheque returned

Claire Brumes

NOTES
Remember to click the Recalculate Taxes tool after changing the overtime hours.

15 **Sales Invoice #104** **Dated Feb. 9/15**

To Capilano Centre Hotel, $2 900 plus $145 GST for weekly contracted linen laundry service. Invoice total $3 045. Terms: 1/15, n/30. Recall stored transaction.

NOTES
Brumes will be entered as the salesperson in the stored transaction.

Allow clients to exceed the credit limit.

16 **Cash Receipt #32** **Dated Feb. 13/15**

From Capilano Centre Hotel, cheque #2314 for $3 014.55 in partial payment of account, including $30.45 discount for early payment. Reference invoice #101.

17 **Sales Invoice #105** **Dated Feb. 13/15**

To Kingsley Inn (use Full Add for the new client), $2 800 plus $140 GST for new contract for daily laundry service with bi-weekly invoices. Invoice total $2 940. Terms: 1/15, n/30. Brumes is the salesperson. Store as recurring bi-weekly entry.

NOTES

Kingsley Inn
(contact Rume Kingsley)
302 Sandman Dr.
Vancouver, BC V8H 1P1
Tel: (604) 259-1881
Fax: (604) 259-1893
Terms: 1/15, n/30
Revenue account: 4020
Tax code: G - GST @ 5%
Credit limit: $5 000
Salesperson: Brumes

18 **Sales Invoice #106** **Dated Feb. 13/15**

To Delta Hotel, $2 900 plus $145 GST for bi-weekly invoice for contracted laundry services. Invoice total $3 045. Terms: 1/15, n/30. Enter Brumes as the salesperson. Store as a bi-weekly recurring transaction.

NOTES

Type –25 in the Loans This Period field for Durtee and –50 for Fretton to recover the loans.

Type 37.62 in the Benefits This Period field for Sissler.

19

Lime Light Laundry
Laundry Services • Pickup & Deliver

Lime Light Laundry
Employee Time Summary Sheet #6

Cheque Date: Feb 14, 2015 Pay period end: Feb 14, 2015

Employee	M. Durtee	I. Sissler	C. Fretton	S. Landings	S. Pott Tran	C. Houseman	C. Brumes
SIN	552 846 826	931 771 620	218 738 631	422 946 541	638 912 634	822 546 859	726 911 134
Week 1	pd	pd	40	40	40		
Week 2	40	40	40	42	40		
Regular hrs	40	40	80	80	80		
Overtime hrs	–	–	–	2			
#sheet sets	370	470	860	950			
Benefits	7.62	37.62	30.69	27.81	30.69		
Loan	-25.00	200.00*	-50.00	–	–		
Sick leave days	–	–	–	–	–		
Personal days	1	–	–	–	–		
Chq/DD #	Chq 79	DD50	DD49	Chq 80	Chq 81		

* to be repaid at $50 per pay

Completed by: Brumes 2/14/15

20 **Payment Cheque #82** **Dated Feb. 14/15**

To Richmond Equipment, $3 360 in payment of invoice #RE-4111.

21 **Cash Purchase Invoice #BCEG-78522** **Dated Feb. 14/15**

From BC Energy Group, $600 plus $30 GST for one month of hydro services. Invoice total $630 due within five days to avoid interest penalty. Paid in full with cheque #83.

22 **Cash Purchase #BCT-11229** **Dated Feb. 14/15**

From BC Telephone, $100 plus $5 GST and $7 PST for one month of telephone services. Invoice total $112. Paid in full with cheque #84.

SESSION DATE – FEBRUARY 21, 2015

23 **Purchase Invoice #FP-2635** **Dated Feb. 16/15**

From Ferndale Paper Products, $200 plus $10 GST and $14 PST for wrapping paper and bags. Invoice total $224. Terms: 1/10, n/30. Recall stored entry.

24 **Sales Invoice #107** **Dated Feb. 16/15**

To Capilano Centre Hotel, $2 900 plus $145 GST for weekly contracted linen laundry service. Invoice total $3 045. Terms: 1/15, n/30. Recall stored transaction.

25 **Cash Receipt #33** **Dated Feb. 18/15**

From Port Moody Resort, cheque #5120 for $5 405.40 in payment of account, including $54.60 discount for early payment. Reference invoice #103.

26 **Cash Receipt #34** **Dated Feb. 18/15**

From Capilano Centre Hotel, cheque #2692 for $3 014.55 in partial payment of account, including $30.45 discount for early payment. Reference invoice #104.

27 **Purchase Invoice #PL-1634** **Dated Feb. 20/15**

From Pacific Laundry Suppliers, $300 plus $15 GST and $21 PST for supply of cleaning products. Invoice total $336. Terms: net 30. Recall stored entry.

28 **Sales Invoice #108** **Dated Feb. 20/15**

To Coquitlam Motel, $3 400 plus $170 GST for contracted bi-weekly laundry services. Invoice total $3 570. Terms: 1/15, n/30. Recall stored transaction. Allow client to exceed credit limit.

29 **Cash Receipt #35** **Dated Feb. 21/15**

From Delta Hotel, cheque #4439 for $3 014.55 in payment of account, including $30.45 discount for early payment. Reference invoice #106.

30 **Purchase Invoice #RE-6998** **Dated Feb. 21/15**

From Richmond Equipment, $2 000 plus $100 GST and $140 PST for new presser. Invoice total $2 240. Terms: 1/10, n/30.

31 **Employee Time Summary Sheet #7** **Dated Feb. 21/15**

For the pay period ending February 21, 2015

Name of Employee	Regular Hours	Overtime Hours	Piece Rate Quantity	Benefits	Loan (Repaid)	Sick Days	Personal Days	Direct Deposit
Durtee, Mouver	40	2	440	$7.62	–$25	1	–	No
Sissler, Iean	40	2	520	$37.62	–$50	–	–	Yes

a. Using Employee Time Summary Sheet #7 and the Employee Information Sheet, complete payroll for the weekly paid employees. Use the Payroll Journal or the Payroll Run Journal.
b. Recover $25 loaned to Mouver Durtee and recover $50 loaned to Iean Sissler.
c. Issue cheque #85 and DD slip #51.

32 **Cash Sales Invoice #109** **Dated Feb. 21/15**

To Burnaby Private Hospital (use Quick Add), $2 400 plus $120 GST for emergency linen and laundry service. Invoice total $2 520. Terms: C.O.D. Received cheque #561 for $2 520 in full payment. There is no discount.

NOTES

Type –25 in the Loans This Period field for Durtee and –50 for Sissler to recover these amounts.

Type 37.62 in the Benefits This Period field for Sissler.

NOTES

Use Quick Add for new cash clients. Remember to enter Brumes as the salesperson.

If you use Full Add for new clients, you can add the salesperson to the new ledger record.

SESSION DATE – FEBRUARY 28, 2015

33

Sales Invoice #110 **Dated Feb. 23/15**

To Capilano Centre Hotel, $2 900 plus $145 GST for weekly laundry service. Invoice total $3 045. Terms: 1/15, n/30. Recall stored entry.

34

Cash Receipt #36 **Dated Feb. 25/15**

From Capilano Centre Hotel, cheque #2974 for $3 014.55 in payment of account, including $30.45 discount for early payment. Reference invoice #107.

35

Cash Receipt #37 **Dated Feb. 25/15**

From Kingsley Inn, cheque #439 for $1 966 in partial payment of account. Reference invoice #105.

36

Cash Receipt #38 **Dated Feb. 25/15**

From Coquitlam Motel, cheque #276 for $3 570 in payment of invoice #102.

37

Payment Cheque #86 **Dated Feb. 26/15**

To Ferndale Paper Products, cheque #86 for $445.76 in payment of invoices #FP-1297 and #FP-2635, including $2.24 discount for early payment.

38

Sales Invoice #111 **Dated Feb. 27/15**

To Delta Hotel, $2 900 plus $145 GST for bi-weekly invoice for linen service. Invoice total $3 045. Terms: 1/15, n/30. Recall stored entry.

39

Sales Invoice #112 **Dated Feb. 27/15**

To Kingsley Inn, $2 800 plus $140 GST bi-weekly bill for laundry service. Invoice total $2 940. Terms: 1/15, n/30. Recall stored entry.

40

Memo #4 **Dated Feb. 28/15**

From Manager: Receipt #37 from Kingsley Inn for $1 966 was entered incorrectly. On Feb. 25, cheque #439 for $2 910.60 was received from Kingsley Inn in full payment of invoice #105, including $29.40 for early payment. Adjust or reverse the original receipt and make the correction.

NOTES

If you use the Adjust Receipt tool to correct the receipt, Sage 50 will automatically make the reversing entry. Delete the original Payment Amount. You will need to enter the amount of discount taken manually. It may be easier to reverse the receipt (refer to page 176) and then enter the client's payment correctly.

When you reverse the receipt, the new receipt number will be updated to #39.

41

Cash Sales Invoice #113 **Dated Feb. 28/15**

To Sleepy Hollow (use Quick Add), $1 100 plus $55 GST for linen and laundry service. Invoice total $1 155. Received cheque #2998 for $1 155 in full payment. There is no discount.

42

Bank Debit Memo #532281 **Dated Feb. 28/15**

From Mountain Heights Bank, $2 045 was withdrawn from the chequing account for the following pre-authorized transactions:

Bank Charges	$ 45
Interest on Bank Loan	120
Reduction of Principal on Bank Loan	880
Interest on Mortgage	750
Reduction of Principal on Mortgage	250

Create new Group account: 5110 Interest Expense

43

Memo #5 **Dated Feb. 28/15**

Complete an adjusting entry for one month of prepaid insurance expired. The one-year insurance policy was purchased on December 31, 2014, for $2 400.

44 **Memo #6** **Dated Feb. 28/15**

Complete month-end adjusting entries for supplies used in February.

Cleaning supplies used	$680
Packaging supplies used	350

45 **Employee Time Summary Sheet #8** **Dated Feb. 28/15**

For the pay period ending February 28, 2015

Name of Employee	Regular Hours	Overtime Hours	Piece Rate Quantity	Benefits	Loan (Repaid)	Sick Days	Personal Days	Direct Deposit
Durtee, Mouver	40	–	510	$7.62	–$25	–	–	No
Sissler, Iean	40	2	510	$37.62	–$50	–	–	Yes
Fretton, Clyne	80	2	1 030	$30.69	–$50	–	–	Yes
Landings, Soffte	80	–	930	$27.81		1	–	No
Tran, S. Pott	80	–		$30.69		–	–	No

a. Using Employee Time Summary Sheet #8 and the Employee Information Sheet, complete payroll for all employees. Use the Payroll Journal or the Payroll Run Journal.
b. Recover $25 loaned to Mouver Durtee, $50 from Clyne Fretton and $50 loaned to Iean Sissler.
c. Issue cheques #87, #88 and #89, and DD #52 and #53.

NOTES

Type –25 in the Loans This Period field for Durtee and –50 for Sissler and Fretton to recover these amounts.

Type 37.62 in the Benefits This Period field for Sissler.

46 **Memo #7** **Dated Feb. 28/15**

Pay Brumes and Houseman their monthly salary. Issue deposit slips #54 and #55. Claire Brumes earned a sales commission of $258 for the month of February and took five days' vacation (use the Vacation Days Taken field, Entitlements tab).

47

Lime Light Laundry
Laundry Services • Pickup & Deliver

Memo #8
From Manager's Desk

Dated Feb. 28/15

Paid Claire Brumes' travel allowance for February 2015.
Issued cheque #90 for $300 to Brumes.
(Added Brumes as supplier and used Travel Allowances Payable account.)

Claire Brumes

NOTES

The travel allowance for Brumes is set up in her ledger record so that the amount is included automatically as an employer expense that debits Travel Allowance Expenses and credits Travel Allowances Payable, just as tuition fees were set up for Sissler. You do not need to enter the expense separately.

This is not a taxable benefit.

In Chapter 16, we set up travel expenses as non-taxable reimbursement income.

48 **Memo #9** **Dated Feb. 28/15**

Clyne Fretton is taking some vacation time. Fretton asked to receive her vacation pay by cheque. Release her retained vacation pay and issue cheque #91.

NOTES

Refer to page 276 if you need help preparing the vacation paycheque.

✓ 49

Memo #10 **Dated Feb. 28/15**

Adjust the paycheque for Brumes. She has returned her deposit pay stub because her earned commission was incorrect. Use the Revenues By Salesperson Report to verify that the correct amount was $385, not $258.

Displaying Salesperson Reports

Click the **Report Centre icon** in the Home window.

Click **Receivables** to open the list of client reports that you can display from the Report Centre.

Displaying the Revenues by Salesperson Report

Two additional reports are available when we add salespersons to journal entries.

Click **Revenues By Salesperson Summary** in the Select A Report list.

Click **Modify This Report** to open the report options:

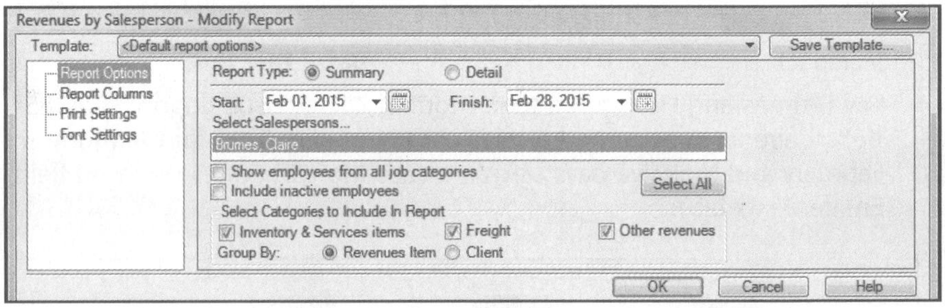

Or choose the Reports menu, then choose Receivables and click Revenues By Salesperson to open the report options screen.

PRO VERSION
The terms Customer and Sales will replace Client and Revenues in the Report Centre.
Click Sales By Salesperson Summary to select the report.

NOTES
You can also access the Revenues by Salesperson Report from the Reports menu under Services Reports. The Services Reports entry will be renamed to match the industry type for other companies. Thus, the Reports menu may show this entry as Business Reports, Retail Reports, Construction Reports and so on.

Brumes is the only employee designated as a salesperson so only her name appears on the list, and she is already selected. You have the option to show all employees, but we do not need them all — we want Brumes' February sales data. The default dates for Start and Finish cover the period we want. You can group the sales information by client or by sales item. You can also include information for freight and other non-inventory sales. For Lime Light, we need to show only the Other Revenues because inventory and freight do not apply. You can also show this report as a **Detail Report** with a line item for each sale, or as a **Summary Report** with totals only for each item or client.

You can exclude amounts that do not apply. Click Freight and Inventory & Services Items to remove the ✓s.

Click **OK** to see the report. The total sales revenue for January was $38 500, so Brumes' commission amount should be changed to $385.

Close the displayed **report**.

NOTES
For both the Revenue by Salesperson and Job Category reports, you can drill down to the Detail Report from the Summary Report. From the Detail Report you can drill down to look up the sales invoices.

Displaying the Sales by Job Category Report

This next report is similar except that it combines the information for all employees in each category. Because we have only one person in the Sales category, reporting by this category should give us the same information as the Revenues By Salesperson Report.

Open the **Report Centre**.

Click **Revenues By Job Category Summary** in the Select A Report list.

Click **Modify This Report** to open the report options:

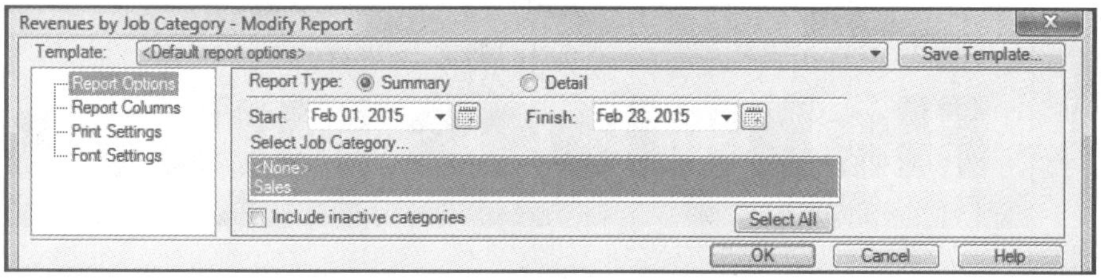

Or choose the Reports menu, then choose Receivables and click Revenues By Job Categories to open the report options screen.

Again the default dates give us the report for the month we need. Categories that do not have salespersons in them are not included in this report. You can create a **Detail Report** with a listing for each individual invoice or a **Summary Report** that provides the total for each selected category.

Click **Sales** to select only this category.

Click **OK** to see the total sales for all persons in the Sales category.

Close the **report** when finished. **Close** the **Report Centre**.

Enter the **remittances for Feb. 28** to complete the application.

50

Memo #11 **Dated Feb. 28/15**

Using the payroll remittance option, remit the following payroll taxes for the pay period ending February 28, including the balance owing from January:

To Receiver General: EI Payable, CPP Payable and Income Tax Payable

To BC Minister of Finance: MSP Payable - Employee and MSP Payable - Employer

To BC Workers' Compensation Board: WCB Payable

To Victoria Trust: RRSP Payable

Issue cheques #92 through #95 in payment.

REVIEW

The Student DVD with Data Files includes Review Questions and Supplementary Cases for this chapter.

PRO VERSION

Click Sales By Job Category Summary to select the report.

CHAPTER TEN

Flabuless Fitness

OBJECTIVES

After completing this chapter, you should be able to

- ***enter*** inventory-related purchase transactions
- ***enter*** inventory-related sale transactions of goods and services
- ***make*** inventory adjustments
- ***assemble*** new inventory items from other inventory
- ***enter*** returns on sales and purchases
- ***create*** credit notes
- ***enter*** sales to preferred customers
- ***enter*** freight on purchases
- ***understand*** the integration of the Inventory Ledger with the Payables, Receivables and General ledgers
- ***create*** new inventory items
- ***display*** and ***print*** inventory reports

COMPANY INFORMATION

Company Profile

Flabuless Fitness, in Winnipeg, Manitoba, sells a wide range of fitness equipment and accessories for home and light commercial use. Stephen Reeves, the owner, opened his business a few years ago after retiring from his career as a professional athlete, gaining business experience with another store and completing some business courses. Reeves has two employees to assist with the work in the store. Reeves works mostly outside the store, promoting the business.

Several of the equipment suppliers offer discounts to the store for early payment. Accounts are also set up for other supplies and services that are provided locally. The store uses a credit card for some of these purchases.

Most customers are located in the Winnipeg region, but Reeves has contacted some colleges and hotels in nearby US cities as potential customers.

All account customers are given discounts for early payment and some preferred customers receive additional discounts. Individual customers who pay by cash, debit or credit card do not receive any discounts and pay for delivery.

NOTES
Flabuless Fitness
199 Warmup Rd., Unit 500
Winnipeg, MB R8T 3B7
Tel 1: (204) 642-2348 (B-FIT)
Tel 2: (800) 448-2348 (B-FIT)
Fax: (204) 642-9100
Business No.: 245 138 121

All items and services sold by the store are set up as inventory so that sales can be monitored. GST is charged on all sales and services. RST is charged on sales of inventory items and equipment assembly, but not on books or on other services. The store pays GST and RST on all taxable purchases, but inventory purchased for resale in the store is exempt from RST.

Reeve's assistant used the following information to convert the accounting records to Sage 50 on February 1, 2015, using the following:

- Chart of Accounts
- Post-Closing Trial Balance
- Supplier Information
- Customer Information
- Employee Information
- Inventory Information
- Accounting Procedures

NOTES

RST, Retail Sales Tax, is the name of the provincial sales tax in Manitoba.

CHART OF POSTABLE ACCOUNTS

FLABULESS FITNESS

ASSETS

Current Assets
1060 Bank Account: Chequing
1080 Bank Account: MasterCard
1090 Bank Account: Visa
1100 Investments
1200 Accounts Receivable
1260 Office Supplies
1265 Linen Supplies
1280 Prepaid Insurance

Inventory Assets
1520 Accessories
1540 Fitness Equipment
1550 Home Gym Equipment
1560 Books

Centre & Equipment
1640 Computer Equipment
1670 Furniture & Fixtures
1700 Retail Premises
1730 Van ▶

▶LIABILITIES

Current Liabilities
2100 Bank Loan
2200 Accounts Payable
2250 Credit Card Payable
2310 EI Payable
2320 CPP Payable
2330 Income Tax Payable
2410 Group Insurance - Employer
2420 Group Insurance - Employee
2460 WCB Payable
2640 RST Payable
2650 GST Charged on Sales
2670 GST Paid on Purchases

Long Term Liabilities
2820 Mortgage Payable

EQUITY
3560 Share Capital
3600 Current Earnings ▶

▶REVENUE

General Revenue
4020 Revenue from Sales
4040 Revenue from Services
4060 Sales Discounts
4150 Interest Revenue
4200 Freight Revenue

EXPENSE

Operating Expenses
5010 Advertising and Promotion
5020 Bank Charges
5030 Credit Card Fees
5035 Promotion Package Services
5040 Damaged Inventory
5060 Cost of Goods Sold
5065 Cost of Services
5070 Cost Variance
5080 Freight Expense
5090 Purchase Discounts
5100 Purchases Returns ▶

▶5130 Depreciation
5190 Delivery Expense
5200 Hydro Expense
5210 Insurance Expense
5220 Interest Expenses
5240 Maintenance of Premises
5250 Supplies Used
5280 Telephone Expenses
5285 Van Maintenance & Operating Expense

Payroll Expenses
5300 Salaries
5310 Commissions
5330 EI Expense
5340 CPP Expense
5350 WCB Expense
5370 Gp Insurance Expense

POST-CLOSING TRIAL BALANCE

FLABULESS FITNESS

Feb. 1, 2015		Debits	Credits
1060	Bank Account: Chequing	$ 77 988.00	
1080	Bank Account: MasterCard	9 350.00	
1090	Bank Account: Visa	8 635.00	
1100	Investments	108 250.00	
1200	Accounts Receivable	14 690.00	
1260	Office Supplies	300.00	
1265	Linen Supplies	450.00	
1280	Prepaid Insurance	4 800.00	
1520	Accessories	7 010.00	
1540	Fitness Equipment	58 500.00	
1550	Home Gym Equipment	15 120.00	
1560	Books	5 200.00	
1640	Computer Equipment	8 000.00	
1670	Furniture & Fixtures	2 000.00	
1700	Retail Premises	200 000.00	
1730	Van	30 000.00	▶
▶ 2100	Bank Loan		$ 50 000.00
2200	Accounts Payable		16 800.00
2250	Credit Card Payable		255.00
2310	EI Payable		363.00
2320	CPP Payable		765.00
2330	Income Tax Payable		1 692.00
2410	Group Insurance - Employer		48.00
2420	Group Insurance - Employee		48.00
2460	WCB Payable		284.00
2640	RST Payable		2 400.00
2650	GST Charged on Sales		3 430.00
2670	GST Paid on Purchases	1 495.00	
2820	Mortgage Payable		180 000.00
3560	Share Capital		295 703.00
		$551 788.00	$551 788.00

SUPPLIER INFORMATION

FLABULESS FITNESS

Supplier Name (Contact)	Address	Phone No. Fax No.	E-mail Web Site	Terms Tax ID
Feelyte Gym Accessories (Stretch Theraband)	7 Onondaga Dr. Vancouver BC V4G 4S5	Tel: (604) 588-3846 Fax: (604) 588-7126	stretch@feelyte.com www.feelyte.com	2/10, n/30 (before tax) 466 254 108
Footlink Corporation (Onna Treadmill)	39 Treadwell St. Winnipeg, MB R6M 3K9	Tel: (204) 777-8133 Fax: (204) 777-8109	onna@footlink.com www.footlink.com	1/15, n/30 (before tax) 274 309 481
Grand Life Insurance				net 1
Manitoba Bell (Annie Heard)	82 Wireless Alley Winnipeg, MB R3B 5R9	Tel: (204) 781-2355	heard@bell.ca www.bell.ca	net 7
Manitoba Energy (Manny Watts)	91 NacNab St. Winnipeg, MB R3R 2L9	Tel: (204) 463-2664	watts@mbengery.ca www.mbengery.ca	net 7
Prolife Exercisers Inc. (C. Glider)	1500 Redmond Rd., Suite 100 Red River MB R4S 1T4	Tel 1: (204) 597-4756 Tel 2: (888) 597-4756	glider@prolife.ex.com www.prolife.ex.com	2/10, n/30 (before tax) 344 566 799
Receiver General for Canada		Tel 1: (800) 561-7761	www.cra-arc.gc.ca	net 1
Riverview Sunoco (Mick Annick)	101 Niska Dr. Winnipeg, MB R3R 2H3	Tel: (204) 622-6181	mick@goodforcars.com www.goodforcars.com	net 21
Trufit Depot (Varry Shapely)	43 Paling Ave. Hamilton, ON L8H 5J5	Tel: (905) 529-7235 Fax: (905) 529-2995	shapely@trufitdepot.ca www.trufitdepot.ca	2/5, n/30 (before tax) 244 573 650
Workers' Compensation Board				net 1

OUTSTANDING SUPPLIER INVOICES

Supplier Name	Terms	Date	Inv/Chq No.	Amount	Tax	Total
Footlink Corporation	1/15, n/30 (before tax)	Jan. 20/15	FC-618	$16 000	$800	$16 800

CUSTOMER INFORMATION

FLABULESS FITNESS

Customer Name (Contact)	Address	Phone No. Fax No.	E-mail Web Site	Terms Credit Limit
Ariandanos Residence (Arianne Ariandanos)	29 Spinning Blvd. Winnipeg, MB R2P 2M2	Tel: (204) 762-8664	arianne@radiantway.com www.radiantway.com	2/5, n/15 $5 000
Botelli & Giroux, Lawyers (Gina Botelli)	30 Court St. Winnipeg, MB R3R 1C7	Tel: (204) 699-2911 Fax: (204) 697-2735	gina@botelli.giroux.com www.botelli.giroux.com	2/5, n/15 $10 000
*Brandon University (Outov Shape)	Kinesiology Dept. Brandon University Brandon, MB R7A 6A9	Tel 1: (204) 529-3000 Tel 2: (204) 529-3198 Fax: (204) 529-3477	oshape@brandonu.ca www.brandonu.ca	2/15, n/30 $10 000
Lavendar Estates (Katherine Harris)	9 Lavender Ct. Winnipeg, MB R2X 3J6	Tel: (204) 782-7300 Fax: (204) 782-8190	harris@lavender.com www.lavender.com	2/5, n/15 $5 000
*Red River College (Phat Nomore)	Physical Education Dept. Red River College Winnipeg, MB R3H 0J9	Tel 1: (204) 622-9250 Tel 2: (204) 622-9238 Fax: (204) 622-9729	nomore@rcc.ca www.rcc.ca	2/15, n/30 $10 000
*The Forks Film Corporation (Francine Despardieu)	6 Gilroy St. Winnipeg, MB R3C 2M2	Tel: (204) 787-1226	fdes@forksfilm.com www.forksfilm.com	2/15, n/30 $10 000

NOTES: The * indicates preferred price list customers. A record is also set up for Cash & Credit Card Sales Customers.

OUTSTANDING CUSTOMER INVOICES

Customer Name	Terms	Date	Inv/Chq No.	Amount	Total
Brandon University	2/10, n/30 (after tax)	Jan. 29/15	2199	$9 040	$9 040
Red River College	2/10, n/30 (after tax)	Jan. 25/15	2194	$5 650	$5 650
				Grand Total	$14 690

EMPLOYEE INFORMATION SHEET

FLABULESS FITNESS

Employee	George Prekor	Asumpta Kisangel
Address	55 Track Rd. Winnipeg, MB R8B 2V7	300 Meditation Circle Winnipeg, MB R4G 4K8
Telephone	(204) 426-1817	(204) 688-5778
Social Insurance No.	532 548 625	488 655 333
Date of Birth (mm-dd-yy)	09/18/70	05/24/76
Federal (Manitoba) Tax Exemption - TD1		
Basic Personal	$11 038 (8 884)	$11 038 (8 884)
Employee Earnings		
Salary (Hours Per Period)	$4 000.00 (150 Hours)	$4 000.00 (150 Hours)
Commission	2% of sales (less returns)	2% of sales (less returns)
Employee Deductions		
Group Insurance	$24	$24
EI, CPP & Income Tax	Calculations are built into Sage 50	

Employee Profiles and TD1 Information

Asumpta Kisangel and **George Prekor** both assist with sales in the store, provide the personal training services to customers and assemble the equipment for customers. Kisangel also does the accounting and teaches yoga classes. Both are salaried employees who receive their $4 000 monthly pay by cheque and contribute $24 each period to a group insurance plan. This amount is matched by the employer — a benefit for the employees. Kisangel and Prekor are single and self-supporting with no dependants and no other deductions, so they have the basic claim amounts for income tax. Instead of vacation pay, they take three weeks of vacation with regular pay each year. Neither has received any payroll advances or loans.

Both employees are listed as salespersons. They receive a sales commission of 2 percent of their net sales (sales less returns) with each paycheque. Their names are entered as salespersons on invoices so that the commissions can be tracked for the Sales by Salesperson Report.

INVENTORY INFORMATION

FLABULESS FITNESS

Code	Description	Min Stock	Prices Reg	(Pref)	Unit	Qty on Hand	Total (Cost)	Taxes
Accessories: Total asset value $7 010 (Linked Accounts: Asset 1520; Revenue 4020, COGS 5050, Variance 5070)								
A010	Body Fat Scale	2	$ 150	($ 130)	unit	20	$1 400	GP
A020	Yoga/Pilates Mat	5	40	(35)	each	60	1 200	GP
A030	Dumbbells	25	2.50	(2.20)	kg	600	540	GP
A040	Jump Rope: Weighted	10	40	(35)	each	20	420	GP
A050	Heart Rate Monitor	4	90	(80)	unit	20	800	GP
A060	Power Blocks	3	300	(250)	set	5	750	GP
A070	Stability Ball	5	12	(10)	each	30	180	GP
A080	Weight/Workout Bench	2	175	(150)	each	10	840	GP
A090	Workout Gloves: all sizes	25	15	(13)	pair	35	280	GP
A100	Aerobic Stepper w/ Risers	5	70	(60)	each	15	600	GP
Fitness Equipment: Total asset value $58 500 (Linked Accounts: Asset 1540; Revenue 4020, COGS 5060, Variance 5070)								
E010	Elliptical Exerciser: AE-200	2	2 100	(1 900)	unit	6	6 600	GP
E020	Elliptical Exerciser: LE-400	2	2 600	(2 300)	unit	6	8 400	GP
E030	Bicycle: Dual Action Calorie Counter	2	850	(720)	unit	12	5 400	GP
E040	Bicycle: Recumbent R-80	2	1 100	(960)	unit	12	7 200	GP
E050	Step Master: Adjustable SC-A60	2	1 900	(1 700)	unit	6	5 700	GP
E060	Treadmill: Basic T-800B	3	1 400	(1 220)	unit	12	9 000	GP
E070	Treadmill: Deluxe T-1100D	3	2 800	(2 500)	unit	12	16 200	GP
Home Gyms Total asset value $15 120 (Linked Accounts: Asset 1550; Revenue 4020, COGS 5060, Variance 5070)								
E080	Home Gym: Basic HG-1400	2	1 600	(1 380)	set	6	$5 520	GP
E090	Home Gym: Deluxe Multi HG-1402	2	2 950	(2 700)	set	6	9 600	GP
Books Total asset value $5 200 (Linked Accounts: Asset 1560; Revenue 4020, COGS 5060, Variance 5070)								
B010	Books: Fitness Guide	15	40	(35)	each	208	5 200	G (RST Exempt)
Services (Linked Accounts: Revenue 4040, COGS 5065)								
S010	Personal Trainer: 1 hour		80	(70)	hour			G (RST Exempt)
S020	Personal Trainer: 1/2 day		200	(190)	1/2 day			G (RST Exempt)
S030	Personal Trainer: full day		400	(380)	day			G (RST Exempt)
S040	Yoga Instructor: 1 hour		100	(95)	hour			G (RST Exempt)
S050	Yoga Instructor: 1/2 day		200	(190)	1/2 day			G (RST Exempt)
S060	Equipment Assembly/Demonstration		75	(60)	job			GP (not exempt for RST)

NOTES: Buying units, selling units and stocking units are the same for all items. Inventory is not oversold.

Accounting Procedures

The Goods and Services Tax (GST): Remittances

Flabuless Fitness uses the regular method for remittance of the Goods and Services Tax. GST collected is recorded as a liability in *GST Charged on Sales*. GST paid, recorded in *GST Paid on Purchases*, decreases the liability. The store files its return with the Canada Revenue Agency (CRA) quarterly, either requesting a refund or remitting the balance owing.

Retail (Provincial) Sales Tax (RST)

Retail Sales Tax of 7 percent is applied to all cash and credit sales of goods in Manitoba. Customers do not pay RST on the services provided by Flabuless Fitness, except for equipment assembly. RST on goods is remitted quarterly to the Minister of Finance.

RST at the rate of 7 percent is also paid on purchases that are not inventory items for resale. Because RST paid is not refundable, it is charged to the asset or expense account associated with the purchase, not to a separate account.

NOTES

In July, 2013, Manitoba changed its provincial tax rate to 8 percent. This change was announced too late to be incorporated into the current text.

Sales Invoices

Flabuless Fitness allows customers to pay on account, or by cash, cheque or credit card. The keystrokes for cash and credit card inventory transactions are similar to those for account sales, except for the method of payment. The program will automatically debit the appropriate bank account instead of *Accounts Receivable*.

Source documents for cash and credit card sales are presented as summaries to avoid a large number of small revenue transactions. A record for Cash & Credit Card Sales is set up to track these sales.

You can print and e-mail sales invoices through the program. Before posting the Sales Journal transaction, preview the invoice. Then click the Print button or the E-mail button.

Credit Card Sales and Purchases

Flabuless Fitness has set up its accounts for credit card sales and purchases.

Freight Expenses and Charges

When a business purchases inventory items, the cost of any freight that cannot be directly allocated to a specific item must be charged to *Freight Expense*. This amount is regarded as an expense rather than a charge to an inventory asset account. Freight or delivery charges to customers are allocated to *Freight Revenue*.

Discounts

To encourage customers to settle their accounts early, Flabuless Fitness offers its account customers a 2 percent discount on before-tax amounts if they pay their accounts within five days. Discounts are calculated automatically when the payment terms are set up and the customer is eligible for the discount. These new terms begin on February 1. There are no discounts on cash or credit card sales.

In addition, some customers have preferred price list status that entitles them to reduced prices. Regular and preferred prices are set up in the Inventory Ledger so the prices are entered automatically. For preferred customers, the discount period is extended to 15 days.

Promotional Packages

Each February, Flabuless Fitness offers special promotional packages that include a variety of accessories, one exercise bicycle and either yoga training or personal trainer time. Assembly of these packages incur additional costs for the service time.

Returns

Returned goods are a normal part of retail businesses. Flabuless Fitness provides full refunds on unused items returned within 14 days. Some items such as gloves cannot be returned for hygienic reasons. Returned items are debited to the contra-revenue account *Sales Returns* so that the returns can be tracked. Refer to page 381.

Returns on purchases also occur regularly. Refer to page 383.

INSTRUCTIONS

1. **Record entries** for the source documents in Sage 50 using the Chart of Accounts, Trial Balance, and Supplier, Customer, Employee and Inventory Information provided. The procedures for entering each new type of transaction are outlined step by step in the Keystrokes section with the source documents.
2. **Print** the **reports** indicated on the following printing forms after finishing your entries. Instructions for inventory reports begin on page 389.

REPORTS

Accounts
- ☐ Chart of Accounts
- ☐ Account List
- ☐ General Journal Entries

Financial
- ☑ Balance Sheet date: Feb. 28
- ☑ Income Statement: Feb. 1 to Feb. 28
- ☑ Trial Balance date: Feb. 28
- ☑ All Journal Entries: Feb. 1 to Feb. 28
- ☑ General Ledger accounts: 1520 1540 1550 4020 4040 from Feb. 1 to Feb. 28
- ☐ Statement of Cash Flows
- ☐ Cash Flow Projection Detail Report
- ☑ Gross Margin Income Statement: Feb. 1 to Feb. 28

Tax
- ☐ Report on

Banking
- ☐ Cheque Log Report

Payables
- ☐ Supplier List
- ☐ Supplier Aged
- ☐ Aged Overdue Payables
- ☐ Purchases Journal Entries
- ☐ Payments Journal Entries
- ☐ Supplier Purchases

Receivables
- ☐ Customer List
- ☐ Customer Aged
- ☐ Aged Overdue Receivables
- ☐ Sales Journal Entries
- ☐ Receipts Journal Entries
- ☐ Customer Sales
- ☑ Sales by Salesperson: Feb. 1 to Feb. 28
- ☐ Customer Statements

Payroll & Employees
- ☐ Employee List
- ☑ Summary: All employees
- ☐ Deductions & Expenses
- ☐ Remittances
- ☐ Payroll Journal Entries
- ☐ T4 Slips
- ☐ Record of Employment
- ☐ Year End Review (PIER)

Inventory & Services
- ☐ Inventory & Services List
- ☑ Summary
- ☐ Quantity
- ☐ Inventory Statistics
- ☑ Sales Summary for all Services: from Feb. 1 to Feb. 28
- ☑ Transaction Summary for A020 Yoga/Pilates Mat, all journals: Feb. 1 to Feb. 28
- ☐ Price Lists
- ☑ Item Assembly Journal Entries: Feb. 1 to Feb. 28
- ☑ Adjustments Journal Entries: Feb. 1 to Feb. 28

Mailing Labels
- ☐ Labels

Forecast & Analysis
- ☐ Forecast
- ☐ Customer Analysis
- ☐ Product Analysis
- ☑ Sales Analysis Report: Feb. 1 to Feb. 28

Management Reports
- ☐ Ledger

GRAPHS
- ☐ Payables by Aging Period
- ☐ Payables by Supplier
- ☐ Receivables by Aging Period
- ☐ Receivables by Customer
- ☐ Sales vs Receivables
- ☐ Receivables Due vs Payables Due
- ☐ Revenues by Account
- ☐ Expenses by Account
- ☑ Expenses and Net Profit as % of Revenue

NOTES
If you are working from backups, restore the backup file SageData13\flabuless1.CAB or flabuless1 to SageData13\Flabuless\flabuless.
Refer to the instructions in Chapter 1, page 22, if you need assistance with restoring files from backups.

KEYSTROKES

Accounting for Inventory Sales

Open **SageData13\Flabuless\flabuless** to access the data files for Flabuless Fitness.

Type 2 7 15 or **choose Feb. 7** from the calendar and **click OK**.

This will enter the session date February 7, 2015. The familiar Receivables module window appears. Inventory & Services has been added to the Modules pane list. Inventory sales are entered in the Sales Journal.

The first transaction involves the sale of inventory items. Many of the steps are identical to those you used for sales in previous applications. You will be using the inventory database and all the Sales Invoice fields to complete this transaction.

✓ 1

Sales Invoice #3000 **Dated February 1, 2015**

Sold by Kisangel to Botelli & Giroux, Lawyers,

3	A050	Heart Rate Monitor	$ 90 /unit
40	A030	Dumbbells	2.50 /kg
1	E010	Elliptical Exerciser: AE-200	2 100 /unit
1	E020	Elliptical Exerciser: LE-400	2 600 /unit
2	E060	Treadmill: Basic T-800B	1 400 /unit
5	B010	Books: Fitness Guide (tax code G)	40 each
6	S040	Yoga Instructor: 1 hour (tax code G)	100 /hour
		Delivery (tax code G)	50
		GST	5%
		RST	7%

Terms: 2/5, n/15.

Click the **Sales Invoices icon**  to open the familiar Sales Journal:

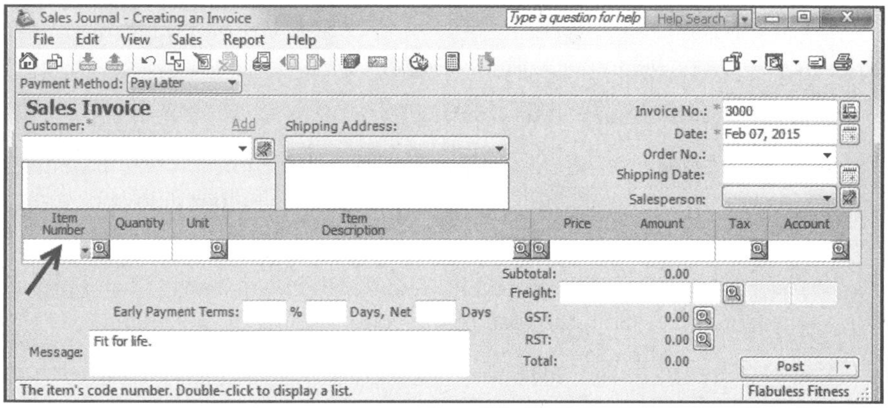

The Sales Journal looks the same as in earlier data files, except for the Sales Journal we customized for Phoebe's Photo Studio in Chapter 6. All the invoice fields are used when we sell inventory. Pay Later is correctly selected as the payment method.

Click the **Customer field list arrow** to display the list of customers.

Click **Botelli & Giroux, Lawyers** to enter the customer's name and address on the form.

The Shipping Address fields, Invoice number, payment terms and tax code defaults are all correct. If necessary, you can edit them. The Order No. is not used for invoices.

Click the **Date field Calendar icon**  to advance the cursor. The default session date is incorrect.

Click **1** on the February calendar.

Click the **Salesperson field** and **choose Kisangel** as the salesperson.

One line is used for each inventory item or service sold by the business. A separate line would also be used for non-inventory sales and to enter returns or allowances.

NOTES

We have selected Retail as the type of industry for Flabuless Fitness because they sell inventory items. The Division (Project) module and fields are hidden.

NOTES

Use the bookmark attached to the back cover to mark the page with the source document.

CLASSIC VIEW

Click the Sales icon to open the Sales Journal.

PRO VERSION

The invoice does not include Order No. or Shipping Date fields.

NOTES

Remember that you can customize the columns and tabbing order and columns. Refer to page 162.

Click the **Item Number field List icon**, or **click** the **field** and **press** *enter* or **double-click** to access the inventory list:

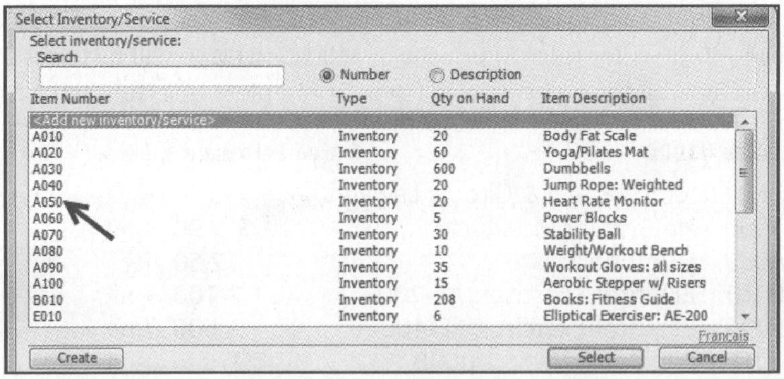

Notice that you can add new inventory items from the Select Inventory/Service screen. The inventory items are listed in order by number or code. For inventory items, the quantities available are also included in this display for reference.

The cursor is in the Search field. We will bypass the search field so that future references to this list will place the cursor in the list rather than in the Search field.

Click **Bypass Search Field** so that the next time the cursor will start in the item list.

Click in the list and type the first letter of a code if you want to advance the list to the codes beginning with that letter.

Click **A050 Heart Rate Monitor** from the list.

Click **Select** to add the inventory item to your form. If you have made an incorrect selection, return to the Item Number field and reselect from the inventory list.

You can also type the code number in the Item Number field and press *tab*, but you must match the case of the code number in the ledger.

The cursor moves to the Quantity field. Notice that the program adds information in each field automatically, based on the inventory record information. All the information except quantity and amount is added by default as soon as you enter the inventory item number. If you select a preferred customer, the default price is the preferred customer price instead of the regular selling price (see the screens on pages 380 and 381).

You should enter the number of units of this item sold in the Quantity field.

Type 3 **Press** *tab*.

If your company settings do not allow inventory levels to go below zero, the program prevents you from continuing when you enter a quantity greater than the available stock, more than 20 in this case, with this warning:

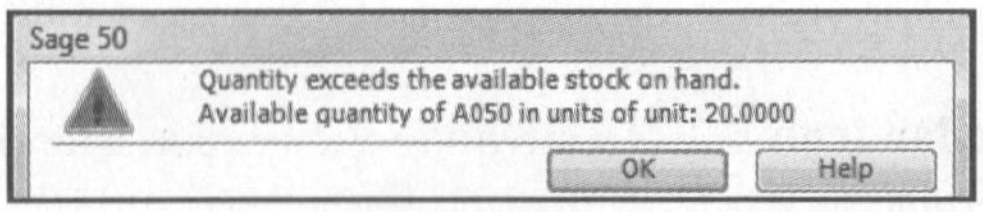

Click OK to return to the journal so you can reduce the quantity.

Since the remaining default information is correct, you do not need to change it. The default tax code — GP — is the code entered for the customer because the customer pays both GST at 5 percent and RST at 7 percent. Services have been set up in the Inventory Ledger so that by default RST is not applied.

The program automatically calculates an amount based on the selling price per unit. This figure appears in the Amount field.

NOTES

If you want to search for items by description, you can type a letter in the Item Description field to see the list of items including the letter you typed and sorted alphabetically by description.

To see the items sorted by description instead of by item number, click the list icon in the Description field.

The option to sort items by number or description in the Inventory Settings applies only to lists in the Adjustments and Item Assembly journals.

NOTES

Inventory codes are case sensitive – you must type A050 in the journal (match the upper-case A in the item code) to enter the item directly in the journal. To use the list of items, you can type a lower-case letter to advance to a later part of the list.

NOTES

Inventory items can be oversold, but you must change the Inventory Ledger settings to allow the quantity on hand to go below zero. This setting is explained in the setup for VeloCity (Chapter 16).

No quantities are shown for services because they are not held in stock.

NOTES

If your company settings allow, you may want to oversell the items if the customer is purchasing backordered inventory stock.

NOTES

The default tax code for the first line is the customer's code.

The default revenue account for the item appears but can be accepted or changed. You would change the account for returns and allowances or unusual entries. Accept the default revenue account for this sale.

You can select another tax code from the Tax Code list if necessary. You can also edit the price to change the selling price for a particular item or customer. To change the account, click the Account field List icon, press *enter* or double-click in the Account field to obtain a list of accounts.

NOTES
If you have entered a default revenue account for the customer that is different from the one for the item, the account for the item replaces the customer's revenue account.

Press *tab* **repeatedly** to advance to the next invoice line and update the first line because all the default record information is correct.

WARNING!
If you click the second line and it is used for part of the description for the first item, you will select and replace the first item instead.

Or you can click the Item Number field on the second line. Click the third line if the item description wraps around to the second invoice line.

Type a

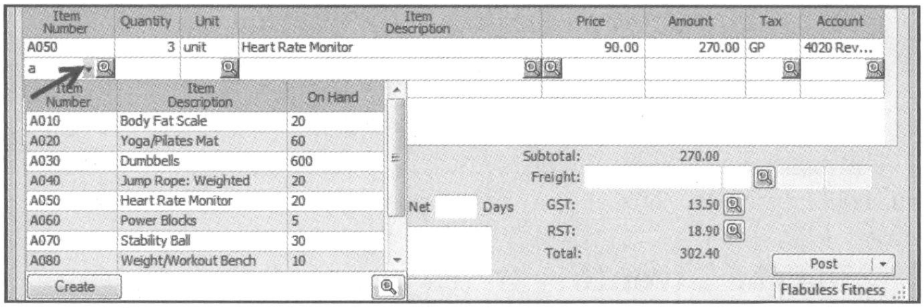

Item Number | Quantity | Unit | Item Description | Price | Amount | Tax | Account
A050 | 3 | unit | Heart Rate Monitor | 90.00 | 270.00 | GP | 4020 Rev...
a
Item Number | Item Description | On Hand
A010 | Body Fat Scale | 20
A020 | Yoga/Pilates Mat | 60
A030 | Dumbbells | 600
A040 | Jump Rope: Weighted | 20
A050 | Heart Rate Monitor | 20
A060 | Power Blocks | 5
A070 | Stability Ball | 30
A080 | Weight/Workout Bench | 10
Create
Subtotal: 270.00
Freight:
Net Days
GST: 13.50
RST: 18.90
Total: 302.40
Post
Flabuless Fitness

NOTES
If you type the entire code in lower-case letters (or upper-case letters), this list will show the single item. You can click it and press *tab* to advance to the Quantity field.

The Item Number field now provides a drop-down item list. Click to select an item from this list. When you type the first letter or number of the code (a), the drop-down list shows the items starting with A. Eight items can be displayed at one time, but you can scroll down to see more items.

Click **A030** and **press** *tab* to advance to the Quantity field. **Type** 40

A new invoice line opens automatically.

Enter the **remaining sale items** using the steps above.

NOTES
The inventory list is also available when you type in the Item Description field, but it is sorted by description instead of by item number.

As you complete each line and advance to the next, the totals and tax amounts at the bottom of the form are updated to include the last item entered.

GP is entered as the tax code for the books and service items, but only GST is added to the invoice total — the RST amount does not increase when you add these items. We will confirm this when we review the journal entry.

To include more invoice lines on your screen, drag the lower frame of the Sales Journal window or maximize the window.

WARNING!
The cursor does not advance to the Quantity field when you select from the drop-down lists, so if you type the quantity before pressing *tab*, you will enter an incorrect code.

At this stage, before adding delivery (freight) charges, the invoice portion of your journal should look like this:

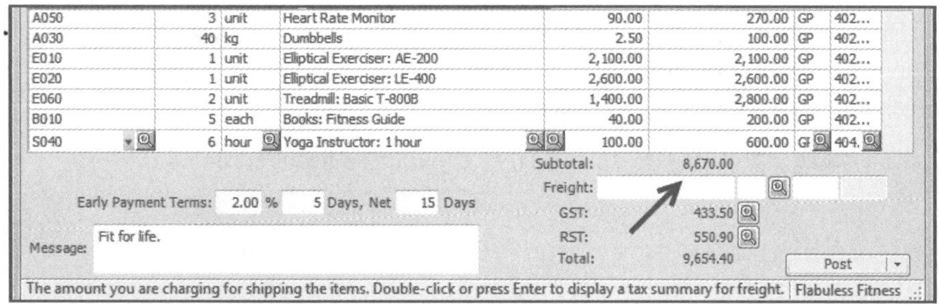

A050 | 3 | unit | Heart Rate Monitor | 90.00 | 270.00 | GP | 402...
A030 | 40 | kg | Dumbbells | 2.50 | 100.00 | GP | 402...
E010 | 1 | unit | Elliptical Exerciser: AE-200 | 2,100.00 | 2,100.00 | GP | 402...
E020 | 1 | unit | Elliptical Exerciser: LE-400 | 2,600.00 | 2,600.00 | GP | 402...
E060 | 2 | unit | Treadmill: Basic T-800B | 1,400.00 | 2,800.00 | GP | 402...
B010 | 5 | each | Books: Fitness Guide | 40.00 | 200.00 | GP | 402...
S040 | 6 | hour | Yoga Instructor: 1 hour | 100.00 | 600.00 | GP | 404.
Subtotal: 8,670.00
Freight:
Early Payment Terms: 2.00 % 5 Days, Net 15 Days
GST: 433.50
Message: Fit for life.
RST: 550.90
Total: 9,654.40
Post
The amount you are charging for shipping the items. Double-click or press Enter to display a tax summary for freight.
Flabuless Fitness

NOTES
If you want to type in the item codes instead of using the selection list for each item, turn on Caps Lock for your keyboard. This will speed up your data entry and ensure that you are using the correct case.

Click the **first Freight field**, the amount field, below the Subtotal.

Type 50 **Press** *tab*.

The customer's tax code, GP, is entered as the default so you must change it.

- **Press** *enter* to see the familiar list of tax codes. **Click G** and then **click Select**.

This completes the journal entry and it should look like the one shown here:

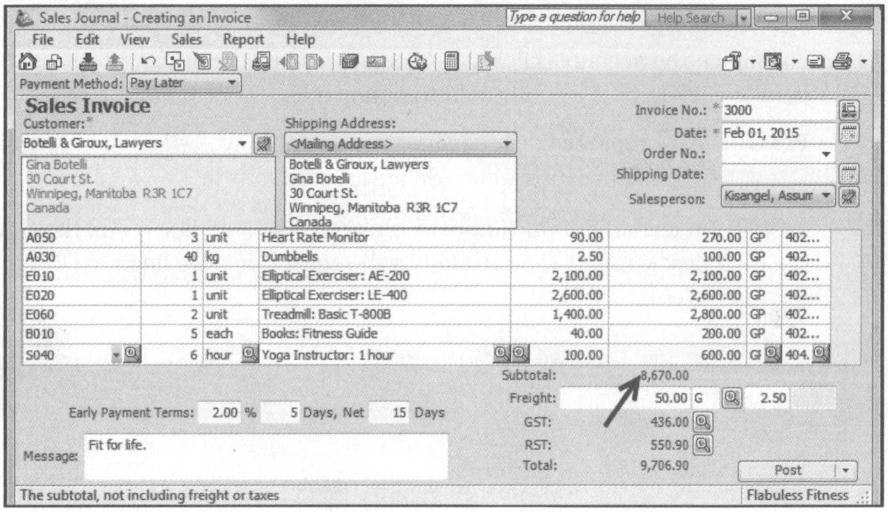

You should review the journal entry before posting it.

Reviewing the Inventory Sales Journal Transaction

> **NOTES**
> Pressing *ctrl* + J will also open the journal display.

Choose the **Report menu** and **click Display Sales Journal Entry**:

Flabuless Fitness
Sales Journal Entry 02/01/2015 (J1)

Account Number	Account Description	Debits	Credits
1200	Accounts Receivable	9,706.90	-
5060	Cost of Goods Sold	4,281.00	-
1520	Accessories	-	156.00
1540	Fitness Equipment	-	4,000.00
1560	Books	-	125.00
2640	RST Payable	-	550.90
2650	GST Charged on Sales	-	436.00
4020	Revenue from Sales	-	8,070.00
4040	Revenue from Services	-	600.00
4200	Freight Revenue	-	50.00
Additional Date:	Additional Field:	13,987.90	13,987.90

> **WARNING!**
> You should always check that the taxes are correct. If you are unsure, you can change the tax code for the books and service items to G. This extra step is required in Chapters 16, 17 and 18.

The tax amounts show that RST is not charged on the sale of books or services — 7% × \$7 870 = \$550.90 — while GST is charged on sales and services plus freight — 5% × \$8 720 = \$436. Both taxes are calculated correctly because of the tax codes and exemptions assigned in the Inventory Ledger records. Books and services are marked as exempt for RST.

Notice that all relevant accounts have been updated automatically because the Inventory and Receivables ledgers are linked to the General Ledger. Therefore, the linked asset, revenue and expense accounts defined for each inventory item have been debited or credited as required. In addition, the linked Receivables accounts we saw earlier are used — *RST Payable*, *GST Charged on Sales* and *Accounts Receivable*. The inventory database and customer record are also updated.

> **NOTES**
> Flabuless uses a single cost of goods sold account for all inventory items.
> In the Premium version you can choose the first-in, first-out (FIFO) method of costing.

Flabuless Fitness uses the average cost method to determine the cost of goods sold. If the stock for an inventory item was purchased at different times and prices, the average of these prices would be used as the cost of goods sold.

Close the **display** to return to the journal input screen.

CORRECTING THE INVENTORY SALES ENTRY

To **correct** an **item** on the inventory line, **click** the **incorrect field** to move the cursor and highlight the field contents. **Press** *enter* to display the list of inventory items, tax codes or accounts. **Click** the **correct selection** to highlight it, then **click Select**, or for the remaining fields, **type** the **correct information**. **Press** *tab* to enter the change.

If you **change** the **inventory** item, **re-enter** the **quantity sold** in the Quantity field. **Press** *tab* to update the totals.

To **insert** a **line**, **click** the **line below** the one you want to add. **Choose** the **Edit menu** and **click Insert Line**. To **remove** a **line**, **click** the **line** you want to delete; **choose** the **Edit menu** and **click Remove Line**.

To correct errors after posting, **click** the **Adjust Invoice tool** in the Sales Journal or **choose** the **Sales menu** and **click Adjust Invoice**. Or **choose Adjust Invoice** from the **Sales Invoices icon drop-down shortcuts list**. Refer to page 181.

If this is a recurring inventory sale, you can store it just like other sales.

Posting

When all the information in your journal entry is correct, you must post the transaction.

Click **Post** [Post] to save the transaction. **Click OK**.

Close the **Sales Journal** to exit to the Home window.

Create **shortcuts** as described in the following memo.

2

Memo #1 **Dated February 1, 2015**

Create shortcuts for transactions in other modules (Create Purchase Invoice, Pay Purchase Invoices, Create General Journal and Payroll Cheque Run).

Accounting for Inventory Purchases

The third transaction involves the purchase of inventory items. Inventory purchases are entered in the Purchases Journal, and many of the steps are the same as those for other credit purchases. Now the inventory database will provide the additional information.

✓ 3

Purchase Invoice #PE-364 **Dated February 2, 2015**

From Prolife Exercisers Inc.

4	E010	Elliptical Exerciser: AE-200	$ 4 600.00
4	E020	Elliptical Exerciser: LE-400	5 600.00
		Freight	100.00
		GST	515.00
		Total	$10 815.00

Terms: 2/10, n/30.

NOTES

For corrections of other, non-inventory invoice details, refer to page 162

WARNING!

If you adjust a posted invoice to correct for selecting the wrong customer, the customer options, such as payment terms, price list or tax codes, are not updated and may be incorrect. For these errors, you should reverse the entry.

NOTES

Transaction confirmation is turned on, so you should click OK when you post or record each transaction. We will not continue the reminder for this step.

NOTES

You can add shortcuts for Pay Expenses and View Accounts if you want.

CLASSIC VIEW
Click the Purchases Journal icon to open the journal.

NOTES
If you did not create shortcuts, click Payables in the Modules pane list to open the Payables window. Then click the Purchase Invoices icon to open the journal.

PRO VERSION
The term Vendor will replace Supplier.

NOTES
If you want to search for items by description, you can type the first letter in the Item Description field to see a list of all items that include the letter you typed. The list will be sorted alphabetically by description.

NOTES
Remember that you can customize the tabbing order.

NOTES
The next time you purchase this item, the new price, $1 150, will be entered as the default.

Click **Create Purchase Invoice** in the Shortcuts pane to display the familiar Purchases Journal input form window:

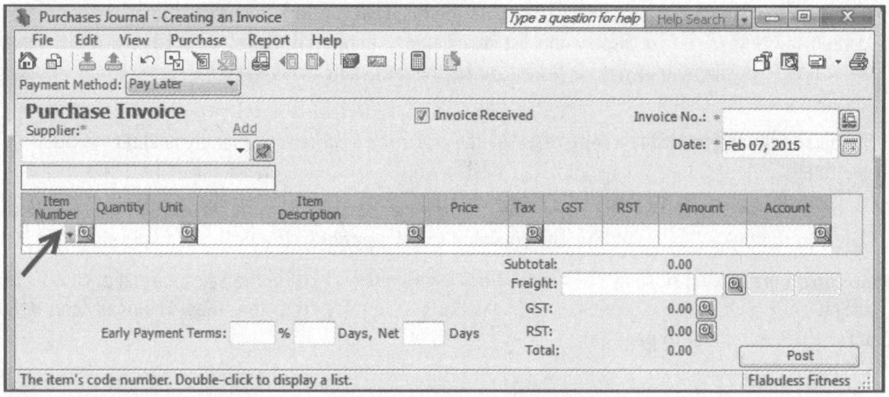

Pay Later is correctly selected as the method of payment.

Click the **Supplier field list arrow** to display the list of suppliers.

Click **Prolife Exercisers** from the list to add it to your input form.

Check your selection. If you chose an incorrect supplier, select again from the supplier list. If you selected correctly, proceed by entering the invoice number.

Click the **Invoice No. field**.

Type PE-364 **Press** tab **twice**.

The cursor advances to the Date field, where you should enter the invoice date.

Type Feb 2

Click the **Item Number field**.

Press enter or **click** the **List icon** to see the list of inventory items.

Notice that you can add new inventory from the Select Inventory/Service window.

Scroll down and **click** **E010 Elliptical Exerciser: AE-200** from the list to highlight it.

Press enter. If you have made an incorrect selection, return to the Item Number field and select again.

You can also click the list arrow to see the entire inventory item list, or a partial list if you type the first letter of the item code, just as you did in the Sales Journal. Press tab to move to the next field.

The cursor advances to the Quantity field. The Item Description field should now show the name, Elliptical Exerciser: AE-200. The default price is the most recent purchase price. Now enter the quantity for this item.

Type 4 **Press** tab.

The cursor advances to the Unit field. The Unit and Description are correct based on Inventory Ledger records.

The Price field records the most recent unit price paid for the purchase of the inventory items. This amount should not include any GST paid that can be used as an input tax credit. The price has changed since the previous purchase, so it is now incorrect. We will update the price by changing the total amount.

Click **4,400.00**, the Amount entered as the default.

Type 4600 **Press** tab to update the unit Price to $1 150.

The correct tax code — code G — is entered by default from the supplier record. Flabuless pays only GST on purchases of inventory items that will be resold.

If a tax code is incorrect, you can change it by selecting from the tax code list.

When purchasing new inventory, no price is recorded. You should enter the quantity and, in the Amount field, enter the total purchase amount. Press (tab) to advance the cursor. Sage 50 will calculate the price per unit.

Press (tab) **repeatedly** to advance to the next line, with the cursor blinking in the Item Number field again, or **click** the **Item Number field** in the next line.

Notice that the cursor skips the RST amount field because the supplier tax code does not include RST. The Account field was also skipped over, because you cannot change the entry for inventory purchases. The account number is dimmed and the Account field is not available. The Asset account for the inventory purchase is defined in the Inventory Ledger as the linked account for purchases and sales. To change the account, you must edit the Inventory Ledger record. The default account for the supplier does not apply to the inventory purchase.

Enter the **second item** from the source document, using the same steps that you used to record the first item. The default price and amount are correct.

Your journal looks like the following when you are ready to enter the freight charge:

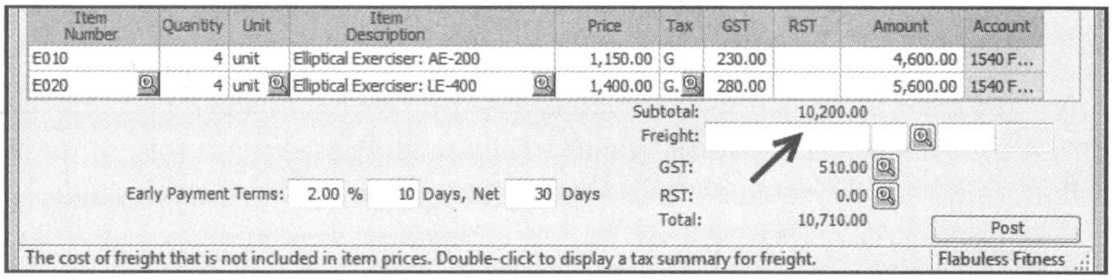

The Freight fields are used to enter any freight charges that cannot be allocated to the purchase of a specific item and to enter the taxes paid on the freight charges. There are four Freight fields: the base amount of the freight charge, tax code, GST amount and, finally, the RST amount. Because GST is paid on freight you must enter a tax code if the supplier charges freight.

Click the **first Freight field**, the amount field, below the Subtotal.

Type 100 **Press** (tab).

The tax code for the supplier, code G, should be entered by default.

If the tax code for freight is not entered automatically, press (enter) to see the familiar list of tax codes. Click G and then click Select.

You do not need to enter amounts for the taxes on freight; they are calculated as soon as you enter the amount of freight charged and the tax code.

Sage 50 calculates the amount of GST (and RST if it is paid) and updates all the totals.

NOTES

RST is not paid on items that are purchased for resale because the store is not the final customer.

NOTES

RST is not charged on freight in Manitoba when it is applied to an RST-exempt purchase. The correct tax code for freight is code G - GST @ 5%.

Your input form is complete and should appear as follows:

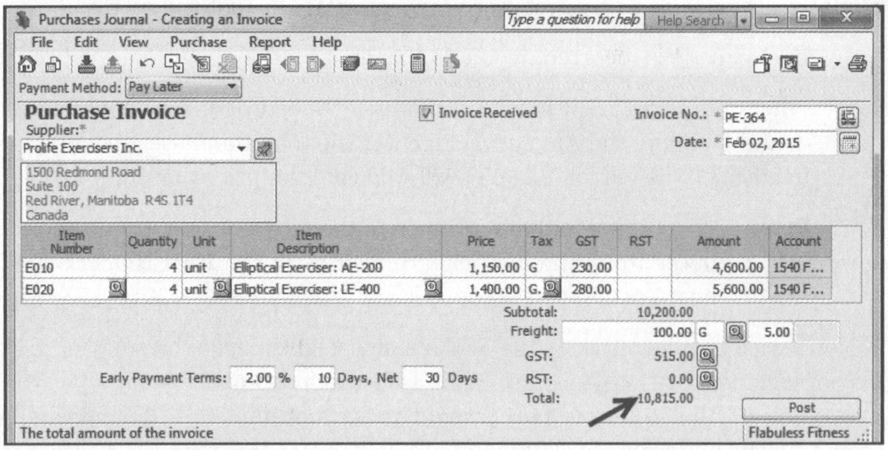

The Subtotal includes all items purchased but does not include freight or taxes.

Reviewing the Inventory Purchase Transaction

NOTES
Pressing ctrl + J will also open the journal display.

As usual, we will review the journal entry before posting it.

Choose the **Report menu** and **click Display Purchases Journal Entry**:

Flabuless Fitness
Purchases Journal Entry 02/02/2015 (J2)

Account Number	Account Description	Debits	Credits
1540	Fitness Equipment	10,200.00	-
2670	GST Paid on Purchases	515.00	-
5080	Freight Expense	100.00	-
2200	Accounts Payable	-	10,815.00
Additional Date:	Additional Field:	10,815.00	10,815.00

The program has automatically updated all accounts relevant to this transaction. The appropriate inventory asset account (*Fitness Equipment*), *Accounts Payable*, *GST Paid on Purchases* and *Freight Expense* have been updated as required because the ledgers are linked — the inventory purchase uses only predefined linked accounts. The inventory database and the supplier record are also updated.

Close the **display** to return to the Purchases Journal input screen.

NOTES
If this is a recurring purchase, you can store it, just like other recurring purchases.

CORRECTING THE INVENTORY PURCHASES JOURNAL ENTRY

If the inventory item is incorrect, **reselect** from the **inventory** list by **pressing** enter while in this field. **Click Select** to add the item to your form. **Type** the **quantity** purchased and **press** tab to update the totals.

Account numbers cannot be changed for inventory items on the purchase invoice. They must be edited in the Inventory Ledger.

To **insert** a new **line**, if you have forgotten a complete line of the invoice, **click** the **line below** the one you have forgotten. **Choose** the **Edit menu** and **click Insert Line** to add a blank invoice line to your form. To **remove** a complete **line**, **click** the **line** you want to delete, **choose** the **Edit menu** and **click Remove Line**.

For assistance with correcting other invoice details, refer to page 114.

To correct an inventory purchase after posting, use the **Adjust Invoice tool** or **choose** the **Purchase Menu** and **click Adjust Invoice**. Refer to page 127. If you selected the wrong supplier, you can reverse the purchase transaction (page 139).

WARNING!
If you adjust a posted invoice to correct for selecting the wrong supplier, the supplier options, such as payment terms and tax codes, are not updated and may be incorrect. For these errors, you should reverse the entry.

Posting

When all the information in your journal entry is correct, you must post the transaction.

Click Post Post. **Close** the **Purchases Journal**.

The Inventory Module

Click **Inventory & Services** in the Modules pane list:

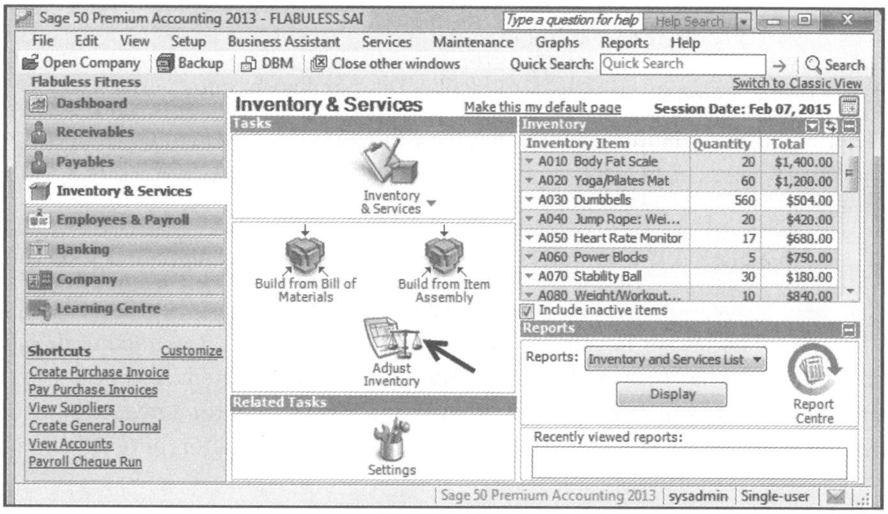

The Inventory module has icons for the ledger records, journal entries and settings. Records are listed in the Inventory Item list pane as they are for other modules so you can access them directly. The Reports pane includes all inventory reports in the Reports list, updated for the recent sale and purchase quantities.

Making Inventory Adjustments

Sometimes inventory is lost, stolen or damaged and adjusting entries are required to reflect the expenses. These inventory adjustments are made in the Inventory Adjustments Journal in the Inventory & Services window. This journal is also used to record lost inventory that is recovered and inventory that is used by the business instead of being sold to customers.

✓ 4

Memo #2 **Dated February 2, 2015**

From Owner: Adjust inventory records for Stability Balls, item A070. Three balls were punctured and are unusable. Charge losses to Damaged Inventory.

Click the **Adjust Inventory icon** 

, the one with the arrow in the previous Home window screen, to open the blank Adjustments Journal:

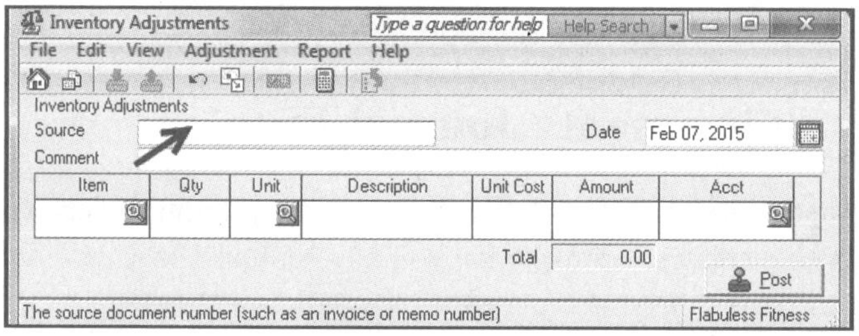

The cursor is in the Source field. The source for an adjustment will normally be a memo from a manager or owner.

Type Memo 2 **Press** tab.

The cursor is in the Date field, with the session date entered and highlighted.

Type 02-02 **Press** tab **twice**.

PRO VERSION

The Inventory module in the Pro version does not include the Build From Bill Of Materials icon.

You will see only two journal icons: Build From Item Assembly and Adjust Inventory.

NOTES

You can hide the Quantity and Total inventory details in the Inventory list pane just as you can hide customer and supplier details. For services, these fields are blank.

Click [open icon] to open the list. Click a detail to remove it.

Click [refresh icon] to refresh or update inventory details.

Click [hide icon] to hide the list.

CLASSIC VIEW

Click the Inventory Adjustments icon: 

PRO VERSION

The Pro version does not include the Refresh tool.

NOTES
Stores that sell inventory frequently use some inventory stock in the store. Use the Adjustments Journal to record these transfers by choosing the appropriate asset or expense account to replace the default linked account. Enter negative quantities because the inventory stock is reduced. Because the store has become the final customer – it has bought the items from itself – it is responsible for reporting the purchase and paying RST on the cost price of these internal sales.

The cursor is now in the Comment field, where you can enter a brief explanation for this transaction.

Type `Stability balls punctured` **Press** (tab).

The cursor advances to the Item field.

Press (enter) or **click** [icon] to display the familiar inventory list.

Notice that the quantities on the list have been updated to include the previous sale and purchase. Services are not included in the list because they have no quantities in stock and cannot be lost or damaged.

Double-click A070 Stability Ball from the list to select and enter it on the form.

The item description, Stability Ball, the unit, unit cost and account have been added automatically. The cursor advances to the Quantity (Qty) field. You need to indicate that the inventory has been reduced because of the damaged item. You do this by typing a **negative** number in the field. Remember always to enter a negative quantity when there is an inventory loss. If lost inventory is recovered later, enter the adjustment with a positive quantity.

Type `-3` **Press** (tab).

The cursor advances to the Unit field. The rest of the journal line is completed automatically. In the Amount field, a negative amount, reflecting the inventory loss, automatically appears as a default based on the average cost. In the Account field, *Damaged Inventory*, the default linked account for inventory losses, appears for this entry. This is the correct account.

If you need to choose another account, press (enter) to display the list of accounts and select the account as usual. You can also edit the unit cost or amount if you know that the price of the unit was different from the default price, the average of all inventory in stock. You can store and recall Adjustments Journal entries just as you do entries in other journals.

Your entry is complete as shown and you are ready to review it:

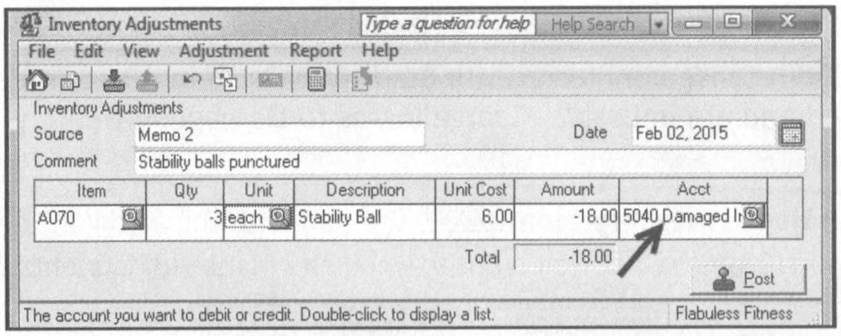

Reviewing the Adjustments Journal Entry

NOTES
Pressing (ctrl) + J will also open the journal display.

Choose the **Report menu** and **click Display Inventory Adjustments Journal Entry** to display the transaction you have entered as shown here:

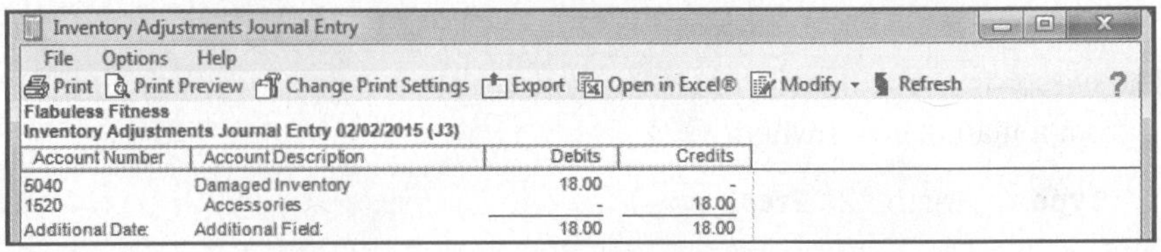

NOTES
The second Inventory Ledger linked account is used for item assembly costs in the Item Assembly Journal. Item assembly is introduced in the next transaction.

You can see that Sage 50 has automatically updated all relevant accounts for this transaction. The appropriate inventory asset defined for this inventory item, *Accessories*, and the inventory database have been reduced to reflect the loss at the average cost price. *Damaged Inventory*, the Inventory linked expense account that was defined for inventory losses or adjustments, has been debited or increased.

Close the **display** to return to the Adjustments Journal input screen.

CORRECTING THE ADJUSTMENTS JOURNAL ENTRY

Move to the field that has the error. **Press** tab to move forward or **press** shift and tab together to move back to a previous field. This will highlight the field information so you can change it. **Type** the **correct information** and **press** tab to enter it.

You can also use the mouse to **point** to a field and **drag** through the **incorrect information** to highlight it. **Type** the **correct information** and **press** tab to enter it.

If the inventory item is incorrect, **reselect** from the **inventory** list by **pressing** enter while in this field. **Click Select** to add it to the form. **Type** the **quantity** and **press** tab. After changing any information on an inventory item line, **press** tab to update the totals.

You can insert and remove lines by selecting these options from the Edit menu.

To start over, **click** [X] or [undo] (or **choose** the **Edit menu** and **click Undo Entry**). **Click Yes** when asked to confirm that you want to discard the transaction.

WARNING!
You cannot adjust or look up an inventory adjustment after posting, so check the entry carefully before posting.

Posting

When all the information in your journal entry is correct, you must save the transaction.

Click **Post** [Post].

Close the **Adjustments Journal** to return to the Inventory window. The next keystroke transaction creates and assembles new inventory items.

Adding a New Inventory Item

Before entering the item assembly transaction, we will create the necessary new inventory items. Memo #3 has the inventory item details.

✓ 5

Memo #3 **Dated February 2, 2015**

Create two new inventory items for winter promotions. Create a new Group asset account, 1570 Promotional Offers, to use as linked account for the items.

Number	Description	Unit	Min Level	Regular Price	Preferred Price	Linked Accounts Asset	Revenue	COGS	Tax
P010	Yoga Training Package	pkg	1	$1 400	(1 250)	1570	4020	5060	GP
P020	Training Workout Package	pkg	1	$1 600	(1 400)	1570	4020	5060	GP

Variance account not required

NOTES
The image files YP01.bmp and TP01.bmp (or YP01 and TP01) were copied to the SageData13\Logos folder when you installed your other data files.

Inventory items can be added from any inventory item field in a journal, from the Inventory & Services icon (that opens the Inventory & Services window) or from the icon's Add Inventory & Service shortcut as shown:

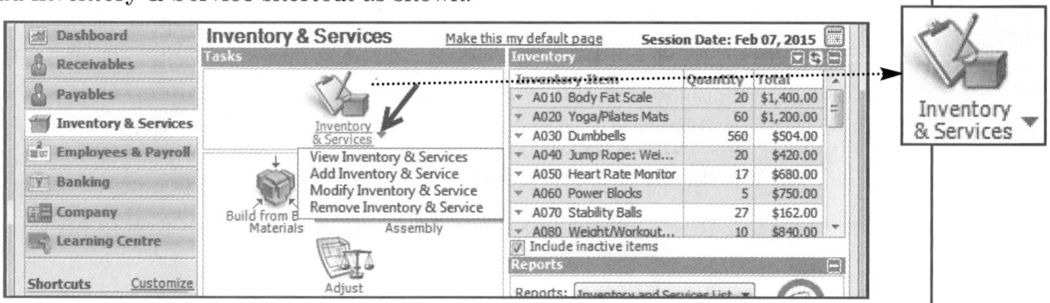

NOTES

You can add inventory items from any journal inventory field when the selection list is available, that is, in the Sales, Purchases Adjustments and Item Assembly journals. Click the List icon in the Item field to open the selection list. Click Add New Inventory/ Service and press *enter* or click the Create button to open the Inventory Ledger window.

Click the **Inventory & Services icon** to open the Inventory & Services window:

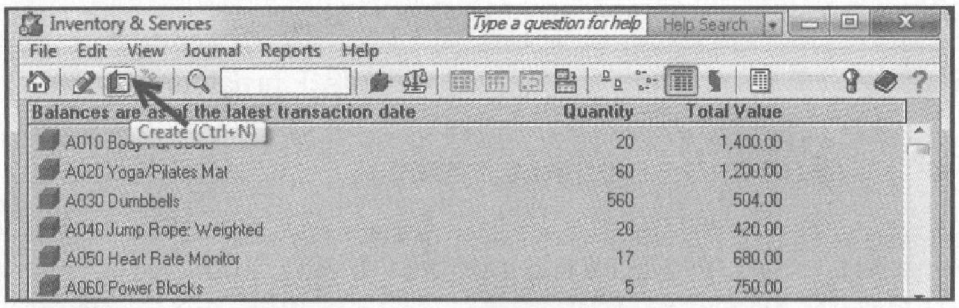

This window is like the Accounts, Suppliers, Customers and Employees windows in other modules and it lists all inventory items and services. If you choose the Add Inventory shortcut, you will open a new ledger record directly and skip this Inventory & Services window.

Click the **Create tool**, **choose** the **File menu** and **click Create** or **press** *ctrl* **+ N.**

Each of these methods opens the Inventory & Services Ledger:

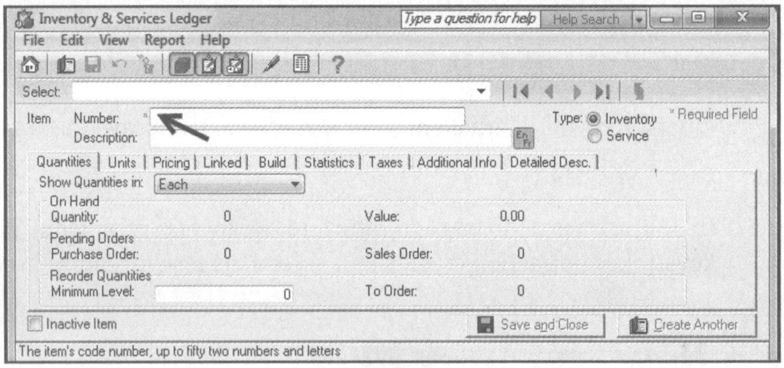

PRO VERSION

The Pro version does not have the Build tab. It applies to the Build From Bill Of Materials option in the Bill of Materials & Item Assembly Journal. This feature is not available in the Pro version.

The Inventory & Services Ledger record has many of the tools that are available in other ledgers, including the Refresh tool. The **Show** tool icons allow you to limit the Select field list to inventory items, services or activities (for time and billing). If all three tools are selected, the list includes all three kinds of items. All Show tools are selected for Flabuless Fitness, so all records are included in the Select list.

NOTES

As in other ledgers and journals, the Refresh tool applies when you work in multi-user mode. Clicking the tool will update the record with changes made by other users who are accessing the data file at the same time.

You can enter both inventory and service items in the Inventory Ledger. You can designate a service as an activity with time and billing information attached. Activities are available for the time and billing features and for selection as internal services — services that are provided by one department to another within the company and can be tracked as expenses. The Time & Billing function will be covered in Chapter 18.

PRO VERSION

The Time & Billing function is not available in the Pro version. The Pro version has only two Show tools – one for inventory items and one for service items. The Refresh tool is also not on the Pro version tool bar.

The packages are inventory, so as a result, the type selection is correct and the fields we need are included. The Quantities tab information is displayed because it is the first tab screen. As usual, required fields are marked with *.

The setup option we selected for inventory sorts the items by code or number.

Therefore, the Item Number field is the first item field. When you choose to sort by description, the longer Description field will come first. (See Chapter 16, page 662.)

From the source document information, you must enter the item code and description. The first Item field contains the code or number of the inventory item — the only required field on this screen; the second Item field contains the description or item name.

Click the **Item Number field.**

Type `P010` **Press** *tab* to advance to the Item Description field.

Type `Yoga Training Package`

Click the **Minimum Level field** in the Reorder Quantities section.

Here you must enter the stock level at which you want to reorder the item in question, or in this case, assemble more packages.

Type 1

NOTES

When you print inventory reports, items that have fallen below the minimum level will be flagged.

The Quantity On Hand, Value, and Order fields are updated from journal entries. Before the Inventory Ledger history is finished, you can add this information as historical data.

The dimmed entry for **Units** on this screen is taken from the Units tab screen.

Click the **Units tab**:

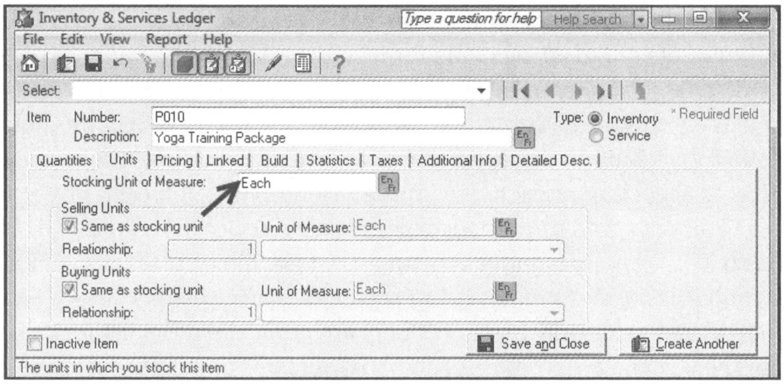

Units show the way in which goods are stored, bought and sold (e.g., by the dozen, by the tonne or by the item). These units may be different if, for example, merchandise is purchased in bulk packages and sold in individual units. When a store buys or stocks inventory in different units from those it sells, you also enter the relationship between the sets of units, for example, 12 units per carton.

Flabuless Fitness measures all units the same way so only one entry is needed.

Double-click **Each** in the Stocking Unit Of Measure field. **Type** pkg

Click the **Pricing tab**:

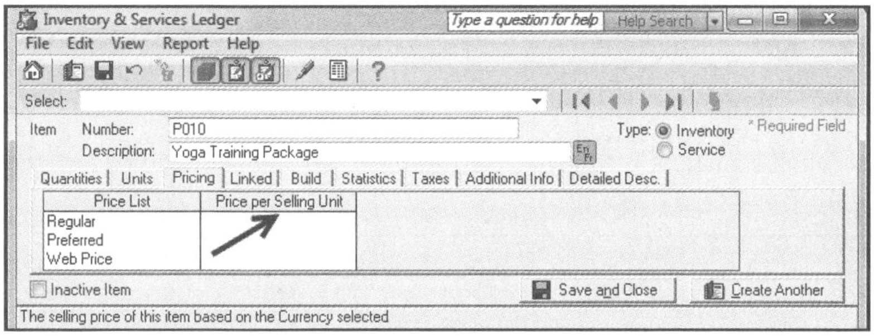

NOTES

You can also select the price list in the Sales Journal from the Price field select list icon. By adding it to the customer's record, the correct price is selected automatically in the journal.

A business may have different price lists. Each item may be assigned a regular price, a selling price for preferred customers and a Web price. Flabuless Fitness has three customers with preferred customer status. Regular, preferred and Web selling prices can also be entered in foreign currencies when other currencies are used.

NOTES

The Premium version allows you to create additional price lists. The Pro version does not include this feature. When you create additional price lists (Inventory Ledger Settings), they will be added to this screen, and you can enter prices for them.

Click the **Price Per Selling Unit column** beside Regular.

Type 1400

Press *tab* to advance to the Price Per Selling Unit field for preferred prices.

The regular price is entered as the default Preferred and Web Price.

Type 1250 to replace the default entry.

NOTES
For other ledgers, the linked accounts are defined for the entire ledger. For example, there is only one Accounts Receivable account.

Click the **Linked tab** to access the linked accounts for the inventory item:

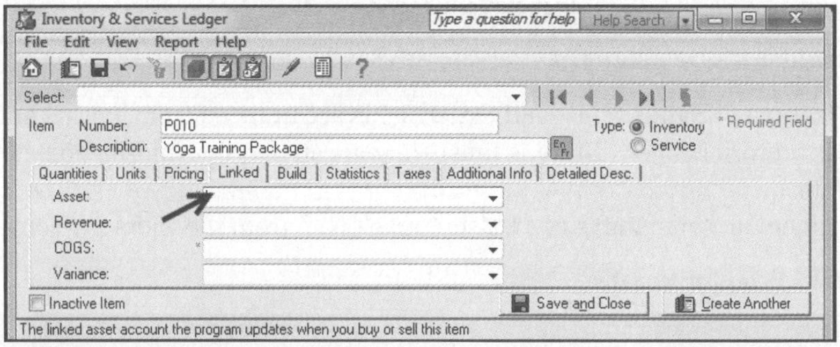

There are two sets of linked accounts for inventory: those that apply to the entire ledger — the default accounts for inventory adjustments and item assembly costs — and those that apply to specific inventory items. The ones in the ledger are item specific and are used as the default accounts whenever inventory items are sold or purchased. By defining linked accounts for each item in the Inventory Ledger, each inventory item can be related to separate asset, revenue, expense and variance accounts.

In the **Asset** field, you must enter the number of the linked asset account affected by purchases and sales of this item. A list of accounts is available from the drop-down list arrow in the Asset field. Only asset accounts are available in the list for the Asset field. Because the account we need does not exist yet, we cannot choose it from the account list for the field. We can create it here. The linked asset account is a required field. You cannot choose or change it in the Purchases Journal.

Click the **Asset field.**

Type `1570 Promotional Offers` **Press** *tab*.

NOTES
When you type the account name in the field at the same time and then press *tab*, the wizard will add both the number and the name for the account. Not all account fields allow you to enter both the number and name for new accounts.

You will see the screen that allows you to create the new account:

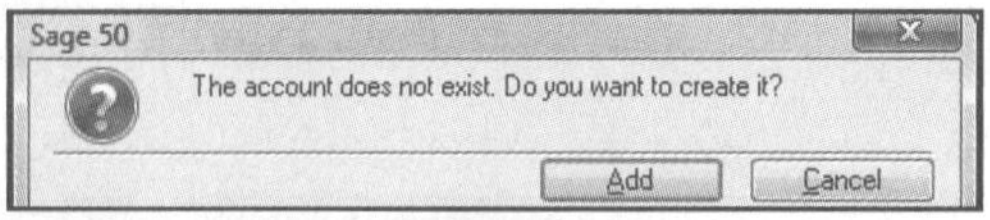

Click **Add** to proceed to the Add An Account wizard. **Click Next** to continue.

Accept the **remaining** account **settings** and **finish** creating the account.

After you click Finish, you will see another message advising you of an account class change for the linked account:

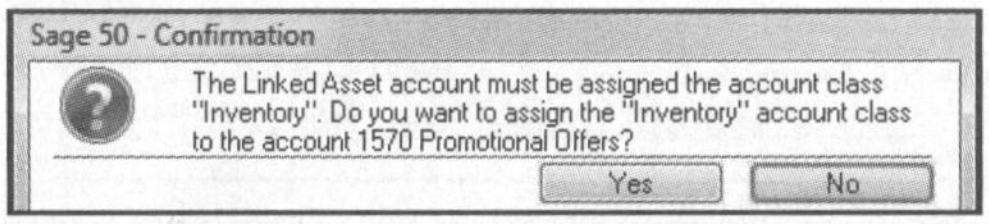

Click **Yes** to accept the change. Clicking No will return you to the Linked Accounts screen so you can select a different account.

NOTES
If necessary, you can create new linked revenue and expense accounts in the same way you created the new asset account.

In the **Revenue** field, you must enter the linked revenue account that will be credited when this inventory item is sold. You can type the account number or select from the list. Only revenue accounts are available for the Revenue field.

NOTES
The linked revenue account is not a required account – you can choose an account in the Sales Journal when you sell inventory. The linked asset and COGS accounts are required – you cannot choose these accounts in the journals.

Click the **Revenue field list arrow** to see the revenue accounts available.

Click **4020 Revenue from Sales** to enter it on your form.

Click the **COGS field list arrow** (Cost of Goods Sold expense) to see the expense accounts available.

In the **COGS** field, you must enter the linked expense account that will be debited when this inventory item is sold. Only expense accounts are available for the COGS field and the Variance field. Flabuless uses the single *Cost of Goods Sold* account for all inventory items. The linked COGS account is also required.

Click **5060 Cost of Goods Sold** from the list.

The **Variance** field contains the linked variance expense account used when the inventory sold is on order, before the goods are in stock. At the time of the sale, *Cost of Goods Sold* is debited for the average cost of the inventory on hand, based on previous purchases. When the goods are received, the actual purchase price may be different from this historical average cost. The price difference is charged to the variance account. Flabuless Fitness does not allow inventory to be oversold so you can leave the Variance account field blank.

Click the **Build tab**:

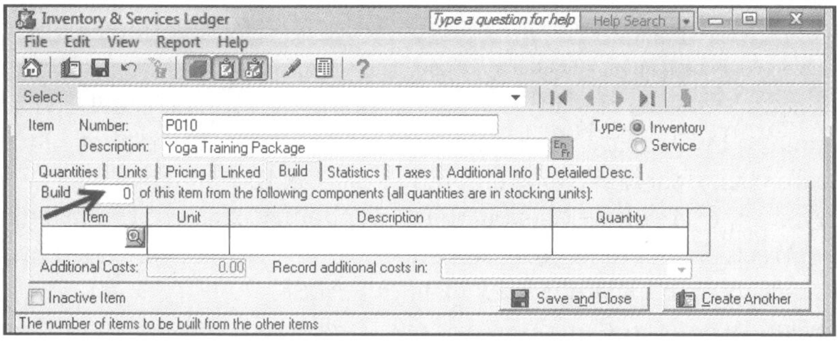

On the Build tab screen, you enter the inventory components that are needed to make the item. You identify the number of items you are building at one time and the required component items. This process is similar to the one found in the Components section of the Item Assembly Journal (see page 376). When it is time to build the item (in the Bill of Materials & Item Assembly Journal), you indicate how many items you are building — the Assembled Items section of the Item Assembly — and the rest of the details are taken from the Build screen of the ledger record. We will use the Build feature in Chapter 18.

Click the **Statistics tab**:

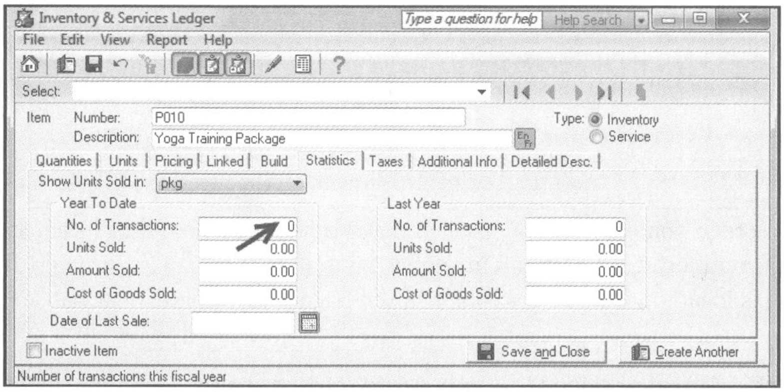

This screen applies to historical data. Since this is a new inventory item, there are no previous sales, and you should leave all entries at zero. The **Date Of Last Sale** shows the most recent date that this item was sold. The **Year To Date** section refers to historical information for the current fiscal period, and the **Last Year** fields apply to the previous year. Inventory Statistics are added to inventory tracking reports.

The **No.** (number) **Of Transactions** refers to the total number of times the item was sold. For example, if one customer bought the item on three separate dates, there would be three transactions. If four customers bought the item on one day, there would be four transactions. If one customer bought four of the same item at one time, there would be one transaction. The **Units Sold** counts the total number of items that were

WARNING!

Check the linked account numbers carefully. If they are incorrect, corresponding journal entries will be posted incorrectly. If you discover the error when you are reviewing the journal entry, you should delete the journal entry line and then edit the Inventory Ledger record before posting.

NOTES

Variance accounts are used in the Truman Tires application in Chapter 13.

PRO VERSION

Click the Statistics tab at this stage.

The Pro version does not have a Build tab because this screen applies to Build From Bill Of Materials, a function not available in the Pro version.

NOTES

You can define multiple levels of building – one item may be made from other items that in turn are made from multiple inventory items.

NOTES

You can enter the historical dates using any of the usual date formats, with or without the year.

sold on all occasions to all customers in the relevant period. The **Amount Sold** field holds the total sale price of all items sold in the period, and the **Cost Of Goods Sold** field records the total purchase price of all items sold.

If you have historical data for the item, you can add it. Sage 50 continually updates the Statistics tab fields from journal entries.

Click the **Taxes tab**:

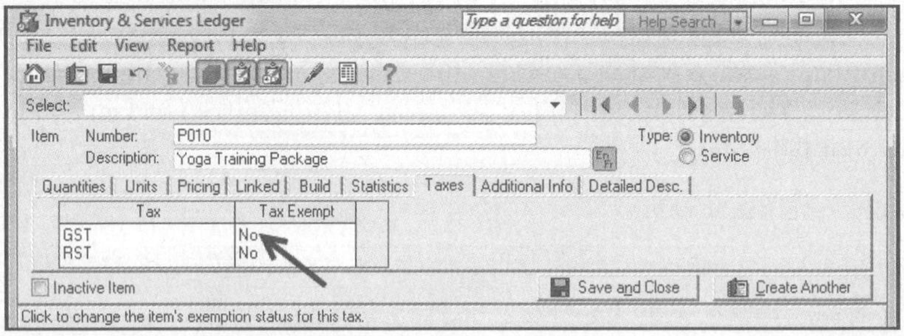

> **NOTES**
> The tax exemption in the ledger record will ensure that a tax is not applied. Books and Service items were marked as Tax Exempt for RST on this screen so that RST does not apply to their sales. The default tax code shown in the journal is taken from the customer ledger record.

All taxes set up for the company will appear on this screen. RST and GST may be charged or omitted by default. Because most goods have these taxes applied to the sale, the default is to charge them — No is entered in the Tax Exempt column. The **Tax Exempt** entry is a toggle switch. Clicking the current entry changes it. The default settings are correct — both taxes are charged. Books and services provided by Flabuless Fitness were designated as tax exempt for RST.

When inventory items are imported and duty is charged, you can enter the duty rate on this screen as well.

The **Additional Info** tab allows for custom-defined information fields relating to the item, just like the Additional Info tabs in other ledgers. It is not used by Flabuless Fitness.

Click the **Detailed Desc. tab**:

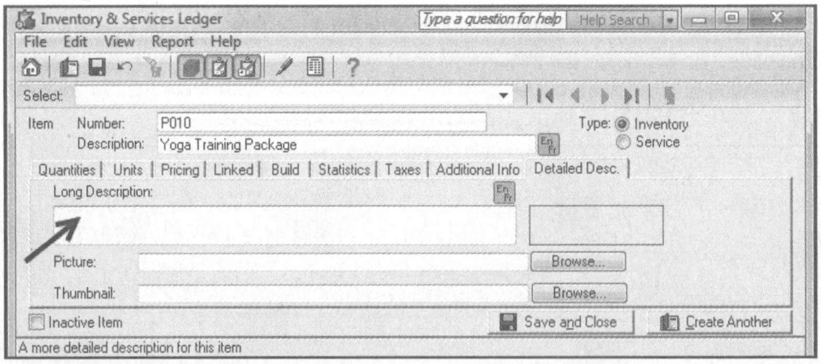

On this screen you can enter a detailed description of the inventory item and the name of a file and location where an image of the item is stored. The bitmap (.bmp) file for this item is located in the Logos folder in the SageData13 folder that has your other data files.

> **NOTES**
> When you first click Browse, the default location may be Documents and Settings. Because we do not know how you have organized your files and folders, we continue to use C:\SageData13 as the location for all the files for this text. This allows us to give clear file path instructions.

Click **Browse** beside the Picture field to open the file location window.

Locate and **open** the **SageData13 folder**.

Double-click **Logos** to open this folder.

Double-click **YP01** (or **YP01.bmp**) to add the image and file name:

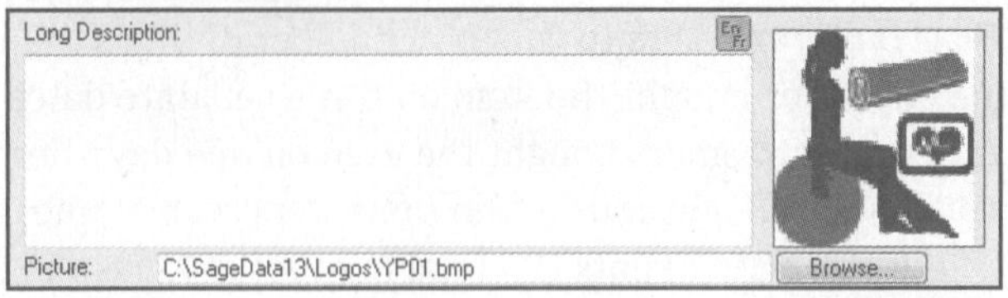

When all the information is correct, you must save your information.

Click **Create Another** to save the new record. The ledger remains open so you can add the second new item.

Click the **Quantities tab**.

> **CORRECTING THE INVENTORY ITEM BEFORE CREATING THE RECORD**
>
> Correct the information if necessary by **clicking** the field that contains the **error**. **Click** the appropriate **tab** to change information screens if necessary. **Highlight** the **error** and **type** the **correct information**. **Press** *tab* to enter the correction.

Enter all the details for item **P020** from page 369.

Click **Save And Close** to save the new record. Both items are added to your ledger list of inventory items.

> **EDITING AN INVENTORY ITEM AFTER CREATING THE RECORD**
>
> You cannot edit an Inventory Ledger record while you are using the item in a journal. You must first **delete** the **journal line containing the item**. **Click** the **journal line**, **choose** the **Edit menu** and **click Remove Line**. Then **click** the journal's **Home window tool** to return to the Home window. **Click Inventory & Services** in the Modules pane list. **Click** the name of the **inventory item** that you need to change in the Inventory pane Item list to open the item's record. **Click** the **tab** you need. **Highlight** the **information** that is incorrect, and then **type** the **correct information**. **Close** the **Ledger window**. **Click** the **Home window journal icon you need** (or the task bar icon/button for the journal) to return to the journal.

Close the **Inventory & Services window** to return to the Home window.

Assembling Inventory Items

Inventory item assembly can be used to build new inventory from other inventory items, to create package offers of two or more regular items for sale at a special price or to reserve inventory for a special project or contract. Flabuless's new inventory items, the promotional packages, are offered at reduced prices, and the cost is the sum of the original component costs. Flabuless Fitness uses the inventory Bill of Materials & Item Assembly Journal to create the promotional packages. The journal can be used to build from Item Assembly or from the Bill of Materials.

The journal's two methods are shown by separate Home window icons. We will use the Item Assembly approach:

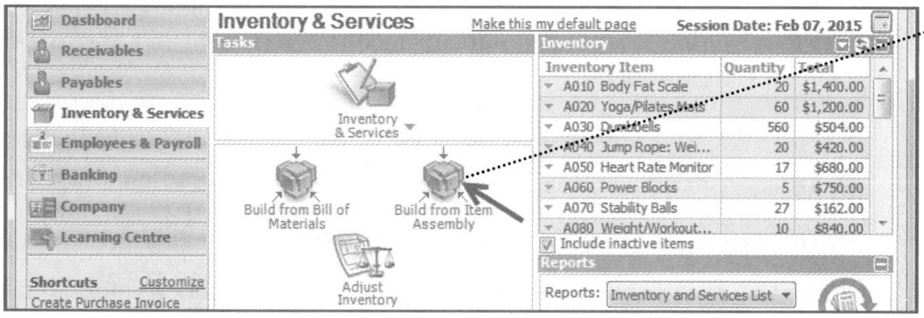

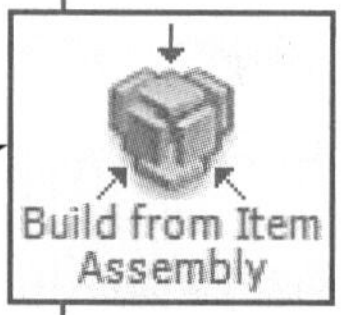

PRO VERSION

In the Pro version, only the Item Assembly approach is available.

CLASSIC VIEW
Click the Bill of Materials & Item Assembly icon

to open the journal.

NOTES
We will use the Item Assembly Journal to refer to the Bill of Materials & Item Assembly Journal.

PRO VERSION
The drop-down list is not available. The cursor will be in the Source field.

CLASSIC VIEW
Click Build From Item Assembly in the Build drop-down list if necessary to open the journal form we need.

NOTES
You could also add the new inventory items, the packages, and the new asset account, 1570 Promotional Offers, directly from the journal while entering the assembly transaction.

Click the **Build From Item Assembly icon** to open the Journal:

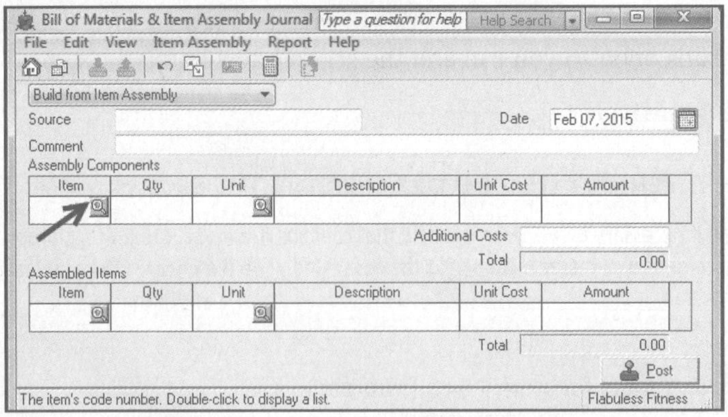

There are two ways to assemble items in the Premium version of Sage 50: Item Assembly or Build From Bill Of Materials defined in the ledger on the Build tab screen (see page 373). When you build items from the bill of materials, the journal has only the assembled items part — the components information is drawn from the ledger record. The bill of materials method will be covered in Chapter 18. We will use the Item Assembly method now. You can access both methods from the Build drop-down list in the journal as shown:

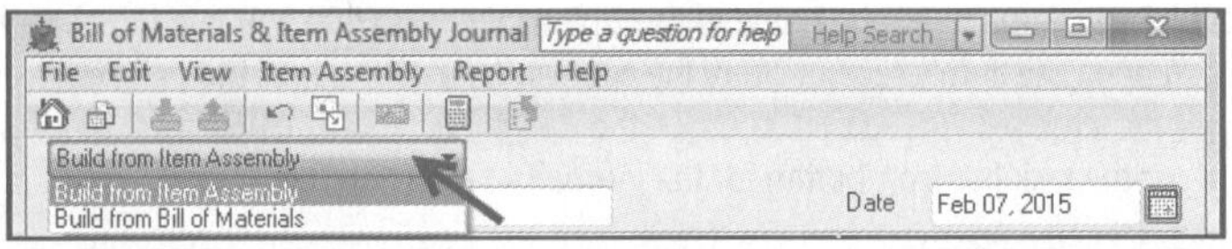

We are using the item assembly method, so you do not need to modify the journal.

✓ 6

Item Assembly #IA-01 **Dated February 3, 2015**

Create five (5) Yoga Training Packages. Transfer 5 of each component item as follows:

5	A020	Yoga/Pilates Mat	$ 20 each
5	A050	Heart Rate Monitor	40 /unit
5	A070	Stability Ball	6 each
5	A080	Workout/Weight Bench	84 each
5	E040	Bicycle: Recumbent R-80	600 /unit

Additional Costs (for Yoga Instructor: 1/2 day) 450

Assembled Items

5	P010	Yoga Training Package	$840 /pkg

Click the **Source field**, where you should enter the reference or form number.

Type IA-01 **Press** tab to advance to the Date field. Enter the date of the transfer.

Type 02-03 **Press** tab **twice** to advance to the Comment field.

Type `Assemble yoga training packages`

Press tab to advance to the first line in the Item field.

You are in the **Assembly Components** section. This first section refers to the items that are being removed from inventory, the "from" part of the transfer or assembly. These items will form the gift package.

Press enter or **click** the **List icon** to display the familiar inventory selection list.

Notice that you can add new inventory items from the Select Inventory list in the Item Assembly Journal. Services are not on this list because they cannot be assembled.

Click **A020 Yoga/Pilates Mat** to select the first item needed.

Click **Select** to add the item to the item assembly form and advance to the Quantity (Qty) field. You must enter the quantity.

Type 5 **Press** *tab* to advance the cursor to the Unit field and to update the Amount.

The unit cost is correct, but it can be edited if you know it is incorrect.

Drag the **lower frame of the journal window** to add input lines so you can see your entire entry on the screen at once.

Click the **next line** in the Item column.

Select the next **inventory item** to be transferred, **enter** the **quantity** and then continue to **enter** the **remaining inventory** for the package.

At this stage, your screen should look like the one shown here:

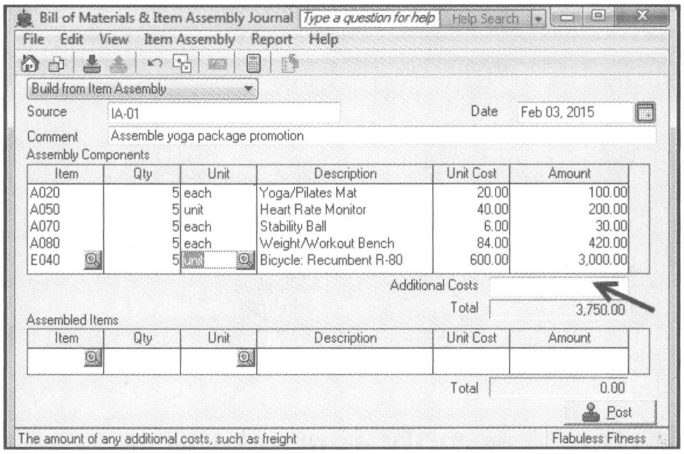

The middle part of the item assembly form contains two fields: Additional Costs and Total. **Additional costs** may come from shipping or packaging involved with assembling, moving or transferring the inventory. Services involved in the package may also be entered as additional costs. The extra costs for all items transferred should be entered into the Additional Costs field. The **Total** is calculated automatically by Sage 50 to include the individual costs of all items transferred — the assembly components — plus any additional costs. Flabuless Fitness has additional costs of $450 ($90 per package) for the personal yoga training.

Click the **Additional Costs field**.

Type 450 **Press** *tab* to update the total.

The cursor advances to the first line in the Item column of the **Assembled Items** section. This section refers to the new or reserved inventory, the item being assembled or the "to" part of the transfer.

Press *enter* or **click** the **List icon** to display the familiar inventory selection list.

Click **P010 Yoga Training Package** to select the item we created.

Click **Select** or **press** *enter* to add the item to the item assembly form and advance to the Quantity (Qty) field.

Type 5

NOTES

The unit cost may be different when the cost of transferred items is lower than the default because older stock is being transferred and it was purchased at a lower price. If you change the unit cost, press *tab* to update the amount.

The Unit Cost and Amount fields are blank because the cost of the new item is still unknown. The unit cost of the assembled items is the total cost of all assembly components, plus additional costs, divided by the quantity or number of units assembled. When a single type of item is assembled and the quantity is greater than one, it is simpler to enter the quantity and amount (the Total in the assembly components portion in the top half of the form) and let the program calculate the unit cost. You can also enter the individual item cost in the Unit Cost field and allow the program to calculate the Amount (Qty times Unit Cost). We will enter the total from the upper portion of the journal.

Click the **Amount field.**

Type 4200 **Press** tab to enter the cost and update the unit cost and total.

NOTES
Because the two totals must be the same, entering the total cost and allowing the program to determine the unit cost ensures this balance.

The totals in the two parts of the assembly form should be the same. If they are not, you will be unable to post the entry.

Your completed form should now resemble the following:

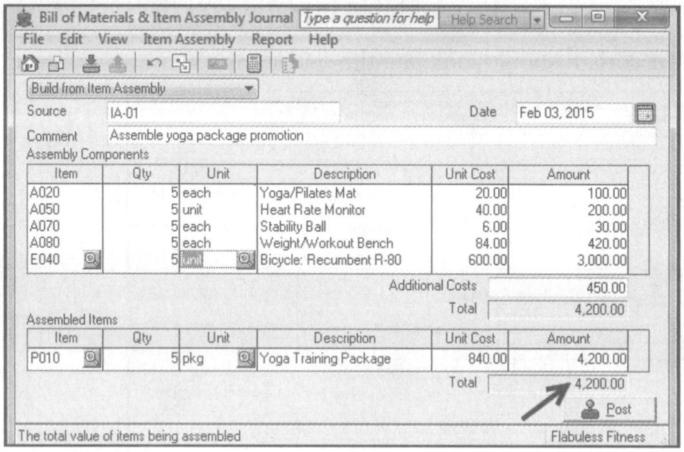
Bill of Materials & Item Assembly Journal
File Edit View Item Assembly Report Help
Build from Item Assembly
Source IA-01 Date Feb 03, 2015
Comment Assemble yoga package promotion
Assembly Components

Item	Qty	Unit	Description	Unit Cost	Amount
A020	5	each	Yoga/Pilates Mat	20.00	100.00
A050	5	unit	Heart Rate Monitor	40.00	200.00
A070	5	each	Stability Ball	6.00	30.00
A080	5	each	Weight/Workout Bench	84.00	420.00
E040	5	unit	Bicycle: Recumbent R-80	600.00	3,000.00

Additional Costs 450.00
Total 4,200.00

Assembled Items

Item	Qty	Unit	Description	Unit Cost	Amount
P010	5	pkg	Yoga Training Package	840.00	4,200.00

Total 4,200.00
Post
The total value of items being assembled — Flabuless Fitness

Reviewing the Item Assembly Journal Entry

PRO VERSION
In the Pro version, you will choose the Report menu and then click Display Item Assembly Journal Entry to see the transaction.

Choose the **Report menu**, then **click Display Bill Of Materials & Item Assembly Journal Entry** to display the transaction you have entered:

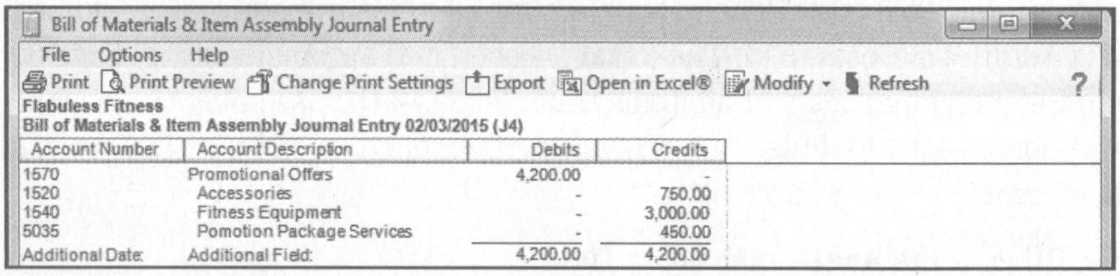
Bill of Materials & Item Assembly Journal Entry
File Options Help
Print Print Preview Change Print Settings Export Open in Excel® Modify Refresh
Flabuless Fitness
Bill of Materials & Item Assembly Journal Entry 02/03/2015 (J4)

Account Number	Account Description	Debits	Credits
1570	Promotional Offers	4,200.00	-
1520	Accessories	-	750.00
1540	Fitness Equipment	-	3,000.00
5035	Pomotion Package Services	-	450.00
Additional Date:	Additional Field:	4,200.00	4,200.00

NOTES
Pressing ctrl + J will also open the journal display.

Notice that Sage 50 has moved the inventory items from their original asset accounts (credit entries to *Accessories* and *Fitness Equipment*) to the newly created inventory account (debit entry to *Promotional Offers*). When you display inventory selection lists or quantity reports, you will see that the quantities for all items involved have been updated. The necessary items are taken out of their regular individual item inventory account and transferred to the new account. Thus the quantities of the original items are reduced because they have been transferred to the new account. Additional Costs are assigned to *Promotion Package Services*, the linked account defined for these costs. This is a contra-expense account — the credit entry for the expense account is added (debit amount) to the inventory value of the assembled inventory asset.

Close the **display** to return to the Item Assembly Journal input screen.

CORRECTING THE ITEM ASSEMBLY JOURNAL ENTRY

Move to the field that has the error. **Press** tab to move forward through the fields or **press** shift and tab together to move back to a previous field. This will highlight the field information so you can change it. **Type** the **correct information** and **press** tab to enter it. You must advance the cursor to the next field to enter a change.

You can also use the mouse to **point** to a field and **drag** through the **incorrect information** to highlight it. **Type** the **correct information** and **press** tab to enter it.

If an inventory item is incorrect, **press** enter while the cursor is in the Item field to **display** the appropriate **list**. **Double-click** the **correct inventory item**. **Re-enter** the **quantity** and **press** tab to update the totals.

Because the item assembly is a complex transaction, it is very easy to make a mistake, so check your work carefully. You may also want to store the original entry. If you discover later that you have made an error, you can recall the entry and add a minus sign to each quantity and to the Additional Costs amount to create a reversing entry.

Click the **Store button**  to display the familiar Store Recurring Transaction screen:

Because this is not a regular recurring transaction, we will use the Random frequency. Choosing the Random frequency for recurring entries enters the session date as the default transaction date when you recall the journal entry.

Click **Monthly** to display the Frequency options.

Click **Random** to select this frequency.

Click **OK** to save the entry and return to the Item Assembly Journal. Notice that the Recall button is now active.

WARNING!
When you recall an Item Assembly transaction, the unit costs and amounts for assembly components may be different from the original entry. The average cost may have changed since you posted the entry if you purchased new components at different prices. The new average cost price will be displayed. The quantities will be correct.
Correcting entries may also change the average unit cost.

Posting

Click **Post** when you are certain that all the information is correct.

Enter the next **assembly transaction**.

7 **Item Assembly #IA-02** **Dated February 3, 2015**

Create five (5) Training Workout Packages. Transfer 5 of each component item as follows:

5	A020	Yoga/Pilates Mat	$ 20 each
5	A040	Jump Rope	21 each
5	A050	Heart Rate Monitor	40 /unit
5	A060	Power Blocks	150 /set
5	A070	Stability Ball	6 each
5	A080	Workout/Weight Bench	84 each
5	A090	Workout Gloves: all sizes	8 /pair
5	A100	Aerobic Stepper w/ Risers	40 each
5	E030	Bicycle: Dual Action Calorie Counter	450 /unit

Additional Costs (for Personal Trainer: 1/2 day) 450

Assembled Items

5	P020	Training Workout Packages	$909 /pkg

Store the assembly as a recurring transaction with random frequency.

NOTES
Do not forget to save the item assembly as a recurring transaction with Random as the period.

When you post the second assembly entry, you will see the low inventory message:

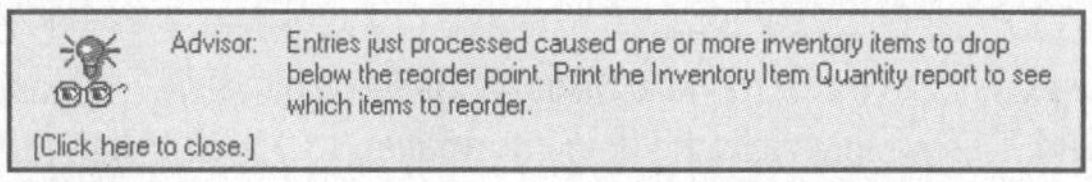
Advisor: Entries just processed caused one or more inventory items to drop below the reorder point. Print the Inventory Item Quantity report to see which items to reorder.
[Click here to close.]

Read the **Advisor message** and then **click** to close it.

Close the **Journal** to return to the Inventory & Services module window.

Click **Receivables** in the Modules pane list to restore this window.

Add **shortcuts** for **Item Assembly** and **Inventory Adjustments** from the Inventory & Services list in the Customize Shortcuts window.

Selling to Preferred Customers

Sage 50 allows you to record multiple inventory prices and to identify customers by the prices they will pay (preferred, regular, Web or a user-defined price). Sales for each group of customers are entered the same way since the program automatically enters the correct price depending on the customer selected and the price option in their ledger record.

✓ 8

Sales Invoice #3001 **Dated February 3, 2015**

Sold by Prekor to Red River College (Preferred customer)

80	A030	Dumbbells	$2.20 /kg
3	E040	Bicycle: Recumbent R-80	960 /unit
3	E080	Home Gym: Basic HG-1400	1 380 /unit
	GST		5%
	RST		7%

Terms: 2/15, n/30. Free delivery. Allow customer to exceed credit limit.

Red River College is a preferred customer — Preferred is entered as the Price List on the customer's Options tab screen.

Click the **Sales Invoices icon** [Sales Invoices] to open the Sales Journal.

Pay Later is the correct selection for this sale to Red River College. The Invoice number is also correct by default.

Choose **Red River College** from the customer list.

Type `Feb 3` in the Date field and **choose** **Prekor** as the salesperson.

Type `a` in the **Item Number field** and **click** **A030 Dumbbells** to add it. **Press** *tab* to advance to the Quantity field.

Type `80` **Press** *tab* to add the first item at the preferred customer price of $2.20 instead of $2.50, the regular price.

Click the **Price field List icon** to open the Select Price list:

NOTES
The price for each price list you have, including the ones you created, will be shown on this list.

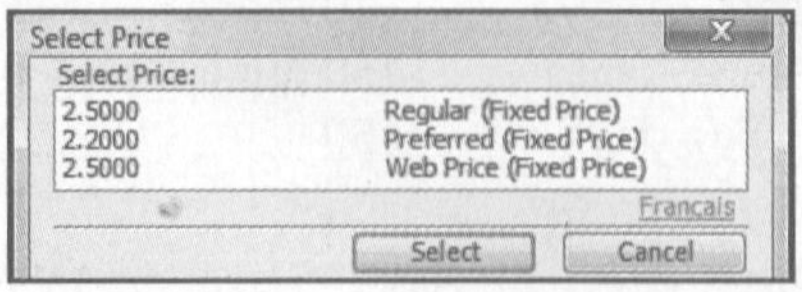
Select Price
Select Price:
2.5000 Regular (Fixed Price)
2.2000 Preferred (Fixed Price)
2.5000 Web Price (Fixed Price)
Français
Select
Cancel

You can also select the item price you need from this screen.

Click the price you want and then click Select to use it in the journal.

Click **Cancel** because the correct price has already been entered.

Enter the **remaining items** sold to this customer to complete the entry:

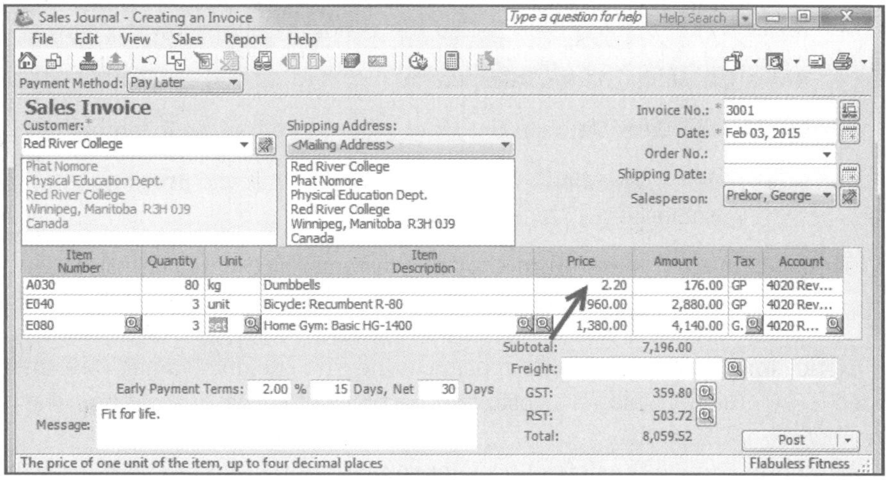

Choose the **Report menu** and **click Display Sales Journal Entry** to review:

Flabuless Fitness
Sales Journal Entry 02/03/2015 (J6)

Account Number	Account Description	Debits	Credits
1200	Accounts Receivable	8,059.52	-
5060	Cost of Goods Sold	4,632.00	-
1520	Accessories	-	72.00
1540	Fitness Equipment	-	1,800.00
1550	Home Gym Equipment	-	2,760.00
2640	RST Payable	-	503.72
2650	GST Charged on Sales	-	359.80
4020	Revenue from Sales	-	7,196.00
Additional Date:	Additional Field:	12,691.52	12,691.52

This entry looks the same as a regular non-discounted sale. Revenue is reduced because of the change in selling price, but this change is not recorded as a discount.

Close the **display** when finished. **Make corrections. Post** the **entry. Click Yes** to allow the customer to exceed the credit limit.

Entering Sales Returns

Customers may return purchases for many different reasons. For example, the size, colour or quality may have been other than expected. Stores have different policies with respect to accepting and refunding returns. Most stores place reasonable time limits on the period in which they will give refunds. Some stores offer credit only and some charge a handling fee on goods returned. Flabuless Fitness will provide full refunds for purchases within two weeks of the sale if the items have not been used or opened. Sales returns are entered in the Sales Journal and are very similar to sales, but the quantity is entered with a minus sign — a negative quantity is sold. Different accounts may be used.

✓ 9

Sales Return #3000-R **Dated February 3, 2015**

Returned to Kisangel by Botelli & Giroux, Lawyers,

−1	E060	Treadmill: Basic T-800B	$1 400 /unit
	GST		5%
	RST		7%

Terms: net 60 days. Create new Subgroup revenue account: 4050 Sales Returns.

Open the **Sales Journal.**

The return must use the same customer and payment method as the original sale. Pay Later is correctly selected.

Choose Botelli & Giroux, Lawyers from the Customer list.

You should use a different invoice number so that the return can be differentiated from a normal sale.

> **NOTES**
> Most stores have separate forms for returns with their own number sequences.

> **NOTES**
> The salesperson should be entered for sales returns because commissions are calculated on total sales less returns.

Click the **Invoice No. field** and **type** `3000-R`

Enter **Feb. 3** in the Date field if this is not the date shown already.

Enter **Kisangel** as the salesperson.

Click the **Item Number field** and **type** `e` to see the inventory list.

Click **E060 Treadmill: Basic T-800B** to enter it and **press** *tab* to move the cursor to the Quantity field.

This adds the first item returned by the customer at the regular price.

Type `-1` **Press** *tab*.

Notice that a positive amount appears in the Price field and a negative amount is added to the Amount field — a positive price times the negative quantity. The tax amounts are also negative.

We should change the default account so that returns can be tracked separately.

Click the **Account field List icon** and **type** `4050`

Press *tab* and **add** **Sales Returns**, the new account. Do not forget to change the account type to **Subgroup** (the account balance is included in a Subtotal).

Enter additional items returned, if there are any, in the same way.

Change the payment **terms** for this entry to **Net 60 Days**.

Your finished journal entry should look like the following one:

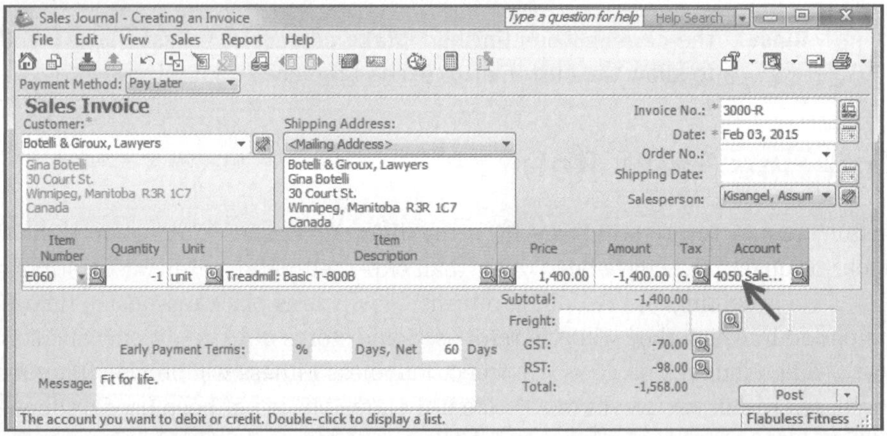

> **NOTES**
> In the Comment field, you could add the reason for the return. The customer's name and address could be added to the Ship To field or the Comment field.

Choose the **Report menu** and **click** **Display Sales Journal Entry** to review it:

Flabuless Fitness
Sales Journal Entry 02/03/2015 (J7)

Account Number	Account Description	Debits	Credits
1540	Fitness Equipment	750.00	-
2640	RST Payable	98.00	-
2650	GST Charged on Sales	70.00	-
4050	Sales Returns	1,400.00	-
1200	Accounts Receivable	-	1,568.00
5060	Cost of Goods Sold	-	750.00
Additional Date:	Additional Field:	2,318.00	2,318.00

Notice that the entry is the reversal of a regular sale. The inventory asset account has been debited because inventory is added back. *Sales Returns* — a contra-revenue account — is debited, reducing revenue, and *Accounts Receivable* is credited because money has been returned to the customer's account to reduce the balance owing. Similarly, *RST Payable* and *GST Charged on Sales* are debited because the tax liabilities have decreased and finally, the expense account *Cost of Goods Sold* is credited because this expense has been reversed.

For Credit Card sales, the return entry will also reverse credit card fees expenses.

Close the **display** when finished. **Make corrections** if necessary.

Post the **entry**. **Close** the **Sales Journal**.

When you open the Receipts Journal for this customer, you will see a negative amount entered for the return:

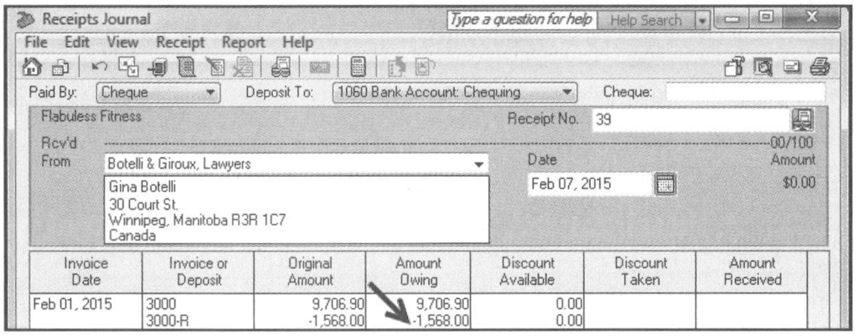

When the customer makes the final payment, accept the Amount Received field for the return to subtract the amount for the return from the original invoice.

Enter the **payment to Prolife Exercisers**.

10 **Payment Cheque #251** **Dated February 3, 2015**

To Prolife Exercisers Inc., $10 609 in payment of account including $206 discount for early payment. Reference invoice #PE-364.

Entering Purchase Adjustments and Credit Notes

Returns on purchases also occur for a variety of reasons: for example, the goods may be damaged or the wrong items may have been shipped. Purchase returns are entered in the same way as sales returns — by adding a minus sign to the quantity so that all the amounts become negative. The supplier and payment method must be the same as the original purchase. You cannot change the default asset account for inventory purchases or returns.

When you review the journal entry you will see that it is a reversed purchase entry. The inventory asset account and *GST Paid on Purchases* will be credited to decrease the inventory and restore the tax liability. *Accounts Payable* will be debited to reduce the amount owing to the supplier. Freight charges, when entered as a negative amount, will also be reversed.

Adjustments for purchases of inventory are made in the same way as other purchase adjustments. However, differences occur when the invoice has already been paid.

✓ 11 **Adjust Purchase Invoice #PE-364-R** **Dated February 4, 2015**

From Prolife Exercisers, Credit Note

3	E010	Elliptical Exerciser: AE-200	$3 450.00
3	E020	Elliptical Exerciser: LE-400	4 200.00
		Freight	100.00
		GST Paid	387.50
Total Invoice			$8 137.50
Total Credit amount			$2 471.50

Terms: net 60 days.

Open the **Purchases Journal**. **Click** the **Adjust Invoice tool** and **select** invoice **PE-364** from **Prolife Exercisers Inc.**

Type `PE-364-R` as the invoice number.

Click **4**, the Quantity for E010 Elliptical Exerciser: AE-200 and **type** 3

Click 4, the Quantity for E020 Elliptical Exerciser: LE-400 and **type** 3

Change the **payment terms** to **net 60** to complete the entry as shown:

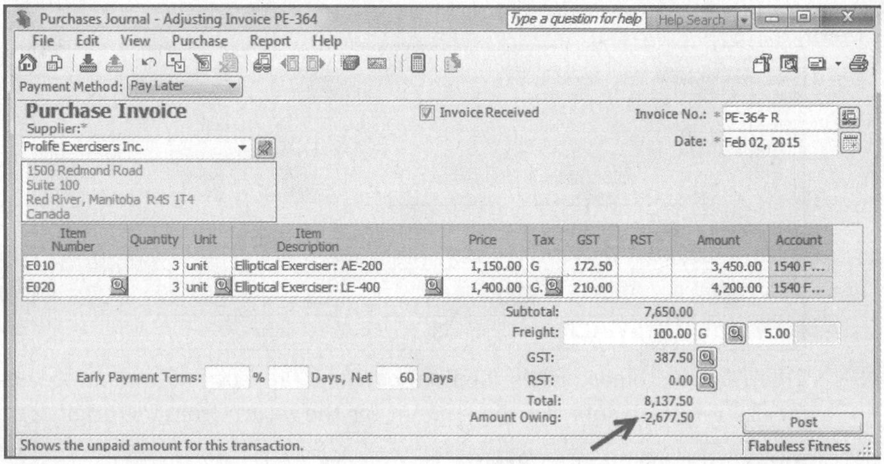

The amount owing appears as a negative amount on the invoice, but unlike the sales return, all other amounts are still positive.

Review the **journal entry** to see that it looks like a normal purchase entry.

Close the **display**. **Make corrections** if needed and **click post**. You may see the following message:

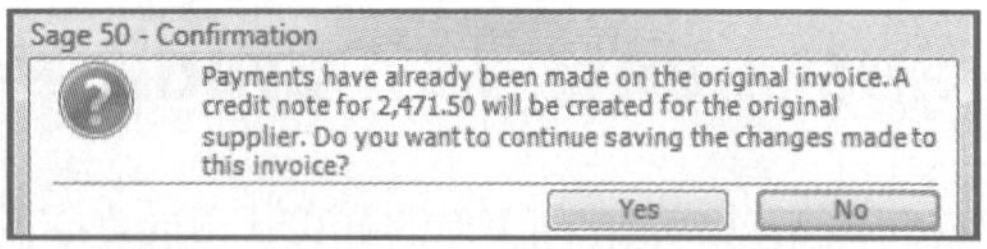

You are advised that payments have been applied to the invoice.

Click **Yes** to continue.

Creating Automatic Credit Notes from Returns

When you reverse or adjust an invoice after an account has been paid, and the original purchase was a "pay later" transaction, as in this example, Sage 50 can automatically create a credit note for the adjustment or reversing entry.

Clicking Yes to continue will result in an additional message about the credit note:

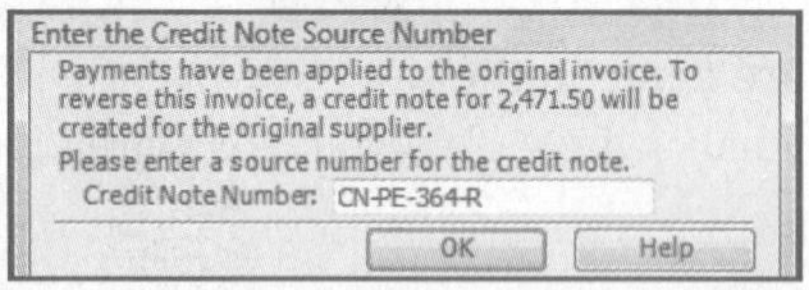

You can accept or change the default note number — the original invoice number preceded by CN that designates this as a credit note — and click OK to continue.

In the Payments Journal, the credit note is entered as an invoice with a negative amount that you can accept to reduce the amount you pay for future purchases:

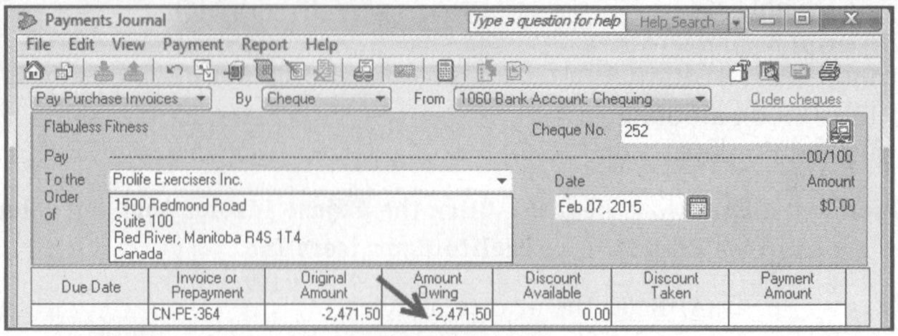

NOTES

You may see this screen immediately when you post the adjustment, instead of the preceding one that does not include the Credit Note Number.

NOTES

The return creates three journal entries: the reversal or cancellation of the discount, the reversing entry and the final correct purchase entry. The net result is a credit balance of \$2 471.50, not \$2 677.50 as shown in the journal.

Automatic Credit Notes from Sales Returns

If you are entering an adjustment or a return for a sales invoice that has been paid, you will see a similar notice when you click Post:

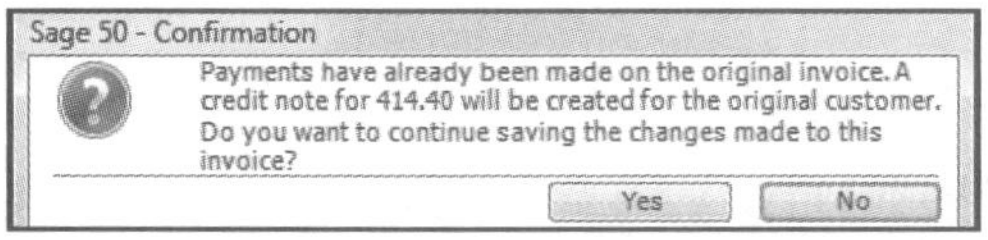

Again, clicking Yes shows the information about the credit note that is created:

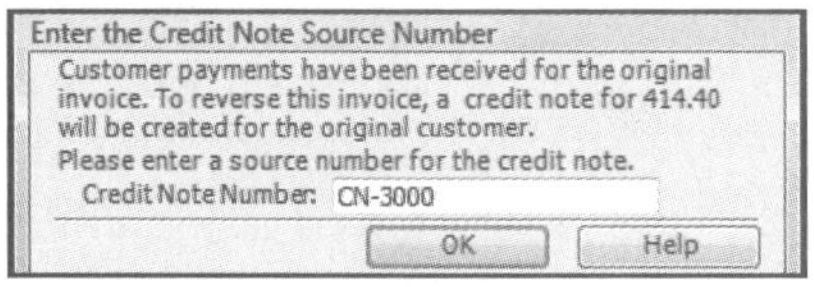

You can accept the default note number — the original invoice number preceded by CN that designates this as a credit note. Click OK to confirm the entry. The credit note for the customer is a negative invoice — in the Receipts Journal for the customer, it appears as a negative amount that you can accept with the next customer payment to reduce the amount owing by the customer.

Enter the **remaining transactions** for February.

12 **Payment Cheque #252** **Dated February 4, 2015**

To Footlink Corporation, $16 640 in payment of account including $160 discount for early payment. Reference invoice #FC-618.

13 **Cash Receipt #39** **Dated February 4, 2015**

From Red River College, cheque #4782 for $5 537 in payment of account including $113 discount for early payment. Reference invoice #2194.

14

To:
Customer: **Flabuless Fitness**
Address: 199 Warmup Ave., #500
Winnipeg, MB R8T 3B7
Reg # 245138121

Feelyte Gym Accessories
7 Onandaga Dr., Vancouver, BC V4G 4S5
Tel: (604) 588-3846 Fax: (604) 588-7126
www.feelyte.com

Invoice #: FG-4100
GST # 466 254 108

Feb. 6, 2015

qty	code	item		total
5	A050	Heart rate monitor @ $40		200.00
10	A060	Power blocks @ $150		1500.00
10	A080	Weight/workout bench @ $84		840.00
5	A100	Aerobic stepper w/risers @ 40		200.00
			Freight	100.00
			GST	142.00
			Invoice Total	2,982.00

Terms: 2/10, n/30 ST

15

Receipt #40 **Dated February 7, 2015**

From Brandon University, cheque #14701 for $8 859.20 in payment of account including $180.80 discount for early payment. Reference invoice #2199.

16

Flabuless Fitness

INVOICE # 3002
Flabuless Fitness
199 Warmup Ave., Suite 500
Winnipeg, MB R8T 3B7
#245138121

Sold to: Lavendar Estates
Address: 9 Lavender Ct.
Winnipeg, MB R2X 3J6
ATTN: Katherine Harris

Salesperson: Kisangel

Date: Feb. 7/15

QTY	CODE	DESCRIPTION	PRICE/UNIT	TAX CODE	TOTAL
4	A070	Stability ball	12 /each	1	48.00
1	B010	Books: fitness guide	40/each	2	40.00
1	E020	Elliptical exerciser: LE-400	2600/unit	1	2,600.00
1	E060	Treadmill: basic T-800B	1400/unit	1	1,400.00
4	S040	Yoga instructor: 1 hour	100/hour	2	400.00
1	P020	Training workout pkg	1600/pkg	1	1600.00
			Delivery	2	50.00

Authorization to exceed credit limit SR

Terms: 2/5, n/15

GST 5%	306.90
RST 7%	395.36
Invoice Total	6,840.26

Tel 1: (204) 642-B-FIT or (800) 448-B-FIT Fax: (204) 642-9100
www.flabulessfitness.com
fit for life

SESSION DATE – FEBRUARY 14, 2015

17

Purchase Invoice #TD-6891 **Dated February 9, 2015**

From Trufit Depot

2	E080	Home Gym: Basic HG-1400	$2 100.00
2	E090	Home Gym: Deluxe Multi HG-1402	3 200.00
	Freight		100.00
	GST		270.00
	Total		$5 670.00

Terms: 2/5, n/20.

NOTES
The price for E080 has changed.

18

Memo #4 **Dated February 9, 2015**

Edit the selling price to reflect increase in purchase price for item E080 Home Gym: Basic HG-1400. The new regular and Web price will be $1 750 and the preferred price will be $1 600.

WARNING!
You will need to add the tax code and the account for the new supplier in the journal. Alternatively, you can use Full Add and enter these details in the supplier's record.

19

Cash Purchase Invoice #WD-114 **Dated February 11, 2015**

From Winnipeg Daily (use Quick Add for new vendor), $1 200 plus $60 GST and $84 RST for ads to run for 12 weeks. Purchase invoice total $1 344 paid in full by Cheque #253. Create new Group account: 1290 Prepaid Advertising.

20

Purchase Invoice #RS-6112 **Dated February 12, 2015**

From Riverview Sunoco, $130 including GST and RST for gasoline purchase for delivery vehicle. Terms: net 21. Store as a recurring bi-weekly entry.

21

Flabuless Fitness

INVOICE # 3003
Flabuless Fitness
199 Warmup Ave., Suite 500
Winnipeg, MB R8T 3B7
#245138121

Sold to: The Forks Film Corp.
Address: 6 Gilroy St.
Winnipeg, MB R3C 2M2
ATTN: Francine Despardieu

Salesperson: Prekor

Date: Feb. 14/15

QTY	CODE	DESCRIPTION	PRICE/UNIT	TAX CODE	TOTAL
2	A010	Body fat scale	130/unit**	1	260.00
80	A030	Dumbbells	2.20/kg	1	176.00
3	A060	Power blocks	250/set	1	750.00
8	A070	Stability ball	10 /each	1	80.00
2	A080	Weight/workout bench	150/each	1	300.00
2	A100	Aerobic stepper w/risers	60 /each	1	120.00
2	E060	Treadmill: basic T-800B	1220/unit	1	2440.00
1	E080	Home gym: basic HG-1400	1600/set	1	1600.00

** *preferred customer discounts & free delivery GP*

Terms: 2/15, n/30

GST 5%	286.30
RST 7%	400.82
Invoice Total	**6,413.12**

Tel 1: (204) 642-B-FIT or (800) 448-B-FIT Fax: (204) 642-9100
www.flabulessfitness.com
fit for life

SESSION DATE – FEBRUARY 21, 2015

22

Sales Invoice #3004 **Dated February 17, 2015**

Sold by Prekor to Brandon University

2	A010	Body Fat Scale	$ 130 /unit
100	A030	Dumbbells	2.20 /kg
2	A040	Jump Rope: Weighted	35 each
4	A080	Weight/Workout Bench	150 each
10	B010	Books: Fitness Guide	35 each
2	E020	Elliptical Exerciser: LE-400	2 300 /unit
2	E030	Bicycle: Dual Action Calorie Counter	720 /unit
2	E060	Treadmill: Basic T-800B	1 220 /unit
2	E080	Home Gym: Basic HG-1400	1 600 /set
	GST		5%
	RST		7%

Terms: 2/15, n/30. Allow customer to exceed credit limit.

23

Receipt #41 **Dated February 17, 2015**

From Brandon University, cheque #19664 for $5 000 in partial payment of invoice #3004.

24

Cash Purchase Invoice #MB-59113 **Dated February 19, 2015**

From Manitoba Bell, $140 plus $7.00 GST paid and $9.80 RST for phone service. Purchase invoice total $156.80 paid by cheque #254 in full payment.

25

Cash Purchase Invoice #ME-34910 **Dated February 19, 2015**

From Manitoba Energy, $210 plus $10.50 GST paid for hydro service. Purchase invoice total $220.50 paid by cheque #255.

26

Receipt #42 **Dated February 20, 2015**

From Lavender Estates, cheque #584 for $6 840.26 in payment of invoice #3002.

27

Sales Invoice #3005 **Dated February 21, 2015**

Sold by Kisangel to Ariandanos Residence

2	A070	Stability Ball	$ 12 each
1	A080	Weight/Workout bench	175 each
2	A090	Workout Gloves	15 /pair
1	B010	Books: Fitness Guide	40 each
1	E080	Home Gym: Basic HG-1400	1 750 /set
1	P020	Training Workout Package	1 600 /pkg
	GST		5%
	RST		7%

Terms: 2/5, n/15. Includes complimentary delivery.

28

Receipt #43 **Dated February 21, 2015**

From Red River College, cheque #5961 for $4 000 in partial payment of invoice #3001.

SESSION DATE – FEBRUARY 28, 2015

29

Sales Invoice #3006 **Dated February 23, 2015**

Sold by Kisangel to Red River College

4	A060	Power Blocks	$ 250 /set
2	A080	Weight/Workout Bench	150 each
3	E040	Bicycle: Recumbent R-80	960 /unit
	GST		5%
	RST		7%

Terms: 2/15, n/30.

30

Memo #5 **Dated February 25, 2015**

Create new inventory item:

Number	Description	Unit	Min Level	Regular Price	Preferred Price	Linked Accounts Asset	Revenue	COGS
E100	Home Gym: Free Weight HG-1403	set	1	$3 200	(2 900)	1550	4020	5060

31

Purchase Invoice #TD-9133 **Dated February 25, 2015**

From Trufit Depot, new inventory item purchase

2	E100	Home Gym: Free Weight HG-1403	$3 000.00
	GST		150.00
	Invoice total		$3 150.00

Terms: 2/5, n/20. Free delivery.

32

Purchase Invoice #RS-7533 **Dated February 26, 2015**

From Riverview Sunoco, $130 including GST and RST for gasoline. Terms: net 21. Recall the stored entry.

33

Bank Debit Memo #91431 **Dated February 28, 2015**

From Red River Credit Union, authorized withdrawals were made from the chequing account on our behalf for the following:

Bank service charges	$ 35
Mortgage interest payment	1 880
Mortgage principal reduction	220
Bank loan interest payment	420
Bank loan principal reduction	480

34

Flabuless Fitness

INVOICE # 3007
Flabuless Fitness
199 Warmup Ave., Suite 500
Winnipeg, MB R8T 3B7
245138121

Sold to: Visa Sales Summary
Address: Cash Customers

Salesperson: Kisangel

Date: Feb. 28/15

QTY	CODE	DESCRIPTION	PRICE/UNIT	TAX CODE	TOTAL
3	A010	Body fat scale	150/unit	1	450.00
15	A020	Yoga/pilates mat	40/each	1	600.00
40	A030	Dumbbells	2.50/kg	1	100.00
5	A050	Heart rate monitor	90/unit	1	450.00
10	A090	Workout gloves: all sizes	15/pair	1	150.00
3	P020	Training workout package	1600/pkg	1	4800.00
10	S010	Personal trainer: 1 hour	80/hour	2	800.00
4	S060	Equipment assembly/instruction	75/job	1	300.00
10	B010	Books: fitness guide	40/each	2	400.00

Direct deposit to Visa account AK

Terms: Visa

GST 5%	402.50
RST 7%	479.50
Total	**8,932.00**

Tel 1: (204) 642-B-FIT or (800) 448-B-FIT Fax: (204) 642-9100
www.flabulessfitness.com
fit for life

35

MasterCard Sales Invoice #3008 **Dated February 28, 2015**

Sold by Prekor to Cash & Credit Card Sales (sales summary)

2	A010	Body Fat Scale	$150 /unit	$ 300.00
5	A020	Yoga/Pilates Mat	40 each	200.00
4	A040	Jump Rope: Weighted	40 each	160.00
3	A060	Power Blocks	300 /set	900.00
6	A090	Workout Gloves: all sizes	15 /pair	90.00
8	B010	Books: Fitness Guide	40 each	320.00
8	S020	Personal Trainer: 1/2 day	200 /1/2 day	1 600.00
4	S030	Personal Trainer: full day	400 /day	1 600.00
8	S050	Yoga Instructor: 1/2 day	200 /1/2 day	1 600.00
	GST		5%	338.50
	RST		7%	115.50
	Total paid by MasterCard			$7 224.00

36

Memo #6 **Dated February 28, 2015**

Prepare the payroll for the two salaried employees, Prekor and Kisangel. Add 2 percent of revenue from sales and services for February as a commission to their salaries. Issue payroll cheques #256 and #257.

Displaying Inventory Reports

Most inventory reports can be displayed from the Reports menu in the Inventory & Services window, from the Home window Reports menu, from the Inventory & Services module window Reports pane drop-down list and from the Report Centre. We will access the reports from the Report Centre.

NOTES
Choose Cash & Credit Card Sales for the Visa and MasterCard sales summaries.

NOTES
Use the Sales by Salesperson Summary Report (by Customer) to find the net sales for each employee. Do not include freight or other sales in the report.

NOTES
If you click the Report Centre icon in the Inventory & Services window, you will open the list of Inventory & Services reports with the first report selected and its sample displayed.

PRO VERSION
Item Assembly Journal Entries replaces Bill Of Materials & Item Assembly Journal Entries in the Select A Report Type list.

The Grouped Inventory and Services List is not available.

CLASSIC VIEW
Right-click the Inventory & Services icon 

. Click the Display tool  to open the Modify Report window.

PRO VERSION
The Pro version does not have the option to Include Internal Service Activities.

PRO VERSION
Grouped lists are not available in the Pro version.

NOTES
You can drill down to the Inventory Transaction Detail Report from the Inventory List and from the Grouped Inventory List.

PRO VERSION
In the Report Centre list, click Item Assembly Journal Entries. Or choose the Report menu, then choose Journal Entries and click Item Assembly.

Click the **Report Centre icon** 

in any window.

Click **Inventory & Services** to open the list of inventory reports:

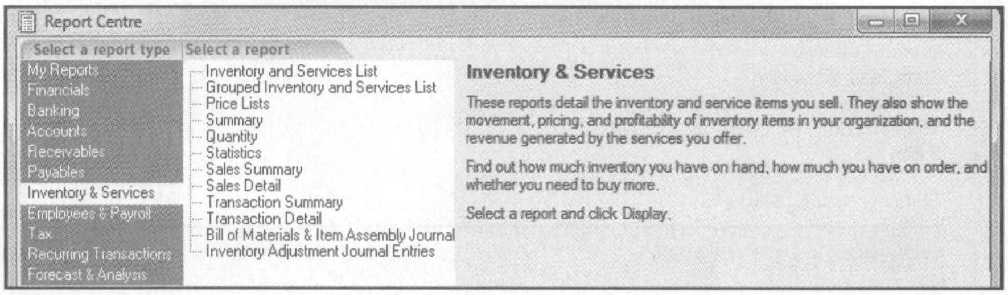

Displaying Inventory Lists

Click **Inventory And Services List**. **Click** **Modify This Report**:

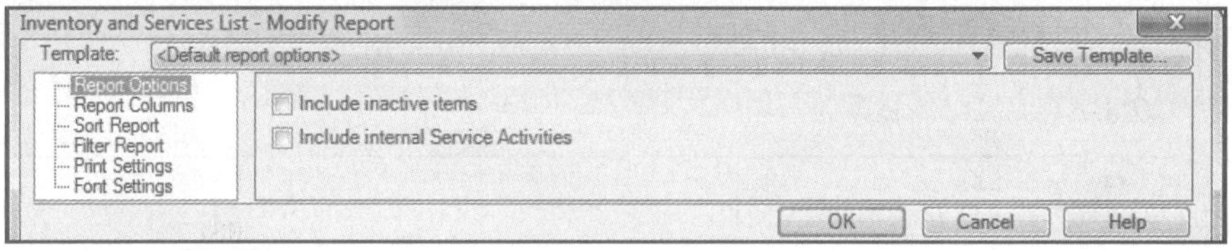

Or you can choose the Reports menu and choose Lists, then click Inventory & Services to see the report options.

The default report shows the item number, description, type, quantity, total value and average cost. To select the fields for the report, choose Report Columns.

Click **OK** to see the list. **Close** the **display** when you have finished.

Displaying Grouped Inventory Lists

Click **Grouped Inventory And Services List**. **Click** **Modify This Report**.

Click **Type** in the Group By field:

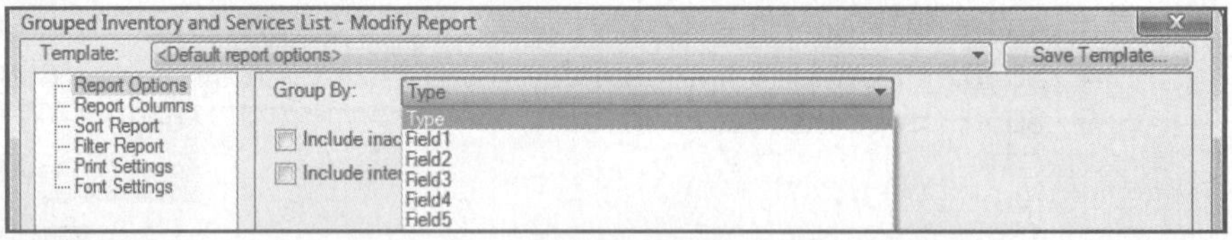

From this list, choose the way you want to sort the list. You can organize by Type (inventory and services are separated) or by any of the additional information fields you created for the ledger. To select the fields for the report, choose Report Columns.

Click **OK** to see the list. **Close** the **display** when you have finished.

Displaying the Item Assembly Journal

Click **Bill Of Materials & Item Assembly Journal Entries** to see the report sample and description.

Click **Modify This Report** to open the report options window:

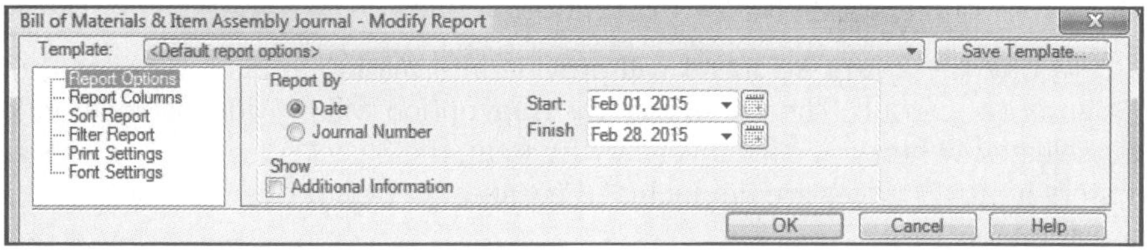

Or choose the Reports menu, then choose Journal Entries and click Bill Of Materials & Item Assembly.

As usual, the earliest transaction date, session date and Report By Date options are provided by default. The sorting, filtering and column options are the same for all journal reports. There is no option to show corrections because these entries cannot be adjusted or reversed automatically.

Enter the **Start** and **Finish dates** you want for the report.

Click **OK**. **Close** the **display** when you have finished.

CLASSIC VIEW
Right-click the Bill Of Materials & Item Assembly icon

. Click , the Display tool .

NOTES
Additional Information for journal entries is covered in Chapter 11.

Displaying the Adjustments Journal

Click **Inventory Adjustment Journal Entries** to see the sample.

Click **Modify This Report** to open the report options window:

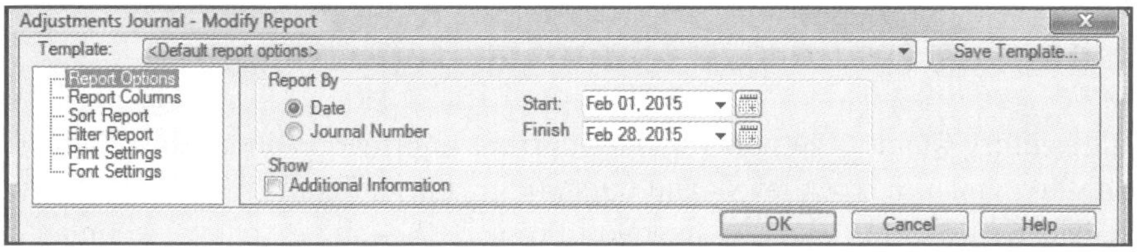

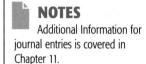

Or you can choose the Reports menu, then choose Journal Entries and click Inventory Adjustments.

As usual, the earliest transaction date, session date and Report By Date options are provided by default.

Enter the **Start** and **Finish dates** you want for the report.

Click **OK**. **Close** the **display** when you have finished.

CLASSIC VIEW
Right-click the Inventory Adjustments icon

. Click , the Display tool .

NOTES
You can drill down to the General Ledger reports from the Item Assembly Journal and from the Adjustments Journal.

Displaying Inventory Summary Reports

The Inventory Summary Report provides detailed quantity and cost information for the inventory you have in stock.

Click **Summary** from the Select A Report list to see the sample.

Click **Modify This Report** to open the report options window:

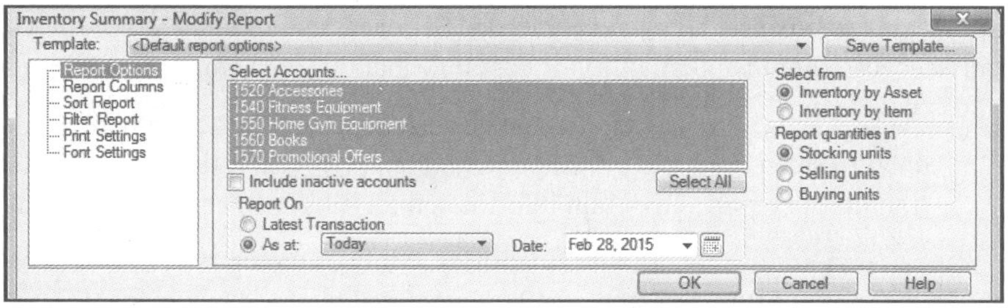

> **NOTES**
> You can customize Summary reports by selecting any of the columns usually included in the report. You can sort and filter by item or description.

You can also choose the Reports menu, then choose Inventory & Services and click Summary to display the report options.

Selecting **Inventory By Asset** will provide information for all inventory items in the asset group(s) chosen. The **Inventory By Item** option will provide information for all the items selected. When you click Inventory By Item, the Select Accounts box lists all inventory items. Services are not included because there is no quantity or cost information for them.

> **NOTES**
> Select All acts as a toggle switch. When all items are selected, clicking Select All will remove all selections. When one or a few items are selected, clicking Select All will select all the entries on the list.

Click a single asset or item to change selections or provide a report for that item only. To select multiple items, press and hold ctrl and then click the items you want in the report. To obtain information for all items, choose Select All.

The **Summary** Report lists the quantity on hand, the unit cost of the inventory and the total value or cost of inventory on hand for the items requested. The total value of the inventory in an asset group is also provided when you select one asset group. You can view the Summary Report for the Latest Transaction Date, or for another date that you enter in the **As At** Date field.

> **NOTES**
> When you display the report with the Latest Transaction option, it includes the profit for each item – either the markup or margin, as selected in the Inventory Ledger Settings.

You can prepare the report with quantities in any of the units you use for the item if these are different, that is, the stocking, buying or selling units (see page 371).

Choose the **options** you need for your report.

Press and **hold** ctrl and **click** the **items** or **assets** you want included.

Click **OK**. **Close** the **display** when you have finished.

> **NOTES**
> You can drill down to the Inventory Transaction Detail Report from the Inventory Summary or Quantity reports.

Displaying Inventory Quantity Reports

The Inventory Quantity Report provides current information about the quantity on hand, the minimum stock levels and outstanding purchase and sales orders. The report also displays the order quantity needed to restore the minimum level when an item has fallen below the minimum level.

Click **Quantity** from the Select A Report list. **Click** **Modify This Report**:

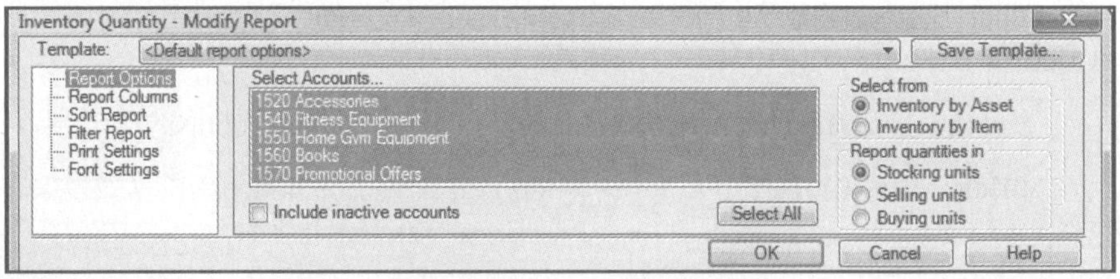

Or choose the Reports menu, then choose Inventory & Services and click Quantity to display the report options.

> **NOTES**
> You can customize Quantity Reports by selecting any of the columns usually included in the report. You can sort and filter by most of the columns usually included in the report.

You can select the items for the report in the same way you did for the Inventory Summary Report. Selecting **Inventory By Asset** will provide information for all inventory items in the asset group(s) chosen. The **Inventory By Item** option will provide information for all the items selected. When you click Inventory By Item, the Select Accounts box lists all inventory items. Services are not included in the Quantity Report because there is no quantity or cost information for them.

Click a single asset or item to change selections or provide a report for that item only. To select multiple items, press and hold ctrl and then click the items you want in the report. To obtain information for all items, choose Select All.

You can prepare the report with quantities in any of the units you use for the item if they are different, that is, the stocking, buying or selling units (see page 371).

Choose the **options** you need for your report.

Press and **hold** *ctrl* and **click** the **names** of all the items or asset groups you want to include in the report.

Click **OK** and **close** the **display** when you have finished.

Displaying Inventory Price Lists

The different inventory prices — regular, preferred, Web and customized prices — are not available in the other inventory reports, but you can see all of these prices together on the Price Lists Report.

NOTES
You cannot sort or filter the Price List Report, but you can select or omit the Item and Description columns. You must select at least one.
There are no drill-down reports from Price Lists.

Click **Price Lists** from the Select A Report list. **Click** **Modify This Report**:

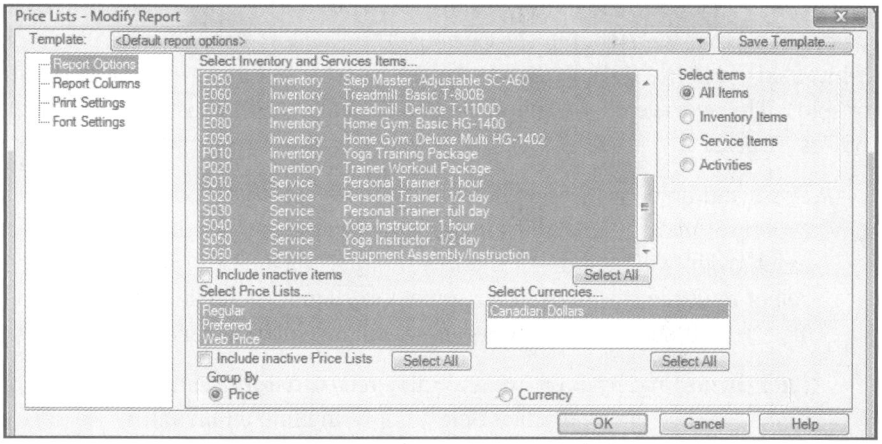

You can also choose the Reports menu, then choose Inventory & Services and click Price Lists to display the report options.

You can choose the item or items that you want on the price list by selecting them from the list, just as you select items for other inventory reports. You can include Regular, Preferred, Web prices and any customized price lists you created.

NOTES
If you have created other price lists or use additional currencies, they will be listed in the Modify Report screen and you can include them in the report.
If you use other currencies, you can also add the price lists in these currencies and then group your lists by currency or by price list.

Click the **Price Lists** you want to report on.

Click **OK** to see the price lists and **close** the **display** when you have finished.

Displaying Inventory Tracking Reports

Several reports provide information about the turnover of inventory products. These reports show whether items are selling well and are profitable and how the sales are distributed over time and customers.

Inventory Statistics Reports

Click **Statistics** from the Select A Report list. **Click** **Modify This Report** to open the report options window:

NOTES
For Inventory Statistics Reports, you can sort and filter by most of the columns usually included in the report.
You can customize Statistics Reports by selecting any of the columns usually included in the report.

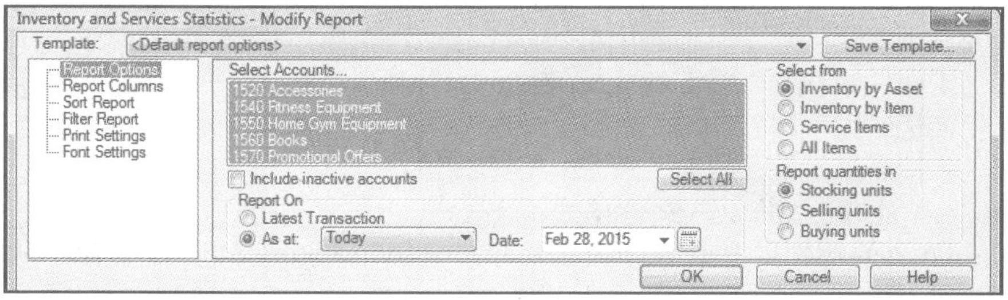

NOTES
You can drill down to the Inventory Sales Detail Report from the Inventory Statistics Report.

NOTES
When you display the report with the Latest Transaction option, it includes the statistics for the previous year as well.

NOTES
You can also choose the FIFO (first-in, first-out) method of determining inventory costs. You make this choice in the Inventory Settings screen. This method is not available for the Pro version.

NOTES
Remember that Select All acts as a toggle switch – when all items are already selected, clicking Select All clears the selection. Clicking Select All when no items are selected, or when one or more items (but not all items) are selected, will select all items.

Or choose the Reports menu, then choose Inventory & Services and click Statistics to display the report options.

The Statistics Report summarizes transactions for the year to date and the previous year, the same historical information that is contained in the Inventory Ledger record (see page 373). For example, the report can show whether a large volume of sales resulted from a single sale for a large quantity or from a large number of smaller sales. Comparing the Statistics Report with the Statistics tab content in a ledger record for the same item will show the similarities.

You can prepare the report for the session date (**Latest Transaction**) or for another date (**As At Date**). When you choose As At, the Date field is available. The report will show the statistics you request as at the date you enter.

The report shows the **Number Of Transactions** (the number of separate sales invoices that included the inventory item); **Units Sold** (the total number of individual items of a kind that were sold in the period); the **Amount Sold** (the total sale price for all items sold); and the **Cost Of Goods Sold** (the total purchase cost of all the items that were sold). The average cost method is used to calculate the cost of goods sold for Flabuless Fitness.

Press and hold *ctrl* and click one or more asset groups to include them in the report, or click Select All to include all asset groups in the report. Selecting an asset group will include all the inventory items in that group in the report. To select multiple assets or items, press *ctrl* and then click the items you want. The default selection — By Asset — will not include services in the report.

Click **Inventory By Item** to list individual inventory items. Select one or more items for the report, or click Select All to include all inventory items. Click **Service Items** to list individual services. Press *ctrl* and hold and click services to include them, or click Select All to include all services. Click **All Items** to include both individual inventory items and individual services in the report. Press *ctrl* and hold and click the items and services to include them in the report, or click Select All to include all items and services.

The list of items will expand according to your selection, and you can choose single or multiple items for inclusion. **Quantities** can be reported in any of the units on record — the units for stocking the inventory, for buying and for selling — if these are different.

Choose the **items** you want in the report.

Choose the **date** for the report (Latest Transaction or As At Date). **Enter** a **date** in the Date field if you chose the As At option.

Click **OK** to display the report. **Close** the **display** when you have finished.

Inventory Sales Reports

Click **Sales Summary** from the Select A Report list. **Click** **Modify This Report**:

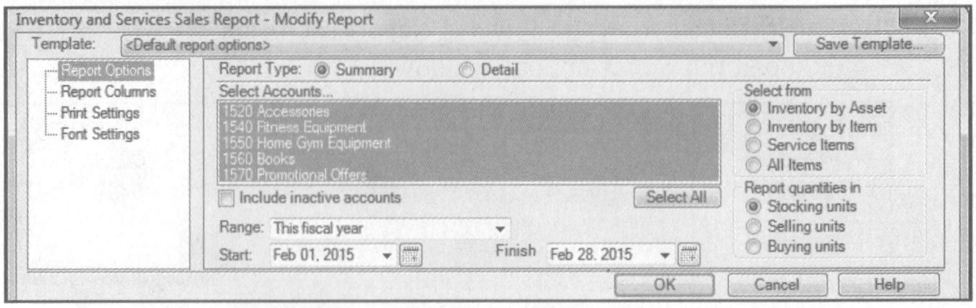

NOTES
To see the Inventory Sales Summary Report on Services, you must click Select From Service Items or choose All Items. Inventory By Item and Inventory By Asset – the default selection – include only inventory items.

Or choose the Reports menu, then choose Inventory & Services and click Sales.

The reports include the number of transactions (Summary option), the quantity of items sold, the revenue per item, the cost of goods sold and the profit for each item. Non-inventory sales are not included. The **Summary** option, selected by default, shows the total for each detail for the selected inventory items organized by item. The **Detail** option provides the same information listed by individual journal entry, including the source document numbers and journal entry numbers. Click Detail to add these details.

As usual, you can choose to report on inventory items, services or both. To report only on all services, click **Service Items** and then Select All. Click **All Items** to include both inventory and services. The list of items will expand accordingly, and you can choose single or multiple items for inclusion. Select All at this stage will provide a report on all inventory and service items.

Again, **quantities** may be reported in stocking, buying or selling units.

> **NOTES**
> You cannot sort or filter the Sales Report, but you can customize the report by selecting the columns you want to include.

> **NOTES**
> You can drill down to the Inventory Sales Detail Report from the Inventory Sales Summary Report. You can display the Customer Aged, Inventory Ledger, Journal Report and view Sales Invoices from the Inventory Sales Detail Report.

Enter the **Start** and **Finish dates** you want for the report, or choose from the Range drop-down list.

Choose the **items** to include in the report.

Choose the **Summary** or **Detail** option.

Click **OK**. **Close** the **display** when you have finished.

Inventory Transaction Reports

The Transaction Report summarizes inventory activity according to the journal used to record the transaction.

> **PRO VERSION**
> Item Assembly is the Journal name in the Pro version instead of Bill of Materials & Item Assembly, and Adjustments replaces Adjustments and Transfers.

Click **Transaction Summary**. **Click Modify This Report**:

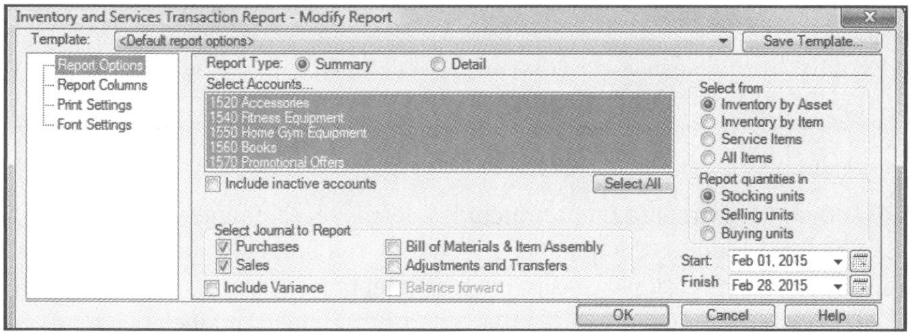

Or choose the Reports menu, then choose Inventory & Services and click Transaction to display the report options.

The report includes details on the number of transactions (Summary option only), the **Quantity In** (increases to inventory from purchases, sales returns, recovery of lost items or assembled items) and **Out** (decreases in inventory from sales, purchase returns, losses and adjustments or assembly components used) and the **Amount In** and **Out** (cost price) for each item chosen in each of the selected journals.

The **Summary** option, the default, includes totals for the selected inventory items organized by item. The **Detail** option provides the same information listed by individual journal entry, including the source document numbers and journal entry numbers.

As in the Sales Report, you can prepare a report for one or more asset groups, one or more inventory items, one or more service items or a combination of services and items (All Items). Clicking the appropriate entry in the Select From list will expand the selection list accordingly.

Quantities may be reported in stocking, buying or selling units. Variances can also be added to the report when they are used.

> **NOTES**
> You can drill down to the Transaction Detail Report from the Transaction Summary Report. You can display the Inventory Ledger and Journal Report from the Transaction Detail Report. You can also view invoices from the Detail Report.

You can choose to show the Balance Forward and include opening balances or to Include Variance and add cost variances for each item.

Click **Detail** to include individual transaction details.

Enter the **Start** and **Finish dates** you want for the report. By default, the earliest transaction and session date appear.

Click the **journals** to include in the report.

Click **OK**. **Close** the **display** when you have finished.

Supplier Purchases Reports

The next two reports combine inventory information with supplier or customer details to show how purchases are spread among suppliers and how sales are divided among customers. The Supplier Purchases and Customer Sales reports also allow you to include information for non-inventory purchases or sales.

Click **Payables** in the Select A Report Type list.

Click **Supplier Purchases Summary**. **Click** **Modify This Report**:

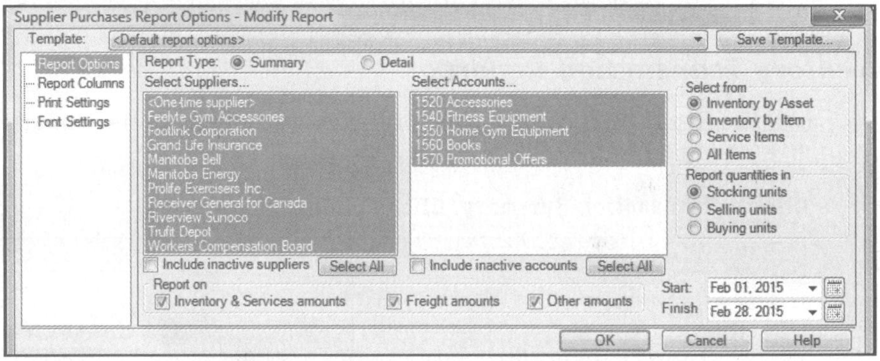

Or choose the Reports menu and choose Payables and click Supplier Purchases.

The Supplier Purchases report includes details on the number of transactions (Summary option only), the quantity purchased, the unit cost and the total cost of the purchase. Non-inventory purchases, such as telephone services, are listed as **Other**.

The **Summary** option organizes the report by supplier and includes totals for the selected categories and items or asset group. The **Detail** option provides the same information by individual journal entry, including the source document numbers and journal entry numbers. Click Detail to choose the Detail option.

When other currencies are used, amounts for foreign suppliers may be shown in either the home currency or the foreign currency.

The selection of inventory, services or asset groups is the same as for the other inventory reports. Reports can be prepared for either stocking, buying or selling units if these are different.

All items and suppliers are selected initially.

Click a **supplier name** or item to begin a new selection.

Enter the **starting** and **ending dates** for the report in the Start and Finish fields.

Click a purchase category — Inventory & Services, non-inventory (Other Amounts) and Freight Amounts — to remove the ✓ and deselect it for the selected supplier and item transactions. Click it again to select it.

Click **OK**. **Close** the **display** when you have finished.

PRO VERSION
This report is named the Vendor Purchases Report.

NOTES
You cannot sort or filter the Supplier Purchases Report, but you can select the columns you want in the report.

NOTES
You can drill down to the Inventory Purchases Detail Report from the Purchases Summary Report. You can view invoices or display the Supplier Aged and Purchases Journal Report from the Purchases Detail Report.

NOTES
To select multiple items, press and hold ctrl and then click the items or suppliers you want to add to the report.

NOTES
Inventory & Services Amounts will be automatically selected whenever you select an item.

Customer Sales Reports

The Customer Sales Report provides the same details as the Inventory Sales Report, but organizes the details by customer as well as by item. Customer Sales reports also have the option to include non-inventory sales.

Click **Receivables** in the Select A Report Type list.

Click **Customer Sales Summary**. **Click** **Modify This Report**:

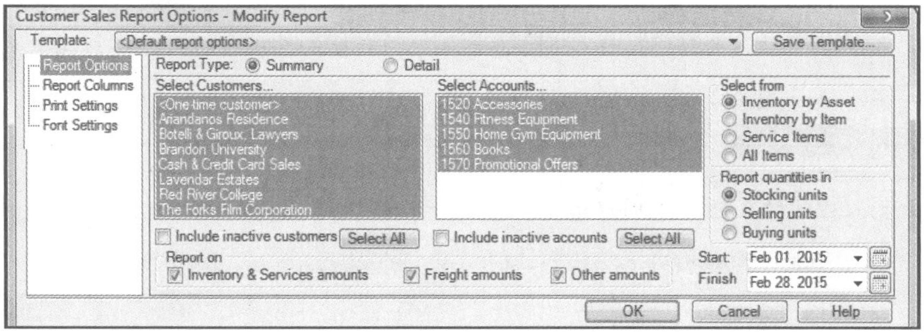

Or choose the Reports menu and choose Receivables and click Customer Sales.

The report includes the number of transactions (Summary option only), the quantity of items sold, the total revenue per item, the cost of goods sold, the profit on the item's sales and the markup or margin. Non-inventory sales, such as sales allowances or non-inventory services, are listed as **Other Amounts**. In Chapter 6, only the customer list was included because there were no inventory items (see page 192).

The **Summary** option organizes the report by customer and includes totals for the selected categories and items or asset groups. The **Detail** option provides the same information listed by individual journal entry, including the source document numbers and journal entry numbers. Click Detail to choose the Detail option. Reports can be prepared for stocking, buying or selling units if these are different. All customers and items are selected initially.

Select **assets**, **inventory** or **services**, **customers**, **dates** and **categories** as you do for Supplier Purchases reports.

Click **OK**. **Close** the **display** when you have finished.

Gross Margin Income Statement

This financial report becomes relevant when a business sells inventory. The report shows the income after inventory costs have been deducted from revenue and before operating expenses are included. This report is available from the Financials report types list.

Click **Financials** in the Select A Report Type list.

Click the ⊞ beside **Income Statement** to expand the list.

Click **Gross Margin - Standard (under Income Statement)**.

Click **Modify This Report** to open the report options window:

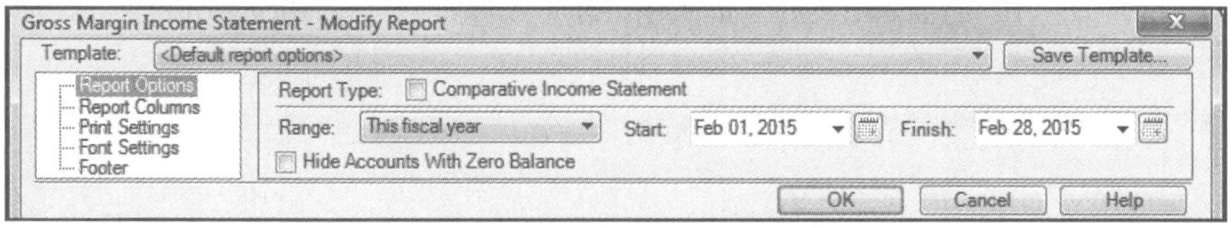

Or choose the Reports menu, then choose Financials and click Gross Margin Income Statement to display the report options.

NOTES
You cannot sort or filter the Customer Sales Report, but you can select the columns you want in the report.

NOTES
If any item is selected, Inventory & Services Amounts will be automatically selected.

NOTES
You can drill down to the Inventory Sales Detail Report from the Customer Sales Summary Report. You can drill down to the Customer Aged and Journal reports from the Detail Report and look up the sales invoice.

WARNING!
You must assign the correct account classes to expense accounts to generate the Gross Margin Income Statement. Cost of Goods Sold accounts must be correctly identified and separated from other types of expenses.

NOTES
Refer to page 56 for details on the Comparative Income Statement.

The report will include different income amounts: gross margin (revenue minus cost of goods sold, before taking into account the other operating expenses), income from operations (operating expenses are deducted from the gross margin) and net income (non-operating revenue and other expenses are entered).

The options for this Income Statement are the same as for regular Income Statements, including the option to generate a Comparative Income Statement.

Enter the **Start** and **Finish dates** you want for the report.

Click **OK**. **Close** the **display** when you have finished.

Displaying Forecast & Analysis Reports

PRO VERSION
Forecast and Analysis Reports and Retail Reports (in the Reports menu) are not available in the Pro version.

This group of reports provides more detailed information about performance and trends.

Click **Forecast & Analysis** in the Select A Report Type list:

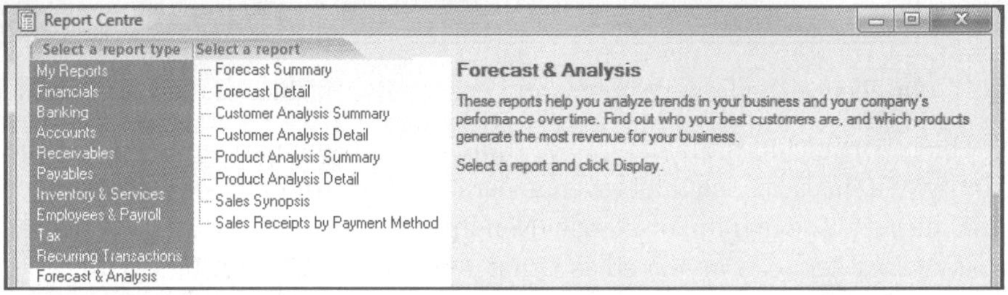

Displaying the Forecast Report

The report will provide monthly forecasts for revenues and expenses, based on the same month in the previous year. This report requires data for more than one year, so you will be unable to view this report for Flabuless Fitness data.

Click **Forecast Summary** and then **click** **Modify This Report**:

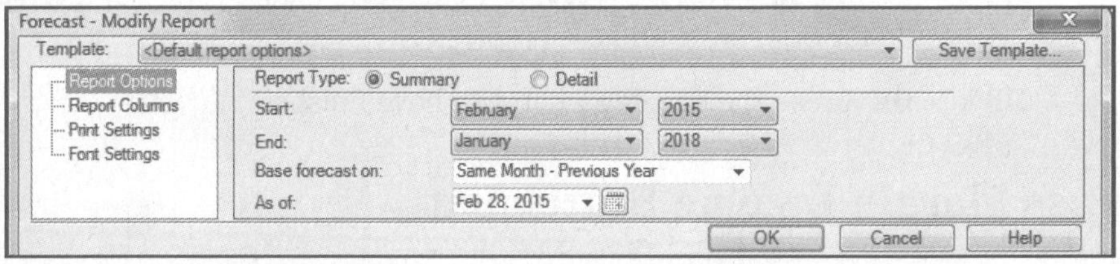

Choose the **months** for which you want the forecast and the date for the report.

Click **OK**. **Close** the **display** when you have finished.

Displaying the Customer Analysis Report

From this report, you can observe the customer sales for the fiscal year to date to see which customers account for the most sales. You can show the customers in the top or bottom x percent, rank them according to revenue, profit, quantity or return on investment (ROI), and you can select the items you want to report on.

Click **Customer Analysis Summary** and then **click Modify This Report**:

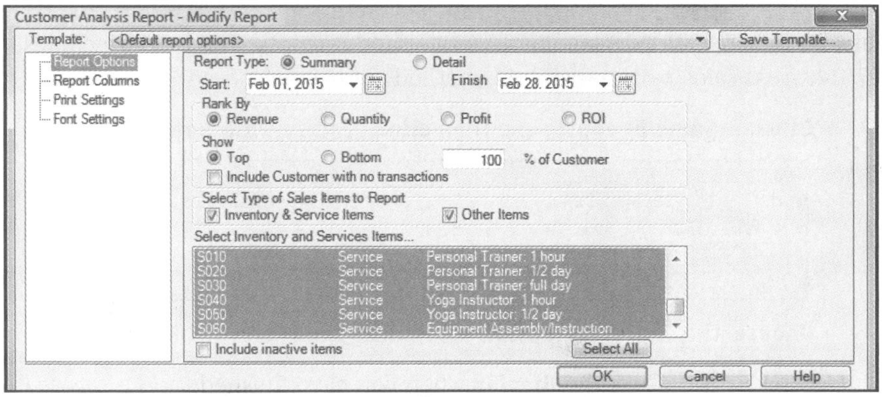

The Detail Report shows individual journal entries while the summary has total amounts.

Choose the **reporting period**, **ranking criteria**, **percentage** and **items**.

Click **OK**. **Close** the **display** when you have finished.

Displaying the Product Analysis Report

The Product Analysis Report is similar to the Customer Analysis Report but organized primarily by product (items and services). You can select the customers to include. Again, you can rank the sales according to revenues, quantity sold, profit and return on investment. You can choose whether to report on the top x percent or the bottom x percent of items.

Click **Product Analysis Summary** and then **click Modify This Report**:

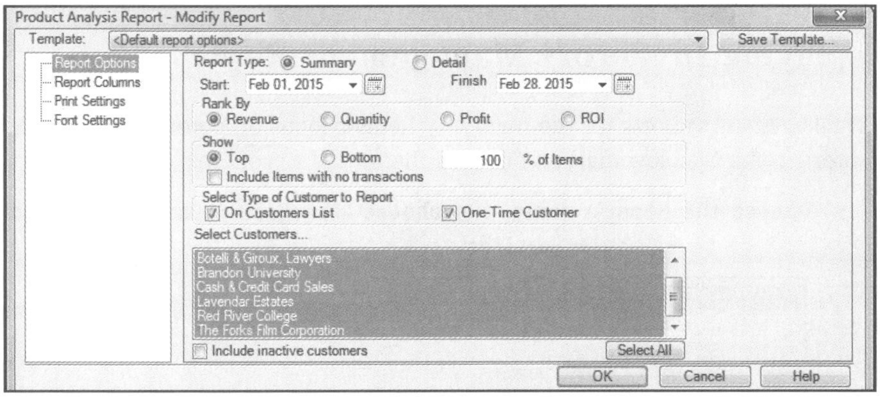

This report also has both a Summary and Detail version. Detail Reports shows individual journal entries while the summary has total amounts.

Choose **reporting period**, **ranking criteria**, **percentage** and **customers**.

Click **OK**. **Close** the **display** when you have finished.

NOTES

From the Home window Reports menu, you can choose Retail Reports (or the <industry type> Reports) and click either Customer Analysis – Top 20% By Profit, or Customer Analysis – Bottom 30% By Profit to see the report options.

The options screen will show the selections named in the menu report title (e.g., top 20%), but you can change the selections as you do in any report options window.

NOTES

You can drill down to the Detail Report from the Customer Analysis Summary Report. From the Detail Report, you can drill down to the Customer Sales Detail Report.

NOTES

From the Home window Reports menu, you can choose Retail Reports (or the <industry type> Reports) and click either Product Analysis – Top 20% Of Active Sales By ROI, or Product Analysis – Bottom 30% Of Sales Including Zero Sales By ROI to see the report options.

The options screen will show the selections named in the menu report title (e.g., top 30%), but you can change the selections as you do in any report options window.

In the Product Analysis Report, ROI (return on investment) is measured as the profit divided by the average inventory value.

NOTES

You can drill down to the Detail Report from the Product Analysis Summary Report. From the Detail Report, you can drill down to the Inventory & Services Sales Detail Report.

Displaying the Sales Synopsis Report

The Sales Synopsis Report summarizes sales and receipts. The report includes the items sold, the gross sales per item and the methods of payment used.

Click **Sales Synopsis** and then **click Modify This Report**:

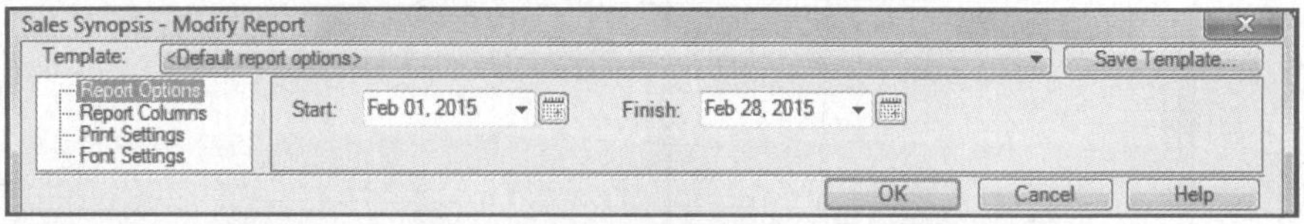

Choose the **reporting period**. Customize the report columns to select details.

Click **OK**. **Close** the **display** when you have finished.

Displaying Sales Receipts by Payment Method Reports

The final forecast and analysis report summarizes the sales according to the customer payment methods, that is, by cash, by credit card or on account (pay later).

Click **Sales Receipts by Payment Method** and then **click Modify This Report**:

Choose the **reporting period**. Customize the report columns to select details.

Click **OK**. **Close** the **display** when you have finished. **Close** the **Report Centre**.

Displaying Inventory Management Reports

The management reports for the Inventory Ledger focus on potential problem items, inventory items with low markup or items that are not profitable.

Choose the **Reports menu**, then **choose Management Reports** and **click Inventory & Services**:

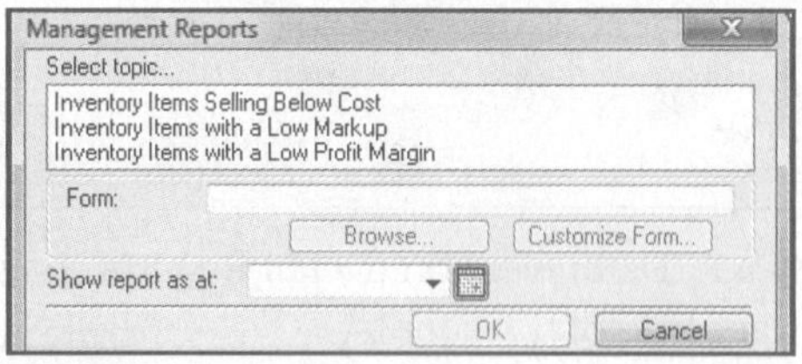

Select a **report** from the list and choose the report form if necessary.

Click **OK** to view the report. **Close** the **display** when you have finished.

NOTES
From the Home window Reports menu, choose Retail Reports and click Daily Sales Summary to see the report options window.
You can drill down to the Inventory & Services Transaction Report from the Sales Synopsis Report.

NOTES
From the Home window Reports menu, choose Retail Reports and click Daily Sales Receipts to see the report options window.

NOTES
To print inventory reports, display the report you want.
Click the Reports & Forms Settings tool to check your printer settings.
Choose the File menu and click Print. Close the display when finished.

NOTES
You cannot access Management Reports from the Report Centre.

CLASSIC VIEW
You can also access Management Reports from the Advice tool in the Classic view Home window tool bar.

NOTES
Flabuless currently has no products that meet the Inventory Management Reports' criteria, so there will be no data included in these reports.

REVIEW

The Student DVD with Data Files includes Review Questions and Supplementary Cases for this chapter.

CHAPTER ELEVEN

Andersson Chiropractic Clinic

OBJECTIVES

After completing this chapter, you should be able to

- ***track*** additional information for receipts, sales and purchases
- ***place*** and ***fill*** supplier orders and quotes
- ***enter*** and ***fill*** sales quotes and orders
- ***convert*** sales and purchase quotes to orders
- ***adjust*** orders and quotes
- ***enter*** debit card sale transactions
- ***make*** payments and deposits using multiple bank accounts and a line of credit
- ***enter*** deposits from customers and prepayments to suppliers
- ***enter*** deposits and prepayments on orders
- ***delete*** stored transactions
- ***remove*** quotes
- ***enter*** transactions from the Daily Business Manager

COMPANY INFORMATION

Company Profile

NOTES
Andersson Chiropractic Clinic
4500 Rae St.
Regina, SK S4S 3B4
Tel 1: (306) 577-1900
Tel 2: (306) 577-2199
Fax: (306) 577-1925
Business No.: 459 556 291

Andersson Chiropractic Clinic is a private clinic owned by Maria Andersson, who practises her profession in Regina, Saskatchewan. This is her second year in private practice after graduating with D.C. (Doctor of Chiropractic) and D.Ac. (Doctor of Acupuncture) degrees. She used some bank loans and her line of credit to consolidate her student loans and set up the clinic.

Andersson specializes in sports injuries and has some sports teams as clients. To treat patients, she uses chiropractic treatments and adjustments for back pain, and physiotherapy, massage, ultrasound, laser treatments, electrical stimulation and acupuncture for other joint and soft tissue injuries. Individual regular patients usually come two or three times per week, although some come daily. These patients settle their accounts bi-weekly. Sports teams have contracts and are billed monthly. Contract customers are offered a discount if they settle their accounts within 10 days. Cash, cheques and debit cards are accepted in payment.

A single assistant in the clinic divides her time between reception, administration and some basic treatments such as laser and ultrasound under the chiropractor's supervision. Andersson designates the precise area to be treated and the time and intensity settings for the equipment.

The office space that Andersson rents has a reception area and four treatment rooms with tables. The monthly rent includes heat but not hydro or telephone. One of the four treatment rooms doubles as Andersson's office and another room has the potential to accommodate a whirlpool. She is considering adding a whirlpool for hydrotherapy and deep water massage treatments because some sports injuries respond well to hydrotherapy.

For new sports team contracts, Andersson prepares sales quotes. When new customers accept a contract, they pay a deposit that is applied to the first month's payment.

Andersson has two bank accounts and a line of credit she uses to pay her bills. The limit on her line of credit is $50 000, and she has already borrowed $15 000 against it. A third bank account is used exclusively for debit card transactions.

Accounts for regular suppliers of treatment equipment, linens, laundry services, office maintenance and so on are set up. Some of these suppliers also offer discounts for early payments and some require Andersson to make prepayments with purchase orders.

No taxes are charged for medical treatment and supplies. Because GST is not charged to customers the business is not eligible for a GST refund. Therefore tax amounts are not tracked — they are included with the expense or asset amounts. Andersson pays both PST and GST for other goods and services.

To convert her accounting records to Sage 50 on October 1, 2015, she used the following information:

- Chart of Accounts
- Trial Balance
- Supplier Information
- Patient/Customer Information
- Accounting Procedures

CHART OF POSTABLE ACCOUNTS

ANDERSSON CHIROPRACTIC CLINIC

ASSETS
1060 Bank: Regina Chequing
1080 Bank: Eastside Chequing
1100 Bank: Interac
1200 Accounts Receivable
1220 Prepaid Insurance
1240 Prepaid Subscriptions
1280 Purchase Prepayments
1300 Linen Supplies
1320 Office Supplies
1340 Other Supplies
1420 Computer Equipment
1430 Accum Deprec: Computers
1450 Treatment Equipment
1460 Accum Deprec: Equipment
1520 Office Furniture ▶

▶1530 Accum Deprec: Furniture
1550 Treatment Tables
1560 Accum Deprec: Tables
1580 Vehicle
1590 Accum Deprec: Vehicle

LIABILITIES
2100 Loans Payable
2200 Accounts Payable
2250 Prepaid Sales and Deposits
2300 Line of Credit Payable

EQUITY
3400 M.A. Capital
3450 M.A. Drawings
3600 Net Income ▶

▶**REVENUE**
4100 Revenue from Services
4150 Sales Discounts
4200 Interest Income

EXPENSE
5010 Bank Charges and Interac Fees
5030 Purchase Discounts
5050 Office Supplies Used
5060 Other Supplies Used
5080 Subscriptions and Books
5090 Insurance Expense
5100 Interest Expense
5110 Freight Expense
5120 Clinic Maintenance ▶

▶5140 Laundry Services
5150 Professional Dues
5180 Depreciation Expenses
5200 Hydro Expense
5240 Telephone Expense
5260 Rent
5300 Vehicle Expenses
5500 Wages Expense
5520 Payroll Services

NOTES: The Chart of Accounts includes only postable accounts and the Net Income or Current Earnings account.

TRIAL BALANCE

ANDERSSON CHIROPRACTIC CLINIC

September 30, 2015		Debits	Credits
1060	Bank: Regina Chequing	$33 530	
1080	Bank: Eastside Chequing	19 100	
1100	Bank: Interac	3 430	
1200	Accounts Receivable	12 500	
1220	Prepaid Insurance	1 600	
1240	Prepaid Subscriptions	480	
1300	Linen Supplies	1 300	
1320	Office Supplies	270	
1340	Other Supplies	530	
1420	Computer Equipment	4 200	
1430	Accum Deprec: Computers		$ 1 050
1450	Treatment Equipment	12 600	
1460	Accum Deprec: Equipment		2 100
1520	Office Furniture	9 600	
1530	Accum Deprec: Furniture		800
1550	Treatment Tables	8 400	
1560	Accum Deprec: Tables		1 400
1580	Vehicle	22 000	
1590	Accum Deprec: Vehicle		5 500
2100	Loans Payable		45 000
2200	Accounts Payable		7 290
2300	Line of Credit Payable		15 000
3400	M.A. Capital		36 355 ▶
▶ 3450	M.A. Drawings	18 000	
4100	Revenue from Services		114 000
4150	Sales Discounts	140	
4200	Interest Income		160
5010	Bank Charges and Interac Fees	390	
5030	Purchase Discounts		210
5050	Office Supplies Used	350	
5060	Other Supplies Used	1 130	
5080	Subscriptions and Books	2 400	
5090	Insurance Expense	8 000	
5100	Interest Expense	2 500	
5110	Freight Expense	120	
5120	Clinic Maintenance	2 100	
5140	Laundry Services	1 800	
5150	Professional Dues	1 495	
5180	Depreciation Expenses	10 850	
5200	Hydro Expense	1 200	
5240	Telephone Expense	1 100	
5260	Rent	23 000	
5300	Vehicle Expenses	3 300	
5500	Wages Expense	21 000	
5520	Payroll Services	450	
		$228 865	$228 865

SUPPLIER INFORMATION

ANDERSSON CHIROPRACTIC CLINIC

Supplier Name (Contact)	Address	Phone No. Fax No.	E-mail Web Site	Terms
Canadian Chiropractic Association (O. Fisshal)	33 Backer Road Toronto, Ontario M4T 5B2	Tel 1: (416) 488-3713 Tel 2: (888) 488-3713	www.cca.ca	net 10
Cleanol and Laundry Services (Bessie Sweeps)	19 Duster Road Regina, Saskatchewan S4R 4L4	Tel: (306) 398-0908 Fax: (306) 398-8211	bsweeps@cls.com www.cls.com	net 30
Grasslands Fuel				net 1 (cash)
Medical Linen Supplies (Oll Whyte)	500 Agar St. Saskatoon, Saskatchewan S7L 6B9	Tel: (306) 662-6192 Fax: (306) 662-4399	owhyte@medsupplies.com www.medsupplies.com	2/10, n/30
OnLine Books			www.onlinebooks.com	net 1 (cheque)
Prairie Power Corp. (M. Jouls)	48 Powers Bay Regina, Saskatchewan S4X 1N2	Tel: (306) 395-1125	www.prairiepower.ca	net 1
Pro Suites Inc. (Kendra Walls)	19 Tenant Cr. Regina, Saskatchewan S4N 2B1	Tel: (306) 396-6646 Fax: (306) 396-5397	walls@prosuites.com www.prosuites.com	net 1 (first of month)
Sonartek Ltd. (T. Waver)	390 Retallack St. Regina, Saskatchewan S4R 3N3	Tel: (306) 579-7923 Fax: (306) 579-8003	twaver@sonartek.com www.sonartek.com	2/15, n/30
The Papery				net 15
Thera-Tables Inc. (Li Flatte)	60 Flatlands Cr. Saskatoon, Saskatchewan S7K 5B1	Tel: (306) 662-6486 Fax: (306) 662-7910	www.theratables.com	2/5, n/30
Western Communications (V. Du Parler)	99 Listener St. Regina, Saskatchewan S4R 5C9	Tel: (306) 395-5533	www.westcom.ca	net 1

OUTSTANDING SUPPLIER INVOICES

ANDERSSON CHIROPRACTIC CLINIC

Supplier Name	Terms	Date	Invoice No.	Amount	Total
Cleanol and Laundry Services	net 30	Sep. 14/15	CLS-2419	$90	
	net 30	Sep. 28/15	CLS-2683	90	
			Balance owing		$180
Medical Linen Supplies	2/10, n/30	Sep. 26/15	MLS-102		$690
Sonartek Ltd.	2/15, n/30	Sep. 22/15	SL-3456		$6 420
			Grand Total		$7 290

PATIENT INFORMATION

ANDERSSON CHIROPRACTIC CLINIC

Patient Name (Contact)	Address	Phone No. Fax No.	E-mail Web Site	Terms Credit Limit
Albert Blackfoot	16 Prairie Bay Regina, Saskatchewan S4N 6V3	Tel: (306) 582-1919	ablackfoot@shaw.ca	net 15 $500
Canadian Royals (K. Player)	1910 Buckingham St. Regina, Saskatchewan S4S 2P3	Tel: (306) 578-4567 Fax: (306) 578-7382	kplayer@canroyals.com www.canroyals.com	1/10, n/30 $5 000
Interplay Ballet School (S. Lightly)	2755 Flamenco St. Regina, Saskatchewan S4V 8C1	Tel: (306) 396-6190 Fax: (306) 396-8186	lightly@lighterthanair.com www.lighterthanair.com	1/10, n/30 $5 000
Roughrider Argos (B. Ball)	2935 Fowler St. Regina, Saskatchewan S4V 1N5	Tel: (306) 399-8000 Fax: (306) 399-8115	www.proball.com/ra	1/10, n/30 $5 000
Suzanne Lejeune	301 Pasqua St. Regina, Saskatchewan S4R 4M8	Tel: (306) 573-6296	slejeune@hotmail.com	net 15 $500

OUTSTANDING PATIENT INVOICES

ANDERSSON CHIROPRACTIC CLINIC

Patient Name	Terms	Date	Invoice No.	Amount	Total
Canadian Royals	1/10, n/30	Sep. 29/15	#638	$4 500	$4 500
Interplay Ballet School	1/10, n/30	Sep. 26/15	#632	$3 100	$3 100
Roughrider Argos	1/10, n/30	Sep. 29/15	#639	$4 900	$4 900
			Grand Total		$12 500

Accounting Procedures

Taxes

Since medical services are not taxable, patients do not pay GST or PST on the treatments and GST paid is not refundable. Therefore, no taxes have been set up in the data files, and no tax options are available in the journal Tax fields. Andersson pays provincial tax at the rate of 5 percent and GST at 5 percent on normal purchases — medical equipment is not taxed. All prices are shown with taxes included, but taxes are not recorded separately — they are included with the expense or asset part of purchases.

Cash and Debit Card Sales

Andersson's individual patients frequently pay by Interac or debit card. Sales invoice amounts are deposited directly to the linked bank account. For this service, Andersson pays a small fee to the bank for each transaction, as well as a monthly rental fee for the terminal. These fees are deducted from the account periodically and are not deducted from deposits for individual transactions. Debit card transactions are summarized and recorded every two weeks.

Payroll

Andersson's assistant is paid a monthly salary through arrangements with the bank. In lieu of a salary, Andersson draws $2 500 per month from her net income.

Discounts

Customers (sports teams) who have contracts with Andersson are offered a 1 percent discount if they pay their accounts in full within 10 days. Full payment is requested within 30 days. Individual patients are asked to pay their accounts every two weeks. Some suppliers also offer discounts for early payments.

All discount terms are set up in the customer and supplier records.

Deposits

When sports team managers sign new contracts for regular monthly billing for treating the team members, they pay a deposit to Andersson. Similarly, some suppliers ask for a deposit or prepayment when Andersson places a large order.

Revenue and Expense Accounts

The customer records for Andersson Chiropractic Clinic are set up with *Revenue from Services* as the default account. For suppliers, the account most often associated with purchases for a supplier has been entered as the default for that supplier.

Bank Accounts and Line of Credit

Andersson has two chequing accounts for deposits and payments. A third bank account is used for all Interac or debit card payments.

Andersson also uses her line of credit when making payments by cheque. At the end of each month, Andersson makes a payment for the interest owing on the line of credit used. When she has the funds, she also pays down the principal owing.

All cheque numbers are updated automatically when the correct account is selected.

INSTRUCTIONS

1. **Record entries for the source documents** in Sage 50 using the Chart of Accounts, Supplier Information, Patient Information and Accounting Procedures for Andersson Chiropractic Clinic. The procedures for entering each new type of transaction in this application are outlined step by step in the Keystrokes section with the source documents.
2. **Print** the **reports and graphs** indicated on the following printing form after you have finished making your entries.

NOTES

The terms Patient and Customer will be used interchangeably in this chapter. Sage 50 applies the label Patient for Customer in medical companies. For sports teams, we will use the term Customer unless the program displays the term Patient on the screen.

NOTES

All discounts are calculated on the full invoice amounts. For purchases, these amounts include taxes.

NOTES

The line of credit is set up as a liability account (the money is owed to the bank), but the Bank class is applied so that the account can be selected in journals to write cheques and deposit receipts. The amount of credit available does not appear on the Balance Sheet or Trial Balance. It is usually added as a Note to the financial statements.

REPORTS

Accounts
- ☐ Chart of Accounts
- ☐ Account List
- ☐ General Journal Entries

Financials
- ☑ Comparative Balance Sheet: amounts only for Oct. 31, 2015, and Nov. 30, 2015
- ☑ Income Statement from Dec. 1, 2014, to Nov. 30, 2015
- ☑ Comparative Trial Balance: amounts only for Nov. 30 and Dec. 1, 2015
- ☑ All Journal Entries: Oct. 1 to Nov. 30
- ☐ General Ledger
- ☑ Statement of Cash Flows from Oct. 1 to Nov. 30
- ☑ Cash Flow Projection Detail Report for accounts 1060 and 1080 for 30 days

Taxes
- ☐ Tax

Banking
- ☐ Cheque Log Report

Payables
- ☐ Supplier List
- ☑ Supplier Aged Detail for all suppliers
- ☐ Aged Overdue Payables
- ☐ Expenses Journal Entries
- ☐ Payments Journal Entries
- ☑ Pending Supplier Orders as at Jan. 15, 2016

Receivables
- ☐ Patient List
- ☑ Patient Aged Detail for all customers
- ☐ Aged Overdue Receivables
- ☐ Patient Statements
- ☐ Fees Journal Entries
- ☐ Receipts Journal Entries
- ☑ Pending Patient Orders as at Jan. 15, 2016

Mailing Labels
- ☐ Labels

Management Reports
- ☐ Ledger

GRAPHS
- ☐ Payables by Aging Period
- ☐ Payables by Supplier
- ☐ Receivables by Aging Period
- ☐ Receivables by Patient
- ☑ Fees vs Receivables
- ☑ Receivables Due vs Payables Due
- ☐ Revenues by Account
- ☐ Expenses by Account
- ☑ Expenses and Net Profit as % of Revenue

NOTES

From the backup file, restore SageData13\andersson1.CAB or andersson1 to SageData13\Andersson\andersson to open the data files for Andersson. Refer to Chapter 1, page 22, if you need assistance.

NOTES

The Payroll, Inventory and Project modules are not included in the Modules pane – they are hidden because these ledgers are not used and are not set up.

PRO VERSION

Vendors replaces the term Suppliers. Purchase Quotes, Purchase Orders and Purchase Invoices are used as the Home window icon labels for tasks.

Click the Purchase Quotes icon to open the journal.

KEYSTROKES

Opening Data Files

Open **SageData13\Andersson\andersson** to access the data files for Andersson. **Enter** **Oct 7, 2015** as the Session date.

Entering a Purchase Quote

On October 1, Andersson received two quotes for a treatment table that will be delivered later in the month. A quote usually provides a guaranteed price for some work or products. The offer is often limited to a stated time period. If the business chooses to accept the offer, the quote may be filled as a purchase for immediate delivery or converted to a purchase order for future delivery. When the goods are received, or the work is completed, the quote is filled and the purchase is completed. Supplier quotes are entered and filled in the Expenses or Purchases Journal.

✓ 1 **Purchase Quote #TT-44** **Dated October 1, 2015**

Delivery date October 10, 2015
From Thera-Tables Inc., $4 000 including taxes for custom-built adjustable height treatment table with drop ends. Terms: 2/5, n/30. Deposit of 10 percent required on accepting quote.

Click **Payables** in the Modules pane list. Icons are added for quotes and orders.

Click the **Supplier Quotes icon** shown in the following screen:

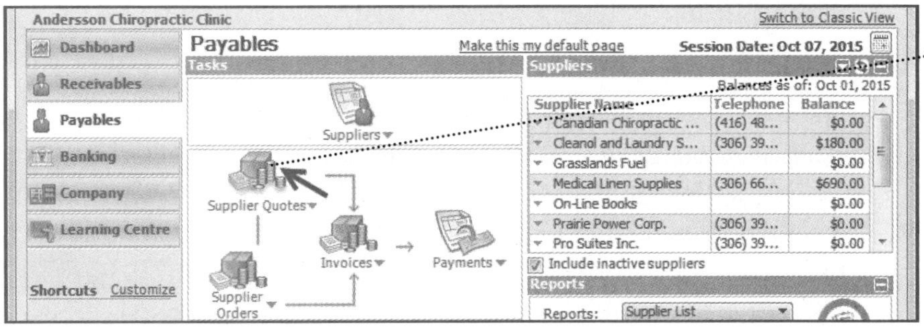

The Expenses Journal – Creating A Quote window opens:

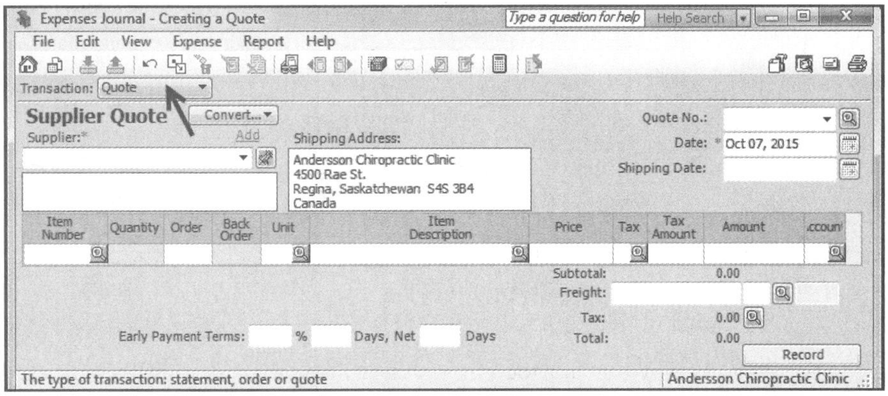

Quote is selected in the Transaction field.

Click the **Supplier field** and **select Thera-Tables Inc.**

Click the **Quote No.** field to advance the cursor and skip the address fields.

Type TT-44

Press tab **twice** to advance to the Date field.

Type 10-1-15

Press tab **twice** to advance to the Shipping Date field.

This is the date on which the order is to be received or the work is to be completed. Sometimes, instead of shipping date, we use the term delivery date for services or starting date for a contract because these terms are more appropriate for quotes and orders for services.

Type 10-10

The Item Number field refers to the code for inventory items. The Quantity (quantity received with this purchase) field will remain blank because this is not a purchase and no goods are received. However, you must enter the number of units that are ordered. You cannot leave the Order field blank. One table is being ordered.

Click the **Order field.**

Type 1

Press tab to advance to the Unit field that also applies to inventory.

Press tab to advance to the Item Description field.

Type custom-built treatment table

Press tab to advance to the Price field. This field refers to the unit price of the items. You must enter a price in order to fill the order later.

CLASSIC VIEW

Click the Expenses, Orders & Quotes icon 

to open the journal. Choose Quote from the journal's Transaction drop-down list.

NOTES

For Medical companies, Sage 50 uses the term Expenses Journal instead of Purchases Journal.

NOTES

Notice that Andersson's address is in the Shipping Address field for the quote.

NOTES

You must choose the supplier before entering the quote number because the supplier issues the quote number.

PRO VERSION

Purchases Journal – Creating A Quote appears in the journal's title bar. The term Vendor replaces Supplier.

The default tabbing order after the Vendor address fields is Date, Quote No. and Shipping Date. After entering the quote number, the cursor advances to the Shipping Date.

NOTES

You cannot access the Quantity field for quotes. This field and the Back Order field are dimmed.

NOTES

In a purchase order, the Back Order quantity field is filled in automatically with the order quantity. In a quote, this field remains blank.

NOTES
If you want, you can customize the journal by removing the columns that are not required. Refer to page 162.
You can remove (do not show) the Item Number, Unit, Tax Code and Tax Amount fields because they are not needed.

Type 4000

Press tab to advance to the Tax field.

Because taxes are not used in this data set, we can skip the tax fields. The amount is entered automatically as the quantity on order times the unit price.

The account is also entered automatically from the supplier's ledger record, so the quote is complete as shown:

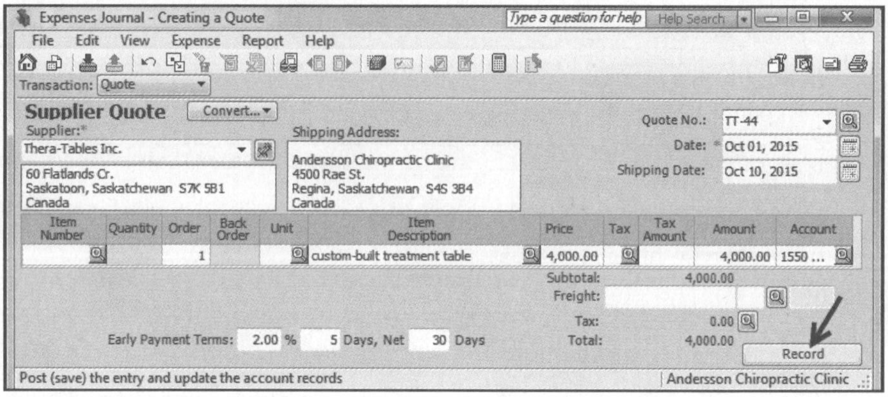

NOTES
Refer to page 114 if you need help correcting the entry.

Check your **work** carefully and **make** any **corrections** necessary just as you do for Purchases Journal entries.

If you try to display the Journal entry, you will see that there is no journal entry associated with the quote. The Record button replaces Post for quotes (and orders). The related journal entry will be completed when the quote is filled and the purchase is completed. When you are sure that the entry is correct, you should record it.

NOTES
The Record button label replaces Post for quotes and orders because no journal entry is posted.

Click the **Record button** Record or **choose** the **Expense menu** and **click** **Record** to save your transaction. **Click OK** to confirm successful recording.

If you forgot to enter the quantity ordered, you will see the following warning:

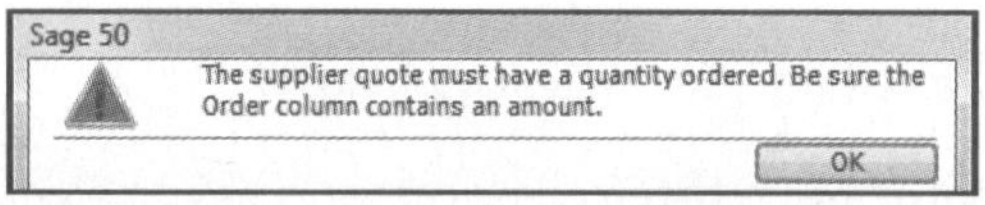

Click OK. Enter the quantity in the Order field and try again to record.

Enter the **second purchase quote** from a new supplier. Remember to add the account number and payment terms to the quote.

NOTES
Notice that Continue is not an option when you add a new supplier for a quote.

2	**Purchase Quote #MT-511**	**Dated October 1, 2015**
	Delivery date October 20, 2015 From Medi-Tables (use Quick Add for the new supplier), $4 550 including all taxes for custom-built treatment table. Terms: net 20. Deposit of 20 percent required on accepting quote.	

Placing a Purchase Order from a Quote

NOTES
We will use the terms purchase order and supplier order interchangeably, unless the term appears in the Sage 50 screen.

Sometimes purchase orders are entered without a quote and sometimes they are converted from a purchase quote. Entering a purchase order directly, without the quote, is the same as entering a purchase quote except that you choose Order as the type of transaction instead of Quote.

The purchase order to Thera-Tables Inc. is a quote converted to an order. The Expenses Journal should still be open and Quote is selected as the Transaction type.

✓ 3

Purchase Order #TT-44 **Dated October 2, 2015**

Delivery date October 10, 2015
To Thera-Tables Inc., $4 000 including taxes for custom-built treatment table.
Terms: 2/5, n/30. Convert quote #TT-44 to purchase order #TT-44.

Click the **Quote No. field list arrow** as shown:

The drop-down list includes all unfilled purchase quotes and purchase orders. The two quotes entered above are listed.

Click **TT-44** to select it.

Press *tab* to select the quote and place it on-screen.

You can change the order to a quote in different ways.

Click the **Convert list arrow** to see conversion options as shown:

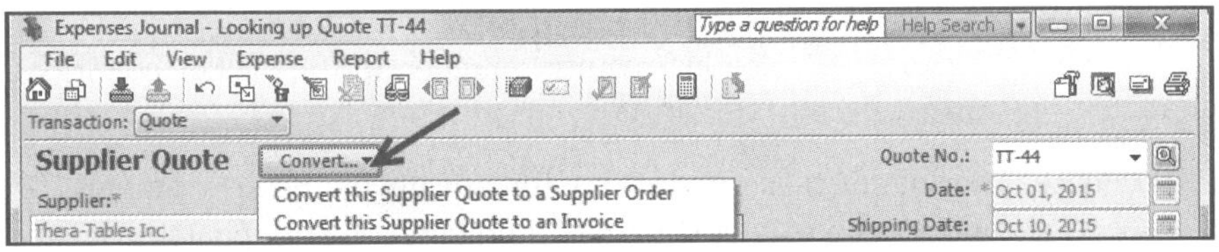

You can convert the quote to an order or directly to an invoice from this menu. Or

Click the **Transaction list arrow** to see the transaction types as shown:

Click **Convert This Supplier Quote To A Supplier Order** from the Convert drop-down list, or

Click **Order** from the Transaction type drop-down list.

The quote screen changes to an order. Order No. replaces Quote No. as the field label:

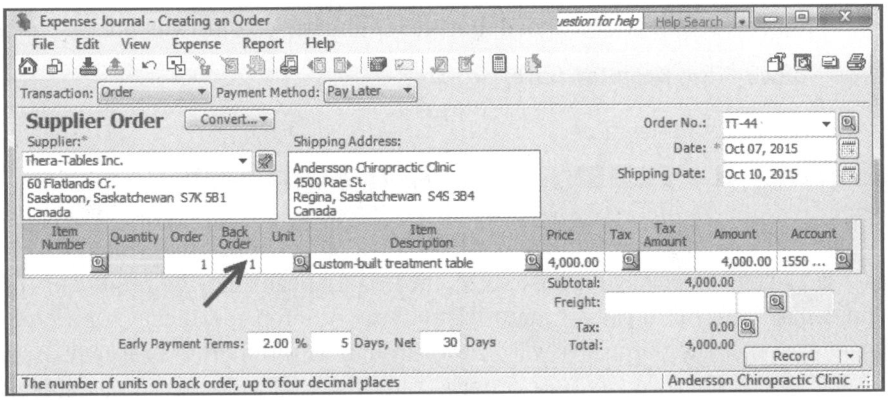

Notice that the purchase order includes a Payment Method field. You can enter prepayments with the order. We show this method of entering prepayments on page 420.

The Order quantity has been copied to the Back Order field. Creating An Order replaces Looking Up Quote in the title bar.

PRO VERSION

Click Convert This Purchase Quote To A Purchase Order from the Convert drop-down list.

NOTES

The Project/Division module is hidden for Andersson because it is not needed, but when used, the term Partner will replace Division or Project for medical companies.

NOTES

The Record button replaces Post because the order does not generate a journal entry.

The session date is entered on the revised form, so we need to change it. If you try to change the quote number, you will see the warning (see margin Notes):

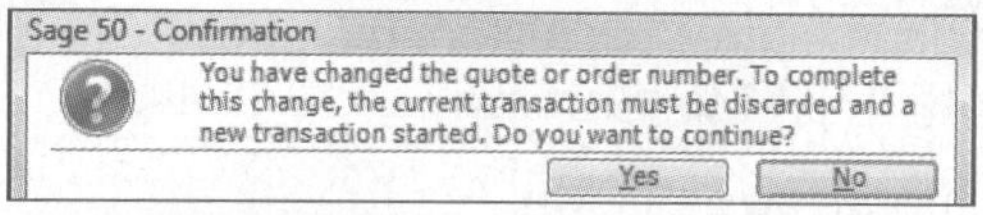

Click No to restore the original quote number.

Click the **Date field Calendar icon**. **Choose October 2**. **Press** tab.

Click the **Record button** Record.

The Record button now includes the option to print on its drop-down list. Print & Record may be selected as the default, just like the Post & Print option for cash purchases and sales.

The program displays the warning message:

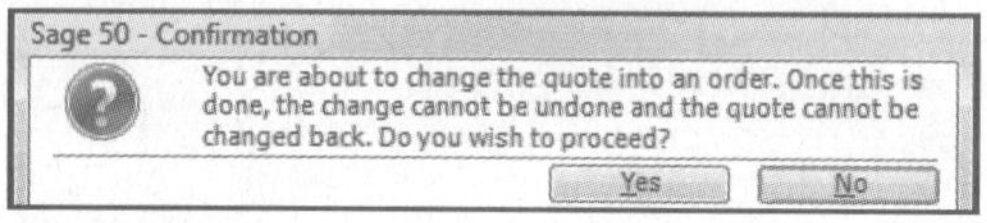

Since we want to convert the quote to an order, we can proceed. The order will replace the quote.

Click **Yes** and **OK**. No journal entry number appears in the confirmation message.

Purchase order numbers are updated automatically by the program, just like sales invoice and cheque numbers. (Alphanumeric numbers are not updated.) If the number for the quote that you are converting is larger than the next purchase order sequence number, a second warning will appear when you record the order because the number is out of sequence. Sage 50 will ask if you want to update your sequence starting number:

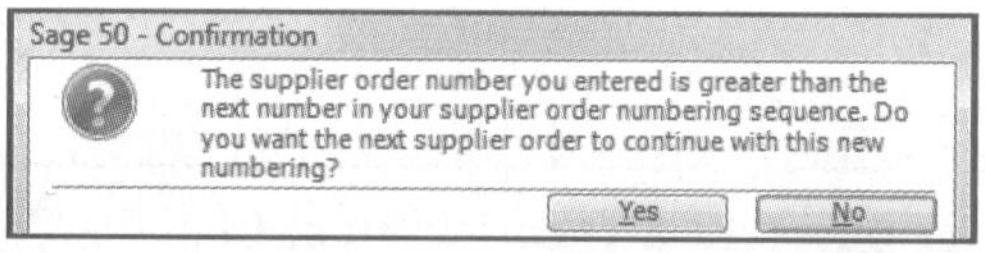

This does not apply to the alphanumeric number we used.

Click Yes if you want to reset the numbering sequence for future purchase orders. Click No to avoid resetting the automatic sequence to the higher number. When you choose No, the higher purchase order number will still be recorded, and later skipped, but the automatic counter will not be changed.

Close the **Supplier Order window**.

Making a Prepayment to a Supplier

Businesses frequently request a deposit — down payment or prepayment — when an order is placed, especially for customized orders. Deposits may be refundable or not. A deposit may be used to pay for materials that are ordered specifically for a project; it may ensure that the purchaser will follow through with the order or it may provide the supplier with some revenue if the order is cancelled and part of the deposit is not refundable.

Prepayments can be made in the Payments Journal or in the Supplier Order Journal window. If the prepayment accompanies the order, you should enter it on the Order form. This prepayment is made later, so we will enter it in the Payments Journal.

NOTES
To change the number of a purchase order to match the number sequence on preprinted forms, you should
- Recall the quote
- Choose the Adjust Quote tool (adjust purchase quotes in the same way as sales quotes – see page 416)
- Change the quote number
- Record the revised quote
- Recall the quote
- Convert the quote to an order by choosing Order from the Transaction list or by choosing Convert to an Order from the Convert drop-down list
- Record the purchase order
- Confirm the conversion
- Check that the order sequence number is correct and update the next order number if necessary

NOTES
We will not continue the instruction to confirm successful posting or recording.

WARNING!
The order will be posted whether you choose Yes or No in the message about updating the order number.

NOTES
If you choose not to reset the number sequence, the higher order number will be skipped in the automatic numbering sequence when you reach it.

NOTES
Entering a prepayment on the Supplier Order form is shown on page 420.

✓ 4

Payment Cheque #567 **Dated October 3, 2015**

To Thera-Tables Inc., $400 from Regina Chequing account as prepayment in acceptance of quote #TT-44 and to confirm order #TT-44.

Click the **Payments icon** to open the Payments Journal.

Click the **Enter Supplier Prepayments tool** or **choose** the **Payment menu** and **click Enter Prepayments**.

This tool button/menu option acts as a switch that opens the fields for deposits:

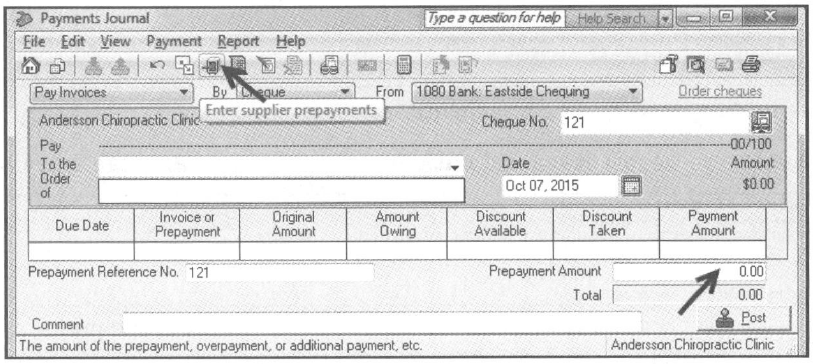

You can leave this tool selected so that the optional fields will always be available.

Two new fields are added to the journal: one for the **prepayment reference number** and one for the **amount**. The reference number is the next cheque number in sequence for the selected bank account and is updated automatically by the program. The rest of the journal is the same as before, but the invoice payment lines are not used. Outstanding invoices, if there are any, will be included in the journal.

When the payment is made by cheque, the **From** field has the list of bank accounts you can choose. The default bank account and cheque number for this payment are not correct. We must change them.

Click the **From field list arrow** to see the list of available bank accounts:

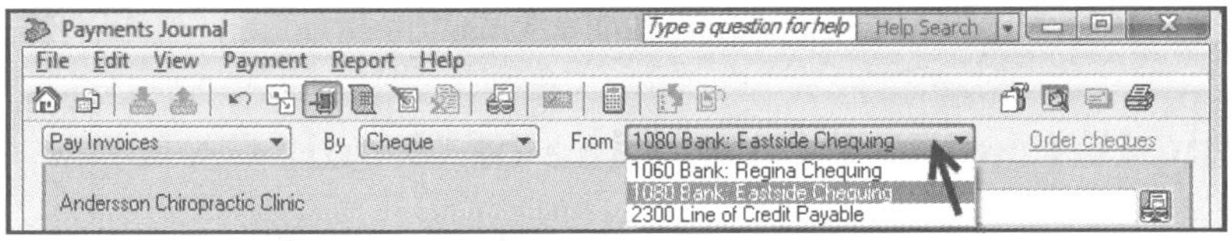

Click **Bank: Regina Chequing**. The cheque number changes.

When you select a different bank account, the cheque number is updated for the new account. Each bank account has its own cheque number sequence, and these numbers are updated as you make payments from each account.

Choose **Thera-Tables Inc.** as the supplier from the drop-down list.

Enter **October 3** as the date of the cheque.

Click the **Prepayment Amount field**.

Type `400`

Click the **Comment field**. Advancing the cursor updates the Total.

Type `Prepayment for order #TT-44`

If an outstanding invoice is paid with the same cheque, enter the invoice payment in the usual way in addition to the deposit amount.

PRO VERSION
Click the Enter Vendor Prepayments tool.

WARNING!
Two bank accounts and the line of credit are available for receipts and payments. Before posting a transaction, check carefully that you have selected the right account.

NOTES
Processing the advance in this way ensures that the advance will appear in the correct supplier account in the Payables Ledger. The manual approach, a General Journal entry that credits the bank account and debits Prepaid Expenses, an asset account, does not show this link with the supplier – the supplier's ledger is updated separately.

> **NOTES**
> You can also use the Prepayment Amount field if you are paying more than the full amount owing for an invoice. You cannot enter an amount in the Payment Amount field greater than the amount owing, but you can record this excess amount as a prepayment.

> **NOTES**
> Notice that the journal entry number (J1) has not increased because of the quotes and order.

> **NOTES**
> For corrections to deposits or prepayments after posting, use the Adjust tool or refer to Appendix C. They can also be reversed, just like receipts. (See page 176.)

> **NOTES**
> The Credit Card account class is assigned to Bank: Interac, so it does not appear with the list of banks.
> The Bank account class is available for all Balance Sheet accounts from the Options tab in the General Ledger. Account classes were introduced in Chapter 7, page 220.

The entry is complete and the journal looks like the one shown here:

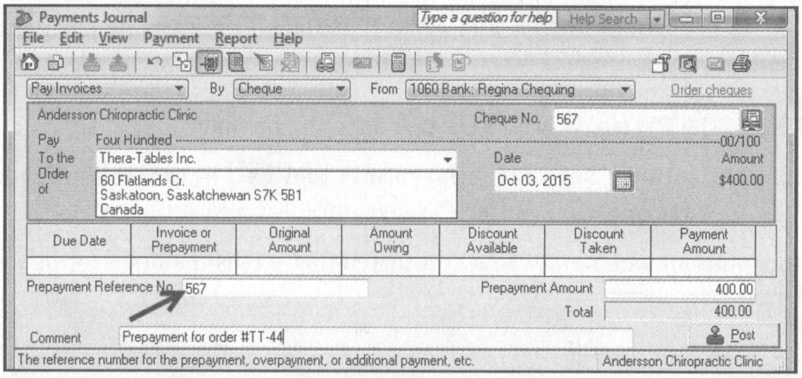

You are ready to review the journal entry.

Choose the **Report menu** and **click Display Payments Journal Entry**:

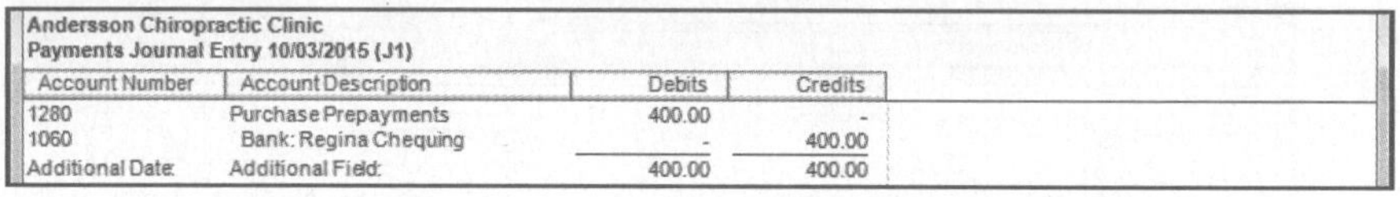
Andersson Chiropractic Clinic
Payments Journal Entry 10/03/2015 (J1)

Account Number	Account Description	Debits	Credits
1280	Purchase Prepayments	400.00	-
1060	Bank: Regina Chequing	-	400.00
Additional Date:	Additional Field:	400.00	400.00

As for other payments, the bank account is credited. However, the prepayment creates an asset until the order is filled, so *Purchase Prepayments*, the linked contra-asset account, is debited — the supplier owes something to us. If there is no previous balance owing to the supplier, the prepayment creates a debit balance for the account. After the purchase, when you pay the supplier, the prepayment will be displayed in red under the heading "Prepayments" and you "pay" it by accepting the amount, just as you do to pay the invoice itself.

Close the **display** when you have finished and **make corrections** to the journal entry if necessary.

Click **Post** [Post] to save the transaction.

Click the **Enter Supplier Prepayments tool** again to close the prepayment fields if you want to close these optional fields.

Entering Payments from a Line of Credit

Choose **Sonartek** from the Supplier list to prepare for the next payment.

✓ 5

Payment Cheque #103 **Dated October 3, 2015**

To Sonartek Ltd., $6 291.60 from the line of credit in payment of account including $128.40 discount for early payment. Reference invoice #SL-3456.

This payment is made from Andersson's line of credit. However, *Bank: Regina Chequing* is still selected as the bank account in the From field.

Click the **From list arrow** to select a different account as shown:

The line of credit is a liability account — it has a credit balance — but it operates like a bank account. By defining it as a Bank class account, it can be used to write cheques in the Payments Journal, just as it would be in an ongoing business.

Choose **Line of Credit Payable** to select this account and to update the cheque number for the new account.

Enter the cheque **date**, the **discount** amount and the **payment amount**.

Entering Additional Information for Transactions

The tool bar in journals has an icon for the option of adding information to a journal report. This **Additional Information tool** allows tracking of one additional date and one other field for transactions in all journals. Andersson has chosen to enter the number of the invoice paid as additional information so it will be included in journal reports.

Click the **Enter Additional Information tool** or **choose** the **Payment menu** and **click Enter Additional Information**:

You can enter one additional date for the transaction and additional text. Both will be available for journal reports when you show the Additional Information (page 451). You can rename these fields as part of the company setup.

Click the **Additional Field** text box.

Type `Ref: inv #SL-3456`

Click **OK** to return to the journal.

Adding the additional details does not change the appearance of the journal. You are ready to review the transaction before posting it.

Press *ctrl* + **J** to open the journal display:

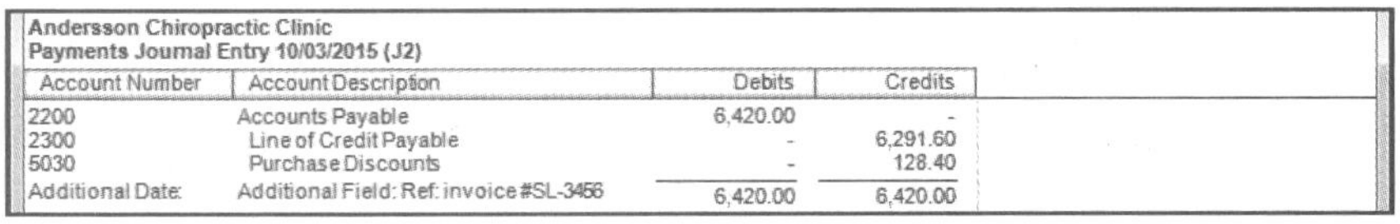

Andersson Chiropractic Clinic
Payments Journal Entry 10/03/2015 (J2)

Account Number	Account Description	Debits	Credits
2200	Accounts Payable	6,420.00	-
2300	Line of Credit Payable	-	6,291.60
5030	Purchase Discounts	-	128.40
Additional Date:	Additional Field: Ref: invoice #SL-3456	6,420.00	6,420.00

One difference between this entry and the earlier payment entries is the use of *Line of Credit Payable* as the account that is credited. This increases the business liability — more money has been borrowed against the line of credit available.

In addition to the usual debit and credit details, the invoice number entered as additional information is included in the display so that you can check it as well.

Close the **journal display**. **Check** your transaction **details** carefully.

Post the **payment** when you are certain the details are correct.

Enter the **next three transactions**. Remember to change bank accounts, modules and journals as needed, or add the shortcuts for these entries.

6 **Cash Purchase #R2015-10** **Dated October 3, 2015**

To Pro Suites Inc., cheque #121 for $2 300 from Eastside Chequing account to pay rent for October. Store the transaction as a monthly recurring entry.

7 **Payment Cheque #568** **Dated October 4, 2015**

To Medical Linen Supplies, $676.20 from Regina Chequing account in payment of account including $13.80 discount for early payment. Reference invoice #MLS-102.

Click **Receivables** in the Modules pane.

NOTES
You can click the Invoice Or Prepayment field and press *tab* to accept the discount and payment amounts.

NOTES
You can name the additional fields in the Company Settings Names window.

WARNING!
Because the additional information is optional, the program does not warn you if you forget to enter it. Therefore, you should make reviewing the journal entry routine practice.

NOTES
Details you enter in the Comment field are also added to the journal report but not to the journal display.

NOTES
You can modify the tabbing order by placing the cheque number after the customer.

8

Cash Receipt #58 **Dated October 4, 2015**

From Interplay Ballet, cheque #447 for $3 069 in payment of account including $31 discount for early payment. Reference invoice #632. Deposited to Eastside Chequing account. Add the invoice number as additional information.

Entering a Sales (Patient) Quote

Sales quotes are like purchase quotes. They offer a customer a guaranteed price for a limited time for merchandise or for work to be completed. The customer may choose to accept or reject the offer.

Quotes are entered from the Patient Quotes icon shown in the Enhanced view Receivables window:

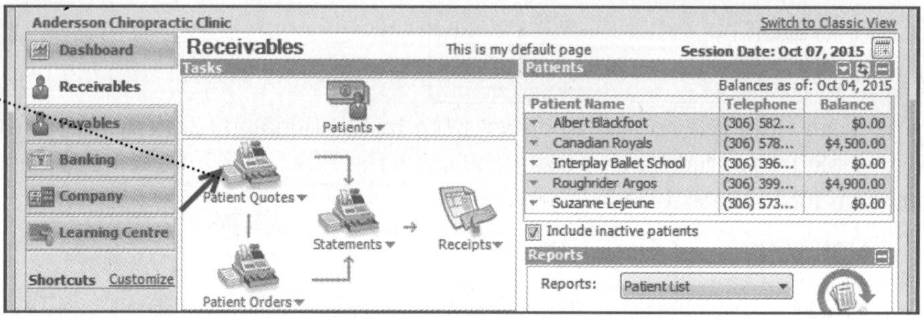

Separate icons are added for orders and quotes, just as they are for the suppliers.

PRO VERSION
Sales Quotes, Sales Orders and Sales Invoices will replace the icon labels Patient Quotes, Patient Orders and Statements.

Click the Sales Quotes icon to open the form you need.

✓ 9

Sales Quote #51 **Dated October 4, 2015**

Starting date October 15, 2015

To Giant Raptors (use Full Add for the new customer), a local basketball team, $3 500 per month for unlimited chiropractic services during the regular six-month training and playing season. Andersson will attend or be on call for all home games. If the team enters the playoffs, the contract may be extended for $1 200 per week. Terms: 1/10, n/30. A deposit of $2 000 will be required on acceptance of the contract. Enter 6 as the number ordered. Each month, the sales invoice for Giant Raptors will be entered as partially filling the order.

NOTES
For services such as those provided by Andersson, the term Shipping Date is not appropriate. In the source documents, we use Starting Date instead.

Click the **Patient Quotes icon**  to open the Fees Journal.

The invoice screen changes to the form for a patient quote:

CLASSIC VIEW
Click the Fees, Orders & Quotes icon  to open the journal, and choose Quote from the journal's Transaction drop-down list.

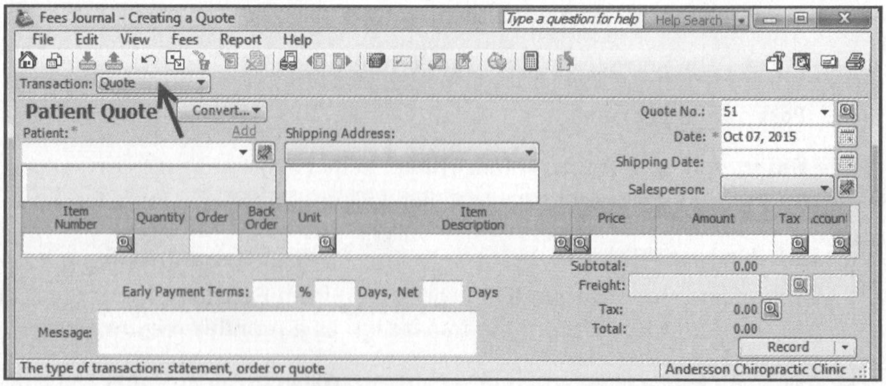

PRO VERSION
Sales Journal – Creating A Quote will appear in the journal's title bar instead of Fees Journal – Creating A Quote.

NOTES
Statement replaces the term Invoice for a medical company. Fees Journal replaces Sales Journal.

WARNING!
You must choose Quote as the Transaction type before entering the customer. Otherwise, a blank quote screen will open.

The quote is completed in much the same way as the sales invoice. However, you must enter a quantity in the Order field, just as you did for purchase quotes and orders. The quote number is entered and updated automatically from the defaults for the Receivables Ledger. As for purchase quotes, the Record button replaces Post.

Additional fields are not available for quotes and orders. The tool is dimmed.

Click the **Patient field**.

Type `Giant Raptors` **Click** the **Add link** above the Patient field to open the ledger directly.

Patient Name (Contact)	Address	Phone No. Fax No.	E-mail Web Site	Revenue Account	Terms Credit Limit
Giant Raptors (Rex Saurus)	550 Tyrannus Dr. Regina, Saskatchewan S4R 5T1	Tel 1: (306) 398-8753 Tel 2: (306) 398-5338 Fax: (306) 398-5339	rex@raptors.com www.raptors.com	4100	1/10, n/30 (change default terms) $5 000

If you type the new name and press *tab* you will notice that Continue is not an option for a quote. You must create at least a partial ledger record.

Click **Save And Close** [Save and Close] after entering all the customer details.

You will return to the quote screen with the account and payment terms added.

Drag through the **date** in the **Date field**.

Type `10 4 15`

Click the **Shipping Date field** to move the cursor because the shipping address and quote number are correct.

Type `10 15`

Click the **Order field**.

Instead of entering the quote as the monthly rate and filling it in the first month, we will enter it as a six-month contract with monthly unit prices. After each month of service, the quote will be partially filled with one month of service.

Type `6`

Click the **Item Description field**.

Type `monthly fee for treatment`

Press *tab* to move to the Price field. You must complete the Price field.

Type `3500`

Press *tab* to advance to the Amount field. The program enters the amount correctly as the quantity times the price.

Press *tab* to move to the Tax field. The Tax field is not used and the account is entered, so the quote is complete:

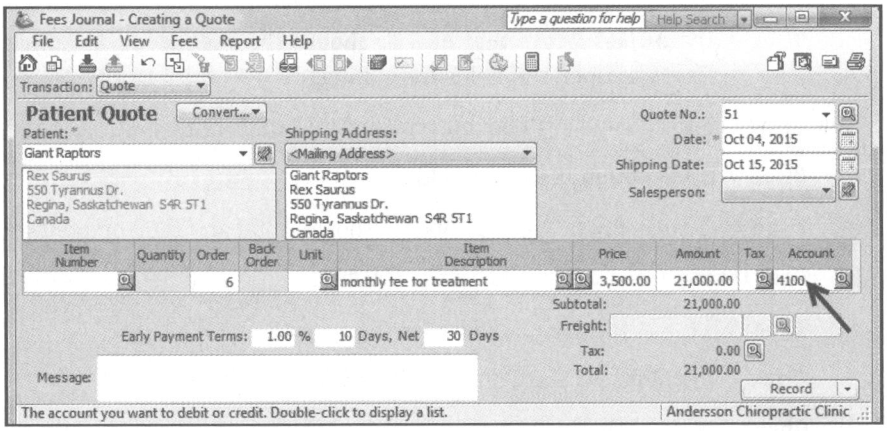

Check the **quote** carefully and **correct mistakes** just as you do in sales invoices. Refer to page 162 for assistance if needed.

WARNING!
If you do not enter a price in the Price field, you cannot fill the quote or order. When you choose this option, the form will remain incomplete.

NOTES
You can choose Print & Record or Record as the default action for the quote by selecting your preference from the Record button drop-down list.

There is no journal entry to display. When a quote is filled by making a sale, the journal entry will be created.

Click **Record** [Record] to save the quote. No journal entry results from the quote.

Leave the **Fees Journal open** to adjust the quote.

Adjusting a Sales Quote

Sometimes a quote contains an error or must be changed if prices are renegotiated. You can adjust sales and purchase quotes and orders after recording them just as you can adjust sales and purchase invoices after posting.

✓ 10

Memo #1 **Dated October 5, 2015**

After some negotiations with the Giant Raptors, Andersson agreed to reduce the contract price to $3 300 per month for the playing season. Playoff games will be billed at $1 100 per week. Adjust the sales quote to change the price.

The Fees Journal – Creating A Quote screen should still be open.

WARNING!
If Quote is not selected as the Transaction type, you will convert the quote to a sales order, or fill the quote when you bring the quote on to the screen.

Click the **Quote No. field list arrow** to see the list of quotes on file.

Click **51** to select the quote you just entered.

Press tab to add the quote to the screen:

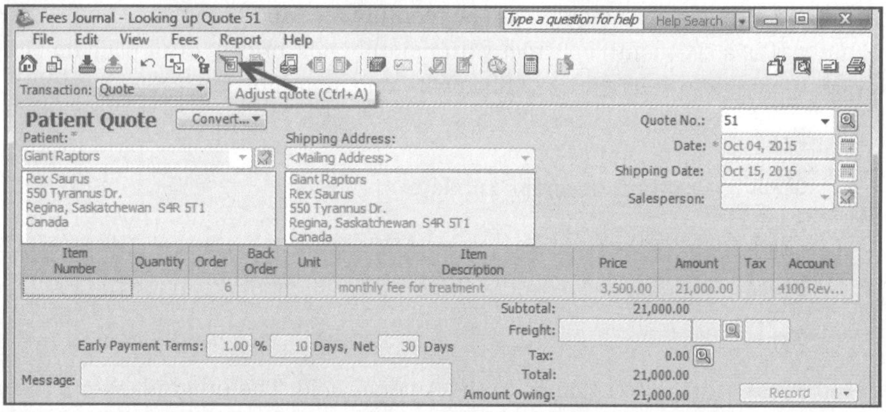

NOTES
To view and adjust orders and quotes, you do not need to use the lookup or search features we used to adjust purchase and sales invoices after posting. Orders and quotes are available directly from the Order/Quote No. field.

The List icon beside the Quote No. field opens the Search window for all quotes. With a large number of quotes, it may be easier to find a quote on this list.

At this stage, you cannot edit the quote. All fields are dimmed.

Click the **Adjust Quote tool** or **choose** the **Fees menu** and **click Adjust Quote** to open the fields for editing.

NOTES
Pressing ctrl + A will open the quote fields for editing. In other journals, pressing ctrl + A opens the Adjust/Search window.

Adjusting Quote 51 replaces Looking Up Quote 51 in the title bar.

Click **3,500.00** in the Price field.

Type `3300` **Press** tab to update the subtotal and total amount to $19 800.

Drag through the **date in the Date field**.

Type `10-5` to enter the date for the revised quote.

Click the **Message field** and **type** `Revised quote`

Check your **work** carefully.

Click **Record** [Record] to save the revised quote. Keep the journal open.

NOTES
All fields in a quote can be edited, except name and address details. To change the name, you must remove the quote and re-enter it for the correct customer. However, you cannot use the same quote number twice.

Converting a Sales Quote to a Sales Order

Sales quotes can be converted to orders just as purchase quotes can be converted to purchase orders.

✓ 11

Sales Order #51 **Dated October 5, 2015**

Starting date October 15, 2015
The Giant Raptors have accepted the modified sales quote #51. Convert the quote to a sales order. All terms and dates are unchanged from the revised quote for $3 300 per month.

The Fees Journal should be open with Quote selected as the transaction type.

Click the **Quote No.** field drop-down list.

Click **51**, the quote number we want, and **press** tab to recall the quote.

There are different ways to convert the quote to an order, as there were for supplier quotes.

Click **Convert This Patient Quote To A Patient Order** from the Convert drop-down list. Or

Click **Quote** in the Transaction field and then **click Order**.

These options are shown in the following two screens:

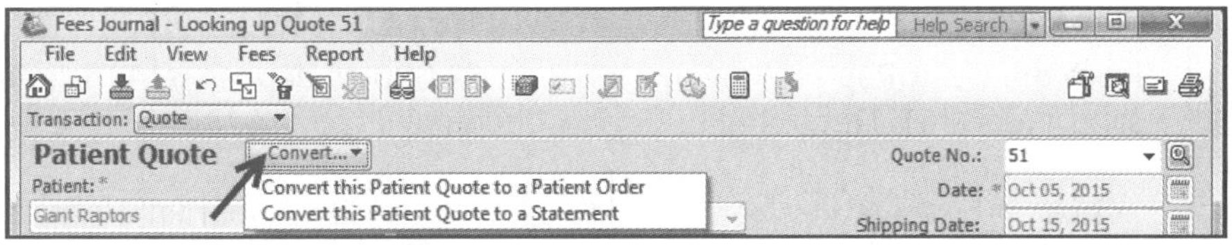

The patient order replaces the revised quote with Creating An Order in the title bar:

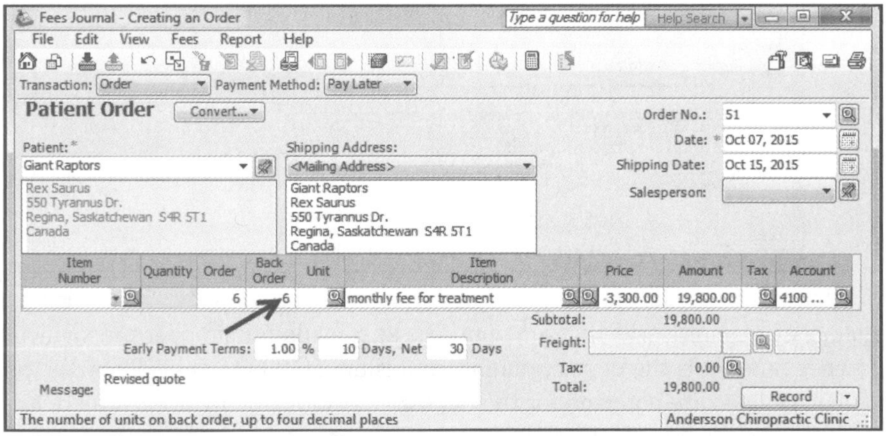

You can also choose Order from the Transaction list first, or click the Home window Patient Orders icon, then choose #51 from the Order/(Quote) No. drop-down list. Press tab to place the quote on-screen as an order.

The order quantity — 6 — has been added to the Back Order field.

Enter **Oct 5** as the order date to replace the session date.

PRO VERSION
Choose Convert This Sales Quote To A Sales Order from the Convert drop-down list or choose Order in the Transaction field.
The term Invoice will replace Statement in the Transaction list.

PRO VERSION
You will see Sales Journal – Creating An Order in the journal title bar.

NOTES
The Quote No. field is labelled Order No. as soon as you convert the quote.

Check all the **details** carefully because there is no journal entry to review.

All other details should be correct for the order because they have not changed. The order can be edited at this stage if needed. We will revise the comment.

Click the **Message field**. **Type** `Order based on revised quote`

Click **Record** to save the sales order and see the warning:

NOTES
You can make Print & Record the default action for the Record button by choosing this from the button's drop-down list.

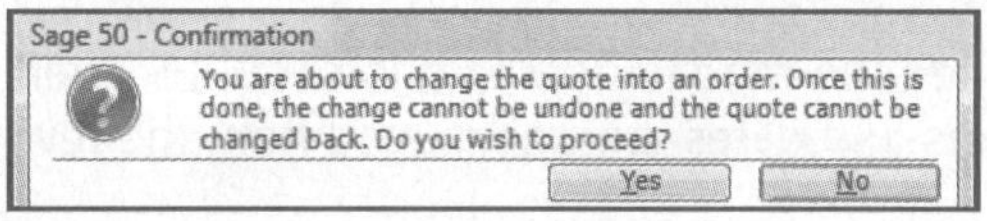

Since we want to change the quote to an order, we should proceed.

Click **Yes**.

Close the **Fees Journal** so that you can enter the customer's deposit.

Entering Customer Deposits

NOTES
We will enter the next customer deposit directly in the sales order (see page 427).

Andersson also requests deposits from her customers when they place orders. Deposits can be entered in the Receipts Journal in the same way as supplier prepayments are entered in the Payments Journal. The customer deposit tool opens fields for a reference number and an amount.

✓ 12

Cash Receipt #59 **Dated October 6, 2015**

From the Giant Raptors, cheque #838 for $2 000 as deposit #14 to confirm sales order #51. Deposited to Regina Chequing account.

Click the **Receipts icon** to open the Receipts Journal.

Click the **Enter Patient Deposits tool** or **choose** the **Receipt menu** and **click Enter Deposits**.

PRO VERSION
Click the Enter Customer Deposits tool – Customer replaces the term Patient in the Pro version.

This tool button/menu option acts as a switch that opens the fields for deposits:

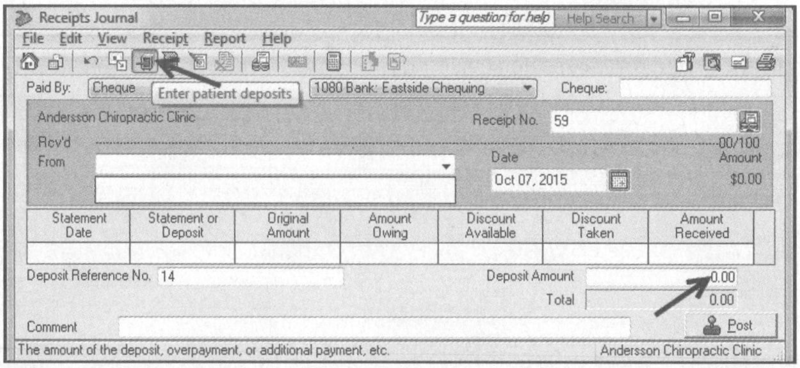

The two new fields added to the journal for the **deposit reference number** and for the **deposit amount** serve the same purpose as they do for supplier prepayments. The reference number is the deposit number and is updated automatically by the program. The invoice lines are not used for the deposit. Outstanding invoices, if there are any, will be included in the journal. If they are being paid with the same customer cheque, enter the receipt in the usual way in addition to the deposit amount.

The receipt number is updated and correct, but we need to change the bank account.

Choose **Giant Raptors** in the From drop-down list.

Click the **Cheque field**.

Type 838

Enter **October 6** as the date of the cheque.

Click the **Deposit To list arrow** to see the list of bank accounts:

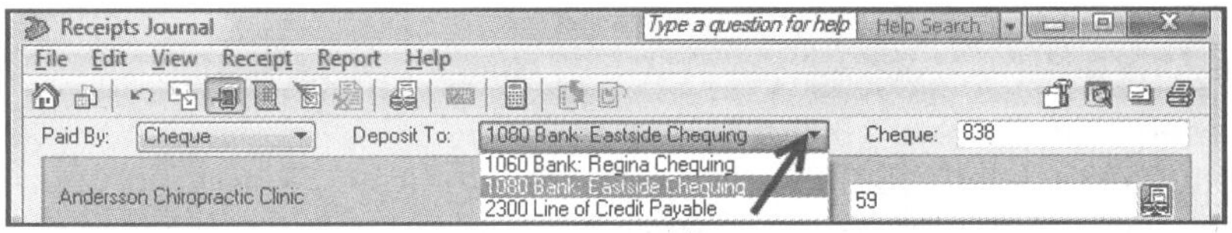

Just as we can pay from any of the accounts that we identify as Bank class accounts, we can deposit to any bank account, including the line of credit.

Choose **Bank: Regina Chequing** to change the account selection.

Click the **Deposit Amount field** at the bottom of the journal.

Type 2000 **Press** tab.

Click the **Enter Additional Information tool**, or **choose** the **Receipt menu** and **click** **Enter Additional Information**.

Click the **Additional Field** text box.

Type Deposit for SO #51

Click **OK** to return to the journal so you can review the transaction.

Choose the **Report menu** and **click** **Display Receipts Journal Entry**:

Andersson Chiropractic Clinic
Receipts Journal Entry 10/06/2015 (J6)

Account Number	Account Description	Debits	Credits
1060	Bank: Regina Chequing	2,000.00	-
2250	Prepaid Sales and Deposits	-	2,000.00
Additional Date:	Additional Field: Deposit for SO #51	2,000.00	2,000.00

As for other receipts, the bank account is debited. The account credited is *Prepaid Sales and Deposits*, a contra-liability account linked to the customer deposits field. If the customer has no previous outstanding balance, the deposit creates a credit entry for the account. Until the sale is completed, the deposit creates a liability — we owe the customer this amount until the order is filled. After the sale, when the customer pays the invoice, the deposit will be displayed in red under the heading "Deposits" and it is "paid" by accepting its amount, just as you enter receipts for the invoice itself.

Close the **display** when you have finished and **make corrections** to the journal entry if necessary.

Click **Post** to save the transaction.

Click the **Enter Patient Deposits tool** again to close the deposit fields.

Close the **Receipts Journal** to return to the Receivables module window.

Change the **session date** to **October 14** and **make** a **backup**. **Enter** the **next two receipts** and then **close** the **journal**.

13

Cash Receipt #60 **Dated October 8, 2015**

From Roughrider Argos, cheque #1122 for $4 851 in payment of account including $49 discount for early payment. Reference sales invoice #639. Deposited to Eastside Chequing account.

14

Cash Receipt #61 **Dated October 8, 2015**

From Canadian Royals, cheque #3822 for $4 455 in payment of account including $45 discount for early payment. Reference sales invoice #638. Deposited to Regina Chequing account.

NOTES

If you modified the tabbing order, pressing tab after selecting the customer will place the cursor in the Cheque field.

NOTES

The Credit Card account class is assigned to Bank: Interac; it does not appear with the list of banks.

Line of Credit Payable has been defined as a Bank class account. Therefore, it appears on the list of bank accounts.

Cash class accounts will also appear on this list. We will use the Cash class in Chapter 15.

NOTES

If a customer overpays an invoice, you can enter the overpayment – the difference between the amount owing and the cheque amount – in the Deposit Amount field to create the required credit balance.

NOTES

Processing the advance in this way ensures that the advance will appear in the correct customer account in the Receivables Ledger. The manual approach, a General Journal entry that debits the bank account and credits Unearned Revenue, a liability account, does not show this link with the customer – the customer's ledger is updated separately.

NOTES

Closing or hiding the Deposit fields is not required.

NOTES

Remember to change the selected bank account when necessary.

Placing a Purchase Order with Prepayment

Placing a purchase order directly without the quote is similar to entering a purchase quote. For this order, a prepayment is included so we will enter it on the order.

✓ 15

Purchase Order #44 and Cheque #104 **Dated October 9, 2015**

Delivery date October 19, 2015

From Sonartek Ltd., $6 000 including taxes for ultrasound machine with multiple frequencies and interchangeable wands. Terms: 2/15, n/30. Deposit of $1 500 paid with cheque #104 from Line of Credit Payable account to confirm order.

Click **Payables** in the Modules pane list to open the Payables window.

Click the **Supplier Orders icon** 

to open the Expenses Journal with Order selected as the transaction type.

The Order No. is entered automatically (Forms Settings), and it will be incremented automatically because purchase orders are generated within your business.

Choose **Sonartek Ltd.** from the supplier list.

Enter **Oct 9 15** as the order date and **Oct 19 15** as the shipping date.

Click the **Order field.**

Type 1 **Press** tab.

The program automatically completes the Back Order field with the quantity on order. The entire order quantity is considered as backordered.

Click the **Item Description field.**

Type ultrasound machine **Press** tab to move to the Price field.

Type 6000 **Press** tab.

If the account number is not entered by default, or if it is incorrect for this order, choose the correct account from the Account field selection list.

We will now enter the prepayment details.

Click the **Payment Method field list arrow** to see the payment options:

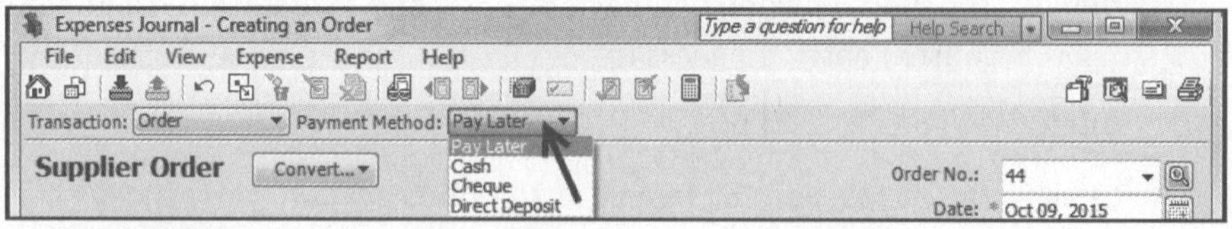

The options are the same as they are for other payments.

Click **Cheque** to open the Paid From bank account field. *Bank: Eastside Chequing*, the default bank account, is entered.

Click the **Paid From list arrow** to see the familiar list of Bank class accounts:

Choose **Line of Credit Payable** to open the cheque number field with the next cheque number for this account.

CLASSIC VIEW
Click the Expenses, Orders & Quotes icon 

to open the journal, and choose Order from the journal's Transaction drop-down list.

PRO VERSION
Click the Purchase Orders icon to open the Purchases Journal with Order selected as the transaction type.

NOTES
You must choose the type of transaction before selecting the supplier or customer. If you do not, the supplier or customer field will be cleared when you select a different type of transaction.

A **Prepayment Applied** field has also been added below the invoice lines on the order form. By default the entire order amount is entered so we need to change it; $1 500 is being paid at this time.

Double-click the **Prepayment Applied field** to select the default amount.

Type 1500 **Press** *tab* to complete the order form as shown:

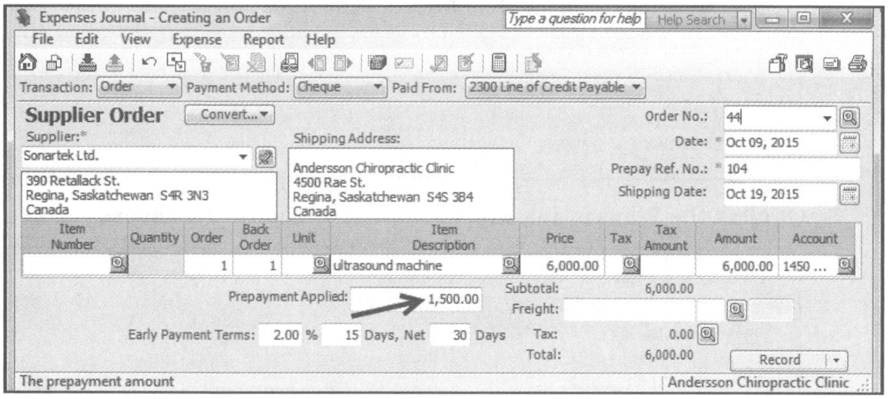

Check the **order** details carefully.

Because we have now actually entered a transaction that affects our account balances, there is a journal entry to review for the order.

Choose the **Report menu** and **click Display Expenses Journal Entry**:

Andersson Chiropractic Clinic
Expenses Journal Entry 10/09/2015 (J9)

Account Number	Account Description	Debits	Credits
1280	Purchase Prepayments	1,500.00	-
2300	Line of Credit Payable	-	1,500.00
Additional Date:	Additional Field:	1,500.00	1,500.00

This prepayment journal entry is the same as the one we made earlier from the Payments Journal (page 412). Only the bank account used is different.

Close the **journal display** to return to the order.

Make **corrections** if necessary. **Click Record** to save the order. Leave the journal open for the next transaction.

Entering a Sales Order

Sales orders are entered in the same way as sales quotes, except that you start with the Patient or Sales Order form instead of the Patient or Sales Quote form.

Click Receivables in the Modules pane and click the Patient Orders icon. Then choose the customer and complete the order details. The Order field cannot be left blank. Sales order numbers are generated by the customer; they are not entered or updated by the program. Enter the customer's sales order number.

Filling a Purchase Order

When an ordered item is received, or work is completed, you must complete a purchase invoice entry to record the transaction. Andersson will record the purchase order number in the Additional Field for the journal reports.

✓ 16 **Purchase Invoice #TT-4599** **Dated October 10, 2015**

From Thera-Tables Inc., to fill purchase order #TT-44 for $4 000 including taxes for custom-built treatment table. Terms: 2/5, n/30.

PRO VERSION

Choose Display Purchases Journal Entry from the Report menu.

NOTES

You can choose Print & Record as the default action for the supplier order by making this selection from the Record button's drop-down list.

CLASSIC VIEW

Click the Fees, Orders & Quotes icon  to open the journal, and choose Order from the journal's Transaction drop-down list.

The Expenses Journal should still be open with Order selected as the Transaction type. Again, there are different ways to turn the order into an invoice.

Choose **TT-44** from the Order No. field drop-down list. **Press** `tab` to recall the order.

Choose **Convert This Supplier Order To An Invoice** from the Convert drop-down list. This is the only conversion option available now:

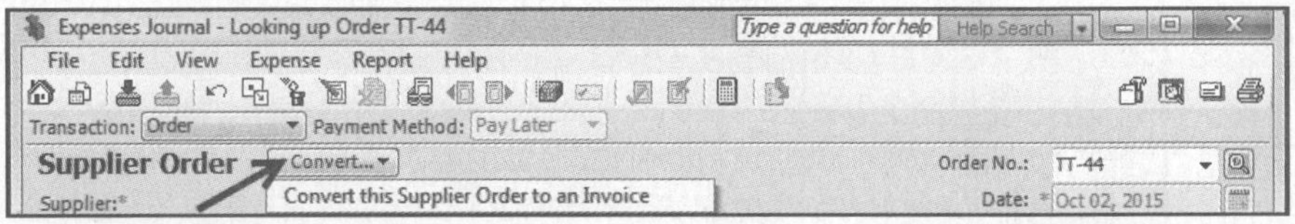

Or **click** the **Transaction drop-down list** as shown and **choose Invoice**:

Or choose Invoice from the Transaction list and then choose TT-44 from the Order/Quote No. drop-down list and press `tab`.

You will see the purchase order details from October 2 entered on the invoice:

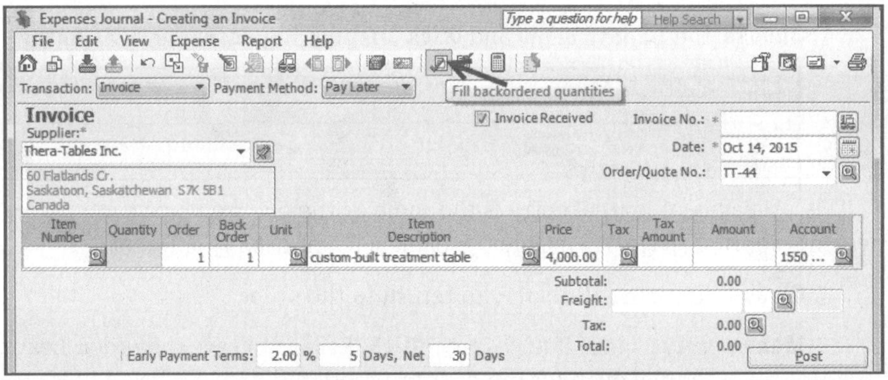

Pay Later, the default selection in the Payment Method field, is correct because this is a credit purchase. Creating An Invoice now shows in the title bar.

Click the **Invoice field**. **Type** `TT-4599`

Press `tab` **twice** to advance to the Date field.

Type `10-10`

The invoice is still incomplete because the quantity displays as backordered and the invoice amount is zero. We need to "fill" the order.

Click the **Fill Backordered Quantities tool** (as shown on the previous screen) or **choose** the **Expense menu** and **click Fill Supplier Order**.

If you did not enter the price for the order, you must edit the invoice to add the missing details. Your invoice should now look like the one that follows:

PRO VERSION
The Purchases Journal is open with Purchase Order as the transaction type. Choose Invoice as the transaction type or choose Convert This Purchase Order To An Invoice.
You will see Purchases Journal – Creating An Invoice in the journal's title bar.

NOTES
After you choose the purchase order number, the order does not appear until after you press `tab` or advance to the next field.

NOTES
The Project/Division module is hidden for Andersson because it is not needed, but when used, the term Partner will replace Division or Project for medical companies.

PRO VERSION
Choose the Purchase menu and click Fill Purchase Order.

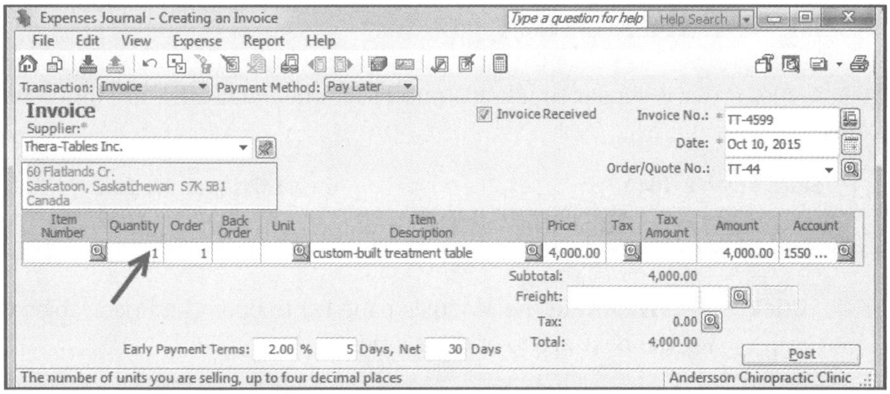

The Back Order quantity has been moved to the Quantity column to reflect the completion of the order. Notice that the prepayment made in the Payments Journal does not show on the invoice and that the full amount is invoiced. When the prepayment is added to the order form, it does appear on the invoice (page 431).

Click the **Enter Additional Information tool** or **choose** the **Expense menu** and **click Enter Additional Information**:

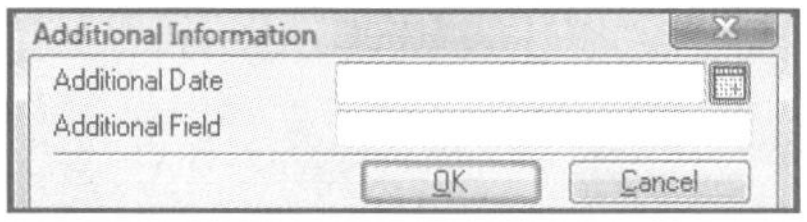

This data entry screen is the same for all journals.

Click the **Additional Field** text box.

Type `Ref: fill P.O. #TT-44`

Click **OK** to return to the journal.

Check the **entry** carefully to be sure that it is correct.

Choose the **Report menu** and **click Display Expenses Journal Entry**.

You can see that this is a normal journal entry with the order number as additional information. Prepayment amounts are not included.

Close the **display**. When the information is correct,

Click the **Post button** Post or **choose** the **Expense menu** and **click Post** to see the following message:

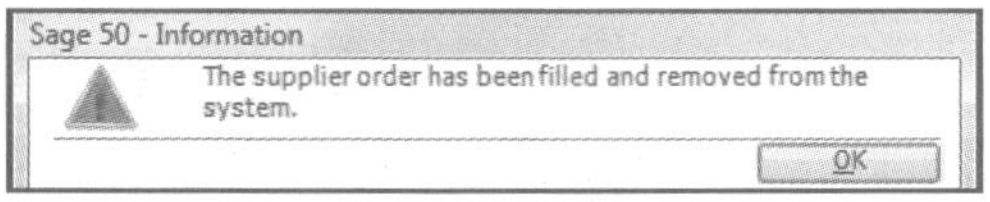

Filled orders and quotes are not saved, but their numbers cannot be used again.

Click **OK** to display a new Expenses Journal invoice form.

Close the **Expenses Journal**.

Filling a Purchase Quote

Filling a purchase quote is similar to filling an order. Choose Invoice, select the quote number and press *tab* to place the quote on-screen as an invoice. The quantity automatically moves to the Quantity column and the total Amount is added. You do not need to choose Fill Backordered Quantities for quotes. Again, you can record the quote number as an additional field for the journal.

NOTES
If the order is partially filled, the backordered quantity will be reduced as in the sales order on page 425.

PRO VERSION
Choose the Purchase menu and click Enter Additional Information.

NOTES
To fill the quote, you can also start with the quote on-screen. Then choose Invoice from the Transaction drop-down list or Convert This Supplier/Purchase Quote To An Invoice from the Convert drop-down list.

Filling a Sales Order

Filling a sales order is similar to filling a purchase order, and there are different ways to do this.

✓ 17

Sales Invoice #649 **Dated October 10, 2015**

To Giant Raptors, to fill the first month of the contract on sales order #51 for $3 300. Terms: 1/10, n/30.

Click **Receivables** in the Modules pane list to open the Receivables window for the next group of transactions.

Click the **Patient Orders icon** to open the Fees Journal.

Click the **Order No. list arrow** to see the available orders.

Click **51. Press** tab to display the original sales order on the screen.

Click **Convert This Patient Order To A Statement** from the Convert drop-down list as shown. This is the only conversion option for orders:

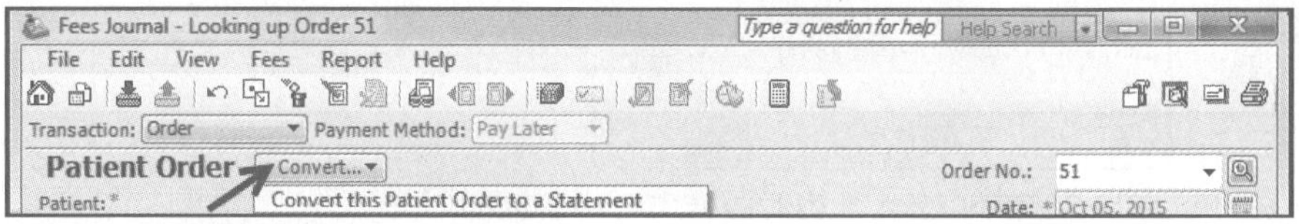

Or **click** the **Transaction drop-down** list as shown and **choose Statement**:

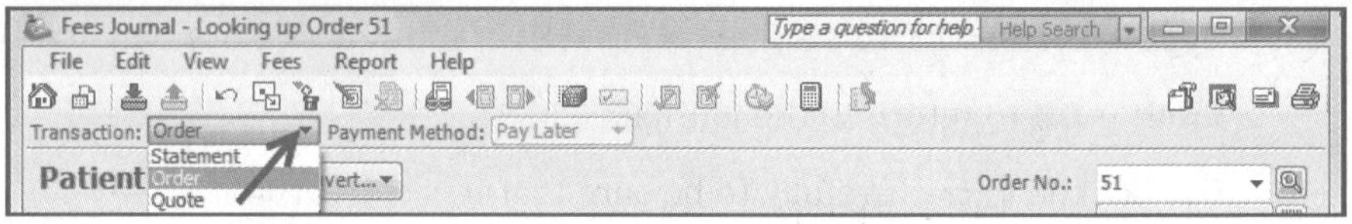

Or choose the Statements icon from the Receivables module Home window. Then choose #51 from the Order/Quote field drop-down list and press tab.

Each of these three approaches will replace the order with an invoice as shown:

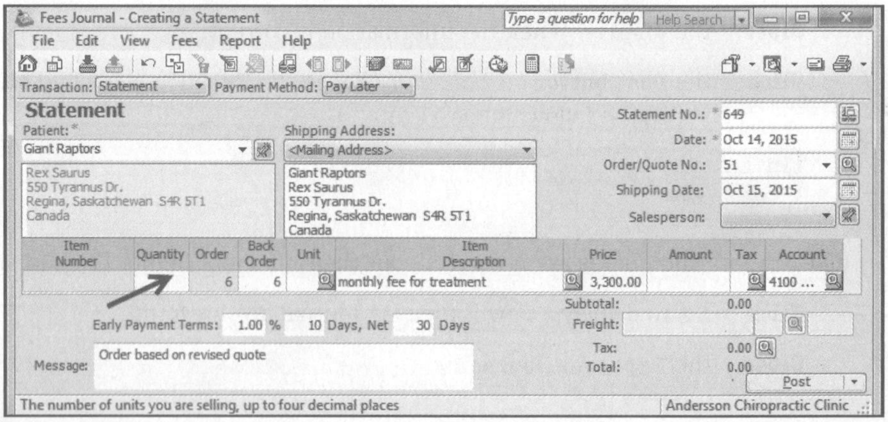

Sometimes only part of the order is received and the order is not completely filled at once, as in this case.

Pay Later should be selected as the payment option for the Statement transaction.

Enter **October 10** as the transaction date.

Click the **Quantity field**. Only one month is being billed at this time.

Type 1 **Press** tab to update the invoice as shown:

PRO VERSION
Click the Sales Orders icon to open the Sales Journal. Choose Order #51 and press tab. You will see Sales Journal – Looking Up Order 51 in the journal's title bar.

Choose Convert This Sales Order To A Sales Invoice from the Convert drop-down list or choose Invoice from the Transaction list.

NOTES
Only one conversion option is possible from the order screen, that is, changing the order to an invoice.

NOTES
If you customized the columns for the Quote form, they will be restored for the Order. In the Premium version, Quote, Order and Invoice forms are customized separately.

PRO VERSION
If you customized the columns for the Quote form, you will see the same changes applied on the Order and Invoice forms. You cannot customize them differently.

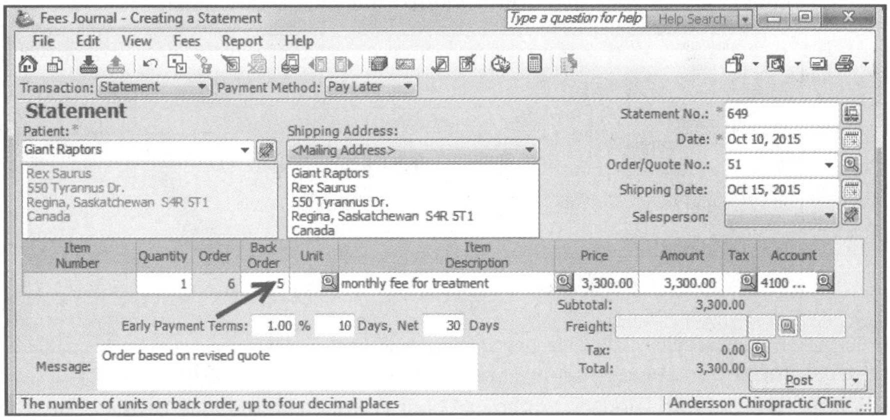

The Amount entered is the fee for one month of service and the Back Order quantity is reduced to five. When the sixth and final month is completed, the order will be filled and removed.

Click the **Enter Additional Information tool** or **choose** the **Fees menu** and **click Enter Additional Information**.

Click the **Additional Field** text box.

Type `Ref: S.O. #51`

Click **OK** to return to the journal. We should also modify the comment.

Click the **Message field**.

Type `Invoice based on revised quote`

Review the **journal entry** and **check** your **work** carefully.

Choose the **Report menu** and **click Display Fees Journal Entry**.

Close the **display** to return to the invoice. **Make corrections** if necessary.

Click **Post** [Post] to record the invoice. The order is not filled, so you do not see the message that the order will be removed.

Close the **Fees Journal**.

NOTES
You could also fill the invoice and then edit the number in the Quantity field from 6 to 1.

PRO VERSION
Choose the Sales menu and click Enter Additional Information.

NOTES
You can double-click the single word Order in the Message field and type Invoice to replace it.

Filling a Sales Quote

Filling a sales quote is similar to filling an order. Choose Statement (or Invoice), select the quote number and press *tab* to place the quote on-screen as an invoice. The order quantity automatically moves to the Quantity column and the total Amount is added. You do not need to choose Fill Backordered Quantities for quotes.

NOTES
To fill the quote, you can also start with the quote on-screen. Then choose Statement from the Transaction drop-down list or Convert This Patient Quote To A Statement from the Convert drop-down list.

Entering Receipts on Accounts with Deposits

The next receipt pays the balance of an account for a customer who has made a deposit.

✓ 18

Cash Receipt #62 **Dated October 13, 2015**

From the Giant Raptors, cheque #939 for $1 267 in full payment of account including $33 discount for early payment. Reference sales invoice #649 and deposit #14. Deposited to Eastside Chequing account.

Click the **Receipts icon** [Receipts] to open the Receipts Journal.

Choose **Giant Raptors** from the customer drop-down list:

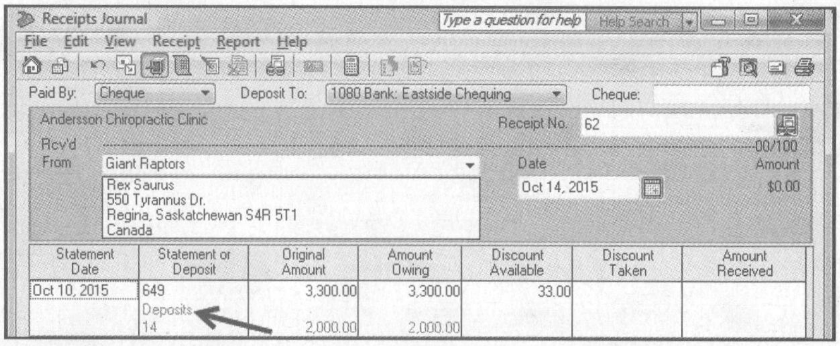

> **NOTES**
> If necessary, drag the lower frame of the journal to include the deposit on the screen or maximize the window.

Customer deposits are displayed in red below the outstanding invoices. The colour indicates that they are negative invoices that reduce the balance owing. The invoice line shows the full amount owing and the full discount amount available.

Enter **939** as the Cheque number and **enter** **Oct 13** in the Date field.

Click the **Discount Taken field** for invoice #649 to accept the discount.

Press *tab* to accept the Amount Received and add the Deposit amount.

Press *tab* to accept the Deposit amount and update the receipt.

Enter the **invoice number** as additional information.

The discount and deposit are subtracted from the full invoice amount so that the total amount now matches the cheque amount as shown in the completed receipt:

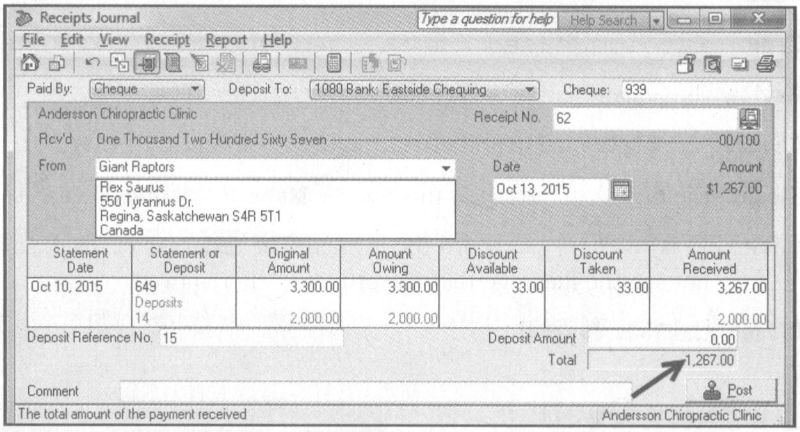

Choose the **Report menu** and **click** **Display Receipts Journal Entry**:

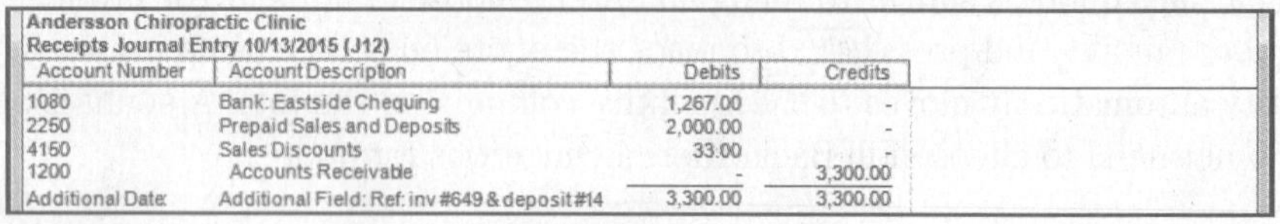

Andersson Chiropractic Clinic
Receipts Journal Entry 10/13/2015 (J12)

Account Number	Account Description	Debits	Credits
1080	Bank: Eastside Chequing	1,267.00	-
2250	Prepaid Sales and Deposits	2,000.00	-
4150	Sales Discounts	33.00	-
1200	Accounts Receivable	-	3,300.00
Additional Date:	Additional Field: Ref: inv #649 & deposit #14	3,300.00	3,300.00

> **NOTES**
> The initial deposit creates a liability. The customer has paid us and we have not provided anything yet. When the order is filled, the liability is removed, so the Accounts Receivable balance debit is offset by the initial liability. When the customer pays the invoice for the balance owing, the initial credit entry must be removed from the record.

Accounts Receivable has been credited for the full invoice amount to clear the invoice. The *Sales Discounts* contra-revenue account has been debited to record the reduction to sales revenue. The *Prepaid Sales and Deposits* contra-liability account has been debited for the full deposit amount to clear its credit balance, and the bank account is debited for the amount of the cheque.

Close the **journal display window**. **Make corrections** if necessary. **Post** the **receipt** and then **close** the **Receipts Journal**.

Enter **sales quote #52** for the new customer.

☐ 19

Quote: 52
Date: Oct 13, 2015
Starting date: Oct 25, 2015
Customer: Veronica Kain
Veronica Kain School of Dance
35 Lady Slipper Rd.
Address: Regina, SK S3V 4H7
Phone No: (306) 376-3218

Andersson Chiropractic Clinic
www.betterbacks.com
4500 Rae St.
Regina, SK S4S 3B4
Tel 1: (306) 577-1900
Tel 2: (306) 577-2199
Fax: (306) 577-1925

QUOTE

Treatment description	Amount
Chiropractic services for the school year (Sep-Jun) Monthly contract rate $1 000 deposit when contract accepted Contract may be extended for summer months	2 500.00

Terms: 1/10, n/30
Signed: *Maria Andersson* **Customer Initials:** VK **TOTAL** 2 500.00

Entering Deposits with Sales Orders

Just as you can enter prepayments to suppliers in the Supplier Order window, you can enter customer deposits on the Patient Order form. When the deposit accompanies the order, this method is recommended.

✓ 20

Sales Order #52 and Deposit #15 **Dated October 14, 2015**

Starting date October 25, 2015
From Veronica Kain School of Dance, acceptance of quote #52. Convert the quote to a sales order leaving all terms and amounts unchanged. Received cheque #865 for $1 000 as deposit #15 to confirm sales order #52. Deposited to Eastside Chequing account.

The Fees Journal should still be open with Quote selected as the transaction type.

Choose **52** from the Quote No. field list and **press** *tab*.

Choose **Order** as the transaction type or **choose** **Convert This Patient Quote To A Patient Order** from the Convert list to convert the quote to an order.

Click the **Payment Method list arrow** to see the payment options:

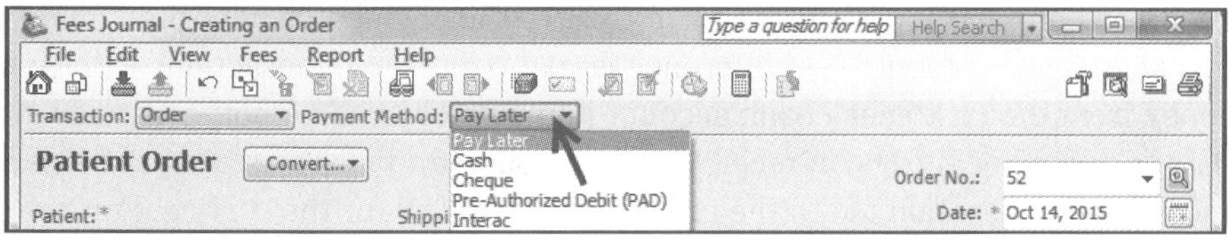

The same customer payment types are available here as in the Receipts Journal.

NOTES

Use Full Add for the new customer.
Email: vkain@dancestudio.ca
Revenue account: 4100
Credit limit: $4 000
Use the source document for the remaining customer details.
Remember to change the default payment terms.
Enter 1 as the Order quantity.

PRO VERSION

Choose Order from the Transaction list in the Sales Journal, or choose Convert This Sales Quote To A Sales Order from the Convert drop-down list.

PRO VERSION

Your screen's title bar will show Sales Journal – Creating An Order.

Click **Cheque** in the Payment Method list to open the extra payment fields:

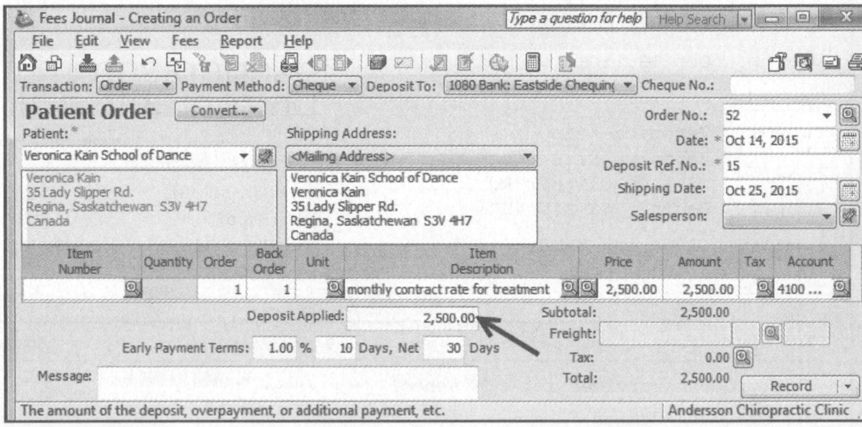

The default bank account is selected for the Deposit To field at the top of the order form. A Cheque number field has also been added to the top of the form and a **Deposit Applied** amount field has been added to the bottom of the order form, as it is for cash sales. The **Deposit Reference Number** field with the next deposit number has also been added.

The session date and bank account are correct so we can add the payment details.

Click the **Cheque No. field**.

Type 865

Double-click the **Deposit Applied field**. The full amount of the order is entered as the default amount and we need to change it.

Type 1000

Press *tab* to update and complete the form.

Choose the **Report menu** and **click** **Display Fees Journal Entry**:

Andersson Chiropractic Clinic
Fees Journal Entry 10/14/2015 (J13)

Account Number	Account Description	Debits	Credits
1080	Bank: Eastside Chequing	1,000.00	-
2250	Prepaid Sales and Deposits	-	1,000.00
Additional Date:	Additional Field:	1,000.00	1,000.00

You can see that this journal entry is identical to the journal entry for deposits entered in the Receipts Journal (page 419). Only the bank account is different. The prepayment or deposit with the sales order creates a journal entry, although the sales order itself does not.

Close the **display** and **click** **Record** to save the transaction.

Click **Yes** to confirm that you are changing the quote to an order.

PRO VERSION
Choose the Report menu and click Display Sales Journal Entry.

Entering Debit Card Sale Transactions

Customers pay for purchases using cash, cheques, credit cards or debit cards. Debit and credit card purchases are similar for a store — the payment is deposited immediately to the linked bank account. The difference is that debit card transactions withdraw the money from the customer's bank account immediately while credit cards advance a loan that the customer repays on receipt of the credit card bill. The store pays a percentage discount or transaction fee to the credit card company for the service. For debit card transactions, the store pays a flat fee for each transaction. Both involve a setup fee and a monthly rental charge for the terminal that communicates electronically with the card-issuing company. Andersson uses the name Interac for all debit card transactions.

NOTES
Fees for debit cards can be lower than credit card fees because the risk of non-payment is eliminated. Debit card payments require the customer's bank balance to cover the amount before the payments are approved.

For Andersson, we set up the debit card as a credit card with a 0.0% transaction fee.

The Fees Journal should be open from the previous transaction. If it is not, open it by clicking the Statements icon. The session date is correct as the invoice date.

✓ 21

Debit Card Sales Summary Invoice #650 Dated October 14, 2015

To various one-time patients, $260 for initial assessments for new patients and $450 for follow-up treatment sessions. Total amount deposited in Interac bank account, $710. Store as a recurring bi-weekly transaction.

Choose **Statement** from the Transaction list.

Choose **One-Time Patient** from the Patient list and **press** tab.

PRO VERSION
Choose Invoice from the Transaction list. Choose One-Time Customer from the Customer list.

For one-time customers, Cash replaces Pay Later as the default option — Pay Later is not an option for one-time customers. The Net Days field is removed to match the immediate payment option and the default bank account is selected. The terms for new customers offer no discount, so the discount fields are blank.

Click the **Payment Method list arrow** as shown to see the payment options:

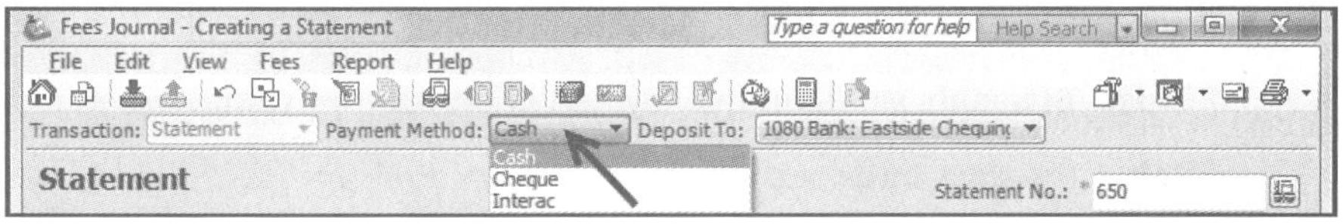

Click **Interac** as the method of payment to modify the invoice.

NOTES
Pay Later is not an option for one-time customers, so the Cash Amount (amount received) field is added automatically.

PRO VERSION
You will see Sales Journal – Creating An Invoice in the journal's title bar.

There is no bank account field or cheque number field as there is when the payment is made by cheque. Interac is linked automatically to a dedicated bank account as part of the company file setup, just like credit cards. Interac Amount replaces Cash Amount as the label for the amount received.

Type `Debit Card Sales Summary` (in the Address field).

Complete the rest of the **invoice** in the same way as credit card or cash sales.

Click the **Item Description field** and **type** `initial assessments`

Click the **Amount field** and **type** `260`

The account is added automatically because we entered it as the default linked revenue account for the Receivables Ledger.

Click the **Item Description field** on the second line of the invoice.

Type `follow-up treatments`

Click the **Amount field** and **type** `450`

Press tab to complete the invoice:

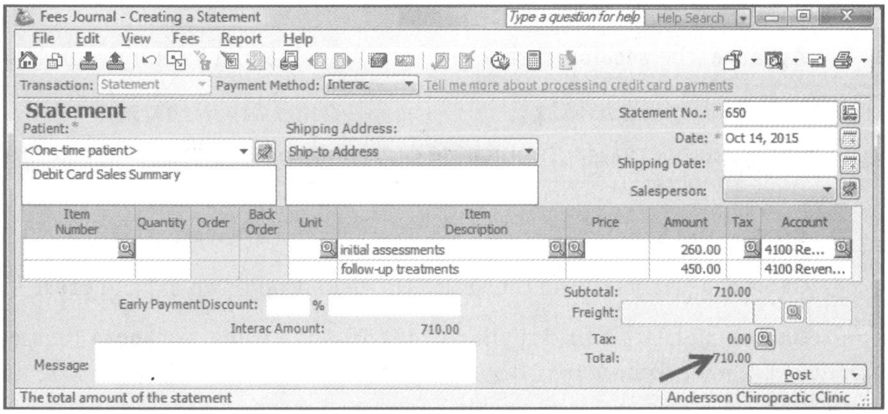

PRO VERSION
Choose the Report menu and click Display Sales Journal.

Choose the **Report menu** and **click Display Fees Journal Entry** to review the entry before posting:

Andersson Chiropractic Clinic
Fees Journal Entry 10/14/2015 (J14)

Account Number	Account Description	Debits	Credits
1100	Bank: Interac	710.00	-
4100	Revenue from Services	-	710.00
Additional Date:	Additional Field:	710.00	710.00

NOTES
The third-party provider that processes the Interac transactions does charge fees, but these would be entered at the time of account reconciliation when the statement is received.

Notice the new linked account for this transaction. The debit card account — *Bank: Interac* — replaces the usual bank account for other cash sales and *Accounts Receivable* for account sales. Unlike credit card sales, no additional fees are entered.

Close the **display** to return to the Fees Journal input screen.

Make **corrections** if necessary, referring to page 162 for assistance.

We can store the entry and use it to enter the debit card summaries every second week. When you recall the transaction, you can edit the amounts. You will not need to save the changes and store the transaction again.

Click the **Store tool** to save the transaction for repeated entries.

Choose **Biweekly** as the frequency and **click OK** to save the stored entry.

Click the **Post button** Post.

Close the **Fees Journal**. **Click Payables** in the Modules pane list.

Enter the **next three transactions** for October 14.

22 **Payment Cheque #122** **Dated October 14, 2015**
To Cleanol and Laundry Services, $90 from Eastside Chequing account in payment of account. Reference invoice #CLS-2419.

NOTES
You may need to scroll down to see the line for the prepayment amount.

23 **Payment Cheque #123** **Dated October 14, 2015**
To Thera-Tables Inc., $3 520 from Eastside Chequing account in full payment of account including $80 discount for early payment. Reference invoice #TT-4599 and cheque #567. Remember to "pay" the prepayment.

24 **Purchase Invoice #CLS-3926** **Dated October 14, 2015**
From Cleanol and Laundry Services, $120 for contracted twice weekly laundry service. Terms: net 30. Store the transaction as a bi-weekly recurring entry.

Filling Purchase Orders with Prepayments

When a prepayment is added directly to the purchase order, the payment details remain on the invoice when you fill the order.

Advance the **session date** to **October 21, 2015** and **back up** your **data**.

✓ 25 **Purchase Invoice #SL-4622** **Dated October 17, 2015**
From Sonartek Ltd., to fill purchase order #44, $6 000 including taxes for multi-frequency ultrasound machine. Terms: 2/15, n/30.

PRO VERSION
Click the Purchase Orders icon to open the journal.

CLASSIC VIEW
Click the Expenses, Orders & Quotes icon.
Choose Order from the Transaction drop-down list.

Click the **Supplier Orders icon** to open the Expenses Journal.

Choose **order #44** from the Order No. field drop-down list and **press** tab.

Choose **Convert This Supplier Order To An Invoice**, or **choose Invoice** from the Transaction drop-down list.

This will add the order details to the invoice form:

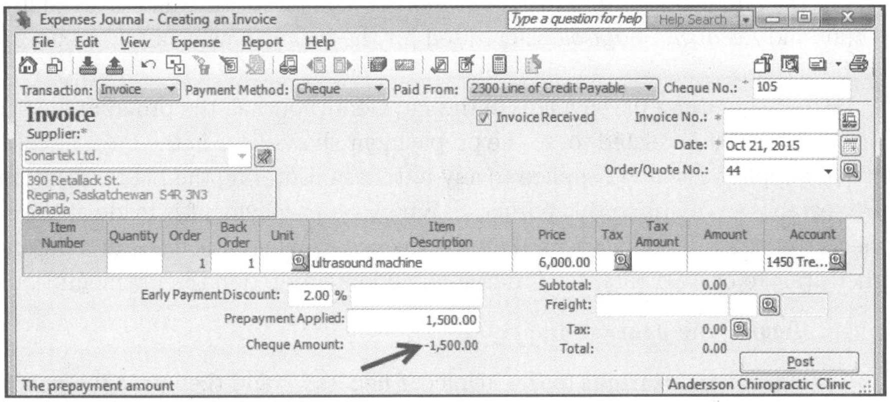

Notice that Cheque is still selected as the Payment Method. The prepayment information from the order is entered as the amount in the **Prepayment Applied** field. The cheque amount is negative because no invoice amount has been added yet.

Click the **Fill Backordered Quantities tool** in the tool bar or **choose** the **Expense menu** and **click Fill Supplier Order**.

Now the cheque amount is $4 380.00 — the total invoice amount minus the prepayment and 2 percent discount. This is not a cash purchase, so we need to change the payment method.

Choose **Pay Later** from the Payment Method drop-down list.

The form is updated — the bank, cheque number and cheque amount fields have been removed. The amount owing changes to $4 500 ($6 000 minus the $1 500 prepayment).

Add the **invoice number** and **purchase date** to the form:

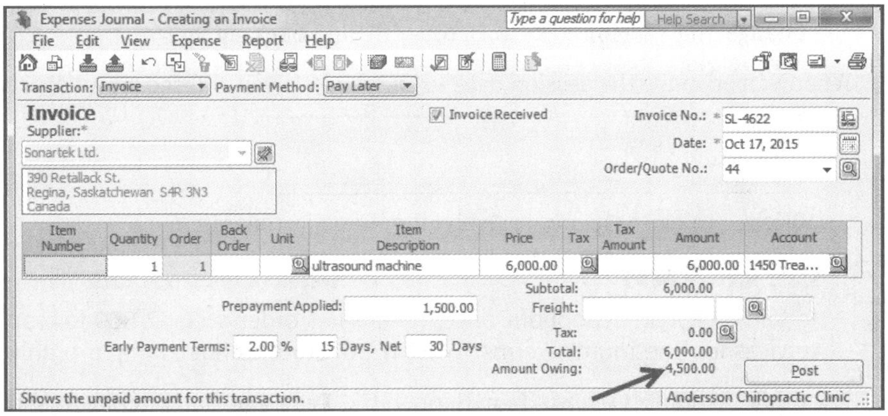

Click the **Additional Information tool**. **Click** the **Additional Information field**.

Type `Ref: fill PO #44` **Click** **OK** to return to the journal.

Press *ctrl* + **J** to open the journal display:

Andersson Chiropractic Clinic
Expenses Journal Entry 10/17/2015 (J18)

Account Number	Account Description	Debits	Credits
1450	Treatment Equipment	6,000.00	-
1280	Purchase Prepayments	-	1,500.00
2200	Accounts Payable	-	4,500.00
Additional Date:	Additional Field: Ref: fill PO #44	6,000.00	6,000.00

The entry differs from the standard purchase entry because of the amount for *Purchase Prepayments*. Because the purchase is complete, the credit with the supplier is removed and the prepayment is treated like a partial payment toward the invoice.

PRO VERSION
You will choose the Purchase menu and click Fill Purchase Order.

WARNING!
If you do not change the method of payment, the purchase amount owing will be posted to the Line of Credit Payable account (a payment by cheque) instead of to Accounts Payable.

PRO VERSION
You will choose the Purchase menu and click Enter Additional Information.

NOTES
If the deposit is made after the order is entered, you can edit (adjust) the order to add the prepayment, using the cheque date for the revised order.

Thus, *Purchase Prepayments* has been credited to reduce this account's balance to zero for the supplier. *Treatment Equipment* is debited for the full purchase invoice amount and *Accounts Payable* is credited for the balance owing after the prepayment is subtracted.

When you enter a prepayment in the Payments Journal, the program does not know which purchase it is related to, so the prepayment shows later in the Payments Journal for that supplier. It can be applied to any purchase. Entering the prepayment on the order establishes a link to this purchase. When the prepayment is made at the same time as the order, it should be entered on the order. When it is made at a different time, either prior to or later than the order, it should be entered in the Payments Journal.

Close the **Journal display**.

Make **corrections** to the invoice if necessary and then **post** the **purchase**.

Click **OK** to confirm that the order has been filled.

Enter the **next two transactions**. **Change** **modules** as needed.

26

Cash Purchase #GF-2641 **Dated October 18, 2015**

From Grasslands Fuel, $62 for gasoline for business vehicle. Invoice total $62 paid in full by cheque #569 from Regina Chequing account. Store as a bi-weekly recurring entry.

27

Cash Sales Invoice #651 **Dated October 20, 2015**

To Albert Blackfoot, $315 for seven treatment sessions. Invoice total paid in full by cheque #426 and deposited to Regina Chequing account. Store as a monthly recurring entry.

Filling Sales Orders with Deposits

Change the **session date** to October 31 and **back up** your **data**.

When you advance the session date to October 31, you will see an Advisor message:

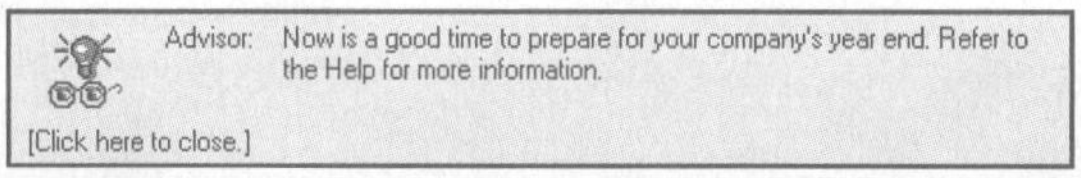
Advisor: Now is a good time to prepare for your company's year end. Refer to the Help for more information.
[Click here to close.]

Click to close the message about year-end preparation.

✓ 28

Sales Invoice #652 **Dated October 25, 2015**

To Veronica Kain School of Dance, to fill sales order #52, $2 500 for contracted services for one month. Terms: 1/10, n/30. Store as a recurring monthly entry.

Click the **Statements Icon** to open the **Fees Journal**. Statement should be selected as the transaction type.

Select **Sales Order #52** from the Order/Quote No. list and **press** *tab* to recall the order as a statement or invoice:

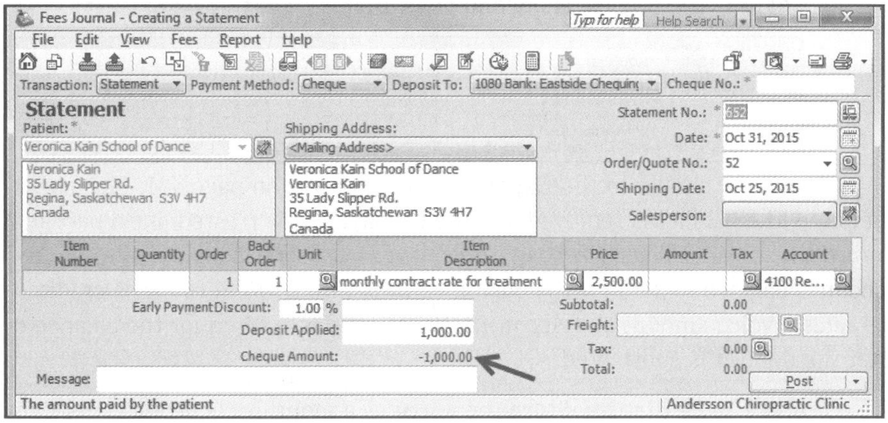

Or click the Patient Orders icon to open the Order form of the journal. Choose #52 from the Order No. drop-down list and press *tab* to recall the order. Then choose Convert This Patient Order To A Statement from the convert drop-down list, or choose Statement from the Transaction drop-down list to change the order to a statement.

Information about the deposit is included in the invoice. Since the deposit was paid by cheque, this is also the default payment method for the invoice, and we need to change it.

Click the **Payment Method list arrow** and **choose Pay Later**.

In the modified form the bank and cheque number fields have been removed. The deposit applied amount field is not available for entering an amount.

Click the **Fill Backordered Quantities tool** in the tool bar or **choose** the **Fees menu** and **click Fill Patient Order**.

With this step, you will update the amounts and fill the order:

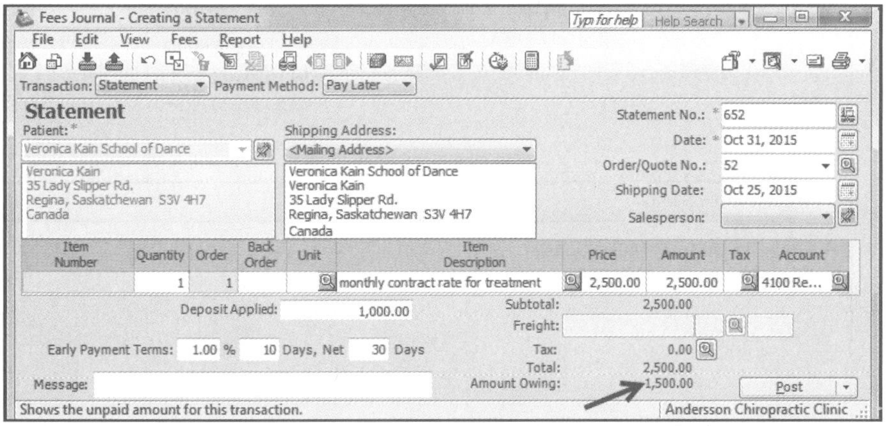

The Cheque Amount field has been removed but the Deposit Applied details remain. The Amount Owing is reduced by the $1 000 deposit.

Enter **Oct 25** as the date for the sale.

Click the **Enter Additional Information tool** or **choose** the **Fees menu** and **click Enter Additional Information**.

Enter `Ref SO #52 & deposit #15` in the Additional Field.

Click **OK** to return to the journal.

PRO VERSION

Open the Sales Journal. Invoice will be selected as the transaction type.

NOTES

When the deposit for a sales order is entered as a receipt separately from the sales order, the deposit amount does not appear in the sales journal when you fill the order.

PRO VERSION

Choose the Sales menu and click Fill Sales Order.

PRO VERSION

Choose the Sales menu and click Enter Additional Information.

> **NOTES**
> When the deposit for a sales order is entered as a receipt separately from the sales order, the deposit amount does not appear in the journal entry for the sale that fills the order.

Choose the **Report menu** and **click Display Fees Journal Entry**:

Andersson Chiropractic Clinic
Fees Journal Entry 10/25/2015 (J21)

Account Number	Account Description	Debits	Credits
1200	Accounts Receivable	1,500.00	-
2250	Prepaid Sales and Deposits	1,000.00	-
4100	Revenue from Services	-	2,500.00
Additional Date:	Additional Field: Ref: SO #52 & de...	2,500.00	2,500.00

The entry is similar to the Expenses Journal entry on page 431. Because the sale is complete, the liability is removed and the prepayment is treated like a partial payment toward the invoice. Thus, *Prepaid Sales and Deposits* has been debited to reduce this account's balance to zero for the customer, *Revenue from Services* is credited for the full sales invoice amount and *Accounts Receivable* is debited for the balance owing after the deposit is subtracted.

Close the **display**. **Store** the **entry** as a monthly recurring transaction.

Click **Post** to save the invoice. **Click OK** to confirm the removal of the order.

Enter the **next group of transactions** up to Cash Receipt #64. **Change modules** as needed, or **create shortcuts**.

29 **Sales Invoice #653** **Dated October 25, 2015**

To Interplay Ballet School, $2 500 for contracted services for one month. Terms: 1/10, n/30. Store transaction as a recurring monthly entry.

30 **Purchase Invoice #CLS-4723** **Dated October 28, 2015**

From Cleanol and Laundry Services, $120 for contracted laundry service. Terms: net 30. Recall stored transaction.

> **NOTES**
> Recall the stored transaction but do not store the changed transaction. When you post the transaction, you will see the message that the transaction has changed and the next due date will be updated. Click Yes to continue. Refer to page 185.

31

Sales Invoice: 654
Date: Oct 28, 2015

Andersson Chiropractic Clinic
www.betterbacks.com
4500 Rae St.
Regina, SK S4S 3B4
Tel 1: (306) 577-1900
Tel 2: (306) 577-2199 Fax: (306) 577-1925

Customer: Debit card sales summary
Address:
Phone No:

Treatment description	Amount
Initial assessments	130.00
Follow-up treatments	630.00

Terms: paid by Interac
Direct deposit to Interac account
Signed: *Maria Andersson* **Customer Initials:** **INVOICE TOTAL** 760.00

32 **Cash Purchase Invoice #WC-83825** **Dated October 28, 2015**

From Western Communications, $125 including taxes for one month of telephone and Internet service. Invoice total paid by cheque #124 from Eastside Chequing account. Store as a monthly recurring entry.

33 **Sales Invoice #655** **Dated October 28, 2015**

To Canadian Royals, $4 500 for contracted services for one month. Terms: 1/10, n/30. Store transaction as a recurring monthly entry.

34 **Sales Invoice #656** **Dated October 28, 2015**

To Roughrider Argos, $4 900 for contracted services for one month. Terms: 1/10, n/30. Store transaction as a recurring monthly entry.

35 **Cash Receipt #63** **Dated October 29, 2015**

From Interplay Ballet School, cheque #501 for $2 475 in payment of account including $25 discount for early payment. Reference sales invoice #653. Deposited to Regina Chequing account.

36 **Payment Cheque #570** **Dated October 29, 2015**

To Cleanol and Laundry Services, $210 from Regina Chequing account in payment of account. Reference invoices #CLS-2683 and #CLS-3926.

37 **Bank Debit Memo #477211** **Dated October 29, 2015**

From Eastside Trust, $2 100 for monthly payroll and $45 payroll service fee withdrawn from chequing account. Store payroll transaction as a monthly recurring entry. Use the General Journal for this payroll transaction.

Entering Receipts for Sales with Deposits on Orders

When a customer makes the final payment toward an invoice that had a deposit with the sales order, the journal entry is different from an entry with a separate deposit.

Open the **Receivables module window**.

✓ 38 **Cash Receipt #64** **Dated October 29, 2015**

From Veronica Kain School of Dance, cheque #878 for $1 475 in payment of account including $25 discount for early payment. Reference sales invoice #652 and deposit #15. Deposited to Eastside Chequing account.

Open the **Receipts Journal** and **select Veronica Kain School of Dance**:

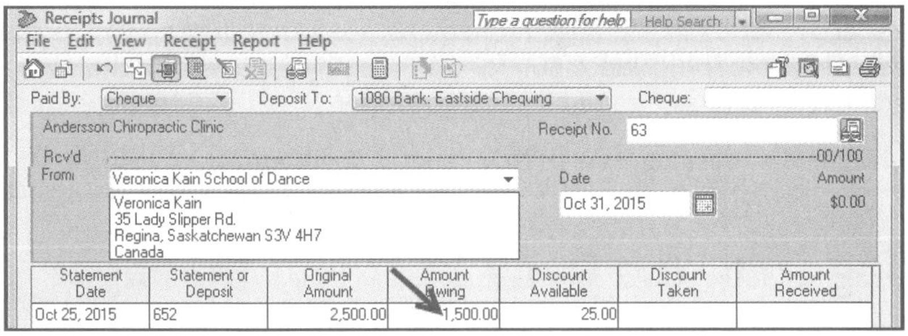

Because the prepayment was cleared at the time of the sale, it does not appear in the Receipts Journal. Instead, the Amount Owing has been reduced, so this is a standard receipt entry. The discount is based on the full invoice amount, or 1 percent of $2 500.

Enter the **remaining transaction details** to complete the entry. **Review** the **transaction** and then **post** it.

> **NOTES**
> Change modules as needed, or create and use shortcuts to enter transactions.

Enter the **remaining transactions** for the Oct. 31 session date.

39 **Purchase Quote #FS-644** **Dated October 29, 2015**
Starting date November 1, 2015
From Fresh Spaces (use Quick Add for the new supplier), $125 per week for daily laundry service. Terms: net 30.

40

PURCHASE QUOTE #45

Cleanol and Laundry Services
19 Duster Road
Regina, SK S4R 4L4
(306) 398-0908

Date: Oct 29, 2015
Starting date: Nov 1, 2015

For: Andersson Chiropractic Clinic
Address: 4500 Rae St.
Regina, SK S4S 3B4
Phone No: (306) 577-1900
Fax No: (306) 577-1925
Contact: Maria Andersson

Order description	Amount
Contract for daily laundry service bi-weekly rate including GST terms: net 30 days	210.00
Quote Total	210.00
Deposit	—
Total Amount	210.00

Authorization: *Bessie Sweeps*

41 **Purchase Order #45** **Dated October 29, 2015**
Starting date November 1, 2015
Convert quote #45 from Cleanol and Laundry Services to an order. The order confirms the price at $210 every two weeks for daily service. Terms: net 30.

> **NOTES**
> To transfer the funds, you should debit the Line of Credit Payable and Interest Expense accounts and credit the bank account.

42 **Memo #2** **Dated October 31, 2015**
Transfer $1 060 from the Regina Chequing account to pay down the line of credit. This amount includes $60 for one month of interest on the amount of credit used. Store as a monthly recurring entry. (Use the General Journal.)

Advance the **session date** to November 7. **Back up** your **data file**.

Working from the Daily Business Manager

> **WARNING!**
> Back up your data file before entering transactions from the Daily Business Manager.

Sage 50 helps a business monitor its performance and cash flow by generating several of the reports that you have seen so far. It also keeps track of recurring transactions, payments and receipts with the Daily Business Manager lists. These lists offer an additional method of internal control. In addition to these lists, the Daily Business Manager can compile financial performance data for the company.

You should be in the Home window after changing the session date to November 7. You can enter many transactions directly from the Daily Business Manager.

You can open the Daily Business Manager from the Company window Daily Business Manager icon, the Business Assistant menu or the Daily Business Manager (DBM) tool:

Click the **Daily Business Manager icon** in the Company module window or **choose** the **Business Assistant menu** and **click Daily Business Manager** or **click** the **DBM tool**:

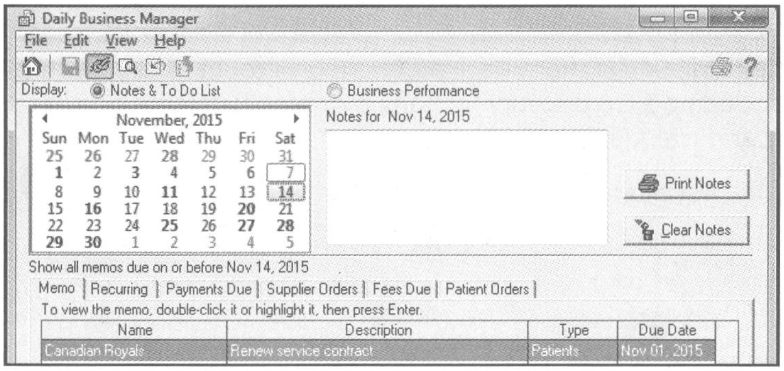

In any journal, you can access the Daily Business Manager from the tool icon or from the View menu Daily Business Manager option.

You can show Daily Business Manager lists automatically each time you advance the session date, each time you start the program or both. Choose the Setup menu, then choose User Preferences and click View (see page 82). Click At Startup and After Changing Session Date below Daily Business Manager to select these options. Menu and tool bar access to the lists are always available.

By default, Sage 50 chooses a date that is one week past the current session date for its Daily Business Manager. The date can be changed by clicking a new date on the calendar. Lists will be updated to reflect the change in date.

Each tab screen includes instructions for accessing journals or selecting an entry.

You can also type notes for a date directly into the Notes box. They will remain on-screen for that date until you choose Clear Notes. You can print these notes and clear them when they are no longer needed.

The Memo tab screen opens with a note for one of the customers about renewing the contract. This memo was entered in the customer's ledger Memo tab screen with a due date and the option to display it in the Daily Business Manager.

✓ 43 **Memo #3** **Dated November 1, 2015**

Review and update memos and enter the next transactions from the Daily Business Manager.

Double-click Canadian Royals to open the memo in the customer's ledger record:

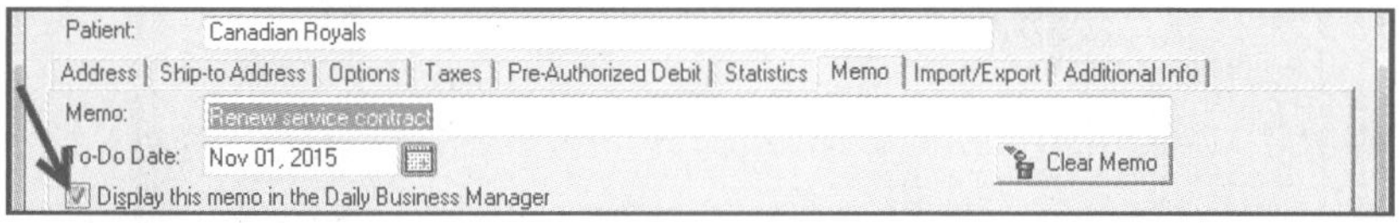

The customer's record opens at the Memo tab screen. You now have the option to edit the memo, remove it if it no longer applies or to change the date for its appearance in the Daily Business Manager. You can see that we have checked the option to display the memo.

NOTES

In the Company module window, the Daily Business Manager icon is in the upper Tasks pane beside Data Management.

CLASSIC VIEW

Click the Daily Business Manager tool in the tool bar, or click the Daily Business Manager icon in the My Business column.

PRO VERSION

The tabs are labelled Purchase Orders, Sales Due and Sales Orders instead of Supplier Orders, Fees Due and Patient Orders.

NOTES

Refer to page 82 to see the Daily Business Manager Settings on the User Preferences View screen.

NOTES
After editing the due date for the memo in the ledger, its date is beyond the display period for the Daily Business Manager.

Change the **date** in the To-Do Date field to **Nov. 1, 2016**.

Click **Save And Close** [Save and Close] to return to the Daily Business Manager. The memo has been removed from the list.

Payments Due

The first entry for November is a cheque issued for an outstanding invoice. To be certain that all outstanding invoices are paid in a timely fashion, we can enter payments from the Daily Business Manager.

✓ 44

Payment Cheque #571 **Dated November 1, 2015**

To Sonartek Ltd., $4 380 from Regina Chequing account in full payment of account including $120 discount for early payment. Reference purchase invoice #SL-4622 and cheque #104 (prepayment).

Click the **Payments Due tab**:

PRO VERSION
Vendor replaces Supplier as the column heading.

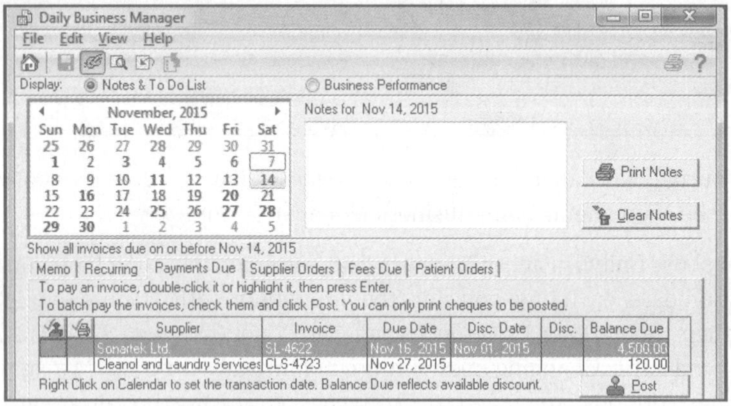

The list includes payments due and any applicable discounts. To see the payments due in a longer period, and to be sure that all discounts available will be included, you can select a later date on the calendar. You might use this list to plan a payment schedule. We want to be able to take advantage of purchase discounts.

The list includes the Supplier name, Invoice number, payment Due Date, Discount Date, Discount availability and the Balance Due (owing). The Discount Date shows when the discount period ends. You can pay the invoices directly from this screen when no changes are needed. You can also open the Payments Journal by double-clicking an invoice line or by clicking an invoice and pressing (enter).

NOTES
No payments are due in the later part of November, so changing the calendar date will not change the display in this example.

If you pay from the Daily Business Manager, the session date is the default, so the discount is no longer available. To change the cheque date, right-click the date you want in the calendar.

Right-click **Nov 1** on the calendar. The discount for Sonartek is now available.

In the November calendar section, 1 now has an open box framing it to indicate it will be the transaction posting date. The Disc. column now has a ✓ and the Balance Due for invoice #SL-4622 has been updated to include the discount:

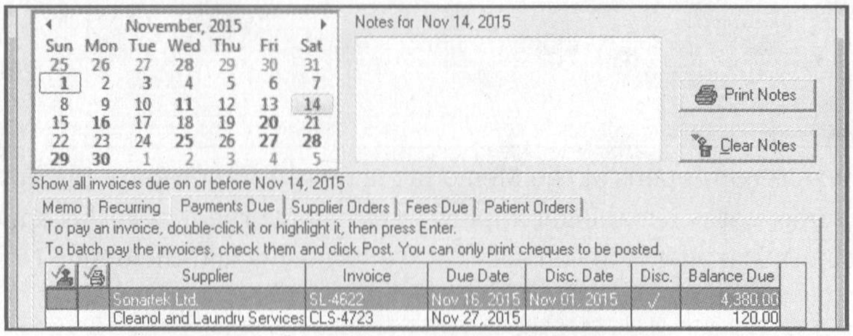

If we post from the Business Manager now, the date and discount will be correct, but the bank account will not. The default amount and bank account (Bank: Eastside Chequing) will be entered when you pay from the Business Manager and you cannot change these fields. Therefore, we must open the journal to pay the invoice.

Double-click the **entry for Sonartek** to open the Payments Journal:

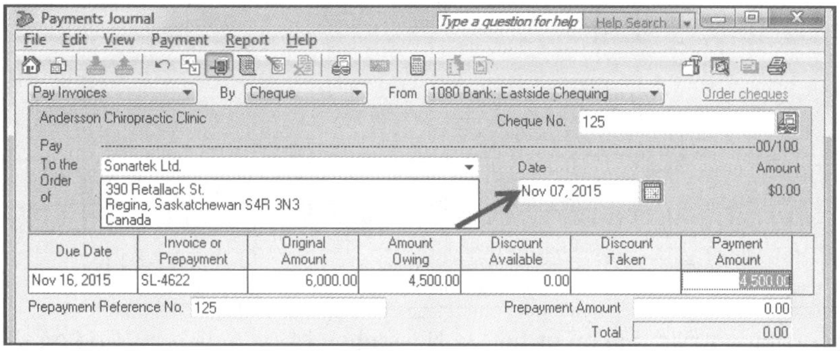

> **NOTES**
> The prepayment was entered on the order and cleared when we filled the order, so it does not appear in the Payments Journal.

Notice that the journal tool bar includes the Daily Business Manager tool.

The session date is now entered again as the default, so the full amount owing is entered by default without the discount. We must change both these details. First we will delete the payment amount because it is already selected.

Press *del* to remove the amount.

Enter **Nov 1** as the date for the payment. **Press** *tab* to make the discount available.

Choose **Bank: Regina Chequing** in the From field to update the cheque number.

Click the **Discount Taken field** and then the **Payment Amount field.**

Press *tab*. **Enter** the **Invoice Number** as Additional Information to complete the payment. **Check** your **entry**.

Click the **Post button** Post to save the entry when you are certain it is correct.

Close the **Payments Journal** to return to the Daily Business Manager.

The Sonartek Ltd. entry has been removed from the list.

Recurring Transactions Due

The next transaction is the recurring cash purchase.

Another advantage to using the Daily Business Manager is that the recurring entries for all journals are listed together. You can open a journal and recall a stored transaction in a single step. You can also post and print sales invoices, individually or in batches, directly from this screen, but you cannot preview them.

Right-click **Nov 7** on the calendar to reset the session date as the posting date.

Click the **Recurring tab**:

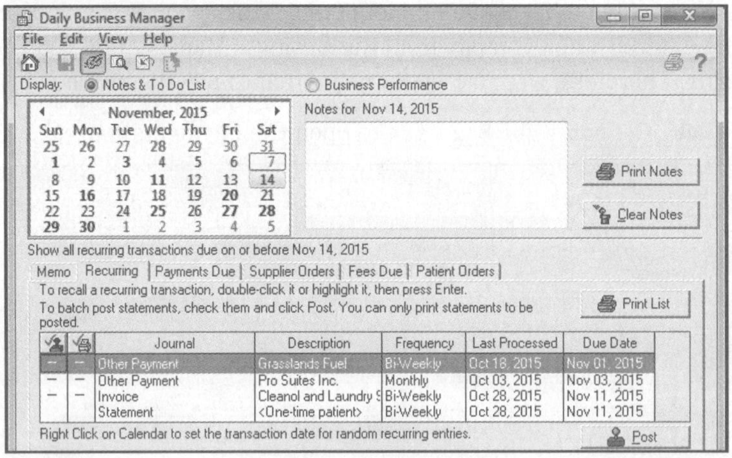

NOTES
If you entered the purchases from Grasslands Fuel and Pro Suites in the Expenses Journal, that will be listed as the journal in the Daily Business Manager window and it will open instead of the Payments Journal. In this case, you should enter the transaction in the Expenses Journal.
The instructions here used the Make Other Payment option in the Payments Journal.

All recurring entries due on or before November 14 (the date marked on the calendar) should be listed, together with the Journal used for the original entry, the entry name (Description) and its recurring Frequency. The most recent posting date (Last Processed) and the Due Date are also included. The entries are listed according to the Due Date, with the earliest date at the top of the list.

The first entry — the fuel purchase from Grasslands Fuel — is due Nov. 1. Recurring purchases require an invoice number as additional information so we need to open the journal first. This payment does not use the default bank account selection.

✓ 45

Cash Purchase Invoice #GF-3677 **Dated November 1, 2015**

From Grasslands Fuel, $62 for gasoline for business vehicle. Invoice total paid in full from Regina Chequing account by cheque #572. Recall stored entry.

NOTES
You may need to scroll up in the transaction section of the Payments Journal to see the original entry. The transaction detail area of the journal may appear blank.

Double-click **Grasslands Fuel**, the cash purchase entry, to open the journal with this transaction on-screen. (**Click** **30** in the November calendar if you do not see all the transactions listed.)

Bank: Regina Chequing is preselected as the bank account in the From field because we stored the transaction with this selection. This is another advantage to storing a transaction.

Enter **GF-3677** in the Invoice/Ref. field. If you are using the Make Other Payment approach, you should update the Comment as well.

Post the **transaction** when you are sure it is correct.

Close the **journal** to return to the Daily Business Manager. The entry for Grasslands Fuel has been removed.

NOTES
Click anywhere in the Daily Business Manager window to update the list if necessary.

✓ 46

Cash Purchase #R2015-11 **Dated November 3, 2015**

To Pro Suites Inc., cheque #125 for $2 300 from Eastside Chequing account to pay rent for November. Recall stored entry.

Double-click **Pro Suites**, the next cash purchase entry, to open the journal.

Enter **R2015-11** in the Invoice/Ref. field. Copy this number to the Comment line as well if you are using the Make Other Payment method.

Post the **transaction** after making certain it is correct.

Close the **Payments Journal**.

The Recurring Transactions list has been updated again — the Pro Suites transaction has been removed.

The remaining list items are not due this week, so we can proceed to another list in the Daily Business Manager. We want to process some receipts next.

Fees (Sales) Due

✓ 47

Cash Receipt #65 **Dated November 5, 2015**

From Canadian Royals, cheque #4011 for $4 455 in payment of account including $45 discount for early payment. Reference sales invoice #655. Deposited to Regina Chequing account.

Click the **Fees Due tab** to see the list of Invoices due within the week:

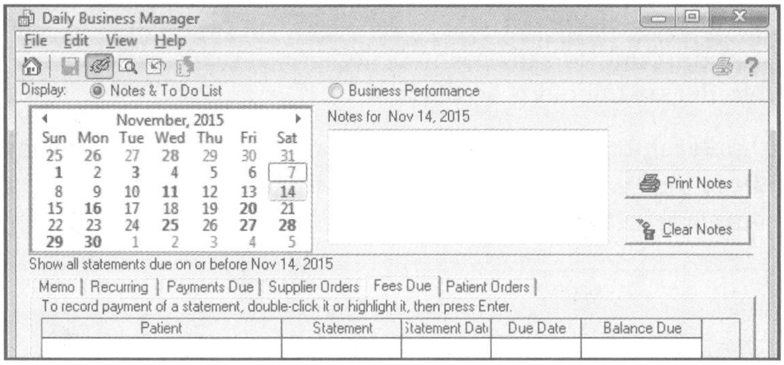

PRO VERSION
Click the Sales Due tab. Customer, Invoice and Invoice Date replace Patient, Statement and Statement Date as the column headings.

The Fees Due list is easy to use as well. It can be used to locate customers with outstanding debts. The list shows the Patient's name, Statement number and Date, payment Due Date and Balance Due (owing) on the due date without the discount. Invoices displayed can be matched against receipts on hand, and you can open the Receipts Journal directly from this window. No invoices are listed because they are not due in the next week. However, most of Andersson's customers take advantage of sales discounts, so we should look at sales due over a longer span than one week. Payments were received from Canadian Royals and Roughrider Argos. These payments are not due until late November, but the customers are paying early to take the discounts.

We cannot post receipts from the Daily Business Manager because customer cheque numbers should be added. We also need to change the bank account for the deposit when it is different from the default.

Click **30** on the November calendar to see all sales invoices due this month:

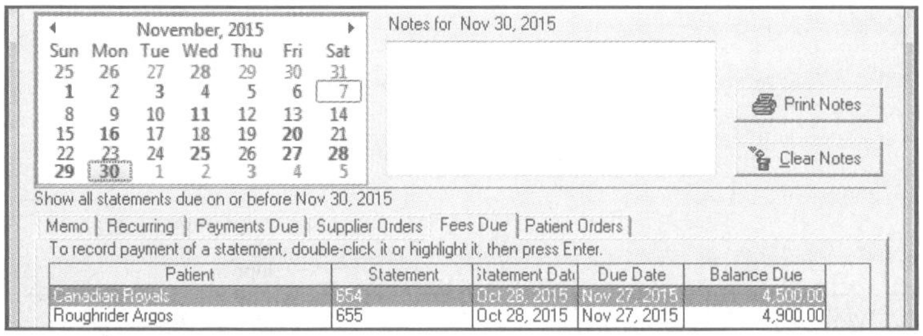

The invoices we need now appear on the list so we can enter receipts for them.

To open the journal, you can double-click any part of the line for the entry you want or click the line and press *enter*.

Double-click the **Canadian Royals** (Invoice #654) to open the Receipts Journal for the selected customer.

Press *tab* to accept the discount and amount for the first invoice. The amount should appear in the Total field and the upper cheque portion.

WARNING!

If the discount had expired by November 7, the session date, you would change the date first, as we did for the payment entry. Then delete the default amount and re-enter the discount taken and payment amount.

NOTES

If you return to the Daily Business Manager, the default date is correct for the receipt from Roughrider Argos, but you must change the bank account because the default account is incorrect. If you remain in the Receipts Journal, you must change the date.

NOTES

Use Full Add for new supplier:

Web: www: gbw.com

Expense account: 1480 Whirlpool (create new account)

Use the source document for the remaining supplier details.

Choose **Bank: Regina Chequing** as the bank account in the Deposit To field.

Add the customer's **cheque number** (#4011) in the Cheque field.

Enter **Nov 5** as the date. **Add** the **invoice number** as additional information.

Display the **journal entry** to review your work. **Close** the **display** and **make corrections** if necessary.

Click **Post** Post to record the transaction.

Enter the next **receipt** from the Receipts Journal because it is already open.

48

Cash Receipt #66 **Dated November 7, 2015**

From Roughrider Argos, cheque #1636 for $4 851 in payment of account including $49 discount for early payment. Reference sales invoice #656. Deposited to Regina Chequing account.

Close the **Receipts Journal**. Both Sales Due entries have been removed. **Close** the **Daily Business Manager window** and **enter** the next **Purchase Order**.

49

PO#:	46
Date:	Nov 7, 2015
Shipping date:	Dec 28, 2015
Ordered from:	Get Better Whirlpools
Address:	35 Eddy Circle Saskatoon, SK S7K 6E3
Phone No:	(306) 665-7210 or (877) 699-1270
Fax No:	(306) 663-6281
Contact:	Ira Spinner

Andersson Chiropractic Clinic
www.betterbacks.com
4500 Rae St.
Regina, SK S4S 3B4
Tel 1: (306) 577-1900
Tel 2: (306) 577-2199 Fax: (306) 577-1925

PURCHASE ORDER

Order description	Amount
therapeutic whirlpool (Model WP-299X) including GST and PST terms: net 20 days	24 000.00
Deposit: $2 000 paid by cheque #573 (Regina Chequing Account)	

Order Total	24 000.00
Deposit	2 000.00
Balance Owing	22 000.00

Authorization: *Maria Andersson*

Patient (Sales) Orders Due

Two more lists are available: Supplier Orders and Patient Orders. To see outstanding items, click the corresponding tab. Lists for orders show unfilled orders due within the next week. You can access the journal windows for items on these lists just as you did for payments and fees due. We can enter the sale from order #51 on November 9 from the Daily Business Manager.

Advance the **session date** to November 14.

✓ 50 **Sales Invoice #657** **Dated November 9, 2015**

To Giant Raptors, to fill one month of the contract in sales order #51 for $3 300. Terms: 1/10, n/30.

Open the **Daily Business Manager window**.

Click the **Patient Orders tab** to see the list:

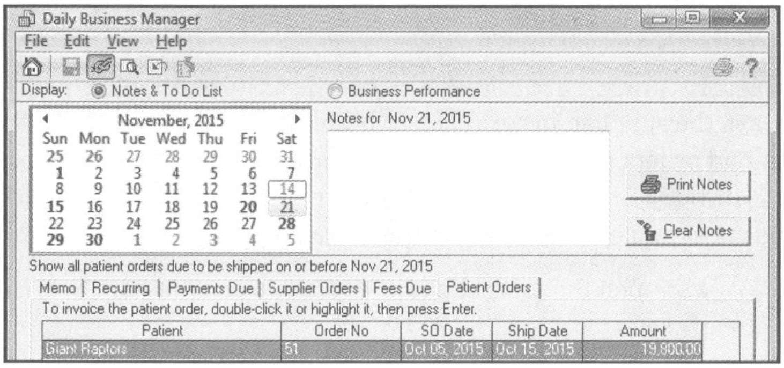

The list displays the patient, order number, order date (SO Date), shipping date and amount.

The order we want is listed. You can turn the order into an invoice from the Daily Business Manager by opening the journal with the order on-screen. As usual, double-clicking will open the transaction window we need.

Double-click **Giant Raptors** (Order #51).

The Fees Journal opens with the order converted to a statement or invoice. Notice that the backordered amount is 5. One month of the contract has been completed.

Enter **Nov 9** in the Date field.

Click the **Quantity field** and **type** 1

Press tab to update the amount. The backordered amount changes to 4.

Check your **entry** and when it is correct, **click** **Post**.

Close the **Fees Journal** to return to the Daily Business Manager.

The order remains on the list because it has not been completely filled and because the initial shipping date is before the session date.

PRO VERSION
Click the Sales Orders tab. Customer replaces Patient as the column heading.

Purchase Orders Due

The next transaction fills the order from Cleanol and Laundry Services.

✓ 51 **Purchase Invoice #CLS-6543** **Dated November 11, 2015**

From Cleanol and Laundry Services, to fill purchase order #45, $210 for contracted daily laundry service. Terms: net 30. Store as a bi-weekly recurring entry. Remove the old stored entry then store the new one.

NOTES
Advance the calendar date selection in the Daily Business Manager if you do not see the recurring transaction listed.

PRO VERSION
Click the Purchase Orders tab. Vendor replaces Supplier as the column heading.

Click the **Supplier Orders tab** to see the list:

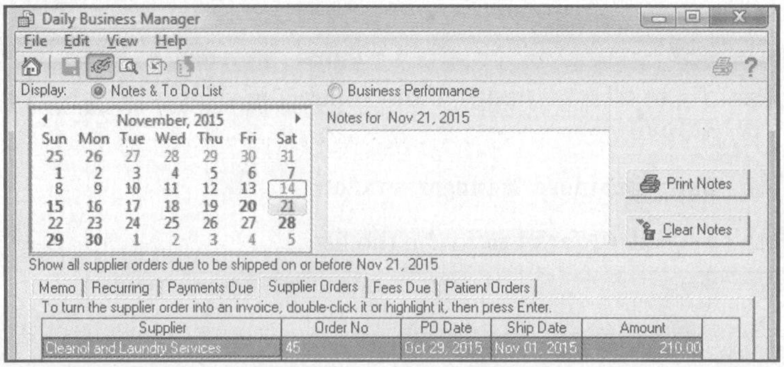

The list displays the supplier, order number, order date, shipping date and amount, making it easy to find orders that you need to track or follow up with the supplier.

Again, we can turn the order from Cleanol and Laundry Services into an invoice from the Daily Business Manager by opening the journal with the order on-screen.

Press *enter* to open the journal entry — Cleanol and Laundry Services is already selected.

Enter **CLS-6543** as the invoice number.

Enter **Nov 11** as the invoice date.

Click the **Fill Backordered Quantities tool**.

Enter the **order number** as additional information.

Do not post the **transaction** yet because we want to store it.

Removing Recurring Transactions

Sometimes a recurring transaction is no longer required, or it needs to be replaced. If you try to store the new purchase invoice from Cleanol and Laundry Services before removing the old entry, the program will not allow you to continue because the name duplicates the entry on file.

NOTES
This is different from recalling a transaction, editing it and then storing it again. In that situation, you can replace the older version. In this situation, we have created a new journal entry first.

Click the **Store tool**. **Choose Biweekly** as the frequency for the transaction and **click OK**.

You will see the Duplicate Entry warning:

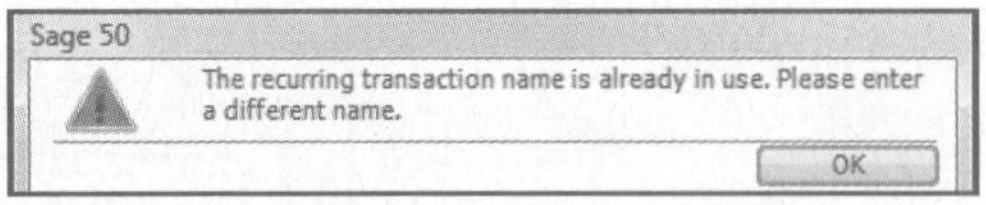

Click **OK** to return to the Store Recurring Transaction screen.

Click **Cancel** to return to the journal. We need to remove the old stored transaction first.

Click the **Recall tool** to open the Recall Recurring Transaction list:

WARNING!
When we complete the entry in this way, we cause the next due date to advance, so the date in the Daily Business Manager and on the Recall screen will be incorrect – we have chosen Store twice. You can edit the date in the journal.

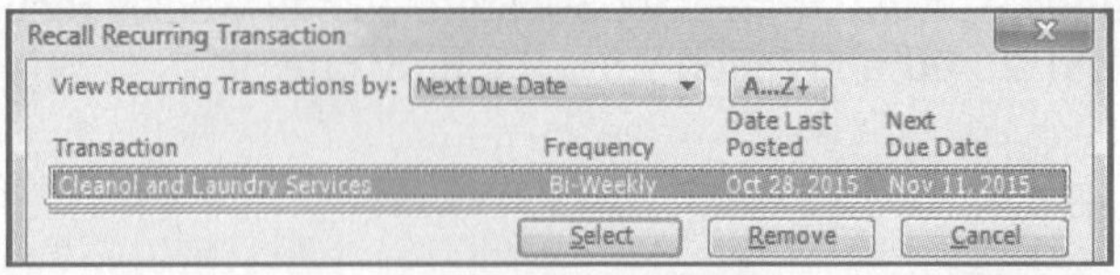

Cleanol and Laundry Services should be selected. If you entered the rental payment to Pro Suites in the Purchases Journal instead of the Payments Journal as an Other Payment, it will be listed in this window as well. The entry for Cleanol should still be selected because it is the next entry that is due. If it is not selected, click to select it.

Click **Remove** to see the confirmation warning:

Click **Yes** to confirm the removal if you have selected the correct entry.

Click **Cancel** if the Recall Transaction window is still open. (Read the margin Notes.)

Click the **Store tool** .

Choose **Biweekly** as the frequency for the new recurring invoice. **Click OK**.

Post the **purchase transaction**.

Click **OK** to confirm that the filled order has been removed.

Close the **Expenses Journal** to return to the Daily Business Manager. The order is no longer listed.

52 **Debit Card Sales Summary Invoice #658** **Dated November 11, 2015**

To various one-time patients, $260 for initial assessments and $450 for follow-up treatment sessions. Total amount deposited in Interac bank account, $710. Enter the stored transaction from the Daily Business Manager.

Close the **Daily Business Manager**. **Enter** the **next of group of transactions**, including the **recurring purchase from Cleanol and Laundry Services** on November 25.

53 **Cash Purchase Invoice #TP-1188** **Dated November 12, 2015**

From The Papery, $230 for paper supplies for treatment rooms and $60 for office supplies. Invoice total $290 paid in full from Eastside Chequing account by cheque #126.

SESSION DATE – NOVEMBER 21, 2015

54 **Cash Receipt #67** **Dated November 18, 2015**

From the Giant Raptors, cheque #1334 for $3 267 in full payment of account including $33 discount for early payment. Reference sales invoice #657. Deposited to Eastside Chequing account.

55 **Purchase Order #47** **Dated November 19, 2015**

Starting date January 1, 2016
From HydraTub Care (use Full Add for new supplier), $200 per month, including taxes for one-year service contract. The contract includes weekly maintenance of whirlpool and repairs. Parts required for repairs will be billed separately. Terms: net 20. Remember to enter 2016 as the year for the starting date.

56 **Purchase Quote #SU-5532** **Dated November 19, 2015**

Starting date December 1, 2015
From Space Unlimited (use Quick Add), $2 250 per month for rent of office space for the next 12 months. Rent does not include heat or hydro. Terms: net 1. Rent payment is due on the first of each month. Security deposit of one month's rent required in advance. Postdated cheques will be accepted.

NOTES

If you have only one recurring transaction, the window closes after you remove it. If there are more transactions, the window stays open and you must click Cancel to close it.

WARNING!

You must enter the year for order #47. If you do not, the program will enter 2015 as the default.

NOTES

HydraTub Care
550 Splash St.
Regina, SK S4T 7H5
Tel: (306) 578-2996
Terms: net 20
Expense account: 5220
(Create a new Group account: 5220 Whirlpool Maintenance.)

57 **Purchase Quote #48** **Dated November 19, 2015**

Starting date December 1, 2015
From Pro Suites Inc., $2 350 per month for rent of office space for the next 12 months. Rent includes heat and hydro. Rent payment is due on the first of each month. A series of postdated cheques will be accepted.

58 **Purchase Order #48** **Dated November 20, 2015**

Starting date December 1, 2015
From Pro Suites Inc., $2 350 per month for rent of office space for the next 12 months. Convert purchase quote #48 to a purchase order.

SESSION DATE – NOVEMBER 28, 2015

NOTES
The year-end Advisor appears when you advance the session date. Read the message and close the Advisor.

59 **Debit Card Sales Summary Invoice #659** **Dated November 25, 2015**

To various one-time customers, $260 for initial assessments and $630 for follow-up treatment sessions. Total amount deposited in Interac bank account, $890. Recall the stored transaction and edit the amounts.

60 **Purchase Invoice #CLS-8210** **Dated November 25, 2015**

From Cleanol and Laundry Services, $210 for contracted laundry service. Terms: net 30. Recall the stored transaction. (Read the margin Notes.)

NOTES
If you recall the recurring transactions from the Daily Business Manager, advance the calendar date selection in the Daily Business Manager if you do not see the recurring transaction listed. If the next due date is incorrect, you can edit the date when you recall the entry. Store it again to correct the next due date.

Posting Directly from the Daily Business Manager

All the Daily Business Manager transactions we have shown so far have been posted after opening the journals. Cheques (payments) and recurring sales invoices can also be posted directly from the Daily Business Manager, if you can accept the default information, that is, the bank account used.

Posting Sales Directly

Although you can post several sales invoices at the same time, you should open the journal and review the entry to verify it is correct. However, to demonstrate the method we will post one sale without opening the journal.

WARNING!
When you post directly from the Daily Business Manager, you cannot review the journal entry or make other changes.
Opening the journal entry before posting allows you to review the entry and correct errors, if there are any.
If you want to post directly from the Daily Business Manager, back up your data file first and check the journal entries to be sure that they are correct.

✓ 61 **Sales Invoice #660** **Dated November 25, 2015**

Enter the recurring sale to Interplay Ballet School, $2 500 for contracted services for one month, directly from the Daily Business Manager. Terms: 1/10, n/30.

Open the **Daily Business Manager**. **Click** the **Recurring tab** if necessary.

If you need to print the invoices, click the Print column beside the invoice.

We will post the next recurring sale directly without opening the journal. It is due on November 25, so we must change the date. The calendar shows the week ending December 5. We must choose the posting (sale) date on the November, not the December, calendar.

Click the **left arrow** ◀ at the top of the December calendar to access the November calendar.

Right-click **25** in the November calendar to select this as the posting date.

Click (left-click) **28** to reset the session date. (When you first returned to the November calendar, November 1 was the session date and the recurring entries were removed.)

NOTES
If you have set the dates correctly, November 25 on the calendar should have an open box framing it and November 28 should appear in a solid coloured box.

Click the **Post column** (the first column) **beside** the sale for **Interplay Ballet** to add a ✓.

Click **Post** Post.

A message appears asking if there is additional information to enter before posting:

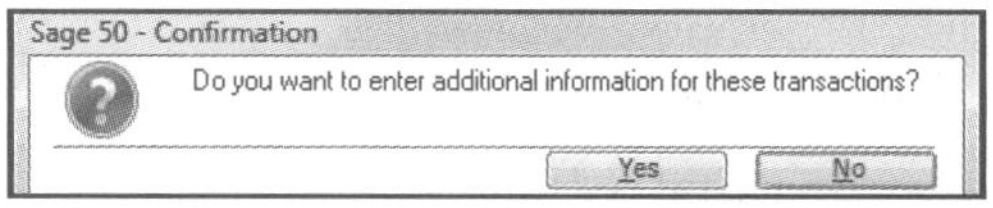

If you want to add details, click Yes to open the Additional Information screen. This screen will not open the journal itself for any other changes. There are no details to add to the Sales Journal entry. We can continue.

Click **No**. You will see a message naming the invoices that are currently being processed and the confirmation:

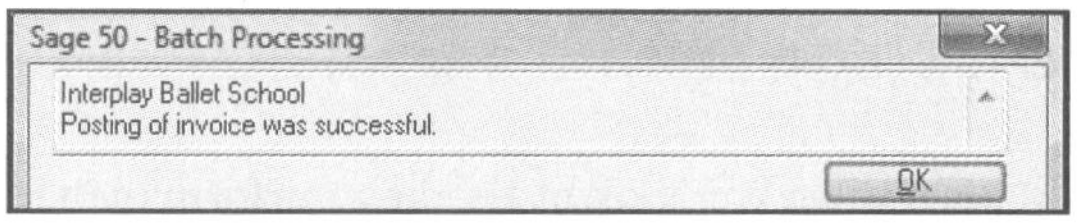

All the invoices that were processed will be listed.

Click **OK** to return to the list of recurring entries. The sale we posted has been removed.

If the entry did not post successfully, Sage 50 will provide that information. Check the journal report for the transaction. If it is not included, open the Fees (Sales) Journal to enter the transaction.

Close the **Daily Business Manager**. **Enter** the next **four recurring transactions**. If you enter these from the Daily Business Manager, open the journals and review each journal entry to be certain they will be posted correctly.

NOTES

Advance the Daily Business Manager date to Dec. 31 if necessary to see all recurring transactions.

62 **Sales Invoice #661** **Dated November 25, 2015**

To Veronica Kain School of Dance, $2 500 for contracted services for one month. Terms: 1/10, n/30. Recall the stored transaction.

63 **Sales Invoice #662** **Dated November 28, 2015**

To Canadian Royals, $4 500 for contracted services for one month. Terms: 1/10, n/30. Recall the stored transaction.

64 **Sales Invoice #663** **Dated November 28, 2015**

To Roughrider Argos, $4 900 for contracted services for one month. Terms: 1/10, n/30. Recall the stored transaction.

65 **Cash Purchase Invoice #WC-122022** **Dated November 28, 2015**

From Western Communications, $125 including taxes for telephone and Internet service. Invoice total paid from Eastside Chequing account by cheque #127. Recall the stored transaction.

Posting Payments Directly

The payment to Cleanol can be posted directly without opening the journal because it uses the default account. The cheque is posted on the session date.

✓ 66 **Payment Cheque #128** **Dated November 28, 2015**

To Cleanol and Laundry Services, $330 from Eastside Chequing account in payment of account. Reference invoices #CLS-4723 and CLS-6543.

WARNING!

Remember that when you pay from the Daily Business Manager, the default amount and bank account are selected. You cannot change them.

Opening the journal entry before posting allows you to review the entry and correct errors, if there are any.

Open the **Daily Business Manager** if necessary. **Click** the **Payments Due tab**.

Click the **Post column** beside **Inv #CLS-4723 and CLS-6543 (Cleanol and Laundry Services)** to add two ✓s.

Click **Post** .

You will be asked if you want to enter additional information for the cheque.

Click **Yes** to open the additional information window or **click No** to continue.

After a brief period, you will see the successful posting confirmation:

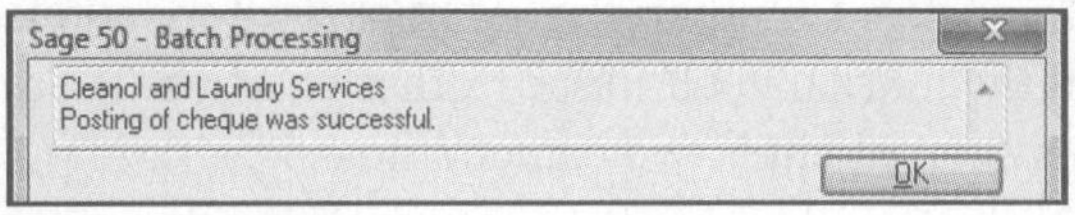

Click **OK**.

Business Performance

Before closing the Daily Business Manager, we will look at the key performance indicators.

Click **Business Performance**:

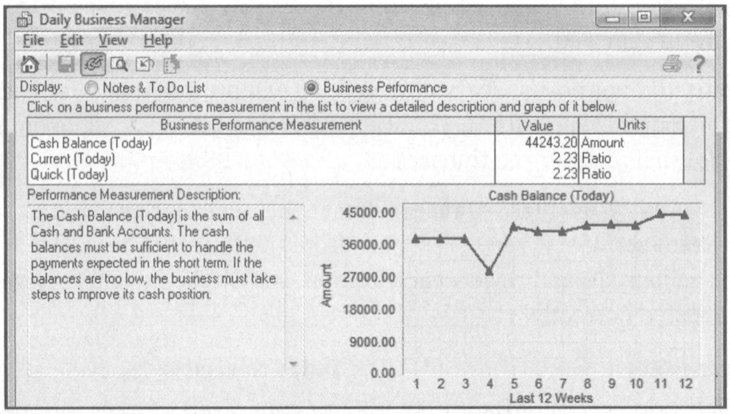

> **NOTES**
> As indicated on the screen, the cash balance is the total for cash and bank accounts. Thus, the balance for Bank: Interac (a Credit Card Receivable Class account) is not included. The Line of Credit liability Bank class account balance is subtracted from the total of the two chequing accounts.

Performance information includes the current bank account balance, the current ratio and the quick ratio at the session date. The information is provided numerically and graphically. Detailed descriptions explain the indicators and guidelines for these financials. Clicking an indicator will display the results.

Click **Notes & To Do List** to restore the lists.

Click to close the Daily Business Manager and return to the Home window.

Advance the **session date** to November 30.

Enter the **remaining transactions** for November 30, including memo #8.

67 **Cash Receipt #68** **Dated November 29, 2015**
From Interplay Ballet, cheque #553 for $2 475 in payment of account including $25 discount for early payment. Reference invoice #660. Deposited to Eastside Chequing account.

68 **Bank Debit Memo #747721** **Dated November 29, 2015**
From Eastside Trust, $3 000 for monthly payroll and $45 payroll service fee withdrawn from chequing account 1080. Recall, edit and store the transaction.

> **NOTES**
> After editing the wage amount, store the changed entry to replace the previous one because this will be the new monthly salary.

69 **Bank Debit Memo #120022** **Dated November 29, 2015**
From Regina Trust, $36 withdrawn from account for service charges.

70 **Memo #4** **Dated November 29, 2015**

Transfer $1 060 from the Regina Chequing account to pay down the line of credit. This amount includes $60 for one month of interest on the amount of credit used. Recall the stored transaction.

71 **Bank Debit Memo #747937** **Dated November 29, 2015**

From Eastside Trust, pre-authorized withdrawals from chequing account:
For bi-monthly loan repayment, $1 370 principal and $230 interest
For bank service charges and debit card fees, $108

72 **Cash Purchase Invoice #PPC-76511** **Dated November 30, 2015**

From Prairie Power Corp., $380 including taxes for two months of hydro service. Invoice total paid from Regina Chequing account by cheque #574.

73 **Memo #5** **Dated November 30, 2015**

From Manager: Record the adjusting entries for supplies used in the previous two months:

Office Supplies	$105
Paper and Other Supplies	260

74 **Memo #6** **Dated November 30, 2015**

From Manager: Record the accumulated depreciation for the two-month period for all fixed assets as follows:

Computer Equipment	$ 230
Treatment Equipment	420
Office Furniture	160
Treatment Tables	280
Vehicle	1 100

75 **Payment Cheque #129 & Memo #7** **Dated November 30, 2015**

To M. Andersson (use Quick Add), $5 000 from Eastside Chequing account for drawings to cover personal expenses.

76 **Memo #8** **Dated November 30, 2015**

From Manager: Close out the M.A. Drawings account by transferring the balance to M.A. Capital.

NOTES
Enter the drawings cheque in the Expenses (Purchases) Journal or as an Other Payment in the Payments Journal. You can add a memo number as the source if you want.

NOTES
To close the Drawings account, credit Drawings and debit Capital. You can find the amount in the Trial Balance, Balance Sheet or General Ledger.

Removing Quotes and Orders

Quotes and orders that will not be filled should be removed so that they are not confused with active quotes and orders.

✓ 77 **Memo #9** **Dated November 30, 2015**

From Manager: Three purchase quotes that are on file are no longer valid. Remove quote #MT-511 from Medi-Tables, quote #FS-644 from Fresh Spaces and quote #SU-5532 from Space Unlimited.
Remove the recurring transactions for Grasslands Fuel (cash purchase) and Albert Blackfoot (sale) because they will no longer be used.

Click the **Invoices icon** in the Payables module window or **click** the **Create Invoice shortcut** if you added one to open the Expenses Journal.

Choose **Quote** from the Transaction list.

Choose **quote #MT-511** and **press** tab to place the quote on-screen.

PRO VERSION
Click the Purchases icon or click the Create Purchase Invoice shortcut if you created shortcuts.

> **NOTES**
> If you click the Adjust tool, the Remove tool and option will not be available.

Click the **Remove tool**

Or **choose** the **Expense menu** and **click Remove Supplier Order Or Supplier Quote** to see the usual warning message:

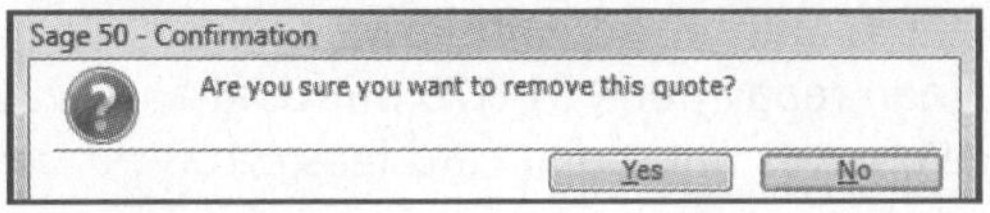

Click **Yes** to confirm.

> **NOTES**
> Instead of using the Remove tool, you can choose the Expense menu in the Expenses (Purchases) Journal and click Remove Supplier Quote or Supplier Order, or the Fees menu in the Fees (Sales) Journal and click Remove Patient Quote or Patient Order.

To remove purchase orders, open the Expenses (Purchases) Journal. Choose Supplier Order from the Transaction list. Choose the order number and press *tab* to put the order on-screen. Click (the Remove Supplier Order tool). Click Yes to confirm deletion.

To remove sales quotes or sales orders, open the Fees (Sales) Journal. Choose Quote (or Patient Order) as the transaction and then select the Quote or Order No. from the list. Press *tab* to bring the quote or order onto the screen. Click (the Remove Patient Quote or Patient Order tool). Click Yes to confirm.

Remove the **other two quotes** and the recurring entries that are not needed.

Close the **journal** and then **enter Memo #10**.

> **NOTES**
> Refer to page 101 for assistance with starting a new fiscal period if needed.

78

Memo #10 **Dated November 30, 2015**

From Manager: Print all financial reports. Back up the data files and start a new fiscal period on December 1, 2015.

Displaying Reports

> **NOTES**
> The Home window Reports menu has an entry for Medical/Dental Reports. This replaces the entry for Service or Retail Reports we saw in previous chapters for those industry types.

Displaying Pending Supplier (Purchase) Orders

Any purchase orders that are not yet filled can be displayed in a report. You can also use this report to check for orders that are delayed or should be removed.

> **PRO VERSION**
> The report is named Pending Purchase Orders Summary By Vendor.

Open the **Report Centre**. **Click Payables** in the Select A Report list.

Click **Pending Supplier Orders Summary By Supplier** and **click Modify This Report**:

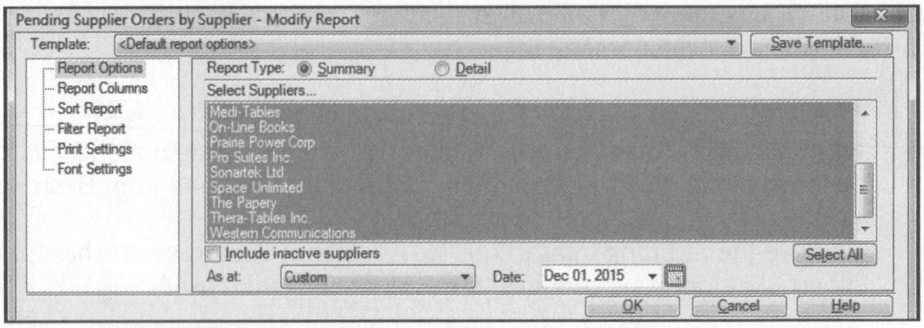

> **NOTES**
> From the Home window Reports menu, choose Payables and Pending Supplier Orders and click By Supplier to see the report options.

Press and **hold** *ctrl* and **click** the appropriate **names** in the supplier list.

Enter **Dec. 31, 2015** as the date for the report. **Click OK** to view the report.

> **NOTES**
> The Pending Supplier/Patient Orders reports can be sorted and filtered by Order No., Order Date, Ship Date and Amount.

All orders due in the next month should be included in the report. The purchase order with HydraTub Care is not included because its starting date is January 1.

Click the **Modify Report tool**.

Display the **report** again using January 15, 2016, as the date to see all outstanding orders. **Close** the **display** when you have finished.

Displaying Pending Patient (Sales) Orders

Any sales orders that are not yet filled can be displayed in the Pending Sales Orders Report. You can also use this report to check for orders that should be removed.

Click **Receivables** in the Select A Report list.

Click **Pending Patient Orders Summary By Patient** to open the sample.

Click **Modify This Report** to open the report options window:

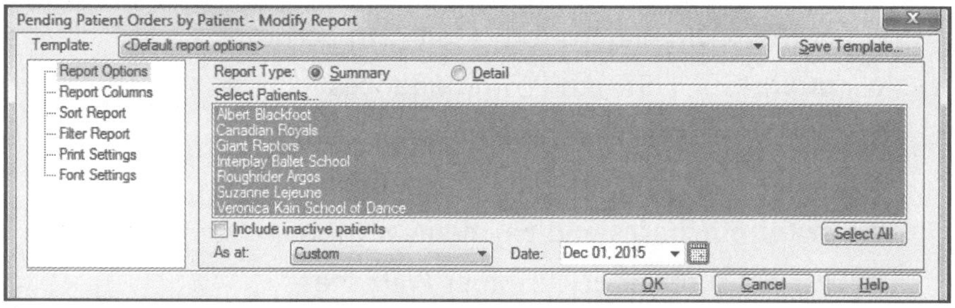

Press and **hold** *ctrl* and **click** the appropriate **names** in the patient list.

Enter **Dec 31, 2015** as the report date to see orders for the next month.

Click **OK** to view the report. One sales order is listed, the partially filled order for the Giant Raptors' contract. **Close** the **display** when finished.

Displaying Additional Information in Journal Reports

When you choose to include additional fields in the journal entries, you can include these details in the journal reports.

Click **Financials** in the Select A Report list. **Click** **All Journal Entries** and **click** **Modify This Report**:

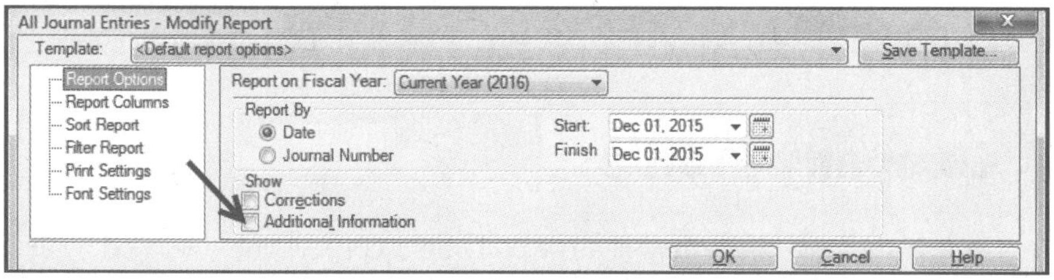

Click **Additional Information** to add a ✓. **Click** **Corrections**.

Enter the **Start** and **Finish dates** for the report. **Click** **OK** .

REVIEW

The Student DVD with Data Files includes Review Questions and Supplementary Cases for this chapter.

NOTES
From the Pending Orders reports, you can drill down to the Supplier/Patient Aged Report and to the order form.
If you drill down to the order, you can fill the order directly by choosing Invoice as the type of transaction and then filling the order as usual. Confirm your intention to change the order to an invoice.

PRO VERSION
The report is named Pending Sales Orders By Customers.

NOTES
You can also choose the Reports menu, then choose Receivables and Pending Patient Orders and click By Patient to view the report options.

NOTES
You can also choose the Reports menu, then choose Journal Entries and click All to see the report options.

CHAPTER TWELVE

OBJECTIVES

After completing this chapter, you should be able to

- ***make*** payments toward credit card accounts
- ***make*** GST, HST and PST remittances
- ***apply*** sales taxes to interprovincial sales
- ***enter*** sales and receipts for foreign customers
- ***enter*** purchases and payments for foreign suppliers
- ***access*** supplier or customer Web sites
- ***e-mail*** invoices to customers
- ***look up*** invoices after posting them
- ***track*** shipments to customers
- ***transfer*** funds between different currency bank accounts
- ***monitor*** business routines with Checklists
- ***create*** an Accountant's Copy of data for adjustments
- ***import*** Accountant's Copy journal entries

COMPANY INFORMATION

Company Profile

Maple Leaf Rags Inc. is a privately held corporation operated by Jaz Bands. After a few years on the East coast, he missed the mountains and moved his small home office from Summerside, Prince Edward Island, to Nanaimo, British Columbia. Bands first considered starting his own business while studying fine arts at Concordia University and business administration at Queen's University. During these years he worked part time in local music stores, dealing with customers who were sometimes frustrated that they had to look in every department to find a variety of types of music by Canadians. With his knowledge and contacts in the music industry, and careful business research he was ready to establish Maple Leaf Rags Inc., a store specializing in Canadian recording artists. He also sells the book that he wrote and published — *A Guide to Canadian Music*.

NOTES

Maple Leaf Rags Inc.
2642 Coldstream Avenue
Nanaimo, BC V9T 2X2
Tel 1: (250) 63M-USIC
Tel 2: (888) 63M-USIC
Fax: (250) 633-4888
Business No.: 128 488 632

Rag is a style of music set in ragtime. Many of Scott Joplin's tunes, including "Maple Leaf Rag," are examples of ragtime music.

Maple Leaf Rags Inc. sells CDs by Canadian artists over the Internet to individuals. It also sells to music stores throughout Canada and the United States, usually to American stores that serve a large Canadian resident and tourist clientele. These stores rely on Bands as a convenient source of Canadian artists' recordings, including native and ethnic music produced by A.B. Original Sounds, which is Bands' recording company. Bands hopes to expand the business to other countries where pockets of Canadian populations can be found, such as countries with Canadian Armed Forces bases. His recent book has also been popular with these customers.

Bands is fortunate to be able to rely on the advice of his friend Dave Manga, whose Outset Media boardgame business distributes its products in a similar way to Maple Leaf Rags. His friend also shares information about suppliers who might be able to provide some of Bands' supplies.

Maple Leaf Rags has expanded rapidly, though Bands is still able to operate out of his own home because the demands for inventory storage space are small. He pays himself rent for use of his home office space.

Bands buys CDs from various recording studios. He buys CD masters from A.B. Original Sounds, and suppliers across Canada copy and package the CDs for his company at competitive prices. He has accounts set up for all his regular suppliers, many of whom offer discounts for early payments. Bands also has set up accounts for his wholesale customers with discounts for early payment.

At the end of each fiscal year, Bands creates a copy of the data files for the accountant, who checks the accuracy of the accounting records and adds the outstanding adjusting entries.

Bands converted his accounting records to Sage 50 after working carefully through a comprehensive Sage 50 textbook by Purbhoo. The following company information summarizes the conversion after the first nine months of the current fiscal period:

- Chart of Accounts
- Trial Balance
- Supplier Information
- Customer Information
- Accounting Procedures

CHART OF POSTABLE ACCOUNTS

MAPLE LEAF RAGS INC.

ASSETS
1020 Bank: Savings Account
1040 Bank: Chequing Account
1060 Bank: Visa
1080 Bank: MasterCard
1140 Bank: USD
1200 Accounts Receivable
1240 Purchase Prepayments
1280 Office Supplies
1300 CD Inventory
1340 Book Inventory
1380 Prepaid Expenses
1410 Computers
1420 Accum Deprec: Computers
1450 Furniture & Equipment
1480 Accum Deprec: Furn & Equip ▶

▶1500 Automobile
1520 Accum Deprec: Automobile

LIABILITIES
2100 Bank Loan
2180 Prepaid Sales and Deposits
2200 Accounts Payable
2250 Amex Payable
2260 Visa Payable
2460 PST Payable
2650 GST Charged on Sales
2660 HST Charged on Sales
2670 GST Paid on Purchases
2680 HST Paid on Purchases
2850 Long Term Loan ▶

▶EQUITY
3560 Common Stock
3600 Retained Earnings
3800 Current Earnings

REVENUE
4100 Revenue from CD Sales
4140 Revenue from Book Sales
4180 Sales Discounts
4200 Freight Revenue
4250 Interest Revenue
4280 Sales Tax Compensation
4300 Exchange Rate Differences

EXPENSE
5100 Advertising & Publicity
5150 Bank Charges & Card Fees ▶

▶5200 Depreciation Expense
5220 Freight & Shipping Expenses
5260 Purchase Discounts
5280 Interest Expense
5300 Internet & Web Site Expenses
5320 Storage Expense
5340 Cost of Books Sold
5360 Materials and Assembly Costs
5380 Cost of CDs Sold
5400 Office Rent
5500 Office Supplies Used
5520 Research Expenses
5560 Telephone Expenses
5580 Travel Expenses

NOTES: The Chart of Accounts includes only postable accounts and the Net Income or Current Earnings account.

TRIAL BALANCE

MAPLE LEAF RAGS INC.

June 30, 2015		Debits	Credits
1020	Bank: Savings Account	$ 76 675	
1040	Bank: Chequing Account	41 000	
1060	Bank: Visa	1 800	
1080	Bank: MasterCard	2 350	
1140	Bank: USD ($720 USD)	760	
1200	Accounts Receivable	71 680	
1280	Office Supplies	600	
1300	CD Inventory	180 350	
1340	Book Inventory	44 840	
1380	Prepaid Expenses	5 900	
1410	Computers	8 200	
1420	Accum Deprec: Computers		$ 1 100
1450	Furniture & Equipment	9 100	
1480	Accum Deprec: Furn & Equip		1 500
1500	Automobile	16 800	
1520	Accum Deprec: Automobile		9 800
2100	Bank Loan		12 000
2200	Accounts Payable		1 540
2250	Amex Payable		390
2260	Visa Payable		860
2460	PST Payable		450
2650	GST Charged on Sales		1 450
2660	HST Charged on Sales		3 634
2670	GST Paid on Purchases	500	
2680	HST Paid on Purchases	1 800	▶
▶ 2850	Long Term Loan		60 000
3560	Common Stock		160 000
3600	Retained Earnings		30 561
4100	Revenue from CD Sales		389 000
4140	Revenue from Book Sales		61 000
4180	Sales Discounts	6 840	
4200	Freight Revenue		5 460
4250	Interest Revenue		2 150
4280	Sales Tax Compensation		45
5100	Advertising & Publicity	18 800	
5150	Bank Charges & Card Fees	1 980	
5220	Freight & Shipping Expenses	4 810	
5260	Purchase Discounts		850
5280	Interest Expense	3 960	
5300	Internet & Web Site Expenses	2 540	
5340	Cost of Books Sold	32 400	
5360	Materials and Assembly Costs	1 800	
5380	Cost of CDs Sold	194 250	
5400	Office Rent	7 200	
5500	Office Supplies Used	800	
5520	Research Expenses	1 200	
5560	Telephone Expenses	905	
5580	Travel Expenses	1 950	
		$741 790	$741 790

SUPPLIER INFORMATION

MAPLE LEAF RAGS INC.

Supplier Name (Contact)	Address	Phone No. Fax No.	E-mail Web Site	Terms Tax ID
A.B. Original Sounds (Marie Raven)	380 Abbey Rd. Vancouver, BC V3P 5N6	Tel: (778) 882-6252 Fax: (778) 882-1100		1/10, n/30 (before tax) 129 646 733
Federal Express (DayLee Runner)	59 Effex Road Nanaimo, BC V9R 6X2	Tel: (800) 488-9000 Fax: (250) 488-1230	www.fedex.com	n/1
Grandeur Graphics (Kathy Grandeur)	26 Drawing Way Victoria, BC V8C 3D1	Tel: (250) 665-3998 Fax: (250) 665-3900	www.wedesignit.com	2/20, n/30 (before tax) 459 112 341
Let 'm Know (Jabber Jaws Lowder)	599 Broadcast Rd. Nanaimo, BC V9S 7J8	Tel: (250) 604-6040 Fax: (250) 604-4660	www.wetellit.com	2/20, n/30 (before tax) 453 925 376
Miles 'R on Us (N. Gins)	522 Drivers St. Saskatoon, SK S7F 5E3	Tel: (800) 592-5239 Fax: (306) 591-4929		n/1
Minister of Finance			www.gov.bc.ca/fin	n/1
Purolator (Speedy Carriere)	46 Shipping Mews Nanaimo, BC V9S 6S2	Tel: (800) 355-7447 Fax: (250) 355-7000	www.purolator.com	n/1
Receiver General for Canada	Summerside Tax Centre Summerside, PE C1N 6L2	Tel: (902) 821-8186	www.cra-arc.gc.ca	n/1
Western Tel (Manny Voyses)	45 Nexus Ave. Nanaimo, BC V9R 3D1	Tel: (250) 679-1011 Fax: (250) 679-1000	www.westerntel.ca	n/7
Wrap It (Able Boxer)	80 Cubit Road Richmond Hill, ON L5R 6B2	Tel: (905) 881-7739 Fax: (905) 881-7000		1/5, n/30 (before tax) 634 529 125

OUTSTANDING SUPPLIER INVOICES

MAPLE LEAF RAGS INC.

Supplier Name	Terms	Date	Invoice No.	Amount	Tax	Total
Grandeur Graphics	2/20, n/30 (before tax)	6/28/15	GG-1304	$ 400	$ 20	$ 420
Let 'm Know	2/20, n/30 (before tax)	6/30/15	LK-692	$1 000	$120	$1 120
			Grand Total			$1 540

CUSTOMER INFORMATION

MAPLE LEAF RAGS INC.

Customer Name (Contact)	Address	Phone No. Fax No.	E-mail Web Site	Terms Credit Limit
Canadian Sounds (X. Pats)	46 Ontario St. Tampa, Florida 33607 USA	Tel: (813) 930-4589 Fax: (813) 930-7330	XPats@cansounds.com www.cansounds.com	3/30, n/60 (before tax) $20 000 USD
CDN Music (Michelle Strings)	230 Nightingale Pl. Vancouver, BC V4R 9K4	Tel: (778) 288-6189 Fax: (778) 288-6000	mstrings@upbeat.com www.cdn.music.ca	3/30, n/60 (before tax) $20 000
Entertainment House (Rob Blinde)	101 Booker St. Toronto, ON M4F 3J8	Tel: (647) 484-9123 Fax: (647) 488-8182	www.ent.house.com	3/30, n/60 (before tax) $150 000
It's All Canadian (Leaf Mapleston)	39 Federation Ave. Victoria, BC V8W 7T7	Tel: (250) 598-1123 Fax: (250) 598-1000	www.canstuff.com	3/30, n/60 (before tax) $20 000
Music Music Music (M. Porter)	10 Red Rock Canyon Sedona, Arizona 86336 USA	Tel: (520) 678-4523 Fax: (520) 678-4500	mporter@music3.com www.music3.com	3/30, n/60 (before tax) $10 000 USD
Total Music (Goode Sounds)	93 Waterside Rd. Fredericton, NB E3B 4F4	Tel: (506) 455-7746 Fax: (506) 455-7000	goode@totalmusic.com www.totalmusic.com	3/30, n/60 (before tax) $50 000
Treble & Bass (Bea Flatte)	399 Chord Blvd. Nanaimo, BC V9R 5T6	Tel: (250) 557-5438 Fax: (250) 557-5550	bflatte@t&b.com www.t&b.com	3/30, n/60 (before tax) $30 000
Web Store Customers				Prepaid by Credit Card

OUTSTANDING CUSTOMER INVOICES

MAPLE LEAF RAGS INC.

Customer Name	Terms	Date	Invoice No.	Amount	Tax	Total
CDN Music	3/30, n/60 (before tax)	6/25/15	591	$ 4 500	$ 225	$ 4 725
Entertainment House	3/30, n/60 (before tax)	1/4/15	233	$56 000	$7 280	$63 280
It's All Canadian	3/30, n/60 (before tax)	6/6/15	589	$ 3 500	$ 175	$ 3 675
			Grand Total			$71 680

Accounting Procedures

NOTES
In 2013, British Columbia reverted to collecting and charging PST and GST separately.
Because Maple Leaf Rags is not registered for HST, it is not required to pay HST on purchases from suppliers in provinces that charge HST. For these purchases he pays GST, unless the goods or services are used or "consumed" in that province.

GST and HST

Maple Leaf Rags Inc. uses the regular method of calculating GST. The GST charged and collected from customers is recorded as a liability in *GST Charged on Sales*. Customers in New Brunswick, Newfoundland and Labrador and Ontario pay HST at the rate of 13 percent instead of GST, Nova Scotia customers pay HST at 15 percent and Prince Edward Island customers pay HST at 14 percent. These HST amounts are recorded in *HST Charged on Sales*. Customers in British Columbia pay GST at 5 percent and PST at 7 percent. In the remaining provinces and territories, customers pay the 5 percent GST on all their purchases. Bands has set up both GST and HST as taxes with appropriate codes. GST (or HST) paid to suppliers is recorded in *GST Paid on Purchases* (or *HST Paid on Purchases*) as a decrease in tax liability. The balance owing is the difference between the GST plus HST charged and GST plus HST paid. Customers who buy books pay only GST at the rate of 5 percent on their purchases — books are exempt from PST and HST in all provinces.

Cash Sales of Services

Cash transactions for Bands are limited to credit card sales since most of his business is with wholesale customers who have accounts. He has merchant Visa and MasterCard arrangements with two financial institutions. Maple Leaf Rags pays a percentage of each sale directly to the credit card companies (the fee is withheld from the sale amount). To simplify the transaction entries, we provide summaries of these credit card sales as if they were to a single customer called Web Store Customers.

Bands uses a Visa gold card and an American Express card for some business purchases and pays annual user fees for these cards.

NOTES
The sales tax rules for discounts are complex and may vary from province to province. Rules for federal taxes may also be different from those for provincial taxes. Sage 50 calculates sales discounts as before or after tax but applies the same formula to GST and retail sales taxes. Adjusting General Journal entries may be required to adjust the amount of tax owing and calculate the tax remittance. We have omitted the tax adjustments for sales discounts.

Discounts

Discounts are calculated automatically by the program when the discount terms are entered as part of the invoices. If the payments are made before the discount term has expired, the discount appears in the Payments and Receipts journals automatically. All discounts are calculated on before-tax amounts. Bands offers a 3 percent discount to wholesale customers to encourage them to pay their accounts on time. Customers who purchase from the Web store and pay by credit card do not receive discounts.

Some suppliers offer before-tax discounts to Maple Leaf Rags as well. These discount terms are set up in the supplier and customer records.

NOTES
Wholesale customers in HST provinces do pay HST on all purchases from Maple Leaf Rags except books.

PST

PST, also called Revenue Tax, is charged at the rate of 7 percent on the base price of goods in British Columbia. Wholesale customers do not pay PST on merchandise they buy for resale. Thus, when Bands sells directly to stores, he charges only GST. He does not charge PST to stores because they are not the final consumers of the product. Individual retail customers in BC pay GST and PST on the purchase of CDs but only GST on books. Customers in other provinces pay GST at 5 percent or HST at the rate for their province. When Maple Leaf Rags makes the PST remittance, it reduces the amount of the remittance by 6.6 percent, the rate of sales tax compensation when the amount collected is greater than $333.33 for the reporting period.

Freight

Customers who order through the Internet pay a shipping rate of $5 for the first CD or book and $2 for each additional item. Wholesale customers pay the actual shipping costs. GST is charged on freight in British Columbia. Bands has accounts set up with his three regular shippers so that he can track shipments online. Their Web site addresses are included in the shipping setup data.

Sales Orders and Deposits

When a customer places a sales order, Bands requests a deposit as confirmation of the order. Deposits are entered on the Sales Order form (see page 427) or in the Receipts Journal (see page 418).

Foreign Customers and Suppliers

Customers outside Canada do not pay GST, HST or PST on goods imported from Canada. Therefore, sales outside the country do not have taxes applied to them. These customers also do not pay any taxes on their shipping charges.

Purchases from suppliers outside of Canada are subject to GST when the goods are used in Canada.

NOTES
For Maple Leaf Rags' retail business type, the terms Customer and Supplier are used. Sales and Purchases are used as icon labels in journal names and in reports.

INSTRUCTIONS

1. **Record entries for the source documents** in Sage 50 using the Chart of Accounts, Supplier Information, Customer Information and Accounting Procedures for Maple Leaf Rags. The procedures for entering each new type of transaction in this application are outlined step by step in the Keystrokes section with the source documents.

   Change module windows as needed, or create shortcuts for journals in other modules.
2. **Print** the **reports for the end of the fiscal period** suggested by the Sage 50 checklists after you have finished making your entries. Refer to the Keystrokes section, pages 489–491. If you have started a new fiscal period, choose **Previous Year** to see the reports you need.

PRO VERSION
Vendors will replace Suppliers for icon, field and report names.

KEYSTROKES

Opening Data Files

Open **SageData13\Maple\maple** to access the data files.

Enter **July 15, 2015** as the first session date for this application.

Click **OK** and then **click OK** to bypass the session date warning.

Session dates are advanced semi-monthly for Maple Leaf Rags, and the backup frequency is set at two-week intervals. The Receivables Home window opens.

PRO VERSION
Restore the backup file SageData13\maple1.CAB or maple1 to SageData13\Maple\maple. Refer to Chapter 1, page 22, if you need assistance with restoring backup files.

NOTES
Payroll, Inventory and Project do not appear in the Modules pane list because these ledgers are not set up.

Tracking Sales Shipments

Businesses that ship goods to customers in other provinces usually have accounts set up with shipping companies so they can track shipments. First we enter the sale.

✓ 1

Visa Credit Card Sales Invoice #593 **Dated July 2/15**

To various Web Store customers, for CDs sold during previous three months

CD sales to BC customers	$ 800 plus 5% GST and 7% PST
CD sales to PEI customers	200 plus 14% HST
CD sales to NS customers	300 plus 15% HST
CD sales to other HST customers	2 280 plus 13% HST
CD sales to other GST customers	900 plus 5% GST
Book sales	3 000 plus 5% GST
Shipping	680 plus 5% GST
(Shipped by Purolator #PCU773XT)	
Invoice total $8 854.40. Paid by Visa.	

Click the **Sales Invoices icon** to open the Sales Journal.

Choose **Web Store Customers** from the Customer list. Leave the transaction type as Invoice. Web Store purchases are usually paid by credit card.

Click the **Payment Method list arrow**:

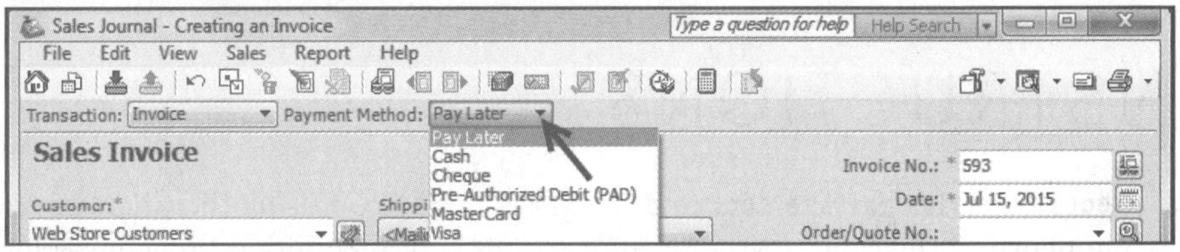

Internet customers have been set up without discounts so the discount fields are blank. Two credit cards are accepted as methods of payment.

Click **Visa** as the method of payment.

Type `July 2` (as the transaction date).

Click the **Item Description field** and **type** `CD sales - BC`

Click the **Amount field** and **type** `800`

Press *tab* to advance to the Tax field and **press** *enter* to see the tax codes:

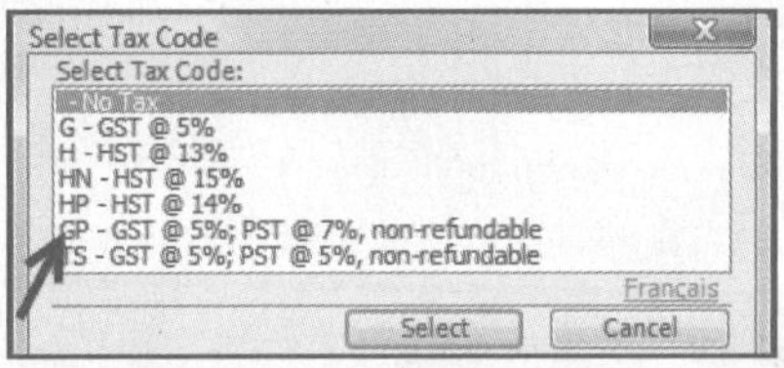

No default tax code is entered for Internet sales because multiple codes are required. We have created tax codes to accommodate interprovincial sales to customers who pay HST (**code H**, or **HN** for NS, or **HP** for PEI customers) and to customers in other provinces who pay only GST (**code G**). For the first sale, to BC customers, the **code GP** is used (GST rate at 5 percent and PST rate at 7 percent).

Click **GP - GST @ 5%, PST @ 7%, non-refundable**.

Click **Select** to return to the sales invoice and advance to the Account field. Account 4100 is correctly entered as the default revenue account.

Click the **Item Description field** on the second invoice line.

Type `CD sales - PEI` **Enter 200** in the Amount field. **Press** *tab*.

Customers in PEI pay 14 percent HST, for which we created the tax code HP.

Press *enter* or **click** the **List icon** to see the Tax Code list.

Double-click **HP - HST @ 14%** to add the code and the account.

NOTES

Usually the same tax code would apply for all invoice lines for a single customer and it can be entered from the customer's record.

NOTES

We have used the tax name PST for provincial sales tax. Two codes apply only to purchases – TS for Saskatchewan (GST @ 5%, PST @ 5%) and Q, which includes 5 percent GST and 7.975 percent QST. Purchases in Manitoba, where the PST rate is also 7 percent, use the code GP.

Goods and services consumed in a province are subject to the PST for that province. Goods shipped to other provinces are exempt from the PST, but not from HST or GST.

Click the **Item Description field** on the next invoice line.

Type `CD sales - NS`

Click the **Amount field**. **Type** `300` **Press** *tab*.

The HST rate at 15 percent applies to sales to customers in Nova Scotia – code HN.

Press *enter* or **click** the **List icon** to see the Tax Code list.

Double-click **HN - HST @ 15%** to add the code and move to the Account field.

Click the **Item Description field** on the next invoice line.

Type `CD sales to other provinces - HST`

Click the **Amount field** and **type** `2280` **Press** *tab*.

The HST rate at 13 percent applies to these sales — tax code H.

Choose **H - HST @ 13%** as the code.

Type `CD sales to other provinces - GST` in the **Item Description field** on the next invoice line.

Type `900` in the Amount field and **press** *tab*.

We now need to enter GST at 5 percent. This rate applies to the remaining provinces that do not apply HST.

Open the **Tax Code list** and **double-click G - GST @ 5%** to add the code and advance to the Account field.

Click the **Item Description field** on the next line. **Type** `Book sales`

Click the **Amount field** and **type** `3000` **Press** *tab*.

Tax code G is also applied to the sale of books in all provinces.

Open the **Tax Code list** and **double-click G - GST @ 5%**.

The cursor advances to the Account field. Book sales are recorded in a separate revenue account so we must change the default entry.

Type `4140`

There are two freight entry fields in the Sales Journal, below the subtotal amount:

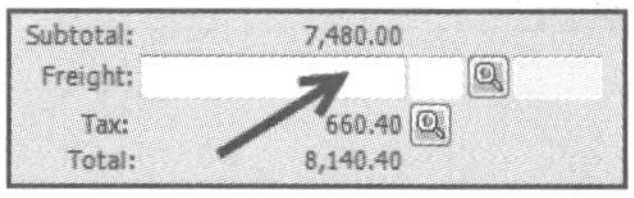

The first field is for the freight amount and the second is for the tax code. Because taxes are paid on freight you must enter a tax code if the customer pays freight. In British Columbia, only GST applies to freight.

Click the **first Freight field**.

Type `680` **Press** *tab* to advance to the tax code field for Freight.

Click the **List icon** to see the Tax Code list and **select Code G**.

The tax amount is calculated as soon as you enter the amount of freight charged and the tax code. This amount is added to the Tax total.

We will now enter the shipping information so that the shipments can be traced if they are not delivered within the expected time. To track a shipment, you must have the tracking number for the package. To arrange for tracking shipments online, most businesses have an account with the shipper and a PIN (personal identification number)

NOTES

Remember that you can change the width of a column by dragging its border in the title line of the column. You can customize the journal by removing the Item and Unit columns.

NOTES

You can also type in the tax codes.

to access the account. When an invoice for these shipments is received from the shipper, it will be entered as a purchase to record the expense to Maple Leaf Rags.

Click the **Track Shipments tool** or **choose** the **Sales menu** and **click Track Shipments** to open the shipping data entry window:

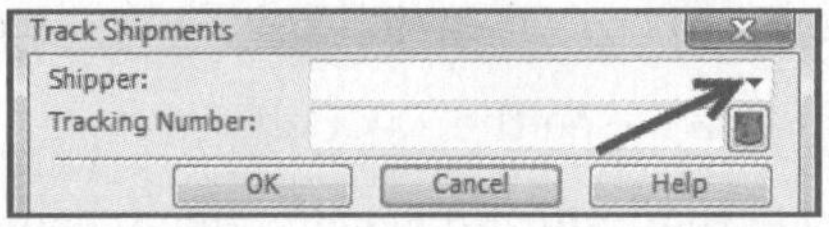

Click the **Shipper field list arrow** to see the list of shippers:

Click **Purolator**. **Press** tab to advance to the Tracking Number field.

Type PCU773XT

Click **OK** to return to the completed invoice. The tracking details do not appear on the invoice form.

All taxes are combined on the invoice as a single entry in the Tax field below Freight. To see the breakdown of individual taxes paid by the customer,

Click the **List icon** beside the Tax field to see the tax details:

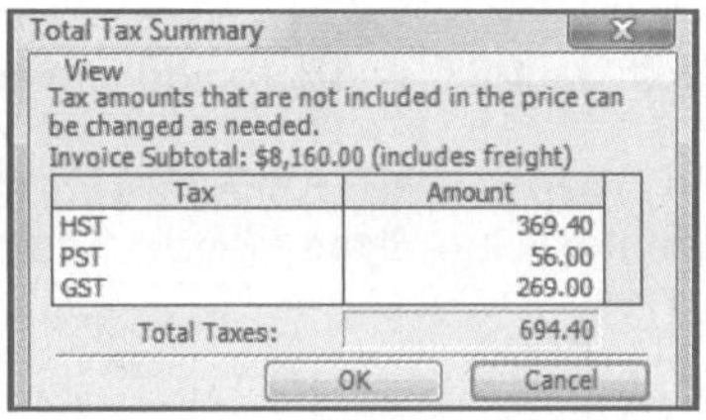

Individual amounts are shown for the three taxes applied to the sale. You can edit these tax amounts if they are incorrect.

Click **OK** to return to the Sales Journal.

Before posting the entry, you should review it.

Choose the **Report menu** and **click Display Sales Journal Entry**:

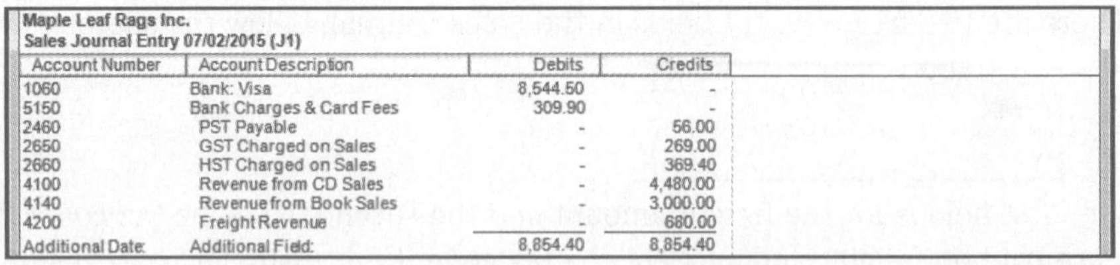

Maple Leaf Rags Inc.
Sales Journal Entry 07/02/2015 (J1)

Account Number	Account Description	Debits	Credits
1060	Bank: Visa	8,544.50	-
5150	Bank Charges & Card Fees	309.90	-
2460	PST Payable	-	56.00
2650	GST Charged on Sales	-	269.00
2660	HST Charged on Sales	-	369.40
4100	Revenue from CD Sales	-	4,480.00
4140	Revenue from Book Sales	-	3,000.00
4200	Freight Revenue	-	680.00
Additional Date:	Additional Field:	8,854.40	8,854.40

Several linked accounts are used for this transaction. The credit card account — *Bank: Visa* — is debited for the total invoice amount minus the transaction discount fees withheld by the credit card company. These fees are debited to the linked fees expense account — *Bank Charges & Card Fees.* Both the *GST* and *HST Charged on Sales* accounts are credited to show the increase in the tax liability to the Receiver General. PST collected from customers is credited to the *PST Payable* account to show the increased liability to the Minister of Finance for BC. Freight charged to customers is credited automatically to the linked *Freight Revenue* account.

Close the **display** to return to the Sales Journal input screen. **Make corrections** if necessary, referring to page 162 for assistance.

Click **Store** and **choose Random** as the frequency. **Add Visa** to the description.

NOTES

Pressing ctrl + K will also open the Track Shipments screen from the journal.

NOTES

Tax amounts may be incorrect because rounded off amounts are added together. If tax is calculated for each line, the total may be different from the tax calculated on a single subtotal amount.

NOTES

When you recall the Visa sales summary, you need to change only the amounts. You will not need to re-enter the descriptions, accounts and tax codes.

The next transaction is also a summary sale to Web Store customers. We can choose to use the same customer next time so that the customer is selected automatically.

Click the **Use The Same Customer Next Time tool** beside the customer name.

The Use The Same Customer Next Time tool has changed shape to indicate it is selected. Clicking the tool again will turn off the selection.

Click the **Post button** Post. We will not repeat the reminder to click OK.

Create **shortcuts** to enter purchases, payments and General Journal transactions or **change** **modules** as needed.

Enter the second credit card **sale** and the Visa car rental **purchase**.

2 **MasterCard Credit Card Sales Invoice #594** **Dated July 2/15**

To various Web Store customers, for CDs sold during previous three months

CD sales to BC customers	$ 700 plus 5% GST and 7% PST
CD sales to PEI customers	200 plus 14% HST
CD sales to NS customers	340 plus 15% HST
CD sales to other HST customers	1 840 plus 13% HST
CD sales to other GST customers	920 plus 5% GST
Book sales	2 700 plus 5% GST
Shipping	630 plus 5% GST

Invoice total $7 944.70. Paid by MasterCard.

3 **Visa Purchase Invoice #MR-1699** **Dated July 2/15**

To Miles 'R on Us, $520 plus 5% GST and 5% PST for two-week car rental while attending Trade Show in Saskatoon. Invoice total $572. Paid by Visa.

Entering Credit Card Bill Payments

Click **Payables** in the Modules pane to open this Home window, if necessary.

✓ 4 **Visa Payment Cheque #761** **Dated July 2/15**

To Visa, $723.50 in payment of credit card account, including $609 for purchases charged from May 16 to June 15, $105 for annual renewal fee and $9.50 in interest charges on the unpaid balance from a previous statement.

Credit card payments are entered in the Payments Journal. You can access the bill payment window from the Pay Credit Card Bills shortcut in the Payments icon drop-down shortcuts list as shown:

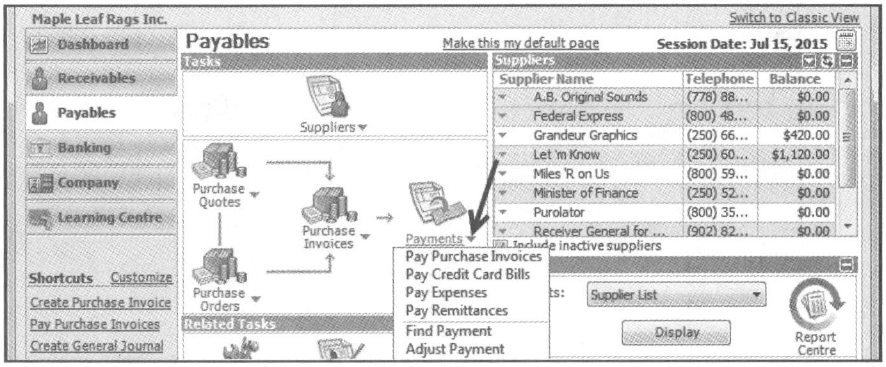

NOTES
When you close the Sales Journal, the Use The Same Customer Next Time tool is automatically turned off or deselected.

NOTES
You can also recall the stored Visa sale to enter the MasterCard sales summary. Change the method of payment and the amounts. Store this entry by adding MC to the description.

NOTES
Remember to select the correct credit card name.
You do not need to enter shipping information for the remaining Web Store sales.

NOTES
Because the car rental is purchased and used in Saskatchewan, the Saskatchewan Provincial Sales Tax rate applies. Use tax code TS (GST plus Saskatchewan PST) – the default code for the supplier.

NOTES
If you changed modules for the previous transaction, the Payables window will be open. If you created and used the shortcut, you will need to change the module window.

Click **Pay Credit Card Bills** in the Payments icon shortcuts list:

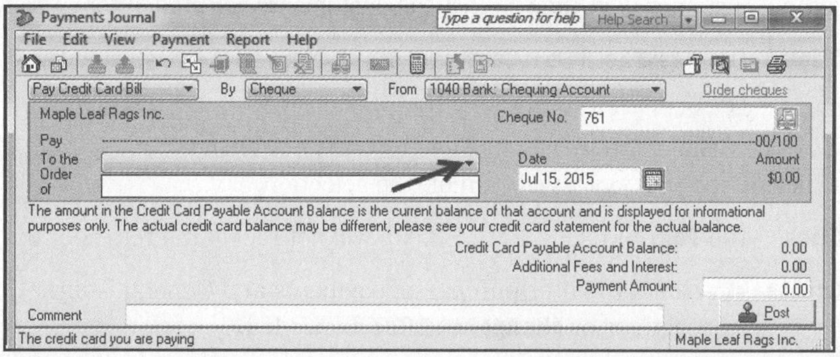

Pay Credit Card Bill is selected as the transaction type in the Pay field. The Pay list in the journal allows you to choose between paying suppliers, paying credit card bills, making cash purchases (other payments) and making payroll remittances. You can make these choices from the Pay field drop-down list or from the Home window.

To access the form you need, you can also click the Payments icon and select Pay Credit Card Bill from the transaction (Pay) drop-down list as shown:

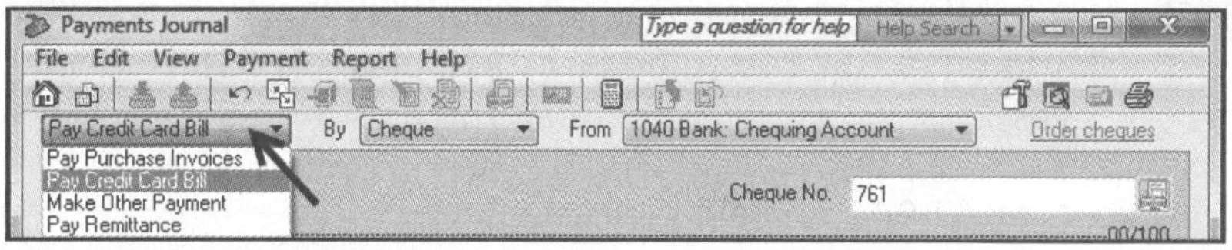

NOTES

All accounts defined as Bank class accounts are on the From list. Bank class is explained in Chapter 7.

Credit Card accounts are not designated as Bank class accounts in the data files for Maple Leaf Rags.

When you choose a different Bank class account from the From list, the cheque number changes to match the numbering sequence set up for that account.

The **By** field (method of payment) has the same options as other journals — payment by cash, cheque or any of the credit cards set up. The **From** field allows you to select a bank account from which to pay because more than one bank account is defined as a Bank class account. The default payment is by cheque. The From list has three bank accounts. The bank account and the cheque number — the next one in the sequence for this account — are correct.

Click the **To The Order Of field list arrow** to access the list of credit cards Maple Leaf Rags has set up for purchases:

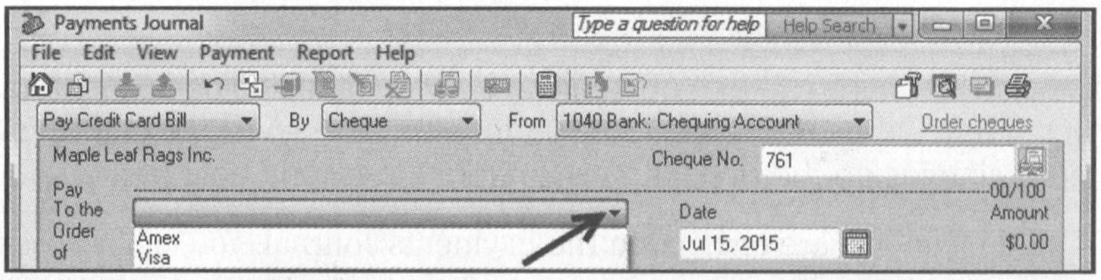

Credit card accounts are set up for Visa and Amex (American Express).

Click **Visa** to update the journal with the Visa account information:

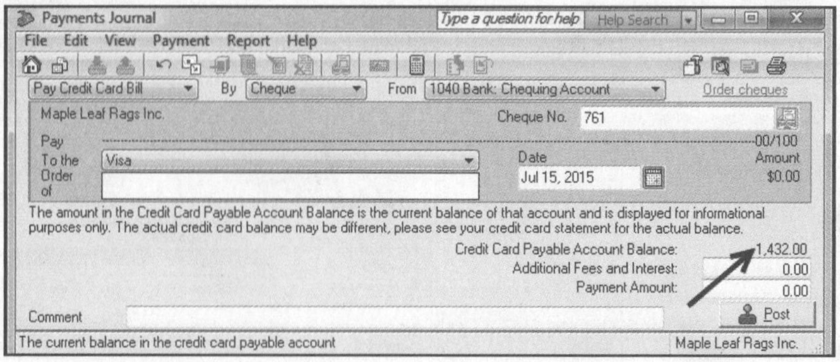

The Account Balance shows the accumulation of all unpaid purchases to date according to the General Ledger *Visa Payable* account balance. This amount is not usually the same as the balance that appears on the credit card statement. Purchases after the statement date will not appear on the statement, and interest charges or renewal fees are not included in the General Ledger account balance.

Drag through the **date in the Date field**. **Type** Jul 2

Click the **Additional Fees And Interest field**.

This field is used to record interest charges on previous unpaid amounts as well as other fees associated with the use of the card. These amounts usually appear on the statement. You must add these amounts together and enter the total in the Additional Fees And Interest field. Maple Leaf Rags owes $105 for the annual card renewal fee and $9.50 in accumulated interest for a total of $114.50.

Type 114.50 **Press** tab to advance to the Payment Amount field.

In the **Payment Amount** field you should enter the total amount of the cheque that is written in payment, including interest, fees and purchases. This will match the balance owing on the statement if the full amount is being paid, or some other amount if this is a partial payment. The remaining balance in the General Ledger *Visa Payable* account reflects current charges or purchases made after the statement date that will be included in the balance owing on the next statement and paid at that time.

Type 723.50

Press tab to update the journal and complete the cheque amount in the upper portion of the journal.

The updated journal should look like the following:

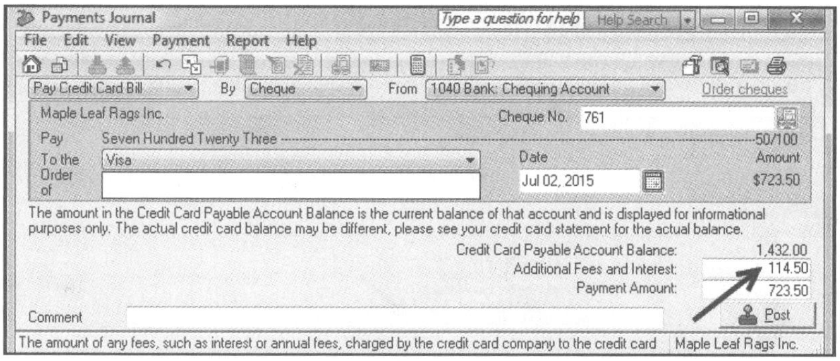

You can add a comment to the journal entry in the Comment field.

You should review the journal entry before proceeding.

Choose the **Report menu** and **click Display Payments Journal Entry** to display the transaction:

Maple Leaf Rags Inc.
Payments Journal Entry 07/02/2015 (J4)

Account Number	Account Description	Debits	Credits
2260	Visa Payable	609.00	-
5150	Bank Charges & Card Fees	114.50	-
1040	Bank: Chequing Account	-	723.50
Additional Date:	Additional Field:	723.50	723.50

Notice that the linked Payables bank account is credited for the full amount of the payment. The payment amount is divided between the debit to *Visa Payable* to reduce the liability for prior purchases and the debit to *Bank Charges & Card Fees*, the linked expense account for additional credit card expenses.

Close the **display** when you have finished reviewing it to return to the Payments Journal.

Make **corrections** by reselecting from a drop-down list or by highlighting an incorrect entry and typing the correct amount. Press tab after changing an amount to update the totals.

NOTES
Credit card companies charge interest on cash advances and on statement balances that are unpaid by the due date.

NOTES
When a partial payment is made to a credit card bill, the payment is applied first to interest and additional fees before reducing the outstanding balance from current purchases.

Click **Post** . A message appears about the cheque number:

> **NOTES**
> This message appears only for credit card bill payments.

Click **Yes** to continue processing the payment.

Close the **Payments Journal** to return to the Payables window.

> **NOTES**
> If you choose Visa in the journal after posting the payment, you will see that the balance matches the General Ledger account balance.

Accessing a Supplier's Web Site

Before making the GST remittance, we will search the Canada Revenue Agency Web site to see whether there are any recent tax changes that affect this business.

✓ 5

Memo #43 **Dated July 3/15**

From J. Bands: Access the Web site for the Canada Revenue Agency to see whether any recent announcements about GST affect the business.

> **PRO VERSION**
> Remember that the term Vendor will replace Supplier.

There are a number of ways to access a supplier record. Because the principles for finding records are the same in all ledgers, we will illustrate different methods.

Click **Receiver General** in the Suppliers pane list in the Payables module window to open the record directly. **Close** the **ledger record**.

You can type text in the Search field or use the Search tool (or Search menu option).

Click the **Quick Search field** in the upper-right section of the Home window.

Type `rec` and **click** —> (click the arrow, not the Search tool):

> **NOTES**
> The Search field is not case sensitive, so the results from the Search field entry will display all uses of the text you entered in the data file (both Rec and rec). The Search tool allows you to choose the search area, either records or transactions.

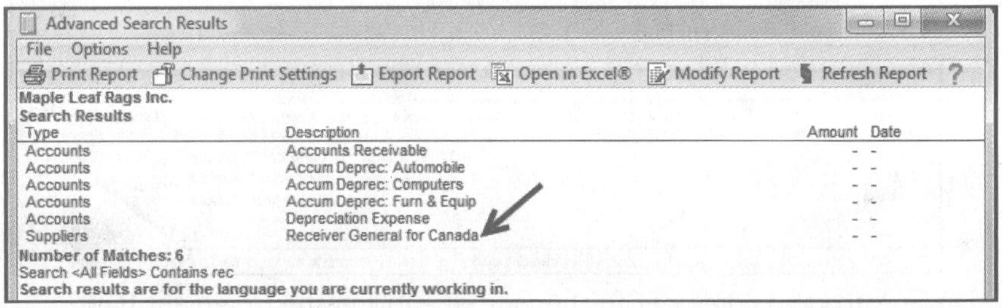

Several account names include this text as well as the supplier record we want.

Double-click the supplier **Receiver General for Canada** to open the record.

Close the **ledger record** and **Search window**.

Click the **Search tool** , or **choose** the **Edit menu** and **click Search**:

> **PRO VERSION**
> The Advanced Search tab and option are not available in the Pro version.

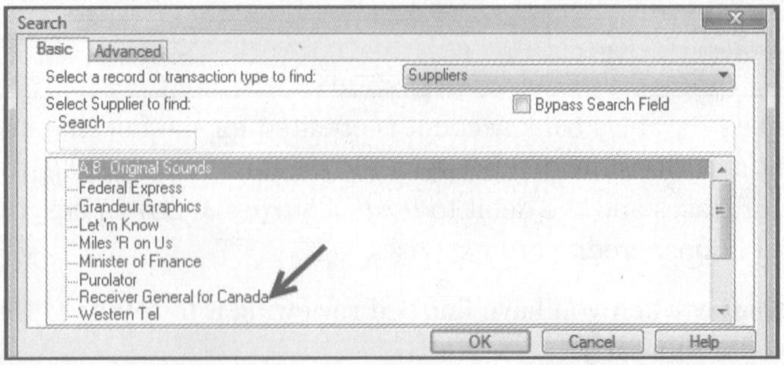

> **NOTES**
> If the last window you had open was a Supplier Ledger, the search area will be Suppliers. The search area would show Payments if you last used the Payments Journal.
> You can type a letter in the Search field to advance the list if you have many suppliers.
> The Advanced Search feature allows you to define additional search parameters.

The Search window opens. The default list depends on your previous transaction. In any Search window, you can select the search area from the Select A Record Or Transaction Type To Find drop-down list as shown:

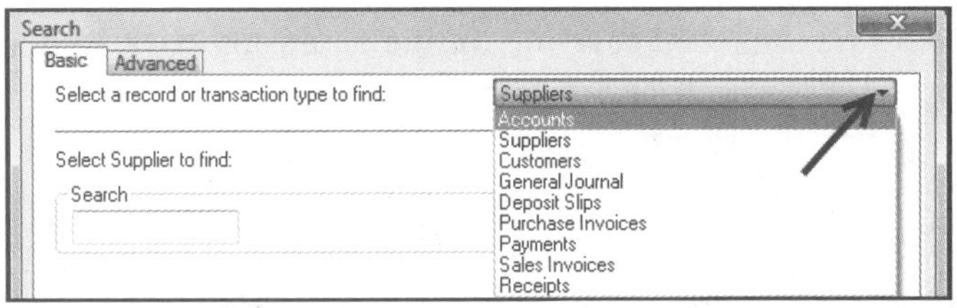

Clicking Suppliers will display the list of suppliers. Click the Search field and type r to advance to that part of the list. Receiver General for Canada will be selected because it is the first record beginning with r.

Double-click Receiver General to open the record. **Close** the **ledger record**.

Another option is to start from the Suppliers icon shortcuts list.

Choose Modify Supplier from the Suppliers (Payables window) drop-down shortcuts list to open the Search window:

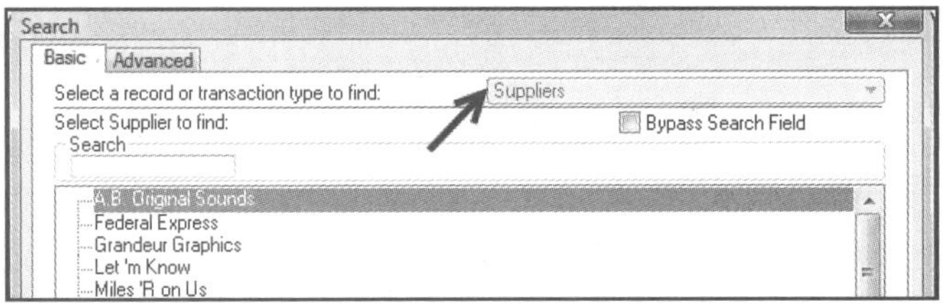

This Search screen looks the same, but **Supplier**, the entry for Select Record Or Transaction To Find, is dimmed.

Double-click Receiver General to open the record. **Close** the **ledger record**.

You can also access the record from the Suppliers window.

Click the **Suppliers icon** 

to open the Suppliers window:

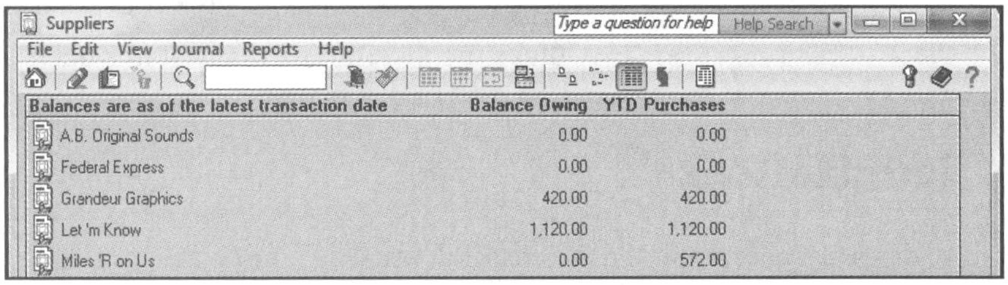

All suppliers are listed with their balances and total year-to-date purchases.

Start your **Internet connection**.

Double-click Receiver General for Canada to open the supplier's ledger:

You can access the Web site directly from this supplier ledger page.

Depending on how your Internet connection is set up, you may access the Web site directly or you may see a screen asking you to connect at this stage. You may need to enter the user ID and password for your Internet provider (if they are not set up to be saved and allow automatic connection). Again, your setup may be different.

NOTES

If you click the Search tool after entering a transaction, you will open the search for a transaction screen. If you click the Search tool after viewing a ledger record, you will list the records for that module.

The Search field is not case-sensitive.

WARNING!
If you have a network connection to access the Internet, such as for high-speed access, you must start your Internet connection before clicking the Web tool in the Payables Ledger window.

Click the **Web tool** or **choose** the **Online menu** and **click Web Site**:

NOTES
Web sites are continually updated, so the screens and sequence of steps may be different from the ones we provide.

You should see the home page for the Canada Revenue Agency.

Choose your language preference.

Click the **Forms And Publications** option.

Click the **Listed By Document Type** option.

You should see a list of types of publications with several types of GST publications included. Select one to list the items for that type.

NOTES
When we selected Business Information and typed HST + BC + PEI in the Search field, we found documents describing changes to taxes in these provinces in 2013.

Find the information about recent changes to HST and PST for BC and PEI.

Close your **Internet browser** when you have found the information you need or when you have finished. You will return to the supplier's ledger.

Close the **Ledger window**. **Close** the **Suppliers window** if it is open.

Tax Remittances

NOTES
Electronic filing of GST/HST returns is covered in Appendix K.

Tax remittances are entered in the Purchases Journal as non-taxable purchase invoices with payment by cheque, or as Other Payments in the Payments Journal. There are two parts to a GST/HST remittance — accounting for the GST (and HST) collected from customers and accounting for the GST (and HST) paid for purchases. The first is owed to the Receiver General while the second part — the input tax credit — is refunded or used to reduce the amount owing. Refer to Chapter 2 for further details. The GST/HST Report can be used to help prepare the return, but the ledger account balances for the date of the filing period should be used as a final check in case there are opening balance amounts that were not entered in the journals. For Maple Leaf Rags, the opening or historical balance is needed. These amounts were not entered through journal transactions so we cannot use built-in Tax Reports.

NOTES
The Pay Remittances shortcut for the Payments icon is used only to remit payroll taxes.

PST remittances also have two parts — accounting for the PST collected from customers and reducing the tax remitted by the sales tax compensation for filing the return on time.

Display or **print** the **General Ledger Report** for the tax accounts for June 30, 2015, to see the amounts you must enter. (Refer to page 57.)

The General Ledger balances you need are the GST, HST and PST amounts in the Trial Balance on page 454. You can also display or print the Trial Balance or Balance Sheet for June 30 to see the amounts for the following tax accounts:

- 2460 PST Payable
- 2650 GST Charged on Sales
- 2660 HST Charged on Sales
- 2670 GST Paid on Purchases
- 2680 HST Paid on Purchases

Making GST Remittances

Choose **Pay Expenses** from the Payments icon shortcuts list.

✓ 6

Memo #44 **Dated July 5/15**

From J. Bands: Refer to June 30 General Ledger balances to remit GST and HST to the Receiver General. Issue cheque #762 for $2 784 from Chequing Account.

Choose **Receiver General for Canada** as the supplier.

Choose **July 5** from the pop-up calendar as the transaction date.

Click the **Account field List icon** to display the account list.

Choose **2650 GST Charged on Sales** to advance to the Description field.

Type `Debiting GST Charged on Sales`

Press *tab* to advance to the Amount field. **Type** `1450`

No Tax should be entered as the default tax code. If it is not, select the correct code from the Tax field list icon.

Click the **Account field List icon** on the next journal line.

Choose **2660 HST Charged on Sales** and advance to the Description field.

Type `Debiting HST Charged on Sales`

Press *tab* to advance to the Amount field. **Type** `3634`

Click the **Account field List icon** on the next journal line.

Choose **2670 GST Paid on Purchases**. In the Description field,

Type `Crediting GST Paid`

Press *tab* to advance to the Amount field.

Type `-500` (Use a **minus sign** or hyphen. The minus sign is necessary to enter a negative amount that credits the liability account.)

Click the **Account field List icon** on the next journal line.

Choose **2680 HST Paid on Purchases**. In the Description field,

Type `Crediting HST Paid`

Press *tab* to advance to the Amount field. **Type** `-1800`

Click the **Invoice/Ref. field**.

Type `Memo 44` **Press** *tab*.

Type `Memo 44, GST/HST remittance for June`

NOTES

Tax amounts that you enter on the Sales Taxes screen in the General Journal are included in the tax reports, but opening balance amounts are not.

NOTES

If the Payments Journal is already open, choose Make Other Payment from the Pay transactions drop-down list.

CLASSIC VIEW

Click the Payments icon to open the journal and select Make Other Payment from the Pay drop-down list.

NOTES

No default account was entered for the Receiver General because four different accounts are required.

This completes your entry as shown here:

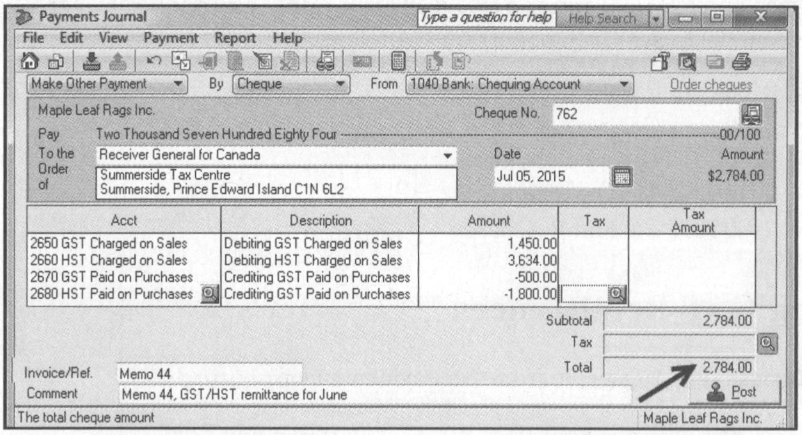

A review of the journal entry will help to clarify the transaction.

Choose the **Report menu** and **click Display Payments Journal Entry**:

Maple Leaf Rags Inc.
Payments Journal Entry 07/05/2015 (J5)

Account Number	Account Description	Debits	Credits
2650	GST Charged on Sales	1,450.00	-
2660	HST Charged on Sales	3,634.00	-
1040	Bank: Chequing Account	-	2,784.00
2670	GST Paid on Purchases	-	500.00
2680	HST Paid on Purchases	-	1,800.00
Additional Date:	Additional Field:	5,084.00	5,084.00

NOTES

GST paid and HST paid are input tax credits that reduce the amount of the remittance.

Normally, a positive amount will create a debit entry in the Payments Journal for an expense or an asset purchase. *GST/HST Charged on Sales* are GST payable accounts with a credit balance. Therefore, entering a positive amount will reduce the GST payable balance by debiting the accounts, as we do when we pay suppliers. The negative entries or credits for the refundable *GST Paid on Purchases* and *HST Paid on Purchases* will offset the debit balance in the ledger for these contra-liability accounts and will reduce the total amount that is paid to the Receiver General. The net cheque amount is credited to the bank account.

Close the **display** window when you have finished. **Make corrections** if necessary.

Click **Post** [Post]. You are now ready to make the PST remittance.

Making PST Remittances

You should still be in the Payments Journal with Make Other Payment selected as the type of transaction.

✓ 7

Memo #45 **Dated July 5/15**

From J. Bands: Refer to the June 30 General Ledger balance to remit PST Payable to the Minister of Finance. Reduce the payment amount by the sales tax compensation of 6.6%. Issue cheque #763 for $420.30 from Chequing Account.

Choose **Minister of Finance** as the supplier. Accept the default bank account.

Accept **July 5** as the date and **accept** the default **account**, *2460 PST Payable*.

Click the **Description field**.

Type `Debiting for PST collected`

Press (tab) to move the cursor to the Amount field. **Type** `450`

You are now ready to enter the revenue from sales tax compensation, 6.6 percent of the *PST Payable* amount.

Click the **Account field List icon** on the second journal line.

Choose **4280 Sales Tax Compensation**. The cursor advances to the Description field.

Type `Sales Tax Compensation` **Press** tab.

Type `-29.70` (Use a **minus sign**. The minus sign will reduce the total amount that is paid to the Minister of Finance.)

Click the **Invoice/Ref. number field.**

Type `Memo 45` **Press** tab to advance to the Comment field.

Type `Memo 45, PST remittance for June`

Choose the **Report menu** and **click** **Display Payments Journal Entry**:

Maple Leaf Rags Inc.
Payments Journal Entry 07/05/2015 (J6)

Account Number	Account Description	Debits	Credits
2460	PST Payable	450.00	-
1040	Bank: Chequing Account	-	420.30
4280	Sales Tax Compensation	-	29.70
Additional Date:	Additional Field:	450.00	450.00

The full *PST Payable* amount is debited to reduce the entire liability by crediting the bank account for the amount of the cheque and the *Sales Tax Compensation* revenue account for the amount of the tax reduction.

Close the **display** when you have finished. **Make corrections** if needed.

Click **Post** Post. **Close** the **Payments Journal**.

> **NOTES**
> Click the Calculator tool to access the calculator if you need to calculate the sales tax compensation amount.

Entering Sales to Foreign Customers

Click **Receivables** in the Modules pane list to open the Receivables window.

Click the **Sales Invoices icon** Sales Invoices to open the Sales Journal. Invoice and Pay Later, the default selections, are correct.

✓ 8

Sales Invoice #595 **Dated July 5/15**

To Canadian Sounds, $2 190 USD for CDs and $300 USD for books. Shipped by Federal Express (#F19YTR563) for $140. Invoice total $2 630 USD. Terms 3/30, n/60. The exchange rate is 1.031.

Choose **Canadian Sounds** from the Customer drop-down list:

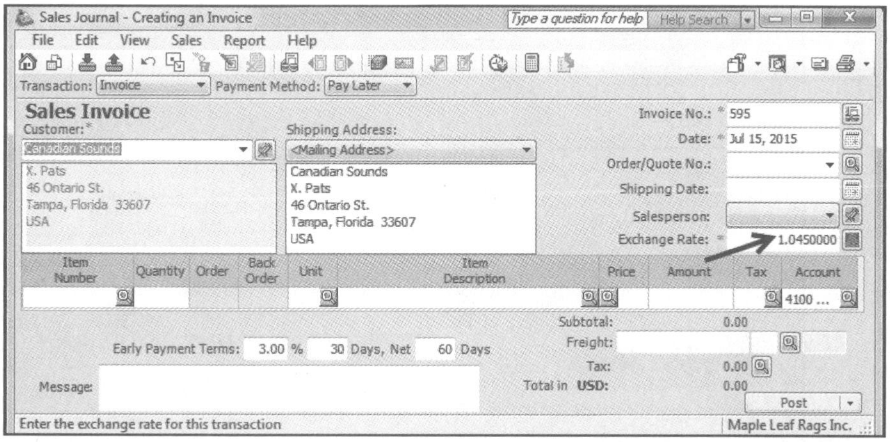

The invoice is modified for the foreign customer. A field for the exchange rate has been added, and the Total is expressed in USD (United States dollars) rather than in

WARNING!
Always check that the date on the Exchange Rate screen matches the transaction date.

Canadian dollars. An exchange rate button provides a list of exchange rates already entered for various dates. There is no rate for July 5.

Choose **July 5** from the Date field calendar.

The Exchange Rate screen opens because the exchange rate on record is more than one day old and no rate has been recorded for this date:

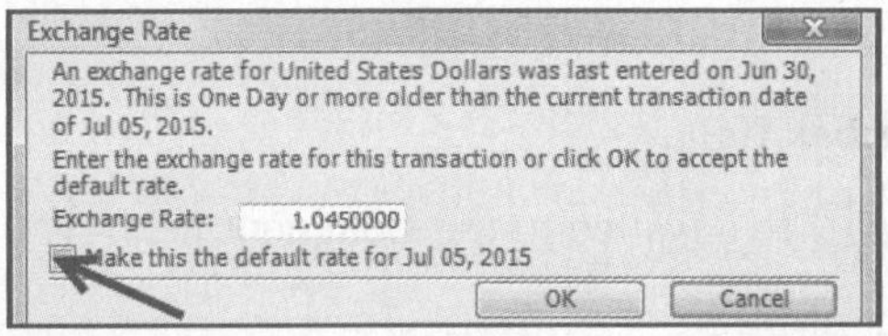

The Exchange Rate setting for the company file warns when the exchange rate on record is more than one day old so that an incorrect old rate is not accepted in error. The most recent exchange rate is entered and selected for editing. You can also edit the exchange rate directly in the journal screen, just as you enter information in other fields.

Type 1.031

Click **Make This The Default Rate For Jul 05, 2015**. **Press** *enter* or **click** **OK** to return to the Sales Journal.

Click the **Item Description field**. **Type** CDs

Click the **Amount field**. **Type** 2190 The default revenue account is correct.

Click the **Item Description field** on the next invoice line. **Type** books

Click the **Amount field**. **Type** 300

Click the **Account field List icon** and **select** account **4140**.

Exported goods are not taxable because they are "consumed" outside of Canada. The No Tax code (blank) is entered as the default and it is correct.

Click the **Freight field**. **Type** 140 **Press** *tab* to update the amounts. Maple does not charge taxes on freight for exported goods.

Click the **Track Shipments tool**.

Choose **Federal Express** as the shipper from the Shipped By list.

Press *tab* to advance to the Tracking Number field.

Type F19YTR563 **Click OK** to return to the completed journal entry:

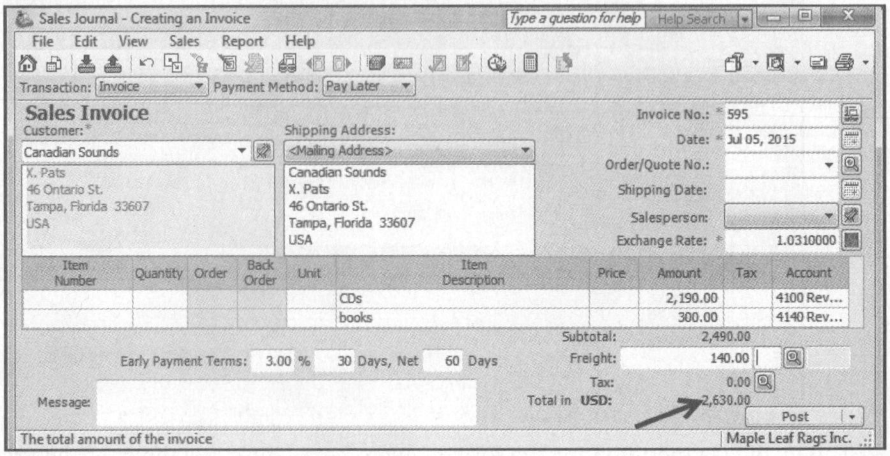

Choose the **Report menu** and **click** **Display Sales Journal Entry**:

Maple Leaf Rags Inc.
Sales Journal Entry 07/05/2015 (J7)

Account Number	Account Description	Foreign A...	Debits	Credits
1200	Accounts Receivable	US$2,630.00	2,711.53	-
4100	Revenue from CD Sales	US$2,190.00	-	2,257.89
4140	Revenue from Book Sales	US$300.00	-	309.30
4200	Freight Revenue	US$140.00	-	144.34
1 United States Dollars equals 1.0310000 Canadian Dollars			2,711.53	2,711.53

Although the journal itself looks the same as for regular invoices — with amounts in US dollars — the journal entry has both the Canadian amounts and the US amounts as well as the exchange rate applied to the transaction. Otherwise, the entry is the same as it would be for sales to Canadian customers. No new accounts are used.

Close the **display** when finished and **make corrections** if necessary.

Click **Post** [Post] to save the transaction. **Close** the **Sales Journal**.

Enter the **next three transactions**.

> **NOTES**
> You can use the Additional Field for the invoice number.
> Use the default bank account 1040 for receipts from Canadian customers.

9

Cash Receipt #125 **Dated July 5/15**

From It's All Canadian, cheque #884 for $3 570 in payment of account including $105 discount taken for early payment. Reference invoice #589.

> **NOTES**
> Wholesale customers who will be selling the product to their own customers do not pay PST.
> Remember to change the revenue account for book sales.

10

Sales Order #TB-04 & Deposit #14 **Dated July 5/15**

Shipping date July 10/15
From Treble & Bass, $10 300 for CDs and $900 for books plus 5% GST. Enter one (1) as the order quantity for each invoice line. Shipping by Purolator for $120 plus GST. Invoice total $11 886. Terms 3/30, n/60. Received cheque #911 for $2 000 as deposit #14 to confirm the order. Refer to page 427.

> **WARNING!**
> Remember to change the payment method to Pay Later for invoice #596. Cheque remains selected from the Sales Order. Refer to page 433. The balance owing is $9 886.

11

Sales Invoice #596 **Dated July 10/15**

To Treble & Bass, to fill sales order #TB-04, $10 300 for CDs and $900 for books plus 5% GST. Shipped by Purolator (#PCU899XT) for $120 plus GST. Invoice total $11 886. Terms 3/30, n/60. Enter the shipper so you can track the shipment.

Entering Foreign Customer Receipts

Click the **Receipts icon** [Receipts] to open the Receipts Journal.

✓ 12

Cash Receipt #126 **Dated July 15/15**

From Canadian Sounds, cheque #2397 for $2 551.10 USD in payment of account less $78.90 discount for early payment. Reference invoice #595. The exchange rate for July 15 is 1.042.

Choose **Canadian Sounds** from the customer list:

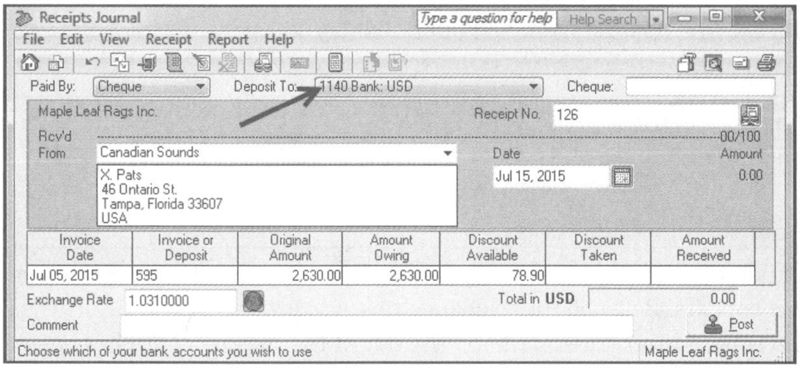

The journal is modified for the foreign customer. The outstanding invoice appears on the screen and the currency is marked as USD. An Exchange Rate field also becomes available.

NOTES
If the correct bank account is not selected by default, you can choose it from the Deposit To drop-down list of bank accounts.

Deposits from US customers are made to the USD bank account. This account is set up as the default bank account for foreign currency transactions.

Click the **Cheque field**. **Type** 2397

Click the **Date field**. The session date is correct as the transaction date.

Click **15** and **press** tab to open the Exchange Rate screen.

If the rate has not changed, you can accept it by clicking Make This The Default Rate For Jul 15, 2015 and clicking OK.

NOTES
The Exchange Rate screen does not open until you "touch" the date field in some way. If the Exchange Rate screen does not open when you enter a date, you can type the exchange rate directly in the Exchange Rate field.

Again, because the last exchange rate we entered was for July 11, the rate is out of date, and we must enter a new one. The previous rate is highlighted.

Type 1.042

Click **Make This The Default Rate For Jul 15, 2015**.

Click **OK** to return to the Receipts Journal. The cursor is on the calendar icon.

Click the **Discount Taken field**.

Press tab to accept the discount because the full invoice is being paid. The cursor advances to the Amount Received field.

Press tab to accept the amount and update the cheque portion of the form.

Click the **Enter Additional Information tool**.

The Total and cheque amount fields are updated in the background journal window.

Click the **Additional Field text box** to move the cursor.

Type Ref: inv #595

Click **OK** to return to the completed journal entry:

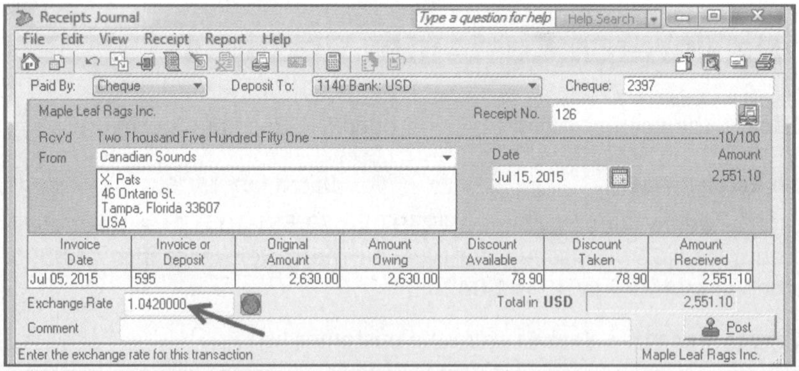

Choose the **Report menu** and **click** **Display Receipts Journal Entry** to review the entry:

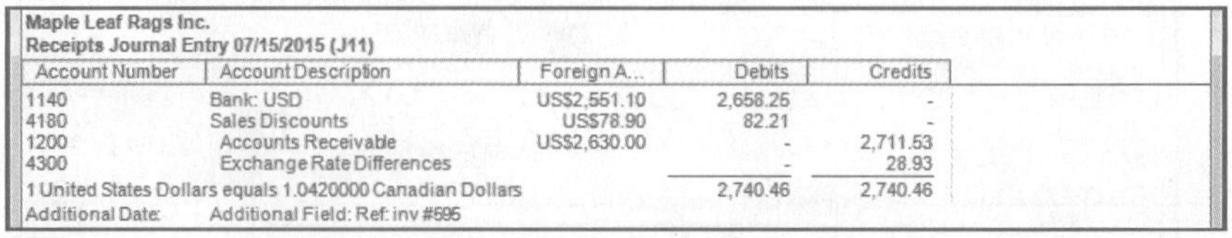
Maple Leaf Rags Inc.
Receipts Journal Entry 07/15/2015 (J11)

Account Number	Account Description	Foreign A...	Debits	Credits
1140	Bank: USD	US$2,551.10	2,658.25	-
4180	Sales Discounts	US$78.90	82.21	-
1200	Accounts Receivable	US$2,630.00	-	2,711.53
4300	Exchange Rate Differences		-	28.93
1 United States Dollars equals 1.0420000 Canadian Dollars			2,740.46	2,740.46
Additional Date:	Additional Field: Ref: inv #595			

NOTES
The gain/loss situation is reversed for payments to foreign suppliers. When the rate increases, the purchased goods cost more and money is lost. A decrease in exchange rate creates a gain.

In addition to the usual linked accounts for receipts, an entry for *Exchange Rate Differences* appears. Because the exchange rate was lower on the day of the sale, the date the revenue was recorded, than on the day of the receipt, there has been a credit to the account. Maple Leaf Rags has gained money on the delay in payment — more Canadian dollars are received for the same US dollar amount when the exchange rate is higher. When the rate decreases, there is a loss. As for foreign customer sales, amounts are given in both currencies along with the exchange rate.

Close the **display** to return to the journal and **make corrections** if necessary.

Click **Post** [Post] to save the transaction.

Close the **Receipts Journal** and **enter** the next **sales transaction**.

13 **Sales Invoice #597** **Dated July 15/15**

To Music Music Music, $1 630 USD for CDs plus $450 USD for books. Shipped by Federal Express (#F27CGB786) for $110. Invoice total $2 190 USD. Terms 3/30, n/60. The exchange rate is 1.042.

NOTES
The Exchange Rate screen does not open for the sale because we already entered a rate for July 15.

Looking Up Invoices to Track Shipments

Lookup provides an exact copy of the posted invoice that you can store, print or e-mail if you have forgotten to do so before posting. This feature can be useful if a customer has an inquiry about a purchase or needs a copy of the invoice. Once a sales or purchase invoice is posted with details about the shipping company, you can look up the invoice to track the shipment to see when delivery is expected. You can use the Find Invoice approach or the Search feature (see the margin Notes).

✓ 14 **Memo #46** **Dated July 16/15**

From J. Bands: Treble & Bass called to inform you that they have not received their shipment of CDs. Look up invoice #596, e-mail a copy of the invoice to the customer and check the delivery status.

Advance the **session date** to **July 31**. **Back up** your data set.

Choose **Find Invoice** from the Sales Invoices shortcuts list as shown:

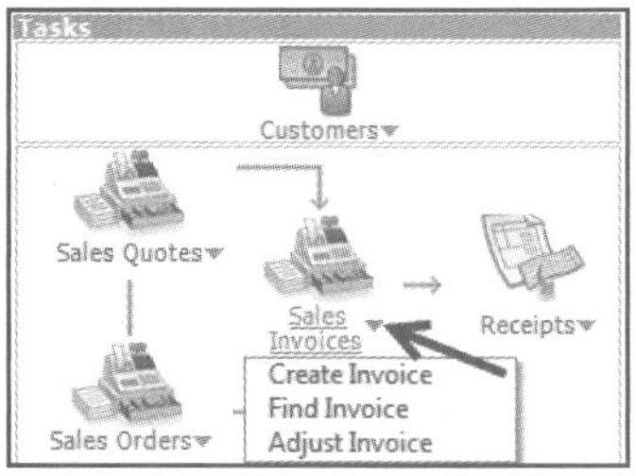

You will open the Search dialogue window:

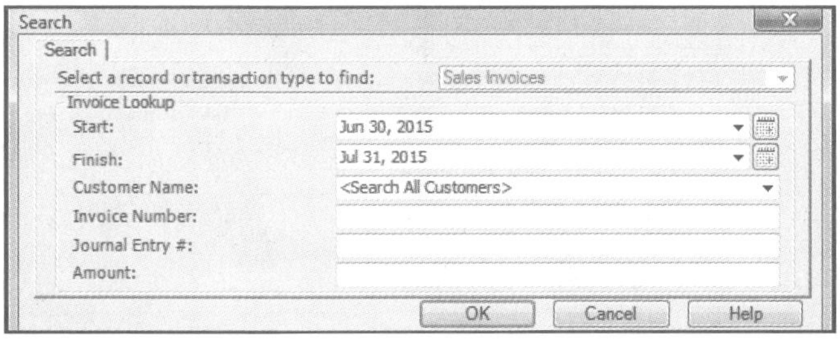

If the Sales Journal is open, you can click the **Look Up An Invoice tool** on the tool bar or beside the Invoice field, or choose the Sales menu and click Look Up Invoice to open this Search window.

NOTES
You can also type Treble in the Search field and click —>.
The result will list the record for the customer and the sales invoice. Double-click the sales invoice entry to open the Lookup screen for this transaction.
The Next and Previous tools will not be available because this sales invoice is the only one that meets the criterion.

The Search screen options for Look Up are like those for adjusting an invoice. You can search through all invoices for the fiscal year to date (or for the previous year if you have not cleared the transactions and lookup data) or enter a narrower range of dates; you can search through invoices for all customers or for a specific customer; or you can search for a specific invoice, journal entry number or amount. Your search strategy will depend on how much information you have before you begin the search and how many invoices there are altogether.

The default displayed Start date in this case shows the earliest transaction date. The Finish date is the most recent session date. You can change these dates to narrow the search, just as you would edit any other date fields, or you can choose dates from the drop-down list or calendar. We want to include all invoices in the search, beginning with the earliest transaction date in the data file, so we can accept the default range of dates.

The Customer Name option allows you to Search All Customers, the default setting, or a specific customer's invoices. You can also look up the invoices for one-time customers.

To display the list of customers, click the Customer Name field or its drop-down list arrow and click the name you need to select a specific customer.

If you know the Invoice Number or the Journal Entry number, you can enter the detail in the related field and click OK. You can also search for a specific Amount.

In this case we will look at all invoices by choosing the default to Search All Customers.

Click **OK** to display the list of invoices that meet the search conditions of date and customers:

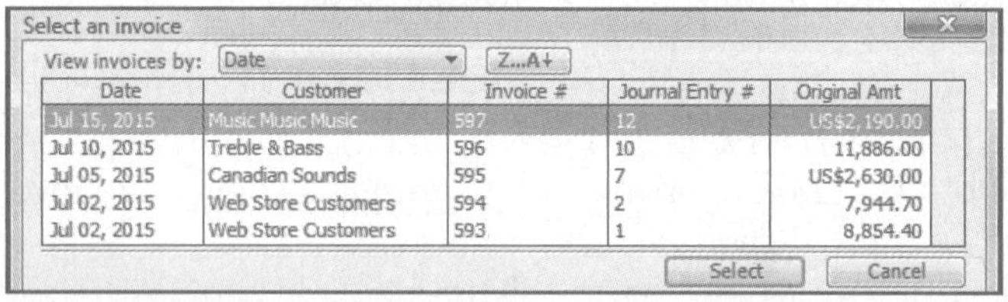

You can sort the list by order of posting date, customer, journal entry number, invoice number and amount. You can also reverse the order of the entries in the list by clicking the Z...A+ button.

Click **Treble & Bass, Invoice Number 596** for $11 886.00 to select it. Click anywhere on the line.

Click **Select** to display the requested invoice as follows:

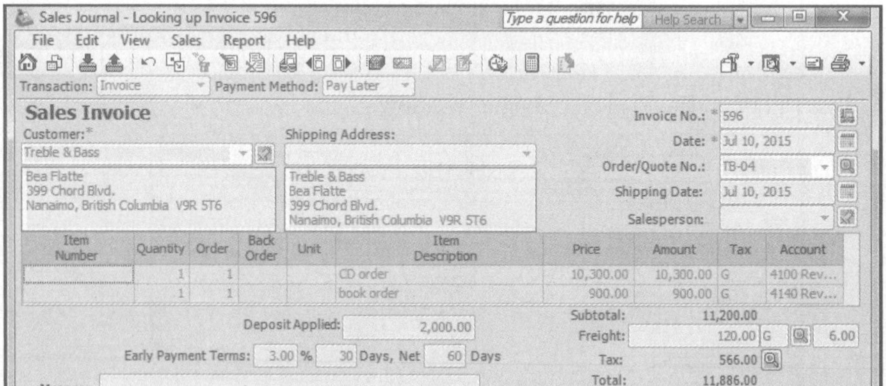

Notice that this is an exact copy of the original invoice, except that you cannot edit or post it. All fields are dimmed, but several familiar tool options are available. You can store, e-mail or print the invoice. Although you cannot adjust an invoice from the Lookup window directly, the Adjust Invoice tool is available. When you click Adjust Invoice, the journal screen changes and the fields become available for editing. You can use the Lookup method to locate the invoice you need to adjust. You can also reverse a transaction directly from the Lookup screen.

If you have selected the wrong invoice, or if you want to view other invoices from this one, you can access them from any Lookup window. If there are no invoices in one or both directions, the corresponding tools will be dimmed.

Click **Look Up Next Invoice** or **Look Up Previous Invoice** or choose Previous or Next Invoice from the Sales menu to display other invoices. You can browse through the invoices in this way until you find the one you need. You should practise viewing other invoices by clicking the Look Up Next and Previous Invoice tools.

Click the **Track Shipments tool** or **choose** the **Sales menu** and **click Track Shipments** to see the shipping details for the sale.

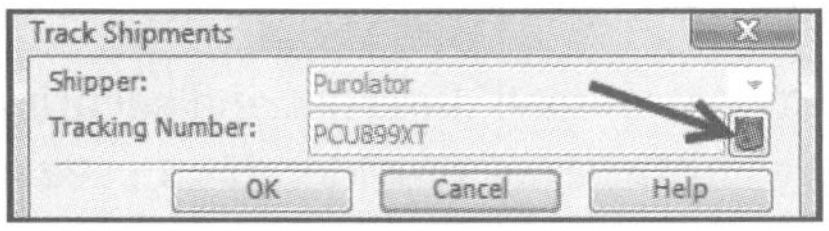

If you need to add or edit the shipping information, click Cancel to close the tracking details window. Click the Adjust Invoice tool in the journal and then the Track Shipments tool.

Click the Web icon to close the shipping details screen and continue:

If you have actually shipped an item and have entered the number provided by the shipper, you can choose Yes and save the number for entering on the Web site tracking page. However, we do not have an actual tracking number or account with Purolator.

Click **No** to continue to the Internet connection.

Your screen at this stage will depend on your Internet setup — you may connect and access the Web site directly, or you may need to enter your account and password first.

Continue as you would for your **usual Internet connection**.

You will access the Web site for Purolator.

Enter the **Tracking Number** in the Track field, **click Track** and follow the instructions provided to continue tracking the shipment.

Close the **Web Site screen** when finished to return to the Lookup screen

Close the **Track Shipments screen** by clicking OK.

We are now ready to e-mail a copy of the invoice to the customer as notice of the shipping date and carrier. (Read the Warning margin note.)

Click the **E-mail tool** or **choose** the **File menu** and **click E-mail**.

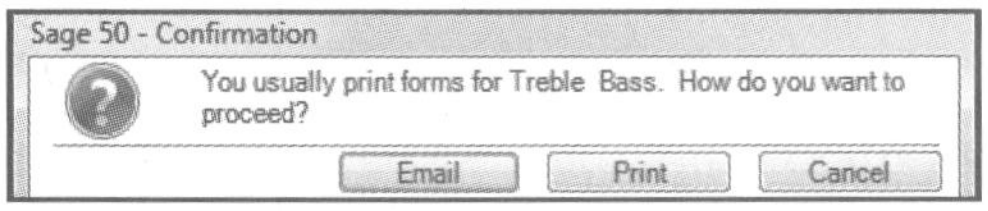

Since printing invoices is the default setting in the customer's ledger record, you are asked if you want to continue, just in case you clicked the wrong button.

Click **E-mail** to continue to the E-mail Information screen:

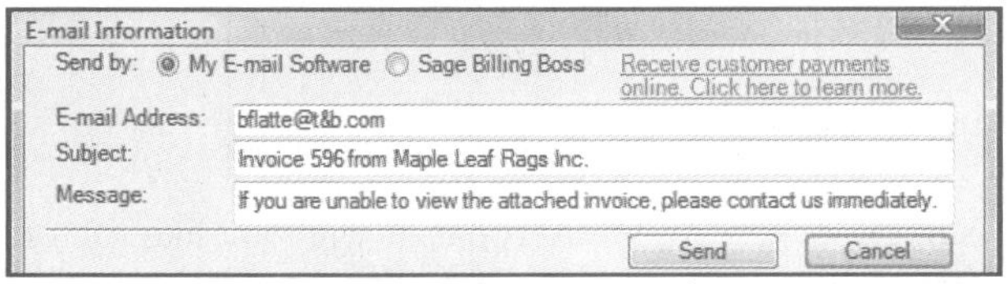

If the e-mail address is missing, you can enter it here. You should replace the address with your own e-mail address if you want to test the e-mail feature.

NOTES

If you entered other Search parameters, the Next and Previous tools will show you all invoices that meet those criteria.

WARNING!

If you have a network connection, such as high-speed access, you must start the Internet connection before clicking the Track Shipments tool.

WARNING!

Web sites are continually updated, so your screens and the sequence of steps may be different from the ones we provide.

NOTES

You do not need an account to track shipments, but you do need the tracking number.

WARNING!

You must have a valid form file reference in the Reports & Forms Settings for E-mail (Invoice forms). If you have used different computers for your data file, the default form reference may be incorrect. If you see an error message about an invalid form, close the e-mail message. In the Sales Journal, click the Change Form Options For Invoices tool. Choose the Sage 50 Form and the generic entry Invoices and be sure that your form location shows Sage 50 Premium Accounting 2013\Forms.

Type (Type your own e-mail address in this field, or that of a classmate.)

You can add a message in the Message field about the shipment tracking details to inform the customer of the expected delivery date.

Click **Send**.

You will see another advisory screen asking whether you want to update the e-mail address in the ledger record.

Click **Yes** to update the ledger record and proceed.

At this stage, your screens will depend on your e-mail, Internet and security program setups. You should be connected to your Internet provider. If you see a message requesting permission to send a message:

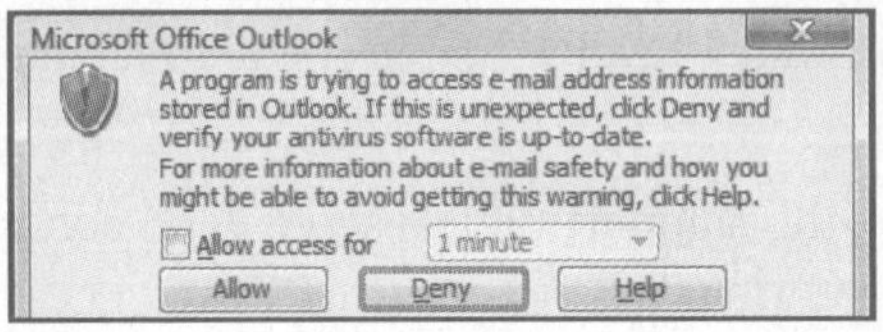

Click **Allow Access For** and then **click** the **Allow button**. You may see the progress screen as the message is transmitted:

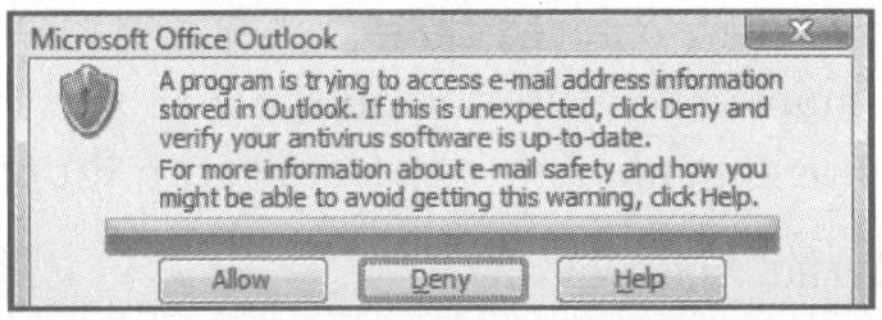

Click **Allow** again if you see this message. **Close** your **e-mail** and **Internet connections** to return to the Sales Journal – Invoice Lookup window.

Close the **Lookup window** to return to the Receivables window.

If you open your Outlook e-mail program, you will see the message indicating the attached invoice document Invoice.PDF, as shown below:

If you have another e-mail program as your default, you may see the single PDF invoice page included directly in your message along with the attached PDF document, as shown in this example:

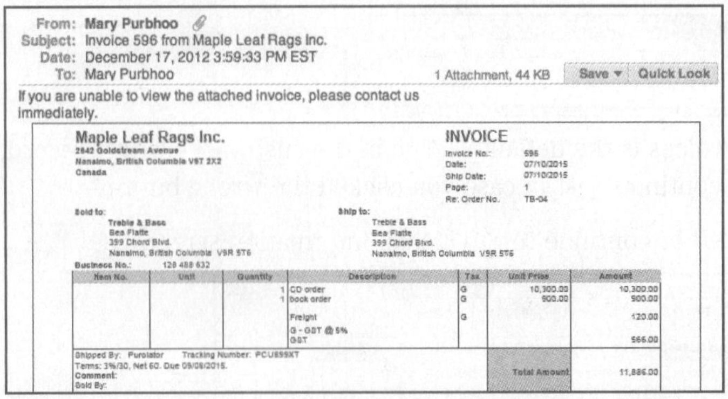

When the attachment is opened with Adobe Acrobat, it will look like the one shown in the screen above. The invoice shows the date of the invoice as well as the shipping and tracking details.

NOTES

The Sage 50 E-mail feature works best when Microsoft Outlook is set up as your default e-mail program.

If you are using a program other than Outlook as your default e-mail program, you may be asked to enter additional settings before you can e-mail the invoice.

Start your Outlook program before starting the e-mail process if the e-mail is not sent.

The Sage Billing Boss program is no longer available.

NOTES

If you see a permission screen with the Yes and No buttons replacing Allow and Deny, you should click Yes.

NOTES

You may have to enter your ID and password before your e-mail program starts.

If necessary, click Allow again when the progress bar has finished to send the message.

Looking Up and Tracking Purchases

You can look up purchase invoices in the same way you look up sales invoices. You can look up purchase invoices from the Purchases Journal and from the Payments Journal.

> Open the Purchases or Payments Journal, click Look Up An Invoice, decide whether you want to restrict the search dates or suppliers and click OK. Choose an invoice from the displayed list and click Select. If you know the invoice number, you can enter it directly and click OK to display the requested invoice.
>
> From the Payments Journal, choose Make Other Payment then click (Look Up An Invoice) to see cash invoices posted in the Payments Journal.

NOTES
You can also look up Purchases Journal invoices from the Payments Journal, Pay Purchase Invoices screen.

Once you look up a purchase invoice, you can track shipments and look up other invoices in the same way as you do for sales. You can also adjust the invoice. Tracking is not available for cash purchases entered as Other Payments in the Payments Journal.

Entering Purchases from Foreign Suppliers

Purchases from foreign suppliers are entered in much the same way as purchases from other suppliers. Once you choose a supplier who uses a different currency, the Purchases Journal changes to add the appropriate fields.

Open the **Payables module window**.

Click the **Purchase Invoices icon** to open the Purchases Journal. Invoice and Pay Later are correctly selected.

✓ 15 **Purchase Invoice #DA-722** **Dated July 16/15**

From Design Anything (use Full Add for new US supplier), $3 200 plus 5% GST for design of labels and CD case inserts for new CDs. Invoice total $3 360 USD. Terms: net 30. The exchange rate is 1.045.

NOTES
Use Full Add so you can enter the correct currency.
Design Anything
(contact Joy Pikchur)
900 Park St., Unit 5
Seattle, Washington 98195
USA
Tel: (800) 639-8710
Fax: (206) 755-8852
Currency: USD
Terms: net 30
Expense account: 5360
Tax code: G

Click the **Supplier field**. **Type** `Design Anything`

Entering a Foreign Supplier Record

Click the **Add link** above the Supplier field to open the Payables Ledger supplier input screen.

Type the supplier address details from the margin Notes.

Enter **July 16** as the date for the Supplier Since field.

Click the **Options tab**. Notice the additional field for currency.

Choose **5360 Materials and Assembly Costs** as the default expense account.

Click the **Currency list arrow** as shown:

WARNING!
You must choose Full Add for new foreign currency suppliers so that you can choose USD as the currency.

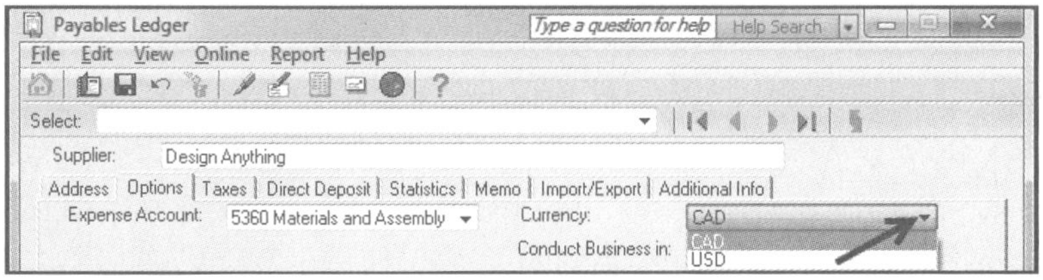

Choose **USD**. A Balance Owing in USD amount is added to the record.

Enter **net 30 days** as the payment terms.

Click the **Taxes tab** to see the default settings.

Click the **Tax Code list arrow** to see the options:

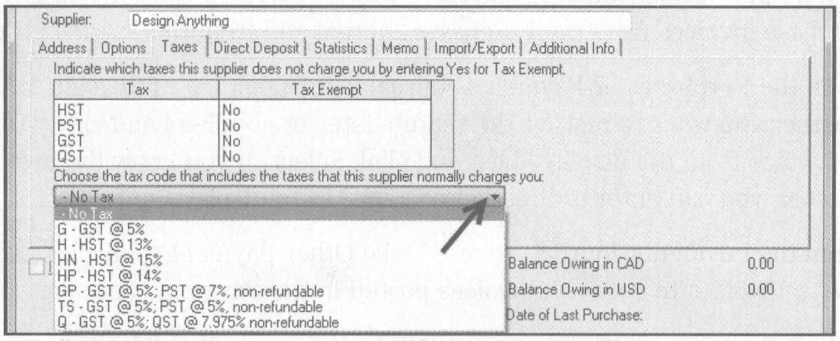

Maple Leaf Rags is not exempt from paying taxes on purchases from Design Anything, and that is the default selection. All tax codes will be available. Most purchases from US suppliers are subject to GST, so we should choose G - GST @ 5% as the default tax code. Maple pays GST on imported goods.

NOTES

The two additional tax codes, TS and Q, are available for purchases in Saskatchewan and Quebec. Provincial taxes on purchases are added to the expense or asset part of the purchase, just like other PST paid amounts. Tax code Q is not shown in the Sales Journal because no linked account was entered for taxes charged on sales.

WARNING!

Leave all Tax Exempt settings at No in case other tax codes are required for taxes on other purchases or on freight.

NOTES

GST is paid directly to the Receiver General at the time the goods arrive in Canada. The foreign supplier does not collect these taxes.

To simplify the exercises, we do not show this aspect of the tax collection and instead include the GST on foreign purchases with the invoices.

Click **Code G - GST @ 5%**.

Click **Save And Close** [Save and Close] to return to the modified invoice:

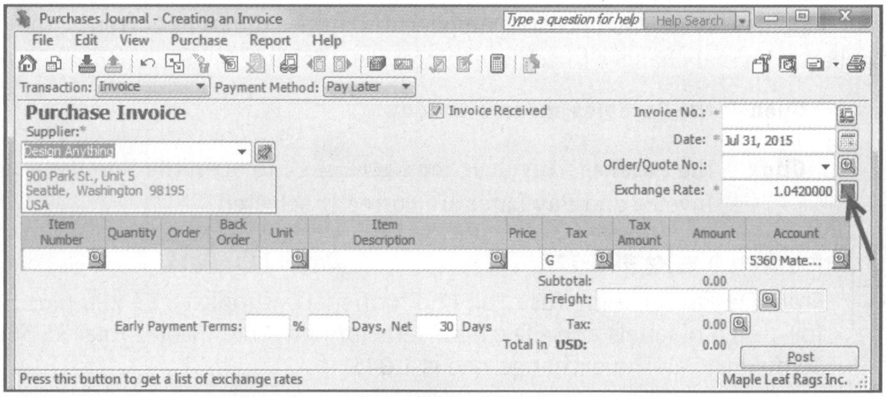

The invoice currency is now shown as USD and exchange rate fields are added. The default terms, expense account and tax code are also on the invoice.

Enter the **Invoice number** and **Date**. **Do not press** tab. If the Exchange Rate update screen opens, click Cancel.

Click the **Exchange Rate tool** to open the list of rates we have already used so that we can choose from this list:

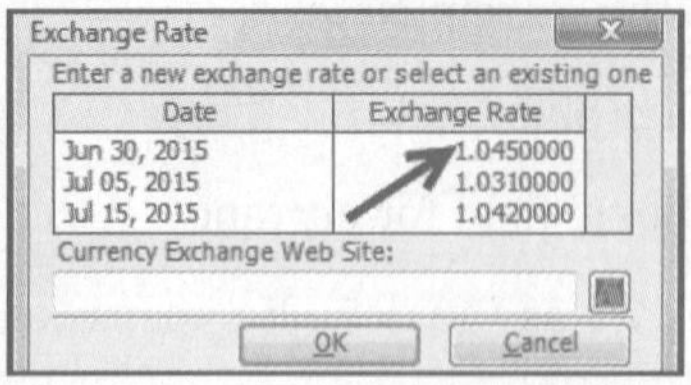

Click **1.045**, the rate for June 30. **Click OK** to return to the journal.

Enter the **Amount** and **Description** to complete the invoice as shown:

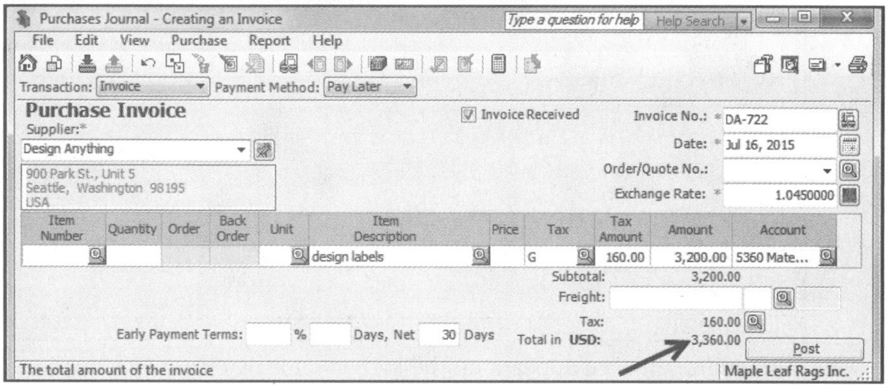

Choose the **Report menu** and **click Display Purchases Journal Entry** to review the entry:

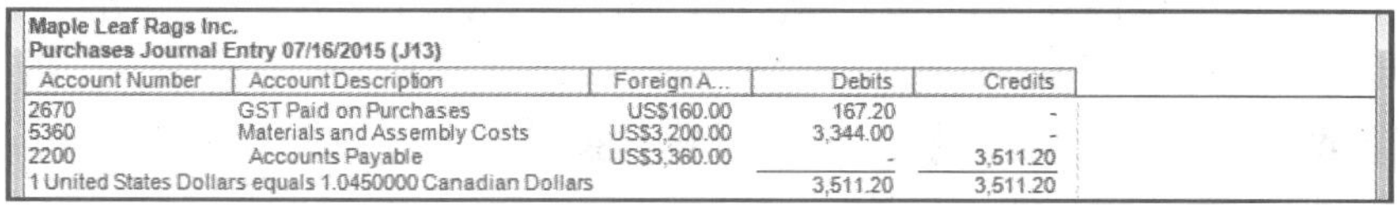

Maple Leaf Rags Inc.
Purchases Journal Entry 07/16/2015 (J13)

Account Number	Account Description	Foreign A...	Debits	Credits
2670	GST Paid on Purchases	US$160.00	167.20	-
5360	Materials and Assembly Costs	US$3,200.00	3,344.00	-
2200	Accounts Payable	US$3,360.00	-	3,511.20
1 United States Dollars equals 1.0450000 Canadian Dollars			3,511.20	3,511.20

The only difference between this and other purchase entries is the addition of the USD currency amounts and exchange rate.

Close the **display** to return to the journal and **make corrections** if necessary.

Click **Post** [Post]. **Close** the **Purchases Journal**.

Enter the **next four transactions**.

16 **Amex Payment Cheque #764** **Dated July 16/15**

To Amex, $335 in payment of credit card account, including $290 for purchases charged from May 25 to June 25 and $45 for annual renewal fee.

17 **Payment Cheque #765** **Dated July 18/15**

To Grandeur Graphics, $412 in full payment of account, including $8 discount for early payment. Reference invoice #GG-1304.

18 **Payment Cheque #766** **Dated July 18/15**

To Let 'm Know, $1 100 in full payment of account, including $20 discount for early payment. Reference invoice #LK-692.

19 **Cash Receipt #127** **Dated July 20/15**

From CDN Music, cheque #28563 for $4 590 in payment of account including $135 discount taken for early payment. Reference invoice #591.

Entering Payments to Foreign Suppliers

Click the **Payments icon** [Payments] or use the shortcut to open the Payments Journal.

✓ 20 **Payment Cheque #284** **Dated July 30/15**

To Design Anything, $3 360 USD in full payment of account. Reference invoice #DA-722. The exchange rate is 1.038.

Choose **Design Anything** from the Supplier list to modify the journal:

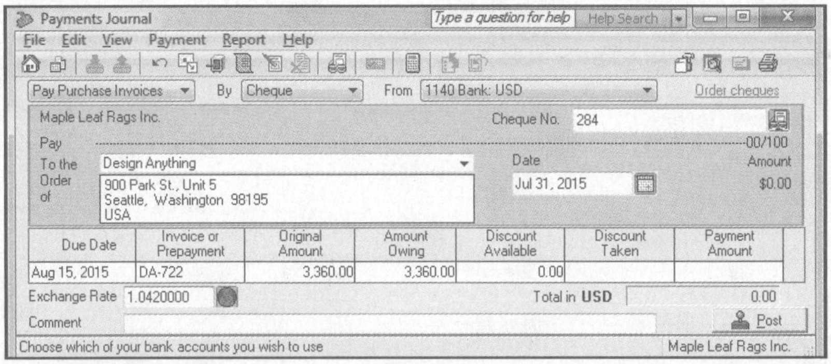

The outstanding invoice appears on the screen and the currency is marked as USD. An Exchange Rate field also becomes available.

Payments to US suppliers are made from the USD bank account. This account is set up as the default bank account for foreign currency transactions. The cheque number is the next in sequence for this account.

Click the **Calendar icon** and **choose July 30** as the transaction date.

The Exchange Rate screen should open automatically — the rate is out of date.

Type 1.038 **Click** **Make This The Default Rate For Jul 30, 2015**.

Press *enter* to return to the Payments Journal. The cursor is on the calendar icon.

Click the **Payment Amount field**. There is no discount.

Press *tab* to accept the amount and complete the entry as shown:

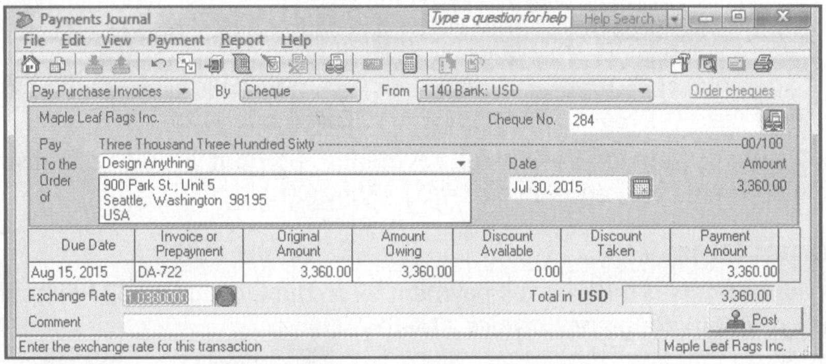

Press *ctrl* + **J** so you can review the journal entry:

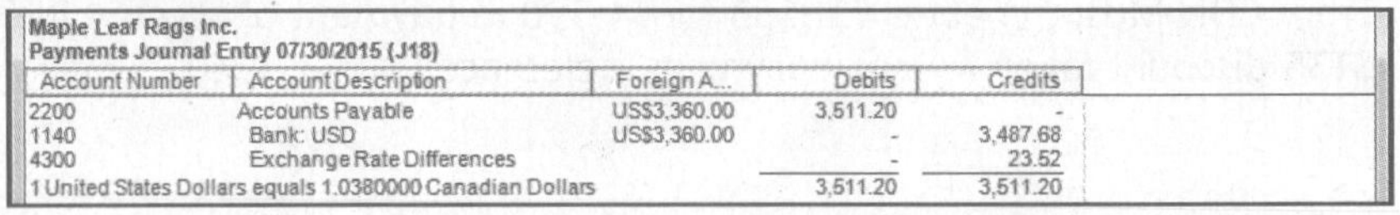
Maple Leaf Rags Inc.
Payments Journal Entry 07/30/2015 (J18)

Account Number	Account Description	Foreign A...	Debits	Credits
2200	Accounts Payable	US$3,360.00	3,511.20	-
1140	Bank: USD	US$3,360.00	-	3,487.68
4300	Exchange Rate Differences		-	23.52
1 United States Dollars equals 1.0380000 Canadian Dollars			3,511.20	3,511.20

A credit entry for *Exchange Rate Differences* appears because the exchange rate was higher on the day of the purchase (the date the purchase was recorded) than on the day of the payment. However, because this is a payment, Maple Leaf Rags has gained on the payment delay as shown by the credit entry for a revenue account — fewer Canadian dollars are needed to pay the same US dollar amount. As for other foreign currency transactions, amounts are given in both currencies and the exchange rate is included.

Close the **display** to return to the journal. **Make corrections** if necessary.

NOTES

If the Exchange Rate screen stays open after you click OK with the session date replacing the transaction date, you may enter an incorrect rate. Click Cancel to close the screen and select the correct exchange rate from the Exchange Rate select list.

Click the Exchange Rate tool beside the field to open the list of rates. You can also type the rate directly in the Exchange Rate field.

Click **Post** [Post] to see this message:

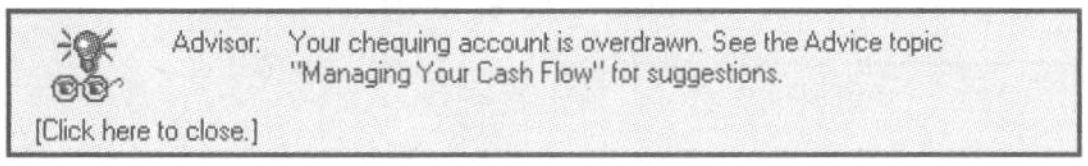

Advisor: Your chequing account is overdrawn. See the Advice topic "Managing Your Cash Flow" for suggestions.
[Click here to close.]

The message indicates that the bank account is overdrawn. We will transfer funds to the USD account to cover the cheque before the supplier has a chance to cash it.

Click the **Advisor icon** to close the message. **Close** the **Payments Journal**.

Transferring Foreign Funds

Click **Banking** in the Modules pane list to open this module window:

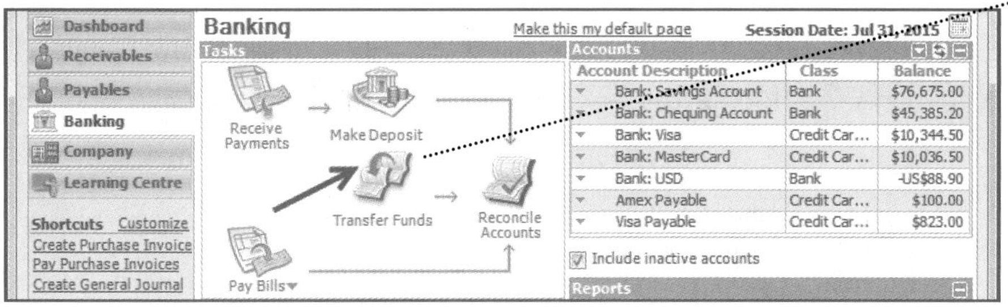

Click the **Refresh icon** in the Accounts pane to update the account balances.

You can see that *Bank USD* is overdrawn — it has a negative balance amount.

The Banking module window has no ledger icons, although it does allow direct access to the ledger records for all accounts involved in making or receiving payments (cash, bank and credit card class accounts). Three journal icons — Make Deposit, Transfer Funds, Reconcile Accounts — are for bank account transactions. The Receive Payments and Pay Bills icons open the Receipts and Payments journals and are duplicated from Receivables and Payables modules.

We use the Transfer Funds Journal to move money from one bank account to another.

✓ 21 **Memo #47** **Dated July 30/15**

From J. Bands: Transfer $1 000 USD from Bank: Chequing Account to Bank: USD. The exchange rate is 1.038.

Click the **Transfer Funds icon** to open the journal we need:

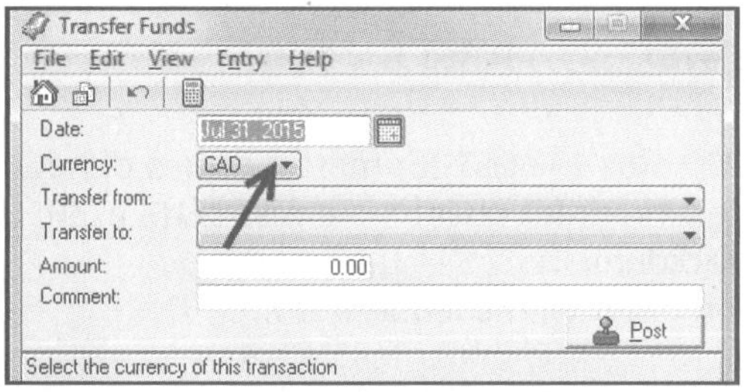

Type July 30 (as the Date).

Click the **Currency list arrow** to see the currency options as shown:

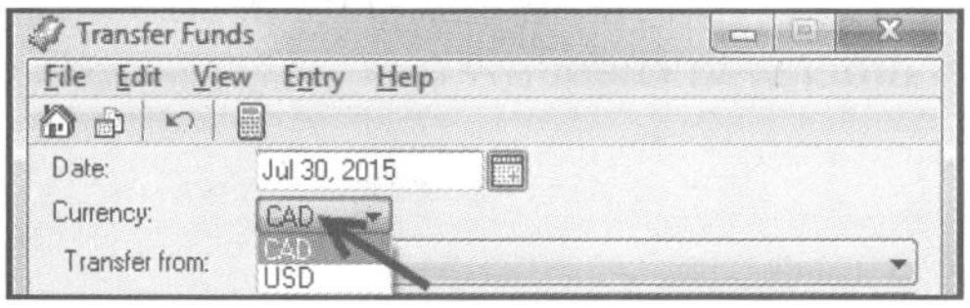

Both currencies are available for Transfer Funds transactions.

NOTES

Access to the Payments and Receipts journals from the Banking module allows all bank-related activities to be completed from this screen.

Account reconciliation and deposits are covered in Chapter 15.

Make Other Payment (Pay Expenses) is the default type of transaction from the Pay Bills icon.

CLASSIC VIEW

The Transfer Funds Journal is not available in the Classic view.

WARNING!

You must choose USD as the currency for the transfer of funds. The CAD bank account will be available for the foreign currency transaction. If you choose CAD as the currency, you cannot access the USD bank account.

NOTES

The Exchange Rate window does not open because we have already entered a rate for July 30. You can still change the rate if needed by editing the amount in the Exchange Rate field.

Click **USD**. The exchange rate is entered correctly for this date.

Click the **Transfer From list arrow** to see the list of available accounts:

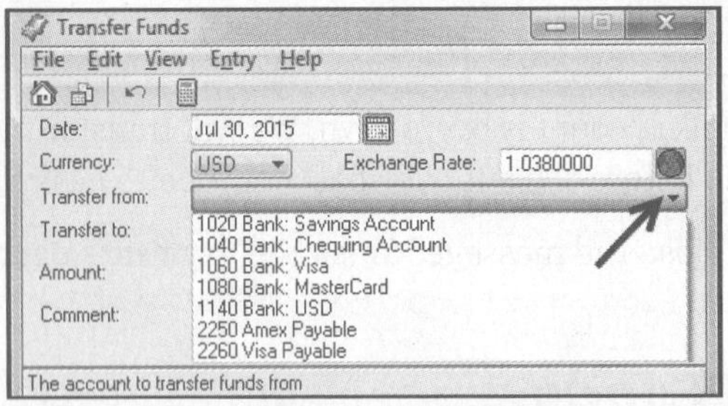

Choose **1040 Bank: Chequing Account** in the Account field. **Press** *tab*.

Click the **Transfer To list arrow** to see the same list of available accounts.

Choose **1140 Bank: USD** and **press** *tab* to advance to the Amount field.

Type `1000` **Press** *tab* to advance to the comment field.

Type `Memo 47: Transfer funds to cover cheque`

Adding the comment will complete the entry:

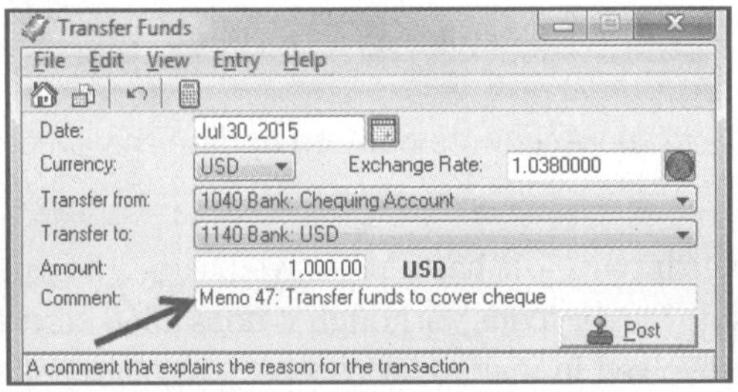

Check your transaction carefully. You cannot display the journal entry before posting. To make corrections after posting, adjust or reverse the transfer in the General Journal.

When you display the Journal Entries Report, the transfer is entered as a typical debit and credit entry, with the exchange rate added and amounts given in both currencies as for other foreign currency transactions.

Click **Post** [Post] to save the transaction.

Close the **Transfer Funds Journal**. The Banking Home window balances are updated.

Enter the **remaining transactions** up to memo #58 on September 30.

22

Purchase Order #204 & Cheque #767 **Dated July 31/15**

Shipping date Aug. 15/15
To A.B. Original Sounds, $50 000 plus 5% GST for master copies of new CDs. Invoice total $52 500. Enter 1 as the order quantity. Terms: 1/10, n/30. Use Materials and Assembly Costs account.
Paid $10 000 as prepayment on order with cheque #767.

23

Purchase Order #205 & Cheque #768 **Dated July 31/15**

Shipping date Aug. 15/15
To Super Dupers (use Full Add for the new supplier), $15 000 to duplicate CDs and books plus 5% GST. Invoice total $15 750. Terms: 1/10, n/30.
Paid $4 000 as prepayment on order with cheque #768.

NOTES
All Asset Bank and Cash class accounts and credit card accounts that are used to make and receive payments are available in the Transfer Funds journal.

NOTES
The funds transfer may also be entered in the General Journal. Both currencies are available for transactions. Again, you must choose the currency before selecting accounts.

WARNING!
Check your transaction carefully because you cannot display the journal entry before posting. You can adjust or reverse the transfers from the General Journal.

NOTES
Transfer Funds entries are included in General Journal Entry Reports. You can also adjust transfers from the General Journal.

NOTES
You can add a shortcut for Transfer Funds from the Banking Shortcuts list. View Accounts is also on the list of Banking module shortcuts.

NOTES
Super Dupers
777 Copiers Ave.
Richmond Hill, ON L4T 6V2
Terms: 1/10, n/30 before tax
Tax code: G
Expense Account: 5360

24

Maple Leaf Rags

www.mapleleafrags.com

2642 Coldstream Avenue
Nanaimo, BC V9T 2X2
Tel 1: (250) 63M-USIC
Tel 2: (888) 63M-USIC Fax: (250) 633-4888

PURCHASE ORDER

PO#:	206
Date:	July 31, 2015
Shipping date:	Aug 15, 2015
Ordered from:	Wrap It
Address:	80 Cubit Road Richmond Hill, ON L5R 6B2
Phone No:	(905) 881-7739
Fax No:	(905) 881-7000
Contact:	Able Boxer

Order description		Amount
Provide CD cases add labels and inserts terms: 1/5, n/30		6 300.00
	Freight (Canada Post)	120.00
	GST	321.00
	HST	--
Deposit: chq #769 for $2 000	**Order Total**	6 741.00
	Deposit	2 000.00
Approved by: *Jaz Bands*	**Balance Owing**	4 741.00

25 **Purchase Invoice #LK-2303** **Dated July 31/15**

From Let 'm Know, $1 500 plus 5% GST and 7% PST for series of ads to run for the next five months (prepaid expense). Invoice total $1 680. Terms: 2/20, n/30.

> **NOTES**
> Change the default account to Prepaid Expenses for the invoice from Let 'm Know.

26 **Cash Purchase Invoice #WT-6632** **Dated July 31/15**

From Western Tel, $205 plus 5% GST and 7% PST for telephone services for two months. Invoice total $229.60. Terms: payment on receipt of invoice. Paid by cheque #770.

27 **Cash Purchase Invoice #PE-49006** **Dated July 31/15**

From Purolator, $1 400 plus 5% GST for shipping services used from May 25 to July 25. Invoice total $1 470. Terms: payment on receipt of invoice. Paid by cheque #771.

28 **Visa Purchase Invoice #PC-34992** **Dated July 31/15**

From Petro-Canada (use Quick Add), $120 plus 5% GST for gasoline for business use. Invoice total $126 paid by Visa.

> **NOTES**
> Use Quick Add for the new supplier. Include gasoline costs with Travel Expenses. Use tax code G – GST @ 5%. The remaining provincial and federal taxes are already included in the price.

SESSION DATE – AUGUST 15, 2015

29 **Visa Payment Cheque #772** **Dated Aug. 2/15**

To Visa, $823 in payment of balance shown on Visa account statement for purchases before July 15, 2015.

30 **Cash Receipt #128** **Dated Aug. 7/15**

From Music Music Music, cheque #8531 for $2 124.30 USD in payment of account less $65.70 discount for early payment. Reference invoice #597. The exchange rate for Aug. 7 is 1.039. Deposit to Bank: USD account.

31 **Payment Cheque #773** **Dated Aug. 8/15**

To Let 'm Know, $1 650 in full payment of account, including $30 discount for early payment. Reference invoice #LK-2303.

32 **Cash Receipt #129** **Dated Aug. 9/15**

From Treble & Bass, cheque #1144 for $9 546.40 in payment of account including $339.60 discount taken for early payment. Reference invoice #596 and deposit #14. Deposit to Bank: Chequing Account.

33 **Sales Order #TM-05** **Dated Aug. 9/15**

Shipping date Aug. 22/15

From Total Music, $28 000 plus HST for CDs and $9 000 for books plus 5% GST – items purchased by major music store chains. Shipping charges $200 plus GST. Invoice total $41 300. Terms 3/30, n/60.

34

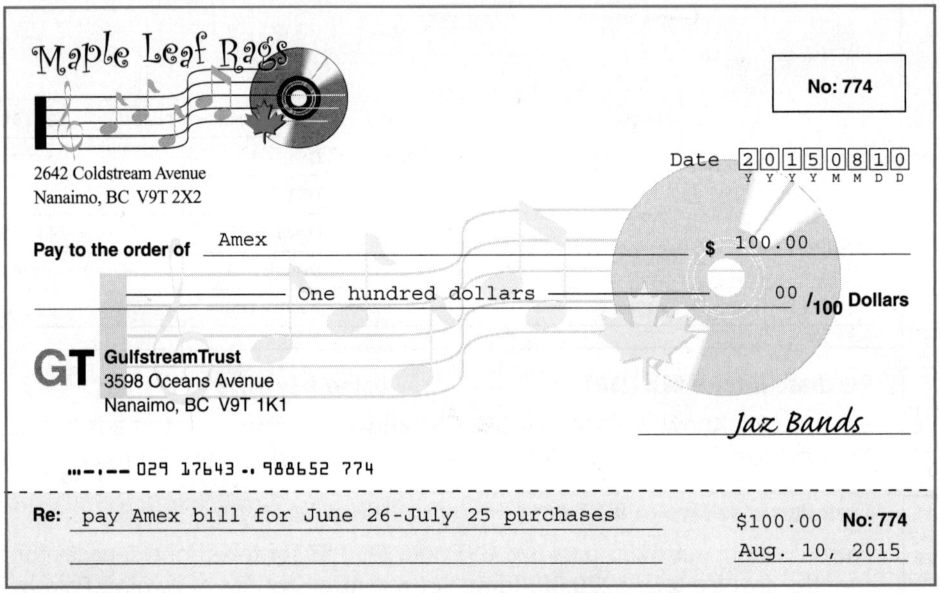

Maple Leaf Rags
2642 Coldstream Avenue
Nanaimo, BC V9T 2X2

No: 774

Date 20150810
Y Y Y Y M M D D

Pay to the order of Amex $ 100.00

One hundred dollars 00 /100 Dollars

GT GulfstreamTrust
3598 Oceans Avenue
Nanaimo, BC V9T 1K1

Jaz Bands

⑈⑆⑈ 029 17643 ⑆ 988652 774

Re: pay Amex bill for June 26-July 25 purchases $100.00 No: 774
Aug. 10, 2015

35 **Cash Receipt #130** **Dated Aug. 11/15**

From Total Music, cheque #502 for $5 000 as down payment, deposit #15, to confirm sales order #TM-05.

36 **Purchase Invoice #CA-7998** **Dated Aug. 12/15**

From Cars for All (use Quick Add for new supplier), $20 000 plus 5% GST and 7% PST for new automobile less $5 000 as a trade-in allowance on old car. Invoice total $16 800. The entry to write off the old car will be made by the accountant at year-end.

37 **Purchase Invoice #ABO-8823** **Dated Aug. 12/15**

From A.B. Original Sounds, to fill purchase order #204, $50 000 plus 5% GST for CD masters. Invoice total $52 500. Terms: 1/10, n/30. (Balance is $42 500.)

WARNING!
Remember to change the payment method to Pay Later for invoices that fill purchase orders with prepayments.

SESSION DATE – AUGUST 31, 2015

38 **Purchase Invoice #SD-9124** **Dated Aug. 18/15**

From Super Dupers, to fill purchase order #205, $15 000 to duplicate CDs and books plus 5% GST. Invoice total $15 750. Terms: 1/10, n/30. (Balance owing is $11 750.)

NOTES
When you advance the session date to Aug. 31, you should see an Advisor message that it is time to prepare for year-end. Read and then close the advisory statement to proceed.

39 **Purchase Invoice #WI-3719** **Dated Aug. 18/15**

From Wrap It, to fill purchase order #206, $6 300 plus 5% GST to prepare CDs for sale. Shipped by Canada Post (#75 553 789 249) for $120 plus 5% GST. Invoice total $6 741. Terms: 1/5, n/30. (Balance owing is $4 741.)

40 **Memo #48** **Dated Aug. 20/15**

From J. Bands: Owner invests $50 000 personal capital to finance production of new inventory. Amount deposited to Bank: Savings Account and credited to Common Stock.

41 **Sales Invoice #598** **Dated Aug. 21/15**

To Total Music, to fill sales order #TM-05, $28 000 plus HST for CDs and $9 000 plus 5% GST for books. Shipping charges $200 plus GST. Invoice total $41 300. Terms 3/30, n/60.

42 **Payment Cheque #775** **Dated Aug. 21/15**

To A.B. Original Sounds, $42 000 in full payment of account, including $500 discount for early payment. Reference invoice #ABO-8823 and prepayment by cheque #767.

43 **Payment Cheque #776** **Dated Aug. 23/15**

To Wrap It, $4 676.80 in full payment of account, including $64.20 discount for early payment. Reference invoice #WI-3719 and prepayment by cheque #769.

44 **Payment Cheque #777** **Dated Aug. 23/15**

To Super Dupers, $11 600 in full payment of account, with the $150 discount for early payment. Reference invoice #SD-9124 and prepayment by cheque #768.

45 **Memo #49** **Dated Aug. 23/15**

From J. Bands: Transfer $60 000 CAD from Bank: Savings Account to Bank: Chequing Account to cover cheques because the chequing account is overdrawn.

46 **Purchase Invoice #JH-0875** **Dated Aug. 25/15**

To J. Henry & Associates (use Quick Add), $1 500 plus $75 GST for legal fees to recover money owed by Entertainment House. Invoice total $1 575. Terms: net 30. Create new Group account 5240 Legal Fees.

47 **Visa Purchase Invoice #PC-49986** **Dated Aug. 28/15**

From Petro-Canada, $128 plus 5% GST for gasoline for business use. Invoice total $134.40 paid by Visa.

NOTES

Close the Advisor warnings about the overdrawn chequing account. The funds transfer in memo #49 will cover the cheques.

SESSION DATE – SEPTEMBER 15, 2015

48 **Memo #50** **Dated Sep. 2/15**

When his Visa bill arrived, Bands realized that he had entered the purchase from Cars for All as a Pay Later invoice instead of a Visa payment. Adjust invoice #CA-7998 from Cars for All. Change the method of payment to Visa.

49 **Visa Payment Cheque #778** **Dated Sep. 2/15**

To Visa, $16 926 in payment of account for purchases from July 16 to August 15, 2015.

50 **Sales Invoice #599** **Dated Sep. 5/15**

To Canadian Sounds, $4 500 USD for CDs and $750 for books. Shipped by Federal Express (#F36FYT863) for $170. Invoice total $5 420 USD. Terms: 3/30, n/60. The exchange rate is 1.037.

NOTES

If you do not change the date for the purchase invoice adjustment, you will see a warning that the transaction date precedes the session date because the transaction was dated in a previous month. Click Yes to proceed.

51

Maple Leaf Rags
www.mapleleafrags.com
2642 Coldstream Avenue
Nanaimo, BC V9T 2X2
Tel 1: (250) 63M-USIC
Tel 2: (888) 63M-USIC Fax: (250) 633-4888
GST # 128 488 632

Sales Invoice: #600
Date: September 10, 2015

Customer: Music Music Music
Address: 10 Red Rock Canyon, Sedona, Arizona 86336 USA
Phone No: (520) 678-4523
Fax No:
Contact: M. Porter

INVOICE

Item description	Amount
150 CDs	1 500.00 USD
25 Books	750.00 USD
Freight	140.00 USD
GST	—
PST	—
HST	—
Invoice Total	2 390.00 USD

Shipped by: Federal Express

Payment: 3/30, n/60
Exchange rate for Sep 10 was 1.036 – JB

Sold by: Jaz Bands

SESSION DATE – SEPTEMBER 29, 2015

NOTES
When you advance the session date to Sep. 29, you may see an Advisor message about the year-end adjustments required. Read and then close the advisory statement to proceed.

52 **Cash Receipt #131** **Dated Sep. 18/15**
From Total Music, cheque #574 for $35 184 in payment of account including $1 116 discount taken for early payment. Reference invoice #598 and deposit #15. Deposit to Bank: Chequing Account.

53 **Cash Purchase Invoice #WT-9810** **Dated Sep. 29/15**
From Western Tel, $245 plus 5% GST and 7% PST for telephone services for two months. Invoice total $274.40. Terms: payment on receipt of invoice. Paid by cheque #779.

54 **Cash Purchase Invoice #PE-62331** **Dated Sep. 29/15**
From Purolator, $1 200 plus 5% GST for shipping services. Invoice total $1 260. Terms: payment on receipt of invoice. Paid by cheque #780.

55 **MasterCard Credit Card Sales Invoice #601** **Dated Sep. 29/15**
To various Web Store Customers, for CDs sold during previous three months

CD sales to BC customers	$1 740 plus 5% GST and 7% PST
CD sales to PEI customers	150 plus 14% HST
CD sales to NS customers	280 plus 15% HST
CD sales to other HST customers	2 100 plus 13% HST
CD sales to other GST customers	1 020 plus 5% GST
Book sales	2 800 plus 5% GST
Shipping	650 plus 5% GST

Invoice total $9 508.30. Paid by MasterCard.

56 **Cash Purchase Invoice #FE-46678** **Dated Sep. 29/15**

From Federal Express, $2 100 plus 5% GST for shipping services. Invoice total $2 205. Terms: payment on receipt of invoice. Paid by cheque #781.

57

Maple Leaf Rags
www.mapleleafrags.com
2642 Coldstream Avenue
Nanaimo, BC V9T 2X2
Tel 1: (250) 63M-USIC
Tel 2: (888) 63M-USIC Fax: (250) 633-4888
GST # 128 488 632

Sales Invoice: #601
Date: September 29, 2015

Customer: Web Store Customers
Address:

Phone No:
Fax No:
Contact:

INVOICE

Description	Amount
Sales summary for 3 months	
CDs sold to BC customers (add GST and PST)	1 800.00
CDs sold to PEI customers (add 14% HST)	100.00
CDs sold to NS customers (add 15% HST)	120.00
CDs sold to customers in other HST provinces (add 13% HST)	1 500.00
CDs sold to customers in other GST provinces (add 5% GST)	1 050.00
Books sold in all provinces (add 5% GST)	2 500.00
Freight (add GST)	690.00
GST	302.00
PST	126.00
HST	227.00
Invoice Total	8 415.00

Shipped by: Purolator

Payment: Visa
Direct deposit to Visa bank account JB

SESSION DATE – SEPTEMBER 30, 2015

58 **Memo #51** **Dated Sep. 30/15**

From J. Bands: Refer to the Sep. 30 General Ledger balance to remit PST Payable to the Minister of Finance. Reduce the $352.80 payment by $23.28, the sales tax compensation of 6.6% of the balance owing. Issue cheque #782 for $329.52 from Bank: Chequing Account.

59 **Memo #52** **Dated Sep. 30/15**

From J. Bands: Prepare for closing the books by completing adjusting entries for prepaid expenses and supplies used

Office Supplies	$ 280
Prepaid Internet Expenses (3 months)	135
Prepaid Rent (3 months of 6)	2 400
Prepaid Advertising (2 months of 5)	663

60 **Memo #53** **Dated Sep. 30/15**

From J. Bands: Complete an adjusting entry for goods sold during the quarter

CDs	$36 500	(Debit Cost of CDs Sold and credit CD Inventory)
Books	$12 600	(Debit Cost of Books Sold and credit Book Inventory)

61 **Memo #54** **Dated Sep. 30/15**

From J. Bands: Complete an adjusting entry to transfer $76 444 in completed inventory. Transfer $67 944 to CD Inventory and $8 500 to Book Inventory. Debit the inventory asset accounts and credit Materials and Assembly Costs.

NOTES
Bands pays only interest on the loans. Both amounts are deducted from the Bank: Chequing Account.

NOTES
To use the Transfer Funds Journal for the transfer, you must enter the transfer for each account as a separate transaction. To complete the funds transfer entry as a single journal entry, you must use the General Journal.

62

Memo #55 **Dated Sep. 30/15**

From J. Bands: Received debit memo from Gulfstream Trust regarding pre-authorized withdrawals from Bank: Chequing Account for quarterly interest payments on loans. Complete adjusting entries for quarterly interest paid

On bank loan	$ 200
On long term loan	1 100

63

Memo #56 **Dated Sep. 30/15**

From J. Bands: The following transfers of funds were completed
$15 000 from Bank: Chequing Account to Bank: Savings Account
$12 000 from Bank: Visa to Bank: Savings Account
$12 000 from Bank: MasterCard to Bank: Savings Account

64

Memo #57 **Dated Sep. 30/15**

From J. Bands: Record Interest Revenue as follows

Bank: Savings Account	$300
Bank: Chequing Account	20

Creating an Accountant's Copy

Many businesses rely on professional accountants to assist them with their accounting. The accountants will check the data entered by the business for errors and make corrections. They also may add the adjusting entries required at the end of a fiscal period to bring the books up to date and to prepare for filing tax returns. The business then begins the new year with a complete and accurate data file.

Sage 50 allows a data file to be saved as an Accountant's Copy. This backup data file can only be restored and opened in the Accountant Edition of Sage 50. The accountant makes journal entries in the file that can be added back to the original business data file. The business may continue with day-to-day journal entry and even start a new fiscal period while the accountant is preparing the additional entries.

✓ 65

Memo #58 **Dated Sep. 30/15**

From J. Bands: Create an Accountant's Copy of the data files so the accountant can review the accounting entries and add the final adjustments for depreciation and the trade-in on the automobiles.

You can create an Accountant's Copy from the File menu or from the Company window Accountant's Tasks pane Accountant's Copy icon shortcuts.

Click **Company** in the Modules pane list to open that module window.

Choose the **File menu**, then **choose Accountant's Copy** and **click Create Accountant's Copy** or **choose Create Accountant's Copy** from the Accountants' Copy icon shortcuts drop-down list as shown:

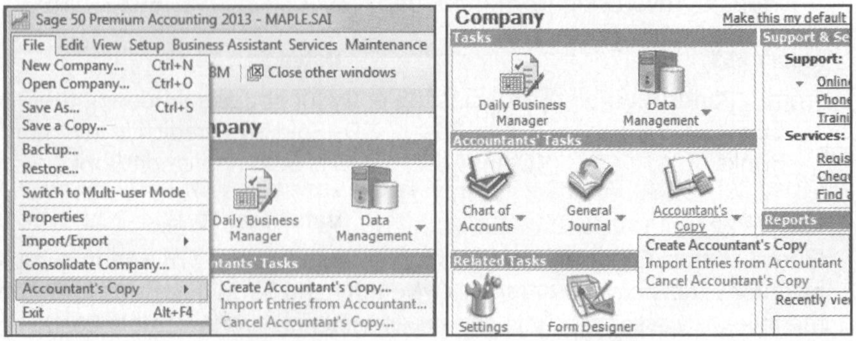

You will be asked to choose a location for the new backup file:

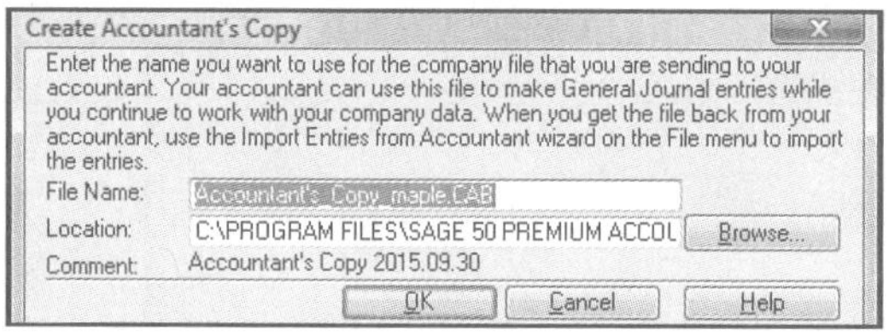

The default name for the file adds Accountant's_Copy_ to the original name so it will not be confused with your other backup files. The default location is a new ACCOUNTANT folder inside the Data folder (in the Sage 50 program folder).

To choose another folder, click Browse and click the folder you want to use. Enter a different name for the file if you want.

Click **OK** to begin making the specialized backup.

When the copy is complete, you will see the following information window:

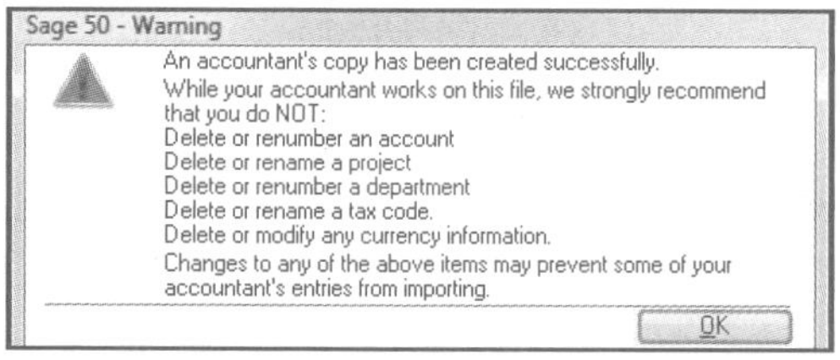

Read this message carefully as it warns what changes you can and cannot make to your working file while the accountant is working with the Accountant's Copy of your file.

Click **OK** to return to your data file.

PRO VERSION
The warning message does not include the details about project and department.

Monitoring Routine Activities

The end of September is the end of Bands' fiscal year. There are a number of steps to complete before beginning the new year. Sage 50 provides assistance with these steps in its checklists.

✓ 66

Memo #59 **Dated Sep. 30/15**

From J. Bands: Review the year-end checklists. Print all reports for the fiscal period ended. Back up the data files. Check data integrity. Advance the session date to October 1, the first day of the next fiscal period.

CLASSIC VIEW
Click (the Checklists tool) to open the Checklists window.

Choose the **Business Assistant menu** and **click** **Checklists** to see the lists available:

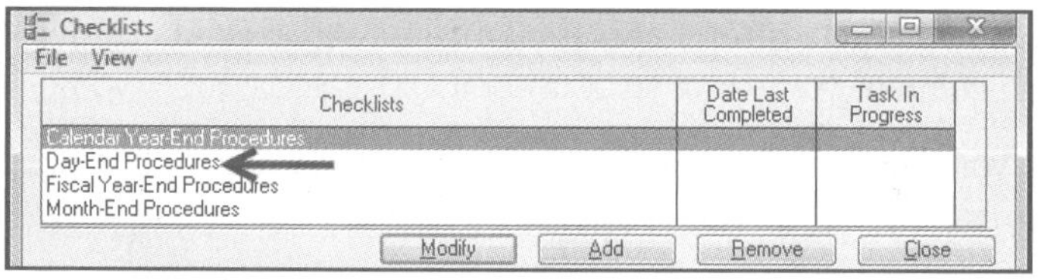

Checklists are available for different periods — end of a fiscal period, end of a business day, end of a month and end of a calendar year for payroll.

You can also create your own checklists, add procedures to one of the predefined checklists and print the checklists for reference.

Before checking the fiscal year-end procedures, we will add a reminder to the daily tasks checklist.

NOTES
You cannot modify (edit) checklists in multi-user mode.

Click **Day-End Procedures** and then **click Modify** to open the list:

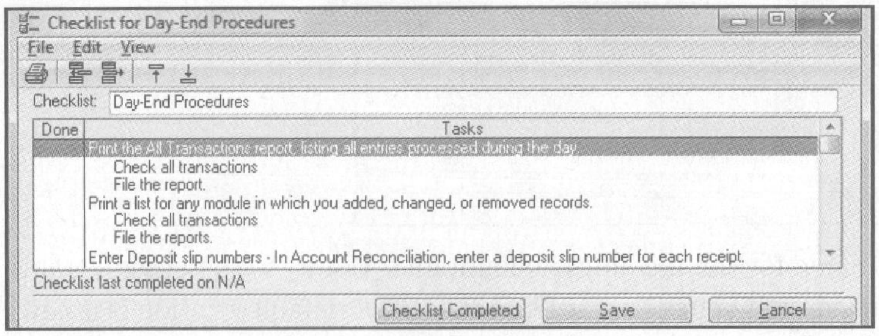

Each checklist can be customized for a company by using the tool buttons or the Edit menu items to insert tasks, delete them or rearrange them.

Click the **Insert Item tool** or **choose** the **Edit menu** and **click Insert** to add a blank line at the top of the task list.

Press *tab* to advance to the Tasks field.

Type `Check bank balances for possible overdrafts`

Click **Save** to return to the Checklists window.

Double-click **Fiscal Year-End Procedures** to see the checklist we need:

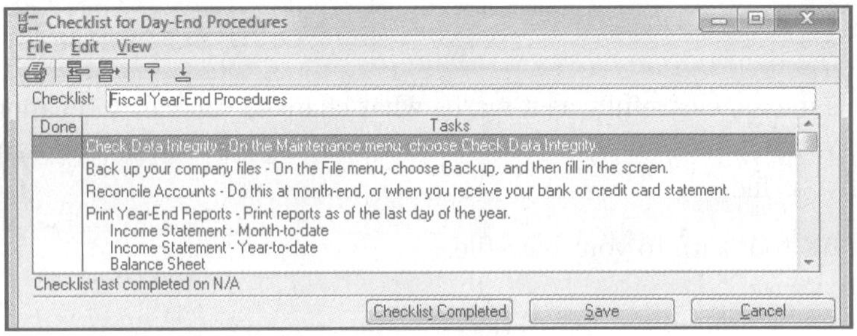

NOTES
Reconciling accounts will be explained in Chapter 15 and budgeting is covered in Chapter 14.

Maple Leaf Rags does not use the budgeting feature of the program so we can remove these tasks from the checklist.

NOTES
In Chapter 15, we describe how to clear data from company files.

Scroll down and **click** **Print Budget Reports**.

Click the **Remove Item tool** or **choose** the **Edit menu** and **click Remove**.

Click **Yes** to confirm that you want to continue with the deletion.

Click the **Print tool** to print the checklist for reference.

Back up the **data files** and **print reports**. These are the most important elements on this list. There are no reports for Payroll, Inventory or Projects. You can remove these reports from the list if you want.

Click the **Done column** after completing a task — a ✓ will be added to the Done column.

Click Save if you want to leave the list and return later. A ✓ will appear in the Task In Progress column on the Checklists screen.

Complete all the **tasks** listed, except printing the reports for the modules that are not used. After finishing all the tasks,

Click **Checklist Completed**. The session date will be added to the Date Last Completed column on the Checklists screen.

Open the remaining checklists to see the tasks to be completed at the end of each month and at the end of a calendar year. Print these lists for reference.

Click **Close** to leave the Checklists window when you have finished.

Start the **new fiscal year** on October 1, 2015.

Displaying Exchange Rate Reports

When a business has foreign currency transactions, Sage 50 will generate reports related to exchange rate gains and losses.

Open the **Report Centre** and **click Financials**:

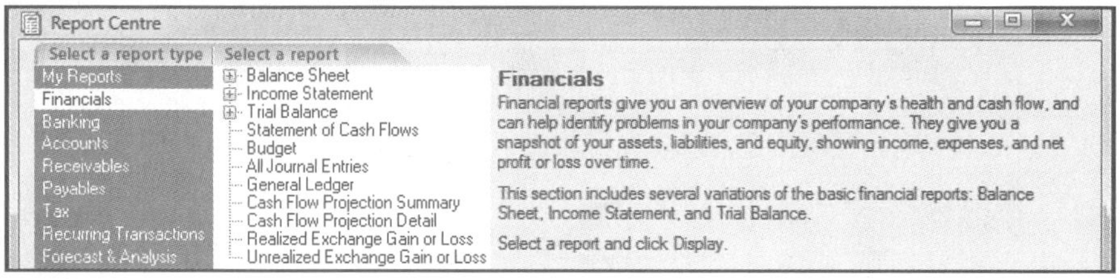

Click **Realized Exchange Gain Or Loss**.

Click **Modify This Report**:

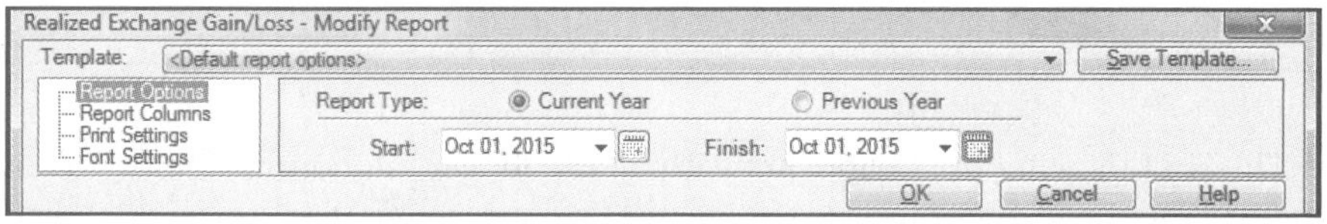

This first exchange rate report includes the gains or losses already realized or recorded because the payment has been made or received and the exchange rate difference is known.

Click **Previous Year** to see reports for this application.

Enter the **dates** for the report (including the year) and **click OK**.

Close the **display** when finished.

To access the second exchange rate report,

Click **Unrealized Exchange Gain Or Loss** in the Select A Report list.

Click **Modify This Report**:

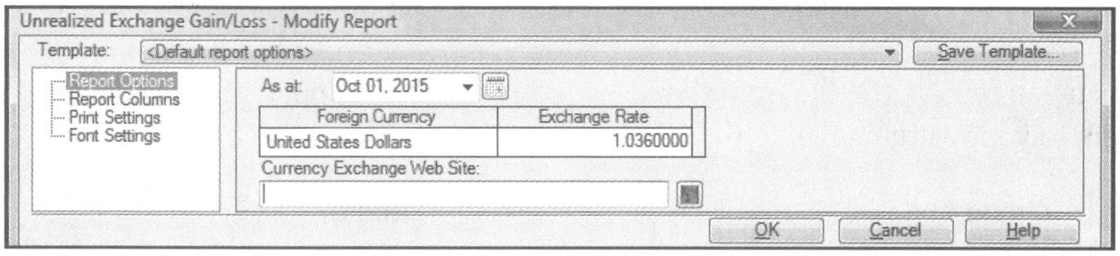

The second report includes the gains or losses that have not yet been realized or recorded — the payment has not been made but the exchange rate is known to have changed since the purchase or sale. When the payment is made or received, the actual gain may be different if the rate has changed again.

The report also revalues existing account balances and previous payments and receipts for the new exchange rate.

Enter the **date** for the report (including the year) and an **Exchange Rate** for that date. **Click OK**.

Close the **display** when finished. **Close** the **Report Centre**.

NOTES
Refer to page 101 for assistance with starting a new fiscal period.

NOTES
From the Home window, choose the Reports menu, then choose Financials and click Realized Exchange Gain/Loss to see the report options.

NOTES
You cannot sort or filter the Exchange Rate reports. You can choose the columns for the Realized Exchange Rate Report.

NOTES
From the Home window, choose the Reports menu, then choose Financials and click Unrealized Exchange Gain/Loss to see the report options.

The Accountant Works with Your Data

When the accountant opens the file you sent, it will be restored in the same version of Sage 50 that you used — Pro, Premium and so on. Only the General Journal, the one used for adjusting entries, is available to the accountant. The following two screens show your data file as it will open for the accountant using the special Accountant Edition version of Sage 50.

The Classic view Home window in the Accountant Edition file is shown here:

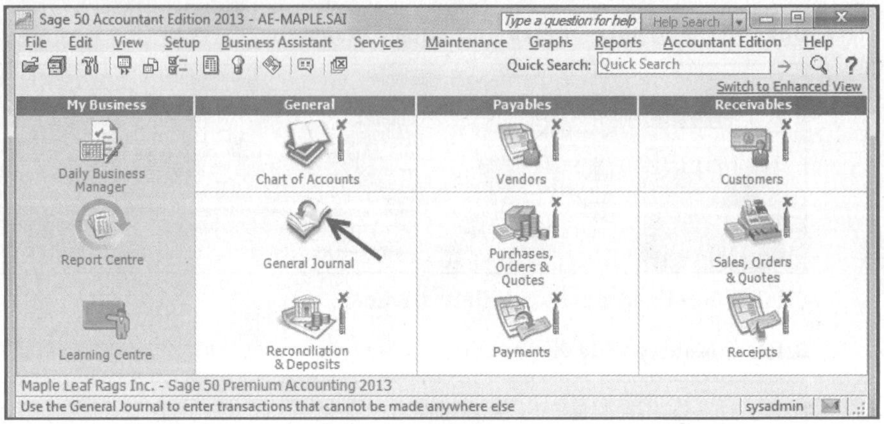

The No Edit symbol  appears with all the ledger and journal icons except for the General Journal. The accountant can view, but not change, the information in the other journals and ledgers.

After adding the required adjustments, the accountant exports the new journal entries to a text file. This option is available from the Accountant Edition menu by choosing Accountant's Copy and then Export Entries For Client as shown:

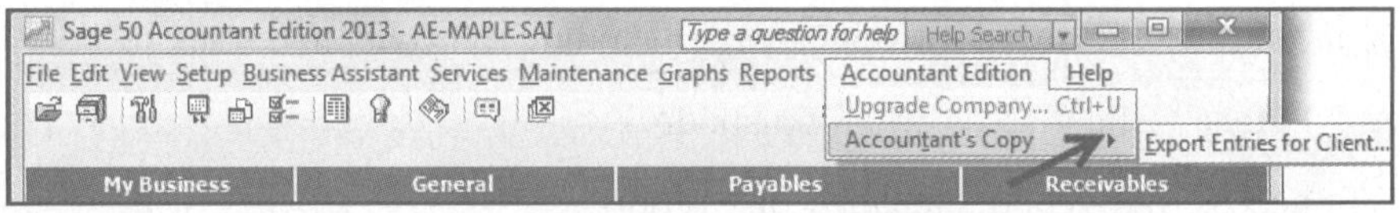

The exported text file of journal entries is sent back to you, the client.

> **NOTES**
> The accountant works with a special version of the program – the Accountant Edition. This program must be used to restore the Accountant's Copy backup file you created.
> The Accountant Edition allows full access to regular data files created in any version (Pro, Premium, First Step and Quantum). The Accountant's Copy data file, however, restricts access to the General Journal in all versions.

> **NOTES**
> You will not see this screen or the next one in your own version of Sage 50. We show these screens for reference only.

> **NOTES**
> We show the Classic view Home window so that you can see the restrictions (the No Edit symbols).

> **NOTES**
> Year-end adjusting entries are typically General Journal entries.

Importing the Accountant's Journal Entries

When you receive the file from the accountant, you must import the journal entries to add them to your working file.

✓ 67

Memo #60 **Dated Oct. 1/15**

From J. Bands: Import the adjusting entries completed by the accountant.

Restore the data file **SageData13\ACCOUNTANT\AE-maple1.CAB** for this step.

Choose the **File menu**, then **choose Accountant's Copy** and **click Import Entries From Accountant**. Or **choose Import Entries From Accountant** from the Accountant's Copy icon shortcuts list:

> **WARNING!**
> You must use the special file we created for this part of the exercise because it matches the imported entries.
> You must use the same file for creating the Accountant's Copy and importing the accountant's entries. You will not be able to import the accountant's entries to your own working file.

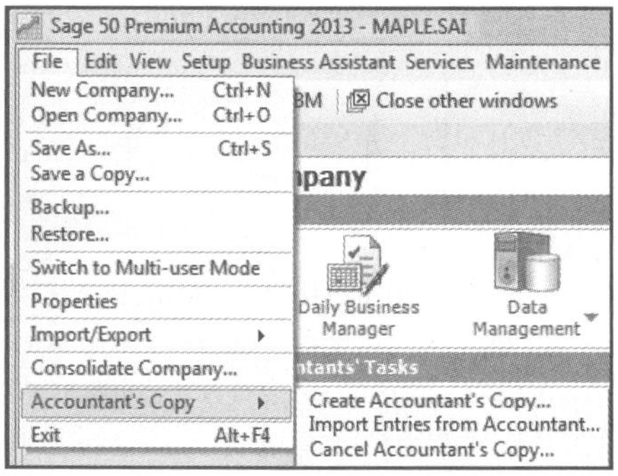

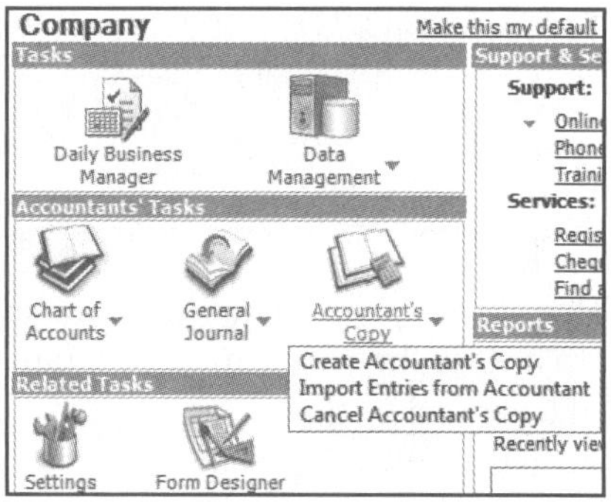

Both the file menu options and the shortcuts list for Accountant's Tasks in the Company module window have changed. Once you create an Accountant's Copy, the other submenu options become available. The program stores the information that there is an outstanding Accountant's Copy for the file so you can import the journal entries later. This menu option remains available until the entries have been imported. You cannot create another Accountant's Copy while there is one outstanding. If you discover an error after you create the Accountant's Copy, you can cancel that version and then create a new Accountant's Copy. The option to **Cancel Accountant's Copy** is used for this purpose. After cancelling, the option to create becomes available again.

The Import Entries wizard begins:

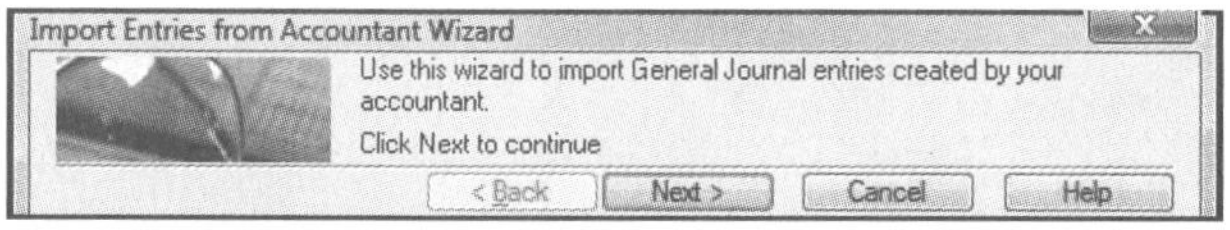

Click **Next**:

You are asked to make a backup before proceeding. Since the step of importing entries cannot be reversed, you should back up the data file first.

Click **Backup** and follow the backup wizard steps. **Click Next** to continue:

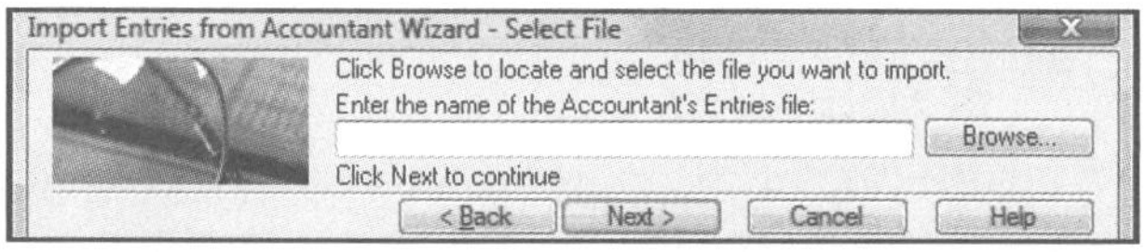

Now you must locate the file the accountant sent. We have added the file you need to the SageData13\ACCOUNTANT folder where the AE-Maple backup is stored.

Click **Browse**.

Locate **SageData13\ACCOUNTANT\Accountant's_Entries_AE-maple.TXT** and **click** to select it.

Click **Open** to add the file name to the wizard screen and then **click Next**.

If you try to import the journal entries to your own Maple Leaf Rags data file, or any other file that is different from the one used to create the Accountant's Copy, you will see the following error message:

Click **OK**. You must use the data file in the Accountant folder for this step.

NOTES

The accountant cannot create new accounts in your data file, so we added the account 5600 Losses on Disposal of Assets for the additional data file AE-maple.

NOTES

The procedure for importing entries from the accountant is similar to importing other General Journal entries. Refer to Appendix J.

WARNING!

Do not use your own data file for this section.

The file you need is Accountant's_Entries_AE-maple.TXT. It is located in the SageData13\ACCOUNTANT folder.

If you are using the correct matching data file, you will see this screen:

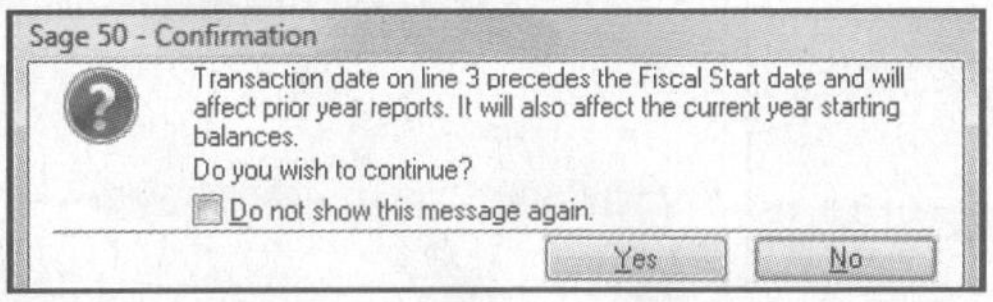

This warning appears because the entries are dated in the previous fiscal year. We want to accept the dates the accountant used because they are correct and the entries should be added to the financial reports for the previous year. We have already changed the settings for this file to allow transactions dated before October 1. Sage 50 still provides this warning whenever you are posting to a previous month. We need to allow all these entries and do not want the message to appear for each one.

> **NOTES**
> If your system settings do not allow transactions in the previous year, you must first change this setting. Refer to page 104.

Click **Do Not Show This Message Again**.

Click **Yes** to display the summary of entries added to your data file:

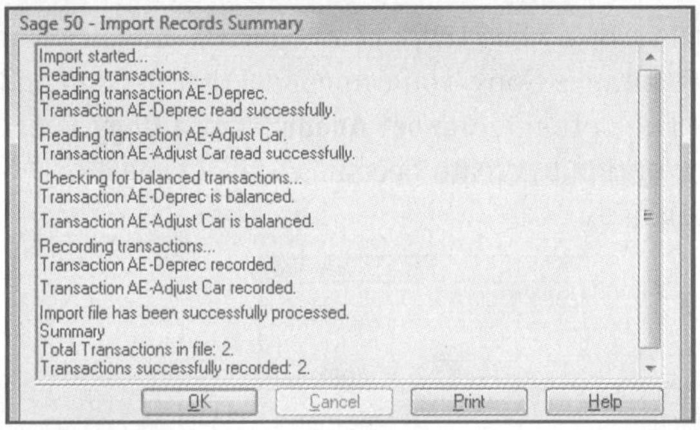

Click **OK**:

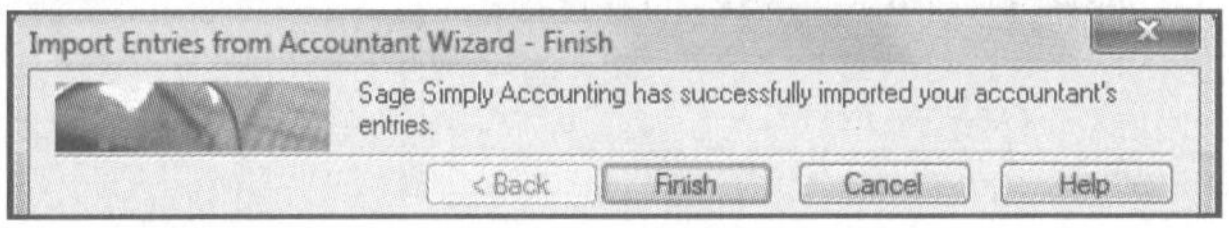

Click **Finish**. The process is now complete.

> **NOTES**
> For this report, we selected the journal options to show Previous Year and Only Entries Posted After Year End. The All Journal Entries Report for the previous year will include these two transactions at the end.

The General Journal report for September 30 will include the accountant's entries:

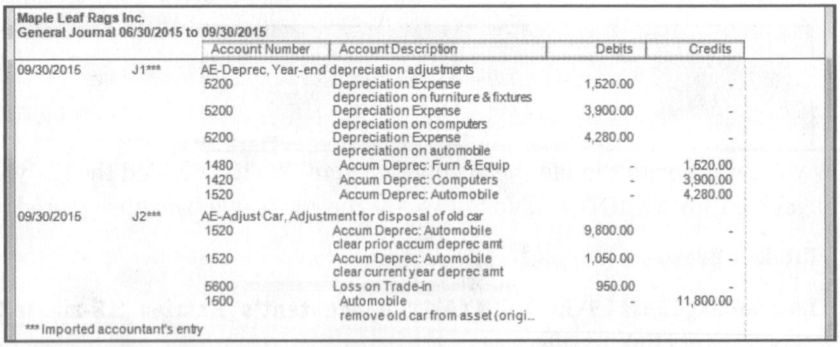

Maple Leaf Rags Inc.
General Journal 06/30/2015 to 09/30/2015

		Account Number	Account Description	Debits	Credits
09/30/2015	J1***	AE-Deprec, Year-end depreciation adjustments			
		5200	Depreciation Expense depreciation on furniture & fixtures	1,520.00	-
		5200	Depreciation Expense depreciation on computers	3,900.00	-
		5200	Depreciation Expense depreciation on automobile	4,280.00	-
		1480	Accum Deprec: Furn & Equip	-	1,520.00
		1420	Accum Deprec: Computers	-	3,900.00
		1520	Accum Deprec: Automobile	-	4,280.00
09/30/2015	J2***	AE-Adjust Car, Adjustment for disposal of old car			
		1520	Accum Deprec: Automobile clear prior accum deprec amt	9,800.00	-
		1520	Accum Deprec: Automobile clear current year deprec amt	1,050.00	-
		5600	Loss on Trade-in	950.00	-
		1500	Automobile remove old car from asset (origi...	-	11,800.00

*** Imported accountant's entry

The journal entry numbers are marked *** with a note that they were created outside the regular file by the accountant.

> **NOTES**
> The journal report shows journal entry numbers 1 and 2. The AE-Maple file you are using has no other journal entries. It is provided only to demonstrate the step of importing the accountant's entries.
> When you import entries, the journal entry numbers may be out of sequence if you have added transactions while the accountant was working with the file.

R E V I E W

The Student DVD with Data Files includes Review Questions and Supplementary Cases for this chapter, including a case with stock transactions that can be completed in the General Journal.

CHAPTER THIRTEEN

TRUMAN TT TIRES

OBJECTIVES

After completing this chapter, you should be able to

- ***enter*** transactions in all journals
- ***create*** new divisions
- ***change*** the Division Ledger name
- ***enter*** import duty on purchases from foreign suppliers
- ***allocate*** revenues and expenses in the General, Sales, Purchases, Payroll and Inventory journals
- ***make*** import duty remittances
- ***enter*** purchases with cost variances
- ***process*** credit card sales transactions
- ***set up*** records for direct payments and pre-authorized debits
- ***enter***, ***upload*** and ***review*** pre-authorized debits and direct deposits and payments
- ***display*** and ***print*** transactions with division details
- ***display*** and ***print*** division reports

COMPANY INFORMATION

Company Profile

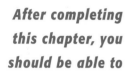

NOTES
Truman Tires
600 Westminster St.
London, ON N6P 3B1
Tel: (519) 729-3733
Fax: (519) 729-7301
Business No.: 230 192 821

Truman Tires, located in London, Ontario, sells tires and wheels for all types of passenger cars, including taxis and service fleets for other businesses. Tyrone Truman completed an auto mechanics program at the local community college and then worked for an auto repair shop in Windsor for several years. He studied business administration part time to prepare him for starting his own business, which he now has operated for several years.

Although he sells all kinds of tires, throughout the year most people buy all-season radial tires. In December, the month in this application, Truman Tires sells mainly winter tires. All tire sales include free installation. The service centre, with its four service bays, also provides a limited range of services for automobiles, including oil changes, brake repairs and replacements, shocks replacements and wheel alignments. Four employees work on the cars while a manager and assistant manager handle all customer contacts and schedule appointments.

PRO VERSION
The term Vendors will be used instead of Suppliers throughout the program.

Truman Tires has a number of regular suppliers of inventory and other parts and supplies. Truman has accounts with most of these suppliers and some offer discounts for early payment. Some of the tires and wheels are imported from Japan, and Truman pays import duties on these items.

Regular customers also have accounts with Truman Tires and are offered a 2 percent discount if they settle their accounts within 10 days. Some customers receive additional discounts through the preferred pricing schedule for all inventory sales and services.

In preparation for expanding his business, Tyrone Truman has decided to apply project costing for his two divisions, Sales and Service. He hopes to assess the profitability of each aspect of the company.

At the end of November 2015, Truman remitted all the company payroll taxes and deductions and closed his books. To convert his accounting records to Sage 50, he used the following:

- Chart of Accounts
- Post-Closing Trial Balance
- Supplier Information
- Customer Information
- Employee Information
- Employee Profiles and TD1 Information
- Inventory Information
- Division Information
- Accounting Procedures

CHART OF ACCOUNTS

TRUMAN TIRES

ASSETS

Current Assets
1050 Bank: Chequing CAD
1060 Bank: Foreign Currency
1070 Bank: Visa
1080 Bank: MasterCard
1090 Bank: Interac
1200 Accounts Receivable
1220 Purchase Prepayments
1240 Brakes & Shocks Parts
1250 Supplies: Garage
1260 Supplies: Office

Inventory Assets
1360 Wheels
1380 Wheel Nuts & Locks
1400 Winter Tires

Plant & Equipment
1650 Cash Register
1660 Computer Equipment
1670 Garage Equipment
1680 Machinery & Tools
1690 Shop & Garage Bays ▶
▶1700 Tow Truck
1710 Yard

LIABILITIES

Current Liabilities
2100 Bank Loan
2150 Prepaid Sales and Deposits
2200 Accounts Payable
2220 Import Duty Payable
2250 Credit Card Payable
2300 Vacation Payable
2310 EI Payable
2320 CPP Payable
2330 Income Tax Payable
2390 EHT Payable
2400 CSB Payable
2410 Union Dues
2460 WSIB Payable
2650 HST Charged on Sales
2670 HST Paid on Purchases

Long Term Liabilities
2850 Mortgage Payable ▶

▶**EQUITY**

Owner's Equity
3560 T. Truman, Capital
3580 T. Truman, Drawings
3600 Net Income

REVENUE

Revenue
4020 Revenue from Sales
4040 Revenue from Services
4100 Other Revenue
4150 Sales Discounts

EXPENSE

Operating Expenses
5020 Advertising & Promotion
5030 Bank Charges
5035 Exchange Rate Differences
5040 Credit Card Fees
5045 Assembly Costs
5050 Cost of Goods Sold
5055 Variance Costs ▶
▶5060 Cost of Services
5065 Freight Expense
5070 Hydro Expense
5080 Interest Expense - Loan
5090 Interest Expense - Mortgage
5100 Inventory Adjustment
5110 Tool Rentals
5120 Inventory Parts Used
5130 Purchase Discounts
5140 Repairs & Maintenance
5150 Telephone Expense

Payroll Expenses
5300 Management Wages
5310 General Wages
5320 Piece Rate Wage Expense
5330 Commissions and Bonuses
5410 EI Expense
5420 CPP Expense
5430 WSIB Expense
5460 EHT Expense

NOTES: The Chart of Accounts includes only postable accounts and Net Income. WSIB (Workplace Safety and Insurance Board) is the name for WCB (Workers' Compensation Board) in Ontario.

POST-CLOSING TRIAL BALANCE

TRUMAN TIRES

November 30, 2015

		Debits	Credits
1050	Bank: Chequing CAD	$20 765	
1060	Bank: Foreign Currency (¥154 000)	2 000	
1070	Bank: Visa	8 000	
1080	Bank: MasterCard	5 000	
1090	Bank: Interac	2 500	
1200	Accounts Receivable	4 181	
1240	Brakes & Shocks Parts	6 800	
1250	Supplies: Garage	2 400	
1260	Supplies: Office	600	
1360	Wheels	9 136	
1380	Wheel Nuts & Locks	738	
1400	Winter Tires	15 480	
1650	Cash Register	2 500	
1660	Computer Equipment	2 500 ▶	
▶ 1670	Garage Equipment	75 000	
1680	Machinery & Tools	25 000	
1690	Shop & Garage Bays	175 000	
1700	Tow Truck	40 000	
1710	Yard	25 000	
2100	Bank Loan		$ 12 000
2200	Accounts Payable		6 048
2250	Credit Card Payable		235
2300	Vacation Payable		6 943
2650	HST Charged on Sales		6 300
2670	HST Paid on Purchases	2 960	
2850	Mortgage Payable		140 000
3560	T. Truman, Capital		254 034
		$425 560	$425 560

SUPPLIER INFORMATION

TRUMAN TIRES

Supplier Name (Contact)	Address	Phone No. Fax No.	E-mail Web Site	Terms Tax ID
Bell Canada (Louis Gossip)	100 Ring Road London, Ontario N5W 2M3	Tel: (519) 387-2355	www.bell.ca	n/10
CAW Union				n/30
Equity Life				n/30
Gulf Oil Company (Petro Crewd)	30 Refinery Cr. London, Ontario N4R 6F1	Tel: (519) 641-6277	pc@gulfoil.com www.gulfoil.com	n/30
London Hydro (Les Current)	755 Ohm Blvd. London, Ontario N6C 1P9	Tel: (519) 649-8100	lesc@londonhydro.on.ca www.londonhydro.on.ca	n/10
London Tool Rentals (Roto Tiller)	239 Pneumatics Rd. London, Ontario N5X 2S4	Tel: (519) 633-7102 Fax: (519) 635-8191	roto@getitfromus.com www.getitfromus.com	n/20 325 622 934
Minister of Finance	Box 620, 33 King St. W Oshawa, Ontario L1H 8H5	Tel: (905) 443- 8200	www.gov.on.ca/fin	n/30
MoTech Auto Parts (Moe Torrs)	2 Revving Parkway Windsor, Ontario N7T 7C2	Tel: (519) 722-1973 Fax: (519) 725-3664	moe@motech.com www.motech.com	2/10, n/30 (after tax) 163 482 977
Receiver General for Canada	PO Box 20004, Station A Sudbury, Ontario P3A 6B4	Tel: (705) 821-8186	www.cra-arc.gc.ca	n/30
Snowmaster Tire Company (I.C. Winters)	86 Sleet St. Tokyo, Japan 162-0829	Tel: (81-3) 5249 7331 Fax: (81-3) 5261 6492	icw@snowmaster.com www.snowmaster.com	net 15
Sylverado Wheels (Roy Rimmer)	100 Round Rd., Unit 2 Tokyo, Japan 100-7227	Tel: (81-3) 3643 8459 Fax: (81-3) 3663 5188	royrimmer@sylverado.com www.sylverado.com	n/30
TuffArm Shocks (Sally Shockley)	489 Spring St. Toronto, Ontario M4Z 3G3	Tel: (416) 699-2019 Fax: (416) 699-3854	Sal@tuffarm.shocks.com www.tuffarm.shocks.com	n/30 263 495 687
Western Hydraulic Repairs (Otto Raizer)	109 Lift St. London, Ontario N6F 8A5	Tel: (519) 645-6722 Fax: (519) 646-1145	o_raizer@whydraulics.com www.whydraulics.com	n/30 466 345 291
Workplace Safety & Insurance Board				n/30

OUTSTANDING SUPPLIER INVOICES

TRUMAN TIRES

Supplier Name	Terms	Date	Invoice No.	Amount CAD	Amount JPY
MoTech Auto Parts	2/10, n/30 (after tax)	Nov. 27/15	MT-1142	$678	
Snowmaster Tire Company	net 15	Nov. 26/15	ST-842	$2 544	¥195 700
Sylverado Wheels	n/30	Nov. 10/15	SW-724	$1 696	¥130 400
TuffArm Shocks	n/30	Nov. 4/15	TS-699	$1 130	
		Grand Total		$6 048	

CUSTOMER INFORMATION

TRUMAN TIRES

Customer Name (Contact)	Address	Phone No. Fax No.	E-mail Web Site	Terms Credit Limit
*Airport Taxi Service (Jett Plane)	100 Runway Rd. London, Ontario N5G 3J7	Tel: (519) 643-6182 Fax: (519) 645-1772	jett@gofly.com www.gofly.com	2/10, n/30 $4 000
Cash Customers				n/1
City Cab Company (Able Driver)	890 Transport St. London, Ontario N5W 1B3	Tel: (519) 641-7999 Fax: (519) 641-2539	driver@wetakeyou.com www.wetakeyou.com	2/10, n/30 $4 000
*London Car Leasing (Nick Borrow)	44 Fleet St. London, Ontario N6T 7V2	Tel: (519) 788-2538 Fax: (519) 789-3264	borrow@whybuy.com www.whybuy.com	2/10, n/30 $4 000
Lovely U Cosmetics (N.O. Blemish)	450 Phare Skinn Cr. London, Ontario N6B 3H3	Tel: (519) 782-4477 Fax: (519) 781-4372	blemish@lovelyU.com www.lovelyU.com	2/10, n/30 $4 000
*Polly Maid Services (Polly Mayden)	92 Scouring St. London, Ontario N6T 2K6	Tel: (519) 648-3645 Fax: (519) 648-2774	polly@pollymaid.com www.pollymaid.com	2/10, n/30 $4 000
Pronto Pizza & Delivery (Wayte Nott)	52 Marguerite St. London, Ontario N5B 2R5	Tel: (519) 784-7287 Fax: (519) 785-8220	waytenott@pronto.com www.pronto.com	2/10, n/30 $4 000

NOTES: Preferred price list customers are marked with an asterisk (*) beside their names. All discounts are after tax.

OUTSTANDING CUSTOMER INVOICES

TRUMAN TIRES

Customer Name	Terms	Date	Invoice No.	Amount	Total
City Cab Company	2/10, n/30 (after tax)	Nov. 26/15	120	$1 808	$1 808
Lovely U Cosmetics	2/10, n/30 (after tax)	Nov. 24/15	116	$1 356	$1 356
Polly Maid Services	2/10, n/30 (after tax)	Nov. 29/15	124	$1 017	$1 017
		Grand Total			$4 181

EMPLOYEE INFORMATION SHEET

TRUMAN TIRES

	Trish Tridon	Joy Fram	Shockley Monroe	Karlby Holley	Troy Niehoff	Albert C. Delco
Position	Manager	Asst Manager	Auto Worker	Auto Worker	Auto Worker	Auto Worker
Social Insurance No.	464 375 286	572 351 559	398 577 619	821 887 114	618 524 664	404 535 601
Address	59 Pond Mills Rd. London, Ontario N5Z 3X3	8 Rington Cres. London, Ontario N6J 1Y7	36 Artisans Cres. London, Ontario N5V 4S3	44 Lockyer St. London, Ontario N6C 3E5	98 Novello Ave. London, Ontario N6J 2A5	18 Ravenglass Cres. London, Ontario N6G 4K1
Telephone	(519) 645-6238	(519) 738-5188	(519) 784-7195	(519) 648-1916	(519) 641-6773	(519) 788-2826
Date of Birth (mm-dd-yy)	09-28-71	02-03-83	05-21-82	08-08-80	05-28-78	08-19-84
Federal (Ontario) Tax Exemption - TD1						
Basic Personal	$11 038 (9 574)	$11 038 (9 574)	$11 038 (9 574)	$11 038 (9 574)	$11 038 (9 574)	$11 038 (9 574)
Other Indexed	$15 506 (8 129)	–	–	–	$13 272 (8 129)	–
Other Non-indexed	–	–	–	$10 720 (11 120)	–	–
Total Exemptions	$26 544 (17 703)	$11 038 (9 574)	$11 038 (9 574)	$21 758 (20 694)	$24 310 (17 703)	$11 038 (9 574)
Employee Earnings						
Regular Wage Rate	–	–	$18.00	$18.00	$18.00	$18.00
Overtime Wage Rate	–	–	$27.00	$27.00	$27.00	$27.00
Regular Salary	$3 800/mo	$2 800/mo	–	–	–	–
Pay Period	monthly	monthly	bi-weekly	bi-weekly	bi-weekly	bi-weekly
Hours per Period	150	150	80	80	80	80
Piece Rate	–	–	$10/job	$10/job	$5/job	$5/job
Commission	1% (Sales – Returns)	–	–	–	–	–
Vacation	4 weeks	3 weeks	4% retained	4% retained	4% retained	4% retained
Vacation Pay Owed	–	–	$1 793	$1 486	$1 811	$1 853
WSIB Rate	3.40	3.40	3.40	3.40	3.40	3.40
Employee Deductions						
CSB	$200	$100	$50	$50	–	–
Union Dues	–	–	1%	1%	1%	1%
EI, CPP & Income Tax	Calculations built into Sage 50 program.					

Employee Profiles and TD1 Information

All Employees All employees are allowed 10 days per year for illness and five for personal reasons. All employees have their paycheques deposited directly into their bank accounts. There are no other company benefits. All payroll remittances are due at the end of each month.

Trish Tridon As the manager at Truman Tires, Tridon supervises the other employees, resolves customer problems and assists with sales. Her salary of $3 800 per month is supplemented by a commission of 1 percent of sales, less returns. Tridon is entered as the salesperson on all sales invoices to calculate the commission. She is paid at the end of each month and is allowed four weeks of vacation with pay. Tridon is married with two children under 12 and claims the basic, spousal and child (federal only) tax claim amounts. She has $200 deducted from each paycheque to buy Canada Savings Bonds.

Joy Fram As assistant manager, Fram helps Tridon with all her duties and also manages the accounting records for the business. She is paid a monthly salary of $2 800 and is allowed three weeks of vacation with pay. She has only the basic tax claim amount because she is single and self-supporting. She has chosen to buy Canada Savings Bonds by having $100 deducted from each paycheque.

Hourly Paid Employees The four hourly paid employees — Monroe, Holley, Niehoff and Delco — share the work of servicing vehicles. Every two weeks, they are paid $18 per hour for the first 40 hours each week and $27 per hour for additional time for performing the full range of services provided by Truman Tires: installing, repairing and rotating tires, brake work, shocks and oil service. However, each hourly employee has one area of specialization and the piece-rate supplement is based on the number of jobs in this area. All receive 4 percent vacation pay that is retained until they take time off. All are union members and pay 1 percent of their wages as union dues.

Shockley Monroe specializes in brake work. He is single and pays $50 from each paycheque toward the purchase of Canada Savings Bonds.

Karlby Holley also buys Canada Savings Bonds through payroll deductions. Her specialty is shocks. As a recent graduate, she has $7 000 tuition and eight months of full-time study to increase her basic single tax claim amount.

Troy Niehoff is married with one child under 12 years of age, so he has the basic, spousal and child (federal only) tax claim amounts. He is not enrolled in the Canada Savings Bonds plan. His area of specialization is tire installation and wheel alignment.

Albert C. Delco is single and does not purchase Canada Savings Bonds through payroll. His area of specialization is oil service and winter preparation.

INVENTORY INFORMATION

TRUMAN TIRES

Code	Description	Min Stock	Selling Price Reg	(Pref)	Unit	Qty on Hand	Total (Cost)	Duty	Taxes
Winter Tires (Linked Accounts: Asset 1400; Revenue: 4020; COGS: 5050; Var: 5055)									
T101	P155/80R14 Tires	4	$ 70	($ 65)	each	20	$ 560	7.0%	HST
T102	P175/70R14 Tires	4	85	(80)	each	20	680	7.0%	HST
T103	P195/75R15 Tires	4	95	(88)	each	20	760	7.0%	HST
T104	P205/75R15 Tires	8	100	(92)	each	28	1 120	7.0%	HST
T105	P185/70R15 Tires	4	105	(96)	each	20	840	7.0%	HST
T106	P195/65R15 Tires	4	110	(100)	each	20	880	7.0%	HST
T107	P185/65R15 Tires	4	115	(105)	each	20	920	7.0%	HST
T108	P185/60R15 Tires	4	120	(110)	each	20	960	7.0%	HST
T109	P195/60R16 Tires	8	125	(115)	each	28	1 400	7.0%	HST
T110	P195/65R16 Tires	8	130	(120)	each	28	1 456	7.0%	HST
T111	P205/65R16 Tires	8	135	(124)	each	28	1 512	7.0%	HST
T112	P205/60R16 Tires	8	140	(127)	each	28	1 568	7.0%	HST
T113	P215/60R16 Tires	8	145	(132)	each	28	1 624	7.0%	HST
T114	P225/60R17 Tires	4	150	(136)	each	20	1 200	7.0%	HST
							$15 480		
Wheels (Linked Accounts: Asset 1360; Revenue: 4020; COGS: 5050; Var: 5055)									
W101	Aluminum R14 Wheels	4	180	(165)	each	16	$1 152	6.0%	HST
W102	Aluminum R15 Wheels	4	195	(187)	each	16	1 248	6.0%	HST
W103	Aluminum R16 Wheels	8	210	(190)	each	20	1 680	6.0%	HST
W104	Aluminum R17 Wheels	4	225	(207)	each	16	1 440	6.0%	HST
W105	Chrome-Steel R14 Wheels	4	70	(65)	each	16	448	6.0%	HST
W106	Chrome-Steel R15 Wheels	4	80	(75)	each	16	512	6.0%	HST
W107	Chrome-Steel R16 Wheels	8	90	(83)	each	20	720	6.0%	HST
W108	Chrome-Steel R17 Wheels	4	100	(92)	each	16	640	6.0%	HST
W109	Steel R14 Wheels	4	40	(38)	each	16	256	6.0%	HST
W110	Steel R15 Wheels	4	45	(42)	each	16	288	6.0%	HST
W111	Steel R16 Wheels	8	50	(46)	each	20	400	6.0%	HST
W112	Steel R17 Wheels	4	55	(50)	each	16	352	6.0%	HST
							$9 136		

▶

INVENTORY INFORMATION CONTINUED

TRUMAN TIRES

Code	Description	Min Stock	Selling Price Reg	(Pref)	Unit	Qty on Hand	Total (Cost)	Duty	Taxes
Wheel Nuts & Locks (Linked Accounts: Asset 1380; Revenue: 4020; COGS: 5050; Var: 5055)									
WN01	Chrome Wheel Nuts	4	$ 10	($ 10)	pkg	24	$ 96	6.0%	HST
WN02	Chrome Wheel Locks	4	25	(23)	pkg	24	240	6.0%	HST
WN03	Nickel/Chrome Wheel Nuts	4	10	(10)	pkg	24	114	6.0%	HST
WN04	Nickel/Chrome Wheel Locks	4	30	(28)	pkg	24	288	6.0%	HST
							$738		
Services (Linked Accounts: Revenue: 4040; COGS: 5060)									
SRV01	Alignment - standard		75	(70)	job				HST
SRV02	Alignment - w/caster replacement		130	(120)	job				HST
SRV03	Brake Service - standard pkg		140	(130)	job				HST
SRV04	Brake Service - complete pkg		175	(163)	job				HST
SRV05	Oil Service - standard pkg		30	(28)	job				HST
SRV06	Oil Service - premium pkg		40	(37)	job				HST
SRV07	Shocks - economy gas-charged		100	(92)	job				HST
SRV08	Shocks - premium gas-matic		140	(130)	job				HST
SRV09	Tire Repairs		30	(28)	job				HST
SRV10	Tire Rotation		10	(10)	job				HST
SRV11	Winter Prep. Service		60	(55)	job				HST

Division Information

Truman Tires uses two divisions — one for sales of tires and wheels and their installation and one for services. Fram will set up these divisions at the beginning of December and Tridon will keep track of the percentage of time each employee works in each division. Because these times vary from one vehicle to another, the percentage allocation is included with each source document. Allocation details for other expenses and revenues are also included with the source documents. Amounts for asset, liability and equity accounts are not allocated.

Accounting Procedures

The Employer Health Tax (EHT)

The Employer Health Tax (EHT) is paid by employers in Ontario to cover the costs of health care for all eligible residents in the province. The EHT rate depends on the total annual remuneration paid to employees (gross wage expense). For employers with total payroll less than $200 000, the EHT rate is 0.98 percent. Sage 50 will calculate the employer's liability to the Ontario Minister of Finance automatically once the information is set up correctly in the payroll defaults and linked accounts. In Chapter 16, we will show the keystrokes necessary for setting up the EHT information. The EHT can be remitted monthly or annually, depending on the total payroll amount.

NOTES
The EHT rate increases to a maximum of 1.95 percent for employers with payroll greater than $450 000.

Taxes: HST

Truman Tires pays HST on all goods and services that it buys, including the imported products, and charges HST on all sales and services. It uses the regular method for remittance of the Harmonized Sales Tax. HST collected from customers is recorded as a liability in *HST Charged on Sales*. HST paid to suppliers is recorded in *HST Paid on Purchases* as a decrease in liability to the Canada Revenue Agency. The report is filed with the Receiver General for Canada by the last day of the month for the previous quarter, either including the balance owing or requesting a refund.

In Ontario, PST is harmonized with GST. The provincial portion of HST is 8 percent.

NSF Cheques

> **NOTES**
> The Sales Journal entry will credit Bank: Chequing CAD for the full amount of the sale including taxes and debit Accounts Receivable for the customer.

> **NOTES**
> If you created a customer record by using Quick Add, or used an existing record (e.g., Cash Customers), you can adjust the sales invoice by changing the method of payment from Cheque to Pay Later. You cannot choose Pay Later as the payment method for one-time customers.

When a bank returns a customer's cheque because there were insufficient funds in the customer's bank account to cover the cheque, the payment must be reversed. If the payment was processed through the Receipts Journal, the reversal should also be processed through the Receipts Journal (see page 176). If the sale was a cash sale to a one-time customer, the reversal must be processed through the Sales Journal. Create a customer record for the customer and process a credit (Pay Later) sale for the full amount of the NSF cheque. Enter No Tax in the Tax Code field to show that the amount is non-taxable because taxes for the sale were recorded at the time of the original sale. Enter the amount as a **positive** amount in the Amount field and enter *Bank: Chequing CAD* in the Account field. On a separate invoice line, enter the amount of the handling charge for the NSF cheque in the Amount field with *Other Revenue* in the Account field. Again, the handling charge is non-taxable.

Returns

When customers return merchandise, they are charged a 20 percent handling charge. In the Sales Journal, enter the quantity returned with a **minus** sign at the regular sale price, add the tax code and enter *Sales Returns & Allowances* in the Account field. The amounts will automatically be negative because of the minus sign in the quantity field, so that *Accounts Receivable* will be credited automatically as well. On a separate invoice line, enter the amount withheld — the handling charge — as a positive amount and credit *Other Revenue*. *Accounts Receivable* will be debited automatically for the amount of the handling charge.

If the original sale was a credit sale, and the account is not yet paid, the return should also be entered as a credit sale so that *Accounts Receivable* will be credited. If the original sale was paid in cash or by credit card, or the account has been paid, the return should be entered as a cash sale or credit card sale so that the appropriate bank account will be credited. (See page 381.)

Reserved Inventory for Divisions

When customers sign a contract, the inventory items needed to complete the work are set aside or reserved by transferring them through the Item Assembly Journal to a designated account. (Refer to page 375.) In this way, these items cannot be sold to other customers because the inventory quantities are already reduced. The minimum stock level for reserved inventory will be zero.

Cash, Credit and Debit Card, and Pre-Authorized Debit (PAD) Sales

> **NOTES**
> We use the term Cash Sales and Purchases for cash and cheque transactions.
> You can also enter the name in the Customer field and choose Continue when prompted. The name is then added to the journal report without creating a customer record.

Most types of businesses accept these different methods of payment. The program handles these transactions automatically through the Sales Journal when you choose the appropriate method of payment. For cash and debit and credit card sales, choose Cash Customers from the Customer list, and add the new customer's name in the Ship To or Address fields if this is not a regular customer. If payment is by cheque, a Cheque Number field opens. Truman Tires accepts Visa, MasterCard and Interac debit cards from customers for store sales. Instructions for setting up credit card processing (page 515) and for pre-authorized debits (page 522) are provided.

The program will debit the appropriate bank account instead of the *Accounts Receivable* control account. All other accounts for this transaction will be appropriately debited or credited.

Cash Purchases and Direct Payments

Choose the supplier from the Supplier list or add the supplier using Quick Add and then choose the correct method of payment. Cash purchases may be entered in the Payments Journal as Other Payments or in the Purchases Journal. For cheque payments, a Cheque Number field opens with the next cheque number entered. Complete the remainder of the cash transaction in the same way you would enter other transactions. Instructions for setting up direct payments are provided (page 531).

The program will credit *Chequing CAD* instead of *Accounts Payable*, the control account. All other accounts for the transaction will be appropriately debited or credited.

PRO VERSION
Remember that you will see the term Vendors when we use the term Suppliers.

Electronic Funds Transfers (EFT)

Pre-authorized debits, direct payments and direct deposits use electronic transfers. Money is taken directly from the customer bank account and deposited to the business bank account, or taken from the business bank account and deposited to supplier and employee bank accounts. Truman Tires has an account set up with a third-party supplier to make these bank account transfers from the program.

NOTES
After completing the entry as usual in Sage 50, the payments are uploaded and the funds transferred through an account with a third-party supplier.

Freight Expense

When a business purchases inventory items, the cost of any freight that cannot be directly allocated to a specific item must be charged to *Freight Expense*. This amount will be regarded as an expense rather than charged to an inventory asset account.

Printing Invoices, Orders and Quotes

To print the invoices, purchase orders or sales quotes through the program, complete the journal transaction as you would otherwise. Before posting the transaction, preview the invoice. If the invoice is correct, you can print it from the preview window, or from the invoice by choosing the File menu and then Print or by clicking the Print tool on the tool bar for the invoice form. Printing will begin immediately, so be sure you have the correct forms for your printer before you begin. If you and the customer or supplier have e-mail, click the E-mail tool to send the invoice or order.

NOTES
To preview, print or e-mail invoices, you must have the correct forms selected for invoices in the Reports & Forms Settings. You can access these settings from the journal tool bar.

Foreign Purchases

Truman Tires imports some inventory items from companies in Japan. The currency for these transactions is Japanese yen (JPY) and the currency symbol is ¥. Truman Tires pays HST and import duties on these purchases. Duty rates are set up in the Inventory Ledger for the individual items and the amounts are calculated automatically by the program.

INSTRUCTIONS

1. **Record entries** for the source documents for December 2015 in Sage 50 using the Chart of Accounts, Trial Balance and other information. The procedures for entering each new type of transaction are outlined step by step in the Keystrokes section with the source documents.
2. **Print** the **reports** and **graphs** indicated on the following printing form after you have finished making your entries.

NOTES
The transactions in this exercise provide a comprehensive practice set. If you want to use it only for review, you can complete the transactions without setting up divisions and entering allocations.

REPORTS

Accounts

- ☐ Chart of Accounts
- ☐ Account List
- ☐ General Journal Entries

Financials

- ☑ Comparative Balance Sheet: Dec. 1 and Dec. 31, difference in percentage
- ☑ Income Statement from Dec. 1 to Dec. 31
- ☑ Trial Balance date: Dec. 31
- ☑ All Journals Entries: Dec. 1 to Dec. 31 with division allocations and foreign amounts
- ☑ General Ledger accounts: 1400 4020 4040 from Dec. 1 to Dec. 31
- ☐ Statement of Cash Flows
- ☑ Cash Flow Projection Detail Report for account 1050 for 30 days
- ☑ Gross Margin Income Statement from Dec. 1 to Dec. 31

Tax

- ☑ Report on HST from Dec. 1 to Dec. 31

Banking

- ☐ Cheque Log Report

Payables

- ☐ Supplier List
- ☐ Supplier Aged
- ☐ Aged Overdue Payables
- ☐ Purchases Journal Entries
- ☐ Payments Journal Entries
- ☐ Supplier Purchases

Receivables

- ☐ Customer List
- ☐ Customer Aged
- ☐ Aged Overdue Receivables
- ☐ Sales Journal Entries
- ☐ Receipts Journal Entries
- ☐ Customer Sales
- ☑ Sales by Salesperson
- ☐ Customer Statements

Payroll

- ☐ Employee List
- ☑ Employee Summary for all employees
- ☐ Deductions & Expenses
- ☐ Remittance
- ☐ Payroll Journal Entries
- ☑ T4 Slips for all employees
- ☐ Record of Employment
- ☑ Year End Review (PIER)

Inventory & Services

- ☐ Inventory & Services List
- ☐ Inventory Summary
- ☐ Inventory Quantity
- ☐ Inventory Statistics
- ☑ Inventory Sales Summary for Winter Tires from Dec. 1 to Dec. 31
- ☑ Inventory Transaction Summary for Wheels, all journals from Dec. 1 to Dec. 31
- ☐ Item Assembly Journal Entries
- ☐ Adjustment Journal Entries
- ☐ Inventory Price Lists

Division

- ☐ Division List
- ☑ Division Income Summary: all divisions, all accounts from Dec. 1 to Dec. 31
- ☐ Division Allocation Report

Mailing Labels

- ☐ Labels

Management Reports

- ☐ Ledger

GRAPHS

- ☐ Payables by Aging Period
- ☐ Payables by Supplier
- ☐ Receivables by Aging Period
- ☐ Receivables by Customer
- ☐ Sales vs Receivables
- ☐ Receivables Due vs Payables Due
- ☐ Revenues by Account
- ☐ Expenses by Account
- ☑ Expenses and Net Profit as % of Revenue

KEYSTROKES

Creating New Divisions

Sage 50 allows allocations for all accounts. Each account ledger record has a check box to allow division allocations for the account (refer to page 93). If this box is checked, the allocation option is available for that account in any journal entry. If it is not checked, you cannot allocate an amount for that account. If you are unable to allocate an amount, check the ledger record for the account you are using to be sure that the option to Allow Division Allocations is selected. Truman Tires will allocate amounts for all revenue and expense accounts. This is the default for new income statement accounts. The option to allow allocations is already turned on for all these accounts in your data file.

Open **SageData13\Truman\truman**. **Enter Dec 7, 2015** as the session date.

Click **OK** to enter the session date. The Receivables Home window appears.

Before entering any transactions with allocations, you should create the divisions as instructed in memo #1.

NOTES
If you are working with backups, you should restore SageData13\truman1.CAB or truman1 to SageData13\Truman\truman.

PRO VERSION
The ledger record option is to Allow Project Allocations.

NOTES
For Truman Tires, the option to allow allocations is not selected in the ledger records for Balance Sheet accounts.

✓ 1

Based on memo #1 from Owner on December 1, create two new divisions: Sales Division and Service Division. Both divisions begin Dec. 1, 2015, and are active. Allocations will be made by percentage.

Click **Divisions** in the Modules pane list to change the Home window:

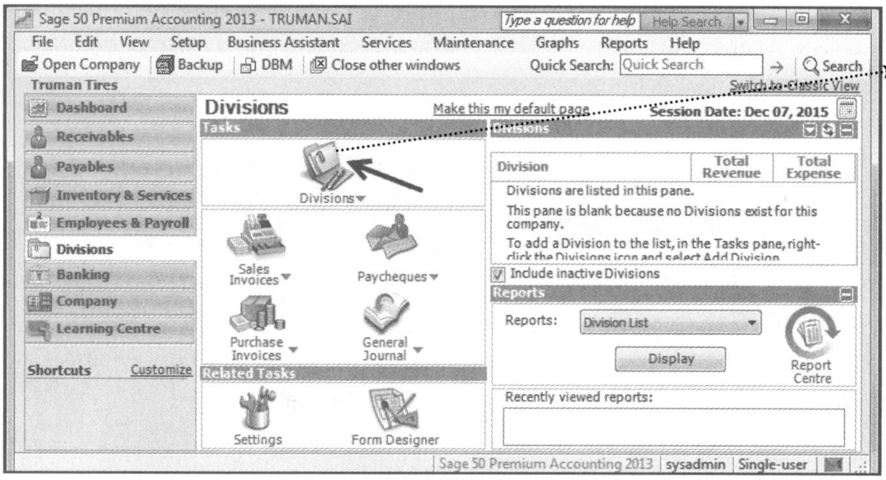

Click **Make This My Default Page** to keep this as the Home window.

The Divisions module window has access to the Divisions ledger records, as well as to four journals that most often have allocated amounts. Divisions are created from the Divisions icon that opens the Division window. The Division window can also be accessed from the Company, Receivables, Payables and Employees & Payroll modules:

These four modules, as shown above, include the Divisions icon in the Tasks panes. These modules have journals that use allocations.

Click the **Divisions icon** to open the Division window:

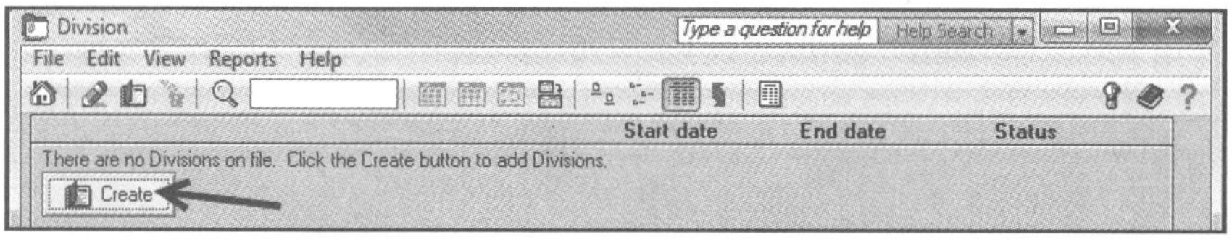

Click **Create**. The new Division Ledger screen appears:

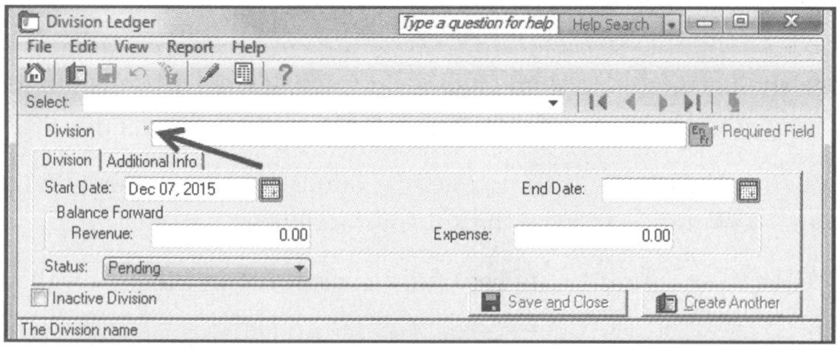

The cursor is in the Division name field, the only required field for the new record. You must enter the name of the first division.

Type `Sales Division` **Press** *tab* **twice** to skip the language button.

The cursor moves to the Start Date field. Enter the date on which you want to begin recording division information, December 1, 2015, to replace the default session date.

NOTES

We have used a straight text format for source documents in this chapter.

PRO VERSION

Click Projects in the Modules pane list. The ledger is named Projects instead of Divisions. We will change this name on page 507.

NOTES

For the Retail company type, Projects are named Divisions. For other industry types, the term Project, Fund, Job Site, Partner, Crops or Property will be applied. Refer to Appendix B in this text.

NOTES

You can also enter allocations in the Inventory Adjustments Journal, but the Divisions icon is not included in the Inventory module window.

PRO VERSION

Click the Projects icon. You will see Project and Project Ledger as the headings in the Title bar for these screens instead of Division and Division Ledger.

NOTES

You can enter division names in French and English when you choose to use both languages.

Type 12-01

You can enter an **Ending Date** for the division if this is appropriate. The ledger also has a **Balance Forward** field for **Revenue** and **Expense**. These fields can be used to enter historical information — the amount of revenue and expense generated by the division before the records were converted to Sage 50 or before the Division Ledger was used. The balances are zero for Truman Tires because a new fiscal period is just beginning.

The next field shows the Status for the division.

Click the **Status field** or list arrow to see the status options:

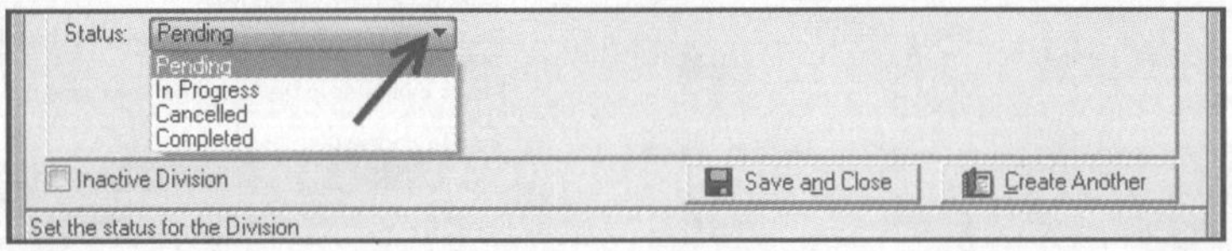

The division may be Pending (not yet started), In Progress or ongoing, Cancelled or Completed. Both divisions at Truman Tires are In Progress or active.

Click **In Progress** from the Status drop-down list.

Click **Create Another** [Create Another] to save the new division.

Enter the **Service Division**, using the steps described above for the Sales Division; **use Dec 1, 2015** as the starting date and **select In Progress** as the Status.

Click **Save And Close** [Save and Close] to save the second division.

You will return to the Division window. Notice that Sage 50 has created a listing for each division including the name, starting and ending dates and status.

Close the **Division window** to return to the module window. The two divisions are added to the Divisions pane in the module window.

NOTES
You can list divisions by icon in the Divisions window by choosing the View menu and icon.
You can re-sort the division icons if they are out of order by choosing the View menu and Re-sort Icons.

Changing Division Settings

Click the **Settings icon** [Settings] to display the Settings window as shown:

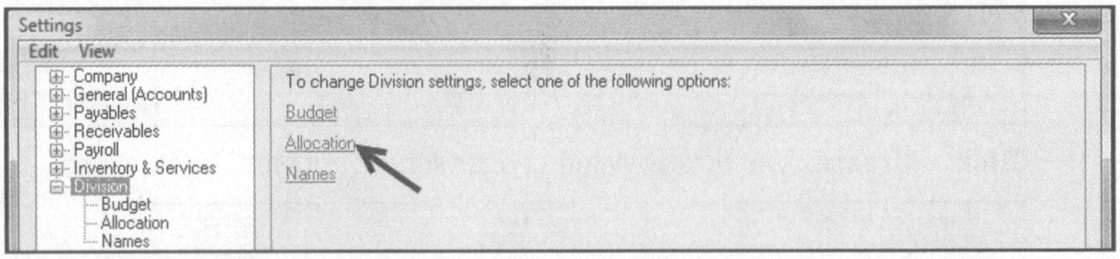

Or choose the Setup menu, then choose Settings. If the Divisions module window is open, the Division Settings screen should open directly.

CLASSIC VIEW
Click the Setup tool. If the Divisions icon is not selected, choose Division from the Select Setup drop-down list and click Select.

NOTES
You cannot change Division settings in multi-user mode.

PRO VERSION
Project will replace Division in the list of modules.

The Division Ledger has settings for budgeting, allocation and names. Budgeting is covered in Chapter 14. We need to view the setting for allocations.

Click **Allocation** either in the list under Division or in the list on the right:

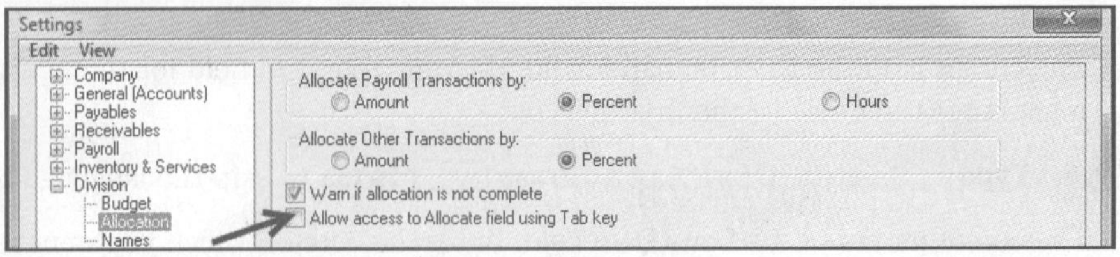

You can enter the allocation in different ways — by Amount, by Percent or by Hours (payroll only). The option to Allocate By Amount requires you to enter the exact dollar amount for each division. Division work for payroll purposes is often recorded by time spent on the division. This is the third option for payroll allocations.

Sage 50 includes a warning for incomplete allocations. It is easy to miss an allocation because you must complete the allocation procedure even if 100 percent of the costs are allocated to a single division, and you must allocate each account line in the journals. You can choose to be warned if you try to post an entry that has not been fully allocated. If you are using divisions, you should always leave the warning turned on. The warning should be selected by default.

If this option is not selected, click Warn If Allocation Is Not Complete. The default setting to allocate expenses by percentage is correct.

You can also choose to access Allocate fields in journals with the tab key. Without this option, you must click the Divisions field to access it or click the Allocate tool to open the Allocation window. Using the tab key allows you to use the keyboard to enter the transaction and allocation. You can still click the field to move the cursor if you want.

Click **Allow Access To Allocate Field Using Tab Key**.

NOTES

If you are not using the allocation feature, do not select the option to Allow Access To Allocate Field Using Tab Key so that the cursor will skip the unused Divisions column.

Changing Division Names

In any version, you can change the name of the ledger to Project, Department, Profit Centre, Cost Centre or something that is more appropriate for a business. The new name will replace Division in all windows and reports. Division as the ledger name for Truman Tires' Sales and Service Departments is appropriate.

Pro version users should change the name from Project to Division.

PRO VERSION

These steps are included so that Pro version users will see the same names as the Premium version users.

Click **Names** under the Division heading:

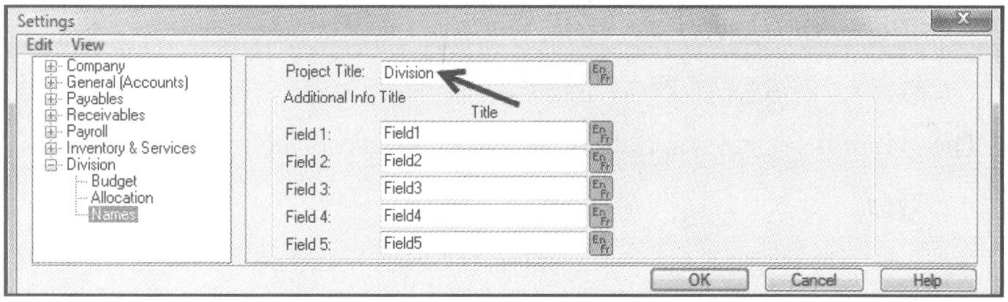

Double-click the Project Title field to select the default name. Type Division (or the name you want to use).

NOTES

We are not renaming Divisions as Departments because Sage 50 has a departmental accounting feature that is different from division allocation (see Chapter 19).

The remaining input fields allow you to add your own user-defined fields for the ledger. The new fields will appear on the Additional Info tab screen in the ledger record. The ledger name can be changed at any time by repeating this step.

Click **OK** to save the Division settings and display a confirmation message:

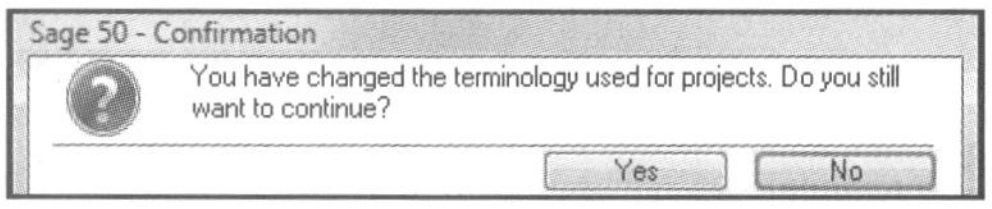

NOTES

Once the project is renamed by changing the Names setting, the new name will apply for all industry types. You must change the name on the Settings screen again if you want to use a different term.

We are warned to ensure that we want the name changed — all labels for the ledger icons, field names and report names will be changed.

Click **Yes** to confirm the change in name and return to the Home window.

Most of the journals we need for Truman are accessible from the Divisions module window; therefore, we will work from here. We can create shortcuts for the other journals used.

NOTES
All transactions can be completed from these shortcuts and journal windows. For example, other payments and payroll remittances are completed from the Payments Journal. Orders and Quotes are entered from the Sales Invoices or Purchase Invoices windows by selecting from the transactions drop-down list in the journal.

NOTES
You can allow allocations for Balance Sheet accounts, but we have not done so for Truman Tires.

Create **shortcuts** for **Pay Purchase Invoices** (Payables), **Create Receipt** (Receivables), **Transfer Funds** and **View Accounts** (Banking), **Item Assembly** and **Inventory Adjustments** (Inventory & Services) and **Payroll Cheque Run** (Employees & Payroll).

Entering Cost Allocations

Costs (or expenses) and revenues are allocated after the regular journal details are added but before the entry is posted. In a journal entry, whenever you use an account for which you have allowed division allocations in the General Ledger, the allocation option is available. For Truman Tires, all revenue and expense accounts allow division allocations.

Click the **Purchase Invoices icon** [Purchase Invoices] to open the Purchases Journal and prepare for entering the first transaction.

✓ 2 On December 1, received invoice #L-4441 for specialty tool rental contract from London Tool Rentals. The rental agreement amount was $280 plus $36.40 HST for a total of $316.40. Terms: net 20 days. Charged 20% of the expenses to Sales Division and 80% to Service Division. This was a one-year contract, stored as a monthly recurring entry.

The journal has not changed with the setup of allocations, and we enter the purchase details the same way.

The first transaction does not involve the purchase of inventory items, so you will not use the inventory database to complete this transaction. Invoice is correct as the transaction type, and Pay Later is the correct payment method.

From the list of suppliers,

Click **London Tool Rentals**.

Click the **Invoice No. field**.

Type `L-4441` **Press** tab **twice**.

The cursor moves to the Date field. You need to replace the default session date.

Type `dec 1`

The tax code H and the account number 5110 should be added as the default. If they are not, you can add them or edit them as needed.

Enter a **description**.

Click the **Amount field** or press tab repeatedly to advance the cursor.

Type `280`

Press tab **twice** to enter the amount of the invoice and the tax amounts and to advance to the Divisions column.

The journal still looks like a regular completed purchase transaction:

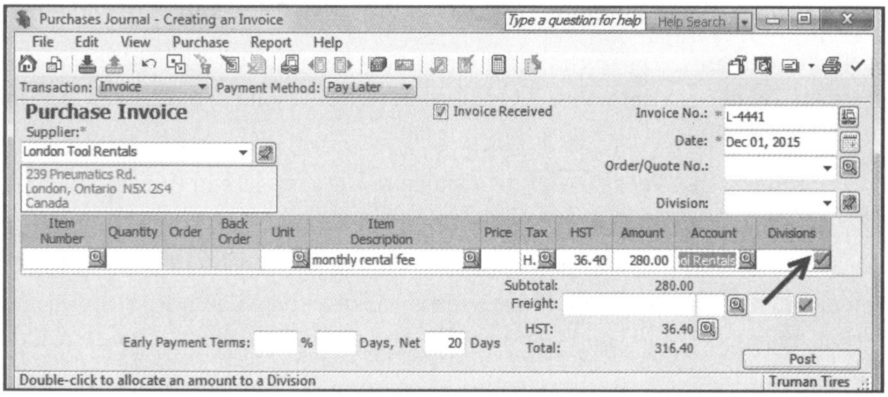

To access the Division Allocation window, the cursor must be on an invoice line with an account that allows allocation. If the account does not allow allocation or if the cursor has advanced to an invoice line without an account, the Allocate tool and menu option will be unavailable.

NOTES
If you try to allocate for an account that does not allow it (in the ledger record), you will see the message that the account is not set up for allocation.

Click the invoice line for the amount you want to allocate to activate the Allocate option. Only accounts that have selected the option to Allow Division Allocations will activate the Allocate tool.

Click the **Allocate tool** in the tool bar or in the Divisions column, or **double-click** the **Divisions column** beside the account or **choose** the **Purchase menu** and **click Allocate**.

NOTES
You can also press ctrl + shift + A to open the Division Allocation window.

You will see the Division Allocation window for the Purchases Journal:

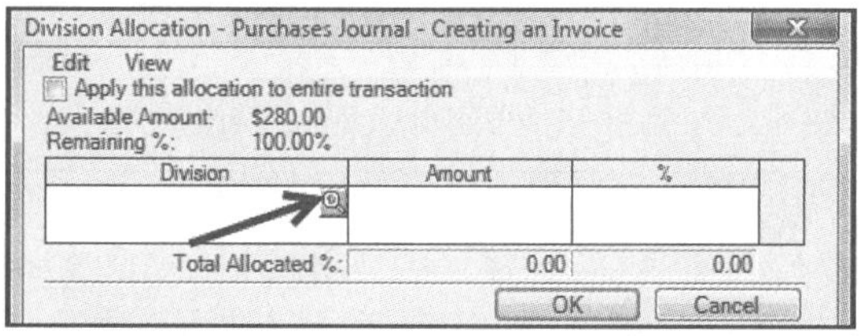

The cursor is in the Division field. The full amount to be allocated, $280 (the base expense amount), is shown at the top for reference together with the proportion remaining to be allocated, 100.00%. Amounts can be allocated by percentage or by actual amount. This choice is made in the Division Settings window shown on page 506. (Choose the Setup menu, click Settings and then click Division and Allocation.) The setting can be changed as needed. Truman Tires uses the Percentage allocation method as indicated in the Division Information.

NOTES
When you change the ledger name, the new name you entered will appear in the screen and column headings in the allocation windows instead of Division.

You must complete the allocation process even if 100 percent of the revenue or expense is assigned to a single division. You must complete the allocation process for each account or invoice line on your input form.

NOTES
The HST amount is not allocated because it is not part of the expense.

Click the **Division List icon** to display the Divisions in alphabetic order:

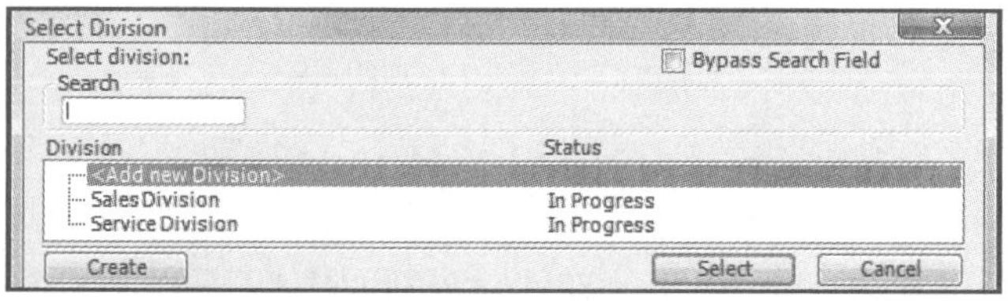

The first division is Sales, which incurs 20 percent of the total rental expense according to the source document information. Notice that you can add a new division from the Select Division window.

Choose Add New Division or click the Create button to open the Division Ledger if you need to create a new division.

Click **Sales Division**, the first one we need. **Click Select** to add it on the form.

The cursor advances to the Percentage field because we selected this method of allocation. By default the unallocated portion (100%) is indicated in this field and selected for editing.

Type 20 **Press** *tab* to advance to the next line in the Division field.

The program calculates the dollar amount for this division automatically based on the percentage entered. The percentage remaining at the top of the input form has been updated to 80.00%. Now you are ready to enter the amount for the remaining division, 80 percent. You need to repeat the steps above to allocate the remainder of the expense.

Press *enter* to open the Select Division window.

Double-click **Service Division** to add the division.

The cursor is in the Percentage field again, with 80.00 as the default because this was the unallocated percentage remaining. Since this amount is correct, we can accept it.

Press *tab* to enter it and complete the allocation with 0.00% remaining to be allocated, as shown here:

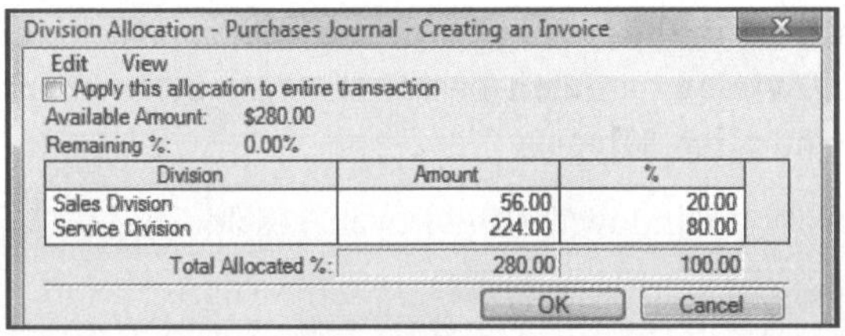

Click **OK** to return to the completed Purchases Journal entry:

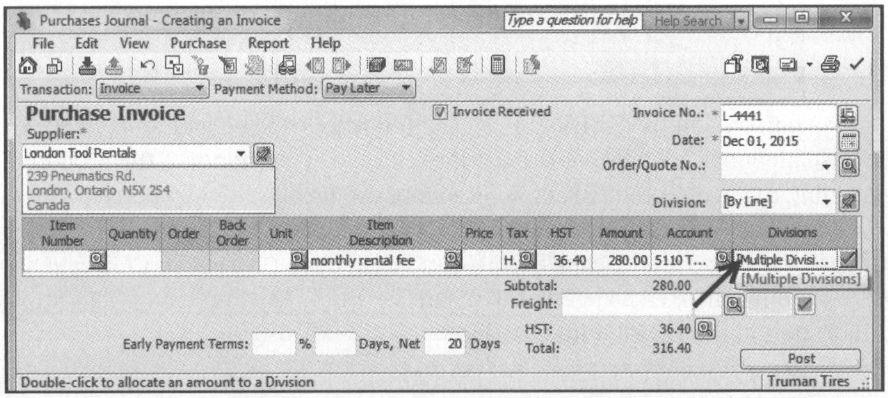

The journal appears unchanged, except for the entry in the Divisions column indicating that the amount has been allocated. The Division name is entered, but because more than one division was used, the entry is Multiple Divisions. The [By Line] entry in the Division field above the invoice lines indicates that more than one division has been applied to the purchase.

Reviewing the Purchases Journal Allocation

Choose the **Report menu** and **click Display Purchases Journal Entry**:

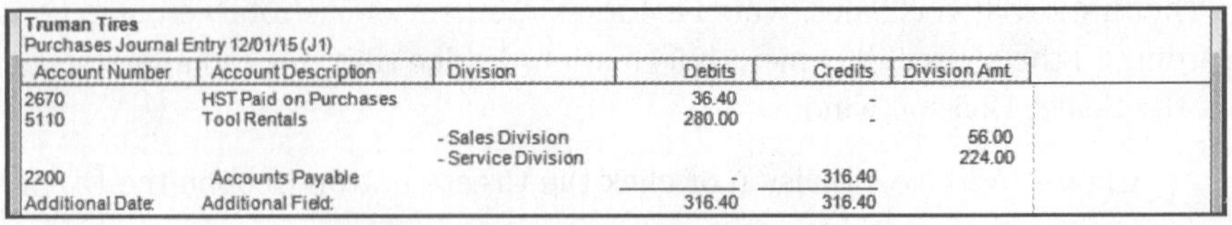
Truman Tires
Purchases Journal Entry 12/01/15 (J1)

Account Number	Account Description	Division	Debits	Credits	Division Amt
2670	HST Paid on Purchases		36.40	-	
5110	Tool Rentals		280.00	-	
		- Sales Division			56.00
		- Service Division			224.00
2200	Accounts Payable		-	316.40	
Additional Date:	Additional Field:		316.40	316.40	

Sage 50 has automatically updated the *Accounts Payable* control account because the Payables and General ledgers are fully integrated. Notice also that the rental expense has been allocated to the two divisions. Only the amount for the expense account *Tool Rentals* is allocated because the other accounts are Balance Sheet accounts that are not set up to allow allocations.

Close the **display** to return to the Purchases Journal input screen.

> **NOTES**
> When PST is paid separately from GST, it will be included with the expense amount and fully allocated with it.

CORRECTING THE PURCHASES JOURNAL ENTRY ALLOCATION

Correct the Purchases Journal part of the entry as you would correct any other purchase invoice. Refer to page 114 if you need assistance.

If you have made an error in the allocation, **click** the **Allocate tool** to return to the Allocation window. **Click** the **line** for the amount being allocated to activate the Allocate tool if necessary. **Click** an **incorrect division** to highlight it. **Press** *enter* to access the Division list. **Click** the **correct division** and **click Select** to enter the change. **Click** an **incorrect percentage** and **type** the **correct information**. **Press** *tab* to save the correction. **Click OK** to return to the Journal window.

Click the **Store tool**. Accept the supplier **name** and **Monthly** as the frequency. **Click OK** to return to the journal.

When you store a transaction with allocations, allocation information is also stored.

To see the allocation again, click the Allocate tool when the cursor is on the relevant line or click the ✓ in the Divisions column.

Posting

When you are certain that you have entered all the information correctly,

Click Post to save the entry. **Click OK** to confirm posting.

> **NOTES**
> You should click OK for the successful posting message each time you record or post a transaction. We will not repeat this instruction.

If you have not allocated 100 percent of the amounts, you will see the warning:

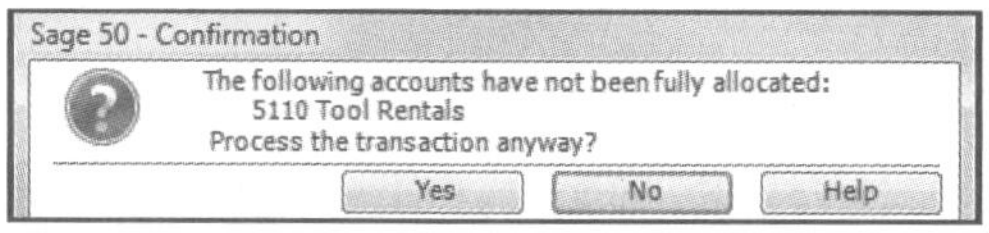

You will see a message like this one if you have not fully allocated a journal amount. If the warning option is not selected (page 506) you may post a transaction incorrectly.

If you made an error, click No to return to the invoice in the Purchases Journal. Click the Divisions column beside the account that is not fully allocated to return to the Allocation screen. Make the changes, click OK and then post.

If you do not want to allocate the full amount, or if the account that was not fully allocated was one for which you cannot access the allocation procedure, such as *Variance Costs* (see the screenshots on page 529), you should click Yes to continue.

> **NOTES**
> Later in the chapter, we will see that cost variances are not allocated.
> You may want to proceed with an incomplete allocation when part of the amount applies to none of the divisions or it applies to an earlier time period before division recording was started.

Close the **Purchases Journal**. The Divisions list pane total expense amounts have been updated with amounts from this transaction. Click the list pane refresh tool if necessary to update division amounts.

Enter the next **two payments** and the **receipt transaction**.

3 Sent cheque #200 for $1 130 to TuffArm Shocks on Dec. 1 to pay invoice #TS-699.

> **NOTES**
> Allocation is not available for invoice payments or receipts.

4 On Dec. 2, sent cheque #201 to MoTech Auto Parts to pay invoice #MT-1142. Cheque for $664.44 allowed for $13.56 discount for early payment.

5 Received cheque #4887 for $1 328.88 on Dec. 2 from Lovely U Cosmetics. Receipt #80 was applied to invoice #116 with early payment discount of $27.12.

Entering Import Duties

Governments may apply import duties that raise the price of imported goods to encourage the local economy. Duty rates or tariffs vary for different kinds of items and for different countries. The duty is collected by the Canada Revenue Agency when the goods first enter Canada, before they are released to the buyer.

In Sage 50, before you can enter duty amounts with the purchase, you must change the Payables settings to charge and track import duties (see page 651). You must also indicate in the foreign supplier's record (Options tab screen) that duty is applied to purchases from that supplier (see page 664). In the Inventory Ledger records (Taxes tab screen), you can enter the duty applied as a percentage (see pages 682–683), or you can enter the rates in the Purchases Journal. For non-inventory purchases, you must enter the rate directly in the Purchases Journal.

The purchase invoice from Snowmaster Tire Company has import duties applied.

NOTES

Edit the purchase amounts.

HST is charged on freight expenses.

Amounts for Balance Sheet accounts are not allocated so, except for the freight amount, there is no allocation for inventory purchases.

✓ 6 Recorded invoice #ST-916 from Snowmaster Tire Company for tires and parts on Dec. 2/15. Payment is due in 15 days. The exchange rate on Dec. 2 was 0.0132. Total import duty charged was ¥14 746 (CAD $194.65). The freight expense was allocated entirely to the Sales Division.

items purchased			amount	duty rate
	Miscellaneous parts		¥ 50 000	6%
20	T110	P195/65R16 Tires	82 000	7%
20	T111	P205/65R16 Tires	85 800	7%
	Freight		6 500	
	HST Paid		29 159	
Invoice Total			¥253 459	

Open the **Purchases Journal**. **Choose Snowmaster Tire Company**. **Press** *tab*:

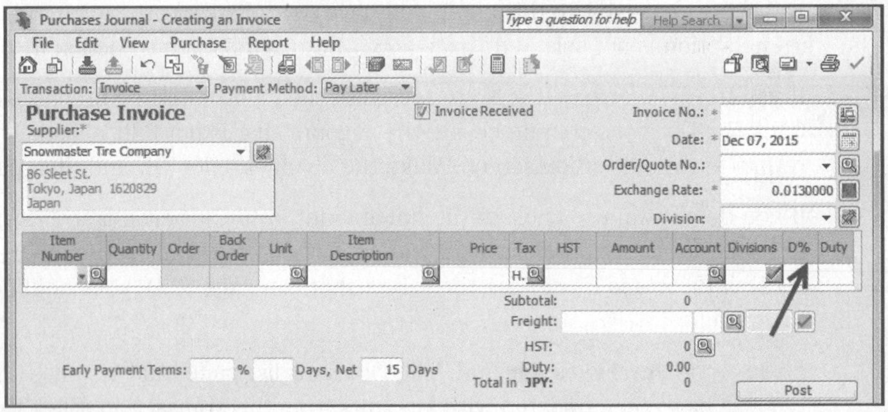

The company settings and the Supplier and Inventory Ledger records for Truman Tires are set up to apply duty.

In addition to the Exchange Rate field and the indication that Japanese yen (JPY) is the currency for this supplier, the duty fields are added because we selected a supplier for whom duty applies. The extra fields are used for the duty percentage and for the duty amount. Duty is charged on all items purchased from Snowmaster Tire Company.

Click the **Invoice field** and **type** ST-916

Enter **Dec 2-15** in the Date field and **press** tab to open the Exchange Rate screen with the most recent rate highlighted.

Type .0132 **Click Make This The Default Rate For Dec. 2, 2015**.

Click **OK** to return to the journal.

Click the **Item Description field**. **Type** miscellaneous parts

Click the **Amount field**. **Type** 50000 **Press** tab.

Choose **1240 Brakes & Shocks Parts** from the Account list. **Press** tab **twice**.

You will advance the cursor to the D% (duty rate) field where you should enter the rate that the government applies to this type of product.

Type 6 **Press** tab to enter the duty amount.

Press tab again to advance to the next line in the Item field. You can now add the inventory item purchases.

Double-click the **Item Number field** to open the Inventory Selection screen.

Double-click **T110** to add this item to the invoice:

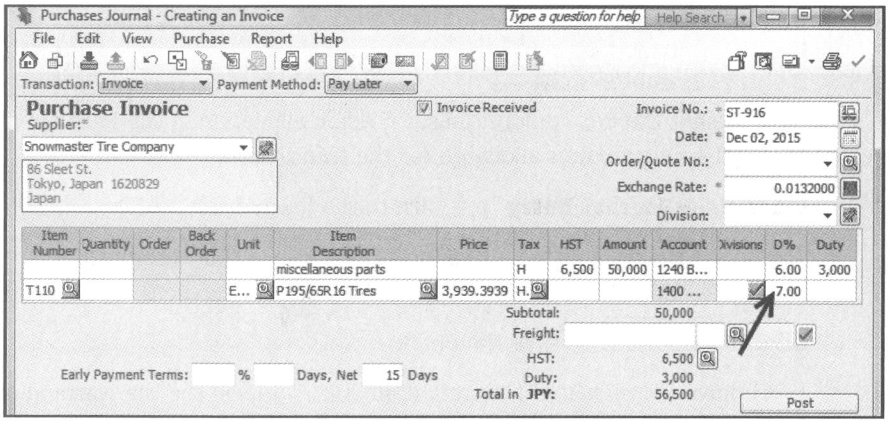

This time the duty rate is added automatically because the rate is recorded in the ledger record for the item.

Type 20 to enter the quantity. **Type** 82000 as the Amount.

Enter the **second inventory item** in the same way.

Click the **first Freight field**, the freight amount field.

Type 6500 and **press** tab.

The tax code H should be entered as the default. The freight tax amount and total are updated.

Allocating Freight Expenses

When you purchase inventory items, the Allocate tool and menu option are not available because the asset accounts were not set up to allow allocations. However, the freight expense for these purchases can be allocated.

The Freight field has an **Allocate button** ☑ (to the right of the freight amount field), so that freight amounts may be allocated separately from other amounts in the entry.

NOTES

When you update exchange rates in the Purchases Journal, the Exchange Rate screen may stay open after you click OK with the session date replacing the transaction date. Click Cancel to close the screen and select the correct exchange rate from the Exchange Rate select list. Click the Exchange Rate tool beside the field to open the list.

NOTES
The Allocate button beside the Freight fields is the same as the main Allocate tool but it applies only to the amount for freight.

NOTES
Freight is allocated by amount – the cursor advances to the Amount field on the Allocation screen after you select the Division. You cannot change this setting.

NOTES
You can allocate freight revenue amounts in the same way. Simply click the Allocate tool beside the Freight fields.

This allocate tool, with the pointer in the following screen, is used for this purpose:

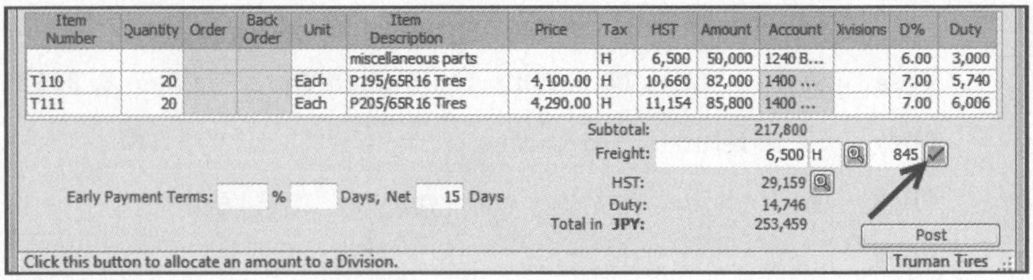

Item Number	Quantity	Order	Back Order	Unit	Item Description	Price	Tax	HST	Amount	Account	Divisions	D%	Duty
					miscellaneous parts		H	6,500	50,000	1240 B...		6.00	3,000
T110	20			Each	P195/65R16 Tires	4,100.00	H	10,660	82,000	1400 ...		7.00	5,740
T111	20			Each	P205/65R16 Tires	4,290.00	H	11,154	85,800	1400 ...		7.00	6,006

Subtotal: 217,800
Freight: 6,500 H 845
Early Payment Terms: % Days, Net 15 Days
HST: 29,159
Duty: 14,746
Total in JPY: 253,459
Post
Click this button to allocate an amount to a Division. Truman Tires

Click the **Allocate tool button** to the right of the Freight fields.

The Division Allocation screen opens. It is the same as the one we saw earlier. The Freight amount, ¥6 500, is entered as the amount to be allocated.

Choose the **Sales Division** and **accept** the **amount** and percentage allocation.

Click **OK** to return to the journal. The journal has not changed in appearance.

Choose the **Report menu** and **click Display Purchases Journal Entry**:

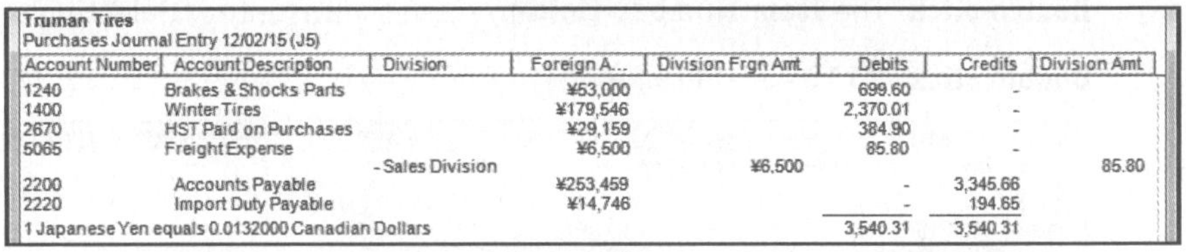

Truman Tires
Purchases Journal Entry 12/02/15 (J5)

Account Number	Account Description	Division	Foreign A...	Division Frgn Amt	Debits	Credits	Division Amt
1240	Brakes & Shocks Parts		¥53,000		699.60	-	
1400	Winter Tires		¥179,546		2,370.01	-	
2670	HST Paid on Purchases		¥29,159		384.90	-	
5065	Freight Expense		¥6,500		85.80	-	
		- Sales Division		¥6,500			85.80
2200	Accounts Payable		¥253,459		-	3,345.66	
2220	Import Duty Payable		¥14,746		-	194.65	
1 Japanese Yen equals 0.0132000 Canadian Dollars					3,540.31	3,540.31	

Only the Freight Expense amount has a division allocation in the journal entry because it was the only amount allocated for the transaction.

Close the **Journal Entry** to return to the journal.

To correct the freight expense allocation, click the Allocate button beside the field to open the Division Allocation screen and make the needed changes.

Click Post to save the entry.

If you have not allocated the freight amount, you will see the warning on page 511 about incomplete allocations.

Enter the following **purchase transaction** from Sylverado Wheels.

7

Recorded invoice #SW-876 from Sylverado Wheels for wheels on Dec. 2, 2015, at the exchange rate of 0.0132. Payment is due in 30 days. Total import duty assessed was ¥11 160 (CAD $147.31). Freight was charged to the Sales Division.

items purchased			amount	duty rate
20	W103	Aluminum R16 Wheels	¥130 000	6%
20	W107	Chrome-Steel R16 Wheels	56 000	6%
	Freight		5 000	
	HST Paid		24 830	
Invoice Total			¥215 830	

Close the **Purchases Journal**.

Allocating in the Sales Journal

Amounts for revenue accounts in the Sales Journal are allocated in the same way as amounts for expense accounts in the Purchases Journal. Each revenue amount in the journal must be allocated completely, but you can assign the same allocation percentages to all accounts in the journal rather than repeating the allocation entry for each invoice line. We will demonstrate this method by showing the steps involved in the Visa sale to Scinto on December 4.

✓ 8

Tridon made sale #125 to Bruno Scinto on Dec. 4/15. Scinto paid by Visa. 100% of revenue and expenses for inventory items was allocated to Sales Division and for the service item to Service Division. Create a new record for Scinto. Set up the data files to process credit card transactions before entering the sale.

items sold			amount	total
4	T104	P205/75R15 Tires	$100 each	$ 400.00
4	T105	P185/70R15 Tires	105 each	420.00
4	W102	Aluminum R15 Wheels	195 each	780.00
1	SRV06	Oil Service - premium pkg	40 /job	40.00
		Harmonized Sales Tax	13%	213.20
Total paid by Visa #4111 1111 1111 1111				$1 853.20

Because this is a credit card sale, we will first set up the data files to allow credit card processing. You cannot enter the credit card processing settings when the Sales Journal is open, so we must complete this step first.

If you do not have an Internet connection, you can skip this section and proceed to the Sales Journal Allocation section. You will also skip the steps for processing the transaction after entering the sales details.

Setting Up Credit Card Processing

When credit card processing details are added to the Company Credit Card Settings, the credit card transaction can be processed directly. You must have a merchant account set up with the processing company. Sage 50 links with Sage Exchange and all kinds of credit cards are processed through this single company. Merchants pay a fee for this service that is separate from the transaction fees charged by the credit card company. The advantage is that the transaction is processed directly as a bank transfer to the merchant.

You must have the Sage Exchange program installed and running on your computer to complete this next step.

You can download this program from the Company Credit Card Settings screen.

Click the **Settings icon**, then click **Company**, **Credit Cards** and **Processing Service** to open the Settings screen you need:

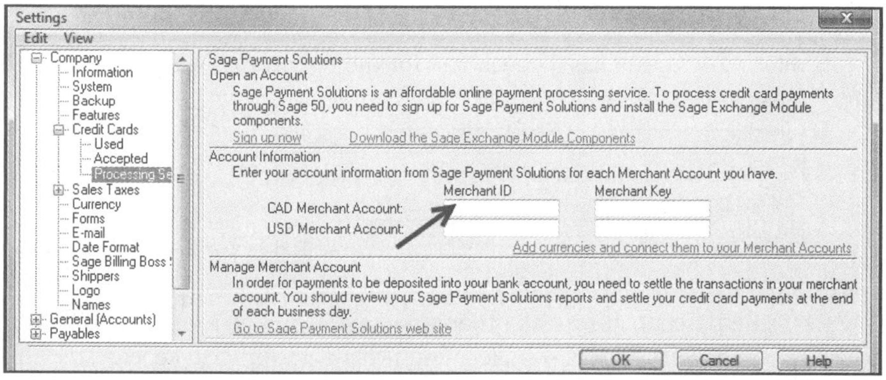

Start your **Internet connection**.

Click the **Download The Sage Exchange Module Components link** on the Settings screen. Follow the instructions to complete the installation.

You must add the Merchant ID number and Key (password) provided for this text by Sage Payment Solutions to activate the feature.

NOTES

Bruno Scinto lives at
35 Highland Rd.
London, ON N3T 1G7
Terms: net 1

NOTES

You can add Tridon as the salesperson in all customer records.

For all cash, credit card or debit card sales, you can type the new customer name and choose Continue or choose Cash Customers and use the Additional Field for the customer name or credit card number.

There is no discount for cash, credit card or debit card sales (Visa, MasterCard and Interac).

NOTES

The Sage Exchange program can be downloaded and installed from the Sage 50 link on the Company Credit Card Settings screen. You may need to change your firewall settings for the program after installing it to allow access.

NOTES

For illustration purposes, we will show the steps to complete this process and the screens that you would see. If you do not want to complete this step, you should complete and post the transaction without entering the Sage Payment Solutions account information. You can also add these details and process the transaction manually as described on page 520.

> **NOTES**
> These merchant numbers are connected to a test account, courtesy of Sage Payment Solutions. They will permit you to practise entering and authorizing credit card transactions.

Click the **Merchant ID field**. This is the number provided by Sage.

Type 651259884634

Press *tab* to advance to the Merchant Key field. This field holds the password for your account.

Type B8B904S6E2K2 As you type, the characters are replaced by *. (The sequence is letter, number, letter, number and so on.)

Click **OK** to close the Settings screen.

> **WARNING!**
> If the Sage Exchange program does not start properly, your firewall may be blocking it. Change the firewall setting to allow this program.

Start the **Sage Exchange program**. It will be running in the background.

You are now ready to enter the sales transaction for Scinto.

Allocating the Revenue Amounts

> **NOTES**
> You can leave the Sales Journal open in the background while you complete transactions in other journals. The salesperson will remain selected until you change the session date. If you use this approach, ensure that you update the dates and payment methods for each sale.
> You can also add Tridon as the salesperson in customer records. Remember to add the salesperson for new customers.

Click the **Sales Invoices icon** to open the Sales Journal.

Enter **Bruno Scinto** in the Customer field. **Click Add** and **enter** the customer's **address** and **terms** to the ledger record. **Click Save And Close**.

Choose **Visa** as the method in the Payment Method field.

Enter **Dec 4 15** as the invoice date.

Choose **Tridon** as the salesperson in the Sold By field.

Click the **Use The Same Salesperson tool** .

Choose **T104** from the inventory selection list as the first item for the sale. The cursor advances to the Quantity field.

Type 4 **Press** *tab* repeatedly to advance to the Divisions column.

Double-click the **Divisions column** or **click** in the Divisions column to open the Division Allocation window.

> **NOTES**
> You can also press *ctrl* + *shift* + A to open the Division Allocation window.

As long as the cursor is anywhere on the invoice line you are allocating, the allocate function is available. Click the Allocate tool button in the tool bar or choose the Sales menu and click Allocate to open the Division Allocation screen.

Choose the **Sales Division** for 100% of the revenue amount.

The allocation screen has a check box for the option Apply This Allocation To Entire Transaction as shown:

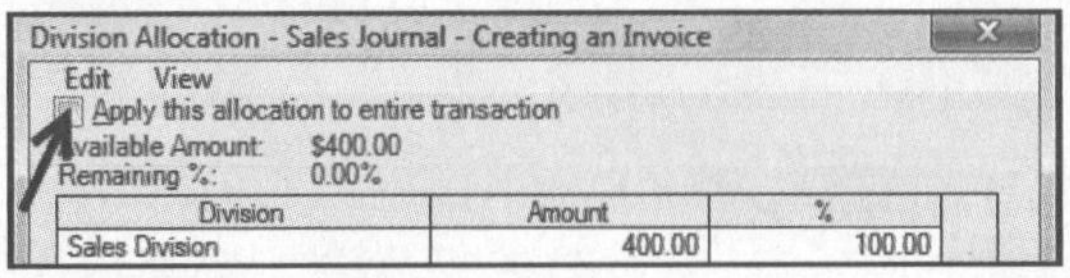

This option allows you to enter the allocation for one amount and have the program apply the same percentages for all other amounts, including freight, automatically. Otherwise you need to repeat the allocation procedure for each account in the journal.

Click **Apply This Allocation To Entire Transaction** to open the message about this selection:

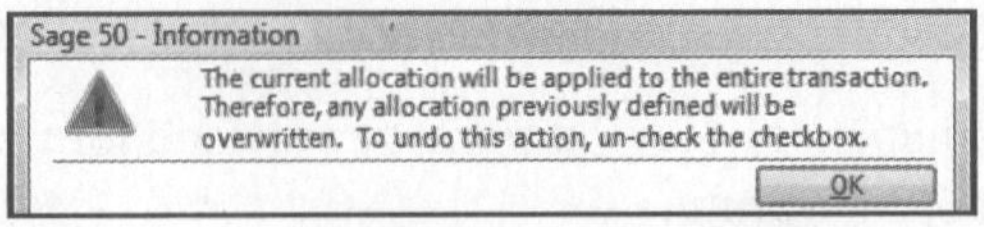

Read the **message** and then **click OK** to return to the allocation screen.

If you do not want to continue with this selection, click the check box again.

The Division Allocation screen has changed as shown:

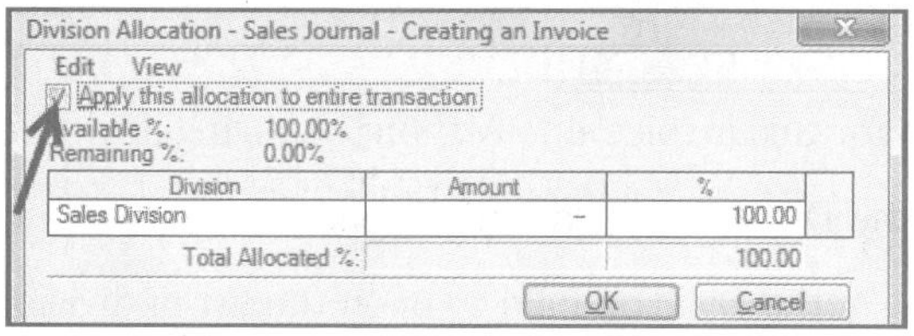

No amounts are entered at this time because the same percentages will be applied and the amounts will be different.

Click **OK** to save the allocation and return to the journal.

Enter the **remaining inventory** and **service items** for the sale.

The division name is added to the Divisions column automatically as you complete the invoice:

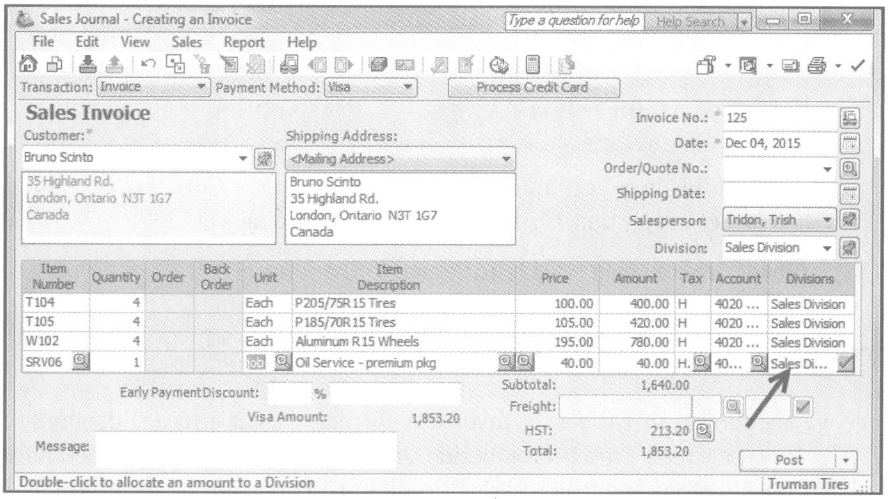

The invoice has been completely allocated, but the allocation is not correct, as you will see when you review the journal entry for the transaction.

Press ctrl + **J** to open the journal display:

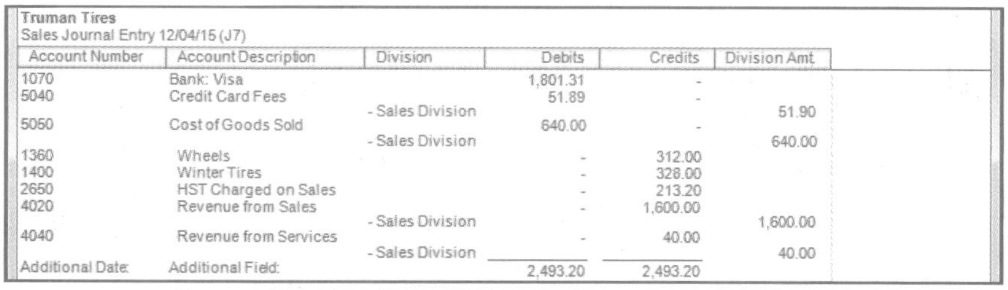

Truman Tires
Sales Journal Entry 12/04/15 (J7)

Account Number	Account Description	Division	Debits	Credits	Division Amt
1070	Bank: Visa		1,801.31	-	
5040	Credit Card Fees		51.89	-	
		- Sales Division			51.90
5050	Cost of Goods Sold		640.00	-	
		- Sales Division			640.00
1360	Wheels		-	312.00	
1400	Winter Tires		-	328.00	
2650	HST Charged on Sales		-	213.20	
4020	Revenue from Sales		-	1,600.00	
		- Sales Division			1,600.00
4040	Revenue from Services		-	40.00	
		- Sales Division			40.00
Additional Date:	Additional Field:		2,493.20	2,493.20	

All amounts are allocated to the Sales Division. However, the service revenue should be allocated to the Service Division, so we must change it.

Close the displayed **report** to return to the journal.

Click anywhere on the line for **item SRV06**.

Click the **Allocate tool**, **double-click** **Sales** in the Divisions column or **choose** the **Sales menu** and **click** **Allocate** to open the Allocation screen.

Click **Apply This Allocation To Entire Transaction**.

NOTES

The credit card fees and allocation amounts differ due to rounding the amounts.

NOTES

You can also press ctrl + shift + A for the selected item to open the Division Allocation screen.

> **NOTES**
> This message appears only for the first allocation you change, You can now change the allocation for additional amounts without seeing the message again.

> **NOTES**
> After you change this setting, you can change allocations for other amounts individually as well without affecting the remaining allocations.
> The Division field in the Journal (above the invoice lines) shows By Line as the entry. SRV06 has Service in the invoice line Division field while the other lines still show Sales.

You will see this message about changing the allocation selection::

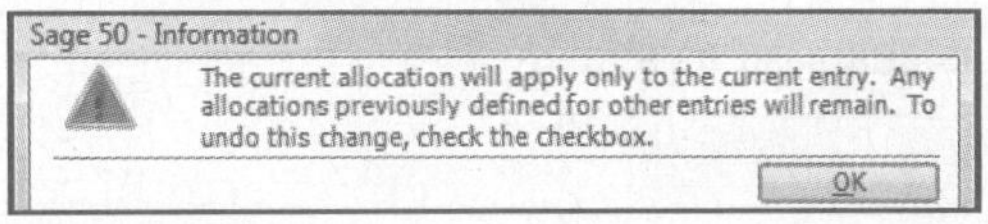

We can change the allocation for this invoice line without changing any other line.

Click **OK** to return to the Division Allocation screen.

Click the **List icon** in the Division field to open the list of divisions.

Double-click **Service Division** to add it to the Division Allocation screen.

Click **OK** to save the change. Service has been entered in the Journal.

Choose the **Report menu** and **click** **Display Sales Journal Entry**:

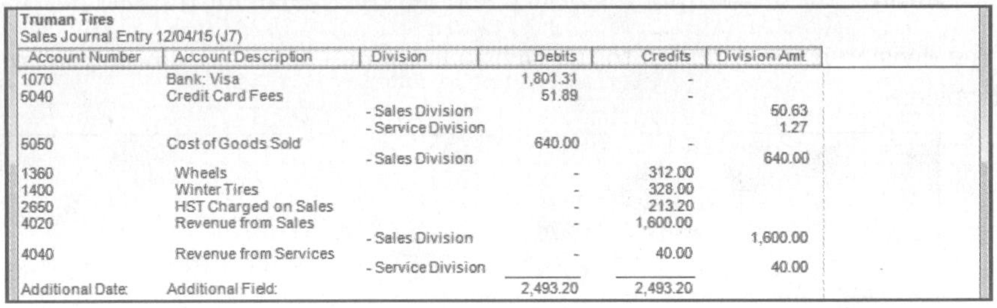

Truman Tires
Sales Journal Entry 12/04/15 (J7)

Account Number	Account Description	Division	Debits	Credits	Division Amt
1070	Bank: Visa		1,801.31	-	
5040	Credit Card Fees		51.89	-	
		- Sales Division			50.63
		- Service Division			1.27
5050	Cost of Goods Sold		640.00	-	
		- Sales Division			640.00
1360	Wheels		-	312.00	
1400	Winter Tires		-	328.00	
2650	HST Charged on Sales		-	213.20	
4020	Revenue from Sales		-	1,600.00	
		- Sales Division			1,600.00
4040	Revenue from Services		-	40.00	
		- Service Division			40.00
Additional Date:	Additional Field:		2,493.20	2,493.20	

The allocation is now correct. The allocation for *Credit Card Fees* is automatically split in the correct proportion. *Cost of Goods Sold* is also allocated.

Close the **Journal Entry** to return to the journal.

Processing a Credit Card Transaction

Once we are certain that the sales invoice is correct, we can process the credit card.

The Process Credit Card button beside the Visa Payment Method selection replaces the link (Tell Me More About Processing Credit Card Payments — see page 181).

> **NOTES**
> You can enter address information at this stage if you did not enter it in the ledger record.

Start the **Sage Exchange program** and your **Internet connection** if you have not already done so.

Click the **Process Credit Card button**:

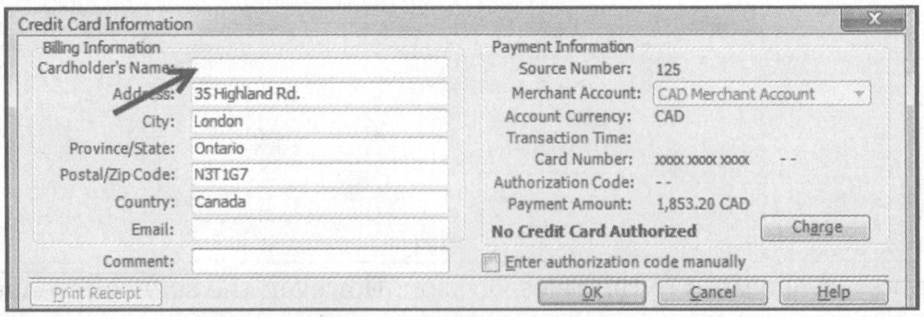

> **NOTES**
> If you enter your own e-mail address, you should receive a message confirming the sale and credit card charge.
> If you did not complete the address fields in the customer's record, you must add the details here.

> **NOTES**
> The name on the credit card may be different from the customer account name, so it is not added automatically.

The screen you see holds the customer information. If you select a customer for whom you have a complete ledger record, the address information will be added from the record. You must fill in the name and address fields to continue.

Card information may be processed/authorized manually or automatically. If you have an account set up with Sage, you can complete the processing automatically. You should have the Sage Exchange program and your Internet connection running.

Click the **Cardholder's Name field** and **type** `Bruno Scinto`

Click the **Charge button** in the lower right-hand corner of the Credit Card Information screen to link to the Sage Exchange Payment site:

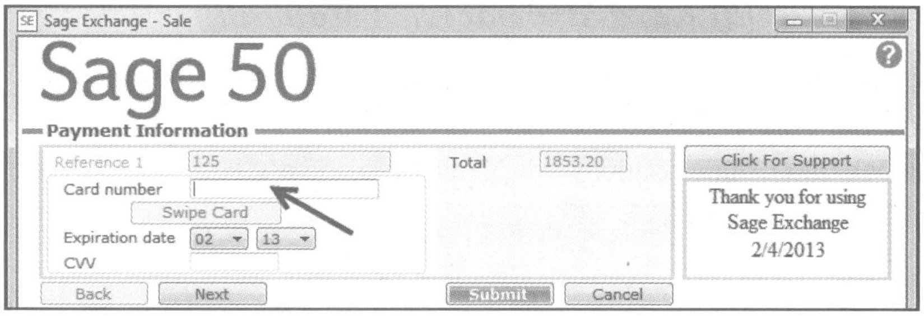

You are now connected to a secure site so that you can provide the credit card information. The cursor is in the Card Number field.

Type 4111111111111111 the 16-digit credit card number.

Select the **month** and **year** for the Expiration Date from the drop-down lists. The date must be later than the current calendar date on your computer system — the card must not be expired.

Entering the CVV code (the code located on the back of the credit card) is optional.

Click **Next** to review the information:

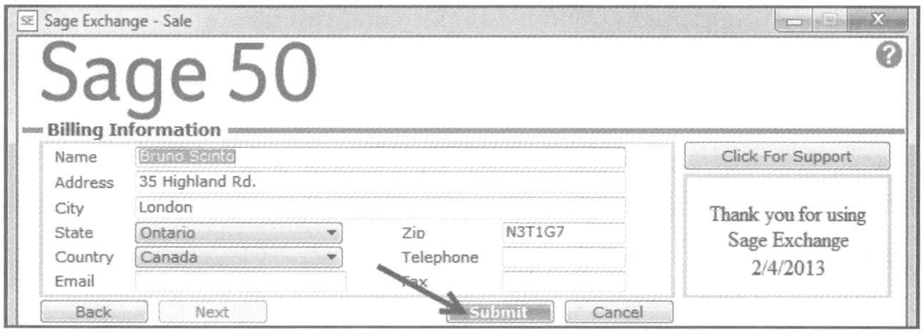

Make corrections by clicking the Back button to return to previous screens.

Click **Submit** to begin the processing. You may see the Processing message progress bar if there is any delay.

After the sale has been authorized, you will receive confirmation with the code:

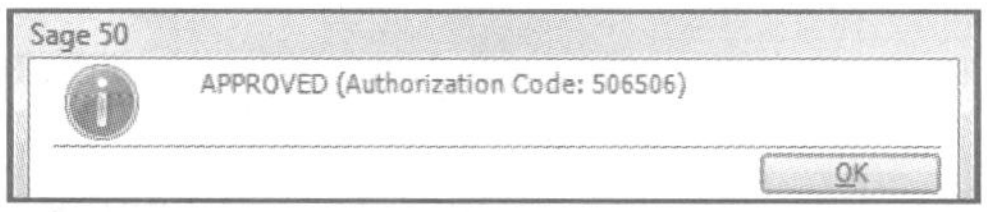

Record the **authorization** number with the sale for reference.

Click **OK**. **Click** **OK** again to return to the Sales Journal.

The Sales Journal Credit Card button label has changed to **Credit Card Details**:

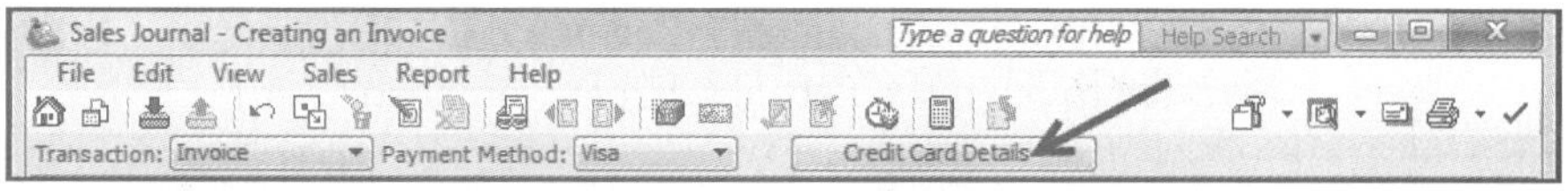

You can click the Credit Card Details button to review the details.

Click 

to save the entry.

If you do not post the transaction after processing the credit card, that is, you discard the transaction, you will see the following message:

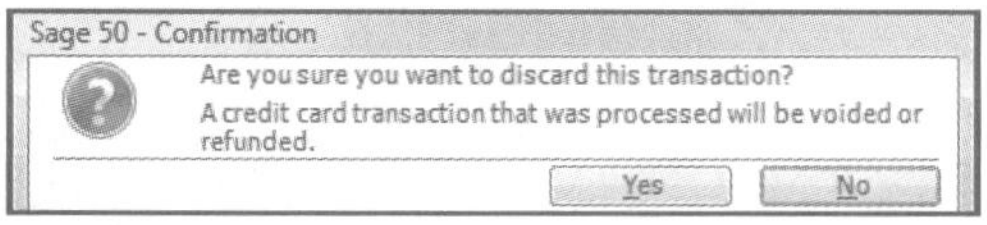

Click **Yes** to continue, discard the transaction, and void or reverse the charges.

NOTES
The system date from your computer will show as the date below the Thank You note and as the starting point for the card expiry date.

NOTES
This is the only Visa number that will be accepted in the test account for processing.

NOTES
If you omit any essential information, the program will warn you and prevent you from continuing until you provide the missing details.

NOTES
To process MasterCard sales automatically in our test account, enter 5499740000000057 as the credit card number.

NOTES
When you return to the Billing Information screen after authorizing the transaction, the option to Void the transaction appears. Clicking this will immediately reverse the charge to the customer's credit card.

NOTES
If you need to change credit card details after processing, you should reverse the sale. You may need to do this manually in order to reverse the credit card charges. Before posting, closing the journal will automatically void the credit card amount.

> **NOTES**
> If you did not add the address details in the customer's record, you can enter them here – or use your own address for practice.

Processing Credit Card Transactions Manually

If you do not have a direct Internet connection, you can process the credit card transaction manually. On the Billing Information screen,

Click Enter Authorization Code Manually to add a ✓:

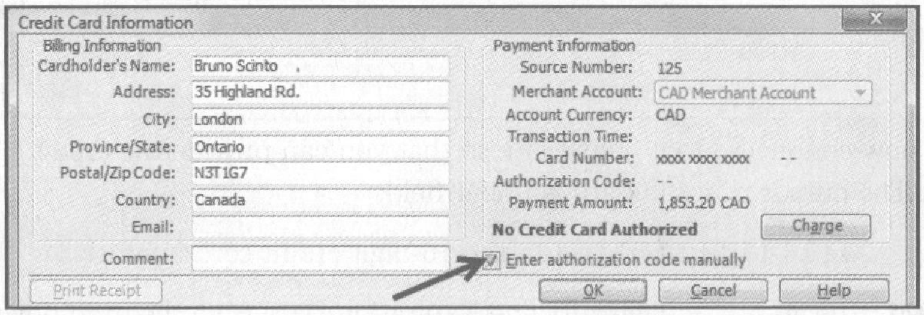

The Card Number field and the Authorization Code fields on this screen become available.

Click the Card Number field. Enter the last four digits of the card number.

Type 1111

Click the Authorization Code field. This code can be obtained by telephone or may be given automatically when the card is swiped on a terminal.

Type 488922

Click OK to return to the Sales Journal. Post the transaction.

Removing Credit Card Processing Settings

When entering a sale while you have account information in your credit card processing settings, you must process the transaction before you can post the sale. If you try to post the sale without the processing step, you will be blocked with this message:

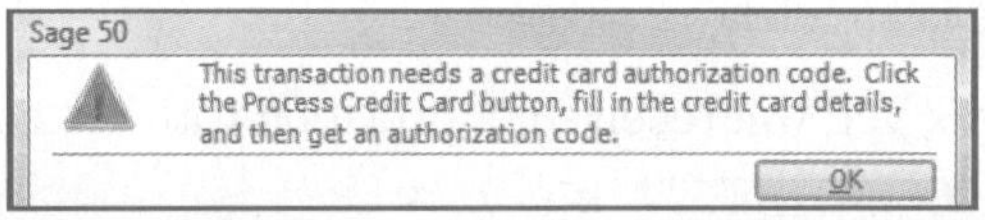

Click **OK**.

Close the **Sales Journal**. You cannot access the merchant account settings while the journal is open.

You need to remove the credit card processing account information, unless you want to process all credit card sales and generate authorization codes.

Click the **Settings icon**, then click **Company**, **Credit Cards** and **Processing Service** to open the Settings screen you need:

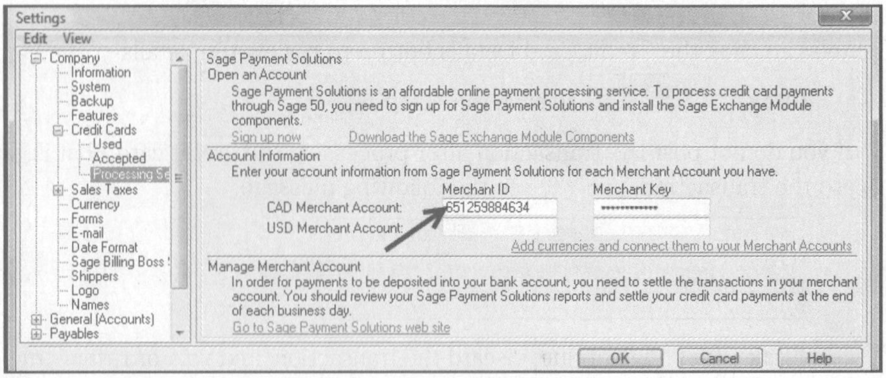

Double-click the **Merchant ID number** and **press** del.

Double-click the **Merchant Key password** and **press** del.

Click **OK** to save the changed settings.

Entering Allocations from the Sales Journal Window

Both the Sales Journal and the Purchases Journal have a Division field with a drop-down list of divisions. By using this selection list, you can quickly apply the same division to all invoice lines.

When you enter allocations with the methods we showed earlier, this field shows the entry [By Line] because we entered different or multiple allocations for one or more individual lines on the invoice, as in the Purchase Invoice on page 510. The Sales Invoice on page 517 shows Sales Division in this field because at that stage, we had allocated the entire transaction to the Sales Division.

When the entire transaction is to be allocated to one division, you can select the division from the Division field drop-down list. We will show this method for the next sale.

✓ 9

Tridon completed MasterCard sale #126 to Alice Ferante on Dec. 4, 2015, and allocated 100% of revenue to Sales Division.

items sold			amount	total
4	T114	P225/60R17 Tires	$150 each	$ 600.00
4	W104	Aluminum R17 Wheels	225 each	900.00
		Harmonized Sales Tax	13%	195.00
Total paid by MasterCard #5499 7400 0000 0057				$1 695.00

NOTES
Alice Ferante lives at
10 Highland Rd.
London, ON N2T 3R2

Open the **Sales Journal**.

Enter **Alice Ferante** as the customer, **press** tab and **click Continue**.

Choose **MasterCard** from the Payment Method drop-down list.

Enter **Dec 4** as the date for the sale.

Choose **Tridon** as the Salesperson.

Enter the first **inventory item** and **quantity**. **Press** tab to update the amount.

Click the **Division field list arrow** as shown:

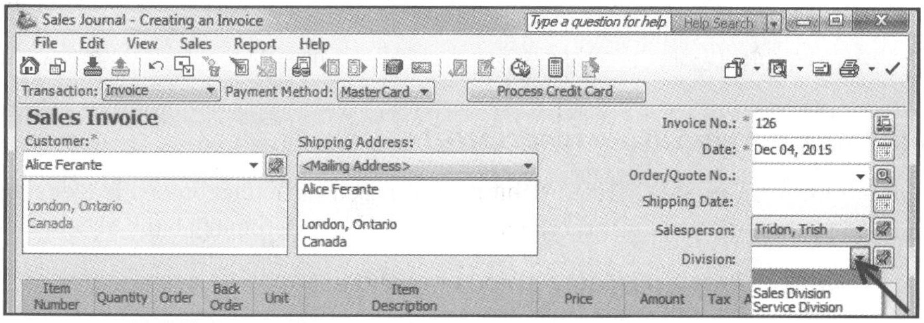

Both divisions are available for selection.

Click **Sales Division**. This division will be added to the first invoice line.

Enter the **second item** and **quantity**. Sales Division is added automatically.

NOTES
You must process the MasterCard credit card sale if you have not removed the processing service account details. Use the card number provided in the source document – this is the only MasterCard number accepted in the test account.

NOTES
You can use the journal's Division field to allocate freight amounts as well. In the Purchases Journal for inventory purchases, the allocation entry will apply only to freight.

If you open the Division Allocation window for either line on the invoice, you will see that the journal selection applies the same allocation to the entire transaction:

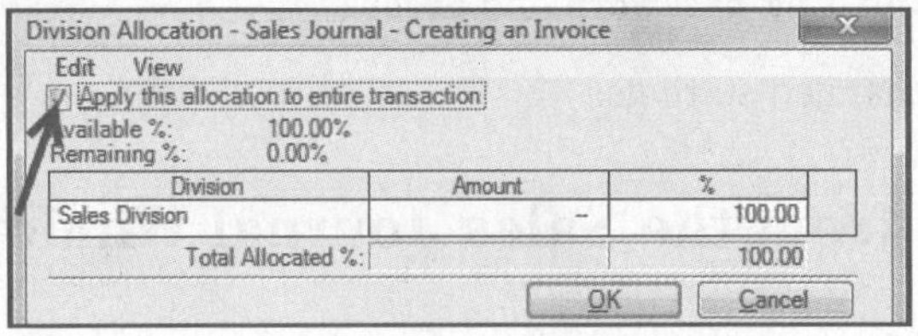

If you need to change the allocation for individual line amounts, you can do so from this window as we did for the previous sale. Click OK to close this window.

> **NOTES**
> If you see the message that the credit card fees are not fully allocated, you must accept the incomplete allocation to continue.

Review your **journal entry** display and **make corrections** if necessary.

Click Post to save the entry.

Pre-Authorized Payments and Deposits

Businesses may have bills paid directly from their bank accounts by allowing suppliers to make automatic withdrawals. Customers may also permit automatic withdrawals for bill payments, and many businesses arrange for paycheques to be deposited directly to employee bank accounts. For these transactions, funds are transferred electronically, directly from one bank account to another. Funds may be transferred between different banks and branches.

Third-party solution providers manage these electronic funds transfers (EFTs). Sage Payment Solutions, PayPal and Beanstream are providers whose services can be linked with features in Sage 50 for these transfers.

We have a test account set up with Beanstream to illustrate the processes involved.

> **NOTES**
> The customer is still responsible for ensuring that the bank account has sufficient funds to pay the bill to avoid overdraft or NSF charges.

Pre-Authorized Debits (PAD)

When customers allow a business to withdraw funds directly to pay their accounts, usually for recurring bills, their method of payment is Pre-Authorized Debit. This arrangement removes concerns about lost cheques and overdue bills.

✓ 10

Received memo #2 from Owner: Two customers have authorized debits. Set up the permission in the customer records and enter bank account details as follows:

customer	branch number	institution (bank) number	account number
City Cab Company	87654	003	655743211
London Car Leasing	38876	002	19928374

Setting Up Pre-Authorized Debits

Before entering a pre-authorized debit sale or receipt, the customer's ledger must be updated to authorize the transactions and to add the customer's bank account details.

Click **Receivables** in the Modules pane to switch to this window.

Click **City Cab Company** in the Customers List pane to open this record.

Click the **Pre-Authorized Debit tab** to access the screen we need:

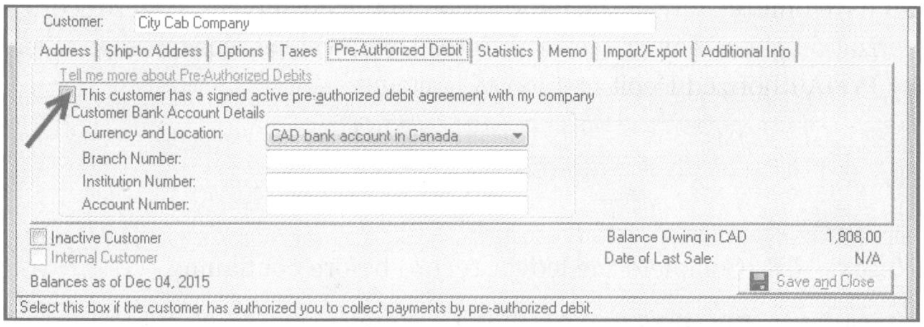

All the fields on this screen are required. The customer must complete and sign a form or agreement including the bank account details and authorizing the withdrawals. Often a blank void cheque accompanies the form to provide the bank account information. Withdrawals may be made in Canadian or United States dollars from bank accounts in Canada or the United States. The **Currency And Location** drop-down list allows you to make this selection.

Click **This Customer Has A Signed Active Pre-Authorized Debit Agreement With My Company** to add a ✓.

Click the **Branch Number field**. **Type** 87654

Press tab to advance to the Institution (bank) Number field.

Type 003 **Press** tab to advance to the Account Number field.

Type 655743211

Click the **next record button** to open the record for London Car Leasing.

Click the **authorized agreement check box** and **enter** the **bank account details**.

Click Save and Close.

Entering Pre-Authorized Debits

Pre-authorized debit is available as a method of payment for both receipts and sales invoices from the Paid By/Method Of Payment drop-down lists respectively. Receipts and sales are entered in the same way as regular receipts and sales. Only the method of payment selection differs.

✓ 11 Entered pre-authorized payment from City Cab Company on Dec. 6 for $1 771.84 including $36.16 discount. Receipt #81 was applied to invoice #120.

Open the **Receipts Journal**.

Choose **City Cab Company** as the customer.

Enter **Dec 6** as the transaction date.

Click the **Paid By list arrow** to see the options:

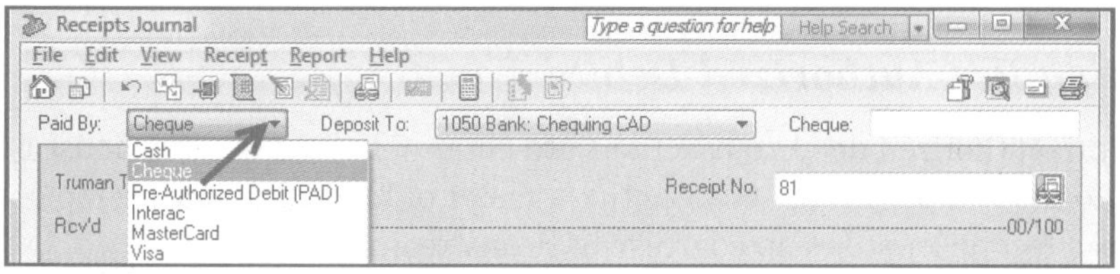

Click **Pre-Authorized Debit (PAD)**.

PAD number replaces the Cheque number field and CP1 (customer payment #1) is entered in this field as the reference number.

NOTES

As soon as you click the check box, you will see a reminder that the data file does not have a user password. Strong passwords are essential when bank details are included in your data files.

NOTES

The bank account information is similar to that entered for employees who have paycheques deposited directly to their bank accounts (see page 336).

Each bank has a unique three-digit bank or institution number, with unique five-digit branch numbers for their different branch locations. The account number is unique for the accountholder and varies in length from bank to bank.

NOTES

You can edit the starting reference number for Pre-Authorized Debits on the Forms screen of Company Settings.

If you have omitted any of the information in the customer's ledger record, either the authorization check box or the bank details, you will see this message when you select the Pre-Authorized Debit method of payment:

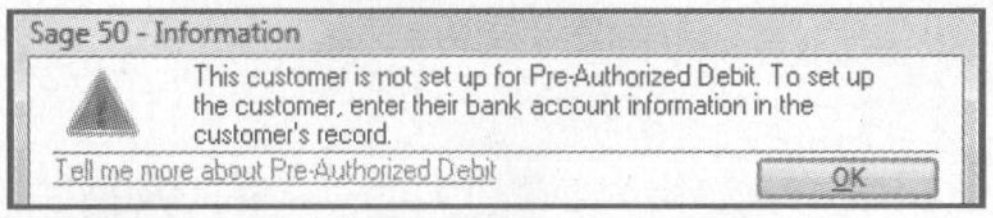

Click **OK**. Complete the ledger record before continuing.

Accept the **Discount** and **Amount** to complete the receipt.

Press ctrl + **J** to review the transaction.

WARNING!
You must remove the customer's name from the journal before you can modify the ledger record.

It looks like a normal receipt — the bank account is debited for the amount received because EFT transactions withdraw the money directly from the customer's account. *Sales Discounts* and *Accounts Receivable* are credited as usual.

NOTES
PAD reference numbers, CP1, CP2 and so on, are automatically updated.

Close the **journal entry** and **Post** the receipt.

Close the **Receipts Journal**.

Open the **Sales Journal** so you can enter the sale to London Car Leasing.

✓ 12

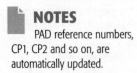

Tridon made sale #127 to London Car Leasing on Dec. 6. The preferred customer has pre-authorized debits and is entitled to the 2% discount for immediate payment. All revenue was allocated to Sales Division.

items sold			amount
12	T101	P155/80R14 Tires	$ 65 each
12	T106	P195/65R15 Tires	100 each
12	W106	Chrome-Steel R15 Wheels	75 each
12	W109	Steel R14 Wheels	38 each
		Harmonized Sales Tax	13%

$3 694.29 was uploaded to our bank account (reference number CP2).

Choose **London Car Leasing** as the customer for the sale.

Enter **Dec 6** as the transaction date.

Click the **Payment Method drop-down list**. The options are the same as those in the Receipts Journal.

Click **Pre-Authorized Debit (PAD)** to update the form with a PAD number; CP2 is entered automatically.

Enter the **remaining details** for the sale, including the division allocations.

Review the **journal entry** — it looks like a regular sale paid by cash or cheque. The bank account is debited for the full amount (minus the 2 percent discount) instead of *Accounts Receivable*.

Close the **journal entry** and **Post** the invoice.

Close the **Sales Journal** to return to the Receivables module window.

Uploading Pre-Authorized Debits

After the pre-authorized debit transactions are entered in Sage 50, they must be uploaded to the company that manages the transfer of funds. For our example, the author has a test account set up courtesy of Beanstream.

✓ 13

Received memo #3 from Owner: Upload pre-authorized customer receipts.

There are two methods you can use to upload pre-authorized debits.

Click the **Upload Pre-Authorized Debits icon** in the Receivables module window Related Tasks pane as shown:

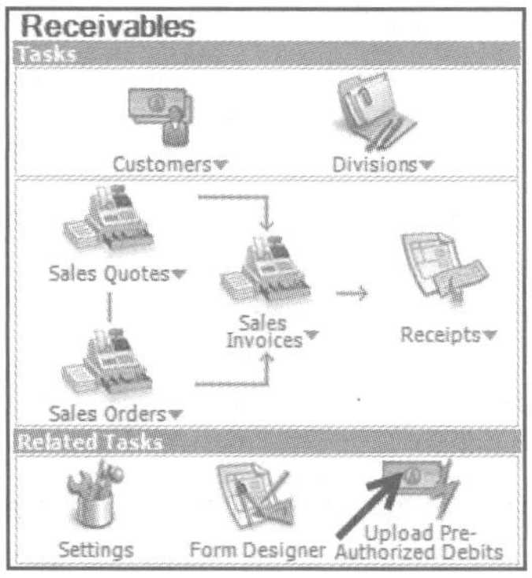

If you are not working in the Receivables module window, you can also upload the transactions from the Home window File menu.

Choose the **File menu** and **Import/Export**, then click **Upload Direct Payments** and **Pre-Authorized Debits** as shown here:

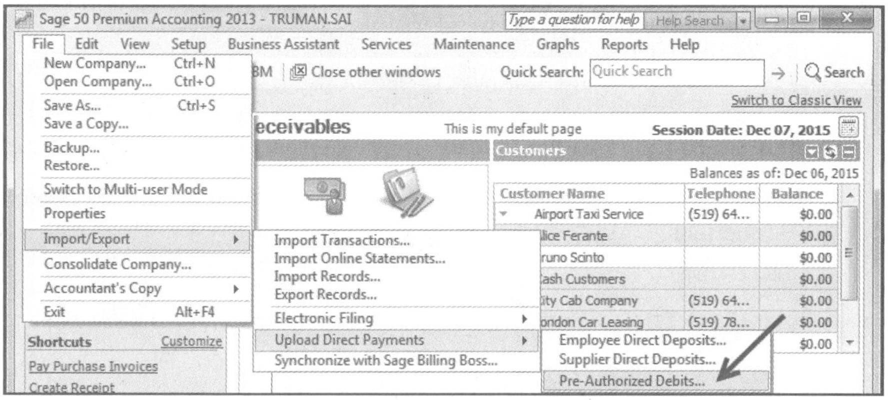

The Upload Transactions window opens, listing the pre-authorized debits entered:

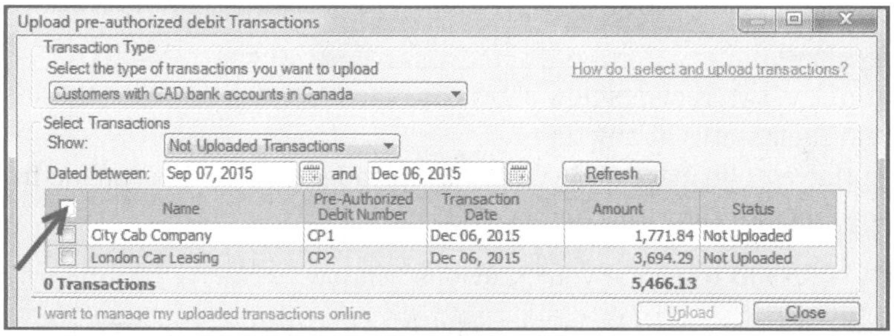

In this window, you can **Select Transactions** to include in the list from the drop-down list for the **Show** field. The default setting is for **Not Uploaded Transactions**. Therefore we see the two receipts we entered. You can also show only transactions already uploaded (see page 526) or all transactions — those uploaded and not yet uploaded.

Each transaction has a check box for selection.

You can select payments individually by clicking the box beside a transaction or all together by clicking the check box in the column heading (marked with the arrow in the previous screen).

Click the **column heading check box** to add checkmarks for both receipts. The Upload button is no longer dimmed.

NOTES
Because of the way this account is set up, you will not be able to follow through with uploading any direct payments.
To cancel the uploading process, click Close to return to the Upload Transactions screen and then click Close to return to your starting point.

Click the **Upload button** to open the authorization screen:

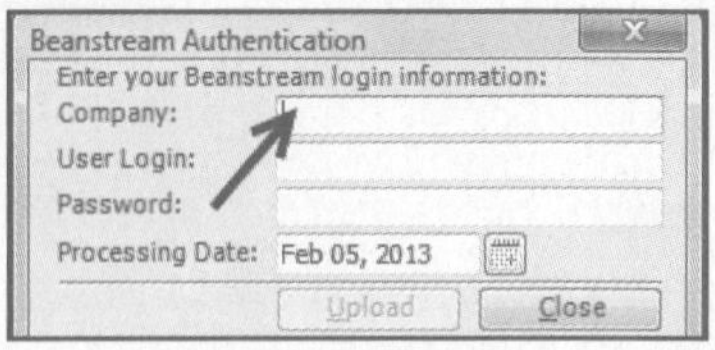

The screens we show for the rest of the process are for illustration purposes only. You will require a Beanstream (or other direct payment) account to continue.

Enter your Beanstream Company name, User Login and Password. Choose the date you want these payments to be processed. The default will be the current calendar date with the money deposited to your account two days after that (see page 535).

Click Upload to begin processing. Depending on the speed of your Internet service, you may see the progress bar.

After the transfer is completed, you will receive a message that the transactions have been uploaded successfully:

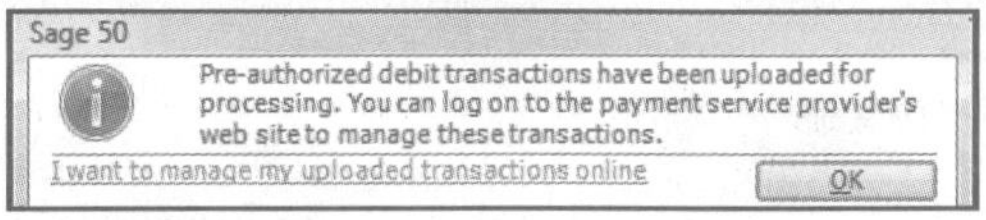

Click OK to return to the Upload Transactions screen.

Choose Uploaded Transactions from the Show drop-down list for Select Transactions:

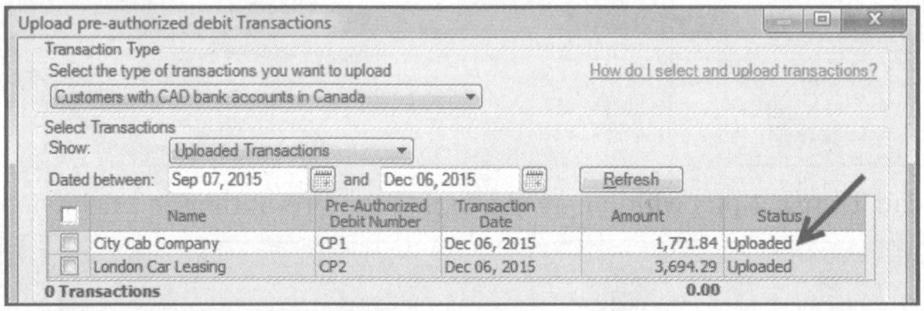

NOTES
You can view transactions for the previous three months.

The status of the two receipts now shows as uploaded. You can view these transactions and their status at any time.

Another option is to manage and view your uploaded transactions online from your Beanstream account. We show this on page 535.

Click **Close** to return to your previous window.

Continue entering the **transactions** up to purchase invoice #ST-1141.

14

Recorded Tridon's Sales Summary as sale #128 for one-time Cash Customers on Dec. 7, 2015. Allocated 100% of revenue and expenses for inventory items to Sales Division and for service items to Service Division.

items sold			amount	total
12	T101	P155/80R14 Tires	$ 70 each	$ 840.00
8	T103	P195/75R15 Tires	95 each	760.00
2	W103	Aluminum R16 Wheels	210 each	420.00
6	SRV02	Alignment - w/caster replacement	130 /job	780.00
2	SRV03	Brake Service - standard pkg	140 /job	280.00
8	SRV06	Oil Service - premium pkg	40 /job	320.00
3	SRV08	Shocks - premium gas-matic	140 /job	420.00
		Harmonized Sales Tax	13%	496.60
Total cash received and deposited to bank account				$4 316.60

NOTES
You will see the Advisor message that inventory items have dropped below the re-order point. Close the Advisor message to continue.
If you click the Item Number List icon in the Sales Journal, you will see that the stock for item T101 is –4 – oversold by four units.

15 Received memo #4 from Owner. Created two new inventory records for winter special packages, both including four tires and wheels and a winter preparation service. One included alignments. A new asset Group account was used for the packages: 1420 Winter-Holiday Tire Packages. The other linked accounts used were Revenue from Sales (account 4020) and Cost of Goods Sold (account 5050). Both items are taxed for HST. Import Duty does not apply.

new item	description	min amt	selling price/unit regular	(preferred)
WHP1	Tires/Wheels/Winter Pkg	0	$ 900 /pkg	($850)
WHP2	Tires/Wheels/Alignment/Winter Pkg	0	$1 400 /pkg	($1 300)

16 Used Form ITA-1 dated Dec 7/15 to assemble five WHP1 Tires/Wheels/Winter Pkg. using 20 tires and 20 wheels as follows:

components			unit cost	total
20	T110	P195/65R16 Tires	$54.4619 each	$1 089.24
20	W107	Chrome-Steel R16 Wheels	37.5888 each	751.78
Additional Costs (for services)				$250.00
assembled items (package)			**unit cost**	**total**
5	WHP1	Tires/Wheels/Winter Pkg	$418.204 each	$2 091.02

17 Used Form ITA-2 dated Dec 7/15 to assemble five WHP2 Tires/Wheels/Alignment/Winter Pkg using 20 tires and 20 wheels as follows:

components			unit cost	total
20	T111	P205/65R16 Tires	$56.7467 each	$1 134.93
20	W103	Aluminum R16 Wheels	87.4739 each	1 749.48
Additional Costs				$500.00
assembled items (package)			**unit cost**	**total**
5	WHP2	Tires/Wheels/Alignment/Winter Pkg	$676.882 each	$3 384.41

SESSION DATE – DECEMBER 14, 2015

18 Recorded purchase order #21 from Snowmaster Tire Company on Dec. 8 at the exchange rate of 0.0135. Payment is due 15 days after delivery on Dec 13.

items purchased			amount
16	T101	P155/80R14 Tires	¥ 36 000
16	T103	P195/75R15 Tires	48 960
8	T106	P195/65R15 Tires	27 280
8	T107	P185/65R15 Tires	28 640
	Freight		6 620
	HST		19 175
Invoice Total			¥166 675

19 Recorded purchase order #22 from Sylverado Wheels on Dec. 8 at the exchange rate of 0.0135. Payment is due 30 days after delivery on Dec 13.

items purchased			amount
16	W106	Chrome-Steel R15 Wheels	¥40 000
8	W109	Steel R14 Wheels	10 800
8	W110	Steel R15 Wheels	12 400
	Freight		5 000
	HST Paid		8 866
Invoice Total			¥77 066

20 On Dec. 9, deposited receipt #82 from Polly Maid Service, cheque #2189 for $996.66 for invoice #124. A discount of $20.34 for early payment was allowed.

NOTES
Packages will not be oversold, so the variance account is not required.

WARNING!
The unit costs change continually as new inventory is purchased at different prices.
Accept the default prices for assembly components and copy the total to the assembled items total. The totals for assembly components (including additional costs) and assembled items must be exactly the same.

NOTES
The services are included as additional costs. You cannot assemble the service items with the inventory to create the package because no purchase costs are associated with the services. Accept the default prices for assembly components and copy the total to the assembled items total. There is no allocation in the Item Assembly Journal.

NOTES
The duty rate does not appear on purchase orders or quotes.

NOTES
Close the Advisor message about the overdrawn account. The transaction, memo #5, will transfer funds to cover the overdraft.

NOTES
Remember to change the currency setting to JPY for the bank transfer.

NOTES
You will see the Advisor message that inventory items have dropped below the re-order point. Close the Advisor message to continue.

21 Entered 0.013 as the exchange rate on Dec. 9 to pay invoices. Paid #ST-842 from Snowmaster Tire Company with cheque #330 for ¥195 700.

22 Paid #SW-724 from Sylverado Wheels with cheque #331 for ¥130 400 in payment.

23 Owner authorized bank transfer of ¥400 000 on memo #5, dated Dec 9/15 to cover cheques written. Money was taken from Chequing account and deposited to Foreign Currency account. The exchange rate for the transfer was 0.013.

24 Tridon made sale #129 to Pronto Pizza & Delivery on Dec. 11. Terms for the sale were 2/10, n/30. 100% of revenues and expenses for inventory items was allocated to Sales Division and for service items to Service Division.

items sold			amount
12	T108	P185/60R15 Tires	$120 each
12	W106	Chrome-Steel R15 Wheels	80 each
4	SRV03	Brake Service - standard pkg	140 /job
4	SRV07	Shocks - economy gas-charged	100 /job
		Harmonized Sales Tax	13%

25 Tridon completed sale #130 to Airport Taxi Service on Dec. 13. Terms for the preferred customer were 2/10, n/30. The Owner has approved the over–credit limit sale. 100% of revenue and expenses for inventory items was allocated to Sales Division and for service items to Service Division.

items sold			amount
8	T103	P195/75R15 Tires	$ 88 each
8	W102	Aluminum R15 Wheels	187 each
8	WN04	Nickel/Chrome Wheel Locks	28 /pkg
6	SRV04	Brake Service - complete pkg	163 /pkg
6	SRV08	Shocks - premium gas-matic	130 /job
		Harmonized Sales Tax	13%

Creating Cost Variances

If items are sold to a customer when the inventory stock is too low to fill the sale completely, the levels in inventory fall below zero and the outstanding items are backordered. The estimated cost of goods for the sale is based on the average cost for the items in stock at the time of the sale. When the items are received, the price may have changed, and the items that fill the rest of the customer's order will have a different cost price from the one recorded for the sale. The difference is the cost variance and is assigned to the linked variance account for the inventory item. The amount of the variance shows in the journal entry for the purchase. Thus two conditions are required for a variance to occur: the inventory is oversold and the cost has changed.

Normally, you do not have to do anything to record a cost variance other than entering the linked account. The program makes the calculations automatically and assigns the amount to the linked variance account for the inventory item.

Enter purchase invoice #ST-1141 from Snowmaster Tire Company.

WARNING!
The exchange rate from the order will be the default and you will need to change it.

✓ 26 Received all items ordered from Snowmaster Tire Company purchase order #21 on Dec. 13/15 with invoice #ST-1141 with payment terms of net 15. Used the exchange rate of 0.0135. Total import duty charged was ¥9 862 (CAD $133.14). The freight expense was allocated entirely to Sales Division. ▶

▶

items purchased			amount	duty rate
16	T101	P155/80R14 Tires	¥ 36 000	7%
16	T103	P195/75R15 Tires	48 960	7%
8	T106	P195/65R15 Tires	27 280	7%
8	T107	P185/65R15 Tires	28 640	7%
	Freight		6 620	
	HST		19 175	
Invoice Total			¥166 675	

Display the **journal entry**. It should match the one shown here:

Truman Tires
Purchases Journal Entry 12/13/15 (J20)

Account Number	Account Description	Division	Foreign A...	Division Frgn Amt	Debits	Credits	Division Amt
1400	Winter Tires		¥149,409		2,017.02	-	
2670	HST Paid on Purchases		¥19,175		258.86	-	
5055	Variance Costs		¥1,333		18.00	-	
5065	Freight Expense		¥6,620		89.37	-	
		- Sales Division		¥6,620			89.37
2200	Accounts Payable		¥166,675		-	2,250.11	
2220	Import Duty Payable		¥9,862		-	133.14	
1 Japanese Yen equals 0.0135000 Canadian Dollars					2,383.25	2,383.25	

There was insufficient stock left for item T101 on Dec. 7 when the cash summary sale was recorded, so the average historic cost for 12 tires, $336, was credited to *Cost of Goods Sold*. Only eight tires were in stock at the time of the sale, with an average cost of $28 ($112 for four tires). When the purchase of item T101 was recorded, the total cost for 16 tires was $520.02, or $130.005 for four tires. The difference, $18.00, between the new cost and the cost in the sales transaction for the four out-of-stock tires is the cost variance.

When you post the transaction, you will see the following warning:

Sage 50 - Confirmation
The following accounts have not been fully allocated:
5055 Variance Costs
Process the transaction anyway?
Yes No Help

Variance costs cannot be allocated, so you must accept the incomplete allocation.

Click **Yes** to continue posting the purchase.

Enter the next group of **transactions** up to memo #6.

27 On Dec. 13, all items ordered from Sylverado Wheels on purchase order #22 arrived. Invoice #SW-1024 confirmed payment terms of net 30 days. Used the exchange rate of 0.0135 for the invoice. Total import duty charged was ¥3 792 (CAD $51.19). The freight expense was allocated entirely to Sales Division.

items purchased			amount	duty rate
16	W106	Chrome-Steel R15 Wheels	¥40 000	6%
8	W109	Steel R14 Wheels	10 800	6%
8	W110	Steel R15 Wheels	12 400	6%
	Freight		5 000	
	HST Paid		8 866	
Invoice Total			¥77 066	

28 Recorded purchase invoice #MT-1521 from MoTech Auto Parts for shipment of wheel nuts received on December 13. Terms for the purchase were 2/10, n/30. The freight amount was allocated to Sales.

items purchased			amount
2 dozen	WN01	Chrome Wheel Nuts	$ 96.00
2 dozen	WN02	Chrome Wheel Locks	240.00
2 dozen	WN03	Nickel/Chrome Wheel Nuts	114.00
2 dozen	WN04	Nickel/Chrome Wheel Locks	288.00
	Freight		20.00
	HST Paid		98.54
Invoice Total			$856.54

NOTES
If you have not closed the journal after entering the order, the duty fields may be omitted from the journal. Close and re-open the journal. They should now be included. You can then add the rates manually if needed.

NOTES
When a purchase entry creates a variance and you have not set up the linked account for variances, you will be prompted to select or create a variance account.

NOTES
The calculated price for the four tires includes the import duty at the rate of 7 percent.

The 16 tires cost ¥36 000 (ST-1141 on pages 528–529) plus duty for a total cost of ¥38 520. This amount is multiplied by the exchange rate of 0.0135 for a cost of CAD $520.02.

NOTES
You may also see this message for rounding errors for currency conversions or credit card fees.

NOTES
Invoice #SW-1024 also creates a cost variance that is not allocated.

NOTES
Enter 2 as the quantity for the purchases from MoTech Auto Parts and edit the amount if necessary.

The wheel locks and nuts have different buying and selling units. They are purchased in boxes of one dozen packages and sold as individual packages.

NOTES
This is a non-inventory sales order. Credit Revenue from Sales.

29 Tridon received sales order #13-1 on Dec. 13 from Lovely U Cosmetics. Contract required five sets of tires and wheels to be installed on Dec. 21/15. The contract price for the job was $5 100 plus $663 HST. Lovely U Cosmetics provided cheque #9754 for $1 800 as a deposit (#13) for the contract. Terms for the balance of the payment were 2/10, n/30 on completion of installation.

Making Import Duty Remittances

Paying the import duty owing on imported merchandise is like paying other taxes. Normally, duty must be paid before the package is released by Customs.

✓ 30 Dec. 14 memo #6 from Owner requested payment of import duty charged on purchases to date to Receiver General. Wrote cheque #202 for $526.29 to pay duty on invoices #ST-916, ST-1141, SW-876 and SW-1024.

NOTES
You can also enter the remittance in the Purchases Journal by choosing Cheque as the method of payment.

Open the **Payments Journal**. The cheque number, bank account and date are correct.

Choose **Make Other Payment**.

Choose **Receiver General for Canada** as the supplier.

Choose **2220 Import Duty Payable** as the account from the Selection list.

You should record the corresponding purchase invoice numbers in the journal as well.

Type `Duty re ST916, ST1141, SW876, SW1024`

Press *tab* to move to the Amount field.

Type `526.29`

Click the **Invoice/Ref. field** and **type** `Memo 6` **Press** *tab*.

Type `Memo 6, Import duty remittance`

Review the **journal entry**. **Close** the **display**. **Make corrections** if needed and then **post** the **transaction**.

Enter the remaining **transactions** up to memo #8.

WARNING!
The unit costs change continually as new inventory is purchased at different prices.
Accept the default prices for assembly components and copy the total to the assembled items total. The totals for assembly components (including additional costs) and assembled items must be exactly the same.

31 Used Form RIF-1001 dated Dec 14/15 to reserve contract items for Lovely U Cosmetics. Free installation included in contract. All items entered at average cost prices. New inventory record was created for the contract using a new linked inventory asset Group account 1440 Reserved Inventory for Workorders and existing accounts 4020 and 5050 for linked Revenue and COGS. HST is charged on the sale and duty does not apply.

new item	description	min amt	regular selling price
LC1	Lovely U Cosmetics Inventory	0	$5 100/contract

reserved (assembly) components		unit cost	total
20 T111	P205/65R16 Tires	$56.7468 each	$1 134.94
20 W107	Chrome-Steel R16 Wheels	37.5885 each	751.77
20 WN04	Nickel/Chrome Wheel Locks	12 /pkg	240.00
contract (assembled) item		**unit cost**	**total**
1 LC1	Lovely U Cosmetics Inventory	$2 126.71 each	$2 126.71

NOTES
Refer to page 416 for assistance with editing the sales order. Editing orders is like editing quotes. Choose Sales Order as the transaction type before choosing the order to adjust. Do not edit the prepayment.
The Divisions column may be hidden in the Sales Journal after entering the order. You can close and then re-open the journal to restore it or use the Allocate tool.

32 Dec. 14 memo #7 included reminder to edit sales order #13-1 from Lovely U Cosmetics. Changed the contract item by entering LC1 as the item number. The quantity ordered (one), price and terms are unchanged.

33 Recorded Tridon's Sales Summary as sale #131 for one-time Cash Customers on Dec. 14, 2015. The following allocations were applied: 100% of service revenue to Service Division; 95% of revenue for WHP1 to Sales and 5% to Service; 90% of revenue for WHP2 to Sales and 10% to Service.

items sold			amount	total
6	SRV01	Alignment - standard	$ 75 /job	$ 450.00
8	SRV03	Brake Service - standard pkg	140 /job	1 120.00
6	SRV05	Oil Service - standard pkg	30 /job	180.00
7	SRV06	Oil Service - premium pkg	40 /job	280.00
12	SRV11	Winter Prep. Service	60 /job	720.00
1	WHP1	Tires/Wheels/Winter Pkg	900 /pkg	900.00
2	WHP2	Tires/Wheels/Alignment/Winter Pkg	1 400 /pkg	2 800.00
	Harmonized Sales Tax		13%	838.50
Total cash received and deposited to bank account				$7 288.50

Direct Deposits – Paying Suppliers

Direct deposits are usually set up for regular bills such as insurance or utilities. The process for suppliers is similar to the one for customers. You need to modify the supplier record (authorize the withdrawal of funds from your bank account and enter your bank account details), choose Direct Deposit as the method of payment for the transactions, enter and post the transactions and upload the payments.

Memo # 8 requests that we modify two supplier records to set up direct deposits.

✓ 34 Memo #8 from Owner: Authorized direct payments and set up of bank account details for London Hydro and Bell Canada:

branch number	institution (bank) number	account number
34809	004	298763

Open the **Payables module window**.

Click **London Hydro** in the Suppliers list pane to open the ledger.

Click the **Direct Deposit tab** to access the screen we need to edit:

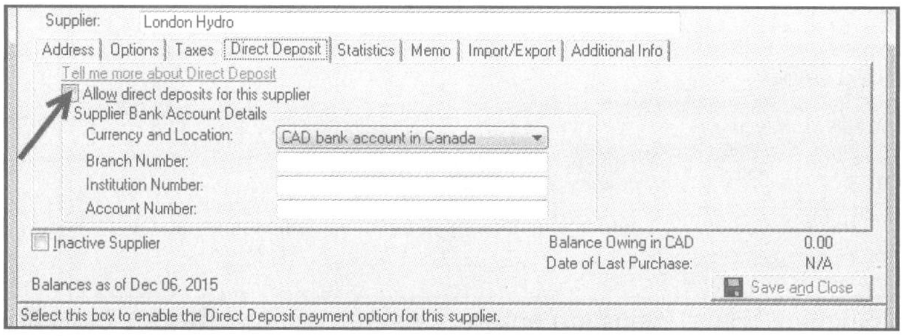

Click **Allow Direct Deposits For This Supplier.**

Enter the **Branch**, **Institution** and **Account numbers**.

Click **Save And Close**.

Open the record for **Bell Canada** and **make** the **same changes** for this supplier record. **Click** **Save And Close**.

You are now ready to enter the hydro bill for which we set up direct deposits.

✓ 35 London Hydro notified us on invoice #LH-31421 of the withdrawal of $293.80 from our account on Dec. 14 to pay $260 for hydro services plus $33.80 HST. The expense was allocated to Sales – 30% and to Service Division – 70%.

NOTES
The same chequing bank account is used for all Payables transactions, so we need to enter the same details for both supplier records. These suppliers will have customer records for Truman Tires authorizing the direct withdrawals.

NOTES
As soon as you click the Allow check box, you will see a note recommending user passwords.

Open the **Purchases Journal** (or the Payments Journal with Make Other Payment selected as the transaction type).

Choose **Direct Deposit** from the Payment Method field to modify the journal:

NOTES
You can edit the starting reference number for Direct Deposits on the Forms screen of Company Settings.

The bank account is entered in the From field and the Cheque No. field label has been replaced by Direct Deposit No. with VP1 (vendor payment #1) entered as the reference.

Enter the **remaining invoice details**, including allocations, in the usual way.

When you review the transaction, you will see that it looks like a regular cash or cheque purchase — the bank account has been credited for the total invoice amount.

Post the **entry**. **Enter** the next **direct deposit invoice** and **close** the **journal**.

36 Invoice #BC-64261 marked as PAID was received from Bell Canada for $90 plus $11.70 HST for telephone services on Dec. 14. $101.70 was withdrawn from our account. 40% of the expense was charged to Sales and 60% to Service Division.

✓ 37 Memo #9 from Owner: Upload the two direct payments to London Hydro and Bell Canada.

Choose the **File menu** and **Import/Export** in the Home window and then **click** **Upload Direct Payments** and **Supplier Direct Deposits**. Or,

Click the **Upload Direct Deposit icon** in the Related Tasks pane of the Payables module window:

These two methods will open the screen we need for the next step, uploading the payments:

NOTES
You may display up to three months of transactions.

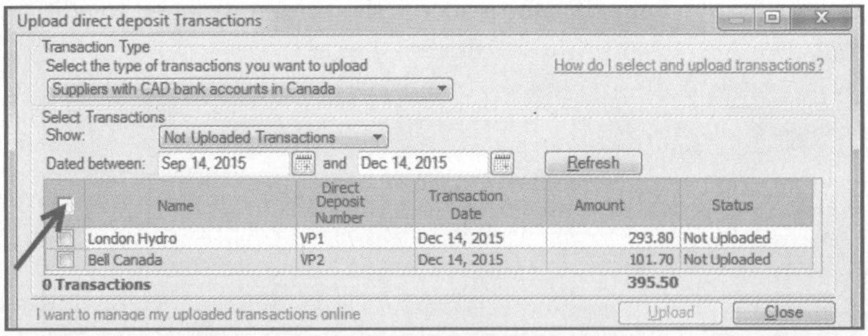

The two payment transactions are entered. As for receipts, we can show Not Uploaded Transactions (the default), Uploaded Transactions or All Transactions — both those uploaded and those not yet uploaded. The selection of payments is also the same. You can select all transactions or individual ones.

Click the **Select check box** in the column heading to add ✓s to both transactions.

Click the **Upload button** to open the Beanstream authorization window:

NOTES
Remember that unless you have a valid account with Beanstream (or another provider), you cannot follow through with uploading the deposits.
To cancel the uploading process, click Close to return to the Upload Transactions screen and then click Close to return to your starting point.

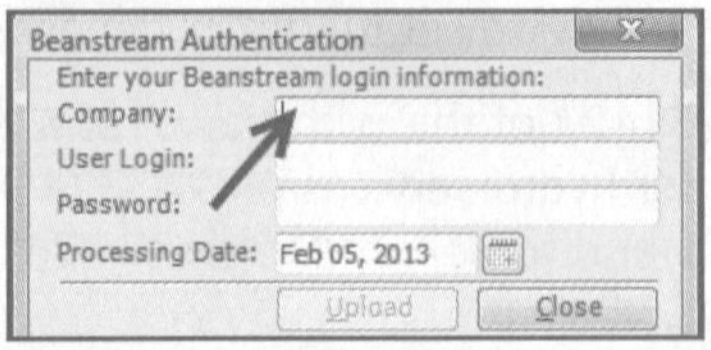

Enter your Beanstream account Company name, User Login and Password and choose the date you want the payments to be processed. Click Upload.

After the uploading has been completed, you will receive a confirmation message:

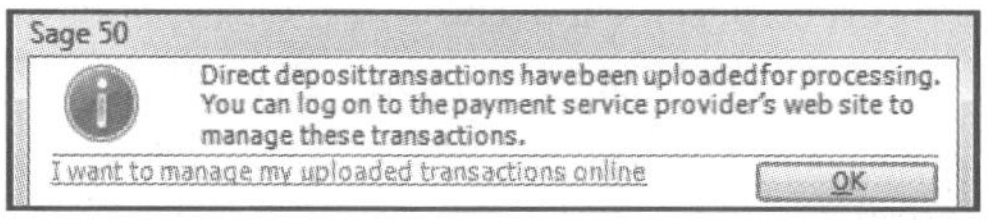

Click OK to return to the Upload Transactions window.
Choose All Transactions from the Show drop-down list:

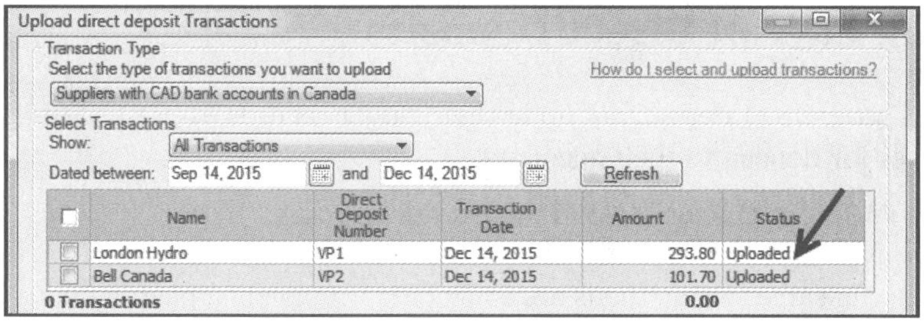

The change in status to Uploaded confirms that we uploaded both deposits.

Click **Close** to return to your previous window.

Complete the **Payroll for Dec 14.** You can use the Payroll Run Journal or enter the individual paycheques in the Paycheques Journal. **Do not post** until you have allocated all amounts.

✓ 38

Complete a payroll cheque run for the hourly employees using Time Summary Sheet #51. The pay period ending date is December 14/15. Allocate 100% of payroll expenses to Service for all employees. Issue deposit slips #112 to #115.

EMPLOYEE TIME SUMMARY SHEET #51 DATED DEC. 14/15

Name of Employee	Week 1	Week 2	Regular Hours	Overtime Hours	No. of Piece Rate Jobs	Sick Days	Personal Days
Delco	40	40	80	0	34	1	–
Holley	40	42	80	2	13	–	1
Monroe	42	40	80	2	20	–	–
Niehoff	40	42	80	2	12	–	–

Allocating in the Payroll and Other Journals

The same principles outlined above to allocate revenues and expenses also apply to the General Journal and Adjustments Journal, and the same Division Settings apply. Payroll allocations have their own setting: by amount, percentage or hours (see page 506).

Once you have entered the journal information for an account that allows allocation, the Allocate tool ☑ will be available. You can use it to enter the allocation information.

In the **Paycheques Journal**, click the Allocate tool ☑.

To correct allocations, click ☑ to re-open the allocation screen.

In the setup for Payroll allocations, you can choose to allocate expenses according to the number of hours worked on each division (see page 506).

In the **Payroll Cheque Run Journal**, use the Division column for the employee who is selected from the list. You can allocate for one employee at a time. Click the employee's name. Then double-click the Division column or choose the

NOTES

Instead of clicking the Division column ✓ beside an employee's name in the Payroll Run Journal, you can click the employee name and then click the Allocate tool button.

You can apply an allocation to the entire transaction (all employees) in the Payroll Run Journal.

Payroll menu and click Allocate To Division to begin the allocation. You can also apply the same allocation to the entire transaction, just as we did in the Sales Journal.

In the Payroll journals, the total payroll expense, not the net pay, is allocated. This includes employer contributions such as EI, CPP, WSIB/WCB and EHT. When you review the journal entry, you will see that all the payroll-related expenses are divided among the divisions according to the percentages you entered. They are shown under the Division column. You may have to scroll to see all the information.

NOTES
All the amounts for an employee will be allocated the same way.

Uploading Payroll Direct Deposits

All employees have direct deposit set up in their ledger records, so we can upload the payroll cheques for deposit to their accounts.

✓ 39 Memo #10 from Owner: Upload the payroll deposits.

Again, the same two methods are available for uploading payroll deposits.

Click the **Upload Direct Deposit icon** 

in the Related Tasks pane of the Employees and Payroll module window. Or,

Choose the **File menu** and **Import/Export** in the Home window and then **click Upload Direct Payments** and **Employee Direct Deposits**:

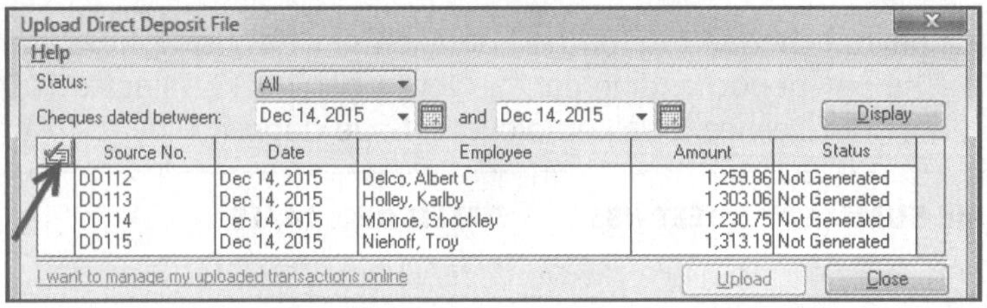

NOTES
The Status drop-down list options are to show Generated deposits, Not Generated deposits or All deposits.

The four employees we paid are listed. **All** is entered as the Status selection with the range of dates for the cheques we are uploading. All deposits are not generated yet.

Click , the **Select check box** in the column heading, to add ✓s for all employees.

Click the **Upload button** to open the Beanstream authorization window.

Enter your Beanstream account Company name, User Login and Password and choose the date you want the payments to be processed. Click Upload.

NOTES
The Upload button becomes available as soon as you select an employee.

After the uploading has been completed, you will receive a confirmation message:

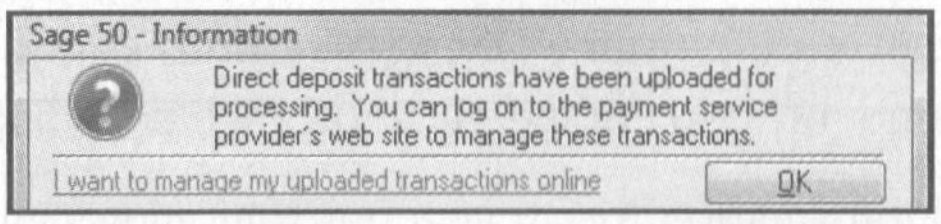

Click OK. Choose Generated from the drop-down list for Status:

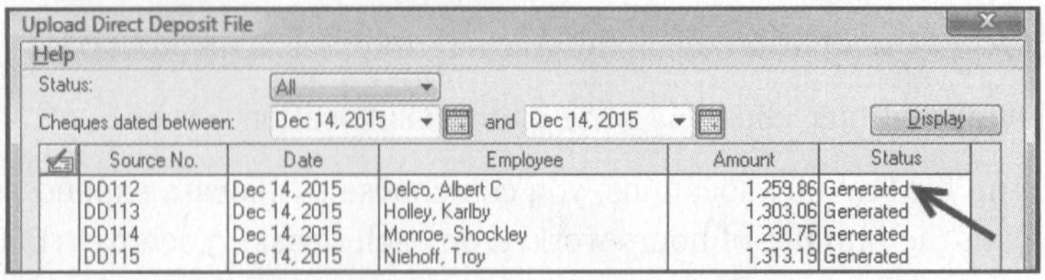

All transactions now have Generated as their status.

Click Close to finish your uploading session.

Reviewing Your Uploaded Transactions

At any time you can review your uploaded transaction online.

Click I Want To Manage My Uploaded Transactions Online in any upload window to review your transactions. You will be connected to the Beanstream login page. Enter your Beanstream account Company name, User Login and Password. Click Processing and Employee Direct Deposit to see your employee transactions:

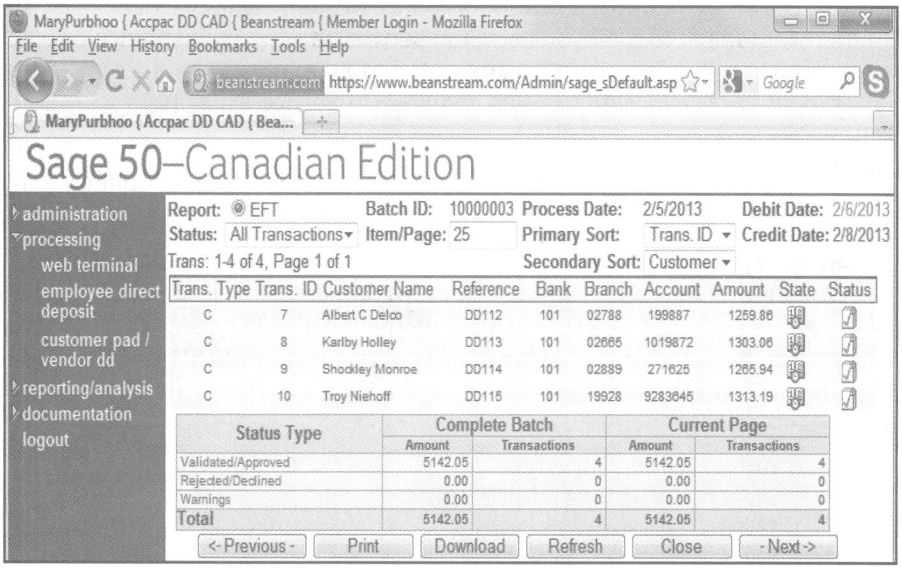

Click Customer PAD/Vendor DD and any line in the summary to see the details:

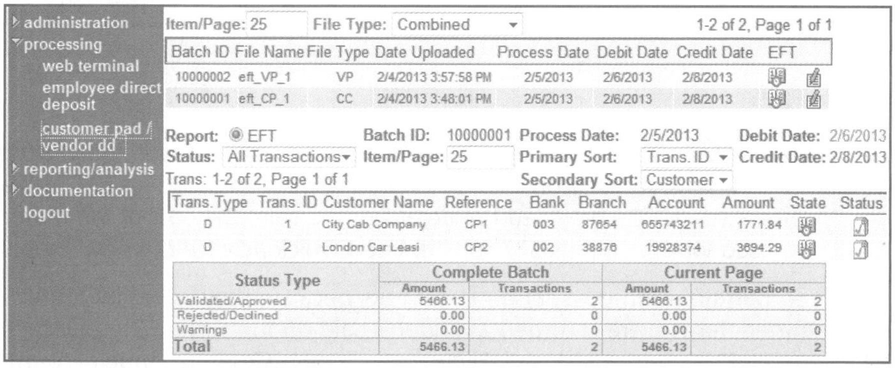

From your account, you can edit the transactions you have uploaded.

Click the Edit tool in a Summary line of the review page, that is, CP1, VP1 or EFT1 to open the options for editing:

You can change the processing date or delete the batch of all items you uploaded at the same time. If you choose Delete, you will be asked to confirm your decision:

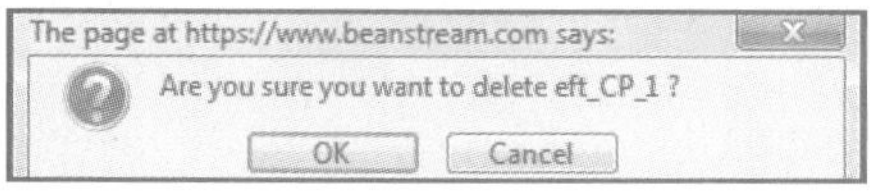

Click OK to continue. Click Logout when finished, to end the session safely.

Enter the remaining **transactions** for December.

NOTES
Our test account with Beanstream will not permit you to follow through with the uploading and reviewing of transactions.

NOTES
The option to manage transactions online is available from all Upload Transactions windows as well as from the uploading confirmation message.

NOTES
Remember that your debits are the bank's credits and vice versa.

NOTES
If you upload a payment that you previously uploaded, you will see the warning about the duplicate entry when you log into the account and view that item.

NOTES
Clicking a summary line such as eft1_CP_1 (for customer pre-authorized debits) will show the details for all the items you uploaded in that single batch.

NOTES
Notice that there is a delay between the date of processing and the date that funds will be withdrawn. This allows time for corrections if necessary.

SESSION DATE – DECEMBER 21, 2015

40 Paid invoice #ST-916 from Snowmaster Tire Company with cheque #332 for ¥253 459 on Dec. 16 in payment of account. The exchange rate was 0.0131.

41 On memo #11 dated Dec 16/15, Owner authorized transfer of ¥400 000 to cover cheques written. Money was taken from Chequing account and deposited to Foreign Currency account. The exchange rate for the transfer was 0.0131.

42 On December 17, wrote cheque #203 to Western Hydraulic Repairs for $452 to pay for repairs to the hydraulic lift in service bay and maintenance of other lifts. Repairs on invoice #WH-690 amounted to $400 plus $52 HST. 20% of the expense was allocated to Sales and 80% to Service Division.

43 Deposited receipt #83 from Pronto Pizza & Delivery on Dec. 19/15. Applied cheque #399 for $3 720.86 to invoice #129 with $75.94 discount for early payment.

44 Recorded Tridon's sale #132 to Efren Barrato on Dec. 20. Barrato paid by MasterCard. Allocations for the sale were applied as follows: 100% of the revenue and expenses for inventory items to Sales Division; 100% of revenue for service items to Service Division; 95% of revenue for WHP1 to Sales and 5% to Service Division; and 90% of revenue for WHP2 to Sales and 10% to Service.

items sold			amount	total
4	WN01	Chrome Wheel Nuts	$ 10 /pkg	$ 40.00
1	SRV04	Brake Service - complete pkg		175.00
5	SRV05	Oil Service - standard pkg	30 /job	150.00
5	SRV06	Oil Service - premium pkg	40 /job	200.00
2	SRV08	Shocks - premium gas-matic	140 /job	280.00
1	WHP1	Tires/Wheels/Winter Pkg		900.00
1	WHP2	Tires/Wheels/Alignment/Winter Pkg		1 400.00
	Harmonized Sales Tax		13%	408.85
Total paid by MasterCard #5809 8213 6238 1601				$3 553.85

45 Cleaning fluids, cleaning cloths and other garage supplies were purchased from Motor Supply Company on Dec. 21 and paid for with cheque #204 for $237.30. Invoice #MS-40002 provided the details of the sale: the cost of the materials purchased was $210 plus $27.30 HST. Used Quick Add for the new supplier.

NOTES
Remember to enter the quantity returned with a minus sign and to change the default account.
Enter Tridon as the salesperson so that her net sales revenue will be calculated correctly for the sales commission.

46 Efren Barrato returned a set of wheel nuts because they were not required. The returned items were recorded as Tridon's sale on form #R-132 on Dec. 21 using account 4130 Sales Returns & Allowances, a new Group revenue account. The handling charge was recorded to Other Revenue and all amounts were allocated to Sales. With the Owner's permission, the refund was paid in cash.

items returned			amount	total
–4	WN01	Chrome Wheel Nuts	$10 /pkg	–$40.00
	Handling charge (20% of total sales price)			9.04
	Harmonized Sales Tax		13%	–4.02
Total cash paid to customer				–$34.98

WARNING!
When filling the sales order, change the method of payment to Pay Later.

47 Sales order #13-1 for Lovely U Cosmetics was filled by Tridon on Dec. 21 and recorded as sale #133. Terms of sale were 2/10, n/30 with $3 963 as the balance owing. Revenue from the sale was allocated entirely to the Sales Division.

items sold			amount
1	LC1	Lovely U Cosmetics Inventory	$5 100
	Harmonized Sales Tax		13%

48 Deposited receipt #84, cheque #9902 from Airport Taxi Service for $4 631.15 in payment of invoice #130 on Dec. 21. $94.51 discount allowed.

49 Recorded invoice #TS-817 for shocks and parts for service work from TuffArm Shocks on Dec. 21. Cost of the parts was $2 000 plus $260 HST. Invoice total $2 260 is due in 30 days.

SESSION DATE – DECEMBER 28, 2015

50 Wrote cheque #205 to MoTech Auto Parts for $839.41 to pay invoice #MT-1521 on Dec. 22 and take early payment discount of $17.13.

51 Tridon made an Interac sale (sale #134) to Cedric Ng on Dec. 22, 2015. 100% of the revenue from the sale of inventory items was allocated to the Sales Division; 100% of revenue for the service item to Service Division; and 90% of revenue for WHP2 to Sales and 10% to Service Division.

items sold			amount	total
4	T111	P205/65R16 Tires	$ 135 each	$ 540.00
4	W103	Aluminum R16 Wheels	210 each	840.00
2	WHP2	Tires/Wheels/Winter Pkg	1 400 /pkg	2 800.00
2	SRV03	Brake Service - standard pkg	140 /job	280.00
		Harmonized Sales Tax	13%	579.80
Total paid in full by debit card #5300 5291 6730 8161				$5 039.80

52 Received invoice #SW-1159 from Sylverado Wheels with shipment on Dec. 22 with payment terms of net 30 days. Total import duty for the purchase was ¥1 440 (CAD $19.30). The purchase was recorded with an exchange rate of 0.0134 and the freight was charged to Sales.

items purchased			amount	duty rate
8	W107	Chrome-Steel R16 Wheels	¥24 000	6%
	Freight		1 000	
	HST Paid		3 250	
Invoice Total			¥28 250	

53 Purchased brake hoses, cables, pads and other brake parts and hardware from MoTech Auto Parts on December 24. Invoice #MT-1894 showed $800 for the parts plus $104 HST. Total amount of $904 due in 30 days; 2% discount if full amount is paid in 10 days.

54 One Chrome-Steel R17 Wheel (W108) that was dented beyond repair by machinery was written off on Dec. 26. Details of the accident were recorded in memo #12. 100% of the write-off was allocated to the Sales Division.

55 Memo #13 from the Owner on Dec. 27 requested that the HST owing be remitted as of November 30, 2015. Issued cheque #206 for $3 340 in full payment. (Use Trial Balance amounts on page 497.)

56 Complete a payroll cheque run for the hourly employees using Time Summary Sheet #52. The pay period ending date is December 28/15. Use the Bonus field for the holiday bonus amount. Allocate 100% of the payroll expenses to Service for all employees. Issue deposit slips #116 to #119.

EMPLOYEE TIME SUMMARY SHEET #52 DATED DEC. 28/15

Name of Employee	Week 1	Week 2	Regular Hours	Overtime Hours	No. of Piece Rate Jobs	Bonus	Sick Days	Personal Days
Delco	40	42	80	2	10	200	–	–
Holley	42	40	80	2	5	200	–	–
Monroe	42	40	80	2	6	200	1	–
Niehoff	40	44	80	4	5	200	–	2

NOTES

If you have difficulty accessing the Divisions column in the Payroll Run Journal, you can click an employee name and then click the Allocate tool button.

57 Pre-authorized withdrawals from the chequing account were recorded on Dec. 28. Debit memo #92564 from Universal Bank itemized the transaction details. The mortgage payment of $1 000 included an interest amount of $790 and the loan payment of $1 200 included $200 for interest. The remaining amounts for these withdrawals were principal. Bank charges of $65 were also on this memo. The expense amounts were shared equally between Sales and Service Divisions.

58

TRUMAN TIRES

ITEM ASSEMBLY COMPLETION FORM ITA-#3

Dated 12/28/15

			Unit cost	Total
Assembled items				
3	WHP2	Tires/Wheels/Alignment/ Winter Pkg.	676.8733 each	2 030.62
Components used				
12	T111	P205/65R16 Tires	56.745 each	680.94
12	W103	Aluminum R16 Wheels	87.4736 each	1 049.68
Additional Costs for service				$300.00

NOTES

Accept the default prices for assembly components and copy the Total to the assembled items Amount field.

59 On Dec. 28, 2015, Tridon sold winter packages to City Cab Company (sale #135). $5 094.04 was uploaded to our bank account from PAD sale with 2% discount. For WHP1, 95% of revenue was allocated to Sales and 5% to Service Division. For WHP2, 90% of revenue was allocated to Sales and 10% to Service Division.

items sold			amount
2	WHP1	Tires/Wheels/Winter Pkg	$ 900 /pkg
2	WHP2	Tires/Wheels/Alignment/Winter Pkg	1 400 /pkg
	Harmonized Sales Tax		13%

60 Tire purchase from Snowmaster Tire Company was received on Dec. 28 with invoice #ST-1383. Payment is due in 15 days. Total import duty for the purchase was ¥13 650 (CAD $180.18). The purchase was recorded with an exchange rate of 0.0132 and the freight amount was charged to Sales.

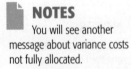

items purchased			amount	duty rate
12	T108	P185/60R15 Tires	¥ 42 000	7%
20	T111	P205/65R16 Tires	85 000	7%
8	T112	P205/60R16 Tires	32 000	7%
8	T114	P225/60R17 Tires	36 000	7%
	Freight		4 660	
	HST Paid		25 956	
Invoice Total			¥225 616	

NOTES

You will see another message about variance costs not fully allocated.

61 Recorded invoice #SW-1419 from Sylverado Wheels on Dec. 28. Payment is due in 30 days. Total import duty for the purchase was ¥17 520 (CAD $231.27). The purchase was recorded with an exchange rate of 0.0132 and the freight amount was charged to Sales.

items purchased			amount	duty rate
8	W102	Aluminum R15 Wheels	¥ 48 000	6%
16	W103	Aluminum R16 Wheels	108 000	6%
8	W104	Aluminum R17 Wheels	56 000	6%
8	W106	Chrome-Steel R15 Wheels	20 000	6%
20	W107	Chrome-Steel R16 Wheels	60 000	6%
	Freight		5 000	
	HST Paid		38 610	
Invoice Total			¥335 610	

62

TRUMAN TIRES

Truman Tires
600 Westminster St., London, ON N6P 3B1
Tel: (519) 729-3733 Fax: (519) 729-7301

Date of sale: Dec. 28/15

To: Summary
One-time cash customers

INVOICE 136

No.	Item		Price	Total	Division*
8	T102	P175/70R14 Tires	85	680.00	Sales
16	T112	P205/60R16 Tires	140	2 240.00	Sales
8	W101	Aluminum R14 Wheels	180	1 440.00	Sales
2	W103	Aluminum R16 Wheels	210	420.00	Sales
8	W105	Chrome-Steel R14 Wheels	70	560.00	Sales
12	WN02	Chrome Wheel Locks	25	300.00	Sales
10	SRV01	Alignment - standard	75	750.00	Service
6	SRV03	Brake Service - standard pkg	140	840.00	Service
6	SRV07	Shocks - economy gas-charged	100	600.00	Service

Terms: Cash			
*** Internal use only**	**Salesperson:** Tridon	**HST# 230 192 821** **13%**	1 017.90
Total cash deposited to bank 12/28/15 T Tridon			**8 847.90**

63 Paid invoice #ST-1141 from Snowmaster Tire Company with cheque #333 for ¥166 675 on Dec. 28. The recorded exchange rate was 0.0132.

SESSION DATE – DECEMBER 31, 2015

64 Memo #14 from Owner on Dec. 31 requested a payroll run for Fram and Tridon, salaried employees, with holiday bonus amounts ($300 for Fram and $500 for Tridon) added. Deposit slips #120 and 121 were issued. 50% of Tridon's pay was allocated to Sales and 50% to Service. 60% of Fram's pay was allocated to Sales and 40% to Service.

NOTES
Use the Bonus field for the bonus amounts.

NOTES
Credit card fees may not be fully allocated because of rounding the amounts.

65

TRUMAN TIRES

Truman Tires
600 Westminster St., London, ON N6P 3B1
Tel: (519) 729-3733 Fax: (519) 729-7301

Date of sale: Dec. 31/15

To: Louise Binder
One-time customer

INVOICE 137

No.	Item		Price	Total	Division*
8	T114	P225/60R17 Tires	150	1 200.00	Sales
8	W104	Aluminum R17 Wheels	225	1 800.00	Sales
8	WN04	Nickel/Chrome Wheel Locks	30	240.00	Sales
2	SRV04	Brake Service - complete pkg	175	350.00	Service
2	SRV08	Shocks - premium gas-matic	140	280.00	Service

Terms: Visa (4515 7827 4563 8900)			
*** Internal use only**	**Salesperson:** Tridon	**HST# 230 192 821** 13%	503.10
Total deposited to bank 12/31/15 T Tridon			4 373.10

66

TRUMAN TIRES

MEMO #15

Date 12/31/2015
From: T. Tridon
To: T. Truman

Paid import duty charged to Receiver General on all outstanding purchases (#SW-1159, ST-1383, SW-1419).

Wrote cheque #207 for $430.75 to pay balance in full.

Trish Tridon

NOTES
Use the Paycheques Journal for Tridon's commission so that you can change the tax amounts. Remove the salary hours and amounts. Click the Taxes tab. Choose the Enter Taxes Manually tool to open the tax fields for editing. Enter 42.04 in the Income Tax field. Do not remove the CPP amount. Remove the CSB deduction on the Deductions tab screen and the number of hours worked on the Entitlements tab screen.

The Sales by Salesperson Report includes revenue from services. The sales commission is based only on the sales revenue.

67 Issued cheque $208 for $420.40 to Tridon as her sales commission (1% of sales less returns based on December Income Statement amounts). Memo #16 from the Owner on Dec. 31 authorized the payment. Allocated 100% of the commission to Sales. 10% income tax was withheld. (Refer to margin Notes.)

68 Memo #17 included a reminder to record payroll remittances for the pay period ending December 31. Entered Memo #17a, 17b, etc., as the reference. Cheques #209 to 213 were submitted in payment.

Receiver General: Canada for EI, CPP and Income Tax
Minister of Finance: EHT
Equity Life: CSB Payable
CAW Union: Union Dues
Workplace Safety & Insurance Board: WSIB

69 Received credit memo #65925 from Universal Bank on Dec. 31. $215 interest was deposited to chequing account. This entry required a new Group account 4200 Revenue from Interest. 50% of the interest revenue was allocated to Sales and 50% to the Service Division.

70 Memo #18 from Owner on Dec. 31 reminded that adjusting entries were needed for supplies and parts used. Allocated 90% of the Parts and Garage supplies to Service and 10% to Sales. Allocated 50% of the Office Supplies to Service and 50% to Sales. Inventory counts were used for the following entries:

part/supplies used	amount	new account required
Brakes and Shocks Parts	$1 900	5160 Brakes & Shocks Parts Used
Supplies: Garage	420	5170 Supplies Used: Garage
Supplies: Office	130	5180 Supplies Used: Office

Displaying Division Reports

Division reports can be displayed from the Division window, from the Division module window Reports pane drop-down list, from the Home window Reports menu and from the Report Centre. We will continue to show reports from the Report Centre.

Click the **Report Centre icon** 

in the Home window.

Click **Division** to open the list of division reports:

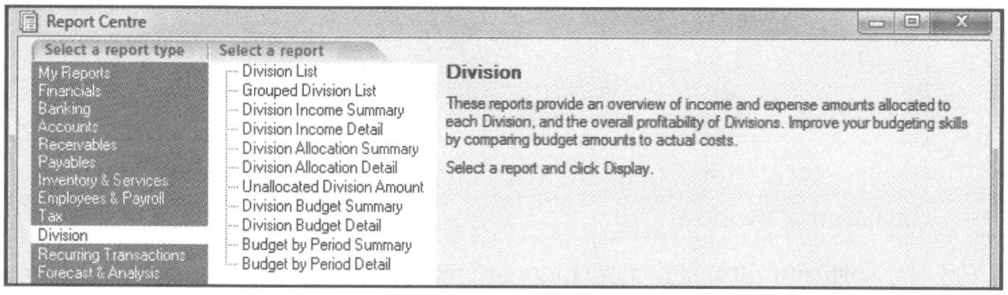

Displaying the Division List

Click **Division List**. **Click Modify This Report** to open the report options:

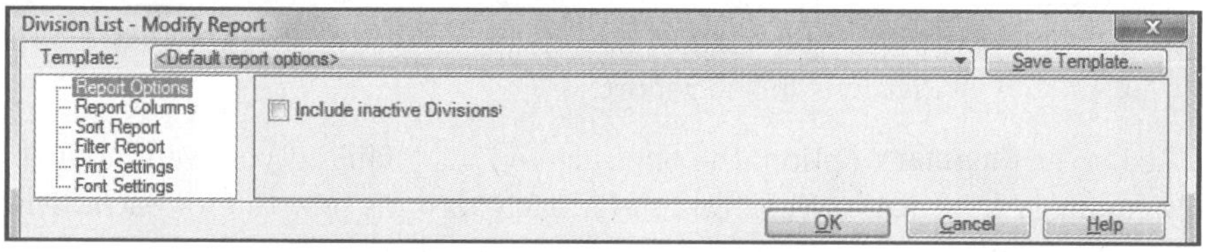

Or choose the Reports menu, then choose Lists and click Division.

Click Report Columns to customize the fields shown on the report.

Click **OK**. **Close** the **display** when you have finished viewing the report.

NOTES
Allocation for the new revenue and expense accounts should be the default setting.

PRO VERSION
Remember that if you have not changed the ledger name, you will see Project instead of Division throughout the report menus and options.
For other company types, Division may be replaced by a name that is appropriate for that type of company. Refer to Appendix B in this text.

NOTES
The terms used for other types of industries will replace Division in all report titles and fields.

PRO VERSION
The Pro version does not have Grouped Division Lists or Unallocated Division Amount Reports.

CLASSIC VIEW
Right-click the Divisions icon 

to select it. Click the Display tool .

NOTES
You can display the Division Allocation Detail Report from the Division List.

Displaying the Grouped Division List

Click **Grouped Division List**. **Click Modify This Report** to see the options.

Click the **Grouped By drop-down list arrow** to see the ways you can organize the report:

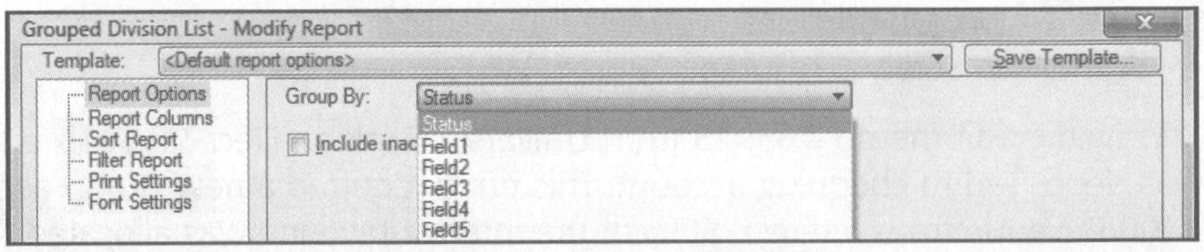

You can group the divisions by division status (e.g., pending, in progress and so on) or by any of the additional fields you added for the ledger.

Choose the **criterion** for grouping.

Click **OK**. **Close** the **display** when you have finished viewing the report.

Displaying Division Income Reports

NOTES

You can drill down to the Division Income Detail Report from the Division Income Summary Report. You can drill down to the Division Ledger, Journal Report, General Ledger, Customer or Supplier Aged or Employee report or look up the transaction from the Division Income Detail Report.

The Division Income Report provides an income statement with revenue, expenses and net income for each division you select for the report.

Click **Division Income Summary**. **Click Modify This Report**:

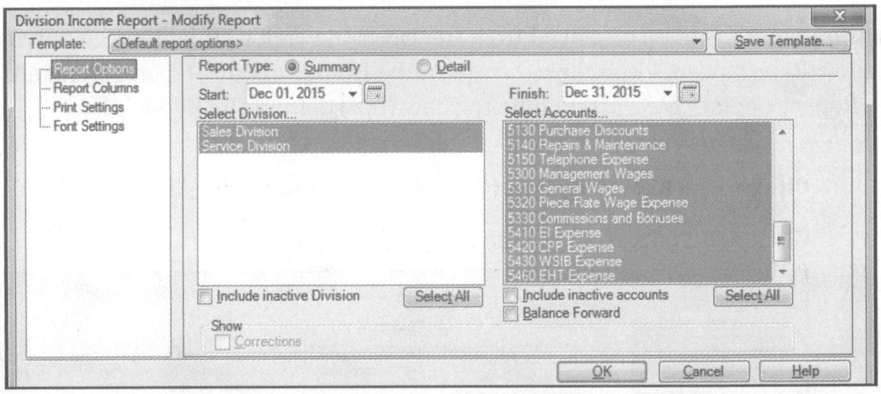

Or choose the Reports menu, then choose Division and click Income to display the Options window.

You can sort and filter Division Income Detail reports by date, comment, source, journal number and amount per transaction. As usual, the fiscal start and session dates are the defaults. All divisions and accounts are selected initially.

Enter the **beginning** and **ending dates** for the report.

Click a **division** to change the selection. **Press** and **hold** ctrl and **click** the **divisions** you want to include in the report. **Click Select All** to include all divisions in the report.

Leave the **Summary** option, the one selected by default, if you want your report to show summary information (i.e., totals) for each account selected for each division. The **Detail** option provides complete journal information for each account for each division selected, including the names of all customers, suppliers and employees, as well as the document's reference number, journal entry number and date. Both options provide a calculation for revenue minus expense.

Next you should select the revenue and expense accounts you want in the report.

Click an **account** to change the selection. **Press** and **hold** ctrl and **click** the **accounts** you want to include in the report or **click Select All** to include them all.

Click **OK** to display the report. **Close** the **display** when finished.

Displaying Division Allocation Reports

When you allow allocation for Balance Sheet accounts and enter allocation amounts for them, they are reported in the Division Allocation Report together with Income Statement accounts. The Division Income Report has only revenue and expense accounts.

NOTES
You must allow allocations for the Balance Sheet accounts to see all the accounts in this report. Without this change, the Account list will include only the revenue and expense accounts.

Click **Division Allocation Summary**. **Click Modify This Report**:

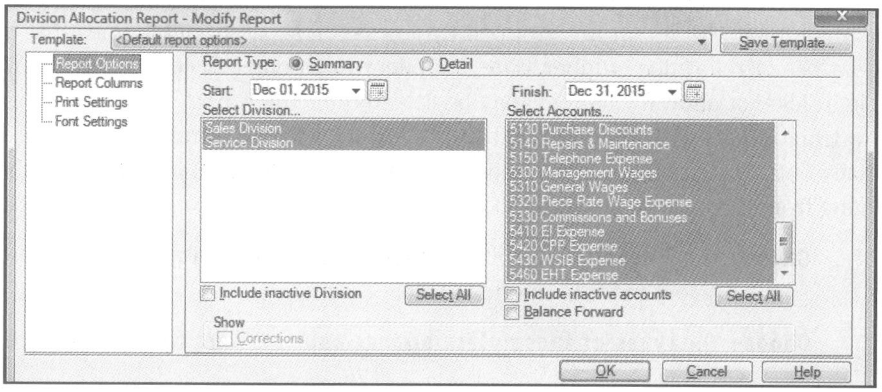

From any Home window, choose the Reports menu, then choose Division and click Allocation to display the Division Allocation Report Options window.

NOTES
Drill-down reports from the Allocation Report are the same as the reports from the Division Income Report.

The Division Allocation Report shows the breakdown of amounts for each division by account. It is similar to the Division Income Report, but the total revenue and expense and the net division income are omitted. Instead, a single total for all accounts is provided for each division.

Although the report options look the same as for the Income Report, if you scroll up the list of accounts you will see that Balance Sheet accounts are included. All reports for which you have allowed allocation will be on the list.

Enter the **Start** and **Finish dates** for the report.

Click a **division** to change the selection. **Press** and **hold** ctrl and **click** the **divisions** you want to include in the report or **click Select All**.

Like the Income Report, the Summary option will show totals and the Detail option provides complete journal information for each account for each division.

After you have indicated which options you want, choose the accounts.

Press and **hold** ctrl and **click** the **accounts** you want or **click Select All**.

Click **OK** to display the report. **Close** the **display** when you have finished.

Displaying the Unallocated Division Amounts Report

If you have any journal transactions with amounts that were not fully allocated, you can show all these transactions in the Unallocated Division Amounts Report. The incomplete allocation may have occurred because you did not add the allocation details or because the program did not allow you to enter them (such as for cost variance amounts).

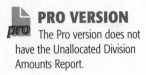

Click **Unallocated Division Amount**. **Click** **Modify This Report** to see the options:

PRO VERSION

The Pro version does not have the Unallocated Division Amounts Report.

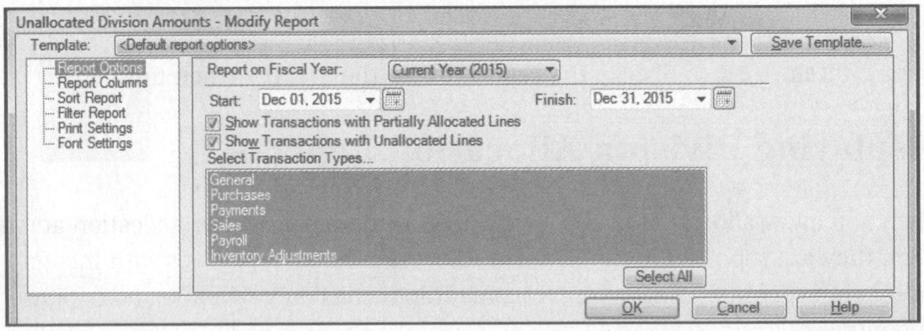

Or choose the Reports menu, then choose Division and click Unallocated Amounts.

Amounts in the report are grouped by journal on separate detail lines that include the invoice or reference number, date, supplier or customer, account and amount. All journals that allow allocations may be selected for the report. You can also choose to show transactions with amounts that were partially allocated, fully unallocated or both. Initially both types of incomplete allocations are selected for all journals with the dates ranging from the earliest transaction to the session date.

Choose the **journals** you want included in the report. **Press** *ctrl* and **click** to select more than one journal.

Choose the **types of incomplete allocations** you want to show — partial or full.

Enter the **Start** and **Finish dates** for the report

Click **OK** to display the report. **Close** the **display** when finished.

Adding Division Details to Journal Reports

When you have entered division information in a journal, you can include the allocation details in any journal report.

Click **Financials** in the Select A Report Type list.

Click **All Journal Entries**. **Click** **Modify This Report**:

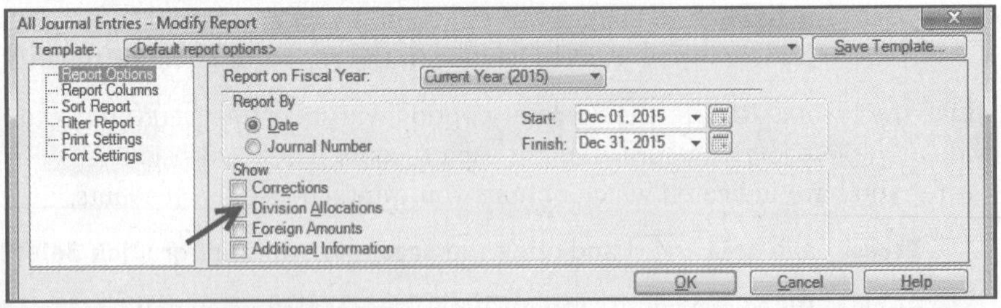

The Journal Report Options window includes a check box for division allocations under the Show heading. For a complete Journal Report, you should also show foreign amounts, corrections and additional information.

NOTES

If you include all the details in the journal report, you should print the report in landscape orientation.

Click **Division Allocations** to include division information in journal reports. By default, journal reports do not include division details.

Choose the **other details** that you want to include in the report and **click** **OK**.

Close the **display** when finished. **Close** the **Report Centre**.

Printing Division Reports

To print division reports, display the report you want using the instructions above.

Click the Print tool or choose the File menu and click Print.

Displaying Division Management Reports

There are management reports for the Division Ledger, just as there are for other ledgers in Sage 50. Management Reports can be displayed only from the Home window Reports menu.

Choose the **Reports menu**, then **choose Management Reports** and **click Division** to see the list of management reports:

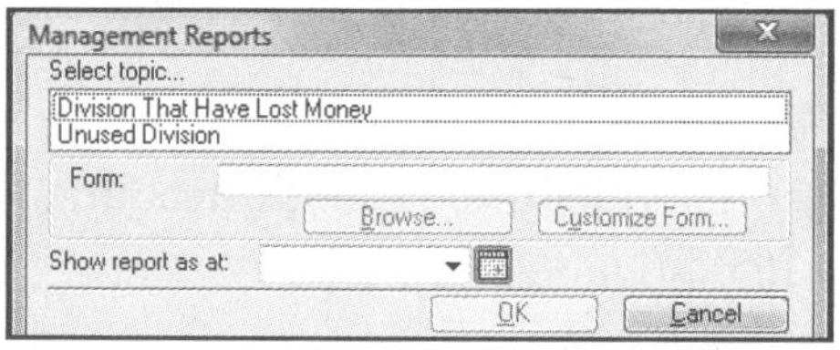

Click the **topic** for the report. **Click OK** to display the report. **Close** the **display** when you have finished.

R E V I E W

The Student DVD with Data Files includes Review Questions and Supplementary Cases for this chapter.

CLASSIC VIEW
You can also access Management Reports from the Advice tool in the Classic view Home window tool bar.

WARNING!
Check that the file location for the form used by the report is correct for your program settings.

NOTES
The Service Division is operating at a loss according to the Management Report.

CHAPTER FOURTEEN

Village Galleries

OBJECTIVES

After completing this chapter, you should be able to

- ***turn on*** the budgeting feature in Sage 50
- ***determine*** and ***enter*** budgeting periods and amounts
- ***allocate*** budget amounts to revenue and expense accounts
- ***enter*** transactions involving Quebec Sales Tax
- ***display*** and ***print*** income statements with budget comparisons
- ***graph*** budget reports
- ***analyze*** budget reports
- ***print*** invoices in batches

COMPANY INFORMATION

Company Profile

NOTES
Village Galleries
509 Boul. Rouin
Montreal, QC H3F 5G5
Tel: (514) 529-6391
Fax: (514) 529-7622
Business No.: 236 412 540

Village Galleries, located in Outremont, an upscale area of Montreal, is owned and operated by Renée and Gilles Montand, a husband-and-wife partnership. The small family-run business recently hired one employee, who will earn a commission on sales. She works in the store several days a week but the Montands maintain the regular operation of the business. Renée performs the accounting duties for the business. Other jobs are occasionally subcontracted.

The store, more like a furniture boutique, carries a limited range of high-quality inventory, selling to clients who are selective in their furniture and accessory preferences. Accessories and furniture for living rooms, bedrooms, dining rooms and kitchens compose the major inventory items in the boutique. The brass furniture pieces are imported from Italy, and some items are high-quality reproductions of antiques made in small Quebec furniture factories by respected artisans. Most of the furniture is made of wood or wood frames covered with fine fabrics. The choice of wood includes mahogany, oak, cherry, ash and, of course, maple and pine. Rich select woods of the highest quality are used to create solid wood pieces, but sometimes expensive veneers are used to complement the designs. In addition, the furniture boutique sells home accessories such as lamps, a small selection of handmade Persian and Oriental rugs made of wool and silk, mirrors and original framed numbered prints imported from Italy.

Most customers are local but, occasionally, customers from abroad who visit Montreal ask for furniture to be shipped to them. Delivery (shipping or freight) is charged on most orders and exported items. Preferred price list customers do not pay for delivery, and they receive discounted inventory prices. All account customers are entitled to a before-tax 2 percent discount if they settle their accounts within 10 days. After 30 days, interest charges accrue at the rate of 1.5 percent per month. Customer deposits from 20 to 25 percent of the total sale are required on all orders. Customers may pay by cheque, cash or credit card.

Some suppliers with whom Village Galleries has accounts require deposits to accompany purchase orders, and some suppliers offer after-tax purchase discounts for early payments. The store has a business credit card account with American Express.

The currency for all foreign transactions, including the purchases from Italy and the sales to European customers, is the euro (€). Foreign prices for inventory are calculated from the exchange rate at the time of sale, so foreign prices are not entered in the inventory ledger. Village Galleries pays import duties on the imported furniture but not on original art work such as the numbered prints.

Renée Montand used the following to set up the accounting files for Village Galleries in Sage 50:

- Chart of Accounts
- Post-Closing Trial Balance
- Supplier Information
- Customer Information
- Employee Information
- Inventory Information
- Accounting Procedures

CHART OF ACCOUNTS

VILLAGE GALLERIES

ASSETS

Current Assets
1060 Chequing Bank Account
1070 Visa Bank Account
1080 MasterCard Bank Account
1090 Bank Account - Euro
1100 Investment Portfolio
1150 Purchase Prepayments
1200 Accounts Receivable
1220 Office Supplies
1240 Furniture Supplies
1260 Prepaid Insurance

Inventory Assets
1320 Bedroom Furniture
1340 Home Accessories
1360 Kitchen & Dining Room Furniture
1380 Living Room Furniture

Fixed Assets
1420 Cash Register ▶
▶1440 Computer Equipment
1460 Equipment & Tools
1480 Gallery Fixtures
1500 Gallery

LIABILITIES

Current Liabilities
2200 Accounts Payable
2220 Prepaid Sales and Deposits
2250 Credit Card Payable
2260 Import Duty Payable
2330 Income Tax Payable
2350 QPP Payable
2360 Quebec Income Tax Payable
2370 QHSF Payable
2460 CSST Payable
2650 GST Charged on Sales
2670 GST Paid on Purchases
2800 Refundable QST Paid
2810 QST Charged on Sales ▶

▶Long Term Liabilities
2950 Mortgage Payable - Gallery

EQUITY

Owner's Equity
3560 Montand, Capital
3580 Montand, Drawings
3600 Current Earnings

REVENUE

4020 Revenue from Sales
4040 Sales Discount
4060 Freight Revenue
4100 Investment Revenue
4120 Interest Revenue

EXPENSE

Operating Expenses
5020 Advertising & Promotion
5030 Exchange Rate Differences
5040 Bank Charges
5050 Credit Card Fees ▶
▶5060 Cost of Goods Sold
5070 Variance Costs
5080 Furniture Supplies Used
5100 Damaged Inventory
5120 Purchase Discounts
5130 Freight Expense
5140 Delivery Expense
5160 Hydro Expense
5180 Insurance Expense
5190 Mortgage Interest Expense
5200 Office Supplies Used
5220 Telephone Expenses

Payroll Expenses
5300 Commissions
5330 CSST Expense
5340 QPP Expense
5350 QHSF Expense
5380 Subcontractor Fees

NOTES: The Chart of Accounts includes only postable accounts and Current Earnings. QPP (Quebec Pension Plan) replaces CPP in Quebec. QHSF (Quebec Health Services Fund) is an employer-funded provincial health and services tax program.
Linked payable and expense accounts for EI, CPP and QPIP (Quebec Parental Insurance Plan) are also included because they are essential linked accounts, but they are not used in this example.

POST-CLOSING TRIAL BALANCE

VILLAGE GALLERIES

June 30, 2015

		Debits	Credits
1060	Chequing Bank Account	$ 51 792.25	
1070	Visa Bank Account	5 445.00	
1080	MasterCard Bank Account	3 555.00	
1090	Bank Account - Euro (€ 1 560)	2 100.00	
1100	Investment Portfolio	50 000.00	
1200	Accounts Receivable	5 748.75	
1220	Office Supplies	400.00	
1240	Furniture Supplies	600.00	
1260	Prepaid Insurance	250.00	
1320	Bedroom Furniture	35 200.00	
1340	Home Accessories	30 900.00	
1360	Kitchen & Dining Room Furniture	24 995.00	
1380	Living Room Furniture	41 925.00	
1420	Cash Register	1 200.00 ▶	
▶ 1440	Computer Equipment	2 800.00	
1460	Equipment & Tools	1 500.00	
1480	Gallery Fixtures	1 000.00	
1500	Gallery	150 000.00	
2200	Accounts Payable		$ 11 395.00
2250	Credit Card Payable		240.00
2260	Import Duty Payable		240.00
2650	GST Charged on Sales		1 680.00
2670	GST Paid on Purchases	980.00	
2800	Refundable QST Paid	90.00	
2810	QST Charged on Sales		1 926.00
2950	Mortgage Payable - Gallery		145 000.00
3560	Montand, Capital		250 000.00
		$410 481.00	$410 481.00

SUPPLIER INFORMATION

VILLAGE GALLERIES

Supplier Name (Contact)	Address	Phone No. Fax No.	E-mail Web Site	Terms Tax ID
Domo Carvaggio (Arturo Dessini)	8 Via Artistes Forli, 47100 Italy	Tel: (39-0543) 457 882 Fax: (39-0543) 457 113	www.domocarvaggio.com	net 30
Énergie Québec (Marie Nuclaire)	5010 Ave. Atomique Montreal, Quebec H2B 6C9	Tel: (514) 782-6101	www.energie.quebec.ca	net 1
L'Ascension Mobiliers (Suzie LaChaise)	RR #2 Jonquière, Quebec G7S 4L2	Tel: (450) 821-1029 Fax: (450) 822-1927	suzie@lascension.com www.lascension.com	1/5, n/30 (after tax) 322 749 610
Montreal Persia Emporium (Perse Moquette)	40 Rue de Tapis Longueuil, Quebec J4K 2L7	Tel: (450) 288-4334 Fax: (450) 288-8201	moquette@MPE.com www.MPE.com	2/5, n/30 (after tax) 473 540 911
Normandin Meubles (Normand Armoire)	RR #3 Nicolet, Quebec J3T 1H5	Tel: (450) 371-7273 Fax: (450) 371-7229	na@normand.meubles.com www.normand.meubles.com	2/10, n/30 (after tax) 136 492 446
Papineau Delivery (Martin Camion)	56 Papineau Ave. Outremont, Quebec H1M 3B3	Tel: (514) 690-2810 Fax: (514) 691-7283	martin@papineau.com www.papineau.com	net 10 288 344 566
Receiver General for Canada	Sudbury Tax Services Office PO Box 20004 Sudbury, Ontario P3A 6B4	Tel 1: (800) 561-7761 Tel 2: (800) 959-2221	www.cra-arc.gc.ca	net 1
Staples (Hélène Magazinier)	777 Ave. de Bureau Montreal, Quebec H4K 1V5	Tel: (514) 759-3488 Fax: (514) 758- 3910	www.staples.com	net 15 128 634 772
Telébec (Robert Bavarde)	84 Rue Causerie Montreal, Quebec H3C 7S2	Tel: (514) 488-2355	www.bell.ca	net 1

NOTES: All supplier discounts are calculated on after-tax amounts.

OUTSTANDING SUPPLIER INVOICES

VILLAGE GALLERIES

Supplier Name	Terms	Date	Invoice	Amount CAD	Total
L'Ascension Mobiliers	1/5, n/30 (after tax)	June 29/15	LM-2114	$4 558.00	$4 558.00
Normandin Meubles	2/10, n/30 (after tax)	June 28/15	NM-192	$6 837.00	$6 837.00
			Grand Total		$11 395.00

CUSTOMER INFORMATION

VILLAGE GALLERIES

Customer Name (Contact)	Address	Phone No. Fax No.	E-mail Web Site	Terms Credit Limit
Caisse Metropolitain (Tomas Monaire)	50 Rue Berri Montreal, Quebec H1B 6F4	Tel: (514) 466-2991 Fax: (514) 468-1826	tmonaire@caissemetro.ca www.caissemetro.ca	2/10, n/30 $5 000
Cash Customers				cash or credit card
Deon Estates (Kaline Deon)	600 Rue St. Denis Montreal, Quebec H2K 7C9	Tel: (514) 729-8217 Fax: (514) 729-9283	kaline.deon@istar.com	2/10, n/30 $5 000
*St. Leonard's Homebuilders (Félice Charpentier)	31 Boul. St. Joseph Montreal, Quebec H4N 2M1	Tel: (514) 788-3645 Fax: (514) 787-7114	felice@stleonards.com www.stleonards.com	2/10, n/30 $10 000
*Westmount Primrose Condos (M.T. Sweets)	121 Rue Notre Dame Montreal, Quebec H3K 4G5	Tel: (514) 499-7117 Fax: (514) 498-2889	sweets@wpcondos.com www.wpcondos.com	2/10, n/30 $10 000

NOTES: All customer discounts are calculated on amounts before tax. Customers pay 1.5% interest on accounts over 30 days. Asterisk (*) indicates preferred price list customer.

OUTSTANDING CUSTOMER INVOICES

VILLAGE GALLERIES

Customer Name	Terms	Date	Invoice	Amount	Tax	Total
Deon Estates	2/10, n/30 (before tax)	June 24/15	168	$5 000	$748.75	$5 748.75

Employee Profile and TD1 Information

Lianne Décor started working for the boutique on July 1, 2015. Using her interior decorating and design skills, she visits homes for consultations to assess needs and suggest furniture from the store that matches the home style and customer taste. She is paid a commission of 20 percent of her monthly sales and takes four weeks of vacation each year. Décor is single and self-supporting. Her tax claim amounts are $14 400 federal and $13 645 provincial for basic and education amounts. She works for the store part time and supplements her sales commission with her independent business as an interior design consultant.

Other employee details:

SIN:	566 811 014	Address:	45 Rue Collage
Date of birth:	August 26, 1979		Montreal, QC H2G 4R5
CSST (WCB) rate:	2.04	Tel:	(514) 639-9202

NOTES

As an employer, Village Galleries makes contributions to the Quebec Health Services Fund equal to 2.7 percent of the total payroll amount for the provincial health care plan. This amount is entered in the Payroll Settings.

CSST (La Commission de la Santé et de la Sécurité du Travail) is the Workers' Compensation Board agency in Quebec.

Employer and employee deductions for the Quebec Parental Insurance Plan are not required because Décor is not EI-insurable.

INVENTORY INFORMATION

VILLAGE GALLERIES

Code	Description	Unit	Min Qty	Selling Price Reg	Selling Price (Pref)	Qty on Hand	Total (Cost)	Duty (Taxes)
Bedroom Furniture: Total asset value $35 200 (Linked accounts: Asset 1320; Revenue 4020; COGS 5060; Variance 5070)								
BF-01	Armoire: dark oak	1-pc	0	$3 100	$3 000	2	$4 400	9.975%
BF-02	Armoire: light ash	1-pc	0	3 000	2 900	2	4 000	9.975%
BF-03	Bed: 3 piece oak	set	0	2 000	1 900	2	2 400	9.975%
BF-04	Bed: 5 piece light ash/oak	set	0	3 000	2 900	2	3 600	9.975%
BF-05	Bed: brass/silver	1-pc	0	1 800	1 700	3	3 300	8.0%
BF-06	Chest: cherry	1-pc	0	1 000	950	3	1 800	9.975%
BF-07	Dresser: cashmere, burl-maple	1-pc	0	1 600	1 500	5	4 500	9.975%
BF-08	Dresser: highboy - dark oak	1-pc	0	1 900	1 800	5	5 500	9.975%
BF-09	Wardrobe: light ash	1-pc	0	2 800	2 700	2	3 600	9.975%
BF-10	Wardrobe: pine	1-pc	0	1 750	1 650	2	2 100	9.975%
Home Accessories: Total asset value $30 900 (Linked accounts: Asset 1340; Revenue 4020; COGS 5060; Variance 5070)								
HA-01	Framed Art: prints 45 x 60cm	each	0	200	180	40	4 000	0.0%
HA-02	Framed Art: prints 75 x 100cm	each	0	300	270	30	4 500	0.0%
HA-03	Lamp: floor solid brass	1-pc	0	400	360	10	2 200	7.0%
HA-04	Lamp: table solid brass	1-pc	0	600	550	10	3 500	7.0%
HA-05	Mirror: oval dark oak	1-pc	0	500	450	5	1 500	9.975%
HA-06	Mirror: square ash/mahogany	1-pc	0	550	500	5	1 900	9.975%
HA-07	Rugs: Persian Isfahan 185 x 275cm	each	0	1 250	1 150	10	6 000	n/a
HA-08	Rugs: Persian Kashan 185 x 275cm	each	0	990	950	10	4 500	n/a
HA-09	Rugs: Persian Tabriz 90 x 160cm	each	0	650	600	10	2 800	n/a
Kitchen & Dining Room Furniture: Total asset value $24 995 (Linked accounts: Asset 1360; Revenue 4020; COGS 5060; Variance 5070)								
KD-01	Buffet: oak	1-pc	0	1 750	1 650	2	2 000	9.975%
KD-02	Buffet: cherry	1-pc	0	2 250	2 150	2	2 200	9.975%
KD-03	Chairs: 4 piece cherry	set	0	1 100	1 000	5	3 000	9.975%
KD-04	Chairs: 4 piece oak	set	0	975	950	5	2 375	9.975%
KD-05	China Cabinet: walnut	1-pc	0	2 100	2 000	2	2 100	9.975%
KD-06	China Cabinet: cherry	1-pc	0	850	800	2	800	9.975%
KD-07	Credenza: maple	1-pc	0	1 675	1 575	2	1 950	9.975%
KD-08	Extension Table: oak	1-pc	0	1 825	1 725	2	2 050	9.975%
KD-09	Huntboard: white pine	1-pc	0	725	650	2	850	9.975%
KD-10	Server: fruitwood	1-pc	0	980	950	2	1 000	9.975%
KD-11	Sideboard: cherry	1-pc	0	1 625	1 525	2	1 850	9.975%
KD-12	Table: brass with glass	1-pc	0	1 780	1 680	4	3 520	8.0%
KD-13	Table: ivory lacquer/pine	1-pc	0	625	550	4	1 300	9.975%
Living Room Furniture: Total asset value $41 925 (Linked accounts: Asset 1380; Revenue 4020; COGS 5060; Variance 5070)								
LR-01	Bookcase: oak/walnut solid	1-pc	0	1 150	1 050	3	1 950	9.975%
LR-02	Chair: various patterns cotton	1-pc	0	525	500	10	2 750	9.975%
LR-03	Cocktail Table: cherry	1-pc	0	925	850	5	2 375	9.975%
LR-04	Console Table: oak	1-pc	0	950	900	5	2 500	9.975%
LR-05	Curio Cabinet: walnut/oak	1-pc	0	1 450	1 350	3	2 400	9.975%
LR-06	Desk: mahogany	1-pc	0	1 840	1 740	5	4 400	9.975%
LR-07	End Table: brass with glass	1-pc	0	610	550	5	1 400	8.0%
LR-08	Lamp Table: ash/oak solid	1-pc	0	825	750	5	2 625	9.975%
LR-09	Loveseat: chenille	1-pc	0	1 325	1 225	5	3 625	9.975%
LR-10	Ottoman & Slipcover: grey leather	2-pc	0	380	350	5	1 000	9.975%
LR-11	Recliner & Ottoman: brown leather	2-pc set	0	1 020	950	5	3 100	9.975%
LR-12	Sectional Sofa: charcoal linen	3-pc	0	2 300	2 200	3	4 200	9.975%
LR-17	Settee: light ash	1-pc	0	850	800	3	1 650	9.975%
LR-18	Sofa & Slipcover: celadon	2-pc	0	1 475	1 375	5	4 375	9.975%
LR-19	Swivel Chair & Slipcover: cotton	2-pc	0	640	600	5	1 950	9.975%
LR-20	Wing Chair: pastel	1-pc	0	575	525	5	1 625	9.975%
Total Inventory Value							$133 020	

Accounting Procedures

The Goods and Services Tax (GST) and Quebec Sales Tax (QST)

Village Galleries uses the regular method for remittance of sales taxes. GST collected from customers is recorded as a liability in *GST Charged on Sales*. GST paid to suppliers is recorded in *GST Paid on Purchases* as a decrease in the liability collected provincially for remittance to the Canada Revenue Agency.

Provincial sales tax (Quebec Sales Tax, or QST) of 9.975 percent is applied to all cash and credit sales of goods and services in the province of Quebec. The Quebec Sales Tax is applied to the base amount of the invoice. QST collected from customers is recorded as a liability in *QST Charged on Sales*. QST paid to suppliers — recorded in *Refundable QST Paid* — decreases the liability to the Ministère du Revenu du Québec.

GST is administered provincially in Quebec, so Montand files returns for both GST and QST with the Ministre de Revenu du Québec. Returns are remitted by the last day of the month for the previous quarter, either requesting a refund or remitting the balance — the difference between *QST Charged on Sales* and *Refundable QST Paid*.

PRO VERSION
You will see the term Vendor instead of Supplier throughout the program.

NOTES
In this chapter, insurance is the only item for which QST is not refundable. GST is not applied to insurance. The QST on all other purchases and services in this chapter is refundable.

Deposits on Custom Orders

When customers place a sales order for furniture, they pay an advance of 20 percent to 25 percent of the price. The deposit may be entered in the Receipts Journal or on the Sales Order form. The Accounts Receivable Ledger for the selected customer will be credited for the advance and *Chequing Bank Account* will be debited. When the work is complete, fill the sales order to make a Sales Journal entry for the full amount of the contract, including relevant taxes. When the customer settles the account, mark the invoice amount and the deposit (if you used the Receipts Journal) as paid. The balance in the Receipts Journal should then match the amount of the customer's cheque.

Partially filled quotes are automatically converted to orders for the backordered items by the Sage 50 program.

NOTES
Processing the advance in this way ensures that the advance will appear in the correct customer account in the Receivables Ledger. The manual approach, a General Journal entry that debits the bank account and credits Unearned Revenue, a liability account, does not show this link with the customer – the customer's ledger is updated separately.

Freight Expenses

When a business purchases inventory items, the cost of freight that cannot be directly allocated to a specific item purchased must be charged to *Freight Expense*. This amount will be regarded as an expense and will not be part of the costs of any inventory asset account.

Printing Sales Invoices

If you want to print sales invoices through the program, complete the Sales Journal transaction as you would otherwise. Preview the transaction before posting it. You can print from the preview window or from the journal (click the Print tool button or choose the File menu and then Print). Before printing, check that you have selected the correct printer and forms. To e-mail an invoice, click the E-mail tool.

NOTES
Remember that if you want to preview or print invoices, you must select the correct printing form. Click the Change Print Forms tool in the Sales Journal to access the settings.

Foreign Purchases and Import Duty

Goods imported from Italy are subject to GST and QST and to import duties at various rates. These taxes are collected at the time the goods are received and are usually paid directly to the Ministre de Revenu du Québec. To simplify the transactions in Sage 50, we have set up the foreign supplier record so that the supplier collects GST, just like suppliers in Canada.

Import duties are handled separately in the program. Duty is calculated automatically because the rates are entered in the Inventory Ledger records. The amount is credited to the linked *Import Duty Payable* account instead of *Accounts*

Payable so the duty is not added to the balance owing to the supplier. The linked asset account is debited.

On receiving the merchandise, the business writes a cheque to the Receiver General to pay the import duties on the purchase. This payment is just like any other tax remittance — enter the duty payable as a positive amount for a cash purchase from the Receiver General and choose *Import Duty Payable* as the account. The amount is the current General Ledger account balance.

INSTRUCTIONS

1. **Open** the data files and set up the **budget** for Village Galleries on July 1, 2015, using Sage 50. Detailed keystroke instructions to assist you follow these instructions.
2. **Enter** the **source documents** for July 2015 in Sage 50 using all the company information provided.
3. **Print** the following **reports** and **graphs**:
   - Balance Sheet as at July 31
   - Journal Entries for all journals from July 1 to July 31
   - Inventory Sales Detail Report for Bedroom Furniture
   - Inventory Quantity Report for all items to check re-order requirements
   - Income Statement, Budget Report with Difference in Percentage: July 1 – July 31
   - Sales vs Budget graph for accounts 4020 and 4040
   - Expenses vs Budget graph for accounts 5060, 5120 and 5300

NOTES
Instructions for the Budget Report begin on page 557. Instructions for budget income reports and graphs begin on page 567.

KEYSTROKES

Setting Up Budgets

It is important for a business to gauge its performance against some standards. These standards can be provided through comparisons with other companies that are in the same line of business or by comparing the same company over several time periods. It is common for a business to set goals for the future based on past performance. For example, there may be an expectation that profits will increase by 10 percent over the previous year or that expenses will be reduced because of the introduction of new cost-reduction methods. If a business waits until the end of the year to assess its progress toward its goals, it may be too late to make necessary corrections if things are not proceeding according to plan. Budgets offer a realistic financial plan for the future that can be used to assess performance.

Before analyzing a budget report, you must turn on the option and enter the budget amounts for the relevant accounts.

Turning On the Budgeting Feature

NOTES
If you are working from backups, restore the backup file SageData13\village1.CAB or village1 to SageData13\Village\village.

Open **SageData13\Village\village**. Do not advance the session date until you have finished the budget setup.

Click the **Settings icon** Settings. **Click General (Accounts)** to open the General Settings list:

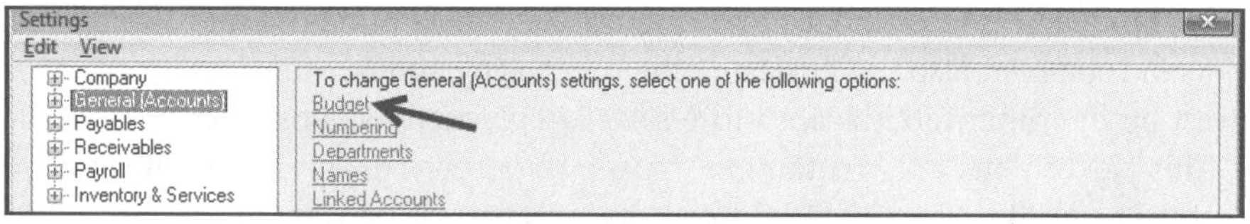

Click **Budget** to open the budgeting options:

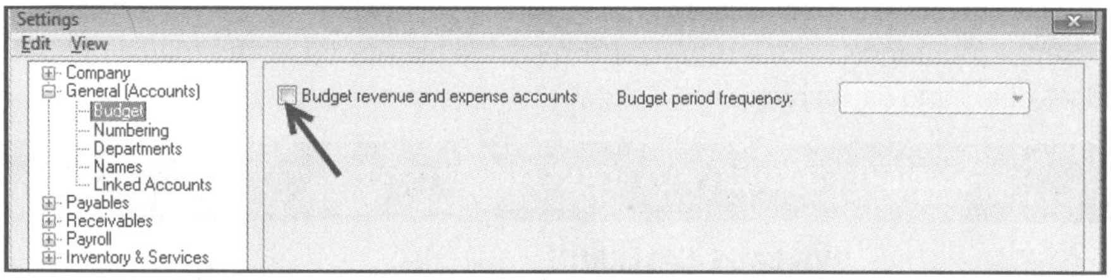

Click **Budget Revenue And Expense Accounts** to turn on the budget feature.

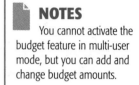

The first decision after choosing the budgeting feature involves a budget period. Whether a business chooses to budget amounts on a yearly, quarterly or monthly basis depends on the needs and nature of the business. Monthly budget reports will be appropriate if the business cycle of buying and selling is short, but not appropriate if long-term projects are involved. The period chosen must provide meaningful feedback about performance. If the periods are too short, there may be insufficient information to judge performance; if the periods are too long, there may be no opportunity to correct problems because they will not be detected soon enough. Village Galleries will use monthly budget periods initially because the Montands want frequent progress reports.

Click the **Budget Period Frequency field** to see the period options:

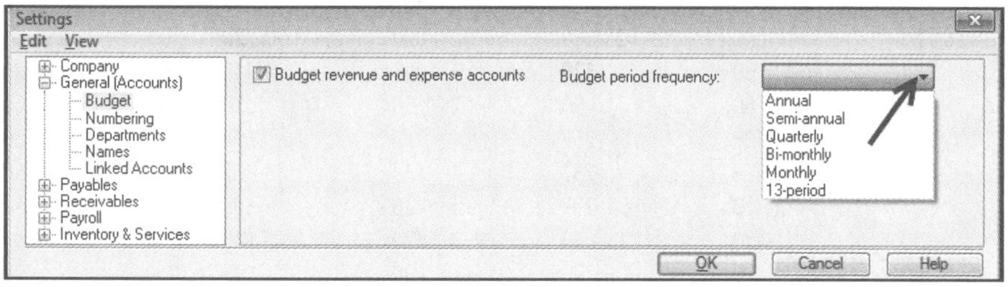

Click **Monthly**.

Click **OK** to return to the Home window and save the settings.

Setting a Budget

The next step is to enter the budget amounts for all expense and revenue accounts.

Budgets can be determined in several different ways. The most common methods are zero-based and incremental budgeting. With the zero-based method, a forecast is made for each revenue and expense account based on expectations about specific planned activities and expenditures. Each budget item must be justified. More commonly, last year's budgets and income statements are used as the starting point and a specific percentage change is applied. Thus, a company might expect to improve its performance over last year by 10 percent, either by increasing sales or by decreasing expenses. Planned special events such as annual month-long sales, new customer drives, and peak or slow periods can be built into the changes in budgeted amounts from one period to the next. Whatever method is used, it is important that the budget be realistic.

Renée Montand examined previous income statements and business practices to see where they could make improvements and to get a realistic forecast. The business has been growing by about 10 percent per year. The corresponding expenses, sales discounts, cost of goods sold and so on also increased by about the same amount. Sales are not divided

PRO VERSION

pro Departments (for departmental accounting) are not available in the Pro version.

NOTES

You cannot activate the budget feature in multi-user mode, but you can add and change budget amounts.

evenly throughout the 12-month period. Most customers purchase new furniture in the spring and summer, also the busiest home purchasing and moving seasons. Sales are slowest in the winter months and store sales are planned for those months.

This pattern has led Montand to expect 12 percent of the year's sales to occur each month from April to August, 10 percent in January during the store sales and 5 percent in each of the remaining months. The recent hiring of an interior consultant should also boost sales over last year's results.

Renée Montand's detailed budget forecast is presented in the following item-by-item budget chart and rationale:

MONTHLY BUDGET FORECAST FOR 2015

VILLAGE GALLERIES

Account	Jul–Aug	Sep–Dec	Jan	Feb–Mar	Apr–Jun	Total for 12 months
REVENUE						
Revenue from Sales	$50 454	$21 023	$42 042	$21 023	$50 454	$420 450
Sales Discount	–504	–210	–420	–210	–504	–4 200
Freight Revenue	1 010	420	830	420	1 010	8 400
Investment Revenue	638	638	638	638	638	7 656
Interest Revenue	22	22	22	22	22	264
TOTAL REVENUE	$51 620	$21 893	$43 112	$21 893	$51 620	$432 570
EXPENSES						
Advertising & Promotion	$ 288	$ 120	$ 240	$ 120	$ 288	$ 2 400
Exchange Rate Differences	0	0	0	0	0	0
Bank Charges	29	12	23	12	29	240
Credit Card Fees	252	105	210	105	252	2 100
Cost of Goods Sold	30 720	12 800	25 600	12 800	30 720	256 000
Variance Costs	144	60	120	60	144	1 200
Furniture Supplies Used	50	50	50	50	50	600
Damaged Inventory	307	128	257	128	307	2 560
Purchase Discounts	–307	–128	–257	–128	–307	–2 560
Freight Expense	307	128	257	128	307	2 560
Delivery Expense	1 010	420	830	420	1 010	8 400
Hydro Expense	90	90	90	90	90	1 080
Insurance Expense	300	300	300	300	300	3 600
Mortgage Interest Expense	1 270	1 270	1 270	1 270	1 270	15 240
Office Supplies Used	65	65	65	65	65	780
Telephone Expenses	80	80	80	80	80	960
Commissions	3 000	1 250	2 500	1 250	3 000	25 000
CSST Expense	61	26	49	26	61	510
QPP Expense	125	52	103	52	125	1 040
QHSF Expense	144	60	120	60	144	1 200
Subcontractor Fees	600	250	500	250	600	5 000
TOTAL EXPENSES	$38 535	$17 138	$32 407	$17 138	$38 535	$327 910
NET INCOME	$13 085	$ 4 755	$10 705	$ 4 755	$13 085	$104 660

BUDGET RATIONALE FOR 2015

VILLAGE GALLERIES

Estimates used to create budget forecasts

Revenue from Sales: increase by 10% over previous year. January, 10% of annual sales; February and March 5%; April, May, June, July and August, 12%; September, October, November and December, 5% each
Sales Discount: expect about 1% of sales on average; most sales are not discounted
Freight Revenue: this has averaged around 2% of sales; most customers request delivery
Interest and Investment Revenue: constant monthly income; same as previous year
Cost of Goods Sold: 60% of net sales (based on markup)
Variance Costs: estimated from price variations in previous years
Damaged Inventory: 1% of Cost of Goods Sold
Purchase Discounts: average 1% of Cost of Goods Sold
Delivery: same amount as Freight Revenue
Freight Expense: average at about 1% of sales
Insurance and Mortgage Interest: same amount each month; small decrease from previous year
Furniture Supplies Used: for maintaining store inventory; constant amount each month
Commissions: estimate, will pay 20% of direct contributions to sales
EI, CPP and QPIP: these do not apply; do not choose Budget This Account
QPP, CSST (WCB) and QHSF: straight percentage of commissions (QPP replaces CPP for Quebec)
Subcontractors' Fees: estimated additional assistance needed for peak periods
Bank Charges & Credit Card Fees: increase over last year for increased credit card usage
Exchange Rate Differences: zero – these are expected to cancel each other over time
Other Expenses: constant each month; no change over last year

Entering Budget Amounts in the General Ledger

Click **Company** in the Modules pane list to change windows.

Click the **Chart of Accounts shortcuts list arrow** and **click Modify Account** to open the Search window. Accounts is selected as the record type:

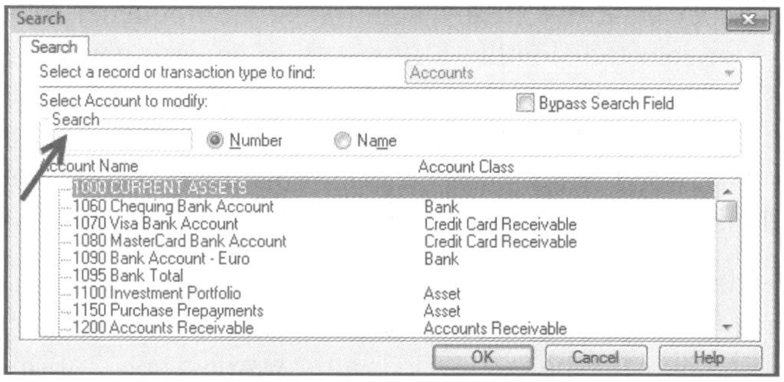

Click the **Search field**.

Type 4 to advance the cursor to the beginning of the 4000-level Revenue accounts.

Click **4020 Revenue from Sales** to highlight the first postable revenue account.

NOTES

You can also click the Chart of Accounts icon and then double-click the account to open the ledger record. Or create and use the View Accounts shortcut (Banking module) to open the Accounts window.

Click **OK** to open the Account Ledger window as shown:

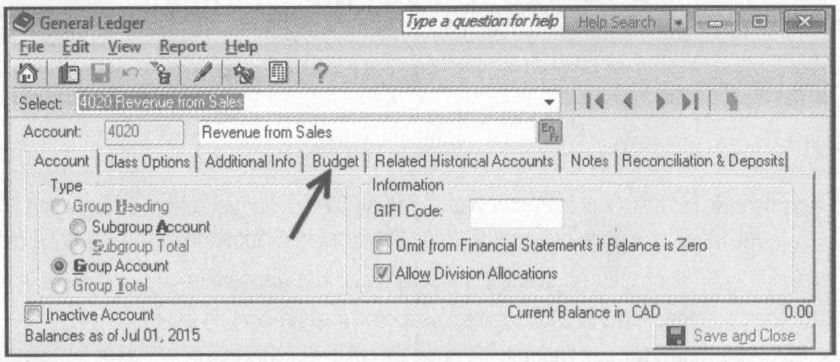

PRO VERSION
The Refresh tool is not available in the Pro version.

NOTES
Budgeting applies only to the postable revenue and expense accounts on the Income Statement. Budget reports are Income Statement reports.

Because we turned on the Budgeting feature in the General Settings window, the Budget tab has been added. This tab will appear only for Income Statement — revenue and expense — accounts.

Click the **Budget tab** to open the budget activation window as shown:

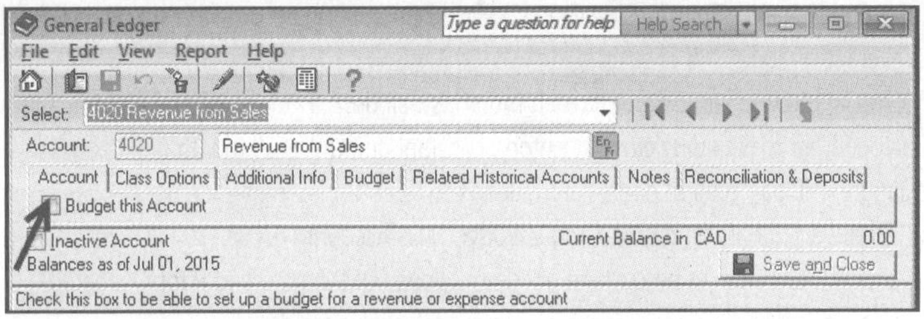

Click **Budget This Account** to open the Budget amount fields as shown:

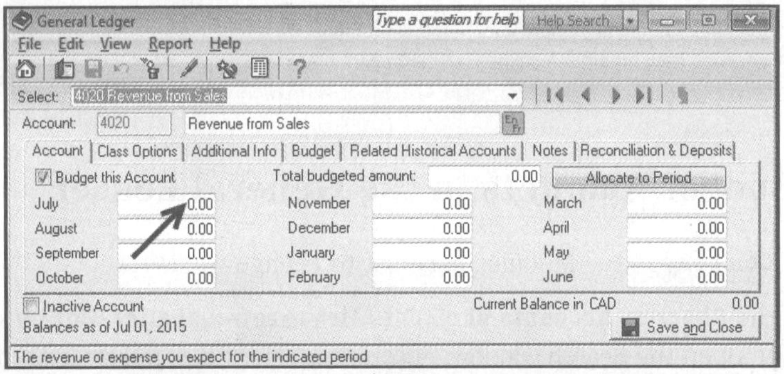

The budget periods displayed at this stage match the period frequency selected in the setup stage. Because we selected Monthly, a 12-month calendar is given, beginning with July, the first month of the fiscal year as entered in the Company Information window. If we had selected Quarterly, four input fields would be provided. You can enter the budget amounts for one period or for more, if the information is available. For Village Galleries, we will enter the amounts determined earlier for each month.

You can change the budget frequency at any time in the General Settings Budget option window. The program will reallocate the previously budgeted amounts proportionately for the new periods after warning you that this will be done and giving you a chance to confirm that you want to proceed.

Refer to the chart on page 554 for budget amounts.

For each revenue and expense, you can add or omit budget amounts. Including budget details for all accounts will, of course, provide the most meaningful budget reports.

Click the **July field** to select the amount.

Type 50454 **Press** *tab*.

The cursor advances to the August field and highlights the entry for editing.

Enter the **amounts** for the **remaining 11 months** according to the budget forecast on page 554 by **typing** the **amount** and **pressing** *tab* to move to the next month.

You can use the **Copy** and **Paste** commands (Edit menu) to copy amounts from one field to another and save some data entry time.

The **Total Budgeted Amount** is updated continually as you enter amounts for each period. After entering all individual monthly amounts, use this Total Budgeted Amount to check your work. It should equal the total for 12 months in the chart of page 554.

When you have entered the amounts for each month,

Click the **Next button** to advance to the next revenue account in the budget tab screen.

Turn on the **budget feature** and **enter budget amounts** for the **remaining** revenue and expense **accounts** by following the steps outlined above. Use the amounts determined for each account in the chart on page 554.

Remember to enter **negative** budget amounts for accounts that decrease the total in a Group or Section (e.g., *Sales Discount* and *Purchase Discounts*).

For some accounts, when the budget amounts for each month are equal, you can use a shortcut to enter the amounts. For example, for *4100 Investment Revenue*,

Click the **Total Budgeted Amount field**.

Type 7656 **Click Allocate To Period** to divide the amount evenly among all budget periods (638 is entered for each month, 7656/12).

After entering the budget amounts for all accounts,

Close the **account's General Ledger window** to return to the Home window.

Display or **print** the **Budget Report** for July to June to check your amounts.

Displaying Budget Reports

You can check the budget amounts you entered for accounts from the Budget Report. Budget reports are available from the Financials report list in the Report Centre.

Open the **Report Centre** and **click Financials** in the Select A Report Type list.

Click **Budget** and then **click Modify This Report**:

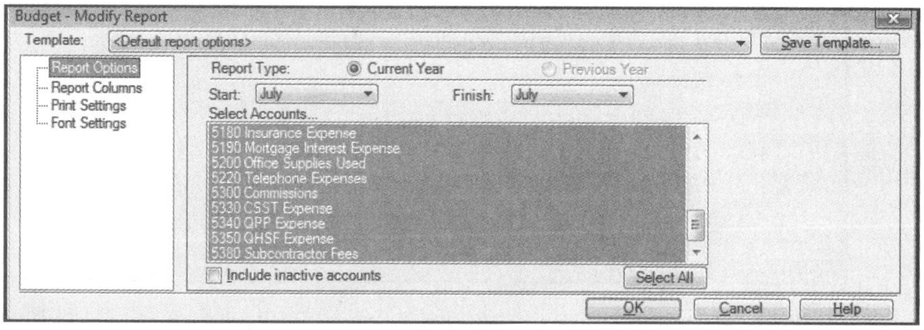

Select the **accounts** you want in the report. To check your entries at this stage, you should accept the default to **Select All** accounts.

Choose the **budget periods** in the Start and Finish fields and **click OK** to see the amounts.

Close the **display** when you have finished.

NOTES

You can also use keyboard shortcuts to copy budget amounts. Highlight the amount you need to copy and press *ctrl* + C. Then click the field you are copying to and press *ctrl* + V.

NOTES

Non-postable accounts, such as subtotals, headings and totals, do not have budget fields.

Do not enter budget amounts for CPP Expense, QPIP Expense and EI Expense. These accounts are not used by Village Galleries, but they are required as essential linked accounts by the program.

NOTES

Because we accessed the ledger record from the Modify Account shortcut Search window, we bypassed the Accounts window. Closing the ledger record therefore returns you directly to the Home window.

NOTES

You can also choose the Reports menu, then choose Financials and click Budget to open the report options screen.

NOTES

From the Budget Report, you can drill down to the General Ledger for the account so you can edit the budget amounts if necessary.

You can select report columns for the Budget Report, but you cannot sort or filter the report.

> **NOTES**
> If you want to see the next group of screens or to enter budget amounts for divisions, you must first view the module (Setup menu, User Preferences, View option; click the check box for Division).

> **PRO VERSION**
> Click Project instead of Division. The module label does not change when you select a different company type.

Adding Budget Amounts to Divisions

If you are using division allocations, you can also enter budget amounts for each division. You must first turn on the budgeting feature and then choose a budget period or frequency. The following steps will illustrate this procedure.

Click the Settings icon and click Division to open the Division Settings:

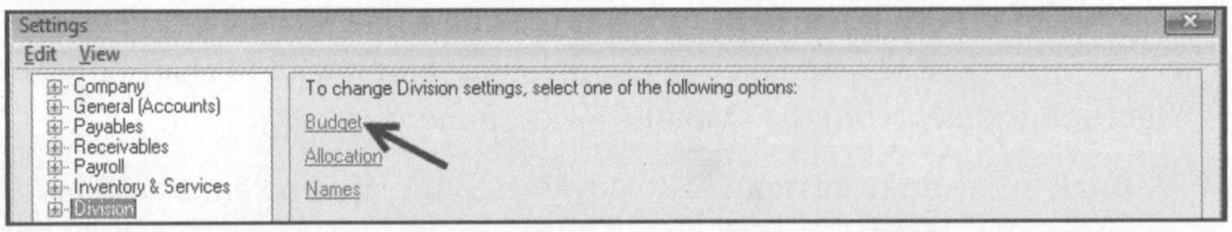

Click Budget to see the division budget activation screen with the familiar options:

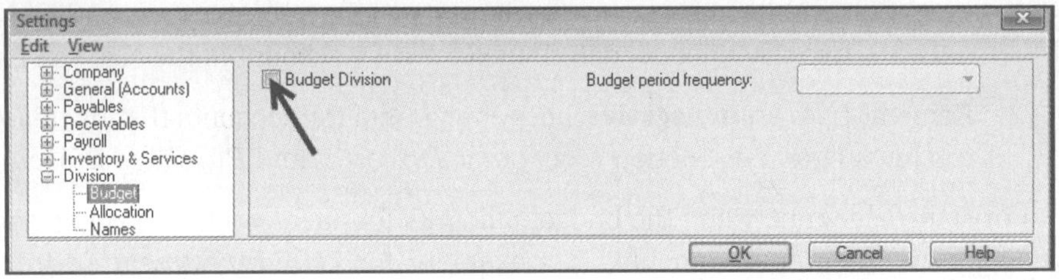

Click Budget Division. Choose a frequency from the Budget Period Frequency drop-down list. Click OK to save the settings.

Click the Divisions icon to open the Division window. Create the divisions if you have not already done so. Open the Division Ledger. A Budget tab has been added. Click the Budget tab to open the budget activation window:

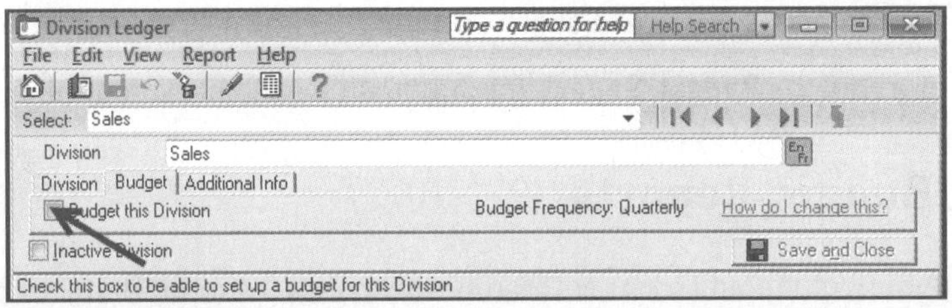

Click Budget This Division to open the budget amount fields. Quarterly periods have been selected for this illustration:

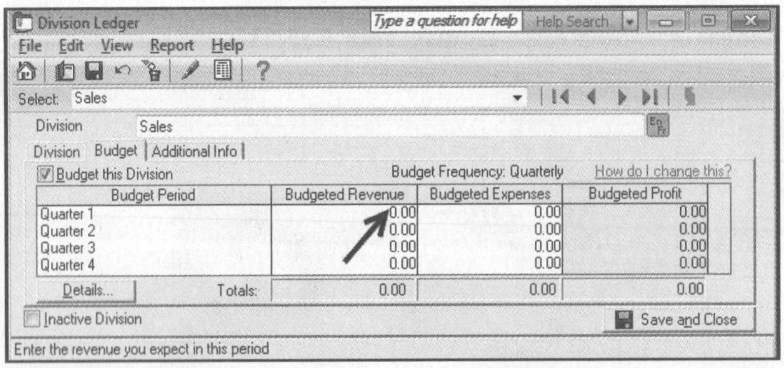

Enter the budgeted Revenue and Expense amounts for each period for this division. Click Details to enter division budget amounts for individual accounts:

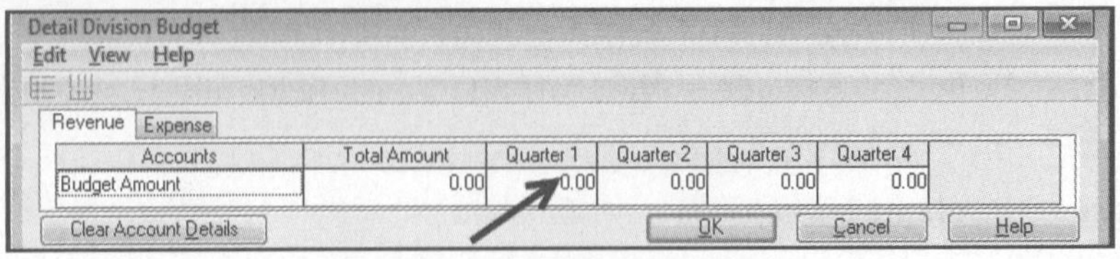

> **PRO VERSION**
> The Pro version does not have the option to enter account details.

On the first line, enter the total revenue or expense amounts and the amounts for each period. The Select list button will become available as shown:

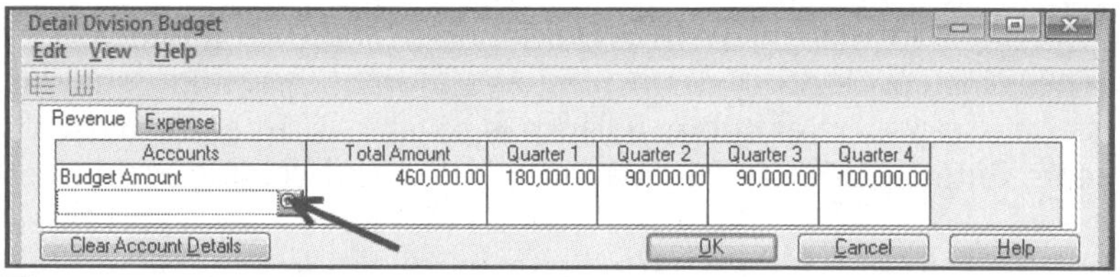

Then enter these details for individual accounts. Click OK to save the details and return to the ledger record. Open the ledger for the next division and enter the budget amounts.

Close the ledger when you have finished and enter the allocations as usual in the journals. Division budget reports will be available.

SOURCE DOCUMENTS

SESSION DATE – JULY 7, 2015

1 **Memo #1** **Dated July 2/15**

From Owner: Pay import duties owing to the Receiver General on June 30. Issue cheque #125 for $240 in full payment of duty owing.

2

Village Galleries

509 Boul. Rouin
Montreal, Quebec
H3F 5G5

Telephone: (514) 529-6391
Fax: (514) 529-7622

Date: July 2/15
To be delivered: July 15/15
For: Caisse Metropolitain
(Tomas Monaire)
50 Rue Berri
Montreal, QC H1B 6F4

QUOTE #71

Description	Qty	Price	Total
HA-03 Lamp: floor solid brass	2	400	800.00
HA-09 Rugs: Persian Tabriz 90 x 160cm	2	650	1300.00
LR-01 Bookcase: oak/walnut solid	2	1150	2300.00
LR-12 Sectional Sofa: charcoal linen	2	2300	4600.00

Sale Terms: 2/10, n/30	Delivery	N/C
GST # 236 412 540	GST 5.0%	450.00
QST # 3344992	QST 9.975%	897.76
Prices quoted will remain valid for 15 days	Total	10347.76

3 **Memo #2** **Dated July 2/15**

From Owner: Convert sales quote #71 to sales order #71. All amounts, dates and terms are unchanged.

NOTES

Create shortcuts for the journals from other modules, or change module windows as needed.

NOTES
The tax on insurance is included. GST is not charged on insurance premiums.

4 **Purchase Quote #224** **Dated July 2/15**
Policy Start date July 5/15
From Quebecor Insurance Co. (use Quick Add), $3 600 for a one-year extension of business insurance policy. Terms: first two months' premium required as deposit on acceptance of quote. Balance is payable in 10 equal monthly payments. Enter 1 (one) as the quantity ordered and debit Prepaid Insurance.

5 **Purchase Order #224 & Cheque #126** **Dated July 2/15**
Convert purchase quote #224 from Quebecor Insurance Co., $3 600 for a one-year extension of business insurance policy, to a purchase order. Issue cheque #126 for $600 as deposit to confirm the order.

6 **Purchase Invoice #QI-7711** **Dated July 3/15**
From Quebecor Insurance Co., to fill purchase order #224, $3 600 for a one-year extension of business insurance policy. The premium balance is due in 10 equal monthly payments. Change the payment method to Pay Later.

7 **Cash Receipt #43** **Dated July 3/15**
From Deon Estates, cheque #118 for $5 648.75 in payment of account, including $100 discount for early payment. Reference invoice #168.

NOTES
You may need to update the cheque number to 127 and then accept the new numbering.

8 **Payment Cheque #127** **Dated July 3/15**
To L'Ascension Mobiliers, $4 512.42 in payment of account, including $45.58 discount for early payment. Reference invoice #LM-2114.

NOTES
Edit the sales prices. Prices for foreign transactions are taken from the exchange rate rather than from the Inventory Ledger records.

Vasco Cardigos
Rua Mariella 36
1207 Lisbon, Portugal
Tel: (351-21) 347 6273
Terms: net 1
Currency: EUR
Revenue account: 4020
Tax code: no tax

9 **Cash Sales Invoice #170** **Dated July 4/15**
To Vasco Cardigos (use Full Add for the new Portuguese customer)

1	BF-02	Armoire: light ash	€ 2 200.00
1	HA-06	Mirror: square ash/mahogany	400.00
		Shipping	200.00

Received cheque #4322 for €2 800 in full payment.
The exchange rate is 1.350.

10 **Credit Card Purchase Invoice #A-1141** **Dated July 4/15**
From Antoine's Hardware Store (use Quick Add for the new supplier), $50 plus $2.50 GST and $4.99 QST for computer screen cleaning kit (office supplies). Purchase invoice total $57.49 paid in full by Amex credit card.

11 **Credit Card Purchase Invoice #PD-211** **Dated July 5/15**
From Papineau Delivery, $180 plus $9.00 GST and $17.96 QST for contracted delivery of furniture. Purchase invoice total $206.96. Paid in full by Amex.

NOTES
You can choose Continue or Quick Add for new customers.

12 **Interac Sales Invoice #171** **Dated July 6/15**
To Catherine Geneve (choose Continue)

1	LR-04	Console Table: oak		$ 950.00
1	LR-05	Curio Cabinet: walnut/oak		1 450.00
		Delivery		100.00
		Goods and Services Tax	5.0%	125.00
		Quebec Sales Tax	9.975%	249.38
Invoice total				$2 874.38

Paid by debit card #7695 4559 0062 0103.

13 **Payment Cheque #128** **Dated July 7/15**
To Normandin Meubles, $6 700.26 in payment of account including $136.74 discount for early payment. Reference invoice #NM-192.

SESSION DATE – JULY 14, 2015

14

Memo #3 **Dated July 8/15**

From Owner: Adjust inventory for one HA-02 Framed Art Print dropped and damaged beyond repair. Charge to Damaged Inventory account.

15

Credit Card Purchase Invoice #QA-197 **Dated July 10/15**

From Quik-Ads (use Quick Add), $200 plus $10.00 GST and $19.95 QST for promotional cards and flyers to advertise home design gallery. Purchase invoice total $229.95 paid in full by Amex credit card.

16

Cash Purchase Invoice #EQ-979764 **Dated July 13/15**

From Énergie Québec, $100 plus $5.00 GST and $9.98 QST for hydro service for one month. Purchase invoice total $114.98 paid in full by cheque #129.

17

Cash Sales Invoice #172 **Dated July 13/15**

To Marie Broussard

1	LR-18	Sofa & Slipcover: celadon		$1 475.00
		Goods and Services Tax	5.0%	73.75
		Quebec Sales Tax	9.975%	147.13
	Invoice total			$1 695.88

Received cheque #339 in full payment. Customer to arrange own delivery.

18

Sales Invoice #173 **Dated July 14/15**

To Marie Broussard (use Quick Add), $50 plus $2.50 GST and $4.99 QST for delivery of sofa. Sales invoice total $57.49. Terms: net 10.

NOTES

Credit Freight Revenue for the delivery to Broussard.

19

Visa Sales Invoice #174 **Dated July 14/15**

To Allysa Morel

1	KD-10	Server: fruitwood		$ 980.00
1	KD-12	Table: brass with glass		1 780.00
1	LR-09	Loveseat: chenille		1 325.00
		Goods and Services Tax	5.0%	204.25
		Quebec Sales Tax	9.975%	407.49
	Invoice total			$4 696.74

Paid by Visa #4185 4458 6712 8405.

20

Credit Card Purchase Invoice #QD-980 **Dated July 14/15**

From Quickie Delivery Service (use Quick Add), $50 plus $2.50 GST and $4.99 QST for emergency delivery of sofa to Marie Broussard. Purchase invoice total $57.49 paid in full by Amex. (Charge to Delivery Expense.)

21

Purchase Invoice #MPE-664 **Dated July 14/15**

From Montreal Persia Emporium (Create new inventory)

2	HA-10	Rugs: Mashad 170 x 240cm	$1 000.00
2	HA-11	Rugs: Qum silk 80 x 150cm	1 600.00
		Goods and Services Tax	130.00
		Quebec Sales Tax	259.35
	Invoice total		$2 989.35

Terms: 2/5, n/30.

New inventory items

Number	Description	Unit	Min	Prices Reg.	(Pref.)
HA-10	Rugs: Mashad 170 x 240cm	1-pc	1	$ 800	($ 750)
HA-11	Rugs: Qum silk 80 x 150cm	1-pc	1	1 500	(1 400)

Linked Accounts: Asset 1340 **Revenue** 4020 **Cost of Goods Sold** 5060 **Variance** 5070

Taxes: GST exempt No **QST exempt** No **Duty Rate** Not applicable

NOTES
Allow the customer to exceed the credit limit.

SESSION DATE – JULY 21, 2015

22

Village Galleries
509 Boul. Rouin
Montreal, Quebec
H3F 5G5

Telephone: (514) 529-6391
Fax: (514) 529-7622

Date: July 15/15

To: Caisse Metropolitain
(Tomas Monaire)
50 Rue Berri
Montreal, QC H1B 6F4

#175

Description	Qty	Price	Total
HA-03 Lamp: floor solid brass	2	400	800.00
HA-09 Rugs: Persian Tabriz 90 x 160cm	2	650	1300.00
LR-01 Bookcase: oak/walnut solid	2	1150	2300.00
LR-12 Sectional Sofa: charcoal linen	2	2300	4600.00
Ref: quote/order #71 Authorization to exceed credit limit GM			

Sale Terms: 2/10, n/30	**Delivery**	N/C
GST # 236 412 540	**GST 5.0%**	450.00
QST # 3344992	**QST 9.975%**	897.76
	Sales Total	10347.76

23 **Memo #4** **Dated July 17/15**

From Owner: Adjust purchase invoice #MPE-664. Montreal Persia Emporium sent a revised invoice for MPE-664 that included a freight charge of $50 plus $2.50 GST and $4.99 QST. New purchase invoice total $3 046.84.

24 **Payment Cheque #130** **Dated July 19/15**

To Montreal Persia Emporium, $2 985.90 in payment of account including $60.94 discount for early payment. Reference revised invoice #MPE-664.

25 **MasterCard Sales Invoice #176** **Dated July 20/15**

To Jacques Altain

1	LR-06 Desk: mahogany		$1 840.00
1	LR-11 Recliner & Ottoman: brown leather		1 020.00
1	LR-20 Wing Chair: pastel		375.00
	Delivery		100.00
	Goods and Services Tax	5.0%	166.75
	Quebec Sales Tax	9.975%	332.68
Invoice total			$3 834.43

Paid by MasterCard #5145 0559 0062 3612.
Edit the selling price of LR-20. The price was reduced because the chair legs were scratched.

26 **Credit Card Bill #AM-07020** **Dated July 20/15**

From American Express (Amex), $791.89 for new purchases before the billing date, July 14, plus $10.50 monthly fee. Total payment required to avoid interest charges is $802.39. Issue cheque #131 for $802.39 to pay Amex balance in full.

27

Village Galleries
509 Boul. Rouin
Montreal, Quebec
H3F 5G5

Telephone: (514) 529-6391
Fax: (514) 529-7622

Date: July 20/15
To be delivered: July 21/15
From: St. Leonard's Homebuilders
(Félice Charpentier)
31 Boul. St. Joseph
Montreal, QC H4N 2M1

QUOTE #72

Description	Qty	Price	Total
BF-01 Armoire: dark oak	2	3000	6000.00
BF-05 Bed: brass/silver	2	1700	3400.00
HA-08 Rugs: Persian Kashan 185 x 275cm	2	950	1900.00
LR-09 Loveseat: chenille	2	1225	2450.00
Telephone request for quote 7/20/15 GM			
Sale Terms: 2/10, n/30		Delivery	N/C
GST # 236 412 540		GST 5.0%	687.50
QST # 3344992		QST 9.975%	1371.57
		Total	15809.07

28

Village Galleries
509 Boul. Rouin
Montreal, Quebec
H3F 5G5

Telephone: (514) 529-6391
Fax: (514) 529-7622

Date: July 21/15

To: St. Leonard's Homebuilders
(Félice Charpentier)
31 Boul. St. Joseph
Montreal, QC H4N 2M1

#177

Description	Qty	Price	Total
BF-01 Armoire: dark oak	1	3000	3000.00
BF-05 Bed: brass/silver	1	1700	1700.00
HA-08 Rugs: Persian Kashan 185 x 275cm	1	950	950.00
LR-09 Loveseat: chenille	1	1225	1225.00
Quote partially filled Balance of quote converted to order #72 Ref: sales quote #72 GM			
Sale Terms: 2/10, n/30		Delivery	N/C
GST # 236 412 540		GST 5.0%	343.75
QST # 3344992		QST 9.975%	685.78
		Total	7904.53

NOTES

Enter 1 in the Quantity field for each item. When you post the sale, allow Sage 50 to generate the sales order automatically by clicking Yes.

29 **Cash Purchase Invoice #T-55612** **Dated July 21/15**

From Telébec, $75 plus $3.75 GST and $7.48 QST for telephone service. Purchase invoice total $86.23 paid in full by cheque #132.

30 **Cash Receipt #44** **Dated July 21/15**

From Caisse Metropolitain, cheque #967 for $10 167.76 in payment of account including $180 discount for early payment. Reference invoice #175.

SESSION DATE – JULY 31, 2015

31 **Sales Invoice #178** **Dated July 23/15**

To Westmount Primrose Condos (preferred customer)

1	KD-02	Buffet: cherry	$2 150	
1	LR-12	Sectional Sofa: charcoal linen	2 200	
2	LR-19	Swivel Chairs & Slipcovers: cotton	600	each
		Goods and Services Tax	5.0%	
		Quebec Sales Tax	9.975%	

Terms: 2/10, n/30.

32 **Cash Receipt #45** **Dated July 28/15**

From Marie Broussard, cheque #357 for $57.49 in payment of account. Reference invoice #173.

33 **MasterCard Sales Invoice #179** **Dated July 28/15**

To Pierre Binoche

1	KD-04 Chairs: 4 piece			$ 975.00
1	KD-08 Extension Table: oak			1 825.00
	Delivery			100.00
	Goods and Services Tax		5.0%	145.00
	Quebec Sales Tax		9.975%	289.28
Invoice total				$3 334.28

Paid by MasterCard #5555 8445 5900 6236.

34 **Credit Card Purchase Invoice #PD-304** **Dated July 30/15**

From Papineau Delivery, $400 plus $20 GST and $39.90 QST for contracted delivery of furniture. Purchase invoice total $459.90 paid in full by Amex.

35 **Bank Debit Memo #643177** **Dated July 30/15**

From Bank of Montreal, $30 for bank service charges for one month and $1 700 for mortgage payment that included $1 425 interest and $275 principal.

36 **Bank Credit Memo #46234** **Dated July 30/15**

From Bank of Montreal, $638 interest earned on investment securities deposited to chequing account.

37 **Cash Receipt #46** **Dated July 30/15**

From St. Leonard's Homebuilders, cheque #3199 for $7 767.03 in payment of account including $137.50 discount for early payment. Reference invoice #177.

38 **Memo #5** **Dated July 31/15**

From Owner: Make adjusting entries for July.

Office supplies used	$ 75
Furniture supplies used	50
Prepaid insurance expired	300

39 **Memo #6** **Dated July 31/15**

From Owner: Lianne Décor earned $5 200 in commissions on her share of sales in July. Issue cheque #133 to pay Décor's commissions.

40 **Memo #7** **Dated July 31/15**

From Owner: Issue cheque #134 for $300 – the premium for one month – to Quebecor Insurance Co. in partial payment of invoice #QI-7711. Repeat the entry five times to prepare the remaining payments for the year as postdated cheques. Issue cheques #135 to 139, dated August 31, September 30, October 31, November 30 and December 31.

Updating Budgets

Changing Budget Amounts

Budget amounts can be updated if needed based on feedback from earlier budget reports. They should not, of course, be changed without good reason.

If you discover that your budget forecasts are incorrect, you can update the amounts for each account individually by repeating the process described above for entering initial budget amounts. Or you can globally update all amounts by a fixed percentage. At the end of July, we are asked to update all budget amounts by 10 percent.

✓ 41 **Memo #8** **Dated July 31/15**

From Owner: Decrease all revenue and expense budget amounts by 10%.

Choose the **Maintenance menu** in the Home window and **click Update Budget Amounts** to see the Update Budget window:

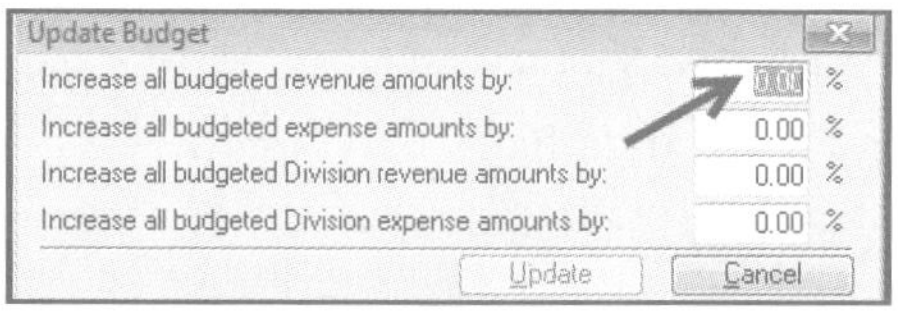

You can change the budgets for revenue and expense accounts separately. You can change division revenue and expense amounts by a different percentage. Use negative numbers to indicate a decrease in amounts and positive numbers for increases.

The entry for Increase All Budgeted Revenue Amounts By is selected.

Type -10 **Press** *tab*.

Type -10 **Click Update** to apply the change.

The screen that follows asks you to confirm that you want to update the budget:

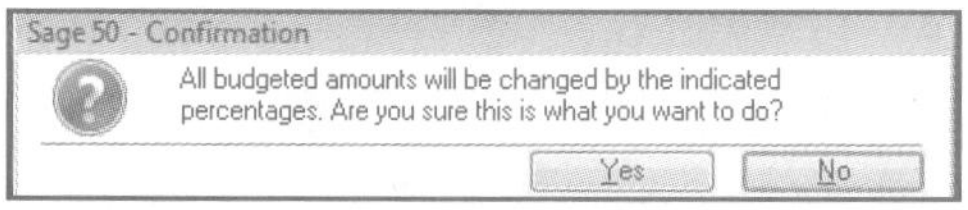

Click **Yes** to apply the changes and return to the Home window.

When you review the account's budget information in the account ledger, you will see that the change has been applied. All budget amounts will be updated.

Changing Budget Frequencies

You can also change the budget frequency. This change is made in the General Ledger Settings screen. For example, to change the period from monthly to quarterly,

Choose the Setup menu, then click Settings. Click General (Accounts) and Budget. Then choose Quarterly from the Budget Period Frequency drop-down list and click OK.

When you have a quarterly budget with different amounts for each quarter and you change the frequency to monthly, each month will have the same budget amount — the total for the four quarters divided by 12. You must edit the amounts if they are incorrect.

For example, a quarterly budget of $1 000, $3 000, $2 000 and $6 000 for the four quarters becomes $1 000 each month if the frequency is changed to monthly ($12000/12).

Before applying the new budget settings, Sage 50 generates the following warning each time you change a budget frequency:

NOTES
If you change the frequency to quarterly, the budget amount you entered for Revenue from Sales will become $105 112.50 for each quarter – the total budget for the year, or 12 months, will be divided by 4 ($420 450/4).

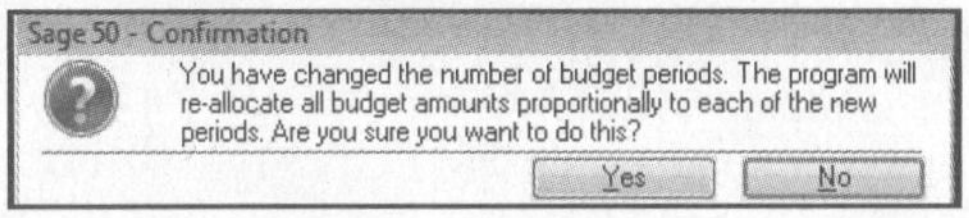

The statement warns that previous budget amounts will be reallocated evenly among the new number of periods. If you change a monthly budget to quarterly, each quarter will have the same budget amount. You can accept or cancel the change.

Printing in Batches

In addition to printing invoices, orders, quotes and cheques at the time of a transaction, you can print them in batches at the end of a period, such as the end of a business day. Batch printing makes it easier to share printers. Any forms that can be printed individually can be printed in batches.

Memo #9 asks us to print all sales invoices.

✓ 42

Memo #9 **Dated July 31/15**

From Owner: Print all sales invoices for July.

First you need to allow batch printing for the data file.

Choose the **Setup menu** and **click Settings**.

Click **Company** and then **click Forms** to open the Settings screen for Forms:

NOTES
To set up for printing in batches, you must work in single-user mode.

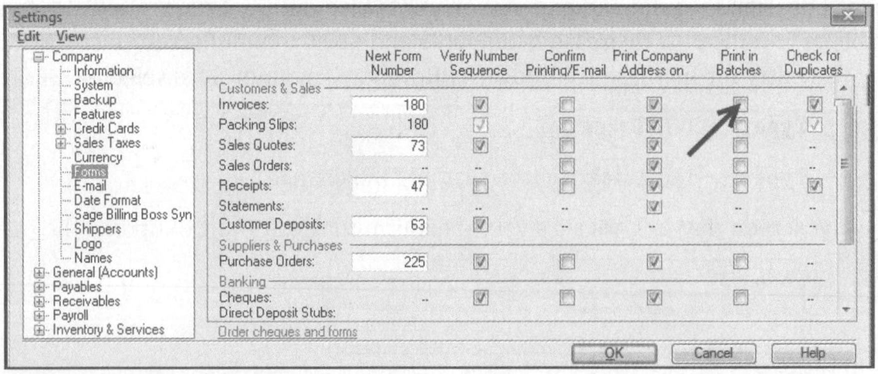

Click the **Print In Batches check box for Invoices**, the first form listed.

Click the **check box for the other forms** that you want to be able to print in batches.

Click **OK** to save the changes.

Now, the Reports menu in the Home window has a Print Batches menu option.

Choose the **Reports menu** then **choose Print Batches** and **click Sales Invoices** to see the printing options:

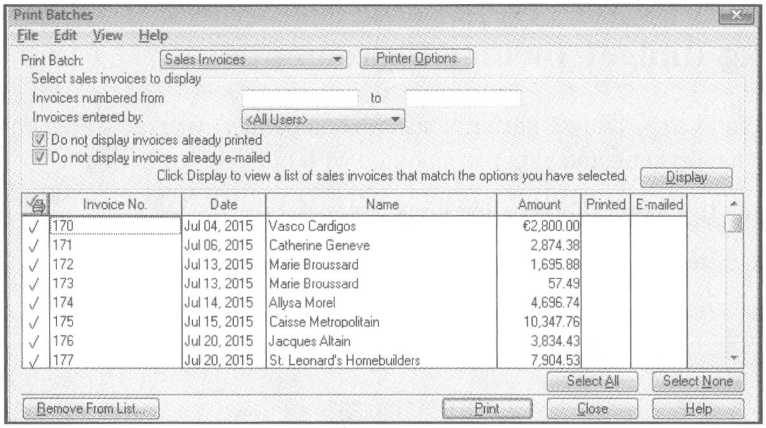

From this screen, you can choose other forms to print in batches. These are available from the **Print Batch** drop-down list. If some invoices have already been **Printed** or **E-mailed**, they will be displayed with a ✓ in the corresponding column. You can remove them from the display by clicking the appropriate check boxes. You can choose a **range of Invoice Numbers** or a specific **User** as selection criteria. After making these selections, click **Display** to show only the requested invoices.

Initially, the ✓s in the Print column indicate all invoices are selected for printing. Clicking **Select None** will remove all the ✓s and clicking **Select All** will select all listed invoices. You can also select invoices individually by clicking Select None and then clicking the invoices you want to print.

Choose the **invoices** you want to print so that only those invoices have a ✓.

Click **Print**. Printing begins immediately, so be sure that you have loaded the forms you need (or use plain paper for practice).

Click **Close** or select another form from the Print Batch list to print other forms.

Printing in Batches from Journals

When you allow batch printing from the Forms Settings screen, you can print these forms in batches directly from the related journal.

All the journals that have a Print tool will have a **Print Batches tool** added to the tool bar for this purpose, that is, the Sales, Purchases, Payments and Paycheques journals.

Budget Reports

Effective use of budget reports involves more than merely observing whether budgeted targets were met or not. Sometimes more information is gained when targets are not met, because the differences can lead to important questions:

- Were the targets realistic? What items were not on target and why?
- If performance exceeds the targets, how can we repeat the success?
- If performance did not meet the targets, were there factors that we failed to anticipate?
- Should we revise future budgets based on the new information?

The problem-solving cycle is set in motion. Even an Income Statement that is on target should be reviewed carefully. There may be room for improvement if the budget

NOTES

Remember that you can customize invoices before printing them. Refer to Appendix E on the Student DVD.

You cannot preview the invoices from the Print Batches window.

NOTES

To print the invoices, you must choose Custom Form and Sage 50 Form in the Reports & Forms settings on the Invoices screen. Choose Invoice in the Description field for invoices and e-mail.

NOTES

The Budget Report that shows budget amounts was described on page 557.

was a conservative estimate. Or you may want to include new information that will affect future performance and was unknown when the budget was drawn up.

Displaying Budget Income Statements

Reports used to analyze budget performance are comparative income statements, comparing actual revenue and expense amounts with budgeted amounts.

Open the **Report Centre** and **click Financials**.

Click the ⊞ **beside Income Statement** to expand the list.

Click Comparative 2 Period and then **click Modify This Report**:

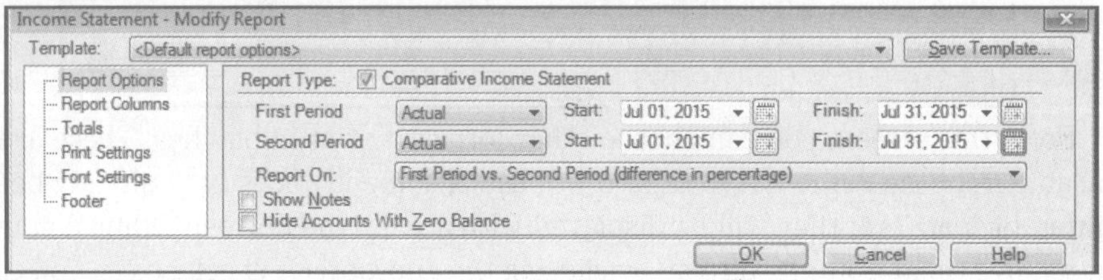

Click Actual in the **Second Period field** to see the budget-related option:

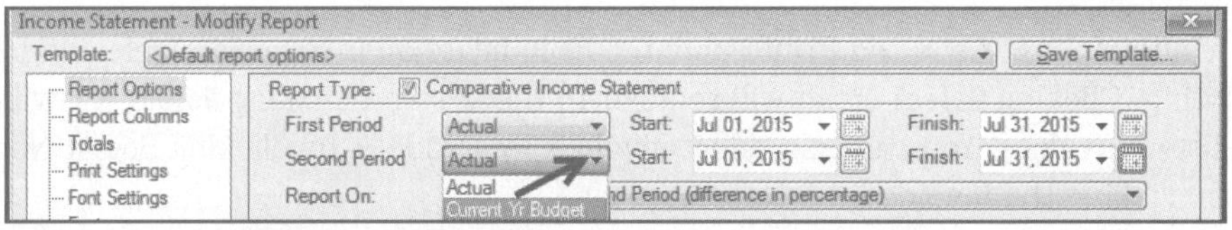

Click Current Yr Budget to change the option.

Budget income statements compare budgeted to actual amounts.

The **Report On** options are the same as the options for regular comparative income statements, but now the Second Period refers to budgeted amounts. Three types of reports are available. The first, **First** (actual) **Period Vs. Second** (budget) **Period (Amounts Only)**, lists the amounts that were budgeted for the revenue and expense accounts for the period indicated and the revenues and expenses actually obtained for the same period. The second, **First** (actual) **Period Vs. Second** (budget) **Period (Difference In Percentage)**, gives these two amounts as well as the percentage that the actual amount is above or below the budgeted amount. The third option, **First** (actual) **Period Vs. Second** (budget) **Period (Difference In Amounts)** provides budget and actual as base amounts, plus the difference between them as a dollar amount.

For the dollar difference and the percentage difference reports, a positive difference means that the budget was exceeded; a negative difference indicates that the results came in under budget. Remember that for revenues, a positive difference (first period amounts are greater than second period amounts) means results were better than expected, but for expenses, a positive difference means that results were poorer than expected (expenses were higher than budgeted). Cost of goods sold will increase directly with sales, so positive differences can mean either improved sales or higher costs, or both.

Click the **budget report** you want. **Close** the **display** when finished.

When you add budget details for divisions, you can also create **division budget reports**. Choose the Reports menu, then choose Division and click Budget. Choose the Report Type, dates and divisions and click OK.

NOTES
You can also choose the Reports menu, then choose Financials and click Income Statement to display the Income Statement options. Click the Report Type field and click Comparative Income Statement.

NOTES
You can choose to show the budget amounts in either the first or the second period.
In our example, we have the budget data in the second period.

Printing Budget Reports

Display the **report** you want to print. **Click** the **Print button** or **choose** the **File menu** in the report window and **click Print**.

Close the **displayed report** when you have finished. **Close** the **Report Centre**.

NOTES
Remember to check your printer selection before you print reports.

Graphing Budget Reports

When the Budgeting option is activated and set up, two budget-related graphs are added to the Graphs menu: Sales vs Budget and Expenses vs Budget. Graphs are available only from the Home window.

Sales vs Budget Graphs

Choose the **Graphs menu** in the Home window and **click Sales Vs Budget** to display the set of revenue accounts:

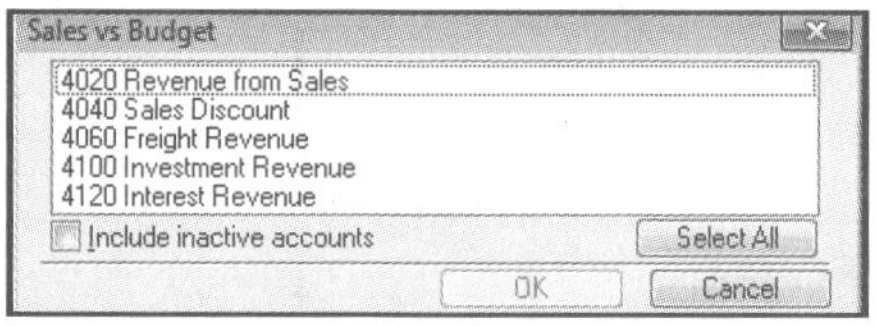

Press and **hold** ctrl and **click** the **accounts** you want to include in the graph or **click Select All**.

Click **OK** to display the graph as a bar chart:

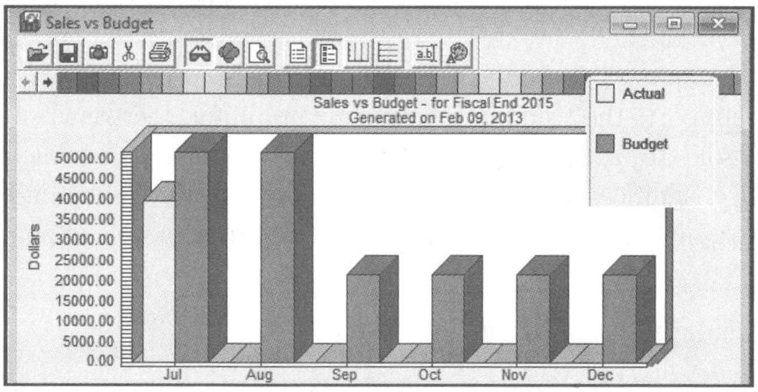

The options for displaying, editing, printing and copying budget graphs and so on are the same as those for other graphs.

The displayed graph includes all revenue accounts **before** the 10 percent budget decrease at the end of July. The amounts for the selected revenue accounts are added together in the single bar labelled Actual. The other bar represents the budgeted amount for the same accounts together. Revenue was much lower than expected, indicating a decline in performance. Budgeted amounts are shown for the remaining months of the fiscal period. There are no actual sales amounts after July.

Close the **displayed graph** when you have finished.

Expenses vs Budget Graphs

Choose the **Graphs menu** in the Home window and **click Expenses Vs Budget** to display the set of expense accounts:

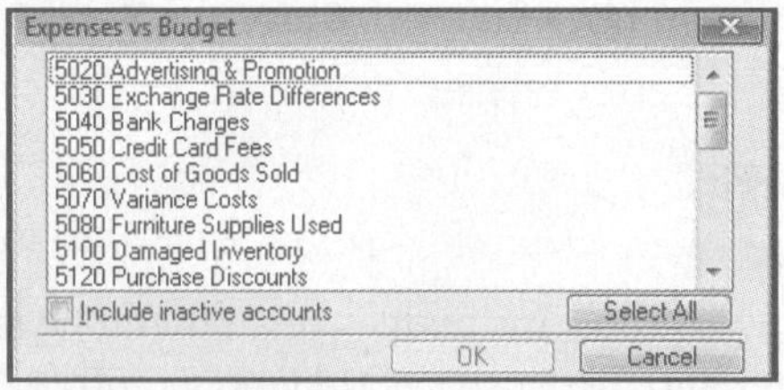

Press and **hold** *ctrl* and **click** the **accounts** you want to include in the graph or **click Select All**.

Click **OK** to display the bar chart:

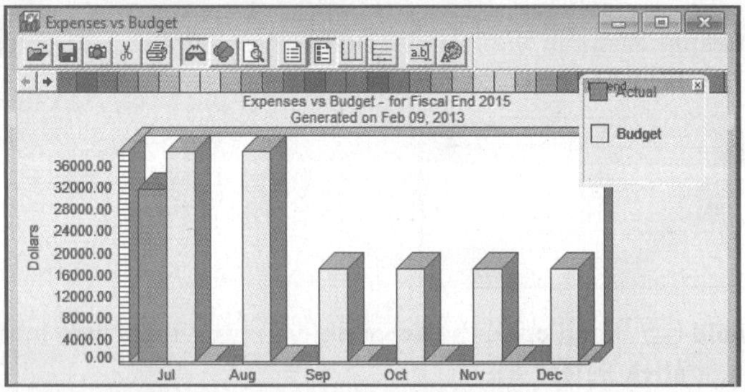

The displayed graph includes all expense accounts at the end of July, before changing the budgeted amounts. The amounts for the selected expense accounts are added together in the bar labelled Actual. The second bar represents the budgeted amount for the same accounts. The graph shows that expenses were also lower than expected. This result supports the trend in the revenue graph for decreased sales because cost of goods sold, the largest expense, is directly proportional to sales. Net income for July was also significantly below the budget forecast. Budgeted amounts are shown for the remaining months of the fiscal period. There are no actual expense amounts after July.

Close the **displayed graph** when you have finished.

R E V I E W

The Student DVD with Data Files includes Review Questions and Supplementary Cases for this chapter.

CHAPTER FIFTEEN

Tesses Tresses

OBJECTIVES

After completing this chapter, you should be able to

- ***prepare*** bank deposit slips
- ***print*** Transaction Reports for bank accounts
- ***compare*** bank statements with Transaction Reports
- ***turn on*** the account reconciliation feature
- ***create*** new linked accounts for reconciliation
- ***set up*** the account reconciliation information
- ***reconcile*** the bank account statement with the General Ledger
- ***reverse*** NSF cheques manually
- ***display*** and ***print*** account reconciliation reports
- ***clear*** paid invoices and ***remove*** accounts

COMPANY INFORMATION

Company Profile

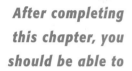

NOTES
Tesses Tresses
55 Salon Rd.
Charlottetown, PE C1A 6D3
Tel: (902) 729-6211
Fax: (902) 728-4821
Business No.: 136 422 374

Tesses Tresses, a hair salon in Charlottetown, Prince Edward Island, is a family business owned by Tess Dubois, her husband, Ian, and her daughter, Felicia. All three had both professional and business management training to prepare them for running the salon. Together they provide a full range of hair care services to clients, most of whom return regularly. Unlike many salons where the price depends on the stylist and client, Tesses Tresses charges one price for each service regardless of client gender or stylist. They also sell a limited range of high-quality hair care products.

The salon building they own includes two apartments that are rented to students. These tenants provided postdated cheques for three months at the beginning of January.

Instead of hiring a maintenance, cleaning and laundry company to take care of the premises, the Dubois family shares this responsibility to reduce expenses. Cleaning is required almost continually to meet hygiene standards for health and safety.

The salon's regular suppliers provide inventory products, including those used in the salon for client services; office supplies; cleaning supplies for the salon; linens such as towels, capes and gowns; and hairdressing equipment. Supplier records are set up for all of these suppliers as well as for utility service companies and government agencies to which Tesses Tresses remits taxes. The salon pays HST on all purchases.

Although most clients are one-time clients who pay by cash and credit card, some repeat clients have accounts and are entitled to a 2 percent discount if they pay within five days. Net payment is due in 15 days. The cash clients do not receive a discount. A record called Cash Customers is set up for the weekly summaries of cash and credit card sales. Clients pay HST at 14 percent on merchandise they buy from the salon and on all services. The tax rates and codes are entered into client and inventory records, so the program automatically calculates taxes.

Tesses Tresses also provides hair styling services to local theatre companies, cutting and styling hair for cast members before performances, re-styling throughout the show for cast character changes and styling wigs. These evening commitments do not conflict with the usual daytime salon business hours. The theatre companies pay preferred prices at about 20 percent off regular prices in addition to the discount for early payment.

At the beginning of February, some unfilled purchase orders will provide the inventory for the additional purchases anticipated for Valentine's Day.

The accounting records for Tesses Tresses were converted to Sage 50 at the beginning of January, and the transactions for January have been completed. The files are ready for January bank account transactions (deposits and account reconciliation) and February transactions. The current accounting records include:

- Chart of Accounts
- Trial Balance as at January 31, 2015
- Supplier Information
- Client Information
- Inventory Information
- Accounting Procedures

CHART OF ACCOUNTS

TESSES TRESSES

ASSETS
- 1030 Undeposited Cash and Cheques
- 1060 Bank: Chequing Account
- 1080 Bank: Credit Cards
- 1200 Accounts Receivable
- 1240 Prepaid Insurance
- 1260 Prepaid Subscriptions
- 1300 Towels and Capes
- 1320 Office Supplies
- 1340 Washroom & Cleaning Supplies
- 1360 Salon Supplies
- 1420 Hair Care Products ▶
- ▶1520 Computer and Cash Register
- 1540 Furniture and Fixtures
- 1560 Salon Equipment
- 1580 Salon and Building

LIABILITIES
- 2100 Bank Loan
- 2150 Credit Card Payable
- 2200 Accounts Payable
- 2750 HST Charged on Sales
- 2760 HST Paid on Purchases
- 2850 Mortgage Payable ▶

▶EQUITY
- 3100 TT Capital
- 3150 TT Drawings
- 3600 Net Income

REVENUE
- 4100 Revenue from Sales
- 4120 Revenue from Services
- 4140 Rental Income
- 4160 Sales Discounts
- 4220 Interest Revenue
- 4240 Other Revenue ▶

▶EXPENSE
- 5020 Advertising and Promotion
- 5040 Bank Charges
- 5060 Credit Card Fees
- 5080 Cost of Services
- 5180 Inventory Losses
- 5200 Cost of Goods Sold
- 5220 Purchase Discounts
- 5240 Insurance Expense
- 5260 Subscriptions Expense
- 5300 Supplies Used
- 5320 Utilities
- 5340 Interest Expense

NOTES: The Chart of Accounts includes only postable accounts and Net Income.

TRIAL BALANCE

TESSES TRESSES

January 31, 2015

		Debits	Credits
1030	Undeposited Cash and Cheques	$ 14 478.11	
1060	Bank: Chequing Account	35 312.22	
1080	Bank: Credit Cards	8 587.26	
1200	Accounts Receivable	22.80	
1240	Prepaid Insurance	750.00	
1260	Prepaid Subscriptions	270.00	
1300	Towels and Capes	530.00	
1320	Office Supplies	130.00	
1340	Washroom & Cleaning Supplies	565.00	
1360	Salon Supplies	255.00	
1420	Hair Care Products	1 567.50	
1520	Computer and Cash Register	4 200.00	
1540	Furniture and Fixtures	7 600.00	
1560	Salon Equipment	4 600.00	
1580	Salon and Building	220 000.00	
2100	Bank Loan		$ 23 520.00
2150	Credit Card Payable		79.80
2200	Accounts Payable		1 459.20 ▶
▶ 2750	HST Charged on Sales		3 022.32
2760	HST Paid on Purchases	484.12	
2850	Mortgage Payable		149 750.00
3100	TT Capital		103 839.00
4100	Revenue from Sales		4 699.00
4120	Revenue from Services		16 889.00
4140	Rental Income		945.00
4160	Sales Discounts	55.18	
5060	Credit Card Fees	315.98	
5200	Cost of Goods Sold	1 860.50	
5220	Purchase Discounts		60.35
5240	Insurance Expense	150.00	
5260	Subscriptions Expense	30.00	
5300	Supplies Used	840.00	
5320	Utilities	290.00	
5340	Interest Expense	1 370.00	
		$304 263.67	$304 263.67

SUPPLIER INFORMATION

TESSES TRESSES

Supplier Name (Contact)	Address	Phone No. Fax No.	E-mail Web Site	Terms Tax ID
Air Pro (Curly Locks)	390 Brows Lane Charlottetown, PE C1A 6M3	Tel: (902) 722-0217 Fax: (902) 723-8100	curly@airpro.com www.airpro.com	net 15 137 456 199
All U Need	Maypoint Plaza #64 Charlottetown, PE C1E 1E2	Tel: (902) 728-4314	www.alluneed.com	net 1 382 732 162
Atlantic Power Corp.	16 Lektrik Rd. Charlottetown, PE C1C 6G1	Tel: (902) 726-1615	www.apc.ca	net 1
Charlottetown City Treasurer	78 Fitzroy St. Charlottetown, PE C1A 1R5	Tel: (902) 725-9173	www.charlottetown.ca/fin	net 1
Eastern Tel (I.D. Caller)	36 Nassau St. Charlottetown, PE C1A 7V9	Tel: (902) 723-2355		net 1
Fine Brushes (Harry Bristle)	13 Ave. Costey Dorval, QC H9S 4C7	Tel: (514) 457-1826 Fax: (514) 457-1883	bristle@finebrushes.com www.finebrushes.com	net 20 188 462 457
Lookin' Good (N. Vayne)	18 Vivanle Cr. Summerside, PE C1N 6C4	Tel: (902) 829-4763 Fax: (902) 829-7392	vayne@lookingood.com www.lookingood.com	net 10 192 721 214
Pro-Line Inc. (Awl Fluff)	190 Rue Mutchmore Hull, QC J8Y 3S9	Tel: (819) 658-7227 Fax: (819) 658-7192	awl.fluff@proline.com www.proline.com	2/10, n/30 (after tax) 621 372 611
Receiver General for Canada	Summerside Tax Centre	Tel: (902) 821-8186		net 1
Seaside Papers (Fyne Pulp)	40 Harbour View Dr. Charlottetown, PE C1A 7A8	Tel: (902) 720-1623 Fax: (902) 720-1639	pulp@seasidepapers.com www.seasidepapers.com	net 1 810 721 011
Sharp Scissors (S. Cutter)	22 Bellevue Ave. Summerside, PE C1N 2C7	Tel: (902) 923-1995 Fax: (902) 923-1726	cutter@sharp.com www.sharp.com	net 10 138 221 100
Zines Inc. (Buetee Tipps)	344 Lepage Ave. Summerside, PE C1N 3E6	Tel: (902) 553- 6291 Fax: (902) 553-7155	tipps@zines.com www.zines.com	net 10 205 602 301

OUTSTANDING SUPPLIER INVOICES

TESSES TRESSES

Supplier Name	Terms	Date	Inv/Chq No.	Amount	Discount	Total
Fine Brushes	net 20	Dec. 20/14	FB-4321	$330.00		$330.00
		Jan. 09/15	CHQ 411	330.00		330.00
	net 20	Jan. 17/15	FB-6219	547.20		547.20
			Balance owing			$547.20
Pro-Line Inc.	2/10, n/30	Dec. 28/14	PL-1002	$ 945.00		$ 945.00
		Jan. 4/15	CHQ 410	926.10	$18.90	945.00
	2/10, n/30	Jan. 4/15	PL-1012	2 072.52		2 072.52
		Jan. 14/15	CHQ 413	2 031.07	41.45	2 072.52
Sharp Scissors	net 10	Jan. 24/15	SS-432	$912.00		$912.00
			Grand Total			$1 459.20

NOTES: Cash and Credit Card Purchases are not included in the chart of supplier invoices.

CLIENT INFORMATION

TESSES TRESSES

Client Name (Contact)	Address	Phone No. Fax No.	E-mail Web Site	Terms Credit Limit
Atta Schule (tenant)		Tel: (902) 724-2996	atta.schule@undergrad.upei.ca	first of month
Brioche Bridal Party (Bonnie Brioche)	75 Marital Way Charlottetown, PE C1E 4A2	Tel: (902) 723-1194 Fax: (902) 726-1921	brioche@weddingbells.com	2/5, n/15 $1 000
Cash Customers				cash/credit card
Conn Seted	14 Hi Brow St. Charlottetown, PE C1E 3X1	Tel: (902) 723-0099	conn.seted@aol.com	net 15 $1 000
Irma Vannitee	77 Makeover Cr. Charlottetown, PE C1B 1J5	Tel: (902) 726-7715	irma.van@skindeep.com	2/5, n/15 $1 000
*On Stage Theatre Company (Marvelle Stage)	100 Marquee Blvd. Charlottetown, PE C1A 2M1	Tel: (902) 727-8201 Fax: (902) 727-0663	marvelle@onstage.com www.onstage.com	2/5, n/15 $2 000
Proud Family	98 Proud St. Charlottetown, PE C1B 3C1	Tel: (902) 721-1113	theprouds@shaw.ca	net 15 $1 000
Stu Dents (tenant)		Tel: (902) 724-7103	stu.dents@undergrad.upei.ca	first of month
*Twilight Theatre (Ona Roll)	55 Footlights Dr. Charlottetown, PE C1B 6V2	Tel: (902) 728-4661 Fax: (902) 724-1556	ona.roll@twilight.com www.twilight.com	2/5, n/15 $2 000

NOTES: All client discounts are calculated on after-tax amounts.
* Indicates preferred customer.

OUTSTANDING CLIENT INVOICES

TESSES TRESSES

Client Name	Terms	Date	Inv/Chq No.	Amount	Discount	Total
Atta Schule	rent payment	Jan. 2/15	CHQ 415			$395.00
	rent payment	Feb. 2/15	CHQ 416 (postdated rent payment)			395.00
	rent payment	Mar. 2/15	CHQ 417 (postdated rent payment)			395.00

▶

OUTSTANDING CLIENT INVOICES CONTINUED

TESSES TRESSES

Client Name	Terms	Date	Inv/Chq No.	Amount	Discount	Total
Brioche Bridal Party	2/5, n/15	Jan. 9/15	468	$121.98		$121.98
		Jan. 14/15	CHQ 206	119.54	$2.44	121.98
Conn Seted	net 15	Jan. 24/15	477			$45.60
		Jan. 29/15	CHQ 238			$45.60
Irma Vannitee	2/5, n/15	Dec. 28/14	452	$120.00		$120.00
		Jan. 2/15	CHQ 46	117.60	$2.40	120.00
	2/5, n/15	Jan. 2/15	464	92.34		92.34
		Jan. 7/15	CHQ 918	90.49	1.85	92.34
	2/5, n/15	Jan. 7/15	467	126.54		126.54
		Jan. 17/15	CHQ CC-61	126.54		126.54
	2/5, n/15	Jan. 16/15	471	67.26		67.26
		Jan. 20/15	CHQ 74	65.91	1.35	67.26
	2/5, n/15	Jan. 27/15	478	22.80		22.80
			Balance owing			$22.80
On Stage Theatre Company	2/5, n/15	Dec. 29/14	455	$250.00		$250.00
		Jan. 3/15	CHQ 382	245.00	$ 5.00	250.00
	2/5, n/15	Jan. 20/15	474	948.48		948.48
		Jan. 24/15	CHQ 429	929.51	18.97	948.48
	2/5, n/15	Jan. 28/15	479	948.48		948.48
		Jan. 31/15	CHQ 498	929.51	18.97	948.48
Stu Dents	rent payment	Jan. 2/15	CHQ 161			$550.00
	rent payment	Feb. 2/15	CHQ 162 (postdated rent payment)			550.00
	rent payment	Mar. 2/15	CHQ 163 (postdated rent payment)			550.00
Twilight Theatre	2/5, n/15	Dec. 28/14	453	$210.00		$210.00
		Jan. 2/15	CHQ 5121	205.80	$4.20	210.00
			Grand Total			$22.80

INVENTORY ITEM INFORMATION

TESSES TRESSES

Item Code	Item Description	Unit	Min Qty	Selling Price Reg	(Pref)	Qty on Hand	Total (Cost)	Tax
Hair Products: Total asset value $1 886.50 (Asset account: 1420, Revenue account: 4100, Expense account: 5200)								
BRS1	Hair Brush: natural bristle	each	2	$28	(24)	16	$ 192.00	HST
BRS2	Hair Brush: styling	each	2	24	(21)	28	224.00	HST
CN1	Pro-Line Conditioner: 150 ml	bottle	3	26	(22)	14	154.00	HST
CN2	Pro-Line Hot Oil Treatment 75 ml	tube	3	29	(25)	33	313.50	HST
FRZ1	Pro-Line Defrizzer: cream 100 ml	jar	3	14	(12)	29	174.00	HST
GEL1	Pro-Line Spray Gel: shaper 150 ml	can	5	22	(18)	21	189.00	HST
SHM1	Pro-Line Shampoo: 225 ml	bottle	5	21	(17)	17	153.00	HST
SPR1	Pro-Line Hair Spray: gentle 150 ml	can	5	17	(14)	28	168.00	HST
							$1 567.50	
Salon Services (Revenue account: 4120, Expense account: 5080)								
SRV1	Colour	each		$ 45	($36)			HST
SRV2	Conditioning Treatment	each		20	(16)			HST
SRV3	Cut and Style	each		40	(32)			HST
SRV4	Highlights	each		100	(80)			HST
SRV5	Perm	each		80	(64)			HST
SRV6	Wash and Style	each		20	(16)			HST
SRV7	Wig Wash, Set and Style	each		30	(24)			HST

NOTES
In 2013, PEI modified its taxation rates and methods, adopting the single 14 percent HST to replace the separate 5 percent GST (on goods and services) and 10 percent PST on goods only. Before the change, the non-refundable PST was charged on the base price of goods plus GST – GST was taxable.

WARNING!
You need to enter a negative receipt for these NSF cheques. You cannot reverse the receipt because different accounts are involved. The original receipt was deposited to Undeposited Cash and Cheques, but the NSF cheque credits the Bank: Chequing Account, after the deposit was entered.

Accounting Procedures

Taxes

HST at 14 percent is charged on all goods and services sold by the salon. Tesses Tresses remits the HST owing — *HST Charged on Sales* less *HST Paid on Purchases* — to the Receiver General by the last day of each month for the previous month.

Sales Summaries

Most salon sales are to one-time clients who do not have accounts. These sales are summarized weekly according to payment — by cash or by credit card — and entered for the client named Cash Customers. By choosing Cash Customers as the client for these sales, the default tax codes and terms should be correct.

Receipts and Bank Deposits

Cash and cheques received in payment are held for weekly deposits in the temporary bank clearing account, *Undeposited Cash and Cheques*. Therefore, Tesses Tresses uses this account as the default Receivables linked bank account for all receipts.

NSF Cheques

If a cheque is deposited from an account that does not have enough money to cover it, the bank returns it to the depositor as NSF (non-sufficient funds). To record the NSF cheque, enter a negative receipt in the Receipts Journal. Select *Bank: Chequing Account* as the Deposit To account. Turn on the option to Include Fully Paid Invoices and enter a negative payment amount. Enter the bank debit number as the receipt and add NSF to the original cheque number in the Cheque field. If a discount was taken for early payment, reverse this amount as well. Then enter a Sales Journal invoice for the amount of the handling charge. Refer to page 605 and A–25 if you need more help.

Cost of Supplies

Instead of buying separate salon supplies for regular client services, Tesses Tresses uses its inventory stock of shampoos, conditioners, gels and so on. Inventory Adjustment entries are completed to make these transfers at cost from the inventory asset account to the supplies account.

INSTRUCTIONS

1. **Enter** the **deposit slips** and **set up** and **complete** the **account reconciliation** for January using the Chart of Accounts, Trial Balance, Supplier, Client and Inventory information provided and using the keystrokes with the source documents as a guide. The journal transactions for January have been completed for you.
2. **Enter** the **source documents** for February, including the account reconciliation.
3. **Print** the **reports** indicated on the following chart after completing your entries.

REPORTS

Accounts
- [ ] Chart of Accounts
- [ ] Account List
- [ ] General Journal Entries

Financials
- [x] Comparative Balance Sheet dates: Feb. 1 and Feb. 28 with difference in percentage
- [x] Income Statement from Jan. 1 to Feb. 28
- [x] Trial Balance date: Feb. 28
- [x] All Journal Entries: Feb. 1 to Feb. 28
- [x] General Ledger: for accounts 1060 and 1080 from Jan. 1 to Feb. 28
- [ ] Statement of Cash Flows
- [x] Cash Flow Projection Detail Report for account 1060 for 30 days
- [ ] Gross Margin Income Statement

Tax
- [ ] Report on

Banking
- [x] Account Reconciliation Summary Report: for 1060 and 1080 from Jan. 1 to Feb. 28
- [ ] Bank Transaction Report
- [ ] Reconciliation Transaction Report
- [x] Deposit Slip Detail Report for account 1060 from Jan. 1 to Feb. 28
- [x] Account Reconciliation Journal Entries: Jan. 1 to Feb. 28
- [x] Deposit Slip Journal Entries: Jan. 1 to Feb. 28
- [ ] Cheque Log Report

Payables
- [ ] Supplier List
- [ ] Supplier Aged
- [ ] Aged Overdue Payables
- [ ] Expenses Journal Entries
- [ ] Payments Journal Entries
- [ ] Supplier Expenses

Receivables
- [ ] Client List
- [ ] Client Aged
- [ ] Aged Overdue Receivables
- [ ] Revenues Journal Entries
- [ ] Receipts Journal Entries
- [ ] Client Revenues
- [ ] Client Statements

Inventory & Services
- [ ] Inventory & Services List
- [ ] Inventory Summary
- [ ] Inventory Quantity
- [x] Inventory Statistics: all items and all details
- [ ] Inventory Sales Summary
- [ ] Inventory Transaction Summary
- [ ] Item Assembly Journal Entries
- [ ] Adjustment Journal Entries
- [ ] Inventory Price Lists

Management Reports
- [ ] Ledger

GRAPHS
- [ ] Payables by Aging Period
- [ ] Payables by Supplier
- [ ] Receivables by Aging Period
- [ ] Receivables by Client
- [ ] Revenues vs Receivables
- [ ] Receivables Due vs Payables Due
- [ ] Revenues by Account
- [ ] Expenses by Account
- [ ] Expenses and Net Profit as % of Revenue

KEYSTROKES

Entering Bank Deposit Slips

Previously, we recorded receipts directly as deposits to the linked bank accounts. In this chapter, we show the procedure for recording receipts and deposits separately. The deposits for the cash and cheques received in January have not yet been recorded.

Open **SageData13\Tess\tess**. **Accept** **January 31** as the session date.

Click **Banking** in the Modules pane list.

Deposits are made using the Make Deposit icon marked with the arrow:

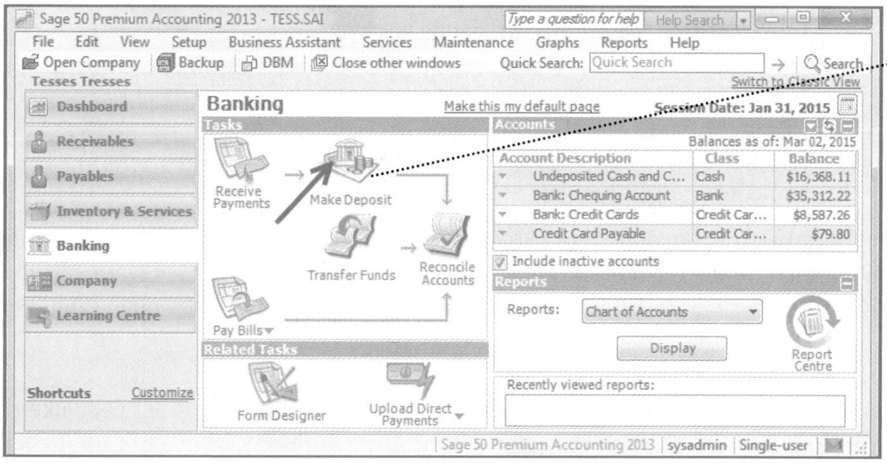

NOTES

If you are using backup files, restore SageData13\tess1.CAB or tess1 to SageData13\Tess\tess.

NOTES

Home window ledger record balances for Tesses Tresses are shown as at March 2, the latest transaction date (for the postdated rent cheques).

Remember that Make Other Payment is the default type of transaction from the Pay Bills icon in the Banking module window.

The first memo requires us to record the deposits for January.

✓ 1 **Memo #7** **Dated Jan. 31/15**

Use the deposit information slips to prepare deposit slips #1 to #5. All amounts were deposited to Bank: Chequing Account.

✓ **DEPOSIT SLIP # 1** **JANUARY 7, 2015**

Date	Cheque #	Client	Amount
Jan 2	46	Irma Vannitee	$ 117.60
Jan 2	5121	Twilight Theatre	205.80
Jan 2	161	Stu Dents	550.00
Jan 2	415	Atta Schule	395.00
Jan 3	382	On Stage Theatre Company	245.00
Jan 7	918	Irma Vannitee	90.49
		Total Cheques	$1 603.89
		Cash	$2 299.38
		(Consisting of 3 × $5; 18 × $10; 25 × $20; 12 × $50; 10 × $100; Coin $4.38)	
		Total Deposit	$3 903.27

Click the **Make Deposit icon** to open the Reconciliation & Deposits journal:

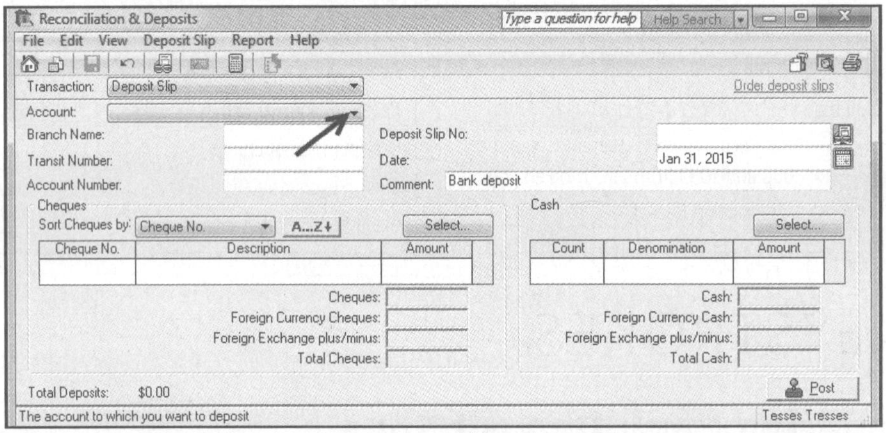

WARNING! You cannot adjust deposit slips or account reconciliation after posting, except with General Journal entries. Back up your data files before beginning the banking transactions.

The journal is named Reconciliation & Deposits because both types of transactions are entered here. You can choose from the **Transaction** drop-down list to change the type. Deposit Slip is selected in the Transaction field because we selected this Home window icon.

The deposit transaction has two parts: the Deposit To component that we see here and the Deposit From portion. All cash and cheques were debited to *Undeposited Cash and Cheques*, a Cash class **clearing account** that is the default account for all receipts. Now we need to transfer these receipts to the *Bank: Chequing Account* as deposits.

First we choose the bank account receiving the deposit.

Click the **Account list arrow** as shown:

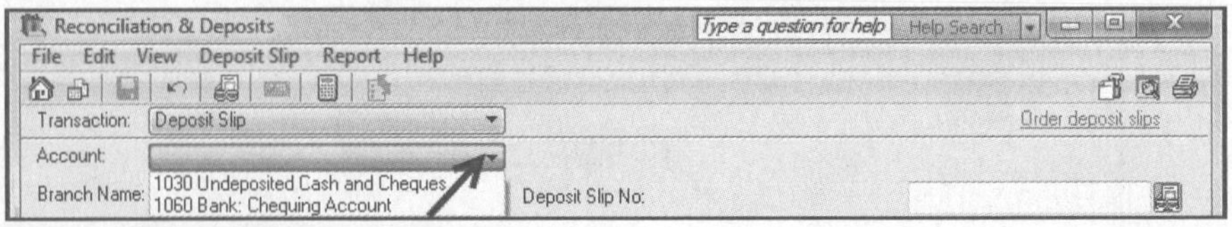

CLASSIC VIEW Click the Reconciliation & Deposits icon

to open the journal and choose Deposit Slip from the Transaction drop-down list.

Both banking accounts are listed: *Undeposited Cash and Cheques* (the default linked Receivables Cash class account) and the Bank class *Bank: Chequing Account*. We must select *Bank: Chequing Account*, the account that is receiving the deposit.

Click **Bank: Chequing Account**.

NOTES Undeposited Cash and Cheques is set up as a Cash class account so that we can use it as the default linked principal bank account for the Receivables Ledger. You could also choose Bank as the class for this account. Both Bank and Cash class accounts can be selected as the default Receivables Bank account.

The deposit slip number is entered and will be updated automatically like the other forms in Sage 50.

Tesses Tresses makes weekly deposits to the bank account of all cash and cheques received during the week. We need to enter the date of the first deposit.

Enter **January 7, 2015** in the Date field for the first deposit.

Next, we must select the outstanding cheques and cash that will be deposited. The Deposit Slip has cheques on the left and cash on the right. There are separate **Select buttons** for these two types of currency. We will add the cheques first by using the Select button in the centre of the journal, above the field for listing the cheques.

The Select button we need is shown with the arrow pointer on it:

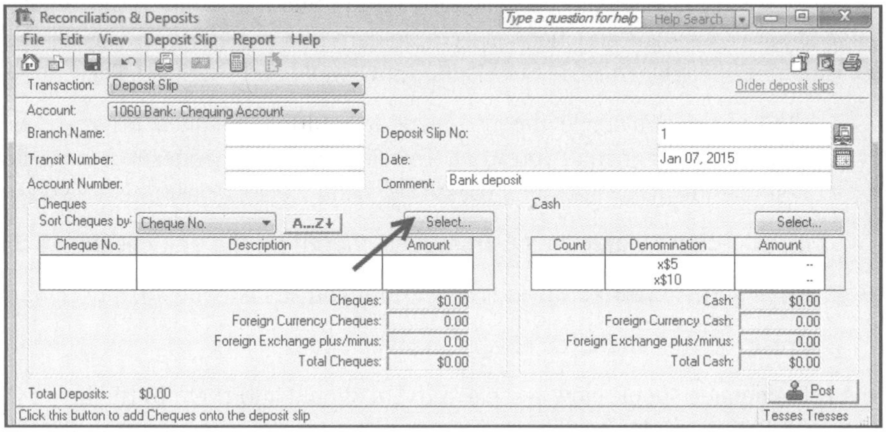

You can drag the column heading margins to change column sizes if you are unable to see all the information. Or you can maximize the journal.

Click the **Select button for Cheques** to open the list of outstanding cheques:

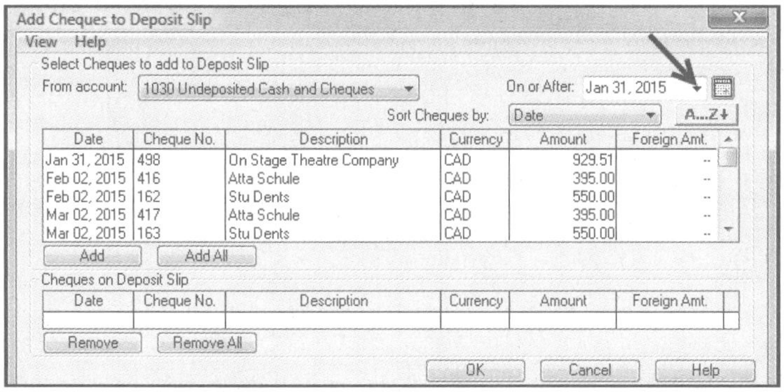

The first banking account, *Undeposited Cash and Cheques*, is selected as the default **From Account** and this is the one we want. Cheques are listed by date in ascending order, but you can choose a different order from the **Sort Cheques By** drop-down list. Cheques may be sorted by any of the column headings for the list of cheques (cheque number, currency, amount, description, foreign amount or foreign exchange amount). You can click the A...Z+ button — changing it to Z...A+ — to sort in descending order.

The session date, January 31, is entered in the **On Or After date** field, so only the cheques for January 31 and the postdated rent cheques are listed. We need to show all cheques that are dated on or after January 1, so this is the date we should enter.

Click the **On Or After field Calendar icon** and **click Jan 1** as the date.

NOTES

You do not need to type the year in the Reconciliation & Deposits Journal date fields. It will be added correctly by the program.

NOTES

When the bank account is set up for online reconciliation, the branch, transit and account numbers are required information in the ledger record and will be added to the Deposit Slip Journal. Online banking is illustrated in Appendix I on the Student DVD.

NOTES

Once the list is in descending order, the order button label changes to Z...A+. Clicking this button again restores the list to ascending order.

NOTES

You can also choose Jan 1 from the On Or After date field drop-down list. You can choose this date for all deposit slip transactions in this chapter if you want.

All the cheques received by the salon are now listed:

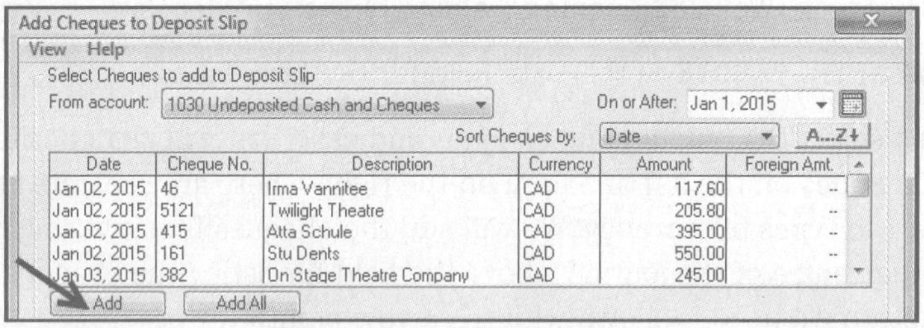

The next step is to select the cheques we want and add them to the deposit.

We should select the six cheques that are dated on or before January 7, cheques from Vannitee, Twilight Theatre, Stu Dents, Atta Schule and On Stage Theatre Company.

Click to select a single cheque. To select multiple cheques, press and hold *ctrl* and click each cheque you want. To select several cheques in a row, click the first cheque you want, then press *shift* and click the last cheque you need.

Click **cheque number 46 from Irma Vannitee**, the first cheque on the list.

Click the **down scroll arrow** until you see cheque #918 from Vannitee.

Press *shift* and **click** **cheque number 918**.

All six cheques should now be selected. We should add them to the list of Cheques On Deposit Slip in the lower half of the form.

Click the **Add button** to place the selected six cheques on the deposit slip:

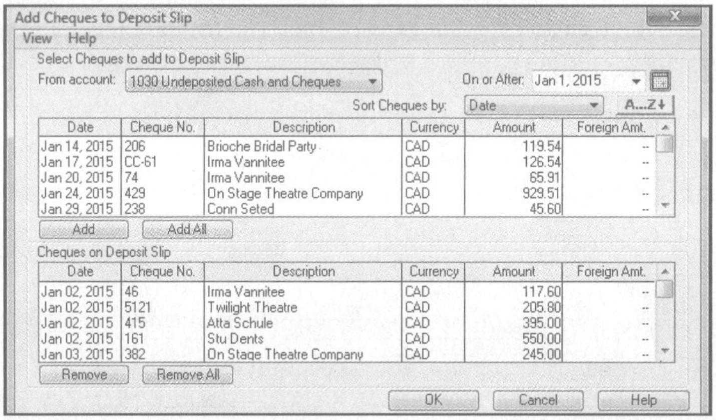

You can also add the cheques one at a time. Click a cheque and then click the Add button to move the cheque. Then click the next cheque and click Add. Repeat until all the cheques you want are in the Cheques On Deposit Slip list. If all cheques are deposited together, you can click Add All.

To **change a selection**, click a cheque in the Cheques On Deposit Slip list and click Remove. To start again, click Remove All to clear the list.

Click **OK** to return to the updated Reconciliation & Deposits Journal:

NOTES

You may prefer to select cheques one at a time when the ones you are depositing are not in sequence.

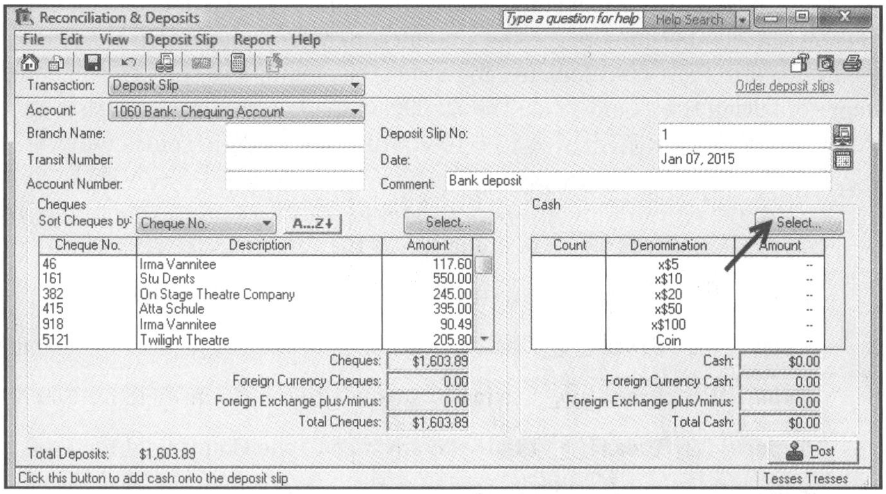

The selected six cheques are added and their total should match the amount on the Deposit Slip source document. If it does not, click the Select button again to correct the cheque selection. If a cheque amount is incorrect, close the journal without saving the changes and correct the original receipt transaction.

The next step is to add the cash portion of the deposit. Tesses Tresses has one cash sale summary amount to deposit, $2 299.38.

Click the **Select button for Cash** to open the deposit form for cash:

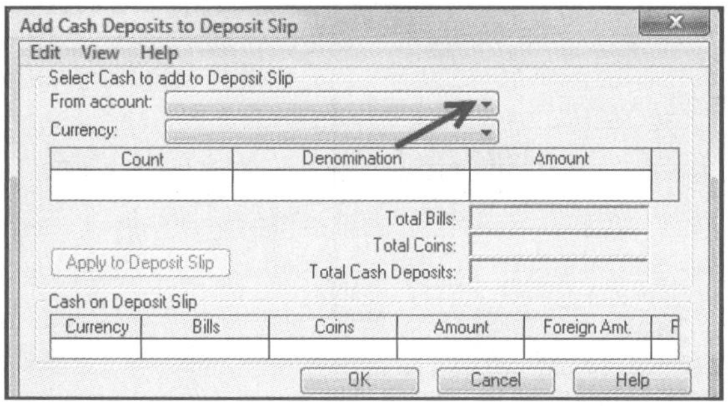

Cash receipts are not listed individually because they are usually combined in the store and held in the cash drawers or safe. When deposits are made, some cash is usually kept in the store to provide change for future clients. This balance may be transferred from *Undeposited Cash and Cheques* to a *Cash on Hand* account, recorded as a General Journal or Transfer Funds transaction. Similarly, the denominations of notes and coins that are received from clients may be different from the deposited ones. To keep the exercise simple, we deposit the full amount of cash received each week.

Since no account is entered by default, we first need to select the account that we are depositing from.

Choose **Undeposited Cash and Cheques** from the From Account drop-down list to modify the deposit form:

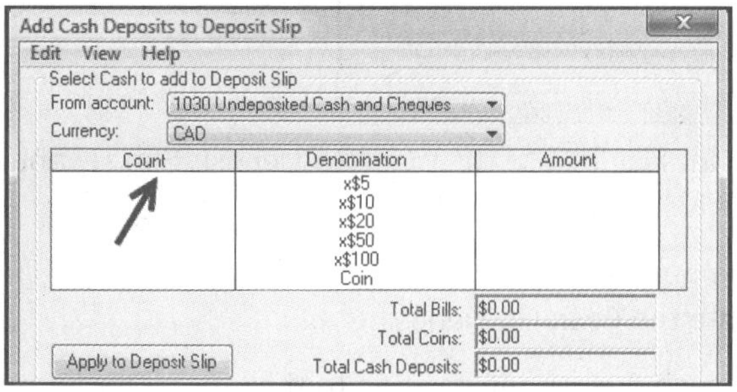

NOTES

The cheques on the deposit slip are sorted by cheque number. You can reverse the order (A...Z+ button) or sort the cheques by description or amount by making the selection from the Sort Cheques By drop-down list.

NOTES

The procedure for depositing partial amounts of cash is the same as the one we describe in this chapter.

NOTES

After selecting the From account, the currency is added – the denomination of the notes will be known and added to the deposit form.

The Cash Deposit form is completed in the same way as a deposit slip at the bank. You enter the number of notes or the amount for each denomination and the total amount of coins. Sage 50 calculates and totals the amounts as soon as you enter the number of bills in the Count field. The $2 299.38 in deposited cash consists of 3 × $5; 18 × $10; 25 × $20; 12 × $50; 10 × $100; and $4.38 in coins.

NOTES

Instead of pressing (tab) twice, you can press (↓) to move the cursor to the next Count line on the form.

Instead of entering the count for each denomination, you can enter the amount and Sage 50 will enter the corresponding count.

Click the **Count field beside** × **$5**.

Type 3 **Press** (tab) to enter $15 as the Amount.

Press (tab) **again** to move to the Count field for $10 notes.

Type 18 **Press** (tab) **twice** to advance to the Count field for $20 notes.

Type 25 **Press** (tab) **twice** to advance to the Count field for $50 notes.

Type 12 **Press** (tab) **twice** to advance to the Count field for $100 notes.

Type 10 **Press** (tab) **twice** to advance to the Count field for coins.

The amount for coins is entered as a total amount in the Amount field. You cannot type in the Count field for Coin.

Press (tab) to advance to the Amount field for coins.

Type 4.38 (You must enter the decimal for amounts less than one dollar.)

Press (tab) to update the total as shown:

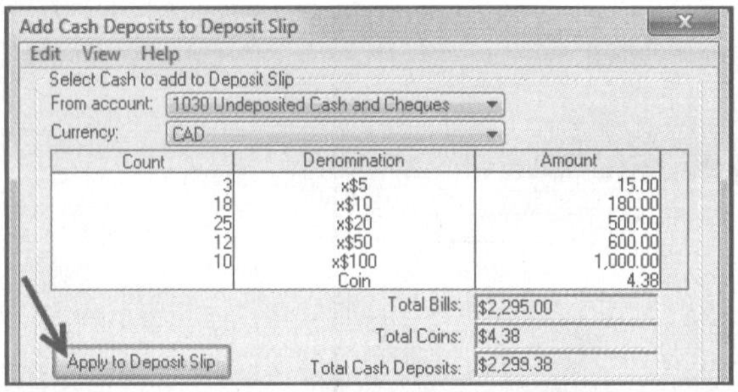

The total amounts for bills and coins remain separated, and the total for the cash deposit is calculated.

The next step is to apply the amount to the deposit slip.

NOTES

Tesses Tresses does not have any foreign currency transactions.

Click the **Apply To Deposit Slip button** to update the form:

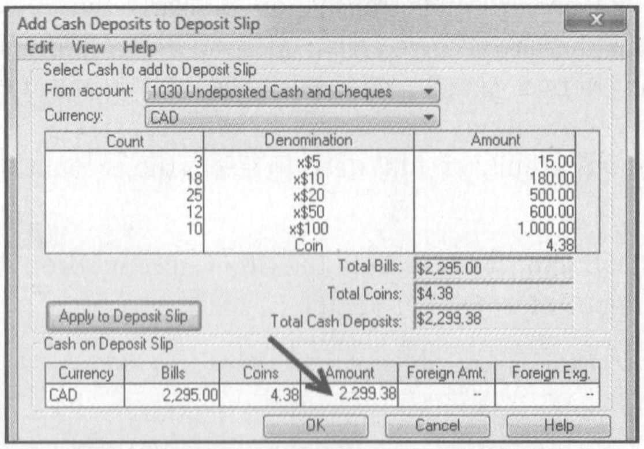

The total cash deposit amount is added to the Cash On Deposit Slip section. The currency for the amount is also included.

To make changes, edit a number in the Count field and press (tab). Click Apply To Deposit Slip to update the Cash On Deposit Slip.

Click **OK** to add this cash deposit information to the journal form:

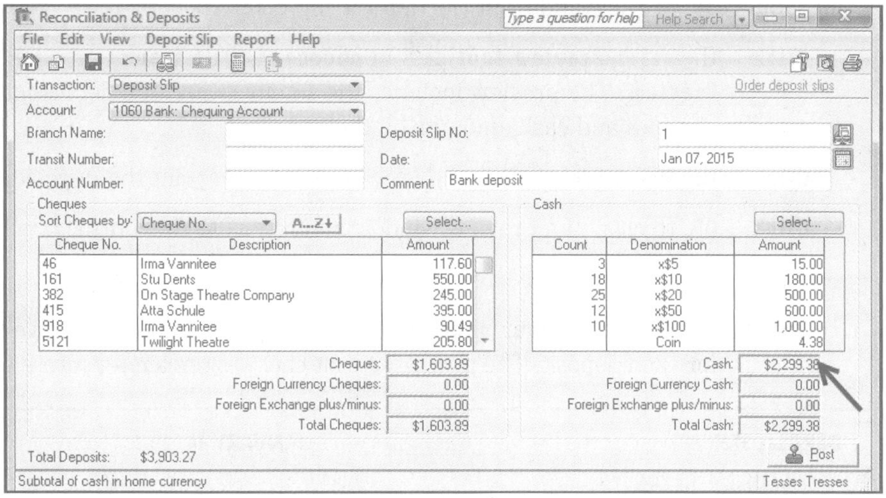

Reconciliation & Deposits

File Edit View Deposit Slip Report Help

Transaction: Deposit Slip — Order deposit slips

Account: 1060 Bank: Chequing Account

Branch Name: — Deposit Slip No: 1

Transit Number: — Date: Jan 07, 2015

Account Number: — Comment: Bank deposit

Cheques — Sort Cheques by: Cheque No.

Cheque No.	Description	Amount
46	Irma Vannitee	117.60
161	Stu Dents	550.00
382	On Stage Theatre Company	245.00
415	Atta Schule	395.00
918	Irma Vannitee	90.49
5121	Twilight Theatre	205.80

Cheques: $1,603.89
Foreign Currency Cheques: 0.00
Foreign Exchange plus/minus: 0.00
Total Cheques: $1,603.89

Cash

Count	Denomination	Amount
3	x$5	15.00
18	x$10	180.00
25	x$20	500.00
12	x$50	600.00
10	x$100	1,000.00
	Coin	4.38

Cash: $2,299.38
Foreign Currency Cash: 0.00
Foreign Exchange plus/minus: 0.00
Total Cash: $2,299.38

Total Deposits: $3,903.27 — Post

Subtotal of cash in home currency — Tesses Tresses

The form is complete. We can accept the default comment "Bank deposit" or change it. The comment will become part of the journal record.

Reviewing the Deposit Slip Entry

Before posting, we should review the journal entry created by the deposit.

Choose the **Report menu** and **click Display Deposit Slip Journal Entry**:

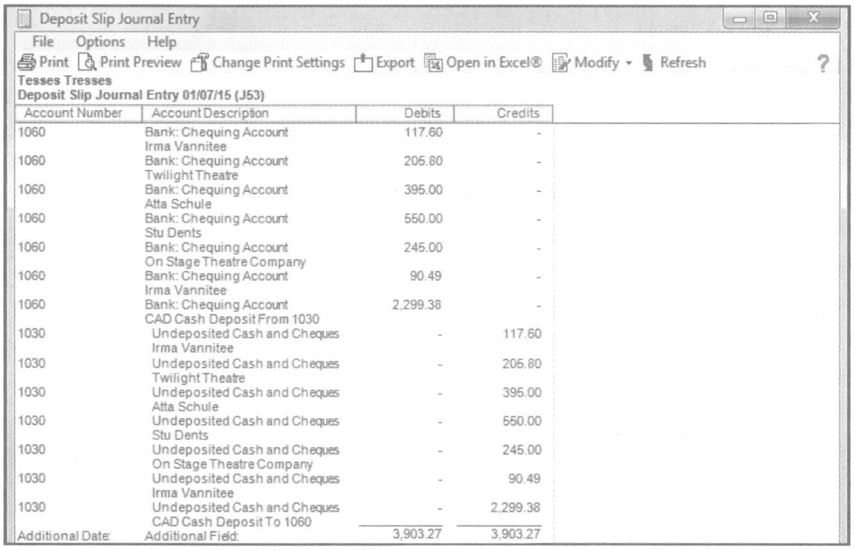

Deposit Slip Journal Entry

File Options Help

Print Print Preview Change Print Settings Export Open in Excel® Modify Refresh

Tesses Tresses

Deposit Slip Journal Entry 01/07/15 (J53)

Account Number	Account Description	Debits	Credits
1060	Bank: Chequing Account Irma Vannitee	117.60	-
1060	Bank: Chequing Account Twilight Theatre	205.80	-
1060	Bank: Chequing Account Atta Schule	395.00	-
1060	Bank: Chequing Account Stu Dents	550.00	-
1060	Bank: Chequing Account On Stage Theatre Company	245.00	-
1060	Bank: Chequing Account Irma Vannitee	90.49	-
1060	Bank: Chequing Account CAD Cash Deposit From 1030	2,299.38	-
1030	Undeposited Cash and Cheques Irma Vannitee	-	117.60
1030	Undeposited Cash and Cheques Twilight Theatre	-	205.80
1030	Undeposited Cash and Cheques Atta Schule	-	395.00
1030	Undeposited Cash and Cheques Stu Dents	-	550.00
1030	Undeposited Cash and Cheques On Stage Theatre Company	-	245.00
1030	Undeposited Cash and Cheques Irma Vannitee	-	90.49
1030	Undeposited Cash and Cheques CAD Cash Deposit To 1060	-	2,299.38
Additional Date:	Additional Field:	3,903.27	3,903.27

In the journal entry, each cheque and cash amount is listed separately. The payer for each cheque is also included. Each deposit item is shown as a debit to *Bank: Chequing Account* and a credit to *Undeposited Cash and Cheques*. This detailed reporting makes it easier to find mistakes if any have been made.

Close the **Journal Entry Display** to return to the journal for corrections.

CORRECTING THE DEPOSIT SLIP JOURNAL ENTRY

To change the cheque part of the deposit, **click** the **Select button** for the **Cheque** part of the journal. To change a selection, **click** a **cheque** in the Cheques On Deposit Slip list and **click Remove**. To start again, **click Remove All** to clear the list. **Click Cancel** to close the Cheques Deposit form without saving changes.

If you need to make changes to the Cash part of the deposit, **click** the **Select button** on the **Cash** side of the Journal. **Click** the **incorrect amount** in the Count field and **type** the **correct amount**. **Press** *tab* to update the total. **Click Apply To Deposit Slip** to update the deposit amount that will be recorded. **Click Cancel** to close the Cash Deposit form without saving changes.

NOTES

The deposit slip entry is J53. Journal entry numbers 1 to 52 are accounted for in the transactions for January.

The order of cheques in the journal report matches the date of receipt as shown on page 580.

WARNING!

You can look up deposit slips after posting them, but you cannot adjust them. You must make the correction with a General Journal entry. For example, you would reverse a deposit slip entry by debiting Undeposited Cash and Cheques and crediting Bank: Chequing Account.

> **NOTES**
> To preview the deposit slip, you must choose Sage 50 Form as the Form Type in the Reports & Forms settings on the Deposit Slips screen. Choose Deposit Slip in the Description field.
> You can check and change the print settings from the Change The Default Printer Settings tool in the journal.

> **NOTES**
> You can also print the deposit slip from the journal's Print tool or File menu, Print option.

> **NOTES**
> Click OK to confirm successful posting of transactions. We will not continue this reminder.

> **NOTES**
> For all deposits, choosing January 1 from the drop-down list in the On Or After field will show all cheques not yet deposited.

> **NOTES**
> At the end of January, the Undeposited Cash and Cheques balance reflects the total of the four postdated rent cheques.

You should also preview and print the deposit slip before posting it.

Click the **Print Preview tool** or **choose** the **File menu** and **click Print Preview**. The preview includes the summary and the details for the cheques and cash amounts on the deposit.

Click the **Print tool** in the Preview window to print the deposit slip.

Click **OK** to close the Preview window and return to the journal.

Click **Post** to save the transaction.

Enter the **remaining four deposits** for January. Remember to change the date for each deposit. The postdated rent cheques remain for future deposits.

☐ **DEPOSIT SLIP # 2** — **JANUARY 14, 2015**

2 Date	Cheque #	Client	Amount
Jan 9	61	Irma Vannitee	$124.01
Jan 14	206	Brioche Bridal Party	119.54
		Total Cheques	$243.55
		Cash	$1 850.22
		(Consisting of 16 × $5; 18 × $10; 22 × $20; 7 × $50; 8 × $100; Coin $.22)	
		Total Deposit	$2 093.77

☐ **DEPOSIT SLIP # 3** — **JANUARY 21, 2015**

3 Date	Cheque #	Client	Amount
Jan 17	CC-61	Irma Vannitee	$126.54
Jan 20	74	Irma Vannitee	65.91
		Total Cheques	$192.45
		Cash	$2 090.76
		(Consisting of 24 × $5; 19 × $10; 14 × $20; 12 × $50; 9 × $100; Coin $.76)	
		Total Deposit	$2 283.21

☐ **DEPOSIT SLIP # 4** — **JANUARY 28, 2015**

4 Date	Cheque #	Client	Amount
Jan 24	429	On Stage Theatre Company	$929.51
		Total Cheques	$929.51
		Cash	$1 861.62
		(Consisting of 24 × $5; 24 × $10; 20 × $20; 8 × $50; 7 × $100; Coin $1.62)	
		Total Deposit	$2 791.13

☐ **DEPOSIT SLIP # 5** — **JANUARY 31, 2015**

5 Date	Cheque #	Client	Amount
Jan 29	238	Conn Seted	$ 45.60
Jan 31	498	On Stage Theatre Company	929.51
		Total Cheques	$975.11
		Cash	$2 431.62
		(Consisting of 6 × $5; 14 × $10; 18 × $20; 14 × $50; 12 × $100; Coin $1.62)	
		Total Deposit	$3 406.73

Close the **Reconciliation & Deposits Journal** and return to the Banking module window.

We are now ready to set up the bank accounts for reconciliation.

Account Reconciliation

For any bank account, the timing of monthly statements is usually not perfectly matched with the accounting entries of the corresponding transactions. Usually some of the cheques written do not appear on the statement, and interest amounts earned on the account or bank charges are not yet recorded because they may be unknown until receipt of the statement. Thus the balance of the bank statement usually does not match the General Ledger balance for the bank account. The process of identifying the differences to achieve a match is the process of account reconciliation.

In Sage 50 you can apply account reconciliation to any Balance Sheet account for which you have regular statements, including credit card payable accounts. For each account you want to reconcile, you must complete the setup procedure.

✓ 6

Memo #8 **Dated Jan. 31/15**

Set up account reconciliation for Bank: Chequing Account and Bank: Credit Cards.

Turning On the Account Reconciliation Feature

Before completing the reconciliation procedure, the General Ledger accounts that will be reconciled must be identified and modified. For the next stage, you will also need a report of all bank account transactions to compare with the bank statement. We will continue to work from the Banking module window to modify the account.

First, we will set up account reconciliation for *Bank: Chequing Account.*

NOTES
Online bank reconciliation is explained in Appendix I on the Student DVD. The Web site for this text is set up for online reconciliation so you can try this feature of the program.

Click **1060 Bank: Chequing Account** in the Banking module Home window Accounts list.

The ledger record for the bank account opens at the Account tab screen:

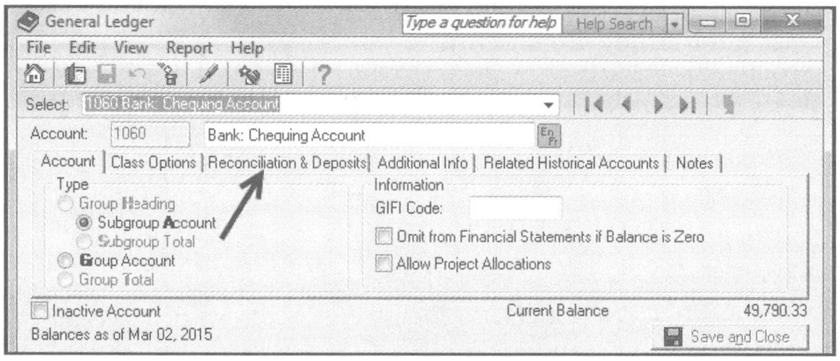

All Balance Sheet accounts have a Reconciliation & Deposits tab, but reconciliation is generally used for accounts with regular statements that summarize all transactions. Usually these are the bank accounts or credit card accounts.

Click the **Reconciliation & Deposits tab**:

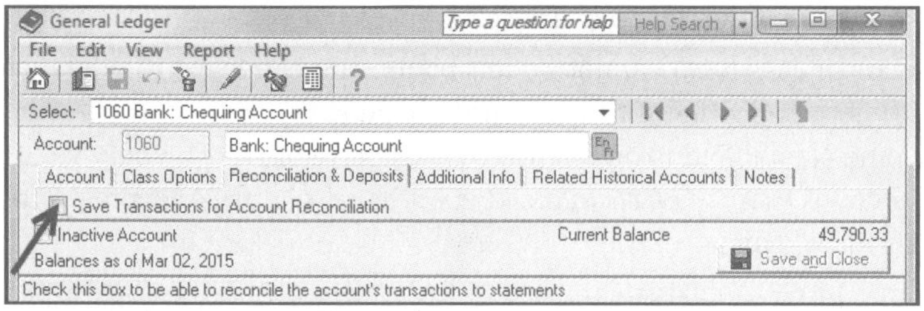

Click **Save Transactions For Account Reconciliation** to add the Set Up button shown in the following screen:

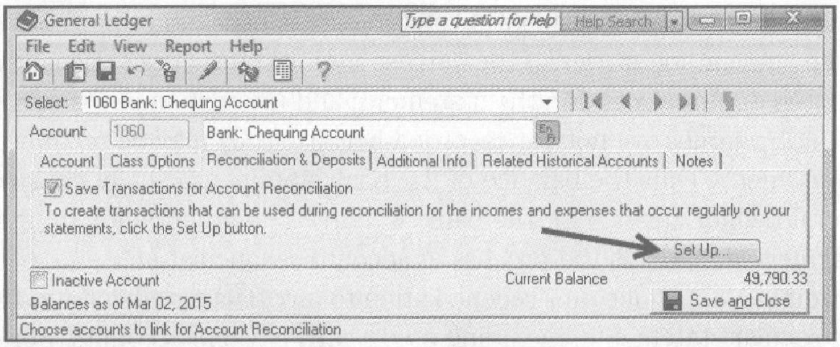

Naming and Linking Reconciliation Accounts

> **NOTES**
> You can save your work and exit at any time. Any changes you have made will be saved and you can continue from where you left off when you are ready.

Most bank statements include monthly bank charges, loan or mortgage payments and interest on deposits. That is, there are usually some regular sources of income and expense. Normally the only source document for these bank account transactions is the bank statement. To use the account reconciliation feature in Sage 50, you should first create the accounts that link to these regular bank account transactions. When you examine the January Bank Statement for Tesses Tresses on page 588, you can see that there is an interest deposit and a withdrawal for service charges. The salon already has accounts for both of these items.

> **NOTES**
> It is always preferable to correct journal entries before completing a reconciliation if you can find the error.

The next step is to name bank statement–related transactions and identify the appropriate General Ledger accounts that link to these transactions. Tesses Tresses has income (interest received) from bank deposits and expenses associated with the bank account, such as bank charges or interest paid on bank loans. An additional account will be needed for adjustments — small discrepancies between the accounting entries and the bank statements, such as amounts entered incorrectly in journal transactions.

You can edit these names and accounts at any time, and you can add other sources of income or expense later if they are needed.

Click **Set Up** to display the following Linked Accounts screen:

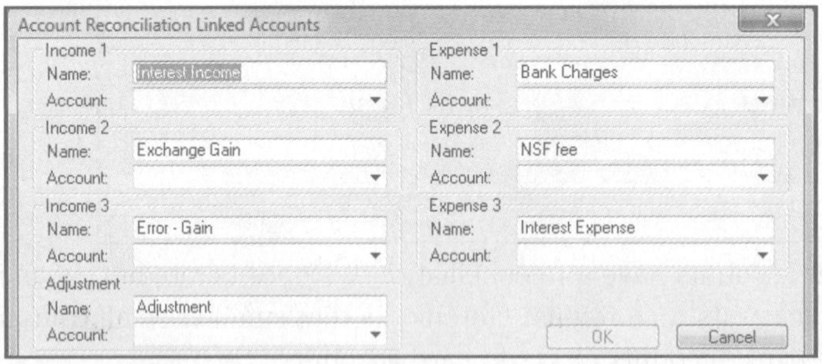

> **NOTES**
> You can enter these accounts at the time of reconciliation, but predefining them here will have them entered automatically in the journal (see page 596).

On this Account Reconciliation Linked Accounts form, you can identify up to three regular sources of income, three types of expenses and one adjustment account for each account you want to reconcile.

The name fields on this form cannot be left blank. You can leave the default names or enter "n/a" for "not applicable" if they are not needed.

The first Income Name field is highlighted, ready for editing. The only source of income for this account that is not recognized elsewhere is interest income. This name is already entered so we can accept it.

> **NOTES**
> Although you can predefine only three income and expense accounts, you can add more income and expense transactions in the Account Reconciliation Journal and select other accounts for them.

Click the **list arrow for the Income 1 Account field** to list the revenue accounts that are available.

Click **4220 Interest Revenue**. **Press** *tab* to advance to the second Income field.

This field and the third Income field are not needed, so we will indicate that they are not applicable.

Type n/a

Press tab **twice** to skip the Account field and advance to the third Income field. **Type** n/a to indicate that it too is not applicable.

Leave the default name for adjustments unchanged.

Click the **Adjustment Account field list arrow**.

Notice that either an expense or a revenue account can be used for adjustments. Tesses Tresses does not have an account for this purpose, so we will create a new expense account.

Type 5050 Reconciliation Adjustments

Press tab. **Click Add** to start the Add An Account wizard.

Accept the **remaining defaults** and **click Finish** to add the account to the Linked Accounts form. **Press** tab to advance the cursor.

The first Expense 1 Name field is highlighted. The salon has one automatic bank account–related expense, bank charges. NSF fee, the second expense, is also used but we do not expect this to be a regular expense. These names are already entered as the default, so we can accept them. Tesses Tresses uses the same account for both expenses.

Click the **Account field list arrow** for **Expense 1** to display the list of expense accounts.

Select **5040 Bank Charges** for this expense account.

Click the **Account field list arrow** for **Expense 2**.

Select **5040 Bank Charges** for this expense account.

Press tab to advance to the third Expense field.

Type n/a to indicate that it is not needed.

Check your **work** carefully. When you are certain that all the names and accounts are correct,

Click **OK** to save the new information. The Set Up button remains available because you can add and change linked accounts.

While the General Ledger is still open, we will set up the linked accounts for *Bank: Credit Cards*.

Click the **Next Account button** ▶ to open the ledger we need.

Click the **Reconciliation & Deposits tab** if necessary.

Click **Save Transactions For Account Reconciliation**.

Click **Set Up**.

Choose **4220** as the linked account for Interest Income.

Choose **5050** as the linked account for Adjustment. **Press** tab to advance to the Expense 1 Name field.

Type Card Fees **Press** tab.

Choose **5060** as the linked account for Card Fees.

NOTES

You can enter "n/a" or leave the default names unchanged for the unused incomes and expenses.

Click **OK** to save the reconciliation accounts.

Close the **Ledger window** to return to the Banking module window.

Reconciling the Bank Statement

Comparing the Bank Statement and Transaction Report

✓ 7

Memo #9 **Dated Jan. 31/15**

Use the following bank statement to reconcile Bank: Chequing Account.

NOTES

The numbers in the Note column correspond to the explanation on page 590.

1 Deposit recorded in December (outstanding prior transaction)

2 Deposit Slips: total amounts from deposit slips

3 Service charges

4 Interest received

5 Scheduled loan payments $2 100 (1 500 + 600)

SAVERS TRUST

321 Queen St., Charlottetown, PE C1A 6D3 www.saverstrust.com

Tesses Tresses
55 Salon Road
Charlottetown, PE C1A 6D3

ACCOUNT STATEMENT
CHEQUING

Transit / Account No
0290 003 433 38-2

Statement period
Jan 1, 2015 to Jan 31, 2015

Date	Note #	Description	Deposits	Withdrawals	Balance
		Balance Fwd			37,238.00
2 Jan	1	Deposit	1,177.00		38,415.00
7 Jan		Cheque #410		926.10	37,488.90
7 Jan	2	Deposit	3.903.27		41,392.17
9 Jan		Cheque #411		330.00	41,062.17
14 Jan	2	Deposit	2,093.77		43,155.94
14 Jan		Cheque #412		216.60	42,939.34
14 Jan		Cheque #413		2,031.07	40,908.27
14 Jan		Transfer 0290 004 123 22-8	5,000.00		45,908.27
15 Jan		NSF Cheque #61		124.01	45,784.26
15 Jan	3	Service Charge – NSF cheque		30.00	45,754.26
17 Jan		Cheque #414		1,830.00	43,924.26
20 Jan		Cheque #415		114.00	43,810.26
21 Jan	2	Deposit	2,283.21		46,093.47
27 Jan		Cheque #416		431.00	45,662.47
27 Jan	5	Scheduled payment: loan		600.00	45,062.47
27 Jan	5	Scheduled payment: mortgage		1,500.00	43,562.47
28 Jan	2	Deposit	2,791.13		46,353.60
31 Jan	3	Service Charges		23.50	46,330.10
31 Jan	4	Interest	52.25		46,382.35
31 Jan		Closing balance			46,382.35

Total Deposits	# 7	$17,300.63
Total Withdrawals	# 12	$8,156.28

We need to compare this bank statement with the Bank Transaction Report provided by the program. Similar to the General Ledger Report, the Bank Account Transaction Report will show all transactions for the account.

Choose the **Reports menu**, then **choose Banking** and **click Bank Account Transactions Report**. The Modify Report window opens:

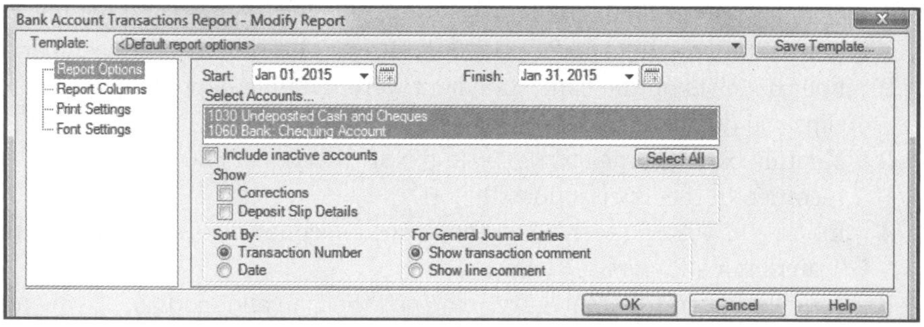

PRO VERSION

The Bank Account Transactions Report is not available in the Pro version.

Use the General Ledger Report for account 1060 for this step. (Choose the Reports Menu, Financials and General Ledger.) You will see the deposit slip total amounts instead of details in the General Ledger Report.

Only Bank and Cash class accounts are listed because the report is available only for bank accounts. The credit card bank account is not shown because it is classified as a Credit Card Receivable account. In order to reconcile the credit card account, you can display or print the General Ledger Report for the period covering the bank statement.

For bank account reports, you can include corrections and deposit slip details or omit them. By default both items are omitted from the report. Since it is easier to work from a report that most closely matches the bank statement, you should omit corrections for this step. The deposit slip details do not appear on the bank statement, but they can be viewed or omitted in the Transactions Report. Because they can help us locate errors, we will include them at this stage.

You can report by date or transaction number and include transaction or line comments.

NOTES

You can also compare the General Ledger Report with the bank statement, but you will not have the option to show individual deposit items on the deposit slips.

You can change the account class for Bank: Credit Cards to Bank. As a result of this change, you can print the Bank Account Transaction Report for it.

Click **1060 Bank: Chequing Account** to select the account.

The default report dates are correct. In an ongoing business, include the date of the oldest outstanding item from your previous bank statement up to the date of the most recent statement.

Click **Deposit Slip Details** to add the ✓.

Click **OK** to view the report:

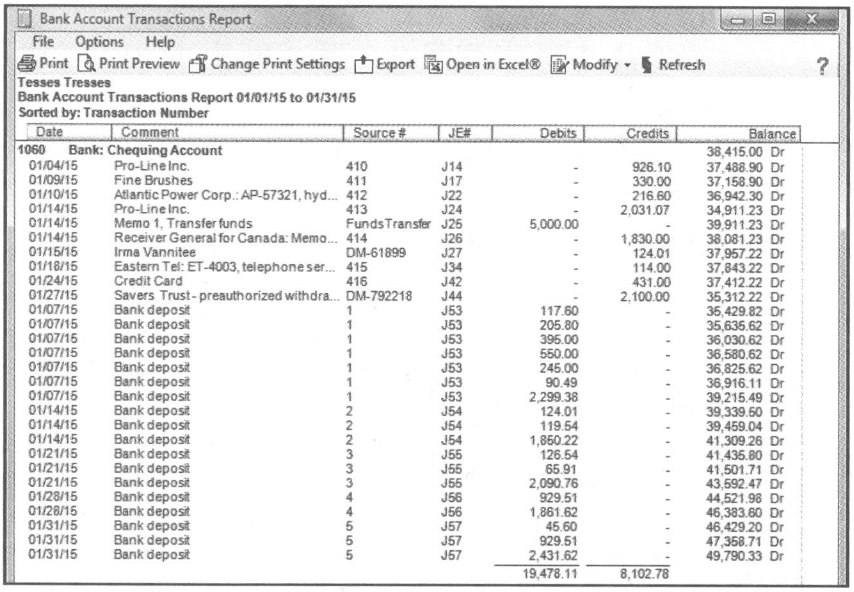
Bank Account Transactions Report

File Options Help

Print Print Preview Change Print Settings Export Open in Excel® Modify Refresh ?

Tesses Tresses
Bank Account Transactions Report 01/01/15 to 01/31/15
Sorted by: Transaction Number

Date	Comment	Source #	JE#	Debits	Credits	Balance
1060	**Bank: Chequing Account**					38,415.00 Dr
01/04/15	Pro-Line Inc.	410	J14	-	926.10	37,488.90 Dr
01/09/15	Fine Brushes	411	J17	-	330.00	37,158.90 Dr
01/10/15	Atlantic Power Corp.: AP-57321, hyd...	412	J22	-	216.60	36,942.30 Dr
01/14/15	Pro-Line Inc.	413	J24	-	2,031.07	34,911.23 Dr
01/14/15	Memo 1, Transfer funds	FundsTransfer	J25	5,000.00	-	39,911.23 Dr
01/14/15	Receiver General for Canada: Memo...	414	J26	-	1,830.00	38,081.23 Dr
01/15/15	Irma Vannitee	DM-61899	J27	-	124.01	37,957.22 Dr
01/18/15	Eastern Tel: ET-4003, telephone ser...	415	J34	-	114.00	37,843.22 Dr
01/24/15	Credit Card	416	J42	-	431.00	37,412.22 Dr
01/27/15	Savers Trust - preauthorized withdra...	DM-792218	J44	-	2,100.00	35,312.22 Dr
01/07/15	Bank deposit	1	J53	117.60	-	35,429.82 Dr
01/07/15	Bank deposit	1	J53	205.80	-	35,635.62 Dr
01/07/15	Bank deposit	1	J53	395.00	-	36,030.62 Dr
01/07/15	Bank deposit	1	J53	550.00	-	36,580.62 Dr
01/07/15	Bank deposit	1	J53	245.00	-	36,825.62 Dr
01/07/15	Bank deposit	1	J53	90.49	-	36,916.11 Dr
01/07/15	Bank deposit	1	J53	2,299.38	-	39,215.49 Dr
01/14/15	Bank deposit	2	J54	124.01	-	39,339.50 Dr
01/14/15	Bank deposit	2	J54	119.54	-	39,459.04 Dr
01/14/15	Bank deposit	2	J54	1,850.22	-	41,309.26 Dr
01/21/15	Bank deposit	3	J55	126.54	-	41,435.80 Dr
01/21/15	Bank deposit	3	J55	65.91	-	41,501.71 Dr
01/21/15	Bank deposit	3	J55	2,090.76	-	43,592.47 Dr
01/28/15	Bank deposit	4	J56	929.51	-	44,521.98 Dr
01/28/15	Bank deposit	4	J56	1,861.62	-	46,383.60 Dr
01/31/15	Bank deposit	5	J57	45.60	-	46,429.20 Dr
01/31/15	Bank deposit	5	J57	929.51	-	47,358.71 Dr
01/31/15	Bank deposit	5	J57	2,431.62	-	49,790.33 Dr
				19,478.11	8,102.78	

PRO VERSION

Remember that the General Ledger Report will show the deposit slip total amounts instead of details.

NOTES

You may want to print the Transaction Report with and without deposit slip details to compare with the bank statement that has only the total deposit amounts.

Print the **report** so that you can compare it with the statement and then **close** the displayed **report**.

Comparing the reports reveals the following differences. The numbers on the following page correspond to the numbers in the margin Notes and the Note # column in the bank statement on page 588.

> **NOTES**
> These numbers correspond to the Note # column of the bank statement on page 588.
> **1** Deposit recorded in December
> **2** Deposit Slips: total amounts from deposit slips
> **3** Service charges
> **4** Interest received
> **5** Scheduled loan payments $2 100 (1 500 + 600)

1 One deposit on January 2 appears on the bank statement and not in the Bank Transaction Report because the deposit was entered late in December.
2 Four deposits on the bank statement were multiple deposits entered on deposit slips and do not match any single entry in the Transactions Report.
3 Monthly bank charges of $23.50 and NSF charges of $30.00 have not been recorded in the Transactions Report.
4 Interest of $52.25 received on the deposit account does not appear in the Transactions Report.
5 A single General Journal entry combined the loan and mortgage payments.

In addition, deposit slip #5 for $3 406.73 in the Report is not listed on the bank statement, and the order of transactions is different.

All discrepancies must be accounted for in order to have the bank statement match the bank balance in the account's General Ledger or on the Balance Sheet.

Reconciling the Account

> **NOTES**
> Remember that you can save your work and exit at any time. Any changes you have made will be saved and you can continue from where you left off when you are ready.

After entering the linked accounts, you can begin the reconciliation. The account reconciliation procedure consists of the following steps to update the General Ledger:

1. Record the opening and ending balances from the bank statement for the account.
2. Add outstanding transactions from prior periods that were not resolved in the previous bank statement (only for the first reconciliation).
3. Identify all the deposits and withdrawals that have been processed by the bank.
4. Complete journal entries for any transactions for which the bank statement is the source document.

The result should be a match between the bank balances in the two statements. If the amounts do not match, the difference will be assigned to the linked Adjustment account. All these steps are completed in the Account Reconciliation Journal.

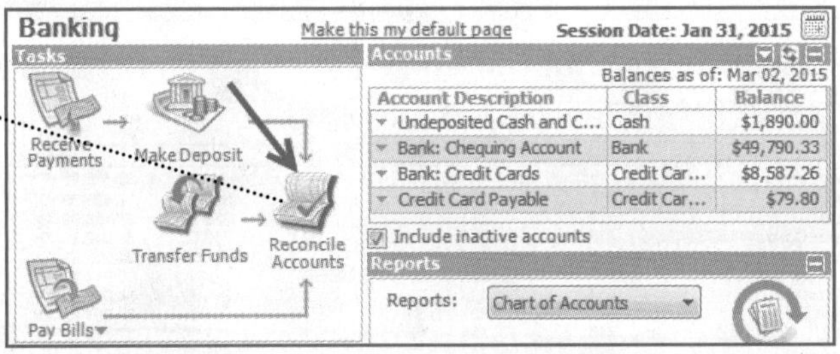

> **CLASSIC VIEW**
> Click the Reconciliation & Deposits icon  to open the journal and choose Account Reconciliation from the Transaction drop-down list if necessary.

Account record balances in the Home window are shown at the latest transaction date, March 2, the date of the postdated rent cheques, as the Accounts pane informs us in the line above the accounts. The postdated cheques account for the *Undeposited Cash and Cheques* balance amount.

If you change User Preferences View Settings to view record balances as at the Session date, as we show here, you will see that the undeposited amount on January 31 is zero:

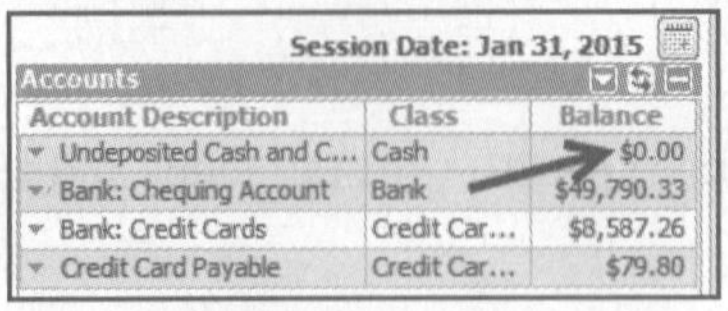

> **NOTES**
> You can also start from the Accounts pane shortcuts list beside the bank account. Click the list arrow beside Bank: Chequing Account and choose Reconcile Accounts. The journal will open with the bank account already entered.

There is no additional information line (Balances As Of) above the accounts in the Accounts pane.

Click the **Reconcile Accounts icon**  to open the Reconciliation Journal:

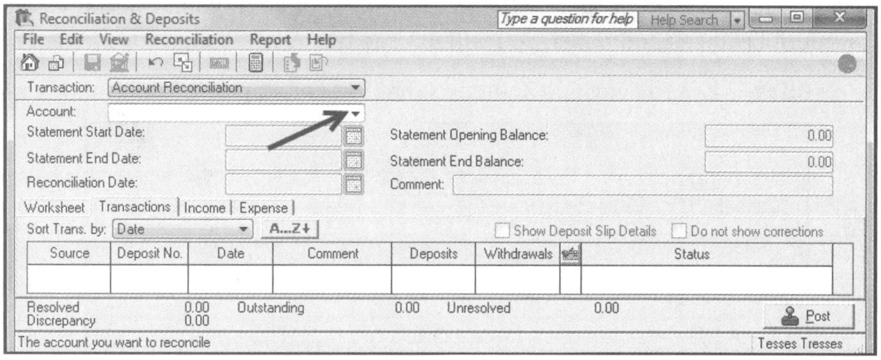

Click the **Account field list arrow**.

The list displays the bank and credit card accounts that we set up for account reconciliation. These are the only accounts available for reconciliation.

> **NOTES**
> There is no allocation option in the Account Reconciliation Journal but additional fields are available, as they are in the other journals.

Select **1060 Bank: Chequing Account** to start the reconciliation:

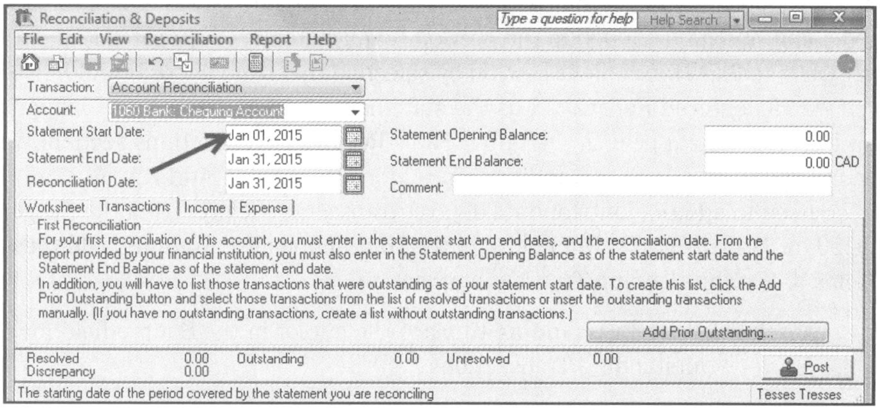

> **NOTES**
> Read the instructions on the screen about the first reconciliation before proceeding. It advises that you must go through the step of adding prior transactions.

The account is entered in the Account field. The first day of the month is entered as the Statement Start Date and the session date is entered automatically in the Statement End Date field and the Reconciliation Date field. These dates will advance by one month — or the length of the reconciliation period of 31 days in this case — when you have finished reconciling the bank account for the current month. The dates are correct, so do not change them.

We need to add the opening and closing bank statement balances from page 588.

Click the **Statement Opening Balance field**.

Type `37238` **Press** tab to advance to the Statement End Balance field.

Type `46382.35` **Press** tab to advance to the Comment field.

Type `January Bank Reconciliation`

For the first reconciliation, we need to add the outstanding transaction from the previous period. A deposit of $1 177 appears on the bank statement but not in the ledger report. The deposit was made at the end of December, too late to be included in the December bank statement, so we need to add it now. Adding prior transactions in the Account Reconciliation Journal does not create a journal entry and does not affect the ledger balance. The step is necessary only to create a match between the bank statement and the current ledger.

> **WARNING!**
> The first time you complete a reconciliation for any account, you must complete this step (click Add Prior Outstanding) even if there are no outstanding prior transactions. If there are no prior transactions to add, click OK from the Add Outstanding Transactions screen.

Click **Add Prior Outstanding** to see the confirmation message:

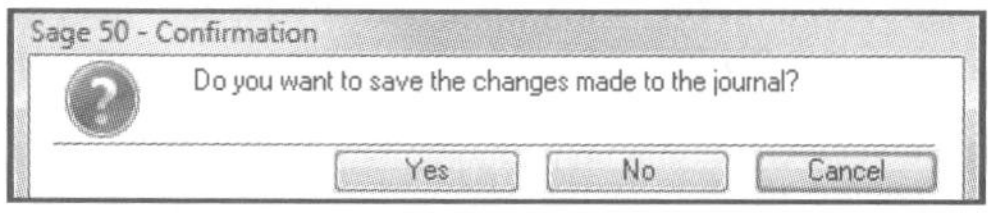

> **NOTES**
> The default date for showing resolved transactions is one month prior to the bank statement start date.

You must save the changes to the journal to continue. If you have not yet entered the account balances and dates, you will not see the Save Changes message.

Click **Yes** to continue and open the Add Outstanding Transactions window:

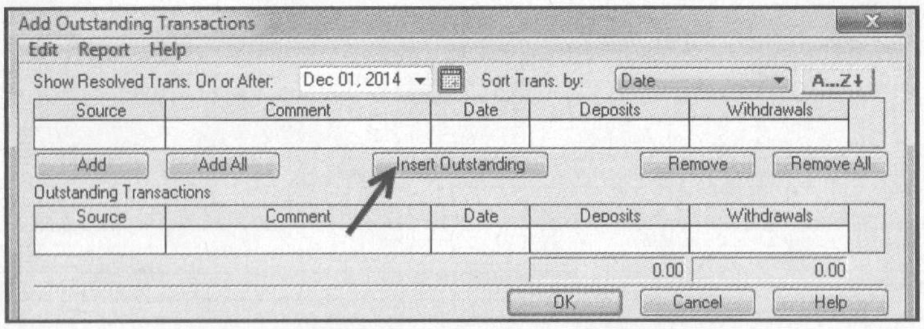

If there are no prior transactions that you need to insert, click OK at this stage to return to the journal.

If you have transactions in Sage 50 that precede the bank statement starting date, they will appear in the upper portion of the screen, in the Resolved Transactions section. If they have been resolved, you can leave them there. If, however, some of them were outstanding, and not included in the previous bank statement, you can add them to the lower Outstanding Transactions section by selecting them and choosing Add.

If we had entered February 1 as the statement starting date, all the January transactions would appear in the upper Show Resolved Transactions section. We would then include them all as outstanding transactions by clicking Add All.

We need to add one outstanding deposit transaction. It preceded the first entry in Sage 50 on January 1 so it will not be in the transactions list. We must add these types of items to the Outstanding Transactions section.

> **WARNING!**
> You cannot access the Outstanding Transactions input fields until you choose Insert Outstanding.

Click **Insert Outstanding** to place the cursor in the Source field for Outstanding Transactions.

Type `5117` to enter the client's cheque number as the Source.

Press *tab* to move to the Comment field. We will enter the client's name.

Type `Twilight Theatre` **Press** *tab* to move to the Date field.

December 31, 2014, is entered as the default date, the last date from the previous statement period. This date is correct, so you do not need to change it. You can enter a different date if necessary.

Press *tab* to move to the Deposits column.

Type `1177` **Press** *tab*.

If there are other outstanding prior transactions, enter them in the same way. For each additional outstanding transaction, you must click Insert Outstanding to move the cursor to the Source field on a new blank line for Outstanding Transactions.

If there are no prior transactions, click OK to return to the journal.

Click **OK** to return to the journal window.

Marking Journal Entries as Cleared

You are now ready to begin processing individual journal entries to indicate whether they have been cleared in this bank statement. That is, you must indicate whether the bank has processed the items and the amounts have been withdrawn from or deposited to the account.

The updated journal window now looks like the following:

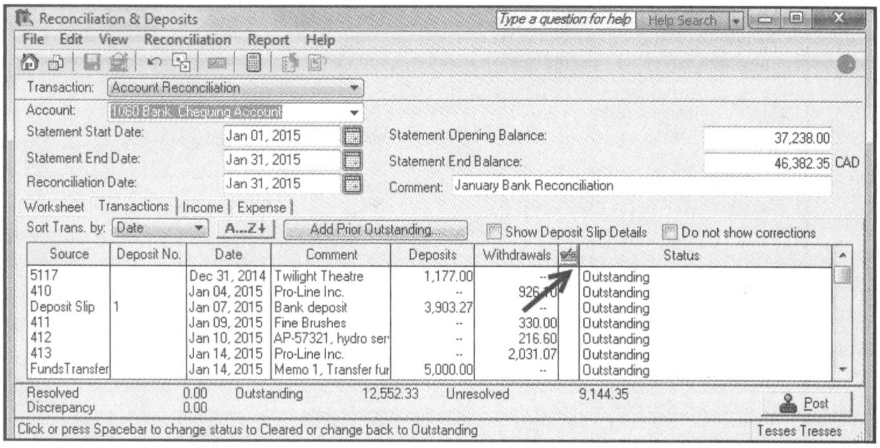

The Transactions tab is selected and all January bank account transactions are now listed, including the one we just added. The bottom section of the screen contains a summary of the transactions. Our goal is to reduce the unresolved amount to zero with no discrepancy. At this stage, a discrepancy may indicate an incorrect account balance.

The Statement End Balance should be correct because we entered it in the previous step. You can add or change it at this stage if necessary.

Showing Corrections

You can hide or show correcting journal entries in the list of transactions by clicking **Do Not Show Corrections**. Removing incorrect and reversing entries can make the reconciliation easier by increasing the match with the statement. When you hide the corrections and then clear transactions, Sage 50 automatically applies the Reversed and Adjustment status to the original incorrect entry (Reversed status) and the reversing entry created by Sage 50 (Adjustment status).

Group Deposits

Sometimes several cheques are deposited as a group, as they were on the weekly deposit slips. Each of these group deposits can now be cleared as a group. If you have not used the deposit slip journal to record deposits, you can define a group deposit by entering the deposit slip number for each item in the Deposit No. field beside the Source. When you clear one item in the group, the others will be cleared at the same time.

You may want to drag the lower frame of the journal window or maximize the journal window to include more transactions on your screen at the same time.

You are now ready to mark the transactions that have been cleared, that is, the ones that appear on the bank statement.

Click the Clear column **for Cheque #5117** (click in the column), the first transaction on the list.

A checkmark appears in the Clear column, the Status has changed from Outstanding to Cleared and the Resolved Amount has increased to $1 177. As you clear each item, the Resolved and Unresolved amounts are updated.

Clear the **remaining journal entries** that appear on the bank statement on page 588 and scroll as necessary to display additional items.

Do not clear deposit slip #5 for $3 406.73.

NOTES

Transactions are sorted by date in ascending order. You can also arrange them by source, comment, deposit amount, withdrawal amount, the order of entry (journal entry number) or deposit number. For any of these, you can choose ascending or descending order with the A...Z+ button. Choosing a different order may make it easier to find a specific transaction.

NOTES

Only the corrections made with the program's adjusting and reversing features will be hidden; manually reversed entries or corrections like the NSF cheque on page 605 will not be hidden.

NOTES

You can click the column heading to clear all entries on the transactions list. Then you can click an individual ✓ to restore the Outstanding status if needed.

NOTES

Remember to clear the withdrawal on Jan. 27 for $2 100 to match the two bank statement entries for $600 and $1 500.

> **NOTES**
> The Outstanding Amount at the bottom of the journal is the amount for the outstanding deposit.

Your transactions list appears as follows:

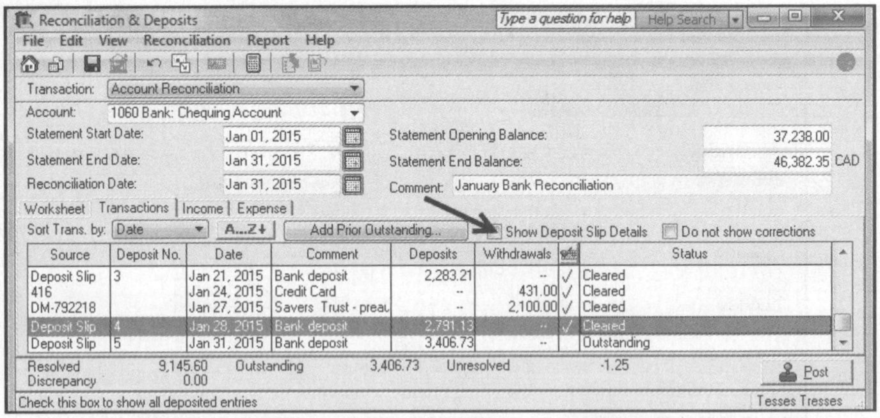

If you mark an item as Cleared by mistake, click the ✓ column again to return the status to Outstanding.

After clearing all transactions from the bank statement, the unresolved amount should be –1.25. This is the net difference for the three unmatched bank statement items: the NSF charge, the service charge and the interest. Journal entries for these items will be added later (page 596).

The next section describes the procedure for clearing transactions that are different in some way, like NSF cheques. By marking their status correctly, you will have a more accurate picture of your business transactions. Cheque #61 for $124.01 from Irma Vannitee was returned as NSF and should be marked as such. This cheque was included on deposit slip #2 (see page 584).

Showing Deposit Slip Details

The NSF cheque we need to mark was part of a group deposit, so it does not appear individually on the Transactions list. First we need to show the details of the deposit slips. Above the Transactions list is the **Show Deposit Slip Details** check box. This check box is a toggle switch; you can hide the details when they are not required or show them if you need to change the status of a single item in the deposit group.

> **NOTES**
> If you sort the transactions by Deposit Number, the deposit slip entries will appear together at the bottom of the list. If you sort by Source, they will appear together at the top of the list in our example.

Click **Show Deposit Slip Details** to add a ✓.

Press the **down scroll arrow** until you see the items for deposit slip #2:

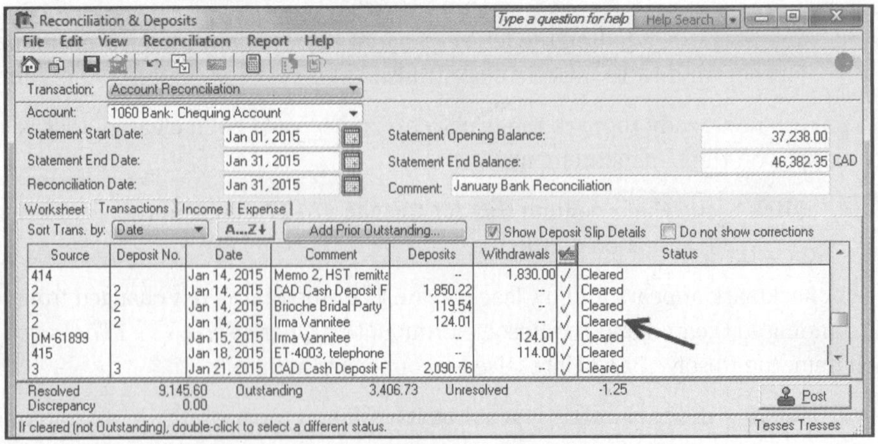

All three deposit slip items, the two cheques and the cash amount on the deposit slip, are marked as Cleared when we clear the deposit.

Marking NSF Cheques

For some items — for example, NSF cheques and their reversing entries — you should add further information because they have not cleared the account in the usual way.

To mark a cheque as NSF,

Click **Cleared** in the Status column for Irma Vannitee's cheque for $124.01 in deposit slip #2, the NSF cheque.

Press *enter* to display the alternatives for the Status of a journal entry:

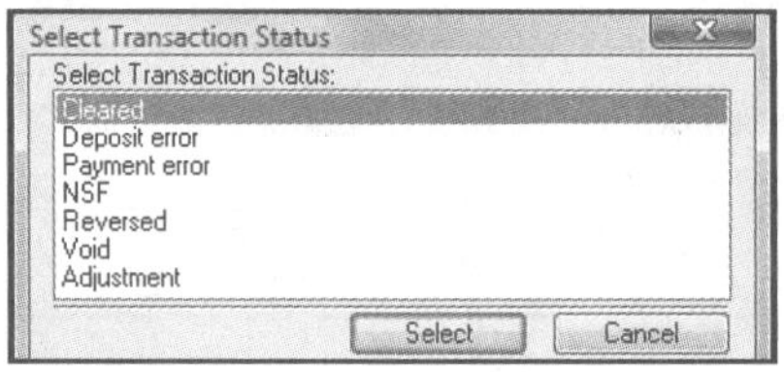

These status alternatives are explained in the Status Options chart that follows.

STATUS OPTIONS

Cleared (C)	for deposits and cheques that have been processed correctly.
Deposit Error (D)	for the adjusting journal entry that records the difference between the amount of a deposit that was recorded incorrectly and the bank statement amount for that deposit. Assign the Cleared status to the original entry for the deposit.
Payment Error (P)	for the adjusting entry that records the difference between the amount of a cheque recorded incorrectly and the bank statement amount for that cheque. Assign the Cleared status to the original entry for the cheque.
NSF (N)	for client cheques returned by the bank because there was not enough money in the client's account. Assign the Adjustment status to the adjusting entry that reverses the NSF cheque.
Reversed (R)	for cheques that are cancelled by posting a reversing transaction entry to the bank account or the Sales or Purchases journals, that is, journal entries that are corrected. Assign the Adjustment status to the reversing entry that cancels the cheque.
Void (V)	for cheques that are cancelled because of damage during printing. Assign the Adjustment status to the reversing entry that voids the cheque.
Adjustment (A)	for the adjusting or reversing entries that are made to cancel NSF, void or reversed cheques. (See the explanations for NSF, Void and Reversed above.)

Click **NSF** to highlight this alternative.

Click **Select** to enter it. The Cleared status changes to NSF for this item.

The final step is to change the status of the entry that reverses the payment or NSF cheque to Adjustment. The final certified cheque received in payment has been cleared normally so its status as Cleared is already correct. Changing the status does not affect the resolved and unresolved amounts. The amounts are just cleared in different ways.

Double-click **Cleared in the Status column for Bank Debit Memo #61899**, the reversing entry (124.01 in the Withdrawals column).

Double-click **Adjustment** to select this as the status.

NOTES

Void cheques are also used to set up automatic payments (direct deposit). Because these do not have amounts or journal entries associated with them, they will not appear in the Reconciliation Journal.

NOTES

The unresolved, resolved and outstanding amounts have not changed.

Your updated transactions list now looks like the one shown here:

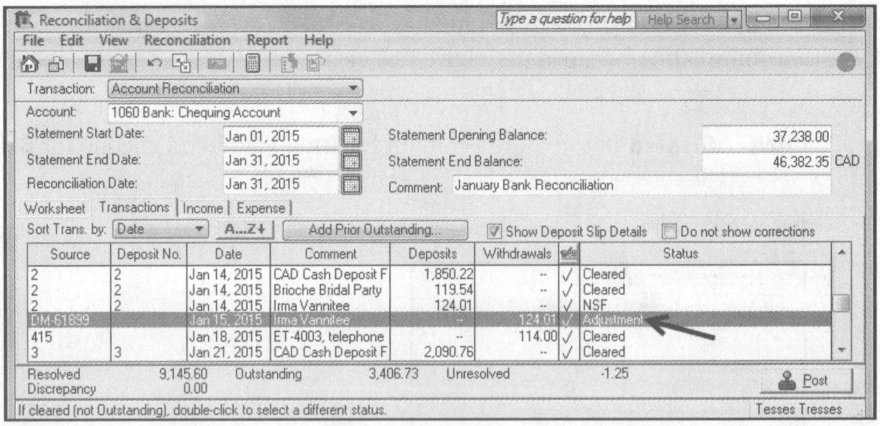

NOTES
Drag the column heading margins if necessary to see all the input columns.

Click **Show Deposit Slip Details** to restore the summary version for deposits.

The status for deposit slip #2 has changed to Cleared again. You can show the details at any time again or if you need to make corrections by clicking the check box for it again.

The resolved, unresolved and outstanding amounts, the net of deposit and withdrawal amounts, are continually updated as you work through the reconciliation procedure. If you display your journal entry from the Report menu at this stage, you will see a credit to *Bank: Chequing Account* and a debit to the expense account *Reconciliation Adjustments* for $1.25, the unresolved amount at this stage — the net amount of interest and all bank charges. The expense amount total is greater than the interest amount by $1.25. The journal entries for these items will reduce the unresolved amount to zero.

Adding Account Statement Journal Entries

Click the **Income tab**.

The Account Reconciliation Journal now includes journal entry fields as shown:

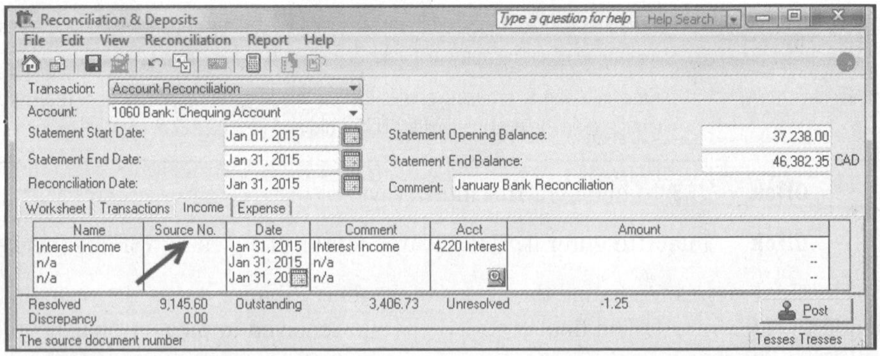

NOTES
You can drag the column heading margins if necessary to see all the input columns.

The entry for Interest Income — the income source we named earlier — is partially completed with the correct default entries for date, comment and account. You can change any of these entries by editing the contents or selecting a different account.

NOTES
You can select a different revenue account in the reconciliation journal for these predefined incomes if this is appropriate.

Click the **Source No. field** beside Interest Revenue to advance the cursor.

Type Bk-Stmt

Click the **Amount field**.

Type 52.25 **Press** *tab*. Notice that the unresolved amount — 53.50 — now matches the amount for the service fee plus the NSF charge.

You can edit these journal entries or transaction status entries at any time before posting. Choosing the **Save tool** will save the work you have completed so far, without posting, and still permit you to make changes later.

If there are other income categories, type the name, source, date, comment, account and amount on the second line. You can enter more than three sources of income on this form and you can choose any revenue account, although you can predefine only three linked accounts.

Click the **Expense tab** to open the input fields for expense transactions:

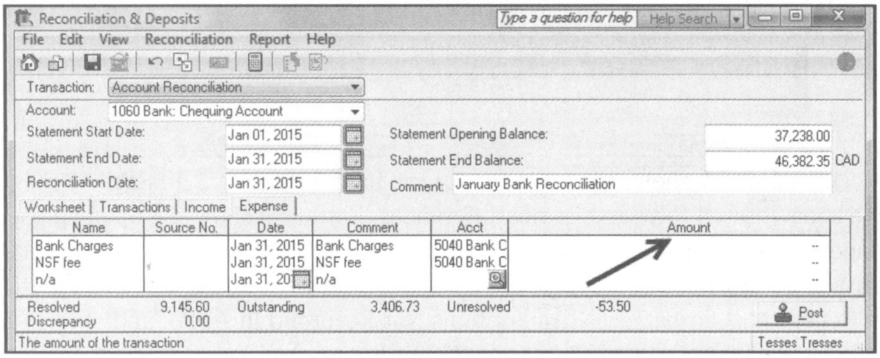

The expense transactions are also partially completed. We need to add the Source No. and the Amount. For the NSF fee, we need to change the date.

You can combine regular service charges with charges for other one-time or unusual services such as stopping a payment on a cheque or NSF fees. We have created a separate category for the NSF charge in order to track this expense. The bank statement contains the amounts for the expenses.

Click the **Source No. field**. Duplicate source document codes are allowed in this journal.

Type Bk-Stmt

Click the **Amount field**.

Type 23.50 **Press** (tab) to advance to the next journal line.

We can now enter the NSF service charges. You can use the same account for more than one journal entry, but you cannot choose the same expense or income category twice. The date for this charge was January 15, so we must also change the default date.

Click the **Source field**. We will enter the debit memo number as the source.

Type DM#61899 **Press** (tab).

Type Jan 15

Click the **Amount field**. **Type** 30 **Press** (tab) to enter the amount.

If there are other expenses, enter the information in the same way. You can enter additional expenses and choose any expense account, although you can predefine only three linked accounts.

At this stage, your unresolved amount and discrepancy should be zero if everything is reconciled. We will look at the Worksheet to see a summary of the changes we made.

NOTES

You can select a different expense account in the reconciliation journal for these predefined expenses if this is appropriate.

Click the **Worksheet tab**:

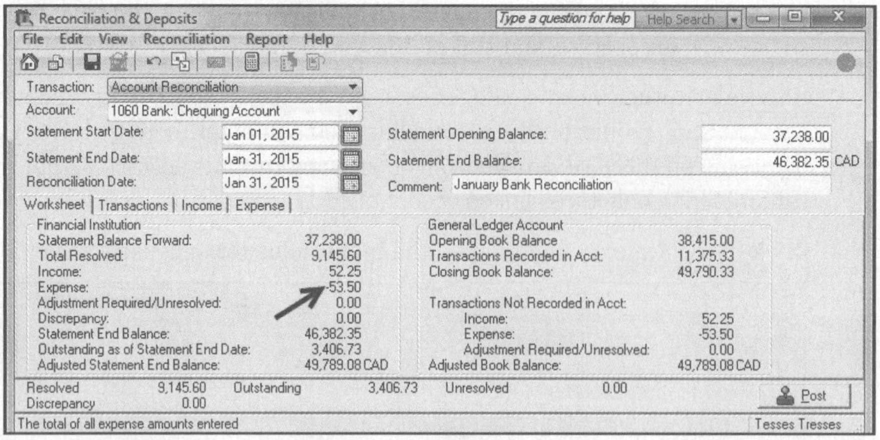

This summary shows the amounts for the bank statement and Sage 50 records that have been entered to reconcile the differences. Both lists show the opening and closing balances and net total transaction amounts. The Account Reconciliation Journal transactions for income and expenses that were not recorded elsewhere are added to the General Ledger balance (Transactions Not Recorded In Acct), and outstanding amounts that were in the General Ledger but not on the bank statement (Outstanding As Of Statement End Date) are added to the Bank Statement balance. The result is a match between the two adjusted balance amounts.

You should also review the reconciliation journal entry before proceeding.

WARNING!

You cannot adjust Account Reconciliation Journal entries, and correcting them after posting is quite difficult.

Do not post the Account Reconciliation Journal transaction until the unresolved amount is zero (or a small discrepancy that you can explain). You can click the Save button to save your work before posting, exit the journal and return later to find the error and make corrections.

Press *ctrl* + **J**:

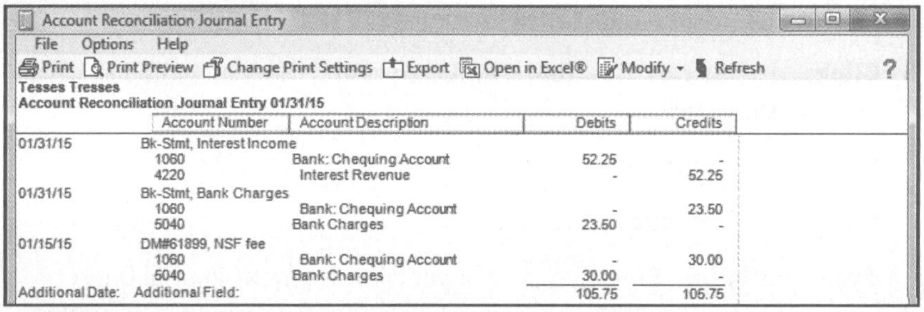

	Account Number	Account Description	Debits	Credits
01/31/15	Bk-Stmt, Interest Income			
	1060	Bank: Chequing Account	52.25	-
	4220	Interest Revenue	-	52.25
01/31/15	Bk-Stmt, Bank Charges			
	1060	Bank: Chequing Account	-	23.50
	5040	Bank Charges	23.50	-
01/15/15	DM#61899, NSF fee			
	1060	Bank: Chequing Account	-	30.00
	5040	Bank Charges	30.00	-
Additional Date:	Additional Field:		105.75	105.75

The income and expense journal entries are listed. In addition, an adjustment entry will be displayed if there is any unresolved amount.

Close the **Report window** when you have finished.

If the unreconciled amount is not zero, you can check your journal entries to see whether you have made an error. Click each option and tab in the journal to show your work for the corresponding part of the reconciliation procedure. Make corrections if necessary. If you still have an unresolved amount, you can save the entry without posting and return later to try to determine whether you made a mistake or whether there was an error on the bank statement.

NOTES

The program will warn you before posting an unresolved amount, allowing you to correct any mistakes before posting the journal entries.

Any discrepancy or unresolved amount will be posted as an adjustment to the reconciliation adjustments expense account created earlier. This account should be used only for small amounts not significant enough to warrant a separate journal entry, such as differences from payroll tax rates in this text.

Click the **Save button**. **Click** to close the journal without posting.

NOTES

The confirmation message shows that three journal entries were posted – the interest and expense transactions.

Back up the **data file**. **Open** the **Account Reconciliation Journal**, **select 1060 Bank: Chequing Account** and resume your work.

Click Post. You are ready to reconcile the next account.

✓ 8 **Memo #10** **Dated Jan. 31/15**

Use the following bank statement to reconcile Bank: Credit Cards.
There is one outstanding item from the previous month:
Sale #457 for $230 to Cash Sales was deposited on Dec. 31, 2014.

SAVERS TRUST

321 Queen St., Charlottetown, PE C1A 6D3 www.saverstrust.com

Tesses Tresses
55 Salon Road
Charlottetown, PE C1A 6D3

ACCOUNT STATEMENT
CREDIT CARD

Transit / Account No
0290 004 123 22-8

Statement period
Jan 1, 2015 to Jan 31, 2015

Date	Description	Deposits	Withdrawals	Balance
	Balance Fwd			1,970.00
2 Jan	Deposit	230.00		2,200.00
2 Jan	Deposit	2,218.44		4,418.44
9 Jan	Deposit	2,506.84		6,925.28
14 Jan	Transfer to 0290 003 433 38-2		5,000.00	1,925.28
16 Jan	Deposit	2,360.42		4,285.70
23 Jan	Deposit	2,251.72		6,537.42
30 Jan	Deposit	2,049.84		8,587.26
31 Jan	Service Charges		11.50	8,575.76
31 Jan	Interest	6.50		8,582.26
31 Jan	Closing balance			8,582.26

Total Deposits # 7 $11,623.76
Total Withdrawals # 2 $5,011.50

Choose **account 1080**.

Enter a **comment** and the **opening** and **closing bank statement balances**.

Enter the **prior outstanding transaction** (see margin Notes).

Clear **all journal entries** to process the statement items.

Add **journal entries** for **service charges** and **interest**. **Review** your **work**, **make corrections** if necessary and then **post** the **transaction**.

Add **Shortcuts** for transactions in other modules, or change modules as needed.

Change the **session date** to **February 7** and then **enter** the **transactions for February** until the NSF cheque on Feb. 25.

9 **Payment Cheque #417** **Dated Feb. 2/15**

To Sharp Scissors, $912.00 in payment of account. Reference invoice #SS-432.

10 **Sales Invoice #482** **Dated Feb. 2/15**

To Irma Vannitee

1	BRS1	Hair Brush: natural bristle	$28
1	CN2	Pro-Line Hot Oil Treatment 75 ml	29
1	SRV3	Cut and Style	40
1	SRV5	Perm	80
		HST	14%

Terms: 2/5, n/15.

NOTES
Refer to keystrokes beginning on page 590 to complete the reconciliation.
There are no deposit slips.

NOTES
HST applies to the purchase and sale of all merchandise sold and services offered by the salon.

NOTES
Ignore the message about late payments for Vannitee because her cheque is on hand.

NOTES
All these inventory items are purchased in units of dozens. Purchase orders were entered in January.

11

Purchase Invoice #PL-1988 **Dated Feb. 4/15**

From Pro-Line Inc., to fill purchase order #52

2	CN1	Pro-Line Conditioner: 150 ml	$ 264.00
2	CN2	Pro-Line Hot Oil Treatment 75 ml	228.00
2	GEL1	Pro-Line Spray Gel: shaper 150 ml	216.00
2	FRZ1	Pro-Line Defrizzer: cream 100 ml	144.00
2	SHM1	Pro-Line Shampoo: 225 ml	216.00
2	SPR1	Pro-Line Hair Spray: gentle 150 ml	144.00
	HST	14%	169.68
Invoice total			$1 381.68

Terms: 2/10, n/30.

12

Cash Purchase Invoice #CCT-15-2 **Dated Feb. 4/15**

From Charlottetown City Treasurer, $220 plus $30.80 HST for water and sewage treatment for three months. Purchase invoice total $250.80 paid by cheque #418 (Utilities account).

13

Sales Invoice #483 **Dated Feb. 4/15**

To Conn Seted

1	FRZ1	Pro-Line Defrizzer: cream 100 ml	$14
1	GEL1	Pro-Line Spray Gel: shaper 150 ml	22
1	SRV1	Colour	45
1	SRV3	Cut and Style	40
	HST		14%

Terms: net 15.

NOTES
Sales Invoice #484 provides services for four theatre performances for six cast members. Do not fill the order. Enter the numbers in the Quantity field. The remainder of the order will be filled later.

14

Sales Invoice #484 **Dated Feb. 5/15**

To Twilight Theatre to partially fill sales order #102

6	SRV3	Cut and Style	$32 each
18	SRV6	Wash and Style	16 each
	HST		14%

Terms: 2/5, n/15.

15

Cash Purchase Invoice CCT-299392 **Dated Feb. 6/15**

From Charlottetown City Treasurer, $4 800 for annual property tax assessment, payable in three equal instalments of $1 600. First instalment is due on receipt of invoice. Remaining two instalments are due May 6 and August 6. Issue cheques #419, 420 and 421 dated February 6, May 6 and August 6 in payment of account. Create new Group account 5380 Property Taxes. Store as a quarterly recurring entry and recall for postdated series.

16

Credit Card Sales Invoice #485 **Dated Feb. 6/15**

Sales Summary for credit card sales (to Cash Customers)

4	BRS1	Hair Brush: natural bristle	$ 28 each	$ 112.00
6	CN1	Pro-Line Conditioner: 150 ml	26 /bottle	156.00
3	FRZ1	Pro-Line Defrizzer: cream 100 ml	14 /jar	42.00
3	GEL1	Pro-Line Spray Gel: shaper 150 ml	22 /can	66.00
8	SHM1	Pro-Line Shampoo: 225 ml	21 /bottle	168.00
26	SRV3	Cut and Style	40 each	1 040.00
5	SRV4	Highlights	100 each	500.00
6	SRV6	Wash and Style	20 each	120.00
	HST		14%	308.56
Invoice total paid by credit cards				$2 512.56

Deposited to credit card bank account.

17 **Credit Card Purchase Invoice #AUN-344** **Dated Feb. 7/15**

From All U Need department store, $300 plus $42 HST for 100 white hand towels for use in the salon. Purchase invoice total $342 paid in full by credit card. Change the default account entry.

18 **Cash Sales Invoice #486** **Dated Feb. 7/15**

Sales Summary for cash sales (to Cash Customers)

6	BRS2	Hair Brush: styling	$24 each	$ 144.00
4	CN2	Pro-Line Hot Oil Treatment 75 ml	29 /tube	116.00
5	GEL1	Pro-Line Spray Gel: shaper 150 ml	22 /can	110.00
5	SPR1	Pro-Line Hair Spray: gentle 150 ml	17 /can	85.00
4	SRV1	Colour	45 each	180.00
24	SRV3	Cut and Style	40 each	960.00
	HST		14%	223.30
	Invoice total paid by cash			$1 818.30

Deposited to Undeposited Cash and Cheques.

19 **DEPOSIT SLIP # 6** **FEBRUARY 7, 2015**

Date	Cheque #	Client	Amount
Feb 2	416	Atta Schule	$395.00
Feb 2	162	Stu Dents	550.00
		Total Cheques	$945.00
		Cash	$1 818.30

(Consisting of 13 × $5; 11 × $10; 12 × $20; 12 × $50; 8 × $100; Coin $3.30)

Total Deposit $2 763.30

SESSION DATE – FEBRUARY 14, 2015

20 **Cash Purchase Invoice #AP-63322** **Dated Feb. 8/15**

From Atlantic Power Corp., $220 plus $30.80 HST for hydro services for one month. Purchase invoice total $250.80 paid by cheque #422.

21 **Sales Invoice #487** **Dated Feb. 8/15**

To Brioche Bridal Party to partially fill sales order #101

3	SRV3	Cut and Style	$40 each
	HST		14%

Terms: 2/5, n/15.

22 **Sales Invoice #488** **Dated Feb. 9/15**

To Irma Vannitee

1	SRV6	Wash and Style	$20
	HST		14%

Terms: 2/5, n/15. Store as a weekly recurring entry.

23 **Purchase Invoice #Z-6775** **Dated Feb. 10/15**

From Zines Inc., $110 plus $15.40 HST to renew subscriptions for one year to hair and fashion magazines (Prepaid Subscriptions account). Purchase invoice total $125.40. Terms: net 10.

24 **Cash Receipt #144** **Dated Feb. 10/15**

From Irma Vannitee, cheque #93 for $246.92 in payment of account including $0.46 discount for early payment. Reference sales invoices #478, 482 and 488.

25

Purchase Order #55 **Dated Feb. 10/15**

Delivery date Feb. 22/15
From Air Pro, $300 for two large hair dryers and $50 for two small hair dryers plus $49 HST. Purchase order total $399. Terms: net 15.

26

Purchase Invoice #FB-27731 **Dated Feb. 10/15**

From Fine Brushes, to fill purchase order #53
To Fine Brushes (stocking up for Valentine's gifts)

30	BRS1	Hair Brush: natural bristle	$360.00
20	BRS2	Hair Brush: styling	160.00
	HST	14%	72.80
Invoice total			$592.80

Terms: net 20.

27

Payment Cheque #423 **Dated Feb. 10/15**

To Pro-Line Inc., $1 354.05 in full payment of account including $27.63 discount for early payment. Reference invoice #PL-1988.

28

Sales Invoice #489 **Dated Feb. 11/15**

To Proud Family

2	BRS1	Hair Brush: natural bristle	$ 28 each
2	BRS2	Hair Brush: styling	24 each
2	SHM1	Pro-Line Shampoo: 225 ml	21 each
4	SRV3	Cut and Style	40 each
1	SRV4	Highlights	100
1	SRV5	Perm	80
	HST		14%

Terms: net 15.

29

Credit Card Sales Invoice #490 **Dated Feb. 13/15**

Sales Summary for credit card sales (to Cash Customers)

8	BRS1	Hair Brush: natural bristle	$28 each	$ 224.00
6	BRS2	Hair Brush: styling	24 each	144.00
8	CN1	Pro-Line Conditioner: 150 ml	26 /bottle	208.00
8	SHM1	Pro-Line Shampoo: 225 ml	21 /bottle	168.00
30	SRV3	Cut and Style	40 each	1 200.00
7	SRV4	Highlights	100 each	700.00
3	SRV5	Perm	80 each	240.00
4	SRV6	Wash and Style	20 each	80.00
	HST		14%	414.96
Invoice total paid by credit cards				$3 378.96

Deposited to credit card bank account.

30

Cash Sales Invoice #491 **Dated Feb. 14/15**

Sales Summary for cash sales (to Cash Customers)

6	BRS2	Hair Brush: styling	$24 each	$ 144.00
8	GEL1	Pro-Line Spray Gel: shaper 150 ml	22 /can	176.00
3	FRZ1	Pro-Line Defrizzer: cream 100 ml	14 /jar	42.00
7	SPR1	Pro-Line Hair Spray: gentle 150 ml	17 /can	119.00
6	SRV1	Colour	45 each	270.00
24	SRV3	Cut and Style	40 each	960.00
2	SRV4	Highlights	100 each	200.00
	HST		14%	267.54
Invoice total paid by cash				$2 178.54

Deposited to Undeposited Cash and Cheques.

31

Purchase Invoice #SS-555 **Dated Feb. 14/15**

From Sharp Scissors, to fill purchase order #54, $600 plus $84 HST for professional high-grade stainless steel stylist scissors. Purchase invoice total $684. Terms: net 10.

32

DEPOSIT SLIP # 7 **FEBRUARY 14, 2015**

Date	Cheque #	Client	Amount
Feb 10	93	Irma Vannitee	$246.92
		Total Cheques	$246.92
		Cash	$2 178.54
		(Consisting of 17 × $5; 18 × $10; 18 × $20; 13 × $50; 9 × $100; Coin $3.54)	
		Total Deposit	$2 425.46

33

Memo #11 **Dated Feb. 14/15**

From Owners: Transfer $10 000 from credit card account to chequing account.

SESSION DATE – FEBRUARY 21, 2015

34

Sales Invoice #492 **Dated Feb. 16/15**

To Irma Vannitee

1	SRV6	Wash and Style	$20
	HST		14%

Terms: 2/5, n/15. Recall stored transaction.

35

Memo #12 **Dated Feb. 17/15**

From Owners: Pay HST owing to the Receiver General for the period ending January 31, 2015. Issue cheque #424 in payment.

NOTES

You can use the Tax Report for HST for January to obtain the HST amounts for the remittance, or you can refer to the General Ledger Report for the two HST accounts.

36

Cash Purchase Invoice #ET-4588 **Dated Feb. 17/15**

From Eastern Tel, $110 plus $15.40 HST for telephone service. Purchase invoice total $125.40 paid in full by cheque #425.

37

Sales Quote #103 **Dated Feb. 19/15**

First performance date Mar. 1/15

To On Stage Theatre Company (for 12 theatre performances for three cast members) at preferred customer prices

3	SRV3	Cut and Style	$32 each
36	SRV6	Wash and Style	16 each
9	SRV7	Wig Wash, Set and Style	24 each
	HST		14%

Terms: 2/5, n/15.

38

Cash Receipt #145 **Dated Feb. 19/15**

From Conn Seted, cheque #269 for $137.94 in payment of account. Reference invoice #483.

39

Cash Receipt #146 **Dated Feb. 19/15**

From Twilight Theatre, cheque #5635 for $547.20 in payment of account. Reference invoice #484.

40

Credit Card Purchase Invoice #SP-399 **Dated Feb. 20/15**

From Seaside Papers, $200 plus $28 HST for office supplies for salon. Purchase invoice total $228 paid in full by credit card.

41

Cash Receipt #147 **Dated Feb. 20/15**

From Brioche Bridal Party, cheque #986 for $136.80 in payment of account. Reference invoice #487.

42

Credit Card Sales Invoice #493 **Dated Feb. 20/15**

Sales Summary for credit card sales (to Cash Customers)

3	BRS1	Hair Brush: natural bristle	$28 each	$ 84.00
2	CN2	Pro-Line Hot Oil Treatment 75 ml	29 /tube	58.00
2	FRZ1	Pro-Line Defrizzer: cream 100 ml	14 /jar	28.00
4	SHM1	Pro-Line Shampoo: 225 ml	21 /bottle	84.00
6	SRV1	Colour	45 each	270.00
21	SRV3	Cut and Style	40 each	840.00
	HST		14%	190.96
	Invoice total paid by credit card bank			$1 554.96

Deposited to credit card bank account

43

Cash Sales Invoice #494 **Dated Feb. 21/15**

Sales Summary for cash sales (to Cash Customers)

5	BRS2	Hair Brush: styling	$24 each	$ 120.00
8	CN1	Pro-Line Conditioner: 150 ml	26 /bottle	208.00
6	GEL1	Pro-Line Spray Gel: shaper 150 ml	22 /can	132.00
7	SPR1	Pro-Line Hair Spray: gentle 150 ml	17 /can	119.00
3	SRV1	Colour	45 each	135.00
26	SRV3	Cut and Style	40 each	1 040.00
10	SRV6	Wash and Style	20 each	200.00
	HST		14%	273.56
	Invoice total paid by cash			$2 227.56

Deposited to Undeposited Cash and Cheques.

44

DEPOSIT SLIP #8 Date: Feb 21, 2015

Tesses Tresses
55 Salon Rd.
Charlottetown PE C1A 6D3

Account No: 0290 3433382

Cheques

No.	Name	Amount
269	Conn Seted	137.94
5635	Twilight Theatre	547.20
986	Brioche Bridal Party	136.80

		Amount	
19	× 5	95	00
27	× 10	270	00
28	× 20	560	00
14	× 50	700	00
6	× 100	600	00
	coin	2	56
Total cash		2227	56
Total cheque		821	94
Subtotal		3049	50
Cash received			
Net Deposit		3049	50

Signature *Tess Dubois*

02/21/15 PW

☐ 45 **Credit Card Purchase Invoice #AUN-478** **Dated Feb. 21/15**

From All U Need department store, $90 plus $12.60 HST for cleaning supplies. Purchase invoice total $102.60 paid in full by credit card.

☐ 46 **Purchase Order #56** **Dated Feb. 21/15**

Shipping date Mar. 3/15
From Lookin' Good, $400 plus $56 HST for 25 polyester and nylon water-resistant monogrammed capes for salon client use. Unit price is $16. Purchase invoice total $456. Terms: net 10.

☐ 47 **Payment Cheque #426** **Dated Feb. 21/15**

To Sharp Scissors, $684 in payment of account. Reference invoice #SS-555.

SESSION DATE – FEBRUARY 28, 2015

☐ 48 **Purchase Invoice #AP-7111** **Dated Feb. 23/15**

From Air Pro, to fill purchase order #55, $350 plus $49 HST for two bonnet-style hair dryers and two handheld hair dryers. Purchase invoice total $399. Terms: net 15.

☐ 49 **Sales Invoice #495** **Dated Feb. 23/15**

To Irma Vannitee

1	SRV6	Wash and Style	$20
	HST		14%

Terms: 2/5, n/15. Recall stored transaction.

☐ 50 **Sales Invoice #496** **Dated Feb. 23/15**

To Brioche Bridal Party to fill remainder of sales order #101

5	SRV6	Wash and Style	$20 each
	HST		14%

Terms: 2/5, n/15.

☐ 51 **Credit Card Bill Payment #2-15** **Dated Feb. 24/15**

From credit card company, $421.80 for purchases made before Feb. 11 and $24 annual card fee. Total payment due to avoid interest penalty $445.80. Issued cheque #427 for $445.80 in full payment.

NOTES
You will see the warning message about using the next cheque number for the credit card payment.

Reversing NSF Cheques on Deposit Slips

In previous chapters, we reversed NSF cheques with the Reverse Receipt shortcut tool in the Adjusting receipt window of the Receipts Journal. In these cases, the bank chequing account was the linked principal bank account for the Receivables module, so the cheque was recorded (deposited) directly to this account. The reversing procedure would select this same account. For Tesses Tresses, *Undeposited Cash and Cheques* is the principal linked bank account for deposits. The NSF cheque, however, is withdrawn from *Bank: Chequing Account* — until we deposit the cheque in the bank its validity is unknown. For this situation, we need to enter a negative receipt for the paid invoice that credits *Bank: Chequing Account*. The following steps describe the procedure for reversing the cheque from Brioche Bridal Party.

✓ 52 **Bank Debit Memo #983321** **Dated Feb. 25/15**

From Savers Trust Co., cheque #986 from Brioche Bridal Party was returned because of insufficient funds. The cheque amount, $136.80, was withdrawn from the chequing account.

WARNING!
Do not reverse the receipt to record this NSF cheque.

Open the **Receipts Journal**.

Choose **Brioche Bridal Party** as the client.

Choose **1060 Bank: Chequing Account** from the drop-down list in the Deposit To field.

Click the **Cheque field** so we can enter the client cheque number.

Type NSF-986

Click the **Receipt No. field**. We will enter the bank debit number here.

Type DM-983321 **Enter February 25** as the date for the transaction.

Click the **Include Fully Paid Invoices/Deposits tool** or **choose** the **Receipt menu** and **click Include Fully Paid Invoices/Deposits**.

The two paid invoices (#468 and 487) are added to the form with the unpaid invoice. Invoice #487 was paid with the NSF cheque, so we need to select it.

Click **487** in the Invoice Or Deposit column.

Press *tab* until the cursor is in the Amount Received column for the line. We need to enter the full amount of the cheque as a negative number.

Type −136.80 **Press** *tab* to enter the amount.

The discount for the unpaid invoice is now selected and we need to remove it.

Press *del* to complete the entry.

Review the **journal entry**.

You will see that *Accounts Receivable* has been debited to restore the amount owing and *Bank: Chequing Account* is credited to reverse the previous deposit. Check that the discount for the unpaid invoice is not included.

Close the **journal display** and then **post** the **receipt**.

Click the **Include Fully Paid Invoices/Deposits tool**

Choose **Brioche Bridal Party** again.

You will see that the invoice amount owing has been fully restored. When the payment is received, you will enter it in the usual way.

Close the **Receipts Journal** and **continue** with the **remaining transactions**.

WARNING!
Remember to delete the selected discounts and amounts for any other invoices.

NOTES
If a discount has been included with the payment, you will need to reverse it as well. Enter the amount of the discount as a negative amount in the Discount Taken field and press *tab*. The cheque amount may be automatically entered as the Amount Received, with the minus sign added. If it is not, enter it as a negative amount.

You should review the entry carefully before posting and then check the Receipts Journal again for the customer to ensure that the invoice has been fully restored.

53 **Memo #13** **Dated Feb. 25/15**
Prepare sales invoice #497 for $30 to charge Brioche Bridal Party for the NSF fee. Credit Other Revenue. Terms: net 15. (Do not charge tax or allow discount.)

54 **Cash Receipt #148** **Dated Feb. 27/15**
From Brioche Bridal Party, certified cheque #RBC7333 for $166.80 in payment of account. Reference invoices #487 and 497 and bank debit memo #983321.

55 **Sales Invoice #498** **Dated Feb. 27/15**
To Twilight Theatre to fill the remainder of sales order #102 (for four nights of theatre performances for four cast members) at preferred customer prices

4	SRV3	Cut and Style	$32 each
16	SRV6	Wash and Style	16 each
4	SRV7	Wig Wash, Set and Style	24 each
	HST		14%

Terms: 2/5, n/15.

NOTES
For Brioche, you will see a warning message about the client often paying late.

56 **Credit Card Sales Invoice #499** **Dated Feb. 27/15**

Sales Summary for credit card sales (to Cash Customers)

6	BRS2	Hair Brush: styling	$24 each	$ 144.00
8	CN1	Pro-Line Conditioner: 150 ml	26 /bottle	208.00
6	FRZ1	Pro-Line Defrizzer: cream 100 ml	14 /jar	84.00
8	SPR1	Pro-Line Hair Spray: gentle 150 ml	17 /can	136.00
3	SRV1	Colour	45 each	135.00
26	SRV3	Cut and Style	40 each	1 040.00
2	SRV5	Perm	80 each	160.00
2	SRV6	Wash and Style	20 each	40.00
	HST		14%	272.58
Invoice total paid by credit cards				$2 219.58

Deposited to credit card bank account.

57 **Cash Sales Invoice #500** **Dated Feb. 28/15**

Valentine's Day sales did not meet expectations, so at the end of the month, all hair brushes were sold at discounted prices. Edit the selling price for BRS1 and BRS2.

Sales Summary for cash sales (to Cash Customers)

20	BRS1	Hair Brush: natural bristle	$18 each	$ 360.00
10	BRS2	Hair Brush: styling	14 each	140.00
28	SRV3	Cut and Style	40 each	1 120.00
4	SRV6	Wash and Style	20 each	80.00
	HST		14%	238.00
Invoice total paid by cash				$1 938.00

Deposited to Undeposited Cash and Cheques.

58

DEPOSIT SLIP #9 Date: Feb 28, 2015

Tesses Tresses
55 Salon Rd.
Charlottetown PE C1A 6D3

Account No: 0290 3433382

Cheques

RBC7333 Brioche Bridal Party 166.80

		Amount	
7	× 5	35	00
22	× 10	220	00
14	× 20	280	00
12	× 50	600	00
8	× 100	800	00
	coin	3	00
Total cash		1938	00
Total cheque		166	80
Subtotal		2104	80
Cash received			
Net Deposit		2104	80

Signature *Tess Dubois*

02/28/15 PW

59

Bank Debit Memo #100121 **Dated Feb. 28/15**

From Savers Trust Co. pre-authorized withdrawals for Mortgage: $1 500 ($1 240 interest & $260 principal) and for Loan: $600 ($115 interest & $485 principal).

60

Memo #14 **Dated Feb. 28/15**

Enter the adjustments for expired prepaid expenses and supplies used:
Prepaid Insurance expired: $150
Prepaid Subscriptions expired: $40
Office Supplies used: $60
Salon Supplies used: $285
Washroom & Cleaning Supplies used: $75

NOTES

Use the Inventory Adjustments Journal to transfer the inventory to the supplies account. Enter **negative** quantities and change the default Inventory Losses account to Salon Supplies for all items. Refer to Accounting Procedures, page 576.

61

Memo #15 **Dated Feb. 28/15**

The following items were transferred from inventory at cost for salon use:

6 CN1 Pro-Line Conditioner: 150 ml
3 CN2 Pro-Line Hot Oil Treatment 75 ml
4 GEL1 Pro-Line Spray Gel: shaper 150 ml
8 SHM1 Pro-Line Shampoo: 225 ml
6 SPR1 Pro-Line Hair Spray: gentle 150 ml

NOTES

Enter Feb. 28 as the Statement and Reconciliation dates to replace March 3 (31 days after the previous reconciliation).

62

Memo #16 **Dated Feb. 28/15**

Use the following statement to reconcile the chequing bank account for February.

SAVERS TRUST

321 Queen St., Charlottetown, PE C1A 6D3 www.saverstrust.com

Tesses Tresses
55 Salon Road
Charlottetown, PE C1A 6D3

ACCOUNT STATEMENT
CHEQUING

Transit / Account No
0290 003 433 38-2

Statement period
Feb 1, 2015 to Feb 28, 2015

Date	Deposit #	Description	Deposits	Withdrawals	Balance
		Balance Fwd			46,382.35
1 Feb	5	Deposit	3,406.73		49,789.08
5 Feb		Cheque #417		912.00	48,877.08
5 Feb		Cheque #418		250.80	48,626.28
7 Feb	6	Deposit	2,763.30		51,389.58
8 Feb		Cheque #419		1,600.00	49,789.58
10 Feb		Cheque #422		250.80	49,538.78
14 Feb	7	Deposit	2,425.46		51,964.24
16 Feb		Cheque #423		1,354.05	50,610.19
18 Feb		Transfer funds from 004 123 22-8	10,000.00		60,610.19
19 Feb		Cheque #425		125.40	60,484.79
21 Feb	8	Deposit	3,049.50		63,534.29
21 Feb		Cheque #424		2,538.20	60,996.09
25 Feb		NSF Cheque #986		136.80	60,859.29
25 Feb		Service Charge - NSF cheque		30.00	60,829.29
26 Feb		Cheque #426		684.00	60,145.29
28 Feb		Scheduled loan payment		600.00	59,545.29
28 Feb		Scheduled mortgage payment		1,500.00	58,045.29
28 Feb		Service Charges - chequing acct		23.50	58,021.79
28 Feb		Interest	47.75		58,069.54
28 Feb		Closing balance			58,069.54

Total Deposits # 6 $21,692.74
Total Withdrawals # 13 $10,005.55

NOTES

You do not need to add linked accounts or prior transactions. Enter the statement ending balance and then mark journal entries as cleared (keystrokes on page 592) to complete the reconciliation.

There are four deposit slips for group deposits.

The loan and mortgage payments were entered together: $1 500 + $600 = $2 100.

Remember to change the status of the NSF cheque from Brioche Bridal Party for $136.80 (in deposit slip #8) to NSF and the status of its reversing entry to Adjustment.

At the end of February, a cheque for $445.80 and one deposit for $2 104.80 are outstanding.

63

Memo #17 **Dated Feb. 28/15**

Use the following statement to reconcile the credit card bank account.

SAVERS TRUST

321 Queen St., Charlottetown, PE C1A 6D3 www.saverstrust.com

Tesses Tresses
55 Salon Road
Charlottetown, PE C1A 6D3

ACCOUNT STATEMENT
CREDIT CARD

Transit / Account No
0290 004 123 22-8

Statement period
Feb 1, 2015 to Feb 28, 2015

Date	Description	Deposits	Withdrawals	Balance
	Balance Fwd			8,582.26
6 Feb	Deposit	2,444.72		11,026.98
13 Feb	Deposit	3,287.73		14,314.71
18 Feb	Transfer funds to 003 433 38-2		10,000.00	4,314.71
20 Feb	Deposit	1,512.98		5,827.69
28 Feb	Service charges		11.50	5,816.19
28 Feb	Interest	8.25		5,824.44
28 Feb	Closing balance			5,824.44

Total Deposits	# 4	$7,253.68
Total Withdrawals	# 2	$10,011.50

NOTES
Enter Feb. 28 as the Statement and Reconciliation dates.

Displaying Banking Reports

Click the **Report Centre icon**  in the Home window.

Click **Banking** to open the list of banking reports in the Report Centre:

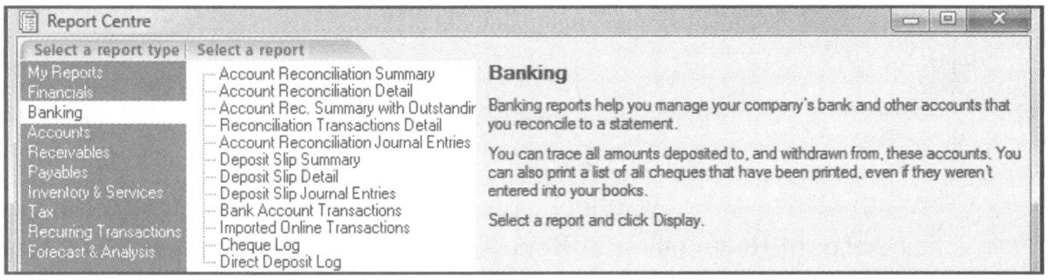

NOTES
The Reports pane list in the Banking module window has Account and Banking reports.

Account Reconciliation Journal

Click **Account Reconciliation Journal Entries**. **Click** **Modify This Report**:

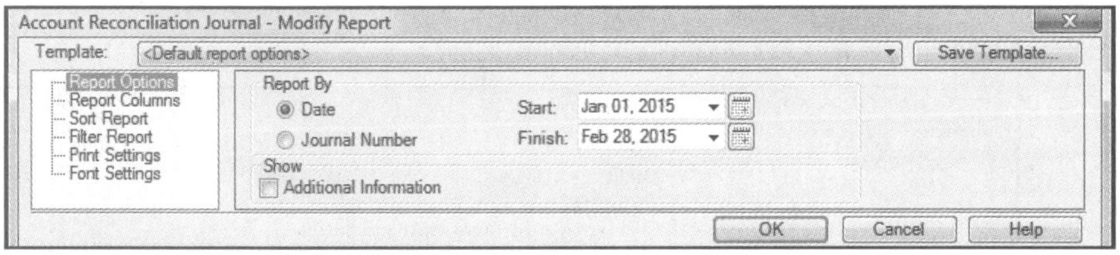

Or choose the Reports menu, choose Journal Entries and click Account Reconciliation to see the report options screen.

The journal can be prepared by selecting journal entry numbers or dates. By default, the report uses posting dates. The usual journal report customizing, sorting and filtering options are available. Notice that there is no option to show corrections.

NOTES
The Cheque Log Report was covered in Chapter 5. Refer to page 148.
For the Bank Account Transactions Report, refer to pages 588–589.
The Direct Deposit Log refers to payroll direct deposits.

CLASSIC VIEW
Right-click the Reconciliation & Deposits icon  to select the journal. Click the Display tool  to open the report options.

Enter the **Start** and **Finish** dates or journal numbers for the report.

Click **OK**. **Close** the **display** when you have finished.

Deposit Slip Journal

Click **Deposit Slip Journal Entries** and **click Modify This Report**:

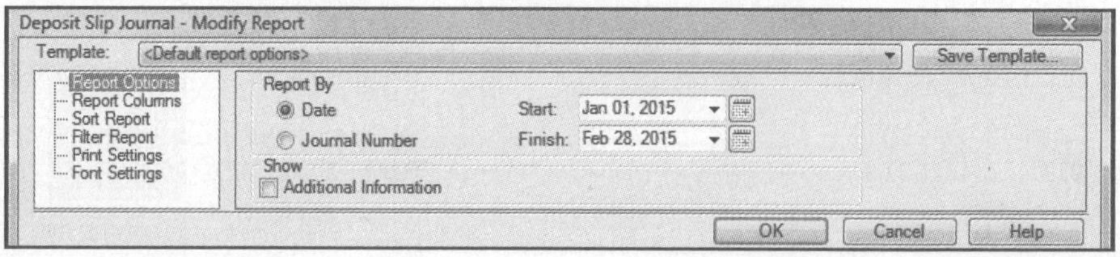

Or, from the Home window, choose the Reports menu, choose Journal Entries and click Deposit Slip to see the report options screen.

The journal can be prepared by selecting journal entry numbers or dates. By default, the report uses posting dates. The usual journal report customizing, sorting and filtering options are available. Notice that there is no option to show corrections.

Enter the **Start** and **Finish** dates or journal numbers for the report.

Click **OK**. **Close** the **display** when you have finished.

Account Reconciliation Report

NOTES

You can display Journal reports, Supplier or Client Aged or Employee reports (if applicable) and look up invoices from the Account Reconciliation Detail Report.

The Reconciliation Report cannot be customized except by choosing columns.

Click **Account Reconciliation Summary** to display the report sample and **click Modify This Report** to see the report options:

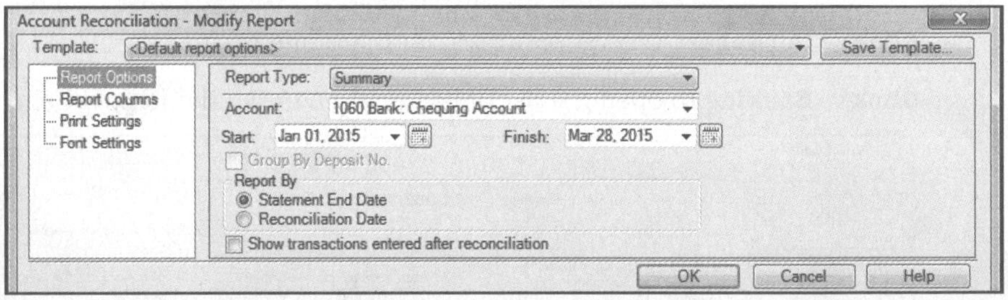

From the Home window, choose the Reports menu, then choose Banking and click Account Reconciliation Report to display the options.

Accept **1060** as the bank account or choose another account from the drop-down list for the Account field.

Enter the **Start** and **Finish** dates. The default Finish date is one month past the latest reconciliation or bank statement date.

Click the **Report Type list arrow**:

From the Report Type drop-down list, you can choose the **Summary** Report to provide totals for deposits, withdrawals, income and expense categories for the bank statements and the General Ledger account, and outstanding amounts that will reconcile the two balances. Unresolved amounts and discrepancies are also reported, if there are any. The **Detail** Report lists all journal entries with their status, such as Cleared, NSF and so on. You can group the Detail Report by Deposit Number. Choose **Summary**

Report With Outstanding Transaction Detail to show only the total outstanding amounts and the adjusted bank and General Ledger balances. You can **report by** either the bank **Statement End Date** or the **Reconciliation Date** recorded in the journal for the report.

Choose the **report type** and **date (Report By) options**.

Click **OK**. **Close** the **displayed report** when you have finished.

Reconciliation Transaction Report

Click **Reconciliation Transactions Detail** and **click Modify This Report** to see the report options window:

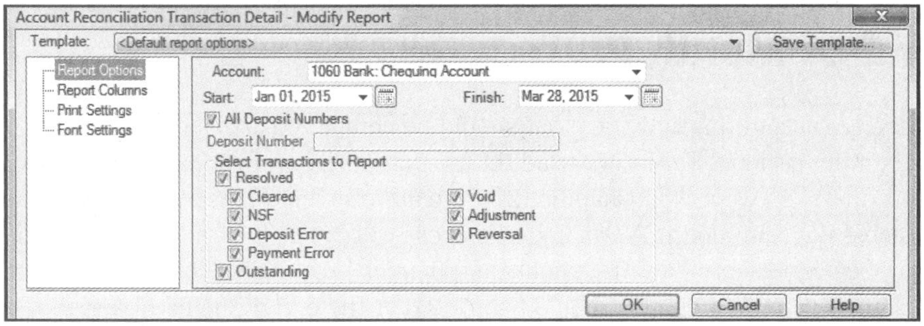

From the Home window, choose the Reports menu, then choose Banking and click Account Reconciliation Transaction Report.

The Reconciliation Transaction Report will list all the transactions with their reconciliation status for the selected bank account for all the status types you chose.

Choose the **account** for the report from the drop-down list.

Enter **Start** and **Finish** dates for the report.

Choose the **Status categories** to include in your reports. By default, all are included, so clicking a category will remove the ✓ from the check box and omit this category from your report.

Click **OK**. **Close** the **displayed report** when you have finished.

Deposit Slip Report

Click **Deposit Slip Summary** and **click Modify This Report**.

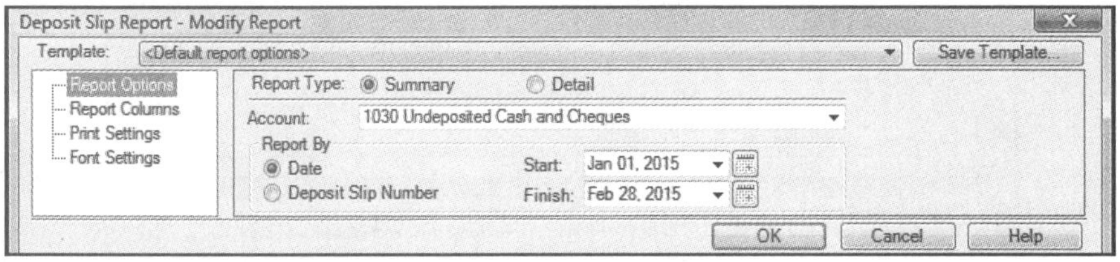

From the Home window, choose the Reports menu, then choose Banking and click Deposit Slip Report to display the options.

The Deposit Slip **Summary** Report shows the total amounts for cash and cheques on each deposit slip, while the **Detail** Report lists all cheque, bill and coin amounts separately for each deposit.

Choose the **account** for the report from the drop-down list.

NOTES
You can drill down to Supplier or Client Aged or Employee reports (if applicable) and look up invoices from the Reconciliation Transaction Detail Report.

NOTES
You can customize the Reconciliation Transaction and Deposit Slip reports by selecting the columns to include, but you cannot sort or filter the reports.
You cannot drill down to other reports from the Deposit Slip Report.

You can display the report for a range of dates or deposit slip numbers. Choose the **Summary** option to see a list of totals for cash and cheques for each deposit slip. Choose **Detail** to see the individual items on each deposit slip and the totals.

Enter **Start** and **Finish** dates for the report.

Click **OK**. **Close** the **displayed report** and the **Report Centre** when finished.

Printing Banking Reports

NOTES
Remember to check your printer selection before you begin printing.

Display the **report** you want to print. **Click** [print tool] or **choose** the **File menu** and **click Print** to print the report. **Close** the **Report window** when finished.

End-of-Month Procedures

There are accounting activities that should be completed at the end of regular accounting periods. Earlier we used the checklists to review fiscal year-end accounting procedures. As we saw in Chapter 12, there are also checklists for the end of each business day and month. Normally, a business will print all journal transactions at the end of each business day. Statements and financial reports will be printed at the end of each month, and all reports should be printed at the end of the fiscal period. T4s should be printed at the end of the calendar year.

Periodically, a business will clear old information from its accounting files to make space. In the manual system, it might store the details in archives or with a secured offsite backup storage provider to keep the current files manageable. Computerized systems should be similarly maintained by making backups of the data files and then clearing the information that is not required. These periodic procedures include clearing journal entries for prior periods, removing paid invoices from client and supplier records and removing suppliers and clients who no longer do business with the company.

Checklists in Sage 50 can assist with these routine procedures.

WARNING!
Back up the data files before proceeding and print all relevant available reports: journals, supplier and client detail reports, inventory tracking reports and the other reports listed in the month-end checklist.

You may want to create a separate copy of the data file to practise clearing data. Use the File menu Save As command, enter a different file name and work with the new file that opens.

✓ 64

Memo #18 **Dated Feb. 28/15**

Back up the data files. Clear journal entries and paid transactions that are no longer needed using January 31 as the date for clearing. Do not clear data for February.

Choose the **Business Assistant menu** in the Home window and **click Checklists** to see the available lists.

Click **Month-End Procedures** to select it and then **click Modify**:

CLASSIC VIEW
You can also click the Checklists button [checklists icon].

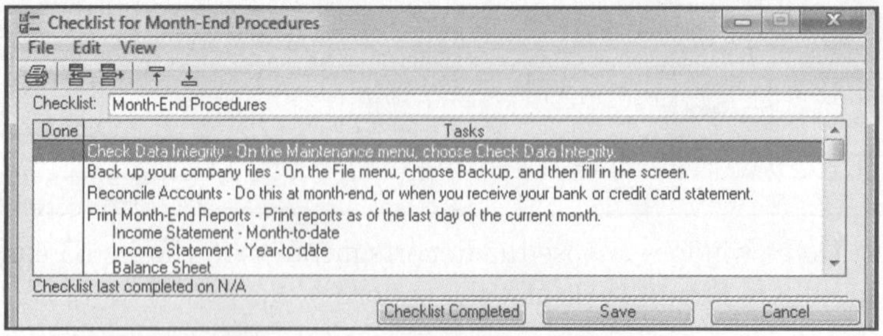

You will see the list of routines that should be completed at the end of a month.

Read the task list. You have already completed some tasks on this list.

Click the **Done column** beside the two tasks that are completed — **Back Up** and **Reconcile Accounts**. We will complete the remaining tasks before marking them.

NOTES
Remember that you can print the task list for reference. Choose the File menu and click Print, click the Print tool or press ctrl + P to print the task list.

Click the **Home window** if part is visible or click the Sage 50 button on the task bar to bring it to the front.

Choose the **Maintenance menu** and **click Check Data Integrity**.

If you do not see the message "Data OK," make a note of any data inconsistencies and return to your most recent backup copy of the file.

Click **OK** to close the Integrity Summary window.

Click the **Done column** beside **Check Data Integrity**.

Click **Save** to return to the main checklists window. A ✓ appears in the Task In Progress column beside Month-End Procedures.

Click **Close** to leave the Checklist window and return to the Home window.

Clearing Paid Supplier Transactions

Choose the **Maintenance menu**, then **choose Clear Data** and **Clear Paid Transactions** and **click Clear Paid Supplier Transactions** to open the list of suppliers:

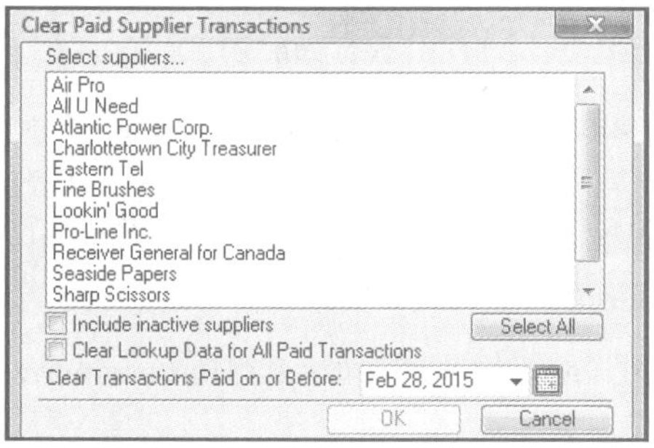

PRO VERSION
You will choose Clear Paid Vendor Transactions. The term Vendor replaces Supplier.

NOTES
You cannot clear data when you are working in multi-user mode.

You can clear invoices for one or more suppliers at the same time. Unpaid invoices are always retained.

Enter **Jan 31** as the last date for which you want to remove invoices.

Click **Select All**. (To select individual suppliers, **press** ctrl and **click** their **names**.) We also have stored lookup details that we no longer need.

Click **Clear Lookup Data For All Paid Transactions**.

Click **OK**. Sage 50 presents the warning shown here:

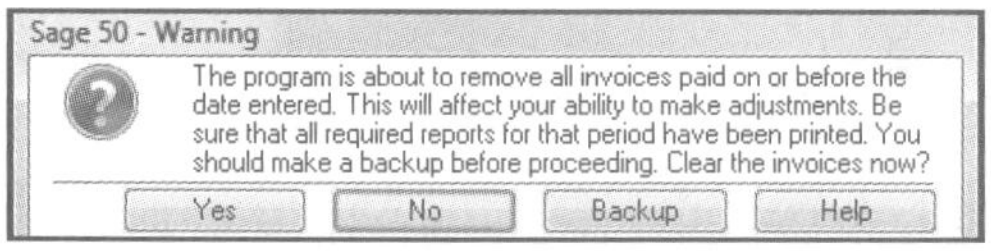

WARNING!
The step of clearing transactions cannot be reversed!

If you have selected correctly and are ready to proceed,

Click **Yes**. When you choose to clear lookup data, you will see this warning:

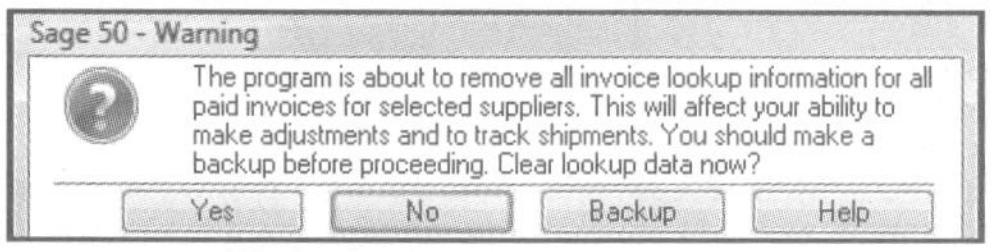

Click **Yes** if you are certain that you should continue.

NOTES
After clearing data, display the relevant reports to see that the information has been cleared. You will be unable to look up and adjust posted invoices if you have removed lookup details for cleared paid transactions.

Clearing Paid Client Transactions

PRO VERSION
You will choose Clear Paid Customer Transactions. The term Customer replaces Client.

Choose the **Maintenance menu**, then **choose Clear Data** and **Clear Paid Transactions** and **click Clear Paid Client Transactions**:

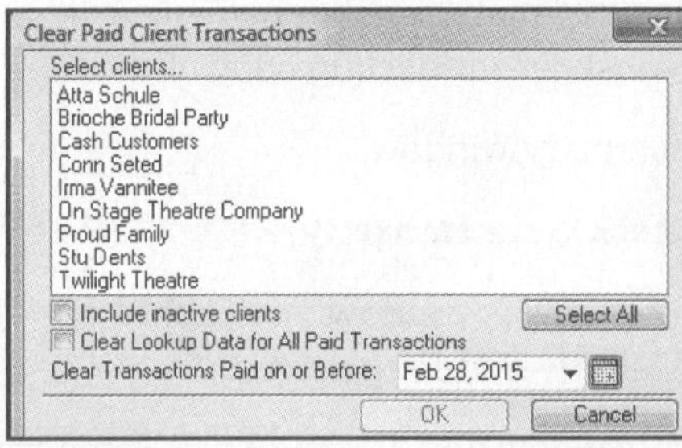

Enter **Jan 31** as the last date for which you want to remove invoices.

Clearing client invoices is similar to clearing supplier invoices.

We will keep all transactions for February. We can clear the invoices and lookup data for Cash Customers and Atta Schule because these are not needed. You can clear paid invoices for all clients by clicking Select All.

Click **Atta Schule**. **Press** ctrl and **click Cash Customers**.

Click **Clear Lookup Data For All Paid Transactions**. **Click OK**.

The next warning is the same as the one we saw for removing supplier invoices. If you are ready, you should proceed.

Click **Yes**. Again, the additional warning for lookup data is shown. If you are certain that you want to continue,

Click **Yes** to remove the lookup data and return to the Home window.

Clearing Tax Reports

You should clear tax reports after filing the tax returns for the period covered by the return so that the next report will include only the current reporting period.

Choose the **Maintenance menu**, then **choose Clear Data** and **click Clear Tax Report** to display the options:

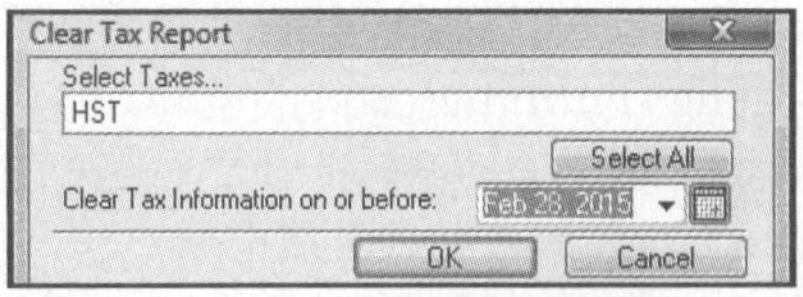

Select the tax or taxes for which you want to clear the reports or click Select All. Then enter the date. Entries on and before the date you enter will be removed.

Click **OK** to see the familiar warning:

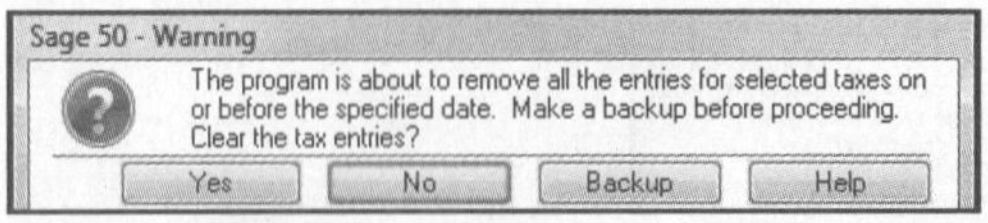

We do not want to remove any tax data because we have not submitted the returns for February.

Click **No** to cancel and return to the Home window.

Clearing Account Reconciliation Data

NOTES
You can clear account reconciliation data for only one account at a time.

Choose the **Maintenance menu**, then **choose Clear Data** and **Clear Account Rec.** and **click Clear Account Rec. Data** to display the options:

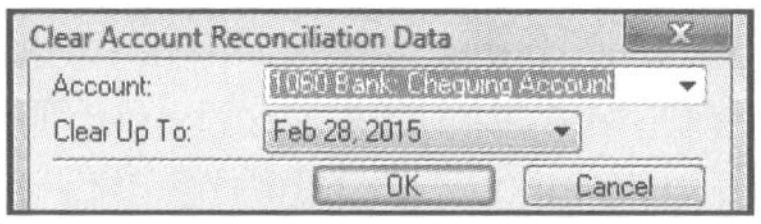

Select the account for which you want to remove the data. Then enter the date. Entries on and before the date you enter will be removed.

We do not want to remove the data at this time. If you choose to continue, you will see the familiar warning before any information is removed.

Click **Cancel** to return to the Home window.

Clearing Inventory Tracking Data

Choose the **Maintenance menu**, then **choose Clear Data** and **click Clear Inventory Tracking Data** to display the following dialogue box:

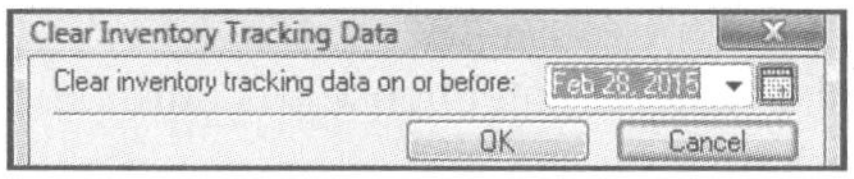

Enter **Jan 31** as the date. Entries on and before Jan. 31 will be removed.

Click **OK**. Again, you see the warning before any data is removed.

If you are certain that you want to proceed,

Click **Yes** to delete the requested information and return to the Home window.

Clearing Lookup Data

You can clear invoice lookup data for both purchase and sales invoices together in a single step or you can clear purchase and sales invoices in separate steps. You can also clear lookup data for remittances from this menu.

PRO VERSION
You will choose Clear Purchase Invoice Lookup Data to clear data for purchase invoices.
You will choose Clear Sales Invoice Lookup Data to clear data for sales invoices.

Choose the **Maintenance menu**, then **choose Clear Data** and **Clear Invoice Lookup Data** and **click Clear Supplier Invoice & Client Invoice Lookup Data** to display the clearing options:

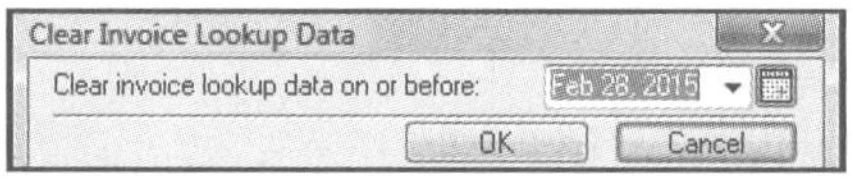

Enter **Jan 31** as the date. Entries on and before Jan. 31 will be removed.

Click **OK**.

NOTES
If you choose to clear invoice lookup data for purchases or sales separately, you can choose to clear the data for one or more suppliers (or clients) or for all of them.

Once again, Sage 50 warns you before removing any data. If you are certain that you want to proceed,

Click **Yes** to continue.

If you cleared the lookup data with the paid transactions, you will see the message stating that there is no invoice data to clear. Click OK to continue.

The requested information is deleted and you will return to the Home window.

To clear only purchase invoice data, choose the Maintenance menu, Clear Data and Clear Invoice Lookup Data and click Clear Supplier Invoice Lookup Data. Choose suppliers for which you want to clear the invoices, enter the date and click OK to see the warning. Click Yes to continue with clearing the data.

To remove only sales invoice data, choose the Maintenance menu, Clear Data and Clear Invoice Lookup Data and click Clear Client Invoice Lookup Data. Select clients for which you want to clear the invoices, enter the date and click OK. Click Yes to continue with clearing the data.

Clearing Deposit Slip Lookup Data

Choose the **Maintenance menu**, **Clear Data** and **Clear Lookup Data**. **Click** **Clear Lookup Data For Deposit Slips** to display the options:

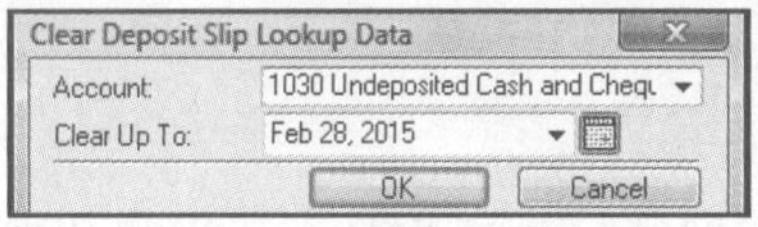

Select the account for which you want to remove the data. Then enter the date. Entries on and before the date you enter will be removed.

We do not want to remove the data at this time. If you choose to continue, you will see the familiar warning before any information is removed.

Click **Cancel** to return to the Home window.

Clearing Lookup Data for Other Payments

NOTES
From the Maintenance menu, Clear Data option, you can also clear lookup data for remittances, notes that you create in the Daily Business Manager, financial history and direct deposits. For each one, you can enter a date after which all data will be retained. You will be warned before any information is removed.

NOTES
If you cleared the lookup data when you cleared the paid transactions, you will see the message stating that there is no lookup data to clear.

Lookup data for other payments are cleared separately from Purchases Journal invoices.

Choose the **Maintenance menu**, **Clear Data** and **Clear Lookup Data**. **Click** **Clear Lookup Data For Other Payments** to display the list of suppliers and the clearing options:

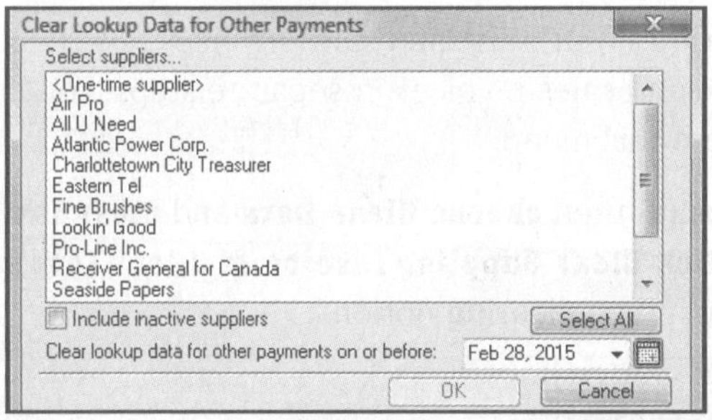

Enter **Jan 31** as the date for the data you want to remove.

Choose the **suppliers**. **Click Select All** to select all suppliers.

Click **OK** to see the warning before any data is removed. To proceed,

Click **Yes**.

The requested information is deleted, and you will return to the Home window.

Automatically Clearing Data

You can also choose to clear data automatically when you start a new fiscal period.

Choose the **Maintenance menu**, then **choose Clear Data** and **click** **Automatically Clear Data** to view your options:

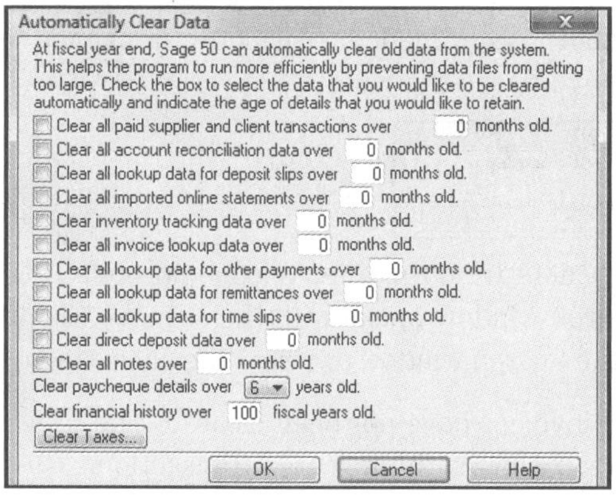

From this screen you can choose what data to clear and how many months of each type of data should be kept when the clearing occurs at the end of the fiscal period.

Click **Cancel** to return to the Home window.

Automatically Clearing Tax Data

Tax information can also be cleared automatically.

Choose the **Maintenance menu**, then **choose Clear Data** and **click Automatically Clear Data**. **Click** the **Clear Taxes button**:

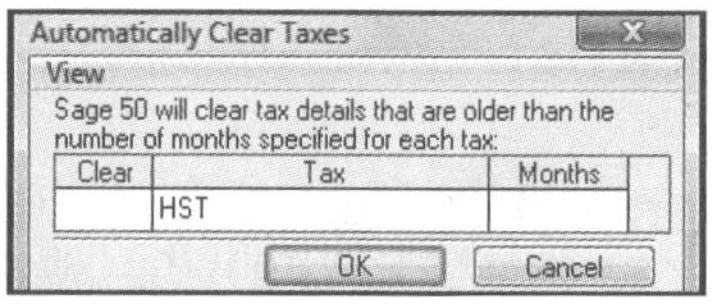

On this screen you can choose what taxes to clear. Data older than the number of months you enter will be removed when the clearing occurs at the end of the fiscal period.

Click the **Clear column** beside the tax and then **enter** the number of **months**. The default is to keep the tax details for 12 months.

Click **Cancel** to return to the Automatically Clear Data screen and **click Cancel** again to return to the Home window.

Removing Supplier and Client Records

Sometimes you know that you will not be doing business with a client or supplier again. Removing their records reduces the length of the lists to scroll through for journal entries and saves on mailing costs. Suppliers are removed from the Suppliers window. Clients are removed from the Clients window. We will remove the client (tenant) Stu Dents because he will be moving out of his apartment after March, the date of his final cheque. First we must clear the paid transactions for this client.

Choose the **Maintenance menu**, then **choose Clear Data** and **Clear Paid Transactions** and **click Clear Paid Client Transactions**.

Click **Stu Dents** on the client list. **Enter February 28, 2015** as the date. **Click** **OK**. When you see the warning,

Click **Yes** to confirm. **Click Yes** to confirm removing lookup data if asked.

Click **Receivables** in the Modules pane list.

Click **Stu Dents** in the Home window Clients list to open the ledger record.

NOTES
Financial history is stored for 100 years in the Premium version and 7 years in the Pro version.

PRO VERSION
The default entry for Clear Financial History Over is 6 Years.

NOTES
When you click the Clear column for a tax, the default number of months is entered and you can change it.

NOTES
An alternative to removing records is to mark clients or suppliers as Inactive and not include them in reports. Inactive clients and suppliers also do not appear in the drop-down lists in journals.
The record will be saved and you can restore it to active status at any time.

Click the **Remove Client tool** in the ledger window, or **choose** the **File menu** and **click Remove** to see the warning:

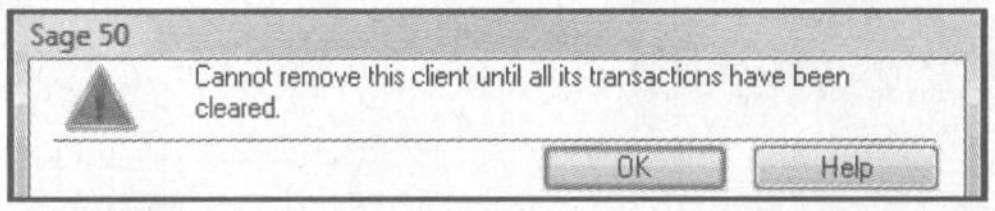
Sage 50
Cannot remove this client until all its transactions have been cleared.
OK
Help

> **NOTES**
> In the ledger window, you can also press ctrl + R to remove the record.

You can also choose Remove Client from the Clients icon shortcuts list in the Receivables window. The Search window opens with the Remove Client option selected. Click Stu Dents in the Search window to select the client and click OK.

> **NOTES**
> There are postdated rent cheques for Stu Dents, so not all the paid transactions were cleared when February 28 was selected as the date.

We selected a client for whom all invoices have not been cleared. The program will not permit you to remove a client, or supplier, with uncleared transactions. Clients with unpaid transactions can never be removed.

> **NOTES**
> You can select March 2 from the Date field drop-down list. (The latest transaction date is usually on the Date field drop-down lists.)

Click **OK** to return to the Receivables module window. Clear the details using March 2 as the date and then remove the client's record. If all transactions are cleared, you will see the familiar warning.

Check that you have selected the client you want before continuing.

Click **Yes** if you have selected correctly.

Click Yes to continue if you see the message about removing lookup data. If you see the message stating that there is no lookup data, click OK to continue.

Completing the Month-End Checklist

> **NOTES**
> Refer to pages 489–490 for more information on removing or adding tasks in checklists.

We will now return to the month-end checklist by marking the remaining tasks as done. The tasks relating to budgeting do not apply so we can delete them from the list and customize the list for Tesses Tresses.

Choose the **Business Assistant menu** and **click Checklists** to see the lists.

Double-click **Month-End Procedures** to open this list.

You can also add tasks to customize the list even further. Just click on the list where you want to add a task, choose the Edit menu and click Insert (or click the Insert Item tool). Then type the task description.

Scroll down the **list** to the budget-related tasks.

Click **Check Your Budget** to select this line.

Click the **Remove Item tool** or **choose** the **Edit menu** and **click Remove**.

Click **Yes** to confirm and select the next task. Remove it and the following one relating to budgets.

Click the **Done column** for the remaining tasks.

Click **Checklist Completed** to return to the opening Checklist window. The session date appears as the Date Last Completed beside Month-End Procedures.

R E V I E W

The Student DVD with Data Files includes Review Questions and Supplementary Cases for this chapter.

CHAPTER SIXTEEN

VELOCITY

OBJECTIVES

After completing this chapter, you should be able to

- ***plan*** and ***design*** an accounting system for a small business
- ***prepare*** procedures for converting from a manual system
- ***understand*** the objectives of a computerized system
- ***create*** company files
- ***set up*** company accounts, ledgers and records
- ***enter*** settings for foreign currency transactions
- ***prepare*** files for foreign currency transactions and importing goods
- ***identify*** preferred customers for reduced prices
- ***enter*** preferred customer prices and import duty rates for inventory
- ***enter*** Inventory Ledger settings and records
- ***finish*** entering the accounting history for all modules
- ***insert*** new accounts, suppliers, customers and employees as required
- ***add*** users, ***create*** passwords and ***enter*** access rights
- ***export*** reports
- ***use*** spreadsheets for analyzing, planning and decision making
- ***enter*** end-of-accounting-period adjustments
- ***perform*** end-of-accounting-period closing routines
- ***analyze*** and ***interpret*** comparative reports

INTRODUCTION

NOTES

If you change the province, remember that rules for the application of the Harmonized Sales Tax (HST), provincial sales taxes and payroll may vary from one province to another, and amounts in the source documents will change.

This application provides a complete accounting cycle for a merchandising business. It is a comprehensive application covering a three-month fiscal period. You will use Sage 50 to convert a manual accounting system to a computerized accounting system and then enter transactions. The routines in this application are common to many small businesses, so they should be useful. The information in this chapter reflects the business realities in Ontario in April 2013.

You may substitute information relevant to other provinces or the latest payroll and tax regulations wherever it is appropriate to do so.

NOTES
Because of the length of the application, group work is encouraged in setting up error-free company files and completing the transactions.

NOTES
VeloCity Inc.
27 Gearing Avenue
Niagara on the Lake
ON L0S 1J0
Tel 1: (905) 468-8356 (velo)
Tel 2: (888) 468-8356 (velo)
Fax: (905) 468-9100
Business No.: 335 677 822

NOTES
In this chapter, the terms Vendors and Suppliers will be used interchangeably, as will the terms Purchases and Expenses, and the terms Sales and Revenues.

NOTES
Foreign customers pay HST when they rent bicycles in Ontario because the services are "consumed" in Canada and not exported.

Because of the length of the setup, instructions for working with the source documents are presented with those documents on page 692.

COMPANY INFORMATION

Company Profile

VeloCity, in Niagara on the Lake, Ontario, sells a small range of bicycles and accessories. Steve Ryder, the owner, a regular participant in bicycle races and competitions, opened the shop in the popular tourist region because of the proximity to trails along the Niagara River and Peninsula. The flat terrain makes this area popular with casual bikers.

All the bicycles are high-quality, light-weight, 27-gear cycles with Shimano gears and derailleurs. The extras, such as the carriage and third-wheel attachments, have attracted touring families with young children and the annual sell-off of all rental bikes appeals to the budget-conscious residents and visitors.

Three employees assist with the work in the store that includes selling and servicing the bicycles, while Ryder spends more time promoting the rental services of the business with theatre and tourism businesses throughout the province.

Several suppliers offer discounts to the store for early payment, including two suppliers in the United States. Accounts are also set up for other supplies and services that are provided locally. The store uses a credit card for some of these purchases.

Most customers are situated in the Niagara region, but Ryder has contracts with some travel companies in New York State to include bicycle rentals with their tour packages. Prices in US dollars are entered in the ledger records so that all prices will be entered automatically in the correct amount and currency when the customer is selected. With the Canadian dollar hovering on par with the US dollar, US dollar prices are currently the same as Canadian dollar prices.

All account customers are given discounts for early payment and some preferred customers receive additional discounts. Individual customers usually pay by cash, debit or credit card and do not receive any discounts. Delivery is provided at a small charge and includes assembly and a brief demonstration on bicycle care.

All items and services sold by the store are set up as inventory so that sales can be monitored. HST is charged on all sales and services, except to foreign customers. The store pays HST on all taxable purchases, including inventory purchased for resale. The exception is books, for which the store pays 5 percent GST on purchases and customers pay 5 percent at the time of sale.

The owner decided to use Sage 50 for record keeping after a consultant prepared the report on the following pages. Ryder found an application in an older Sage 50 textbook by Purbhoo. It appeared similar in complexity and structure to VeloCity and even included complete instructions for creating the data files. Before converting the books for the store, he asked his assistant to work through this application for practice. Next she printed all the relevant business guide information and prepared the following reports to assist with the conversion on May 1, 2015:

- Income Statement
- Business Information
- Chart of Accounts
- Balance Sheet
- Post-Closing Trial Balance
- Supplier Information
- Customer Information
- Employee Information
- Inventory Information
- Accounting Procedures

MANAGER'S REPORT ON SAGE 50

PREPARED FOR VELOCITY

1. Sage 50 allows a business to process all source documents in a secure and timely fashion. It can automatically prepare both single-period and comparative accounting reports for planning, decision making and controlling operations within the business.
2. The software eliminates some of the time-consuming manual clerical functions. For example, it can automatically prepare invoices, cheques and statements, and it can perform all the necessary mathematical calculations. Being freed from these chores, the accountant can extend her role to assume a much higher level of responsibility. For example, the accountant will have more time to spend analyzing reports with the owner and can work directly with the owner in making business decisions.
3. Sage 50 can easily export reports to spreadsheets for further analysis, or link with the Internet, with other software programs and with suppliers and customers for interactive data exchange. When combined with the graphing, account reconciliation and budgeting features, these reports permit the owner to analyze past trends and to make better predictions about the future behaviour of the business.
4. As the business grows, the manager can divide work more meaningfully among new accounting personnel. Since Sage 50 provides subsidiary ledgers that are linked to control accounts in the General Ledger, it automatically coordinates accounting work performed by different individuals. Customizable window backgrounds can even accommodate mood changes of the different users.
5. Sage 50 allows the owner to exercise business controls in a number of areas.

IN GENERAL

- Access to confidential accounting records and editing capability can be restricted to authorized personnel by using passwords.
- Mechanical errors can be virtually eliminated, since journal transactions with unequal debits and credits cannot be posted. Customer, supplier, employee, inventory and project names appear in full on the journal entry input forms, making errors less likely.
- The ability to customize and preview forms, store recurring entries and look up posted invoices makes it possible to avoid errors in repeated information and to double check invoices in response to customer and supplier inquiries.
- Errors in General, Sales, Receipts, Purchases, Payments and Payroll journal entries can be corrected as adjustments or reversed. The software automatically creates and posts the reversing entries.
- Sage 50 provides an audit trail for all journals.
- Bank account, customer, supplier and inventory records can be set up to calculate many foreign currency transactions automatically, including import duties.
- Daily Business Manager lists and checklists provide reminders of upcoming discounts, recurring entries and routine tasks.
- Business advice, management reports and built-in warnings all provide helpful information for running the business.
- Sage 50 provides a directory of customers, suppliers and employees, and can create mailing labels for them.

GENERAL LEDGER

- Sage 50 provides a directory of accounts used by the business, including all linked accounts for the other ledgers.
- The information in these accounts can be used to prepare and analyze financial reports such as the Balance Sheet and Income Statement.

RECEIVABLES LEDGER

- Credit limit entries for each customer should reduce the losses from non-payment of accounts. Customers with poor payment histories can have their credit limits reduced or their credit purchase privileges removed.
- Customers can be linked to price lists so that they automatically receive differential prices.
- Sales quotes and order entries result in automatic Sales Journal entries when the quotes or orders are filled.
- Tax codes, payment terms and accounts are added to the customer record and automatically entered for sales when the customer is selected.
- Accounts receivable can be aged, and each customer's payment behaviour can be analyzed. This feature allows for the accurate calculation of provisions for bad debts.

PAYABLES LEDGER

- The information from the review of transactions with suppliers and from the accounts payable aged analysis can be combined with detailed cash flow reports to make payment decisions. Sage 50 helps to predict short-term cash needs in order to establish priorities for making payments and to schedule payments to suppliers.
- The GST/HST remittance or refund is calculated automatically because of the linked GST/HST accounts in the Payables and Receivables ledgers.
- Sage 50 purchase quotes and order entries result in automatic Purchases Journal entries when quotes or orders are filled.
- The usual tax code, payment terms and expense account for a supplier can be entered in the supplier record so that they are entered automatically for purchases when the supplier is selected.

PAYROLL LEDGER

- Sage 50 maintains employee records with both personal and payment information for personnel files.
- Paycheques for several employees can be processed as a single payroll run entry with direct payroll deposit.
- Once records are set up, the program automatically withholds employee deductions including income tax, CPP (Canada Pension Plan) and EI (Employment Insurance) and is therefore less prone to error. Updated tax tables can be obtained from Sage.

▶

Manager's Report on Sage 50 Page 2

PAYROLL LEDGER CONTINUED

- Payroll summaries permit easy analysis of compulsory and optional payroll expenses and benefits, employee contributions and entitlements.
- Different kinds of income can be linked to different expense accounts. In addition, the wages for different employees can be linked to different expense accounts, again permitting better tracking of payroll expenses.
- Sage 50 automatically links payroll with control accounts in the General Ledger. Remittance amounts are tracked and linked with the corresponding payroll authorities for monthly or quarterly remittance.

INVENTORY LEDGER

- The software provides an inventory summary or database of all inventory items.
- Services can be set up as inventory and tracked the same way as inventory items.
- Inventory reports flag items that need to be re-ordered, and the reports can be used to make purchase decisions.
- Import duty rates and different prices in home and foreign currencies can be set up in the ledger so they appear automatically in the journals. Additional price lists can be added.
- Inventory codes can be matched to the supplier and customer item codes so that common order forms are created automatically.
- The software calculates inventory variance costs when the items sold are out of stock and later purchased at different prices.
- Sage 50 automatically updates inventory records for multiple locations when inventory is purchased, sold, transferred, lost, recovered or returned. It warns when you try to oversell inventory.
- Different units for stocking, selling and buying items can be saved for inventory items so that prices are automatically entered correctly for both sales and purchases. Reports can be prepared for any of the units on record.
- Inventory tracking reports can monitor sales and purchase activity on individual inventory items to see which ones are selling well and which are not. These reports can be used to determine optimum inventory buying patterns to reduce storage costs.

6. In summation, Sage 50 provides an integrated management accounting information system with extensive built-in controls.

INCOME STATEMENT

VELOCITY

February 1 to April 30, 2015

Revenue			
4000	GENERAL REVENUE		
4020	Revenue from Sales	$69 520.00	
4040	Revenue from Services	28 430.00	
4060	Sales Discounts	–965.00	
4100	Net Sales		$96 985.00
4120	Exchange Rate Differences		–12.00
4150	Interest Revenue		980.00
4200	Freight Revenue		245.00
4390	TOTAL GENERAL REVENUE		$98 198.00
TOTAL REVENUE			$98 198.00
Expense			
5000	OPERATING EXPENSES		
5010	Advertising and Promotion		$ 830.00
5020	Bank Charges		169.00
5030	Credit Card Fees		780.00
5040	Damaged Inventory	$ 210.00	
5050	Cost of Goods Sold: Accessories	4 535.00	
5060	Cost of Goods Sold: Bicycles	11 710.00	
5070	Cost of Goods Sold: Books	4 300.00	
5080	Cost Variance	64.00	
5090	Freight Expense	432.00	
5100	Purchase Discounts	–620.00	
5110	Purchases Returns & Allowances	–425.00	
5120	Net Cost of Goods Sold		20 206.00
5130	Depreciation: Computer Equipment	910.00	
5140	Depreciation: Furniture & Fixtures	80.00	
5150	Depreciation: Service Tools	120.00	
5160	Depreciation: Van	190.00	
5170	Depreciation: Retail Premises	2 740.00	
5180	Net Depreciation		4 040.00
5190	Delivery Expense		63.00
5200	Hydro Expense		828.00
5210	Insurance Expense		1 800.00
5220	Interest on Loan		1 240.00
5230	Interest on Mortgage		5 200.00
5240	Maintenance of Premises		1 055.00
5250	Supplies Used		265.00
5260	Property Taxes		2 700.00
5270	Uncollectable Accounts Expense		500.00
5280	Telephone Expense		795.00
5285	Van Maintenance & Operating Expense		1 638.00
5290	TOTAL OPERATING EXPENSES		$42 109.00
5295	PAYROLL EXPENSES		
5300	Wages		10 303.00
5305	Salaries		23 400.00
5310	Commissions & Bonuses		360.00
5320	EI Expense		790.00
5330	CPP Expense		1 548.00
5340	WSIB Expense		403.00
5360	EHT Expense		332.00
5370	Gp Insurance Expense		306.00
5380	Employee Benefits		930.00
5490	TOTAL PAYROLL EXPENSES		$38 372.00
TOTAL EXPENSE			$80 481.00
NET INCOME			$17 717.00

BUSINESS INFORMATION

VELOCITY

USER PREFERENCES: Options

Use Accounting Terms
Automatically save changes to records
Calculate record balances by session date
Automatically refresh balances

View Daily Business Manager and Checklists off
Show Company name, Advice, Session date at startup, and Paid stamps

Pop-Ups Your own preferences

Transaction Confirmation Turned on

COMPANY SETTINGS: Information

Address	27 Gearing Avenue Niagara on the Lake, ON L0S 1J0
Tel 1	(905) 468-8356 (VELO)
Tel 2	(888) 468-8356 (VELO)
Fax	(905) 468-9100
Industry	Retail
Business No.	335 677 829 RT0001
Business Province	Ontario
Fiscal Start	May 01, 2015
Earliest Transaction	May 01, 2015
Fiscal End	Jul 31, 2015

System Warn if accounts not balanced

Backup Semi-monthly; Display reminder
Scheduled, automatic backup off

Features All used

Forms Settings (Next Number)

Sales Invoices No. 2470
Sales Quotes No. 56
Receipts No. 812
Customer Deposits No. 21
Purchase Orders No. 38
Employee Direct Deposits No. 25
Check for duplicates
Print in batches

Date Format mm-dd-yyyy and Long Dates

Logo SageData13\logos\velo.bmp

Names Additional Field Ref. Number

Credit Card Information

Used: Visa
Payable 2250 Expense 5030

Accept:	Visa	Interac
Fee	2.5%	0%
Expense	5030	5030
Asset	1120	1120

Sales Taxes

Tax	ID on forms	Track: Purch	Sales
HST	335 677 829	2670	2650
GST	335 677 829	2670	2650

	Exempt?	Taxable?	Report?
HST	No	No	Yes
GST	No	No	Yes

Tax Codes
H: HST, taxable, 13%, not included, refundable
G: GST, taxable, 5%, not included, refundable
IN: HST, taxable, 13%, included, refundable

Foreign Currency

USD United States Dollars
Tracking Account 4120
Exchange Rate on 05/01/15 1.015

GENERAL SETTINGS No changes

PAYABLES SETTINGS

Address Niagara on the Lake, Ontario, Canada

Options: Aging periods 15, 30, 60 days
Discounts before tax Yes

Import Duty

Track import duty
Linked account 2220

RECEIVABLES SETTINGS

Address Niagara on the Lake, Ontario, Canada

Options: Aging periods 10, 30, 60 days
Interest charges 1.5% after 30 days
Statements include invoices for 31 days
Use tax code H for new customers

Discount: Payment terms 2/10, n/30
Discounts before tax No
Line Discounts Not used

Comments

On Sales Invoice Interest @ 1.5% per month charged on accounts over 30 days.

PAYROLL SETTINGS

Names: Income and Deduction

Income 1 Salary
Income 2 Commission
Income 3 No. Clients
Income 4 Bonus
Income 5 Tuition
Income 6 Travel Exp
Deduction 1 RRSP
Deduction 2 CSB Plan
Deduction 3 Garnishee

Names: Additional Payroll

Field 1 Emergency Contact
Field 2 Contact Number
User Expense 1 Gp Insurance
Entitlement 1 Vacation
Entitlement 2 Sick Leave
Entitlement 3 PersonalDays

Incomes

Income	Type	Taxable	Vac. Pay
Regular	Hourly rate	Yes	Yes
Overtime 1	Hourly rate	Yes	Yes
Salary	Income	Yes	No
Bonus	Income	Yes	No
Commission	Income	Yes	No
No. Clients	Piece Rate	Yes	Yes
Tuition	Income	Yes	No
Travel Exp	Reimburse	No	No

Deductions

RRSP Before tax, after other deductions
CSB Plan After tax and other deductions
Garnishee After tax and other deductions

Taxes

EI factor 1.4
WSIB rate 1.29
EHT factor 0.98
QHSF Not applicable

Entitlements

Name	Track %	Max Days	Clear
Vacation	8.0%	25	No
Sick Leave	5.0%	15	No
PersonalDays	2.5%	5	No

Remittance

Payroll Liability	Remittance Supplier
EI, CPP, Income Tax	Receiver General
WSIB	Workplace Safety & Insurance Board
EHT	Minister of Finance
Gp Insurance, RRSP	Welland Insurance
CSB	Escarpment Investments
Garnishee	Receiver General

End of next remitting period: May 1

Job Categories

Sales: employees are salespersons
All employees are in Sales category

INVENTORY SETTINGS

Profit evaluation by markup
Sort inventory by number
Foreign prices from inventory records
Allow inventory levels to go below zero

ACCOUNT CLASS SETTINGS

Bank
1060 Bank: Niagara Trust Chequing (CAD)
Next cheque no. 101
Next deposit no. 18
1080 Bank: Niagara Trust Savings (CAD)
1140 Bank: USD Chequing (USD)
Next cheque no. 346

Cash
1030 Undeposited Cash and Cheques

Credit Card Receivable
1120 Bank: Visa and Interac

Credit Card Payable
2250 Credit Card Payable

Operating Expense Class
All postable expense accounts except COGS subgroup (accounts 5040–5110)

LINKED ACCOUNTS FOR LEDGERS

See pages 650–655, 660–661

CHART OF ACCOUNTS

VELOCITY

ASSETS
1000 CURRENT ASSETS [H]
1010 Test Balance Account
1030 Undeposited Cash and Cheques [A]
1060 Bank: Niagara Trust Chequing [A]
1080 Bank: Niagara Trust Savings [A]
1120 Bank: Visa and Interac [A]
1140 Bank: USD Chequing [A]
1150 Net Bank [S]
1200 Accounts Receivable [A]
1210 Allowance for Doubtful Accounts [A]
1220 Advances & Loans Receivable [A]
1230 Interest Receivable [A]
1240 Net Receivables [S]
1250 Purchase Prepayments
1260 Prepaid Advertising
1270 Prepaid Insurance
1280 Office Supplies
1290 Bicycle Repair Parts
1300 Rental Bicycles
1400 TOTAL CURRENT ASSETS [T]

1500 INVENTORY ASSETS [H]
1520 Accessories
1540 Bicycles
1560 Books
1580 TOTAL INVENTORY ASSETS [T]

1600 CENTRE & EQUIPMENT [H]
1610 Computer Equipment [A]
1620 Accum Deprec: Computer Equipment [A]
1630 Net Computer Equipment [S]
1640 Furniture & Fixtures [A]
1650 Accum Deprec: Furniture & Fixtures [A]
1660 Net Furniture & Fixtures [S]
1670 Service Equipment & Tools [A]
1680 Accum Deprec: Service Tools [A]
1690 Net: Service Tools [S]
1700 Van [A]
1710 Accum Deprec: Van [A]
1720 Net Van [S]
1730 Retail Premises [A]
1740 Accum Deprec: Retail Premises [A]
1750 Net Retail Premises [S]
1890 TOTAL CENTRE & EQUIPMENT [T] ▶

▶LIABILITIES
2000 CURRENT LIABILITIES [H]
2100 Bank Loan
2200 Accounts Payable
2210 Prepaid Sales and Deposits
2220 Import Duty Payable
2250 Credit Card Payable
2280 Accrued Wages
2300 Vacation Payable
2310 EI Payable [A]
2320 CPP Payable [A]
2330 Income Tax Payable [A]
2350 Receiver General Payable [S]
2380 EHT Payable
2400 RRSP Payable
2410 CSB Plan Payable
2420 Group Insurance Payable
2430 Garnisheed Wages Payable
2460 WSIB Payable
2500 Business Income Tax Payable
2650 GST/HST Charged on Sales [A]
2670 GST/HST Paid on Purchases [A]
2750 GST/HST Owing (Refund) [S]
2790 TOTAL CURRENT LIABILITIES [T]

2800 LONG TERM LIABILITIES [H]
2820 Mortgage Payable
2890 TOTAL LONG TERM LIABILITIES [T]

EQUITY
3000 OWNER'S EQUITY [H]
3560 S. Ryder, Capital
3600 Current Earnings [X]
3690 TOTAL OWNER'S EQUITY [T]

REVENUE
4000 GENERAL REVENUE [H]
4020 Revenue from Sales [A]
4040 Revenue from Services [A]
4060 Sales Discounts [A]
4100 Net Sales [S]
4120 Exchange Rate Differences
4150 Interest Revenue
4200 Freight Revenue
4390 TOTAL GENERAL REVENUE [T] ▶

▶EXPENSE
5000 OPERATING EXPENSES [H]
5010 Advertising and Promotion
5020 Bank Charges
5030 Credit Card Fees
5040 Damaged Inventory [A]
5045 Item Assembly Costs [A]
5050 Cost of Goods Sold: Accessories [A]
5060 Cost of Goods Sold: Bicycles [A]
5070 Cost of Goods Sold: Books [A]
5075 Cost of Services [A]
5080 Cost Variance [A]
5090 Freight Expense [A]
5100 Purchase Discounts [A]
5110 Purchases Returns & Allowances [A]
5120 Net Cost of Goods Sold [S]
5130 Depreciation: Computer Equipment [A]
5140 Depreciation: Furniture & Fixtures [A]
5150 Depreciation: Service Tools [A]
5160 Depreciation: Van [A]
5170 Depreciation: Retail Premises [A]
5180 Net Depreciation [S]
5190 Delivery Expense
5200 Hydro Expense
5210 Insurance Expense
5220 Interest on Loan
5230 Interest on Mortgage
5240 Maintenance of Premises
5250 Supplies Used
5260 Property Taxes
5270 Uncollectable Accounts Expense
5280 Telephone Expense
5285 Van Maintenance & Operating Expense
5290 TOTAL OPERATING EXPENSES [T]

5295 PAYROLL EXPENSES [H]
5300 Wages
5305 Salaries
5310 Commissions & Bonuses
5320 Travel Expenses
5330 EI Expense
5340 CPP Expense
5350 WSIB Expense
5360 EHT Expense
5370 Gp Insurance Expense
5380 Employee Benefits
5490 TOTAL PAYROLL EXPENSES [T]

NOTES: The Chart of Accounts includes all accounts and Net Income. Group account types are not marked. Other account types are marked as follows: [H] Heading, [A] subgroup Account, [S] Subgroup total, [T] Total, [X] Current Earnings.

BALANCE SHEET

VELOCITY

April 30, 2015

Assets

1000	CURRENT ASSETS		
1060	Bank: Niagara Trust Chequing	$ 52 744.00	
1080	Bank: Niagara Trust Savings	118 110.00	
1120	Bank: Visa and Interac	5 925.00	
1140	Bank: USD (9 350 USD)	9 500.00	
1150	Net Bank		$186 279.00
1200	Accounts Receivable	17 110.00	
1210	Allowance for Doubtful Accounts	−800.00	
1220	Advances & Loans Receivable	100.00	
1230	Interest Receivable	420.00	
1240	Net Receivables		16 830.00
1260	Prepaid Advertising		480.00
1270	Prepaid Insurance		4 800.00
1280	Office Supplies		300.00
1290	Bicycle Repair Parts		1 150.00
1300	Rental Bicycles		7 520.00
1400	TOTAL CURRENT ASSETS		$217 359.00
1500	INVENTORY ASSETS		
1520	Accessories	6 540.00	
1540	Bicycles	40 840.00	
1560	Books	5 000.00	
1580	TOTAL INVENTORY ASSETS		$ 52 380.00
1600	CENTRE & EQUIPMENT		
1610	Computer Equipment	7 000.00	
1620	Accum Deprec: Computer Equip	−3 000.00	
1630	Net Computer Equipment		4 000.00
1640	Furniture & Fixtures	2 000.00	
1650	Accum Deprec: Furn & Fixtures	−400.00	
1660	Net Furniture & Fixtures		1 600.00
1670	Service Equipment & Tools	3 000.00	
1680	Accum Deprec: Service Tools	−900.00	
1690	Net: Service Tools		2 100.00
1700	Van	30 000.00	
1710	Accum Deprec: Van	−5 000.00	
1720	Net Van		25 000.00
1730	Retail Premises	200 000.00	
1740	Accum Deprec: Retail Premises	−5 000.00	
1750	Net Retail Premises		195 000.00
1890	TOTAL CENTRE & EQUIPMENT		$227 700.00
	TOTAL ASSETS		$497 439.00 ▶

Liabilities

▶ 2000	CURRENT LIABILITIES		
2100	Bank Loan		$ 50 000.00
2200	Accounts Payable		12 510.40
2250	Credit Card Payable		220.00
2280	Accrued Wages		760.00
2300	Vacation Payable		706.00
2310	EI Payable	$ 639.00	
2320	CPP Payable	1 307.00	
2330	Income Tax Payable	2 210.00	
2350	Receiver General Payable		4 156.00
2380	EHT Payable		331.00
2400	RRSP Payable		350.00
2410	CSB Plan Payable		350.00
2420	Group Insurance Payable		102.00
2430	Garnisheed Wages Payable		200.00
2460	WSIB Payable		403.00
2500	Business Income Tax Payable		3 600.00
2650	GST/HST Charged on Sales	6 860.00	
2670	GST/HST Paid on Purchases	−2 990.00	
2750	GST/HST Owing (Refund)		3 870.00
2790	TOTAL CURRENT LIABILITIES		$ 77 558.40
2800	LONG TERM LIABILITIES		
2820	Mortgage Payable		180 000.00
2890	TOTAL LONG TERM LIABILITIES		$180 000.00
	TOTAL LIABILITIES		$257 558.40

Equity

3000	OWNER'S EQUITY	
3560	S. Ryder, Capital	$222 163.60
3600	Current Earnings	17 717.00
3690	TOTAL OWNER'S EQUITY	$239 880.60
	TOTAL EQUITY	$239 880.60
	LIABILITIES AND EQUITY	$497 439.00

POST-CLOSING TRIAL BALANCE

VELOCITY

April 30, 2015

		Debits	Credits
1060	Bank: Niagara Trust Chequing	$ 52 744.00	
1080	Bank: Niagara Trust Savings	118 110.00	
1120	Bank: Visa and Interac	5 925.00	
1140	Bank: USD Chequing (9 350 USD)	9 500.00	
1200	Accounts Receivable	17 110.00	
1210	Allowance for Doubtful Accounts		$ 800.00
1220	Advances & Loans Receivable	100.00	
1230	Interest Receivable	420.00	
1260	Prepaid Advertising	480.00	
1270	Prepaid Insurance	4 800.00	
1280	Office Supplies	300.00	
1295	Bicycle Repair Parts	1 150.00	
1300	Rental Bicycles	7 520.00	
1520	Accessories	6 540.00	
1540	Bicycles	40 840.00	
1560	Books	5 000.00	
1610	Computer Equipment	7 000.00	
1620	Accum Deprec: Computer Equipment		3 000.00
1640	Furniture & Fixtures	2 000.00	
1650	Accum Deprec: Furniture & Fixtures		400.00
1670	Service Equipment & Tools	3 000.00	
1680	Accum Deprec: Service Tools		900.00
1700	Van	30 000.00	
1710	Accum Deprec: Van		5 000.00
1730	Retail Premises	200 000.00	
1740	Accum Deprec: Retail Premises		5 000.00
2100	Bank Loan		50 000.00
2200	Accounts Payable		12 510.40
2250	Credit Card Payable		220.00
2280	Accrued Wages		760.00
2300	Vacation Payable		706.00
2310	EI Payable		639.00
2320	CPP Payable		1 307.00
2330	Income Tax Payable		2 210.00
2380	EHT Payable		331.00
2400	RRSP Payable		350.00
2410	CSB Plan Payable		350.00
2420	Group Insurance Payable		102.00
2430	Garnisheed Wages Payable		200.00
2460	WSIB Payable		403.00
2500	Business Income Tax Payable		3 600.00
2650	GST/HST Charged on Sales		6 860.00
2670	GST/HST Paid on Purchases	2 990.00	
2820	Mortgage Payable		180 000.00
3560	S. Ryder, Capital		239 880.60
		$515 529.00	$515 529.00

SUPPLIER INFORMATION

VELOCITY

Supplier Name (Contact)	Address	Phone No. Fax No.	E-mail Web Site	Terms Tax ID	Expense Acct Tax Code
Complete Cycler Inc. (Strate Spokes) (USD supplier)	1500 Redmond Road Suite 100, Woodinville Washington 98072 USA	Tel: (425) 628-9163 Fax: (425) 629-7164	sspokes@cycler.com www.cycler.com	2/10, n/30 (before tax)	H
Energy Source (Manny Watts)	91 Power Rd. Niagara Falls, ON L2H 2L9	Tel: (905) 463-2664	watts@energysource.ca www.energysource.ca	net 1	5200 H
Escarpment Investments (P. Cuniary)	122 King St. W. Hamilton, ON L8P 4V2	Tel: (905) 462-3338 Fax: (905) 461-2116	pc@escarp.invest.ca www.escarp.invest.ca	net 1	2410 no tax (exempt)
Lakeshore Sunoco (Mick Annick)	101 Lakeshore Rd. Niagara on the Lake ON L0S 1J0	Tel: (905) 622-6181 www.goodforcars.com	mick@goodforcars.com	net 1 IN	5285
Minister of Finance (N.O. Money)	631 Queenston Rd. Hamilton, ON L8K 6R5	Tel: (905) 462-5555	www.gov.on.ca/fin	net 1	no tax (exempt)
Niagara Bell (Noel Coller)	100 Parkway Ave. Niagara Falls, ON L2E 2K5	Tel: (905) 525-2355	www.bell.ca	net 1	5280 H
Pro Cycles Inc. (C. Glider)	7 Trackway Dr. Waterloo, ON N2G 4S5	Tel: (519) 588-3846 Fax: (519) 588-7126	glider@procycles.com www.procycles.com 466 254 108	1/15, n/30 (before tax)	H
Receiver General for Canada		Tel: 1 (800) 561-7761	www.cra-arc.gc.ca	net 1	no tax (exempt)
Welland Insurance (Feulle Cuvver)	718 Montgomery Dr. Welland, ON L3B 3H5	Tel: (905) 588-1773 Fax: (905) 588-1624	fc@welland.insur.ca www.welland.insur.ca	net 1	no tax (not exempt)

SUPPLIER INFORMATION CONTINUED

Supplier Name (Contact)	Address	Phone No. Fax No.	E-mail Web Site	Terms Tax ID	Expense Acct Tax Code
Wheel Deals (Onna Roller) (USD supplier)	4900 Tubular Circle El Cerrito, California 94533 USA	Tel 1: (510) 525-4327 Tel 2: (800) 567-9152 Fax: (510) 526-1135	onna@wheeldeals.com www.wheeldeals.com	2/10, n/30 (before tax)	H
Workplace Safety & Insurance Board (I.M. Hurt)	PO Box 2099 Oshawa, ON L1J 4C5	Tel: (800) 525-9100 Fax: (905) 523-1824	www.wsib.on.ca	net 1	2460 no tax (exempt)

OUTSTANDING SUPPLIER INVOICES

VELOCITY

Supplier Name	Terms	Date	Inv/Chq No.	Amount	Rate	Tax	Total
Complete Cycler Inc.	2/10, n/30 (before tax)	Apr. 28/15	CC-914	$4 000 USD	@1.02	$520 USD	$4 610.40 CAD
		Apr. 28/15	Chq 344	2 000 USD	@1.02		2 000.00 USD
							2 570.40 CAD
Pro Cycles Inc.	1/15, n/30 (before tax)	Apr. 20/15	PC-618	$8 000		$1 040	$9 040.00
		Apr. 21/15	Chq 96	3 000			3 000.00
			Balance Owing				$ 6 040.00
Wheel Deals	2/10, n/30 (before tax)	Apr. 30/15	WD-391	$3 400 USD		$442 USD	$ 3 900.00 CAD
				Grand Total			$12 510.40

CUSTOMER INFORMATION

VELOCITY

Customer Name (Contact)	Address	Phone No. Fax No.	E-mail Web Site	Terms Tax Code	Credit Limit
*Americas Vinelands Tours (B. Bacchus)	75 Graperie Ave. Buffalo, New York 14202 USA	Tel: (716) 367-7346 Fax: (716) 367-8258	bbacchus@avt.com www.avt.com Currency: USD	2/10, n/30 no tax	$15 000 ($15 000 USD)
*Backstage Tours (G. O. Rideout)	13 Wellspring Dr. Stratford, ON N5A 3B8	Tel: (519) 526-3344 Fax: (519) 525-1166	rideout@backstagetours.ca www.backstagetours.ca	2/10, n/30 H	$15 000
Festival Tours (Bea Player)	62 Ibsen Court Niagara Falls, New York 14301 USA	Tel: (716) 399-1489 Fax: (716) 399-2735	bplayer@festivaltours.com www.festivaltours.com Currency: USD	2/10, n/30 no tax	$15 000 ($15 000 USD)
*Niagara Rapids Inn (Eddy Currents)	339 Picton St. Niagara on the Lake ON L0S 1J0	Tel 1: (905) 468-3000 Tel 2: (905) 468-3198 Fax: (905) 468- 3477	currents@niagararapids.ca www.niagararapids.ca	2/10, n/30 H	$15 000
*Park 'N Ride Tours (G. O. Carless)	4900 Airport Rd, Toronto, ON M9P 7F2	Tel 1: (416) 622-9250 Tel 2: (416) 622-9238 Fax: (416) 622-9729	carless@parknride.ca www.parknride.ca	2/10, n/30 H	$15 000
Shavian B & B (G. B. Shaw)	93 Workout Rd. Niagara on the Lake ON L0S 1J0	Tel: (905) 468-1800 Fax: (905) 468-1278	gbshaw@shavianBB.com www.shavianBB.com	2/10, n/30 H	$15 000
Cash and Interac Customers	Terms: net 1	Tax code: H			
Visa Sales (for Visa customers)	Terms: net 1	Tax code: H			

NOTES: Preferred price list customers are marked with an asterisk (*). The ship-to address is the same as the mailing address for all customers.

OUTSTANDING CUSTOMER INVOICES

VELOCITY

Customer Name	Terms	Date	Inv/Chq No.	Amount	Total
Backstage Tours	2/10, n/30 (after tax)	Apr. 30/15	2199	$9 040	
		Apr. 30/15	Chq 488	2 100	
			Balance Owing		$6 940
Niagara Rapids Inn	2/10, n/30 (after tax)	Apr. 26/15	2194	$5 650	$5 650
Shavian B & B	2/10, n/30 (after tax)	Apr. 23/15	2191	$4 520	$4 520
				Grand Total	$17 110

EMPLOYEE INFORMATION SHEET

VELOCITY

Employee	Dunlop Mercier	Pedal Schwinn	Shimana Gearie
Position	Service/Sales	Sales/Tour Guide	Sales/Accounting
Address	55 Trailview Rd. Niagara on the Lake, ON L0S 1J0	2 Fallsview Drive Niagara Falls, ON L2J 4F8	300 Vineland Rd. Niagara on the Lake, ON L0S 1J0
Telephone	(905) 468-1817	(905) 489-4412	(905) 468-5778
Social Insurance No.	532 548 625	783 455 611	488 655 333
Date of Birth (mm-dd-yy)	09/18/82	03/15/79	05/24/82
Date of Hire (mm-dd-yy)	01/06/10	02/15/08	08/25/11
Federal (Ontario) Tax Exemption - TD1			
Basic Personal	$11 038 (9 574)	$11 038 (9 574)	$11 038 (9 574)
Other Indexed	–	–	$17 568 (12 642)
Other Non-Indexed	–	–	$3 070 (3 126)
Total Exemptions	$11 038 (9 574)	$11 038 (9 574)	$31 676 (25 342)
Additional Federal Tax	–	$50.00	–
Employee Taxes			
Historical Income tax	$1 668.29	$3 022.96	$1 835.46
Historical EI	$207.73	$283.72	$262.07
Historical CPP	$547.31	$761.00	$760.39
Deduct EI; EI Factor	Yes; 1.4	Yes; 1.4	Yes; 1.4
Deduct CPP	Yes	Yes	Yes
Employee Income			
Loans: Historical Amount	$100.00	(use) ✓	(use) ✓
Benefits Per Period	$16.00	$35.00	$35.00
Benefits: Historical Amount	$128.00	$140.00	$140.00
Vacation Pay Owed	$706.00	(do not use)	(do not use)
Vacation Paid	$386.00	(do not use)	(do not use)
Regular Wage Rate (Hours per Period)	$18.00/hr (80 hours)	(do not use)	(do not use)
Regular Wages: Historical Amount	$11 520.00	(do not use)	(do not use)
Overtime 1 Wage Rate	$27.00/hr	(do not use)	(do not use)
Overtime 1 Wages: Historical Amount	$486.00	(do not use)	(do not use)
Salary (Hours Per Period)	(do not use)	$4 100.00 (150 hours)	$3 700.00 (150 hours)
Salary: Historical Amount	(do not use)	$16 400.00	$14 800.00
Commission	(do not use)	(do not use)	(use) ✓ 2% (service revenue)
Commissions: Historical Amount	(do not use)	(do not use)	$348.00
No. Clients (piece rate)	$10	$10	$10
Bonus:	(use) ✓	(use) ✓	(use) ✓

▶

EMPLOYEE INFORMATION CONTINUED			
Employee	**Dunlop Mercier**	**Pedal Schwinn**	**Shimana Gearie**
Employee Income continued			
Tuition: Per Period	(use) ✓	(use) ✓	$310
Tuition: Historical Amount	–	–	$1 240
Travel Exp.: Historical Amount	(use) ✓	$120.00	(use) ✓
Pay Periods	26	12	12
Vacation Rate	6% retained	0% not retained	0% not retained
Record Wage Expenses in	Linked Accounts	Linked Accounts	Linked Accounts
Deductions			
RRSP (Historical Amount)	$50.00 ($450.00)	$100.00 ($400.00)	$100.00 ($400.00)
CSB Plan (Historical Amount)	$50.00 ($450.00)	$100.00 ($400.00)	$100.00 ($400.00)
Garnishee (Historical Amount)	(do not use)	$200.00 ($800.00)	(do not use)
WSIB and Other Expenses			
WSIB Rate	1.29	1.29	1.02
Group Insurance (Historical Amount)	$16.00 ($128.00)	$35.00 ($140.00)	$35.00 ($140.00)
Entitlements: Rate, Maximum Days, Clear? (Historical Amount)			
Vacation	–	8%, 25 days, No (15)	8%, 25 days, No (15)
Sick Leave	5%, 15 days, No (12)	5%, 15 days, No (10)	5%, 15 days, No (8)
Personal Days	2.5%, 5 days, No (4)	2.5%, 5 days, No (2)	2.5%, 5 days, No (3)
Direct Deposit			
Yes/No	Yes	Yes	Yes
Branch, Institution, Account No.	89008, 102, 2998187	94008, 102, 3829110	89008, 102, 2309982
Percent	100%	100%	100%
Additional Information			
Emergency Contact & Number	Adrian Ingles (905) 548-0301	Alex Schwinn (905) 688-2973	Martha Gearie (905) 458-5778
T4 and RL-1 Reporting			
EI Insurable Earnings	$12 392.00	$16 400.00	$15 148.00
Pensionable Earnings	$12 520.00	$16 540.00	$16 528.00
Withheld	$3 323.33	$5 667.68	$3 657.92
Net Pay	$9 168.67	$10 852.32	$12 730.08

Employee Profiles and TD1 Information

All Employees VeloCity pays group insurance premiums for all employees. They also are reimbursed for tuition fees when they successfully complete a university or college course. These two benefits are taxable. In addition, when they use their personal vehicles for company business, they are reimbursed for car expenses.

All employees are entitled to three weeks' vacation, ten days' sick leave and five personal days of leave per year. All three employees have sick leave and personal days that they can carry forward from the previous year. The two salaried employees take three weeks' vacation as paid time and the hourly employee receives 6 percent of his wages as vacation pay when he takes his vacation.

Starting in May, as an incentive to provide excellent customer service, all employees will receive a quarterly bonus of $10 for every completed satisfactory customer survey.

Dunlop Mercier is responsible for shipping, receiving, delivery and assembly for customers. He also does all the repair work in the store. He is single, so he uses only the basic tax claim amount. Every two weeks his pay, at the rate of $18 per hour, is deposited to his account. For the hours beyond 40 hours in a week, he receives an overtime rate of $27 per hour. He is owed four months of vacation pay. He contributes to his RRSP and Canada Savings Bond plan through payroll deductions. He still owes $100 from a loan of $200 for which he will pay back $50 in each of the next two pay periods.

Pedal Schwinn is the store manager for VeloCity, and she assists with store sales. Her monthly salary of $4 100 is deposited directly into her bank account. Schwinn is married with one child but uses the basic single claim amount because her husband is also employed and he uses the federal child tax claim amount. Her payroll deductions include additional federal income tax for other income, wages garnisheed to pay for prior taxes owing and regular contributions to her Registered Retirement Savings Plan and Canada Savings Bonds.

NOTES
Wages may be garnisheed by any creditor, but the most common one is the Receiver General to pay back-taxes owing.

Shimana Gearie does the accounting and manages the Payables, Receivables and Payroll in addition to sales in the store. Although she is single, she supports her infirm mother so she has the spousal equivalent claim and a caregiver amount in addition to the basic single claim and tuition amounts. A commission of 2 percent of revenue from services supplements her monthly salary of $3 700, which is deposited directly into her bank account. She has RRSP and CSB contributions withheld from her paycheques.

INVENTORY INFORMATION

VELOCITY

Code	Description	Min Stock	CAD Reg	Prices (Pref)	USD Reg.	Prices (Pref)	Stock/Sell Unit	Buying Unit	Relationship	Qty on Hand	Total (Cost)
Accessories: Total asset value $6 540 (Linked Accounts: Asset 1520; Revenue 4020, COGS 5050, Variance 5080) Charge HST											
AC010	Bicycle Pump: standing model	5	$ 50	($ 45)	$ 50	($ 45)	unit	box	4/box	10	$ 300
AC020	Bicycle Pump: hand-held mini	5	80	(70)	80	(70)	unit	box	10/box	10	500
AC030	Helmet	15	120	(105)	120	(105)	helmet	carton	10/carton	40	2 400
AC040	Light: halogen	10	25	(22)	25	(22)	unit	box	10/box	20	200
AC050	Light: rear reflector	20	15	(12)	15	(12)	unit	box	10/box	30	210
AC060	Lock: kryptonite tube	10	70	(65)	70	(65)	lock	box	5/box	15	600
AC070	Pannier: front wicker clip-on	3	80	(75)	80	(75)	basket		same	6	300
AC080	Pannier: rear mesh	3	60	(55)	60	(55)	basket		same	10	380
AC090	Trailer: 2-child closed	1	620	(570)	620	(570)	unit		same	4	1 200
AC100	Trailer: third-wheel rider	1	260	(235)	260	(235)	unit		same	3	450
Books: Total asset value $5 000 (Linked Accounts: Asset 1560; Revenue 4020, COGS 5070, Variance 5080) HST exempt, charge GST only											
BK010	Books: Complete Bicycle Guide	10	40	(35)	40	(35)	book		same	110	2 200
BK020	Books: Endless Trails	10	40	(35)	40	(35)	book		same	140	2 800
Bicycles: Total asset value $40 840 (Linked Accounts: Asset 1540; Revenue 4020, COGS 5060, Variance 5080) Charge HST											
CY010	Bicycle: Commuter Steel frame CX10	3	640	(590)	640	(590)	bike		same	12	3 720
CY020	Bicycle: Commuter Alum frame CX90	3	960	(850)	960	(850)	bike		same	12	6 480
CY030	Bicycle: Racer Ultra lite RX480	1	3 100	(2 800)	3 100	(2 800)	bike		same	4	6 200
CY040	Bicycle: Trail Alum frame TX560	4	1 220	(1 090)	1 220	(1 090)	bike		same	16	9 920
CY050	Bicycle: Mountain Alum frame MX14	2	1 850	(1 650)	1 850	(1 650)	bike		same	6	5 580
CY060	Bicycle: Mountain Carbon frame MX34	1	2 950	(2 600)	2 950	(2 600)	bike		same	2	3 440
CY070	Bicycle: Youth YX660	4	460	(420)	460	(420)	bike		same	16	3 520
CY090	Stationary Converter	2	870	(800)	870	(800)	unit		same	6	1 980

NOTES: No duty is charged on items imported from the United States. The duty rate is 0%.
Stocking and selling units are the same for all items.
Buying units and the relationship to stocking units are entered only when these are different from the stocking/selling units.
"Same" is entered in the relationship column when the same unit is used for all measures.

INVENTORY INFORMATION CONTINUED

Code	Description	CAD Prices Reg	CAD Prices (Pref)	USD Prices (Reg)		Unit	Taxes
Services (Linked Accounts: Revenue 4040, Expense 5075)							
S010	Boxing for shipping	$ 75	($ 70)	$ 75	($ 70)	job	HST (not exempt)
S020	Maintenance: annual contract	110	(100)	110	(100)	year	HST (not exempt)
S030	Maintenance: complete tune-up	70	(65)	70	(65)	job	HST (not exempt)
S040	Rental: 1 hour	10	(9)	10	(9)	hour	HST (not exempt)
S050	Rental: 1 day	30	(25)	30	(25)	day	HST (not exempt)
S060	Repairs	45	(40)	45	(40)	hour	HST (not exempt)

Accounting Procedures

Harmonized Sales Taxes: HST, GST and PST

HST at the rate of 13 percent is applied to all goods and services offered by VeloCity, except books. The Harmonized Sales Tax includes the provincial sales tax of 8 percent. Goods that are exempt for PST, such as books, have a different tax code applied (code G – GST @ 5%).

VeloCity uses the regular method for remittance of the Harmonized Sales Tax. HST and GST collected from customers are recorded as liabilities in *GST/HST Charged on Sales*. HST and GST paid to suppliers are recorded in *GST/HST Paid on Purchases* as a decrease in liability to the Canada Revenue Agency (CRA). These two postable accounts are added together in the subgroup total account *GST/HST Owing (Refund)* because a single return is remitted for both taxes. The balance of HST and GST to be remitted or the request for a refund is sent to the Receiver General for Canada by the last day of the current month for the previous month.

Tax calculations will be correct only for customers and suppliers for whom the tax exempt option was set as No. The GST and HST Reports available from the Reports menu will include transactions completed in the Sales, Purchases and General journals, but the opening historical balances will not be included. Therefore, the amounts shown in the tax reports may differ from the balances in the General Ledger accounts. You should use the General Ledger accounts to verify the balance owing (or refund due) and make adjustments to the report manually as necessary.

After the report is filed, clear the HST and GST Reports up to the last day of the previous month. Always back up your files before clearing the tax details.

NOTES
Because VeloCity also sells books that are exempt for HST but not GST, the name GST/HST is applied to accounts.

PRO VERSION
The term Vendors replaces Suppliers throughout the program.

NOTES
To clear the tax report, choose the Maintenance menu, then Clear Data. Click Clear Tax Report and select HST and GST.

The Employer Health Tax (EHT)

The Employer Health Tax (EHT) is paid by employers in Ontario to provide Ontario Health Insurance Plan (OHIP) coverage for all eligible Ontario residents. The EHT is based on the total annual remuneration paid to employees. Employers whose total payroll is less than $200 000 pay EHT at the rate of 0.98 percent. The EHT rate increases with total payroll to a maximum of 1.95 percent for payroll amounts of $450 000 and more. In this application, EHT will be remitted quarterly. *EHT Payable* is set up as a liability owing to the supplier, Minister of Finance. The Remittance Payments Journal will provide you with the balance owing to the Minister of Finance when the liability is linked to this supplier.

Aging of Accounts

VeloCity uses aging periods that reflect the payment terms it provides to customers and receives from suppliers. For customers, this will be 10, 30 and 60 days, and for suppliers,

15, 30 and 60 days. Interest at 1.5 percent is charged on customer accounts that are not paid within 30 days. Regular customer statements show interest amounts, and invoices are then prepared to add the interest to the amount owing in the ledger record.

Discounts

VeloCity offers a 2 percent discount to regular account customers if they settle their accounts within 10 days. Full payment is requested within 30 days. These payment terms are set up as defaults. When the receipt is entered and the discount is still available, the program shows the amount of the discount and the net amount owing. No discounts are given on cash or credit card sales. Customer discounts are calculated on after-tax amounts.

NOTES
Daily Business Manager lists are helpful for making sure that you take advantage of available discounts.

Some customers receive preferred customer prices that are approximately 10 percent below the regular prices. These customers are identified in the ledger records and the preferred prices are set up in the inventory ledger records.

Some suppliers also offer discounts for early settlement of accounts. Again, when the terms are entered for the supplier and payment is made before the discount period expires, the program displays the discount as available and automatically calculates a net balance owing. Payment terms vary from supplier to supplier. Supplier discounts may be calculated on before-tax amounts or after-tax amounts.

Freight

When a business purchases inventory items, the cost of any freight that cannot be directly allocated to a specific item must be charged to *Freight Expense* — a general expense that is not charged to the costs of any inventory asset account. Customers also pay for delivery. HST is charged on freight for both sales and purchases (tax code H).

Bank Deposits

Deposit slips are prepared weekly when cash and cheques are received. Receipts are debited to *Undeposited Cash and Cheques* and transferred weekly to *Bank: Niagara Trust Chequing*.

Imported Inventory

Some inventory items are imported from the United States. The bank accounts, supplier records and inventory records are modified to accommodate the foreign currency transactions and import duties automatically.

NOTES
Although import duties are not charged on the items imported by VeloCity from the United States, we show the setup of import duties and set the rates at zero so that no tax will be charged.

Business Income Tax

VeloCity pays income tax in quarterly instalments to the Receiver General based on its previous year's net income.

Purchase Returns and Allowances

A business will sometimes return inventory items to suppliers because of damage, poor quality or shipment of the wrong items. Usually a business records these returns after it receives a credit note from a supplier. The return of inventory is entered in the Purchases Journal as an inventory purchase:

- Select the item in the Item field and enter the quantity returned as a **negative** amount in the Quantity field. The program will automatically calculate a negative amount as a default in the Amount field. You cannot change the account number.
- Accept the default amount and enter other items returned to the supplier.
- Enter the appropriate tax code for each item returned.

The program will create a negative invoice to reduce the balance owing to the supplier and will reduce the applicable inventory asset accounts, the freight accounts, *GST/HST Paid on Purchases* and the quantity of items in the Inventory Ledger database.

Purchase allowances for damaged merchandise that is not returned are entered as non-inventory negative purchase invoices. Enter the amount of the allowance as a **negative** amount in the Amount field and leave the tax fields blank (i.e., treat it as non-taxable). Enter *Purchases Returns & Allowances* in the Account field.

NOTES
Purchases Returns & Allowances is a contra-expense account with a credit balance. The return creates a credit entry that will reduce total expenses.

Sales Returns and Allowances

Sometimes customers will return inventory items. Usually, a business records the return after it has issued a credit note. The return is entered in the Sales Journal as a negative inventory sale, choosing the same customer and payment method as in the original sale:

- Select the appropriate item in the Item field.
- Enter the quantity returned with a **negative** number in the Quantity field.
- The price of the item appears as a positive number in the Price field, and the Amount field is calculated automatically as a negative amount.
- Enter the tax code for the sale and the account number for *Sales Returns & Allowances.*

The program will create a negative invoice to reduce the balance owing by the customer, and *Cost of Goods Sold* and *GST/HST Charged on Sales*. The applicable inventory asset accounts and the quantity of items in the Inventory Ledger database will be increased.

Sales allowances are entered as non-taxable, non-inventory negative sales invoices, creating a debit entry for *Sales Returns & Allowances* and a credit for *Accounts Receivable*. If the allowance is paid by cheque, enter the allowance in the Payments Journal as an Other Payment paid by cheque.

NOTES
The sales tax rules for credits, allowances and discounts are complex. They may be different for provincial and federal taxes and they may differ from one province to another. Adjusting General Journal entries may be required to adjust the amount of tax owing and calculate the tax remittance. We have chosen to leave out the tax component for transactions of this type. Refer to Chapter 2 for more information about sales taxes.

NOTES
Sales Returns & Allowances is a contra-revenue account with a debit balance. The sales return creates a debit entry that will reduce total revenue and Accounts Receivable.

NSF Cheques

If a cheque is deposited from an account that does not have enough money to cover it, the bank returns it to the depositor as NSF (non-sufficient funds). If the cheque was in payment for a cash sale, you must process the NSF cheque through the Sales Journal because there was no Receipts Journal entry. Create a customer record if necessary and enter a positive amount for the amount of the cheque. Choose *Bank: Niagara Trust Chequing* as the account. Choose Pay Later as the method of payment. If the customer is expected to pay the bank charges, enter these on the second invoice line as a positive amount and select the appropriate revenue account.

NOTES
The Sales Journal entry will credit the bank account and debit Accounts Receivable for the allowance.

If the NSF cheque in payment of an invoice was deposited to a different account than the one used in the Receipts Journal, create a negative receipt to reverse the cheque. Choose Include Fully Paid Invoices. Click the invoice line that this cheque was applied to. Enter the discount taken as a negative amount. Enter the Payment Amount as a negative amount. Choose the correct bank account from the Deposit To field. Refer to page 605 and Appendix C.

Adjustments for Bad Debt

Most businesses set up an allowance for doubtful accounts or bad debts, knowing that some customers will fail to pay. The amount entered for this will be a reasonable guess at how much of the *Accounts Receivable* amount will never be collected. When the allowance is set up, a bad debts or uncollectable accounts expense account is debited and the allowance is credited (effectively reducing the net receivables balance). When a business is certain that a customer will not pay its account, the debt should be written off by crediting *Accounts Receivable* and debiting *Allowance for Doubtful Accounts*. When taxes apply, an extra step is required. Part of the original sales invoice was

NOTES
Allowance for Doubtful Accounts is a contra-asset account that normally has a credit balance. Therefore, a debit entry from the negative amount will reduce this credit balance, reducing both the allowance and the Accounts Receivable balances.

entered as a credit (increase) to *GST/HST Charged on Sales*. By entering the full amount and the code IN for taxes included, the GST/HST payable amount will automatically be correctly reduced. In Sage 50, record the write-off of the debt in the Sales Journal using the following steps:

- Select the customer whose debt will not be paid.
- Enter a source document number to identify the transaction (e.g., memo).
- Enter a **negative** amount for the total unpaid invoice in the Amount field.
- Enter *Allowance for Doubtful Accounts* in the Account field.
- Enter the tax code **IN** (taxes included).

If the customer was also charged for the NSF fees, enter this information on the next invoice line:

- Enter a **negative** amount for the total NSF charge in the Amount field.
- Enter *Allowance for Doubtful Accounts* in the Account field.
- Enter the tax code **No tax**.

Review the transaction. *Accounts Receivable* is credited (reduced) by the full amount of the invoice to remove the balance owing by this customer. *Allowance for Doubtful Accounts* has been debited (reduced) by the amount of the invoice minus taxes. *GST/HST Charged on Sales* has been debited for the tax portion of the invoice to reduce the tax liability.

After recording the write-off, "pay" both the original invoice and the write-off in the Receipts Journal. The balance will be zero and there will be no journal entry. This step removes the items from the Receipts Journal for the customer so that you can clear the paid transactions and later remove the customer's record.

Manually you would complete the entry as follows:

1. Set up the Allowance for Doubtful Account (bad debts).

Date	Particulars	Debit	Credit
04/01	5270 Uncollectable Accounts Expense	1 000.00	
	1210 Allowance for Doubtful Accounts		1 000.00

2. Customer G. Bell declares bankruptcy. Write off outstanding balance, $226, including HST.

Date	Particulars	Debit	Credit
04/30	1210 Allowance for Doubtful Accounts	200.00	
	2650 GST/HST Charged on Sales	26.00	
	1200 Accounts Receivable, G. Bell		226.00

Occasionally, a bad debt is recovered after it has been written off. When this occurs, the above procedure is reversed and the GST/HST liability must also be restored. The recovery is entered as a non-inventory sale in the Sales Journal as follows:

NOTES
You would also follow these steps when only part of the bad debt amount is recovered.

- Select the customer and enter the date and source document number.
- Type an appropriate comment such as "Debt recovered" in the Item Description field.
- Enter a **positive** amount for the total invoice amount in the Amount field.
- Enter the tax code **IN** (taxes included).
- Enter *Allowance for Doubtful Accounts* in the Account field.

Review the transaction. You will see that *Accounts Receivable* has been debited for the full amount of the invoice. *Allowance for Doubtful Accounts* has been credited for the amount of the invoice minus taxes. *GST/HST Charged on Sales* has been credited for the tax portion of the invoice to restore the tax liability.

As the final step, record the customer's payment in the Receipts Journal as you would record any other customer payment.

Remittances

The Receiver General for Canada:

- Monthly EI, CPP and income tax deductions withheld from employees must be paid by the 15th of each month for the previous month.
- Monthly GST/HST owing or requests for refunds must be filed by the end of each month for the previous month.
- Business income tax is paid in quarterly instalments.
- Garnisheed wages are submitted by the 15th of each month for the previous month. A separate cheque is issued for this remittance.

The Minister of Finance:

- Quarterly Employer Health Tax (EHT) deductions must be paid by the 15th of May, July, October and January for the previous quarter.

The Workplace Safety and Insurance Board:

- Quarterly Workplace Safety and Insurance Board (WSIB) assessment for employees must be paid by the 15th of the month for the previous quarter.

Escarpment Investments:

- Monthly Canada Savings Bond Plan (CSB Plan) deductions withheld from employees must be paid by the 15th of the month for the previous month.

Welland Insurance:

- Monthly Registered Retirement Savings Plan (RRSP) deductions withheld from employees must be paid by the 15th of the month for the previous month.
- Group insurance contributions paid by the employer must be paid by the 15th of the month for the previous month.

For all remittances, the next payment is due May 1 for the pay period ending April 30. Because May 1 is the earliest transaction date, we cannot enter a date before this. Therefore, May 1 will be the first end of remitting period date for all remittances.

NOTES

In practice, a business would make these four federal tax remittances to different federal offices. Separate supplier accounts would be needed for each remittance. For this application, one supplier account and address has been used for the Receiver General to reduce the length of the supplier list.

INSTRUCTIONS FOR SETUP

Set up the **company accounts** in Sage 50 using the Business Information, Chart of Accounts, Balance Sheet, Income Statement, Post-Closing Trial Balance and Supplier, Customer, Employee and Inventory Information provided above for April 30, 2015. Instructions to assist you in setting up the company accounts follow. The setup of the Inventory Ledger is given in detail. Abbreviated instructions are included for the remaining steps. Refer to the Toss for Tots (Chapter 4), Air Care Services (Chapter 7) and Lime Light Laundry (Chapter 9) applications if you need more detailed explanations for other ledgers. Page references for the coverage of these topics in earlier chapters are included in this chapter.

KEYSTROKES FOR SETUP

Creating Company Files

We will create the company files from scratch. Once we create the files and define the defaults, we will add the accounts, define linked accounts for all ledgers, set up

NOTES

Refer to page 208 for detailed instructions on creating company files.

additional features, create supplier, customer, employee and inventory records and add historical data.

Start the **Sage 50 program**. You should see the Select Company window.

Click **Create A New Company**.

Click **OK**. You will see the Setup wizard welcome screen.

Click **Next** to open the Company Name and Address screen. The cursor is in the Name field.

Type `VeloCity` (and your own name) **Press** tab to advance to the Street 1 address field.

Type `27 Gearing Ave.` **Press** tab. **Press** tab again.

Type `Niagara on the Lake` **Press** tab.

Type `o` to enter the province code (ON) and province (Ontario).

Click the **Postal Code field**.

Type `l0s1j0` **Press** tab.

Type `Canada` **Press** tab.

Type `9054688356` **Press** tab to enter the first phone number.

Type `8884688356` **Press** tab to enter the second phone number.

Type `9054689100` to enter the fax number.

Click **Next** to open the company Dates window.

The cursor is in the Fiscal Year Start field, the date on which the business begins its fiscal year. VeloCity closes its books quarterly and is beginning a new quarter in May. To be certain that you have the correct year, type the date in text style using four digits for the year. Until we change the date format, it is displayed in the short form.

Enter the **fiscal dates** as follows:

- Fiscal Start: May 1, 2015
- Earliest Transaction date: May 1, 2015
- Fiscal End: July 31, 2015

Remember that you can edit the company information and fiscal dates later from the Setup menu, Settings option (choose Company and Information).

Click **Next**.

Click **Let Me Build The List Of Accounts Myself....** **Click Next**.

Click **Yes** to confirm your selection and continue to the industry type list.

Choose **Retail** as the Industry for the business. **Click Next**.

Type `velocity` to replace the default entry for the file name.

Drag through **Tess** in the folder name field (or the folder you last worked with).

Type `Velocity\`

If you are using an alternative location for your company files, substitute the appropriate path, folder or drive in the example.

Click Browse to locate the folder you want or type the complete path in the File Location field (e.g., Type C:\SageData13\Velocity\).

NOTES
Save your work and update your backup file frequently as you complete the setup.

NOTES
You cannot complete the company setup in multi-user mode. Many of the settings options are dimmed and unavailable when you are working in multi-user mode.

NOTES
Add your own name to the company name to personalize your data files.

NOTES
Because we selected Ontario as the province, some defaults will be added to the data file. WCB will be renamed WSIB.

NOTES
If you later change the province, you may have to change some settings linked to the province selection.

NOTES
The default date format for new companies is determined by your own computer system settings and is displayed below the date fields. Day, month or year may be first.

NOTES
You can select another folder by clicking Browse to open the folder path screen and then clicking the folder you want to use. Click OK to return to the File Name screen.
If the folder you want does not yet exist, click the folder into which you want to place the new folder and click OK. Type Velocity\ at the end of the path in the Location field.

Click **Next**.

Click **Yes** to confirm that you are creating a new folder.

Click **Finish** to save the information. **Be patient**, and wait for Sage 50 to finish creating the data files.

Click **Close** to close the Setup wizard screen.

Click **I Will Update My Tax Information Myself**. **Click Finish**.

Click **Show This Window On Startup** in the Welcome/Getting Started window and **click Close** to close the Welcome window.

The Home window has the name Velocity in the title bar and non-accounting term labels for the modules in the Modules pane list. The program will automatically set up defaults based on the information you have just entered.

NOTES
The Welcome/Getting Started screen may be open in the background, behind the Home window. Click its button on the task bar or click the Sage 50 icon on the task bar and then click the Welcome Getting Started pop-up window to bring it to the front. You can then close it.

Preparing the System

The next step involves changing the defaults. Change the defaults to suit your own work environment, such as selecting your printer or choosing forms for cheques, invoices or statements. The keystroke instructions are given for computer-generated cheques, invoices and statements. Refer to the Business Information Chart on page 623 for the company default settings.

NOTES
Use the Backup feature frequently while setting up your files and each time you finish your work session to update your backup copy.

You may finish your session at any time while completing the setup. Simply open the data file, accept the session date and continue from where you left off.

Changing the User Preference Settings

You should make the following changes to the User Preferences from the Setup menu. Refer to Chapter 4, page 81, for assistance if necessary.

Choose the **Setup menu** and **click User Preferences** to open the Options screen.

Click **Use Accounting Terms** and **Automatically Save Changes To Supplier...**.

You can show Home window ledger record balances by the session date or the latest transaction date, and automatically recalculate these balances or refresh them manually when you want. Make the selections you prefer for your own use.

CLASSIC VIEW
Division and Time & Billing are both included in the Module column.

Click **View**.

Click **After Changing Session Date** for **Daily Business Manager** and for **Checklists** to turn off these features and remove the ✓s.

Click **Show Change Session Date At Startup**.

Hiding the Division module and Time & Billing is optional. You can finish the history without this step because they have no linked accounts.

Click Division in the Pages column and Time & Billing in the Features column if you choose to hide them.

Transaction Confirmation should be selected by default.

Click **Pop-ups** and **choose** the **messages** you want to display and hide.

Click **OK** to save the settings and return to the Home window.

After changing these settings, modules have accounting term names. The user preference settings can be modified at any time by repeating these steps.

WARNING!
Do not skip any ledger icon windows before completing the setup.

PRO VERSION
You will see the term Project instead of Division, and you will not see the Time & Billing feature.

CLASSIC VIEW

You can right-click any Home window icon and then click the Setup tool.

When the Settings window opens, click Company and then click Information.

If you select a journal, you will open the Linked Accounts window for the ledger. If you click a ledger icon, you will open the Settings window for the ledger.

The Classic View has no icon that will open the Company Settings directly from the Setup tool.

Changing Company Defaults

Correcting Company Information

The first steps in setting up the company data files apply to the Company module. We will work from that window.

Click OK at any time to save the settings and close the Settings window. To continue later, you can use the Settings icon to access Settings.

Click **Company** in the Modules pane list to change the Home window.

Click the **Settings icon**, or **choose** the **Setup menu** and **click Settings**.

Click **Information**.

Click the **Business No. field**. **Type** 335 677 829 RT0001

Changing System Settings

Click **System**. Use the following System settings:

- Use Cheque No. As The Source Code For Cash Purchases And Sales
- Do Not Allow Transactions Dated Before May 1, 2015
- Allow Transactions In The Future (Beyond The Session Date)
- Warn If Transactions Are More Than 7 Days In The Future
- Warn If Accounts Are Not Balanced When Entering A New Month

Changing Backup Settings

Click **Backup**. Use the following Backup settings:

- Semi-monthly Backup Frequency
- Display a Backup Reminder When Closing This Company

Click **Automatically Back Up This File** to remove the ✓. We do not want to schedule automatic backups for instructional files.

NOTES

If you chose to hide the Division module, Division will not appear in the Features Settings window.

Changing Features Settings

VeloCity uses all features of the program except Divisions — orders, quotes and language options should be selected. Division and Packing Slips may be left unselected.

Click **Features**.

Click **each feature** to change its setting.

NOTES

Credit Cards, Sales Taxes and Currency settings require linked accounts, so we will set them after creating accounts.

Changing Default Settings for Forms

Click **Forms** to display the defaults.

Use the Forms options to set up the automatic numbering and printing of all cheques and invoices. They apply only to numerical invoices.

If you want to use automatic invoice numbering, type the next number from the source documents so the automatic numbering system can take over from the manual system. Using automatic numbering reduces the risk of typing and recording an incorrect invoice or cheque number even when you are not printing cheques and invoices through the program. For VeloCity, the next invoice is #2470.

Click **1** in the **Invoices Next Form Number field**. **Type** 2470

Click the **Sales Quotes Next Form Number field**. **Type** 56

Click the **Receipts Next Form Number field**. **Type** 812

Click the **Customer Deposits Next Form Number field**. **Type** 21

Click the **Purchase Orders Next Form Number field**. **Type** 38

Click the **Employee Direct Deposit Stubs Next Form Number field**.

Type 25

Leave selected the option to verify number sequences for all forms so that the program will warn you if you skip or duplicate a number.

Click a check box to add other features or to turn off an option once it is selected. The ✓ in the appropriate boxes indicates a feature is being used.

The option to Confirm Printing/E-mail will warn you to print before posting a transaction. When printing invoices, statements or cheques you should include the company address, unless it is already printed on your forms.

If you print or e-mail invoices and cheques through the computer, you should turn on the option to Confirm Printing/E-mail.

We want to allow batch printing, printing several forms at once after posting instead of one at a time while entering a transaction.

Click the **Print In Batches check box** for each form to add a ✓ to each box.

We should also check for duplicate numbers. This control is not selected by default.

Click the **Check For Duplicates check box for Invoices and Receipts**.

Changing Date Format Settings

Click **Date Format**.

We want to use the long date form for all dates on the screen to verify that we are entering dates correctly. For the reports, you may use either the long or short form. MM (month) should be the first entry in the Short Date Format field.

Choose **MM-dd-yyyy** from the Short Date drop-down list.

Click **Long Dates** as the setting for On The Screen, Use.

Adding the Company Logo

Click **Logo**. **Click Browse**. **Click Computer** in the folders and links pane on the left-hand side.

Double-click **C:**. Then **double-click SageData13** to open this folder.

Double-click the **Logos folder**.

Double-click **velo.bmp** or **velo** to enter this file name. The picture and file name should be added to the Logo Settings screen.

Changing Default Names

VeloCity uses the additional information fields in journals. You can label these fields. However, you must use the same names for all journals. We will therefore enter a generic label for the Additional Information Field.

NOTES

Many invoices include the alpha or letter portion of the invoice number on the preprinted invoice form. You could then enter the next number from the numeric portion in the Invoices Number field. Alphanumeric invoice numbers, such as VC-399, cannot be increased automatically by the computer.

NOTES

If you hide Time & Billing, the next number for time slips will not be included on the Forms screen. You can leave the field blank if you are not hiding the feature.

WARNING!

Check that the short date format begins with month (MM).

NOTES

The Forms folder in your Sage 50 Program folder may be the default location when you click Browse.

Click **Names**:

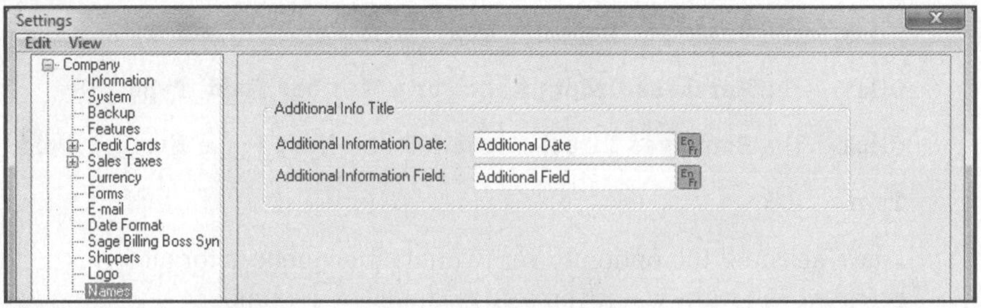

Drag through Additional Field.

Type Ref. Number

Click **OK** to save the new information and return to the Home window.

Many of the other settings require linked accounts. Therefore, we will create all the General Ledger accounts before entering the remaining settings.

Preparing the General Ledger

NOTES
Remember that you can finish your session at any time. To continue, just open the file, accept the session date and start again from where you left off.

The next stage in setting up an accounting system involves preparing the General Ledger for operation. This stage involves

1. organizing all accounting reports and records (this step has been completed)
2. creating new accounts and adding opening balances
3. printing reports to check the accuracy of your records

Creating New Accounts

The next step is to create the accounts, including the non-postable accounts. Remember to enter the correct type of account. For postable accounts, you should also indicate whether you want to omit accounts with zero balances from financial statements. You need to refer to the company Chart of Accounts on page 624 to complete this step. While creating the accounts, keep the Accounts window open in the background for reference.

Current Earnings is the only predefined account, and you do not need to edit it.

Refer to The Format of Financial Statements (page 86) for a review of these topics if needed. Refer to the instructions in the Toss for Tots application, page 92, if you need help with creating accounts.

NOTES
Maximizing the Accounts window allows you to see the list of accounts as well as the new ones you are creating.

Click the **Chart of Accounts icon** to open the Accounts window.

Click to maximize the Accounts window.

If the accounts are not displayed by name or by type, you should change the view. Click the Display By Type tool or choose the View menu and click Type.

NOTES
You can also press *ctrl* + N to open a New Account ledger window and create a new account.

Click the **Create tool** in the Accounts window tool bar or **choose** the **File menu** and **click Create**.

Drag the Ledger window to a screen position so that both the list of accounts in the Accounts window and the Ledger window are visible. This will make it easier to monitor your progress.

Type the **account number**. **Press** *tab* and **type** the **account name**.

Click the correct **account type**. Remember subgroup accounts (A) must be followed by a subgroup total (S).

Click **Omit From Financial Statements If Balance Is Zero** to select this option.

Allow Division Allocations will be selected by default for all postable revenue and expense accounts, so you do not need to change this option, even if you use divisions.

You will enter the account balances in the next stage.

When all the information is correct, you must save your account.

Click **Create Another** [Create Another] to save the new account and advance to a blank ledger account window.

Create the **other accounts** by repeating these procedures.

Close the **General Ledger window** when you have entered all the accounts on page 624, or when you want to end your session.

After entering all the accounts, you should check for mistakes in account number, name, type and order.

Click [✓] or **choose** the **File menu** and **click Check The Validity Of Accounts** to check for errors in account sequence such as missing subgroup totals, headings or totals. The first error will be reported.

Correct the **error** and **check** the **validity** again. Repeat this step until the accounts are in logical order.

Display or **print** your updated **Chart of Accounts** at this stage to check for accuracy of account names and numbers. **Choose** the **Reports menu** and **click Display Chart of Accounts**. Compare the report with the chart on page 624 and make corrections as needed.

NOTES

We will change the account class for expense accounts when we change the class for other accounts that are used as linked accounts.

WARNING!

It is important to have the accounts in logical order at this stage. You will be unable to display some reports when the accounts are not in logical order, so you will not be able to check some of your work. You cannot finish the history if accounts are not in logical order.

Entering Historical Account Balances

The opening historical balances for VeloCity can be found in the Post-Closing Trial Balance dated April 30, 2015 (page 626). All Income Statement accounts have zero balances because the books were closed at the end of the first quarter. Headings, totals and subgroup totals (i.e., the non-postable accounts) do not have balances. Remember to put any forced balance amounts into the *Test Balance Account*.

Open the account information window for **1060 Bank: Niagara Trust Chequing**, the first account requiring a balance.

Click the **Opening Balance field**.

Type the **balance**.

Correct the **information** if necessary by repeating the above steps.

Click the **Next button** [▶] to advance to the next ledger account window.

Enter **negative numbers for accounts that decrease the total** in a group or section (e.g., *Allowance for Doubtful Accounts*, *Accum Deprec*, *GST/HST Paid on Purchases*). These account balances are indicated with a minus sign (–) in the Balance Sheet on page 625.

Repeat these **procedures** to **enter** the **balances** for the remaining accounts in the Post-Closing Trial Balance on page 626. *Test Balance Account* should have a zero balance.

Close the **Ledger window**.

NOTES

If you want to use the Retained Earnings linked account to enter account balance discrepancies, you must delay entering account balances until after you enter General linked accounts (see pages 227–228).

NOTES

For account 1140 Bank: USD Chequing, enter $9 500, the balance in Canadian dollars. The USD balance will be added after we set up currencies.

After entering all account balances, you should display the Trial Balance to check them against the amounts on page 626. You can do this from the Accounts window.

Choose the **Reports menu** and **click Trial Balance**. **Click** the **Print tool**.

Close the **display** when finished. Leave the Accounts window open.

Check all **accounts** and **amounts** and **make corrections** if necessary.

Defining Account Classes

Defining bank accounts involves changing the account class to Bank and indicating the currency for the accounts and the cheque and deposit number sequences. If you use online banking, you must also enter the bank name, account numbers and Web site. We must also change the class for *Undeposited Cash and Cheques* to either Bank or Cash to use it as the linked account for receipts. Cash is the appropriate selection. Remember that the bank account class changes must be saved before we can enter the next cheque numbers. Changes are saved automatically when we open the next ledger record.

NOTES
Refer to the chart on page 623 for bank information and to page 220 for a review of Bank class accounts.

We must also define the account class for the credit card asset and the credit card payable accounts and change the account class for expense accounts. We will make all these changes before continuing the setup.

NOTES
We must define 1030 Undeposited Cash and Cheques as a Bank or Cash class account in order to enter it as the linked bank account for Receivables. Cash is the most appropriate selection.
Both Bank and Cash class accounts are available in the Deposit To field for cash sales and receipts.

Double-click 1030 Undeposited Cash and Cheques to open the ledger.

Click the **Class Options tab**.

Choose **Cash** from the drop-down list of account classes.

Click the **Next Account button** to open the ledger for account **1060**.

Choose **Bank** from the list of account classes.

Click the **Next Deposit Number field**.

Type 18

Click the **Next Account button**.

Choose **Bank** as the account class for *1080 Bank: Niagara Trust Savings*.

Click **Chequing** (Account Type field). **Click Savings** from the list.

Click the **Next Account button** to **open** the ledger for **1120 Bank: Visa and Interac**.

Choose **Credit Card Receivable** as the account class.

Click the **Next Account button** to **open** the ledger for **1140 Bank: USD Chequing**.

Choose **Bank** as the account class.

Click the **Select account list arrow**.

Click **2250 Credit Card Payable** to open its ledger screen at the Class Options tab screen.

NOTES
To open the ledger for Credit Card Payable, you can click the Next Account button repeatedly or choose the account from the Select Account list arrow.

Choose **Credit Card Payable** as the account class. Notice that Credit Card Receivable is not available as a class option for the liability account.

Click the **Select account list arrow** again and **choose 5010 Advertising and Promotion**.

Select **Operating Expense** as the account class.

Click ▶. **Select** the **Operating Expense** class for all postable expense accounts except the cost of goods subgroup accounts (#5040–5110).

Close the **General Ledger window** and the **Accounts window**.

Entering Company Default Settings

Adding a Foreign Currency

VeloCity purchases some inventory items from suppliers in the United States and must set up the company files to allow transactions in USD, United States dollars. We will set up the foreign currency now because we need this information for bank account and supplier and customer settings.

Click the **Settings icon** and **Company**.

Click **Currency** under Company to see the Currency Information window:

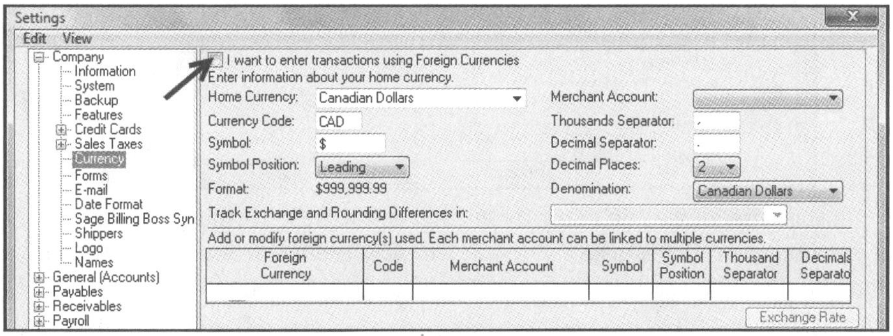

Canadian Dollars is the default in the Home Currency field, and its code, symbol, format and so on are added. You enter the currencies in the columns in the lower half of the screen, but first you must turn on the option to use other currencies.

Click **I Want To Enter Transactions Using A Foreign Currency**.

Exchange rates vary from day to day and even within the day. When purchases and payments are made at different times, they are subject to different exchange rates. We have seen these differences in the Maple Leaf Rags application (Chapter 12). Exchange rate differences may result in a gain — when the exchange rate drops before a payment is made or when the rate increases before a payment is received from a customer — or a loss — when the rate increases before a payment is made or when the rate drops before a customer makes a payment. These differences are tracked in the linked account designated on this screen. Rounding differences may also result in gains and losses because the amounts are recorded with two decimal places and exchange rates usually have several significant digits. The account for these differences may be an expense account or a revenue account. VeloCity uses a revenue account.

Click the **list arrow** for **Track Exchange And Rounding Differences In**.

Both revenue and expense accounts are available for linking.

Click **4120 Exchange Rate Differences** to enter the linked account.

The next step is to identify the foreign currency or currencies.

Click the **Foreign Currency field**. **Type** U

NOTES
Leave the account class for accounts 5040 to 5110 unchanged (set to Cost of Goods Sold class) so that you can create Gross Margin Income Statements.

NOTES
Remember that you can finish your session at any time. To continue, just open the file, accept the session date and start again from where you left off.

NOTES
After allowing transactions in a foreign currency, you can change the column sizes by dragging the heading margins so that all headings appear clearly.

PRO VERSION
After you click Allow Transactions In A Foreign Currency, the screen expands with the fields you need to add the currency. Choose the account for tracking exchange rate differences. Then select United States Dollars from the Foreign Currency field drop-down list. Click the Exchange Rate button and enter the date and exchange rate in the Date and Exchange Rate columns.

PRO VERSION
The Pro version of Sage 50 allows only two currencies – the home currency plus one foreign currency.

NOTES
You can add a new account at this stage if necessary. Type the new account number and press *tab*. Click Add to start the Add An Account wizard.

Click the **List icon** for the field to open the list of currencies:

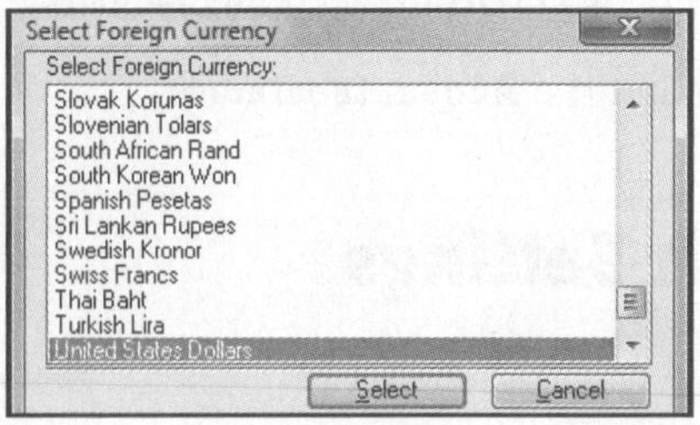

The list of currencies opens and United States Dollars should be selected.

Scroll down if necessary, and **double-click United States Dollars** to add it to the Currency Information screen, if necessary. The currency code, symbol and format are added for the selected currency. Accept the defaults.

Click the **Exchange Rate button**:

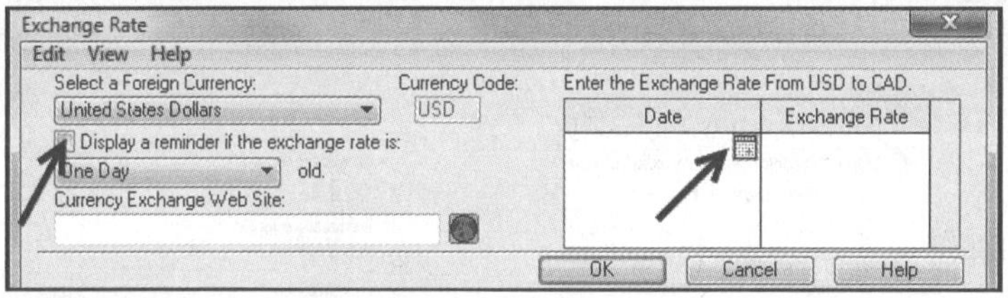

On this screen, we can enter the exchange rates for various dates for each currency. The selected currency is listed in the Select A Foreign Currency field. All currencies you created will be listed in the drop-down list for this field.

Click the **Date field**.

Type 05 01 **Press** *tab* to advance to the Exchange Rate field.

Type 1.015

If you know the rates for other dates, you can enter them as well. Otherwise, you can enter current rates in the journals as we did in the previous chapters. These rates will be added to the list on this screen.

To ensure that you do not use an old exchange rate that is no longer accurate, you should turn on the reminder that warns if the rate is out of date. A one-day period for updating should be sufficient.

Click **Display A Reminder If The Exchange Rate Is**.

Accept **One Day Old** as the time interval.

Now every time you change the transaction date to one day past the date of the rate previously used, the program will warn you and give you an opportunity to change the rate. If the rate has not changed, you can accept the old rate.

Click **OK** to return to the Currency Settings screen.

Setting Up Credit Cards

VeloCity accepts Visa credit card payments from customers as well as debit cards (Interac). The store also uses a Visa card to pay for some purchases. Setting up credit cards includes naming them, identifying the linked accounts and entering fees associated with the cards.

Click **Credit Cards** for the next step. You will see the warning message:

NOTES
The Premium version of Sage 50 accepts more than one foreign currency.

NOTES
If you have a Web site that you use for exchange rate information, you can enter it here as well. Then, with your Internet connection active, click the Web tool to access the Web site directly and obtain current rates. The Web tool appears on the Exchange Rate list screen that you access by clicking the Exchange Rate tool beside the Exchange Rate field in the journals.

NOTES
Refer to the Business Information Chart on page 623 for credit card details. To review credit card setup, refer to page 222 for additional information.

Click **Yes**. Currencies are used with other settings so they must first be saved.

Click **Used** to open the Credit Card Information screen for the cards that the business uses.

Click the **Credit Card Name field**.

Type `Visa` **Press** *tab* to move to the Payable Account field.

Press *enter* to see the list of available accounts.

Double-click **2250** to add the account and move to the Expense Account field.

Press *enter* to see the account list.

Double-click **5030**.

Click **Accepted** under Credit Cards to open the Credit Card Information screen for the cards that the business accepts from customers.

Click the **Credit Card Name field**.

Type `Visa` **Press** *tab* to advance to the Discount Fee % field.

Type `2.5` **Press** *tab* to advance to the Expense Account field.

Press *enter* to see the list of accounts available for linking.

Double-click **5030** to choose and enter the account. The cursor advances to the Asset Account field.

Press *enter* to see the list of accounts available for linking.

Double-click **1120** to choose and add the credit card bank account.

Click the **List icon** for the Currency field to open the list of currencies:

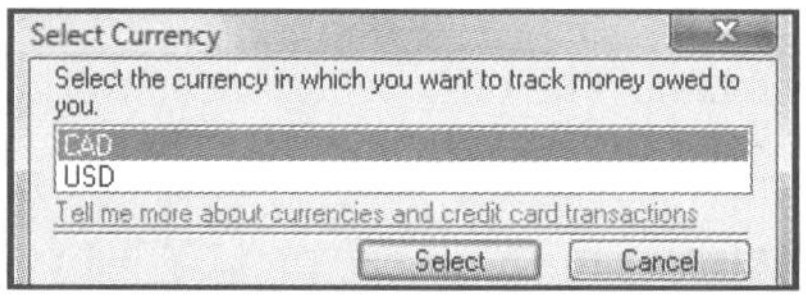

Sage 50 Premium version accepts credit cards in a foreign currency. You must use separate linked accounts for cards in different currencies.

Click **Cancel** to return to the Cards Accepted screen.

Enter **Interac** as the name, **0** as the %, **5030** as the Expense account and **1120** as the Asset account to set up the debit card.

Click Processing Services to open these settings:

WARNING!

You must choose a Credit Card Payable or Bank class account as the Payable Account for cards used.

Although accounts in other classes appear on the Select Account list, selecting them will generate an error message when you save the entries.

NOTES

You must choose a Credit Card Receivable or Bank class account as the Asset Account for cards accepted.

PRO VERSION

The Pro version does not allow credit cards in foreign currencies.

NOTES

You can enter the following account details for processing credit cards:

Merchant ID: 651259884634

Merchant Key: B8B9O4S6E2K2

Remember that when you set up for processing credit cards, you must follow through with the processing for all Visa sales. And you must enter 4111111111111111 as the Visa number and leave your Internet connection on.

For Interac (debit card) sales, process the card transaction manually (see page 520).

If you want to use the **credit card processing** service feature, you can use the merchant ID and key provided in Chapter 13.

Click the Merchant ID field and enter your number. Press Tab. Type your Merchant Key in this field.

Setting Up Sales Taxes

> **NOTES**
> Refer to the Business Information Chart on page 623 for sales tax information. Refer to page 224 for a review of sales taxes.

VeloCity charges and pays GST on books and HST on all other purchases. We will set up codes for these two taxes. We want to generate reports on both taxes.

Both taxes are linked to the GST/HST accounts because a single remittance to the Receiver General for Canada is made for both taxes; only the rates are different.

Click **Sales Taxes** under Company. There are settings for tax names and codes.

Click **Taxes** to access the Sales Tax Information screen:

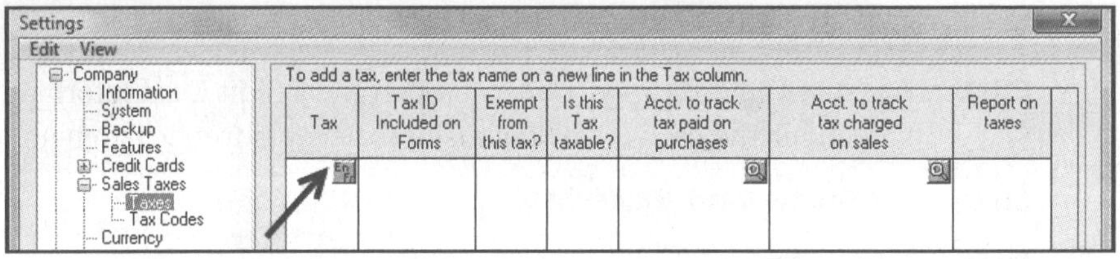

> **PRO VERSION**
> The Terms Purchases and Sales will replace the terms Expenses and Revenues.

Press *tab* to advance to the Tax field on the Taxes screen where you should enter the name of the tax. We will enter the HST first.

Type HST **Press** *tab* to advance to the Tax ID field where we enter the business number.

Type 335 677 829 **Press** *tab* to advance to the **Exempt From This Tax?** column.

VeloCity is not tax exempt for HST, so the default, No, is correct. HST is not taxable in Ontario (no other tax is charged on HST).

> **NOTES**
> PST is still charged separately on insurance in Ontario. Because this tax is not refundable, you do not need to track it or create a tax code for it. It will be included directly in the expense or asset component of the purchase.

Click , the **List icon for Acct. To Track Tax Paid On Purchases**.

Choose **2670 GST/HST Paid on Purchases**. The cursor advances to the field for the Account To Track Tax Charged On Revenues.

Choose **2650 GST/HST Charged on Sales** from the List icon  list of accounts. The cursor advances to the Report On Taxes field.

Click **No** to change the default entry to Yes.

Press *tab* so you can enter the information for GST.

VeloCity is not exempt from GST. The ID number and linked accounts are the same as for HST. GST is not taxable and the tax is refundable.

Type GST **Press** *tab* to advance to the Tax ID field.

Type 335 677 829

Click , the **List icon for Acct. To Track Tax Paid On Purchases**.

Choose **2670 GST/HST Paid on Purchases**. The cursor advances to the field for the Account To Track Tax Charged On Sales.

Choose **2650 GST/HST Charged on Sales** from the List icon  list of accounts. The cursor advances to the Report On Taxes field.

Click **No** in the Report On Taxes column to change the entry to Yes.

Entering Tax Codes

Click **Tax Codes** to open the next information screen:

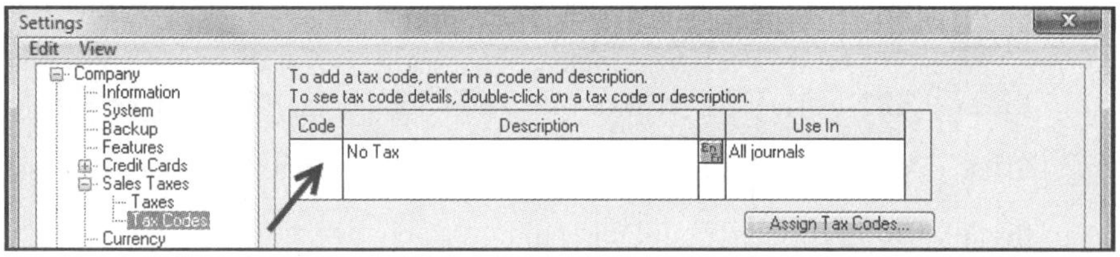

A single code, No Tax, is created as a default.

We need to create tax codes for sales and purchases when HST alone is charged and when only GST applies. There are also purchases with HST included, so we need a code for this situation as well (e.g., gasoline is priced with all taxes included).

Click the **Code column** below the blank on the first line.

Type H **Press** *tab* to move to the Description field.

Press *enter* or **double-click** to open the Tax Code Details screen:

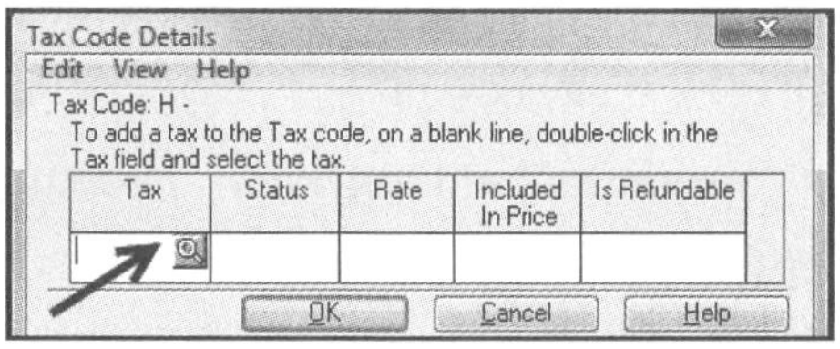

Click the **Tax field List icon** to see the list of taxes entered.

Both taxes from the Taxes screen appear on the list.

Click **Select** because HST is already selected and return to the Details.

Defaults are entered for the remaining fields. The **Status** is **Taxable** and the tax is **not included** — these are correct — tax is calculated and charged and is not included in the price.

Click the **Rate field**. **Type** 13

Click **No** in the Is Refundable column to change the entry to Yes.

Click **OK** to return to the Tax Codes screen for additional codes.

The description HST @ 13% appears beside the code H and the tax is used in all journals. You can edit the description if you want. If the tax were not refundable, non-refundable would be added to the description automatically. We are ready to enter the second code, to apply only GST.

Press *tab* until you advance to the next line in the Code column.

Type G **Press** *tab* to move to the Description field.

Press *enter* to open the Tax Code Details screen.

Click the **Tax field List icon**.

Select **GST**. Taxable and not included are correct.

Type 5 in the **Rate field**.

Click **No** in the Is Refundable column to change the entry to Yes.

Click **OK** to return to the Tax Codes screen. The description GST @ 5% has been added.

NOTES

If you need to remove a tax code detail line, click the line to be removed, choose the Edit menu and click Remove Line.

Press tab until you advance to the next line in the Code column, below G.

Type IN **Press** tab to move to the Description field.

Press enter or **double-click** to open the Tax Code Details screen.

Enter **HST** as the tax, **13%** as the rate. Taxable as the status is correct.

Click **No** in the Included In Price column to change the entry to Yes.

Click **No** in the Is Refundable column to change the entry to Yes.

Click **OK** to return to the Tax Codes screen.

The description "HST @ 13%, included" appears beside the code IN.

Updating Bank Account Settings

Adding Currency to a Bank Account

We need to complete two more steps for bank accounts — identify the currency for the account, and enter the next cheque number. By default, the home currency is selected. We need to change this setting for the USD chequing account.

Click the **Search tool** . The accounts should be listed.

Double-click **1140 Bank: USD Chequing**.

Click the **Class Options tab** to see the current class setting — Bank.

Click the **Currency list arrow**:

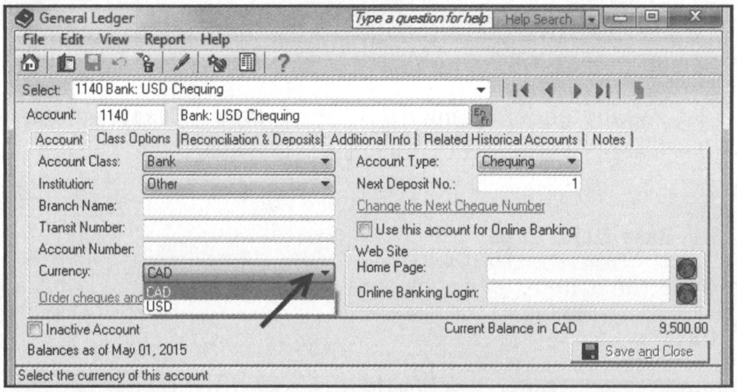

Once we identify an account as a bank account and allow foreign currency transactions, we identify the currency for the account on the Class Options tab screen.

Click **USD**. Zero now appears as the balance amount for the USD currency.

Click **Change The Next Cheque Number**. You will see the following warning:

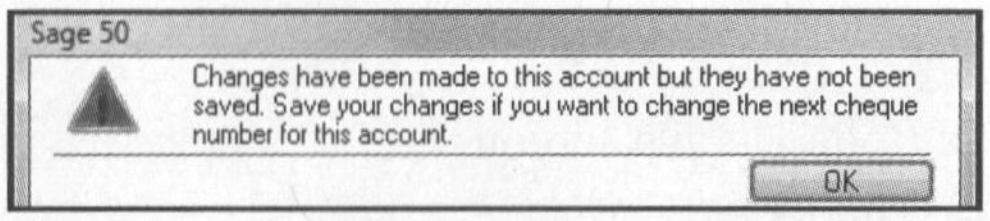

Click **OK** to return to the ledger window so we can save the changes.

Click the **Save tool** or **choose** the **File menu** and **click Save**:

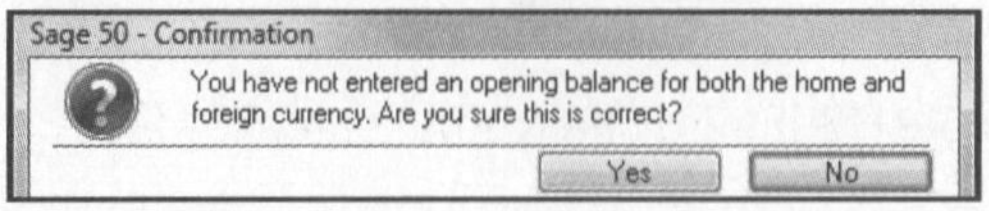

Because we have entered the balance in only the Home currency, we are asked to confirm that this is correct. It is not.

Click **No** to return to the ledger window so we can add the USD balance.

Click the **Account tab** to return to the Opening Balance fields. A second field has been added for the balance in USD.

Click the **Opening Balance In USD field**. **Type** `9350`

Click the **Save tool** .

You should now be able to add the next cheque number in the sequence.

Click the **Class Options tab**.

Click **Change The Next Cheque Number** to open the cheque Form settings:

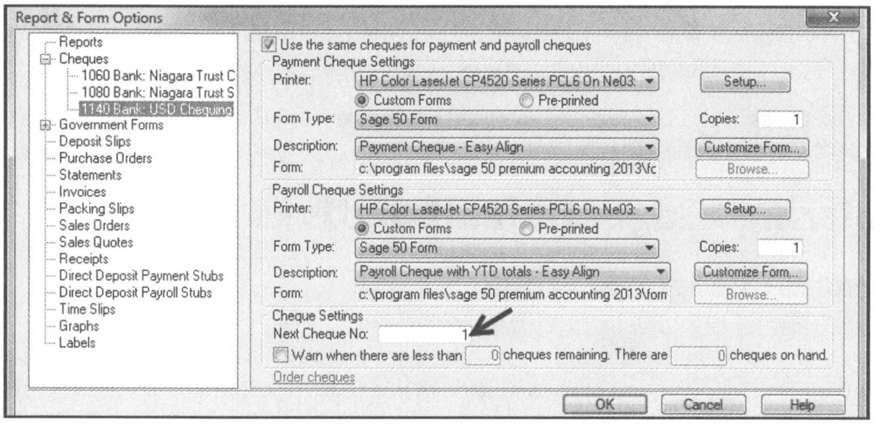

The account we started from is selected, so the cheque number field is available.

Click the **Next Cheque No. field**. **Type** `346`

Click **1060 Bank: Niagara Trust Chequing** in the left panel under Cheques.

Click the **Next Cheque No. field**. **Type** `101`

We will make additional printer setting changes before proceeding, while the Reports & Forms window is open.

Changing Other Printer Settings

Reports and forms settings apply only to the data file that you are using. They must be set for each data file separately and the settings are saved with each file.

Click Reports or click the form for which you want to enter settings.

Choose the printer you will be using for reports. Change the margins if necessary. Choose fonts and type sizes for the report from the lists. Click Setup to choose other options for your printer such as paper size, location, two-sided printing and so on.

Click OK to save your settings and return to the previous Printer setting screen.

Each type of form — cheques, invoices and so on — has its own setup.

Click **Invoices** to see the settings for printing invoices.

Check that the **file locations** for the forms are correct or dimmed.

For **E-mail** and **Printed Forms**, to avoid a file location error message, check that the location in the Form field is the Forms folder in your Sage 50 Premium Accounting 2013 program folder.

As you did for reports, select the printer and set the margins, font and type size to match the forms you are using. Preprinted forms were included as part of

WARNING!
The entries in the Form fields should be valid locations. The Form field references should show the Forms folder in your Sage 50 Premium Accounting 2013 program folder.

NOTES
You can change other printer settings at this stage if you want, or you can change them at any time as needed.

NOTES
From the Home window, choose the Setup menu and click Reports & Forms. The printer setting options for reports are given. More information about changing printer settings is available in Appendix E on the Student DVD.

NOTES

Refer to Appendix F on the Student DVD if you want to customize printed invoices.

the program installation and are located in the Forms folder in the main Sage 50 program folder. You should Print Subtotals In Invoices.

To preview invoices you must select **Custom Form** and **Sage 50 Form**.

If you want to customize the invoice form choose Sage 50 Form and click **Customize Form**.

To print labels, click Labels and enter the size of the labels and the number that are placed across the page.

To set the printer options for cheques or other forms, click the form you want and make the necessary changes.

Click **OK** to save the information when all the settings are correct. You can change printer settings at any time.

Close the **Ledger** and **Accounts windows** to continue entering the settings.

CLASSIC VIEW

You can access the linked accounts screens for any ledger directly. Right-click a journal icon to select it for the ledger you want and then click the Setup tool.

For example, to access General Linked Accounts, right-click the General Journal or the Reconciliation & Deposits icon,

or

.

Click the Setup tool . The General linked accounts screen opens. If no icon is selected, click General in the Select drop-down list.

Follow the same steps for other ledgers. Start with the Sales or Receipts icon to open the linked accounts screen for the Receivables Ledger, and so on.

Entering Ledger Default Settings

General Ledger Settings

Most of the settings for the General Ledger are already correct. VeloCity is not setting up budgets or departments yet, and it does not use the additional ledger record fields. Using and showing numbers for accounts and four-digit account numbers, the default settings, are also correct for VeloCity. We need to add linked accounts.

Choose the **Setup menu** and **click Settings** to continue entering the settings.

Defining Linked Accounts

Linked accounts are General Ledger accounts that are affected by entries in other journals. For example, recording an inventory purchase will update the Inventory Ledger, several General Ledger accounts and the balance owing to the supplier. Refer to page 227 for a review of linked accounts. Refer to page 88 for a review of the Current Earnings Account. Linked accounts are also needed for other features.

NOTES

Refer to page 227 to review General Linked accounts.

Identifying General Linked Accounts

The *Current Earnings* capital account records the changes in net income resulting from sales and expenses. At the end of the fiscal period, the net income (the balance from *Current Earnings*) is transferred to the Retained Earnings capital account — *S. Ryder, Capital* is the Retained Earnings account for VeloCity — and income and expense accounts are reset to zero to prepare for the new fiscal period.

Click **General (Accounts)**.

Click **Linked Accounts under General (Accounts)**.

The General Ledger has two linked accounts. Both must be capital accounts.

GENERAL LINKED ACCOUNTS

Retained Earnings	3560 S. Ryder, Capital
Current Earnings	3600 Current Earnings

NOTES

You can create new accounts from any Linked Accounts screen by typing a new account number in the Account field and pressing tab to start the Add An Account wizard.

Type the **account number** or **select** the **account** from the drop-down list.

Payables Ledger Settings

Click **Payables** and then **click Address**.

Enter **Niagara on the Lake**, **Ontario** and **Canada** as the default city, province and country for suppliers.

Click **Options**.

You should change the intervals for the aging of accounts. Some suppliers offer discounts for payment within 5, 10 or 15 days. Discounts from one-time suppliers are calculated on before-tax amounts.

Set the **aging** intervals at **15**, **30** and **60** days.

Click **Calculate Discounts Before Tax For One-Time Suppliers**.

Setting Up Import Duties

Although most goods imported from the United States are not subject to tariffs or import duties because of NAFTA (the North American Free Trade Agreement), you should know how to set up this feature. We will set up the program to charge duty but set the rate at zero so that no duty will be applied on purchases. You must activate the Duty option before creating supplier records so that you can indicate in the supplier records those suppliers that supply goods on which duty is charged. Without these two steps, the duty fields in the Purchases Journal will be unavailable.

Click **Duty** to access the settings we need:

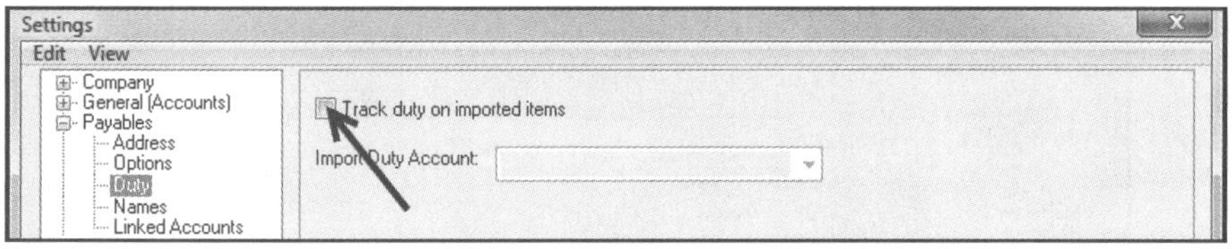

Click **Track Duty On Imported Items** to use the feature and open the linked account field.

A Payables account is linked to import duties for the liability to the Receiver General.

Click **2220 Import Duty Payable** from the Import Duty Account drop-down list.

Changing Payables Terminology

Sage 50 chooses a set of terms that is appropriate for the type of business. These terms can be modified by the user on the Names Settings screen. For the companies in this text, we have accepted the default terms. If you want to change them,

Click Names to open the settings:

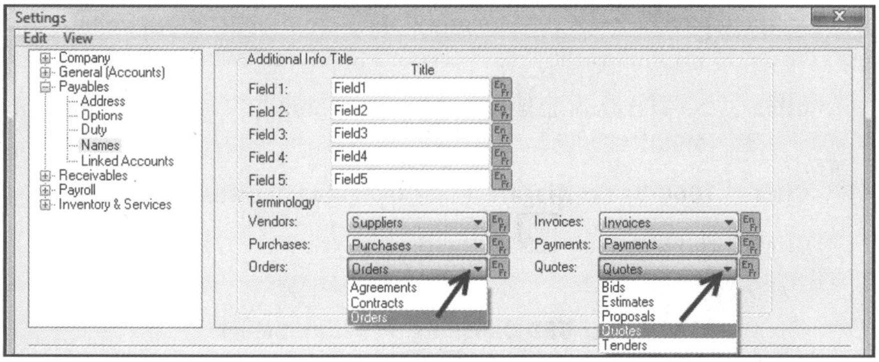

NOTES
Refer to page 228 if you want to review Payables Settings.

PRO VERSION
Remember that the term Vendors will replace Suppliers.

WARNING!
Sage 50 will not allow you to remove an account while it is being used as a linked account. When you try to remove an account, click OK in the Warning window to return to the Accounts window. First, turn the linking function off by deleting the account in the Linked Accounts window. Then remove the account in the Accounts window. You cannot remove an account if it has a balance or if journal entries have been posted to it.

PRO VERSION
The Terminology part of the Names Settings screen is not included in the Pro version because you cannot change the terms used.

NOTES
You can change the terminology used for Vendors, Purchases, Invoices, Orders and Quotes from the Names Settings screen if you want.

NOTES
Refer to Appendix B, page A–18 for a list of the terms used for different types of industry.

CLASSIC VIEW
To add the Payables Ledger linked accounts from the Home window, right-click the Purchases or the Payments Journal icon in the Home window to select it.

Click the Setup tool. Or choose the Setup menu, then choose Settings, Payables and Linked Accounts.

NOTES
Notice that this screen is different from the one on page 230 for Air Care Services that uses only one currency.

WARNING!
You cannot change the currency for an account when it is used as a linked account. You can choose a home currency account as the linked account to use with a foreign currency. If you had not yet changed the currency for 1140 Bank: USD Chequing, you could still choose it as the linked account. However, you would then be unable to change the currency to USD.

The upper part of the screen has five fields for the additional information you can add to the Payroll Ledger records. You can rename these fields if you want to use them.

The lower part of the screen has drop-down lists of terms for the various icons in the module. The names you select here will appear throughout the program as the names for icons, fields and reports. We have shown the drop-down lists of terms for Orders and Quotes. To see the terms you can choose for Vendors, Purchases and Invoices, refer to Chapter 7, page 229.

To change the terms, click the term you want to change and choose a different term from the drop-down list.

Identifying the Payables Linked Accounts

VeloCity uses *Bank: Niagara Trust Chequing* as its principal linked bank account for all home currency cheque transactions in the subsidiary Payables and Payroll ledgers.

PAYABLES	
Bank Account To Use for Canadian Dollars	1060 Bank: Niagara Trust Chequing
Bank Account To Use For United States Dollars	1140 Bank: USD Chequing
Accounts Payable	2200 Accounts Payable
Freight Expense	5090 Freight Expense
Early Payment Purchase Discount	5100 Purchase Discounts
Prepayments and Prepaid Orders	1250 Purchase Prepayments

To enter the Payables Ledger linked accounts,

Click **Linked Accounts** to display the Linked Accounts window:

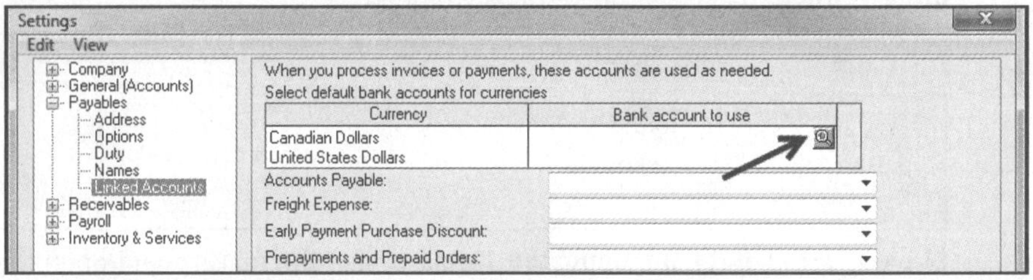

We need to identify the default General Ledger bank accounts used for payments to suppliers. Cash transactions in the Payments Journal will be posted to the bank account you select in the journal window. Bank and Cash class accounts are available in the journals, and the principal linked account defined here will be selected as the default.

You can see the list of accounts available for linking by clicking the drop-down list arrow for any linked account field. Only Bank and Cash class accounts may be used in the bank fields. That is why we needed to classify the bank accounts first.

VeloCity has two bank accounts for payments. The chequing account is the principal bank account for Canadian currency transactions, and the USD account is used for transactions in United States dollars.

You can choose a separate linked account for each currency, or you may use the Canadian dollar account for more than one currency. You can select a Home currency account as the linked account for foreign currency transactions, but you cannot select a foreign currency account as the linked account for Home currency transactions.

Click the **List icon** in the Bank Account To Use column for Canadian Dollars.

Click **1060 Bank: Niagara Trust Chequing** and **click Select**.

Click the **List icon** in the Bank Account To Use column for United States Dollars.

Click **1140 Bank: USD Chequing** and **click Select**.

Enter the **remaining linked accounts** from the chart on the previous page. **Type** the **account number** or **select** the **account** from the drop-down list.

Check the linked accounts carefully. To delete a linked account, click it to highlight it and press *del*. You must complete this step of deleting the linked account before you can remove the account in the General Ledger from the Accounts window.

NOTES
The remaining Payables linked accounts were introduced in Chapter 7. Refer to page 230 if you need to review these accounts.

Receivables Ledger Settings

NOTES
Refer to page 231 if you need to review Receivables Ledger settings.

Click **Receivables** and then **click Address**.

Enter **Niagara on the Lake**, **Ontario** and **Canada** as the default address.

Click **Options**.

VeloCity prints the salesperson's name on all customer forms for the customer's reference in case a follow-up is required. Most customers (and inventory items) use the tax code H, so we will use this as the default for new customers. The default tax code will be selected when we enter the customer records.

VeloCity charges 1.5 percent interest on overdue accounts after 30 days, includes paid invoices on customer statements for 31 days — this is appropriate for the monthly statements — and uses the payment terms to set the aging intervals.

Enter **10**, **30** and **60** days as the **aging** periods.

Click **Interest Charges** to add a ✓ and turn on the calculation.

Press *tab* to advance to the % field for Interest Charges.

Type 1.5 **Press** *tab*.

Type 30

Click the **Tax Code For New Customers field** to see the list of tax codes.

Click **H - HST @ 13%**.

Click **Print Salesperson On Invoices, Orders And Quotes**.

Entering Discount Settings

VeloCity offers its account customers a 2 percent after-tax discount for 10 days; full payment is due in 30 days. VeloCity does not use the line discount feature.

Click **Discount** to open the next Receivables settings screen.

Click the **% field** of the **Early Payment Terms** section.

Type 2 **Press** *tab*.

Type 10 **Press** *tab*.

Type 30

Click **Calculate Line Discounts On Invoices ...** to turn off the feature. You will see the warning:

PRO VERSION
Line Discounts are not available in the Pro version.

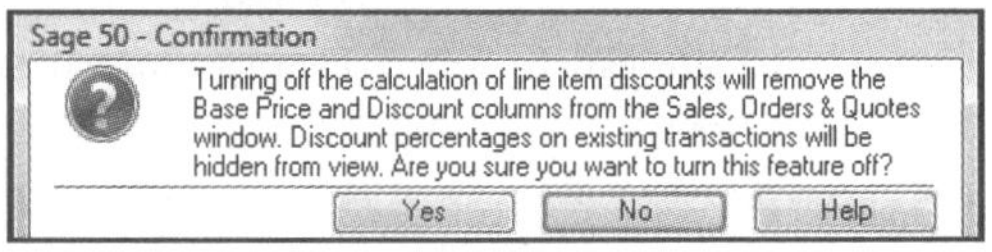

Click **Yes** to confirm your selection.

Changing Default Comments

Click **Comments** under Receivables.

You may add a comment or notice to all your invoices, quotes and order confirmations. You could use this feature to include payment terms, a company motto or notice of an upcoming sale. Remember that you can change the default message any time you want. You can also edit it for a particular sale or quote when you are completing the invoice. The cursor is in the Sales Invoices field.

Type `Interest @ 1.5% per month on accounts over 30 days.`

Repeat this procedure to enter comments for the other forms.

Changing Receivables Terminology

Click **Names** under Receivables:

PRO VERSION
The Terminology part of the Names Settings screen is not included in the Pro version because you cannot change the terms used.

NOTES
You can change the terminology used for Customers, Invoices, Sales, Orders and Quotes from the Names Settings screen if you want.

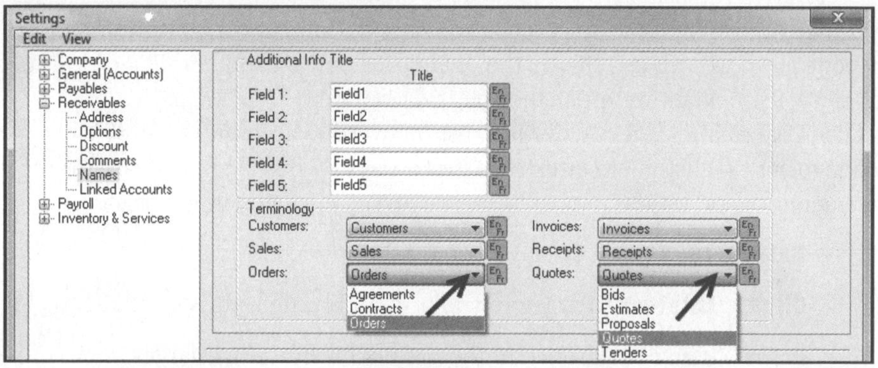

This screen has the same structure as the one for Payables additional information field names and ledger terminology.

In the screen above, we have shown the drop-down lists of terms for Orders and Quotes. The names you select here will appear throughout the program as the names for icons, fields and reports. To see the terms you can choose for Customers, Sales and Invoices, refer to Chapter 7, page 233.

To change the terms, click the term you want to change and choose a different term from the drop-down list.

Defining the Receivables Linked Accounts

CLASSIC VIEW
To add the Receivables Ledger linked accounts from the Home window, right-click the Sales, Orders & Quotes or the Receipts Journal icon in the Home window to select it.
Click the Setup tool. Or choose the Setup menu, then choose Settings, Receivables and Linked Accounts.

The Receivables Ledger linked accounts parallel those for the Payables Ledger.

Click **Linked Accounts** under Receivables:

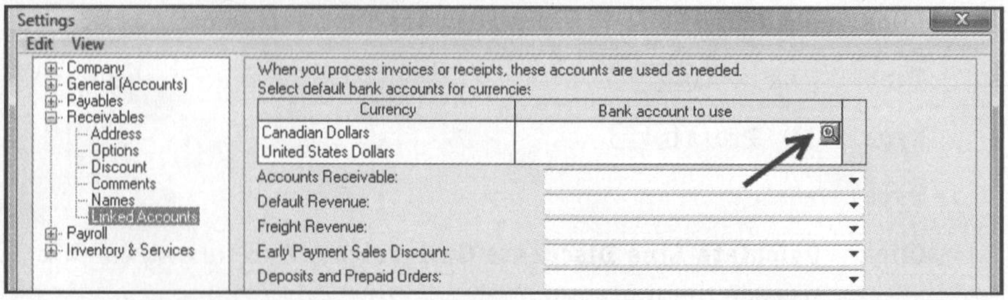

NOTES
Notice that this screen has changed because of the second currency. You can compare it with the one on page 234 for Air Care Services.

We need to identify the default General Ledger bank account used to receive payments from customers. Cash transactions in the Sales and Receipts journals will be posted to the bank account you select in the journals. The linked account will be the default, but any Bank or Cash class account may be selected in the journals.

VeloCity has several bank accounts. Cheques and cash receipts are held in the *Undeposited Cash and Cheques* clearing account and then deposited weekly to the

Bank: Niagara Trust Chequing account. Therefore, the default Canadian bank account for receipts is *Undeposited Cash and Cheques*. *Bank: USD Chequing* is the default account for foreign currency customer transactions. Although most linked accounts may be used only once, one bank account can be linked to the Payables, Receivables and Payroll ledgers.

The following accounts are required as linked accounts for the Receivables Ledger:

RECEIVABLES LINKED ACCOUNTS

Bank Account To Use for Canadian Dollars	1030 Undeposited Cash and Cheques
Bank Account To Use for United States Dollars	1140 Bank: USD Chequing
Accounts Receivable	1200 Accounts Receivable
Default Revenue	do not use – leave blank
Freight Revenue	4200 Freight Revenue
Early Payment Sales Discount	4060 Sales Discounts
Deposits and Prepaid Orders	2210 Prepaid Sales and Deposits

NOTES
The linked revenue account from the Inventory Ledger record will be added as the default for sales.

Click the **List icon** in the Bank Account To Use column for Canadian Dollars.

Click **1030 Undeposited Cash and Cheques** and **click Select**.

Click the **List icon** in the Bank Account To Use column for United States Dollars.

Click **1140 Bank: USD Chequing** and **click Select**.

Enter the **remaining linked accounts** from the chart on this page. **Type** the **account number** or **select** the **account** from the drop-down list.

NOTES
The remaining linked accounts were introduced in Chapter 7. Refer to page 234 if you need to review these accounts.

Payroll Ledger Settings

At this stage, we will change the settings for Payroll Names, Income, Deductions, Taxes and Entitlements. After creating supplier and employee records, we can change the Remittance and Job Category settings.

NOTES
Refer to pages 319–325 to review payroll settings if necessary.

Entering Payroll Names

Because the names we use will appear on the remaining payroll setting screen, we will define them first.

Click **Payroll** and then **click Names** in the list of Payroll options.

Click **Incomes & Deductions** to access the first group of payroll names.

Many of the standard income types are mandatory and cannot be changed. These fields are shown on a shaded background. Some of the other default names are also correct so you do not need to redefine them. You can leave Income 1 and Income 2, labelled "Salary" and "Commission," unchanged because VeloCity has two salaried employees and pays a sales commission to one employee. There is allowance for 20 different kinds of income in addition to the compulsory fields and 20 different payroll deductions. Each income and deduction label may have up to 12 characters.

VeloCity uses the additional income fields for bonuses, piece rate pay and taxable benefits (tuition fee payments) so that these incomes can be identified by name on the paycheque. The piece rate pay is based on completed favourable client surveys for the employees. Travel expenses repaid directly to employees are also entered as income, but they are reimbursements and will not be taxed.

NOTES
Reimbursements are added to net pay (the amount of the paycheque), but are not added to gross pay to calculate taxes.

VeloCity also has three payroll deductions at this time: RRSP — the Registered Retirement Savings Plan; CSB Plan — the Canada Savings Bond Plan; and Garnishee — the wages that are withheld and submitted to the Receiver General for prior years' taxes.

Click **Income 3 in the Name Column** to highlight the contents.

Type No. Clients **Press** tab to advance to the Income 4 field.

Type Bonus **Press** tab to advance to the Income 5 field.

Type Tuition **Press** tab to advance to the Income 6 field.

Type Travel Exp. **Press** tab to advance to the Income 7 field.

Press del to remove the entry. **Press** tab to select the next field.

Delete the **remaining Income names** until they are all removed.

Press tab after deleting Income 20 to select Deduction 1 in the Deductions column.

Press tab again if necessary to select Deduction 1 in the Name column.

Type RRSP **Press** tab to advance to the second deduction Name field.

Type CSB Plan **Press** tab to highlight the next field.

Type Garnishee **Press** tab to highlight the next field.

Press del. VeloCity does not have other payroll deductions.

Press tab to select the next field. **Delete** the **remaining deductions**.

NOTES
If clicking does not highlight the field contents, drag through an entry to select it. Double-clicking may open the language labels screen.

NOTES
In Chapter 9, we created Travel Expenses as a user-defined expense and issued separate cheques to the employee for them and used the generic Benefits field to enter all employee benefits.

NOTES
You can also press ↓ to access the next Deduction Name field instead of pressing tab.

NOTES
You can add names to any of these fields later if you need to.

Entering Additional Payroll Names

VeloCity keeps an emergency contact name and phone number for each employee as additional information in the personnel files. We will name these extra fields for the Payroll Ledger.

On this next screen, we also name the additional payroll expenses for VeloCity and the entitlements for employees. VeloCity has group insurance as a user-defined expense and offers sick leave and personal leave days for all employees as well as vacation days for salaried employees.

We will briefly review income, benefits and user-defined expenses.

Group insurance is classified as a benefit for employees because the premiums are paid to a third party rather than to the employee. The employer's expense for the benefit is entered as a user-defined expense. Tuition is classified as an income because it is paid to the employee through regular paycheques. The employer's expense for this benefit is recorded in the expense account linked to the income, just like wage expenses. Reimbursements may also be entered as income or as user-defined expenses, depending on how the payment is made. If we entered travel expenses as a user-defined expense, we would create a linked payable account and then issue a separate cheque to the employee to provide the reimbursement. If we repay the expense on the payroll cheque, we define it as an income — reimbursement — that is not taxable.

The Prov. Tax field is used for Quebec payroll taxes. Since we will not choose Quebec as the employees' province of taxation or enter linked accounts for them, the program will automatically skip the related payroll fields. WSIB is entered as the name for WCB (Workers' Compensation Board) because we selected Ontario as the business province. The field has a drop-down list of alternative names for WCB and other taxes you may use as an employer expense.

NOTES
HST is one alternative on the WCB drop-down list because some employee benefits are taxable.

Click **Additional Payroll**.

Double-click **Field1**. **Type** Emergency Contact

Press tab **twice** to highlight the next field. (Read margin Notes.)

Type Contact Number

Delete the **names for fields 3 to 5**.

Drag through **User Exp 1**, the Expense 1 field, to highlight the contents.

Type Gp Insurance

Delete the **remaining expenses**.

Drag through **Days 1**, the Entitlement 1 field, to highlight the contents.

Type Vacation **Press** tab **twice** to highlight the next entitlement name.

Type Sick Leave **Press** tab **twice** to highlight the next name.

Type PersonalDays

Delete the **remaining entitlement names**.

Entering Settings for Incomes

Click **Incomes** under Payroll.

This screen designates the types of income and the taxes that apply. By deleting the names we do not need this list becomes easier to work with. As we did for Lime Light Laundry (Chapter 9), we can modify this screen by hiding the columns that apply to Quebec so that only the columns we need are on-screen at the same time.

Point to the **right column heading margin for Calc. Tax (Que.)** until the pointer changes to a two-sided arrow.

Drag the **margin to the left** until the column is hidden.

Remove the **column for Calc. QHSF** and **Calc. QPIP** in the same way.

For each type of income, you must indicate what taxes are applied and whether vacation pay is calculated on the income. Most of the information is correct. Regular and overtime hours are paid on an hourly basis, while salary and commissions are paid at designated income amounts per period. All taxes apply to these types of income at VeloCity, so these default settings are correct. Vacation pay and EI, however, are not calculated on all incomes so some of these checkmarks should be removed. In addition, we should designate the type of income for the income names that we created and the taxes that apply to them. First, we should choose the type of income because that will change the defaults that are applied.

By default, all new incomes are assigned to the Income type. This assignment is correct for Bonus, the extra annual holiday payment. The tuition fee payment is a taxable benefit paid directly to the employee, so it is also classified as an Income. The generic Benefits field in journals is used for items that the employer pays directly to a third party on behalf of the employee. The monetary value of the premiums would be added as a benefit to the employee's gross wages to determine taxes and then subtracted again to determine the net pay. The employee does not receive the actual dollar amount. If a benefit is added to net pay, it should be classified as an Income. Therefore, in this example tuition is an Income.

Travel Expenses are **Reimbursements** and No. Clients is the name for the **Piece Rate** basis of paying bonuses. **Differential Rates** apply to different hourly rates paid at different times and are not used by VeloCity.

NOTES

On the Additional Payroll screen, you need to press tab twice to skip the Fr/Eng language button. If you are not using both languages (Company Settings, Features), press tab once to move to the next field. On the Incomes & Deductions screen, the language button is automatically skipped when you press tab.

NOTES

You can use up to 12 characters for User-Defined Expense and Entitlement names including spaces – that is why we omitted the space for the Personal Days entitlement name.

You can use the language button to enter labels in the second language.

NOTES

If necessary, scroll to the right to see the column margin you need.

NOTES

When you close and re-open the Payroll Settings screen, the hidden and resized columns will be restored.

QPIP (Quebec Parental Insurance Plan) provides parental leave benefits to EI-insurable employees. Both employers and employees pay into the plan.

NOTES

Tuition is defined as a type of income because it is paid directly to the employee. It is not a reimbursement because it is taxable.

Using the generic Benefits requires a linked Expense account and Payable account (paid to the third party, as for Lime Light Laundry in Chapter 9) while Income type and Reimbursements require only linked Expense accounts (paid directly to the employee on the paycheque).

If you select the Benefit income type, the expense will not be included in the journal entry – it must be recorded separately as an adjustment.

Click **No. Clients** to place the cursor on the correct line.

Press tab to move to the Type column. A List icon is added.

Click the **List icon** to see the income types.

Click **Piece Rate** to select this type for No. Clients.

Click **Select** to add the Type to the Settings screen. **Press** tab.

The cursor advances to the Unit of Measure field and the entry has changed to Item. The amount paid to employees is based on the number of completed surveys. Notice that the Insurable Hours checkmark was removed when we changed the type.

Type Surveys

Click **Travel Exp** to select this income line. **Press** tab.

Click the **List icon**. **Double-click** **Reimbursement** to enter this income type. All taxes are removed because this type of payment is not taxable.

Many of the changes are made automatically when we select the income type. We need to make more modifications. Insurable Hours, the number of work hours, is used to determine eligibility for Employment Insurance benefits. Regular, overtime and salary paid hours are counted but commissions, bonuses and tuition are not. No time can be accurately attached to them so they are not counted. EI is not calculated on benefits, so we also need to remove the Calc. EI ✓ for Tuition.

NOTES
A full-time employee whose only source of income is commissions and who is eligible for EI benefits may have a regular number of hours attached to the pay period and entered in the ledger.

Click **Commission** to select this income line.

Press tab **repeatedly** until the cursor is in the **Calc. Ins. Hours field**.

Click to remove the ✓, or **press** the **space bar**.

Press ↓ **twice** to place the cursor in the **Calc. Ins. Hours field for Bonus**.

Click to remove the ✓, or **press** the **space bar**.

Press ↓ **again** to place the cursor in the **Calc. Ins. Hours field for Tuition**.

Click to remove the ✓, or **press** the **space bar**.

Press ← to place the cursor in the **Calc. EI field for Tuition**.

Click to remove the ✓, or **press** the **space bar**.

We still need to modify the entries for vacation pay. In Ontario, vacation pay is calculated on all performance-based wages. This includes the regular wages, overtime wages and piece rate pay. We need to remove the remaining ✓. The ✓ for Travel Exp has already been removed. Salaried workers receive paid time off rather than a percentage of their wages as vacation pay. We do not need to remove the ✓ for Overtime 2. If it is used later, vacation pay will be calculated on it as well.

NOTES
Vacation pay is calculated on all wages. This calculation includes the piece rate pay – number of client evaluations – because it is a performance-based wage or income. Bonuses are not based on measurable performance; therefore, vacation pay is not applied to these amounts or to the other benefits.
The regulations governing vacation pay are set provincially.

Click **Salary** in the Income column.

Press tab **repeatedly** until the cursor is in the **Calc. Vac. column**.

Click to remove the ✓, or **press** the **space bar**.

Remove the ✓ for **Calc. Vac.** for **Commission**, **Bonus** and **Tuition**.

We do not need to change the Quebec tax settings (the hidden columns). They will not be applied when we select Ontario as the province for employees. The option to **track tips** applies to payroll in Quebec, so we do not need to choose this option.

Your completed Income Settings screen should look like the following one we show:

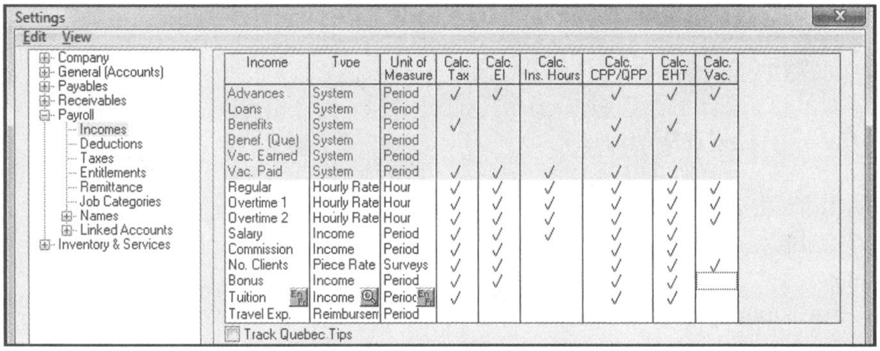

Entering Tax Settings for Deductions

Click **Deductions** under Payroll:

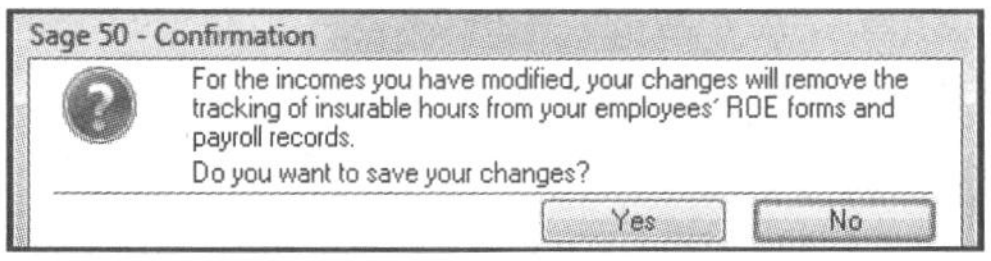

Click **Yes** when prompted to save the settings and confirm that ROE information connected to the deleted incomes will not be tracked.

Only the deduction names you entered earlier appear on this screen. You can calculate deductions as a percentage of the gross pay or as a fixed amount. Some deductions, like union dues, are usually calculated as a percentage of income. The Amount settings are correct for VeloCity.

All deductions are set by default to be calculated after all taxes (Deduct After Tax is checked). For CSB Plan and Garnishee, this is correct — they are subtracted from income after income tax and other payroll taxes have been deducted. However, RRSP contributions qualify as tax deductions and will be subtracted from gross income before income tax is calculated, but not before EI, CPP and so on, so you must change its setting.

Click the **Deduct After Tax column** for RRSP to remove the ✓ and change the setting to Before Tax.

The remaining settings are correct. RRSP is deducted after the other payroll taxes and vacation pay because these deductions are based on gross wages.

Defining Default Tax Rates

Click **Taxes** under Payroll.

This group of fields refers to the rate at which employer tax obligations are calculated. The factor for Employment Insurance (**EI Factor**) is correct at 1.4. The employer's contribution is set at 1.4 times the employee's contribution. In the next field, you can set the employer's rate for **WSIB** (Workplace Safety and Insurance Board) premiums. On this screen, you can enter 1.29, the rate that applies to the majority of employees. You can modify rates for individual employees in the ledger records.

The next field, **EHT Factor**, shows the percentage of payroll costs that the employer contributes to the provincial health plan. The rate is based on the total payroll costs per year; the percentage for VeloCity is 0.98 percent because the total payroll is less than $200 000.

The **QHSF Factor** (Quebec Health Services Fund) applies to Quebec employees so we do not need to enter a rate for it. QHSF is similar to EHT.

Click the **WSIB Rate field**. **Type** `1.29`

NOTES

You can modify this screen as we modified the Incomes Settings screen so that only the columns we need are on-screen. You can remove the Deduct After Tax (Que.), QHSF and QPIP columns.

NOTES

Garnisheed wages for family support may be exempt for taxes when the family receiving them must claim the amount as taxable income.

WARNING!

If you later change the province in the Company Information screen, the name entered for WCB does not change. You must enter the correction manually on the Additional Payroll names screen.

NOTES

WSIB is the name for WCB in Ontario.

QHSF was used for Village Galleries (Chapter 14).

Press tab to advance to the EHT Factor field.

Type .98

Defining Entitlements

Click **Entitlements** under Payroll.

On this screen you can enter the rules for entitlements that apply to all or most employees. These will be added to new employee records as defaults.

Entitlements are usually linked to the number of hours worked. Employees at VeloCity are not entitled to take vacation time until they have worked for a certain period of time or to take paid sick leave immediately after being hired. The **Track Using % Hours Worked** determines how quickly entitlements accumulate. For example, 5 percent of hours worked yields about one day per month or 12 days of leave per year. VeloCity has **Maximums** for the number of days per year that an employee can take or accumulate. And finally, the days unused are not **cleared at the end of a year**. The number of days carried forward is still limited by the Maximum number of days available. The calculations are based on an eight-hour day as the default.

VeloCity gives salaried workers three weeks of vacation (8 percent) and allows a maximum of 25 days. Sick leave at 10 days per year is earned at the rate of 5 percent to the maximum of 15 days. Personal leave days (five days) accrue at the rate of 2.5 percent for a maximum of five days per year. VeloCity allows two of the three weeks of vacation time and five of the ten days of sick leave to be carried over to the following year; that is, they are not cleared at the end of the year. Personal leave days cannot be carried forward — the maximum is the same as the yearly allotment.

NOTES
Entitlements may also be given directly as a number of days without tracking hours by entering the number of days in the Maximum Days field.

NOTES
When the number of days accrued reaches the maximum, the Days Earned entries on the paycheques Entitlements tab screen will be zero.

Click the **Track Using % Hours Worked field for Vacation**.

Type 8 **Press** tab to advance to the Maximum Days field.

Type 25 **Press** tab.

Click the **Track Using % Hours Worked field for Sick Leave**.

Type 5 **Press** tab to advance to the Maximum Days field.

Type 15 **Press** tab.

Click the **Track Using % Hours Worked field for PersonalDays**.

Type 2.5 **Press** tab to advance to the Maximum Days field.

Type 5 **Press** tab.

Entering Payroll Linked Accounts

There are many linked accounts for payroll because each type of income, tax, deduction and expense that is used must be linked to a General Ledger account.

Click **Linked Accounts** under Payroll then **click Incomes**.

The names here are the ones you entered in the Names windows. If you deleted a name, it will not appear here.

The linked accounts for all types of income appear together on this first screen. You must identify a wage account for each type of employee payment used by the company, even if the same account is used for all of them. Once the Payroll bank account is identified as the same one used for Payables, the program will apply a single sequence of cheque numbers for all cheques prepared from the Payables and Payroll journals.

The following linked accounts are used by VeloCity for the Payroll Ledger:

NOTES
Refer to page 325 to review payroll linked accounts if necessary.

CLASSIC VIEW
To add payroll linked accounts, you can right-click the Paycheques or the Payroll Cheque Run Journal icon in the Home window to select it.

Click the Setup tool. Or choose the Setup menu, and then choose Settings, Payroll and Linked Accounts.

If no Home window icon is selected, you can use the Setup tool's Select Setup drop-down list, choose Payroll and click Select.

PAYROLL LINKED ACCOUNTS

INCOMES

Principal Bank	1060 Bank: Niagara Trust Chequing		
Vac. Owed	2300 Vacation Payable	Advances & Loans	1220 Advances & Loans Receivable
Income			
Vac. Earned	5300 Wages	Commission	5310 Commissions & Bonuses
Regular	5300 Wages	No. Clients	5310 Commissions & Bonuses
Overtime 1	5300 Wages	Bonus	5310 Commissions & Bonuses
Overtime 2	Not used	Tuition	5380 Employee Benefits
Salary	5305 Salaries	Travel Exp.	5320 Travel Expenses

DEDUCTIONS	**Linked Account**	**Payment Adjustment Account**
RRSP	2400 RRSP Payable	2400 RRSP Payable
CSB Plan	2410 CSB Plan Payable	2410 CSB Plan Payable
Garnishee	2430 Garnisheed Wages Payable	2430 Garnisheed Wages Payable

TAXES	**Payables**	**Expenses**	**Payment Adjustment**
EI	2310 EI Payable	5330 EI Expense	5330 EI Expense
CPP	2320 CPP Payable	5340 CPP Expense	5340 CPP Expense
Tax	2330 Income Tax Payable		2330 Income Tax Payable
WSIB	2460 WSIB Payable	5350 WSIB Expense	5350 WSIB Expense
EHT	2380 EHT Payable	5360 EHT Expense	5360 EHT Expense
Not used	Tax (Que.), QPP, QHSF, QPIP	**Not used** QPP, QHSF, QPIP	**Not used** Tax (Que.), QPP, QHSF, QPIP

USER-DEFINED EXPENSES

	Payables	**Expenses**	**Payment Adjustment**
Gp Insurance	2420 Group Insurance Payable	5370 Gp Insurance Expense	5370 Gp Insurance Expense

Type the **account number** or **select** the **account** from the drop-down list.

Choose **1060 Bank: Niagara Trust Chequing** for the Principal Bank field.

Press *tab* to advance to the next linked account field.

Choose **2300 Vacation Payable** for the Vac. Owed field.

Choose **1220 Advances & Loans Receivable** for the Advances & Loans field.

Choose **5300 Wages** for Vacation Earned, Regular and Overtime 1.

Choose **5305 Salaries** for Salaries.

Choose **5310 Commissions & Bonuses** for Commission, No. Clients and Bonus.

Choose **5380 Employee Benefits** for Tuition.

Choose **5320 Travel Expenses** for Travel Exp.

Click **Deductions** to see the next set of Payroll accounts.

Enter the **linked payable** and **payroll adjustment accounts** for **RRSP**, **CSB Plan** and **Garnishee** from the chart above.

Click **Taxes** to see the next set of Payroll linked accounts.

Enter the **linked payables**, **expenses** and **payment adjustment accounts** for **EI**, **CPP**, **Tax**, **WSIB** and **EHT** from the chart above.

Click **User-Defined Expenses** to see the final Payroll accounts.

Enter the **linked payable**, **expense** and **payment adjustment accounts** for **Gp Insurance** from the chart above.

Check the **linked** payroll **accounts** against the chart above.

WARNING!

Sage 50 will not allow you to remove a linked account while it is being used as a linked account. When you try to remove an account, click OK in the Warning window to return to the Accounts window. First, turn the linking function off by deleting the account in the Linked Accounts window. Then remove the account in the Accounts window. You cannot remove an account if it has a balance or if journal entries have been posted to it.

NOTES

The deleted income and deduction names do not appear on the screens for linked accounts.

NOTES

You can add accounts from the Linked Accounts windows. Type a new number, press *enter* and choose to add the account.

NOTES

If you can use an account for more than one link, the account will be available in the drop-down list. Otherwise, once an account is selected as a linked account, it is removed from the list.

Inventory & Services Ledger Settings

Click **Inventory & Services** to see the options for this ledger:

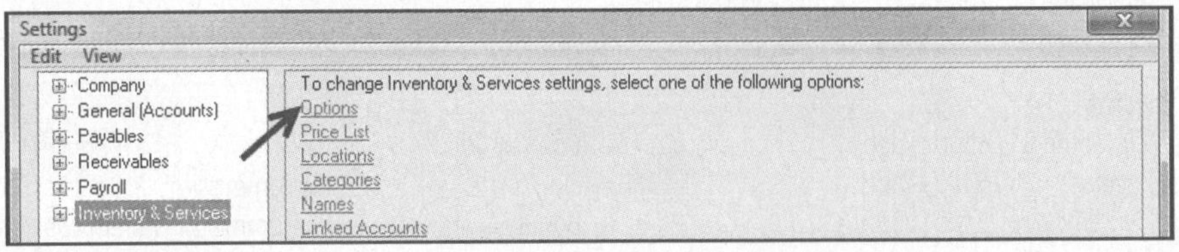

Click **Options**:

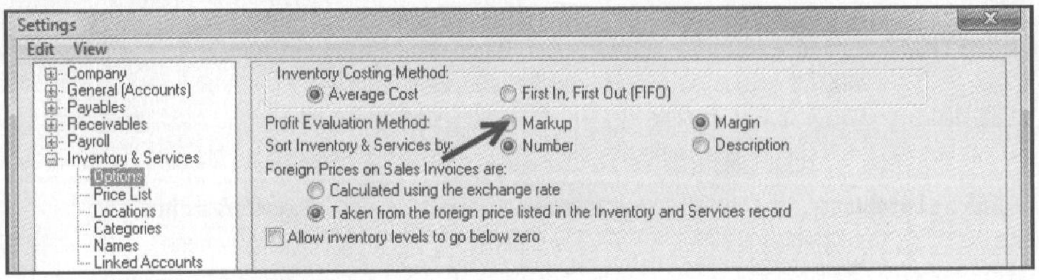

PRO VERSION
The Price List, Locations and Categories options are not available in the Pro version.
The FIFO method of costing is also not available in the Pro version.

Inventory costs may be calculated in two ways. In the average cost method, costs are continually updated as you buy and sell at different prices. With the FIFO method, costs are tracked with the items and do not change for any one item — its historic purchase price remains as the cost price at the time of sale. VeloCity uses average costs.

Profits may be calculated on the basis of margin or markup. You can change the setting at any time, so you can prepare reports using both evaluation methods. The formulas for profit evaluation by Margin and Markup are as follows:

Margin = (Selling Price – Cost Price) x 100%/Selling Price

Markup = (Selling Price – Cost Price) x 100%/Cost Price

VeloCity uses the markup method of evaluating the profit on inventory sales, so we need to change the default setting.

Click **Markup** to change the calculation method.

NOTES
The list of items you see in the Item Description field in the Sales and Purchases journals is always sorted by description. The Item Number field list in these journals is always sorted by number.
The choice you make on the Inventory Settings screen affects the selection lists only in the Adjustments and Item Assembly journals.

If you choose to sort Inventory Ledger items by description, the product name field will appear before the product number in the Inventory Ledger input forms, and inventory selection lists will be sorted alphabetically by name (see margin Notes). When item numbers are not used, sorting by description will make it easier to find the item you want.

Because we added a foreign currency, the option to take foreign prices for sales from the Inventory Ledger or from the exchange rate is added. The default setting to use the foreign price in the Inventory Ledger Record is correct for VeloCity. With this option, you can switch pricing methods for individual items. If you choose the exchange rate method, you cannot choose different methods for different items.

The final option is to Allow Inventory Levels To Go Below Zero. VeloCity will choose this option to permit customer sales for inventory that is backordered.

Click **Allow Inventory Levels To Go Below Zero** to select the option.

NOTES
Price lists are used in Chapter 18 to update prices. You can change one price relative to another for all items in a single step. Inventory locations are also covered in Chapter 18.

In the Premium version, you can create additional price lists and modify price lists from this settings screen. You can also set up the locations for inventory if you have more than one place where inventory is stored or sold.

Inventory Linked Accounts

VeloCity currently uses both linked accounts for inventory, the one for inventory adjustments or damaged merchandise and the one for additional item assembly costs. The linked accounts for the Inventory Ledger are listed here:

INVENTORY	
Item Assembly Costs	5045 Item Assembly Costs
Adjustment Write-off	5040 Damaged Inventory

Click **Linked Accounts** under Inventory & Services:

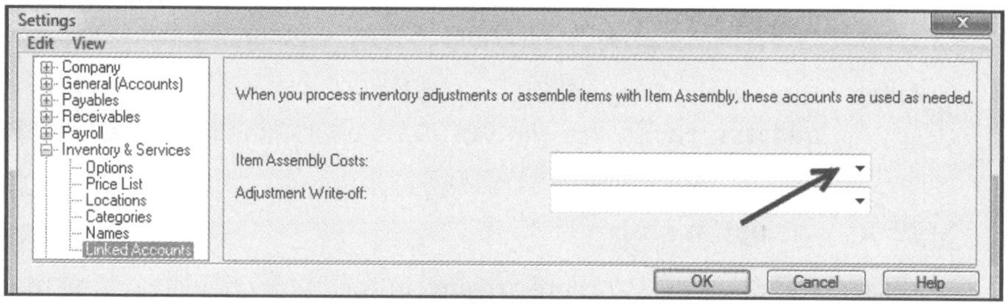

Type the **account number** or **select** the **account** from the drop-down list.

Choose **Item Assembly Costs** as the Item Assembly Costs linked account.

Press *tab*. **Choose** **5040 Damaged Inventory** as the Adjustment Write-off linked account.

Settings options for the Division module will be hidden if you chose to hide the module (User Preferences, View settings). Time and Billing, introduced in Chapter 18, has no settings options.

Click **OK** to save the new settings.

You will see several warnings. Because we deleted some payroll names, we are being warned that any accounts linked to these deleted fields will also be removed. The next message refers to the additional payroll names, and we are again being warned that their linked accounts will be removed. Refer to Chapter 9, page 328.

A second group of warnings relates to required account class changes for linked accounts. Refer to Chapter 7, page 234.

Read **each message carefully** and **click** **Yes** in response to return to the Home window.

Preparing the Subsidiary Ledgers

We have now completed the General Ledger setup, including

1. organizing all accounting reports and records
2. creating new accounts
3. identifying linked accounts for all ledgers
4. activating additional features and entering their linked accounts

The remaining steps involve setting up the records in the subsidiary ledgers:

5. inserting supplier, customer, employee and inventory information
6. entering historical startup information
7. printing reports to check the accuracy of your records

Preparing the Payables Ledger

Use VeloCity's Supplier Information on pages 626–627 to create the supplier records and add the outstanding historical invoices. If any information is missing for a supplier, leave that field blank. The first supplier, Complete Cycler Inc., is a foreign currency supplier.

CLASSIC VIEW

To add inventory linked accounts, you can also right-click the Item Assembly or the Inventory Adjustments Journal icon in the Home window to select it.

Click the Setup tool. Or choose the Setup menu, and then choose Settings, Inventory & Services and Linked Accounts.

NOTES

To see the Division module options, refer to page 506.

WARNING!

Check your work carefully. Although you can change the designated linked accounts at any time, journal entries will be posted incorrectly if you do not have the correct linked accounts.

NOTES

For a review of the Payables Ledger setup, refer to page 235.

PRO VERSION
Remember that the term Vendors will replace Suppliers.

Entering Supplier Accounts

Click **Payables** in the Modules pane list.

Click the **Suppliers icon** to open the Suppliers window.

Click the **Create button** or **choose** the **File menu** and **click Create** or **press** ctrl + **N**. The cursor is in the Supplier field.

Enter the supplier's **name**. On the Address tab screen, enter the **contact**, **address**, **phone**, **fax** and **tax ID** numbers, and the **e-mail** and **Web site** addresses from page 626.

Click the **Options tab**.

Enter the **discounts**, if there are any, in the Terms fields, and the number of days in which the net amount is due. **Click Calculate Discounts Before Tax** if the discounts are before tax. Otherwise, leave the box unchecked.

WARNING!
You cannot change the currency for a supplier or customer after entering historical invoices, so you must select the currency first. Otherwise, you must pay the invoices, clear paid transactions, remove the supplier and then re-create the supplier record from scratch.

After you enter historical invoices for a foreign supplier or customer, you cannot change the currency setting for the company, even if you delete the supplier.

You cannot access the duty fields in the Purchases Journal unless Charge Duty On Items Purchased is checked in the supplier's ledger.

Identifying Foreign Suppliers

Foreign suppliers are also identified on the Options tab screen.

Click the **Currency field list arrow**:

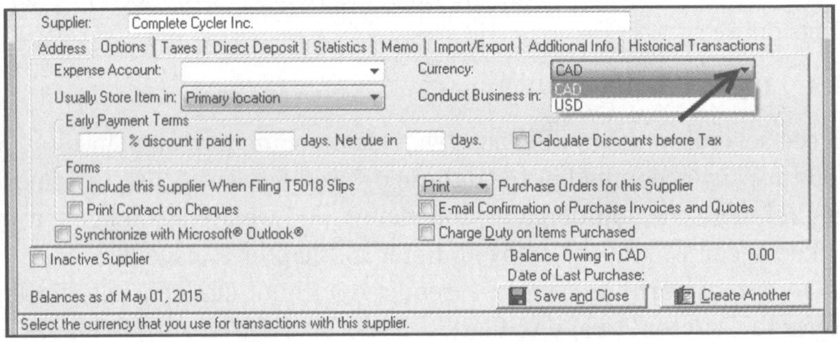

Click **USD**.

Click **Charge Duty On Items Purchased**.

You must change this duty setting to make the duty fields in the Purchases Journal available for this supplier.

You can print the contact on cheques if this is appropriate for the supplier.

Enter the **default expense account** for the supplier if there is one.

NOTES
Leaving the code as No Tax and leaving the exempt status set at No will permit you to charge taxes if needed.

If taxes are not calculated correctly for a supplier or customer, check that the Ledger entries for Tax Exempt are set to No.

Do not enter a default expense account for inventory suppliers — the linked asset account from the Inventory Ledger record is selected automatically by the program.

We will enter tax codes for all suppliers and customers later using the Assign Tax Codes feature in the Company Sales Tax Codes Settings (page 677). It is not necessary to change Tax Exempt entries. Leaving the setting at No will make all tax codes available. As long as the tax code in the journal is correct, taxes will be calculated correctly.

You do not need to enter any details on the Statistics, Memo and Import/Export tab screens.

The Balance Owing will be entered automatically by the program once you have entered historical invoices.

NOTES
Year-to-date purchases and payments are not recorded because this is a new fiscal period.

Correct any **errors** by returning to the field with the mistake, highlighting the errors and entering the correct information.

Entering Historical Supplier Transactions

The chart on page 627 provides the information you need to complete this stage. Complete Cycler has an outstanding balance so we must enter the historical transactions.

Click the **Historical Transactions tab**. **Click Save Now**. **Click Invoices**:

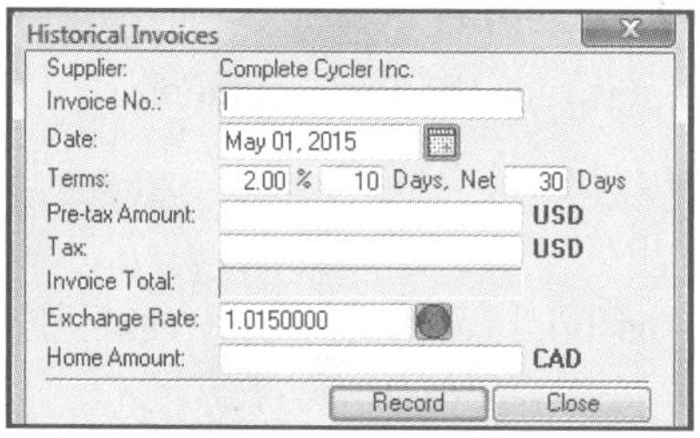

The Historical Invoices input screen for foreign suppliers has additional fields for the second currency information.

You can edit the payment terms for individual invoices if needed.

Because Complete Cycler Inc. discounts are calculated before taxes, there are separate fields for pretax and tax invoice amounts.

Enter **CC-914** as the **Invoice Number** and **Apr 28** as the invoice **Date**.

Press tab. The Exchange Rate screen opens.

Enter **1.02** as the exchange rate and **click Make This The Default Rate For April 28**. **Click OK**.

Click the **Pretax Amount field for USD**.

Type 4000 **Press** tab to advance to the Tax amount field for USD.

Type 520 **Press** tab.

In the Home Amount field, $4,610.40 should be entered correctly automatically.

Click **Record**.

Repeat these steps to **enter other invoices** for this supplier, if there are any.

When you have recorded all outstanding invoices for a supplier,

Click **Close** to save the invoice.

You will return to the Historical Transactions tab screen. The invoices you entered have been added to the Balance fields. Balances are displayed in both currencies.

Historical Invoices for Home currency suppliers are recorded in the same way, except for the entry of the exchange rate.

We will continue by entering historical payments to this supplier.

Historical Payments

Click **Payments** on the Historical Transactions tab screen:

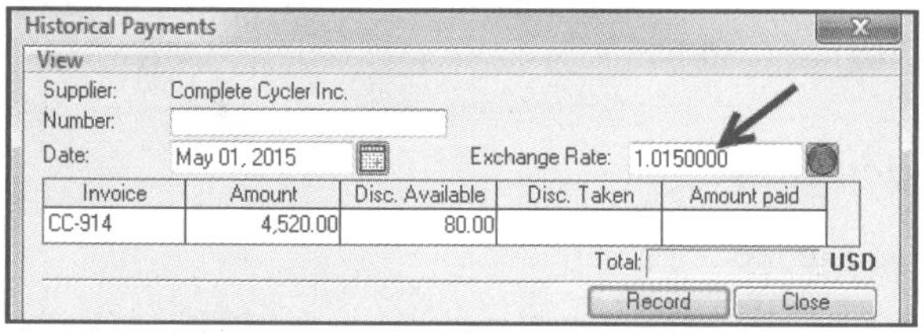

NOTES
You can refer to page 239 to review entering historical supplier invoices and payments if necessary.

WARNING!
If you save an incorrect invoice amount, you must pay the invoice, clear paid invoices for the supplier (Home window, Maintenance menu), reset the payments for the year to zero (supplier's ledger, Statistics tab) and re-enter the outstanding invoices. Refer to page 250.

NOTES
For Wheel Deals, enter $3 900 as the Home Amount after you enter the USD amount and allow the program to recalculate the exchange rate. Do not save the revised exchange rate when prompted.

Historical payments for foreign suppliers have one additional field, the one for the exchange rate. You must enter an exchange rate for these payments — there is no field for the home currency amount.

Click the **Number field**.

Type 344 (the **cheque number** for the first payment).

Press tab and **enter** the **payment date** for the first payment.

The exchange rate, 1.02, should be entered automatically because we made it the default rate for April 28 when we entered the invoice.

Skip the **Discount fields** because discounts are taken only when the early payment is a full payment.

Click the **Amount Paid column** (on the line for the invoice being paid).

Type 2000 for the **payment amount**.

Press tab to advance to the next invoice if there is one. Delete any amounts or discounts that are not included in the payment.

WARNING!
Remember not to include any discounts taken in the historical payments. If you do include them, the Payables Ledger will not be balanced and you will be unable to finish the history.

Click **Record** to save the information and to display an updated statement for this supplier.

Repeat these steps to **enter other payments** to this supplier.

When you have recorded all outstanding payments for a supplier,

Click **Close** to return to the Payables Ledger for the supplier. Notice that the payment you have just entered has reduced the Balance field.

Click the **Create tool** to display a new blank Payables Ledger screen.

Click the **Address tab**.

Repeat these procedures to **enter** the **remaining suppliers** and their **historical transactions** from pages 626–627.

NOTES
The Statistics tab screen shows the summary amounts in both Canadian and US dollars.

If there are no historical invoices and payments,

Click **Create Another** to save the record and open a blank Payables Ledger window. **Click** the **Address tab**.

Display or **print** the **Supplier List** and the **Supplier Aged Detail Report**, including terms, historical differences and foreign amounts. Compare these reports with the information on pages 626–627 to check the accuracy of your work.

NOTES
The historical invoices and payments will be entered on the Statistics tab screen as Last Year's Purchases and Payments because we are starting a new fiscal period.

Preparing the Receivables Ledger

Use VeloCity's Customer Information on pages 627–628 to create the customer records and add the outstanding historical invoices. Revenue accounts are added from the inventory records so they are not needed in the customers' records. If any information is missing for a customer, leave that field blank.

NOTES
For a review of the Receivables Ledger setup, refer to page 242.

Entering Customer Accounts

Click **Receivables** in the Modules pane list.

Click the **Customers icon** to open the Customers window.

Click the **Create button** [Create] or **choose** the **File menu** and then **click Create**. The cursor is in the Customer field.

Enter the customer's **name**. On the Address tab screen, enter the **contact**, **address**, **phone** and **fax numbers**, and the **e-mail** and **Web site addresses** according to page 627.

You can edit the default payment terms for individual customers or for individual historical invoices if necessary.

Click the **Ship-To Address tab**.

The Mailing Address is already selected as the default ship-to address, so the same address will apply to both fields on invoices, orders and quotes.

Click the **Options tab**.

Most entries on the Options tab screen are correct. Terms are entered from the default Receivables settings. Customer statements should be printed. Americas Vinelands Tours and Festival Tours are USD customers. All other customers are Canadian and use the Home currency (CAD).

Choose **USD** from the Currency list for Americas Vinelands Tours (and for Festival Tours).

Choose **Preferred** from the Price List field list for **Americas Vinelands Tours** and for other preferred customers (the ones marked with * in the customer information chart on page 627) to change the price list for these customers.

Change the payment **terms** to **net 1** for **Cash and Interac**, and **Visa Sales customers**.

The default code H is entered as the default tax code for all customers. We will change the codes for the USD customers from the Assign Tax Codes option.

Click the **Statistics tab**.

Enter the **credit limit**. Enter both CAD and USD limits for USD customers.

This is the amount that the customer can purchase on account before payments are required. If the customer goes beyond the credit limit, the program will issue a warning before posting an invoice.

The balance owing will be included automatically once you have provided the outstanding invoice information. If the customer has outstanding transactions, proceed to the next section on historical information. Otherwise,

Click **Create Another** [Create Another] to save the information and advance to the next new Receivables Ledger input screen.

Click the **Address tab**.

NOTES

The preferred customers are:
Americas Vinelands Tours
Backstage Tours
Niagara Rapids Inn
Park 'N Ride Tours

WARNING!

Do not forget to remove the discount terms for cash and credit card customer sales. Changing the ledger records will make the sales invoice terms correct automatically.

Entering Historical Customer Information

The chart on page 628 provides the information you need to complete this stage.

Enter the customer's **name**, **address**, **options**, **taxes** and **credit limit**.

Click the **Historical Transactions tab**. **Click Save Now**.

Click **Invoices**.

NOTES

You can refer to page 245 to review entering historical customer invoices and payments if necessary.

WARNING! If you save an incorrect invoice amount, you must pay the incorrect invoice, clear paid transactions for the customer, then re-enter the customer's outstanding invoices. Refer to page 250.

Enter the **invoice number**, **date** and **amount** for the first invoice. The default terms should be correct.

Press *tab* to advance to the next field after entering each piece of information.

When all the information is entered correctly, you must save the customer invoice.

Click **Record** to save the information and to display another blank invoice for this customer.

Repeat these procedures to **enter** the **remaining invoices** for the customer, if there are any.

When you have recorded all outstanding invoices for a customer,

Click **Close** to return to the Historical Transactions window for the customer.

The invoices you entered have been added to the Balance field. Continue by entering payments received from this customer, if there are any, or proceed to enter the next customer.

Click **Payments** on the Historical Transactions tab screen.

Click the **Number field**.

Enter the **cheque number** for the first payment.

WARNING! Remember not to include any discounts taken in the historical payments. If you do include them, the Receivables Ledger will not be balanced and you will be unable to finish the history.

Press *tab* and **enter** the **payment date** for the first payment. Again, discounts apply only to full payments made before the due dates, so you should skip the Discount fields.

Click the **Amount Paid column** (on the line for the invoice being paid).

Enter the **payment amount**.

Press *tab* to advance to the next amount if other invoices are being paid. Delete any amounts or discounts that are not included in the payment.

Click **Record** to save the information and to display the updated balance for this customer.

Repeat these procedures to **enter** the **remaining payments** from the customer.

When you have recorded all outstanding receipts from a customer,

Click **Close** to return to the Receivables Ledger window for the customer.

The payment you entered has updated the customer's Balance field amount.

Click the **Create tool** to open a new Receivables Ledger input screen.

Click the **Address tab** to prepare for entering other customers. After entering all customer records and historical data,

Click **Save And Close** [Save and Close] (or [X]) after adding the last customer. **Close** the **Customers window** to return to the Home window.

Display or **print** the **Customer List** and the **Customer Aged Detail Report**, including terms and historical differences. Compare these reports with the information on pages 627–628 to check your work.

Preparing the Payroll Ledger

> **NOTES**
> For a review of the Payroll Ledger setup, refer to pages 328–338.

Use the VeloCity Employee Information Sheet, Employee Profiles and Additional Payroll Information on pages 628–630 to create the employee records and add historical information.

We will enter the information for VeloCity employee Dunlop Mercier.

Click **Employees & Payroll** in the Modules pane list.

Click the **Employees icon** in the Home window.

Click the **Create button** or **choose** the **File menu** and **click Create**.

Entering Personal Details for Employees

The Payroll Ledger new employee information form will open at the Personal information tab screen so you can begin to enter the employee record.

The Payroll Ledger has a large number of tabs for the different kinds of payroll information. The cursor is in the Employee field. By entering the surname first, your employee lists will be in correct alphabetic order.

Type `Mercier, Dunlop` **Press** *tab*.

Type `55 Trailview Rd.` to enter the Street address.

The default city and province, those for the store, are correct.

Click the **Postal Code field**.

Type `l0s1j0` **Press** *tab*.

The program corrects the postal code format and advances the cursor to the Phone 1 field.

Type `9054681817`

The default **Language Preference** is correctly set as English.

Click the **Social Insurance Number (SIN) field**. You must use a valid SIN. The program has corrected the telephone number format.

> **NOTES**
> Social Insurance Number is not a required field. If you enter it, you must enter a valid number.
> Birth Date is a required field – it is used to determine CPP eligibility and requirements.

Type `532548625` **Press** *tab*.

The cursor advances to the Birth Date field. Enter the month, day and year using any accepted date format. Birth Date is a required field and it must be correct because it is linked to CPP calculations.

Type `9-18-82` **Press** *tab* **twice**.

The cursor moves to the Hire Date field, which should contain the date when the employee began working for VeloCity.

Type `1-6-10`

> **NOTES**
> Refer to page 298 for more information about employee terminations.

The next two fields will be used when the employee leaves the job — the date of termination and the reason for leaving that you can select from the drop-down list. The final option designates employees as active or inactive. All employees at VeloCity are active, so the default selection is correct.

We have not yet created Job Categories to identify salespersons, so we will assign employees to them later. The program will automatically enter the Date Last Paid.

NOTES
Refer to page 330 to review entering employee tax details.

WARNING!
Enter employee historical payroll details carefully. You will be unable to edit these fields after finishing the history or after making Payroll Journal entries for the employee.

They must also be correct because they are used to create T4s for tax reporting.

NOTES
The program skips the Quebec tax fields because you selected Ontario as the province of taxation and no linked accounts were entered for them.

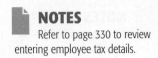

Entering Employee Tax Information

Click the **Taxes tab** to advance to the next set of employee details.

This screen allows you to enter income tax–related information for an employee, including the historical amounts for the year to date. Tax Table is a required field.

Click the **Tax Table list arrow** to see the list of provinces and territories.

Click **Ontario**, the province of taxation for VeloCity employees.

Press *tab* to advance to the **Federal Basic Personal Amount field.**

Type 11038

Press *tab* to advance to the **Provincial Basic Personal Amount field.**

Type 9574

Gearie is the only employee with additional claim amounts. Schwinn is the only employee who chooses to have additional taxes withheld.

For **Gearie**, entering the **three federal and provincial claim amounts** from page 628 in their respective fields will provide the correct total, indexed and non-indexed amounts.

For **Schwinn**, click the **Additional Fed. Tax** field and type **50**.

If an employee is insurable by EI, you must leave the box for **Deduct EI** checked. The default EI contribution factor, 1.4, for VeloCity is correct. We entered it in the Payroll Taxes Settings window (page 659).

All employees at VeloCity make CPP contributions so leave this check box selected. We will enter the historical income tax amounts next.

Click the **Historical Amount field** for **Income Tax**.

Type 1668.29 **Press** *tab* to advance to the EI Premiums Historical Amount field.

Type 207.73 to enter the amount of EI paid to date. **Press** *tab* to move to the CPP Contributions Historical Amount field.

Type 547.31

Entering Income Amounts for Employees

We defined all the types of income for VeloCity in the Names, Incomes & Deductions setup (page 655). All employees use the following types of income, although not all will have regular amounts and not all will be used on all paycheques:

- Loans
- Benefits
- No. Clients
- Bonus
- Tuition
- Travel Exp.

For Mercier the following incomes are also used: Vacation (Vac.) Owed, Vacation (Vac.) Paid, Regular and Overtime 1.

For Gearie and Schwinn, Salary is used. For Gearie, Commission is also used. Because Quebec is not selected as the province of taxation, Benefits (Que) is not preselected. Checkmarks for Advances, Loans, Benefits and Vacation cannot be removed.

All the details you need to complete the Income tab chart are on pages 628–629.

Click the **Income tab**.

On the Income chart you can indicate the types of income that each employee receives (the **Use** column), the usual rate of pay for that type of income (**Amount Per Unit**), the usual number of hours worked (**Hours Per Period**), the usual number of pieces for a piece rate pay base (**Pieces Per Period**) and the amounts received this year before the earliest transaction date or the date used for the first paycheque (**Historical Amount**). The **Year-To-Date (YTD) Amount** is added automatically by the program based on the historical amounts you enter and the paycheques entered in the program.

Checkmarks should be entered in the Use column so that the fields will be available in the Payroll journals, even if they will not be used on all paycheques.

Click **Regular** in the Income column to select the line.

Press tab to advance to the Amount Per Unit field where we need to enter the regular hourly wage rate.

Type 18 **Press** tab to advance the Hours Per Period field.

The usual number of work hours in the bi-weekly pay period is 80. You can change the default amount in the Payroll journals. Salaried workers normally work 150 hours each month.

Type 80 **Press** tab to advance to the Historical Amount field.

Historical income and deduction amounts for the year to date are necessary so that taxes and deductions can be calculated correctly and T4 statements will be accurate.

Type 11520 **Press** tab.

The amount is entered automatically in the YTD column and the cursor advances to the Use column for Overtime 1.

Press tab so you can enter the overtime hourly rate.

Type 27

Press tab **twice** to advance to the Historical Amount field. There is no regular number of overtime hours.

Type 486

The next three income types do not apply to Mercier, so they should not be checked. The next income that applies is No. Clients, the piece rate method of pay. There is no historical amount, but we need to enter the rate or amount per unit (survey). The remaining incomes (No. Clients, Bonus and Travel Exp.) are correctly checked. There is no fixed amount per unit or period and there are no historical amounts.

Pressing the space bar when you are in the Use column will also add a ✓ or remove one if it is there. Pressing ↓ will move you to the next line in the same column.

Click the **Use column beside Salary** to remove the ✓.

Click the **Use column beside Commission** to remove the ✓.

Click **No. Clients** in the Income column to select the line. **Press** tab.

Type 10 to enter the amount received for each completed survey.

If employees have received vacation pay, enter this amount in the **Vac. Paid** field. Vacation pay not yet received is entered in the **Vac. Owed** field. Any loans (or advances) paid to the employees and not yet repaid are recorded in the **Loans** or (**Advances**) **Historical Amount** field. There is no record of advance or loan amounts recovered.

NOTES
Refer to page 331 if you need to review entering employee income details.

NOTES
In the chart on pages 628–629, the incomes that are used by an employee have a ✓ or an amount in the employee's column.

NOTES
Checkmarks are added by default for all incomes, deductions and expenses that have linked accounts.

WARNING!
Do not click the Use column beside Regular or No. Clients as that will remove these checkmarks.

NOTES
If you added a linked account for Overtime 2, it will have a ✓ in the Use column and you should remove it for all employees.

NOTES
Remember that commissions must be calculated manually and entered in the Payroll journals. The Commission field in the Payroll Ledger allows only a fixed amount, not a percentage of sales, as the entry.

WARNING!
The totals for all employees for advances paid, loans paid and vacation pay owing must match the corresponding General Ledger account balances before you can finish entering the history.

We need to add the historical loans, benefits and vacation amounts for Mercier. Mercier has $100 in loans not yet repaid, and he has not received all the vacation pay he has earned this year.

Scroll **to the top** of the list so that the information for Loans is available.

Click the **Historical Amount column beside Loans**.

Type 100

Press tab to move to the Amount Per Unit column for Benefits. The group insurance premiums paid by the employer are employee benefits.

Type 16 **Press** tab to move to the Historical Amount for Benefits.

Type 128 **Press** tab to advance to the Historical Amount for Vac. Owed.

Type 706 **Press** tab to advance to the Historical Vac. Paid Amount.

Type 386

For **Schwinn**, click the Use column for Regular, Overtime 1 and Commission to remove the ✓. Enter the monthly salary and press tab. Enter 150 as the number of hours worked in the pay period. Press tab and enter the historical amount. For No. Clients, enter 10 as the amount per unit. For Travel Exp., enter 120 as the historical amount. You cannot remove the ✓ for Vac. Owed and Vac. Paid, even if they are not used.

For **Gearie**, repeat these steps but leave Commission checked and enter the historical amount. For Tuition, enter the per period and historical amounts.

NOTES
Employees may be paid yearly (1), semi-annually (2), monthly for 10 months (10), monthly (12), every four weeks (13), every two weeks for a 10-month year (22), twice a month (24), every two weeks (26) or weekly (52).

Pay Periods Per Year, another required field, refers to the number of times the employee is paid, or the pay cycle. Mercier is paid every two weeks, so 26 times per year.

Click the **list arrow** beside the field **for Pay Periods Per Year**.

Click **26**.

Retaining Vacation pay is normal for full-time hourly paid employees. Part-time and casual workers often receive their vacation pay with each paycheque because their work schedule is irregular. You will turn off the option to retain vacation when an employee receives the vacation pay, either when taking a vacation or when leaving the company (see page 276). If the employee is salaried and does not receive vacation pay, the option should also be turned off. For Mercier, or any employee who receives vacation pay, leave the option to Retain Vacation checked and type the vacation pay rate in the % field.

NOTES
When you select a specific account, all payroll expenses for that employee will be linked to the same account – the one you identify in this field. If you want to use different accounts for different wage expenses, you must use the linked accounts.

Double-click the **% field beside Vacation Rate**.

Type 6

For **Schwinn** and **Gearie**, click Retain Vacation to remove the ✓.

Employee wages may all be linked to their individual and different linked expense accounts or to one single account. Wage expenses for all VeloCity employees are linked to the default accounts shown on page 661.

Entering Default Payroll Deduction Amounts

NOTES
Refer to page 334 to review entering employee deductions.

Click the **Deductions tab** to open the screen for payroll deductions.

On this screen, you can indicate which deductions apply to the employee, the amount normally deducted and the historical amount — the amount deducted to date this year. All deductions are selected in the Use column. These are the deductions you entered previously (page 656).

By entering deduction amounts here, they will be included automatically on the Payroll Journal input forms. Otherwise, you must enter them manually in the Journal for each pay period. Since all three employees participate in the RRSP and CSB plans, you can enter the information here so that the deductions are made automatically. You should make permanent changes by editing the employee ledger record.

If you choose to calculate deductions as a percentage of gross pay in the Payroll Settings, the Percentage Per Pay Period fields will be available.

Click **RRSP** in the Deduction column to select the line.

Press (tab). You should enter the amount that is withheld in each pay period.

Type 50 **Press** (tab) to advance the cursor to the Historical Amount field.

Type 450 **Press** (tab) to advance the cursor to the Use column for CSB Plan.

Press (tab). Enter the amount that is to be withheld in each pay period.

Type 50 **Press** (tab) to advance the cursor to the Historical Amount field.

Type 450 **Press** (tab) to update the YTD Amount and advance to the Use column for Garnishee.

Click the **Use column for Garnishee** to remove the ✓. Mercier does not have wages withheld.

For **Schwinn**, enter 200 as the Amount and 800 as the YTD amount for Garnishee.

The remaining deductions are not used by VeloCity. The names were deleted (page 656) so they do not appear on the chart.

> **NOTES**
> For one-time changes, you can edit deduction amounts in the Payroll journals on the Deductions tab or the Deductions Details screen.
> The Use column in the ledger record must be checked for the field to become available in the journal.

Entering WSIB and Other Expenses

Click the **WSIB & Other Expenses tab**.

The user-defined expenses we created in the Additional Payroll Names screen (page 657) and the default WSIB rate (page 659) are entered on this screen.

In Ontario, WSIB (Workplace Safety and Insurance Board) is the name for Workers' Compensation Board, so the tab is labelled WSIB. In other provinces, the tab label will be WCB & Other Expenses or the name selected on the Additional Payroll Names screen.

The default WSIB rate is entered from our setup information, but you can enter a different rate for an individual employee in this field. The rate is correct for Mercier.

For **Gearie**, enter 1.02 as the WSIB rate.

Other user-defined expenses are also added on this screen. VeloCity has only group insurance as a user-defined expense.

Click the **Gp Insurance Amt. Per Period**. Enter the amount that the employer contributes in each pay period.

Type 16 **Press** (tab) to advance to the Historical Amount field.

Type 128

The remaining expense fields are not used by VeloCity.

> **NOTES**
> Refer to page 335 to review entering WSIB (WCB) details.

> **NOTES**
> The name WSIB in Ontario emphasizes safety rather than compensation for accidents. WSIB (or WCB) pays workers when they have been injured on the job and are unable to work.

Entering Employee Entitlements

We entered the default rates and amounts for entitlements as Payroll Settings (page 660), but they can be modified in the ledger records for individual employees.

> **NOTES**
> Refer to page 335 if you need to review entering employee entitlements.

We must also enter the historical information for entitlements. This historical number will include any days carried forward from the previous periods. The number of days accrued cannot be greater than the maximum number of days defined for the entitlement for an employee. The number of Net Days Accrued, the amount unused and available for carrying forward, is updated automatically from the historical information and current payroll journal entries. Entitlements information is included in the chart on page 629.

Click the **Entitlements tab**.

> **NOTES**
> If employees take days before the sufficient number of hours worked have been accrued, the program will warn you. Then you can allow the entry for entitlements or not. This entry is similar to allowing customers to exceed their credit limits.

You cannot enter information directly in the Net Days Accrued fields on the Entitlements tab screen.

Mercier receives vacation pay instead of paid time off so the vacation entitlements details should be removed. The defaults for sick leave and personal days are correct.

Click **8.00** in the **Track Using % Hours Worked field for Vacation**.

Press del to remove the entry.

Press tab to advance to the Maximum Days field.

Press del to remove the entry.

Click the **Historical Days field for Sick Leave**.

Type 12

Press ↓ to advance to the Historical Days field for PersonalDays. The number of days is added to the Net Days Accrued.

Type 4 **Press** tab to enter the amount.

For **Gearie** and **Schwinn**, the default entries for tracking and maximum days are correct, but you must enter the Historical Days for each entitlement.

Entering Direct Deposit Information

> **NOTES**
> Refer to page 336 if you need to review entering direct deposit details.

Click the **Direct Deposit tab**.

All three employees have elected to have their paycheques deposited directly to their bank accounts. On this screen, we need to enter the bank account details. For each employee who has elected the direct deposit option, you must turn on the selection in the Direct Deposit Paycheques For This Employee check box. Then you must add the five-digit **Transit Number**, the three-digit **Bank Number**, the bank **Account Number** and finally the amount that is deposited, or the percentage of the cheque. Direct Deposit information is included in the chart on page 629.

> **NOTES**
> All banks in Canada are assigned a three-digit bank number and each branch has a unique five-digit transit number. Account numbers may range from five to twelve digits.

Click the **Direct Deposit Paycheques For This Employee check box** to add a ✓.

Click the **Branch No. field**.

Type 89008 **Press** tab to advance to the Institution No. field.

Type 102 **Press** tab to advance to the Account No. field.

Type 2998187 **Press** tab **twice** to advance to the Percentage field.

Type 100

> **NOTES**
> The paycheque deposit may be split among multiple bank accounts by entering different percentages for the accounts.
> To delete bank account details, click the Direct Deposit check box, change the deposit status to Inactive and then delete the bank information.

The Memo tab will not be used at this time. You could enter a note with a reminder date to appear in the Daily Business Manager, for example, a reminder to issue vacation paycheques on a specific date or to recover advances.

Entering Additional Information

VeloCity has chosen to enter the name and phone number of the person to be contacted in case of an emergency involving the employee at work. We added the names for these fields in the Payroll Settings (page 657).

Click the **Additional Info tab** to access the fields we added for the ledger when we entered Names.

You can indicate whether you want to display any of the additional information when the employee is selected in a transaction. We do not need to display the contact information in the Payroll Journal. Refer to the chart of page 629 for contact details.

Click the **Emergency Contact field**.

Type Adrian Ingles

Press tab **twice** to move to the Contact Number field.

Type (905) 548-0301

Entering T4 and RL-1 Reporting Amounts

The next information screen allows you to enter the year-to-date EI insurable and pensionable earnings. By adding the historical amounts, the T4 slips prepared for income taxes at the end of the year and the record of employment termination reports will also be correct.

Because there are yearly maximum amounts for CPP and EI contributions, these historical details are also needed. Totals for optional deductions are also retained in the employee record. The amounts you need are in the chart on page 629.

Click the **T4 and RL-1 Reporting tab** to open the next screen we need.

In the **Historical EI Ins. Earnings** field, you should enter the total earned income received to date that is EI insurable. The program will update this total every time you make payroll entries until the maximum salary on which EI is calculated has been reached. At that time, no further EI premiums will be deducted.

Pensionable Earnings are also tracked by the program. This amount determines the total income that is eligible for Canada Pension Plan. CPP deductions will stop automatically when the maximum has been reached. The Pension Adjustment amount is used when the employee has a workplace pension program that will affect the allowable contributions for personal registered pension plans and will be linked with the Canada Pension Plan. Workplace pension income is reduced when the employee also has income from the Canada Pension Plan. Since VeloCity has no company pension plan, the Pension Adjustment amount is zero.

The T4 Employee Code applies to a small number of job types that have special income tax rules.

Click the **Historical Amounts field for EI Ins. Earnings**.

Type 12392

Click the **Historical Amounts field for Pensionable Earnings**.

Type 12520

Correct any employee information **errors** by returning to the field with the error. **Highlight** the **error** and **enter** the **correct information**. **Click each tab** in turn so that you can check all the information.

When all the information is entered correctly, you must save the employee record.

NOTES
Refer to page 337 to review entering employee additional information details.

NOTES
Additional information for other ledgers may also be displayed or hidden in journal transactions.

WARNING!
The Contact Number field is not predefined as a telephone number, so its format will not be corrected automatically by the program.

NOTES
Refer to page 337 if you need to review entering T4 and RL-1 reporting details.

NOTES
The EI Insurable amount is the total of gross wages, including overtime wages and vacation pay, but not benefits.

Pensionable earnings include these same incomes plus benefits.

NOTES
We will not use the remaining tax information fields for VeloCity. VeloCity does not have a company pension plan with regular payroll deductions, so there is no plan registration number. The Pension Adjustment amount is used when an employee contributes to a company pension plan and these payments reduce the amount the employee can contribute to a private registered pension plan. Income from company pension plans may also be reduced when CPP is collected at retirement.

CPP contribution rates are set federally.

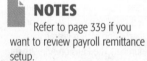

Click **Create Another** [Create Another] to save the record and to open a new blank employee information form.

Click the **Personal tab** so that you can enter address information.

Repeat these procedures to **enter** other employee **records**.

Click **Save And Close** [Save and Close] after entering the last record to save the record and close the Payroll Ledger.

NOTES
You can print these reports from the Reports menu in the Employees window.

Display or **print** the **Employee List** and the **Employee Summary Report**. Compare them with pages 628–630 to check the accuracy of your work.

Close the **Employees window** to return to the Home window.

Entering Job Categories

NOTES
Refer to page 340 if you want to review the setup for job categories.

Now that we have entered all the employees, we can set up job categories and indicate which employees are in each category.

Click the **Settings icon** [Settings]. Then **click Payroll** and **Job Categories**.

On the Job Categories screen, you enter the category names and indicate whether the employees in each category submit time slips and whether they are salespersons.

Categories may be active or inactive. We need a new category called Sales.

Notice that if you do not create categories, the employees in the default selection <None> are salespersons so they can still be selected in the Sales Journal.

Click the **Job Category field below <None>**.

Type Sales **Press** tab to add checkmarks to the next two columns and set the status to Active.

Click **Assign Job Categories** to change the screen.

The Sales category is selected and the screen is updated with employee names. Initially, all are Employees Not In This Job Category.

You can add employee names to the category by choosing an employee and clicking **Select** or by choosing **Select All**. Once employees are in a category (the column on the right), you can remove them. Select an employee and click **Remove** or click **Remove All** to move all names at the same time.

Click **Select All** to place all employees in the Sales category. **Click OK**.

Setting Up Payroll Remittances

NOTES
Refer to page 339 if you want to review payroll remittance setup.

Because we have entered all payroll settings and all suppliers, we can set up the payroll remittances information. This process has three steps: linking the suppliers to the taxes or deductions they receive, entering remittance frequency and entering the pay period end date for the next remittance. Refer to the chart on page 623 and the Accounting Procedures on page 635.

Click **Remittance** under **Payroll**.

All the payroll items that are linked to liability (remittance) accounts are listed: taxes, deductions and user-defined expenses. For each liability, we can select a supplier and enter the payment frequency and due date for the next payment.

Click the **List icon** in the Remittance Supplier column on the line for EI.

Click **Receiver General for Canada** in the list of suppliers that opens.

Click **Select** or **press** *enter* to return to the Remittance Settings screen with the cursor in the Remitting Frequency field for EI.

Choose **Monthly** from the Frequency drop-down list. **Press** *tab*.

Type May 1

Enter the remaining **Remittance Suppliers**, **Frequencies** and dates for the **End Of Next Remitting Period**. Refer to the chart on page 623.

For **EHT** and **WSIB**, select the **Quarterly Remitting Frequency**.

Assigning Sales Tax Codes

Instead of entering tax codes in the individual ledger records, we can assign them in groups with the Assign Tax Codes feature. You can use this feature to enter initial tax code settings, as we do here, or to update tax codes at any time.

Click **Company**, **Sales Taxes** and **Tax Codes** to open the Settings:

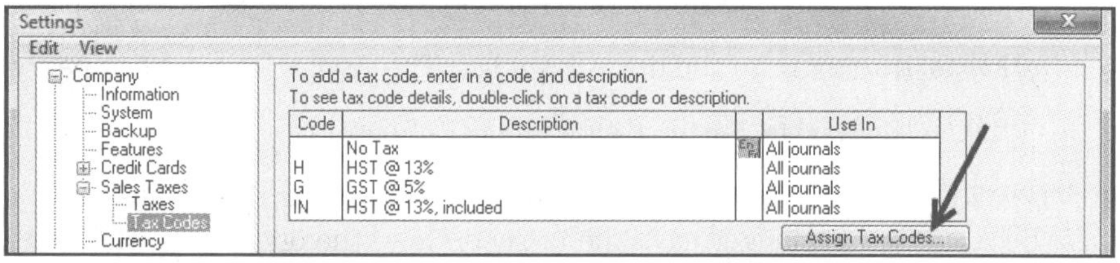

Click the **Assign Tax Codes** button below the list of codes:

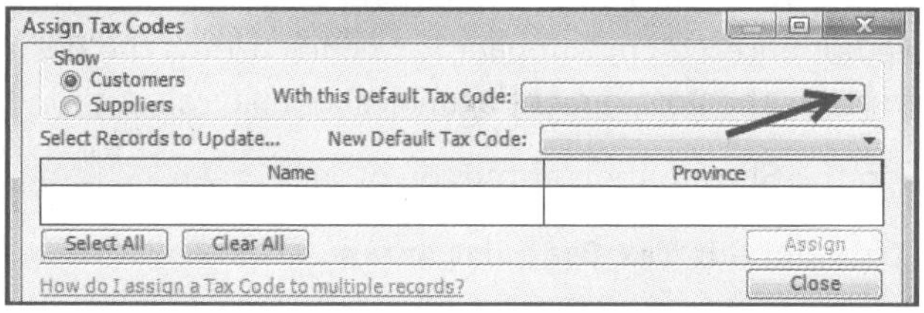

You can assign codes for suppliers and for customers. Customers are selected initially. None are listed because no tax code is selected. All customers were assigned the tax code H as part of the setup for the Receivables Ledger. As a result, showing all customers With This Default Tax Code will include all customers.

Choose **H - HST @ 13%** from the With This Default Tax Code drop-down list:

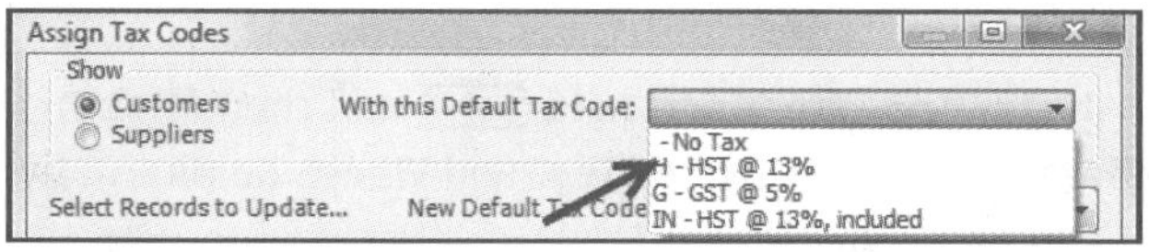

This will include all customers in the selection list:

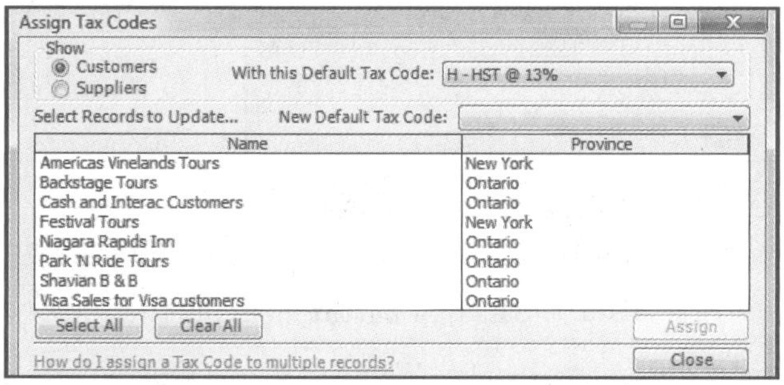

The next step is to select the customers that require a different tax code.

NOTES

All payroll remittances are made monthly except those for EHT to the Minister of Finance and WSIB to the Workplace Safety and Insurance Board. These two remittances are made quarterly.

The end of the next remitting period for all suppliers is May 1.

NOTES

If you already entered No Tax for the USD customers, they will not appear on this list.

You can select one customer by clicking the name, all customers by clicking Select All or more than one customer. We need to select the two USD customers.

Click **Americas Vinelands Tours**.

Press and **hold** ctrl and then **click** **Festival Tours**. Both names are now highlighted and we are ready to choose a new default code for them.

Click the **New Default Tax Code list arrow** as shown:

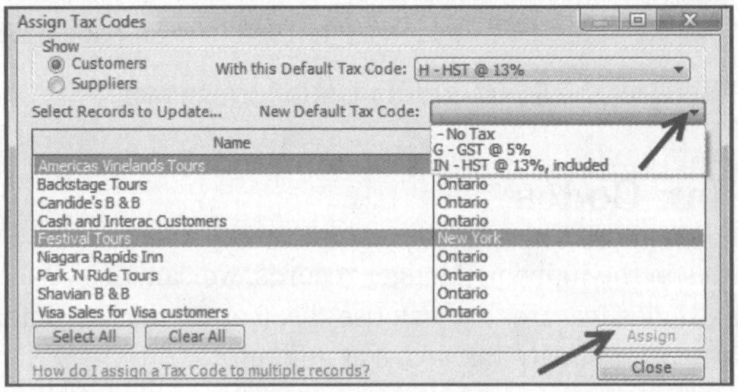

Our options are to change from code H to one of the codes not already applied. We can choose from No Tax, G and IN. USD customers do not pay taxes on exported goods.

Choose **No Tax** from the drop-down list. The Assign button becomes available.

Click the **Assign button** below the list of names.

This will change the code for these two customers. Their names are removed from the list because they no longer have the tax code H — the one we are showing.

The remaining customers stay on the list so you can assign other tax codes if necessary. Tax code H is correct for the other customers, so we can continue by applying supplier tax codes. We have not entered any supplier tax codes yet, so the default entry will be No Tax. This is correct for the government agencies and payroll authorities.

WARNING!
You must click the Assign button before proceeding to apply the changes.

NOTES
If you already entered tax codes for the suppliers, your list of suppliers at this stage will be different.

Click **Suppliers** in the Show option at the top of the screen.

Click the **With This Default Tax Code list arrow**.

Select **No Tax** from this list to display all our suppliers:

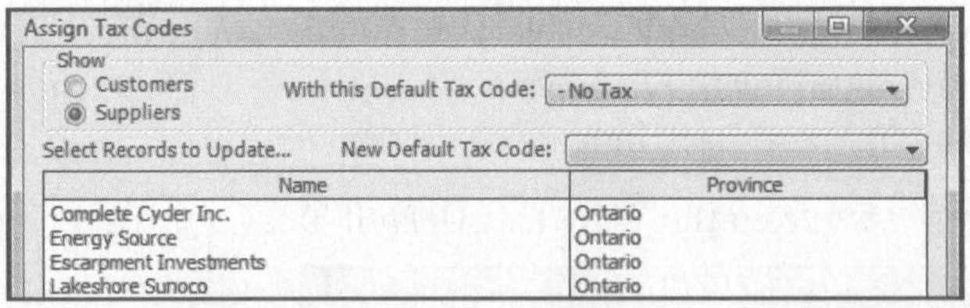

Click **Complete Cycler Inc.** **Press** and **hold** ctrl and then **click** **Energy Source**, **Niagara Bell**, **Pro Cycles Inc.** and **Wheel Deals**. All five names should remain highlighted (selected).

Click the **New Default Tax Code list arrow**:

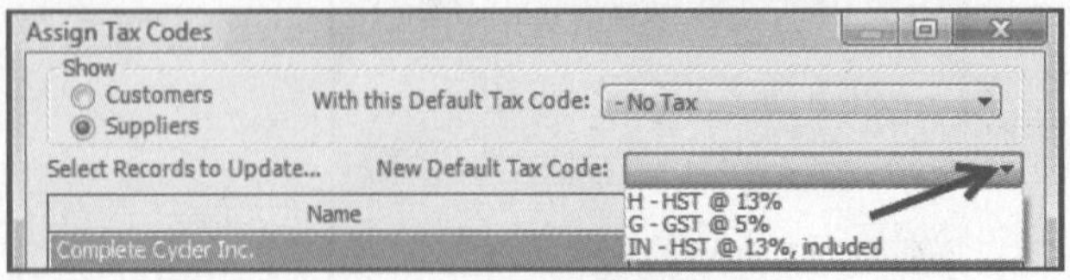

We are changing from the code No Tax, so this is not on the drop-down list.

Click **H - HST @ 13%**. **Click** the **Assign button** to apply the code.

The five names are removed from the display. We need to make one more change.

Click **Lakeshore Sunoco**, which requires the IN tax code.

Click the **New Default Tax Code list arrow**.

Click **IN - HST @ 13%, included**. **Click** **Assign** to apply the code and remove the supplier's name from the display.

The remaining five suppliers are government agencies and payroll authorities for which the default No Tax code is correct.

Click **Close** to save all the changes and return to the Tax Codes Settings.

Click **OK** to save all the new settings and return to the Home window.

Preparing the Inventory Ledger

Use the VeloCity Inventory Information and chart on pages 630–631 to record details about the inventory items on hand.

Entering Inventory Records

The following keystrokes will enter the information for VeloCity's first inventory item, Bicycle Pump: standing model.

Click **Inventory & Services** in the Modules pane list.

Click the **Inventory & Services icon**. Again, with no inventory items on file, the icon window is empty.

Click the **Create button** or **choose** the **File menu** and **click** **Create**:

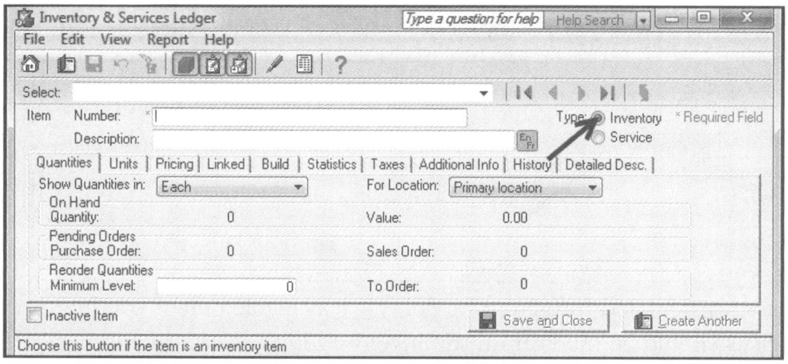

The cursor is in the Item Number field. Use this field for the code or number for the first item. When you sort inventory by description, the two item fields shown here will be reversed — the Description field will appear first. Item Number is a required field.

Type `AC010` **Press** *tab* to advance to the Item Description field, the field for the name of the inventory item.

Type `Bicycle Pump: standing model`

The Type is set correctly for this item as Inventory rather than Service.

The Show Quantities In field allows you to select the units displayed in the ledger. If you have entered different units for stocking, selling and buying, these will be available from the drop-down list. The Quantity On Hand and Value fields are updated by the program as are the Purchase Orders and Sales Orders Pending.

Click the **Minimum Level field**. Here you should enter the minimum stock level or re-order point for this inventory item.

Type 5

PRO VERSION

There isn't a Build tab in the Pro version, and only two show icons will be included in the tool bar. The Show Activities tool applies only to Premium features, and the Refresh tool is used with the multi-user option in Premium.

NOTES

If you hide the Inventory icon window (Setup menu, User Preferences, View), you will see this Inventory Ledger immediately when you click the Inventory & Services icon.

NOTES

The Item Description is not a required field.

Click the **Units tab** to see the next information screen:

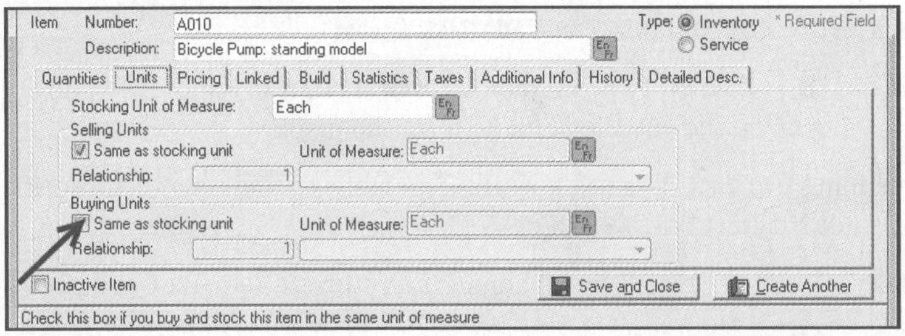

You can enter different units for items when the units for buying, stocking and selling differ. VeloCity uses the same units for stocking and selling but some buying units are different. For example, if items are purchased in dozens and stocked individually, the relationship is 12 to 1. The Stocking Unit must be changed. The bicycle pumps are purchased in boxes of 4 pumps and stocked and sold individually (unit).

Double-click the default entry **Each** for the Stocking Unit Of Measure.

Type Unit

Click **Same As Stocking Unit** in the **Buying Units section** to remove the ✓ and open the relationship fields. Here you should indicate how many stocking units are in each buying unit.

Press *tab* to advance to the Unit Of Measure field.

Type Box **Press** *tab* **twice** to advance to the Relationship field.

Type 4 **Press** *tab*. Check that the entry is 4 Unit Per Box. If it is not, click the drop-down list and choose this relationship.

Click the **Pricing tab** to open the next group of inventory record fields:

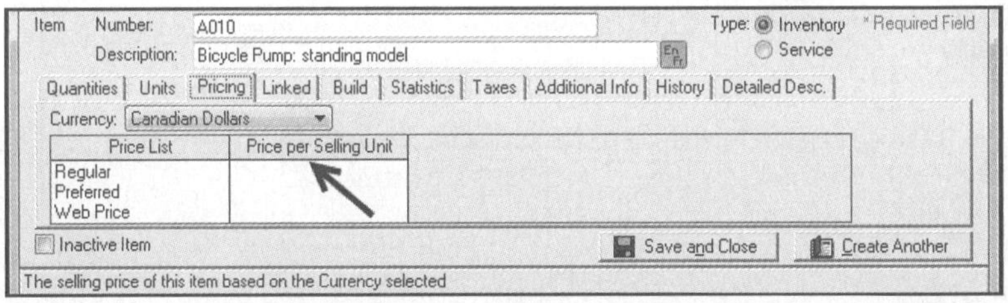

The Currency field and foreign price fields are available only if you indicated that inventory prices should be taken from the Inventory Ledger record and not calculated using the exchange rate. The pricing option appears on the Inventory Settings screen only after you enter foreign currency information. Therefore, you must add and save currency information first. Taking prices from the ledger record is the default setting.

On the Pricing tab screen, you can enter regular, preferred and Web prices in the currencies that you have set up. If you created additional price lists, their names will also appear on this screen. The home currency (Canadian Dollars) is selected first.

Click the **Regular Price Per Selling Unit field**. Here you should enter the selling price for this inventory item.

Type 50 **Press** *tab* to advance to the Preferred Selling Price field.

The regular price is also entered as the default Preferred and Web Price. We do not have Web sales so we can accept the default entry for Web prices. Preferred selling prices are shown in brackets in the Inventory Information chart on page 630.

Type 45 to replace the default entry.

Choose **United States Dollars** from the Currency list to open USD price fields:

WARNING!
Enter inventory details very carefully. You cannot remove an inventory record or change the Type if there is a quantity on hand. You must edit the History fields to reduce the quantity and value to zero. Then remove the item and re-enter all the details correctly.

Changing the Type requires an additional step. Close the ledger to save the changes in the history (with zero quantity). When you open the ledger again, you may edit the Type.

WARNING!
You must enter the unit relationship information before entering the history for inventory so that purchase prices and average costs will be calculated correctly.

NOTES
By working from the Inventory Ledger Settings, Price Lists screen, you can create new price lists and update all prices from one screen. In Chapter 18, we update inventory prices using this approach.

NOTES
The Inventory Ledger Settings screen is shown on page 662. You cannot change these settings while the Inventory Ledger is open.

PRO VERSION
You cannot create additional price lists or update them globally in the Pro version.

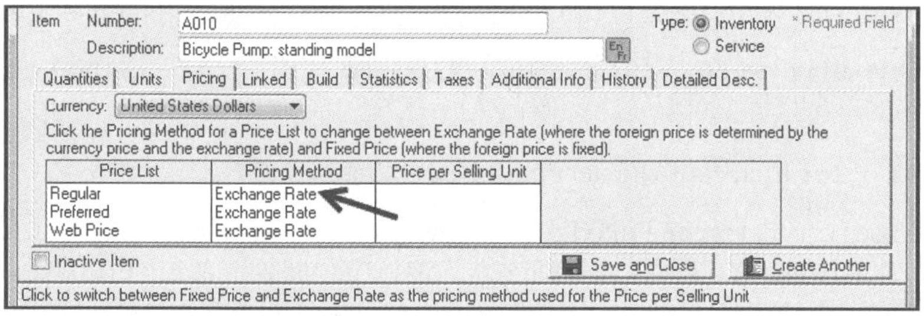

The pricing method is entered separately for each price. You can choose either Exchange Rate or Fixed Price for Regular, Preferred and Web prices.

Click **Exchange Rate** beside Regular to change the entry to Fixed Price.

Press *tab* to advance to the Regular Price Per Selling Unit field.

Type 50 **Press** *tab* to advance to the Pricing Method field.

Click **Exchange Rate** to change the entry to Fixed Price.

Press *tab* to advance to the Preferred Price Per Selling Unit field.

Type 45 **Press** *tab*.

Click the **Linked tab** to open the linked accounts screen for the item:

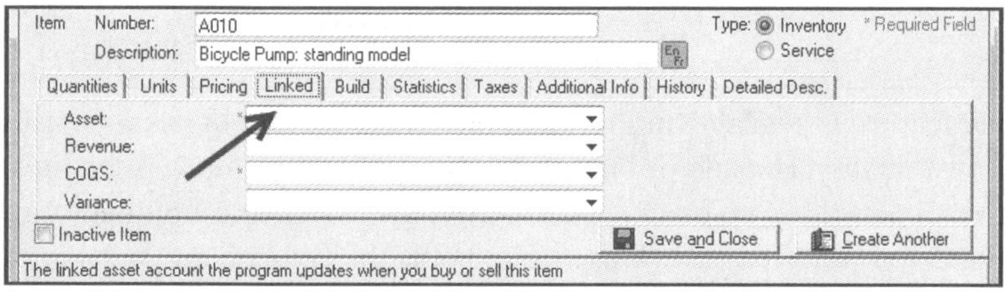

Click the **Asset field list arrow**.

Here you must enter the **asset** account associated with the sale or purchase of this inventory item. The Inventory chart on page 630 shows that all accessories use account *1520*. All bicycles use *1540* and the books use *1560* as the asset account. All available asset accounts are in the displayed list. Asset account is a required field.

Enter the account by clicking the list arrow and choosing from the drop-down account list, or

Type 1520 **Press** *tab*.

The program asks you to confirm the account class change for account 1520:

Click **Yes** to accept the change.

The cursor advances to the **Revenue** field. Here you must enter the revenue account that will be credited with the sale of this inventory item.

Again, you can display the list of revenue accounts by clicking the list arrow. Or,

Type 4020 **Press** *tab*.

The cursor advances to the **COGS** field. Here you must enter the expense account to be debited with the sale of this inventory item, normally the *Cost of Goods Sold* account. VeloCity keeps track of each inventory category separately and has different expense accounts for each category. The appropriate expense account is updated automatically when an inventory item is sold. The COGS account is another required field.

NOTES

The record option to change the way foreign prices are calculated is available only when you selected Foreign Prices Are Taken From The Foreign Price Listed In The Inventory And Services Record as your Inventory Setting (page 662).

NOTES

Revenue and Variance accounts are not required fields for inventory items. Entering them in the ledger will add them automatically in the journal when the item is sold.

NOTES

If you add a new account at this stage, you can include an Opening Balance using the Add An Account wizard. Because the history is not finished, the Opening Balance field is added to the wizard.

NOTES

If you did not change the account class for expense accounts, you will not see the message about account class changes for 5050 and 5070. However, if all expense accounts are designated as Cost of Goods Sold accounts, you cannot produce an accurate Gross Margin Income Statement.

Click the list arrow beside the field to display the available expense accounts.

Double-click **5050** or **type** 5050 **Press** *tab* to advance to the Variance field.

Click **Yes** to accept the account class change.

Sage 50 uses the **Variance** linked account when you restock oversold items. If there is a difference between the historical average cost of goods remaining in stock and the actual cost when the new merchandise is received, the price difference is charged to the variance expense account at the time of the purchase. If you have not indicated a variance account, the program will ask you to identify one when you are entering the purchase that has a variance.

Type 5080 or **click** the **list arrow** and **choose** the **account**.

Click the **Build tab**.

Click **Yes** to accept the account class change and access the Build screen:

PRO VERSION

The Build tab screen is not included in the Pro version. Click the Statistics tab as the next step.

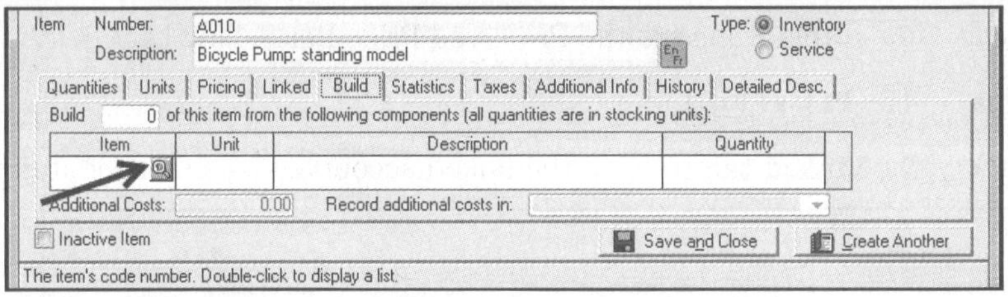

NOTES

Building an item from a bill of materials is covered in Chapter 18.

The Build feature is available in Premium but not in the Pro version. On this screen you define how this item is made or built from other inventory items. Then, in the journal, you can build the item by choosing it from the available list and entering the number of units you want to build. This screen holds the components portion of the Item Assembly Journal.

Click the **Statistics tab** to open the next tab information screen:

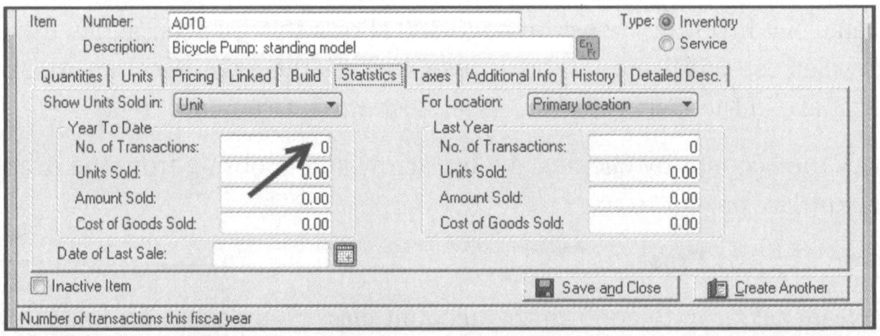

On this screen, you can enter historical information about the sale of the product. It would then be added to the inventory tracking information for reports.

The first activity field, the Date Of Last Sale, refers to the last date on which the item was sold. The next two sections contain information for the Year To Date and the previous year. Since VeloCity has not kept this information, you can skip these fields. Refer to page 373 in the Flabuless Fitness application (Chapter 10) for a more detailed description of these historical Statistics fields.

Click the **Taxes tab** to input the sales taxes relating to the inventory item:

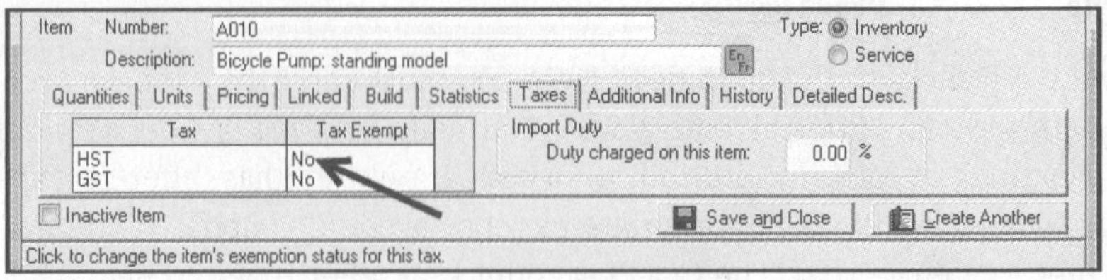

You can indicate whether the item is taxable for all the taxes you set up, GST and HST in this case. HST is charged on sales of all inventory items except for books, so the default entry No for **Tax Exempt** is correct for bicycle pumps.

The exemption settings in the ledger record do not control the tax code entered in the Sales Journal. They prevent a tax from being applied.

For **Books: Complete Bicycle Guide** and **Books: Endless Trails**, items BK010 and BK020, **click No** beside **HST** for Tax Exempt to change the entry to Yes. This will leave the Tax code field blank in the journal so you can add code G.

Duty is also entered on this screen. You must activate the duty tracking option (page 651) before the duty rate field becomes available. Since no duty is charged on the imported inventory, you can leave the duty rate at 0%.

We have not added fields to the ledger record as we did for Payroll so we can skip the **Additional Info** screen.

The next step is to add the opening historical balances for the inventory items.

Click the **History tab**:

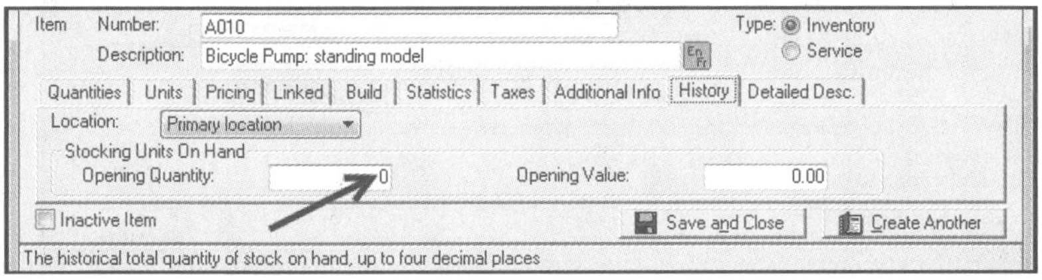

This screen has information about the starting quantities for the item at the time of conversion to Sage 50. The opening quantities and values are added to the quantity on hand and value on the Quantities tab screen. History is entered in stocking unit quantities (the same as selling units for VeloCity).

Click the **Opening Quantity field** to enter the opening level of inventory — the actual number of items available for sale.

Type 10 **Press** *tab*.

The cursor advances to the **Opening Value** field, where you should enter the actual total cost of the inventory on hand.

Type 300 **Click** the **Detailed Desc. tab**:

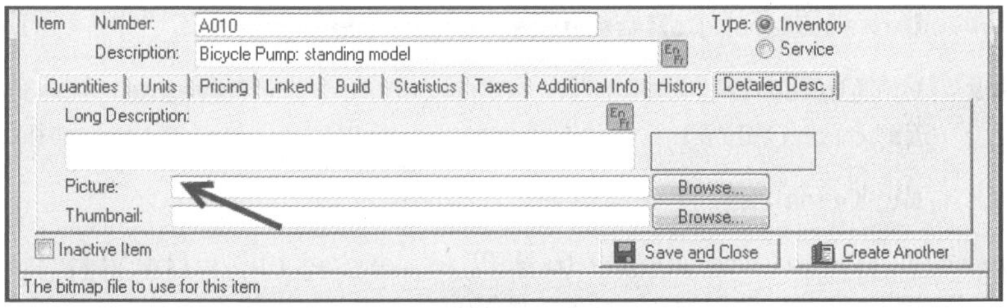

The final tab screen allows you to enter further descriptive information. This optional information provides a detailed description of the inventory item (about 500 characters) as well as a picture in image file format.

Type the detailed item description in the Long Description text box.

Click **Browse** beside Picture. **Click Computer**. **Double-click C:**, **SageData13**, **Logos** and **pump.bmp** or **pump** to add the file name and picture.

Correct any **errors** by returning to the field with the mistake. **Highlight** the **error** and **enter** the **correct information**. **Click** the different **tabs** to see all the information that you entered.

NOTES

To open the duty fields in the Purchases Journal, you must activate tracking of duty information and indicate in the supplier record that duty is charged on purchases from the supplier. Rates entered in the Inventory Ledger records will appear automatically in the Purchases Journal for those items. Duty rates can also be entered in the journal if you have not entered them in the ledger records.

NOTES

When you set up multiple locations, you can enter the quantity and value for items at each location. The Primary location is the default. In Chapter 18, we add a second location for VeloCity's second store, Ryder's Routes.

WARNING!

Enter inventory history details carefully. To change historical quantities, you must delete the history entries, save the item, then remove the item and re-enter it. Otherwise the cost information in journal entries will be incorrect.

The total opening value amounts for all items in an asset group must match the General Ledger asset account balance before you can finish entering the history.

NOTES

A picture file for the Bicycle Pump: standing model has been added to the SageData13\Logos folder with your other data files. We have not provided picture files for the remaining inventory items.

NOTES

Other picture file formats may be used.

When all the information is entered correctly, you must save your inventory record.

Click **Create Another** [Create Another] to save the record and advance to a new input screen.

Click the **Quantities tab** to prepare for entering the next item.

Repeat these procedures to **enter other** inventory **records** on page 630.

Entering Inventory Services

The final items on the inventory chart (page 631) are services that VeloCity provides. Entering services is similar to entering inventory, but there are fewer details.

You should have a blank Inventory & Services Ledger window open at the Quantities tab screen.

Click **Service** in the upper-right section of the screen to change the Type:

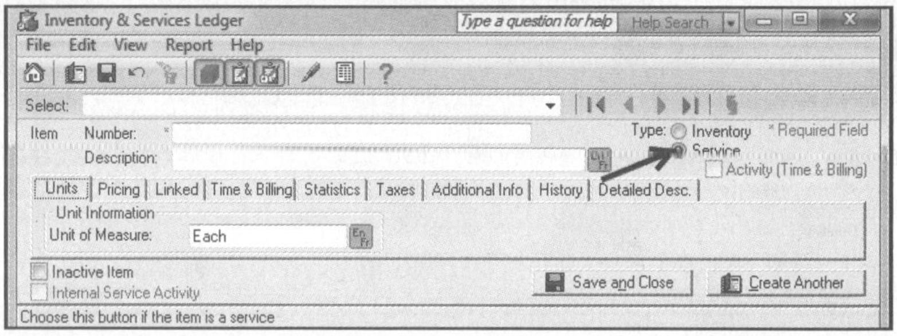

> **PRO VERSION**
> The Time & Billing tab screen is used to set up Time & Billing, a feature that is not available in the Pro version. The Activity setting and Internal Service Activity also apply to the Time & Billing feature, so they do not appear on the Pro version screen.

There are fewer tabs and fields for services because some item details do not apply. The Unit Of Measure and Selling Price have the same meaning for services as they do for inventory items. Because service items are not kept in stock or purchased, only the selling unit is applicable, there is no minimum quantity and the History tab and fields are removed. Only expense and revenue accounts are linked for services. The other two linked account fields do not apply and are removed for services. Remember to use *Revenue from Services* and *Cost of Services* as the linked accounts for inventory services.

Item Number is the only required field for service items.

Enter the **Item Number** and **Description** and the **Unit Of Measure**.

Click the **Pricing tab** and add **Regular** and **Preferred prices** in Canadian dollars. Select Canadian Dollars as the currency if necessary.

Select **United States Dollars** and **enter** the **fixed prices** for this currency.

Click the **Linked tab**. **Enter** the linked accounts for **Revenue (4040)** and **Expense (5075)**. Accept the account class change if prompted.

Click the **Taxes tab**.

> **NOTES**
> Enter USD prices because United States customers who use these services in Canada will pay taxes.

> **NOTES**
> Notice that linked accounts for services are not required. However, adding them to the ledger record will have them entered into the journal automatically.

Most services in Ontario are subject to HST. All services offered by VeloCity are not exempt from HST, so the default is correct at No.

Click **Create Another** [Create Another].

Click the **Units tab**. **Repeat** these procedures to **enter other service records**.

Click **Save And Close** [Save and Close] after entering the last service record.

Close the **Inventory & Services window** to return to the Home window.

Display or **print** the **Inventory List**, **Summary**, **Quantity** and **Price Lists** reports. Compare them with the information on pages 630–631 to check them for accuracy.

Finishing the History

The last stage in setting up the accounting system involves finishing the history for each ledger. Before proceeding, you should check the data integrity (Home window, Maintenance menu) to see whether there are any out-of-balance ledgers that will prevent you from proceeding. Correct these errors and then make a backup copy of the files.

You may also want to create a complete working copy of the not-finished files.

Making a Backup of the Company Files

Choose the **File menu** and **click Backup**, **click** the **Backup tool** or **click Backup** in the **Data Management icon shortcuts list** (Company module window) to start the Backup wizard.

Click **Browse** and **choose** the **data folder you want** for the not-finished backup of the data file.

Double-click the **File name field** in the Backup wizard screen.

Type `nf-velo`

Click **OK** to create a backup copy of all the files for VeloCity.

The "NF" designates files as not finished to distinguish them from the ones you will work with to enter journal transactions. You will return to your working copy of the file so you can finish the history.

Changing the History Status of Ledgers to Finished

Refer to page 95 and page 250, respectively, for assistance with finishing the history and correcting history errors.

Choose the **History menu** and **click Finish Entering History**.

If your amounts, account types and linked accounts are correct, you will see the warning about this step not being reversible and advising you to back up the file first.

Click **Proceed** when there are no errors and you have backed up your files.

If you have made errors, you will not see the warning message. Instead you will see a list of errors.

Click **Print** so that you can refer to the list for making corrections.

Click **OK** to return to the Home window. **Make** the **corrections**, and then **try again**.

Click **Proceed**.

The VeloCity files are now ready for you to enter transactions. The ledger icons in all module windows now appear without the open history icons. All the ledgers are ready for transactions.

Congratulations on reaching this stage! This is a good time to take a break.

Finish your **session**. This will give you an opportunity to read the next section and the instructions before starting the source document transactions.

WARNING!

Before you finish entering the history, make a backup copy of the VeloCity company files. This is necessary if you find later that you need to correct some of the historical information. Remember, once you finish entering the history, you cannot add information for any period before the earliest transaction date.

NOTES

To make a new folder, type NF-Velo in the path for the location to replace Backup.

You can also click Make New Folder in the Browse window and type NF-Velo when the New Folder name appears. Click OK to return to the Backup wizard.

To make a complete working copy backup, choose Save A Copy from the File menu to start the save procedure. Your current working copy will remain open when you have finished.

NOTES

If modules are hidden and then later unhidden, they will appear with the open history quill pen icon, as we saw when we added the Payroll Ledger for Lime Light Laundry in Chapter 9. When you later view these modules and choose the History menu, open or unfinished modules will be listed individually so you can set them as finished one at a time.

Project and Time & Billing do not have not-finished (open history) symbols.

> **WARNING!**
> Before adding passwords for practice, make a backup of your data file without passwords. You can restore this file to continue working if you forget your password or lock yourself out of the data file.
> We strongly advise you not to set passwords for your working copy data files used for tutorial purposes.

> **NOTES**
> Passwords have not been added to any data files for this text.

> **NOTES**
> You must work in single-user mode to set up passwords and users.

Entering Users and Security Passwords

Sage 50 allows you to set up passwords for different users. The password for the system administrator (sysadmin) controls access to the system or program. Passwords for other users control viewing and editing privileges for different ledgers, journals and reports. For example, if different employees work with different accounting records, they should have different passwords.

Restricting access by setting passwords is different from hiding ledgers using the Setup menu, User Preferences, View screen. Since the View preferences are unrestricted user settings, these hidden ledgers can be restored at any time. Ledgers hidden by restricted access passwords can be accessed and restored only by opening the files with the system administrator (sysadmin) password and changing access rights.

Users and passwords are entered from the Setup menu in the Home window.

Choose the **Setup menu** and **click Set Up Users** to display the control window:

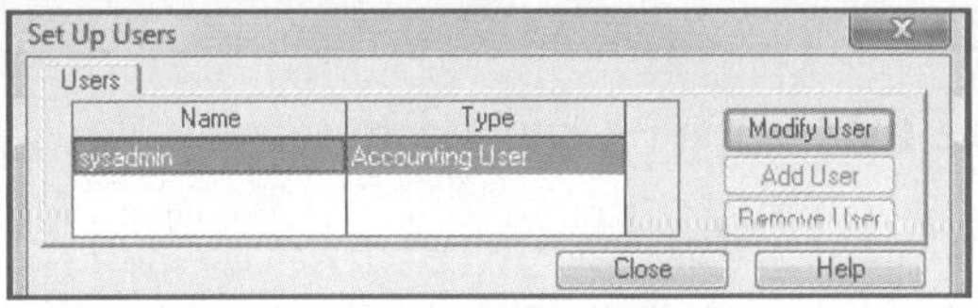

This Set Up Users window lists all users currently set up in the data files. Initially, the only user is sysadmin (system administrator). The highest level of access comes with the sysadmin password that allows the user to enter, use or modify any part of the data files, including creating users and setting passwords. The sysadmin password must be set before any other passwords can be set, so this user is selected initially. You can set up passwords for additional users to allow them access to different parts of the program. Begin by adding a password for sysadmin.

> **WARNING!**
> If you have forgotten your password, you will be unable to open the files. For this reason, you should
> - keep the code in a safe place.
> - choose a code that is unique to you but easy for you to remember.
> - keep a backup copy of the unprotected files in a safe place.

> **PRO VERSION**
> Time & Billing access rights are not shown in the Pro version.

Click **Modify User** to open the Modify User password entry screen:

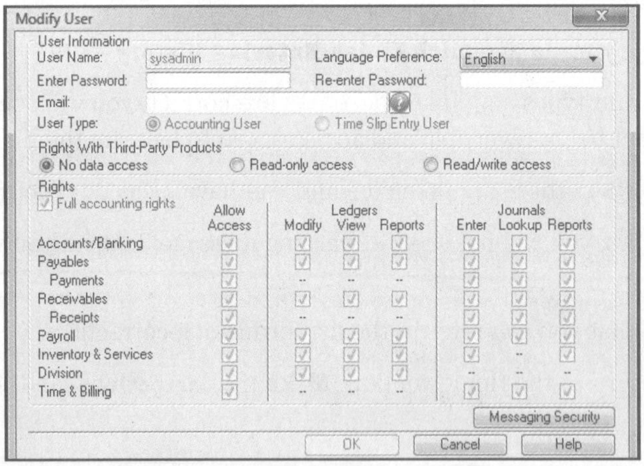

You cannot modify access privileges for the sysadmin because someone (the system administrator) must have full access to the data. All the Accounting Rights options are dimmed. The cursor is in the Enter Password field.

If you want **e-mail messages** from Sage also to go to an address other than the primary one connected with your Sage account, enter it in the E-mail field.

> **NOTES**
> Passwords must be different for each person in order to serve their purpose of restricting access.

You can use up to seven letters and/or numbers as the code. Passwords are case-sensitive. That is, ABC is different from Abc. If you enter a password with an upper-case (capital) letter, you must use an upper-case letter each time.

Type the **word** or **code** that you want as your password. For practice, choose a simple password such as your first name or your initials.

Press tab to advance to the next field, Re-enter Password.

For security reasons, the password is never revealed on the screen — you will see an asterisk (*) or some other symbol for each letter or number that you type. As an additional precaution, Sage 50 requires you to enter the code twice in exactly the same way.

Type the **password** or **code** again.

If the two entries do not match, Sage 50 generates an error message.

Click OK and try re-entering the code again. If you still do not have a match, go back to the Enter Password field and type in the code. You may have mistyped the first entry. Then re-enter the password in the Re-enter Password field.

The **Messaging Security** button opens a screen with different types of Sage communications:

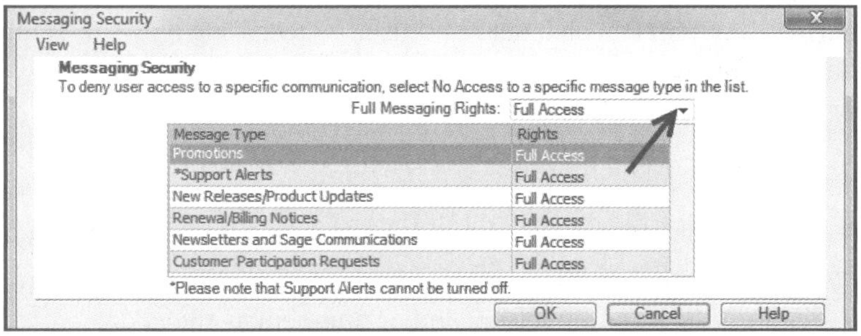

The drop-down list beside Full Messaging Rights has two options for each user: full access or no access. Support messages are always displayed. Click OK to return to the Add User screen. By default, the system administrator has full access to all types of messages.

Access to **third-party products** can also be limited — the read/write access option provides the fullest level of access. It is not selected by default.

Click **OK**. You will return to the Modify User screen. **Click OK** again to return to the Set Up Users screen.

If you have allowed read and write access to third-party products, and the password you entered is weak, the program will recommend selecting a more secure password.

For practice, you can click No to continue with the easy password.

The remaining user setup option buttons are now available. If you return to the Home window, there will be one password for the data files, the one for sysadmin.

You can now enter additional users.

Click **Add User** to open the new user setup screen:

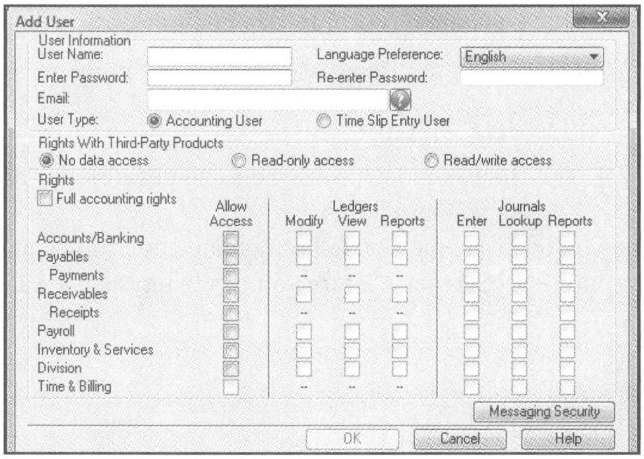

NOTES
Additional information about users and passwords is provided in Appendix G on the Student DVD.

NOTES
After choosing No Access for Full Messaging Rights, you can choose access rights for each message separately.

NOTES
Access to third-party products is required to link the accounting data with the Microsoft Office Word and Excel documents (refer to Appendix L on the Student DVD).

Weak passwords are ones that may be easy to guess. Strong passwords combine upper- and lower-case letters and numbers without using real words or simple number patterns.

PRO VERSION
The option to set up an Accounting Entry User or a Time Slip Entry User is not available in the Pro version. The Time & Billing module is also not listed because this is a Premium feature.

If you see a message about updating to multi-user Premium or Quantum versions, click Do Not Show This Message Again (unless you want to upgrade).

Adding Other Users

After you have added a password for the system administrator (sysadmin), you can set up additional users with unique passwords.

Each user can be allowed access to all parts of the program (full accounting rights) or access to only some of the ledgers and journals. Access to ledgers, journals and reports can be controlled separately. The Add User window should be open.

To give a user full access, click Full Accounting Rights below the Password section. For each ledger and journal, you can allow any of the following access levels: no access (no ✓ for Allow Access); modifying (editing) rights that include viewing; viewing rights only; or access to ledger reports. For journals, you can allow no access, enter rights (enter and look up transactions), lookup only or access to journal reports. Rights for each ledger and journal can be controlled separately, and each user may have different access rights. Each user must have a unique name and password.

Initially, the Add User options are shown for an Accounting User for access to the ledgers and journals, but you can also restrict a user to accessing only the Time Slips. Refer to Appendix G for setting up time slip users.

The cursor should be in the User Name field.

Type the **name** of the first user.

Press *tab* **twice** to advance to the Enter Password screen.

Type the **word** or **code** that you want as your restricted usage password. You can use up to seven letters and/or numbers as the code.

Press *tab* to advance to the next field, Re-enter Password.

Type the **password** or **code** again.

Again, for security purposes, to be sure you entered the password that you intended, you must enter the same code twice. When the two entries match, you can define access rights for the first user.

To allow access, click the check boxes beside the ledger name in the appropriate columns. For example, to allow viewing access only for the General Ledger, click the Allow Access check box beside Accounts/Banking. The program adds ✓s for all columns beside Accounts/Banking. Click Modify and Reports to remove those ✓. To allow no access, leave the Allow Access check box in the first column empty.

Similarly, you can restrict access to third-party information and messages for each user. Passwords do not serve their purpose if the user cannot view reports in Sage 50 but can access and modify those reports in another program.

Click **OK** to save the new user and return to the Set Up Users screen.

After entering all the users, return to the Home window to save all the changes.

Click **Close** to return to the Home window.

Nothing has changed yet. The Home window looks the same because you are using the program as the sysadmin (system administrator).

However, the next time you open the file, the following dialogue box will appear, and you will be required to enter the password before you can open the data file:

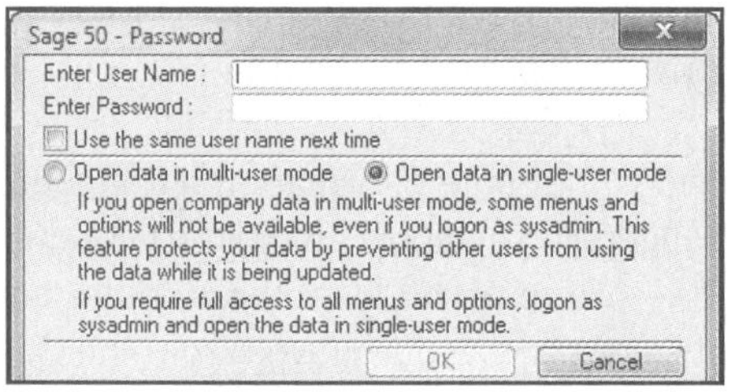

Type the **user name**, either sysadmin or another user name. **Press** *tab*.

Type the **password** or **code** for this user.

Choose the **Single-User** or **Multi-User mode** for accessing the file. **Click OK**.

If you enter an incorrect code, nothing happens — the Password dialogue box remains open. If you enter the sysadmin password, you will have full access to all parts of the program, including the security settings. If you have set passwords, you must enter the program using the sysadmin password in order to change the security settings and passwords. Individual users, other than the sysadmin, can change their own passwords at any time. They cannot access the passwords for other users.

If you enter as a user other than the sysadmin, and do not have full accounting rights, you will see a restricted view of the Home window, like the one on the following page. The Classic view Home window shows restrictions for a user, together with the access rights allocated to that user.

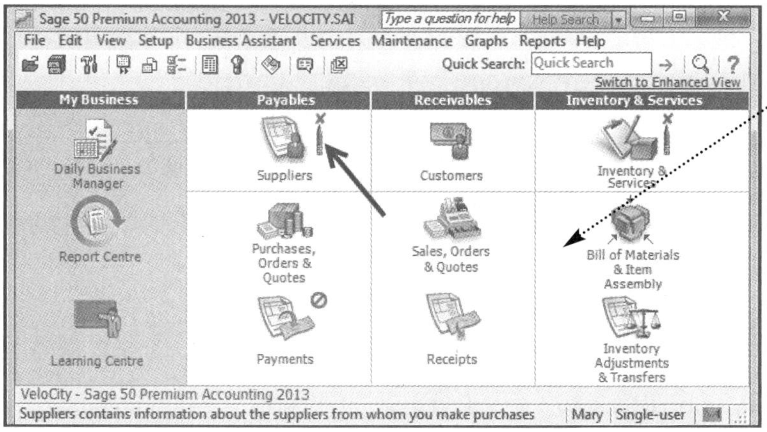

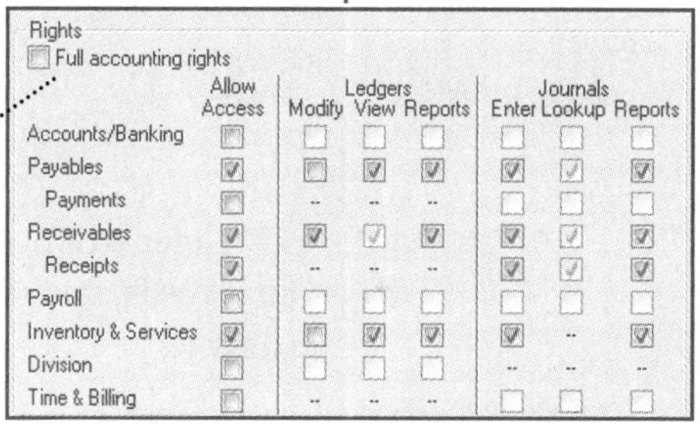

The user above can input normal sales journal entries and inventory entries, accept payments from customers and enter purchases. He/she cannot write cheques to suppliers, pay employees, reconcile accounts, make deposits or make General Journal entries.

The user does not have access to the General Ledger or journals, the Payroll Ledger or journals or to the Division Ledger — their icons are missing (no ✓ appears for these ledgers in the Allow Access settings).

Only the Customers Ledger in this example can be modified. The **No Edit** symbol  beside the Suppliers and Inventory & Services ledger icons means that these ledgers can be viewed but not edited (✓ for View, but not for Modify). If you open these ledgers, all fields will be dimmed.

The **No Entry** symbol  on the Payments Journal indicates no access is permitted (the user cannot write cheques — there is no ✓ for Allow Access). The Receivables (Customers & Sales) and Inventory journals are not restricted — no extra icon appears with them (✓ for Enter, Lookup and Reports).

When access to reports is restricted for any journal or ledger (no ✓ for reports), those report menu options will be dimmed.

PRO VERSION

The Pro version is a single-user program. The Password screen does not have the option to open in single- or multi-user mode. You will need to enter your user name and password (and, if appropriate, the option to use the same user name next time).

STUDENT VERSION

The Student Premium Version is also a single-user program.

CLASSIC VIEW

The Classic view Home window shows all access rights on a single screen.

PRO VERSION

You will not see the Time Slips entry in the Pro version, and the name of the inventory journals will be Item Assembly and Inventory Adjustments.

NOTES

Changing passwords is covered in Appendix G on the Student DVD.

NOTES
Restricted menu options are directly related to the user's access rights.
The same set of access right restrictions is applied as in the previous illustration.

NOTES
Although users can change their own passwords, the sysadmin retains final control. He/she can still reset all passwords and remove users when necessary.

Several main menu options are also restricted. Only the system administrator can access the Set Up Users menu option after passwords are set. All users can change their own passwords.

The Enhanced view shown below provides the same information but in a different way. The Home window icons have not changed (no symbols are added). Modules the user cannot access — Banking and Payroll — are removed from the Modules pane list. The General Journal and Chart of Accounts icons are also removed from the Company window because the user is not permitted to access them. Access to the Payables module is limited, as we can see from the three drop-down shortcuts lists in the illustration. The user can view the supplier records but not change them — only the View shortcut is available. The user's access to the Purchases Journal is unrestricted — all menu options are still available. Access to the Payments Journal is completely denied — the user cannot write cheques and all menu options are dimmed. The Receivables module (not shown) is unchanged because access to it is unrestricted.

We can see these user restrictions in the following illustration of two Enhanced view module windows:

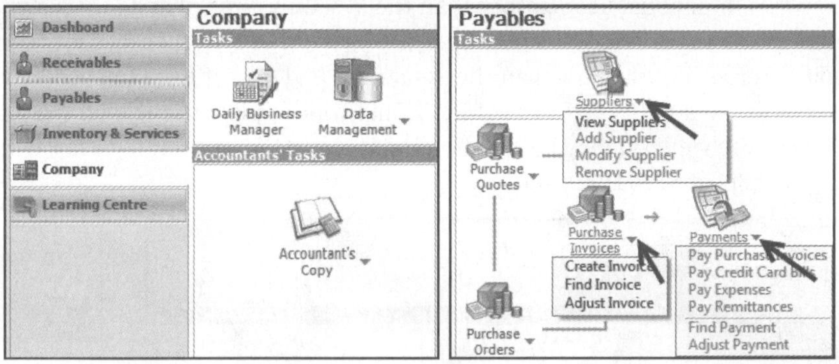

Refer to Appendix G on the Student DVD for information on changing and removing passwords, and using the wizard to create time-slip entry and accounting users and passwords.

Exporting Reports

NOTES
Integration with Microsoft Office software, including Sage 50 Intelligence, is described further in Appendix L on the Student DVD.

Sage 50 allows you to export reports to a specified drive and path. The files created by the program may then be used by spreadsheet or word processing programs. Exporting files will allow you to perform additional calculations and interpret data for reporting purposes. This process of integrating Sage 50 files with other software is an important step in making the accounting process meaningful.

The following keystrokes will export the opening Balance Sheet for VeloCity to a spreadsheet.

NOTES
Depending on your previous export selection, your default format and folder may be different from the ones we show here.
Logos may be entered in the Save In field if you did not change folder selections after adding the picture file.

NOTES
By default your working folder is selected, or the folder you used for the previous exported report.

Display the **Balance Sheet** or the report you want to export.

Click the **Export Report tool** or **choose** the **File menu** and **click Export** to display the following screen:

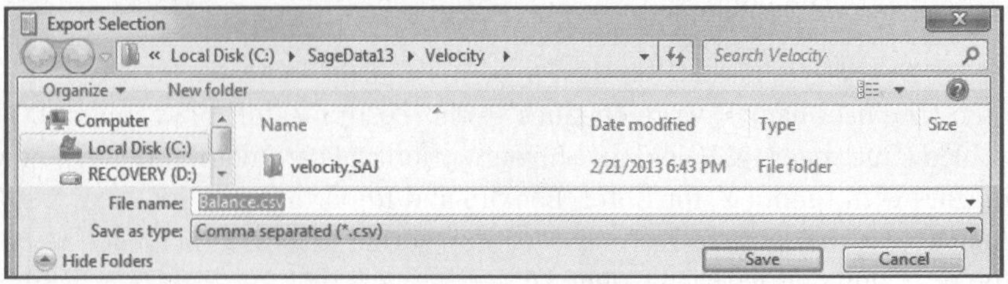

Click the **Save As Type list arrow** to see the types of files you can create:

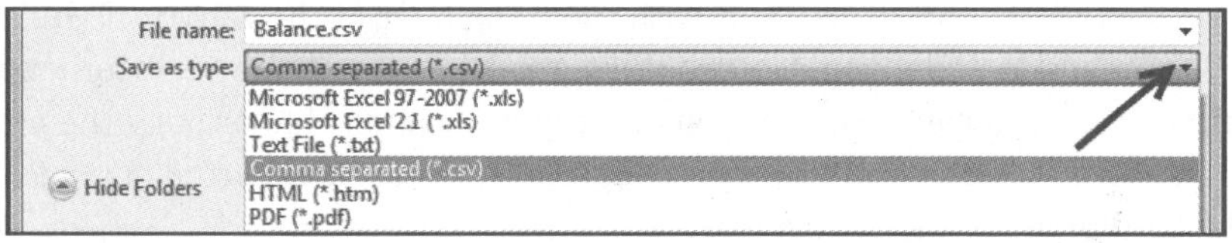

File formats available for export purposes include HTML for Web pages, Text for a word processing format file, Microsoft Excel Versions 97–2007 and 2.1, Comma Separated and PDF.

Click **Microsoft Excel 97-2007** as the type for the Balance Sheet in the Save As Type field. Use the field list arrow to display the file type options if needed.

Choose the **location** for your exported file.

Click the **File Name field list arrow** to access the folder you want.

Accept the default **file name**, or **type** the **name** you want for your file. The program assigns an extension to the file name so that Microsoft Excel will recognize the new file as an Excel file.

Click **Save**. You will return to your displayed report.

To create a text file, click Text File. To generate a file that you can view with Acrobat Reader, but not modify, click PDF.

Any Sage 50 report that you have on display can also be opened directly as a Microsoft Excel spreadsheet. Formulas for totals and so on are retained and you can then use the spreadsheet file immediately.

Display the **Sage 50 report** you want to use in Excel.

Click the **Open In Excel tool** or **choose** the **File menu** and **click** **Open In Microsoft Excel** to see the file name window:

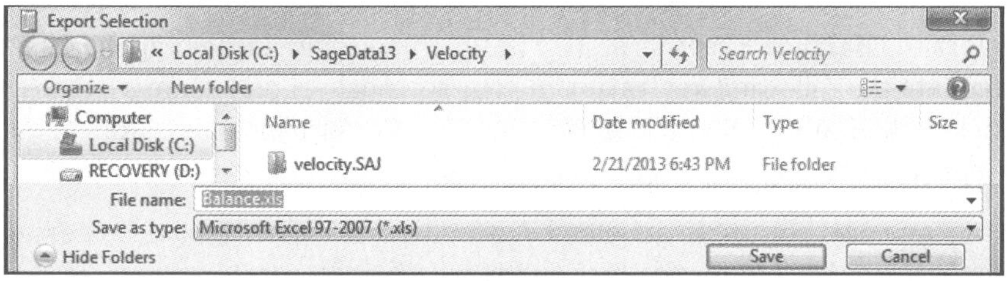

Choose a **location** for your spreadsheet data file.

Click **Save** to open the spreadsheet. Your Sage 50 data file will remain open.

Close the **Excel file** when finished.

You can now work with a report that you have exported.

Using Your Data Files and Reports with Other Software

Finish the session using Sage 50. Start the program you want to use with the exported file. Open the file you exported.

Some spreadsheet programs can open and convert a file that was saved in the format of a different program. For example, Microsoft Excel can open (or save) text files or Comma Separated Files. Simply choose the alternative file type in your Open File (or Save File) window. Click OK. Your exported file should replace the blank document screen.

Once you have exported a financial statement as a text file, you can include it in a written report prepared with any word processing program. You can then use the features of the word processing software to enhance the appearance of the statement

NOTES
The bank statements for Chapter 15, Chapter 16 – Case 8 in Appendix D on the Student DVD – and Chapter 17 – Case 2 in Appendix D on the Student DVD – were created by exporting the General Ledger reports as .CSV files to a spreadsheet, modifying the data and then copying the results to a word processing file.

NOTES
This feature saves the Excel file before opening it, so you can return to it later.

NOTES
Be sure that the selected file type also matches the format of your exported file (e.g., .txt for a text file, or .xls for Excel).
Refer to the built-in help or program manuals if necessary for assistance with the third-party program.

NOTES
Comma Separated (*.csv) format files opened in Excel and resaved as *.xls files provide the best format and view for working with the files in Excel if you need to modify the file or add formulas.

using format styles that are consistent with the remainder of the report. If you have exported a spreadsheet file, you can use the spreadsheet program to perform additional calculations. Then you can save the modified report as a text file or copy the cells you want to be incorporated in a word processing report. We used exported spreadsheets to create the bank statements for this text.

When working with a spreadsheet program, you can use the calculation capabilities of the spreadsheet program to make comparisons between statements from different financial periods. You might also want to use the charting or graphing features to prepare presentation materials.

Exporting reports offers advantages over re-creating the statements — you save the time of retyping, and you ensure greater accuracy by avoiding errors while retyping.

SOURCE DOCUMENT INSTRUCTIONS

Instructions for May

1. **Enter** the **transactions** for May using all the information provided.
2. **Print** the following **reports**:
   a. Journal Entries (All Journals) for May, including foreign amounts, corrections and additional transaction details
   b. Customer Aged Detail Report for all customers for May
   c. General Ledger account reports for
      - Bank: Niagara Trust Chequing
      - Revenue from Sales
      - Sales Returns and Allowances
   d. Supplier Purchases Summary for Wheel Deals, all items, for May
3. **Export** the **Balance Sheet** as at May 31, 2015, to a spreadsheet application. **Calculate** the following **key ratios** in your spreadsheet and compare them with the ratios in the Daily Business Manager Business Performance indicators:
   a. current ratio b. quick ratio
4. **Set up** a **budget** for use in June and July and **enter amounts** based on expenses and revenues for May and for the first quarter.

Instructions for June

1. **Enter** the **transactions** for June using all the information provided.
2. **Print** the following **reports**:
   a. Journal Entries (All Journals) for June, including foreign amounts, corrections and additional transaction details
   b. Supplier Aged Detail Report for all suppliers for June
   c. Employee Summary Report for all employees for the pay period ending June 30, 2015
   d. Inventory Sales Summary Report (observe and report items that have not sold well over the two-month period)
   e. Customer Sales Summary (all customers, items and categories) for June
3. **Export** the **Comparative Balance Sheet** for May 31 and June 30, 2015, to a spreadsheet application to use for three-month comparisons at the end of July.
4. **Compare** June's **performance against** May's budget **forecast**.

Instructions for July

1. **Enter** the **transactions** for July using all the information provided.
2. **Print** the following **reports**:
   a. Journal Entries (All Journals) for July, including foreign amounts, corrections and additional transaction details
   b. Trial Balance, Balance Sheet and Income Statement on July 31
   c. Inventory Statistics Report for Bicycles (All Journals) for July
   d. Bank Transaction Report for all bank accounts from May 1 to July 31
3. **Export** the **Balance Sheet** and **Income Statement** to a spreadsheet application. Combine the Balance Sheet with the comparative one for May and June. **Compare** first- and second-quarter figures, item by item, to assess the performance of VeloCity. You may want to use Multi-period reports for this comparison.
4. **Make** a **backup copy** of your data files. **Advance** the **session date** to August 1, 2015.
5. **Print** the **Trial Balance**, **Balance Sheet** and **Income Statement** for August 1. **Compare** the end of July and the first of August **statements** and note the changes that result from Sage 50 closing the books for the new fiscal period.

PRO VERSION
Print the General Ledger Report for the bank accounts instead of the Bank Transaction Report.

WARNING!
Chapter 16, Case 8, in Appendix D on the Student DVD, has the data you need to complete the bank account reconciliation for VeloCity. You must use your data files for July 31 to complete the reconciliation, so be sure to make a backup copy before you advance the session date to the new fiscal year. (Or use the file provided by your instructor.)

SOURCE DOCUMENTS

SESSION DATE – MAY 15, 2015

1 **Memo #5-1** **Dated May 1, 2015**
Reverse the Accrued Wages adjustment from previous quarter. (Debit Accrued Wages and credit Wages expense account.)

2 **Cash Receipt #812** **Dated May 1, 2015**
From Shavian B & B, cheque #147 for $4 429.60 in payment of account including $90.40 discount for early payment. Reference invoice #2191.

NOTES
Remember that receipts are deposited to Undeposited Cash and Cheques. This should be the default account.

3 **Payment Cheque #101** **Dated May 2, 2015**
To Pro Cycles Inc., $5 960 in payment of account including $80 discount for early payment. Reference invoice #PC-618.

4 **Purchase Order #38** **Dated May 2, 2015**
Shipping date May 25, 2015
From Wheel Deals

25	CY020	Bicycle: Commuter Alum frame CX90	$13 000.00 USD
4	CY070	Bicycle: Youth YX660	900.00 USD
3	AC100	Trailer: third-wheel rider	450.00 USD
		Freight	200.00 USD
		HST	1 891.50 USD
		Total	$16 441.50 USD

Terms: 2/10, n/30. The exchange rate is 1.015.

NOTES
Edit the default purchase cost entered in the Amount field.

5 **Cash Receipt #813** **Dated May 2, 2015**
From Niagara Rapids Inn, cheque #73 for $5 537 in payment of account including $113 discount for early payment. Reference invoice #2194.

NOTES
Fallsview Riverside Resort
Contact: T. Player
190 Water St.
Niagara Falls, ON L8C 2V8
Tel: (905) 466-5576
Fax: (905) 466-7284
E-mail: tplayer@frr.ca
Web: www.frr.ca
Terms: 2/10, n/30
Credit limit: $15 000
Tax code: H

6

Sales Order #5-1-FRR **Dated May 2, 2015**

Delivery date May 6, 2015
To Fallsview Riverside Resort (use Full Add for new customer)

1	AC010	Bicycle Pump: standing model	$ 50/ unit
2	AC020	Bicycle Pump: hand-held mini	80/ unit
10	AC030	Helmet	120/ helmet
9	AC040	Light: halogen	25/ unit
18	AC050	Light: rear reflector	15/ unit
9	AC060	Lock: kryptonite tube	70/ lock
2	AC070	Pannier: front wicker clip-on	80/ basket
2	AC080	Pannier: rear mesh	60/ basket
1	AC090	Trailer: 2-child closed	620/ unit
1	AC100	Trailer: third-wheel rider	260/ unit
1	CY010	Bicycle: Commuter Steel frame CX10	640/ bike
4	CY020	Bicycle: Commuter Alum frame CX90	960/ bike
4	CY040	Bicycle: Trail Alum frame TX560	1 220/ bike
2	CY090	Stationary Converter	870/ unit
	Freight	(tax code H)	50
	HST		13%

Terms: 2/10, n/30.
Received cheque #96 for $3 000 as down payment (deposit #21) to confirm sales order.

7

Payment Cheque #346 **Dated May 5, 2015**

To Wheel Deals, $3 774 USD in payment of account including $68 discount for early payment. Reference invoice #WD-391. The exchange rate is 1.018.

8

Memo #5-2 **Dated May 5, 2015**

Re Damaged Inventory: Two (2) wicker panniers, item AC070, were crushed and damaged beyond repair. Adjust the inventory to recognize the loss.

NOTES
Remember to change the payment method to Pay Later for the sales invoice that fills the order.
If you want, you can enter Gearie as the salesperson for all sales.

9

Sales Invoice #2470 **Dated May 5, 2015**

To Fallsview Riverside Resort, to fill sales order #5-1-FRR

1	AC010	Bicycle Pump: standing model	$ 50/ unit
2	AC020	Bicycle Pump: hand-held mini	80/ unit
10	AC030	Helmet	120/ helmet
9	AC040	Light: halogen	25/ unit
18	AC050	Light: rear reflector	15/ unit
9	AC060	Lock: kryptonite tube	70/ lock
2	AC070	Pannier: front wicker clip-on	80/ basket
2	AC080	Pannier: rear mesh	60/ basket
1	AC090	Trailer: 2-child closed	620/ unit
1	AC100	Trailer: third-wheel rider	260/ unit
1	CY010	Bicycle: Commuter Steel frame CX10	640/ bike
4	CY020	Bicycle: Commuter Alum frame CX90	960/ bike
4	CY040	Bicycle: Trail Alum frame TX560	1 220/ bike
2	CY090	Stationary Converter	870/ unit
	Freight	(tax code H)	50
	HST		13%

Terms: 2/10, n/30.

NOTES
Niagara Courier
Contact: Dawn Spokesman
28 Torstar St. N.
Niagara Falls, ON L2E 5T8
Tel: (905) 577-1800
E-mail: spokesman@niagaracourier.ca
Web: www.niagaracourier.ca
Terms: net 10
Tax code: H
Expense account: 1260

10

Credit Card Purchase Invoice #NC-114 **Dated May 6, 2015**

From Niagara Courier (use Full Add for new vendor), $500 plus $65 HST for prepaid advertisement to run over the next 12 weeks. Purchase invoice total $565 paid in full by Visa.

11 **Payment Cheque #347** **Dated May 6, 2015**

To Complete Cycler Inc., $2 440 USD in payment of account including $80 discount for early payment. Reference invoice #CC-914. The exchange rate is 1.014.

12 **Memo #5-3** **Dated May 7, 2015**

From Visa, received monthly credit card statement for $240 including $220 for purchases up to and including May 3 and $20 annual renewal fee. Submitted cheque #102 for $240 in full payment of the balance owing.

13 **Deposit Slip #18** **Dated May 7, 2015**

Prepare deposit slip for all receipts for May 1 to May 7 to deposit the funds to Bank: Niagara Trust Chequing from Undeposited Cash and Cheques. The total deposit for the three cheques is $12 966.60.

14 **Cash Receipt #814** **Dated May 9, 2015**

From Backstage Tours, cheque #472 for $6 759.20 in payment of account including $180.80 discount for early payment. Reference invoice #2199.

15 **Credit Card Purchase Invoice #PS-1149** **Dated May 10, 2015**

From Paper & Stuff (use Full Add for new vendor), $150 plus $19.50 HST for stationery and other office supplies for store. Purchase invoice total $169.50 paid in full by Visa.

16 **Credit Card Purchase Invoice #LS-612** **Dated May 14, 2015**

From Lakeshore Sunoco, $92 including HST and PST for gasoline purchase for delivery vehicle. (Use tax code IN.) Purchase invoice total paid in full by Visa.

17 **Employee Time Summary Sheet #14** **Dated May 14, 2015**

For the Pay Period ending May 7, 2015
Dunlop Mercier worked 80 regular hours and 2 hours of overtime in the period. Recover $50 loan. Issue payroll deposit slip #DD25.

18 **Deposit Slip #19** **Dated May 14, 2015**

Prepare deposit slip for all receipts for May 8 to May 14 to deposit the funds. One cheque for $6 759.20 is being deposited.

19 **Memo #5-4** **Dated May 14, 2015**

Payroll Remittances: Use May 1 as the End of Remitting Period date to make the following payroll remittances in the Payments Journal. Read the warning.

a) Record payment for EI, CPP and Income Tax Payable up to May 1 to the Receiver General for Canada. Issue cheque #103 in full payment.
b) Record payment for Garnisheed Wages Payable up to May 1 to the Receiver General for Canada. Issue cheque #104 in full payment.
c) Record payment for EHT Payable up to May 1 to the Minister of Finance. Issue cheque #105 in full payment.
d) Record payment for RRSP Payable up to May 1 to Welland Insurance. Issue cheque #106 in full payment.
e) Record payment for CSB Payable up to May 1 to Escarpment Investments. Issue cheque #107 in full payment.
f) Record payment for Group Insurance Payable up to May 1 to Welland Insurance. Issue cheque #108 in full payment.
g) Record payment for WSIB Payable up to May 1 to Workplace Safety and Insurance Board. Issue cheque #109 in full payment.

WARNING!
You may need to change the bank account for the payment to Visa. The USD bank account may remain selected after the US dollar payment.

NOTES
All deposits are made to Bank: Niagara Trust Chequing from Undeposited Cash and Cheques.

NOTES
Paper & Stuff
Contact: Clip Papers
26 Pulp Ave.
Niagara on the Lake, ON
L0S 1J0
Terms: net 30
Tax code: H
Expense account: 1280

PRO VERSION
You must use the Paycheques Journal because the cheque date is different from the session date.

NOTES
Enter Memo #5-4A, Memo #5-4B and so on in the Reference Number and Comment fields for the payroll remittances.

WARNING!
When you remit the payroll taxes to the Receiver General, the Pay Period date for Garnisheed Wages is updated to June 1 at the same time. You must change the date back to May 1 when making this remittance. Similarly, the first payment to Welland Insurance changes the date for the second one and you must change it back to May 1 before paying the amounts to avoid including the amounts from the May 14 paycheque. Choose Yes to save the new dates when prompted.

Sage 50 groups the remittances to suppliers. To avoid this, you can create separate supplier accounts.

20 **Memo #5-5** **Dated May 14, 2015**

Record payment for GST and HST for the period ending April 30 to the Receiver General for Canada. Issue cheque #110 in full payment.

21 **Cash Purchase Invoice #ES-64329** **Dated May 15, 2015**

From Energy Source, $120 plus $15.60 HST paid for hydro service. Purchase invoice total $135.60. Terms: cash on receipt. Issue cheque #111 in full payment.

22 **Cash Receipt #815** **Dated May 15, 2015**

From Fallsview Riverside Resort, cheque #195 for $13 439.35 in payment of account including $335.50 discount for early payment. Reference invoice #2470 and deposit #21.

23 **Purchase Order #39** **Dated May 15, 2015**

Shipping date May 20, 2015
From Complete Cycler Inc.,

1	AC020	Bicycle Pump: hand-held mini	$ 500.00 USD
7	AC030	Helmet	4 200.00 USD
5	AC040	Light: halogen	500.00 USD
5	AC050	Light: rear reflector	350.00 USD
10	AC060	Lock: kryptonite tube	2 000.00 USD
		Freight	100.00 USD
		HST	994.50 USD
		Invoice total	$8 644.50 USD

Terms: 2/10, n/30. The exchange rate is 1.019.

24 **Purchase Order #40** **Dated May 15, 2015**

Shipping date June 1, 2015
From Wheel Deals

4	AC090	Trailer: 2-child closed	$ 1 200.00 USD
4	AC100	Trailer: third-wheel rider	600.00 USD
20	CY020	Bicycle: Commuter Alum frame CX90	10 800.00 USD
		Freight	120.00 USD
		HST	1 653.60 USD
		Invoice total	$14 373.60 USD

Terms: 2/10, n/30. The exchange rate is 1.019.

SESSION DATE – MAY 31, 2015

25 **Cash Purchase Invoice #NB-59113** **Dated May 19, 2015**

From Niagara Bell, $80 plus $10.40 HST paid for phone service. Purchase invoice total $90.40. Terms: cash on receipt. Issue cheque #112 in full payment.

26 **Purchase Invoice #CC-2014** **Dated May 20, 2015**

From Complete Cycler Inc., to fill purchase order #39

1	AC020	Bicycle Pump: hand-held mini	$ 500.00 USD
7	AC030	Helmet	4 200.00 USD
5	AC040	Light: halogen	500.00 USD
5	AC050	Light: rear reflector	350.00 USD
10	AC060	Lock: kryptonite tube	2 000.00 USD
		Freight	100.00 USD
		HST	994.50 USD
		Invoice total	$8 644.50 USD

Terms: 2/10, n/30. The exchange rate is 1.0178.

27

Credit Card Sales Invoice #2471 **Dated May 20, 2015**

To Visa Sales (sales summary)

5	AC020	Bicycle Pump: hand-held mini	$ 80/ unit	$ 400.00
10	AC030	Helmet	120/ helmet	1 200.00
8	AC040	Light: halogen	25/ unit	200.00
8	AC050	Light: rear reflector	15/ unit	120.00
8	AC060	Lock: kryptonite tube	70/ lock	560.00
4	AC080	Pannier: rear mesh	60/ basket	240.00
1	AC090	Trailer: 2-child closed	620/ unit	620.00
1	AC100	Trailer: third-wheel rider	260/ unit	260.00
20	BK010	Books: Complete Bicycle Guide (code G)	40/ book	800.00
20	BK020	Books: Endless Trails (code G)	40/ book	800.00
1	CY030	Bicycle: Racer Ultra lite RX480	3 100/ bike	3 100.00
3	CY040	Bicycle: Trail Alum frame TX560	1 220/ bike	3 660.00
1	CY060	Bicycle: Mountain Carbon frame MX34	2 950/ bike	2 950.00
2	CY090	Stationary Converter	870/ unit	1 740.00
4	S010	Boxing for shipping	75/ job	300.00
4	S020	Maintenance: annual contract	110/ year	440.00
8	S030	Maintenance: complete tune-up	70/ job	560.00
20	S040	Rental: 1 hour	10/ hour	200.00
18	S050	Rental: 1 day	30/ day	540.00
14	S060	Repairs	45/ hour	630.00
	GST		5%	80.00
	HST		13%	2 303.60
	Total paid by Visa			$21 703.60

28

Deposit Slip #20 **Dated May 22, 2015**

Prepare deposit slip for all receipts for May 15 to May 22 to deposit the funds. The total deposit for the single cheque is $13 439.35.

29

Cash Purchase Invoice #N-2015-1 **Dated May 23, 2015**

From Niagara Area Treasurer (use Full Add), $900 in full payment of first instalment of quarterly property tax assessment. Terms: EOM. Issued cheque #113 in full payment. Store as a monthly recurring entry. Recall the stored transaction to issue cheques #114 and #115 as postdated cheques for the next two instalments, dated June 23 and July 23.

30

Sales Invoice #2472 **Dated May 23, 2015**

To Park 'N Ride Tours (preferred customer)

1	AC010	Bicycle Pump: standing model	$ 45/ unit
2	AC020	Bicycle Pump: hand-held mini	70/ unit
10	AC030	Helmet	105/ helmet
6	AC040	Light: halogen	22/ unit
6	AC050	Light: rear reflector	12/ unit
6	AC060	Lock: kryptonite tube	65/ lock
2	AC070	Pannier: front wicker clip-on	75/ basket
1	AC100	Trailer: third-wheel rider	235/ unit
10	BK020	Books: Endless Trails (code G)	35/ book
2	CY020	Bicycle: Commuter Alum frame CX90	850/ bike
2	CY040	Bicycle: Trail Alum frame TX560	1 090/ bike
2	CY070	Bicycle: Youth YX660	420/ bike
6	S020	Maintenance: annual contract	100/ year
	GST		5%
	HST		13%

Terms: 2/10, n/30.

WARNING!

You must change the tax code for books (items BK010 and BK020) to G so that taxes will be correctly applied for these items.

NOTES

Niagara Area Treasurer
Contact: Budd Jett
53 Price St.
Niagara Falls, ON L2K 2Z3
Tel: (905) 461-0063
Web: www.NAT.ca
Terms: net 1
Tax code: no tax (exempt)
Expense account: 5260
Use N-2015-2 and N-2015-3 as the Invoice numbers for the postdated payments for property taxes.

NOTES

Remember to change the tax code for Books to G.

31

Purchase Invoice #WD-364 **Dated May 26, 2015**

From Wheel Deals, to fill purchase order #38

25	CY020	Bicycle: Commuter Alum frame CX90	$13 000.00 USD
4	CY070	Bicycle: Youth YX660	900.00 USD
3	AC100	Trailer: third-wheel rider	450.00 USD
		Freight	200.00 USD
		HST	1 891.50 USD
		Total	$16 441.50 USD

Terms: 2/10, n/30. The exchange rate is 1.012.

PRO VERSION
Remember that you must use the Paycheques Journal.

32

Employee Time Summary Sheet #15 **Dated May 28, 2015**

For the Pay Period ending May 21, 2015
Dunlop Mercier worked 80 regular hours and 4 hours of overtime. Recover $50 loan. Issue payroll deposit slip #DD26.

NOTES
Remember to change the tax code for Books to G.

33

Sales Invoice #2473 **Dated May 28, 2015**

To Backstage Tours (preferred customer)

20	AC030	Helmet	$105/ helmet
10	BK020	Books: Endless Trails (code G)	35/ book
10	S040	Rental: 1 hour	9/ hour
20	S050	Rental: 1 day	25/ day
	GST		5%
	HST		13%

Terms: 2/10, n/30.

34

Sales Return 2473-R **Dated May 29, 2015**

Backstage Tours returned one damaged helmet (AC030) priced at $105 plus 13% HST. Total sales return amount $118.65 credited to account.
Create new Subgroup Account 4070 Returns and Allowances. Change the terms to net 60; there is no discount. Delete or change the comment.
Create an Adjustments Journal entry to write off the damaged helmet.

35

Memo #5-6 **Dated May 29, 2015**

Transfer $26 000 USD to USD Chequing account from 1120 Bank: Visa and Interac for upcoming payments. The exchange rate is 1.017.

36

Payment Cheques #348 and 349 **Dated May 29, 2015**

To Complete Cycler Inc., $8 491.50 USD in payment of account including $153 discount for early payment. Reference invoice #CC-2014.

To Wheel Deals, $16 150.50 USD in payment of account including $291 discount for early payment. Reference invoice #WD-364.
The exchange rate is 1.017.

NOTES
Pedlar Maintenance Co.
Contact: Moe Pedlar
890 Braker St.
Niagara on the Lake, ON
L0S 1J0
Tel: (905) 468-2331
Terms: net 1
Tax code: H
Expense account: 5240

37

Cash Purchase Invoice #PMC-55 **Dated May 29, 2015**

From Pedlar Maintenance Co. (use Full Add), $300 plus $39 HST paid for cleaning and maintenance of premises. Terms: cash on receipt. Issue cheque #116 for $339 in full payment. The company bills monthly for its services so store the entry as a monthly recurring transaction. You will need to change the bank account if you use the Payments Journal for this entry.

38

Bank Debit Memo #91431 **Dated May 31, 2015**

From Niagara Trust, authorized withdrawals were made from the chequing account on our behalf for the following:
Bank service charges: $35
Mortgage payment: $1 580 interest and $120 principal reduction
Bank loan payment: $420 interest and $480 principal reduction

39 **Credit Card Purchase Invoice #LS-6533** **Dated May 31, 2015**

From Lakeshore Sunoco, $69 including HST for gasoline (tax code IN) and $40 plus $5.20 HST for oil change (tax code H). Purchase invoice total $114.20 charged to Visa account.

40 **Memo #5-7** **Dated May 31, 2015**

Prepare the payroll for the two salaried employees, Pedal Schwinn and Shimana Gearie. Add 2 percent of revenue from services for May as a commission to Gearie's salary. Issue payroll deposit slips #DD27 and #DD28.

SESSION DATE – JUNE 15, 2015

41 **Cash Receipt #816** **Dated June 1, 2015**

From Backstage Tours, cheque #434 for $3 220.41 in payment of account including $68.14 discount for early payment. Reference sales invoice #2473 and 2473-R.

42 **Purchase Invoice #WD-1804** **Dated June 1, 2015**

From Wheel Deals, to fill purchase order #40

4	AC090	Trailer: 2-child closed	$ 1 200.00 USD
4	AC100	Trailer: third-wheel rider	600.00 USD
20	CY020	Bicycle: Commuter Alum frame CX90	10 800.00 USD
		Freight	120.00 USD
		HST	1 653.60 USD
		Invoice total	$14 373.60 USD

Terms: 2/10, n/30. The exchange rate is 1.016.

43 **Sales Invoice #2474** **Dated June 1, 2015**

To Festival Tours (monthly recurring sale)

40	S040	Rental: 1 hour	$10/ hour	USD
20	S050	Rental: 1 day	30/ day	USD
		HST	13%	

Terms: 2/10, n/30. The exchange rate is 1.016.

44 **Cash Purchase Invoice #WI-6921** **Dated June 2, 2015**

From Welland Insurance, $2 592 (including PST) for six months of insurance coverage. Invoice total $2 592. Issued cheque #117 in payment.

45 **Sales Invoice #2475** **Dated June 2, 2015**

To Americas Vinelands Tours (USD preferred customer)

2	AC020	Bicycle Pump: hand-held mini	$ 70/ unit	USD
20	AC030	Helmet	105/ helmet	USD
6	AC040	Light: halogen	22/ unit	USD
6	AC050	Light: rear reflector	12/ unit	USD
8	AC060	Lock: kryptonite tube	65/ lock	USD
20	BK010	Books: Complete Bicycle Guide	35/ book	USD
20	BK020	Books: Endless Trails	35/ book	USD
8	CY010	Bicycle: Commuter Steel frame CX10	590/ bike	USD
		Freight	30	USD

Terms: 2/10, n/30. The exchange rate is 1.014.

46 **Cash Receipt #817** **Dated June 5, 2015**

From Americas Vinelands Tours, cheque #198 for $8 931.72 USD in payment of account, including $182.28 discount for early payment. Reference invoice #2475. The exchange rate is 1.015.

NOTES
Enter the two items purchased from Lakeshore Sunoco on separate lines because you need different tax codes for them.

NOTES
You must calculate the amount of the commission manually and then enter the amount in the journal.
Use the Revenue from Services amount in the Income Statement for the month of May to calculate the commission.

NOTES
Because the services for Festival Tours were provided in Canada, HST is charged. Change the tax code to H.

NOTES
PST is charged on insurance in Ontario. PST paid is not refundable, so there is no need to track it or record it separately. It will be included with the amount for Prepaid Insurance.

NOTES
Taxes are not charged on exported goods or on freight for foreign customers.

47

Deposit Slip #21 **Dated June 5, 2015**

Prepare deposit slip for all receipts for May 29 to June 5 to deposit the funds. The total deposit for the single cheque is $3 220.41.

48

Cash Receipt #818 **Dated June 7, 2015**

From Festival Tours, cheque #1257 for $1 107.40 USD in payment of account, including $22.60 early payment discount. Reference invoice #2474. The exchange rate is 1.012.

49

Credit Card Purchase Invoice #LS-6914 **Dated June 8, 2015**

From Lakeshore Sunoco, $69 including HST for gasoline. Purchase invoice total $69 charged to Visa account.

50

Memo #6-1 **Dated June 9, 2015**

From Visa, received monthly credit card statement for $940.70 for purchases up to and including June 3. Prepare cheque #118 for $940.70 to pay the Visa bill.

NOTES

Remember to change the tax code for Books to G.

51

Credit Card Sales Invoice #2476 **Dated June 9, 2015**

To Visa Sales (sales summary)

1	AC010	Bicycle Pump: standing model	$ 50/ unit	$ 50.00
8	AC030	Helmet	120/ helmet	960.00
8	AC040	Light: halogen	25/ unit	200.00
8	AC050	Light: rear reflector	15/ unit	120.00
8	AC060	Lock: kryptonite tube	70/ lock	560.00
2	AC090	Trailer: 2-child closed	620/ unit	1 240.00
12	BK010	Books: Complete Bicycle Guide (code G)	40/ book	480.00
24	BK020	Books: Endless Trails (code G)	40/ book	960.00
5	CY020	Bicycle: Commuter Alum frame CX90	960/ bike	4 800.00
2	CY050	Bicycle: Mountain Alum frame MX14	1 850/ bike	3 700.00
1	CY070	Bicycle: Youth YX660	460/ bike	460.00
6	S010	Boxing for shipping	75/ job	450.00
12	S020	Maintenance: annual contract	110/ year	1 320.00
20	S040	Rental: 1 hour	10/ hour	200.00
20	S050	Rental: 1 day	30/ day	600.00
20	S060	Repairs	45/ hour	900.00
	GST		5%	72.00
	HST		13%	2 022.80
	Total paid by Visa			$19 094.80

52

Payment Cheque #350 **Dated June 9, 2015**

To Wheel Deals, $14 119.20 USD in payment of account including $254.40 early payment discount. Reference invoice #WD-1804. The exchange rate is 1.014.

53

Sales Order #6-1-SBB **Dated June 12, 2015**

Delivery Date: June 14, 2015

From Shavian B & B

16	AC030	Helmet	$120/ helmet
10	AC040	Light: halogen	25/ unit
10	AC050	Light: rear reflector	15/ unit
10	AC060	Lock: kryptonite tube	70/ lock
1	AC090	Trailer: 2-child closed	620/ unit
1	AC100	Trailer: third-wheel rider	260/ unit
7	CY020	Bicycle: Commuter Alum frame CX90	960/ bike
3	CY070	Bicycle: Youth YX660	460/ bike
10	S020	Maintenance: annual contract	110/ year
	HST		13%

Terms: 2/10, n/30.

54 **Purchase Invoice #PC-1031** **Dated June 12, 2015**

From Pro Cycles Inc.

2	AC010	Bicycle Pump: standing model	$ 240.00
1	AC020	Bicycle Pump: hand-held mini	500.00
6	AC030	Helmet	3 600.00
5	AC040	Light: halogen	500.00
5	AC050	Light: rear reflector	350.00
5	AC060	Lock: kryptonite tube	1 000.00
10	AC070	Pannier: front wicker clip-on	500.00
10	AC080	Pannier: rear mesh	380.00
		Freight	140.00
		HST	937.30
		Invoice total	$8 147.30

Terms: 1/15, n/30.

55 **Employee Time Summary Sheet #16** **Dated June 12, 2015**

For the Pay Period ending June 5, 2015

Dunlop Mercier worked 80 regular hours in the period. He will receive $200 as a loan and have $50 recovered from each of the following four paycheques. Issue payroll deposit slip #DD29.

56 **Cash Receipt #819** **Dated June 13, 2015**

From Shavian B & B, cheque #284 for $2 000 as down payment (deposit #22) in acceptance of sales order #6-1-SBB.

57 **Memo #6-2** **Dated June 14, 2015**

Record payment for GST and HST for the period ending May 31 to the Receiver General for Canada. Issue cheque #119 in full payment. Clear the tax reports up to May 31.

58 **Memo #6-3** **Dated June 14, 2015**

Payroll Remittances: Make the following remittances for the period ending May 31. Choose Pay Remittance for payroll remittances.

a) Record payment for EI, CPP and Income Tax Payable for May to the Receiver General for Canada. Issue cheque #120 in full payment.
b) Record payment for Garnisheed Wages Payable for May to the Receiver General for Canada. Issue cheque #121 in full payment.
c) Record payment for RRSP Payable to Welland Insurance. Issue cheque #122 in full payment.
d) Record payment for CSB Payable to Escarpment Investments. Issue cheque #123 in full payment.
e) Record payment for Group Insurance Payable for May to Welland Insurance. Issue cheque #124 in full payment.

NOTES

Enter Memo #6-3A, Memo #6-3B and so on in the Reference Number and Comment fields for payroll remittances.

WARNING!

Remember to reset the Pay Period date to June 1 for the second remittance to the Receiver General and Welland Insurance to avoid including the amounts from the June 12 paycheque.

59 **Purchase Invoice #WD-3047** **Dated June 15, 2015**

From Wheel Deals

3	AC090	Trailer: 2-child closed	$ 900.00 USD
3	AC100	Trailer: third-wheel rider	450.00 USD
4	CY030	Bicycle: Racer Ultra lite RX480	6 000.00 USD
4	CY060	Bicycle: Mountain Carbon frame MX34	6 880.00 USD
4	CY090	Stationary Converter	1 320.00 USD
		Freight	200.00 USD
		HST	2 047.50 USD
		Invoice total	$17 797.50 USD

Terms: 2/10, n/30. The exchange rate is 1.0155.

60

Sales Invoice #2477 **Dated June 15, 2015**

To Shavian B & B, to fill sales order #6-1-SBB

16	AC030	Helmet	$120/ helmet
10	AC040	Light: halogen	25/ unit
10	AC050	Light: rear reflector	15/ unit
10	AC060	Lock: kryptonite tube	70/ lock
1	AC090	Trailer: 2-child closed	620/ unit
1	AC100	Trailer: third-wheel rider	260/ unit
7	CY020	Bicycle: Commuter Alum frame CX90	960/ bike
3	CY070	Bicycle: Youth YX660	460/ bike
10	S020	Maintenance: annual contract	110/ year
	HST		13%

Terms: 2/10, n/30.

61

Memo #6-4 **Dated June 15, 2015**

Old rental bicycles will be sold and replaced with new ones. Create new inventory item: CY200 Used Bicycles with a selling price of $200 each.
Enter an Inventory Adjustment to add 20 Used Bicycles (CY200) from Rental Bicycles asset account. The unit cost is $375. (Enter 20 as a positive quantity to increase the inventory. Change the default account to 1300.)
Enter an Inventory Adjustment to move 20 Bicycles (CY020) from inventory to Rental Bicycles asset account. Accept the default unit cost. (Enter a negative quantity to decrease the inventory. Change the default account to 1300.)

NOTES

New inventory:
Item: CY200 Used Bicycles
The CAD and USD selling price for all customers will be $200 and the minimum quantity is 0.
Linked accounts:
Asset 1540 Bicycles
Revenue 4020 Revenue from Sales
Expense 5060 Cost of Goods Sold: Bicycles
Variance account is not used.

SESSION DATE – JUNE 30, 2015

62

Cash Purchase Invoice #NB-71222 **Dated June 16, 2015**

From Niagara Bell, $95 plus $12.35 HST paid for phone service. Purchase invoice total $107.35. Terms: cash on receipt of invoice. Issue cheque #125 in full payment.

63

Payment Cheque #126 **Dated June 16, 2015**

To Pro Cycles Inc., $8 075.20 in payment of account including $72.10 discount for early payment. Reference invoices #PC-1031.

64

Deposit Slip #22 **Dated June 19, 2015**

Prepare deposit slip for the single cheque for $2 000 for June 13 to June 19.

65

Payment Cheque #351 **Dated June 20, 2015**

To Wheel Deals, $17 482.50 USD in payment of account including $315 discount for early payment. Reference invoice #WD-3047. The exchange rate is 1.014.

66

Memo #6-5 **Dated June 20, 2015**

Transfer $18 000 USD to Bank: USD Chequing from 1120 Bank: Visa and Interac Account to cover cheque to Wheel Deals. The exchange rate is 1.014.

67

Cash Purchase Invoice #ES-79123 **Dated June 20, 2015**

From Energy Source, $150 plus $19.50 HST paid for hydro service. Purchase invoice total $169.50. Terms: cash on receipt. Issue cheque #127 in full payment.

68

Credit Card Purchase Invoice #M-1034 **Dated June 21, 2015**

From Mountview Delivery (use Quick Add for the new supplier), $80 plus $10.40 HST paid for delivery services. Invoice total $90.40. Full amount paid by Visa. Enter tax code H in the Purchases Journal.

69 **Sales Invoice #2478** **Dated June 22, 2015**

To Candide's B & B (use Full Add for new customer)

2	AC020	Bicycle Pump: hand-held mini	$ 80/ unit
2	AC090	Trailer: 2-child closed	620/ unit
1	AC100	Trailer: third-wheel rider	260/ unit
20	BK020	Books: Endless Trails (code G)	40/ book
40	S050	Rental: 1 day	30/ day
	GST		5%
	HST		13%

Terms: 2/10, n/30.

70 **Cash Receipt #820** **Dated June 24, 2015**

From Shavian B & B, cheque #391 for $12 506.94 in payment of account with $296.06 discount for early payment. Reference invoice #2477 and deposit #22.

71 **Cash Receipt #821** **Dated June 26, 2015**

From Candide's B & B, cheque #532 for $3 990.36 in payment of account including $81.44 discount for early payment. Reference invoice #2478.

72 **Memo #6-6** **Dated June 26, 2015**

Add Charitable Donations as a payroll deduction. Since VeloCity will match employee donations, a user-defined expense is also needed.

Create new Group accounts
- 2440 Charitable Donations - Employee
- 2450 Charitable Donations - Employer
- 5390 Charitable Donations Expense

Add Donations as new name (Setup, Settings, Payroll, Names)
- for Deduction 4 on Names, Incomes & Deductions screen
- for User-Defined Expense 2 on Names, Additional Payroll screen

Change Deduction Settings (Payroll, Deductions)
- Deduct Donations by Amount After Tax, EI, CPP, EHT and Vacation Pay

Add new payroll linked accounts (under Payroll Settings)
- 2440 for Employee Donations (Linked Accounts, Deductions)
- 2450 for Employer Donations (Linked Accounts, User-Defined Expenses, Payables)
- 5390 for Employer Donations (Linked Accounts, User-Defined Expenses, Expenses and for Payment Adjustment)

Enter amounts in Payroll Ledger for Deductions and WSIB & Other Expenses
- Gearie: Check Use for the deduction; enter $20 as the deduction and the expense amount per period
- Schwinn: Check Use for the deduction; enter $25 as the deduction and the expense amount per period

73 **Employee Time Summary Sheet #17** **Dated June 26, 2015**

For the Pay Period ending June 19, 2015

Dunlop Mercier worked 80 regular hours in the period and 2 hours of overtime. Recover $50 loan and issue payroll deposit slip #DD30.

74 **Deposit Slip #23** **Dated June 26, 2015**

Prepare deposit slip for all receipts for June 20 to June 26 to deposit the funds. The total deposit for two cheques is $16 497.30.

75 **Cash Purchase Invoice #PMC-68** **Dated June 29, 2015**

From Pedlar Maintenance Co., $300 plus $39 HST paid for maintenance. Terms: cash on receipt. Issue cheque #128 for $339 in payment. Recall stored transaction.

NOTES

Remember to change the tax code for Books to G.

NOTES

Candide's B & B
Contact: Candide Shaw
190 Playtime Circle
Niagara on the Lake, ON
L0S 1J0
Tel: (905) 468-5576
Terms: 2/10, n/30
Credit limit: $15 000
Tax code: H

NOTES

To add deductions, refer to
page 655 for names
page 659 for payroll deductions settings
page 660 for linked accounts
page 672 for entering the employee deduction
page 673 for WSIB & other expense amounts.

76

Debit Card Sales Invoice #2479 **Dated June 29, 2015**

To Bruno Scinto (cash and Interac customer)

1	AC010	Bicycle Pump: standing model	$ 50/ unit	$ 50.00
2	AC030	Helmet	120/ helmet	240.00
2	AC040	Light: halogen	25/ unit	50.00
2	AC050	Light: rear reflector	15/ unit	30.00
2	AC060	Lock: kryptonite tube	70/ lock	140.00
2	CY030	Bicycle: Racer Ultra lite RX480	3 100/ bike	6 200.00
2	S020	Maintenance: annual contract	110/ year	220.00
		HST	13%	900.90
		Invoice total paid in full		$7 830.90

Debit card #5919 7599 7543 7777. Amount deposited to Visa and Interac account.

77

Credit Card Purchase Invoice #LS-7823 **Dated June 30, 2015**

From Lakeshore Sunoco, $115, including HST, for gasoline and $80 plus $10.40 HST for tire repairs. Purchase invoice total $205.40 paid in full by Visa. (Remember to change the tax code for the tire repairs.)

NOTES
Remember to change the tax code for Books to G.

78

Credit Card Sales Invoice #2480 **Dated June 30, 2015**

To Visa Sales (sales summary)

2	AC010	Bicycle Pump: standing model	$ 50/ unit	$ 100.00
2	AC030	Helmet	120/ helmet	240.00
2	AC040	Light: halogen	25/ unit	50.00
4	AC050	Light: rear reflector	15/ unit	60.00
20	AC060	Lock: kryptonite tube	70/ lock	1 400.00
8	AC080	Pannier: rear mesh	60/ basket	480.00
8	BK010	Books: Complete Bicycle Guide (code G)	40/ book	320.00
40	BK020	Books: Endless Trails (code G)	40/ book	1 600.00
2	CY030	Bicycle: Racer Ultra lite RX480	3 100/ bike	6 200.00
1	CY060	Bicycle: Mountain Carbon frame MX34	2 950/ bike	2 950.00
2	CY090	Stationary Converter	870/ unit	1 740.00
30	S040	Rental: 1 hour	10/ hour	300.00
40	S060	Repairs	45/ hour	1 800.00
		GST	5%	96.00
		HST	13%	1 991.60
		Total paid by Visa		$19 327.60

NOTES
Wellness in Print
Contact: Slim Writer
29 Editorial Circle
Hamilton, ON L6G 2S6
Tel: (905) 488-1000
Terms: net 30
Tax code: G
Business No.: 813 276 490

79

Purchase Invoice #WP-4489 **Dated June 30, 2015**

From Wellness in Print (use Full Add for new supplier)

150	BK010	Books: Complete Bicycle Guide	$3 000.00
200	BK020	Books: Endless Trails	4 000.00
		GST	350.00
		Purchase invoice total	$7 350.00

Terms: net 30 days.

80

Bank Debit Memo #96241 **Dated June 30, 2015**

From Niagara Trust, authorized withdrawals were made from the chequing account on our behalf for the following:

Bank service charges: $35
Mortgage payment: $1 570 interest and $130 principal reduction
Bank loan payment: $400 interest and $500 principal reduction

81

Memo #6-7 **Dated June 30, 2015**

Prepare the payroll salaries for Pedal Schwinn and Shimana Gearie. Gearie took one day of personal leave. Add 2 percent of service revenue for June as a commission to Gearie's salary. Issue payroll deposit slips #DD31 and #DD32.

82 **Memo #6-8** **Dated June 30, 2015**

Print customer statements. Prepare invoice #2481 to charge Park 'N Ride Tours $133.21 interest – 1.5% of the overdue amount. Terms: net 15.

SESSION DATE – JULY 15, 2015

83 **Sales Invoice #2482** **Dated July 1, 2015**

To Festival Tours, recall stored entry

40	S040	Rental: 1 hour	$10/ hour	USD
20	S050	Rental: 1 day	30/ day	USD
	HST		13%	

Terms: 2/10, n/30. The exchange rate is 1.0155.

84 **Employee Time Summary Sheet #18** **Dated July 9, 2015**

For the Pay Period ending July 2, 2015
Dunlop Mercier worked 80 regular hours in the period (no overtime) and took one day of sick leave. Recover $50 loaned and issue payroll deposit slip #DD33.

85 **Cash Receipt #822** **Dated July 9, 2015**

From Park 'N Ride Tours, cheque #1431 for $9 014.13 in payment of account. Reference invoices #2472 and #2481.

86 **Memo #7-1** **Dated July 9, 2015**

From Visa, received monthly credit card statement for $364.80 for purchases made before July 3, 2015. Submitted cheque #129 for $364.80 in full payment of the balance owing.

87 **Deposit Slip #24** **Dated July 9, 2015**

Prepare deposit slip for the single cheque for $9 014.13 being deposited.

88 **Memo #7-2** **Dated July 14, 2015**

Record payment for GST and HST for the period ending June 30 to the Receiver General for Canada. Issue cheque #130 in full payment. Remember to clear the tax report up to June 30 after making the remittance.

89 **Memo #7-3** **Dated July 14, 2015**

Payroll Remittances: Make the following payroll remittances for the pay period ending June 30 in the Payments Journal.

a) Record payment for EI, CPP and Income Tax Payable for June to the Receiver General for Canada. Issue cheque #131 in full payment.
b) Record payment for Garnisheed Wages Payable for June to the Receiver General for Canada. Issue cheque #132 in full payment.
c) Record payment for RRSP Payable to Welland Insurance. Issue cheque #133 in full payment.
d) Record payment for CSB Payable to Escarpment Investments. Issue cheque #134 in full payment.
e) Record payment for Group Insurance Payable for June to Welland Insurance. Issue cheque #135 in full payment.
f) Record payment for Charitable Donations Payable for June to Canadian Cancer Society. Create a new supplier record and select Payroll Authority for the supplier. Choose the new supplier in the Payroll Remittance Settings screen for both Donations entries. Include employee and employer contributions in remittance. Issue cheque #136 in full payment.

NOTES

Remember that if you want to preview the customer statement, you must choose Custom Form, Sage 50 Form and Statements in the Reports and Forms settings on the screen for Statements. Refer to page 163.

NOTES

Enter Memo #7-3A, Memo #7-3B and so on in the Reference Number and Comment fields for the payroll remittances.

WARNING!

Remember to reset the Pay Period date to July 1 for the second remittance to the Receiver General and Welland Insurance to avoid including the amounts from the July 9 paycheque.

NOTES

You cannot create the new supplier from the Pay Remittance form in the Payments Journal – you must close the Remittance Journal.

Refer to page 676 for setting up payroll remittances.

NOTES
Remember to change the tax code for Books to G.

90 **Credit Card Sales Invoice #2483** **Dated July 14, 2015**

To Visa Sales (sales summary)

5	AC020	Bicycle Pump: hand-held mini	$ 80/ unit	$ 400.00
14	AC030	Helmet	120/ helmet	1 680.00
21	AC040	Light: halogen	25/ unit	525.00
36	AC050	Light: rear reflector	15/ unit	540.00
4	AC060	Lock: kryptonite tube	70/ lock	280.00
3	AC080	Pannier: rear mesh	60/ basket	180.00
2	AC100	Trailer: third-wheel rider	260/ unit	520.00
18	BK010	Books: Complete Bicycle Guide (code G)	40/ book	720.00
35	BK020	Books: Endless Trails (code G)	40/ book	1 400.00
2	CY020	Bicycle: Commuter Alum frame CX90	960/ bike	1 920.00
6	CY040	Bicycle: Trail Alum frame TX560	1 220/ bike	7 320.00
2	CY070	Bicycle: Youth YX660	460/ bike	920.00
2	CY090	Stationary Converter	870/ unit	1 740.00
20	CY200	Used Bicycle	200/ bike	4 000.00
30	S020	Maintenance: annual contract	110/ year	3 300.00
	GST		5%	106.00
	HST		13%	3 032.25
	Total paid by Visa			$28 583.25

91 **Cash Receipt #823** **Dated July 15, 2015**

From Festival Tours, cheque #638 for $1 130 USD in payment of account. Reference invoice #2482. The exchange rate is 1.016.

92 **Memo #7-4** **Dated July 15, 2015**

Transfer $30 000 from the Visa bank account to the savings account.
Transfer $20 000 from the Visa bank account to the CAD chequing account.

SESSION DATE – JULY 31, 2015

93 **Memo #7-5** **Dated July 18, 2015**

Pay $8 000 to the Receiver General for Canada for quarterly instalment of business income tax. Issue cheque #137. Create new Group account 5550 Business Income Tax Expense. (Hint: Remember Business Income Tax Payable.)

94 **Memo #7-6** **Dated July 18, 2015**

Create appropriate new Heading and Total accounts around the new Group account 5550 to restore the logical order of accounts.

95 **Cash Purchase Invoice #NB-86344** **Dated July 18, 2015**

From Niagara Bell, $120 plus $15.60 HST paid for monthly phone service. Purchase invoice total $135.60. Terms: cash on receipt of invoice. Issue cheque #138 in full payment.

96 **Cash Purchase Invoice #ES-89886** **Dated July 18, 2015**

From Energy Source, $140 plus $18.20 HST paid for hydro service. Purchase invoice total $158.20. Terms: cash on receipt. Issue cheque #139 in full payment.

97 **Sales Invoice #2484** **Dated July 19, 2015**

To Fallsview Riverside Resort

4	CY020	Bicycle: Commuter Alum frame CX90	$960/ bike
30	S040	Rental: 1 hour	10/ hour
30	S050	Rental: 1 day	30/ day
	HST		13%

Terms: 2/10, n/30.

98

Cash Sales Invoice #2485 **Dated July 19, 2015**

To Jim Ratter (choose Continue)

1	AC030	Helmet	$120/ helmet	$120.00
1	AC070	Pannier: front wicker clip-on	80/ basket	80.00
		HST	13%	26.00
		Invoice total paid in full with cheque #16.		$226.00

99

Deposit Slip #25 **Dated July 23, 2015**

Prepare deposit slip for single cheque totalling $226 to deposit funds.

100

Employee Time Summary Sheet #19 **Dated July 23, 2015**

For the Pay Period ending July 16, 2015
Dunlop Mercier worked 80 regular hours in the period and took 1 day of sick leave. Recover $50 loaned and issue payroll deposit slip #DD34.

101

Memo #7-7 **Dated July 25, 2015**

Issue a cheque to Dunlop Mercier for vacation pay. Dunlop wants to pay for his upcoming vacation. Issue cheque #140. (Read the margin Warning.)

102

Credit Card Sales Invoice #2486 **Dated July 25, 2015**

To Visa Sales (sales summary)

3	AC010	Bicycle Pump: standing model	$ 50/ unit	$ 150.00
14	AC030	Helmet	120/ helmet	1 680.00
12	AC040	Light: halogen	25/ unit	300.00
16	AC050	Light: rear reflector	15/ unit	240.00
8	AC060	Lock: kryptonite tube	70/ lock	560.00
2	AC070	Pannier: front wicker clip-on	80/ basket	160.00
3	AC090	Trailer: 2-child closed	620/ unit	1 860.00
1	AC100	Trailer: third-wheel rider	260/ unit	260.00
18	BK010	Books: Complete Bicycle Guide (code G)	40/ book	720.00
25	BK020	Books: Endless Trails (code G)	40/ book	1 000.00
3	CY010	Bicycle: Commuter Steel frame CX10	640/ bike	1 920.00
6	CY020	Bicycle: Commuter Alum frame CX90	960/ bike	5 760.00
6	CY070	Bicycle: Youth YX660	460/ bike	2 760.00
20	S020	Maintenance: annual contract	110/ year	2 200.00
12	S030	Maintenance: complete tune-up	70/ job	840.00
12	S060	Repairs	45/ hour	540.00
	GST		5%	86.00
	HST		13%	2 499.90
	Total paid by Visa			$23 535.90

103

Memo #7-8 **Dated July 25, 2015**

Received Bank Debit Memo #99142 from Niagara Trust. Cheque #16 from Jim Ratter for $226.00 was returned as NSF. Prepare sales invoice #2487 to charge Ratter for the sales amount and add $30 in service charges for the cost of processing the cheque. Create new Group account 4220 Other Revenue. Terms: net 30. (See margin Notes.)

104

Purchase Order #41 **Dated July 25, 2015**

Shipping date August 10, 2015
From Wheel Deals

10	AC070	Pannier: front wicker clip-on	$ 500.00 USD
10	AC080	Pannier: rear mesh	400.00 USD
		HST	117.00 USD
		Invoice total	$1 017.00 USD

Terms: 2/10, n/30. The exchange rate is 1.013.

WARNING!

Remember to remove all wage and benefit amounts, deductions, user-defined expense amounts and entitlements for the vacation paycheque.

Remember to turn on the Retain option after creating the vacation paycheque.

Refer to page 276.

NOTES

Remember to change the tax code for Books to G.

NOTES

You cannot reverse Ratter's NSF cheque or enter a negative receipt for it because it was a cash sale. You cannot adjust the invoice by changing the method of payment because there is no customer record.

Entering the Bank Account in the Sales Invoice for the amount of the NSF cheque will reverse the bank deposit and restore the accounts payable.

Use Quick Add to create a new partial record for Jim Ratter. For the Ratter invoice, credit chequing account for $226, credit Other Revenue for $30, debit Accounts Receivable for $256. Refer to Accounting Procedures, page 633.

105

Purchase Order #42 **Dated July 25, 2015**

Shipping date August 10, 2015

From Pro Cycles Inc.

6	CY010	Bicycle: Commuter Steel frame CX10	$ 1 860.00
10	CY020	Bicycle: Commuter Alum frame CX90	5 400.00
4	CY030	Bicycle: Racer Ultra lite RX480	6 000.00
4	CY040	Bicycle: Trail Alum frame TX560	2 480.00
3	CY050	Bicycle: Mountain Alum frame MX14	2 790.00
4	CY060	Bicycle: Mountain Carbon frame MX34	6 880.00
6	CY070	Bicycle: Youth YX660	1 350.00
4	CY090	Stationary Converter	1 320.00
		Freight	200.00
		HST	3 676.40
		Invoice total	$31 956.40

Terms: 2/10, n/30. Paid $5 000 deposit with cheque #141.

106

Purchase Order #43 **Dated July 25, 2015**

Shipping date August 10, 2015

From Complete Cycler Inc.

2	AC010	Bicycle Pump: standing model	$ 240.00 USD
1	AC020	Bicycle Pump: hand-held mini	500.00 USD
5	AC030	Helmet	3 000.00 USD
5	AC040	Light: halogen	500.00 USD
5	AC050	Light: rear reflector	350.00 USD
8	AC060	Lock: kryptonite tube	1 600.00 USD
		Freight	120.00 USD
		HST	820.30 USD
		Invoice total	$7 130.30 USD

Terms: 1/15, n/30. The exchange rate is 1.013.

107

Memo #7-9 **Dated July 27, 2015**

Write off Jim Ratter's account because attempts to contact him were unsuccessful. The outstanding amount is considered a bad debt. Improved customer screening for payment by cheque will be implemented for new customers. (See margin Notes.)

NOTES

Use tax code IN for $226, the sale portion of the bad debt. Use No Tax as the code for the $30 handling charge. Remember to "pay" the account. Refer to Accounting Procedures, page 633.

108

Credit Card Purchase Invoice #LS-9855 **Dated July 27, 2015**

From Lakeshore Sunoco, $98 including HST paid for gasoline. Purchase invoice total $98 paid in full by Visa.

109

Cash Purchase Invoice #PMC-89 **Dated July 29, 2015**

From Pedlar Maintenance Co., $300 plus $39 HST paid for cleaning and maintenance of premises. Terms: cash on receipt. Issue cheque #142 for $339 in full payment. Recall stored transaction.

110

Bank Credit Memo #7642 **Dated July 31, 2015**

From Niagara Trust, semi-annual interest was deposited to bank accounts. $155 was deposited to chequing account and $815 to the savings account. Remember interest receivable balance $420.

111

Memo #7-10 **Dated July 31, 2015**

Prepare the payroll for Pedal Schwinn and Shimana Gearie, the salaried employees. Add 2 percent of service revenue for July as a commission to Gearie's salary. Issue payroll deposit slips #DD35 and #DD36.

112 **Memo #7-11** **Dated July 31, 2015**

Prepare separate payroll cheques to pay all employees for completed surveys and quarterly bonuses. Withhold 10 percent income tax. (See margin Notes.)

Gearie	$300 bonus, 20 completed client surveys, $50 income tax
Schwinn	$250 bonus, 28 completed client surveys, $53 income tax
Mercier	$250 bonus, 26 completed client surveys, $51 income tax

Issue cheques #143, #144 and #145.

113 **Memo #7-12** **Dated July 31, 2015**

Increase the allowance for doubtful accounts by $500 (credit entry) in preparation for the next fiscal period.

114 **Bank Debit Memo #143661** **Dated July 31, 2015**

From Niagara Trust, authorized withdrawals were made from the chequing account on our behalf for the following:

Bank service charges: $35
Mortgage payment: $1 550 and $150 principal reduction
Bank loan payment: $380 and $520 principal reduction

115 **Memo #7-13** **Dated July 31, 2015**

Prepare quarterly adjusting entries for depreciation on fixed assets using the following amounts:

Computer equipment	$ 550
Furniture & fixtures	80
Service tools	120
Retail premises	2 450
Van	1 875

116 **Memo #7-14** **Dated July 31, 2015**

Prepare adjusting entries for the following:

Office supplies used	$ 190
Bicycle repair parts used	200
Prepaid insurance expired	2 016
Prepaid advertising expired	680
Payroll liabilities accrued for Mercier	720

Create a new Group expense account 5255 Repair Parts Used.

REVIEW

The Student DVD with Data Files includes Review Questions and Supplementary Cases for this chapter that encourage group work and report analysis. The DVD also includes bank reconciliation and online banking for this chapter.

NOTES

Use the Paycheques Journal to enter the piece rate pay and bonuses.

- Enter the piece rate pay and bonus amounts.
- Click Enter Taxes Manually so that you can edit the income tax amounts.
- On the Income tab screen, remove all hours, wage, salary and benefit amounts. Do not remove Vacation Accrued for Schwinn.
- On the remaining tab screens, remove entitlement hours and deduction and user-defined expense amounts.
- Click the Taxes tab.
- Click Recalculate Taxes.
- Enter the income tax amount. Do not change the EI or CPP amounts.
- Click Enter Taxes Automatically after creating the bonus cheques.

CHAPTER SEVENTEEN

Stratford Country Inn

OBJECTIVES

After completing this chapter, you should be able to

- ***plan*** and ***design*** an accounting system for a small business
- ***prepare*** a conversion procedure from manual records
- ***understand*** the objectives of a computerized accounting system
- ***create*** company files
- ***set up*** company accounts
- ***assign*** appropriate account numbers and account classes
- ***choose*** and ***enter*** appropriate settings for all ledgers
- ***create*** supplier, guest, employee and inventory records
- ***enter*** historical data and account balances in all ledgers
- ***finish*** entering historical data to prepare for journal entries
- ***enter*** accounting transactions from realistic source documents

COMPANY INFORMATION

Company Profile

Stratford Country Inn is situated in Ontario just outside the Stratford city limits, close to Stratford Festival Theatres. The Inn has room for approximately 50 guests, with additional cots available for families who want to share rooms with their children. In addition to the theatre, which attracts most of the guests, the Inn has facilities for rowing and canoeing on the small lake area near the Thames River, and a forested area nearby is used for lovely summer walks or cross-country skiing in winter. Boxed lunches are available for picnics on the waterfront before theatre events or for afternoons in the park and fixed price dinners are offered in the dining room. Many guests stay for several days at a time.

For an additional cost, a private consultant will pamper the guests with aromatherapy sessions. The consultant pays the Inn for use of her studio.

Guests come from near and far, and even a few American theatre groups have become regular visitors. The Inn prepares invoices and accepts payments in United States dollars for US accounts. For groups and clubs, the Inn bills the entire group as a single client. Most individual guests pay by Visa or MasterCard.

NOTES
Stratford Country Inn
100 Festival Road
Stratford, ON
N5A 3G2
Tel 1: (519) 222-6066
Tel 2: (888) 272-6000
Fax: (519) 272-7960
Business No.: 767 698 321

NOTES
For the accommodation business, the terms Guest and Supplier replace Customer and Vendor.

All guests pay HST on the services provided by the Inn and GST on the historic books. Regular guests, clubs, groups or agencies that reserve blocks of theatre tickets and accommodation have credit accounts. Groups place a deposit to confirm their accommodation. For groups that are offered preferred rates, no deposits are required. In the event of overbooking, guests who cannot be placed at the Inn are put up at a nearby bed and breakfast at the Inn's expense.

The grounds of the Inn include conference rooms for discussions and debates about theatre performances and related topics. Buses take guests to the theatre and return them to the Inn on a scheduled basis. Meals can be included for those who want an all-inclusive package. The Inn's dining room caters to its full accommodation guests as well as non-resident guests.

The owner, manager and desk attendant look after the front office. The owner also provides tours of the main theatre district that include backstage access. Five additional staff members cater to the other needs of the guests.

Accounts payable have been set up for food supplies, a maintenance contract (a cleaning crew vacuums the Inn), maintenance and repairs (electrical and carpentry work), linen supplies for kitchen and guest rooms and laundry services for towels and bedding.

By June 30, the Inn was ready to convert its accounting records to Sage 50 and had gathered the following reports to make the conversion:

- Chart of Accounts
- Post-Closing Trial Balance
- Supplier Information
- Guest Information
- Employee Information and Profiles
- Inventory and Services Information

PRO VERSION
The terms Customer and Vendor will replace the terms Guest and Supplier.

CHART OF ACCOUNTS

STRATFORD COUNTRY INN

ASSETS
Bank: Stratford Trust CAD Chequing
Bank: Stratford Trust USD Chequing
Bank: Credit Card
Accounts Receivable
Advances and Loans Receivable
Purchase Prepayments
Prepaid Advertising
Prepaid Insurance
Food Inventory
Linens & Towels
Blankets & Bedding
Supplies: Computer
Supplies: Office
Supplies: Dining Room
Supplies: Washroom
Books
Computer Equipment
Accum Deprec: Computers
Furniture & Fixtures ▶

▶Accum Deprec: Furn & Fix
Vehicle
Accum Deprec: Vehicle
Country Inn & Dining Room
Accum Deprec: Inn & Dining Room
Grounds & Property

LIABILITIES
Bank Loan
Accounts Payable
Prepaid Sales and Deposits
Credit Card Payable
Vacation Payable
EI Payable
CPP Payable
Income Tax Payable
EHT Payable
Group Insurance Payable
Tuition Fees Payable
WSIB Payable
GST Charged on Sales
GST Paid on Purchases ▶

▶HST Charged on Services
HST Paid on Purchases
Mortgage Payable

EQUITY
E. Prospero, Capital
Current Earnings

REVENUE
Revenue from Books
Revenue from Inn
Revenue from Dining Room
Revenue from Tours
Rental Fees
Other Revenue
Exchange Rate Differences

EXPENSE
Advertising & Promotion
Bank Charges and Card Fees
Cost of Books Sold
Cost of Services
COGS: Food ▶

▶Depreciation: Computers
Depreciation: Furn & Fix
Depreciation: Vehicle
Depreciation: Inn & Dining Room
Purchase Discounts
Interest Expense: Loan
Interest Expense: Mortgage
Hydro Expenses
Maintenance & Repairs
Overflow Accommodation
Telephone Expense
Vehicle Expenses
Wages: Management
Wages: General
Wages: Dining Room
EI Expense
CPP Expense
WSIB Expense
EHT Expense
Tuition Fees Expense

NOTES: Use appropriate account numbers and add subgroup totals, headings and totals to organize your Chart of Accounts as necessary. Remember to add a test balance account for the setup.

POST-CLOSING TRIAL BALANCE

STRATFORD COUNTRY INN

June 30, 2015	Debits	Credits		Debits	Credits
Bank: Stratford Trust CAD Chequing	$33 964		▶ Accum Deprec: Vehicle		10 000
Bank: Stratford Trust USD Chequing			Country Inn & Dining Room	400 000	
(2 900 USD)	3 000		Accum Deprec: Inn & Dining Room		20 000
Bank: Credit Card	12 000		Grounds & Property	200 000	
Accounts Receivable (deposit)		$ 1 000	Bank Loan		25 000
Advances and Loans Receivable	250		Accounts Payable		8 068
Prepaid Advertising	50		Credit Card Payable		395
Prepaid Insurance	400		Vacation Payable		4 946
Food Inventory	1 650		EI Payable		1 092
Linens & Towels	2 000		CPP Payable		1 759
Blankets & Bedding	3 000		Income Tax Payable		3 109
Supplies: Computer	400		EHT Payable		577
Supplies: Office	500		Group Insurance Payable		330
Supplies: Dining Room	800		WSIB Payable		1 310
Supplies: Washroom	250		GST Charged on Sales		310
Books	4 000		GST Paid on Purchases	200	
Computer Equipment	4 000		HST Charged on Services		5 970
Accum Deprec: Computers		1 200	HST Paid on Purchases	3 700	
Furniture & Fixtures	38 000		Mortgage Payable		300 000
Accum Deprec: Furn & Fix		4 200	E. Prospero, Capital		368 898
Vehicle	50 000▶			$758 164	$758 164

SUPPLIER INFORMATION

STRATFORD COUNTRY INN

Supplier Name (Contact)	Address	Phone No. Fax No.	E-mail Web Site	Terms Tax ID
Avon Maintenance Services (Ken Sparkles)	66 Kleen Road Stratford, Ontario N5A 3C3	Tel: (519) 272-4611 Fax: (519) 272-4813	www.avonservices.com	net 30 631 393 461
Bard's Linen & Towels (Jason Bard)	21 Venice Street Stratford, Ontario N5A 4L2	Tel: (519) 271-2273 Fax: (519) 271-9333	bard@bards.com www.bards.com	2/10, n/30 after tax 763 271 673
Bell Canada (Bea Heard)	30 Whisper Road Stratford, Ontario N5A 4N3	Tel: (519) 273-2355	bheard@bell.ca www.bell.ca	net 10 634 345 373
Minister of Finance				net 1
Perth County Hydro (Wynd Mills)	66 Power Road Stratford, Ontario N5A 4P4	Tel: (519) 272-6121	www.perthenergy.com	net 10 721 431 214
Receiver General for Canada				net 1
Stratford Service Centre (A.L.L. Ledfree)	33 MacBeth Avenue Stratford, Ontario N5A 4T2	Tel: (519) 271-6679 Fax: (519) 276-8822	ledfree@ssc.com www.ssc.com	net 1 634 214 211
Tavistock Laundry Services (Martin Tavistock)	19 Merchant Road Stratford, Ontario N5A 4C3	Tel: (519) 271-7479 Fax: (519) 271-7888	www.tavistock.com	net 30 639 271 343
Tempest Food Wholesalers (Vita Minns)	35 Henry Avenue Stratford, Ontario N5A 3N6	Tel: (519) 272-4464 Fax: (519) 272-4600	vita@tempest.com www.tempest.com	net 30 673 421 936
Travellers' Life				
Workplace Safety & Insurance Board				
Zephyr Advertising Services (Tom DeZiner)	32 Portia Blvd. Stratford, Ontario N5A 4T2	Tel: (519) 271-6066 Fax: (519) 271-6067	tom@westwinds.com www.westwinds.com	net 1 391 213 919

LIST OF REMITTANCE SUPPLIERS

STRATFORD COUNTRY INN

Remittance Supplier	Payroll Remittance	Frequency	Next Pay Period Ending Date
Receiver General for Canada	EI, CPP and Income Tax	Quarterly	Jul 1
Workplace Safety & Insurance Board	WSIB	Quarterly	Jul 1
Minister of Finance	EHT	Quarterly	Jul 1
Travellers' Life	group insurance	Quarterly	Jul 1

OUTSTANDING SUPPLIER INVOICES

STRATFORD COUNTRY INN

Supplier Name	Terms	Date	Inv/Chq No.	Amount	Total
Avon Maintenance Services	net 30	June 7/15	AM-68	$565	
	net 30	June 14/15	AM-85	565	
	net 30	June 21/15	AM-101	565	
	net 30	June 28/15	AM-127	565	
			Balance owing		$2 260
Tavistock Laundry Services	net 30	June 8/15	TL-693	$904	
	net 30	June 22/15	TL-742	904	
			Balance owing		$1 808
Tempest Food Wholesalers	net 30	June 23/15	TF-113	$2 000	
	net 30	June 30/15	TF-183	2 000	
			Balance owing		$4 000
			Grand Total		$8 068

GUEST INFORMATION

STRATFORD COUNTRY INN

Guest Name (Contact)	Address	Phone No. Fax No.	E-mail Web Site	Terms Credit Limit
Festival Club of Rosedale (Jane Birken)	3 Rosedale Valley Rd. Toronto, Ontario M5G 3T4	Tel: (416) 482-6343	janebir@conundrum.com	net 5 $6 000
Hamlet Holiday Agency (Ron Doleman)	60 Tibault Avenue Stratford, Ontario N5A 3K3	Tel 1: (519) 272-6461 Tel 2: (800) 777-7777	rdoleman@hamlet.com www.hamlet.com	net 5 $6 000
* Metro Arts Appreciation Group (R. Downey)	4400 Yonge St. North York, Ontario M6L 3T4	Tel: (416) 923-8142	RDowney@artnet.com www.artnet.com	net 5 $6 000
* NY Friends of Shakespeare (J. Monte)	33, 16th Avenue Buffalo, NY 13002	Tel 1: (716) 755-4992 Tel 2: (888) 755-5000	monte@aol.com	net 5 $4 000 (USD)
Waterloo University Literary Club (T. Fornello)	88 College Rd. Waterloo, Ontario N2A 3F6	Tel: (519) 431-6343	fornello4@uwo.ca	net 5 $6 000

* Preferred price list guest

OUTSTANDING GUEST INVOICES

STRATFORD COUNTRY INN

Guest Name	Terms	Date	Inv/Chq No.	Total
Hamlet Holiday Agency	net 30	June 30/15	Deposit #40 (Chq 317; enter a negative invoice)	$1 000

EMPLOYEE INFORMATION SHEET

STRATFORD COUNTRY INN

	Owen Othello	Clara Claudius	Mary MacBeth	Hedy Horatio	Juliet Jones	Shelley Shylock	Bud Romeo
Position	Manager	Clerk	Cook	Waiter	Concierge	Waiter	Service
Social Insurance No.	691 113 724	873 863 211	284 682 556	294 654 421	177 162 930	891 263 634	254 685 829
Address	38 Falstaff St. Stratford, ON N5A 3T3	147 King Henry St. Mary's, ON N4X 1B2	3 Bard Cr. Stratford, ON N5A 6Z8	17 Elizabeth St. Stratford, ON N5A 4Z1	5 Capella Cres. Stratford, ON N5A 5M1	29 Avon St. Stratford, ON N5A 5N5	42 Hosteller St. New Hamburg, ON N0B 2G0
Telephone	(519) 272-2191	(519) 373-6495	(519) 277-1338	(519) 278-5343	(519) 273-9122	(519) 273-5335	(519) 381-3738
Date of Birth (mm-dd-yy)	6-29-75	4-21-68	8-3-73	12-3-80	1-25-74	3-12-84	5-27-73
Date of Hire (mm-dd-yy)	3-1-02	5-2-95	6-1-05	6-1-07	1-1-06	1-1-09	12-16-04
Federal (Ontario) Tax Exemption - TD1							
Basic Personal	$11 038 (9 574)	$11 038 (9 574)	$11 038 (9 574)	$11 038 (9 574)	$11 038 (9 574)	$11 038 (9 574)	$11 038 (9 574)
Other Indexed		$4 468	$15 506 (8 129)		$22 382 (17 216)	–	$15 506 (8 129)
Other Non-indexed	$4 920 (5 032)	–		$3 500 (3 612)	–	$10 200 (10 600)	–
Total Exemptions	$15 958 (14 606)	$15 506 (9 574)	$26 544 (17 703)	$14 538 (13 186)	$33 420 (26 790)	$21 238 (20 174)	$26 544 (17 703)
Additional Federal Tax	–	–	–	$50.00	–	$50.00	–
Employee Taxes							
Historical Income Tax	$4 110.12	$2 796.42	$3 029.01	$2 655.52	$3 345.44	$1 013.86	$1 499.66
Historical EI	$501.60	$376.20	$513.51	$329.55	$468.16	$176.36	$325.85
Historical CPP	$989.34	$721.44	$1 014.83	$621.80	$917.87	$294.49	$613.90
Employee Income							
Loans: Historical	–	–	–	$100.00	–	–	$150.00
Benefits: Historical	$3 800.00	–	–	$2 380.00	–	$6 480.00	–
Vacation Pay Owed	–	–	$1 400.57	$898.85	$1 276.85	$480.96	$888.77
Regular Wage Rate	–	–	$22.00/hr	$14.00/hr	$20.00/hr	$12.00/hr	$14.00/hr
No. Hours Per Period	160	160	80	80	80	80	80
Wages: Historical	–	–	$22 880.00	$14 560.00	$20 800.00	$7 872.00	$14 560.00
Overtime 1 Wage Rate	–	–	$33.00/hr	$21.00/hr	$30.00/hr	$18.00/hr	$21.00/hr
Overtime 1: Historical	–	–	$462.00	$420.00	$480.00	$144.00	$252.00
Regular Salary	$3 800/mo.	$2 850/mo.	–	–	–	–	–
Salary: Historical	$22 800.00	$17 100.00	–	–	–	–	–
Commission	1% (Revenue from Inn)		–	–	–	–	–
Pay Periods	12	12	26	26	26	26	26
Vacation Rate	4 weeks	4 weeks	6% retained	6% retained	6% retained	6% retained	6% retained
Wage Account	Management	General	Dining Room	Dining Room	General	Dining Room	General
Deductions							
Group Insurance	$30.00	$60.00	$30.00	$15.00	$30.00	$15.00	$30.00
Insurance: Historical	$180.00	$360.00	$390.00	$195.00	$390.00	$195.00	$390.00
WSIB and User-Defined Expenses							
WSIB Rate	2.55	2.55	1.70	1.70	2.55	1.70	2.55
Tuition: Historical	$3 800.00	–	–	$2 380.00	–	$6 480.00	–
Entitlements (Rate, Maximum Days, Clear, Days Accrued)							
Vacation	8%, 30, No, 20	8%, 30, No, 20	–	–	–	–	–
Sick Leave	5%, 15, No, 9	5%, 15, No, 7	5%, 15, No, 8	5%, 15, No, 9	5%, 15, No, 10	5%, 15, No, 3	5%, 15, No, 8
T4 and RL-1 Reporting							
EI Insurable Earnings	$22 800.00	$17 100.00	$23 342.00	$14 980.00	$21 280.00	$8 016.00	$14 812.00
Pensionable Earnings	$26 600.00	$17 100.00	$23 342.00	$17 360.00	$21 280.00	$14 496.00	$14 812.00
Withheld	$5 781.06	$4 254.06	$4 947.35	$3 801.87	$5 121.47	$1 679.71	$2 829.41
Net Pay	$17 018.94	$12 845.94	$18 394.65	$11 278.13	$16 158.53	$6 336.29	$12 132.59

Payroll Information

General Payroll Information E. Prospero, the owner, has arranged group insurance for his employees, and all employees have elected to join the plan. As entitlements, all staff may take 10 days' sick leave per year, and the vacation allowances are quite generous for the industry — four weeks of paid vacation for salaried staff after three years of service and 6 percent for all hourly paid employees. As an additional benefit, employees are reimbursed for their tuition fees on completion of eligible courses. Salaried employees are paid monthly, and hourly employees are paid every two weeks. All employees are eligible for EI and pay CPP; the EI factor is 1.4. The Inn pays 0.98 percent of payroll for EHT, the provincial health tax. WSIB rates vary for different types of work performed by the employees of the Inn.

Wage expenses for the manager, the dining room staff and the remaining general employees are tracked separately in three different payroll expense accounts.

NOTES

Enter entitlements as Payroll Settings and edit records for each employee as needed.

Tuition is a user-defined payroll expense and taxable benefit. The benefits for Othello, Horatio and Shylock have already been paid, so only historical amounts are entered.

Remember that WSIB is the name for WCB in Ontario.

Employee Profiles and TD1 Information

E. Prospero owns the Inn and oversees all activities. Together with family members, he fills in where needed. He does not collect a salary and is not recorded as an employee.

Owen Othello is the salaried manager for the Inn. He welcomes guests, instructs other employees and discusses issues, problems and plans with the owner. He is single and studies part time in an MBA program. One night a week he commutes to Toronto. An education allowance — $140 per month federal and $154 provincial — and $3 800 for tuition increase his basic tax claim amounts. Othello is the salesperson for all sales, and beginning in July, he will receive a commission of 1 percent of the revenue from the inn.

NOTES

The claim amounts subject to indexing do not include education and tuition amounts. The amount subject to indexing is used by the program to update claim amounts when a new tax table is introduced, based on the government indexing rate.

NOTES

Education amounts include the monthly allowance for textbooks.

Clara Claudius has been with the Inn the longest and works as the desk attendant. Although her primary job is reservations clerk, she also performs the accounting for the Inn. She too is salaried. Because her husband is also fully employed, she uses the basic single tax claim amounts plus the federal claim for two young dependent children.

Mary MacBeth works as the cook in the dining room. As a single parent with three dependent children, she claims the spousal equivalent for tax purposes for one child and the federal child credit for the other two. She is paid at an hourly rate of $22 per hour for the first 40 hours each week and $33 per hour after that.

Hedy Horatio divides her time between waiting tables and helping the cook for her pay at the rate of $14 per hour plus $21 per hour for overtime hours. She studies part time at Conestoga College in the chef training program. The $2 380 tuition fee and the education tax claims — $140 per month federal and $154 provincial — supplement her basic single claim.

Juliet Jones deals with requests from guests, working as the concierge and arranging for room service. She lives with and cares for her father and therefore has the eligible dependant claim plus a caregiver claim. She also has the age deduction transferred from her father ($6 854 federal and $4 490 provincial) to supplement her basic single claim. Her hourly wage rate is $20 for the first 40 hours each week and $30 for additional hours.

Shelley Shylock waits tables in the dining room at the Inn. During the summer and festival months, she works full time for the Inn at the rate of $12 per hour and $18 for hours beyond the first 40 each week. She works part time until summer while she is a full-time student at the University of Waterloo. The education deduction of $465 ($515 provincial) per month plus tuition fees at $6 480 supplement her tax claim amounts.

Bud Romeo takes care of room service requests and also handles the baggage for the guests. He is married with two dependent children, so he has the spousal claim amount in addition to the basic single amount and federal child claim. He too is paid hourly at the rate of $14 per hour and $21 per hour for the time beyond 40 hours per week.

INVENTORY AND SERVICES INFORMATION

STRATFORD COUNTRY INN

Description	Min Stock	Prices Reg	(Pref)	Unit	Qty on Hand	Total (Cost)	Taxes
Books:: Total asset value $4 000 (Linked Accounts: Books; Revenue from Sales, Cost of Books Sold)							
Two Stratfords: England and Ontario	5	$80	($70)	each	20	$1 000	G
Annotated Plays of Shakespeare	5	80	(70)	each	40	2 000	G
History of Stratford Country Inn	5	50	(45)	each	40	1 000	G
Services: Rooms (Linked Accounts: Revenue from Rooms, Cost of Services)							
Single Room		$150	($130)	room/night			H
Double Room		200	(175)	room/night			H
Services: Meals (Linked Accounts: Revenue from Dining Room, Cost of Services)							
Boxed Lunch		$30	($25)	meal			H
Dinner - Prix Fixe		$70	($65)	meal			H
Services: Tours (Linked Accounts: Revenue from Tours, Cost of Services)							
Guided Tour		$500	($450)	tour			H

NOTES: All prices are the same in United States and Canadian dollars.

WARNING!
Save your work and make backups frequently.

WARNING!
Remember to use a test balance account or the Retained Earnings account to check the Trial Balance before finishing the history for the General Ledger. Print the appropriate reports to check your work as you enter the company data.

NOTES
Guests from the United States pay taxes on their Ontario purchases because the services and goods are consumed in Ontario.

PRO VERSION
Remember that the terms Vendors and Customers will replace Suppliers and Guests.

INSTRUCTIONS

1. Use all the information presented in this application to set up the company accounts for Stratford Country Inn in Sage 50 using the following steps:
   a. Create company files in a new data folder for storing the company records.
   b. Enter the company information. Start a new fiscal period on July 1, 2015, and finish the period on September 30, 2015. Choose Accommodation as the industry.
   c. Enter names and printer information.
   d. Prepare the settings by changing the default settings as necessary.
   e. Organize the Balance Sheet and Income Statement accounts.
   f. Create accounts to correspond to your Balance Sheet and Income Statement. Add appropriate account numbers and types.
   g. Set up currency information for the USD transactions. The exchange rate on June 30 is 1.035.
   h. Change the account class for bank and credit card accounts and set up the cheque sequence.
   i. Enter linked accounts for the ledgers and credit cards. The fee is 2.75 percent.
   j. Enter sales tax information and create tax codes for GST @ 5%, refundable and HST @ 13%, refundable. Reports should be available for both taxes.
   k. Enter guest, supplier, employee and inventory information. The tax code for all suppliers and guests is H, except for the payroll remittance suppliers, and for Tempest Food Wholesalers, which supplies tax exempt foods.
   l. Enter historical balances in all ledgers.

m. Create two Job Categories: Sales (employees are salespersons) and Other (employees in this category are not salespersons). Assign Othello to Sales and all other employees to the Other category.
n. Set up Payroll Remittances. Add the supplier and remittance frequency and enter July 1, 2015, as the end date of the next remitting period.
o. Back up your files.
p. Finish entering the history for all ledgers and finish your session.

2. Using the information provided, enter the source documents for July using Sage 50.

3. After you have completed your entries, print the following reports:
   a. Journal Entries (All Journals) from July 1 to July 31, 2015
   b. Supplier Aged Detail Report for all suppliers on July 31, 2015
   c. Guest Aged Detail Report for all guests on July 31, 2015
   d. Employee Summary (all employees) for the pay period ending July 31, 2015
   e. Income Statement for the period ending July 31, 2015

SOURCE DOCUMENTS

Create new accounts or supplier and guest records as needed for the source documents that follow. Change session dates as needed.

☐

Telephone: (519) 271-BARD (2273)
Fax: (519) 271-9333

Bard's Linen & Towels

Website: www.bards.com
E-mail: bard@bards.com

Invoice: BLT-64

Date: July 1, 2015

Sold to: Stratford Country Inn
100 Festival Road
Stratford, ON
N5A 3G2

STOCK NO.	QTY.	DESCRIPTION	PRICE	AMOUNT
1601	20	Satin Sheets	35.00	700.00
1801	100	Bath Towels	10.00	1000.00
2802	100	Face Cloths	3.00	300.00

CUSTOMER COPY	Terms on Account: 2/10, N/30			GROSS	2000.00
Method of payment:	On Account	C.O.D.	Credit Card		
HST #763 271 673	✓			HST 13%	260.00
				TOTAL	2260.00

☐

AVON Maintenance Services
66 Kleen Road, Stratford, ON N5A 3C3
Telephone (519) 272-4611
Fax: (519) 272-4813
www.avonservices.com

Invoice: AM-148
Date: July 1, 2015
Sold to: Stratford Country Inn
100 Festival Road
Stratford, ON
N5A 3G2
Phone: (519) 222-6066

Code	Service Description	Price
KX-55	Vacuum Premises Floor Polishing Washroom Cleaning Maintenance and Repairs Recurring bi-weekly billing	1000.00

Signature: E Prosper
Terms: Net 30 days
HST #631 393 461
HST 130.00
Amount owing 1130.00

☐

100 Festival Road, Stratford, ON N5A 3G2
Tel.: (519) 222-6066 1-888-272-6000
Fax.: (519) 272-7960

Stratford Country Inn

STRATFORD TRUST
80 Sterling Avenue
Stratford, ON N5A 3G3

No: 701

Date 20150705 (YYYYMMDD)

Pay Two Thousand Two Hundred Sixty 00 $ 2,260.00

TO THE ORDER OF
Avon Maintenance Services
66 Kleen Road
Stratford, ON N5A 3C3

PER E Prosper
Treasurer

••‥•• 392451 ••• 22 • 701

Re: Invoices AM-68, 85, 101, 127
$ 2,260.00 **No: 701**
July 5, 2015

WARNING! You must change the tax code for books to G on all sales invoices so that taxes will be correctly applied for these items.

☐

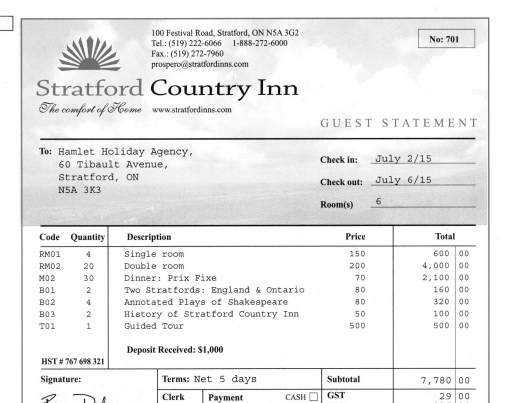

100 Festival Road, Stratford, ON N5A 3G2
Tel.: (519) 222-6066 1-888-272-6000
Fax.: (519) 272-7960
prospero@stratfordinns.com

No: 701

Stratford Country Inn

The comfort of Home www.stratfordinns.com

GUEST STATEMENT

To: Hamlet Holiday Agency,
60 Tibault Avenue,
Stratford, ON
N5A 3K3

Check in: July 2/15
Check out: July 6/15
Room(s) 6

Code	Quantity	Description	Price	Total	
RM01	4	Single room	150	600	00
RM02	20	Double room	200	4,000	00
M02	30	Dinner: Prix Fixe	70	2,100	00
B01	2	Two Stratfords: England & Ontario	80	160	00
B02	4	Annotated Plays of Shakespeare	80	320	00
B03	2	History of Stratford Country Inn	50	100	00
T01	1	Guided Tour	500	500	00
		Deposit Received: $1,000			

HST # 767 698 321

Signature: Ron Dukeman

Terms: Net 5 days

Clerk CC

Payment Method: CASH ☐ CHEQUE ☐ ON ACCOUNT ☑

Subtotal	7,780	00
GST	29	00
HST	936	00
BALANCE	$7,745	00

☐

Waterloo University Literary Club
88 College Road
Waterloo, ON N2A 3F6

No: 413

Date 20150706
YYYYMMDD

Pay to the order of Stratford Country Inn $ 1,000.00

One Thousand 00/100 **Dollars**

Waterloo Trust
550 King Street
Waterloo, ON N2A 3F8

T. Fornello
Chair

⑈⑆ 60431 ⑆ 105 ⑈ 413

Re: Deposit #41 – booking rooms in Inn **No: 413**

$1,000.00 July 6, 2015

☐

100 Festival Road, Stratford, ON N5A 3G2
Tel.: (519) 222-6066 1-888-272-6000
Fax.: (519) 272-7960

Stratford Country Inn

STRATFORD TRUST
80 Sterling Avenue
Stratford, ON N5A 3G3

No: 702

Date 20150707
YYYYMMDD

Pay One Thousand Eight Hundred Eight 00 $ 1,808.00

TO THE ORDER OF
Tavistock Laundry Services
19 Merchant Road
Stratford, ON N5A 4C3

PER E Prospero
Treasurer

⑆⑈ 392451 ⑆ 22 - 702

Re: Invoices TL-693, 742 $ 1,808.00 **No: 702**

July 7, 2015

☐

100 Festival Road, Stratford, ON N5A 3G2
Tel.: (519) 222-6066 1-888-272-6000
Fax.: (519) 272-7960
prospero@stratfordinns.com

Stratford Country Inn
The comfort of Home www.stratfordinns.com

VISA
SALES SUMMARY STATEMENT

No: 702

July 7, 2015

Code	Quantity	Description	Price	Total	
RM01	8	Single room	150	1,200	00
RM02	25	Double room	200	5,000	00
M01	6	Boxed Lunch	30	180	00
M02	10	Dinner: Prix Fixe	70	700	00
B01	2	Two Stratfords: England & Ontario	80	160	00
B02	4	Annotated Plays of Shakespeare	80	320	00
B03	4	History of Stratford Country Inn	50	200	00
T01	2	Guided Tour	500	1,000	00

HST # 767 698 321	**Subtotal**	8,760	00
Approved: E Prospero	**Goods & Services Tax**	34	00
	Harmonized Sales Tax	1,050	40
	VISA Receipts	$9,844	40

☐

Sold to: Stratford Country Inn
100 Festival Road
Stratford, ON
N5A 3G2

Billing Date: July 8, 2015
Invoice No: TF-284
Customer No.: 3423
Customer Copy

TEMPEST Food Wholesalers
35 Henry Avenue
Stratford, ON N5A 3N6

Telephone: (519) 272-4464
Fax: (519) 272-4600
Website: www.tempest.com

Date	Description	Charges	Payments	Amount
July 8/15	Fish and Meats	1000.00		1000.00
	Fresh Fruits	200.00		200.00
	Fresh Vegetables	200.00		200.00
	Dry Goods	200.00		200.00
	Dairy Products	200.00		200.00
	Baking Goods	200.00		200.00
	Recurring bi-weekly billing			

Terms: Net 30 days	**Subtotal**	2000.00
HST #673 421 936		
Signature: E Prospero	**HST 13%**	exempt
Overdue accounts are subject to 16% interest per year	**Owing**	2000.00

☐

Invoice No: TL-798
Date: July 8, 2015
Customer: Stratford Country Inn
100 Festival Road
Stratford, ON
N5A 3G2

Phone: (519) 222-6066

TAVISTOCK LAUNDRY Services
19 Merchant Road
Stratford, ON
N5A 4C3

Phone: (519) 271-7479
Fax: (519) 271-7888
www.tavistock.com

HST #639 271 343

Code	Description	Price	Amount
C-11	10 Loads Sheets	40.00	400.00
C-14	5 Loads Pillow Covers	20.00	100.00
C-20	15 Loads Towels	20.00	300.00
	Recurring bi-weekly billing		

Overdue accounts are subject to a 2% interest penalty per month	**Sub-total**	800.00
Terms: Net 30 days	**HST**	104.00
Signature: E Prospero	**Total**	904.00

☐

100 Festival Road, Stratford, ON N5A 3G2
Tel.: (519) 222-6066 1-888-272-6000
Fax.: (519) 272-7960

Stratford Country Inn

ST **STRATFORD TRUST**
80 Sterling Avenue
Stratford, ON N5A 3G3

No: 703

Date 2 0 1 5 0 7 0 9
Y Y Y Y M M D D

Pay Four Thousand 00 $ 4,000.00

TO THE ORDER OF Tempest Food Wholesalers
35 Henry Avenue
Stratford, ON N5A 3N6

PER E Prospero
Treasurer

392451 22 703

Re: Invoices TF-113, 183 $ 4,000.00 **No: 703**
July 9, 2015

☐

Hamlet Holiday Agency
60 Tibault Avenue,
STRATFORD, ON N5A 3K3

SB **Scotia Bank**
44 Welland Avenue
STRATFORD, ON N5A 3F6

No: 349

Date 2 0 1 5 0 7 1 0
Y Y Y Y M M D D

Pay Seven thousand, seven hundred & forty-five 00 $ 7,745.00

TO THE ORDER OF Stratford Country Inn
100 Festival Road
Stratford, ON N5A 3G2

PER Ron Doleman
Treasurer

64299 168 349

Re: Receipt #56 (Cheque #317)
Invoice #701 $7,745.00 **No: 349**
July 10, 2015

☐

100 Festival Road, Stratford, ON N5A 3G2
Tel.: (519) 222-6066 1-888-272-6000
Fax.: (519) 272-7960

Stratford Country Inn

STRATFORD TRUST
80 Sterling Avenue
Stratford, ON N5A 3G3

No: 704

Date 20150710
YYYYMMDD

Pay Two Thousand Two Hundred Fourteen —— 80 $ 2,214.80

TO THE ORDER OF
Bard's Linen & Towels
21 Venice Street
Stratford, ON N5A 4L2

PER E. Prospero
Treasurer

••—•••••392451•••22•704

Re: Invoice BLT-64, Discount taken $45.20 $ 2,214.80 **No: 704**
July 10, 2015

☐

STRATFORD SERVICE CENTRE
33 MacBeth Avenue
Stratford, ON N5A 4T2
Tel: (519) 271-6679
Fax: (519) 276-8822
www.ssc.com

Date: July 11, 2015 **Invoice:** 1143

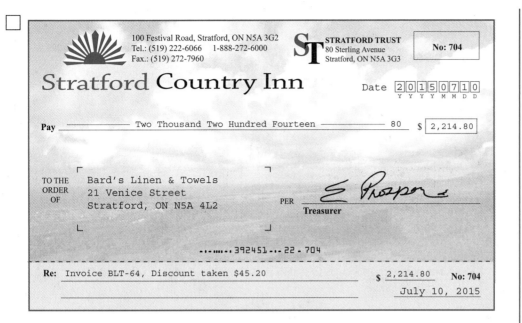

Customer: Stratford Country Inn
100 Festival Road
Stratford, ON
N5A 3G2

Phone: (519) 222-6066

HST #634 214 211

Code	Description	Price	Amount
M-114	Lube, Oil and Filter	40.00	40.00
XF-1	Fuel	120.00	120.00
		Sub-total	160.00
		HST	20.80
		Owing	180.80

APPROVAL EP

CUSTOMER COPY

Cash	VISA	On Account
	✓	

☐

100 Festival Road, Stratford, ON N5A 3G2
Tel.: (519) 222-6066 1-888-272-6000
Fax.: (519) 272-7960

Stratford Country Inn

ST STRATFORD TRUST
80 Sterling Avenue
Stratford, ON N5A 3G3

No: 705

Date 2 0 1 5 0 7 1 2
Y Y Y Y M M D D

Pay —— Two Thousand Three Hundred Eighty —— 00 $ 2,380.00

TO THE ORDER OF
Receiver General for Canada
PO Box 20002, Stn A
Sudbury, ON P3A 5C3

PER
Treasurer

392451 22 705

Re: HST and GST Remittance for June 30 $ 2,380.00 **No: 705**

July 12, 2015

☐

100 Festival Road, Stratford, ON N5A 3G2
Tel.: (519) 222-6066 1-888-272-6000
Fax.: (519) 272-7960

Stratford Country Inn

ST STRATFORD TRUST
80 Sterling Avenue
Stratford, ON N5A 3G3

No: 706

Date 2 0 1 5 0 7 1 2
Y Y Y Y M M D D

Pay —— Five Thousand Nine Hundred Sixty —— 00 $ 5,960.00

TO THE ORDER OF
Receiver General for Canada
PO Box 20002, Stn A
Sudbury, ON P3A 5C3

PER
Treasurer

392451 22 706

Re: EI, CPP and Income tax remittances for June $ 5,960.00 **No: 706**

July 12, 2015

100 Festival Road, Stratford, ON N5A 3G2
Tel.: (519) 222-6066 1-888-272-6000
Fax.: (519) 272-7960
prospero@stratfordinns.com

No: 703

Stratford Country Inn

The comfort of Home www.stratfordinns.com

GUEST STATEMENT

To: Waterloo University
Literary Club,
88 College Road,
Waterloo, ON
N2A 3F6

Check in: July 9/15
Check out: July 13/15
Room(s) 8

Code	Quantity	Description Transaction	Price	Total	
RM01	16	Single room	150	2,400	00
RM02	24	Double room	200	4,800	00
M01	7	Boxed Lunch	30	210	00
M02	16	Dinner: Prix Fixe	70	1,120	00
B01	1	Two Stratfords: England & Ontario	80	80	00
B02	2	Annotated Plays of Shakespeare	80	160	00
B03	1	History of Stratford Country Inn	50	50	00
T01	1	Guided Tour	500	500	00
		Deposit Received: $1,000			

HST # 767 698 321

Signature: T. Fornello

Terms: Net 5 days

Clerk CC

Payment Method: CASH ☐ CHEQUE ☐ ON ACCOUNT ☑

Subtotal	9,320	00
GST	14	50
HST	1,173	90
BALANCE	$9,508	40

---

100 Festival Road, Stratford, ON N5A 3G2
Tel.: (519) 222-6066 1-888-272-6000
Fax.: (519) 272-7960
prospero@stratfordinns.com

Stratford Country Inn

The comfort of Home www.stratfordinns.com

VISA **No: 704**

SALES SUMMARY STATEMENT

July 14, 2015

Code	Quantity	Description	Price	Total	
RM01	7	Single room	150	1,050	00
RM02	12	Double room	200	2,400	00
M01	10	Boxed Lunch	30	300	00
M02	40	Meals	70	2,800	00
B01	2	Two Stratfords: England & Ontario	80	160	00
B02	3	Annotated Plays of Shakespeare	80	240	00
B03	3	History of Stratford Country Inn	50	150	00
T01	1	Guided Tour	500	500	00

HST # 767 698 321

Approved: E Prospero

Subtotal	7,600	00
Goods & Services Tax	27	50
Harmonized Sales Tax	916	50
VISA Receipts	$8,544	00

☐

100 Festival Road, Stratford, ON N5A 3G2
Tel.: (519) 222-6066 1-888-272-6000
Fax.: (519) 272-7960
prospero@stratford.com

ET27

Stratford Country Inn

The comfort of Home www.stratfordinns.com

EMPLOYEE TIME SUMMARY SHEET

Pay period ending: July 14, 2015

Name of Employee	Regular hours	Overtime hours	Sick days
☐ Horatio, Hedy	80	0	0
☐ Jones, Juliet	80	0	1
☐ MacBeth, Mary	80	2	0
☐ Romeo, Bud	80	2	0
☐ Shylock, Shelley	80	2	0

Memo: Issue cheques #707 to #711
Recover $100 loan from Horatio and Romeo

☐

AVON Maintenance Services

66 Kleen Road, Stratford, ON N5A 3C3
Telephone (519) 272-4611
Fax: (519) 272-4813
www.avonservices.com

Invoice No: AM-184
Date: July 15, 2015
Sold to: Stratford Country Inn
100 Festival Road
Stratford, ON
N5A 3G2
Phone: (519) 222-6066

Code	Service Description	Price
KX-55	Vacuum Premises * Floor Polishing Washroom Cleaning Maintenance and Repairs Recurring bi-weekly billing * new price as described in our previous notice	1100.00

Signature: E Prospero	**Terms:** Net 30 days	**HST**	143.00
	HST #631 393 461	**Amount owing**	1243.00

☐

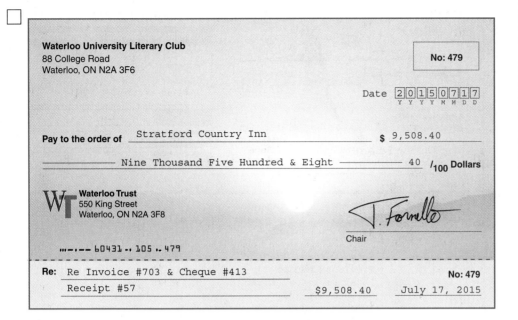

Waterloo University Literary Club
88 College Road
Waterloo, ON N2A 3F6

No: 479

Date 2 0 1 5 0 7 1 7
Y Y Y Y M M D D

Pay to the order of Stratford Country Inn **$** 9,508.40

Nine Thousand Five Hundred & Eight 40 /100 **Dollars**

WT **Waterloo Trust**
550 King Street
Waterloo, ON N2A 3F8

Chair

⑈⑆⑈ 60431 ⑆ 105 ⑆ 479

Re: Re Invoice #703 & Cheque #413
Receipt #57 $9,508.40 **No: 479** July 17, 2015

☐

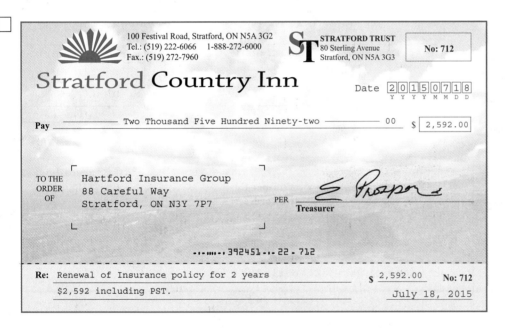

100 Festival Road, Stratford, ON N5A 3G2
Tel.: (519) 222-6066 1-888-272-6000
Fax.: (519) 272-7960

ST **STRATFORD TRUST**
80 Sterling Avenue
Stratford, ON N5A 3G3

No: 712

Stratford Country Inn

Date 2 0 1 5 0 7 1 8
Y Y Y Y M M D D

Pay Two Thousand Five Hundred Ninety-two 00 $ 2,592.00

TO THE ORDER OF
Hartford Insurance Group
88 Careful Way
Stratford, ON N3Y 7P7

PER **Treasurer**

⑆⑈⑆ 392451 ⑆ 22 - 712

Re: Renewal of Insurance policy for 2 years $ 2,592.00 **No: 712**
$2,592 including PST. July 18, 2015

☐

PERTH COUNTY HYDRO
66 Power Road, Stratford, Ontario N5A 4P4
www.perthenergy.com

Customer Care: 272-6121

CUSTOMER NAME / SERVICE ADDRESS	
Stratford Country Inn 100 Festival Road Stratford, ON N5A 3G2	
Date:	July 18, 2015
Account No:	3921 462 513
Invoice No:	37232

Months	Reading	Description		Net Amount
1	86527	Commercial Consumption		300.00
1		Flat Rate Charge – Water Heaters		60.00
1		Rental of Equipment		40.00
		Total Current Charges		400.00
		Previous Charges	385.20	
		Total Payments, Thank You	385.20	
		Balance Forward		0.00
		Adjustments		0.00

Paid in Full with cheque #713 for $452 07/18/15 E Prosper

Average Daily KWh Consumption		HST #721 431 214	Due Date		
Same Period Last Year	This Bill	After due date, a 1.5% monthly late payment interest charge will apply.	July 25/15	HST 13%	52.00
269	258		Pay This Amount	TOTAL	452.00

☐

Bell

30 Whisper Road
Stratford, ON
N5A 4N3

www.bell.ca

Account Inquiries: 273-BELL (2355)

Account Number
519-222-6066

Account Address
Stratford Country Inn
100 Festival Road
Stratford, ON
N5A 3G2

July 18, 2015

ACCOUNT SUMMARY

Current Charges	
Monthly Services (June 12 to July 12)	240.00
Equipment Rentals	50.00
Chargeable Messages	30.00
HST 634 345 373	41.60
Total Current Charges	361.60
Previous Charges	
Amount of Last Bill	323.00
Payment Received June 19 – Thank You	323.00
Adjustments	0.00
Balance Forward	0.00

Paid in Full – chq #714 – 07/18/15 E Prosper

Invoice: BC-66431	PLEASE PAY THIS AMOUNT UPON RECEIPT ⇒	$361.60

100 Festival Road, Stratford, ON N5A 3G2
Tel.: (519) 222-6066 1-888-272-6000
Fax.: (519) 272-7960
prospero@stratfordinns.com

No: 705

Stratford Country Inn
The comfort of Home www.stratfordinns.com

GUEST STATEMENT

To: NY Friends of Shakespeare,
33, 16th Avenue,
Buffalo, NY
13002

Check in: July 17/15
Check out: July 20/15
Room(s) 9

Code	Quantity	Description	Price	Total	
RM01	6	Single room	130	780	00
RM02	21	Double room	175	3,675	00
M01	20	Boxed Lunch	25	500	00
M02	16	Dinner: Prix Fixe	65	1,040	00
B01	2	Two Stratfords: England & Ontario	70	140	00
B03	4	History of Stratford Country Inn	45	180	00
T01	1	Guided Tour	450	450	00
		**Preferred customer - no deposit required			
HST # 767 698 321		Exchange rate: 1.0395 CAD			
			Subtotal	6,765	00
			GST	16	00
			HST	837	85
			BALANCE	USD $7,618	85

Signature: J.Monte

Terms: Net 5 days

Clerk CC

Payment Method: CASH ☐ CHEQUE ☐ ON ACCOUNT ☑

Festival Club of Rosedale
3 Rosedale Valley Rd.
Toronto, Ontario
M5G 3T4

No: 61

Date 20150720 (YYYYMMDD)

Pay to the order of Stratford Country Inn $ 1,000.00

One Thousand 00 /100 **Dollars**

Royal Bank
56 Bloor Street
Toronto, ON M5N 3G7

Jane Birker
Chairperson

⑈--- 34298 ⑆021⑆ 061

Re: Deposit #42 – booking rooms in Inn **No: 61**

$1,000.00 July 20, 2015

☐

ST STRATFORD TRUST
80 Sterling Avenue
Stratford, ON N5A 3G3

VISA

Statement Period M D Y		Account Number	Account Enquiries	Daily Interest Rate	Annual Interest Rate
From	06/15/15	4512 6221 1384 6201	1-800-272-VISA	.05068%	18.5%
To	07/15/15				

Trans. Date	Post Date	Particulars	Amount	Bus. Exp.
06 13	06 16	Stratford Service Centre, Stratford, ON	85.00	EP
06 18	06 21	Office Supplies Unlimited, Stratford, ON	88.00	EP
06 25	06 27	Stratford Service Centre, Stratford, ON	133.00	EP
06 28	06 30	Bullrich Dept. Store #32, Stratford, ON	113.00	EP
06 28	06 30	Bullrich Dept. Store #32, Stratford, ON	-24.00	EP
07 11	07 13	Stratford Service Centre, Stratford, ON	180.80	EP
06 20	06 20	Payment — Thank You	-422.00	EP

Balance $575.80 paid in full by cheque # 715 E Prospero July 21/15

Credit Limit	Opening Balance	Total Credits	Total Debits	Your New Balance
8500.00	422.00	446.00	599.80	575.80

Available Credit	Payment Due Date Month Day Year	Overlimit or Past Due	Current Due	Minimum Payment	Payment Amount
7924.20	07/24/15	-	57.00	57.00	575.80

☐

100 Festival Road, Stratford, ON N5A 3G2
Tel.: (519) 222-6066 1-888-272-6000
Fax.: (519) 272-7960
prospero@stratfordinns.com

Stratford Country Inn
The comfort of Home
www.stratfordinns.com

VISA

No: 706

SALES SUMMARY STATEMENT

July 21, 2015

Code	Quantity	Description	Price	Total	
RM01	4	Single room	150	600	00
RM02	18	Double room	200	3,600	00
M01	8	Boxed Lunch	30	240	00
M02	22	Meals	70	1,540	00
B01	2	Two Stratfords: England & Ontario	80	160	00
B02	5	Annotated Plays of Shakespeare	80	400	00
B03	3	History of Stratford Country Inn	50	150	00
T01	1	Guided Tour	500	500	00

HST # 767 698 321	Subtotal	7,190	00
Approved: E Prospero	Goods and Services Tax	35	50
	Harmonized Sales Tax	842	40
	VISA Receipts	$8,067	90

Sold to: Stratford Country Inn
100 Festival Road
Stratford, ON
N5A 3G2

Billing Date: July 22, 2015
Invoice No: TF-344
Customer No.: 3423
Customer Copy

TEMPEST Food Wholesalers
35 Henry Avenue
Stratford, ON N5A 3N6

Telephone: (519) 272-4464
Fax: (519) 272-4600
Website: www.tempest.com

Date	Description	Charges	Payments	Amount
July 22 /15	Fish and Meats	1000.00		1000.00
	Fresh Fruits	200.00		200.00
	Fresh Vegetables	200.00		200.00
	Dry Goods	200.00		200.00
	Dairy Products	200.00		200.00
	Baking Goods	200.00		200.00
	Recurring bi-weekly billing			
Terms: Net 30 days			**Subtotal**	2000.00
HST #673 421 936				
Signature: E Prosper			**HST 13%**	exempt
Overdue accounts are subject to 16% interest per year			**Owing**	2000.00

Invoice No: TL-841
Date: July 22, 2015
Customer: Stratford Country Inn
100 Festival Road
Stratford, ON
N5A 3G2

Phone: (519) 222-6066

TAVISTOCK LAUNDRY Services
19 Merchant Road
Stratford, ON
N5A 4C3

Phone: (519) 271-7479
Fax: (519) 271-7888
www.tavistock.com

HST #639 271 343

Code	Description	Price	Amount
C-11	10 Loads Sheets *	45.00	450.00
C-14	5 Loads Pillow Covers	20.00	100.00
C-20	15 Loads Towels	20.00	300.00
	Recurring bi-weekly billing * new prices		
Overdue accounts are subject to a 2% interest penalty per month		**Sub-total**	850.00
Terms: Net 30 days		**HST**	110.50
Signature: E Prosper		**Total**	960.50

Zephyr Advertising Services
32 Portia Blvd.,
Stratford, ON
N5A 4T2

Telephone (519) 271-6066
Fax (519) 271-6067
www.westwinds.com
orders: contact tom@westwinds.com

ZA - 6998

Stratford Country Inn
100 Festival Road
Stratford, ON
N5A 3G2

Date	Description	Charges	Amount
July 23, 2015	Brochures & Flyers	100.00	100.00
		HST	13.00
HST # 391 213 919	Terms: Cash on Receipt	Total	113.00

Paid in full
cheque # 716
July 23/15

NY Friends of Shakespeare
33, 16th Avenue,
Buffalo, NY 13002

No: 181

Date 20150724
YYYYMMDD

Pay to the order of Stratford Country Inn $ 7,618.85 (USD)

Seven thousand, six hundred eighteen 85 /100 Dollars

Chase Bank
4, 12th Avenue
Buffalo, NY 13002

J.Monte

⑈—⑆—— 93937 ⑆ 301 ⑆ 181

Re: Re Invoice #705: Receipt #59
U.S. Currency. Currency Exchange 1.031 Cdn. $7,618.85 (USD) July 24, 2015

No: 181

☐

STRATFORD SERVICE CENTRE

33 MacBeth Avenue
Stratford, ON N5A 4T2
Tel: (519) 271-6679
Fax: (519) 276-8822
www.ssc.com

Date: July 25, 2015 **Invoice:** 1207

Customer: Stratford Country Inn
100 Festival Road
Stratford, ON
N5A 3G2

Phone: (519) 222-6066

HST #634 214 211

Code	Description	Price	Amount
R-69	Transmission–overhaul	500.00	500.00
XF-1	Fuel	100.00	100.00
		Sub-total	600.00
		HST	78.00
		Owing	678.00

APPROVAL	CUSTOMER COPY		
	Cash	VISA	On Account
EP		✓	

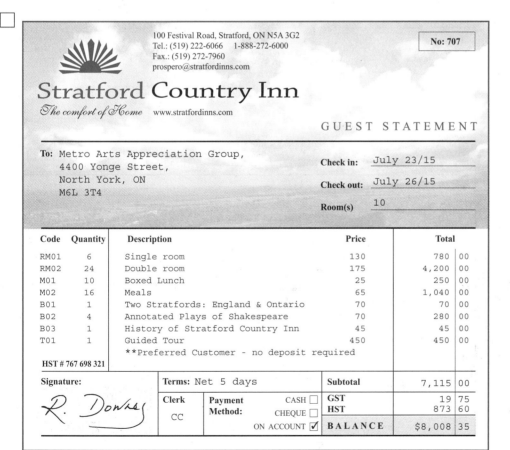

☐

Stratford Country Inn
The comfort of Home

100 Festival Road, Stratford, ON N5A 3G2
Tel.: (519) 222-6066 1-888-272-6000
Fax.: (519) 272-7960
prospero@stratfordinns.com
www.stratfordinns.com

No: 707

GUEST STATEMENT

To: Metro Arts Appreciation Group,
4400 Yonge Street,
North York, ON
M6L 3T4

Check in: July 23/15
Check out: July 26/15
Room(s) 10

Code	Quantity	Description	Price	Total	
RM01	6	Single room	130	780	00
RM02	24	Double room	175	4,200	00
M01	10	Boxed Lunch	25	250	00
M02	16	Meals	65	1,040	00
B01	1	Two Stratfords: England & Ontario	70	70	00
B02	4	Annotated Plays of Shakespeare	70	280	00
B03	1	History of Stratford Country Inn	45	45	00
T01	1	Guided Tour	450	450	00
		**Preferred Customer - no deposit required			
HST # 767 698 321					

Signature:	Terms: Net 5 days		Subtotal	7,115	00
R. Downey	Clerk CC	Payment Method: CASH ☐ CHEQUE ☐ ON ACCOUNT ☑	GST	19	75
			HST	873	60
			BALANCE	$8,008	35

100 Festival Road, Stratford, ON N5A 3G2
Tel.: (519) 222-6066 1-888-272-6000
Fax.: (519) 272-7960
prospero@stratford.com

ET28

Stratford Country Inn
The comfort of Home
www.stratfordinns.com

EMPLOYEE TIME SUMMARY SHEET

Pay period ending: July 28, 2015

Name of Employee	Regular hours	Overtime hours	Sick days
Horatio, Hedy	80	2	0
Jones, Juliet	76	4	0
MacBeth, Mary	80	0	0
Romeo, Bud	80	0	1
Shylock, Shelley	80	2	0

Memo: Issue cheques #717 to #721
Recover $50 loan from Romeo

100 Festival Road, Stratford, ON N5A 3G2
Tel.: (519) 222-6066 1-888-272-6000
Fax.: (519) 272-7960
prospero@stratfordinns.com

VISA

No: 708

Stratford Country Inn
The comfort of Home
www.stratfordinns.com

SALES SUMMARY STATEMENT

July 28, 2015

Code	Quantity	Description	Price	Total	
RM01	7	Single room	150	1,050	00
RM02	14	Double room	200	2,800	00
M01	35	Boxed Lunch	30	1,050	00
M02	20	Dinner: Prix Fixe	70	1,400	00
B01	3	Two Stratfords: England & Ontario	80	240	00
B02	5	Annotated Plays of Shakespeare	80	400	00
B03	6	History of Stratford Country Inn	50	300	00
T01	2	Guided Tour	500	1,000	00

HST # 767 698 321	Subtotal	8,240	00
Approved: E Prospero	Goods and Services Tax	47	00
	Harmonized Sales Tax	949	00
	VISA Receipts	$9,236	00

☐

100 Festival Road, Stratford, ON N5A 3G2
Tel.: (519) 222-6066 1-888-272-6000
Fax.: (519) 272-7960
prospero@stratfordinns.com

No: 709

Stratford Country Inn

The comfort of Home www.stratfordinns.com

GUEST STATEMENT

To: Festival Club of Rosedale,
3 Rosedale Valley Road,
Toronto, ON
M5G 3T4

Check in: July 26/15
Check out: July 30/15
Room(s) 8

Code	Quantity	Description	Price	Total	
RM01	8	Single room	150	1,200	00
RM02	24	Double room	200	4,800	00
M01	28	Boxed Lunch	30	840	00
M02	28	Meals	70	1,960	00
B01	1	Two Stratfords: England & Ontario	80	80	00
B02	2	Annotated Plays of Shakespeare	80	160	00
B03	2	History of Stratford Country Inn	50	100	00
T01	1	Guided Tour	500	500	00
		Deposit Received: $1,000			
HST # 767 698 321					

Signature: Jane Birker	**Terms:**		**Subtotal**	9,640	00
	Clerk CC	**Payment Method:** CASH ☐ CHEQUE ☐ ON ACCOUNT ☑	**GST**	17	00
			HST	1,209	00
			BALANCE	$9,866	00

☐

Hamlet Holiday Agency
60 Tibault Avenue,
STRATFORD, ON N5A 3K3

SB **Scotia Bank**
44 Welland Avenue
STRATFORD, ON N5A 3F6

No: 393

Date 2 0 1 5 0 7 3 1
Y Y Y Y M M D D

Pay One thousand 00 $ 1,000.00

TO THE ORDER OF
Stratford Country Inn
100 Festival Road
Stratford, ON N5A 3G2

PER Ron Doleman

⑈⑆—⑆—— 64299 ⑆ 168 ⑆ 393

Re: Deposit #43 – booking rooms in Inn

No: 393

$1,000.00 July 31, 2015

☐

100 Festival Road, Stratford, ON N5A 3G2
Tel.: (519) 222-6066 1-888-272-6000
Fax.: (519) 272-7960
prospero@stratfordinns.com

Stratford Country Inn

The comfort of Home www.stratfordinns.com

MEMO #31

From: the owner's desk
To: Clara Claudius
July 31, 2015

1. Transfer $35,000 from Credit Card Bank account to CAD Chequing account.
2. Transfer $6,000 USD from USD Chequing account to CAD Chequing account. The exchange rate is 1.041.

☐

100 Festival Road, Stratford, ON N5A 3G2
Tel.: (519) 222-6066 1-888-272-6000
Fax.: (519) 272-7960
prospero@stratfordinns.com

Stratford Country Inn

The comfort of Home www.stratfordinns.com

MEMO #32

From: the owner's desk
To: Clara Claudius
July 31, 2015

1. a) Pay Owen Othello salary and sales commission (1% Revenue from Inn). Issue cheque #722.
   b) Pay Clara Claudius salary. Issue cheque #723.
2. Pay quarterly balances owing as at July 1
   a) To Minister of Finance (EHT), cheque #724
   b) Workplace Safety and Insurance Board (WSIB), cheque #725
   c) Travellers' Life (Group Insurance), cheque #726
3. Prepare adjusting entries for the following:
   a) Food Inventory on hand $1 395
   b) Write off $200 of Prepaid Insurance
   c) Write off $50 of Prepaid Advertising
   d) Depreciation on Country Inn & Dining Room $600
      Depreciation on Computers $200
      Depreciation on Furniture & Fixtures $600
      Depreciation on Vehicles $800

REVIEW

The Student DVD with Data Files includes a comprehensive supplementary case for this chapter and bank reconciliation.

Part 3
Advanced Premium Features

CHAPTER EIGHTEEN

Ryder's Routes

OBJECTIVES

After completing this chapter, you should be able to

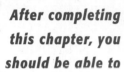

- ***set up*** inventory service activities for time and billing
- ***update*** prices from Inventory Settings
- ***enter*** employee time slips
- ***import*** time slip activities to prepare employee paycheques
- ***import*** time slip activities to prepare customer invoices
- ***display*** and ***print*** time and billing reports
- ***set up*** additional currencies
- ***build*** new inventory from Inventory Ledger record details
- ***set up*** multiple inventory locations
- ***add*** inventory locations to journal entries
- ***transfer*** inventory between locations
- ***understand*** related accounts for multiple fiscal periods
- ***display*** and ***print*** multi-period financial reports

COMPANY INFORMATION

Time and Billing Profile

PRO VERSION
You will be unable to complete this chapter if you are using the Pro version.

You can download and install the Student Premium version program to complete Chapters 18 and 19. You must uninstall your Pro version before you can install the Student version. Refer to page A–10.

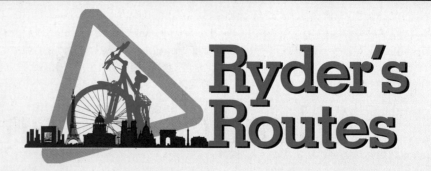

Ryder's Routes, under the management of Steve Ryder and VeloCity, provides bicycle tour guide services in Canada and internationally to travel companies wanting to add cycling to their group package tours. Tour guides will also service the guests' bicycles while on tour. Guests may rent bicycles for their trips or ship their own bicycles. To accommodate this new service, Ryder will invoice customers using the Time & Billing module. After modifying the service records to price the services according to the time taken to complete the work and adding the new services, the company can track the work performed by each employee for each customer.

Additionally, Ryder has contracted with new suppliers and customers in Europe. No duty is charged on imported exercise equipment.

In August, Ryder's Routes began providing guide services in addition to the existing services for the bicycles it sells. These services are billed in three ways:

at an hourly rate, at a flat rate regardless of the time required to complete the work and at no charge for repairs to bicycles under warranty. All tour and service work will be managed from Ryder's Routes, a new store near the VeloCity showroom. For convenience, Ryder's Routes will also sell bicycle accessories. Other inventory can be transferred to Ryder's Routes as needed. Separate inventory locations will be set up for the two stores so that Ryder can track the inventory at each location.

Ryder hired two new employees: Yvonne Leader will serve as tour guide and Moishe Alee will work as the primary sales associate in the new store.

The company's fiscal period will be reduced to one month and cash sales summaries will be entered at the end of the month to reduce the number of source documents in this application.

NOTES
Sales and services provided by Ryder's Routes in Canada will have HST added. Tour guide services that are provided outside of Canada (in Europe or the United States) will not be taxable. The location determines the taxability, not the nationality of the customer.

KEYSTROKES

Modifying Company Information

Changing Fiscal Dates

Open **SageData13\Ryder\ryder** to access the data files for this chapter. and **accept August 1, 2015** as the session date.

NOTES
If you are working from the backup files, restore SageData13\ryder1.CAB or ryder1 to SageData13\Ryder\ryder.

Enter the **adjustment** for accrued wages and then **change** the **fiscal dates**.

1 **Memo #8-1** **Dated August 1, 2015**

Prepare an adjusting entry to reverse the year-end adjustment for $720 for accrued payroll. (Debit Accrued Wages and credit Wages.)

NOTES
The wage expense credit entry that reverses the accrued payroll ensures that the correct amount from this pay period will be assigned to the previous fiscal period, adhering to the principle of recording expenses in the period in which they were incurred.

✓ 2 **Memo #8-2** **Dated August 1, 2015**

Change the company fiscal dates. The new fiscal end is August 31, 2015. Change the company name to VeloCity - Ryder's Routes

Click **Company** in the Modules pane list to open the Company window.

Click the **Settings icon** [Settings], then **click Information**, or **choose** the **Setup menu** and **click Settings**, **Company** and **Information**:

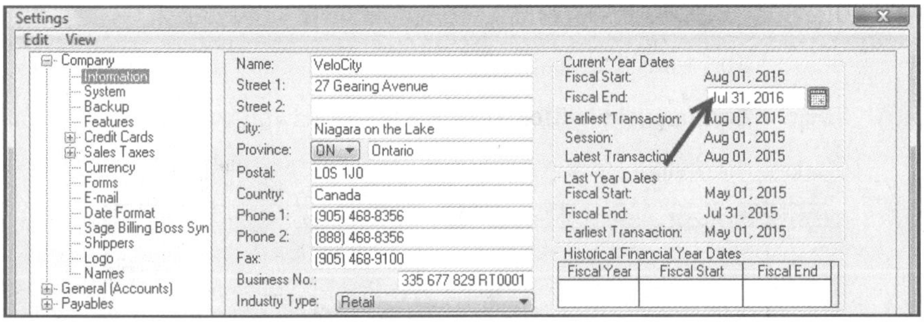

Most fiscal dates cannot be changed. Only the fiscal end can be edited. After starting a new fiscal period, the fiscal end is updated to one year past the new fiscal start because this period is most commonly used. Ryder's Routes, however, will use a one-month fiscal period to allow for more frequent performance review.

Drag through Jul 31, 2016 in the Fiscal End field.

Type 08-31-2015

Drag through VeloCity in the Name field.

Type VeloCity - Ryder's Routes

Leave the Settings window open so you can add the currency.

Adding a Foreign Currency

The Premium version of Sage 50 allows more than one foreign currency. Setting up additional currencies is similar to adding the first one. We will add the euro as the second foreign currency because a new supplier in Germany will provide some inventory items and European tours have been negotiated.

✓ 3

Memo #8-3 **Dated August 1, 2015**

Add the euro as a foreign currency to prepare for transactions with customers and suppliers in Europe. The linked account for exchange rate differences is 4120 and the exchange rate on August 1 is 1.3705.

Change the account number for 1150 Net Bank to 1190 to accommodate the new bank account for foreign currency transactions.

Create a new Subgroup account, 1150 Bank: Euro Chequing. 1150 is a Bank class account and the next cheque number is 101.

Add 1150, the new bank account, as the linked account for Payables and Receivables bank transactions in euros.

Click **Currency** to open the Currency Information window:

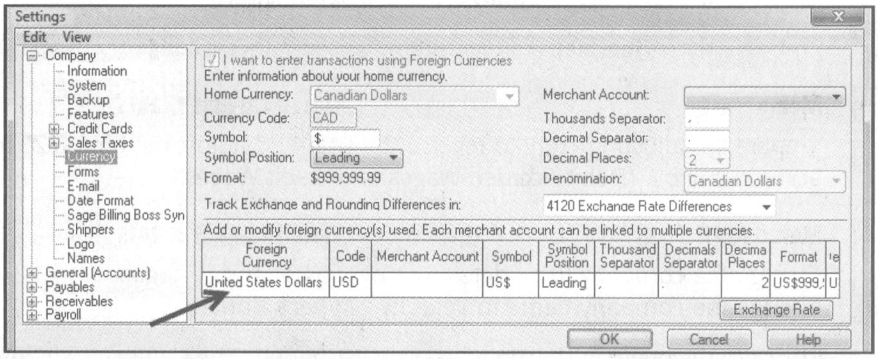

The currency added previously and its linked account for exchange rate differences are entered. You can select a different linked account, but you must use the same linked account for all currencies.

Click the **Foreign Currency column** below United States Dollars. **Click** the **List icon** to see the currency selection list.

Click **Euro** and then **click** **Select**. The codes and symbols for Euro are added.

Click the **Exchange Rate button**:

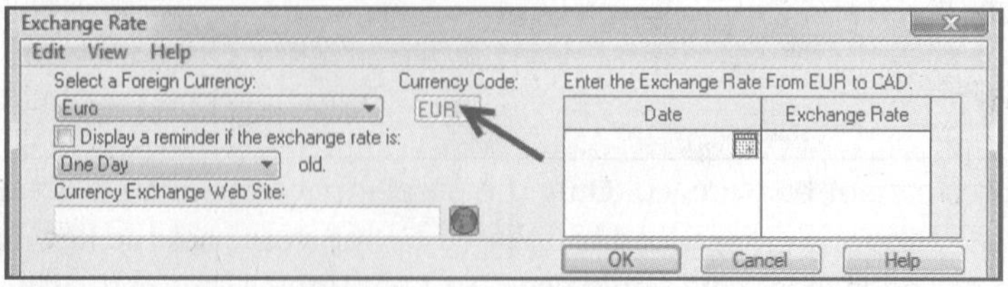

Euro is selected as the currency because the cursor was on this line in the previous screen. All other currencies you entered will be available from the Select A Foreign Currency drop-down list. You can add exchange rates for any of them.

Click the **Date column**. **Type** Aug 1

Press *tab* to move to the Exchange Rate column. **Type** 1.3705

NOTES

If you choose United States Dollars from the Select A Foreign Currency list, you will see a list of all the dates and exchange rates you have already used.

Click **Display A Reminder If The Exchange Rate Is.**

The ✓ is added and we will use the default **One Day** as our reminder period.

Click **OK** to return to the Settings. **Click OK** to return to the Home window.

Adding a Foreign Bank Account

Before using the currency in transactions, we need to create a new bank account for euro transactions.

Click the **Chart of Accounts icon** to open the Accounts window.

Change the **account number for 1150 Net Bank**, the Subtotal account, to **1190**.

Click the **Create tool** to open a new ledger window and **add** the new account **1150 Bank: Euro Chequing**.

Click **Subgroup Account** to change the Type if necessary.

Click the **Class Options tab**.

Choose **Bank** from the Account Class drop-down list.

Click the **Currency list arrow** to see the options:

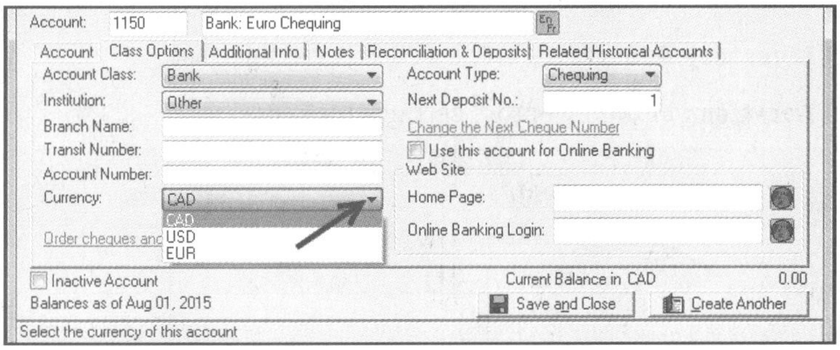

Click **EUR**. **Click** the **Save tool** before adding the cheque number.

Click **Change The Next Cheque Number** to open the Reports & Forms settings.

Click the **Next Cheque No. field** near the bottom of the form.

Type `101` **Click OK** to save the number and return to the ledger window.

Close the **Ledger window** and then **close** the **Accounts windows**.

Adding Linked Bank Accounts

We need to identify the new account as the linked account for euro transactions.

Click the **Settings icon**. Then **choose Payables** and **Linked Accounts**:

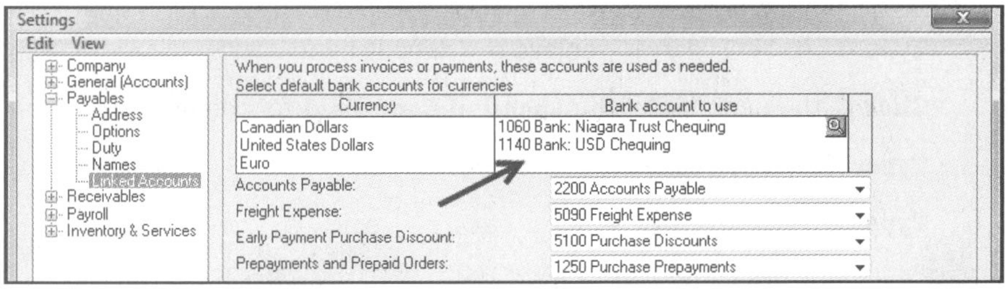

Click the **Bank Account To Use column** beside Euro.

NOTES

You can click the Create tool in the Accounts window or in any ledger account window to open a new account ledger record window.

NOTES
Undeposited Cash and Cheques is defined as a Canadian Cash account so it is included with the linked account selection list for euros. You cannot use the USD chequing account for euro transactions – it is not on the list of available accounts.

Click the **List icon**. Only the Canadian and euro bank accounts can be selected as the euro currency bank account.

Double-click **1150**.

Click **Receivables** and **Linked Accounts**.

Click the **Bank Account To Use column** beside Euro.

Type `1150` **Press** tab. Leave the Settings window open.

Entering Inventory Locations

Before leaving the Settings window, we will add the two stores as the locations for the business and for inventory. Items can be purchased for and sold from either store. Adjustments can also be made for the separate locations. The number of items in each store can, therefore, be monitored. If needed, items can be transferred from one location to another.

✓ 4

Memo #8-4 **Dated August 1, 2015**

Set up inventory locations for the two stores: VeloCity and Ryder. The VeloCity store is the primary location for inventory and the Ryder store is the secondary location for accessories and tour guide services.

NOTES
Click the button beside modules to collapse the expanded lists.

Click **Inventory & Services** in the Settings modules list.

Click **Locations** in the Inventory settings list:

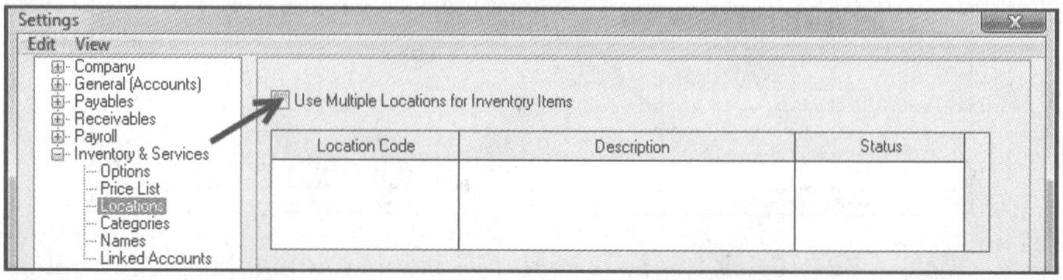

Click **Use Multiple Locations For Inventory Items** to activate the option:

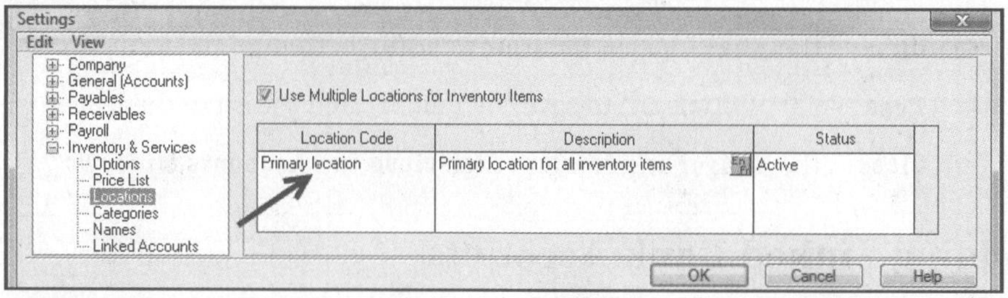

The Code and Description fields are now available; we can enter the two stores. We will accept the default description for the first location.

Press tab **twice** to select Primary Location.

Type `VeloCity` to replace the default name.

Click the next line of the **Location Code field** for the next store.

Type `Ryder` **Press** tab.

Type `Ryder Store for tours and accessories`

Both locations are active.

Click **OK** to return to the Home window.

Click **Inventory & Services** in the Modules pane list.

Click **AC010 Bicycle Pump: standing model** in the Home window Inventory Item list.

The Quantities tab screen includes a For Location field.

Click the **For Location field list arrow** to see the two locations you entered:

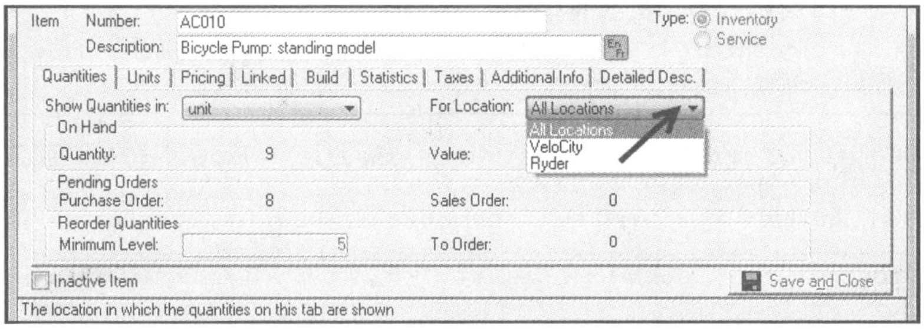

Choose **VeloCity** from the For Location drop-down list to display the quantity at that store. **Choose Ryder** from the For Location drop-down list.

Initially, all the stock is at the primary location, the VeloCity store. The quantity at the VeloCity store is the same as the quantity for the All Locations selection. The quantity at the Ryder store is zero.

Close the **Ledger window** to return to the Inventory & Services module window.

NOTES

You can set separate minimum levels for each location. When you select a location, the Minimum Level field becomes available for that location. When All Locations are shown, the field is dimmed.

Time and Billing

Many businesses that provide services use time as the basis for billing customers. Law firms, consulting businesses and service businesses that complete maintenance and repair work are just a few examples. In addition, these businesses may keep track of how much time each employee spends on a particular job and then compare this with the standard number of hours expected for that type of work. Some jobs can be billed at a flat rate and some, such as warranty repairs or work performed for other departments of the same company, may be provided at no charge. In each of these cases, it is still important to know how much time was spent on the job. Businesses might also want to track non-billable and non-payroll times such as for lunch breaks when an employee is at a customer site.

The Time & Billing module in Sage 50 tracks these kinds of activities by integrating the Payroll, Inventory and Sales ledgers.

Setting Up Time and Billing Activities

Before recording the services provided by employees to customers, that is, filling in time slips, we must modify service records to apply time and billing. First we will create the new services. We will work from the Inventory module. It should still be open.

Choose **Add Inventory & Service** from the Inventory & Services icon drop-down shortcuts list to open a new record for inventory.

✓ 5

Memo #8-5 **Dated August 1, 2015**

Create the new records described in the chart on the following page to add services and include Time & Billing information:

NOTES
Prices for tour guide services are group rates based on groups of 10 to 15 cyclists. Smaller and private groups may be served, but the rates will be the same. USD and euro prices will be added later.

Item	Description	Selling Price Reg	Selling Price (Pref)	Unit	Related to Time?	Billable?	Billing Basis	Rate
S070	Tour Guide: Hour	$150	($120)	Hour	Yes	billable	billable time	per hour
S080	Tour Guide: Day	640	(560)	Day (8 hours)	Yes	billable	billable time	per day
S100	Warranty Repairs	0	(0)	Service Call	No	non-billable		

Linked accounts for tours: Revenue: 4050 Revenue from Tours (new Subgroup account)
Expense: 5075 Cost of Services
Linked accounts for repairs: Revenue: 4040 Revenue from Services and Expense: 5075 Cost of Services
Taxes: Charge HST on services provided in Canada. International tour guide services will be exempt from HST.

Type S070 **Press** *tab*. **Type** Tour Guide: Hour **Press** *tab*.

Click **Service** as the Type of item to modify the form for service items:

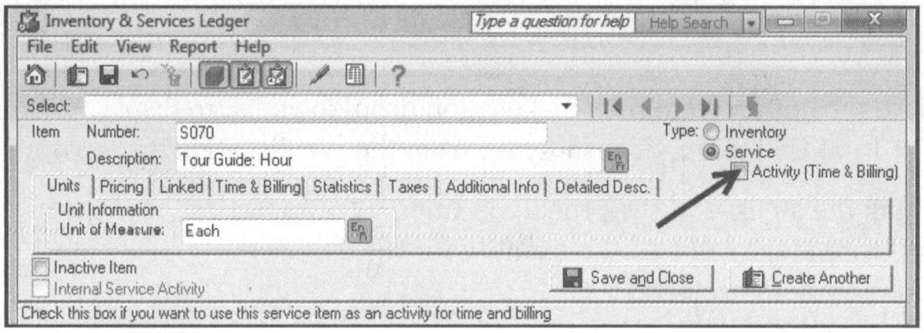

The Units tab window appears and Activity is available as an option under Service.

Click **Activity (Time & Billing)** to add a ✓.

This selection will open the fields related to time and billing on the Time & Billing tab. The Units information is now dimmed and the Required Field indicator (*) is added back to the screen. We will enter units on the Time & Billing tab screen, as instructed by the message that appears on the screen after we choose Activity. The Internal Service Activity option becomes available because this also applies to the Time & Billing module. We will enter the other item information first.

NOTES
Businesses often track the number of hours of service provided internally to other departments in the company as a way of monitoring internal efficiency or tracking departmental costs. They may monitor the time even if there is no charge for the service to the other department.

WARNING!
If you do not change the account type to Subgroup Account, the accounts will not be in logical order, and you will be unable to display some reports.
You can make the correction later from the General Ledger to restore the logical account order.

Click the **Pricing tab** to open the Canadian dollar (home currency) price list.

Click the **Regular Price Per Selling Unit field**.

Type 150 **Press** *tab* to advance to the Preferred Selling Price field.

Type 120

Click the **Linked tab**.

Click the **Revenue account field**. We will add the new account.

Type 4050 Revenue from Tours **Press** *tab* and **click Add** to start the Add An Account wizard with the name and number added.

Click **Next three times** to accept the defaults until you see the **Subgroup And Group Accounts** screen.

Click **Yes** because this account is a Subgroup account.

Accept the **remaining defaults** to finish creating the account.

Click the **Expense field** and **type** 5075

Click the **Time & Billing tab** to see the next group of fields to be set up:

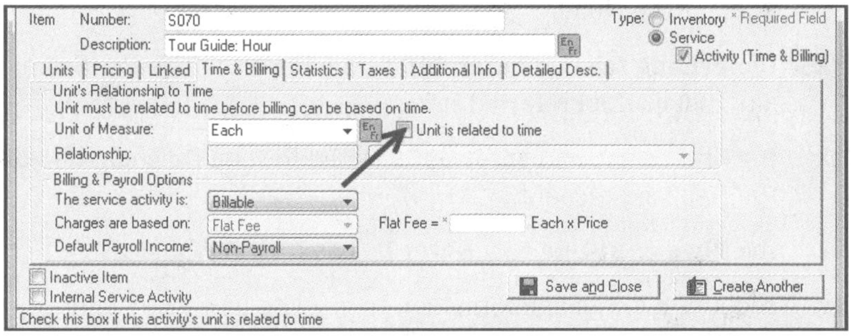

This screen has all the details that relate to the Time & Billing module. On this screen we must define the unit that the price is based on, indicate whether the unit is based on time and then add the relationship between the time and the unit of measure.

Click the **list arrow beside Each** in the Unit Of Measure field.

Click **Hour**.

This Unit is automatically recognized as related to time, and the Relationship fields are now dimmed because we have already indicated a time unit. The next three fields, shown together on the following screen, define the **billing and payroll options**:

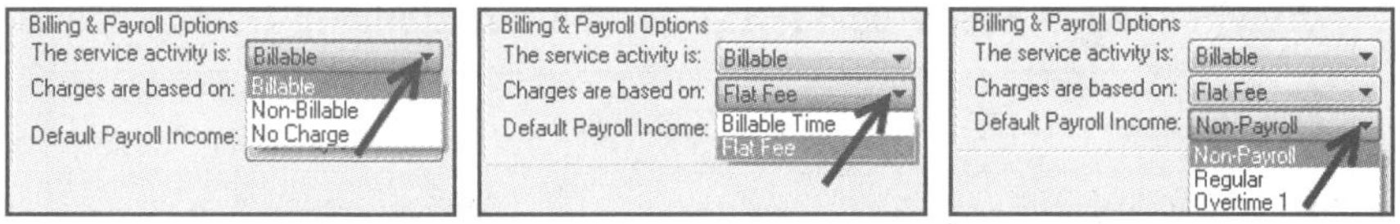

Billable is selected as the default for the service activity and this is correct. The other options are that an activity is Non-Billable or that there is No Charge for the activity. Charges for the service can be based on a Flat Fee or on Billable Time. Tour guide work is based on billable time.

The next option allows the time worked on the activity to be applied to an employee's paycheque. You can choose whether the time should be charged to the default payroll income account or to overtime. The non-payroll option may be selected if the work is completed by salaried employees. All services offered by Ryder's Routes are provided by the regular employees at the regular hourly wage rate.

Click **Flat Fee** in the Charges Are Based On field or its list arrow.

Click **Billable Time** to change the entry.

Click **Non-Payroll** in the Default Payroll Income field or its list arrow.

Click **Regular** to complete the Time & Billing tab screen as shown here:

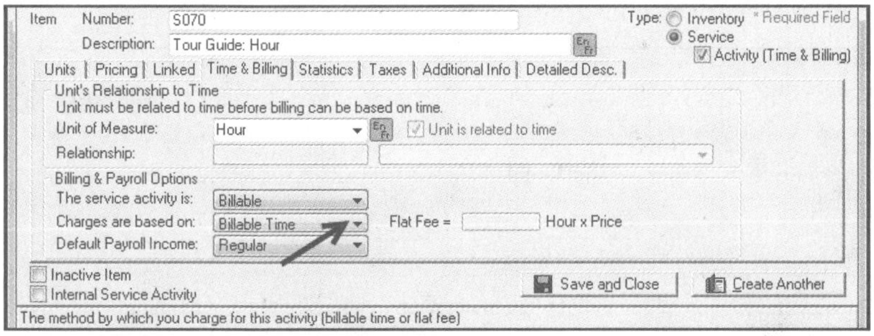

Click the **Taxes tab**. You can accept the defaults. HST is charged, so the service is not tax exempt for HST.

Click **Create Another**  to save the record.

You are now ready to enter the next service. Service and Activity (Time & Billing) remain selected from the previous entry and are correct.

NOTES

A service activity may be non-payroll if salaried workers or managers complete the activity because these individuals are not paid on the basis of hours worked.

Employee lunch hours may also be tracked as non-payroll activities.

NOTES

In Ontario, most services are taxable for HST.

Enter **S080** as the Number and **Tour Guide: Day** as the Description.

Click the **Pricing tab** and **enter 640** as the Regular Price Per Selling Unit and **560** as the Preferred Price.

Click the **Linked tab** and **enter 4050** as the Revenue account and **5075** as the Expense account.

Click the **Time & Billing tab**. **Enter Day** as the Unit Of Measure.

NOTES
Day is not automatically recognized as a unit of time. Only hours and minutes are the default time units in the program.

This service requires additional information to indicate how many hours, or units of time, are in the day. The service will still be billed at an hourly rate, but the rate is lower when a longer time period is purchased. Day as the unit is not automatically recognized as a unit related to time.

Click **Unit Is Related To Time** to add a ✓ and open the Relationship fields.

Each day is based on eight billable hours of activity, so the relationship is entered as eight hours per day. The relationship field is a required field when the unit is not Hour or Minute and you indicate that it is related to time.

Click the **first Relationship field**. **Type** 8

Click the **list arrow beside the second Relationship field** to see the list:

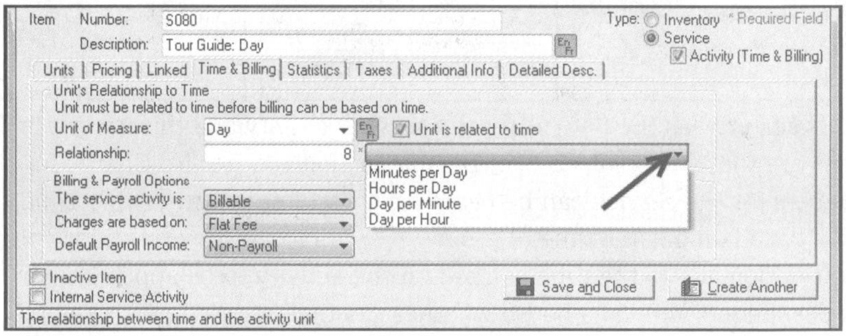

The relationship can be based on the number of hours or minutes per unit, or the number of units per hour or minute.

Click **Hours Per Day**.

The next option is correct — the activity is Billable. However, it is charged on the basis of time, not at a flat rate. We need to change the entry for Charges Are Based On.

Click **Flat Fee** in the Charges Are Based On field or its list arrow.

Click **Billable Time** and then **choose Regular** as the Default Payroll Income category to complete the record as shown:

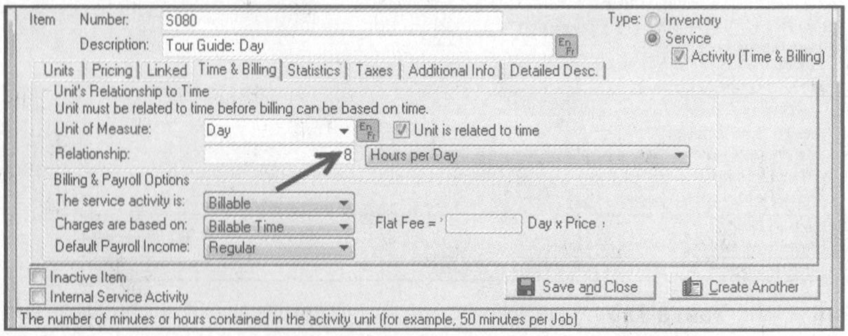

Click **Create Another** 

to save the record.

The final service is provided at no charge to customers, but it is entered as an inventory item so that the time spent on warranty repairs can be monitored. The price will be entered as zero.

Enter **S100** as the Number and **Warranty Repairs** as the Description.

Click the **Pricing tab**. Do not enter any prices for the warranty service so that the prices will remain at zero.

Click the **Linked tab** and **enter 4040** as the Revenue account and **5075** as the Expense account.

Click the **Time & Billing tab**. **Enter Service Call** as the Unit Of Measure.

The service call for warranty work is not related to time because there is no charge for this service. We must indicate that the work is not billable. In addition, employees are paid at their usual wage rate for completing warranty work, even though the customer does not pay, so we must change the payroll category.

Click the **list arrow beside Billable**. **Click Non-Billable** to change the entry.

Choose **Regular** as the Default Payroll Income category to complete the record:

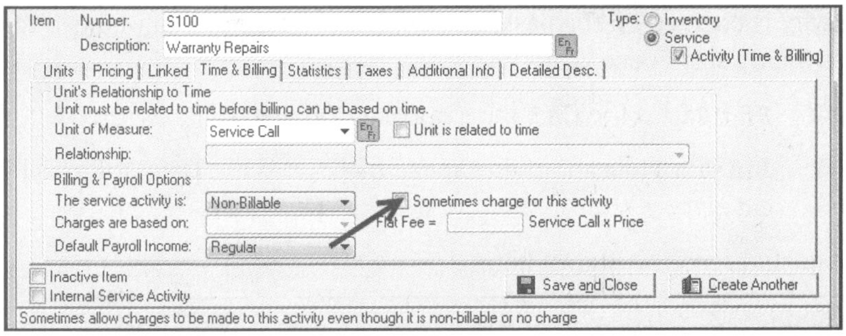

Another option for services that are normally not billed is to **sometimes charge**. When you choose the No Charge or Non-Billable options, this category becomes available. The pricing options are the same as for billable activities. You can relate the unit to time and enter the number of hours or minutes per unit, or enter a flat fee for the exceptional price. Prices are taken from Price fields on the Pricing tab screen.

Click **Save And Close** 

to save the record and return to the Inventory & Services module window.

Adding Time and Billing Information to Services

You are now ready to edit the remaining service records to apply time and billing.

✓ 6

Memo #8-6 **Dated August 1, 2015**

Edit the remaining service inventory records to add Time & Billing information and change the Canadian dollar prices. Add foreign currency prices for services.

Item	Selling Price Reg	(Pref)	Unit	Related to Time?	Relation	Billable?	Billing Basis
S010	$80	($ 70)	box	yes	30 minutes/box	billable	billable time
S030	70	(65)	tune-up	no		billable	flat rate: 1 tune-up x price
S060	50	(40)	hour	yes		billable	billable time

NOTES
Sales of annual service contracts and rentals are not entered as service activities – there is no service time associated with them.

Scroll down the Inventory Item list in the Inventory & Services module window.

Click **S010 Boxing for shipping** in the Home window list of items and services to open the record.

Click the **Time & Billing tab** to open the Time & Billing screen.

All the fields are dimmed because we still need to mark the service as an Activity for time and billing.

Click **Activity (Time & Billing)** to open the extra fields.

Enter **box** as the Unit Of Measure.

Again, as a unit, box is not automatically related to time.

Click **Unit Is Related To Time** to add a ✓ and open the relationship fields.

Each boxing job is based on 30 minutes of billable activity, so the relationship is entered as 30 minutes per box. This is the average time required to box one bicycle.

Click the **first Relationship field**. **Type** 30

Click the **list arrow beside the second Relationship field**.

Click **Minutes per box**.

The activity is charged on the basis of time, not at a flat rate, so we need to change the entry for Charges Are Based On.

Click **Flat Fee** in the Charges Are Based On field or its list arrow.

Click **Billable Time** and then **choose** **Regular** as the Default Payroll Income category.

The completed record is shown here:

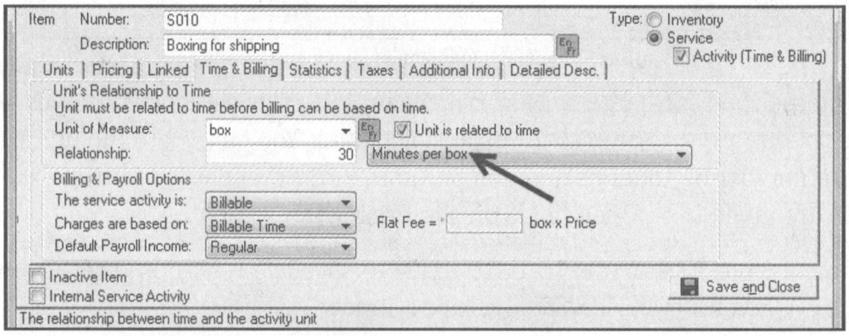

Click the **Next Item tool** **twice** to open the record for S030 Maintenance: complete tune-up.

Click **Activity (Time & Billing)** to change the item type.

Enter **tune-up** as the Unit Of Measure.

The service is priced at a flat rate, so the unit is not related to time. Tune-up is not recognized as a unit of time so the ✓ is not added. Billable is also the correct choice but we need to enter the rate. Notice that Flat Fee = ___ tune-up x Price is entered as the field label. This means that we must enter a number, not a price. The price will be calculated as the number of completed tune-ups multiplied by the price that is taken from the Pricing tab fields.

The flat rate for this service is one times the price; each tune-up is priced at $70 ($65 for preferred customers).

Click the **field beside Flat Fee =**.

Type 1

Choose **Regular** as the Default Payroll Income category.

NOTES

When the relationship entry is 30 minutes per unit with the ledger price based on units, the charge in the Time Slip, which is based on the number of hours, would be for two boxes when you enter one hour.

Your Time & Billing screen should look like the one shown here:

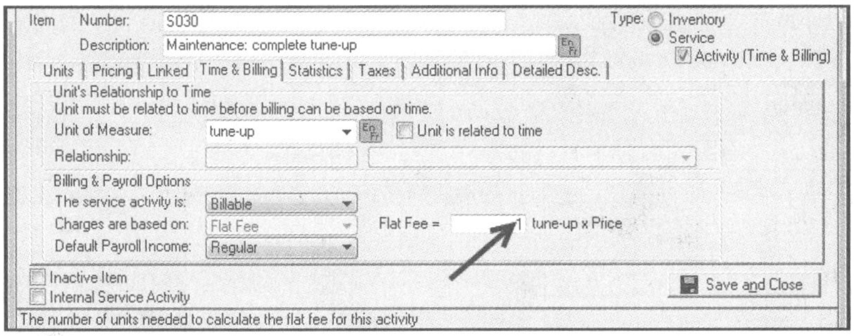

Click the **Next Item tool** (three times) to open the record for **S060 Repairs**.

Click **Activity (Time & Billing)**.

Again, because Hour is the unit, it is automatically related to time and most of the default details are correct.

Choose **Regular** as the Default Payroll Income category.

Click **Save And Close** to save the record and return to the Inventory & Services module window.

We will now edit the prices for these services using the Update Price Lists feature in the Inventory Settings.

Updating Service Activity Prices

The Premium version allows you to define additional price lists and to update all prices from one screen. This feature is available as one of the settings for the Inventory Ledger. You can change individual item prices from this location or, if prices are raised by a fixed percentage for one or more items or services, you can make the price changes globally. You can also set the prices in one list relative to the prices in another list by indicating the increase or decrease. All activity prices that require updating are listed in the following chart:

Item	Canadian Prices		USD Prices			Euro Prices		
	Reg	(Pref)	Reg	(Pref)		Reg	(Pref)	
S010	$ 80	($ 70)	$80	($ 70)	fixed price	€ 55	(€ 50)	fixed price
S060	50	(40)	50	(40)	fixed price	N/A	N/A	
S070	150	(120)	150	(120)	fixed price	110	(85)	fixed price
S080	640	(560)	640	(560)	fixed price	450	(400)	fixed price

Click the **Settings icon**. **Click** **Price List** to see the Price List Settings:

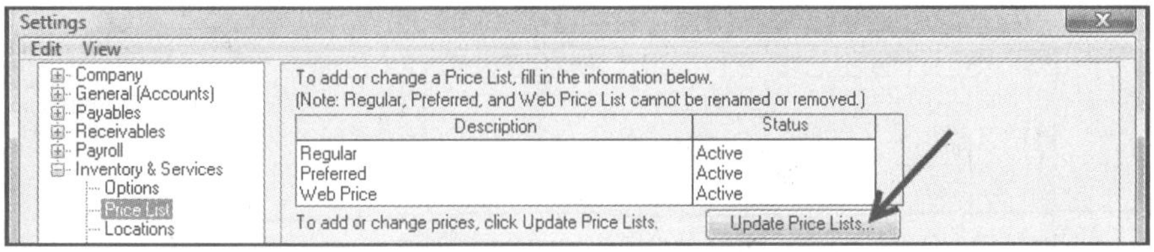

On this screen, you can define new price lists. You cannot remove or modify the three predefined price list names. If you want to create a new price list, you can type the new price list name below Web Price in the Description column and click Update Price Lists to open the item list. We need to update Regular and Preferred prices.

NOTES
The Flat Fee rate is a required field when the Flat Fee method of pricing is selected.

NOTES
The remaining services (rentals and annual service contract) cannot be related to a specific amount of employee time, so they are not marked as activities.

NOTES
Price increases and decreases may be entered as amounts or percentages relative to the reference price.

NOTES
Foreign currency prices are not needed for services provided only in Canada to Canadian customers. The remaining services do not apply to customers in Europe.

Click the **Update Price Lists button**:

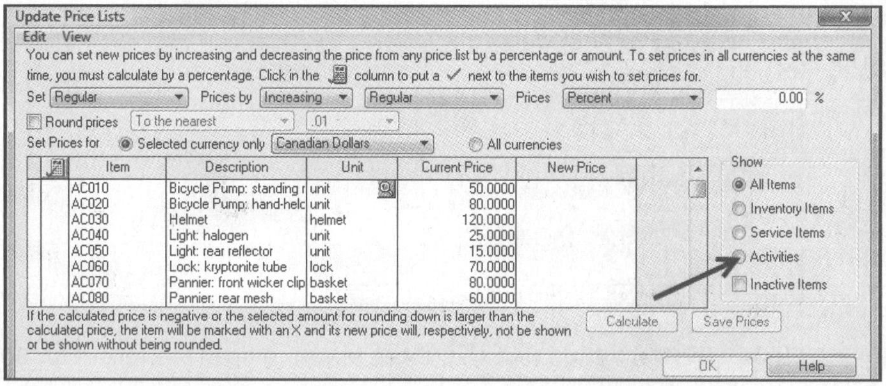

The inventory list opens with all items and services listed. You can display the list of all items, inventory items only, service items only or activities only.

You can select the items whose prices you want to update globally. You can set the prices in one list relative to another list by increasing or decreasing the reference prices by a fixed percentage or amount. Then you can round off the prices to the nearest unit — ranging from 0.0001 dollar to 1 000 dollars. You can make the price changes for one currency or for all currencies at the same time. You can also enter or edit individual prices in the new price column, so you can use this list to enter price changes manually for several inventory items on a single screen, without opening each ledger record separately.

You can Round Prices if you want to work with even amounts. Choose the direction for rounding off the price — up to the nearest, down to the nearest or to the nearest unit. Choose the nearest unit you want to round to from the drop-down list.

We will work from the smaller list of Activities. When you are changing a large number of prices, it is more efficient to work from the Update Price List screen.

Click **Activities** in the Show list on the right-hand side of the screen:

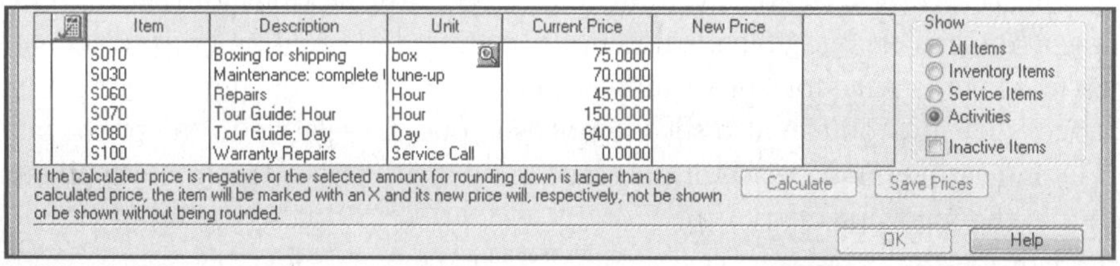
Item Description Unit Current Price New Price
S010 Boxing for shipping box 75.0000
S030 Maintenance: complete tune-up 70.0000
S060 Repairs Hour 45.0000
S070 Tour Guide: Hour Hour 150.0000
S080 Tour Guide: Day Day 640.0000
S100 Warranty Repairs Service Call 0.0000
Show
All Items
Inventory Items
Service Items
Activities
Inactive Items
If the calculated price is negative or the selected amount for rounding down is larger than the calculated price, the item will be marked with an X and its new price will, respectively, not be shown or be shown without being rounded.
Calculate
Save Prices
OK
Help

The Regular prices are shown. We will edit these first. We will change the prices directly by entering the revised price in the New Price column. The prices for S010 and S060 have changed.

Click **S010** and **press** *tab* until the cursor is in the New Price column.

Type 80

Press ↓ **twice** to place the cursor in the New Price column for activity S060.

Type 50 **Press** *tab*. Your price list should now look like the following one:

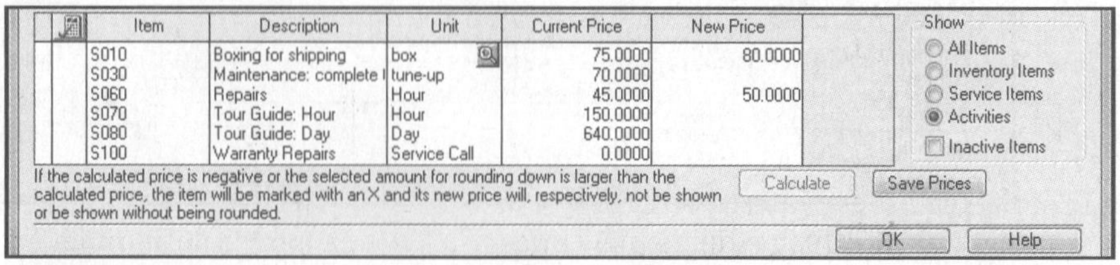
Item Description Unit Current Price New Price
S010 Boxing for shipping box 75.0000 80.0000
S030 Maintenance: complete tune-up 70.0000
S060 Repairs Hour 45.0000 50.0000
S070 Tour Guide: Hour Hour 150.0000
S080 Tour Guide: Day Day 640.0000
S100 Warranty Repairs Service Call 0.0000
Show
All Items
Inventory Items
Service Items
Activities
Inactive Items
If the calculated price is negative or the selected amount for rounding down is larger than the calculated price, the item will be marked with an X and its new price will, respectively, not be shown or be shown without being rounded.
Calculate
Save Prices
OK
Help

Now we will update USD regular prices.

Click **Canadian Dollars** in the Selected Currency Only field as shown in the next screenshot and **select United States Dollars**:

NOTES

If you have different units for stocking and selling, you can select the unit as well. The Unit field has a list icon.

Click an item to select it. Then click the list icon that opens beside the entry in the Unit column to see the different units you can choose.

NOTES

You can select individual items by clicking the Select column beside the item. Click the column for the next item you want to change, and so on. Pressing the space bar when the cursor is in the Select column will also add the checkmark and select an item.

Then apply the change rules you want to only the selected items. For example, you could select items S010 and S060 and then apply the rule to increase these prices by a fixed amount of $5. We apply change rules to edit prices on page 775.

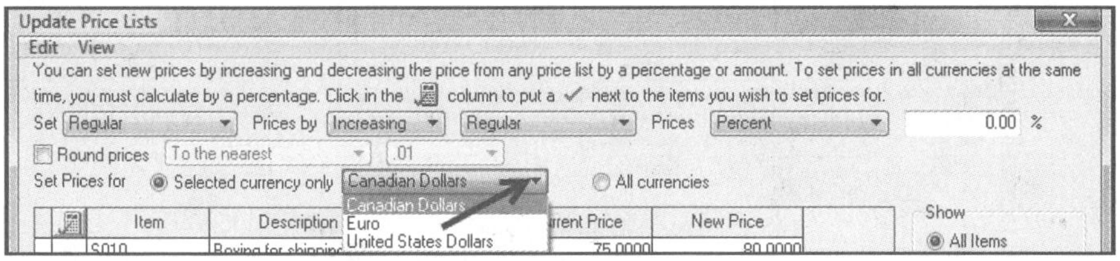

You will be shown a warning:

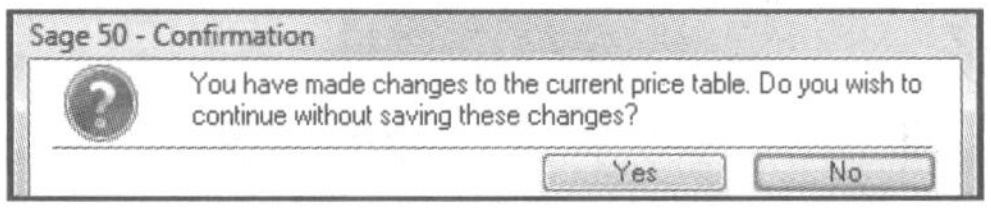

Before we continue, we need to save the new prices.

Click **No** to return to the Canadian Dollars price list. **Click Save Prices**. The new prices move to the Current Price column:

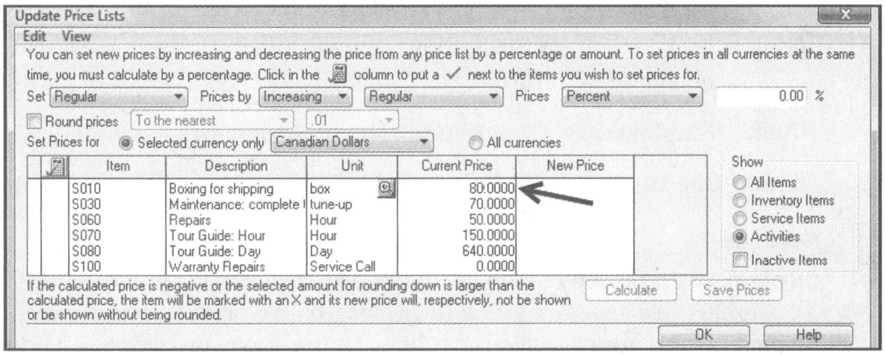

Click **Canadian Dollars** again in the Selected Currency Only field and **select United States Dollars** to view the prices in United States Dollars:

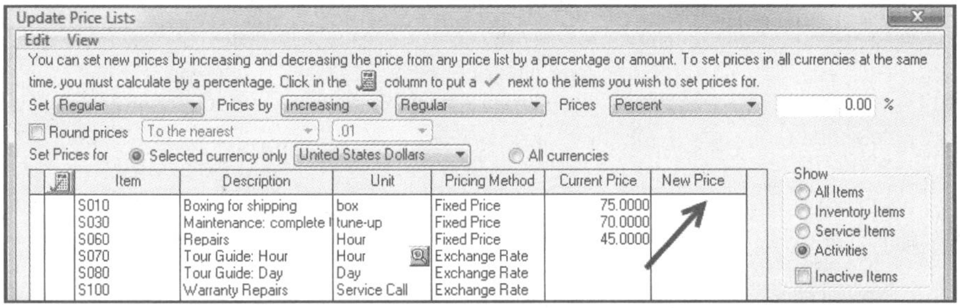

We need to change the prices for S010 and S060 as we did for Canadian Dollar prices, and we need to add prices for the new service activities.

Click **S010** and **press** *tab* until the cursor is in the New Price column.

Type 80

Press ↓ **twice** to place the cursor in the New Price column for activity S060.

Type 50

Click **Exchange Rate** for item S070 to change the entry to Fixed Rate.

Press *tab* to advance to the New Price column. **Type** 150

Click **Exchange Rate** for item S080 to change the entry to Fixed Rate.

Press *tab* to advance to the New Price column. **Type** 640

Click **Save Prices**. The new prices move to the Current Price column.

We can now update the Preferred USD prices.

WARNING!

You must save the new prices by clicking Save Prices. If you click OK first, or choose another price list, you will be shown this confirmation message that asks if you want to continue without saving.

Click **Regular** in the Set field as shown and **click Preferred**:

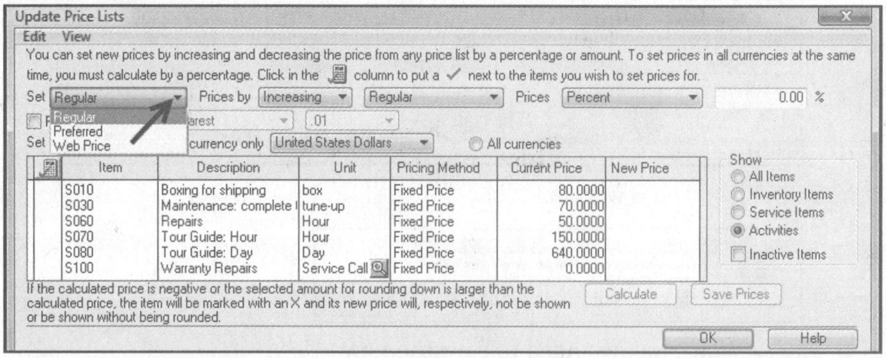

Enter the **preferred prices** for United States dollars next. **Enter** the **regular** and **preferred prices** for euros from the chart on page 749. Remember to **click Save Prices** after each set. Read the margin Notes.

Click **OK** to return to the Settings window. **Click OK** again to save all the changes and return to the Home window.

Click **Employees & Payroll** in the Modules pane list.

Create the **two new employee records**. **Change** the **session date to August 14**.

NOTES

To enter the euro prices, select Euro as the currency and Regular as the price list. Enter the prices on page 749. Click Save Prices. Select Preferred as the price list and enter the preferred prices from page 749. Click Save Prices.

7

Memo #8-7 **Dated August 1, 2015**

Create new employee records for Yvonne Leader and Moishe Alee. Leader will work exclusively as a tour guide (activities), billing on the basis of time. She will be paid for the hours worked, but her minimum pay will be for 20 hours per week. Because Leader will also receive customer tips that she tracks on her own, she will pay additional taxes each pay period. Alee will be paid a monthly salary as a sales assistant in the new store.

	Leader, Yvonne	Alee, Moishe
Address:	499 Itinerant Dr. Mt. Hope, ON L0R 1W0	551 Spoker Dr. St. Catharines, ON L2V 8H3
Telephone	(905) 418-7192	(905) 688-9101
SIN	420 011 009	128 663 887
Birthdate	06-23-82	08-31-84
Date of Hire	08-01-15	08-01-15
Job Category	Sales	Sales
Tax Table	Ontario	Ontario
Basic Indexed: Fed (Prov)	$11 038 ($9 574)	11 038 ($9 574)
Additional Federal Tax	$50 per week	
Regular Wage	$24/hour	NA
# hours:	20 hours (min hours in paycheque)	150 hours
Overtime Wage	$30/hour	NA
Salary	NA	$3 150/month
Do not use	Salary, Commission	Regular, Overtime
Pay Period:	Weekly (52 per year)	Monthly (12 per year)
Vacation:	4% Retained	3 weeks (0%, not retained)
Record Wage	Expenses in: Payroll linked accounts	
WSIB Rate:	1.29	1.29
Vacation	delete entry	8%, 25 days max
Sick Leave	5%, 15 days max	5%, 15 days max
Personal Days	2.5%, 5 days max	2.5%, 5 days max
Direct Deposit	100% of paycheque to branch #89008 institution #102 account #341002	100% of paycheque to branch #67752 institution #102 account #198823

NOTES

Refer to pages 328–339 if you need assistance with entering the new employees. There is no historical information for the new employees.

Leader and Alee will not receive the group insurance benefit or the piece rate pay (No. Clients) or Bonus initially. Those benefits will apply after they finish the probationary work period. They also have no additional deductions at this time for RRSP, CSB, Donations or Garnishee.

Preparing Time Slips

After setting up the service records to mark the activities and enter billing information, you can track the amount of time that each employee works for each customer at each activity by completing Time Slips.

Time slips for employees like the following one for Mercier may be entered from the Receivables module window or from the Employees & Payroll module window. These alternatives are illustrated in the partial Home windows below:

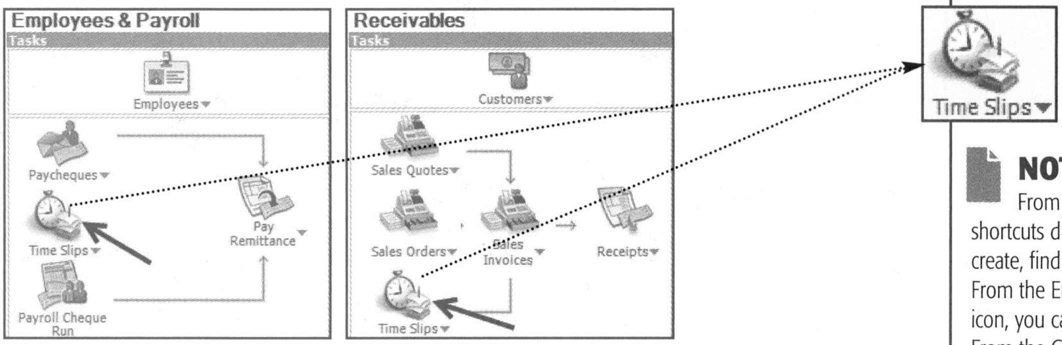

✓ **TIME SLIP #1** **DATED AUGUST 7, 2015**

8 For Dunlop Mercier

Customer	Item	Actual Time	Billable Time	Billable Amount	Taxable	Payroll Time
Cathedral Tours	S010	3 hours	2.5 (5 boxes)	€ 275.00	yes	3 hours
Niagara Rapids Inn*	S060	4 hours	3.5 hours	$140.00	yes	4 hours
Niagara Rapids Inn*	S030	2 hours	2 hours	$65.00	yes	2 hours
Niagara Rapids Inn*	S100	4 hours	–	–	yes	4 hours
Festival Tours	S100	2 hours	–	–	yes	2 hours

Click the **Time Slips icon** in the Receivables module Tasks pane or in the Employees & Payroll module Tasks pane:

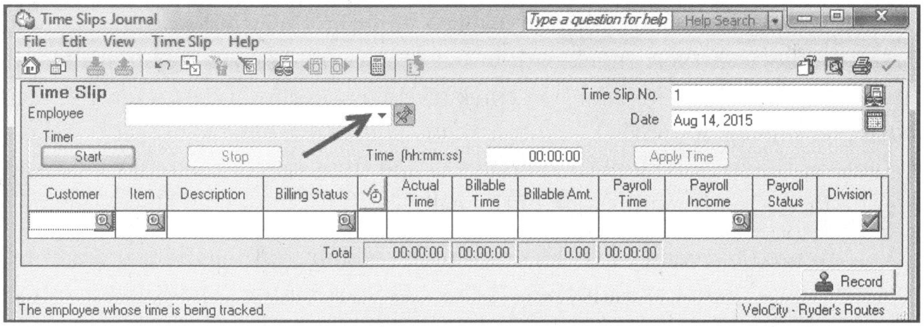

The Time Slips Journal opens. All the tool icons in this window are the same as those found in other journals. Also, as in other journals, employees can be selected from a drop-down list and List icons are available for many of the fields.

Many features in other journals are also available for time slips. You can access these options from the tool buttons as you do in other journals or from the Time Slip menu. For example,

- Click the Store tool  and enter a name and frequency to store the time slip as a recurring transaction.
- Click the Look Up Time Slip tool  to look up a time slip just as you look up purchases or sales invoices.
- Click the Adjust Time Slip tool  to adjust a time slip after recording. You cannot adjust a time slip for selecting the wrong employee.

NOTES
From the Time Slips icon shortcuts drop-down lists, you can create, find and adjust time slips. From the Employees Time Slips icon, you can also pay employees. From the Customers Time Slips icon, you can also create invoices.
You can add a shortcut for Create A Time Slip.

NOTES
The * indicates that preferred customer prices apply.

CLASSIC VIEW
Click the Time Slips icon  in the Time & Billing column.

NOTES
Use Full Add for two new customers in Europe so that you can add the currency and price list:

New Regular price customer
Cathedral Tours
550 Kirchestrasse
1020 Vienna, Austria
Tel: 01 316 521
Currency: Euro
Terms: 2/10, n/30
Tax Code: No tax
Credit Limit: $10 000 CAD
(€ 6 000)

New Preferred price customer
Gallery Tours
21 Via Della Mosca
50122 Florence, Italy
Tel: 055 282 691
Currency: Euro
Terms: 2/10, n/30
Tax Code: No tax
Credit Limit: $10 000 CAD
(€ 6 000)

NOTES
Remember that you can maximize the window, scroll to see additional information or change the width of the columns by dragging.

The Time Slip number is updated automatically by Sage 50. Its starting number is taken from the Forms Settings, just like the next number for other forms. If the Time & Billing module is not hidden, the Next Number field for Time Slips is included in the Forms Settings screen. The number is correct.

The first time slip is for Mercier. His first job was completed for Cathedral Tours, a new regular price customer in Europe. Use Full Add for the new customer.

Click the **Employee list arrow** and **choose Dunlop Mercier**.

Enter **August 7** in the Date field for the Time Slip.

Click the **Customer field** and **type** `Cathedral Tours`

Add the **complete record** details for the new customer.

Click the **Item field List icon** to see the Select Activity list:

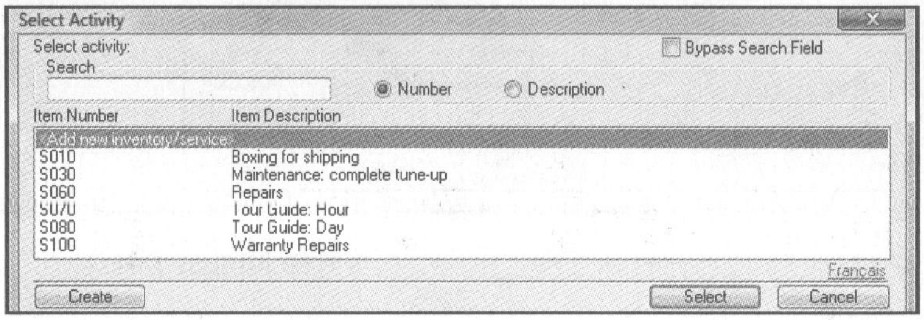

All services for which you selected Activity as the type of Service and added time and billing details will be on this list. Other services and inventory will not be included.

Double-click **S010 Boxing for shipping** to add it to the journal.

The Item and Description fields are the usual ones for inventory and service transactions. The next field, **Billing Status**, is completed from the Time & Billing tab details in the ledger record. Usually the defaults are correct, but you can change them if needed. The Billing Status field has a List icon and a selection list. Activities may be Billable, Non-Billable or provided at No Charge.

NOTES
If there is no checkmark in the Stopwatch column, clicking will add it. Clicking will also remove the checkmark once it is there.

If an activity is billable, you can use the **Timer** in this window to track the time worked on the activity. A checkmark in the **Stopwatch column** indicates that you can use the timer. Some businesses track all time spent for a customer. For example, if a customer phones for advice, and telephone advice is a billable activity, you can start the timer at the beginning of the phone call and then stop at the end to have an accurate measure of the duration of the call.

To use the timer, click the Stopwatch column for the customer and activity if the ✓ is not already there. Click the Start button. The counter will keep time in seconds until you click Stop. You can use this measurement as the actual time for the activity by clicking Apply Time.

NOTES
The best way to learn the formats for entering times is to enter different numbers and observe how Sage 50 records them in the journal.

Time is entered as the number of hours, minutes and seconds (hhmmss). You can also enter the times as decimal amounts, such as 2.75 for two hours and 45 minutes. The simplest way to explain the format for entering time is with a few examples. The following chart summarizes the examples and outlines some of the rules:

EXAMPLES OF TIME ENTRIES IN THE TIME SLIPS JOURNAL

Entering This Number	Records This Time	Displays in Journal as
1 or 01 or 100 or 10000	Records 1 hour	01:00:00
001 or 0001 or 000100	Records 1 minute	00:01:00
00001 or 000001	Records 1 second	00:00:01
130 or 0130 or 013000	Records 1.5 hours (1 hour and 30 minutes)	01:30:00
0110 or 110 or 11000	Records 1 hour and 10 minutes	01:10:00
1030 or 103000	Records 10 hours and 30 minutes	10:30:00
11515 or 011515	Records 1 hour, 15 minutes and 15 seconds	01:15:15
995959	Records 99 hours, 59 minutes and 59 seconds	99:59:59

RULES FOR TIME ENTRIES IN THE TIME SLIPS JOURNAL

- You can enter up to six digits (hhmmss). A one- or two-digit number is always interpreted as the number of hours (zero minutes, zero seconds). The remaining missing digits are always assumed to be zero.
- For a three-digit entry, the first number represents hours and the next two represent the minutes.
- For a four-digit number, the first two numbers represent hours and the next two represent minutes.
- For a five-digit number, the first number represents the number of hours, the next two, minutes, and the final two, seconds.
- For a six-digit entry, the first two numbers represent hours, the next two, minutes, and the last two, seconds.
- You can omit seconds and minutes if they are zero. Leading zeros are not needed for hours.
- The times allowed on a line for one activity range from the shortest time of 1 second, entered as 000001 or 00001, to the longest, 99 hours, 59 minutes and 59 seconds, entered as 995959.

NOTES
Notice that decimals are not used for the display of the time entries.

There are three columns for time: the **Actual Time** spent at the activity; the **Billable Time** or amount of time that the customer pays for; and the **Payroll Time** or hours the employee is paid for. Sometimes the customer is billed for fewer hours than the job actually required. For example, if an estimate has been given and the work is much more complex than anticipated, a business will usually not bill the customer for the full amount in the interest of good customer relations. At other times, the customer may be charged for more time than the activity requires. For example, a job may have a minimum time component, such as one hour of labour. Most companies will want to keep track of all times so that they can revise their prices to reflect their true costs.

Mercier spent three hours packing the five boxes (actual time); the customer will pay for 2.5 hours of work (billable time for five boxes); and Mercier will be paid for three hours of work for this job (payroll time).

NOTES
An employee may be paid for the actual number of hours, the billable number of hours or some other time agreed on between the employee and the employer. For example, the pay may be limited to a maximum number of hours for a specific job to encourage efficient work habits.

Click the **Actual Time field**.

Type 3 **Press** (tab). Your journal now looks like the one below:

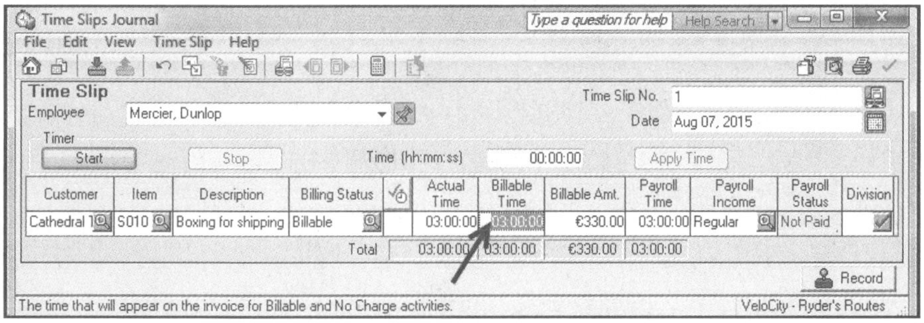

The program enters 03:00:00, the actual time, as the billable time and the payroll time. The price (**Billable Amt.**) is the billable time multiplied by the price from the ledger — € 55 per box (half-hour). The currency is added for foreign currency amounts.

For this customer, five bicycles were packed for shipping. Recall that we entered 30 minutes as the usual number of minutes (or 0.5 hours) for the job. The hourly rate was determined as the Selling Price divided by the usual number of hours, that is, € 55 divided by 0.5, or € 110 per hour. Thus the amount for 2.5 hours is 2.5 x € 110, or € 275.

Notice that the **Payroll Status** is Not Paid. You can edit the billable time, the billable amount, the payroll time and payroll income category for individual activities. We need to change the billable time to 2.5 hours, 2 hours and 30 minutes. The billable time is already selected.

Type 230 or 2.5 **Press** tab to update the billable amount to €275.

Click the **Customer list icon** and **select Niagara Rapids Inn** for the second activity.

Click the **Item list icon** and **select S060 Repairs**.

Click the **Actual Time column**.

Type 4 **Press** tab. **Type** 330 to update the Billable Time and Amount.

Repair service work is billed at a straight hourly rate so the amount is the billable time multiplied by the hourly rate for the preferred customer.

Click the **Customer list icon** on the next line. **Select Niagara Rapids Inn** again.

Click the **Item list icon** and **select S030 Maintenance: complete tune-up**.

Click the **Actual Time column**. **Type** 2 **Press** tab.

This time the flat rate of $65 is entered for the preferred price customer and you cannot edit the billable time. However, you can edit the billable amount.

Click the **Customer list icon** and **select Niagara Rapids Inn** for the fourth activity.

Click the **Item list icon** and **select S100 Warranty Repairs**.

Click the **Actual Time column**.

Type 4 **Press** tab. No amount is entered because the activity is non-billable, but the hours are added to the employee's payroll time.

Click the **Customer list icon** and **select Festival Tours**.

Click the **Item list icon** and **select S100 Warranty Repairs**.

Click the **Actual Time column**.

Type 2 **Press** tab to complete the entry as shown:

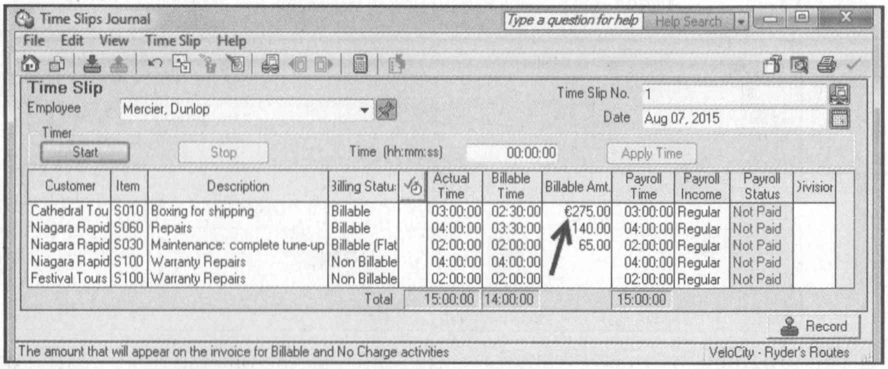

Check the **time slip** carefully before recording and **correct mistakes**.

You can also allocate time slip details to divisions — on the basis of either percent or time (from the ledger settings) and on the basis of actual, billable or payroll time (from the Allocate Based On drop-down list in the next screen).

Click the Division column for the activity line to open the Allocation screen:

NOTES

Remember that a single digit represents the number of hours.

Prices on time slips are shown in the currency of the customer.

WARNING!

There is no journal entry to review the time slip, so check it carefully.

You can adjust the time slip if you find an error after you record it.

You cannot reverse time slips automatically. If you selected the wrong employee, edit the time slip by deleting all time entries. The program will remove the time slip from the system. The time slip number cannot be used again, so you must use the next number.

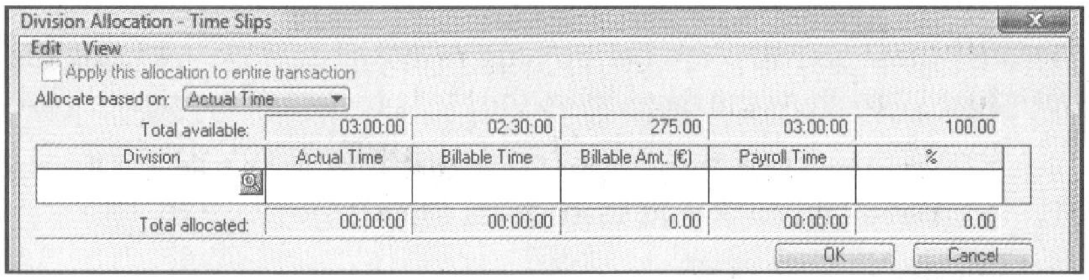

Choose the basis of allocation and division. Enter the time or percentage allocated to the division for that activity. Click OK to return to the journal when finished.

Click the **Record button** [Record] to save the entry.

Complete Time Slip #2 and then **close** the **Time Slips Journal**.

> **NOTES**
> Notice that the successful recording confirmation message does not include a journal entry number.

☐ **TIME SLIP #2** **DATED AUGUST 7, 2015**

9 For Yvonne Leader

Customer	Item	Actual Time	Billable Time	Billable Amount	Taxable	Payroll Time
Cathedral Tours	S080	13 hours	12 hours	€ 675.00	no	13 hours
Cathedral Tours	S070	3 hours	2 hours	€ 220.00	no	3 hours
Festival Tours	S080	8 hours	8 hours	USD 640.00	yes	8 hours
Niagara Rapids Inn*	S070	4 hours	3.5 hours	$420.00	yes	4 hours

> **NOTES**
> Service items S070 and S080 are not taxed when they are provided outside of Canada. They are deemed to be part of the tour. Services provided in Canada are taxable.
> The * indicates that preferred customer prices apply.

Add a **shortcut** for the **Time Slips Journal**. **Choose Create Time Slip** under the Time & Billing heading.

Paying Employees from Time Slips

After filling in the time slips, we use them to prepare paycheques.

✓ 10 **Employee Time Summary Sheet #20** **Dated August 7, 2015**

For the Pay Period ending August 7, 2015
Use time slips to prepare the paycheque for Yvonne Leader. Issue deposit slip #37.
Pay Dunlop Mercier for 80 regular hours in the period and 2 hours of overtime.
Recover $50 loaned and issue deposit slip #38.

Open the **Paycheques Journal**.

Enter August 7 as the Date and the Period Ending date.

Choose Leader from the Employee list and **press** *tab* to enter her information:

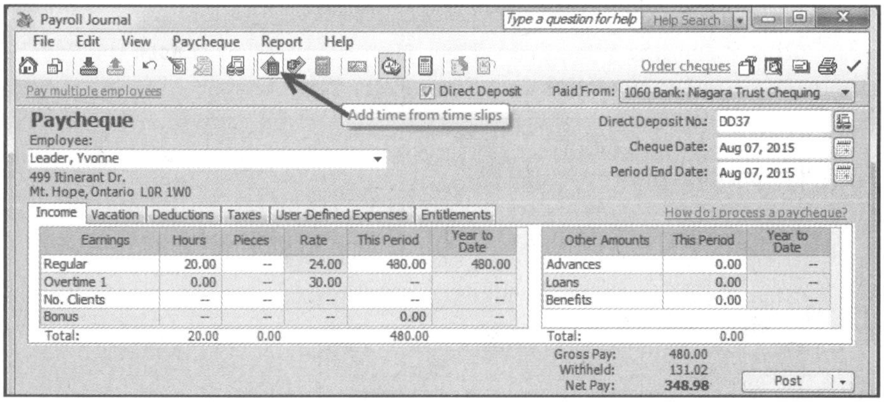

> **NOTES**
> You can also add time slips information in the Payroll Cheque Run Journal by selecting the employees and clicking the Add Time tool button or by choosing Add Time From Time Slips from the Payroll menu. The option to increase the number of hours to those in the ledger record must be applied the same way to all employees or to none of them.

When activities are set up in the Inventory and Services Ledger, and time slips are entered for employees, Sage 50 tracks the hours worked so you can use the summary of these time slips to prepare paycheques.

NOTES
The Time Slip tool remains unavailable until you select an employee.

We will use this method to prepare the paycheque for the new employee, Yvonne Leader, because these activities are her primary responsibility. We are using the Paycheques Journal to show the Sage 50 options for processing the time slips.

Click the **Add Time From Time Slips tool** or **choose** the **Paycheque menu** and **click Add Time From Time Slips**.

The Payroll Hour Selection screen opens:

When you begin from the Employees & Payroll module Time Slips drop-down shortcut (Pay Employee From Time Slip), you will open a Search window. After you select the employee, the Payroll Hour Selection screen opens with the Payroll Journal in the background.

You should enter the dates for the time slips that apply to this pay period. Leader has worked for one week; therefore, you should include the time slips up to August 7.

These dates are entered as the defaults because we already entered August 7 as the period ending date and August 1 is the date Leader was hired.

Click **OK** to return to the journal.

The number of hours is updated as shown in the following completed journal entry:

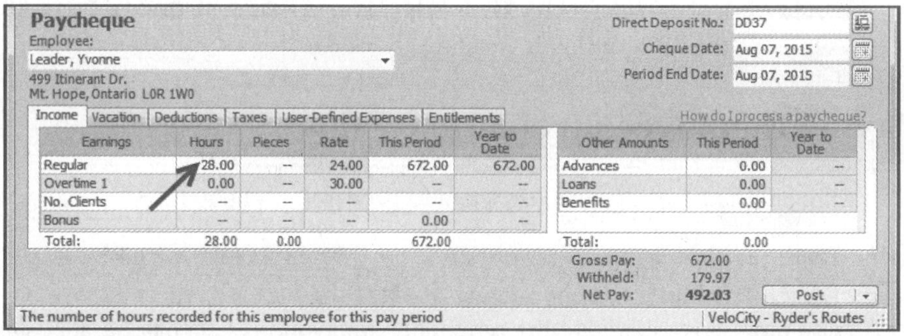

You can edit the number of hours as usual if necessary, and you can add advances or other deductions if they are appropriate.

Review the **journal entry** and, when you are certain that it is correct,

Click **Post** to save the transaction. **Click Yes** to continue.

Choose **Mercier** from the Employee list and press *tab* to enter his default payroll information.

Click the **Add Time From Time Slips tool** or **choose** the **Paycheque menu** and **click Add Time From Time Slips**:

WARNING!
You must complete the step of adding time from the time slips. If you do not, the payroll status for these activities will continue to show as Not Paid and the employee could be incorrectly paid a second time for the same work.

Again, the time slip period matches the pay period for the employee.

Click **OK** to see the warning:

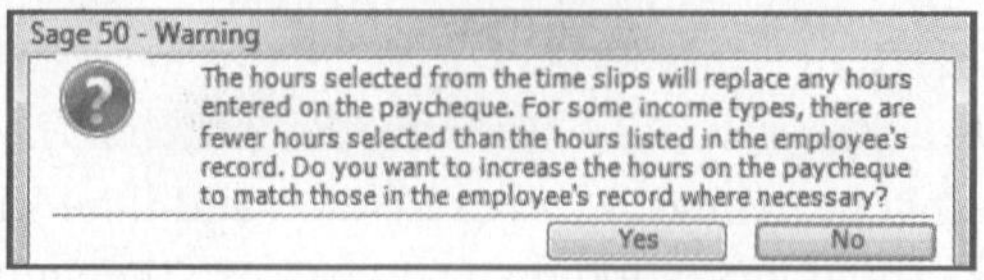

For Mercier, the hours worked exceed the hours on his time slip for the various customer jobs because he also performs other duties at the store. You have the option of accepting the Time Slip information or increasing the hours to match the default in the employee records. For Mercier, the Payroll Ledger entry is the correct one.

Click **Yes** to increase the number of hours and return to the journal. The number of Regular hours remains unchanged at 80 hours.

Click the **Overtime 1 field**. **Type** 2 to add the overtime hours.

Click the **Loans field** and **accept** the **default** $50 remaining to be repaid.

Review the **journal entry** and make corrections if necessary.

Click **Post**. **Click** **Yes** to continue and save the transaction.

Close the **Payroll Journal**.

The program will update the Payroll Hours Selection dates for the next paycheque and the Payroll Status on these Time Slips.

Open the **Time Slips Journal** from the shortcut or from the icon.

Click the **Look Up Time Slips tool** .

Type 2 in the Time Slip Number field and **click** **OK** to see Leader's time slip.

You should see that the employee has been paid — Paid appears in the Payroll Status column for each job completed by this employee. You cannot use this time slip information for payroll again.

Click the **Look Up Time Slips tool** and **enter** **1** in the Time Slip Number field. **Click** **OK** to see Mercier's time slip.

His payroll status is also marked as Paid because we added time from the time slips, even though the hours were not used to determine his pay.

Close the **Time Slips Journal**.

Preparing Sales Invoices from Time Slips

When sales invoices are prepared for mailing to customers, the activities from the time slips can be added directly to the invoices without re-entering each activity.

Click **Receivables** in the Modules pane list, if necessary.

Click the **Sales Invoices icon** Sales Invoices to open the Sales Journal.

✓ 11

Sales Invoice #2488 **Dated August 7, 2015**

To Cathedral Tours: Complete sales invoice for €1 170 plus HST from time slip activities. Include all activities to date. Enter H as the tax code for S010. Sales invoice total €1 205.75. Terms: 2/10, n/30. The exchange rate is 1.38.

Choose **Cathedral Tours** as the customer. Invoice and Pay Later are correct.

Enter **August 7, 2015** as the invoice date and **1.38** as the **exchange rate**.

Time slip activities may be entered using the tool icon or the Sales menu option:

NOTES
When you add time slip hours in the Payroll Run Journal, you must do so for all selected employees. You cannot choose individual employees for this. You will see the confirmation about number of hours being increased, but again, it will apply to all employees.

NOTES
When you use the Time Slip number to look up the time slip, the Previous and Next tools will not be available.
You can Search All Employees in the Search lookup window and click OK to list all the time slips and then select one as we did in other journals.

NOTES
From the Receivables module Time Slips icon shortcuts list, you can choose Create Invoice From Time Slip. When you choose the customer from the Select Customer screen, the Activities Service Selection screen shown on page 760 opens for that customer.

NOTES
If necessary, scroll or change the column width to see all the columns.

NOTES
By showing non-billable activities, you can include Warranty Repair hours on the selection list. Non-billable activities are not added to the sales invoice.

NOTES
Clicking , the Add Activity column heading, will select all the activities in the list. Then you can click any activity to deselect it if you need to.

WARNING!
Enter tax codes on sales invoices for foreign customers carefully. Refer to the Time Slip if necessary.

NOTES
You can edit the amount billed to the customer in the Sales Journal by changing the Amount or the Price. You can also choose a different account number for the sales.

NOTES
If the information in the Time Slip was incorrect, close the Sales Journal without posting the invoice and adjust the Time Slip. Then re-enter the sales invoice.

Click the **Add Time Slip Activities tool** or **choose** the **Sales menu** and **click Add Time Slip Activities** to open the activities list for this customer:

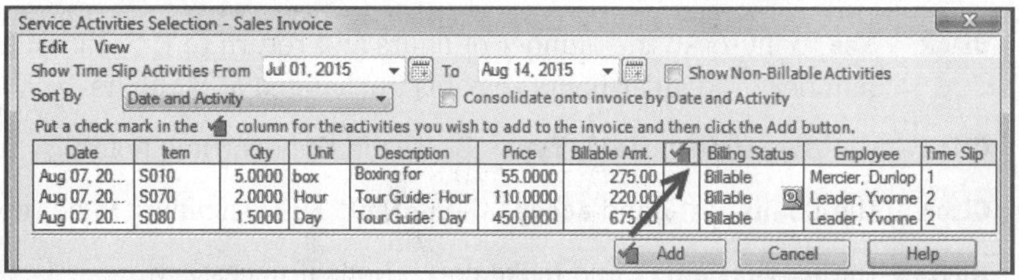

Services provided to the customer by all employees will be listed, and you can also include Non-Billable Activities by clicking its check box. You may need to scroll to see the information in all columns. You can Sort the list By Date And Activity, the default, By Employee And Activity or By Activity. You can also Consolidate the list By Date And Activity, combining the amounts for each activity recorded for the same date. You can select all the activities for the invoice, or omit some if they are incomplete or come after the billing date. All activities should be included in the invoice for Cathedral Tours.

Enter **Aug 1 2015** and **Aug 7 2015** as the date range in the Show Time Slip Activities From and To date fields.

Click the **Add Activity column** for the first activity, S010. Only activities with a ✓ in this column are added to the sales invoice.

Click the **Add Activity column** for the remaining activities.

Click the **Add button** Add to return to the Sales Journal.

The activities are now added to the journal.

Taxes are charged on the boxing service for Canadian customers on European tours because the work was completed in Canada, so we need to change this tax code entry.

Double-click the **blank Tax code field for item S010,** and **choose H** as the code to complete the entry as shown:

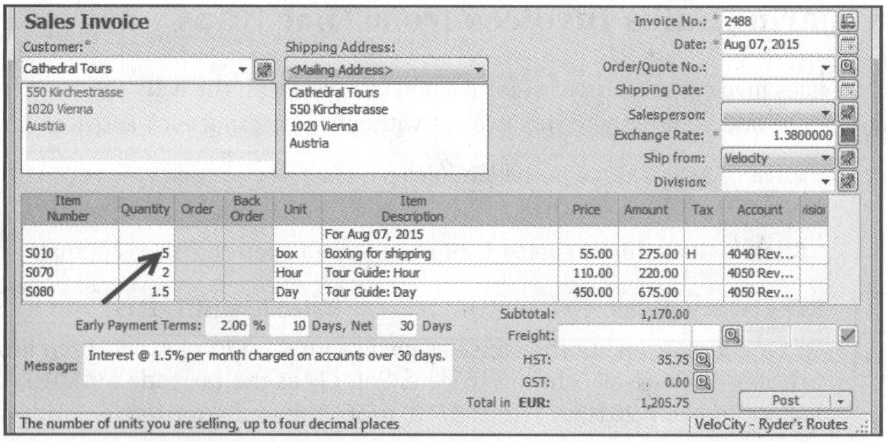

Notice that the Quantity refers to the units in the ledger — for S010, the customer pays for five completed units or boxes at one-half hour each. On the time sheet, we entered 230 (or 2.5) as the billable time. The 12 hours of tour guide service are entered as 1.5 days, the unit in the ledger. You can add other regular services or inventory to the sales invoice if they were sold to the same customer; you do not need to create a separate invoice for them.

You should review the journal entry before posting it.

Choose the **Report menu** and **click Display Sales Journal Entry**:

VeloCity - Ryder's Routes
Sales Journal Entry 08/07/2015 (J4)

Account Number	Account Description	Foreign A...	Debits	Credits
1200	Accounts Receivable	€1,205.75	1,663.94	-
2650	GST/HST Charged on Sales	€35.75	-	49.34
4040	Revenue from Services	€275.00	-	379.50
4050	Revenue from Tours	€895.00	-	1,235.10
1 Euro equals 1.3800000 Canadian Dollars			1,663.94	1,663.94

The journal entry is like other sales journal entries.

Close the **report** when you have finished viewing it and **make corrections** if necessary.

To correct the activities, click [icon] to return to the Service Activities Selection list. Previously selected activities are shown as Invoiced in the Billing Status column. Clicking the Add Activity column [icon] will add the ✓ and restore the status to billable so you can select a different group of activities.

Click Post to save the journal entry.

Enter the next **four transactions**.

☐ 12 **Sales Invoice #2489** **Dated August 7, 2015**

To Niagara Rapids Inn: Complete sales invoice for $625 plus HST from time slip activities. Include all activities to date. Sales invoice total $706.25. Terms: 2/10, n/30.

☐ 13 **Sales Invoice #2490** **Dated August 7, 2015**

To Festival Tours: Complete sales invoice for $640 USD from time slip activities. Include all activities to date. No tax is charged for tours in the United States. Sales invoice total $640 USD. Terms: 2/10, n/30. The exchange rate is 1.018.

☐ 14 **Cash Receipt #825** **Dated August 7, 2015**

From Fallsview Riverside Resort, cheque #1628 for $5 695.20 in full payment of account. Reference sales invoice #2484.

☐ 15 **Memo #8-8** **Dated August 7, 2015**

From Visa, received monthly credit card statement for $98 for purchases made before August 1, 2015. Submitted cheque #146 for $98 in full payment.

Building New Inventory

Instead of assembling inventory using the Item Assembly method, you can set up the inventory assembly components as part of the ledger record and then use this information to build an item using the Bill of Materials method. We will create the new inventory Promotional Safety Package, including the items or materials that make up the package.

✓ 16 **Memo #8-9** **Dated August 7, 2015**

Create a new inventory record for a promotional safety package that bundles several popular accessories. Create new linked Asset account: 1510 Promotions.

Item: AP100 Promotional Safety Package
Unit: package
Minimum: 0
Linked accounts: Asset 1510 Promotions Revenue 4020 COGS 5050

Currency	**CAD**	**USD**	**Euro**
Regular Selling Price	$375	$375	€ 270
Preferred Selling Price	$350	$350	€ 250

Tax exempt: No

NOTES

The regular selling price for the promotional safety package would be $405.

Build Components: use 1 of each AC020 Bicycle Pump: hand-held mini
AC030 Helmet
AC040 Light: halogen
AC060 Lock: kryptonite tube
AC070 Pannier: front wicker clip-on
and 2 of AC050 Light: rear reflector

Choose **Inventory & Services** from the Modules pane list.

Choose **Add Inventory & Service** from the Inventory & Services icon shortcuts list to open the Inventory Ledger for new Service Activity items. The cursor is in the Item Number field.

Type AP100 **Press** tab.

Type Promotional Safety Package

Click **Inventory** as the Type to modify the form for the inventory item.

The Units tab screen is displayed. All units are the same for this package.

Double-click **Each** and **type** package

Click the **Quantities tab**. The Minimum level is correct at 0.

Click the **Pricing tab** to access the price fields.

On the Pricing tab screen, you can enter regular and preferred prices in all the currencies that you have set up. Canadian prices are shown initially.

Click the **Regular Price Per Selling Unit field**.

Type 375 **Press** tab to advance to the Preferred Price field.

Type 350

Choose **United States Dollars** from the Currency list.

Foreign prices for Ryder's Routes are fixed, so we need to change the default setting. Clicking the entry will change the setting.

Click **Exchange Rate** beside Regular to change the setting to Fixed Price.

Press tab to advance to the Regular Selling Price for United States Dollars.

Type 375 **Press** tab to advance to the Preferred Pricing Method.

Click **Exchange Rate** to change the setting to Fixed Price. **Press** tab.

Type 350

Choose **Euro** from the currency list.

Click **Exchange Rate** beside Regular to change the setting to Fixed Price.

Press tab to advance to the Regular Price for Euro.

Type 270 **Press** tab to advance to the Preferred Pricing Method.

Click **Exchange Rate** to change the setting. **Press** tab. **Type** 250

Click the **Linked tab** to open the linked accounts screen.

Click the **Asset field**.

Type 1510 Promotions **Press** tab. We need to add the account.

Click **Add** and **press** tab to open the Add Account wizard.

Accept the remaining **defaults** for the account and **click Yes** to change the account class.

Press (tab) to advance to the Revenue account field.

Type 4020 **Press** (tab) to advance to the COGS account field.

Type 5050

The variance linked account is not needed for this item.

Click the **Taxes tab** to see the sales taxes relating to the inventory.

The default entry No for Tax Exempt is correct — HST is charged on the sale of this item. Duty is not charged on this item because it is not purchased.

Click the **Build tab** to see the information screen we need for entering the assembly or building components for inventory items:

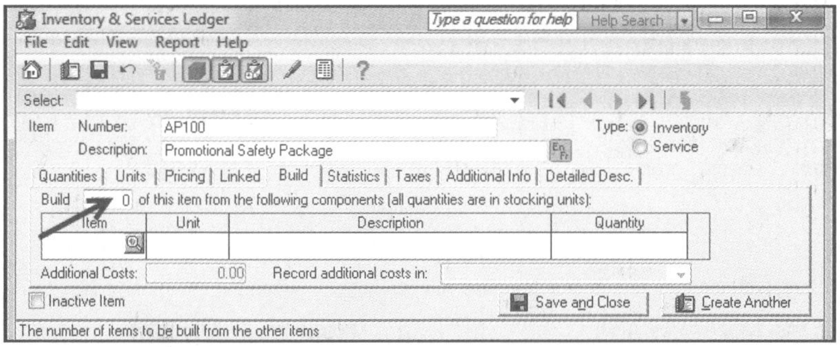

On this screen, we enter the relationship between the new inventory and its components, that is, how many new items we are building and how many of each input item this number of units requires. This is very similar to the Item Assembly Journal, except that we are only defining the building process at this stage. The actual building or assembly still takes place in the journal. One package is created from the set of accessories — we build one package at a time.

Click the **Build field** to enter the default number of packages being assembled from the set of components.

Type 1 **Press** (tab) to advance to the Item (number) field.

Click the **List icon** and **select AC020 Bicycle Pump: hand-held mini** to enter the first item.

The cursor advances to the Quantity field after entering the unit and description. Here you need to enter the number of pumps included in each Promotional Safety Package. We are defining the unit relationship between the assembled item and its components. One component item is used to make the package.

Type 1 **Press** (tab) to advance to the second Item line.

Enter the **next four components** and **enter 1** as the quantity for each. For **A050**, **enter 2** as the quantity.

The **Additional Costs** and its linked account field (**Record Additional Costs In**) became available once we entered the number of units to build. These fields have the same meaning as they do in the Item Assembly Journal. However, in the Bill of Materials method, costs are entered in the ledger record and separate assembly linked accounts can be defined for each item. There are no additional costs associated with creating the package so we should leave these fields blank.

NOTES

You can mark the new inventory as exempt for GST, but you do not need to do so.

NOTES

This screen is similar to the upper Components section of the Item Assembly Journal (page 376), but you cannot enter unit costs for the components.

NOTES

In the Pro version, there is one linked Item Assembly Costs account for the ledger, and it is entered on the Inventory Linked Accounts screen. This linked account is used for all Build From Item Assembly transactions in both Pro and Premium versions.

In the Premium version, you can enter a different linked additional costs account for each item you build. These different linked accounts will be used for Build From Bill Of Materials transactions.

Click the **Quantities tab**. The quantity on hand remains at zero until we build the item in the journal.

Correct any **errors** by returning to the field with the mistake. **Highlight** the **error** and **enter** the **correct information**. **Click** the different **tabs** to see all the information that you entered.

Click **Save And Close** 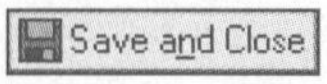 to save the record.

NOTES
Built items may also be purchased if this is appropriate. They are available for selection in the Purchases Journal.

Building an Inventory Item in the Journal

The quantity of Promotional Safety Packages is still zero. In order to create stock of the package for sale, we must build the item in the Bill Of Materials & Item Assembly Journal shown by the hand pointer below:

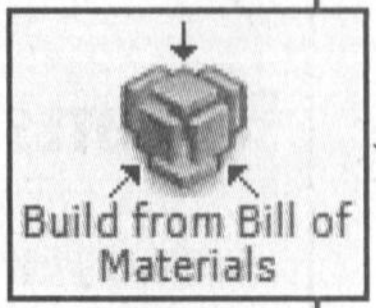

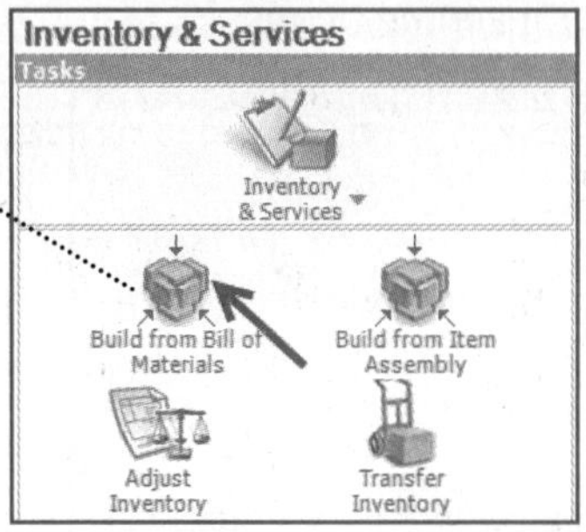

CLASSIC VIEW
Click the Bill Of Materials & Item Assembly icon  to open the journal. Choose Build From Bill Of Materials from the Build drop-down transactions list if necessary.

✓ 17 **Memo #8-10** **Dated August 7, 2015**

Build five (5) packages of the new item Promotional Safety Package (AP100).

Click the **Build From Bill Of Materials icon** to open the journal:

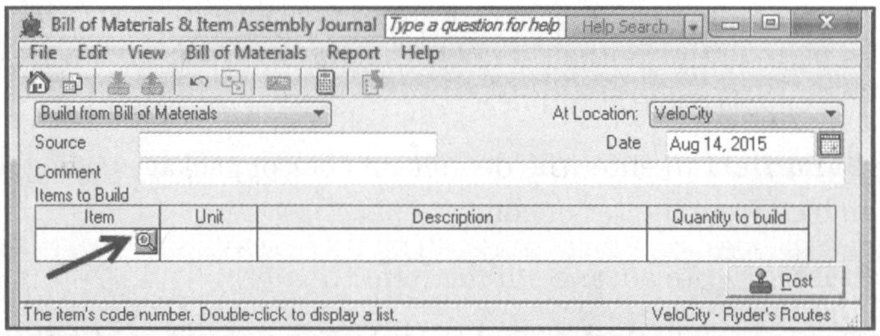

NOTES
Remember that you can choose Build From Item Assembly or Build From Bill Of Materials from the transactions drop-down list once the journal is open (see page 376).

NOTES
The additional costs and the components information are taken from the ledger record – the Build tab screen details. Item cost, as usual, is the average cost for each component because we selected this method for the company file (see page 662).

In the Premium version, you can assemble new inventory items either by using the Item Assembly method that we used in previous applications or the Bill of Materials method that follows.

The journal resembles the lower half of the Build From Item Assembly Journal screen, the Assembled Items section, but without components and costs (see page 376). Information for the upper half of that screen — for components and costs — is located in the ledger record. The default location is VeloCity.

Click the **Source field**.

Type `Memo 8-10` **Press** *tab* to advance to the Date field.

Type `8-7` **Press** *tab* **twice** to advance to the Comment field.

Type `Create promotional packages` **Press** *tab*. The cursor moves to the Item field.

Click the **List icon** to open the selection list:

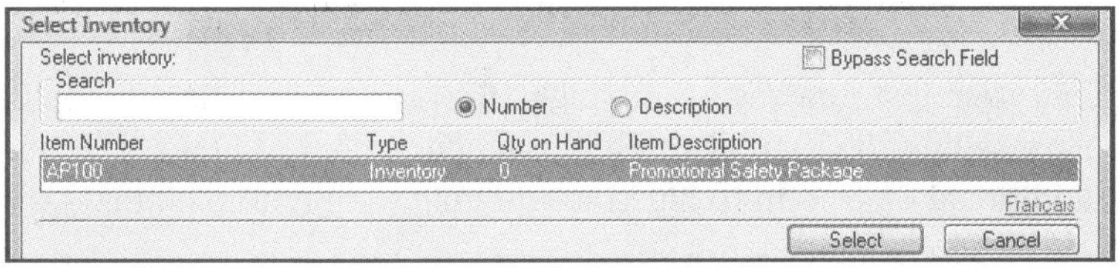

All items for which you have added build information will be listed on this screen. Because we have entered these details only for the Promotional Safety Package, it is the only one listed.

Double-click **AP100** to add it to the journal.

The unit and description are added for the package and the default quantity is 1. These details are taken from the ledger record. The quantity is selected so we can change it. We are creating five packages.

Type 5 to complete the journal entry as shown:

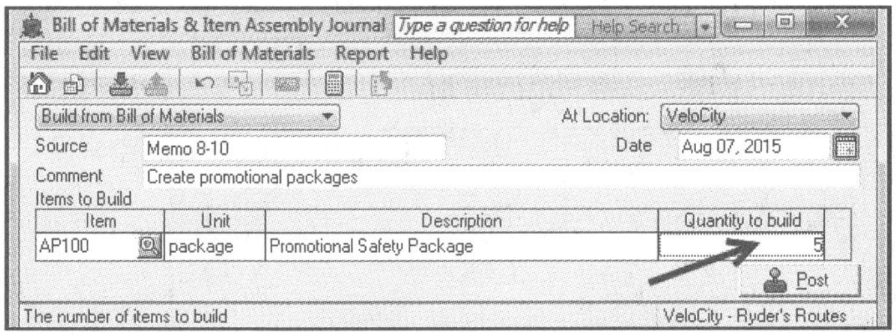

If you have other items to build, you can continue by choosing the items and entering a quantity for each of them.

Review your **work** before posting the transaction.

Choose the **Report menu** and **click** **Display Bill Of Materials & Item Assembly Journal** to display the journal transaction:

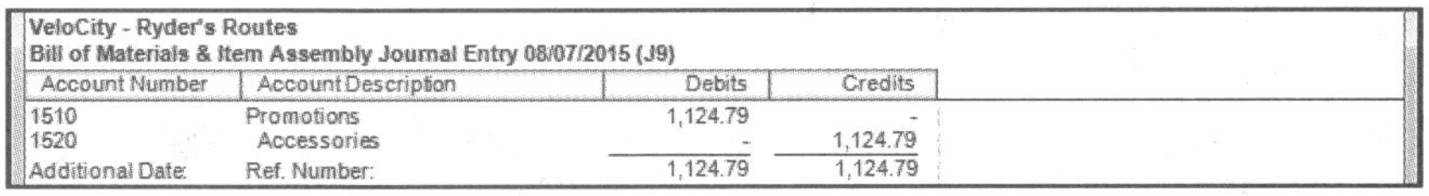

VeloCity - Ryder's Routes
Bill of Materials & Item Assembly Journal Entry 08/07/2015 (J9)

Account Number	Account Description	Debits	Credits
1510	Promotions	1,124.79	-
1520	Accessories	-	1,124.79
Additional Date:	Ref. Number:	1,124.79	1,124.79

The asset account balances have been updated by the transaction, just as they are in an Item Assembly transaction. Compare this journal entry with the one on page 378. The inventory quantities are also updated from the transaction — the quantity of packages increases and the quantities for the other items decrease. Additional costs, if any, would be credited to the linked cost account for the package and debited to the assembled item asset account.

Close the **journal display** and **make corrections** if necessary.

If there is not enough inventory of any item in stock to complete the build, you will see an error message asking you to reduce the quantity to build:

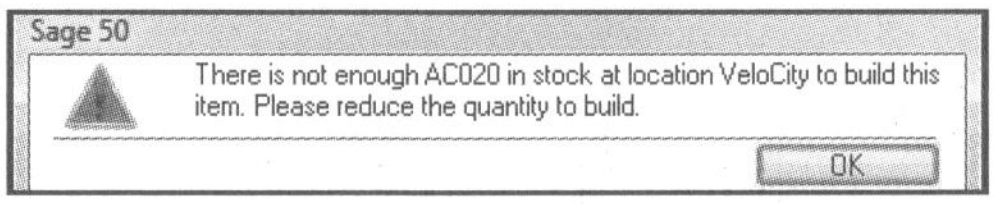

Click OK and reduce the number of units you are building.

Click 

to save the entry. **Close** the **advisor** about low inventory.

Click the Item List icon to see that the number of promotional packages has been changed to five. Click Cancel to close this screen without making a selection.

You can now sell the package just like any other inventory item.

NOTES

You cannot change the unit cost using the Build method. The Cost fields are not available in the journal or in the ledger record.

The default quantity is taken from the ledger record's Build tab screen, where we entered the rule for building one item at a time.

NOTES

When you link the same asset account to the assembled item and its components, you will see the message that no journal entry results from the transaction. However, all inventory quantities are updated by the transaction.

Multiple Levels of Build

You can use a built item just like any other single inventory item. The process is the same when you are selling the item or using it as a component to build other inventory. We created an additional built item to illustrate the following multiple build — you will not see the next two screenshots.

Nested building components are common in construction work. When you use a built item as a component for a second-stage build, you select it on the Build tab screen just like other inventory. When you are building the new second-stage item in the Bill of Materials Journal, the built component may be out of stock. In this case, Sage 50 provides the following message:

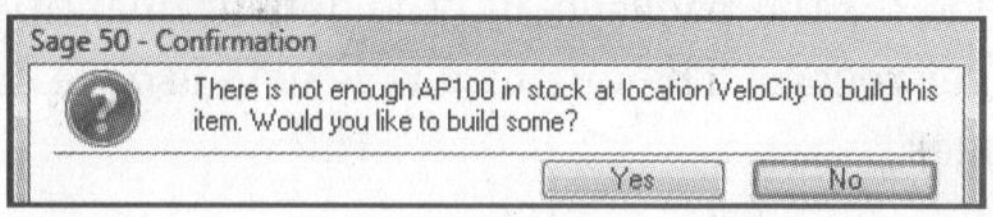

You can now automatically build the primary item, the built component, as part of the same journal transaction.

Click Yes to continue with the additional build:

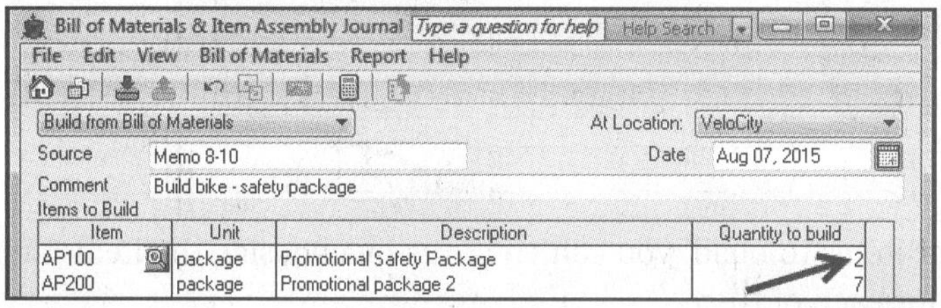

Sage 50 will add the out-of-stock built item to the Bill of Materials Journal as the first item to build. The number of units built will be those required to complete the secondary build.

Close the **Journal**.

> **NOTES**
> If there are further layers of building nested in a transaction, Sage 50 will offer the chance to build the necessary components at each stage in the same way to complete the initial transaction.

Transferring Inventory between Locations

Items can be transferred from one location where the stock is available or stored to another. In Sage 50, the option to transfer items is available in the Inventory Adjustments & Transfers Journal, accessed from the Transfer Inventory icon:

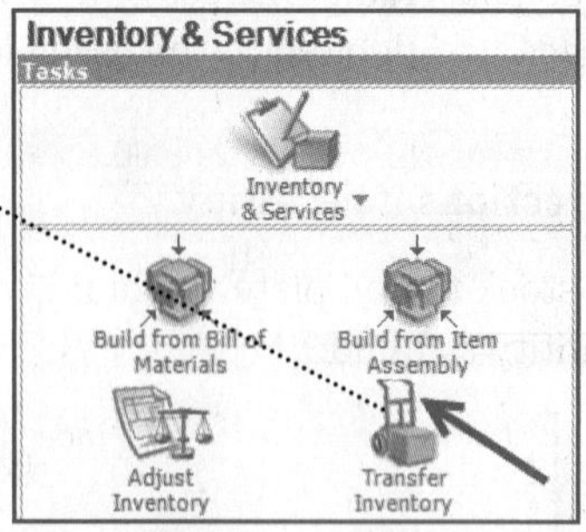

> **NOTES**
> Transfers may also occur when the item a customer wants is not located at the store the customer is visiting.

> **CLASSIC VIEW**
> Click the Inventory Adjustments & Transfers icon
> 
>
> to open the journal. Choose Transfer Between Locations from the drop-down transactions list if necessary.

✓ 18

Memo #8-11 **Dated August 7, 2015**

The Ryder store is preparing for its official opening. Transfer the following inventory items from the VeloCity store to the Ryder store:

5	AP100	Promotional Safety Package
10	AC030	Helmet
10	AC040	Light: halogen
20	BK010	Books: Complete Bicycle Guide
20	BK020	Books: Endless Trails

Click the **Transfer Inventory icon** to open the journal with Transfer Between Locations, the type of transaction we need, already selected:

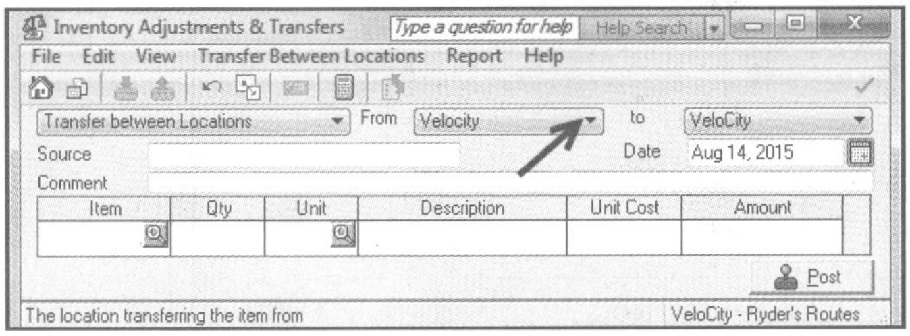

This is the same journal we used for other inventory adjustments in previous chapters, but there is no field for account numbers. When multiple locations are used, transfers between locations are made in this journal as well. You can select the type of transaction from the transactions drop-down list as shown:

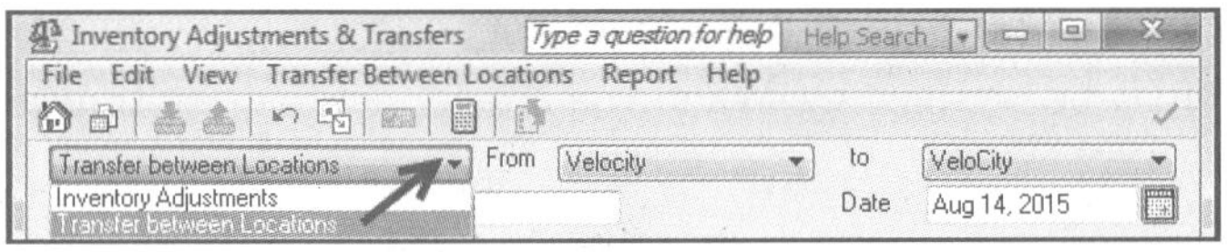

We need to indicate the direction of the transfer, in this case from the VeloCity store to the Ryder store. VeloCity is the default location for both fields because it is the primary location. This is correct as the From location.

Click the **From** drop-down list to see both locations.

Click the **To drop-down list**:

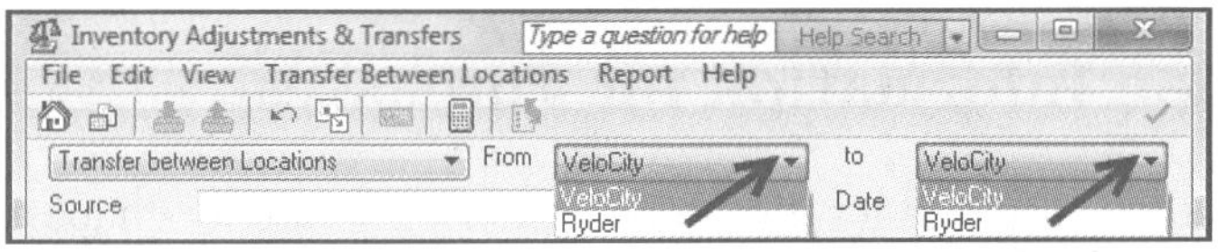

Both locations are available in both lists. You can make transfers to and from either location.

Click **Ryder** to add the second location for the To field.

As for other types of transactions, we need to enter the date, the source and a comment. Then we will enter the items that are being moved.

Click the **Source field**.

Type `Memo 8-11` **Press** tab to move to the Date field.

Enter **August 7** as the date of the inventory move.

Click the **Comment field**.

Type `Move inventory to Ryder store`

Press tab to advance to the Item code field. A list of items is available, as it is for inventory fields in other journals.

You can access the inventory list by pressing enter in the Item field, double-clicking the field or clicking the List icon.

Click the **List icon** and **select AP100**, the first item on the transfer list.

Press tab to move to the Qty (quantity) field.

Type 5

NOTES

Both locations are listed in the From and the To location drop-down lists because items may be transferred from either location to the other.

NOTES
Accept the default cost prices for items transferred.

NOTES
You can store the transfer just like any other transaction. If you need to make a correction later, you can recall the entry to use as a reference for making changes.

NOTES
The successful recording message for the transfer does not include a journal entry number.

WARNING!
You will need to edit the purchase order date before you can fill it. The order quantity for item AC060 has been increased from 8 to 18.

Enter the **remaining items** in the same way to complete the entry as shown:

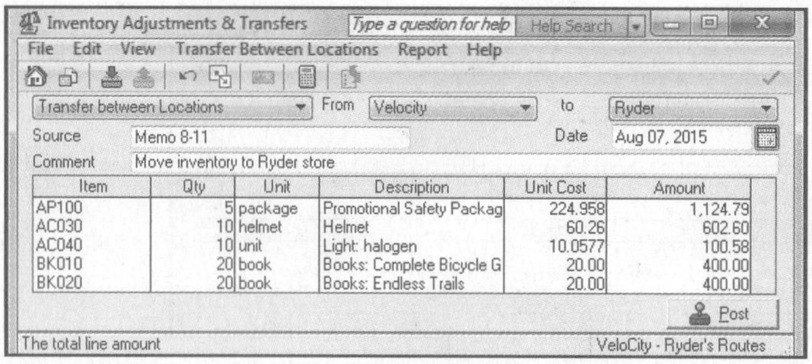

When you record (post) the transfer, the inventory at the two locations will be updated — the quantity at the VeloCity store is reduced and the quantity at the Ryder store is increased. You can see the changes that you made by accessing the ledger records for the items and choosing the locations on the Quantity tab screen. However, no journal entry results from this transaction and you cannot look up or adjust the entry, so check it carefully before posting. When you are certain that the transaction is correct, you must save it.

Click Post to save the entry. **Close** the **journal** to return to the Inventory Home window.

To correct the transfer after posting, you should repeat the transfer but reverse the direction of the movement of goods — enter the original From location in the To location field and the original To location in the From location field. Refer to Appendix C, page A–29.

Adding Location Information for Purchases

Now that we have multiple locations for inventory, we must indicate which location the inventory is taken from or sent to when we make purchases, sales and adjustments. By choosing the correct location, we can accurately keep track of the quantity on hand at each store.

The purchase order from Complete Cycler Inc. was delivered to the Ryder store.

✓ 19

Purchase Invoice #CC-3775 **Dated August 10, 2015**

From Complete Cycler Inc. to fill purchase order #43
All items shipped to Ryder store location

2	AC010	Bicycle Pump: standing model	$ 240.00 USD
1	AC020	Bicycle Pump: hand-held mini	500.00 USD
5	AC030	Helmet	3 000.00 USD
5	AC040	Light: halogen	500.00 USD
5	AC050	Light: rear reflector	350.00 USD
18	AC060	Lock: kryptonite tube	3 600.00 USD
		Freight	120.00 USD
		HST	1 080.30 USD
		Invoice total	$9 390.30 USD

Terms: 1/15, n/30. The exchange rate is 1.02.

Open the **Purchases Journal** (click the Create Purchase Invoice shortcut).

Choose **PO #43** in the order number field and **press** tab.

The order is placed on-screen as an invoice:

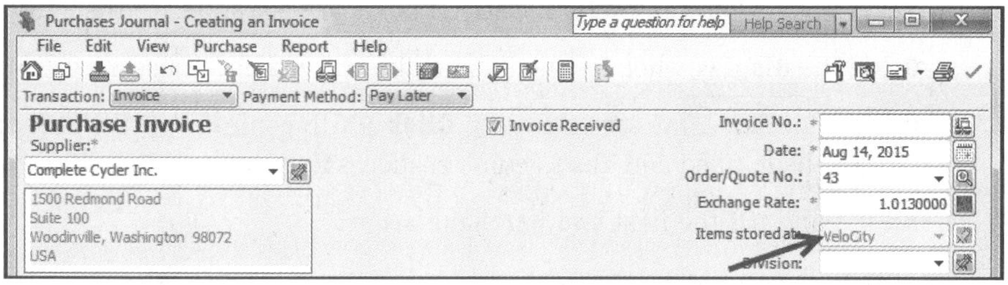

When the order was entered, locations were not set up. The location field (**Items Stored At**) is dimmed and unavailable. VeloCity, the primary location, is entered, and this is not correct. We need to edit the order to change the location before filling it. We must also change the quantity ordered for item A060.

Choose **Order** from the Transaction drop-down list to restore the purchase order. **Click Yes** to confirm that you are discarding the invoice.

Choose **PO #43** in the Order No. field list. **Press** *tab* to place the order on the screen. The fields are still dimmed and cannot be edited.

Click the **Adjust Purchase Order tool**, or **choose** the **Purchase menu** and **click Adjust Purchase Order** or **press** *ctrl* **+ A**. We can now modify the order.

Click the **Items Stored At drop-down list arrow** as shown and **click Ryder**:

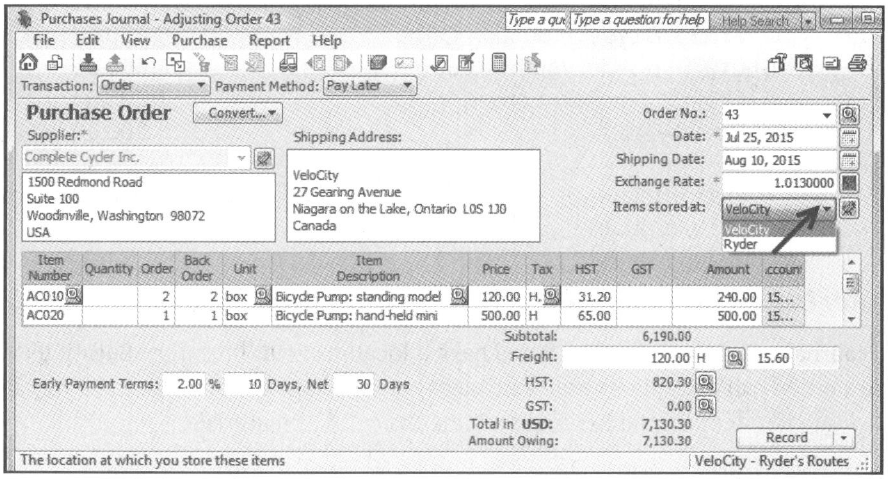

Enter **Aug 10 15** as the purchase order date.

Enter **1.02** as the exchange rate when prompted to change the rate.

Click **8**, the order quantity for AC060 and **type** 18 We can now fill the order.

Choose **Invoice** from the Transaction drop-down list or **choose Convert This Purchase Order To A Purchase Invoice** from the Convert drop-down list.

Sage 50 shows you the familiar confirmation message:

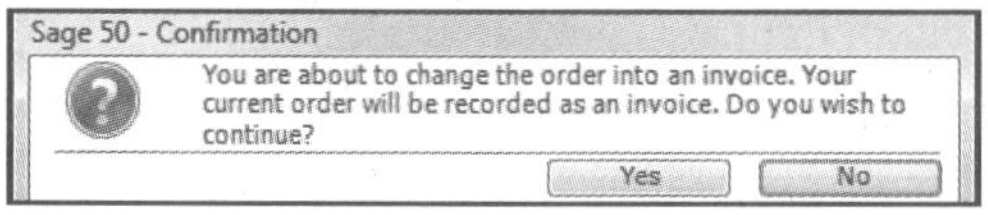

Click **Yes** to confirm that you are changing the order to an invoice.

Click the **Fill Backordered Quantities tool**, or **choose** the **Purchase menu** and **click Fill Backordered Quantities**. **Add CC-3775** as the invoice number and **Aug 10** as the invoice date to complete the transaction.

WARNING!

You must change the date for the purchase order. The original purchase order was placed on July 23. You cannot continue with this date because it precedes August 1, the start of the fiscal period and the date in the Do Not Allow Transactions Dated Before (Company, System Settings) field.

NOTES

If the Exchange Rate screen opens again, click Cancel because we already entered the date for August 10.

NOTES
Location details are not included in the journal entry, but the inventory records will be correctly updated.

Review your **journal entry**. Location details are not added to the journal entry.

Close the **display** when finished and make corrections if necessary.

Click Post to save the entry. **Click OK** to confirm that the order has been filled and **Yes** to confirm successful posting.

Adjust and **fill** the next **two purchase orders**.

NOTES
Add Ryder as the location. Enter August 10 as the Order Date to adjust purchase order #41. Fill the order and add WD-4558 as the invoice number.

20

Purchase Invoice #WD-4558 **Dated August 10, 2015**

From Wheel Deals to fill purchase order #41
All items shipped to Ryder store location

10	AC070	Pannier: front wicker clip-on	$ 500.00 USD
10	AC080	Pannier: rear mesh	400.00 USD
		HST	117.00 USD
		Invoice total	$1 017.00 USD

Terms: 2/10, n/30. The exchange rate is 1.02.

NOTES
Remember to change the payment method to Pay Later when you fill the order from Pro Cycles Inc.

21

Purchase Invoice #PC-3877 **Dated August 10, 2015**

From Pro Cycles Inc. to fill purchase order #42 for VeloCity store

6	CY010	Bicycle: Commuter Steel frame CX10	$ 1 860.00
10	CY020	Bicycle: Commuter Alum frame CX90	5 400.00
4	CY030	Bicycle: Racer Ultra lite RX480	6 000.00
4	CY040	Bicycle: Trail Alum frame TX560	2 480.00
3	CY050	Bicycle: Mountain Alum frame MX14	2 790.00
4	CY060	Bicycle: Mountain Carbon frame MX34	6 880.00
6	CY070	Bicycle: Youth YX660	1 350.00
4	CY090	Stationary Converter	1 320.00
		Freight	200.00
		HST	3 676.40
		Invoice total	$31 956.40

Terms: 2/10, n/30.

Entering Locations in the Sales and Other Journals

NOTES
Location information may also be entered on the Options tab screens in the supplier record (Usually Store Item In field) and customer ledger records (Usually Ship Item From field).

All journals that use inventory items have a location field. Inventory Location information can be added to sales invoices (and orders and quotes), inventory adjustments, item assemblies and building from bill of materials.

✓ 22

Sales Invoice #2491 **Dated August 10, 2015**

To Candide's B & B (from VeloCity store)

8	AC030	Helmet	$120/ helmet
4	AC060	Lock: kryptonite tube	70/ lock
4	CY020	Bicycle: Commuter Alum frame CX90	960/ bike
		HST	13%

Terms: 2/10, n/30.

Open the **Sales Journal** and **click** the **Ship From list arrow**:

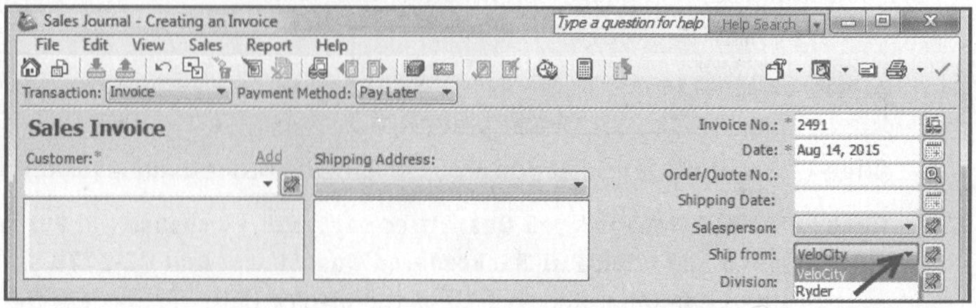

Choose **VeloCity**. **Enter** the remaining details for **Sales invoice #2491**. **Review** and then **post** the **entry**. **Close** the **Sales Journal**.

The next two screens show the location selection in the Inventory Adjustments and Bill of Materials & Item Assembly journals from the At Location drop-down list:

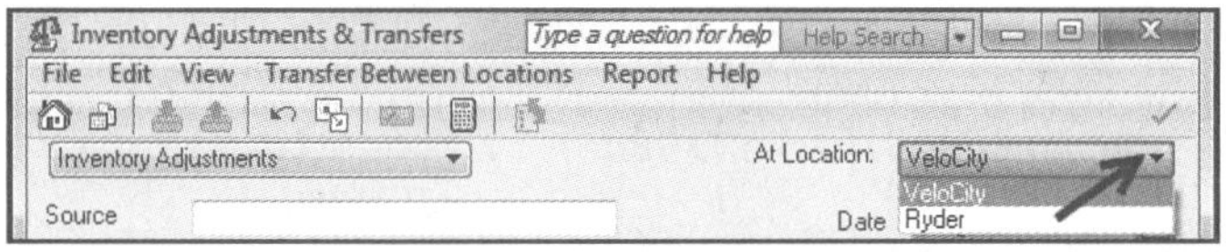

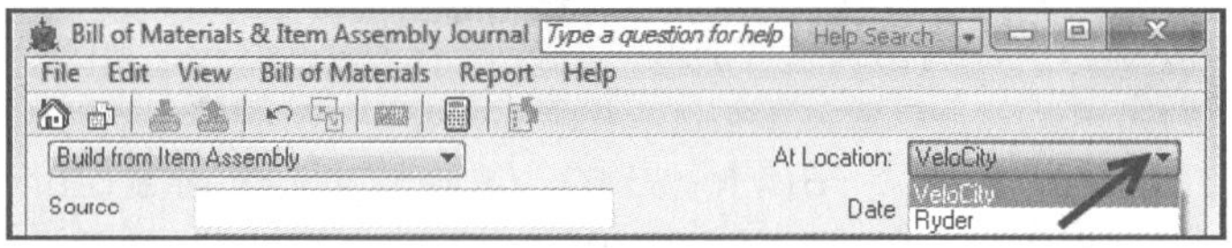

If the location you chose does not have any stock of an item needed to complete the build or assembly, you will see the following message:

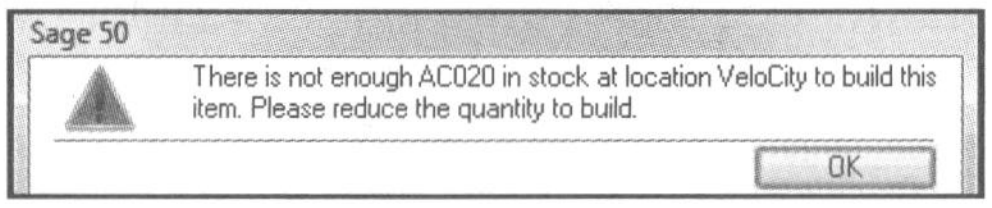

Click **OK**. In this case, you must first transfer or purchase the required item.

Enter the **remaining transactions** for August up to Memo #8-18.

23 **Memo #8-12** **Dated August 14, 2015**

Remittances: Use the August 1 balances to make the following remittances in the Payments Journal. (See margin Notes and Warning.)

a) Record payment for GST and HST for July to the Receiver General for Canada. Issue cheque #147 in payment.
b) Record payment for Garnisheed Wages Payable for July to the Receiver General for Canada. Issue cheque #148 in full payment.
c) Record payment for EI, CPP and Income Tax Payable for July to the Receiver General for Canada. Issue cheque #149 in full payment.
d) Record payment for EHT Payable for the quarter to the Minister of Finance. Issue cheque #150 in payment.
e) Record payment for RRSP Payable to Welland Insurance. Issue cheque #151 in payment.
f) Record payment for CSB Payable to Escarpment Investments. Issue cheque #152 in payment.
g) Record payment for Group Insurance Payable for July to Welland Insurance. Issue cheque #153 in payment.
h) Record payment for Charitable Donations Payable for July to Canadian Cancer Society (employer and employee contributions). Issue cheque #154 in payment.
i) Record payment for WSIB Payable for the quarter to the Workplace Safety & Insurance Board. Issue cheque #155 in payment.

24 **Purchase Invoice #ABS-7597** **Dated August 14, 2015**

From ABS International (use Full Add for new foreign supplier)

10 CY040 Bicycle: Trail Alum frame TX560	€4 000.00
Freight	100.00
HST	533.00
Purchase invoice total	€4 633.00

The duty rate for these items is 0%.
Terms: net 30. The exchange rate is 1.385.
Change the default amounts.
All items shipped to the VeloCity store.

NOTES

Choose Make Other Payment to remit the sales taxes.

Choose Pay Remittance to remit payroll taxes and deductions.

Clear the GST and HST reports for July 31.

WARNING!

Remember to reset the Pay Period date to August 1 for the second remittance to the Receiver General and Welland Insurance to avoid including the amounts from the August 7 paycheque.

NOTES

Use Full Add for the new supplier because you need to add currency information.

ABS International
Contact: Derek Rad
Schumacher Str. 96
55123 Mainz, Germany
Tel: (49-6131) 468 913
Fax: (49-6131) 468 248
Currency: EUR
Terms: net 30
Tax code: H

SESSION DATE – AUGUST 31, 2015

25 **Sales Order #8-1-PNR & Deposit #23** **Dated August 16, 2015**

Delivery date August 24, 2015 (from VeloCity store).
From Park 'N Ride Tours. Special volume discounts will apply.

20	AC030	Helmet	$100/ helmet
10	AC060	Lock: kryptonite tube	60/ lock
10	CY040	Bicycle: Trail Alum frame TX560	900/ bike
	HST		13%

Terms: 2/10, n/30. Change all prices for this order.
Deposit cheque #438 for $5 000 received with order.

26 **Cash Receipt #826** **Dated August 18, 2015**

From Candide's B & B, cheque #614 for $5 625.59 in payment of account including $114.81 discount for early payment. Reference sales invoice #2491.

27 **Cash Purchase Invoice #NB-00124** **Dated August 20, 2015**

From Niagara Bell, $220 plus HST for one month of phone service for two stores. Purchase invoice total $248.60. Terms: cash on receipt of invoice. Issue cheque #156 in full payment.

28 **Deposit Slip #26** **Dated August 21, 2015**

Prepare deposit slip for $16 320.79 for cheques received in previous two weeks.

29 **Cash Purchase Invoice #ES-93215** **Dated August 21, 2015**

From Energy Source, $180 plus HST for hydro service. Purchase invoice total $203.40. Terms: cash on receipt of invoice. Issue cheque #157 in full payment.

30 **Memo #8-13** **Dated August 21, 2015**

Transfer 30 kryptonite tube locks (item AC060) from Ryder to VeloCity store. Build 5 AP100 Promotional Safety Packages at the Ryder store location.

NOTES
The * indicates preferred customer prices apply.

31 **TIME SLIP #3** **DATED AUGUST 21, 2015**

For Dunlop Mercier

Customer	Item	Actual Time	Billable Time	Billable Amount	Taxable	Payroll Time
Cathedral Tours	S010	8 hours	8 (16 boxes)	€ 880.00	yes	8 hours
Gallery Tours*	S010	4 hours	4 (8 boxes)	€ 400.00	yes	4 hours
Park 'N Ride Tours	S100	2 hours	2 hours	–	N/A	2 hours
Backstage Tours*	S030	1.5 hours	1 hour	$65.00	yes	1.5 hours
Backstage Tours*	S060	4 hours	4 hours	$160.00	yes	4 hours
Americas Vinelands Tours*	S080	8.5 hours	8 hours	USD 560.00	yes	8.5 hours

32 **TIME SLIP #4** **DATED AUGUST 21, 2015**

For Yvonne Leader

Customer	Item	Actual Time	Billable Time	Billable Amount	Taxable	Payroll Time
Backstage Tours*	S070	4 hours	4 hours	$480.00	yes	4 hours
Backstage Tours*	S080	9 hours	8 hours	$560.00	yes	9 hours
Gallery Tours*	S080	26 hours	24 hours	€ 1 200.00	no	26 hours
Gallery Tours*	S070	3.5 hours	3 hours	€ 255.00	no	3.5 hours
Cathedral Tours	S080	17 hours	16 hours	€ 900.00	no	17 hours
Cathedral Tours	S070	6 hours	6 hours	€ 660.00	no	6 hours

33

Employee Time Summary Sheet #21 **Dated August 21, 2015**

For the Pay Period ending August 21, 2015

Edit the employee record for Yvonne Leader. Leader will be paid every two weeks (26 pay periods per year) and her minimum number of hours will be 40. If her contract hours from time slips are less than 40 hours, she will be paid for 40 hours. Change the Additional Federal Tax amount to $100.

Use time slips to prepare the bi-weekly paycheque for Yvonne Leader for the actual number of hours worked. Issue deposit slip #39.

Dunlop Mercier worked 80 regular hours in the period and 4 hours of overtime. Issue deposit slip #40 in payment. (Add time from time slips but choose Yes to use regular hours when prompted.)

NOTES

Pay Periods and Hours are entered on the Income tab and Additional Federal Tax on the Taxes tab of the Employee Ledger record.

Use the Paycheques Journal for the payroll transactions so that you can enter the correct cheque and period ending dates. You cannot change the cheque date in the Payroll Cheque Run Journal.

34

Sales Invoice #2492 **Dated August 21, 2015**

To Cathedral Tours: Complete sales invoice for €2 440 plus HST from time slip activities. Include all activities to date. Enter H as the tax code for item S010. Sales invoice total €2 554.40. Terms: 2/10, n/30. The exchange rate is 1.37.

NOTES

Enter tax codes for foreign customers carefully.

35

Sales Invoice #2493 **Dated August 21, 2015**

To Gallery Tours: Complete sales invoice for €1 855 plus HST from time slip activities. Enter H as the tax code for item S010. Include all activities to date. Sales invoice total €1 907. Terms: 2/10, n/30. The exchange rate is 1.37.

36

Sales Invoice #2494 **Dated August 21, 2015**

To Backstage Tours: Complete sales invoice for $1 265 plus HST from time slip activities. Include all activities to date. Sales invoice total $1 429.45. Terms: 2/10, n/30.

37

Sales Invoice #2495 **Dated August 21, 2015**

To Americas Vinelands Tours: Complete sales invoice for $560 USD plus HST from time slip activities. Change the tax code for S080 to H. Include all activities to date. Sales invoice total $632.80 USD. Terms: 2/10, n/30. The exchange rate is 1.02.

NOTES

The tour for Americas Vinelands Tours is taxable because it is provided in Canada for the US customer.

38

Credit Card Purchase Invoice #LS-12331 **Dated August 24, 2015**

From Lakeshore Sunoco, $125 including HST paid for gasoline and $380 plus HST for vehicle repairs. Purchase invoice total $554.40 paid in full by Visa. Use Tax code IN for the gasoline purchase and tax code H for the repairs.

39

Sales Invoice #2496 **Dated August 28, 2015**

To Park 'N Ride Tours, to fill sales order #8-1-PNR (VeloCity store)

20	AC030	Helmet	$100/ helmet
10	AC060	Lock: kryptonite tube	60/ lock
10	CY040	Bicycle: Trail Alum frame TX560	900/ bike
	HST		13%

Terms: 2/10, n/30. Remember to change the payment method to Pay Later.

NOTES

Do not forget to change the payment method for invoice #2496.

TIME SLIP #5 **DATED AUGUST 31, 2015**

40 For Dunlop Mercier

Customer	Item	Actual Time	Billable Time	Billable Amount	Taxable	Payroll Time
Shavian B & B	S010	2 hours	2 (4 boxes)	$320.00	yes	2 hours
Shavian B & B	S100	3 hours	–	–	yes	3 hours
Niagara Rapids Inn*	S030	2 hours	2 hours	$65.00	yes	2 hours
Niagara Rapids Inn*	S060	4 hours	4 hours	$160.00	yes	4 hours
Americas Vineland Tours*	S060	4 hours	4 hours	USD 160.00	yes	4 hours
Americas Vineland Tours*	S010	2 hours	2 (4 boxes)	USD 280.00	yes	2 hours

TIME SLIP #6 **DATED AUGUST 31, 2015**

41 For Yvonne Leader

Customer	Item	Actual Time	Billable Time	Billable Amount	Taxable	Payroll Time
Backstage Tours*	S080	15 hours	16 hours	$1 120.00	yes	15 hours
Backstage Tours*	S070	5 hours	4.5 hours	$540.00	yes	5 hours
Festival Tours	S070	4 hours	3 hours	USD 450.00	yes	4 hours
Festival Tours	S080	12 hours	12 hours	USD 960.00	yes	12 hours
Americas Vinelands Tours*	S070	2.5 hours	2 hours	USD 240.00	yes	2.5 hours
Americas Vinelands Tours*	S080	8 hours	8 hours	USD 560.00	yes	8 hours

42 **Sales Invoice #2497** **Dated August 31, 2015**

To Shavian B & B: Complete sales invoice for $320 plus HST from time slip activities. Include all activities to date. Sales invoice total $361.60. Terms: 2/10, n/30.

43 **Sales Invoice #2498** **Dated August 31, 2015**

To Niagara Rapids Inn: Complete sales invoice for $225 plus HST from time slip activities. Include all activities to date. Sales invoice total $254.25. Terms: 2/10, n/30.

44 **Sales Invoice #2499** **Dated August 31, 2015**

To Americas Vinelands Tours: Prepare sales invoice for $1 240 USD plus HST from time slip activities for all activities to date. All activities are taxable (tax code H). Sales invoice total $1 401.20 USD. Terms: 2/10, n/30. The exchange rate is 1.01.

45 **Sales Invoice #2500** **Dated August 31, 2015**

To Backstage Tours: Sales invoice for $1 660 plus HST from time slip activities for all activities to date. Sales invoice total $1 875.80. Terms: 2/10, n/30.

46 **Credit Card Sales Invoice #2501** **Dated August 31, 2015**

To Visa Sales (sales summary). Sold from VeloCity store.

12	AC040	Light: halogen	$ 25/ unit	$ 300.00
12	AC060	Lock: kryptonite tube	70/ lock	840.00
2	AC100	Trailer: third-wheel rider	260/ unit	520.00
18	BK010	Books: Complete Bicycle Guide (code G)	40/ book	720.00
25	BK020	Books: Endless Trails (code G)	40/ book	1 000.00
6	CY020	Bicycle: Commuter Alum frame CX90	960/ bike	5 760.00
2	CY030	Bicycle: Racer Ultra lite RX480	3 100/ bike	6 200.00
2	CY050	Bicycle: Mountain Alum frame MX14	1 850/ bike	3 700.00
1	CY060	Bicycle: Mountain Carbon frame MX34	2 950/ bike	2 950.00
6	CY070	Bicycle: Youth YX660	460/ bike	2 760.00
2	CY090	Stationary Converter	870/ unit	1 740.00
10	S020	Maintenance: annual contract	110/ year	1 100.00
	GST		5%	86.00
	HST		13%	3 363.10
	Total paid by Visa			$31 039.10

NOTES

Remember to change the tax code for Books to G.

47 **Bank Debit Memo #96241** **Dated August 31, 2015**

From Niagara Trust, authorized withdrawals were made from the chequing account on our behalf for the following:

Bank service charges	$ 35
Mortgage interest payment	1 550
Mortgage principal reduction	150
Bank loan interest payment	380
Bank loan principal reduction	520

48 **Debit Card Sales Invoice #2502** **Dated August 31, 2015**

To Interac customers (sales summary). Sold from Ryder store.

10	AP100	Promotional Safety Packages	$375/ unit	$3 750.00
10	AC030	Helmet	$120/ helmet	1 200.00
6	S030	Maintenance: complete tune-up	70/ job	420.00
6	S060	Repairs	50/ hour	300.00
14	BK020	Books: Endless Trails (code G)	40/ book	560.00
	GST		5%	28.00
	HST		13%	737.10
	Total paid by Interac			$6 995.10

49 **Memo #8-14** **Dated August 31, 2015**

Prepare the payroll for Pedal Schwinn, Shimana Gearie and Moishe Alee, the salaried employees. Add 2 percent of service revenue for August as a commission to Gearie's salary. Issue deposit slips #41, #42 and #43.

50 **Memo #8-15** **Dated August 31, 2015**

Interest earned but not yet received for bank accounts for August is $195.

51 **Memo #8-16** **Dated August 31, 2015**

Prepare month-end adjusting entries for depreciation on fixed assets using the following amounts:

Computer equipment	$180
Service equipment	40
Furniture & fixtures	25
Retail premises	810
Van	625

52 **Memo #8-17** **Dated August 31, 2015**

Prepare end-of-period adjusting entries for the following:

Office supplies used	$ 100
Repair parts used	90
Prepaid insurance expired	812
Prepaid advertising expired	100
Payroll liabilities accrued	1 540

> **WARNING!**
> This is the first sale from the Ryder store, so you must change the default location.

> **NOTES**
> Remember to change the tax code for Books to G.

Updating Inventory Prices

At the end of the month, inventory prices will be increased. Rather than changing each record for regular and preferred prices in both Canadian and US dollars, we will use the Update Price List method that we used earlier to edit the activity prices. This method is more efficient when many prices must be changed or when they are changed by a fixed amount or percentage. In this case, we are increasing regular prices by 10 percent. The feature also allows us to round off the prices automatically.

✓ 53 **Memo #8-18** **Dated August 31, 2015**

With two stores open and increased expenses, the prices for all inventory items will be raised. All regular prices (Canadian and US) will increase by 10 percent. All new preferred prices (Canadian and US) will be 15 percent lower than the new regular prices. Round all prices to the nearest five dollar amount.

Click the **Settings icon** 
.

Click **Inventory & Services** and then **click Price List**.

NOTES
The euro prices are not changing.

Click **Update Price Lists**. **Click** **Inventory Items** to show only items we need.

Click the **select item column heading** to select all items as shown:

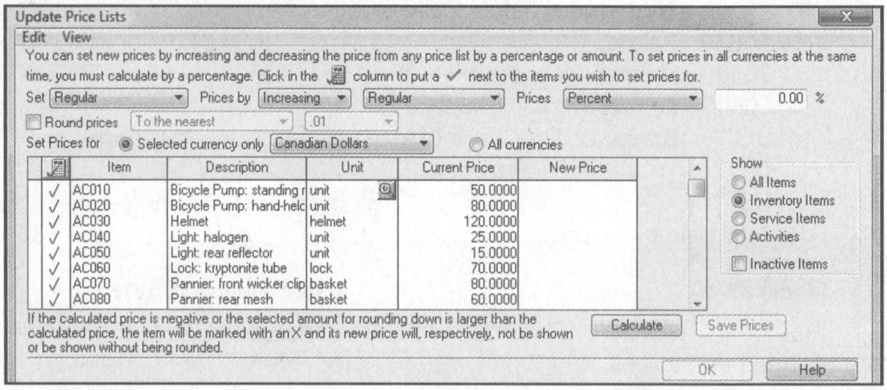

The upper part of the screen has the rules for the change. We can change any price list by increasing or decreasing the prices from another price list by a percentage or a fixed amount. These options are shown in the following screen:

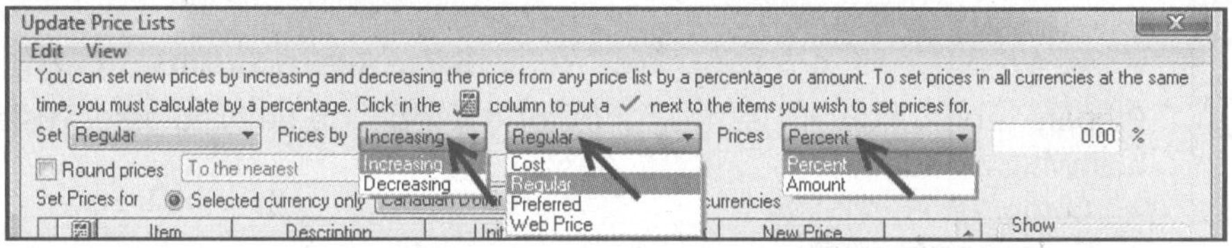

We are increasing Canadian Regular prices by a fixed percentage, so these entries are already correct. We are rounding the new prices up to the nearest five dollar amount. First, we need to enter the percentage of the increase.

NOTES
Prices may be set relative to any of the price lists for the data set, including the ones you created, as well as relative to the cost price.

Click **0.00 in the % field**. **Type** `10`

Press *tab* to move to the check box for rounding.

Click the **Round Prices check box** to add a ✓ and open the field we need.

Again, we have some options. You can round up, round down or round to the nearest amount. We want to round up to the nearest five dollar amount. To the nearest and one cent (.01) are the default entries. The units range from one ten-thousandth of a dollar (.0001) to one thousand dollars (1 000.00). These two selection lists are shown in the following screen image:

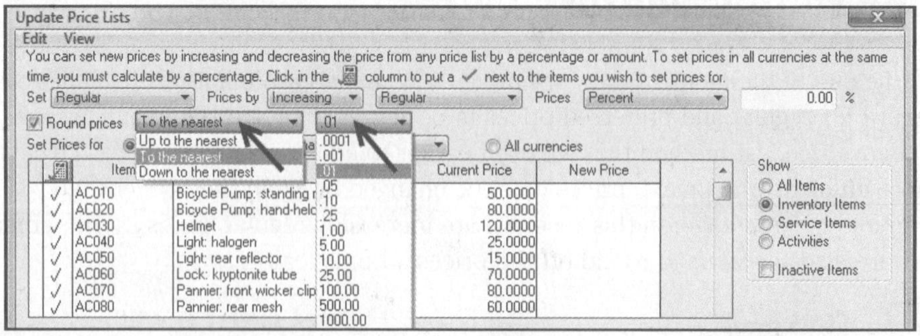

Click **To The Nearest** to open the rounding options list and **choose Up To The Nearest**.

Click **.01** to open the selection list and **choose 5.00** (five dollars) as the amount to complete the selection of options as follows:

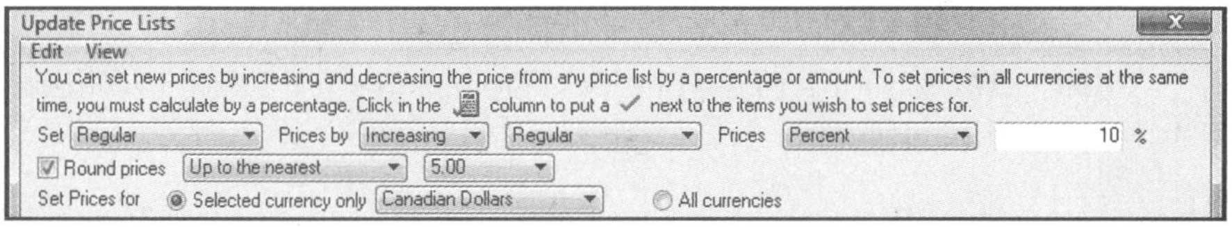

Click **Calculate** to update the prices and add them to the New Price column.

We can now still edit individual prices — they have not yet been saved. For A100 the new price is too high. We also do not want to change the book prices.

Click **415** in the New Price column for AP100. **Type** 400

Press ⬇ to select **45** in the New Price column for BK010 and **type** 40

Press ⬇ to select **45** in the New Price column for BK020 and **type** 40

Click **Save Prices** to transfer the new prices to the Current Price column.

We will set the preferred prices relative to the new regular prices, decreasing them by 15 percent and rounding up to the nearest five dollars. We need to change the selected price list, the direction of the change and the percentage.

NOTES

You could also click the Select column for the book items to remove the ✓ after selecting all items. In this way, the change rules will not apply to these two items.

Click **Regular** in the Set field as shown and then **choose Preferred**:

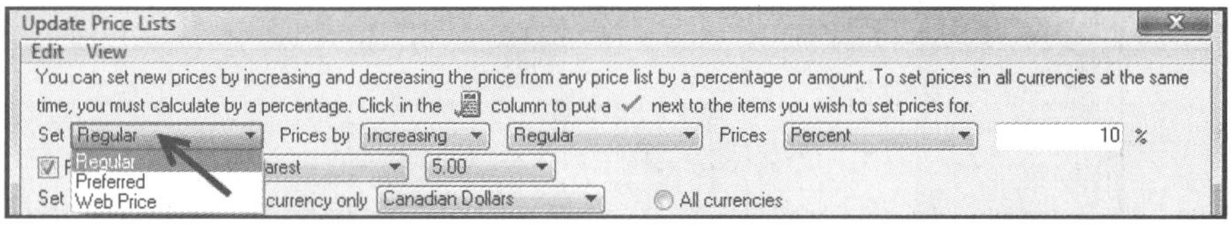

Click **Increasing** in the Prices By field and **choose Decreasing**. Regular is correct as the reference price list.

Click **10** in the % field and **type** 15

The remaining options are correct, so your completed selections should look like the following:

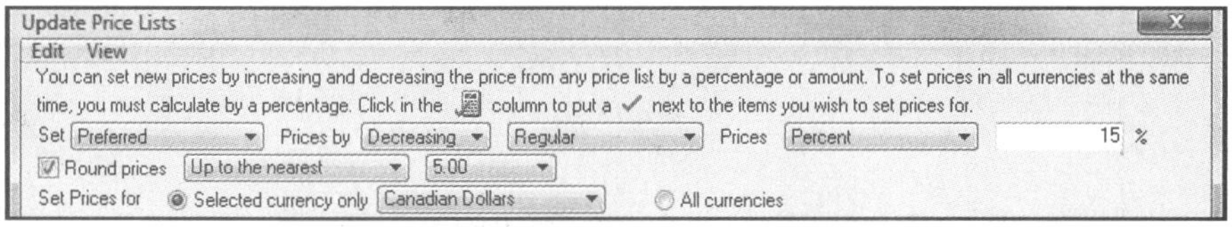

Click **Calculate** to update the prices and add them to the New Price column.

Click **Save Prices** to transfer the new prices to the Current Price column.

You can now change the prices for US dollars.

Click **Canadian Dollars** in the Selected Currency Only field as shown and **choose United States Dollars**:

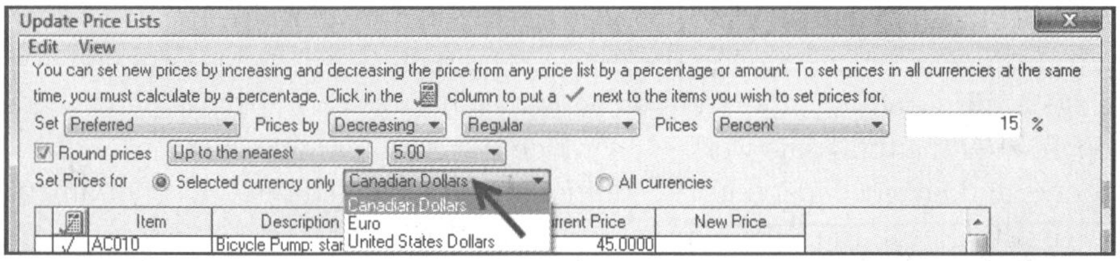

Apply the same changes to the US dollar regular and preferred prices so these prices will match the Canadian prices again. First, increase the regular prices by 10 percent and rounding up to the nearest $5.00 and then adjust the prices for AP100, BK010 and BK020. Then change the preferred prices by decreasing the regular prices by 15 percent, rounding up to the nearest $5.00 amount.

NOTES
You can update the euro prices in the same way, by selecting euro as the currency. You can also update the prices for all currencies at the same time when the same updating rule applies to them all. You can, of course, adjust individual prices after.

Remember to **calculate** and then **save each price set**.

Click **OK** to return to the Settings screen and **click OK** again to return to the Home window.

Displaying Time and Billing Reports

The various Time and Billing reports provide different ways of organizing the same information. You can view the reports by customer, by employee and by activity.

Customer Time and Billing Report

NOTES
Sorting and filtering are not available for Time and Billing reports, but you can choose the columns to include in the report.

Click the **Report Centre icon** in the Home window. **Click Time & Billing**. **Click** the ⊞ beside **Billing**, **Payroll** and **Purchases** to expand the list of available reports:

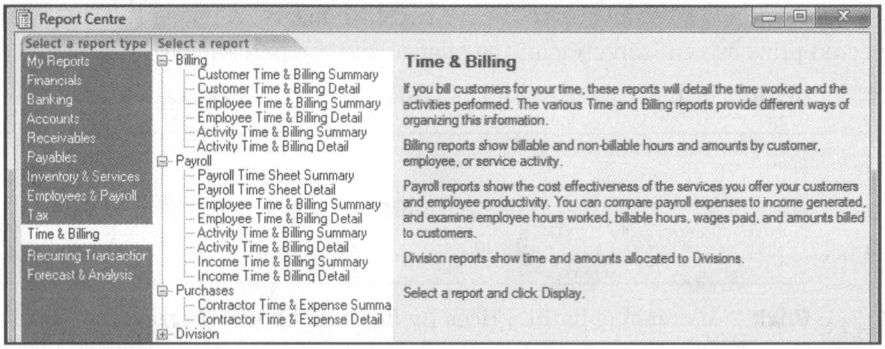

NOTES
Contractor time & billing reports (under Purchases) and Division reports do not apply to Ryder's Routes.

Click **Customer Time & Billing Summary** under **Billing**. **Click Modify This Report**:

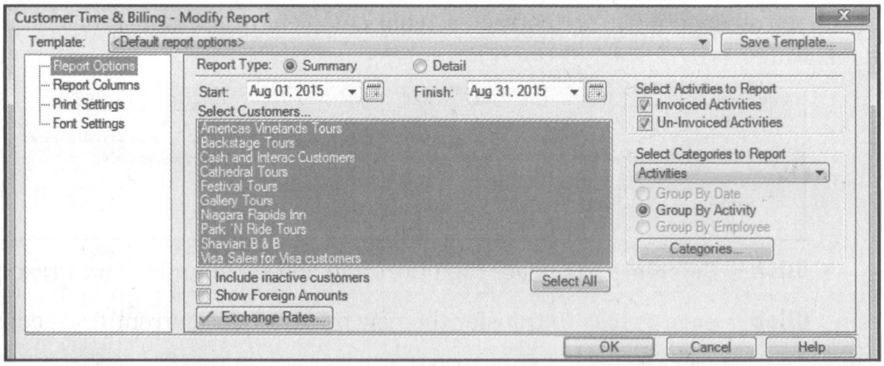

NOTES
From the Home window, choose the Reports menu, then choose Time & Billing. Click Billing and click Time By Customer to see the report options.

NOTES
Time and Billing reports can include a large amount of information. A good way to understand these reports is to prepare a very complete report. For example, select the Detail Report, choose all employees, click all Details and Activities and choose Activities and Customers as the categories for the report. Then choose all service activities from the next list. Print the report. Click the Modify tool or choose Modify Report from the Options menu in the report. Compare this report with the Summary Report for the same details and categories.

Time and Billing reports by customer show the time and billed amounts organized by customer. Summary and Detail reports are available. **Detail** reports include a report line for each activity or employee on each time slip while the **Summary** reports show only the totals for each selected category (activity or employee). You can select one or more customers for inclusion in the report. The reports will include columns for several billing details — actual time spent on activities, billable time, billable percentage (the proportion of the total time worked for which the customer was charged), billable amounts and invoiced amounts. In addition, if you changed the prices for any of the service activities in the Sales Journals, the report will show these changes as amounts written down or up. In the report, the invoiced amounts will then be different from the billable amounts. The effective billable percentage shows the relation between the invoiced amount and the billable amount. The non-billable time, no-charge time and amounts written down or up as percentages of the billable amounts are not in the default report, but you can add them by customizing the report columns. The default columns may also be removed. The report details can also be grouped — by date, by activity or by employee.

You can include **invoiced activities** (bills have been sent) or **uninvoiced activities** (bills have not been created and sent) or both.

The next decision for the report relates to the **categories** you want to include. You can report on the time spent according to the **activities** performed for the customer or according to the **employee** who completed the work or both. In all cases, the categories are shown for each customer you selected.

Enter **Start** and **Finish dates** for the report.

Choose the **customers** for the report. **Press** and **hold** ctrl and **click** the **customer names** to begin a new selection. **Click Select All** to include (or remove) all customers.

Choose the **invoicing details** for the report. **Click** a **detail** to remove a ✓ or to add it.

Click the **Select Categories To Report list arrow** to select activities or employees or both.

Click the **Categories button** to open the secondary selection list.

NOTES
From the Exchange Rates button you can access a window that allows you to enter current exchange rates for showing foreign amounts for foreign customers in the report.

If you choose Activities as the category, you will see the list of activities:

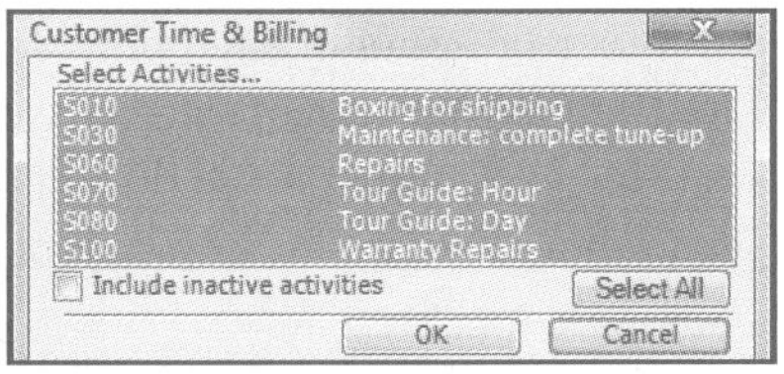

If you choose Employees as the category, you must select from the employee list. If you choose both Activities and Employees, you must choose from lists for both.

Initially, all activities are selected and clicking will change the selection. The Select All button acts like a toggle switch. To begin a new selection of activities,

NOTES
When you select two categories, you can group the report details by either one.

NOTES
Remember that Select All acts as a toggle switch. Initially, all items (or customers) are selected. Clicking Select All will clear the selection. If no items or a few items are selected, clicking Select All will include all items.

Click **Select All** to clear all selections.

Press and **hold** ctrl and **click** the **activities** you want in the report to begin a new selection. **Click Select All** to include (or remove) all activities.

Click **OK** to return to the report options screen.

Click **OK** to see the report.

The report shows the amount of time worked for each customer according to the activity, employee or both, depending on the category you selected.

Close the **report** when you have finished.

Employee and Activity Time and Billing Reports

The other two Time and Billing reports are similar to the Time by Customer Report, except that they organize the amounts by employee or by activity. The first options screen for the **Employee Time & Billing Report** (Summary or Detail) will show the Employee list, and the second selection screen will list the customers, the activities or both, depending on the category you choose. The Time by Employee Report shows the time and billed amounts for each employee for each customer, each activity or both, depending on the categories you choose.

Similarly, the first options screen for the **Activity Time & Billing Report** (Summary or Detail) will show the Activity list, and the second selection screen will list the customers, the employees or both, depending on the category you choose. The Time by Activity Report shows the time and the billed amounts for each activity for each customer or by each employee or both, depending on the category you choose.

Other report options are the same as they are for the Time by Customer Report, and both reports are available as a Summary or a Detail report.

Payroll Time Sheet Reports

The Time Sheet Report provides a summary of the hours of each income category that is on the time sheets. The number of hours of non-payroll, regular payroll and overtime for each employee can be included.

Click **Payroll Time Sheet Summary** under **Payroll**. **Click** **Modify This Report**:

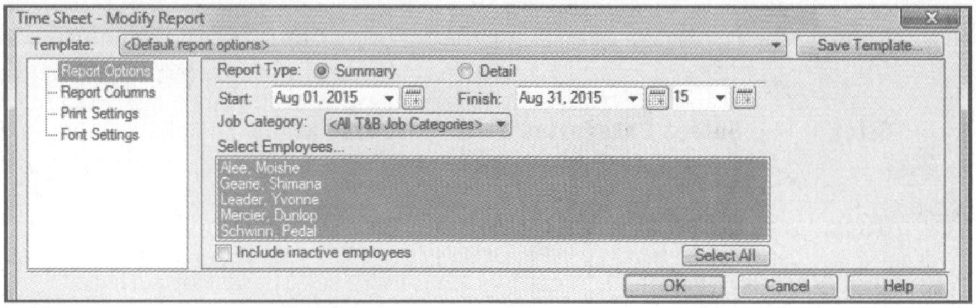

NOTES
From the Home window, choose the Reports menu, then choose Time & Billing. Click Payroll and click Time Sheet to see the report options.

The **Summary** Report will provide the total number of hours in each payroll category (Non-payroll, Regular and Overtime 1 — the payroll category in the ledger record for the activity) for each employee selected for each time period during the report interval. The **Detail** Report will show the number of hours in each payroll category for each time sheet.

You can customize the report by selecting columns for the payroll category. Non-payroll, Regular and Overtime 1 columns may be included or omitted.

Enter **Start** and **Finish dates** for the report.

Choose the **employees** for the report. **Press** and **hold** ctrl and **click** the **employee names** to begin a new selection. **Click** **Select All** to include (or remove) all employees.

Click **OK** to display the report.

Close the **report** when you have finished.

Employee Time and Billing Payroll Reports

The remaining Payroll Time reports provide information about the cost effectiveness of the service activities by comparing the labour costs with the income generated — the amount billed to the customer. Employee productivity is also measured by examining the actual hours, billable hours, payroll hours, wages paid and invoiced amounts.

NOTES
From the Home window, choose the Reports menu, then choose Time & Billing. Click Payroll and click Time By Employee to see the report options.

Click **Employee Time & Billing Summary** under **Payroll**.

Click **Modify This Report**:

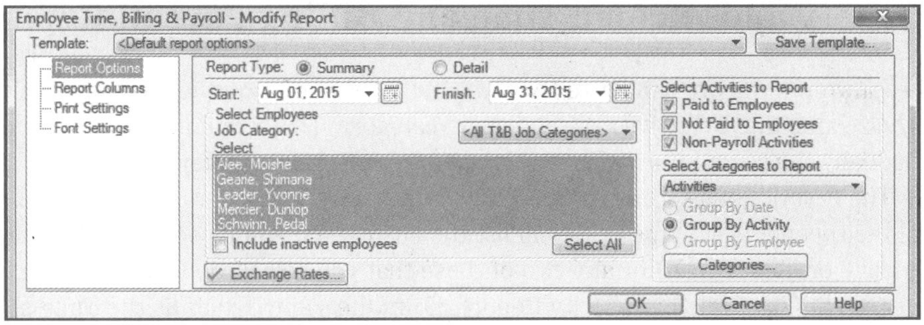

Summary and Detail reports are available. **Detail** reports include a report line for each time sheet entry while the **Summary** reports show only the totals for each selected category. You can select one or more employees for inclusion in the report. The reports will include several time and billing **details** — actual time spent on activities, payroll time, billable time, billable amounts, the actual payroll expense and the productivity ratio (the billable amount compared to the payroll expense) can be included. The effective productivity ratio percentage shows the relation between the invoiced amount and the payroll expense amount. Payroll percentage (payroll time as a proportion of actual time) and billable percentage (the proportion of the total time worked for which the customer was charged) can be added to the report when you customize the report by selecting these time and billing details (report columns). The default report columns may be included or removed.

The report can include **activities** for which you have **paid** the employees, activities that have **not yet been paid**, activities that are **non-payroll** or all three payroll details.

The next decision for the report relates to the **categories** you want to include. You can report on the time spent according to the **activity** performed by the employee, according to the **customer** for whom the work was completed, according to the **income** (that is, regular, non-payroll or overtime) or any two of these three categories. In all cases, the categories are shown for each employee you selected.

When you choose two categories for the report, you can group report details by one of them — select from date, activity, customer or income.

Enter **Start** and **Finish dates** for the report.

Choose the **employees** for the report. **Press** and **hold** ctrl and **click** the **employee names** to begin a new selection. **Click Select All** to include (or remove) all employees.

Choose the **payroll status details**. **Click** a **detail** to add or to remove a ✓.

Choose the **categories** for the report from the Select Categories To Report drop-down list.

Click the **Categories button** to open the secondary selection list.

If you select the Activities category, you will see the complete list of all services defined as activities in the ledger.

Choose the **activities** for the report. **Press** and **hold** ctrl and **click** the **activity names** to begin a new selection. **Click Select All** to include (or remove) activities.

Click **OK** to return to the report options screen.

Click **OK** to see the report. By default the report will print in landscape orientation (sideways on the page) so that all details can fit on a line.

Close the **report** when you have finished.

NOTES

If you select Customers or Income as the category, you will see selection lists for each category. If you selected two categories, you can choose from selection lists for both categories.

NOTES

The August 31 report for Ryder shows that both employees have been partially paid for their time sheet entries – the last time sheet has not yet been added to their paycheques. The same report for August 21 shows all time sheet activities have been paid.

Activity and Income Time and Billing Payroll Reports

These two reports are similar to the Time by Employee Report except that they organize amounts by activity or by income category. The three reports provide essentially the same information but organize the details in different ways.

The first options screen for the **Time by Activity Report** will show the Activity list, and the second selection screen will list the customers, employees, incomes (regular, overtime or non-payroll) or any two of these that you select, depending on the category you choose. The Time by Activity Report shows the same details as the Time by Employee Report but lists them for each activity for each customer, each employee, each income or any two of these, depending on the categories you choose.

Similarly, the first options screen for the **Time by Income Report** will show the income list, and the second selection screen will list the customers, the employees, activities or any two of these three, depending on the category you choose. The Time by Income Report shows the same details as the Time by Employee Report but lists them for each activity for each customer, by each employee, each activity or any two of these, depending on the categories you choose.

Other report options are the same as they are for the Time by Employee Report, and both reports are available as a Summary or a Detail report.

Multiple Fiscal Periods and Reports

After you have accumulated two fiscal periods of financial data, you can produce historical reports for these additional periods. Data for the current and previous years are always available, unless you have cleared the information.

NOTES
Financial reports for August:
- Income Statement
- Balance Sheet
- Trial Balance
- Supplier and Customer Aged reports
- Employee Summary Report
- Inventory Summary and Inventory Quantity Detail reports, including location

✓ 54

Memo #8-19 **Dated August 31, 2015**

Back up the data files and print all financial reports for the August fiscal period.
Start a new fiscal year. Do not clear old data.
Change the fiscal end to September 30, 2015.

Prepare a **list** of inventory items that should be ordered.

Choose the **Maintenance menu** and **click Start New Year** to begin a new fiscal year.

Choose Yes when asked if you want to Back Up Your Data Files Before Beginning The New Fiscal Year and follow the backup instructions.

Choose No when asked if you want to clear the old data.

The Update Locking Date screen opens.

Enter 09/01/15 as the new date. **Click OK** to update the earliest transaction.

Choose the **Setup menu**, then **click Settings**, **Company** and **Information**:

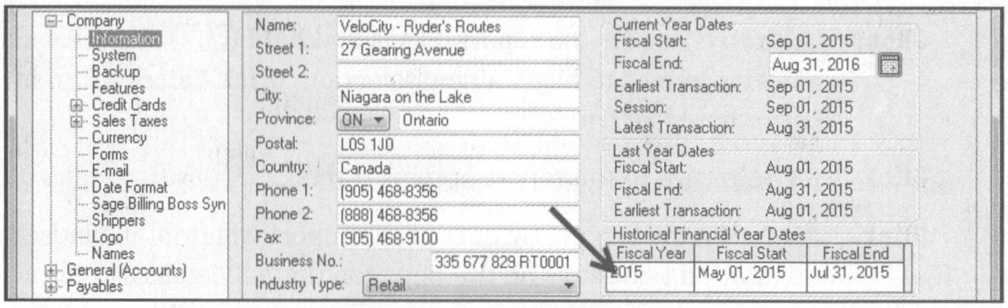

NOTES
The Pro version stores up to seven years of historical financial data; the Premium version stores up to 99 years of data.

Notice that the first fiscal period, May 1 to July 31, 2015, is now listed in the section for Historical Financial Year Dates.

Drag through Aug 31, 2016, the Fiscal End date.

Type 09-30-15 **Click OK** to save the date and return to the Home window.

Multi-Period Financial Reports

Multiple-period reports are available for the Balance Sheet, Income Statement and Trial Balance. All are accessed from the Financials list of reports.

Click the **Report Centre icon**.

Click **Financials** to expand this list of reports.

Click the ⊞ beside **Balance Sheet**, **Income Statement** and **Trial Balance** to expand the Select A Report list. **Click Multi-Period** under **Balance Sheet** as shown:

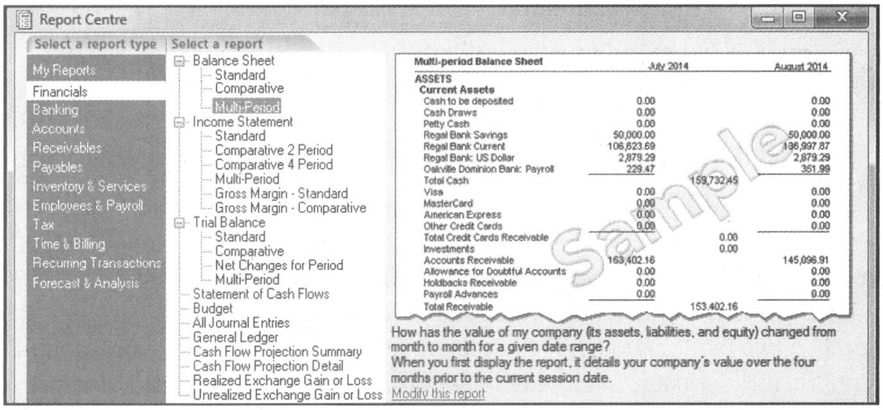

Click **Modify This Report**:

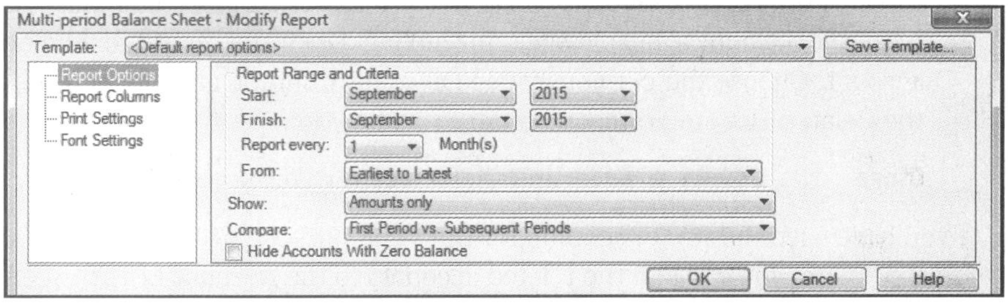

From the Home window, choose the Reports menu, then choose Financials and Multi-Period Reports and click Balance Sheet to see the report options.

The regular financial reports available in comparative form compare two fiscal periods or dates. Reports for the previous fiscal period are also available in regular reports. The multi-period reports show more than two periods and can include multiple fiscal periods before the previous one.

For VeloCity and Ryder's Routes, monthly data can be viewed in a single report for May, the first month for which we entered data in Sage 50, to August.

There are several options for displaying the report. You can show the balances for each month for any interval ranging from one to twelve months. The report can be ordered from the earliest period to the latest or from latest to earliest. You can show Amounts Only, Difference In Percentage or Difference In Amounts, just as you do for regular comparative reports. And you can compare the first period with each subsequent period, or you can compare each period with subsequent periods.

After choosing the options for the report,

Click **OK** to see the report.

NOTES

From the Home window, choose the Reports menu, Financials, Multi-Period Reports, and click Balance Sheet, Income Statement or Trial Balance.

NOTES

Dates before the previous fiscal period that are eligible for the report will show in the Historical Financial Year Dates section of the Company Information screen on page 782.

Close the **report** when you have finished.

The **Income Statement** and **Trial Balance** are available for the same periods as the Balance Sheet. They have the same report options. To see these reports,

Click **Multi-Period** under **Income Statement** (or **Trial Balance**) and then **click Modify This Report**.

Choose the **report options** and **click OK**.

Close the **report** when you have finished. **Close** the **Report Centre**.

Related Historical Accounts

Because we have advanced to the next (third) fiscal period, we can see the list of related accounts. You can see and edit the related historical accounts in the General Ledger record for the account in the Related Historical Accounts tab screen.

Click the **Chart of Accounts icon** in the Company module window.

Double-click an **account** to open its General Ledger record.

Click the **Related Historical Accounts tab** to see the accounts used in previous periods.

If an account currently being used has a different name and number than the account used for the same purpose in a previous period, you can link them.

Each account shows itself as the related historical account if it has been used for more than two fiscal periods. Each account can be related to only one account. Therefore, if the account is already related to itself, you cannot select it again.

Open the record for the (old) previously used account. Delete the account listed as the related account in the Related Historical Accounts tab. This will make the account available again for linking. Open the record for the new account. Choose the previously used account from the account selection list in the Related Historical Accounts tab.

Close the **Ledger window** and then **close** the **Accounts window**.

If you have used different accounts for the same purpose over the periods and you have related them, you can add the related accounts to the Account List. To see the report of related account numbers,

Choose the **Reports menu**, then **choose Lists** and **click Accounts**.

Click **Include Related Historical Accounts** and then **click OK**.

The report will list all General Ledger accounts with the current information and the accounts that were used for those same purposes in previous fiscal periods — the information that is stored in the General Ledger Related Historical Accounts tab fields.

Close the **report** when you have finished.

Close the **Home window** to exit the Sage 50 program.

R E V I E W

The Student DVD with Data Files includes Review Questions and Supplementary Cases for this chapter.

CHAPTER NINETEEN

Able & Associates

OBJECTIVES

After completing this chapter, you should be able to

- ***activate*** departmental accounting
- ***create*** departments
- ***add*** departments to accounts, vendors and clients
- ***add*** departments in journal entries
- ***apply*** line discounts in sales journal entries
- ***display*** and ***print*** department reports

COMPANY INFORMATION

Company Profile

NOTES

Able & Associates Inc.
88 Practice Blvd.
Huntsville, ON P1H 1T2
Tel: (705) 463-2145
Fax: (705) 465-1110
Business No.: 167 344 577

Able & Associates Inc. is a partnership of two chartered accountants, Count and Memor Able. They began their practice in Huntsville, Ontario, two years ago, shortly after receiving their C.A. designations. They each invested capital to start up the office. By relying extensively on electronic communications, remote access to client computers and frequent phone calls, they are able to serve clients throughout a large geographic area. Only occasional on-site meetings are required and local clients often come to their office. Most of their revenue comes from auditing and preparing regular financial statements and income tax returns for small business clients. They share office space and office expenses, including a full-time office assistant. Count works in the office full time, but Memor is there only three days a week, spending the other two days working in a small family business. Thus, they allocate their joint expenses using a 60/40 percent division.

Most of the clients have contracts with Able & Associates and pay fees on a monthly basis. These clients are entitled to a discount of 2 percent of their fees if they pay within 10 days of the invoice date. Full payment is requested within 30 days. One-time clients do not receive discounts. Some regular vendors also offer discounts for early payment.

On March 31, at the end of the fiscal period, they decided to use the departmental accounting feature in Sage 50 to track their financial performance. Payroll taxes were remitted at year-end. To prepare for allocating opening account balances to departments, all opening account balances were transferred

NOTES
For this professional service business, the terms Client and Vendor are used.

to unallocated accounts in the corresponding financial statement section. The following business information was used to set up the accounts:

- Chart of Accounts
- Post-Closing Trial Balance and Statement of Opening Account Balances
- Vendor Information
- Client Information
- Employee Information
- Accounting Procedures

CHART OF POSTABLE ACCOUNTS

ABLE & ASSOCIATES INC.

ASSETS
10800 Bank: Chequing
11000 Investments
11200 Prepaid Association Dues
11400 Prepaid Subscriptions
11600 Prepaid Insurance
12000 Accounts Receivable
13400 Office Supplies
14400 Office Equipment
14800 Office Furniture
15000 Library ▶

▶**LIABILITIES**
21000 Bank Loan
22000 Accounts Payable
22500 Visa Payable
23000 EI Payable
23100 CPP Payable
23200 Income Tax Payable
24200 WSIB Payable
26500 HST Charged on Services
26700 HST Paid on Purchases

EQUITY
34500 Invested Capital: C. Able ▶

▶34800 Invested Capital: M. Able
35500 Retained Earnings
36000 Current Earnings

REVENUE
41000 Revenue from Services
41500 Revenue from Interest
41800 Other Revenue
42000 Sales Discounts

EXPENSE
51200 Association Dues
51300 Bank and Card Fees ▶

▶51400 Interest Expense
51500 Insurance Expense
51600 Publicity and Promotion
51800 Purchase Discounts
52000 Subscriptions
52200 Telephone Expense
52400 Rent
54000 Salaries
54100 EI Expense
54200 CPP Expense
54300 WSIB Expense

NOTES: The Chart of Accounts includes only postable accounts and the Current Earnings account. Able & Associates use five-digit account numbers for the General Ledger accounts.

POST-CLOSING TRIAL BALANCE

ABLE & ASSOCIATES INC.

April 1, 2015		Debits	Credits
10800	Bank: Chequing	$ 21 300	
11000	Investments	44 000	
11200	Prepaid Association Dues	2 800	
11400	Prepaid Subscriptions	1 500	
11600	Prepaid Insurance	4 500	
12000	Accounts Receivable	2 260	
13400	Office Supplies	1 800	
14400	Office Equipment	12 000	
14800	Office Furniture	8 000	
15000	Library	4 800	▶
▶ 21000	Bank Loan		$ 15 000
22000	Accounts Payable		2 260
22500	Visa Payable		1 400
26500	HST Charged on Services		2 200
26700	HST Paid on Purchases	1 640	
34500	Invested Capital: C. Able		33 000
34800	Invested Capital: M. Able		22 000
35500	Retained Earnings		28 740
		$104 600	$104 600

STATEMENT OF ACCOUNT OPENING BALANCES

ABLE & ASSOCIATES INC.

April 1, 2015		Debits	Credits
19500	Unassigned Assets	$102 960	▶
▶ 29500	Unassigned Liabilities		$ 19 220
39500	Unassigned Capital		83 740
		$102 960	$102 960

NOTES: The true account balances are shown for the regular postable accounts in the Trial Balance. The three unassigned accounts in the Statement of Opening Balances are temporary holding accounts. The temporary balance in these accounts is the sum of all balances for that section of the Balance Sheet (which temporarily have zero balances). These balances will be transferred back to the regular accounts to set up the departmental opening balances.

VENDOR INFORMATION

ABLE & ASSOCIATES INC.

Vendor Name (Contact)	Address	Phone No. Fax No.	E-mail Web Site	Terms Tax ID
Bell Canada (Yap Long)	500 Central Line Huntsville, Ontario P1F 2C2	Tel: (705) 466-2355	yap.l@bell.ca www.bell.ca	net 1
Muskoka Maintenance (M. Handimann)	72 Spoiler St. Huntsville, Ontario P1P 2B8	Tel: (705) 469-0808 Fax: (705) 469-6222	handimann@yahoo.com	2/10, n/30 295 416 822
Northlands Office Mgt. (Hi Bilding)	59 Condor St. Huntsville, Ontario P1D 4F4	Tel: (705) 283-9210 Fax: (705) 283-2310	bilding@northlands.com	net 1
Office Plus (B. Laser)	4 Paper Corners Huntsville, Ontario P1E 1G1	Tel: (705) 466-3335	www.officeplus.ca	1/15, n/30 822 101 500
Receiver General for Canada	Sudbury Tax Services Office PO Box 20004 Sudbury, ON P3A 6B4	Tel 1: (800) 561-7761 Tel 2: (800) 959-2221	www.cra-arc.gc.ca	net 1

OUTSTANDING VENDOR INVOICES

ABLE & ASSOCIATES INC.

Vendor Name	Terms	Date	Invoice No.	Amount	Total
Office Plus	1/15, n/30	Mar. 21/15	OP-2339	$2 260	$2 260

CLIENT INFORMATION

ABLE & ASSOCIATES INC.

Client Name (Contact)	Address	Phone No. Fax No.	E-mail Web Site	Terms Credit Limit
Adrienne Aesthetics (Adrienne Kosh)	65 Bytown Ave. Ottawa, Ontario K2C 4R1	Tel 1: (613) 722-9876 Tel 2: (613) 722-8701 Fax: (613) 722-8000	a.kosh@adrienneaesthetics.com www.adrienneaesthetics.com	2/10, n/30 $10 000
Dorfmann Design (Desiree Dorfmann)	199 Artistic Way, Unit 500 Hamilton, Ontario L8T 3B7	Tel: (905) 642-2348 Fax: (905) 642-9100	dd@dorfmann.com www.dorfmann.com	2/10, n/30 $10 000
Gorgeous Gifts (Gitte Gurlosi)	600 First St. Huntsville, Ontario P1L 2W4	Tel: (705) 462-1203 Fax: (705) 462-3394	gg@ggifts.com www.ggifts.com	2/10, n/30 $10 000
Truman Tires (Tyrone Truman)	600 Westminster St. London, Ontario N6P 3B1	Tel: (519) 729-3733 Fax: (519) 729-7301	tt@trumantires.com www.trumantires.com	2/10, n/30 $10 000

OUTSTANDING CLIENT INVOICES

ABLE & ASSOCIATES INC.

Client Name	Terms	Date	Invoice No.	Amount	Total
Adrienne Aesthetics	2/10, n/30	Mar. 25/15	843	$2 260	$2 260

EMPLOYEE INFORMATION SHEET

ABLE & ASSOCIATES INC.

Tryin, Reelie (Office Assistant)

Social Insurance No.	429 535 644	Total Federal (Ontario) Tax Exemption - TD1	$11 38 (9 574)
Address	200 Water St. #301 Huntsville, Ontario P1H 2L8	Employee Income (Reg. hours) Salary	 $3 800 /month (150 hours)
Telephone	(705) 446-2190		
Date of Birth (mm-dd-yy)	04-04-81	WSIB Rate	0.89
EI, CPP & Income Tax	Calculations built into Sage 50 program		

Accounting Procedures

Taxes (HST)

NOTES

Able & Associates Inc. pays GST at the rate of 5 percent on subscriptions to professional journals and other books purchased for the business.

Able & Associates Inc. is a professional service business using the regular method of calculating HST. HST, at the rate of 13 percent, is charged on all services and paid on purchases. The difference between the HST charged and HST paid is remitted to the Receiver General for Canada quarterly.

Departments

Able & Associates has two departments, one for each partner. The division of most assets is 60 percent and 40 percent, to be consistent with their initial investments in the partnership and their time in the office.

Discounts for Early Payments

Able & Associates offers discounts to regular clients if they pay their accounts within 10 days. Full payment is expected in 30 days. No discounts are allowed on partial payments. Additional discounts are applied occasionally for clients in special circumstances. These are entered as line discounts for the sales.

Some vendors with whom Able & Associates has accounts set up also offer discounts for early payments.

INSTRUCTIONS

1. **Set up two departments** for Able & Associates.
2. **Record entries for the source documents** in Sage 50. Transactions indicated with a ✓ in the completion box beside the source document have step-by-step keystroke instructions.
3. **Print** the following **reports and graphs** after you have finished making your entries. Instructions for departmental reports begin on page 803.
   a. Comparative Balance Sheet with Departments for April 1 and April 30.
   b. Income Statement with Departments for April 1 to April 30.
   c. Departmental Income Statement.
   d. Journal Report for April 1 to April 30 for all journals.

KEYSTROKES

Departmental Accounting

Most companies are divided into departments such as sales, marketing, service, finance, human resources and manufacturing. And most companies want to track the costs and performance of these departments separately. The departmental accounting feature in Sage 50 permits more detailed company reporting and analysis.

Unlike projects that work only through journal entries, departments are connected to all ledgers and journals. Departments can be associated with individual accounts, vendors and clients, and you can choose departments for accounts in journal entries.

Each account may be used by only one department or by more than one department. For example, automotive parts in a car dealership will be used by the service department but not by the human resources or sales departments. Other accounts, such as a bank account, may be connected to all departments. Similarly, individual vendors, such as a car-parts vendor, may be linked to a specific department while others, such as utility providers, are linked to all departments. Clients, too, may be connected to specific departments. When you set up these connections, the departmental links are added to journal entries automatically, and you can generate detailed reports with departmental information.

Departmental account balances are generated when you add departmental information to journal entries, but they cannot be added as opening account balances in the ledgers. Therefore, ideally, you will add departmental information when you create company files so that you can have departmental information for all accounts. You can also choose to use departments only for income statement accounts and start using departments at the beginning of a fiscal period when these accounts have zero balances.

Setting Up Departments

Open **SageData13\Able\able**. **Enter April 30, 2015** as the session date.

The history for the company files is not finished. Some linked accounts are missing and the ledgers are not balanced. (See margin Notes.)

Creating Departments

Before using departmental accounting, you must activate the feature and create the departments. The feature is not turned on by default, and you can add departments to an existing Sage 50 data file.

✓ 1 **Memo #1** **Dated April 1/15**

Create two departments for Able & Associates: 1001: C. Able and 2001: M. Able

Click the **Settings icon** and **General (Accounts)** and **Departments**:

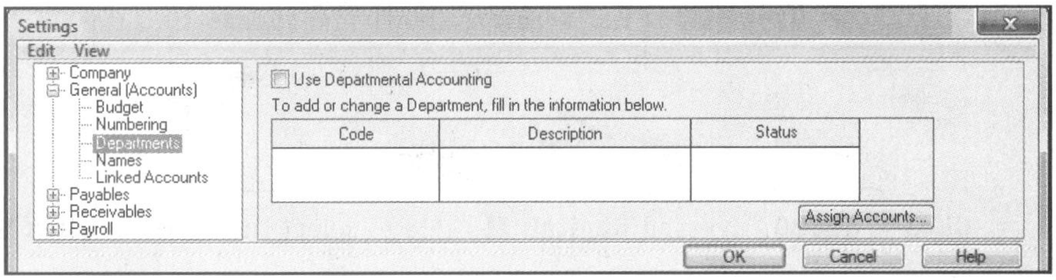

WARNING! You cannot remove departments once you add them and use them, so you should back up data files before adding departments.

NOTES If you are working from backups, you should restore SageData13\able1.CAB or able1 to SageData13\Able\able.

NOTES This exercise has few source documents so we use a single session date for all transactions.

WARNING! Do not attempt to finish the history yet. Essential linked accounts are missing.

NOTES The history for the data set must remain unfinished for now. Accounts Receivable and Accounts Payable accounts are needed in journal entries (to add opening department balances – see page 792), so they have not yet been entered as linked accounts. In addition, Accounts Receivable and Accounts Payable begin with zero balances. As a result, these opening balances do not match the totals of the historical client and vendor invoices.

Click **Use Departmental Accounting** to see the warning:

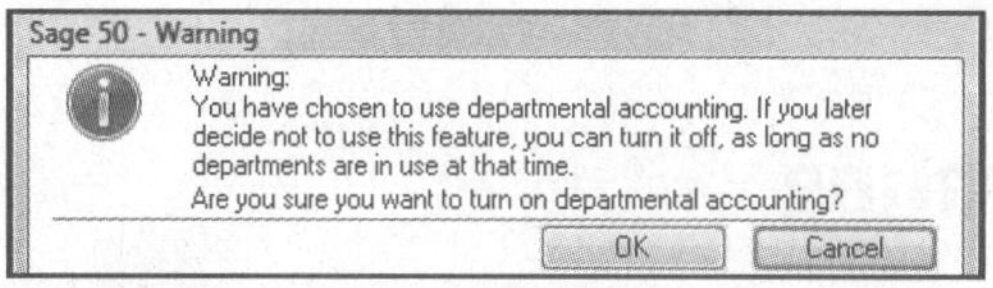

Adding departments is not a reversible step, unless the departments have not yet been used.

Click Cancel if you are not working with a separate copy of the data file. Make a backup first.

Click **OK** to return to the Departments Settings screen.

For each department you want, you must assign a four-digit code and a name.

Click the **Code field**.

Type `1001` **Press** *tab* to advance to the Description field. The Status is automatically set as Active.

Type `C. Able`

Unused departments can have their status set to Inactive by clicking Active.

Click the **Code field** on the next line. **Type** `2001`

Press *tab* to advance to the Description field. **Type** `M. Able`

Click the **Assign Accounts button** to open the next screen:

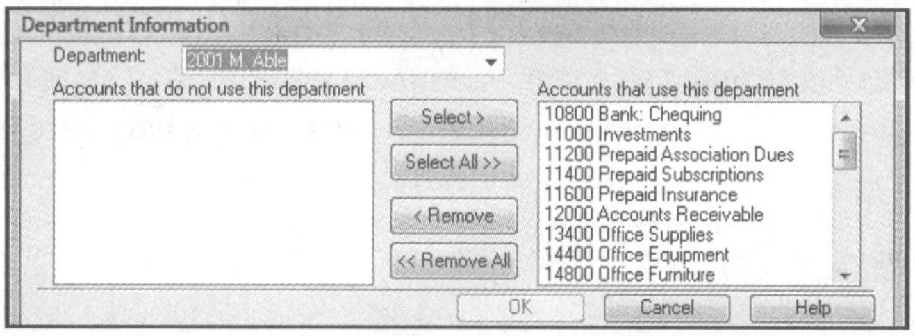

From this screen, you can indicate which accounts use the departments. The cursor was on M. Able in the previous screen, so this department is selected. You can select departments from the drop-down list in the Department field.

Initially, all accounts use all departments. From this window, you can select accounts that are to be removed for a department.

The two investment accounts are separated according to the partner, so we should assign each one only to its correct department. That is, we can remove *34500 Invested Capital: C. Able* for M. Able and remove *34800 Invested Capital: M. Able* for C. Able. We are working with the M. Able department first.

Scroll down the list of Accounts That Use This Department.

Click **34500 Invested Capital: C. Able** to select the account.

Click **Remove**. The account moves to the list of Accounts That Do Not Use This Department on the left-hand side of the screen.

Click the **Department list arrow** as shown and **choose 1001 C. Able**:

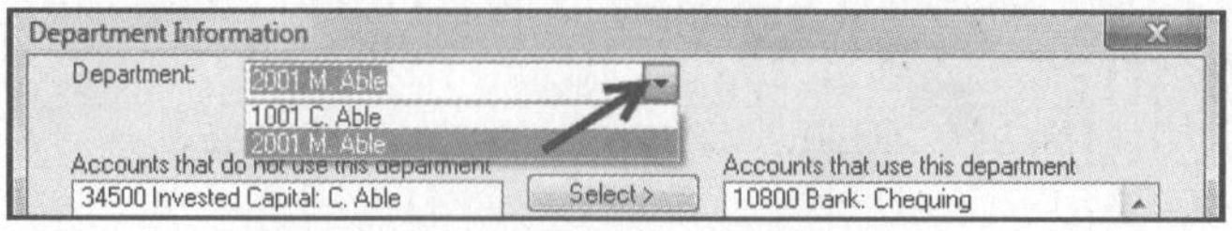

Click **34800 Invested Capital: M. Able** to select the account. **Click** **Remove**.

To move an account back to the "Use" list, click it again and then click Select.

> **WARNING!**
> The Department Code must be a four-digit number. No letters or other characters are allowed.

> **NOTES**
> Able & Associates uses five-digit account numbers. This selection is made from the Settings screen for General (Accounts) Numbering option (see page 80).

Click an account that you want to change and then press and hold ctrl. Click each account you want until all the accounts you want are included.

Click the Remove button to shift the selected accounts to the other column.

Click Remove All to shift all the accounts to the "Do Not Use" column.

If only a few accounts use a department, it is easier to place them all on the "Do Not Use" side and then move the few to the "Use" side.

Reverse this procedure to move an account from the "Do Not Use" to the "Use" side. Click the account on the "Do Not Use" side and then click the Select button.

Click **OK** to return to the Settings window. **Click** **OK** to return to the Home window.

Adding Departments to Accounts

Instead of adding department information to accounts from the Department Information window, you can add departments in the account ledger record directly.

✓ 2

Memo #2 **Dated April 1/15**

Assign accounts to departments. Invested Capital accounts are used by the department named in the account. All other accounts are used by both departments.

NOTES

You can also create a View Accounts shortcut (Banking Module) that will open the Accounts window. Double-click the account you need.

Click **Company** in the Modules Pane list. **Click** the **Chart of Accounts icon**.

Double-click **34500 Invested Capital: C. Able** in the list of accounts to open the General Ledger.

A new tab, Departments, has been added to the ledger record.

Click the **Departments tab** to open the new screen:

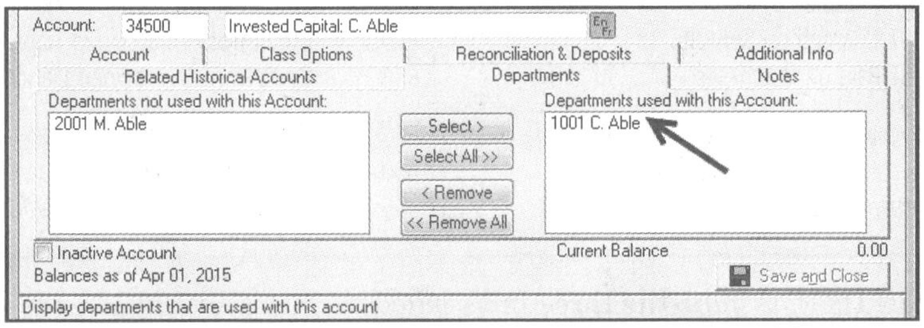

Notice that 2001 M. Able is located on the left-hand side under Departments Not Used With This Account because we moved it earlier on the Settings screen. 1001 C. Able is in the Departments Used With This Account column.

On this screen, you can designate the departments that the account uses. You can modify these selections at any time. You can see that this screen is the same as the one for Department Information, except that now we are "moving" the department instead of the account. However, in the General Ledger, you change the information for only one account at a time.

Click a department to select it or press ctrl and click more than one department if you want to select additional departments. Clicking Select will add the department to the account. Clicking Remove will remove a selected department from the account and place it on the "Not Used" side. Remove All and Select All will move all departments at once to the other side.

Close the **Ledger window**. **Close** the **Accounts window**.

NOTES

An alternative method would be to enter all opening account balances as usual and then make General Journal entries to divide the principal account amount between the two department accounts. Using this method, you would credit 10800 and debit 10800 - 1001 and 10800 - 2001.

In this case, you must still start with the history unfinished and before you enter the linked accounts for Accounts Receivable and Accounts Payable so that you can access these accounts in the journal (see page 794).

NOTES

Remember to reverse the usual liability entries for HST Paid on Purchases because this account normally has a debit balance.

Adding Opening Departmental Balances

When you create a new company data file and add general ledger accounts, you must enter the opening account balances as well, but you cannot split these balances among the departments. However, when you are entering transactions and have set up departments, you can choose a department from any Account field that allows you to select an account. We will use this approach to enter the opening departmental balances for all accounts. Initially we placed the total for all Balance Sheet accounts in the "unassigned" placeholder accounts for each section. When we transfer these amounts back to their appropriate accounts through General Journal entries, we can also assign departments.

✓ 3

Memo #3 **Dated April 1/15**

Assign departmental opening account balances by transferring the unassigned balances from the chart below. Add linked accounts and then finish the history.

Account	Department Amounts		Source
	1001: C. Able	2001: M. Able	
10800 Bank: Chequing	$ 12 780	$ 8 520	Debit from Unassigned Assets
11000 Investments	26 500	17 500	Debit from Unassigned Assets
11200 Prepaid Association Dues	1 400	1 400	Debit from Unassigned Assets
11400 Prepaid Subscriptions	900	600	Debit from Unassigned Assets
11600 Prepaid Insurance	2 700	1 800	Debit from Unassigned Assets
12000 Accounts Receivable	2 260		Debit from Unassigned Asset
13400 Office Supplies	1 080	720	Debit from Unassigned Assets
14400 Office Equipment	7 200	4 800	Debit from Unassigned Assets
14800 Office Furniture	4 000	4 000	Debit from Unassigned Assets
15000 Library	2 400	2 400	Debit from Unassigned Assets
21000 Bank Loan	9 000	6 000	Credit from Unassigned Liabilities
22000 Accounts Payable	1 356	904	Credit from Unassigned Liabilities
22500 Visa Payable	840	560	Credit from Unassigned Liabilities
26500 HST Charged on Services	1 320	880	Credit from Unassigned Liabilities
26700 HST Paid on Purchases	984	656	Debit from Unassigned Liabilities
34500 Invested Capital: C. Able	33 000		Credit from Unassigned Capital
34800 Invested Capital: M. Able		22 000	Credit from Unassigned Capital
35500 Retained Earnings	17 244	11 496	Credit from Unassigned Capital

After entering the transfers, the three unassigned accounts should all have zero balances and your Trial Balance should match the one on page 786.

Click the **General Journal icon**.

Enter **Memo 3A** as the Source, and **enter April 1** as the date.

Click the **Comment field** and **type** `Transfer opening asset account balances to departments`

Click the **Account field List icon** to see the modified Select Account list.

Each account has a ⊞ icon added to indicate additional information is available. When you click the ⊞, all departments used by that account will be listed, so you can select a department for the transaction.

Click the ⊞ **icon** beside **10800 Bank: Chequing**:

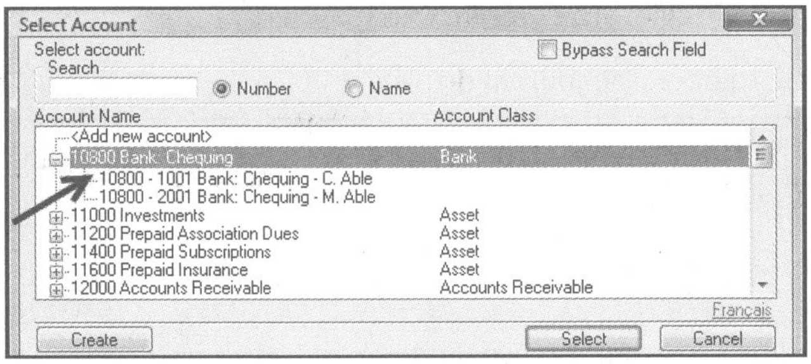

The modified list now shows the departments connected with the account. *Bank: Chequing* has both departments available for a journal transaction. If you click the ⊞ beside *34500 Invested Capital: C. Able*, you will see that you can select only the one department that we assigned to it.

Click **10800 - 1001 Bank: Chequing - C. Able**.

Click **Select** to return to the journal with the cursor in the Debits field.

Type 12780 to enter the portion of the asset for this department.

Click the **Account field list icon** again.

Double-click **10800 - 2001 Bank: Chequing - M. Able**. The cursor advances to the Credits field.

Type –8520 (add a minus sign to the amount). **Press** *tab*. The amount moves to the Debits column because we typed the minus sign.

Click the **Account field** and **type** 19500

Press *tab* to enter the total balance for the asset as a credit entry.

Notice that the accounts with departments all use the same format: account number, space, hyphen, space, department number. We can use this format to enter account numbers directly in a journal without using the Select Account list. You can omit the spaces when typing these numbers. Sage 50 will add them.

Click the **Account field** on the next blank line.

Type 11000-1001

Press *tab* to enter the account and advance to the Debits field.

Type 26500

Click the **Account field** and **type** 11000-2001

Press *tab* and **type** –17500 to move the amount to the Debits field.

Click the **Account field** and **type** 19500 **Press** *tab* to enter the credit amount. **Press** *tab* again to update the totals.

At this stage, your journal entry should look like the one below:

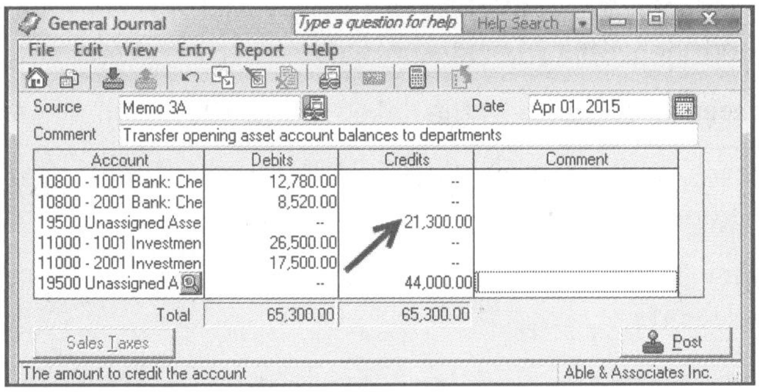

NOTES

You can enter all the debit asset accounts first and then enter a single total for 19500 Unassigned Assets. We have chosen to transfer the balances for one account at a time so we can check our work more easily. For each transfer, the amount from 19500 Unassigned Assets should match the amount for the General Ledger account in the Trial Balance on page 786.

NOTES

Typing the account number may be faster because the Select Account list appears without the department subaccounts expanded. You must click the ⊞ each time.

Before continuing, we will review the journal entry.

Press ctrl **+ J** to open the journal display:

Able & Associates Inc.
General Journal Entry 04/01/2015 (J1)

Account Number	Account Description	Debits	Credits
10800 - 1001	Bank: Chequing - C. Able	12,780.00	-
10800 - 2001	Bank: Chequing - M. Able	8,520.00	-
19500	Unassigned Assets	-	21,300.00
11000 - 1001	Investments - C. Able	26,500.00	-
11000 - 2001	Investments - M. Able	17,500.00	-
19500	Unassigned Assets	-	44,000.00
Additional Date:	Additional Field:	65,300.00	65,300.00

The journal entry is different from the usual one in one significant way — we were able to divide the balance in each asset account between the two departments. These separate amounts can be added to the standard financial reports and will enable us to produce separate reports for each department.

Close the **journal display**.

Enter the **remaining asset account balance transfers** from memo #3 on page 792.

NOTES
Do not enter sales tax information when prompted for the HST accounts.

Review the **journal entry** again to verify that the total debits and credits match the initial account balance for *Unassigned Assets*.

Post the **journal entry** after entering all the asset account balances.

Enter the **liability account balance transfers** from memo #3 on page 792 as the second journal entry.

NOTES
Remember you can adjust General Journal entries after posting. Refer to page 43.

Review the **transaction** and then **post** it when the amounts are correct.

Enter the **capital account balance transfers** from memo #3 on page 792 as the third journal entry.

Review the **transaction** and then **post** it when the amounts are correct.

Close the **General Journal** to return to the Company module window.

Compare your **Trial Balance** with the one on page 786 and make corrections if needed.

WARNING!
If you try to finish the history now, you will see the error message that the essential linked accounts are missing.

If you entered the amounts correctly, the account balances for *Accounts Receivable* and *Accounts Payable* should match the historical invoice balances. However, before we can finish the history, we must add the missing essential linked accounts.

Finishing the History

Because we needed to access *Accounts Receivable* and *Accounts Payable* as postable accounts in the General Journal, we did not enter them as linked accounts. To finish the history, you must add these essential linked accounts.

Click the **Settings icon** 

. **Click Payables** in the left panel of the Settings window and then **click Linked Accounts**.

NOTES
Prepayments and deposits are not used but linked accounts for them are required. Therefore, we can use Accounts Payable and Accounts Receivable.

Enter **22000 Accounts Payable** as the linked account for Accounts Payable.

Enter **22000 Accounts Payable** as the linked account for Prepayments and Prepaid Orders.

Click **Receivables** in the left panel of the Settings window and then **click Linked Accounts**.

Enter **12000 Accounts Receivable** as the linked account for Accounts Receivable.

Enter **12000 Accounts Receivable** as the linked account for Deposits and Prepaid Orders.

Click **OK** to save the settings.

Choose the **History menu** and **click Finish Entering History**.

Click **Backup** and continue to back up the not-finished file. **Click OK** when the backup is complete.

Click **Proceed** to finish the history.

WARNING!
Make a backup copy of the not-finished file so you can correct opening balance amounts later if necessary.

Adding Departments to Client Records

If some clients or vendors deal with only one department, you can add this information to the ledger record. C. Able has Adrienne Aesthetics as an exclusive client, and Dorfmann Design deals only with M. Able.

✓ 4

Memo #4 **Dated April 1/15**

Clients: Assign C. Able to Adrienne Aesthetics and M. Able to Dorfmann Design. The remaining clients are associated with both departments.

Click **Receivables** in the Modules pane list. **Click Adrienne Aesthetics** in the Clients List pane to open the record at the Address tab screen.

A Department field is added to the Address tab screen.

Click the **Department list arrow** to see the drop-down list of departments:

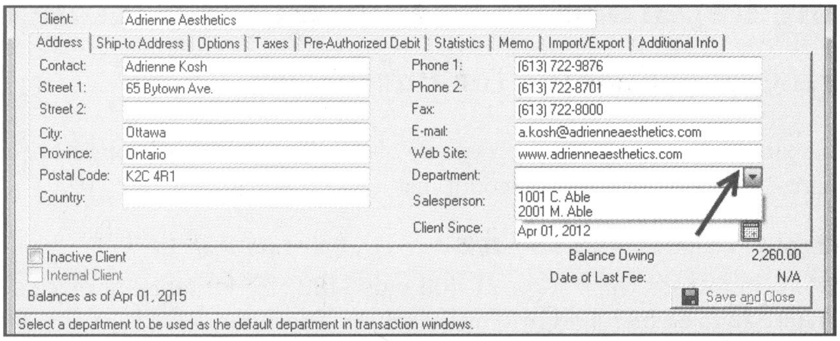

Click **1001 C. Able** to select the department.

Next we need to select the departmental revenue account as the client's default.

Click the **Options tab** so you can change the default revenue account.

Click the **Revenue Account field list arrow** to see the expanded account list:

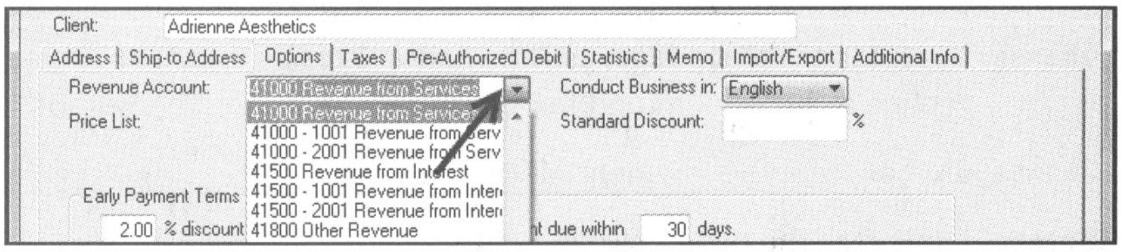

Each account has three numbers associated with it — one for the main account and one for each department. By selecting the departmental account in the ledger record, department information will be added as the default when you sell to this client.

Choose **41000 - 1001 Revenue from Services - C. Able** from the account list.

NOTES
If a client or vendor is used by more than one department, you should not add a department to the record.

NOTES
Notice that another field is added to the ledger record – the Standard Discount field. Entering a rate in this field will add it to the Sales Journal automatically as the line discount rate (see page 799). You can still change the line discount rate in the journal.

Click the **Next Client tool** to open the record for Dorfmann Design.

Choose **41000 - 2001 Revenue from Services - M. Able** from the Revenue Account list.

Click the **Address tab** and **enter 2001 M. Able** in the Department field.

Click **Save And Close** Save and Close.

The remaining clients work with both departments so we cannot add one department exclusively for them.

Adding Departments to Vendor Records

If a vendor is connected exclusively with one department, you can add the department to the vendor record, just as you do for clients. At this time, all vendors are used by both departments so we will not add departments to the records.

If you want to add departments to vendor records, open the Payables module window and then open the vendor record. The Department field has been added to the Address tab screen.

Click the Department field list arrow to see the departments and click the one you want.

On the Options tab screen, choose the departmental account as the default for expenses.

Repeat this procedure for other vendors. Close the last vendor record.

Adding Departments to Journal Transactions

Entering Departments for Purchases

Adding departmental details to purchases involves selecting the appropriate departmental General Ledger subaccount instead of the main one.

NOTES
You can also enter this purchase in the Payments Journal as an Other Payment. Enter the amounts and choose the departmental accounts in the same way as described here.

✓ 5

Cheque Purchase Invoice #NO-2015-4 **Dated April 3/15**

From Northlands Office Mgt., $1 400 plus $182 HST for rental of office suite. Invoice total $1 582 paid by cheque #3011. $840 (60 percent) of the expense should be assigned to C. Able and $560 (40 percent) to M. Able.

Before proceeding, you should create shortcuts for the journals in other modules.

Create **shortcuts** to create and pay vendor invoices, to create paycheques and to create General Journal entries.

Click the **Create Vendor Invoices shortcut** to open the journal.

Choose **Northlands Office Mgt.** as the vendor. **Press** tab. The default general Rent account and tax code are added from the vendor's record.

Choose **Cheque** from the Payment Method list.

Enter **April 3** as the payment date.

Click the **Amount field**. **Type** 840 **Press** tab.

Click the **List icon** beside *Rent* in the Account field to open the Select Account screen. **Click** the ⊞ **icon** beside **52400 Rent**:

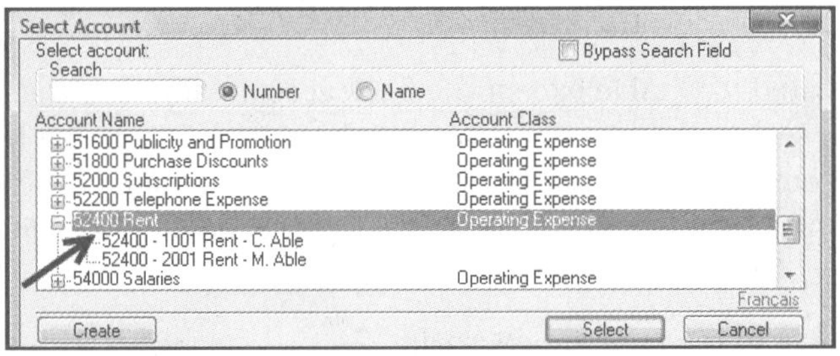

Department subaccounts are added, just as they were in the General Journal.

Click **52400 - 1001 Rent - C. Able**. **Press** (enter) to add the account for C. Able's share.

Click the **Amount field** on the second journal line. **Type** 560

Press (tab). **Click** the **Account field List icon**.

Choose **52400 - 2001 Rent - M. Able**. **Press** (enter) to add the account for M. Able's share.

Enter **line Descriptions** and **Source** to complete the entry.

Choose the **Report menu** and **click** **Display Payments Journal entry**:

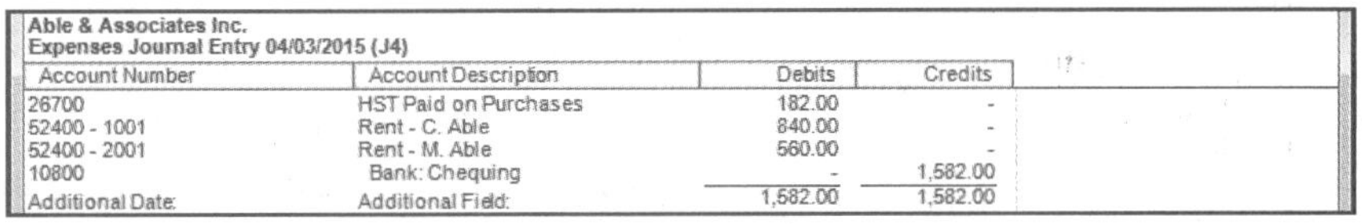

Able & Associates Inc.
Expenses Journal Entry 04/03/2015 (J4)

Account Number	Account Description	Debits	Credits
26700	HST Paid on Purchases	182.00	-
52400 - 1001	Rent - C. Able	840.00	-
52400 - 2001	Rent - M. Able	560.00	-
10800	Bank: Chequing	-	1,582.00
Additional Date:	Additional Field:	1,582.00	1,582.00

The rental expense amount has been shared between the two departments, but the other amounts have not. Because no single department is linked to the vendor, and the other accounts for the transaction are not accessible, they remain unallocated.

Close the **journal display** to return to the journal.

Click the **Paid From bank account list arrow**:

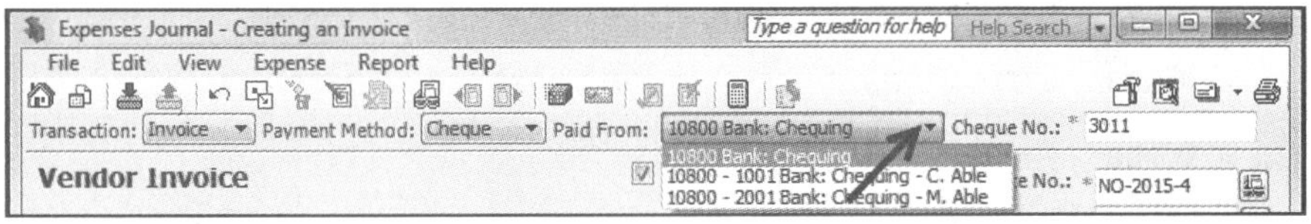

You can change the default bank account for this payment, but you can choose only one account for the single cheque. A complete allocation requires access to both bank department subaccounts. Therefore, you cannot allocate the bank amount.

Make **corrections** if necessary. **Post** the **transaction** and **close** the **journal**.

NOTES

You could also make separate payment journal entries for each department amount. This will allow you to choose the associated departmental bank account number, but not the department for tax accounts.

Entering Departments for Receipts

✓ 6

Cash Receipt #48 **Dated April 4/15**

From Adrienne Aesthetics, cheque #3101 for $2 214.80, including $45.20 discount in full payment of invoice #843. Assign all amounts to C. Able.

Restore the **Receivables module** as the Home window if necessary.

Click the **Receipts Journal icon**  to open the journal.

Choose **Adrienne Aesthetics**. **Press** (tab) to add the outstanding invoice.

Enter **Apr 4 -15** as the date and **enter** **3101** as the client's cheque number.

Accept the **discount taken** and **amount received**.

Press *ctrl* **+ J** to review the transaction.

All amounts are allocated to C. Able except the bank account amount. The accounts are allocated because we set up a unique department link for the client in the ledger record. The allocated amounts are those for the default linked accounts for the journal. In this case, we can also allocate the bank amount because only one department is involved and we can select the account.

Close the **display** to return to the journal.

Click the **Deposit To bank account list arrow**:

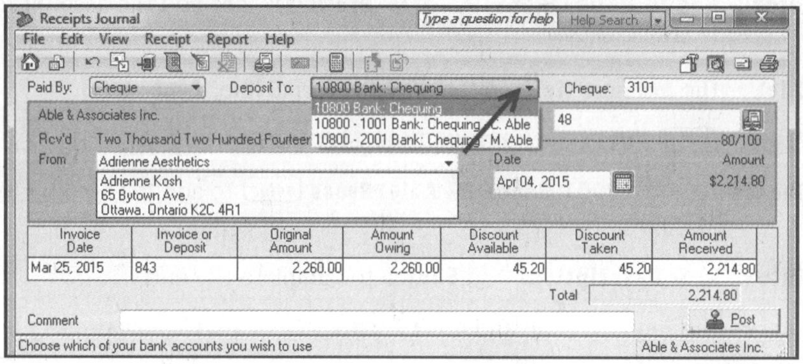

Click **10800 - 1001 Bank Chequing - C. Able** to update the journal entry.

Press *ctrl* **+ J** to review the transaction:

Able & Associates Inc.
Receipts Journal Entry 04/04/2015 (J5)

Account Number	Account Description	Debits	Credits
10800 - 1001	Bank: Chequing - C. Able	2,214.80	-
42000 - 1001	Sales Discounts - C. Able	45.20	-
12000 - 1001	Accounts Receivable - C. Able	-	2,260.00
Additional Date:	Additional Field:	2,260.00	2,260.00

The entry is now completely allocated and it is correct. All amounts, including the discount, are attributed to C. Able's department.

Close the **display** to return to the journal.

Make **corrections** if necessary and **post** the **transaction**.

Close the **Receipts Journal**.

Entering Departments for Sales

Click the **Client Invoices icon**  to open the Fees journal.

✓ 7

Sales Invoice #851 **Dated April 4/15**

To Adrienne Aesthetics, $5 800 plus HST for auditing financial statements and $900 plus HST for monthly accounting fee. Invoice total $7 243.30. Terms: 2/10, n/30. Additional 5 percent discount applies to the fee for auditing, by special arrangement with client. Adrienne Aesthetics is C. Able's client.

Choose **Adrienne Aesthetics**. **Press** *tab* to add the client's record details.

Enter **April 4** as the date. This time the default revenue account is correct:

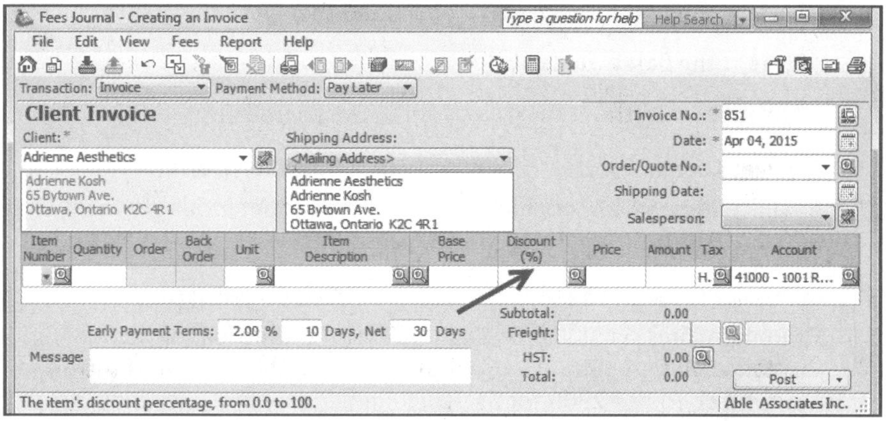

The department subaccount is taken from the record because a single department is linked to the client and we added this as the default revenue account.

Two columns — **Base Price** and **Disc. %** — have been added to the journal. These fields allow us to add discounts that apply only to a single invoice line, so you can enter different discount rates for each invoice line. Able & Associates offers discounts for special circumstances. For part of this invoice, a 5 percent discount applies.

Entering Line Discounts

Click the **Item Description field**.

Type `prepare audited financial statements`

Press *tab* to advance to the Base Price field.

Type `5800`

Press *tab* to advance to the Discount % field.

Type `5`

Press *tab* to apply the amount of the discount — $290.00.

The new discounted unit price, $5 510, has been added to the Price field. To have the amount entered automatically, you can enter the quantity for the line.

Click the **Quantity field**. **Type** `1` **Press** *tab* to update the line.

The discounted amount, $5 510, is now entered as the amount.

Press *ctrl* **+ J** to review the transaction as we have entered it so far:

Able & Associates Inc.
Fees Journal Entry 04/04/2015 (J6)

Account Number	Account Description	Debits	Credits
12000 - 1001	Accounts Receivable - C. Able	6,226.30	-
26500 - 1001	HST Charged on Services - C. Able	-	716.30
41000 - 1001	Revenue from Services - C. Able	-	5,510.00
Additional Date	Additional Field	6,226.30	6,226.30

Again, all amounts are allocated correctly because we have a single department linked to the record. Notice that the discount is taken directly to reduce revenue; it is not linked to the sales discount account used for early payments.

Close the **display** to return to the journal and complete the entry.

Click the **Item Description field**. **Type** `monthly fee`

Click the **Amount field**. No discount applies to this service.

Type `900`

Press *tab* **twice** to add the tax code and advance to the Account field. The default account should be entered automatically.

Review the **entry**, **make corrections** and then **post** the **transaction**.

Close the **Sales Journal**.

Continue with the **transactions** up to the payroll entry on April 30.

NOTES

You will be unable to allocate the payment to Office Plus because more than one department is involved and you cannot select accounts for the payments. As for the cash purchase, you can choose only one bank account, so this amount also remains unallocated.

8

Payment Cheque #3012 **Dated April 5/15**

To Office Plus, $2 237.40, including $22.60 discount in full payment of invoice #OP-2339. (You cannot assign these amounts – see margin Notes.)

9

Cash Sales Invoice #852 **Dated April 10/15**

To Truman Tires, $1 000 plus $130 HST for monthly fee for accounting assistance. Assign $600 (60%) of the fee to C. Able and $400 (40%) to M. Able. Received cheque #2900 for $1 107.40 in full payment, including 2% discount for early payment. (See margin Notes.)

NOTES

For the sale to Truman Tires, enter 600 as the amount for account 41000 - 1001, and on the second line enter 400 as the amount for account 41000 - 2001. The amounts for Bank: Chequing, Sales Discounts and HST will remain unallocated.

10

Sales Invoice #853 **Dated April 14/15**

To Dorfmann Design, $5 000 plus HST for preparing special financial reports for potential investors and $700 plus HST for monthly accounting fee. Invoice total $5 876 (with discount). Terms: 2/10, n/30. Additional 10 percent discount applies to the fee for preparing financial reports. Assign 100% of all amounts to M. Able.

11

Sales Invoice #854 **Dated April 20/15**

To Gorgeous Gifts, $3 000 plus $390 HST for assistance with response to Canada Revenue Agency audit and $500 plus $65 HST for monthly accounting fee. Invoice total $3 955. Terms: 2/10, n/30. Assign $1 800 plus $300 (60%) of revenue amounts to C. Able and $1 200 and $200 (40%) to M. Able.

12

Cash Purchase Invoice #BC-233008 **Dated April 22/15**

From Bell Canada, $400 plus $52 HST for monthly telephone and Internet service for one multi-line office telephone, two mobile phones and networked Internet service. Invoice total $452 paid by cheque #3013. Assign $240 (60%) of expense amount to C. Able and $160 (40%) to M. Able.

NOTES

For the purchase from Office Plus, enter 1800 as the amount for account 14800 - 1001, and on the second line enter 1200 as the amount for account 14800 - 2001. The amounts for Accounts Payable and HST will remain unallocated.

13

Purchase Invoice #OP-5102 **Dated April 25/15**

From Office Plus, $3 000 plus $390 HST for new boardroom table and chairs (Office Furniture account). Invoice total $3 390. Terms: 1/15, n/30. Assign $1 800 (60%) of the asset account amount to C. Able and $1 200 (40%) to M. Able. (See margin Notes.)

14

Memo #5 **Dated April 25/15**

Remit the HST owing to the Receiver General as at March 31. Issue cheque #3014. Assign $1 320 for HST Charged on Services and $984 for HST Paid (60% of HST amounts) to C. Able and $880 for HST Charged on Services and $656 for HST Paid (40%) to M. Able.

15

Cash Sales Invoice #855 **Dated April 30/15**

To various one-time clients, $6 000 plus $780 HST for personal income tax preparation. Total cash received $6 780 deposited to bank account. Assign $3 600 (60%) of revenue amount to C. Able and $2 400 (40%) to M. Able.

Entering Departments for Payroll Transactions

Payroll amounts are allocated to departments differently than amounts in other journals. If an employee works only with one department, you can add the department to the employee's ledger record.

✓ 16

Memo #6 **Dated April 30/15**

Prepare payroll for Tryin, office assistant. Issue cheque #3015. Assign 60% of all amounts to C. Able and 40% to M. Able.

Click the **Create Paycheque shortcut** to open the journal.

Choose **Tryin, Reelie**. **Press** *tab* to add the employee's default record details.

All Payroll Journal accounts are linked accounts, so you cannot choose the department subaccounts to enter allocations. Instead, you can open the Department Allocation screens from the Paycheque menu or from the Departments tool as shown in the following two screen images:

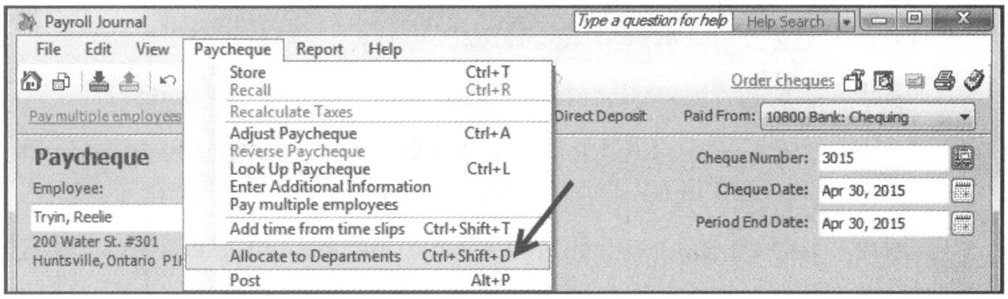

Choose the **Paycheque menu** and **click Allocate To Departments** or **click** the **Allocate Account Amounts To Departments tool**.

Both methods will open the Allocation screen:

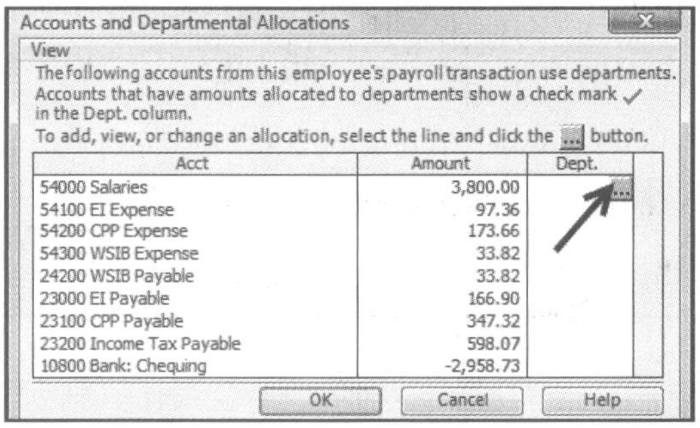

All accounts used in the journal entry are listed, and you can allocate one or more of them, or all, in the same way, or you can use different percentages or amounts.

Click the **Department Detail button** (in the Dept. column) for Salaries:

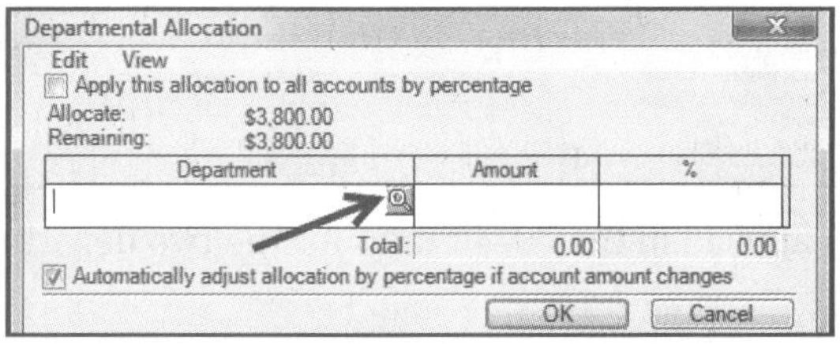

This screen is similar to the one we use to enter division allocations (see page 509). You can select one or more departments for each journal entry amount. And you can apply the same allocation to all accounts, just as we did for divisions in Chapter 13 (pages 516–518). Payroll amounts for the Ables are allocated by percentage, but you can allocate by amount if you prefer. You do not need to allocate the entire amount for an account. We want the same breakdown to apply to all amounts.

NOTES

Allocate To Departments is also available in the Payroll Cheque Run Journal from the Payroll menu. You can allocate for each employee separately.

Click the **Department List icon** to see the selection list for departments:

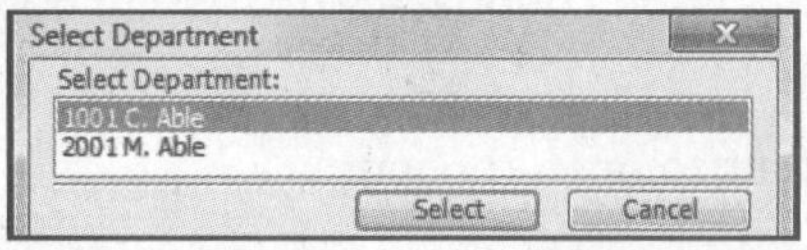

Click **1001 C. Able**. **Click Select** to add the department.

Press *tab* to advance to the % (percentage) field.

Type 60 **Press** *tab* to advance to the Department field again.

Press *enter* and **enter M. Able** for the rest of the allocation.

Press *tab* and **accept** the **default entry** — 40 percent.

Click **Apply This Allocation To All Accounts By Percentage**.

Click **OK** to return to the account list screen. A ✓ has been added to each account in the Dept. column.

Click **10800 Bank Chequing** to select the account line.

Click the **Dept. Detail button** for this account:

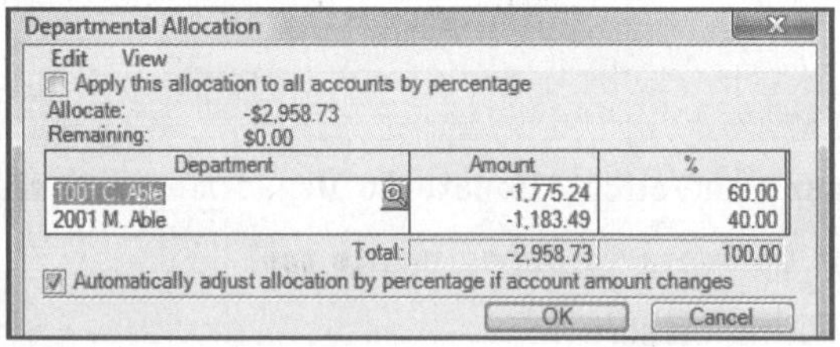

You can see that the same 60–40 allocation is applied. But in this window, you have the option to change the allocation for the single account without affecting the others.

Click **OK** to accept the amounts already entered (or Cancel).

Click **OK** again to return to the journal and review the entry.

Press *ctrl* + **J** to view the journal entry:

Able & Associates Inc.
Payroll Journal Entry 04/30/2015 (J15)

Account Number	Account Description	Debits	Credits
54000 - 1001	Salaries - C. Able	2,280.00	-
54000 - 2001	Salaries - M. Able	1,520.00	-
54100 - 1001	EI Expense - C. Able	58.42	-
54100 - 2001	EI Expense - M. Able	38.94	-
54200 - 1001	CPP Expense - C. Able	104.20	-
54200 - 2001	CPP Expense - M. Able	69.46	-
54300 - 1001	WSIB Expense - C. Able	20.29	-
54300 - 2001	WSIB Expense - M. Able	13.53	-
10800 - 1001	Bank: Chequing - C. Able	-	1,775.24
10800 - 2001	Bank: Chequing - M. Able	-	1,183.49
23000 - 1001	EI Payable - C. Able	-	100.14
23000 - 2001	EI Payable - M. Able	-	66.76
23100 - 1001	CPP Payable - C. Able	-	208.39
23100 - 2001	CPP Payable - M. Able	-	138.93
23200 - 1001	Income Tax Payable - C. Able	-	358.84
23200 - 2001	Income Tax Payable - M. Able	-	239.23
24200 - 1001	WSIB Payable - C. Able	-	20.29
24200 - 2001	WSIB Payable - M. Able	-	13.53
Additional Date:	Additional Field:	4,104.84	4,104.84

All amounts are automatically applied in the 60–40 ratio for the two departments.

Close the **display** to return to the journal.

Make **corrections** if necessary and **post** the **transaction**.

Close the **Paycheques Journal**.

Enter the final **two General Journal entries** with allocations for all accounts.

17 **Memo #7** **Dated April 30/15**

The following transactions appeared on the monthly bank statement for the bank chequing account. Assign 60% of all amounts to C. Able and 40% to M. Able.

	Amounts for C. Able	Amounts for M. Able
Bank charges $60	$ 36	$ 24
Bank loan principal $300	180	120
Bank loan interest $200	120	80
Interest on Chequing account $60	36	24
Interest from investments $180	108	72
Bank net withdrawal $320	192	128

18 **Memo #8** **Dated April 30/15**

Enter the adjustments for supplies used and prepaid expenses expired in April. Assign all amounts as indicated in the following summary. Create new Group Expense account 52600 Supplies Used.

	Amounts for C. Able	Amounts for M. Able
Office Supplies $100	$ 60	$ 40
Prepaid Insurance $500	300	200
Prepaid Association Dues $400	200	200
Prepaid Subscriptions $250	150	100

NOTES
If you credit (or debit) the bank account for each charge (or deposit) amount separately, you will not enter the final net withdrawal amounts.

Handling Unallocated Amounts

We saw that the amounts for some accounts in the journals were not allocated. Most of the affected accounts are Balance Sheet accounts and many users prefer to apply departmental accounting only to Income Statement accounts to avoid these incomplete entries. Unallocated amounts can also leave Departmental Balance Sheets out of balance as some amounts will not be included. For example, in a purchase of assets, the asset account was allocated but the HST account was not.

To prepare complete Departmental reports without unallocated amounts, you can enter General Journal adjusting entries to transfer the balances from the main account to the correct departmental subaccount. You can see that this could be a time-consuming exercise as you would have to first determine all the appropriate amounts. Furthermore, the linked *Accounts Receivable* and *Accounts Payable* accounts are not accessible as postable accounts. You would still be unable to allocate these amounts. For this exercise, we will not enter the adjustments for unallocated amounts.

NOTES
In the Accountant Edition of Sage 50, all accounts are available for posting. Your accountant would be able to make these adjustments for you by working with an Accountant's Copy of your data file. Refer to Chapter 12.

Department Reports

Many of the standard Sage 50 reports can have department information added to them. In addition, the primary financial statements — the Balance Sheet, Income Statement and Trial Balance — are available as departmental reports. As before, we will work from the Report Centre.

Click the **Report Centre icon** in the Home window.

Click **Financials** to open the list of financial reports.

Click the **beside Balance Sheet** to expand this list.

Click the **beside Income Statement** to expand this list.

Click the ⊞ **beside Trial Balance** to expand this list:

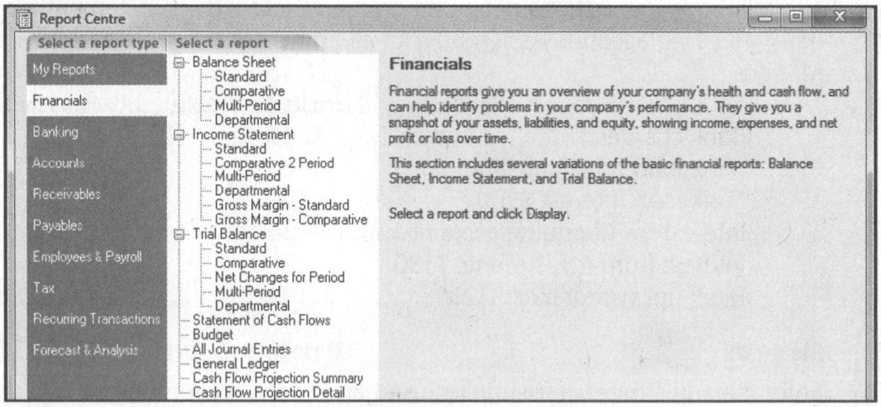

You can prepare a Departmental version of each of these reports.

Displaying Departmental Balance Sheets

If you want Balance Sheet information for each department, you should prepare the Departmental Balance Sheet.

Click **Departmental** under **Balance Sheet**. **Click Modify This Report**:

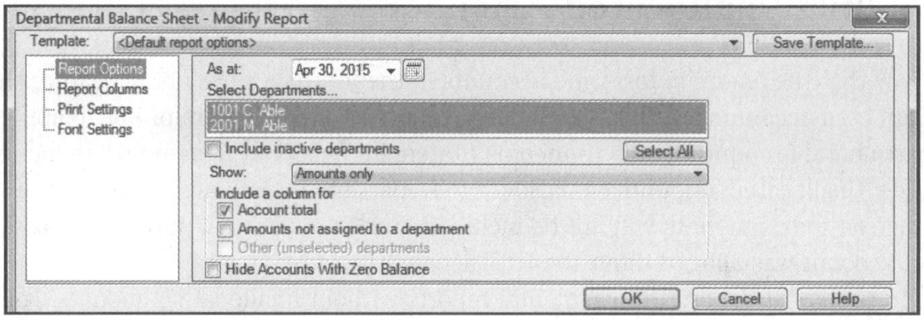

From the Home window, choose the Reports menu, then choose Financials and Departmental Reports and click Balance Sheet to see the report options.

NOTES
Including unallocated amounts – those not assigned to departments – and totals will provide balanced reports.

You can report on one or more departments or all departments. The departments are shown as column headings, so you have a complete Balance Sheet for each department you selected. Remember that the Balance Sheet for each department separately may not balance if some amounts were not allocated.

Reports can include **Amounts** only or each amount as a **Percentage Of The Total**. You can also add **extra columns** for the total amount for each account, for amounts not assigned to any department and for the total amount for other departments not included in the report.

Choose the **departments** you want to include.

Choose the **Amounts** or **Percentage** option.

Choose the **additional columns** you want.

Enter the **date** for the report and **click OK**.

Close the **display** when you have finished.

Departmental Income Statement and Trial Balance Reports

Departmental Income Statements and Departmental Trial Balances are also available. The Departmental Income Statement is probably the most frequently used of these reports.

For both reports, select the departments to include in the report and choose whether you want to include amounts that are not assigned to a department. You can show amounts only or add the percentage of the total amount in your reports. In other respects, these reports are like the standard non-departmental reports.

Adding Departments to Other Reports

Many other reports allow departmental details to be added after you set up and use departments. **Journal reports** automatically include the department number with the account numbers if you have added that information to the journal transaction.

The **Balance Sheet**, **Income Statement**, **Trial Balance** and **General Ledger** all have a **Show Departments** check box added. Division reports also have this option.

Access the **report options** in the usual way from the Report Centre or from the Reports menu.

The Show Departments option is shown in the Balance Sheet Options window:

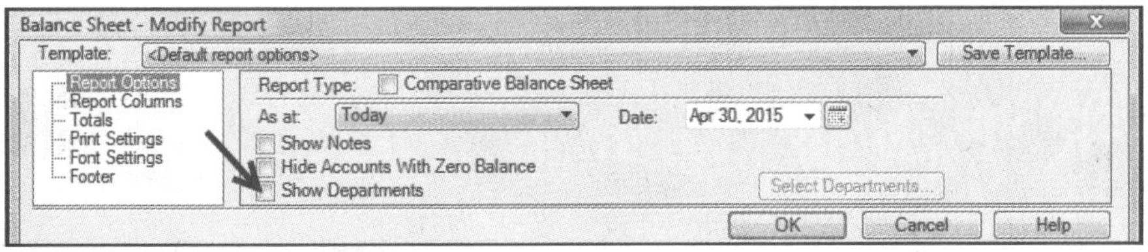

Click **Show Departments** to have the details added to the report.

Click the **Select Departments button** to open the department list:

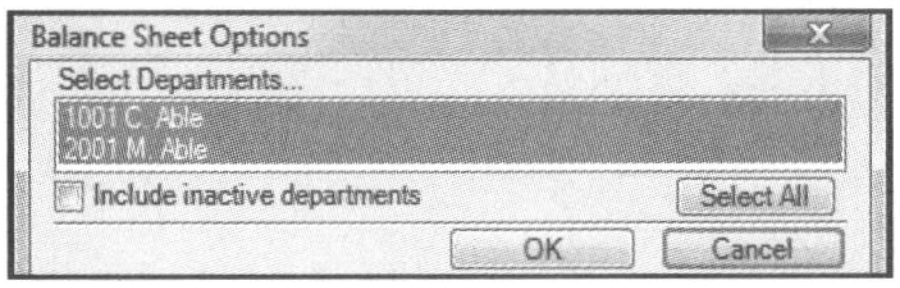

Select the **departments** you want to add to the report.

Click **OK** to return to the initial Balance Sheet Options window.

Choose other **report options** in the usual way and **click OK** to see the report.

Close the **display** when you have finished.

Department information can also be added to client and vendor reports. The Vendor Aged and Aged Overdue reports and the Pending Purchase Order Report allow you to group the vendors by department for the report. The Client Aged and Aged Overdue reports and the Pending Sales Order Report have the same option for grouping clients by department.

The following Vendor Aged Report options screen shows this option:

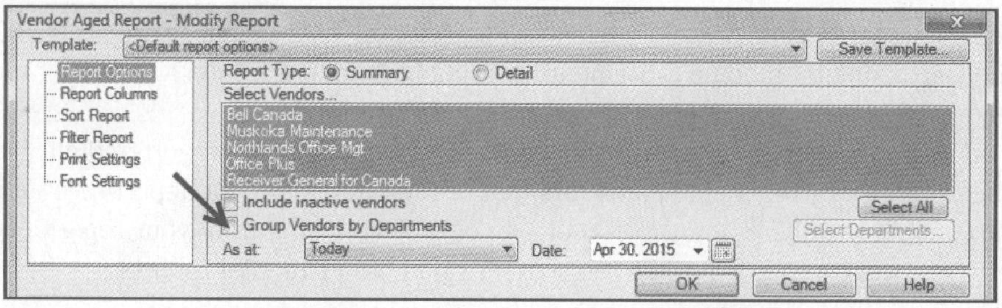

Click **Group Vendors By Departments** to select the option.

Click the **Select Departments button** to open the department list.

Select the **departments** you want to add to the report.

You can include or omit vendors that do not have an assigned department.

Click **OK** to return to the Vendor Aged Report options screen.

Choose other **report options** in the usual way.

Click **OK** to see the report.

Close the **display** when you have finished.

Close the **Report Centre** if it is open.

R E V I E W

The Student DVD with Data Files includes Review Questions and Supplementary Cases for this chapter.

Part 4
Appendices

APPENDIX A

Installing Sage 50

INSTALLING SAGE 50 FROM THE PROGRAM CD

STUDENT VERSION
Instructions for installing from the downloaded program begin on page A–8. Instructions for downloading, installing and activating the Student version begin on page A–10.

The instructions for installation that follow refer to the regular Premium version of the program, but most steps for installing the program are the same for all versions. Margin notes outline the differences for the Pro version and for the Student (Premium) version.

The Sage 50 Student version is available only as a download from the Sage 50 Web site. Special instructions for downloading, installing and activating the Student version begin on page A–10.

Start your **computer** and the **Windows program**.

Insert the **Sage 50 program CD** in the CD/DVD drive.

NOTES
From the Computer window, you can right-click D: and click Open Autoplay and Run Launch.exe to start the auto-run feature and show the Installation screens on this page.

NOTES
You can purchase and download the retail version of Sage 50 from the Web site <na.sage.com/sage-50-accounting-ca>. Be sure that you are selecting the Canadian version of Sage 50 – you will see a Canadian flag icon on the picture of the program box.
Refer to page A–8 for instructions on downloading the program. The installation procedure is the same as from a CD.

The next step will depend on your version of Windows and on your system settings for dealing with CDs. Installation from the CD/DVD drive may begin immediately, or you may see a screen asking what you want to do with this CD with an option or link for **Run launch.exe** included. Clicking the Run launch.exe link will also start the installation. If installation does not begin immediately or the Run option is not displayed, follow the boxed instructions on page A–3.

Many computers have drive D: as the CD/DVD drive, so we will use that in the keystrokes that follow.

The following options screen appears to begin the installation:

If you have any other programs running, click Exit, close the other programs and start again.

If you want to see the French version of this screen, click **Français** in the upper left-hand corner. We show only the English language screens.

Click **Install Sage 50**. Wait for the Select A Language To Use With This Installation screen to appear:

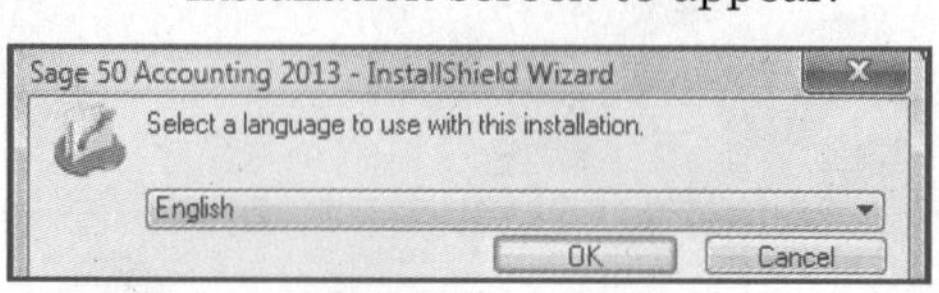

Click your **language preference** from the drop-down list and **click OK**.

IF INSTALLATION DOES NOT BEGIN IMMEDIATELY

You can install the program from the Windows opening screen or desktop. Many computers have drive D: as the CD/DVD drive, so we will use that drive in the keystrokes that follow. (For drive D:, substitute the drive letter for your CD/DVD drive.)

Click the **Start icon**  on the task bar to open the Search field.

Click the **Start Search text box** 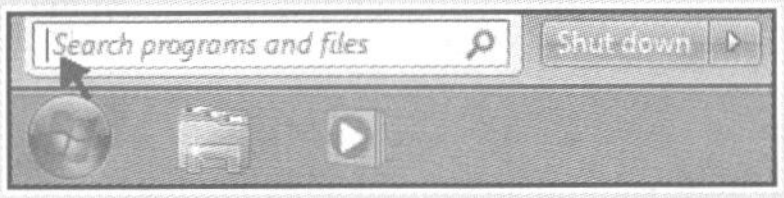

.

Type run and **press** enter to open the Run window:

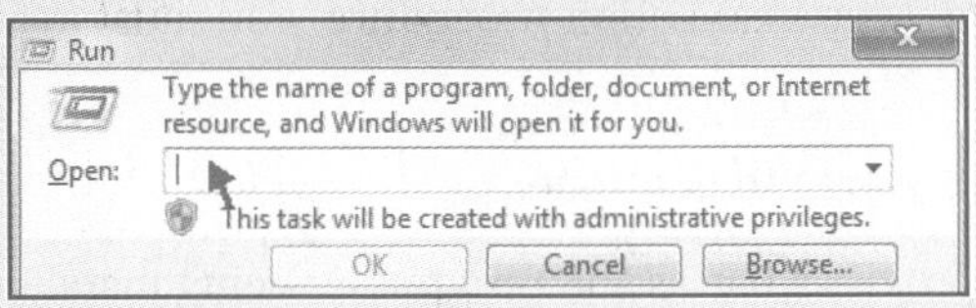

Click the **Open** field if necessary to place the cursor. You can type the name of the program you want directly in the Open field of the Run window.

Type D:\Setup\setup.exe or **D:\launch.exe** in the Open field. **Click OK**.

If you need to locate the program, **click Browse** in the Run window to find the Sage 50 program CD. (Click Computer and double-click the Sage 50 CD.) Then **double-click launch** (or **launch.exe**) or **double-click** the **Setup** folder and then **double-click setup** (or **setup.exe**).

If you start with the **launch** program, you will open the CD home page on the previous page. If you start from the **Setup\setup.exe** program, you will begin the installation immediately and see the Select A Language To Use With This Installation screen – the screen that follows this instruction box.

NOTES
The instructions in the shaded box beside this note apply to Windows 7. For other versions of Windows, the instructions may be different.

You are now ready to begin installing the program:

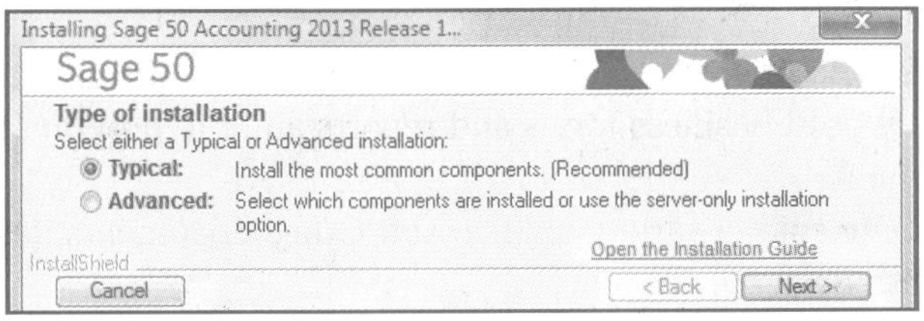

The default option, **Typical**, will provide all the basic components you need. If you want to omit some features, you must choose the Advanced option. Leave the default selection unchanged.

Click **Next**. The next step requires you to enter the Serial Number:

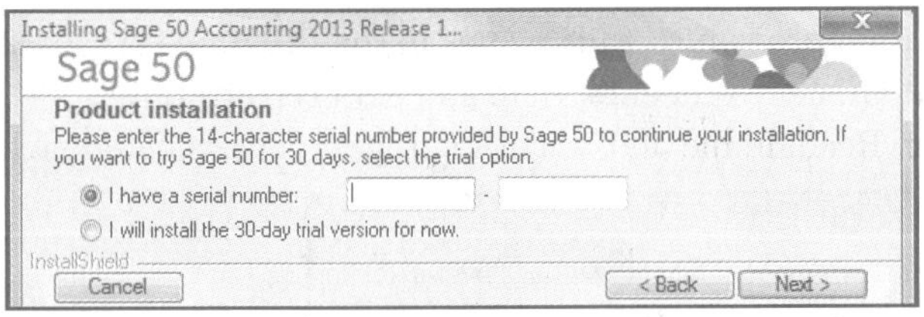

For regular or retail Pro and Premium versions, each copy has a unique serial number. Before you can continue, you must enter the serial number exactly as it appears in the e-mail you received from downloading the program or on the program package or CD case.

The cursor is in the Serial Number field, ready for you to enter the number.

Type your **Serial Number** in the space provided.

STUDENT VERSION
The serial number for all copies of the Student version is 242P1U2-1000004

NOTES
The letters o and i are not used in serial numbers or key codes.

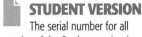

PRO VERSION
The title bar will show Installing Sage 50 Pro 2013 Release 1.

STUDENT VERSION
The title bar will show Installing Sage 50 Premium 2013 - Student Version Release 1.

Click **Next** to advance to the licence agreement:

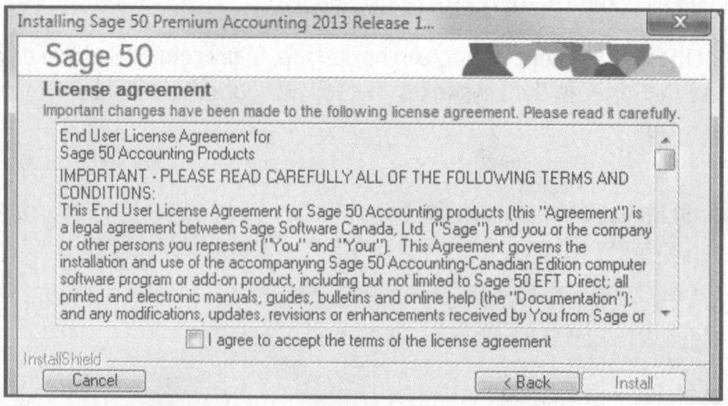

Not accepting the agreement will cancel the installation procedure. You must accept the agreement to install the program.

Read the **agreement** and **click I Agree** to continue.

Click **Install**. You will see the progress bar as the program is being installed:

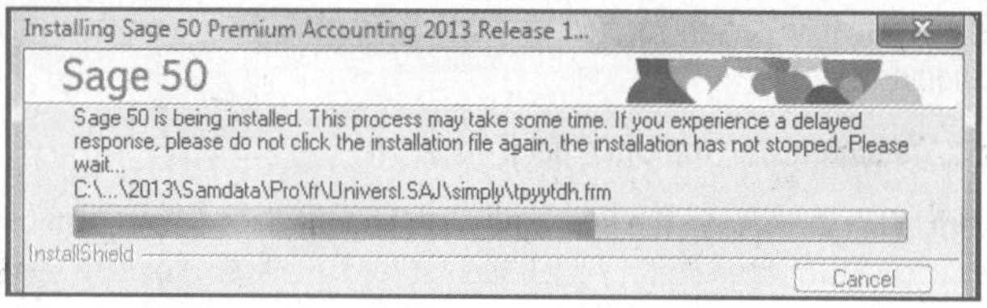

PRO VERSION
The default installation destination folder will be Sage 50 Pro Accounting 2013.

By default, the program and all components will be included as follows:

- **Sage 50 Program**: the program that you will need to perform the accounting transactions for your company (installed to C:\Sage\Sage 50 Premium Accounting 2013).
- **Sample Data**: complete records for a sample company — Universal Construction.
- **Templates**: predefined charts of accounts and settings for a large number of business types.
- **Crystal Reports Print Engine**, **Customizable Forms** and **Management Reports**: a variety of commonly used business forms and reports and the program to access and print them.
- **Microsoft Office Documents**: a variety of Microsoft Office documents designed for integrated use with Sage 50.
- **Manuals & Tutorials**: documentation and videos to help you learn the program.
- **Add-in for Microsoft Outlook**: a program link that connects your data with Microsoft Outlook.
- **Sage 50 Business Intelligence**: a program that allows more extensive customization of reports.

NOTES
The Reports menu has a link for Sage 50 Business Intelligence, but you must purchase the licence to use it after the initial 30-day trial period.

In addition, the installation procedure adds names in the Programs list for the Sage 50 program, Microsoft Office documents, Help and data repair utilities.

The options to view the ReadMe file and start the program are selected next:

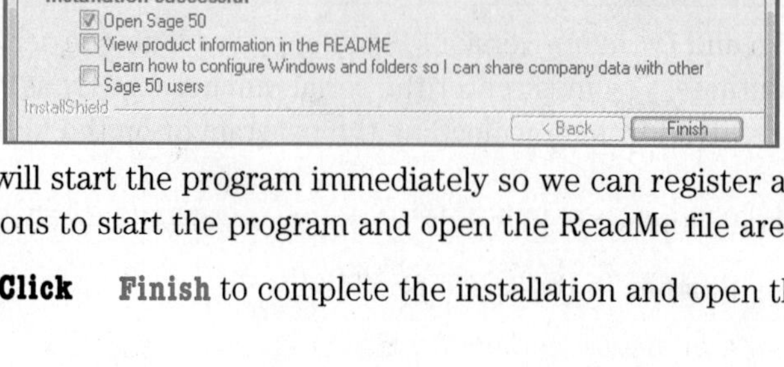

We will start the program immediately so we can register and activate the program. The options to start the program and open the ReadMe file are selected.

WARNING!
Wait for the Setup window to close after you close the ReadMe window. This may take some time.

Click **Finish** to complete the installation and open the ReadMe screen.

Registering and Activating Your Program

Read the **information** about recent changes to the program that may not yet be documented elsewhere.

Close the **ReadMe screen** to see the Registration message:

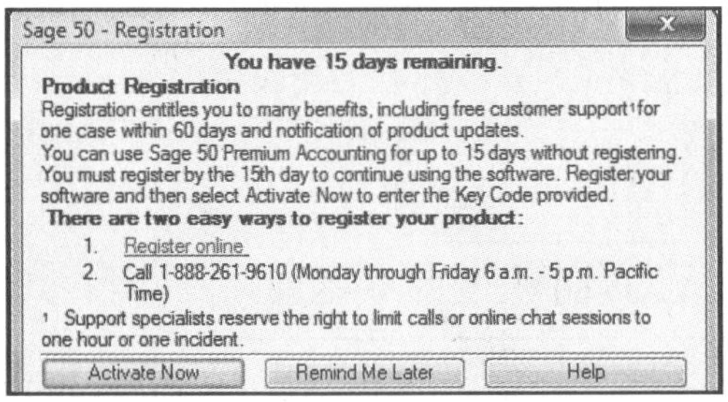

If you choose Remind Me Later, open any data file, choose the Help menu and click Enter Key Code to see the screen shown above. This reminder message will also appear each time you start the program until you complete the activation.

Until you register and activate the program, you will be allowed to use the program for a limited number of days. If you have already registered and have the activation codes, click **Activate Now** and skip the next step.

Have your product serial number ready for the registration. You can register online or by telephone. The telephone number is provided. To register online, start your Internet connection. Click the **Register Online link** on the registration information screen. Follow the instructions provided.

Print a copy of the codes screen for reference.

When you register, you will provide the serial number from the program package or CD and receive an account ID number, a key code number and a payroll ID number. These numbers will be linked to the serial number you provided and cannot be used for a different copy of the program.

Click **Activate Now** to start the activation procedure:

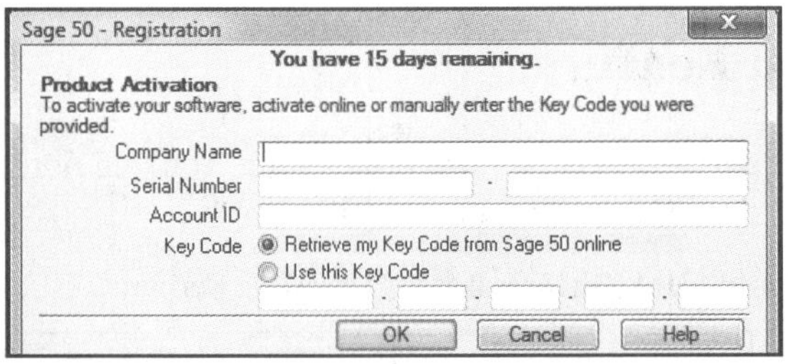

Enter your **Company Name** and the **Account ID** provided by Sage for the program you have registered.

You can retrieve the key code online, the default selection. To do this,

Start your **Internet connection** and **click OK**.

You will be connected to the Sage 50 Web site and the account ID and serial number will be uploaded from your program to create a key code. The key code will be added to your program automatically.

If you already have the key code, you can enter it on this screen manually.

Click **Use This Key Code** to open the Key Code fields.

Enter the **Key Code** provided by Sage for this program.

STUDENT VERSION
You will not see this screen for the Student version.

WARNING!
The Company Name must match the name you used to register the program with Sage.
Enter all numbers exactly as they are given to you, including spaces and punctuation.

STUDENT VERSION
Proceed to page A–12 for assistance with activating the Student version.

NOTES
If you have an existing account with Sage, registration may be completed automatically. You must still activate the program.

> **NOTES**
> If you downloaded the program, your serial number and key codes will be e-mailed to you. You can copy and paste them into the appropriate fields on the activation screen.

Enter all names and numbers exactly as they are given to you, including spaces and punctuation. The key code is not case sensitive. If you make a mistake, the program will warn you and you can re-enter the details.

Click **OK**.

When you have completed the registration, you will see the confirmation screen:

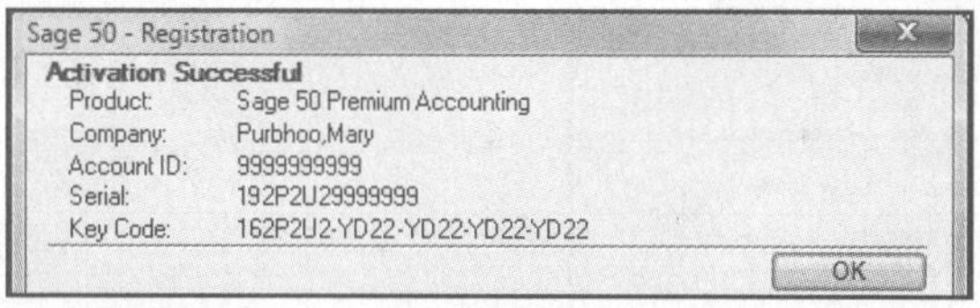

Click **OK** to continue to the Sage 50 Welcome screen:

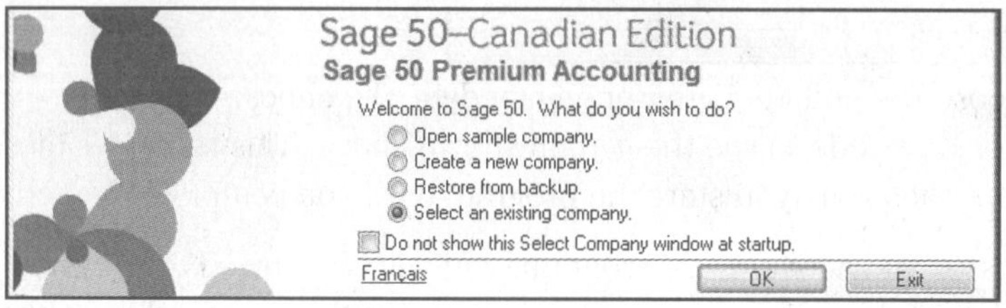

Click **Open Sample Company**. **Click OK** to continue to the Session Date window:

> **NOTES**
> Instructions for starting Sage 50 are included in Chapter 1 of this text, beginning on page 7.

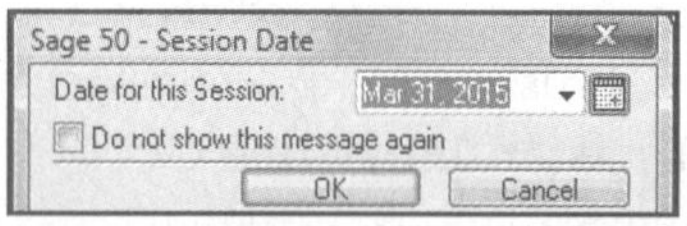

Click **OK** to accept the default session date. The session date will be explained in Chapter 3 when you need to enter transactions.

> **NOTES**
> If this is not the first time you have used Sage 50, including earlier versions, the option to Open The Last Company You Worked On will be added. The file name for that company will be included as shown on page 22.

You can now view a short video to learn more or access this video later from the Help menu. These are some of the options on the Getting Started screen.

Click **Close** to close the Getting Started window.

If you see information screens about Sage services, you can close them.

Unlocking the Payroll Features

We will unlock and activate the Payroll module before proceeding. You will not need to unlock payroll in the Student version of the program.

Choose the **Help menu** and **click Unlock Auto Payroll** as shown:

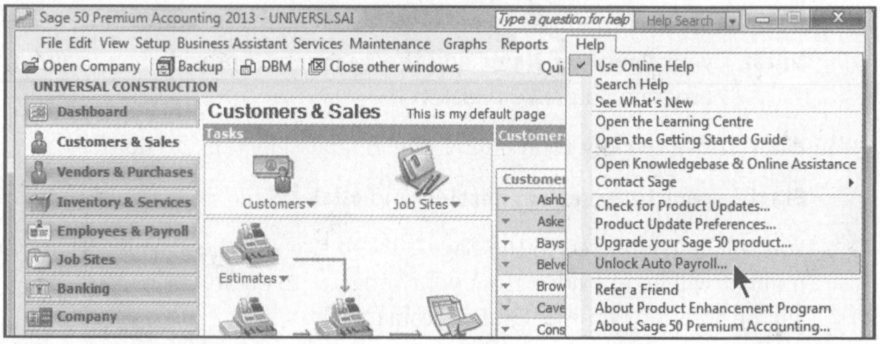

> **STUDENT VERSION**
> You will not see the payroll activation option or screens because payroll is already activated.

An information screen about payroll services for Sage 50 opens:

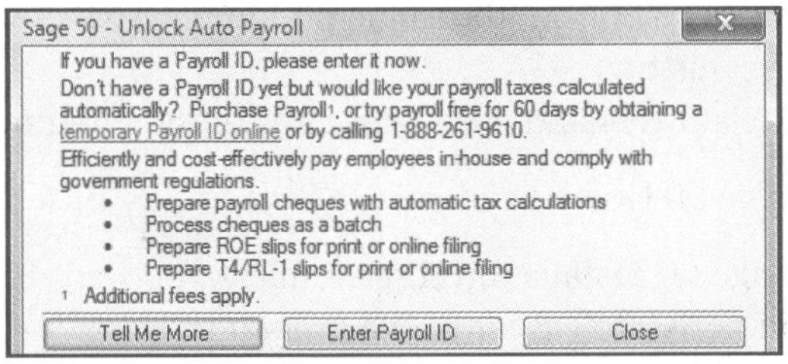

This screen advises you that you need a payroll ID and subscription to the Sage 50 Payroll Plan — a fee-based service — to use the payroll features in the program. To learn more about the payroll plan or to subscribe, click Tell Me More.

Click **Enter Payroll ID**:

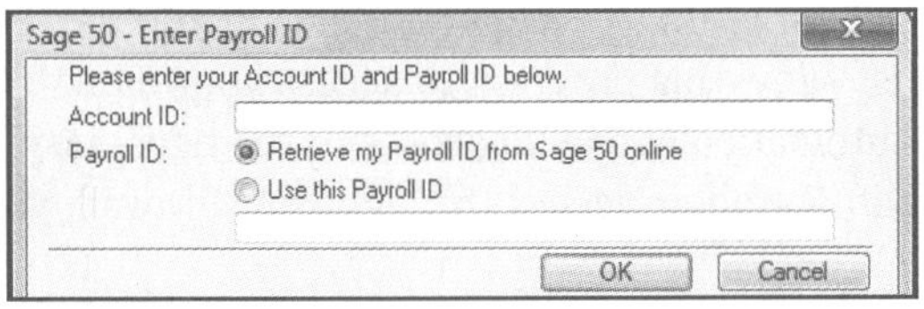

You must enter the account payroll ID numbers provided for your program registration. The default selection is to retrieve the payroll ID online.

Click the **Account ID field** and **type** your **account number**.

Click **OK**. (Be sure that you have started your Internet connection.)

The payroll ID will be downloaded directly to your program.

If you have the number already, you can enter it manually.

Click **Use This Payroll ID** to make this selection.

Click the **Payroll ID field** and **type** the **number** provided, exactly as it is given to you. The code is not case sensitive.

If the activation is successful, you will see the following message:

Click **OK** to continue.

After you have activated your program and unlocked payroll, you can retrieve these codes automatically by selecting the online options if you need to reinstall the program.

Turning Off Automatic Updates

You should not update the program beyond Release 1, the one we used for this text, so that your payroll amounts and screens will match the ones we show.

Choose the **Help menu** and **click** **Automatic Update Preferences** (refer to the Help menu shown on page A–6).

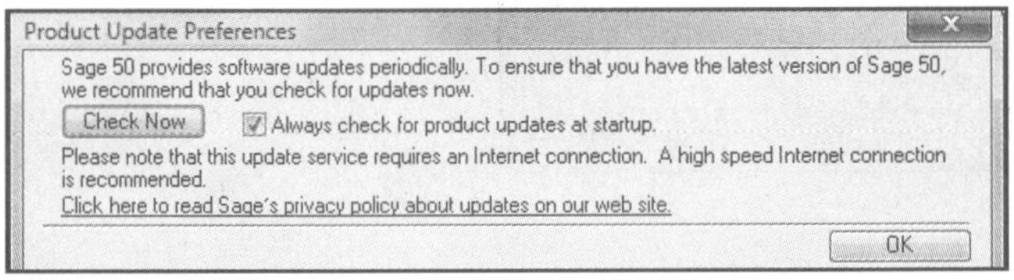

Click **Always Check For Product Updates At Startup** to **remove** the ✓ and turn off the automatic update option.

Click **OK** to continue working with your data files.

NOTES

If you have not activated the program yet, you can do so from the Help menu. Choose Enter Key Code from the Help menu to open the You Have XX Days Remaining screen shown on page A–5.

WARNING!

Do not remove the program CD before clicking Exit on the opening Sage 50 Installation screen (see the illustration on page A–2).

STUDENT VERSION

In the Student version, you will not see the message about updates.

WARNING!

Always Check For Updates At Startup has a ✓ beside it that indicates the automatic update feature is on. Click Always Check For... to remove the ✓ and turn off the option. Click OK to continue.

WARNING!
If you download program updates, you may download a later version than the one we use and your payroll amounts may be different from the ones we show. Payroll tables are updated every six months and the Release (1, 2 and so on) is linked to payroll tax table dates. After updating, you will no longer be able to open these data files with Release 1.

You can turn on automatic updates later from this same preferences window, after you have finished the applications in this text.

You can begin working with the data sets and use all features of the program.

Click to close the Sage 50 Home window.

Click **Exit** to close the Sage 50 Installation screen unless you want to install the guides. You can now safely remove the program CD.

Click to close the Windows Explorer or Computer window if it is open.

Firewall Settings

Sage 50 uses the Connection Manager program to access data files. If you have a firewall installed on your computer, you must allow this program to access your data. In most cases, the installation process will automatically enable access to the necessary components of the program. If you do not allow access through your firewall, you cannot open your data files.

If you are unable to open a data file, you may need to configure your firewall manually to allow access for the following .exe programs: Sage 50, Sage_SA_conv150, Sage_SA_conv160, Sage_SA_conv170, Sage_SA_conv180, Sage_SA_conv190, Sage_SA_conv200, Sage_SA_TST, Sage_SA_upgradejet, Sage_SA_upload, Sage_SA_ErrorLogSubmitter, SimplyConnectionManager, Simply.SystemTrayIcon, mysqld-nt and mysqladmin.

NOTES
If you see a run-time error message about the Connection Manager when you attempt to open a Sage 50 data file, you may need to start the Connection Manager program and/or configure your firewall settings manually to allow access. The programs listed are those required for Windows 7.

A complete list of the programs your firewall must not block is available from the Help menu Search option when you enter Firewall in the Search field (see Chapter 1, page 15).

INSTALLING SAGE 50 FROM DOWNLOAD

Download the **Sage 50 program** from the Sage Web site <na.sage.com>. You may see an initial security warning:

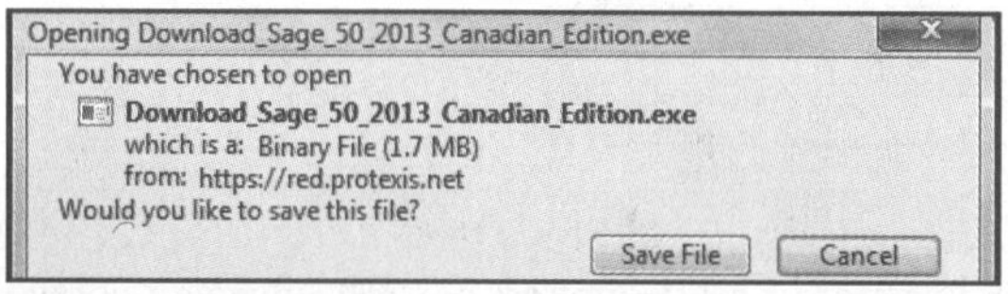

NOTES
The warnings you see will depend on the download and security settings on your computer.

Click **Save File**. An icon for the download is placed on your desktop.

Double-click the **download icon** on your desktop 

.

You may see another security message with a warning about running a program downloaded from the Internet:

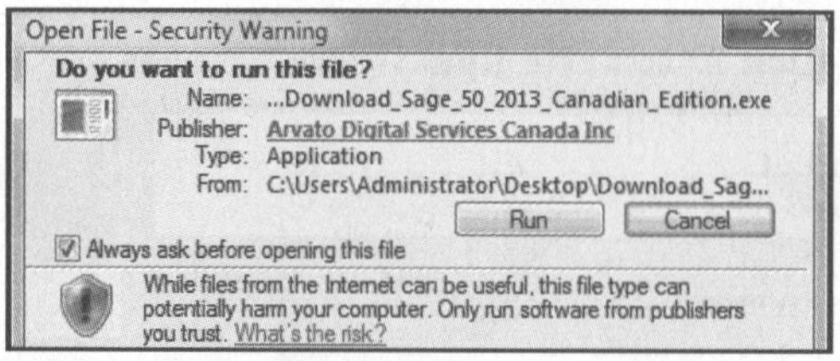

Click **Run**.

The downloaded file must be extracted. You can choose the location for the extracted program files from the screen that follows:

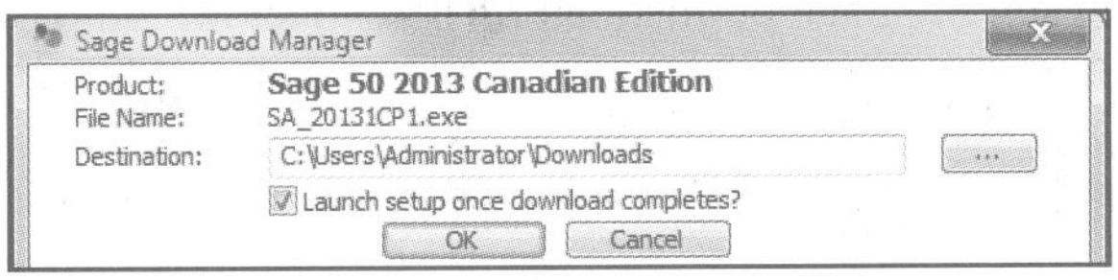

This screen also has the option to launch the program setup immediately after the files have been extracted — the default selection (✓ added) — or to complete the installation later.

Accept the **default location** or **click** the **... button** beside the File Name field and choose another location.

Click **OK** to continue and start the Sage Download Manager:

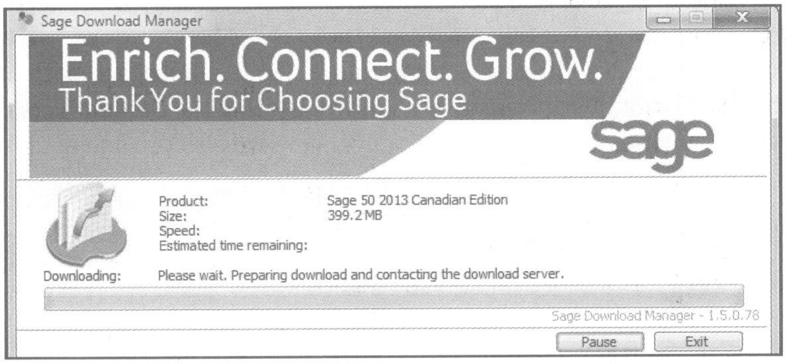

While the files are being downloaded, you will see the progress:

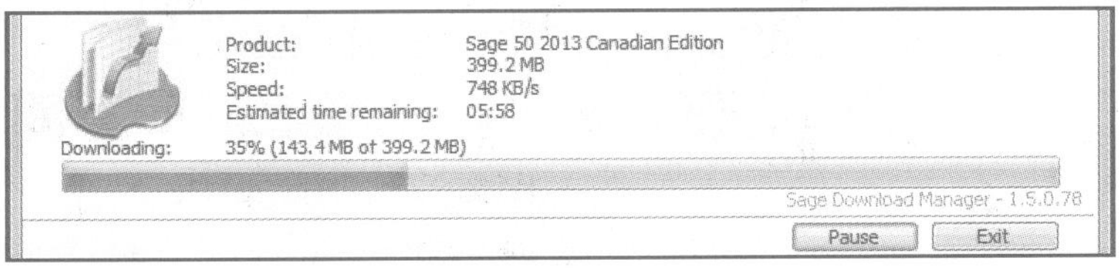

When finished, the Download Manager window has a **Launch** button and that will start the program installation. To install the program later, click **Exit**. When you are ready to install the program, find the file you need. The Desktop under Favorites is shown here as the location for the downloaded file:

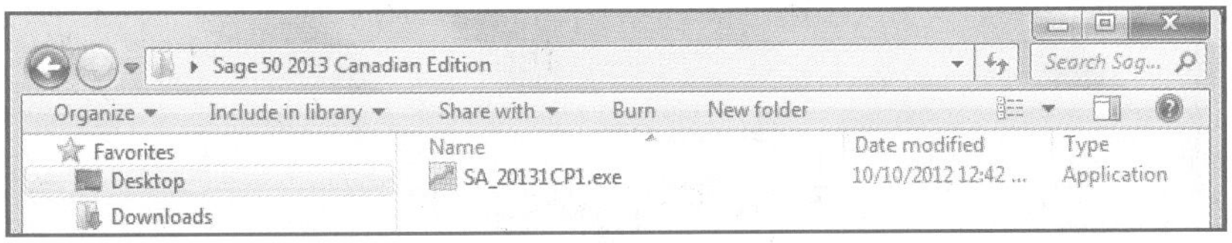

> **NOTES**
> If you change the location, make a note of it so that you can find the program later for installation.

> **NOTES**
> The Downloads folder is also located under Favorites in the Computer window. If you choose this location for your downloaded program file, click Downloads, then double-click Sage 50 2013 Canadian Edition and SA_20131-CP1.exe.

Beginning the Installation

Double-click the **Sage folder** 

and **program icon** 

(or filename **SA_2013CP1.exe**) to begin the installation. Or **click** **Launch** in the Sage Download Manager:

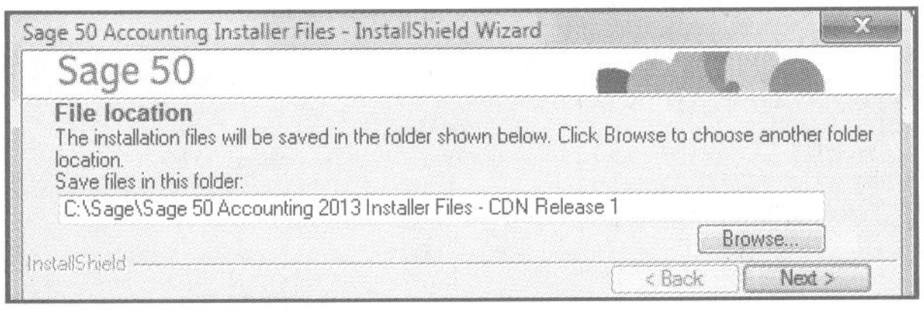

You are now asked to enter the location for the installer control files.

Accept the **default location** or **click** **Browse** and choose another location.

Click **Next**. You will see the Sage 50 Installation screen shown on page A–2.

Click **Install Sage 50** and follow the steps we show on page A–2.

DOWNLOADING, INSTALLING AND ACTIVATING THE STUDENT VERSION

NOTES
Versions of the Sage 50 program before 2013 are named Sage Simply Accounting.

STUDENT VERSION
The Student version is a single-user program.

The Student Premium version of Sage 50 is available only as a download and must be downloaded from the Sage 50 Web site <na.sage.com/sage-50-accounting-ca/download/2013/student>. The actual installation is the same as it is for the regular retail CD version of the program, so we will not repeat those steps here. Instead, we will demonstrate the steps involved in downloading the program and extracting the program files to start the installation. Because activating or registering the Student version is different from the activation of the regular retail version, we also provide detailed instructions for that process. These instructions begin on page A–12.

NOTES
Mozilla Firefox was used as the browser for the screenshots in this section. If you use Windows Internet Explorer, your screens and options may look different.

Downloading the Student Version Program

Start your **Internet connection** and **open** your **Web browser**.

Type `na.sage.com/sage-50-accounting-ca/download/2013/student` in the Web address field. **Press** *enter*:

WARNING!
If you have previously installed Sage 50, or an earlier Sage Simply Accounting Student version, you must uninstall that program before you can install the current Sage 50 2013 program. Use the Control Panel Programs – Uninstall A Program function to uninstall the program properly.

Refer to Using This Book, page xiii, for more information about different versions and the limitations of the Student version.

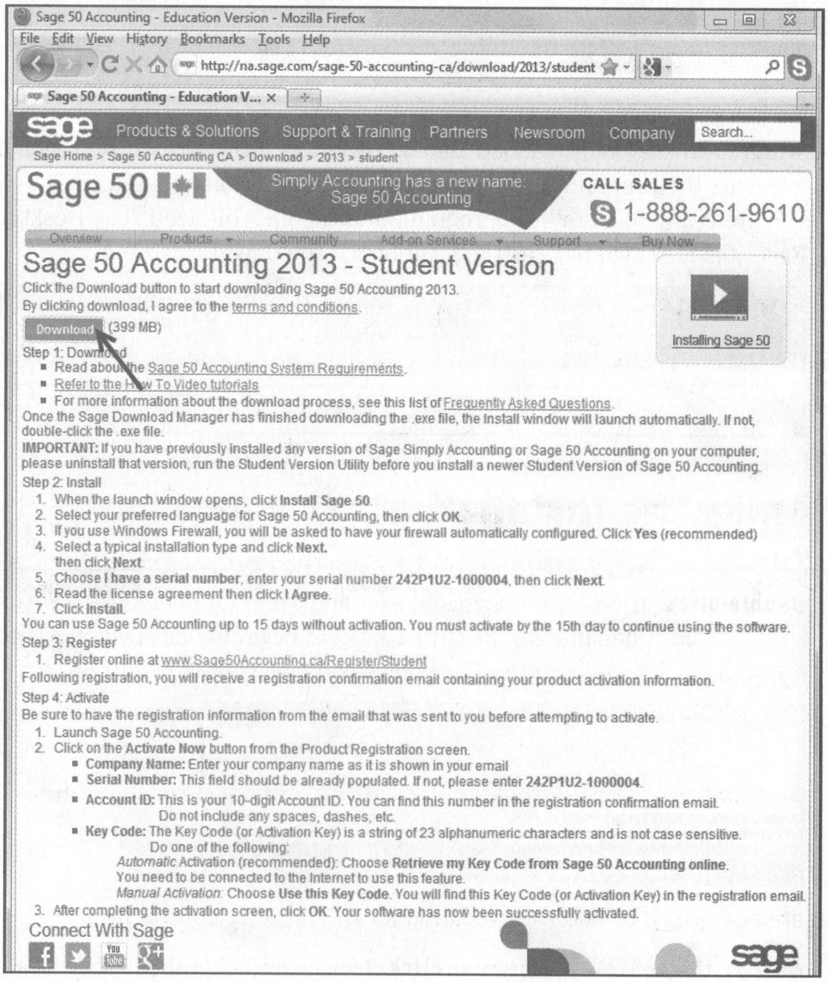

Click the **Download button**.

The next steps are the same as for the download of the retail version (pages A-8 – A-9), except that the download file and folder name include the word Student.

Choose to **Save** the file if asked. The file is saved to your desktop with an icon for it.

Double-click the **download icon** on your desktop 

. You may see another security message with the option to run the program.

Click **Run**. After the file has downloaded it must be extracted. You can choose the location for the installer and program files.

This screen also has the option to launch the program setup immediately after the files have been extracted — the default selection — or to complete the launch and installation later.

Accept the **default location** or **click** the **... button** beside the File Name field and choose another location.

Click **OK** to continue after making your choices. While the files are being downloaded, you will see the progress.

Click **Launch** on the Sage Download Manager window to begin the installation.

If you did not choose to launch immediately, make a note of this location for later and click OK to close the windows. When you are ready to install the program, find the file you need.

NOTES

At this stage you are downloading the Sage Download Manager controller. The program files are actually downloaded in the next stage.

NOTES

Click Run to continue and start the InstallShield Wizard if you see the warning on page A–8 about downloaded Internet files.

Beginning the Installation

Double-click the **Sage folder** 

on your desktop or in the Downloads folder to open it.

Double-click the file **SA_20131CP1.exe** or the **program icon** 

on your desktop or in your Downloads folder to begin the installation. Or **click Launch** in the Sage Download Manager:

You will see the Sage Installation screen — the same screen we show in this appendix on page A–3.

Continue the **installation** by following the instructions on pages A–2 to A–6.

Type `242P1U2-1000004` (see page A–3) when you are prompted to enter the serial number. (This serial number applies to all copies of the Student version program.)

Starting the Sage 50 program immediately is the default selection. You should choose this option so you can activate your program immediately.

STUDENT VERSION

It may take several minutes for all the program files to be extracted from the SA_20131CP1.exe file before you see the installation screens.

NOTES

Your options for opening and saving downloaded files will depend on your own computer settings. You may see a screen with the option to run the program immediately, or one with the options to save the file or cancel the download. The location of the downloaded file will also depend on the settings you have entered for your Internet browser program. Desktop or the Downloads folder are the most common default locations – we show Desktop as the location.

Activating the Student Version

When you start the Student version, you will see this message:

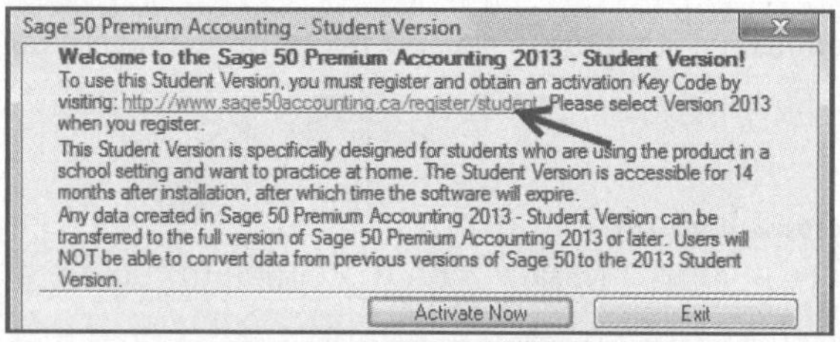

You must activate the program before you can use it. There is no trial period.

Do not click the **Activate Now button** because you do not have the key code.

If you are already at the Activation screen on page A–13 and you do not yet have the key code, click **Cancel** to return to the registration page.

Start your **Internet connection**.

Click **www.sage50accounting.ca/register/student** — the underlined Web address link in the Welcome screen — to open the Student Version Registration window for Sage 50:

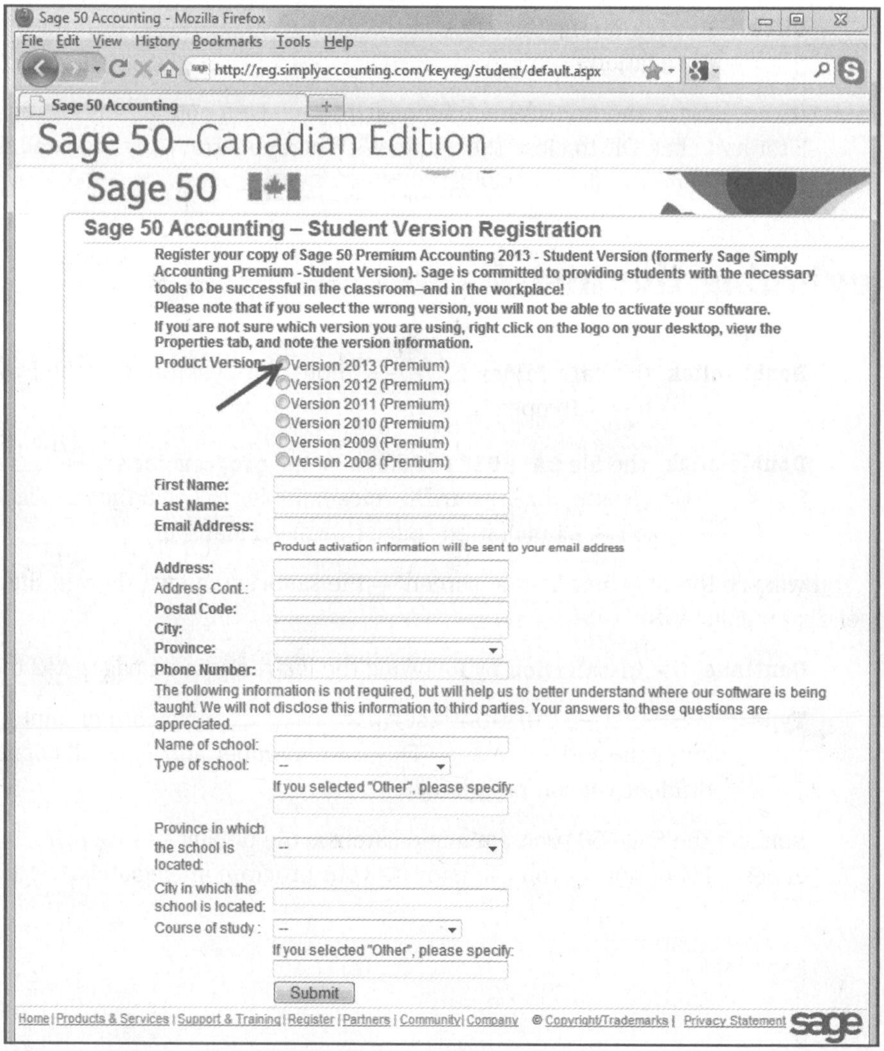

The required fields for your registration are included on the first part of this screen. These field names appear in bold face type.

STUDENT VERSION

The Student version must be registered and activated before you can use the program. Go to <www.sage50accounting.ca/register/student/> to get the key codes for activating the Student version. The Welcome screen has a link to this Web site.

The activation message warns that you can use the program for only 14 months and you will not be able to open data from previous versions of Sage Simply Accounting.

WARNING!

Clicking Activate Now will open the Activation screen that requires you to enter the key code (page A–13). Instead, you should go to the Web site from the previous screen that includes a direct link to the activation site.

If you are already at the Activation screen on page A–13 and you do not yet have the key code, click Cancel to return to the registration page.

NOTES

If your browser is open, you can type the address in the Address bar <www.sage50accounting.ca/register/student> . You must include the www.

WARNING!

Several versions can be activated from this site, so be sure to select the correct version.

Click **Version 2013 (Premium)** to select the version included with this text.

Enter **your own first and last name** in the two Name fields.

Enter your **e-mail address** in the E-Mail Address field.

Enter your **address** (**street**, **postal code**, **city** and **province**) and **phone number** in the appropriate fields.

You will receive an e-mail from Sage with the serial number and key code. Keep these numbers for reference.

The remaining fields are optional, but it is helpful for Sage to have these details.

Click **Submit** when you have finished. You will see a message confirming the successful registration:

Close your **Web browser page** to return to the Welcome registration screen.

Click **Cancel** to close the Activation screen because you do not yet have the key code. Wait for this e-mail.

You will receive an e-mail within the next three days with the key code for the next step.

Write down the **23-character key code** from your e-mail message — you will enter this on the Activation screen.

You can copy and paste the code from your e-mail into the key code fields.

Start the **Sage 50 program** (**double-click** the **Sage 50 Premium 2013 icon** on your desktop) to re-open the Activation window.

Click the **Activate Now button** to open the Student Version Activation screen:

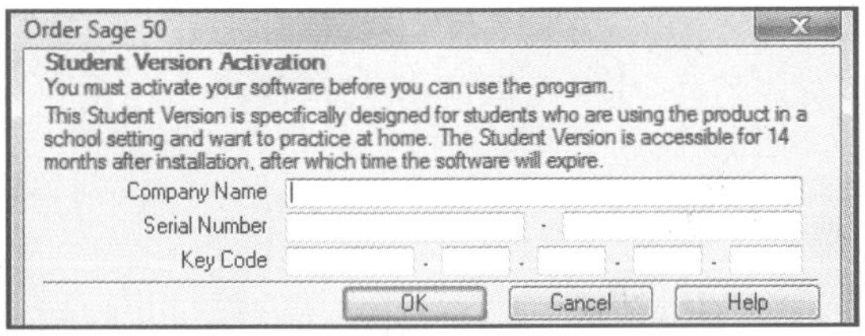

Type **your name** in the Company Name field. **Press** *tab* to advance to the Serial Number field.

Type 242P1U2-1000004 (This is the serial number for all copies of the Student version program.)

Press *tab* to advance to the **first Key Code field**.

Type the **23-character key code** from e-mail message you received.

NOTES

You will not need a payroll ID – payroll is activated as soon as you register.

STUDENT VERSION

The Student version does not have an Account ID field.

Click **OK**. Your Sage 50 Welcome screen opens and you can now use the program for 14 months.

Students needing help with the program should work with their instructor. Additional help for students is available online from the following Web site: **<www.sageforstudents.com/forums>**

Student Version Expired Error Message

WARNING! You must uninstall Sage 50 before you run the CleanUp utility program. And you must run the CleanUp utility program before starting the new installation.

When you try to activate the Student version, you may see a message that the Student version has expired and you can no longer use it.

If you have not used the program for 14 months, the "expired" message may be triggered by registry file information from a previous installation. If you see this message, you may have previously installed a version of the Sage 50 program. You must uninstall that program before you can install the current Sage 50 2013 program.

Click **Exit** to close this window and **uninstall** the **Student 2013 version** and any other version of Sage 50 you have installed.

Use the **Control Panel Programs - Uninstall A Program** function (Add/Remove Programs in Windows XP) to uninstall the program properly.

If you have already uninstalled all other Sage 50 programs and you still see this message when you try to activate the Student version, you will need to uninstall the Student version program again and then run the Student Version Utility.

Uninstall the **Sage 50 2013 Student version program**.

Start your **Internet connection** and **open** your **Web browser** if necessary.

Type `na.sage.com/sage-50-accounting-ca/download/2013/student` in the Web address field. **Press** *enter*.

NOTES You must uninstall any earlier Student versions of Sage Simply Accounting before installing the 2013 Sage 50 program. Then run the Student Version Utility (StudentVerCleanUp.exe) before installing the current version.

Click the **Student Version Utility program link** on this Web page (in the IMPORTANT statement at the end of Step 1 on the Download page) to download this program to your desktop.

Double-click the **desktop icon StudentVerCleanUp.exe** to run this program.

Click **OK** when you see a confirmation when the program has finished.

You should now be able to install and activate Sage 50 version 2013 by following the instructions on page A–9.

APPENDIX B

Shortcuts & Terminology

KEYBOARD SHORTCUTS

Using the Keyboard Instead of a Mouse

NOTES
The illustration in Chapter 1, page 13, shows several keyboard alternative commands in the pull-down Entry menu.

All Windows software applications are designed to be used with a mouse. However, there may be times when you prefer to use keyboard commands. And, if the mouse itself is inoperative, the keyboard alternatives may prevent you from losing data. A few basic principles will help you understand how they work. Some commands are common to more than one Windows software program. For example, ctrl + **C** (press and hold the Control key while you press C) is the copy command and ctrl + **V** is the paste command. Any selected text or image will be copied or pasted when you use these commands.

Pressing alt accesses the first menu bar item. Then press the arrow keys, ↑ and ↓, to move you up and down through the pull-down menu choices of a highlighted menu item or ← and → to go back and forth to other menu items. Some menu choices have direct keyboard alternatives or shortcuts. If the menu item has an underlined letter, pressing alt together with the underlined letter will access that option directly. For example, alt + **F** (press alt, and while holding down alt, press F) accesses the File pull-down menu. Then pressing O (the underlined letter for Open) will give you the dialogue box for opening a new file. Some tool buttons and menu choices in Sage 50 have a direct keyboard command. When available, these direct keystrokes are given with the tool button name or to the right of a menu choice. For example, alt + f4 is the shortcut for closing the active window or exiting from the Sage 50 program when the Home window is the active window.

To cancel a menu display, press esc.

In the Sage 50 Home window, you can use the arrow keys to move among the ledger and journal icons. Press alt, alt and → to highlight the first icon, and then use the arrow keys to change selections. Each icon is highlighted or selected as you reach it and deselected as you move to another icon.

To choose or open a highlighted or selected item, press enter.

When input fields are displayed in a Sage 50 window, press tab to move to the next field or shift and tab together to return to the previous field. The tab key is used frequently in this workbook as a quick way to accept input, advance the cursor to the next field and highlight field contents to prepare for editing. Using the mouse while you input information requires you to remove your hands from the keyboard, while the tab key does not.

NOTES
The same shortcuts in Sage 50 may have different functions, depending on the window you start from.

A summary of keyboard shortcuts used in Sage 50 is included on page A–16. Additional shortcuts using more than two keys, such as ctrl + shift + **A** for Allocate are also available. They are displayed in pull-down menus or with the tools for those commands.

SUMMARY OF BASIC KEYBOARD SHORTCUTS

Shortcut	Resulting Action
ctrl + A	Adjust, begin the Adjust a Posted Entry function.
ctrl + B	Bring the Home window to the front.
ctrl + C	Copy the selected text.
ctrl + E	Look up the previously posted invoice (from a journal lookup window).
ctrl + F	Search, begin the search function.
ctrl + J	Display the journal entry report.
ctrl + K	Track shipment from a previously posted invoice lookup screen.
ctrl + L	Look up a previously posted transaction (from the journal window).
ctrl + N	Look up the next posted invoice (from a journal lookup window).
ctrl + N	Open a new record window (from a ledger icon or ledger record window).
ctrl + P	Print, open the print dialogue box.
ctrl + R	Recall a stored journal entry (from a journal window when an entry is stored).
ctrl + R	Remove the account record, or remove the quote or order (from ledger, quote or order window).
ctrl + S	Access the Save As function from the Home window (Home window, File menu) to save the data file under a new name. Keep the new file open.
ctrl + S	Save changes to a record; keep the ledger window open (from any ledger window).
ctrl + T	Store the current journal entry (open the Store dialogue box).
ctrl + V	Paste the selected text at the cursor position.
ctrl + X	Cut (delete) the selected text.
ctrl + Z	Undo the most recent change.
alt + C	Create another record; saves the record you are creating and opens a new record form to create another new record.
alt + N	Save and close; save the new record and close the ledger.
alt + P	Post the journal entry or record the order or quote.
alt + f4	Close the active window (if it has a close button). Closes the program if the Home window is active.
alt + the underlined character on a button	Select the button's action. An alternative to clicking the button and/or pressing enter.
alt	Access the first item on the menu bar.
tab	Advance the cursor to the next field.
shift + tab	Move the cursor to the previous field.
Click	Move the cursor or select an item or entry.
shift + Click	Select all the items between the first item clicked and the last one.
ctrl + Click	Select this item in addition to ones previously selected.
enter	Choose the selected item or action.
Double-click	Select an entire word or field contents. In fields with lists, open the selection list.
→	Move right to the next icon to select it or to the next character in text.
←	Move left to the next icon to select it or to the next character in text.
↓	Move down to the next icon or entry in a list to select it.
↑	Move up to the previous icon or entry in a list to select it.

ACCOUNTING VS. NON-ACCOUNTING TERMS

We have used accounting terms in this workbook because they are familiar to students of accounting and because we needed to provide a consistent language for the book. The most frequently used non-accounting terms are included here for reference and comparison, in case you want to leave the non-accounting terms selected (Home window, Setup menu, User Preferences, Options screen — see page 81).

The chart shows the terms used for the Pro version and for the Premium version when the Other Industry type is selected. For other industries in the Premium version, the terms in the chart on the following page — Terminology Used for Different Types of Industries — will replace the Non-accounting Terms for Payables and Receivables. For example, you may see Providers and Expenses or Supporters and Revenues. The term Suppliers generally replaces Vendors.

SUMMARY OF EQUIVALENT TERMS

MAJOR TERMS	ACCOUNTING TERMS	NON-ACCOUNTING TERMS
	Journal Entries	Transaction Details
	Payables	Vendors & Purchases
	Receivables	Customers & Sales
	Post	Process

DETAILED LIST: LOCATION	ACCOUNTING TERMS	NON-ACCOUNTING TERMS
Setup menu – Settings screen	Payables	Vendors & Purchases
	Receivables	Customers & Sales
Setup menu, User Preferences, View screen – Modules/Pages	Payables (Classic View)	Vendors & Purchases
	Receivables (Classic View)	Customers & Sales
Graphs menu	Payables	Unpaid Purchases
	Receivables	Unpaid Sales
Reports menu and Report Centre – Financials	General Ledger	Transactions by Account
Report Centre – Financials	All Journal Entries	All Transactions
Reports menu and Report Centre	Payables	Vendors & Purchases
	Receivables	Customers & Sales
Reports menu	Journal Entries	Transaction Details
Reports menu – Management Reports	Payables	Vendors & Purchases
	Receivables	Customers & Sales
All Icon window menus	Journal	Transactions
Accounts ledger window	General Ledger	Chart of Accounts Records
Vendors ledger window	Payables Ledger	Vendor Records
Customers ledger window	Receivables Ledger	Customer Records
All journals (button and menu)	Post	Process

INDUSTRY TYPES AND TERMS

In the Premium version, the terms and labels change when you select different types of industries (Setup menu, Settings, Company, Information screen — see page 75). The chart on the following page summarizes the terms you will see when you apply different industry types. You can change the default industry terminology on the Settings, Names screens for the Payables and Receivables modules.

TERMINOLOGY USED FOR DIFFERENT TYPES OF INDUSTRIES

INDUSTRY	TERMS OR LABELS USED IN RECEIVABLES LEDGER				
	Customers	**Sales Invoices**	**Sales Quotes**	**Sales Orders**	**Sales Journal – Invoice**
Pro version (all)	Customers	Sales Invoices	Sales Quotes	Sales Orders	Sales Journal – Invoice
Premium Version					
Accommodation	Guests	Charges	Sales Quotes	Sales Orders	Sales Journal – Charge
Agriculture	Customers	Customer Invoices	Customer Quotes	Customer Orders	Revenues Journal – Invoice
Construction/ Contractor	Customers	Bills	Estimates	Contracts	Sales Journal – Bill
Educational Service	Clients	Statements	Client Quotes	Client Orders	Fees Journal – Statement
Entertainment	Customers	Sales Invoices	Sales Quotes	Sales Orders	Sales Journal – Invoice
Food & Beverage	Guests	Charges	Sales Quotes	Sales Orders	Sales Journal – Charge
Manufacturing/ Industrial	Customers	Sales Invoices	Sales Quotes	Sales Orders	Sales Journal – Invoice
Medical/Dental	Patients	Statements	Patient Quotes	Patient Orders	Fees Journal – Statement
Non-Profit	Supporters	Statements	Supporter Quotes	Supporter Orders	Revenues Journal – Statement
Other	Customers	Sales Invoices	Sales Quotes	Sales Orders	Sales Journal – Invoice
Personal Service	Clients	Client Invoices	Client Quotes	Client Orders	Revenues Journal – Invoice
Professional Service	Clients	Client Invoices	Client Quotes	Client Orders	Fees Journal – Invoice
Real Estate/Property	Clients	Statements	Client Quotes	Client Orders	Revenues Journal – Statement
Retail	Customers	Sales Invoices	Sales Quotes	Sales Orders	Sales Journal – Invoice
Service	Clients	Client Invoices	Client Quotes	Client Orders	Revenues Journal – Invoice
Transportation	Customers	Sales Invoices	Sales Quotes	Sales Orders	Sales Journal – Invoice

INDUSTRY	TERMS OR LABELS USED IN PAYABLES LEDGER				
	Vendors	**Purchase Invoices**	**Purchase Quotes**	**Purchase Orders**	**Purchases Journal – Purchase Invoice**
Pro version (all)	Vendors	Purchase Invoices	Purchase Quotes	Purchase Orders	Purchases Journal – Invoice
Premium Version					
Accommodation	Suppliers	Invoices	Purchase Quotes	Purchase Orders	Purchases Journal – Invoice
Agriculture	Suppliers	Purchase Invoices	Purchase Quotes	Purchase Orders	Purchases Journal – Invoice
Construction/ Contractor	Suppliers	Invoices	Quotes	Orders	Purchases Journal – Invoice
Educational Service	Suppliers	Invoices	Purchase Quotes	Purchase Orders	Purchases Journal – Invoice
Entertainment	Suppliers	Supplier Invoices	Supplier Quotes	Supplier Orders	Expenses Journal – Invoice
Food & Beverage	Suppliers	Invoices	Purchase Quotes	Purchase Orders	Purchases Journal – Invoice
Manufacturing/ Industrial	Suppliers	Purchase Invoices	Purchase Quotes	Purchase Orders	Purchases Journal – Invoice
Medical/Dental	Suppliers	Invoices	Supplier Quotes	Supplier Orders	Expenses Journal – Invoice
Non-Profit	Providers	Invoices	Provider Quotes	Provider Orders	Expenses Journal – Invoice
Other	Vendors	Purchase Invoices	Purchase Quotes	Purchase Orders	Purchases Journal – Invoice
Personal Service	Suppliers	Supplier Invoices	Supplier Quotes	Supplier Orders	Expenses Journal – Invoice
Professional Service	Vendors	Vendor Invoices	Vendor Quotes	Vendor Orders	Expenses Journal – Invoice
Real Estate/Property	Suppliers	Invoices	Supplier Quotes	Supplier Orders	Expenses Journal – Invoice
Retail	Suppliers	Purchase Invoices	Purchase Quotes	Purchase Orders	Purchases Journal – Invoice
Service	Suppliers	Supplier Invoices	Supplier Quotes	Supplier Orders	Expenses Journal – Invoice
Transportation	Vendors	Purchase Invoices	Purchase Quotes	Purchase Orders	Purchases Journal – Invoice

Terms for Project Project (for Other, Service, Personal Service, Professional Service, Transportation and all industries in Pro version), Division (for Accommodation, Education, Entertainment, Food, Manufacturing and Retail), Crops (for Agriculture), Job Site (for Construction), Partner (for Medical), Fund (for Non-profit), Property (for Real Estate)

APPENDIX C

Correcting Errors after Posting

We all make mistakes. This appendix outlines briefly the procedures you need to follow for those rare occasions when you have posted a journal entry incorrectly and you need to reverse it manually. In most cases, you can use the Adjust Journal Entry or Reverse Entry procedures to make corrections.

Obviously, you should try to detect errors before posting. Reviewing journal entries should become routine practice. The software also has built-in safeguards that help you avoid mistakes. For example, outstanding invoices cannot be overpaid and employee wages and payroll deductions are calculated automatically. Furthermore, names of accounts, customers, vendors, employees and inventory items appear in full, so that you can check your journal information easily.

Before making a reversing entry, consider the consequences of not correcting the error. For example, misspelled customer names may not be desirable, but they will not influence the financial statements. After making the correction in the ledger, the newly printed statement will be correct (the journal will retain the original spelling). Sometimes, however, the mistake is more serious. Financial statements will be incorrect if amounts or accounts are wrong. Payroll tax deductions will be incorrect if a wage amount or linked account is incorrect. GST/HST and PST remittances may be incorrect as a result of incorrect tax codes or sales or purchase amounts. Discounts will be incorrectly calculated if an invoice or payment date is incorrect. Some errors also originate from outside sources. For example, purchase items may be incorrectly priced by the vendor.

NOTES

Adjusting entry procedures are shown on:

page 43 – General Journal
page 127 – Purchases
page 129 – Other Payments
page 137 – Payments
page 182 – Sales
page 274 – Paycheque
page 294 – Payroll Run Entry

Reversing entry procedures are explained on:

page 45 – General Journal
page 139 – Purchases
pages 176 and 605 – Receipts
page 276 – Payroll
page 250 – Historical invoices

For audit purposes, prepare a memo explaining the error and the correction procedure. A complete reversing entry is often the simplest way to make the corrections for a straightforward audit trail. With the one-step reversing entry feature from the Adjust Entry or Lookup window in Sage 50, the reversing entry is made automatically. This feature is available for General Journal entries, paycheques, sales, purchases, receipts and most payments. Choose Adjust Invoice from the pull-down menu under the corresponding transaction menu, or click the Adjust Invoice tool in the journal. Then make the corrections if possible, or choose Reverse Entry from the pull-down menu under the corresponding transaction menu or click the Reverse tool. Under all circumstances, you should follow generally accepted accounting principles. Sage 50 will create the reversing entry automatically. Reports will include the correct entries after you post the adjusted journal entry. Including the original and reversing entries in reports is optional.

However, this feature is not available for all journals. And when the journal entry deposit account for a receipt is not the bank account (because the deposit was made later), you need to reverse a receipt manually to record an NSF cheque. In this appendix we will illustrate the procedure for reversing entries in all journals.

Reversing entries in all journals have several common elements. In each case, you should use an appropriate source number that identifies the entry as reversing (e.g., add ADJ or REV to the original source number). You should use the original posting date and add a comment. Make the reversing entry as illustrated on the following pages. Display the journal entry, review it carefully and, when you are certain it is correct, post it. Next, you must enter the correct version of the transaction as a new journal entry with an appropriate identifying source number (e.g., add COR to the original source number).

Reversing entries are presented for each journal. Only the transaction portion of each screen is shown because the remaining parts of the journal screen do not change. The original and reversing entry screens and their corresponding journal displays are included. Explanatory notes appear beside each set of entries.

GENERAL JOURNAL

Use the same accounts and amounts in the reversing entry as in the original entry.

Accounts that were debited originally should be credited, and accounts that were credited originally should be debited.

Click the Sales Taxes button if you used this screen. Choose the tax code and, if necessary, enter the Amount Subject To Tax with a minus sign.

Repeat the allocation using the original percentages.

The General Journal display is not shown because it basically looks the same as the journal input form.

You can use the Adjust Entry or Reverse Entry features instead. See page 43 and page 45.

GENERAL JOURNAL: Original Entry

Account	Debits	Credits	Comment	Allo
1360 Paint & Supplies	200.00	--	paint supplies	
2670 GST Paid on Purch	10.00	--	GST @ 5%	
2120 A/P - Western Sky	--	210.00	terms: net 20	
Total	210.00	210.00		

Reversing Entry

Account	Debits	Credits	Comment	Allo
2120 A/P - Western Sky	210.00	--	reversing A/P amount	
1360 Paint & Supplies	--	200.00	reversing supplies amount	
2670 GST Paid on Purch	--	10.00	reversing GST @ 5%	
Total	210.00	210.00		

PURCHASES JOURNAL

The only change you must make is that positive amounts in the original entry become negative amounts in the reversing entry (place a minus sign before the amount in the Amount field).

Similarly, negative amounts, such as for GST/HST Paid in GST/HST remittances, must be changed to positive amounts (remove the minus sign).

If freight was charged, enter the amount of freight with a minus sign.

Use the same accounts and amounts in the reversing entry as in the original entry. Tax amounts change automatically.

Repeat the allocation with the original percentages.

You can use the Adjust Invoice and Reverse Invoice options instead (page 127 and page 139). Reversing a paid invoice will generate a credit note.

Remember to "pay" the incorrect and reversing invoices to remove them from the Payments Journal and later clear them.

PURCHASES JOURNAL (NON-INVENTORY): Original Entry

Item Number	Quantity	Order	Back Order	Unit	Item Description	Price	Tax	HST	Amount	Account	Divisions
					lift repairs		H	39.00	300.00	5140 Repair...	[Multiple Divisions]

Subtotal: 300.00
Freight:
HST: 39.00
Total: 339.00

Early Payment Terms: 2.00 % 20 Days, Net 30 Days

Purchases Journal Entry 12/07/15 (J21)

Account Number	Account Description	Division	Debits	Credits	Division Amt
2670	HST Paid on Purchases		39.00	-	
5140	Repairs & Maintenance		300.00	-	
		- Sales Division			90.00
		- Service Division			210.00
2200	Accounts Payable		-	339.00	
Additional Date:	Additional Field:		339.00	339.00	

Reversing Entry

Item Number	Quantity	Order	Back Order	Unit	Item Description	Price	Tax	HST	Amount	Account	Divisions
					reversing lift repairs entry		H	-39.00	-300.00	5140 Repair...	[Multiple Divisions]

Subtotal: -300.00
Freight:
HST: -39.00
Total: -339.00

Early Payment Terms: 2.00 % 20 Days, Net 30 Days

Purchases Journal Entry 12/07/15 (J23)

Account Number	Account Description	Division	Debits	Credits	Division Amt
2200	Accounts Payable		339.00	-	
2670	HST Paid on Purchases		-	39.00	
5140	Repairs & Maintenance		-	300.00	
		- Sales Division			-90.00
		- Service Division			-210.00
Additional Date:	Additional Field:		339.00	339.00	

PAYMENTS JOURNAL – OTHER PAYMENTS: Original Entry

Acct	Description	Amount	Tax	HST	Allo
5150 Telephone Expense	telephone service	180.00	H	23.40	√

Subtotal	180.00
Tax	23.40
Total	203.40

Payments Journal Entry 12/08/15 (J24)

Account Number	Account Description	Division	Debits	Credits	Division Amt
2670	HST Paid on Purchases		23.40	-	
5150	Telephone Expense		180.00	-	
		- Sales Division			72.00
		- Service Division			108.00
1050	Bank: Chequing CAD		-	203.40	
Additional Date:	Additional Field:		203.40	203.40	

Reversing Entry

Acct	Description	Amount	Tax	HST	Allo
5150 Telephone Expense	reversing telephone service entry	-180.00	H	-23.40	√

Subtotal	-180.00
Tax	-23.40
Total	-203.40

Payments Journal Entry 12/08/15 (J26)

Account Number	Account Description	Division	Debits	Credits	Division Amt
1050	Bank: Chequing CAD		203.40	-	
2670	HST Paid on Purchases		-	23.40	
5150	Telephone Expense		-	180.00	
		- Sales Division			-72.00
		- Service Division			-108.00
Additional Date:	Additional Field:		203.40	203.40	

Sage 50 - Confirmation

This cheque does not have a positive amount and is using a cheque number. Do you want to continue anyway?

Yes No

PAYROLL REMITTANCES: Original Entry

Remitting Frequency: Monthly End of Remitting Period: Dec 31, 2015

Remittance	Amount Owing	Payment Adjustment Account	Payment Adjustment	Payment Amount
CSB	400.00	1050 Bank: Chequing CAD		400.00
			Total	400.00

Payments Journal Entry

		Account Number	Account Description	Debits	Credits
12/31/15	(J33)	Memo 44, Equity Life : CSB remittance			
		2400	CSB Payable	400.00	-
		2200	Accounts Payable	-	400.00
12/31/15	(J34)	203, Equity Life : CSB remittance			
		2200	Accounts Payable	400.00	-
		1050	Bank: Chequing CAD	-	400.00
Additional Date:	Additional Field:			800.00	800.00

Reversing Entry

Remitting Frequency: Monthly End of Remitting Period: Dec 31, 2015

Remittance	Amount Owing	Payment Adjustment Account	Payment Adjustment	Payment Amount
CSB	0.00	1050 Bank: Chequing CAD		-400.00
			Total	-400.00

OTHER PAYMENTS

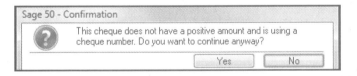

The only change you must make is that positive amounts in the original entry become negative amounts in the reversing entry (place a minus sign before the amount in the Amount field).

Similarly, negative amounts, such as for GST/HST Paid in GST/HST remittances, must be changed to positive amounts (remove the minus sign).

Use the same accounts and amounts in the reversing entry as in the original entry. Tax amounts change automatically.

Repeat the allocation with the original percentages.

You can use the Adjust Invoice and Reverse Invoice options instead (page 129).

If you see a message about using the next cheque number with a negative amount, click No and enter a memo number or other reference in the cheque number field.

PAYROLL REMITTANCES

Payroll remittances are reversed in the same way as other payments. Enter the same cheque date and End Of Remitting Period date as you did for the original transaction and then enter the original amounts with a minus sign added.

Enter a memo number or other reference in the cheque number field to avoid using a cheque number for a negative amount.

You can also adjust and reverse these payments automatically. Open the Remittance Journal and search for the remittance you want. From the Adjust window, you can make changes or use the Reverse tool to reverse the entry completely.

PAYMENTS

Click , the Include Fully Paid Invoices tool button.

The change you must make is that positive amounts in the original entry become negative amounts in the reversing entry.

If a discount was taken, click the Discount Taken field on the invoice line for the payment being reversed. Type the discount amount with a minus sign. Press tab to enter the payment amount. The minus sign will be added.

If no discount was taken, click the Payment Amount field on the invoice line for the payment being reversed. Type a minus sign and the amount.

Click No if you see the warning about posting a negative cheque amount and enter another reference number instead. This will restore the original balance owing for the invoice.

You can also use the Adjust Payment tool or the Reverse Payment feature. (See page 137 and page 176.)

If you have already cleared the paid invoice, prepare a new Purchases Journal entry for the amount of the payment (non-taxable) to restore the balance owing. Enter a positive amount in the Amount field for the amount of the cheque and the Bank account in the Account field (to avoid entering the expense twice). On the next line, enter the discount amount (positive) with the Purchase Discounts account in the Account field. This will debit the Bank and Purchase Discounts accounts and credit Accounts Payable.

CREDIT CARD PAYMENTS

Enter the same amounts as in the original entry.

Add a minus sign to the Additional Fees And Interest amount and to the Payment Amount in the reversing entry.

Enter a memo number or other reference in the cheque number field to avoid using a cheque number for a negative amount.

Payments Journal Entry

		Account Number	Account Description	Debits	Credits
12/31/15	(J35)	Memo 44, Equity Life : reversing CSB remittance			
		2200	Accounts Payable	400.00	-
		2400	CSB Payable	-	400.00
12/31/15	(J36)	203, Equity Life : reversing CSB remittance			
		1050	Bank: Chequing CAD	400.00	-
		2200	Accounts Payable	-	400.00
Additional Date:		Additional Field:		800.00	800.00

PAYMENTS: Original Entry

Due Date	Invoice or Prepayment	Original Amount	Amount Owing	Discount Available	Discount Taken	Payment Amount
Dec 27, 2015	LTR-456	452.00	452.00	9.04	9.04	442.96
					Total	442.96

Payments Journal Entry 12/10/15 (J35)

Account Number	Account Description	Debits	Credits
2200	Accounts Payable	452.00	-
1050	Bank: Chequing CAD	-	442.96
5130	Purchase Discounts	-	9.04
Additional Date:	Additional Field:	452.00	452.00

Reversing Entry

Due Date	Invoice or Prepayment	Original Amount	Amount Owing	Discount Available	Discount Taken	Payment Amount
Dec 21, 2015	L-4441	316.40	0.00	0.00		
Dec 27, 2015	LTR-456	452.00	0.00	0.00	-9.04	-442.96
					Total	-442.96

Payments Journal Entry 12/10/15 (J36)

Account Number	Account Description	Debits	Credits
1050	Bank: Chequing CAD	442.96	-
5130	Purchase Discounts	9.04	-
2200	Accounts Payable	-	452.00
Additional Date:	Additional Field:	452.00	452.00

CREDIT CARD PAYMENTS: Original Entry

Credit Card Payable Account Balance:	235.00
Additional Fees and Interest:	22.00
Payment Amount:	122.00

Payments Journal Entry 12/10/15 (J37)

Account Number	Account Description	Debits	Credits
2250	Credit Card Payable	100.00	-
5040	Credit Card Fees	22.00	-
1050	Bank: Chequing CAD	-	122.00
Additional Date:	Additional Field:	122.00	122.00

Reversing Entry

Credit Card Payable Account Balance:	113.00
Additional Fees and Interest:	-22.00
Payment Amount:	-122.00

Payments Journal Entry 12/10/15 (J38)

Account Number	Account Description	Debits	Credits
1050	Bank: Chequing CAD	122.00	-
2250	Credit Card Payable	-	100.00
5040	Credit Card Fees	-	22.00
Additional Date:	Additional Field:	122.00	122.00

INVENTORY PURCHASES: Original Entry

Item Number	Quantity	Order	Back Order	Unit	Item Description	Price	Tax	HST	Amount	Account	Divisions
T102	20			Each	P175/70R14 Tires	34.00	H	88.40	680.00	1400 Winte...	
T104	20			Each	P205/75R15 Tires	56.00	H	145.60	1,120.00	1400 Winte...	

Subtotal: 1,800.00
Freight: 200.00 H 26.00
HST: 260.00
Early Payment Terms: % Days, Net 30 Days Total: 2,260.00

Purchases Journal Entry 12/09/15 (J39)

Account Number	Account Description	Division	Debits	Credits	Division Amt
1400	Winter Tires		1,800.00	-	
2670	HST Paid on Purchases		260.00	-	
5065	Freight Expense		200.00	-	
		- Sales Division			200.00
2200	Accounts Payable		-	2,260.00	
Additional Date:	Additional Field:		2,260.00	2,260.00	

Reversing Entry

Item Number	Quantity	Order	Back Order	Unit	Item Description	Price	Tax	HST	Amount	Account	Divisions
T102	-20			Each	P175/70R14 Tires	34.00	H	-88.40	-680.00	1400 Winte...	
T104	-20			Each	P205/75R15 Tires	56.00	H	-145.60	-1,120...	1400 Winte...	

Subtotal: -1,800.00
Freight: -200.00 H -26.00
HST: -260.00
Early Payment Terms: % Days, Net 30 Days Total: -2,260.00

Purchases Journal Entry 12/09/15 (J40)

Account Number	Account Description	Division	Debits	Credits	Division Amt
2200	Accounts Payable		2,260.00	-	
1400	Winter Tires		-	1,800.00	
2670	HST Paid on Purchases		-	260.00	
5065	Freight Expense		-	200.00	
		- Sales Division			-200.00
Additional Date:	Additional Field:		2,260.00	2,260.00	

SALES JOURNAL (INVENTORY AND NON-INVENTORY): Original Entry

Item Number	Quantity	Order	Back Order	Unit	Item Description	Price	Amount	Tax	Account	Divisions
T104	4			Each	P205/75R15 Tires	100.00	400.00	H	4020 Rev...	Sales Division
W104	4			Each	Aluminum R17 Wheels	225.00	900.00	H	4020 Rev...	Sales Division
					custom repairs		200.00	H	4040 Rev...	Service Division

Subtotal: 1,500.00
Freight: 100.00 H 13.00
HST: 208.00
Early Payment Terms: % Days, Net 30 Days Total: 1,808.00

Sales Journal Entry 12/14/15 (J41)

Account Number	Account Description	Division	Debits	Credits	Division Amt
1200	Accounts Receivable		1,808.00	-	
5050	Cost of Goods Sold		520.00	-	
		- Sales Division			520.00
1360	Wheels		-	360.00	
1400	Winter Tires		-	160.00	
2650	HST Charged on Sales		-	208.00	
4020	Revenue from Sales		-	1,300.00	
		- Sales Division			1,300.00
4040	Revenue from Services		-	200.00	
		- Service Division			200.00
4180	Freight Revenue		-	100.00	
		- Sales Division			100.00
Additional Date:	Additional Field:		2,328.00	2,328.00	

INVENTORY PURCHASES

Change positive quantities in the original entry to negative ones in the reversing entry (place a minus sign before the quantity in the Quantity field).

Similarly, change negative quantities, such as for returns, to positive ones (remove the minus sign).

Add a minus sign to the freight amount if freight is charged.

Use the same accounts and amounts in the reversing entry as in the original entry. Tax amounts are corrected automatically.

Repeat the allocation using the original percentages.

You can use the Adjust Invoice and Reverse Invoice options instead (page 127 and page 139).

Remember to "pay" the incorrect and reversing invoices to remove them from the Payments Journal and later clear them.

SALES JOURNAL

For inventory sales, change positive quantities in the original entry to negative ones in the reversing entry (place a minus sign before the quantity in the Quantity field). Similarly, change negative quantities, such as for returns, to positive ones (remove the minus sign).

For non-inventory sales, change positive amounts in the original entry to negative amounts in the reversing entry (place a minus sign before the amount in the Amount column).

Add a minus sign to the freight amount if freight is charged. Add the salesperson.

Use the same accounts and amounts in the reversing entry as in the original entry, and the same method of payment.

Repeat the allocation using the original percentages.

You can use the Adjust Invoice and Reverse Invoice options instead (page 182). Reversing a paid invoice will generate a credit note.

Remember to "pay" the incorrect and reversing invoices to remove them from the Receipts Journal and later clear them.

Reversing Entry

Item Number	Quantity	Order	Back Order	Unit	Item Description	Price	Amount	Tax	Account	Divisions
T104	-4			Each	P205/75R15 Tires	100.00	-400.00	H	4020 Rev...	Sales Division
W104	-4			Each	Aluminum R17 Wheels	225.00	-900.00	H	4020 Rev...	Sales Division
					custom repairs		-200.00	H	4040 Rev...	Service Division

Subtotal: -1,500.00
Freight: -100.00 H -13.00
Early Payment Terms: % Days, Net 30 Days
HST: -208.00
Total: -1,808.00

Sales Journal Entry 12/15/15 (J42)

Account Number	Account Description	Division	Debits	Credits	Division Amt
1360	Wheels		360.00	-	
1400	Winter Tires		160.00	-	
2650	HST Charged on Sales		208.00	-	
4020	Revenue from Sales		1,300.00	-	
		- Sales Division			-1,300.00
4040	Revenue from Services		200.00	-	
		- Service Division			-200.00
4180	Freight Revenue		100.00	-	
		- Sales Division			-100.00
1200	Accounts Receivable		-	1,808.00	
5050	Cost of Goods Sold		-	520.00	
		- Sales Division			-520.00
Additional Date:	Additional Field:		2,328.00	2,328.00	

NOTES
The Cost of Goods Sold amounts may have changed if you are using the average cost method and other transactions with different prices have taken place since the original sale.

DEPOSITS or PREPAYMENTS: Original Entry

Invoice Date	Invoice or Deposit	Original Amount	Amount Owing	Discount Available	Discount Taken	Amount Received
Dec 13, 2015	130	4,725.66	4,725.66	94.51		

Deposit Reference No. 13
Deposit Amount 1,500.00
Total 1,500.00

Receipts Journal Entry 12/15/15 (J43)

Account Number	Account Description	Debits	Credits
1050	Bank: Chequing CAD	1,500.00	-
2150	Prepaid Sales and Deposits	-	1,500.00
Additional Date:	Additional Field:	1,500.00	1,500.00

DEPOSITS
You cannot enter a negative amount in the Deposit field, so you must "pay" the deposit.
Click the Payment Amount field for the Deposit line and press *tab*. Deposit amounts are shown in red under the heading Deposits.

Reversing Entry

Invoice Date	Invoice or Deposit	Original Amount	Amount Owing	Discount Available	Discount Taken	Amount Received
Dec 13, 2015	130	4,725.66	4,725.66	94.51		
	Deposits					
	13	1,500.00	1,500.00			1,500.00

Deposit Reference No. 14
Deposit Amount 0.00
Total -1,500.00

Receipts Journal Entry 12/15/15 (J44)

Account Number	Account Description	Debits	Credits
2150	Prepaid Sales and Deposits	1,500.00	-
1050	Bank: Chequing CAD	-	1,500.00
Additional Date:	Additional Field:	1,500.00	1,500.00

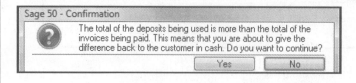

Sage 50 - Confirmation

The total of the deposits being used is more than the total of the invoices being paid. This means that you are about to give the difference back to the customer in cash. Do you want to continue?

Yes No

NOTES
When you post the transaction, you will be asked to confirm that you want to make the payment to the customer – you are returning the deposit. Click Yes to continue.

RECEIPTS WITH DEPOSITS: Original Entry

Invoice Date	Invoice or Deposit	Original Amount	Amount Owing	Discount Available	Discount Taken	Amount Received
Dec 13, 2015	130	4,725.66	4,725.66	94.51	94.51	4,631.15
	Deposits					
	15	1,500.00	1,500.00			1,500.00

Deposit Reference No. 16 Deposit Amount 0.00

Total 3,131.15

Receipts Journal Entry 12/15/15 (J57)

Account Number	Account Description	Debits	Credits
1050	Bank: Chequing CAD	3,131.15	-
2150	Prepaid Sales and Deposits	1,500.00	-
4150	Sales Discounts	94.51	-
1200	Accounts Receivable	-	4,725.66
Additional Date:	Additional Field:	4,725.66	4,725.66

Reversing Entry

Invoice Date	Invoice or Deposit	Original Amount	Amount Owing	Discount Available	Discount Taken	Amount Received
Dec 13, 2015	130	4,725.66	0.00	0.00	-94.51	-4,631.15
	Deposits					
	15	1,500.00	0.00			-1,500.00

Deposit Reference No. 16 Deposit Amount 0.00

Total -3,131.15

Receipts Journal Entry 12/15/15 (J58)

Account Number	Account Description	Debits	Credits
1200	Accounts Receivable	4,725.66	-
1050	Bank: Chequing CAD	-	3,131.15
2150	Prepaid Sales and Deposits	-	1,500.00
4150	Sales Discounts	-	94.51
Additional Date:	Additional Field:	4,725.66	4,725.66

PAYROLL JOURNAL: Original Income Tab Entry

Income | Vacation | Deductions | Taxes | User-Defined Expenses | Entitlements   How do I process a paycheque?

Earnings	Hours	Pieces	Rate	This Period	Year to Date
Regular	80.00	--	18.00	1,440.00	32,960.00
Overtime 1	4.00	--	27.00	108.00	924.00
Piece Rate	--	10.00	5.00	50.00	50.00
Bonus	--	--	--	100.00	100.00
Total:	84.00	10.00		1,698.00	

Other Amounts	This Period	Year to Date
Advances	0.00	--
Loans	100.00	100.00
Benefits	25.00	125.00
Total:	125.00	

Gross Pay: 1,723.00
Withheld: 437.03
Net Pay: **1,360.97**   Post

Reversing Income Tab Amounts

Income | Vacation | Deductions | Taxes | User-Defined Expenses | Entitlements   How do I process a paycheque?

Earnings	Hours	Pieces	Rate	This Period	Year to Date
Regular	-80.00	--	18.00	-1,440.00	30,080.00
Overtime 1	-4.00	--	27.00	-108.00	708.00
Piece Rate	--	-10.00	5.00	-50.00	-50.00
Bonus	--	--	--	-100.00	-100.00
Total:	-84.00	-10.00		-1,698.00	

Other Amounts	This Period	Year to Date
Advances	0.00	--
Loans	-100.00	0.00
Benefits	-25.00	100.00
Total:	-125.00	

Gross Pay: -1,723.00
Withheld: -437.03
Net Pay: **-1,360.97**   Post

RECEIPTS

Click , the Include Fully Paid Invoices tool.

Change positive amounts in the original entry to negative amounts in the reversing entry.

If a discount was taken, click the Discount Taken field on the invoice line for the receipt being reversed. Type the discount amount with a minus sign. Press *tab* to enter the payment amount. The minus sign will be added. Type a minus sign and enter the amount for the deposit.

If no discount was taken, click the Amount Received field on the invoice line for the receipt being reversed. Type a minus sign with the invoice receipt amount and with the deposit amount.

This will restore the original balance owing for the invoice.

You can use the Adjust Receipt and Reverse Receipt options instead (page 176).

If an NSF cheque uses a different bank account from the deposit entry, you must reverse the receipt manually. Choose the Bank account in the Deposit To field (page 605).

If you have already cleared the invoice, make a new Sales Journal entry for the payment amount (non-taxable) to restore the balance owing. Enter both the cheque and discount amounts as positive amounts and enter the Bank and Sales Discounts accounts instead of Revenue.

PAYROLL JOURNAL

Redo the original incorrect entry but DO NOT POST IT!

Click the Enter Taxes Manually tool to open all the deduction fields for editing.

Type a minus sign in front of the number of hours (regular and overtime) or in front of salary, commission and bonus amounts and piece rate quantity. Press *tab* to update all amounts, including vacation pay (change them to negative amounts). ▶

PAYROLL JOURNAL CONTINUED

▶For the Advances and Loans fields, change the sign for the amount. Advances and loans should have a minus sign in the reversing entry and advances and loans recovered should be positive amounts.

Click the Deductions tab and edit each deduction amount by typing a minus sign in front of it.

Click the Taxes tab. Check the amounts for CPP, EI and Tax with the original journal entry because these amounts may be incorrect (the employee may have reached the maximum contribution since the original entry, or may have entered a different tax bracket). Change the amounts to match the original entry if necessary. The Employee Detail Report will provide the amounts entered for each paycheque.

Click the User-Defined Expenses tab. Change the original positive amounts to negative by adding a minus sign.

Click the Entitlements tab. Add a minus sign to the number of hours worked. You cannot enter a negative number for Days Taken and earned. Enter the number of days taken in the Days Earned field. Enter the number of days earned in the Days Taken field.

Repeat the allocation with the original percentages and post.

Remember to click the Calculate Taxes Automatically button before you make the correct payroll entry.

The year-to-date balances will be restored.

You can use the Adjust Cheque option or Reverse Cheque instead to reverse and correct the Paycheque or Payroll Run journal entry (see page 274 and page 294). Using the reverse cheque approach may be safer, as payroll transactions are complex.

Enter a memo number or other reference in the cheque or deposit number field to avoid using a cheque number for a negative amount.

Original Payroll Vacation Tab Entry

Income | Vacation | Deductions | Taxes | User-Defined Expenses | Entitlements — How do I process a paycheque?

Type	This Period Hours	This Period Amount	Year to Date Hours	Year to Date Amount
Balance Forward (as of Jan 01, 2015)	--	--	--	--
Vacation Earned	--	63.92	--	1,974.52
Vacation Paid *	0.00	0.00	--	--
Vacation Owed	--	--	--	1,974.52

* These hours are recorded as EI Insurable Hours

Reversing Vacation Tab Amounts

Income | Vacation | Deductions | Taxes | User-Defined Expenses | Entitlements — How do I process a paycheque?

Type	This Period Hours	This Period Amount	Year to Date Hours	Year to Date Amount
Balance Forward (as of Jan 01, 2015)	--	--	--	--
Vacation Earned	--	-63.92	--	1,846.68
Vacation Paid *	0.00	0.00	--	--
Vacation Owed	--	--	--	1,846.68

* These hours are recorded as EI Insurable Hours

Original Entries for Deductions and Taxes Tabs

Income | Vacation | Deductions | Taxes | User-Defined Expenses | Entitlements

Deduction	This Period	Year to Date
CSB	50.00	350.00
Union Dues	17.23	340.59
Total:	67.23	

Income | Vacation | Deductions | Taxes | User-Defined Expenses | Entitlements

Tax	This Period	Year to Date
CPP	78.63	1,443.50
EI	29.24	735.33
Tax	261.93	5,470.89
Total:	369.80	

Reversing Amounts for Deductions and Taxes Tabs

Income | Vacation | Deductions | Taxes | User-Defined Expenses | Entitlements

Deduction	This Period	Year to Date
CSB	-50.00	300.00
Union Dues	-17.23	306.13
Total:	-67.23	

Income | Vacation | Deductions | Taxes | User-Defined Expenses | Entitlements

Tax	This Period	Year to Date
CPP	-78.63	1,286.24
EI	-29.24	676.85
Tax	-261.93	4,947.03
Total:	-369.80	

Original Entries for User-Defined Expenses and Entitlements Tabs

Income | Vacation | Deductions | Taxes | User-Defined Expenses | Entitlements

Employer-paid payroll expenses

Expense	This Period	Year to Date
Medical Prem	42.00	42.00
Total:	42.00	

Income | Vacation | Deductions | Taxes | User-Defined Expenses | Entitlements

Hours worked this period: 80.00

Entitlement	Days Earned	Days Taken	Net Days Accrued
Vacation	0.00	0.00	0.00
Sick Leave	0.50	1.00	7.50
Personal Day	0.25	1.00	0.75

Reversing Amounts for User-Defined Expenses and Entitlements Tabs

Income | Vacation | Deductions | Taxes | User-Defined Expenses | Entitlements

Employer-paid payroll expenses

Expense	This Period	Year to Date
Medical Prem	-42.00	-42.00
Total:	-42.00	

Income | Vacation | Deductions | Taxes | User-Defined Expenses | Entitlements

Hours worked this period: -80.00

Entitlement	Days Earned	Days Taken	Net Days Accrued
Vacation	0.00	0.00	0.00
Sick Leave	1.00	0.50	8.00
Personal Day	1.00	0.25	1.50

Original Payroll Journal Entry

Payroll Journal Entry 12/15/15 (J46)

Account Number	Account Description	Debits	Credits
1210	Loans Payable	100.00	-
5310	General Wages	1,611.92	-
5320	Piece Rate Wage Expense	50.00	-
5325	Medical Premium Expense	42.00	-
5330	Commissions and Bonuses	100.00	-
5410	EI Expense	40.94	-
5420	CPP Expense	78.63	-
5430	WSIB Expense	58.58	-
5460	EHT Expense	16.89	-
1050	Bank: Chequing CAD	-	1,360.97
2225	Medical Payable	-	42.00
2300	Vacation Payable	-	63.92
2310	EI Payable	-	70.18
2320	CPP Payable	-	157.26
2330	Income Tax Payable	-	261.93
2390	EHT Payable	-	16.89
2400	CSB Payable	-	50.00
2410	Union Dues Payable	-	17.23
2460	WSIB Payable	-	58.58
Additional Date:	Additional Field:	2,098.96	2,098.96

Reversing Payroll Journal Entry

Payroll Journal Entry 12/15/15 (J46)

Account Number	Account Description	Debits	Credits
1050	Bank: Chequing CAD	1,360.97	-
2225	Medical Payable	42.00	-
2300	Vacation Payable	63.92	-
2310	EI Payable	70.18	-
2320	CPP Payable	157.26	-
2330	Income Tax Payable	261.93	-
2390	EHT Payable	16.89	-
2400	CSB Payable	50.00	-
2410	Union Dues Payable	17.23	-
2460	WSIB Payable	58.58	-
1210	Loans Payable	-	100.00
5310	General Wages	-	1,611.92
5320	Piece Rate Wage Expense	-	50.00
5325	Medical Premium Expense	-	42.00
5330	Commissions and Bonuses	-	100.00
5410	EI Expense	-	40.94
5420	CPP Expense	-	78.63
5430	WSIB Expense	-	58.58
5460	EHT Expense	-	16.89
Additional Date:	Additional Field:	2,098.96	2,098.96

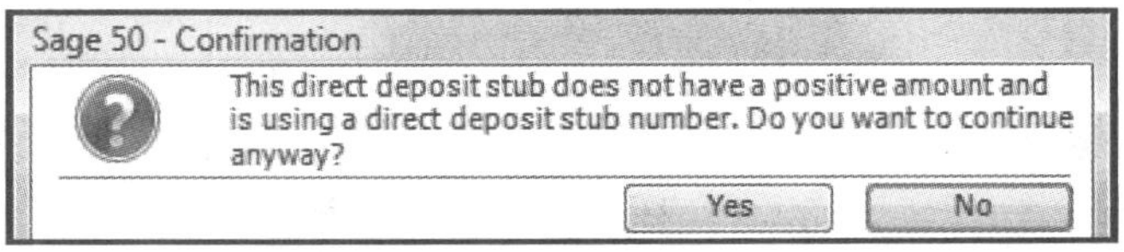

Sage 50 - Confirmation
This direct deposit stub does not have a positive amount and is using a direct deposit stub number. Do you want to continue anyway?
Yes
No

NOTES

When you are reversing a direct deposit entry, you must confirm that a negative amount is entered as the net deposit.

Click No. Enter a memo number or other reference in the cheque or deposit number field to avoid using a deposit stub number for a negative amount.

ITEM ASSEMBLY JOURNAL

Re-enter the assembly as you did originally.

Type a minus sign in front of each quantity in the Qty field in both the Assembly Components and Assembled Items sections.

Also type a minus sign in front of the amount for Additional Costs.

If you know the actual original unit costs and they have changed, you can enter the original cost amounts in the reversing entry.

ITEM ASSEMBLY JOURNAL: Original Entry

Assembly Components

Item	Qty	Unit	Description	Unit Cost	Amount
T110	20	Each	P195/65R16 Tires	55.00	1,100.00
W107	20	Each	Chrome-Steel R16 Wheels	38.00	760.00
				Additional Costs	250.00
				Total	2,110.00

Assembled Items

Item	Qty	Unit	Description	Unit Cost	Amount
WHP1	5	PKG	Tires/Wheels/Winter Pkg	422.00	2,110.00
				Total	2,110.00

Bill of Materials & Item Assembly Journal Entry 12/15/15 (J49)

Account Number	Account Description	Debits	Credits
1420	Winter-Holiday Tire Packages	2,110.00	-
1360	Wheels	-	760.00
1400	Winter Tires	-	1,100.00
5045	Assembly Costs	-	250.00
Additional Date:	Additional Field:	2,110.00	2,110.00

Reversing Entry

Assembly Components

Item	Qty	Unit	Description	Unit Cost	Amount
T110	-20	Each	P195/65R16 Tires	55.00	-1,100.00
W107	-20	Each	Chrome-Steel R16 Wheels	38.00	-760.00
				Additional Costs	-250.00
				Total	-2,110.00

Assembled Items

Item	Qty	Unit	Description	Unit Cost	Amount
WHP1	-5	PKG	Tires/Wheels/Winter Pkg	422.00	-2,110.00
				Total	-2,110.00

Bill of Materials & Item Assembly Journal Entry 12/16/15 (J49)

Account Number	Account Description	Debits	Credits
1360	Wheels	760.00	-
1400	Winter Tires	1,100.00	-
5045	Assembly Costs	250.00	-
1420	Winter-Holiday Tire Packages	-	2,110.00
Additional Date:	Additional Field:	2,110.00	2,110.00

ADJUSTMENTS JOURNAL

Change the sign for the quantity in the Qty field (positive to negative or negative to positive).

If you know the actual original unit costs and they have changed, you can enter the original cost amounts in the reversing entry.

Repeat the allocation using the original percentages.

ADJUSTMENTS JOURNAL: Original Entry

Item	Qty	Unit	Description	Unit Cost	Amount	Acct	Allo
W101	-2	Each	Aluminum R14 Wheels	72.00	-144.00	5100 Invent	✓
				Total	-144.00		

Inventory Adjustments Journal Entry 12/15/15 (J50)

Account Number	Account Description	Division	Debits	Credits	Division Amt
5100	Inventory Adjustment		144.00	-	
		- Service Division			144.00
1360	Wheels		-	144.00	
Additional Date:	Additional Field:		144.00	144.00	

Reversing Entry

Item	Qty	Unit	Description	Unit Cost	Amount	Acct	Allo
W101	2	Each	Aluminum R14 Wheels	72.00	144.00	5100 Invent	√
				Total	144.00		

Inventory Adjustments Journal Entry 12/15/15 (J50)

Account Number	Account Description	Division	Debits	Credits	Division Amt
1360	Wheels		144.00	-	
5100	Inventory Adjustment		-	144.00	
		- Service Division			-144.00
Additional Date:	Additional Field:		144.00	144.00	

TRANSFER FUNDS JOURNAL: Original Entry

Currency:	JPY	Exchange Rate:	0.0131000
Transfer from:	1050 Bank: Chequing CAD		
Transfer to:	1060 Bank: Foreign Currency		
Amount:	40,000	JPY	
Comment:	Transfer to cover cheques		

Reversing Entry

Currency:	JPY	Exchange Rate:	0.0131000
Transfer from:	1060 Bank: Foreign Currency		
Transfer to:	1050 Bank: Chequing CAD		
Amount:	40,000	JPY	
Comment:	reversing funds transfer entry		

General Journal 12/15/15 to 12/15/15

	Account Number	Account Description	Debits	Credits	Foreign A...
12/15/15 J51	Funds Transfer, Transfer to cover cheques				
	1060	Bank: Foreign Currency	524.00	-	¥40,000
	1050	Bank: Chequing CAD	-	524.00	¥40,000
1 Japanese Yen equals 0.0131000 Canadian Dollars					
12/15/15 J52	Funds Transfer, reversing funds transfer entry				
	1050	Bank: Chequing CAD	524.00	-	¥40,000
	1060	Bank: Foreign Currency	-	524.00	¥40,000
1 Japanese Yen equals 0.0131000 Canadian Dollars			1,048.00	1,048.00	

TRANSFER INVENTORY JOURNAL: Original Entry

Transfer between Locations — From: Velocity — to: Ryder

Source: Memo 22 — Date: Aug 22, 2015

Comment: Transfer items to create promotional packages

Item	Qty	Unit	Description	Unit Cost	Amount
AC010	5	unit	Bicycle Pump: standing mo	30.00	150.00
AC030	5	helmet	Helmet	60.00	300.00

Reversing Entry

Transfer between Locations — From: Ryder — to: Velocity

Source: Memo 23 — Date: Aug 22, 2015

Comment: Reverse transfer of items to create promotional packages

Item	Qty	Unit	Description	Unit Cost	Amount
AC010	5	unit	Bicycle Pump: standing mo	30.00	150.00
AC030	5	helmet	Helmet	60.00	300.00

TRANSFER FUNDS JOURNAL

The easiest way to reverse the transfer is to enter the same amounts but switch the bank accounts. Enter the original Transfer From account in the Transfer To field. Enter the original Transfer To account in the Transfer From field.

There is no journal entry to review. You can see the reversal in the General Journal Report. The two related General Journal Report entries are shown here.

For foreign currency transfers, use the same exchange rate for both the original and the reversing transfer.

You can also use the Adjust Entry or Reverse Entry procedure for the transfer in the General Journal. When you look up transactions, the transfer entry is included. You can select it and then adjust it or reverse it like any other General Journal transaction (see page 43 and page 45).

TRANSFER INVENTORY JOURNAL

You cannot enter a negative quantity in the Transfer Inventory Journal.

Enter the transaction in the same way as the original one with one change – switch the locations for the From and To fields. Enter the original From location in the To field and the original To location in the From field.

No journal entry results from this transaction. However, the inventory ledger records will be updated for both locations.

BILL OF MATERIALS JOURNAL

Change the sign for the quantity in the Quantity To Build field (positive to negative or negative to positive).

Notice that the journal entries are the same as those for the Item Assembly Journal transactions on page A–27.

Costs may have changed since you entered the original transaction when you are using the average cost of goods method. You cannot change the unit costs in the Bill of Materials method.

BILL OF MATERIALS JOURNAL: Original Entry

Items to Build

Item	Unit	Description	Quantity to build
AP100	package	Promotional Safety Package	5

Bill of Materials & Item Assembly Journal Entry 08/19/2015 (J12)

Account Number	Account Description	Debits	Credits
1510	Promotions	2,970.00	-
1520	Accessories	-	1,120.00
1540	Bicycles	-	1,100.00
5045	Item Assembly Costs	-	750.00
Additional Date:	Ref. Number:	2,970.00	2,970.00

Reversing Entry

Items to Build

Item	Unit	Description	Quantity to build
AP100	package	Promotional Safety Package	-5

Bill of Materials & Item Assembly Journal Entry 08/19/2015 (J13)

Account Number	Account Description	Debits	Credits
1520	Accessories	1,120.00	-
1540	Bicycles	1,100.00	-
5045	Item Assembly Costs	750.00	-
1510	Promotions	-	2,970.00
Additional Date:	Ref. Number:	2,970.00	2,970.00

INDEX

PAGES A31–A218 ON STUDENT DVD

Appendix D, A-31 – A-70
Appendix E, A-71 – A-84
Appendix F, A-85 – A-94
Appendix G, A-95 – A-106
Appendix H, A-107 – A-134
Appendix I, A-135 – A-140
Appendix J, A-141 – A-150
Appendix K, A-151 – A-166
Appendix L, A-167 – A-176
Appendix M, A-177 – A-186
Appendix N, A-187 – A-206
Appendix O, A-207 – A-218

PAGES A31–A218 ON STUDENT DVD

PAGES A31–A218 ON STUDENT DVD

Appendix D, A–31 – A–70
Appendix E, A–71 – A–84
Appendix F, A–85 – A–94
Appendix G, A–95 – A–106
Appendix H, A–107 – A–134
Appendix I, A–135 – A–140
Appendix J, A–141 – A–150
Appendix K, A–151 – A–166
Appendix L, A–167 – A–176
Appendix M, A–177 – A–186
Appendix N, A–187 – A–206
Appendix O, A–207 – A–218

PAGES A31–A218 ON STUDENT DVD

PAGES A31–A218 ON STUDENT DVD

Appendix D, A–31 – A–70
Appendix E, A–71 – A–84
Appendix F, A–85 – A–94
Appendix G, A–95 – A–106
Appendix H, A–107 – A–134
Appendix I, A–135 – A–140
Appendix J, A–141 – A–150
Appendix K, A–151 – A–166
Appendix L, A–167 – A–176
Appendix M, A–177 – A–186
Appendix N, A–187 – A–206
Appendix O, A–207 – A–218

PAGES A31–A218 ON STUDENT DVD

PAGES A31–A218 ON STUDENT DVD

Appendix D, A-31 – A-70
Appendix E, A-71 – A-84
Appendix F, A-85 – A-94
Appendix G, A-95 – A-106
Appendix H, A-107 – A-134
Appendix I, A-135 – A-140
Appendix J, A-141 – A-150
Appendix K, A-151 – A-166
Appendix L, A-167 – A-176
Appendix M, A-177 – A-186
Appendix N, A-187 – A-206
Appendix O, A-207 – A-218

"AS IS" LICENCE AGREEMENT AND LIMITED WARRANTY

READ THIS LICENCE CAREFULLY BEFORE OPENING THIS PACKAGE. BY OPENING THIS PACKAGE, YOU ARE AGREEING TO THE TERMS AND CONDITIONS OF THIS LICENCE. IF YOU DO NOT AGREE, DO NOT OPEN THE PACKAGE. PROMPTLY RETURN THE UNOPENED PACKAGE AND ALL ACCOMPANYING ITEMS TO THE PLACE YOU OBTAINED THEM. THESE TERMS APPLY TO ALL LICENSED SOFTWARE ON THE DISK EXCEPT THAT THE TERMS FOR USE OF ANY SHAREWARE OR FREEWARE ON THE DISKETTES ARE AS SET FORTH IN THE ELECTRONIC LICENCE LOCATED ON THE DISK:

1. GRANT OF LICENCE and OWNERSHIP: The enclosed computer programs and any data ("Software") are licensed, not sold, to you by Pearson Canada Inc. ("We" or the "Company") in consideration of your adoption of the accompanying Company textbooks and/or other materials, and your agreement to these terms. You own only the disk(s) but we and/or our licensors own the Software itself. This licence allows instructors and students enrolled in the course using the Company textbook that accompanies this Software (the "Course") to use and display the enclosed copy of the Software for academic use only, so long as you comply with the terms of this Agreement. You may make one copy for back up only. We reserve any rights not granted to you.

2. USE RESTRICTIONS: You may not sell or license copies of the Software or the Documentation to others. You may not transfer, distribute or make available the Software or the Documentation, except to instructors and students in your school who are users of the adopted Company textbook that accompanies this Software in connection with the course for which the textbook was adopted. You may not reverse engineer, disassemble, decompile, modify, adapt, translate or create derivative works based on the Software or the Documentation. You may be held legally responsible for any copying or copyright infringement that is caused by your failure to abide by the terms of these restrictions.

3. TERMINATION: This licence is effective until terminated. This licence will terminate automatically without notice from the Company if you fail to comply with any provisions or limitations of this licence. Upon termination, you shall destroy the Documentation and all copies of the Software. All provisions of this Agreement as to limitation and disclaimer of warranties, limitation of liability, remedies or damages, and our ownership rights shall survive termination.

4. DISCLAIMER OF WARRANTY: THE COMPANY AND ITS LICENSORS MAKE NO WARRANTIES ABOUT THE SOFTWARE, WHICH IS PROVIDED "AS-IS." IF THE DISK IS DEFECTIVE IN MATERIALS OR WORKMANSHIP, YOUR ONLY REMEDY IS TO RETURN IT TO THE COMPANY WITHIN 30 DAYS FOR REPLACEMENT UNLESS THE COMPANY DETERMINES IN GOOD FAITH THAT THE DISK HAS BEEN MISUSED OR IMPROPERLY INSTALLED, REPAIRED, ALTERED OR DAMAGED. THE COMPANY DISCLAIMS ALL WARRANTIES, EXPRESS OR IMPLIED, INCLUDING WITHOUT LIMITATION, THE IMPLIED WARRANTIES OF MERCHANTABILITY AND FITNESS FOR A PARTICULAR PURPOSE. THE COMPANY DOES NOT WARRANT, GUARANTEE OR MAKE ANY REPRESENTATION REGARDING THE ACCURACY, RELIABILITY, CURRENTNESS, USE, OR RESULTS OF USE, OF THE SOFTWARE.

5. LIMITATION OF REMEDIES AND DAMAGES: IN NO EVENT, SHALL THE COMPANY OR ITS EMPLOYEES, AGENTS, LICENSORS OR CONTRACTORS BE LIABLE FOR ANY INCIDENTAL, INDIRECT, SPECIAL OR CONSEQUENTIAL DAMAGES ARISING OUT OF OR IN CONNECTION WITH THIS LICENCE OR THE SOFTWARE, INCLUDING, WITHOUT LIMITATION, LOSS OF USE, LOSS OF DATA, LOSS OF INCOME OR PROFIT, OR OTHER LOSSES SUSTAINED AS A RESULT OF INJURY TO ANY PERSON, OR LOSS OF OR DAMAGE TO PROPERTY, OR CLAIMS OF THIRD PARTIES, EVEN IF THE COMPANY OR AN AUTHORIZED REPRESENTATIVE OF THE COMPANY HAS BEEN ADVISED OF THE POSSIBILITY OF SUCH DAMAGES. SOME JURISDICTIONS DO NOT ALLOW THE LIMITATION OF DAMAGES IN CERTAIN CIRCUMSTANCES, SO THE ABOVE LIMITATIONS MAY NOT ALWAYS APPLY.

6. GENERAL: THIS AGREEMENT SHALL BE CONSTRUED AND INTERPRETED ACCORDING TO THE LAWS OF THE PROVINCE OF ONTARIO. This Agreement is the complete and exclusive statement of the agreement between you and the Company and supersedes all proposals, prior agreements, oral or written, and any other communications between you and the company or any of its representatives relating to the subject matter.

Should you have any questions concerning this agreement or if you wish to contact the Company for any reason, please contact in writing: Permissions, Pearson Canada Inc., 26 Prince Andrew Place, Toronto, Ontario M3C 2T8.

HST Charged on Sales

Bank

HST Paid